ISCA 2010

June 19-23, 2010
Saint-Malo, France

The 37th Annual
International Symposium on

COMPUTER ARCHITECTURE

Sponsored by
ACM SIGARCH
IEEE Computer Society TCCA

IEEE computer society

IEEE

CONFERENCE PROCEEDINGS

Association for Computing Machinery

SIGARCH

Association for
Computing Machinery

Advancing Computing as a Science & Profession

The Association for Computing Machinery
2 Penn Plaza, Suite 701
New York, New York 10121-0701

ISBN: 978-1-4503-0052-0

Additional copies may be ordered prepaid from:

ACM Order Department
PO Box 30777
New York, NY 10087-0777, USA

Phone: 1-800-342-6626 (USA and Canada)
+1-212-626-0500 (Global)
Fax: +1-212-944-1318
E-mail: acmhelp@acm.org
Hours of Operation: 8:30 am – 4:30 pm ET

ACM Order Number 415104

Printed in the USA

Message from the General Chair

It is my pleasure to welcome you all to Saint-Malo for the *37th International Symposium on Computer Architecture*. ISCA returns to France for the first time since 1980 when it was hosted in La Baule. 1980 was the first time that ISCA was organized outside the US. Since then, ISCA has supported a tradition of organizing the conference outside of North America every third year. Many other forums have since adopted this tradition.

The success of a conference of this scale requires a lot of work from many people. First of all, many thanks to Uri Weiser and Ronny Ronen, the co-program chairs, for assembling a fantastic program committee and for putting together the technical program. Uri, Ronny and I would like to thank Bill Dally and Olivier Temam for accepting our invitations to deliver the conference keynotes. Thanks also goes to Mark Hill for organizing the panel "La Microarchiture est morte. Longue Vie à la Microarchitecture."

ISCA has a long tradition of having strong workshops and tutorials associated with the conference. Yanos Sazeides, the workshop/tutorial chair made a remarkable job of attracting and selecting workshops and tutorials. I thank all the workshop and tutorial organizers for their investment in the continuous success of the ISCA conference series. For the second year in a row, Gabe Loh accepted the position of publication chair, many thanks to him. I would like to thank Dave Kaeli for administering the student travel grants. I would like to thank Hans Vandierendonck and Mattan Erez, the publicity co-chairs, for making sure that everyone in the community has been informed about ISCA 2010. Uri, Ronny and I would like to thank Zvika Guz who maintained flawlessly the ISCA submission web-site.

I must also thank my colleagues at INRIA/IRISA who "volunteered" to help with the organization, Erven Rohou the web chair, Isabelle Puaut the finance chair and Pierre Michaud, the local arrangement co-chair. Special thanks go to Elisabeth Lebret from INRIA Rennes. Elisabeth is used to running local arrangements for conferences organized by INRIA Rennes. Assisted by Pierre Michaud, she has taken care of all the small details that make a conference a successful social event for the community.

I would like to thank all of the corporate sponsors of ISCA who have provided generous financial support even in tough economic times: Intel, Hewlett-Packard, IBM Research, Microsoft Research, ARM, Thales, Google, STMicroelectronics, Samsung, AMD, VMware and Sun. I would also like to acknowledge the support from various local and national institutions: INRIA, IRISA, Fondation Michel Métivier, Brittany Region, Université of Rennes I and French Ministry of Research. Their contributions allowed us to keep the cost of registration down while still providing the social events required for meetings and exchanges. Our thanks also go to ACM SIGARCH, IEEE TCCA, and the National Science Foundation for providing funding for the student grants. I would also like to thank Microsoft Research and the ACM SIGARCH for their just-in-time support of the Turing Lecture reception.

Finally, despite the fact they both have created extra entropy in the burden of finalizing the technical and social program, I would like to express the gratitude of the whole ISCA research community to Mary Jane Irwin and to Charles P. Thacker. Jane is the recipient of 2010 ACM Athena award. Charles is the recipient of 2009 ACM Turing award. They have both decided to deliver their lectures at ISCA 2010. We are really honored to have both of them with us. Thanks Mary Jane, Thanks Charles.

We hope that you have a stimulating ISCA-37 and enjoy Saint-Malo and its surrounding treasures: the old city, the beaches and the tide, the Mont-Saint-Michel, …

André Seznec
INRIA Rennes

Message from the Program Chairs

On behalf of the Program Committee we are pleased to welcome you to the 2010 International Symposium on Computer Architecture held in Saint Malo, France.

It has been a great honor for us to serve as PC chairs of the prestigious ISCA conference. The ISCA conference is well known in the community as the forerunner in Computer Architecture because of its unique ability to provide, under one roof, maximum exposure for the newest ideas in the field. It is the responsibility of this conference to shape the direction Computer Architecture will take in the future and to promote its enormous potential.

Traditionally, the technical program of ISCA included some of the best research work in Computer Architecture, from the academia and industry. This year's ISCA program is as strong as ever, a testimonial to the continued vitality of Computer Architecture research. This year's program features papers on today's "hot" computer architecture topics, including energy efficiency designs, caches, memory subsystems, accelerator architecture, evaluation techniques, reliability and fault tolerance. This year we feature a unique QOB (Quantitative Out of the Box) session that emphasizes qualitative new innovative papers vs. thorough quantitative analysis papers. We hope you will enjoy and learn from the presentations and the papers.

The conference papers selection is the fruit of a long and rigorous process. The conference is grateful to all of the authors for the time and effort invested in submitting their best work. 245 papers were submitted to the conference, out of which the Program Committee selected 44 papers to be presented in the ISCA 2010 conference (18% acceptance rate).

We have been fortunate to recruit an outstanding Program Committee of 46 members that took the overwhelming task of selecting the best papers. Committee members contributed their time and expertise towards the goal of making this conference a success. We would like to deeply thank each and every Program Committee member. Only now we understand the enormous load they took on themselves: reviewing the submitted papers (we performed a total of 1200 reviews), interacting with other PC members and participating in the full day PC meeting marathon at the O'Hare Airport in Chicago (February 20th 2010).

The success of the paper selection process should be attributed to the many people involved and we would like to thank them all. Thanks to our student Zvika Guz who mastered the submission site and was always ready (although he got married just before the PC meeting) to help/change/respond. Thanks to the 87 External Review Committee members and the 236 secondary reviewers for delivering quality reviews, on time. Thanks to Luiz Barroso and Wen-mei Hwu for their incredible help and responsiveness in answering all our tedious questions and requests. Thanks to the Steering Committee and the general chair, André Seznec, for their ongoing advice and support.

We would like to thank Bill Dally and Olivier Temam for accepting our invitations to deliver the conference keynotes and to Mark Hill for organizing the panel on the future potential of microarchitecture.

It was an interesting period for us — we learned a lot, we feel we acquired a much better vision of our community and some insight on where this community should go.

And to all of you, thank you for coming to ISCA to the beautiful Saint Malo, enjoy the technical program and enjoy life.

Uri Weiser, *Technion*
Ronny Ronen, *Intel*

Table of Contents

Session 3A: Memory Subsystems

Session 3B: Productivity and Debugging

Keynote Address

Session 4A: Acceleration Architecture

Session Chair: Babak Falsafi *(EPFL)*

Session 4B: Threading

Session Chair: Sanjay Patel *(University of Illinois, Chicago)*

Session 5A: Simulation Technologies and Real System Evaluation

Session Chair: Lieven Eeckhout *(Ghent University)*

Session 5B: Cluster and Data Center

Session Chair: David A. Wood *(University of Wisconsin)*

Keynote Address

Keynote Address

Session Chair: André Seznec *(INRIA)*

Session 6A: QOB

Session Chair: Onur Mutlu *(Carnegie Mellon University)*

ISCA 2010 Organization

General Chair: André Seznec *(INRIA Rennes)*

Workshop/Tutorials Chair: Yanos Sazeides *(University of Cyprus)*

Local Arrangements Chairs: Elisabeth Lebret *(INRIA Rennes)*
Pierre Michaud *(INRIA Rennes)*

Finance Chair: Isabelle Puaut *(Université de Rennes I)*

Web Chair: Erven Rohou *(INRIA Rennes)*

Publicity Chairs: Hans Vandierendonk *(University of Ghent)*
Mattan Erez *(The University of Texas at Austin)*

Publication Chair: Gabriel Loh *(Georgia Institute of Technology / Microsoft Research)*

Submission Chair: Zvika Guz *(Technion)*

Student Travel Grants Chair: David Kaeli *(Northeastern University)*

Steering Committee: Luiz André Barroso *(Google)*
Doug Burger *(Microsoft Research)*
Jesse Fang *(Intel)*
Wen-mei Hwu *(University of Illinois at Champaign-Urbana)*
Steve Keckler *(The University of Texas at Austin)*
Kai Li *(Princeton University)*
Josep Torrellas *(University of Illinois at Champaign-Urbana)*
Mateo Valero *(UPC Barcelona)*
Per Stenström *(Chalmers)*

ISCA 2010 Program Committee

Program Chairs: Uri Weiser *(Technion)*
Ronny Ronen *(Intel)*

Committee Members: David Albonesi *(Cornell University)*
Todd Austin *(University of Michigan)*
Bryan Black *(AMD)*
David Brooks *(Harvard University)*
Doug Burger *(Microsoft Research)*
Brad Calder *(Microsoft)*
Doug Carmean *(Intel)*
Tom Conte *(Georgia Institute of Technology)*
Al Davis *(University of Utah / HP Labs)*
Giuseppe Desoli *(ST Microelectronics)*
Sandhya Dwarkadas *(University of Rochester)*
Lieven Eeckhout *(Ghent University)*
Mattan Erez *(The University of Texas at Austin)*
Babak Falsafi *(École Polytechnique Fédérale de Lausanne)*
Paolo Faraboschi *(HP Labs)*
Antonio González *(Intel / UPC Barcelona)*
Michael Gschwind *(IBM)*
Kim Hazelwood *(University of Virginia)*
Wen-mei Hwu *(University of Illinois)*
Hyesoon Kim *(Georgia Institute of Technology)*
Martha Kim *(Columbia University)*
Mikko Lipasti *(University of Wisconsin)*
Gabriel Loh *(Georgia Institute of Technology / Microsoft Research)*
Scott Mahlke *(University of Michigan)*
José F. Martínez *(Cornell University / Carnegie Mellon University)*
Margaret Martonosi *(Princeton University)*
Avi Mendelson *(Microsoft)*
Shubu Mukherjee *(Intel)*
Onur Mutlu *(Carnegie Mellon University)*
Mike O'Boyle *(University of Edinburgh)*
Kunle Olukotun *(Stanford University)*
Emre Özer *(ARM)*
Sanjay Patel *(University of Illinois)*
Li-Shiuan Peh *(MIT)*
Moinuddin Qureshi *(IBM)*
Amir Roth *(University of Pennsylvania)*
Yanos Sazeides *(University of Cyprus)*
Kevin Skadron *(University of Virginia)*
Jim Smith *(Intel)*
Guri Sohi *(University of Wisconsin)*
Per Stenström *(Chalmers University)*
Olivier Temam *(INRIA)*
Josep Torrellas *(University of Illinois)*
Dean Tullsen *(University of California, San Diego)*
Mateo Valero *(UPC Barcelona)*
David Wood *(University of Wisconsin)*

ISCA 2010 Referees

External Review Committee:

Ali-Reza Adl-Tabatabai
Saman Amarasinghe
Krste Asanović
Leonid Azriel
Rajeev Balasubramonian
Michael Behar
Amit Berman
David Bernstein
Francois Bodin
Evgeny Bolotin
Pradip Bose
Anne Bracy
Călin Caşcaval
Derek Chiou
Jaewoong Chung
Albert Cohen
Bob Colwell
Dan Connors
Bill Dally
Chita Das
Veerle Desmet
Assia Djabelkhir
Nathalie Drach
José Duato
Pradeep Dubey
Marc Duranton
Susan Eggers
Matthew Farrens
Krisztián Flautner
Diana Franklin
Georgi Gaydadjiev
Ran Ginosar
Jim Goodman
Dan Hammerstrom
Mark Hill
Sebastien Hily
Glenn Hinton
James Hoe
Ravi Iyer
Quinn Jacobson
Norm P. Jouppi
David Kaeli
Steve Keckler
Isaac Keslassy
Avinoam Kolodny
James Larus
Geoff Lowney
Srilatha Manne
Diana Marculescu
Milo Martin
Sally McKee
Pierre Michaud
Chuck Moore
Tomer Morad
Andreas Moshovos
Todd Mowry
Trevor Mudge
John Nickolls
Yale Patt
Ravi Rajwar
Alex Ramirez
Partha Ranganathan
Lawrence Rauchwerger
Glenn Reinman
Jose Renau
Erven Rohou
Efi Rotem
Eric Rotenberg
Pascal Sainrat
Mike Schlansker
Steve Scott
André Seznec
John Shen
Tim Sherwood
Daniel Sorin
Jared Stark
Marc Tremblay
Dan Truong
Rich Uhlig
Bob Valentine
Hans Vandierendonck
T. Vijaykumar
Zigi Walter
Emmett Witchel
Wei Wu
Cliff Young

Additional Reviewers:

Manuel Acacio
Andrea Acquaviva
Sarita Adve
Jung Ho Ahn
Alaa Alameldeen
Amin Ansari
Remzi Arpaci-Dusseau
Dave Bacon
James Balfour
Brad Beckmann
Ramon Beivide
Jesse G. Beu
Abhishek Bhattacharjee
Raj Bheda
Ricardo Bianchini
Nate Binkert
Thomas Boesch
Rajesh Bordawekar
Demid Borodin
Jeff Brown
Paul Bryan
Ioana Burcea
Brad Burgess
Alper Buyuktosonoglu
Qiong Cai
Trey Cain
Jared Casper
Luis Ceze
Craig Chase
Mainak Chaudhuri
Shimin Chen
Chen-Yong Cher
Hyoun Kyu Cho
Fred Chong
Dave Christie
George Chrysos
Mark Cianchetti
Marcelo Cintra
Nate Clark
Kypros Constantinides
Jean-Philippe Cousin
Chris Craik
Adrian Cristal
Reetuparna Das
Aniruddha Dasgupta
Derek Davis
Koen DeBosschere
André DeHon
Balaji Dhanasekaran
Chen Ding
Haakon Dybdahl
Eiman Ebrahimi
Alexandre Eichenberger
Mootaz Elnozahy

Additional Reviewers (continued):

Natalie Enright-Jerger
Oguz Ergin
Hadi Esmaeilzadeh
Ayose Falcon
Chris Fallin
Kayvon Fatahalian
Alexandra Fedorova
Shuguang Feng
Michael Ferdman
Marco Fiorentino
Carlo Galuzzi
Saugata Ghose
Ruben Titos Gil
Roberto Gioiosa
Jose Gonzalez
Chris Gregg
Brian Greskamp
Dominik Grewe
Boris Grot
Erika Gunadi
Shantanu Gupta
Sudhanva Gurumurthi
Zvika Guz
Heather Hanson
Nikos Hardavellas
Mitchell Hayenga
Mark Heinrich
Andrew Hilton
Hank Hoffmann
Sunpyo Hong
Hemayet Hossain
Wei Huang
Hillary Hunter
Ibrahim Hur
Engin Ipek
Canturk Isci
Aamer Jaleel
Jose A. Joao
Timothy Jones
Russ Joseph
Tejas Karkhanis
Miray Kas
Kamil Kedzierski
Omer Khan
Minjang Kim
Yoongu Kim
Meyrem Kirman
Nevin Kirman
Marios Kleanthous
Christos Kozyrakis
Rakesh Kumar
Eren Kursun
Alan Kyker
Nagesh B. Lakshminarayana
Per Larsson-Edefors
Alvy Lebeck
Benjamin Lee
Hsien-Hsin S. Lee
Chang Joo Lee
Jaekyu Lee
Charles Lefurgy
Shih-Lien Lu
Wayne Luk
Steven S. Lumetta
Marc Lupon
Ken Mai
Rajit Manohar
Pedro Marcuello
Mike Marty
Kevin McGrath
Moray McLaren
Mojtaba Mehrara
Rami Melhem
Bilha Mendelson
Brett Meyer
Rustam Miftakhutdinov
Asit Mishra
Jeff Mogul
Satish Narayanasamy
David Nellans
Chrysostomos Nicopoulos
Mike O'Connor
Mark Oskin
Myrto Papadopoulou
Francesco Papariello
Francesco Paterna
Andrea Pellegrini
Miquel Pericas
Paula Petrica
Timothy M. Pinkston
Jason Poovey
Leo Porter
Michael Powell
Milos Prvulovic
Andrew Putnam
David Ramos
VJ Reddi
Steve Reinhardt
Jude Rivers
Behnam Robatmili
Jonathan Rohrer
Chad Rosier
Juan Rubio
Jeff Rupley
Daniel Sanchez
Hiroshi Sasaki
Daniele Scarpazza
Michael Scott
Larry Seiler
Gadiel Seroussi
Vivek Seshadri
Simha Sethumadhavan
Kai Shen
Arrvindh Shriraman
Yan Solihin
Leonel Sousa
Vilas Sridharan
Viji Srinivasan
Radu Stefan
Karin Strauss
Lixin Su
Lavanya Subramanian
Ed Suh
M. Aater Suleman
Aater Suleman
Steve Swanson
Michael Taylor
Radu Teodorescu
Sasa Tomic
Kuen Hung Tsoi
James Tuck
Osman Unsal
Dan Upton
Enrique Vallejo
Dana Vantrease
Guru Venkataramani
Xavier Vera
Ilya Wagner
M. M. Waliullah
Matthew Watkins
Ian Watson
Robert Weikle
David Wentzlaff
Sudhakar Yalamanchili
Sami Yehia
Donald Yeung
Jason Zebchuk
Wei Zhang
Hongzhou Zhao
Rongrong Zhong
Pin Zhou
Khubaib

ISCA 2010 Sponsors & Supporters

Sponsors:

SIGARCH

IEEE computer society

IEEE TCCA

Supporters:

NSF

AMD

hp invent

ARM

Microsoft Research

SAMSUNG

Google

THALES

IBM Research

intel Leap ahead

intel Israel Processor Architecture

Sun ORACLE

vmware

FONDATION MICHEL MÉTIVIER

INRIA

UNIVERSITÉ DE RENNES 1 ueb

Région BRETAGNE

IRISA

ST

Moving the Needle, Computer Architecture Research in Academe and Industry

William J. Dally
NVIDIA and Stanford University

Abstract: The goal of computer architecture research is to move the needle, that is to affect the future of computing in a positive way. Publications, prototypes, and studies are all just different means to this common end. This talk will address how to move the needle in academic and industrial settings discussing what works and what doesn't. Our work is constrained by applications, technology, and commercial reality. The architecture funnel starts with many concepts that proceed through stages of evaluation and refinement. A relatively few successful concepts make it out the far side to deployment. Most concepts fail, and good researchers cut their losses early. The funnel has many years of latency and good researchers aim for results that are relevant beyond this latency. Academics are best at the early stages of the concept funnel – where their long-term perspective and freedom from constraints are advantages. Industry excels at the later stages of the pipeline where resources and experience are well suited to refining ideas for deployment. Too often good concepts fall into a chasm between the two. Good partnerships are needed to bridge this chasm. This talk will give illustrate this exploration of architecture research with numerous examples of successes and failures. It will give recommended best practices for academic and industrial research. I will close with a glimpse of the future of architecture.

Categories & Subject Descriptors: C.1.0 Computer Systems Organization; PROCESSOR ARCHITECTURES, General.

General Term: Design.

ISCA'10, June 19–23, 2010, Saint-Malo, France.
ACM 978-1-4503-0053-7/10/06.

WiDGET: Wisconsin Decoupled Grid Execution Tiles

Yasuko Watanabe* John D. Davis† David A. Wood*

*Department of Computer Sciences
University of Wisconsin—Madison
1210 W. Dayton Street
Madison, WI 53706
{watanabe, david}@cs.wisc.edu

†Microsoft Research — Silicon Valley Lab
1065 La Avenida
Mountain View, CA 94043
john.d@microsoft.com

ABSTRACT

The recent paradigm shift to multi-core systems results in high system throughput within a specified power budget. However, future systems still require good single thread performance—no longer the predominant design priority—to mitigate sequential bottlenecks and/or to guarantee service-level agreements. Unfortunately, near saturation in voltage scaling necessitates a long-term alternative to dynamic voltage and frequency scaling.

We propose an energy-proportional computing infrastructure, called WiDGET, that decouples thread context management from a sea of simple execution units (EUs). WiDGET's decoupled design provides flexibility to alter resource allocation for a particular power-performance target while turning off unallocated resources. In other words, WiDGET enables dynamic customization of different combinations of small and/or powerful cores on a single chip, consuming power in proportion to the delivered performance.

Over all SPEC CPU2006 benchmarks, WiDGET provides average per-thread performance that is 26% better than a Xeon-like processor while using 8% less power. WiDGET can also scale down to a level comparable to an Atom-like processor, turning off resources to reduce average power by 58%. WiDGET achieves high power efficiency ($BIPS^3/W$), exceeding Xeon-like and Atom-like processors by up to 2x and 21x, respectively.

Categories and Subject Descriptors

C.1.4 [**Parallel Architectures**]: Distributed architectures

General Terms

Performance, Design, Experimentation

Keywords

Power proportional computing, power efficiency, hardware, performance, instruction steering

ISCA'10, June 19-23, 2010, Saint-Malo, France.

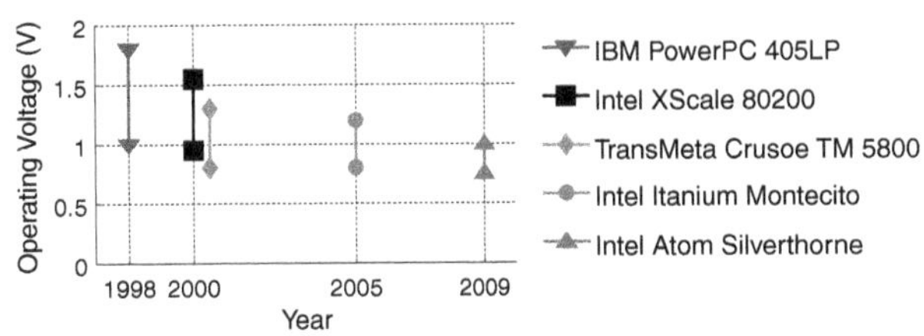

Figure 1. Operating voltage ranges

1. INTRODUCTION

Current trends in microprocessor design have appropriately recast Moore's law from the GHz race to the cores (threads) per die race. Designers trade off design complexity for power and area efficiency. Furthermore, ever increasing wire delays favor many small hardware structures over a few large monolithic structures. As a result, we have observed a paradigm shift to chips with multiple simple in-order cores, such as Intel's Larrabee [32] and Sun's Niagara [20]. Small cores deliver high thread-level parallelism and power efficiency, but Amdahl's Law dictates that we not ignore single thread performance [2,13]. Ignoring Amdahl's Law would lead to systems that are highly susceptible to sequential bottlenecks and/or fail to meet service-level agreements [28].

A key challenge in the multi-core era is developing an energy-proportional computing infrastructure and, at the same time, balancing system throughput and sequential thread performance. An Intel Nehalem processor, for instance, relies on dynamic voltage and frequency scaling (DVFS) to tackle the challenge [15]. By power gating a subset of cores, it can raise the voltage and frequency of the remaining cores to boost their performance without exceeding the power budget. Unfortunately, DVFS is no longer sufficient. Figure 1 shows that while maximum supply voltage has declined over the past decade, minimum supply voltage has remained almost the same (operating in the subthreshold regime is never energy-efficient [40]). This shrinking operating voltage range significantly reduces the benefit of DVFS.

We seek to provide an alternative approach to achieving energy-proportional computing. We propose WiDGET (Wisconsin Decoupled Grid Execution Tiles), a hardware design that decouples thread context management (i.e., instruction engines or IEs) from a sea of simple computation resources (i.e., execution units or EUs), loosely defining core boundaries. Rather than scaling voltage like DVFS, WiDGET scales cores up and down through global resource allocation, varying the number of enabled IEs and the number of EUs assigned to each IE. This decoupled design activates only the

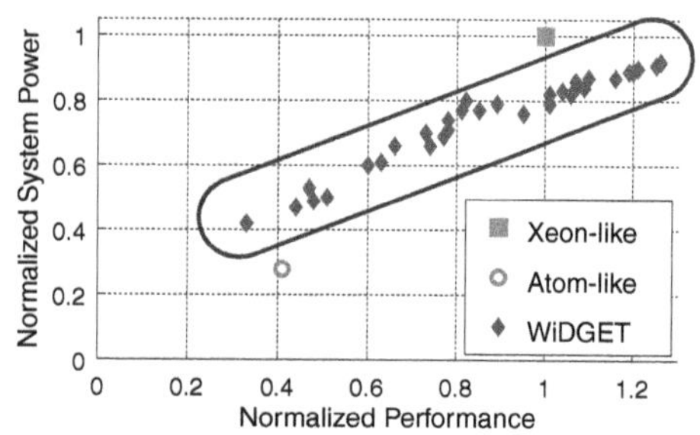

Figure 2. Power proportionality

computation resources needed for a particular power-performance target—turning off the rest to save power—permitting dynamically and individually customized cores on a single chip.

In this paper, we focus on WiDGET's single thread power and performance with emphasis on power proportionality. We define power proportionality as power dissipation in proportion to single thread performance, adapted from Barroso and Hölzle's definition of energy proportionality [4]. WiDGET achieves power proportionality through EU provisioning, under system software control, as demonstrated in Figure 2. With the maximum number of EUs, WiDGET provides 8% power savings for 26% better performance than a high performance Xeon-like processor (Section 5.1 presents configuration details) running SPEC CPU2006 benchmarks. With the minimum number of EUs, WiDGET uses 58% less power, approximating the power and performance of a low power Atom-like processor. In addition, between these two extremes, WiDGET affords a wide power-performance range.

WiDGET's decoupled modular design enables flexible EU configuration, but makes distributing instructions to the disjoint EUs a key challenge. By taking into account communication overheads, we show that simplified steering logic can yield good performance.

The key contributions of this paper are:

- A power proportional design enabled by EU modularity, allowing WiDGET to scale across the power-performance spectrum.
- A unified framework that dynamically exploits programs' parallelism within a power budget. WiDGET decouples thread context management from a sea of computation resources. We trade off complexity for power, replacing the monolithic, power-hungry out-of-order (OoO) issue logic in a conventional OoO machine with simple in-order EUs.
- WiDGET's high power efficiency (BIPS^3/W) exceeds the Xeon-like and Atom-like processors by up to 2x and 21x, respectively.

The rest of the paper first presents a high-level overview of our design and compares it to related proposals (Section 2). We present a cost model that accounts for communication overheads, making a case for an implementable hardware instruction steering design (Section 3). We then present details of the WiDGET microarchitecture (Section 4), and evaluate the power proportionality

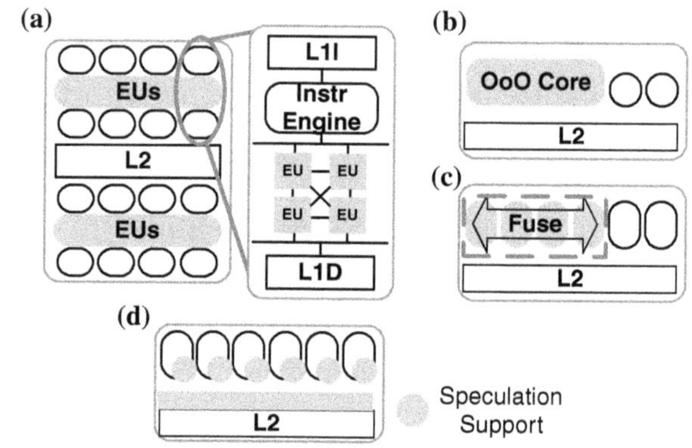

Figure 3. The general paradigm of balancing TLP and ILP
Each system uses the shaded components to accelerate single thread performance. (a)WiDGET. (b) Heterogeneous CMPs. (c) Dynamic multi-core processors. (d) TLS.

(Section 5). Finally, we present our conclusions and future work (Section 6).

2. OVERVIEW AND RELATED WORK

The goal of this work is a power proportional framework, in which cores gracefully transition across the power-performance spectrum. To address this goal, we harness multiple in-order issue resources, instead of relying on power-hungry OoO logic. This design delivers power efficiency, but three constraints must be met to preserve OoO-like performance. First, ready instructions must be exposed to the heads of the in-order issue buffers. Second, stalled instructions must not block the execution of later ready instructions. Third, the design should provide enough buffering capacity to prevent instruction queue clog—a pathologic stall condition in which dispatch is halted while all scheduling resources are occupied by earlier waiting instructions. Satisfying all of these constraints requires intelligent management of in-order issue resources.

Figure 3(a) illustrates WiDGET's sea of resources design. An instruction engine (IE) resembles a conventional OoO core's front-end and back-end pipeline functions with the addition of instruction steering logic for the distributed EUs. Each EU is capable of buffering and executing instructions in order. A hierarchical operand network connects a cluster of four adjacent EUs via full bypass, while a 1-cycle link bridges two adjacent clusters. An IE has an associated EU cluster, which is enough to deliver the performance of a comparable OoO machine (Section 5.2). Yet the decoupled design provides the flexibility to further scale up the core by borrowing up to four EUs from the neighboring IE. The hardware has control paths to distribute instructions and commands to any assigned EU in one cycle.

By varying the number of in-order EUs, which include some amount of instruction buffering, we can select a point on the power-performance spectrum best suited to the current situation. When the workload calls for aggressive exploitation of instruction-level parallelism (ILP), additional EUs can be allocated to service demands. On the other hand, the number of EUs can be reduced to conserve power, e.g., when running many threads.

2.1 Related Work

Table 1 summarizes the key aspects of WiDGET in comparison to the relevant prior proposals. Notably, WiDGET stands out by focusing on scaling both up and down (column 2) to achieve power proportionality (cols. 3-7) while retaining ISA compatibility (col. 8). We are not aware of any earlier work that demonstrates a core that can scale power and performance from close to an Atom to better than a Xeon. We briefly discuss closely related work, referencing Table 1.

2.1.1 Power-Proportional Computing

Chandrakasan et al. are among the first to introduce the concept of power-proportional computing [7]. They pointed out that once computational capability of a design meets service-level agreements, the remaining transistor budget should be devoted to power saving techniques, including DVFS [22] and power gating [14]. Barroso and Hölzle made a case for energy proportionality, especially for servers that rarely reach complete idle or near-peak utilization [4]. Whereas PowerNap proposes system-level techniques for idle-power reduction [25], Thread Motion employs several statically set voltage/frequency domains for non-idle power management [27]. Lastly, previously proposed adaptive cores focus on power savings [1,10,8], and thereby are limited to scaling cores down (col. 2).

2.1.2 Single-Thread Performance Techniques

Heterogeneous CMPs. A heterogeneous CMP (Figure 3(b)) combines a small number of aggressive superscalar cores for ILP with many lightweight cores for thread-level parallelism (TLP) (col. 3) [21]. Due to the statically set core designs for the target class of applications (col. 2), it has limited effectiveness for applications outside of the target class [31].

Dynamic Multi-Core Processors. Dynamic multi-core processors execute independent threads on a collection of small homogeneous cores (col. 3) to provide TLP, but dynamically fuse these cores together to provide greater ILP for a single thread (Figure 3(c)). Core Fusion enlarges the resources in each pipeline stage (col. 4) by aggregating OoO cores (col. 5) [16]. In contrast, Composable Lightweight Processors (CLP) leverages the EDGE ISA (col. 8) to eliminate centralized structures, such as rename logic, even in a fused mode [18], but requires recompilation, unlike WiDGET.

Thread-Level Speculation (TLS). TLS relies on software to divide a dynamic instruction stream into contiguous segments at control-flow boundaries (col. 7) [11,36]. The hardware speculatively executes the resulting chain of control dependent threads, using buffered state to recover from misspeculation (Figure 3(d)). The control driven execution makes TLS susceptible to thread squash propagation [29], which WiDGET avoids by being dataflow driven.

Clustered Architectures. The goal of early clustered architectures was to continue the superscalar trend of wider and deeper pipelines with minimum complexity for performance. Hence, each cluster may utilize complex OoO execution (col. 5). In addition, they trade off inter-cluster communication latencies for load balancing so long as the latencies can be hidden (cols. 6, 7). WiDGET, on the other hand, attacks both performance and power aspects of communication, as the next section explains, by using small units immune to long wire delays and localizing operand transfers.

Table 1: Comparison to Prior Related Work

Design	Scale Up & Down?	Symmetric?	Decoupled Exec?	In-Order?	Wire Delays?	Data Driven?	ISA Compativility?
WiDGET	Y	Y	Y	Y	Y	Y	Y
Adaptive Cores [1,10,8]	N	-	Y/N	Y/N	-	-	Y
Heterogeneous CMPs [21]	N	N	N	Y/N	-	-	Y
Core Fusion [16]	Y	Y	N	N	Y	-	Y
CLP [18]	Y	Y	Y	Y	Y	Y	N
TLS [13]	N	Y	N	Y/N	-	N	Y
Multiscalar [42]	N	Y	N	N	-	N	N
Complexity-Effective [26]	N	Y	Y	Y	N	Y	Y
Salverda & Zilles [31]	Y	Y	N	Y	N	Y	Y
ILDP [19] & Braid [38]	N	Y	Y	Y	-	Y	N
Quad-Cluster [3]	N	Y	Y	N	Y	Y/N	Y
Access/Execute [35]	N	N	N	Y	-	Y	N
Cost-Effective [6]	N	N	Y	N	Y	Y	Y

3. INSTRUCTION STEERING COST MODEL

Limits to CMOS scaling and increasing wire delays prompt a decentralized design, such as WiDGET. In this design regime, the instruction steering policy becomes an integral part of the performance equation. It determines issue time, which is governed by data dependencies, structural hazards, and the EUs' issue policy. As a result of this complex interaction, providing a cost model for instruction steering guides some of the design decisions for our architecture. We extend Salverda and Zilles's cost model by adding communication-latency-awareness [31] and discuss the implications of this new model.

3.1 Extending the Salverda and Zilles Model

Salverda and Zilles evaluated steering cost of an instruction i as a function of the dataflow (i.e., *horizon*) and in-order issue constraints (i.e., *frontier*) [31]. The horizon marks the time when an instruction becomes ready to issue, which is imposed by the dispatch time, *disp(i)*, and computation of the source operands, *data(i)*. Hence, the horizon of i is $h(i) = max\{disp(i), data(i)\}$. Throughout this section, we use Figure 4 to help explain their cost model and our extension. Figure 4(a) shows an example sequence of instructions, each of which takes one cycle to execute on one of the two available EUs. Both `i2` and `i3` depend on `i1` and must execute before `i4`. Assuming all three instructions dispatch in cycle 0, then the horizon of `i3` is 2 because it must wait for the result of `i1` to become available, as the arrow and

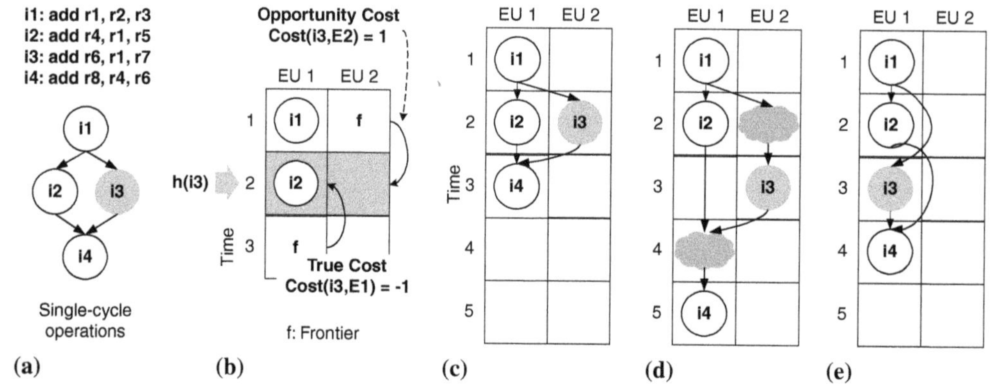

Figure 4. Limitations of the Salverda and Zilles cost model (a) An example instruction sequence and the dataflow graph. (b) Steering cost of i3. (c) Steering under idealized communication assumption. (d) Impacts of adding a 1-cycle latency between EUs using the ideal cost model. (e) Communication-latency-aware cost model under a 1-cycle latency between EUs.

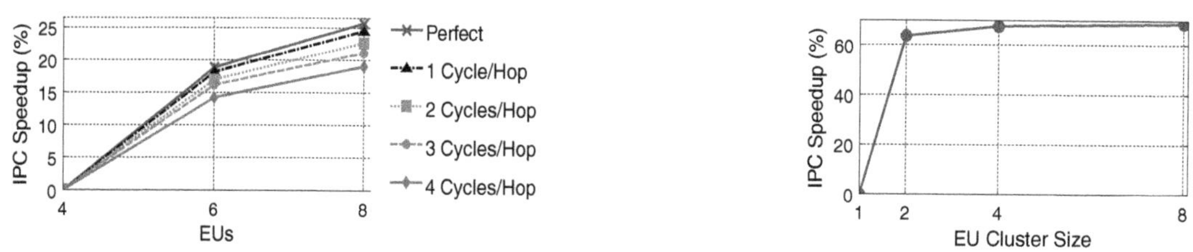

(a) Unclustered EUs: EU count impact on performance

(b) Clustered EUs: Cluster size impact on performance

Figure 5. Performance sensitivity under realistic communication delays

shaded region in Figure 4(b) show. On the other hand, the frontier of an in-order EU *e*, *f(e)*, denotes the earliest time an instruction becomes the head of the FIFO queue. In Figure 4(b), the frontier of EU 1 is 3, whereas that of EU 2 is 1 due to the unutilized resource.

The cost of steering an instruction to an EU becomes: *Cost(i, e) = h(i) - f(e)*. A negative cost indicates a *true cost* of the instruction because earlier instructions in the steered EU delay the issue time. This is the case of steering `i3` to EU 1. Although `i3` becomes ready at cycle 2, it cannot issue until `i2` finishes execution at cycle 3. A positive cost, on the other hand, reflects an *opportunity cost.* The instruction becomes the earliest instruction in the EU while still waiting for the operands, potentially deferring execution of later instructions. Steering `i3` to EU 2 incurs an opportunity cost by leaving EU 2 idle at cycle 1. Thus, an ideal steering occurs when *Cost(i, e)* is zero, issuing the instruction as soon as it becomes ready without lowering EU utilization. This example has no zero-cost steering. The Salverda and Zilles cost model prefers minimal true cost to opportunity cost in order to increase parallelism, steering `i3` to EU 2. `i4` can be steered to either EU 1 or EU 2, but in either case completes in cycle three as illustrated in Figure 4(c).

Although Salverda and Zilles assumed idealized inter-EU communication, the communication cost cannot be ignored as wire delay increasingly dominates with decreasing CMOS feature scaling. If just a single-cycle inter-EU delay is added, Figure 4(d) shows that the same sequence now takes five cycles. The clouds depict the incurred operand transfer delays that did not exist under the idealized communication assumption in Figure 4(c). A cost model that is sensitive to communication overheads will instead keep all four instructions in the same EU, completing the sequence in four cycles as shown in Figure 4(e).

Figure 5 demonstrates the importance of accounting for communication delays. Figure 5(a) shows the harmonic means of IPC speedup for the SPEC CPU2006 benchmark suite by varying the communication delay from zero to four cycles. Each speedup is based on a four-EU configuration with the same delay. The idealized communication enables 26% speedup from four to eight EUs, whereas it drops to 19% under four-cycle delays. Thus, as one would expect, performance gains from increased EU count degrade as communication becomes more expensive.

However, assuming delays between every EU is rather pessimistic. A more realistic design will cluster a few EUs with no intra-cluster delay, while imposing inter-cluster delays. Figure 5(b) plots the performance implications of cluster size. It fixes the EU count to eight and assumes a 1-cycle delay per inter-cluster hop. The speedups are normalized to an unclustered design, in which inter-EU communication increases one cycle. By assigning two EUs per cluster, performance increases 64%. A cluster size of four further improves the speedup by another 4%, but the speedup gain becomes negligible beyond that point. Despite the similar performance of the 2- and 4-EU clusters, WiDGET employs the latter for more scalable power proportionality (Section 5.3).

Our extension of the Salverda and Zilles cost model incorporates the impact of communication delays. Specifically, operand availability is now governed by two variables:

operand computation time by the producer *and* the operand transfer time to reach the consumer EU. We denote the latter as *comm(i, e)*. The horizon is therefore a function of an EU as well: $h(i, e) = max\{disp(i), data(i) + comm(i, e)\}$. In the example of Figure 4, the horizon of `i3` is calculated as the following, provided it is dispatched at time 0 and `i1` is steered to EU 1:

$h(i3, EU\ 1) = max\{0, 2 + 0\} = 2$

$h(i3, EU\ 2) = max\{0, 2 + 1\} = 3$

We call the extended model the Communication-Latency-Aware Cost Model and measure the steering cost: $Cost(i, e) = h(i, e) - f(e)$. An ideal steering decision, therefore, sends an instruction to a different EU from the producer's EU only when the operand transfer latency can be hidden. In contrast, the Salverda and Zilles cost model, assuming no communication penalties, spreads computation across the EUs to minimize true cost, benefiting from higher EU count. Salverda and Zilles therefore conclude that dataflow properties constrain the performance improvement from fusing in-order cores. It requires either a very convoluted steering mechanism that keeps track of each EU's frontier in relation to an instruction's horizon or fusing so many cores that fusion overheads become impractical. Under realistic communication delays, however, our model tends to mitigate the pressure for more EUs and obviate the need for considering distant EUs. This reduces the number of available instruction steering slots, leading to an implementable steering policy.

3.2 Toward Practical Steering

WiDGET approximates the communication-latency-aware cost model by controlling often known variables, *disp(i)* and *comm(i, e)*, and simplifying hard-to-predict variables, *data(i)* and *f(e)*. We try to steer a consumer directly behind the producer, similar to the dependence-based steering proposed by Palacharla et al. [26]. The important difference is accounting for communication, thereby keeping dependent instructions nearby to reduce the latency and power from operand transfers. Hence, WiDGET only considers a subset of the available EUs for a given instruction, making the steering complexity tractable.

4. MICROARCHITECTURE

The current technological trends favor a hardware design based on a sea of resources. This design naturally maps well to TLP, but makes achieving high ILP very challenging. WiDGET addresses this issue by aggregating in-order-issue EUs to approximate OoO-issue capability. We therefore employ steering to distribute instructions, localizing dependent instructions into the same cluster whenever possible. The routing network forwards operands to intra-cluster EUs in time for back-to-back execution, but incurs an additional cycle for each inter-cluster transfer. Conversely, independent instructions are steered to any empty EUs and execute in parallel. When there is a long-latency instruction, the EU that is executing the instruction acts as a buffer for the chain of dependent instructions; other EUs remain in an unblocked state and can continue execution. Thus, our sea of resources design enables independent instructions to run ahead of the earlier stalled instructions in available EUs, extracting ILP and memory-level parallelism from a program. Figure 6 illustrates an example WiDGET chip with eight instruction engines (IEs), each of which consists of front-end and back-end pipeline functions comparable to a conventional OoO core. An IE therefore manages thread specific information, including the register file and the reorder buffer (ROB), for a thread fetched and dispatched from the IE. The following sections provide more details about the IE and EU functionality.

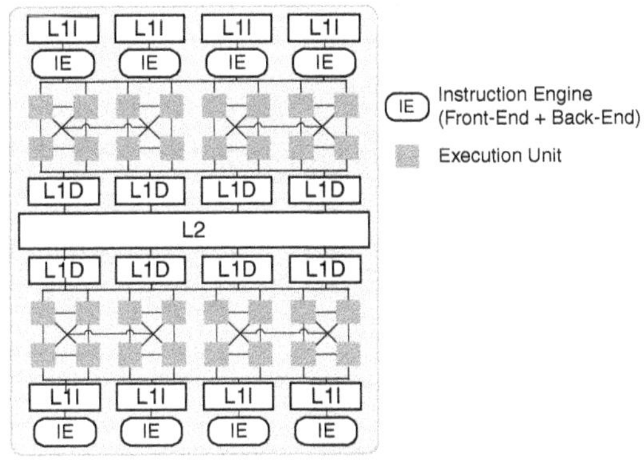

Figure 6. WiDGET microarchitecture

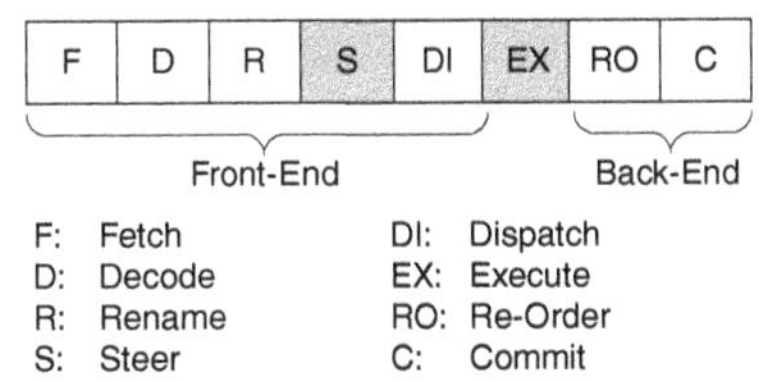

Figure 7. Pipeline Stages

4.1 Pipeline Stages

Figure 7 shows WiDGET's pipeline stages, highlighting those that are unique to WiDGET. The non-shaded stages resemble a conventional OoO design except for the additional NoSQ (short for No Store Queue) support to eliminate a centralized memory disambiguation mechanism during execution [33].

WiDGET makes steering decisions at the Steer Stage so that instructions are dispatched to the appropriate EUs the following cycle. Section 4.2 provides detailed description of our steering heuristic.

The Execute stage can take multiple cycles depending on the operation and the utilization of the selected EU. Each EU independently manages instruction execution and no more than one operation issues at a time per EU. The total issue width is a function of the aggregate EU count, as each EU provides an additional execution engine. Executed instructions are removed from their EUs and forward the results directly to the consumer EUs, if any, and to the register file in the dispatching IE. Section 4.3 describes the detailed implementation.

4.2 Front-End

Figure 8 illustrates the detailed front-end of our architecture, which resembles a conventional OoO core's with the

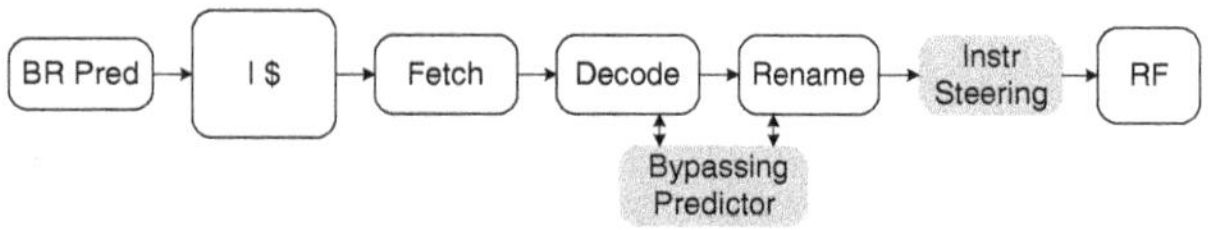

Figure 8. Front-End

```
/*  Let  I  be  an  instruction  under
consideration. Also, let s and EUps be I's
source operand and the producer EU of operand
s, respectively. s is omitted when only a
single operand is outstanding. */

0: switch (numOutstandingOps(I)){
1: case 0:
2:   return getEmptyEU();
3: case 1:
4:   if (!hasInstrBehind(s))
5:     return EUp;
6:   else
7:     return getEmptyEUInCluster(EUp);
8: case 2:
9:   if (!hasInstrBehind(s1))
10:    return EUp1;
11:  else if (!hasInstrBehind(s2))
12:    return EUp2;
13:  else
14:    return getEmptyEUInCluster(EUp1,EUp2);
15:}
```

Figure 9. Pseudo-code for instruction steering

addition of the NoSQ mechanism (*Bypassing Predictor*) and instruction steering. We derive the steering heuristic from the observation made in Section 3 that dependent instructions must be kept nearby, obviating the need for considering every EU each time. Specifically, we send consumers directly behind the producer or to an empty EU in the same EU cluster. If no such EU is found, we simply stall steering until either a desirable EU becomes available or the producer finishes execution. It is through stalling that we ensure steering complexity is manageable and communication overheads do not diminish the benefits from parallelism.

The heuristic requires three pieces of information: a producer's steered EU, whether a producer has another consumer steered to the same instruction buffer, and a list of empty EUs. We employ a Last Producer Table (LPT) and an empty bit vector to keep track of the first two and the last information, respectively. The LPT is indexed by a register and contains two fields. The first field indicates the instruction buffer ID to which the producing instruction of the given register is steered. The second field consists of a single bit; when set, this bit indicates at least one instruction has been steered as a result of the producer-consumer relationship. An LPT entry is updated when an instruction is steered and is invalidated when the register value is written back to the register file. An invalid entry, therefore, indicates that the value has been computed and is available in the register file. The empty bit vector is sized to the total number of instruction buffers, marking the corresponding buffer's occupancy status. We similarly use a full bit vector to ensure a producer instruction buffer still has room for the consumer instruction. Feedback from the EUs updates both of the bit vectors every cycle.

Figure 9 provides pseudo-code for the steering heuristic. The location of a producer (*EUp*) is tracked by accessing LPT with the consumer's source operand. If the indexed entry's buffer ID is null, the producer has already computed the operand. *getEmptyEU()* accesses the empty bit vector and returns an ID whose corresponding entry is set to 1. If more than one entry is set, it randomly chooses an ID from an EU cluster with more empty buffers for load balancing. If all of the entries are set to 0, the function returns -1, indicating a steering stall. *hasInstrBehind(s)* returns true if an LPT entry indexed by *s* has the consumer field set to 1; otherwise, it returns false. Given one or more EU IDs, *getEmptyEUInCluster()* searches the empty bit vector only within the corresponding EU cluster(s). It returns either an available ID similarly to *getEmptyEU()* or -1 if no empty buffers are found in the cluster(s), stalling the steering.

This is best explained with an example, illustrated in Figure 10. Suppose eight EUs spanning two clusters are dedicated to this instruction engine. Further assume all operands are initially available in the register file and all EUs are empty. Figure 10(a) shows a dataflow graph of instructions with each node denoting an instruction sequence number and the destination register in parenthesis.

In the first cycle, instructions `i1` through `i4` are steered. Since `i1` has no data dependencies, it is steered to the empty EU 0 (line 2 in Figure 9). It marks the steered EU ID in the LPT entry for the destination register `r1`, leaving the consumer field unchanged. It also resets the empty bit vector for EU 0. Conversely, `i2` depends on `i1`. An access to the LPT entry for `r1` reveals the producer of `i1` is steered to EU 0 and no other instructions have followed `i1` yet. Hence, `i2` is steered to the producer EU 0 (line 5). It updates the corresponding LPT entry as well as `i1`'s to prevent other consumers of `i1` from steering to EU 0. `i3` begins a new independent chain. It selects the empty EU 4 in Cluster 1 to balance the load (line 2). Both the LPT entry for `r3` and the empty bit vector are updated accordingly. `i4` is analogous to the case of `i2`, following the producer EU 4 (line 5). As both of the head instructions in EUs 0 and 4 are ready, they execute in their EUs. Figure 10(b) shows the steering result at the end of cycle 1.

In the second cycle, `i5` through `i8` are steered. `i5` is sent to the producer EU 0 (line 5), setting the consumer field in the `r2`'s LPT entry. `i6` also depends on `i2`, yet an LPT lookup informs that the slot immediately succeeding `r2` has been claimed. `i6` therefore finds the empty EU 2 in the same Cluster 0 by accessing the Empty Bit Vector (line 7). Note that `i2` will forward the result to EU 2 at the end of the execution, enabling both `i5` and `i6` to execute in parallel. `i7` depends on both `i5` and `i4` which are in EUs 0 and 4, respectively. Although both of the producers have empty slots behind them, `i7` selects the producer EU 0 of the first source operand `r5` (line 10). Finally, `i8` is sent to the producer EU 2 (line 5). Figure 10(c) displays the final state at the end of cycle 2.

The naive implementation of steering is serial, since it is constrained by the serial dependencies among a group of instructions to be steered. However, we utilize a parallel prefix computation. The parallel dependence-check performed in renaming is employed to detect dependencies in the same steering group [30]. Concurrently, each instruction accesses the LPT and the bit vectors to choose a candidate EU. Then

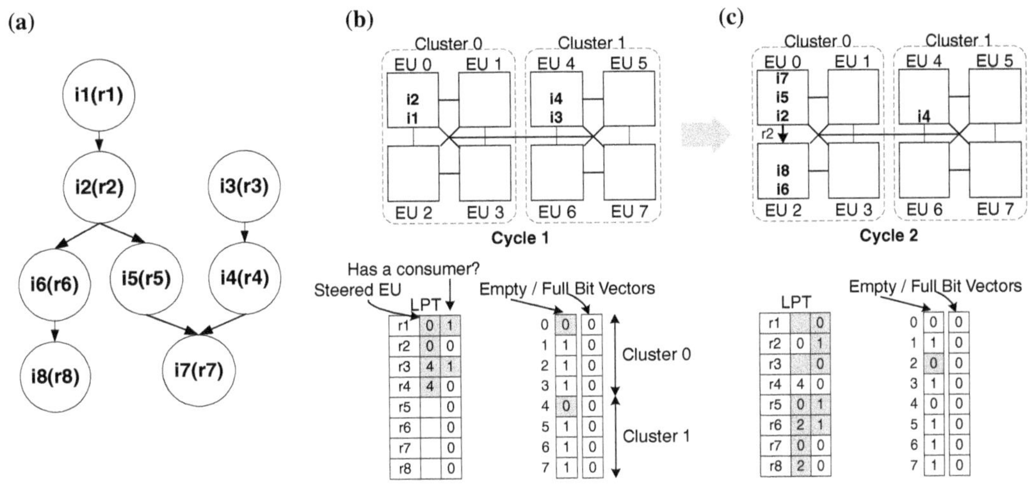

Figure 10. Instruction Steering Example

the candidate EUs are compared and are modified if necessary to reflect the intra-group dependencies, followed by updating the LPT and the bit vectors accordingly.

4.3 Execution Unit

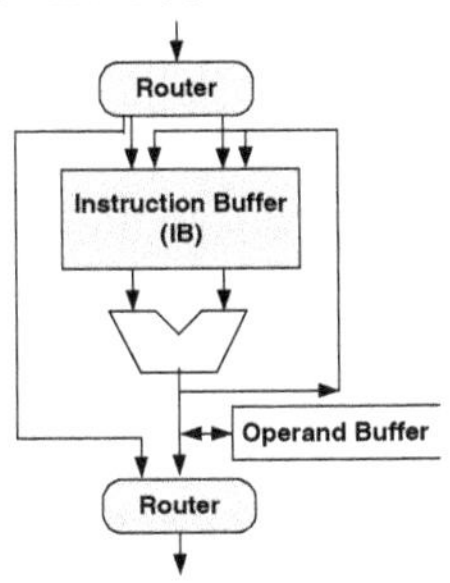

Figure 11. Execution Unit

Figure 11 shows an EU, consisting of a small instruction buffer (IB) FIFO, execution engine (an integer ALU, floating-point unit, and address generation unit), operand buffer, and router connections at the input and output. The IB is configured to be four times larger than the fetch width to minimize front-end stalls. Each entry has four fields: instruction, operand 1, operand 2, and a bit vector of consumer EU IDs. The consumer EU ID field indicates EUs to forward the result to. Although our dynamic instruction steering provides the ability to adjust to dynamic events, the caveat is that consumer EUs are not known until the dependent instructions are steered. Therefore, an instruction has to send its EU ID to the producer EU via control paths after steering is performed. However, a race can occur if a producer has finished execution and has been removed from the IB by the time the consumer reaches the producer EU. To prevent this situation, an operand buffer holds the result of an instruction for a cycle, which is the latency of register file write backs.

The units in the execution engine are pipelined, though an EU can only issue one instruction per cycle. Note that each additional EU increases both issue bandwidth and buffer space for scheduled instructions. This primarily contributes to WiDGET's high single thread performance with simple in-order EUs.

4.4 Back-End

The back-end resembles a conventional OoO core's. The ROB ensures in-order commit, and stores write their values to the data cache at commit as in a traditional pipeline.

5. EVALUATION

This section evaluates the microarchitecture described in Section 4 and the potential for power-proportional computing. Since this paper focuses on single thread performance, we leave the evaluation of parallelism management as future work. Instead, we focus on two crucial properties of power proportionality: wide performance and power ranges.

5.1 Simulation Methodology

We use a full-system execution-driven simulator, composed of three parts: 1) A detailed timing-first microarchitecture-level processor simulator, which models dynamically-scheduled SPARC v9 processors, 2) Wisconsin GEMS [24,39] for memory system timing, and 3) Virtutech Simics [23] for full-system functionality and to verify the timing-first components. Wattch [5] and CACTI [34] are integrated for modeling power.

For the single thread performance evaluation, we use the entire SPEC CPU2006 benchmark suite, which is a collection of sequential workloads. All programs were compiled for the 64-bit SPARC ISA using the Sun Studio 11 compiler with base tuning.

WiDGET's power proportionality can be best assessed by commercial processors on the opposite ends of a design spectrum. Hence, we use two baselines designed after a low power Intel Atom Silverthorne [9] and a high performance Intel Xeon Tulsa [37]. We call the former Mite and the latter Neon. The memory hierarchy of the baselines and WiDGET is configured to emulate Neon's in order to isolate the performance of the three different core designs. We evaluate WiDGET configurations with 1 through 8 EUs allocated to an instruction engine. These initial experiments assume *a priori* static allocation of EUs, as might be done by low-level system software. The mechanisms and policies to trade-off ILP and TLP via EU provisioning are beyond the scope of this paper.

Table 2 lists the key configuration parameters. The area estimate only accounts for a single-threaded core with the listed memory hierarchy. We derived the area of the Neon and Mite from published die area and attributed core com-

Table 2: Machine configurations

	Mite	Neon	WiDGET
LI-I / L1-D	32 KB, 4-way, 1 cycle; Next-line prefetching for L1-I		
BR Predictor	4K-entry Bimodal branch predictor; 16-entry RAS; 64-entry, 4-way BTB		
Instruction Engine	2-wide FE and BE	4-wide FE and BE; 128-entry ROB	
Execution Core	16-entry unified in-order instruction queue; 2 INT, 2 FP, 2 Addr Gen	32-entry unified OoO instruction queue; 3 INT, 3 FP, and 2 Addr Gen; 0-cycle operand bypass to anywhere in core	16-entry in-order IB per EU; 1 INT, 1 FP, and 1 Addr Gen per EU; 0-cycle operand bypass within a cluster of four EUs; 1-cycle inter-cluster link
Disambiguation	NoSQ; 256-entry, 4-way store-load bypassing predictor; 1K-entry T-SSBF		
L2 / L3 / DRAM	1 MB, 8-way, 12 cycles / 4 MB, 16-way, 24 cycles / ~300 cycles, 16-entry MSHR		
Area Estimate (45nm)	~30 mm^2	~41 mm^2	~33 mm^2 (8 EUs)

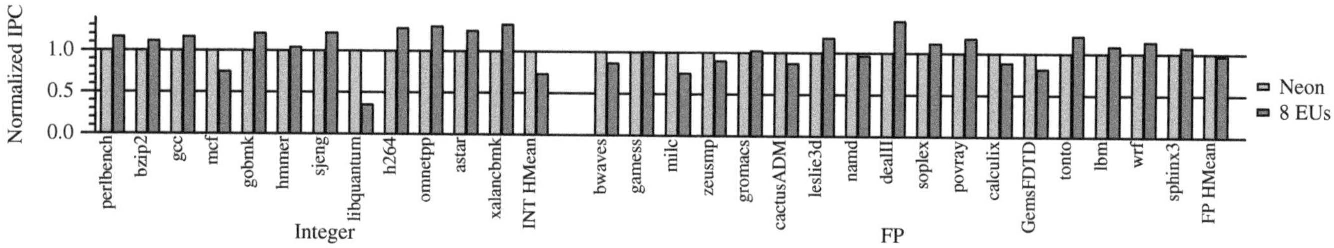

Figure 12. 8-EU performance relative to the Neon

ponent or unit area. The Neon's area was then halved because of the process technology change from 65 and 45nm. Note, our more aggressive memory hierarchy increases Mite's memory die area. WiDGET's area estimate includes an instruction engine, 8 EUs, and the memory hierarchy. We estimate that the Atom's core area is roughly equivalent to WiDGET with 2 EUs due to the similar core structure sizes. The area of an each additional EU is based on a TRIPS processor's Execution Tile [17], which resembles the EU composition. Despite WiDGET's greater ALU resources, our area model concludes that WiDGET is smaller than the Neon, mainly due to WiDGET's simpler structures.

In this evaluation, we fully provision ports on the register file and L1-D cache. When modeling power consumption, we outfit the register file with read ports numbering twice the dispatch width (8), and write ports numbering the commit width (4). A similar simplifying assumption is applied to the L1-D power model.

5.2 Performance Range of WiDGET

A wide performance range is vital for power proportionality, yet WiDGET's in-order issue constraint makes it challenging to match OoO execution performance. Therefore, we first evaluate single thread performance of WiDGET when configured with the maximum number of EUs: 8 EUs with an instruction buffer per EU. Figure 12 presents IPCs relative to the high-performance Neon baseline, with integer benchmarks on the left and floating-point benchmarks on the right. Even with more than double the ALU resources, one third of the benchmarks fail to match the Neon's performance. In particular, WiDGET is only able to produce 35% of the Neon performance for the outlier libquantum, drastically impacting the integer harmonic mean.

Figure 13 demonstrates the average EU utilization, revealing the sources of the performance degradation. *Empty* is when an EU has no instructions in the instruction buffer (IB). *Waiting for Producer* and *Waiting for Op Transfer* are when EU utilization is wasted because the head instruction in the IB has at least one outstanding operand. The former is waiting for the operand to be computed, whereas the latter indicates that the operand has been computed but has not yet reached the EU due to the inter-cluster communication delay. Finally, *Accessing Memory* and *Executing ALU* are when an EU is executing memory and non-memory instructions, respectively. Since instructions reside in IBs until execution is complete, memory-intensive workloads cause EUs to spend much of the time waiting for load data (*Accessing Memory*).

The under-performing benchmarks demonstrate common characteristics: frequent stalls due to memory access and outstanding producers. This increases the pressure on the EUs to buffer more dependent instructions for a longer period of time. As a result, the steering logic becomes more prone to stalls due to the lack of desirable EUs. libquantum is the most prominent example. It spends 62% and 37% of the time on memory accesses and waiting for producers, respectively, leaving non-memory execution to a mere 1%. In contrast, benchmarks that have comparable performance to the Neon have the opposite trends. They have a larger portion of time spent on executing non-memory instructions and are less likely to waste EU utilization by waiting for operands. Hence, fewer EUs are necessary to buffer stalled chains of instructions, leveraging more EUs to execute inde-

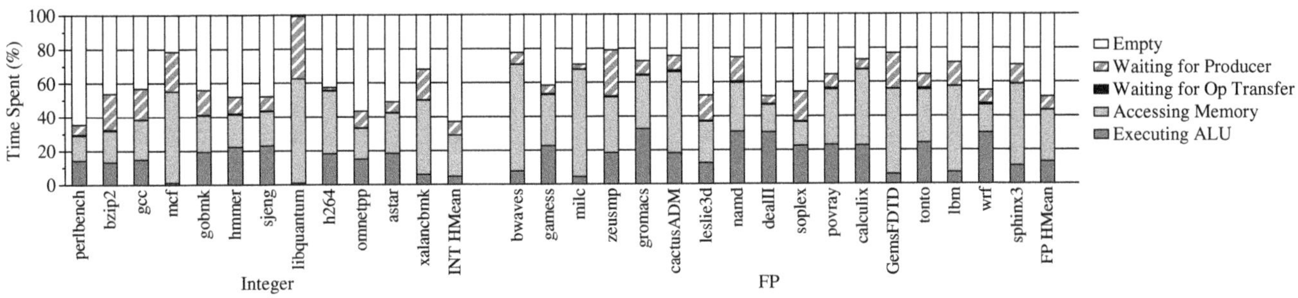

Figure 13. Average cycles spent on each EU state with 8 EUs

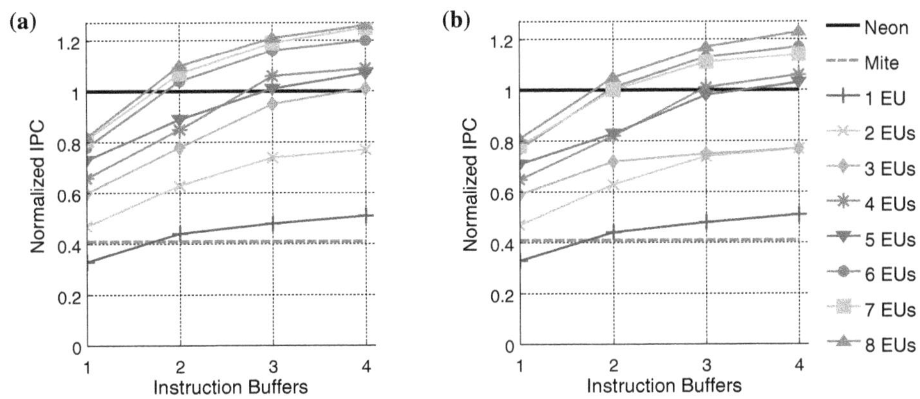

(c)

EUs \ IBs	1	2	3	4
1	0.0	0.0	0.0	0.0
2	0.0	0.0	0.0	0.0
3	***-1.9***	***-8.1***	***-22***	***-24***
4	-1.8	-3.1	-4.3	-2.7
5	***-3.4***	***-7.0***	***-2.3***	***-3.4***
6	-1.5	-3.0	-2.4	-2.0
7	***-3.2***	***-6.6***	***-7.3***	***-8.8***
8	-1.1	-4.1	-3.3	-2.3

Figure 14. Harmonic mean IPCs relative to the Neon (a) 4-EU cluster size. (b) 2-EU cluster size. (c) IPC degradation (%) of the 2-EU cluster size compared to the 4-EU cluster size.

pendent chains. Note that WiDGET's hierarchical operand network in lieu of the Neon's full operand bypass has little effect on the EUs. EUs spend less than 1% of the time on waiting for operands to be transferred, which is accomplished by enforcing cluster affinity at the steering logic.

As Salverda and Zilles observed [31], the limiting factor of WiDGET's performance is the number of independent instruction chains the system can expose, not the issue bandwidth. To overcome this, we expand the buffering capability by allocating multiple IBs to each EU. Despite the same issue bandwidth, an EU can now buffer more than one stalled chain while permitting an independent chain in another IB to utilize the otherwise idle execution engine. This change, however, requires each EU to have simple instruction issue selection logic; we use an oldest-instruction-first policy. Nevertheless, the logic is much less complex than that of a monolithic OoO as long as the number of IBs per EU is kept small. WiDGET's selection logic, with 8 EUs and 4 IBs each, only consumes 3% of the Neon's centralized instruction selection logic power. We also enlarge the size of the empty and full bit vectors in the steering logic to the total number of IBs. The steering complexity is managed by keeping the cluster locality invariant.

Figure 14(a) summarizes the performance benefits of increased buffering. The harmonic mean IPCs of the entire SPEC CPU2006 benchmark suite is presented, normalized to the Neon. WiDGET performs comparably to the Neon with at least 12 IBs, which is explained by the benchmarks' dataflow characteristics. When an ROB has 128 entries, which is our configuration, the integer and floating-point benchmarks have 8 and 12 extractable independent chains, respectively (these results not shown). With 4 IBs per EU, as few as 3 EUs are sufficient, while 8 EUs outperform the Neon by 26%—a sharp contrast to 18% degradation by the 1 IB counterpart. Therefore, mapping chains of dependent instructions to the sufficient number of buffers achieves extraction of ILP and memory-level parallelism despite the in-order issue constraints. WiDGET can also scale down with a single EU and an IB with performance slightly less than the Mite, offering a wide performance range of 3.8.

It is clear that the performance sees diminishing returns after 7 EUs with 4 IBs each, obviating the need for more than 2 clusters. Rather, an interesting comparison is to 8 EUs with 3 IBs, which yield similar performance. 7 EUs with 4 IBs deploy more buffers than 8 EUs with 3 IBs, while the latter uses more ALUs. We evaluate the tradeoff from the power dissipation perspective in Section 5.4.

5.3 Impacts of a Cluster Size

Cluster sizes impact WiDGET performance, making it non-monotonic with increasing EU count. Figure 14(a) illustrates this anomaly for the 5-EU case with three or four IBs, which is caused by the hierarchical operand network that employs a single-cycle link to bridge two adjacent clusters of 4 fully bypassed EUs. Hence, the 5-EU design forms a highly unbalanced system of a cluster of 4 EUs and a single EU. As dependent instructions are steered to the same cluster for locality, instruction chains steered to the single-EU cluster are likely to stall the front-end due to a lack of buffers. Increased buffer count mitigates the stalls, though it also creates opportunities for other independent chains to be steered to the single-EU cluster, causing structural hazards.

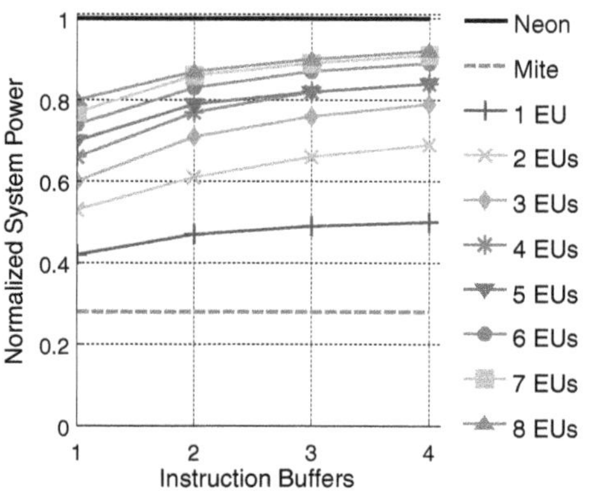

Figure 15. Harmonic mean system power relative to the Neon

mcf, which has a complex dataflow, is primarily responsible for degrading the harmonic mean IPC.

Reducing the cluster size to 2 has more dramatic performance impacts. Even though it can simplify steering logic and intra-cluster full-bypass network, Figure 14(b) demonstrates that the performance becomes highly sensitive to the cluster formation. With 3 or more IBs per EU, the odd EU configurations degrade the performance of the even EU configurations once 2 EUs are assigned. Therefore, under this cluster size, WiDGET must allocate a pair of EUs to gain benefits, resulting in coarser-grained power proportionality. We thus use a cluster size of 4 for the rest of the paper.

5.4 Power Range of WiDGET

Figure 15 presents the harmonic mean system power of the SPEC CPU2006 benchmark suite, normalized to the Neon. We did a best-effort validation of the Neon and Mite power consumption against Atom [9] and Xeon [37] processors, respectively, by first configuring them using the published data. We power down non-provisioned EUs [14].

The shape of WiDGET's curve resembles that of the performance curve in Figure 14, demonstrating the power proportionality. WiDGET, composed of simple building blocks, achieves 8-58% power savings compared to the Neon. Furthermore, WiDGET's EU modularity enables scaling down the power by up to 2.2 to approximate the Mite's low power. The crossing of the 4- and 5-EU lines, unlike the rest of the monotonic power increase with EU count, is due to the relationship of the hierarchical operand network and the steering heuristic as before.

Figure 15 elucidates the previous section's performance and EU provisioning tradeoff. Since power consumption of 7 EUs with 4 IBs and 8 EUs with 3 IBs are almost identical, one can resort to the former, the slightly higher performing configuration. This has additional benefits of stealing less EUs from a neighbor, allowing more threads to run in parallel as the power budget permits.

WiDGET's power increase from dedicating more EUs is not solely due to the additional resources, but is also the result of higher utilization in the existing resources. As Figure 16 shows, the breakdown for harmonic mean system power of the SPEC CPU2006 benchmark suite is divided into two broad categories, each with four subcategories: caches and core logic. *Fetch/Decode/Rename*, which includes a branch predictor and an instruction translation buffer, accounts for most of the front-end logic. WiDGET's instruction steering logic, despite residing in the front-end, and the execution core are included in the *Execution* component to make a fair comparison with Neon and Mite for power stemming from the execution model. Hence, this category encompasses in-order instruction queues for the Mite and WiDGET, an OoO instruction queue for the Neon, operand network, and a data translation lookaside buffer. *Backend* and *ALU* include the commit logic and the ALU resources, respectively.

Enlarging resource allocation has a first-order impact on the ALU and execution power, whereas a second-order impact is increased activity in the system caused by the larger effective window size, resulting in proportional power growth in Fetch/Decode/Rename, L1D, and L2. Yet, WiDGET's considerable power savings compared to Neon comes from the difference in the execution models. WiDGET effectively replaces the Neon's associative search in the OoO issue queue and the full bypass with simple in-order EUs and the hierarchical operand network, resulting in 24-29% reduction in the execution power. This is sufficient to mask out WiDGET's additional power resulting from the higher ALU count, even in the 8-EU case.

The breakdown is also useful to understand the power gap between Mite and WiDGET's 1 EU with 1 IB configuration. WiDGET's OoO support in the instruction engine, namely register renaming and ROB, is primarily responsible for the extra power. Nonetheless, WiDGET achieves a wide power range of 2.2.

Figure 17 puts together the power-performance relationship of the three designs. It is the same graph as Figure 2, except with differentiation of WiDGET's EU count. WiDGET consumes 21% less power than the Neon for the same performance (i.e., 3 EUs with 4 IBs), and yields 8% power savings for 26% better performance (i.e., 8 EUs with 4 IBs). WiDGET dissipates power in proportion to the performance, covering both the high-performance Neon and the low-power Mite on a single chip.

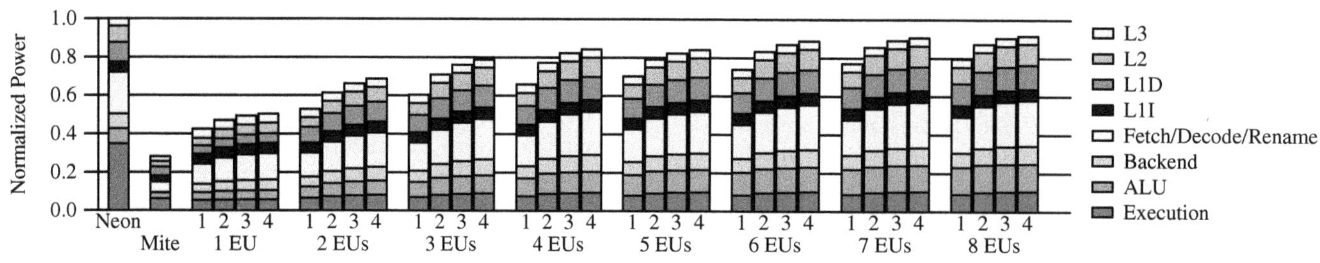

Figure 16. Power breakdown relative to the Neon

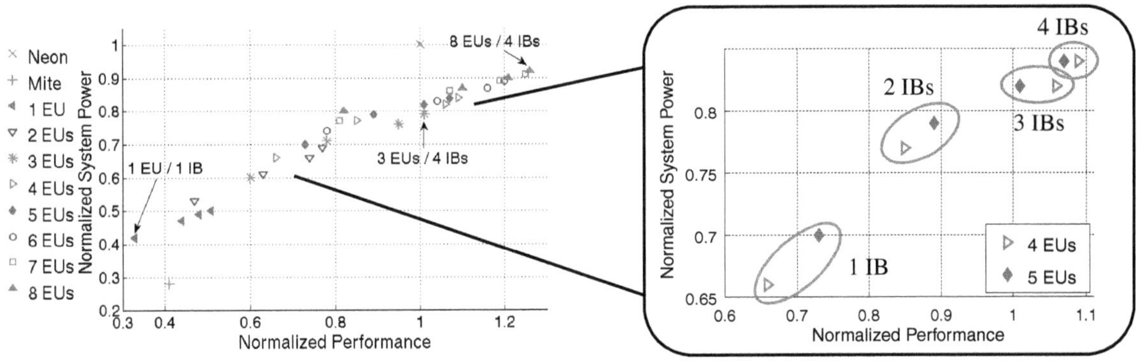

Figure 17. Power Proportionality of WiDGET compared to Neon and Mite

For a more detailed look at Figure 17, we provide a blown-up cutout focusing on the 4- and 5-EU data points that do not follow the rest of the power-performance trend due to the unbalanced clusters. The data points of each EU count correspond to 1 through 4 IBs from left to right. The distance between the 4- and 5-EU points shrinks as the number of IBs per EU increases from 1 to 2. With 3 or 4 IBs, the positions of the 4- and 5-EU points are swapped; the 5-EU points are to the left and lower than their 4-EU counterparts. Hence, it is not beneficial to increase buffers after allocating 2 IBs to the 5-EU configuration.

Finally, Figure 18 compares power efficiency of the three processor designs. We use $BIPS^3/W$ as the metric, which is appropriate for evaluating efficiency differentials caused by microarchitectural designs [12]. Notably, the diagonal line in the figure demarks the seven of WiDGET's configurations below the line that deliver higher power efficiency than the Neon despite the lower performance: 6-8 EUs with 1 IB, 3-5 EUs with 2 IBs, and 3 EUs with 3 IBs. Furthermore, WiDGET is 48% more power efficient than the Neon when achieving the same performance and exceeds the Neon and Mite by up to 2x and 21x, respectively.

6. CONCLUSION

We proposed a power proportional design called WiDGET. The decoupling of the computation resources enables flexibility to provision EUs to meet different power-performance goals. WiDGET can be optimized for high throughput and low power by provisioning a small number of EUs to each instruction engine. When one or more powerful cores are needed to meet service-level agreements, for instance, system software can dedicate more EUs to accelerate single thread performance. By using only as many resources as necessary to deliver target performance, WiDGET achieves power-proportional computing.

Despite the use of in-order EUs to save power, WiDGET yields even higher performance than the aggressive Neon by deploying sufficient buffering for scheduled instructions and steering based on dependences. This distributed instruction buffering was the key to single thread performance and we believe global distributed buffering, if managed well, can yield performance for other forms of parallelism. The distributed instruction buffers improve latency tolerance, allowing independent chains to execute ahead of earlier,

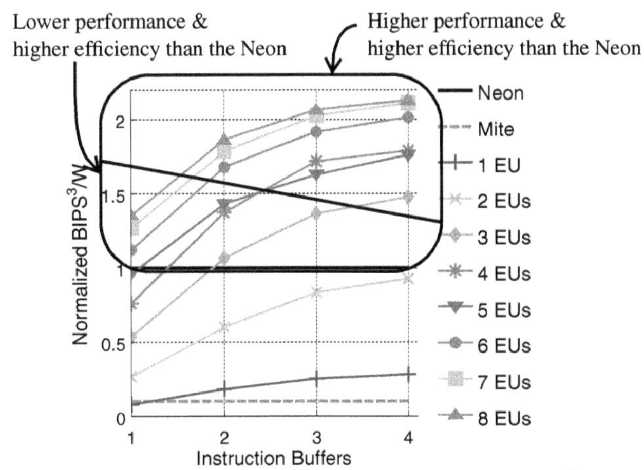

Figure 18. Geometric mean power efficiency ($BIPS^3/W$)

stalled chains, which is our mechanism to extract ILP and memory level parallelism. Furthermore, the removal of OoO execution logic contributes to the primary power savings of WiDGET, resulting in 24-29% reduction in the execution power compared to Neon. We experimentally showed that WiDGET consumes 21% less power than the Neon for the same performance and achieves 8% power savings for 26% better performance than Neon.

This paper focused on the single thread capability of WiDGET. In the future, we will evaluate it in a multi-threaded context, generalizing power proportionality to energy proportionality. Many open questions still remain, including policies for dynamic EU provisioning both within and across instruction engines, guaranteeing service-level agreements in the hardware, and harnessing other shared resources, such as the L2 and off-chip bandwidth. We would also like to explore multithreading the instruction engines for further power savings. A case where this is valuable is multithreaded applications with high cache miss rates. Since instruction engines would spend most of the time idle waiting for the memory requests, it is more energy efficient to consolidate such threads onto a single instruction engine and turn off other instruction engines. In this case, the distributed instruction buffers within an EU could also be used for thread instruction buffers, providing another level of multi-threading beyond what could be available in the IE. EUs may also be specialized to better accommodate different types and phases of applications. An example is a deployment of a few EUs tuned for streaming memory accesses and a computation-intensive EU.

WiDGET is the first step towards a grand goal of a unified framework for extracting parallelism with high energy efficiency. Specifically, we would like to achieve an energy proportional design that reconfigures the cores to meet a power-performance target of a given workload mix.

7. ACKNOWLEDGMENTS

This work is supported in part by the National Science Foundation (NSF), with grants CCR-0324878, CNS-0551401, CNS-0720565, and CCF-0916725, as well as donations from Microsoft and Sun Microsystems/Oracle. The views expressed herein are not necessarily those of the NSF, Microsoft or Sun Microsystems/Oracle. Prof. Wood has a significant financial interest in Microsoft.

We thank Dan Gibson, Steven Kunkel, James Laudon, Charles P. Thacker, Philip M. Wells, and anonymous reviewers for their comments on the paper.

8. REFERENCES

[1] D. Albonesi, R., Balasubramonian, S. Dropsbo, S. Dwarkadas, F. Friedman, M. Huang, V. Kursun, G. Magklis, M. Scott, G. Semeraro, P. Bose, A. Buyuktosunoglu, P. Cook, and S. Schuster. Dynamically tuning processor resources with adaptive processing. *IEEE Computer*, 36(2):49–58, Dec. 2003.

[2] G. M. Amdahl. Validity of the Single-Processor Approach to Achieving Large Scale Computing Capabilities. In *AFIPS Conference Proceedings*, pages 483–485, Apr. 1967.

[3] A. Baniasadi and A. Moshovos. Instruction distribution heuristics for quad-cluster, dynamically-scheduled, superscalar processors. In *Proc. of the 27th Annual Intnl. Symp. on Computer Architecture*, June 2000.

[4] L. A. Barroso and U. Hölzle. The Case for Energy-Proportional Computing. *IEEE Computer*, 40(12), 2007.

[5] D. Brooks, V. Tiwari, and M. Martonosi. Wattch: A Framework for Architectural-Level Power Analysis and Optimizations. In *Proc. of the 27th Annual Intnl. Symp. on Computer Architecture*, pages 83–94, June 2000.

[6] R. Canal, J.-M. Parcerisa, and A. Gonzalez. A Cost-Effective Clustered Architecture. In *Proc. of the Intnl. Conf. on Parallel Architectures and Compilation Techniques*, Oct. 1999.

[7] A. P. Chandrakasan, S. Sheng, and R. W. Brodersen. Low-Power CMOS Digital Design. *IEEE Journal of Solid-State Circuits*, 27(4):473–484, April 1992.

[8] M. S. Floyd, S. Ghiasi, T. W. Keller, K. Rajamani, F. L. Rawson, J. C. Rubio, and M. S. Ware. System power management support in the IBM POWER6 microprocessor. *IBM Journal of Research and Development*, 51(6), 2007.

[9] G. Gerosa, S. Curtis, M. D'Addeo, B. Jiang, B. Kuttanna, F. Merchant, B. Patel, M. Taufique, and H. Samarchi. A Sub-2 W Low Power IA Processor for Mobile Internet Devices in 45 nm High-k Metal Gate CMOS. *IEEE Journal of Solid-State Circuits*, 44(1):73–82, 2009.

[10] J. González and A. González. Dynamic Cluster Resizing. In *Proceedings of the 21st International Conference on Computer Design*, 2003.

[11] L. Hammond, B. Hubbert, M. Siu, M. Prabhu, M. Chen, and K. Olukotun. The Stanford Hydra CMP. *IEEE Micro*, 20(2):71–84, March-April 2000.

[12] A. Hartstein and T. R. Puzak. Optimum Power/Performance Pipeline Depth. In *Proc. of the 36th Annual IEEE/ACM International Symp. on Microarchitecture*, Dec. 2003.

[13] M. D. Hill and M. R. Marty. Amdahl's Law in the Multicore Era. *IEEE Computer*, pages 33–38, July 2008.

[14] Z. Hu, A. Buyuktosunoglu, V. Srinivasan, V. Zyuban, H. Jacobson, and P. Bose. Microarchitectural techniques for power gating of execution units. In *International Symposium on Low Power Electronics and Design*, pages 32–37, Aug. 2004.

[15] Intel and Core i7 (Nehalem) Dynamic Power Management, 2008.

[16] E. Ipek, M. Kirman, N. Kirman, and J. F. Martinez. Core Fusion: Accomodating Software Diversity in Chip Multiprocessors. In *Proc. of the 34th Annual Intnl. Symp. on Computer Architecture*, June 2007.

[17] S. Keckler, D. Burger, K. Sankaralingam, R. Nagarajan, R. McDonald, R. Desikan, S. Drolia, M. Govindan, P. Gratz, D. Gulati, H. H. amd C. Kim, H. Liu, N. Ranganathan, S. Sethumadhavan, S. Sharif, and P. Shivakumar. *Architecture and Implementation of the TRIPS Processor.* CRC Press, 2007.

[18] C. Kim, S. Sethumadhavan, M. S. Govindan, N. Ranganathan, D. Gulati, D. Burger, and S. W. Keckler. Composable Lightweight Processors. In *Proc. of the 40th Annual IEEE/ACM International Symp. on Microarchitecture*, Dec. 2007.

[19] H. S. Kim and J. E. Smith. An instruction set and microarchitecture for instruction level distributed processing. In *Proc. of the 29th Annual Intnl. Symp. on Computer Architecture*, May 2002.

[20] P. Kongetira, K. Aingaran, and K. Olukotun. Niagara: A 32-Way Multithreaded Sparc Processor. *IEEE Micro*, 25(2):21–29, Mar/Apr 2005.

[21] R. Kumar, D. Tullsen, P. Ranganathan, N. Jouppi, and K. Farkas. Single-ISA Heterogeneous Multi-core Architectures for Multithreaded Workload Performance. In *Proc. of the 31st Annual Intnl. Symp. on Computer Architecture*, pages 64–75, June 2004.

[22] G. Magklis, G. Semeraro, D. H. Albonesi, S. G. Dropsho, S. Dwarkadas, and M. L. Scott. Dynamic Frequency and Voltage Scaling for a Multiple-Clock-Domain Microprocessor. *IEEE Micro*, 23(6):62–68, Nov/Dec 2003.

[23] P. S. Magnusson et al. Simics: A Full System Simulation Platform. *IEEE Computer*, 35(2):50–58, Feb. 2002.

[24] M. M. K. Martin, D. J. Sorin, B. M. Beckmann, M. R. Marty, M. Xu, A. R. Alameldeen, K. E. Moore, M. D. Hill, and D. A. Wood. Multifacet's General Execution-driven Multiprocessor Simulator (GEMS) Toolset. *Computer Architecture News*, pages 92–99, Sept. 2005.

[25] D. Meisner, B. T. Gold, and T. F. Wenisch. PowerNap: Eliminating Server Idle Power. In *Proc. of the 14th Intnl. Conf. on Architectural Support for Programming Languages and Operating Systems*, Mar. 2009.

[26] S. Palacharla and J. E. Smith. Complexity-Effective Superscalar Processors. In *Proc. of the 24th Annual Intnl. Symp. on Computer Architecture*, pages 206–218, June 1997.

[27] K. K. Rangan, G.-Y. Wei, and D. Brooks. Thread Motion: Fine-Grained Power Management for Multi-Core Systems. In *Proc. of the 36th Annual Intnl. Symp. on Computer Architecture*, June 2009.

[28] V. J. Reddi, B. Lee, T. Chilimbi, and K. Vaid. Web Search Using Small Cores: Quantifying the Price of Efficiency. *Technical Report MSR-TR-2009-105, Microsoft Research*, Aug. 2009.

[29] J. Renau, K. Strauss, L. Ceze, W. Liu, S. Sarangi, J. Tuck, and J. Torrellas. Energy-Efficient Thread-Level Speculation on a CMP. *IEEE Micro*, 26(1), Jan/Feb 2006.

[30] A. Roth and G. S. Sohi. Register Integration: A Simple and Efficient Implementation of Squash Reuse. In *Proc. of the 33rd Annual IEEE/ACM International Symp. on Microarchitecture*, pages 223–234, Dec. 2000.

[31] P. Salverda and C. Zilles. Fundamental performance constraints in horizontal fusion of in-order cores. In *Proc. of the 14th IEEE Symp. on High-Performance Computer Architecture*, pages 252–263, Feb. 2008.

[32] L. Seiler, D. Carmean, E. Sprangle, T. Forsyth, M. Abrash, P. Dubey, S. Junkins, A. Lake, J. Sugerman, R. Cavin, R. Espasa, E. Grochowski, T. Juan, and P. Hanrahan. Larrabee: a many-core x86 architecture for visual computing. In *Proceedings of the International Conference on Computer Graphics and Interactive Techniques*, 2008.

[33] T. Sha, M. M. K. Martin, and A. Roth. NoSQ: Store-Load Communication without a Store Queue. In *Proc. of the 39th Annual IEEE/ACM International Symp. on Microarchitecture*, pages 285–296, Dec. 2006.

[34] T. Shyamkumar, N. Muralimanohar, J. H. Ahn, and N. P. Jouppi. CACTI 5.1. Technical Report HPL-2008-20, Hewlett Packard Labs, 2008.

[35] J. E. Smith. Decoupled Access/Execute Computer Architecture. In *Proc. of the 9th Annual Symp. on Computer Architecture*, pages 112–119, Apr. 1982.

[36] G. Sohi, S. Breach, and T. Vijaykumar. Multiscalar Processors. In *Proc. of the 22nd Annual Intnl. Symp. on Computer Architecture*, pages 414–425, June 1995.

[37] S. Tam, S. Rusu, J. Chang, S. Vora, B. Cherkauer, and D. Ayers. A 65nm 95W Dual-Core Multi-Threaded Xeon Processor with L3 Cache. In *Proc. of the 2006 IEEE Asian Solid-State Circuits Conference*, Nov. 2006.

[38] F. Tseng and Y. N. Patt. Achieving Out-of-Order Performance with Almost In-Order Complexity. In *Proc. of the 35th Annual Intnl. Symp. on Computer Architecture*, June 2008.

[39] Wisconsin Multifacet GEMS Simulator. http://www.cs.wisc.edu/gems/.

[40] B. Zhai, D. Blaauw, D. Sylvester, and K. Flaunter. Theoretical and Practical Limits of Dynamic Voltage Scaling. In *Proc. of the 41st Annual Design Automation Conference*, pages 868–873, June 2004.

Forwardflow: A Scalable Core for Power-Constrained CMPs

Dan Gibson
Computer Sciences Department
University of Wisconsin—Madison
1210 W. Dayton St.
Madison, WI 53706
gibson@cs.wisc.edu

David A. Wood
Computer Sciences Department
University of Wisconsin—Madison
1210 W. Dayton St.
Madison, WI 53706
david@cs.wisc.edu

ABSTRACT

Chip Multiprocessors (CMPs) are now commodity hardware, but commoditization of parallel software remains elusive. In the near term, the current trend of increased core-per-socket count will continue, despite a lack of parallel software to exercise the hardware. Future CMPs must deliver thread-level parallelism when software provides threads to run, but must also continue to deliver performance gains for single threads by exploiting instruction-level parallelism and memory-level parallelism. However, power limitations will prevent conventional cores from exploiting both simultaneously.

This work presents the Forwardflow Architecture, which can scale its execution logic up to run single threads, or down to run multiple threads in a CMP. Forwardflow dynamically builds an explicit internal dataflow representation from a conventional instruction set architecture, using forward dependence pointers to guide instruction wakeup, selection, and issue. Forwardflow's backend is organized into discrete units that can be individually (de-)activated, allowing each core's performance to be scaled by system software at the architectural level.

On single threads, Forwardflow core scaling yields a mean runtime reduction of 21% for a 37% increase in power consumption. For multithreaded workloads, a Forwardflow-based CMP allows system software to select the performance point that best matches available power.

Categories and Subject Descriptors

C.1: [**Processor Architectures**]: Multiple Data Stream Architectures (Multiprocessors), Other Architecture Styles—*Adaptable architectures*

General Terms

Performance, Design

Keywords

Chip Multiprocessor (CMP), Power, Scalable Core

ISCA'10, June 19–23, 2010, Saint-Malo, France.

If you were plowing a field, which would you rather use: Two strong oxen or 1024 chickens?

—Attributed to Seymour Cray

1 INTRODUCTION

The last several years have witnessed a paradigm shift in the microprocessor industry, from chips holding one increasingly complex out-of-order core to chips holding a handful of simpler cores [13, 32]. While Moore's Law continues to promise more transistors [8], power and thermal concerns have driven the industry to focus on more power-efficient multicore designs. Microarchitects hope to improve applications' overall efficiency by focussing on thread-level parallelism (TLP), rather than instruction-level parallelism (ILP) within a single thread.

At least two fundamental problems undermine this vision. First, microprocessor vendors are already shipping products in which not all cores can simultaneously operate at full speed due to power constraints [14]. This trend is likely to continue, as the fraction of active transistors decreases with each technology generation [6, 34].

Second, Amdahl's Law still applies. Even well-parallelized applications have sequential bottlenecks that limit their parallel speedup, and most applications are not currently parallel at all. A thousand simple cores may maximize performance in an application's parallel section, but simple cores exacerbate sequential bottlenecks by providing limited ILP. Hill and Marty's multicore model [11] leads to the conclusion that "researchers should seek methods of increasing core performance even at high cost." In other words, rather than simply double the number of simple cores when the transistor count doubles, architects should budget some of the additional transistors to increase single-thread performance instead.

Together, these two problems motivate *scalable cores*: cores that can trade off power and performance as the situation merits. Scaling core performance means scaling core resources to extract additional ILP, either by statically provisioning cores differently or by dynamically (de)allocating core resources. Conventional core microarchitectures have evolved largely in the uniprocessor domain, and scaling their microarchitectural structures in the CMP domain poses significant complexity and power challenges.

In a scalable core, resource allocation changes over time. Cores must not rely on powered-off components to function correctly when scaled down, and must not wastefully broad-

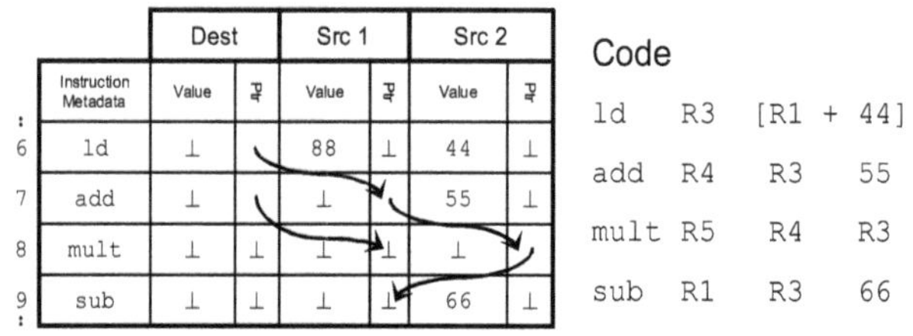

Figure 1. Dataflow Queue Example

cast across large structures when scaled up. Designers of scalable cores should avoid structures that are difficult to scale, like centralized register files and bypassing networks. Instead, they should focus on structures that can be easily disaggregated, and powered-on incrementally to improve core performance independent of other structures.

This work presents the *Forwardflow Architecture*, a scalable core design targeted at power-constrained CMPs leveraging a modular instruction window. Forwardflow represents inter-instruction dependences via a linked list of *forward pointers* [23, 24, 35]. Instructions, values, and data dependences reside in a distributed *Dataflow Queue* (DQ), as illustrated in Figure 1. The DQ is comprised of independent banks and pipelines, which can be activated or de-activated by system software to scale a core's execution resources.

In a Forwardflow-based CMP, single-thread performance can be increased by scaling up a single core (19% runtime reduction on SPEC INT 2006, 25% on SPEC FP 2006, 9% on the Wisconsin Commercial Workload Suite). Other cores can be scaled down (e.g., with DVFS [14]) or disabled to stay within the power budget. Even for multi-threaded workloads, scaling is still valuable when the power consumed does not exhaust the supply. Forwardflow cores can continue to scale performance up until a desired power budget has been reached.

Forwardflow's design delivers both high-performance and energy efficiency. Overall, Forwardflow cores are more efficient than a traditional core baseline in 44 of 47 studied benchmarks. No one configuration is most efficient in all cases, but because Forwardflow cores can scale, they enable system software to optimize a CMP for the desired metric, whether it be performance, energy efficiency, or low chip-wide power consumption.

2 TOWARD SCALABLE CORES

The most important feature of scalable (processor) cores is that they have multiple operating configurations at varied power/performance points. Scalable cores can *scale up*, allowing single-threaded applications to aggressively exploit ILP and MLP to the limits of available power, or can *scale down* to exploit TLP with more modest (and less power-hungry) single-thread performance. To compete with traditional designs, a scalable core should have a nominal operating point at which it delivers performance comparable to a traditional out-of-order core at comparable power, and should offer more aggressive configurations when scaled up. In other words, performance itself should not be sacrificed for performance scaling.

Canonical work in this domain, *Core Fusion* [15] and *Composable Lightweight Processors* [16], compose entire cores to scale all pipeline resources at the same rate. Our work differs by observing that many workloads do not effectively utilize even relatively narrow instruction fetch (e.g., four instructions per cycle). To do so, Little's Law suggests that a core must maintain enough instructions in flight to match the product of fetch width and the average time between dispatch and commit (or squash). These buffered instructions constitute an *instruction window*—the predicted future execution path. As memory latencies increase, cores require large windows to exploit even modest fetch bandwidth. Our work builds on this insight by focusing on scaling window size to expose parallelism in memory-intensive workloads.

However, not all instructions in the window are alike. In a typical out-of-order design, instructions not yet eligible for execution reside in an *instruction scheduler*. The scheduler determines when an instruction is ready to execute (wakeup) and when to actually execute it (selection), based on operand availability. In general, instruction *windows* are easily scalable because they are SRAM-based, while many instruction *schedulers* are not because they rely on CAM-based [36] or matrix-based [10, 27] broadcast for wakeup and priority encoders for selection.

Because many workloads are limited by latency to memory, it is important for high-performance cores—and scalable cores when scaled up—to service as many memory accesses concurrently as possible. However, a non-scalable instruction scheduler limits how much MLP a core can exploit, due to a phenomenon called *IQ (scheduler) clog* [33], in which the scheduler fills with instructions dependent on a long-latency operation (such as a cache miss). Optimizations exist to attack this problem, e.g., by steering dependent instructions into queues [22], moving dependent instructions to a separate buffer [26], and tracking dependences on only one source operand [17]. These proposals ameliorate, but do not eliminate, the poor scalability of traditional instruction schedulers.

Runahead Execution, Waiting Instruction Buffers, and Continual Flow Pipelines address the scheduler problem by draining a scheduler of non-ready instructions (e.g., by buffering instructions [18,31] or by simply discarding them [7, 21]). Drained instructions are no longer eligible for scheduling, and therefore they cannot wake and issue until they are re-inserted into the scheduler.

Another approach to improving scheduler scalability is to name the first successor of a value explicitly with a pointer [23, 24, 35], thereby reducing the likelihood of broadcasts in the scheduling hardware—broadcasts become corner cases but are still necessary. These approaches reduce scheduler complexity and power in fixed-size cores because most instructions have few successors [24, 27]. Our core design exploits this observation ubiquitously, by using

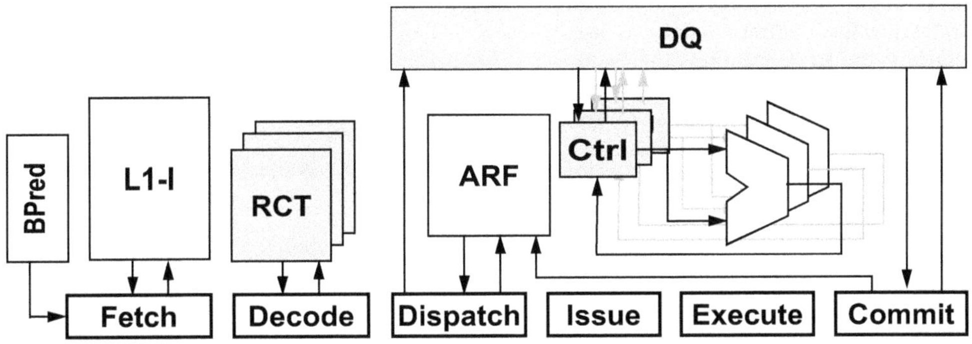

Figure 2. Pipeline diagram of the Forwardflow architecture. Forwardflow-specific structures are shaded.

pointers to represent not only the first register dependency, but *all* register and memory dependences (via NoSQ [28]), thereby *completely eliminating broadcasts*. Like the dataflow architectures that inspired this work [3,25], our design leverages these same dependence pointers to direct data flow within the core itself, rather than relying on a centralized physical register file.

3 FORWARDFLOW ARCHITECTURE

In Forwardflow cores, inter-instruction dependences are represented as linked lists of *forward pointers* [23, 24, 35], instead of using physical register identifiers to label values. These pointers, along with values for each operand, are stored in the *Dataflow Queue* (DQ), shown in Figure 1, which takes the place of the traditional scheduler and centralized physical register file. Instead of broadcasting, DQ update hardware chases pointers to implement instruction wakeup. Though most dependence lists are short, serializing wakeup causes some slowdown. However, the use of pointers throughout the design enables a large, multi-banked DQ implementation, which allows independent lists to be chased concurrently.

At the highest level, the Forwardflow pipeline (Figure 2) is not unlike traditional out-of-order microarchitectures. The Fetch stage fetches instructions on a predicted execution path, and Decode detects and handles potential data dependences, analogous to traditional renaming. Dispatch inserts instructions into the Dataflow Queue (DQ) and instructions issue when their operands become available. When instructions complete, scheduling logic wakes and selects dependent instructions for execution. Instructions commit in-order from the DQ.

3.1 Frontend

In Forwardflow, Fetch proceeds no differently than other high-performance microarchitectures. Decode produces all information needed for Dispatch, which inserts the instruction into the DQ and updates the forward pointer chains. Decode must determine which pointer chains, if any, each instruction belongs to. It does this using the Register Consumer Table (RCT), which tracks the *tails* of all active pointer chains in the DQ. Indexed by the architectural register name, the RCT resembles a traditional rename table except that it records the most-recent instruction (and operand slot) to *reference* a given architectural register. Each instruction that writes a register begins a new value chain, but instructions that read registers also update the RCT to maintain the forward pointer chain for subsequent successors. The RCT also identifies registers last written by a committed instruction, and thus which values can be read at dispatch-time from the Architectural Register File (ARF).

The RCT is implemented as a RAM-based table. Since the port requirements of the RCT are significant, we expect it to be implemented aggressively and with some duplication. Fortunately, the RCT itself is small: each entry requires only $2 \cdot \lceil \log_2 N_{DQEntries} \rceil + 4$ bits.

3.2 The Dataflow Queue (DQ)

The Dataflow Queue (DQ) is the heart of the Forwardflow architecture, and is involved in instruction dispatch, issue, completion, and commit. The DQ is essentially a CAM-free Register Update Unit [30], in that it schedules and orders instructions, but also maintains operand values. Each entry in the DQ holds an instruction's metadata (e.g., opcode, ALU control signals, destination architectural register name), three data values, and three forward pointers, representing up to two source operands and one destination operand per instruction. Value and pointer fields have empty/full and valid bits, respectively, to indicate whether they contain valid information. Dispatching an instruction allocates a DQ entry, but updates the pointer fields of *previously* dispatched instructions. Specifically, an instruction's DQ insertion will update zero, one, or two pointers belonging to *earlier* instructions in the DQ to establish correct forward dependences.

Figure 3 illustrates the dispatch process for a simple code sequence, highlighting both the common case of a single successor (the `R4` chain) and the uncommon case of multiple successors (the `R3` chain). Fields read are bordered with thick lines; fields written are shaded. The bottom symbol (⊥) is used to indicate NULL pointers (i.e., cleared pointer valid bits) and cleared empty/full bits.

In the example, Decode determines that the `ld` instruction is ready to issue at Dispatch because both source operands are available (`R1`'s value, `88`, is available in the ARF, since its busy bit in the RCT is zero, and the immediate operand, `44`, is extracted from the instruction). Decode updates the RCT to indicate that `ld` produces `R3` (but does not add the `ld` to `R1`'s value chain, as `R1` remains available in the ARF).

Dispatch reads the ARF to obtain R1's value, writes both operands into the DQ, and issues the ld immediately. When the add is decoded, it consults the RCT and finds that R3's previous use was as the ld's destination field, and thus Dispatch updates the pointer from ld's destination to the add's first source operand. Like the ld, the add's immediate operand (55) is written into the DQ at dispatch. Dispatching the add also reads the ld's result empty/full bit. Had the ld's value been present in the DQ, the dispatch of the add would stall while reading the value array.

The mult's decode consults the RCT, and discovers that both operands, R3 and R4, are not yet available and were last referenced by the add's source 1 operand and the add's destination operand, respectively. Dispatch of the mult therefore checks for available results in both the add's source 1 value array and destination value array, and appends the mult to R3's and R4's pointer chains. Finally, like the add, the sub appends itself to the R3 pointer chain, and writes its dispatch-time ready operand (66) into the DQ.

Values for instruction operands may be obtained in four ways, each of which are handled differently in Forwardflow:

- Immediate operands, extracted from the instruction itself, are written into the instruction's appropriate operand value array in Dispatch (e.g., the add's second operand, 55).
- The Architectural Register File (ARF) is read in Dispatch to provide committed values to dispatching instructions (e.g., the ld's first source operand, R1). Values from the ARF are written into the instruction's operand value array, to ensure that values are local to instructions and can be accessed at issue-time without consulting potentially distant structures (e.g., a centralized register file).
- Values produced by earlier in-flight instructions that have not yet executed (i.e., values not available at the successor's dispatch) will be delivered to the instruction by the pointer chasing hardware (e.g., this will be the case for the add, mult, and sub instructions).
- Values from earlier in-flight instructions that have already executed (identified via empty/full bits on value arrays) are read from the previous successor's (or producer's) value array and written into the dispatching instruction's value array (does not appear in the example).

3.3 Wakeup, Selection, and Issue

Once an instruction has been inserted into the DQ, it waits until its unavailable source operands are delivered by the execution management logic. Each instruction's DQ entry number (i.e., its address in the RAM) accompanies the instruction though the execution pipeline. When an instruction nears completion in its functional pipeline, pointer chasing hardware reads the instruction's destination value pointer. This pointer defines the value chain for the result value, and, in a distributed manner, locations of all succes-

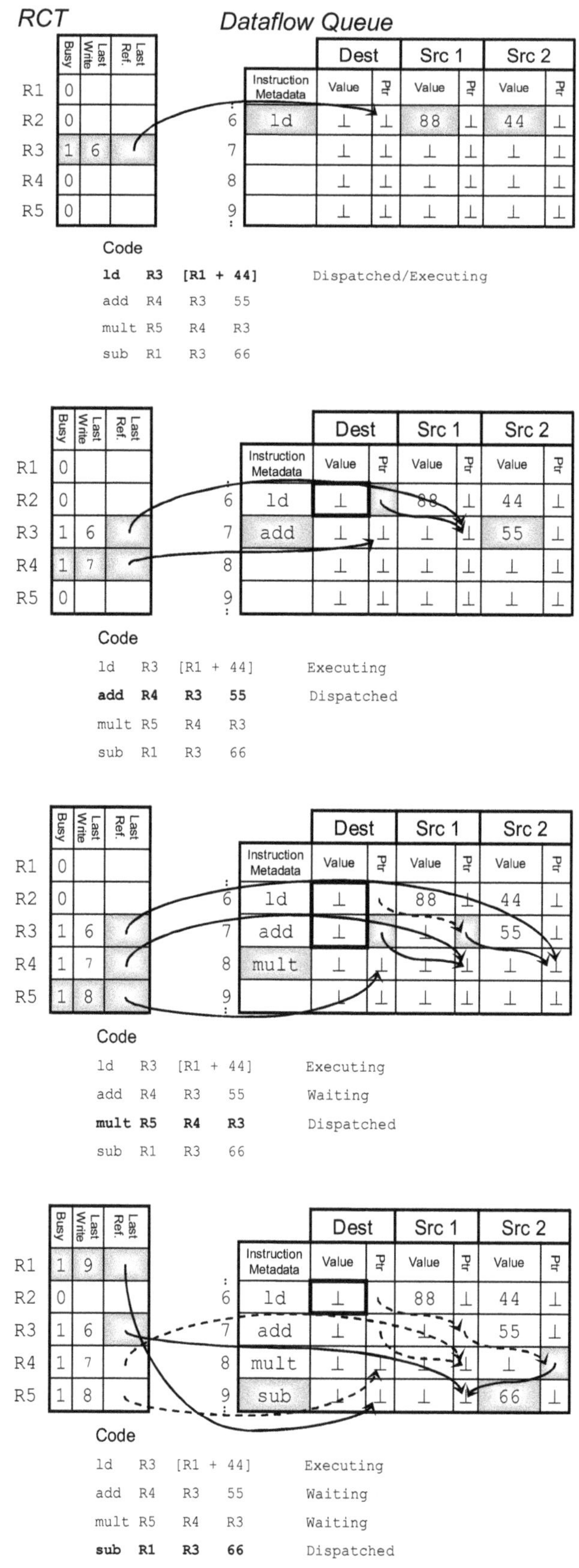

Figure 3. Dispatch Example

sors through transitive pointer chasing. The complete traversal of a chain is a multicycle operation, and successors beyond the first will wakeup (and potentially issue) with delay linearly proportional to their position in the chain.

The wakeup process is illustrated in Figure 4. Upon completion of the `ld`, the memory value (`99`) is written into the DQ, and the `ld`'s destination pointer is followed to the first successor, the `add`. Whenever a pointer is followed to a new DQ entry, available source operands and instruction metadata are read speculatively, anticipating that the arriving value will enable the current instruction to issue (a common case [17]). Thus, in the next cycle, the `add`'s metadata and source 2 value are read, and, coupled with the arriving value of `99`, the `add` may now be issued. Concurrently, the update hardware reads the `add`'s source 1 pointer, discovering the `mult` as the next successor.

As with the `add`, the `mult`'s metadata, other source operand, and next pointer field are read. In this case, the source 1 operand is unavailable, and the `mult` will issue at a later time (when the `add`'s destination pointer chain is chased). Finally, following the `mult`'s source 2 pointer to the `sub` delivers `99` to the `sub`'s first operand, enabling the `sub` to issue. At this point, a NULL pointer is discovered at the `sub` instruction, indicating the end of the value chain.

After instructions have been executed (i.e., when the empty/full bit on the destination operand's field has been set), instructions are removed from the head of the DQ and committed in program order. Commit logic removes the head instruction from the DQ by updating the DQ's head pointer and writes to the ARF where applicable. If the RCT's last writer field matches the committing DQ entry, the RCT's busy bit is cleared and subsequent successors may read the value directly from the ARF. The commit logic is not on the critical path of instruction execution, and the write to the ARF is not timing critical as long as space is not needed in the DQ for instruction dispatch.

As stated above, the pointer chasing hardware is responsible for issuing instructions to functional units during traversal. Should a particular instruction be unable to issue because of a structural hazard (i.e., all functional units are busy), the pointer chase must stall until the instruction can issue normally. Nominally, this condition is only a minor performance overhead. Rarely, a second structural hazard can arise when pointer chain that would normally begin its chase requires the use of stalled pointer-chasing control circuitry. This forms a circular dependence, as the functional unit cannot accept a new operation (i.e., the current result must first be collected from the functional unit) and the pointer-chasing hardware must stall until it can issue the current instruction, resulting in deadlock. The intersection of these two control hazards is rare, and can be ameliorated by modest buffering. Should deadlock still arise, the circular dependence is easily detected (i.e., all functional units are stalled and the update hardware is stalled), and can be resolved with a pipeline flush; ordering

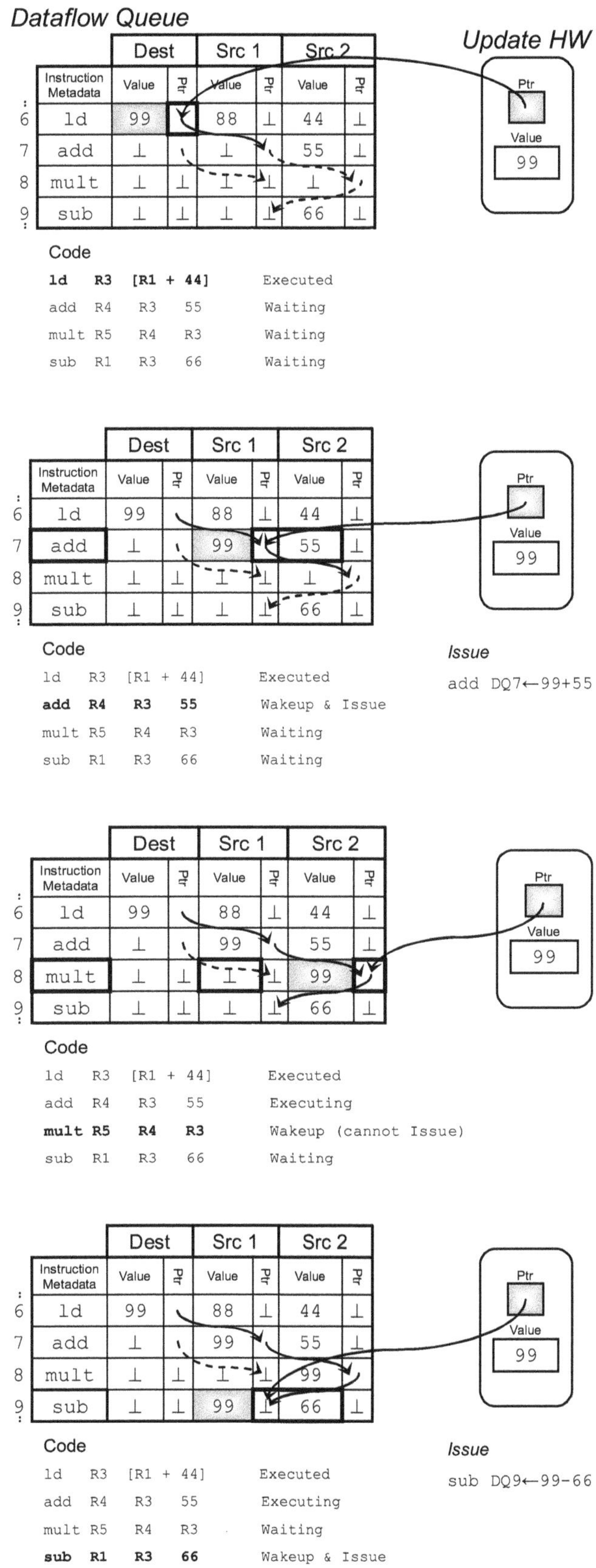

Figure 4. Wakeup Example

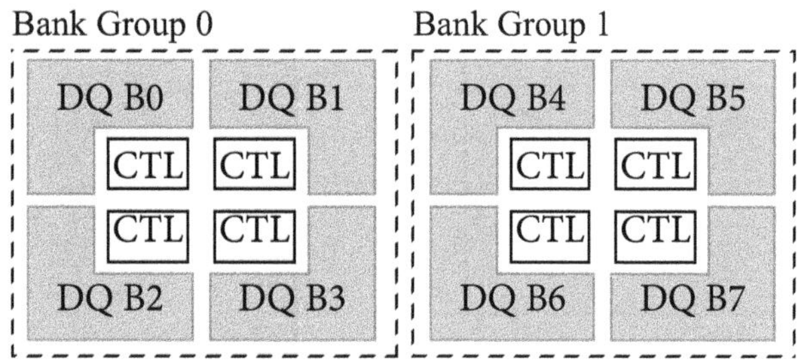

Figure 5. Eight-Bank Hierarchical DQ Floorplan

properties of functional units guarantees forward progress of at least one instruction.

3.4 Distributed Implementation

The number of value chains that may be followed concurrently in a given cycle is bounded by the number of banks (and ports) on the DQ. Pointers that designate operands in a distant bank must traverse a significant chip area. Figure 5 illustrates a conceptual Forwardflow floorplan that arranges eight DQ banks in groups of four; pointers that cross bank groups incur additional latency. Functional pipelines are associated with groups, so execution resources can scale with window size.

The DQ is sub-banked on low-order bits of the DQ entry number to support concurrent access to contiguous elements. Sub-banking delivers ample bandwidth to dispatch and commit logic—which access the DQ contiguously—without adding additional ports. Each field of the DQ is implemented as a separate SRAM (e.g., value fields are separate from each pointer field, etc.), to further simplify the design, and to enable greater concurrency in the DQ management logic.

Since the DQ is built entirely of small SRAMs, it can scale to much larger sizes than a traditional instruction scheduler, yet is accessed at finer granularity than a ROB. Each entry in the DQ requires an estimated $200 + 3 \cdot \lceil \log_2 N_{DQEntries} \rceil$ bits of storage across all fields.

3.5 Pointer Chasing Hardware

In our design, each bank of the DQ is serviced by an independent instance of the pointer chasing hardware shown in Figure 6, consisting of a **`next`** pointer register, a current **`value`** register, a *pending queue* of pointer/value pairs, and buffered ports to the interconnect between the banks of the DQ. The logical behavior is described in the accompanying algorithm, which runs every cycle. Since DQ entry numbers accompany instructions through functional pipelines, pointers to destination fields can be inferred as instructions complete execution.

During a given cycle, the update hardware for a particular bank will attempt to follow exactly one pointer. If no pointer is available (line 8), the DQ is not accessed by the update hardware, thereby conserving power. Otherwise, if `next` designates a non-destination field (i.e., one of the two source operands), the remaining source operand (if present) and instruction opcode are read from the DQ, and the

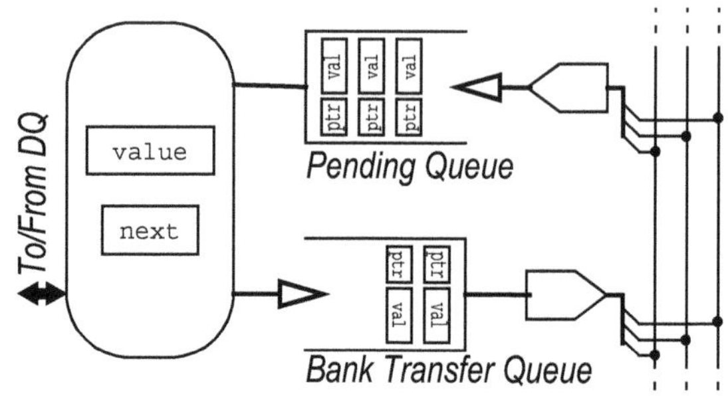


```
1   // Handle pending queue
2   if next == NULL:
3     next = in.ptr
4     value = in.val
5     in.pop()
6
7   if next == NULL:
8     return // No work to do
9
10  // Try to issue, if possible
11  if type(next) != Dest &&
12    dq[next].otherval.isPresent:
13    val2 = dq[next].otherval
14    opcode = dq[next].meta
15    if !Issue(opcode, val, val2):
16      return // Stall
17
18  dq[next].val = value
19  next = dq[next].ptr
20
21  // Handle DQ bank transfer
22  if bank(next) != bank(this):
23    out.push(next,value)
24    next = NULL
```

Figure 6. Pointer Chasing Hardware and Algorithm

instruction is passed to issue arbitration (line 15). If arbitration for issue fails, the update hardware stalls on the current `next` pointer and will issue again on the following cycle.

The update hardware writes the arriving value into the DQ (line 18) and reads the pointer at `next` (line 19), following the list to the next successor. If the pointer designates a DQ entry assigned to a different bank, the pair `<next,value>` is placed in the bank transfer queue (line 23), and will traverse the interconnect in the next cycle.

The inter-DQ-bank interconnect itself is comprised of a first-level crossbar between neighboring banks (refer to Figure 5) for fast communication between logically adjacent DQ entries. A second-level crossbar connects each bank group, with additional communication delay. For maximum performance, the update hardware optimizes the case where `next` is initially NULL, the pending queue is empty, and a new pointer/value pair arrives from the interconnect.

3.6 Control Speculation

Like other out-of-order machines, Forwardflow relies on dynamic branch and target prediction to improve pipeline

Table 1. Configuration Parameters

Component	*OoO*	*F-1*	*F-2*	*F-4*
Window Size	128	128 (One Bank Group)	256 (Two Bank Groups)	512 (Four Bank Groups)
Scheduler Type	Hybrid [12]	Forwardflow		
Scheduler Size	Unified 32-entry	Full Window		
Functional Units	2xI-ALU/2xFP-ALU/ 2xD-MEM	2xI-ALU/2xFP-ALU/ 2xD-MEM	4xI-ALU/4xFP-ALU/ 2xD-MEM	8xI-ALU/8xFP-ALU/ 2xD-MEM
Branch Prediction	YAGS 4K PHT 2K Exception Table, 2KB BTB, 16-entry RAS			
Disambiguation	NoSQ [28] 1024-entry predictor, 1024-entry double-buffered SSBF			
Fetch-Dispatch Time	Min. 7 Cycles			
L1-I Cache	32KB, 4-way, 64B line, 4-cycle pipelined, 2 lines per cycle, 2 processor-side ports			
L1-D Cache	32KB, 4-way, 64B line, 4-cycle LTU, write-through, write-invalidate, included by L2			
L2 Cache	1 MB, 8-way, 4 banks, 64B line, 11 (12) cycle load (store) latency, write back, private			
L3 Cache	8 MB, 16-way, 8 banks, 64B line, 24 cycle latency, shared			
Main Memory	2 QPI-like Links (Up to 64GB/s), 300 cycle latency			
Coherence	MOESI-based Directory Protocol			
On-Chip Interconnect	2D Mesh, 16B bidirectional links, one transfer per cycle, 1-cycle 5-ary routers, 5 virtual channels per link			

utilization. Branch recovery mechanisms must restore the RCT's state as it was before the instructions following the branch were decoded, and invalidate all false-path instructions. The former is accomplished by checkpointing the RCT on predicted branches, a technique identical to the checkpointing of a register rename table. To accomplish the latter, we augment the pointer fields with valid bits, which are checkpointed with RCTs on branch predictions and restored on misprediction events [24].

Not all forms of recovery can be handled by restoring from checkpoints. When exceptions or interrupts occur, it is legal to flush all instructions that follow the excepting instruction and quiesce the pipeline. This allows decode to resume with an empty RCT. So long as recoveries of this type are rare cases, performance impact is limited.

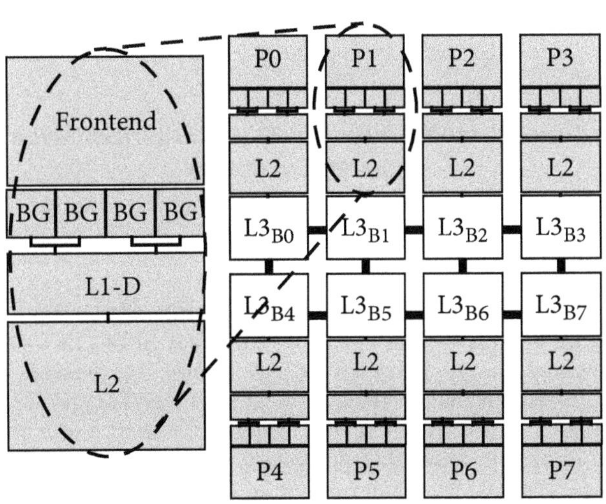

Figure 7. 8-Way CMP Target

3.7 Scaling Forwardflow Cores

The use of pointers throughout the design enables Forwardflow's control logic to handle window size reconfiguration gracefully—pointers are already oblivious of the structure to which they *point*. Since the DQ is managed as a FIFO, it is a simple matter to modify the head and tail pointer wraparound logic to accommodate variable DQ capacities that are powers of two, using simple modulo-2^N logic. DQ size can be abstracted as a power-control state [14], manageable by system software. Unused bank groups can safely be power-gated. While some prior work has examined techniques for dynamically adapting a core's aggressiveness in hardware [2], for now, we leave this policy decision to software. This work is agnostic of the precise mechanism that software might use to make scaling decisions, but many solutions are possible, including static profiling, online monitoring, and dynamic adaptation.

4 METHODOLOGY

Our target machine is an 8-way CMP, pictured in Figure 7. Each node consists of a core, a private L1/L2 cache hierarchy, and one bank of a large, shared L3. We assume each core and private cache hierarchy operates in its own voltage domain, and furthermore that bank groups in the Forwardflow designs can be independently powered off. We evaluate Forwardflow using full-system cycle-accurate simulation, using Virtutech Simics [19], GEMS's Ruby [20], and in-house timing-first processor models. We simulate SPEC CPU 2006 [9], SPEC OMP [4], and Wisconsin commercial workloads [1]. We report ED and ED^2 as our measures of energy efficiency.

We include a traditional out-of-order implementation as our baseline (*OoO*), to show that a nominal Forwardflow core performs comparably to a more traditional architecture. All target machines use NoSQ [28] for memory disambiguation. Our implementation of NoSQ represents memory dependences by inserting artificial register dependences,

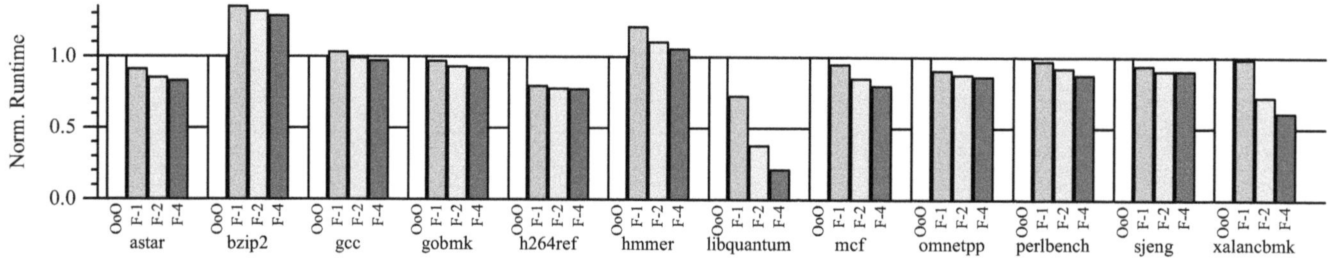

Figure 8. SPEC INT 2006 Runtime

which are enforced by the DQ as though a genuine register dependency existed. NoSQ's predictions are verified via store vulnerability filtering and load replay at commit-time.

We evaluate three Forwardflow configurations with progressively larger DQs: *F-1*, *F-2*, and *F-4*. *F-1* has the same window size and the same number of execution resources as *OoO*. *F-1* has a four-way banked DQ; each bank has 32 entries. With the exception of cache bandwidth and capacity (held constant, as we do not scale the L1-D or D-TLB), *F-2* has twice the execution resources of *F-1*—it represents two *F-1* backends powered-on, similar to Figure 5. *F-4* again doubles backend resources (i.e., four powered-on backends), for an aggregate window size of 512 entries, peak issue rate of 18 (8 INT, 8 FP, 2 MEM).

Our target machines run unmodified SPARCv9 operating systems and binaries. We model hardware-assisted TLB fill and register window exceptions for all target machines. We simulate each benchmark for one hundred million instructions. Multiple runs are used to achieve tight 95% confidence intervals (error bars are not visible in most cases). Benchmarks are fast-forwarded past their initialization phases, during which page tables, TLBs, predictors, and caches are warmed. We have augmented our simulators with Wattch [5] and CACTI 5 [29], which provide architectural-level approximations of power consumed by logic and memory structures in the 32nm process. Our model assumes aggressive clock gating of logic structures not in use, with no reactivation delay. L2 and L3 caches are implemented with variable bias to control leakage and Low Standby Power Devices [29] are used throughout the design, accounting for low overall leakage power.

5 EVALUATION

We first consider the behavior of single threads on single cores of our 8-way CMP. We assume the seven unused cores are in an off state in which they consume no power (this assumption also applies to their private L2 caches, but *not* to their shared L3 banks—single-thread benchmarks observe the full L3 capacity). We believe this mode of operation will not be uncommon in future chips, as commodity multi-threading remains elusive for many workloads.

A scalable core allows core configuration to be customized by system software, so it is possible to have the best of all worlds in most situations. We envision that this capability will complement DVFS in the positive scaling direction (i.e., can be used to scale performance up beyond what frequency scaling alone can provide). However, for due

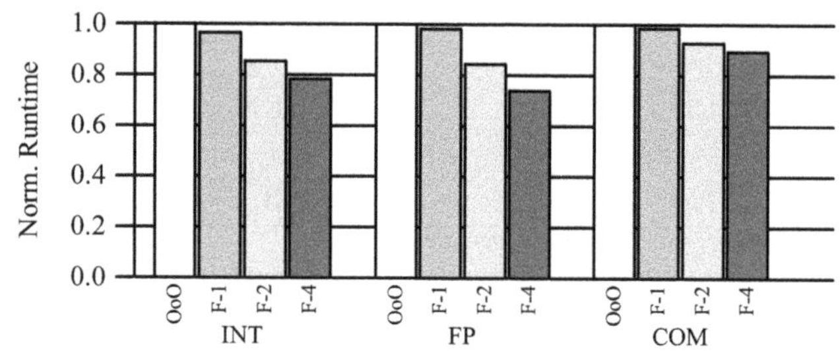

Figure 9. a) INT, FP, and COM Mean Runtime

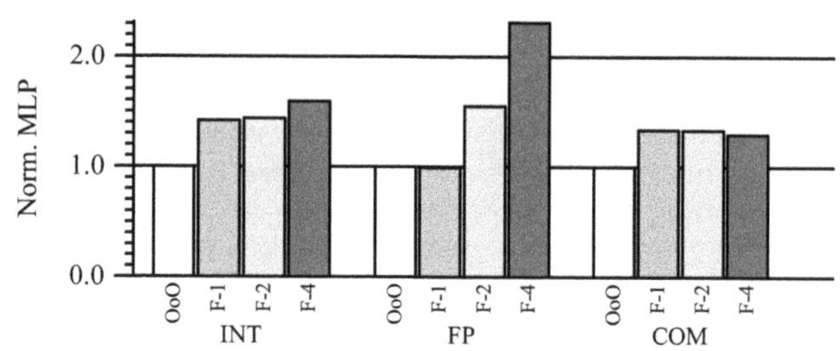

Figure 9. b) INT, FP, and COM Mean MLP

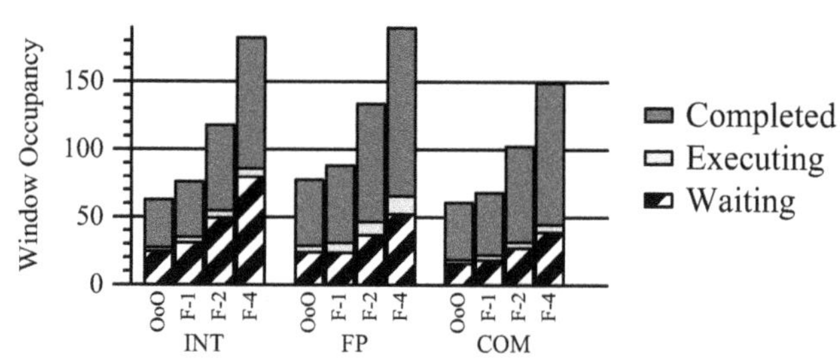

Figure 9. c) INT, FP, and COM Categorized Mean Window Occupancy

diligence, we evaluate all configurations, with the full expectation that not all points will be favorable for all configurations.

5.1 Single-Threaded Performance Results

Figure 8 presents runtimes for individual SPEC INT 2006 benchmarks, normalized to *OoO*. Figure 9.a presents the geometric means for SPEC INT, SPEC FP and single-thread versions of the commercial workloads. Overall, these show the expected result that performance improves as window size increases: the mean runtime of *F-4* is 21% less than *F-1* (23% vs. *OoO*)—indicating that Forwardflow delivers performance scaling for single threaded workloads.

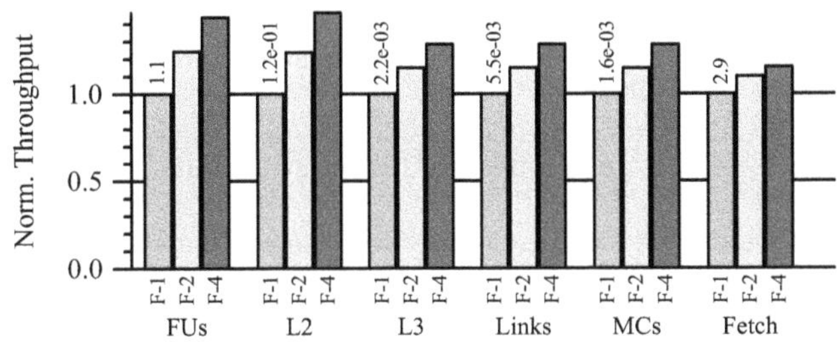

Figure 10. Scaling Effects on Throughput

To gain insight into the behavior of our design, we examine the MLP and categorized window occupancy of each configuration in Figures 9.b and 9.c, respectively. In the latter, we classify post-dispatch instructions into three categories: *Waiting* instructions are not yet eligible to execute because of an unavailable operand (these instructions are scheduler-resident in *OoO*). *Executing* instructions are currently being executed by the functional pipelines, or are outstanding in the memory system. *Completed* instructions have finished execution, but have not yet committed, due to an earlier Waiting or Executing instruction.

MLP and occupancy of Executing instructions (the observed ILP) are of key importance to performance. Across all single-thread benchmarks, univariate regression of Forwardflow runtimes with respect to MLP and Executing occupancy yields median $R^2 = 0.92$ and $R^2 = 0.94$, respectively, suggesting that both play an important role in performance scaling.

OoO suffers from IQ clog in several cases (most dramatically in `libquantum`), limiting performance. Instructions dependent on cache misses fill *OoO*'s scheduler, preventing dispatch—even if ready instructions follow in the subsequent instruction stream. The effect of IQ clog is evident in Figure 9.c: *OoO*'s mean Waiting occupancy is very close to the scheduler size, indicating that the scheduler is often full. The Forwardflow designs, with no disjoint scheduler, do not suffer from scheduler clog (and can therefore accommodate more Waiting instructions). This yields a small runtime reduction of 2.4% for *F-1* versus *OoO*, in spite of the latency of serialized wakeup in Forwardflow cores.

Further insight is offered by considering the throughput of several on-chip structures (Figure 10) as the core is scaled from *F-1* to *F-4*. Not surprisingly, scaling the Forwardflow DQ increases functional unit throughput (*FUs*), but also more aggressively exercises *unscaled* portions of the chip. Throughput at L2 and L3 input ports, on-chip links, memory controllers, and the fetch logic all increase substantially when the core is scaled up. In other words, core scaling enables single threads to better utilize shared chip resources (nominally provisioned for many cores), and to better utilize portions of the core that are not scaled (e.g., *Fetch*).

In three cases, no Forwardflow configuration exceeds the performance of *OoO*. `bzip2` and `hmmer` both exhibit high L1-D hit rates, and thus the latency of serialized wakeup

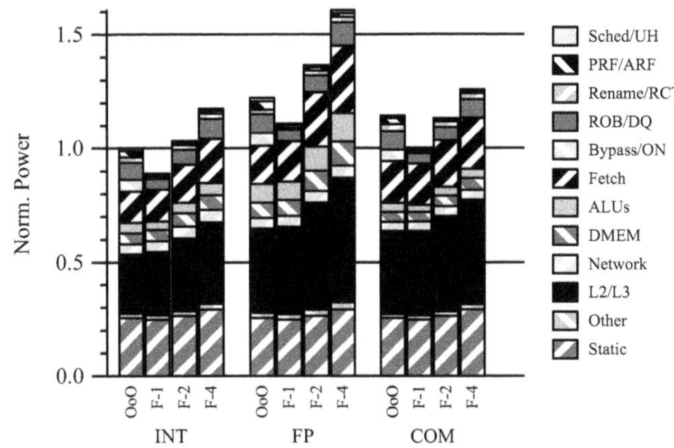

Figure 11. Single-Thread Power Breakdown

cannot be hidden by accesses to memory (`gromacs` from SPEC FP 2006 behaves similarly). Some benchmarks are not particularly sensitive to changes in window size (e.g., `gcc`, `gobmk`, `sjeng`), as these benchmarks are control intensive, and performance gains are quickly lost to branch misprediction. `sjeng`'s performance actually *degrades* as the window size grows beyond a certain point. Forwardflow's performance does not scale perfectly: scaling larger comes at the cost of increased wire delay when communicating with distant DQ elements. Increased operand network delay, and increased delay in dispatching instructions to distant DQ banks can overcome the benefit gained from increased window capacity and issue bandwidth.

5.2 Single-Threaded Power

Figure 11 presents the mean chip-wide power breakdown for each configuration. All power results are normalized to the harmonic mean power consumed by *OoO* when running SPEC INT. We organize power into twelve categories: of those that are not self-explanatory, "Other" includes NoSQ and control logic not suitable for other categories, "Network" refers to the on-chip inter-processor network, "DMEM" includes D-TLBs and L1-D caches, "Fetch" includes I-TLBs and L1-I caches, "Bypass/ON" represents power consumed by *OoO*'s bypassing network or Forwardflow's operand network, and "Sched/UH" represents *OoO*'s scheduler and Forwardflow's update hardware, respectively.

The general trend of power consumption is fairly uniform across all workloads: *F-1* consumes 9.9% less power overall than *OoO*, due to Forwardflow's efficient SRAM-based design. *F-2* and *F-4* tend to exceed *OoO*'s consumption (7.2% and 23% respectively), constituting a dynamic power range of 37% between *F-1* and *F-4*. However, merely exceeding the power consumed by a single active *OoO* core does not imply that the CMP's power budget is exceeded—the power required to operate all cores simultaneously (e.g., Figure 13) is substantially higher than operating *F-4* alone for any one benchmark.

The larger Forwardflow configurations consume more power than *OoO* overall, but much of this increase in power consumption arises because activity increases *elsewhere* on

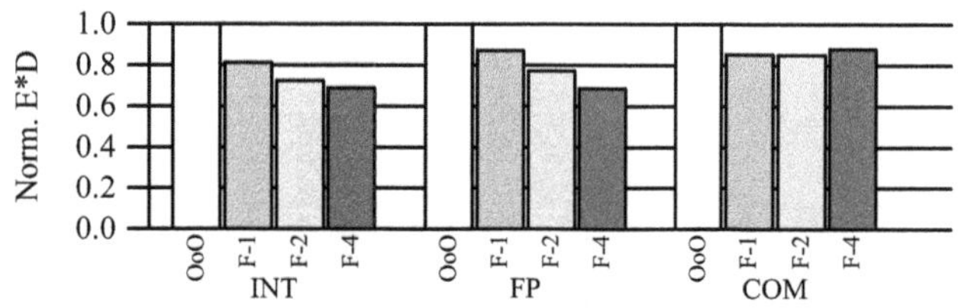

Figure 12. a) Normalized *ED*

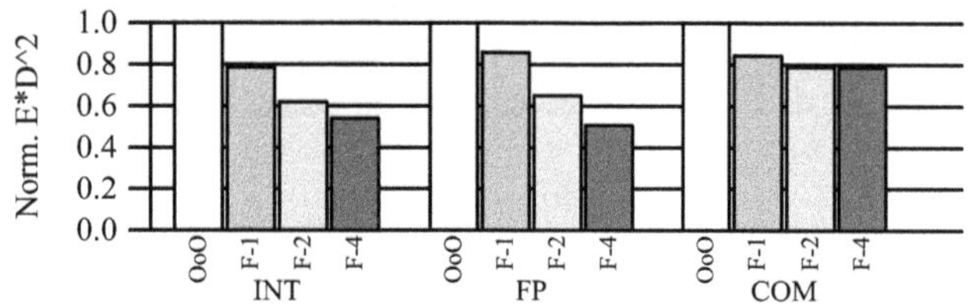

Figure 12. b) Normalized ED^2

the CMP—from the graph, it is evident that the power consumed from Forwardflow-specific components (Sched, RF, RCT, DQ) does not increase as substantially as other core components (e.g., Fetch) or from the on-chip caches (L2/L3). This is a desired result, and follows from the throughputs shown in Figure 10. Forwardflow can scale core performance without concentrating power dissipation in the scaled components.

Figure 12 presents mean *ED* and ED^2. Because *F-1* is both faster and consumes less power than *OoO*, it is not surprising that *F-1* is more efficient overall by these metrics. One of the three Forwardflow configurations minimizes *ED* and ED^2 in 30 of 33 of the single-threaded benchmarks. However, *no single configuration is most efficient for all workloads*—12 benchmarks minimize *ED* with *F-1*, 6 with *F-2*, and 12 with *F-4*. ED^2, with a heavier weight on performance, is optimized in 13 benchmarks by *F-2*, and in 17 by *F-4*. Because no one configuration best suits all workloads, scalable cores in general and Forwardflow cores in particular enable system software to optimize the CMP for peak performance, lowest power consumption, or optimum efficiency, as the situation merits.

5.3 Multithreaded Workloads

We next evaluate the CMP when it is fully utilized by a multithreaded application: either a commercial workload, or one of the SPEC OMP benchmarks. We again evaluate the performance, power, and efficiency of each configuration, but now all eight cores on our CMP are in an active state. In the multithreaded domain, the configuration space becomes significantly more complicated, as the possibility of heterogeneity arises. Though we leave any evaluation of this heterogeneity for future work, we observe that there are a large cross-product of design points between all-*F-1* and all-*F-4*, considering the number of available benchmarks.

Figure 13 plots performance and power of multithreaded benchmarks. Unlike previous runtime graphs, Figure 13 plots speedup normalized to that of *OoO* (*OoO* itself does not explicitly appear on the plots). Each benchmark is represented by a line, beginning with the power/performance point of *F-1*, and continuing to those of *F-2* and *F-4*. Power is normalized to the same scale as Figure 11: Y=1.0 is the power consumed by one *OoO*-core running SPEC INT 2006. Note that SPEC OMP benchmark `art` is absent from the figure, as its behavior is dominated by TLB fill, and does not appear at the chosen scale because of very low overall power consumption.

As with the single-threaded workloads, most of the multithreaded workloads scale in both power consumption and performance from *F-1* to *F-4*, though some benchmarks do not scale at all (e.g., `ammp` and `wupwise` in SPEC OMP). Mean runtime reduction is 12% (8.2%) for OMP (commercial workloads), and is accompanied by an increase in chip power of 32% (40%).

We observe a substantial power range in the objective benchmarks, as each exercises the available resources in a different manner. Depending on the available power budget, it may not be possible to run even scaled-down cores at full speed (e.g., DVFS may be required): *F-1* running `apsi` consumes more than 12x the power of an average single thread of SPEC INT on *OoO*. With the aggressive clock gating used in this study, these ranges are possible, as an individual `apsi` thread is comparable in power consumption to the most power-hungry threads of SPEC CPU (and, of course, there are eight such threads in our OMP benchmarks).

Because we set no quantitative upper bound on our CMP power envelope, we cannot conclude which configurations

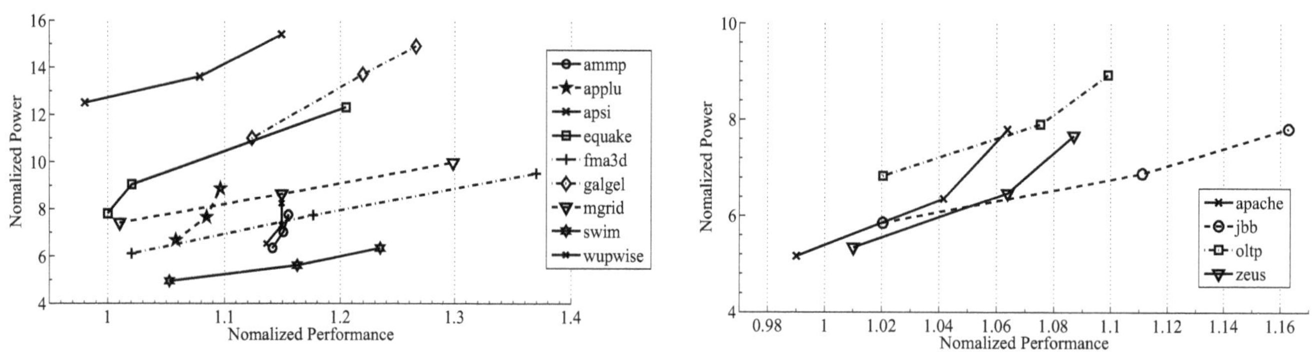

Figure 13. SPEC OMP (left) and Commercial Workload (right) Power vs. Performance

are best. Instead, we briefly consider two hypothetical power budgets. The first is Y=8.0, the power budget at which the CMP is provisioned to allow each core to operate at *OoO*'s power when running SPEC INT. Under this constraint, *OoO* can run 9 of 14 benchmarks at full speed (i.e., without any DVFS to hold power below the accepted maximum). At least one Forwardflow configuration can run without DVFS for all but two of these benchmarks, and several benchmarks (e.g., `equake`, `fma3d`, `jbb`) can safely scale to *F-4*. A second point of interest is Y=14.6, at which all *OoO* configurations can run without employing DVFS. At this power level, all Forwardflow configurations are feasible, except *F-4* running `galgel` or `apsi`. Between these extremes of power budget, Forwardflow configurations—both the evaluated homogeneous and the possible heterogeneous configurations—provide a wealth of dynamic power range for system software to exploit.

As in the single-thread experiments, no single configuration is most efficient for all 14 benchmarks. ED is minimized by *F-1* in 9 cases, by *F-2* in 1, and by *F-4* in the remaining 4. As before, additional performance weight in the ED^2 metric skews the minimum toward more aggressive designs, to *F-1* for 6 benchmarks, *F-2* for 1, and *F-4* for the remaining 7. *OoO* never minimizes ED, nor ED^2.

6 CONCLUSIONS AND FUTURE WORK

Though Moore's Law endures, the fraction of simultaneously active transistors is dropping, and architects must find new methods to deliver both ILP and TLP with a single chip design. Single threads are likely to remain common workloads in many scenarios, but the transition to threading should not be hampered by lack of available parallelism in the hardware. To this end, we have re-evaluated core microarchitecture to design a processor that can scale its execution resources to match the available TLP. Our design, Forwardflow, is a scalable core architecture implementing out-of-order execution with manageable size and complexity. Forwardflow's execution resources can be scaled up to improve single-thread performance by 21% when few threads are available, allowing greater utilization of CMP resources by single threads than a traditional design. We evaluate a Forwardflow design that is ISA-compatible with existing SPARCv9 binaries and operating systems.

The Forwardflow core design itself is efficient and disaggregated. It replaces centralized scheduling logic and register files with a distributed, RAM-based Dataflow Queue (DQ), which can scale gracefully from small to large instruction windows, allowing the system to trade-off power and performance depending on how many DQ banks the system software provisions and enables. This design is more energy-efficient in 44 of 47 studied workloads (by either ED or ED^2 metrics).

Forwardflow joins and, we hope, will be followed by other proposals to address the key issue of single-thread performance in the CMP domain—the design of scalable cores alone is an area worthy of future exploration. Perhaps most importantly, in order for future scalable core designs to flourish, much research remains exploring scaling *policies*. In particular, it is not clear how system software (or some other controlling entity) should go about choosing a core configuration to best match a particular workload in absentia of advance profiling. The complexities of managing power consumption in a CMP are subtle, and as this work has shown, there is no single configuration that will be optimal in all cases. Moreover, benchmark behavior changes in time, and this should be considered in future work addressing these challenges.

ACKNOWLEDGEMENTS

This work is supported in part by the National Science Foundation (NSF), with grants CCR-0324878, CNS-0551401, CNS-0720565, and CCF-0916725, as well as donations from Microsoft and Sun Microsystems/Oracle. The views expressed herein are not necessarily those of the NSF, Microsoft or Sun Microsystems/Oracle. Prof. Wood has a significant financial interest in Microsoft. The authors would like to acknowledge Mark Hill, Yasuko Watanabe, Natalie Enright Jerger, and members of the Multifacet and Multiscalar research groups (past and present), for encouragement, advice, and support. We further acknowledge the attendees of the UW Computer Architecture Affiliates conference for spirited discussion and suggestions, and our anonymous reviewers for their very useful remarks.

REFERENCES

[1] A. R. Alameldeen, C. J. Mauer, M. Xu, P. J. Harper, M. M. K. Martin, D. J. Sorin, M. D. Hill, and D. A. Wood. Evaluating Non-deterministic Multi-threaded Commercial Workloads. In *Proc. of the 5th Workshop on Computer Architecture Evaluation Using Commercial Workloads*, pages 30–38, Feb. 2002.

[2] D. Albonesi, R., Balasubramonian, S. Dropsbo, S. Dwarkadas, F. Friedman, M. Huang, V. Kursun, G. Magklis, M. Scott, G. Semeraro, P. Bose, A. Buyuktosunoglu, P. Cook, and S. Schuster. Dynamically tuning processor resources with adaptive processing. *IEEE Computer*, 36(2):49–58, Dec. 2003.

[3] K. Arvind and R. S. Nikhil. Executing a Program on the MIT Tagged-Token Dataflow Architecture. *IEEE Transactions on Computers*, pages 300–318, Mar. 1990.

[4] V. Aslot, M. Domeika, R. Eigenmann, G. Gaertner, W. Jones, and B. Parady. SPEComp: A New Benchmark Suite for Measuring Parallel Computer Performance. In *Workshop on OpenMP Applications and Tools*, pages 1–10, July 2001.

[5] D. Brooks, V. Tiwari, and M. Martonosi. Wattch: A Framework for Architectural-Level Power Analysis and Optimizations. In *Proc. of the 27th Annual Intnl. Symp. on Computer Architecture*, pages 83–94, June 2000.

[6] K. Chakraborty, P. M. Wells, and G. S. Sohi. Computation Spreading: Employing Hardware Migration to Specialize CMP Cores On-the-fly. In *Proc. of the 12th Intnl. Conf. on Architectural Support for Programming Languages and Operating Systems*, Oct. 2006.

[7] J. Dundas and T. Mudge. Improving Data Cache Performance by Pre-Executing Instructions Under a Cache Miss. In *Proc. of the 1997 Intnl. Conf. on Supercomputing*, pages 68–75, July 1997.

[8] I. T. R. for Semiconductors. ITRS 2006 Update. Semiconductor Industry Association, 2006. http://www.itrs.net/Links/2006Update/2006UpdateFinal.htm.

[9] J. L. Henning. SPEC CPU2006 Benchmark Descriptions. *Computer Architecture News*, 34(4):1–17, 2006.

[10] A. Henstrom. US Patent #6,557,095: Scheduling operations using a dependency matrix, Dec. 1999.

[11] M. D. Hill and M. R. Marty. Amdahl's Law in the Multicore Era. *IEEE Computer*, pages 33–38, July 2008.
[12] M. Huang, J. Renau, and J. Torrellas. Energy-efficient hybrid wakeup logic. In *ISLPED '02: Proceedings of the 2002 international symposium on Low power electronics and design*, pages 196–201, New York, NY, USA, 2002. ACM.
[13] Intel. First the Tick, Now the Tock: Next Generation IntelÆ Microarchitecture (Nehalem). http://www.intel.com/technology/architecture-silicon/next-gen/whitepaper.pd% f, 2008.
[14] Intel. Intel and Core i7 (Nehalem) Dynamic Power Management, 2008.
[15] E. Ipek, M. Kirman, N. Kirman, and J. F. Martinez. Core Fusion: Accomodating Software Diversity in Chip Multiprocessors. In *Proc. of the 34th Annual Intnl. Symp. on Computer Architecture*, June 2007.
[16] C. Kim, S. Sethumadhavan, M. S. Govindan, N. Ranganathan, D. Gulati, D. Burger, and S. W. Keckler. Composable Lightweight Processors. In *Proc. of the 40th Annual IEEE/ACM International Symp. on Microarchitecture*, Dec. 2007.
[17] I. Kim and M. H. Lipasti. Half-price architecture. In *Proc. of the 30th Annual Intnl. Symp. on Computer Architecture*, pages 28–38, June 2003.
[18] A. R. Lebeck, T. Li, E. Rotenberg, J. Koppanalil, and J. P. Patwardhan. A Large, Fast Instruction Window for Tolerating Cache Misses. In *Proc. of the 29th Annual Intnl. Symp. on Computer Architecture*, May 2002.
[19] P. S. Magnusson et al. Simics: A Full System Simulation Platform. *IEEE Computer*, 35(2):50–58, Feb. 2002.
[20] M. M. K. Martin, D. J. Sorin, B. M. Beckmann, M. R. Marty, M. Xu, A. R. Alameldeen, K. E. Moore, M. D. Hill, and D. A. Wood. Multifacet's General Execution-driven Multiprocessor Simulator (GEMS) Toolset. *Computer Architecture News*, pages 92–99, Sept. 2005.
[21] O. Mutlu, J. Stark, C. Wilkerson, and Y. N. Patt. Runahead Execution: An Effective Alternative to Large Instruction Windows. *IEEE Micro*, 23(6):20–25, Nov/Dec 2003.
[22] S. Palacharla and J. E. Smith. Complexity-Effective Superscalar Processors. In *Proc. of the 24th Annual Intnl. Symp. on Computer Architecture*, pages 206–218, June 1997.
[23] S. E. Raasch, N. L. Binkert, and S. K. Reinhardt. A scalable instruction queue design using dependence chains. In *Proc. of the 29th Annual Intnl. Symp. on Computer Architecture*, pages 318–329, May 2002.
[24] M. A. Ramirez, A. Cristal, A. V. Veidenbaum, L. Villa, and M. Valero. Direct Instruction Wakeup for Out-of-Order Processors. In *IWIA '04: Proceedings of the Innovative Architecture for Future Generation High-Performance Processors and Systems (IWIA'04)*, pages 2–9, Washington, DC, USA, 2004. IEEE Computer Society.
[25] K. Sankaralingam, R. Nagarajan, H. Liu, C. Kim, J. Huh, D. Burger, S. W. Keckler, and C. Moore. Exploiting ILP, TLP, and DLP with the Polymorphous TRIPS Architecture. In *Proceedings of the 30th Annual International Symposium on Computer Architecture*, pages 422–433, June 2003.
[26] S. R. Sarangi, W. Liu, J. Torrellas, and Y. Zhou. ReSlice: Selective Re-Execution of Long-Retired Misspeculated Instructions Using Forward Slicing. In *Proc. of the 38th Annual IEEE/ACM International Symp. on Microarchitecture*, Nov. 2005.
[27] P. Sassone, J. R. II, E. Brekelbaum, G. Loh, and B. Black. Matrix Scheduler Reloaded. In *Proc. of the 34th Annual Intnl. Symp. on Computer Architecture*, pages 335–346, June 2007.
[28] T. Sha, M. M. K. Martin, and A. Roth. NoSQ: Store-Load Communication without a Store Queue. In *Proc. of the 39th Annual IEEE/ACM International Symp. on Microarchitecture*, pages 285–296, Dec. 2006.
[29] T. Shyamkumar, N. Muralimanohar, J. H. Ahn, and N. P. Jouppi. CACTI 5.1. Technical Report HPL-2008-20, Hewlett Packard Labs, 2008.
[30] G. S. Sohi and S. Vajapeyam. Instruction Issue Logic for High-Performance Interruptable Pipelined Processors. In *Proc. of the 14th Annual Intnl. Symp. on Computer Architecture*, pages 27–34, June 1987.
[31] S. T. Srinivasan, R. Rajwar, H. Akkary, A. Gandhi, and M. Upton. Continual Flow Pipelines. In *Proc. of the 11th Intnl. Conf. on Architectural Support for Programming Languages and Operating Systems*, Oct. 2004.
[32] M. Tremblay and S. Chaudhry. A Third-Generation 65nm 16-Core 32-Thread Plus 32-Scout-Thread CMT SPARC Processor. In *ISSCC Conference Proceedings*, 2008.
[33] D. M. Tullsen, S. J. Eggers, J. S. Emer, H. M. Levy, J. L. Lo, and R. L. Stamm. Exploiting Choice: Instruction Fetch and Issue on an Implementable Simultaneous Multithreading Processor. In *Proc. of the 23th Annual Intnl. Symp. on Computer Architecture*, pages 191–202, May 1996.
[34] G. Venkatesh, J. Sampson, N. Goulding, S. Garcia, V. Bryksin, J. Lugo-Martinez, S. Swanson, and M. B. Taylor. Conservation Cores: Reducing the Energy of Mature Computations. In *Proc. of the 9th Intnl. Conf. on Architectural Support for Programming Languages and Operating Systems*, Nov. 2000.
[35] R. Vivekanandham, B. Amrutur, and R. Govindarajan. A scalable low power issue queue for large instruction window processors. In *Proc. of the 20th Intnl. Conf. on Supercomputing*, pages 167–176, June 2006.
[36] K. C. Yeager. The MIPS R10000 Superscalar Microprocessor. *IEEE Micro*, 16(2):28–40, Apr. 1996.

Energy-Performance Tradeoffs in Processor Architecture and Circuit Design: A Marginal Cost Analysis

Omid Azizi* Aqeel Mahesri† Benjamin C. Lee* Sanjay J. Patel‡ Mark Horowitz*

*Dept of Electrical Engineering
Stanford University
Stanford, CA
{oazizi,bcclee,horowitz}@stanford.edu

†NVIDIA Corporation
Santa Clara, CA
amahesri@nvidia.com

‡Dept of Electrical and Computer Engineering
University of Illinois at Urbana-Champaign
Urbana, IL
sjp@illinois.edu

ABSTRACT

Power consumption has become a major constraint in the design of processors today. To optimize a processor for energy-efficiency requires an examination of energy-performance trade-offs in all aspects of the processor design space, including both architectural and circuit design choices. In this paper, we apply an integrated architecture-circuit optimization framework to map out energy-performance trade-offs of several different high-level processor architectures. We show how the joint architecture-circuit space provides a trade-off range of approximately 6.5x in performance for 4x energy, and we identify the optimal architectures for different design objectives. We then show that many of the designs in this space come at very high marginal costs. Our results show that, for a large range of design objectives, voltage scaling is effective in efficiently trading off performance and energy, and that the choice of optimal architecture and circuits does not change much during voltage scaling. Finally, we show that with only two designs—a dual-issue in-order design and a dual-issue out-of-order design, both properly optimized—a large part of the energy-performance trade-off space can be covered within 3% of the optimal energy-efficiency.

Categories and Subject Descriptors

C.4 [**Performance of Systems**]: *design studies, modeling techniques*; C.1.0 [**Processor Architectures**]: General

General Terms

Design, Performance

Keywords

Microarchitecture, Energy efficiency, Design trade-offs, Optimization, Design space exploration, Co-optimization

1. INTRODUCTION

Technology scaling has historically been a driving force behind microprocessor performance. As the semiconductor industry has scaled into very small feature sizes, however, the need to control leakage current has prevented further threshold and supply voltage scaling. This break from Dennard scaling [7] has led to rapid increases in power density, and power consumption is now a primary constraint in all microprocessor design [14]. Not only does power dissipation impact battery-life in embedded devices, it also constrains achievable performance in server architectures.

To optimize a microprocessor for energy-efficiency, a designer must consider the cost-benefit trade-offs of all design options, choosing those features and parameter values that offer the best return in terms of performance per unit energy. While this strategy is straightforward in theory, in practice, it has been difficult to automate since the space of processor design options is often extremely large, and one needs to consider trade-offs in the architecture, the circuit design and potentially the technology.

Fortunately, previous research has already created many of the pieces needed to create such an optimization framework. Recent advances in microarchitectural design space modeling through statistical sampling and regression techniques have opened the door to large-scale architectural design space exploration and evaluation [18, 15]. At the circuit level, there also exist numerous tools that can characterize energy-delay trade-offs for a given circuit [22, 6]. Moreover, work over the past few decades has created extremely efficient methods to find the optimal solutions to problems with convex optimization objective functions [3]. We leverage these prior works to characterize a joint circuit-architecture design space; by creating architectural models and circuit trade-off characterizations that have log-convex[1] forms, we use geometric program solvers to optimize our model over this joint design space to map out the overall energy performance trade-off space. We have found that joint architecture and circuit optimization can save between 15% to 150% of the required energy, depending on the design objectives.

In this paper, we use this framework to explore a broad space of designs ranging from a simple single-issue in-order design to an aggressive quad-issue out-of-order machine. The results of the optimization determine the choice of underly-

[1] log-convex functions are convex after applying log transformation.

ing microarchitectural parameters, circuit implementations, and operating voltage. Our results show that, without voltage scaling, the architectural and circuit trade-offs yielded a performance range that was modest: the resulting optimal energy-performance curves tend to have rapidly changing marginal energy costs. Enhancing architecture design parameters to improve performance quickly requires large increases in energy. Conversely, trying to save energy quickly leads to rapid losses in performance. Voltage scaling has more slowly diminishing marginal costs and we find, with voltage scaling, a small subspace of architectures and circuits are efficient for a broad range of performance and energy targets.

2. OPTIMIZATION FRAMEWORK

To evaluate energy-performance trade-offs in the processor design space, we use a circuit-aware architecture optimization framework. In this approach, we first create architectural models using design space sampling and statistical inference, capturing a large multi-dimensional space of microarchitectural parameters. Next, we characterize the energy-delay trade-offs of each of the underlying circuit blocks that are found in processor designs, which we store in a circuit library. The architecture and circuit spaces are then joined together to form an integrated design space model. In this joint model, the architectural models are made aware of the energy-delay trade-offs of the underlying circuits, and any constraints that these circuits may place on the architecture are also enforced. This joint architecture-circuit design space is finally sent to an optimization/exploration engine, which, given an optimization objective and resource budgets, searches the space to find the most efficient design configuration. Figure 1 shows an overview of this co-optimization framework.

The combination of these techniques creates a framework that is both powerful and general. It is powerful since it enables a rigorous study of marginal performance benefits and energy costs of any design decision; with this framework we can identify the parameter values that yield the most energy efficient design for a performance target, or the highest possible performance design for a given energy target. It is general because we can construct architectural models for any system simply by extracting simulation samples from the designer's simulator of choice, and we can include circuit tradeoffs from a broad range of tools. In this framework, building the architectural models and circuit libraries are generally one-time costs, unless new architectures or circuits are being explored. The design space exploration engine, because it uses a convex optimizer, can produce optimized designs in under 30 seconds.

In the following subsections, we provide a brief discussion of each component of this optimization framework. For a more in-depth examination of this framework, we refer the reader to [1].

2.1 Architectural Modeling

At the architectural level, we require models that predict how the architectural performance (CPI) of the overall system changes as we change the underlying parameters. The parameters at this level range from the choice of high-level architecture to the tuning of microarchitectural knobs such as cache sizes and functional unit latencies.

Traditionally, such modeling is done through simulation [2].

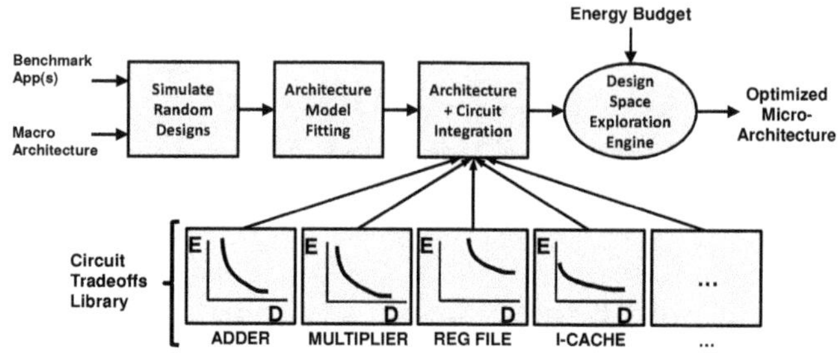

Figure 1: *Overview of the optimization framework. Architectural models are generated using sampling and fitting methods. Energy-delay (E-D) trade-off curves are characterized for each circuit. These design spaces are integrated, and the design space exploration engine finds the optimized design.*

Long run times, however, make simulation intractable for exploring large design spaces. To overcome this restriction, recent works have proposed the use of statistical sampling and inference to create fitted models from a relatively small sample of design points [18, 15, 8]. In these approaches, a small number of random design configurations (with randomly selected design parameter values) are simulated in the traditional manner; the simulation results are then used to infer how the different design parameters interact and affect overall performance. The inference process essentially fits a model to the data through regressions. These approaches produce predictive mathematical models which can be quickly evaluated to estimate the performance in any part of the captured space, and are powerful tools for design space exploration. In previous works, Lee and Brooks used cubic splines [18], whereas Ipek et al. used artificial neural networks [15]; both were shown to produce good fits.

We use similar statistical techniques to create architectural models in our framework. However, instead of the previously suggested functional forms, we use posynomial functions, which are mathematical functions consisting of the sum of any number of positive monomial terms[2] to produce the fits. Using posynomial functions offers the advantage that, as log-convex functions, they can be optimized very efficiently. The potential drawback is that posynomial functions are less general than other forms such as cubic splines, and can have difficulty capturing spaces with complex behaviors involving hills and valleys. Fortunately, the design knobs in the architectural performance space that we are trying to capture usually have a monotonic, diminishing returns profile: for example, reducing a unit's latency or increasing a cache size in the simulator typically only improves performance. It is not expected that turning such knobs would produce hills, valleys or plateaus which would otherwise cause problems. We have compared our fits to cubic spline fits and found them to be of comparable accuracy, thus suggesting that the use of posynomial functions is not generally a restricting factor in the models we produce.

When using a fitting approach to performance modeling, there are still limitations of how much of the design space we can effectively capture. The use of a smooth function such as a posynomial lends itself well to capturing the tunable parameters in the design space. Thus, parameters such as la-

[2] A monomial is a product of powers of variables. For example, $kx^a y^b z^c$ is a monomial in the variables x, y and z with k, a, b, and c as constants.

tencies of units and sizes of structures are often modeled well through posynomial functions. On the other hand, discrete changes to an architecture, such as in-order vs out-of-order execution, or use of centralized vs distributed instruction windows, are less natural to fit with continuous functions. For these these latter design choices—which we refer to as *macro*-architectural design choices—we generate individual models that we optimize separately. Thus, the models we generate predict CPI as a function of the latencies of units and sizes of structures like caches, buffers and queues:

$$CPI = f(..., latency_i, ..., size_j, ...) \qquad (1)$$

Since each application behaves differently, we generate separate models for each benchmark using this approach. The fitted models for each benchmark can then be composed together to produce an overall CPI for a suite of benchmarks.

The number of design space samples required to generate a fit depends on the complexity of the system being modeled. For example, we have found 200 samples often enough for simple in-order processors, and 500 samples to be sufficient for a complex superscalar out-of-order processor. We set aside a fraction of these samples to perform validation. To measure model error, we use the same metric as in [18]: $error = |predicted - actual|/actual$. The average of median errors over different benchmarks range from less than 1% to 6%; more complex macro-architectures such as out-of-order processors tend to be harder to fit.

Figure 2 show three sample fits: a very accurate fit, a typical fit, and a worse fit. Even in the worst case, which is for a particular application running on a complex quad-issue out-of-order processor, the median error is less than 10%. The CDFs of these three fits are also shown to give the reader a sense of the distribution of errors in each of these generated models.

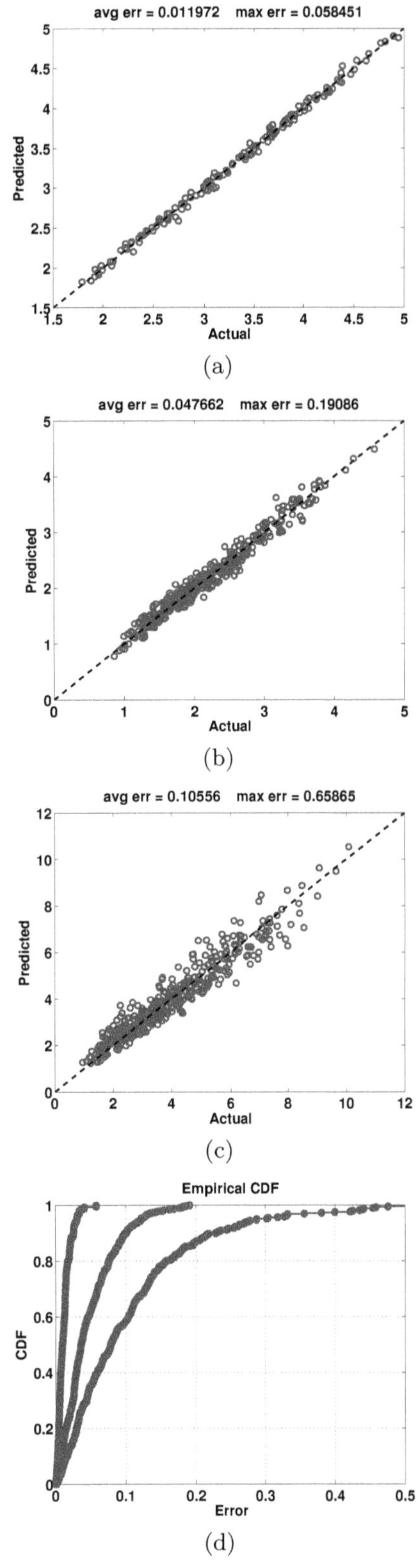

Figure 2: *Validation of three architectural models generated through posynomial design space fitting. (a)-(c) compare model predictions to the results of the simulator. (a) is a very accurate fit, (b) is a typical fit, and (c) is a worse fit. (d) shows the cumulative distribution of errors for these three models. Even in the worst case, the median error is less than 10% for a performance range that spans 10x.*

2.2 Circuit Trade-offs Library

At the circuit/logic level, there is also a large space of design options. A given circuit can be implemented in various ways that trade-off energy and delay. The design space at this level includes the choice of circuit topology (e.g. ripple-carry adders, carry-lookahead adders, etc.), logic synthesis mappings, circuit styles (e.g. static, dynamic, etc.) and the sizing of gates. Because the energy and delay characteristics of these circuits can affect the energy and performance of the higher-level system, we need to explore and characterize this trade-off space for each circuit block.

There are many tools that can help explore the circuit design space [6, 10, 22]. Given a circuit topology, many of these tools can automatically generate energy-delay trade-off curves. By trying different discrete circuit topologies and circuit styles with these tools, one can create a large trade-off space for a circuit [21]. Our optimization framework is not dependent on the particular tool used to explore the circuit design space; it only needs energy-delay points for each circuit. These design points can be annotated so that once a certain circuit energy-delay point is selected, we can back-reference the annotation to determine the specific circuit implementation.

Given a set of design points, our goal is to create a model that predicts the energy cost of a unit per use. For purely logic units, the trade-off is between energy and delay only. For storage structures such as caches, buffers and queues, the delay and energy also depend on their size. Thus, the trade-off characterizations that we produce generally take the form of:

$$Energy = f(Delay), \text{ for logic units} \quad (2)$$

$$Energy = f(Delay, Size), \text{ for memory structures} \quad (3)$$

Just as with the architectural models, we use posynomial functions for $f()$ to produce these characterizations.

We characterize circuits for unpipelined logic. We do this intentionally because cycle time and pipeline depth are parameters in the optimization design space; we account for the energy and delay overheads of inserting pipeline registers during design space integration.

2.3 Design Space Integration

To build the full system model, we need to integrate the architectural and circuit design spaces. This requires making the appropriate links between circuit delays and the pipeline latencies, and then computing the total energy cost from the underlying circuits. For example, one issue with architectural models is that a pipe stage can contain arbitrary amounts of logic. In our integrated model, we make the architectural model aware of the real delays of logic units. We link the physical delays, D_i, of units in the circuit library to the cycle-based latency, N_i, in the architectural model through the cycle time T_{cyc}. The number of pipe stages in a unit is, therefore, the delay of the underlying circuit divided by the clock period T_{cyc} (i.e. cutting the logic into stages). Adding delay overheads for pipeline registers, we get following relationship

$$N_i = D_i/(T_{cyc} - T_{ff}). \quad (4)$$

where T_{ff} includes register setup, clock-to-q times and clock skew overheads.

The optimization framework treats the cycle time, T_{cyc}, as a design space variable (along with D_i and N_i), so it can also explore different pipeline depths for a unit by changing T_{cyc} while holding D_i constant. There is, of course, an energy cost associated with deeper pipelines that comes with an increased number of pipeline registers. This is accounted for in the energy models below.

There may also be certain units that cannot be pipelined. Control units such as the next-PC logic, a processor's instruction scheduler or stall logic may need to compute once a cycle. This is an important consideration as it can place constraints on the cycle time, affecting total performance. In such cases, our framework allows us to specify that these critical logic units cannot be pipelined, accounting for the effects of such circuits on system performance.

We model total energy per instruction (EPI) as the sum of three components: energy spent in logic blocks, in pipeline registers, and in the the clock network. For the logic component, total energy depends on the average energy consumed per use of each circuit, E_i, times its activity rate α_i:

$$EPI_{logic} = \sum_i (\alpha_i \times E_i) \quad (5)$$

The energy cost E_i links directly to the circuit trade-offs. Thus, choosing to use faster circuits will naturally cause an increase in total logic energy.

The energy spent in the registers and the clock network both depend on the number of pipeline registers. We approximate the number of pipeline registers in each unit, R_i, as a function of the number stages, N_i, and the average logic width, W_i. Then, total register energy is the average energy cost of a single register, E_{ff}, times the total number of pipeline registers in that unit, R_i, times the unit's activity factor, α_i. Total clock energy is the total number of registers times the average clock energy, E_{ffclk}, times the cycles per instruction, CPI, to convert it to a per instruction basis.

$$R_i = (N_i)^\eta \times W_i \quad (6)$$

$$EPI_{regs} = \sum_i (\alpha_i \times R_i \times E_{ff}) \quad (7)$$

$$EPI_{clk} = \sum_i (R_i) \times E_{ffclk} \times CPI \quad (8)$$

Here, the parameter η allows for modeling super-linear pipeline register growth, and can be unique for each architectural block. E_{ff} and E_{ffclk} are extracted from real designs. Using these models means that increasing pipeline depth will improve performance, but at an increased energy because of a larger R_i.

For most units, the activity factor α_i, which represents the number of times a unit is used per instruction, can be extracted from the application instruction mix and is constant. With caches, however, the number of times a higher level memory is accessed depends on the miss rate of the cache below it. Thus, we also characterize the miss rate as a function of cache size and use this data in the optimization framework to account for the activity factors of higher level memories as lower level caches change.

3. EXPERIMENTAL METHODOLOGY

We use the optimization framework of Section 2 to explore energy-performance trade-offs in the processor design space. For this study, we examine six different processor architectures: single-issue, dual-issue and quad-issue designs with both in-order and out-of-order execution. This covers a large range of the traditional architecture space, from a simple lower-energy, low-performance single-issue in-order processor to an aggressive higher-energy, high-performance quad-issue out-of-order processor. We note that this set of architectures builds in scope on those examined by previous works [19, 15, 8], all of which looked at superscalar, out-of-order designs only.

For each of these high-level architectures, there are also many tunable microarchitectural parameters that trade-off energy and performance. Table 1 lists these parameters for the design space we explore. This microarchitectural space includes billions of possible design configurations, without even taking into account the circuit design space we explore.

We use a large 8MB L2 cache with a fixed access time in this study. Because the clock cycle time of the core is an optimization parameter, the relative access latency in cycles can still vary, and so the L2 access latency is included in the design space. The DRAM latency is likewise included in the design space because the core frequency can change. The large L2 cache was used because it reduces costly accesses (both energy and delay-wise) to the main memory and lets us focus on the energy-efficiency of the processing core.

We use a YAGS branch predictor [9] in all architectures except the single-issue in-order design, where we use simple 2-bit counters instead. We tried both predictors on all architectures. From an energy-performance perspective, the performance return of the YAGS predictor was usually worth the small increase in total energy. We found the 2-bit coun-

Table 1: *Micro-architectural design space parameters.*

Parameter	Range
Branch predictor	0-1024 entries
BTB size	0-1024 entries
I-cache (2-way) size	2-32KB
D-cache (4-way) size	4-64KB
Fetch latency	1-3 cycles
Decode/Reg File/Rename lat.	1-3 cycles
Retire latency	1-3 cycles
Integer ALU latency	1-4 cycles
FP ALU latency	3-12 cycles
L1 D-cache latency	1-3 cycles
ROB size	4-32 entries
IW (centralized) size	2-32 entries
LSQ size	1-16 entries
L2 cache latency	8-64 cycles
DRAM latency	50-200 cycles
Cycle Time	unrestricted
Supply Voltage	0.7-1.4 V

ters were still useful for very low energy budgets, so we use this simpler predictor for the single-issue in-order design. The lower CPI of these simple designs also means that more aggressive predictors are not as important.

As benchmark suites, we use a subset of SPEC CPU benchmarks. We simulate 500 randomly generated design configurations per benchmark, from which we then generate our architectural models through statistical inference. We set aside a percentage of these these samples for validating our models. Median fitting errors are listed in Table 2; on average, our models have errors of 6.0% or less.

To create the circuit energy-delay characterizations for our circuit libraries, we use a mixed approach. For logic units and small memory structures (queues, register files, etc.), we build Verilog implementations, and use Synopsys Design Compiler to synthesize each of these blocks. The synthesis is based on a CMOS 90nm technology standard cell library. By sweeping the timing constraint on these blocks, Design Compiler produces different logic topologies, synthesis mappings and gate sizings that trade-off energy and delay. Designs with tighter delay constraints use more aggressive mappings and larger gates, resulting in higher energy per use.

For larger memories such as the memory caches and the BTB, we use CACTI 6.0 [20] to characterize the energy-delay trade-off space. CACTI searches the space of possible SRAM memory organizations to evaluate access time and power characteristics of design points. We use CACTI to extract all energy-delay points in this search space, which we then use to construct energy-delay trade-off models.

We use this approach to characterize the energy-delay trade-offs for all the major blocks in the processor: the ALUs, the caches, the reorder buffer, the instruction window, etc. While we have taken care to include all major components in a processor, there are often numerous smaller units and state registers that are present in commercial designs that we are not including. Moreover, while characterizing energy-delay trade-offs for individual circuit blocks is straightforward, accounting for the communication and control in a processor is more difficult, and is often done with empirical data. We have created first-order models of these effects, but we expect others, with more data to draw on, to improve our models in the future. While the detailed results will change as the underlying models improve, we believe that the general trends and conclusions in our study will still hold true.

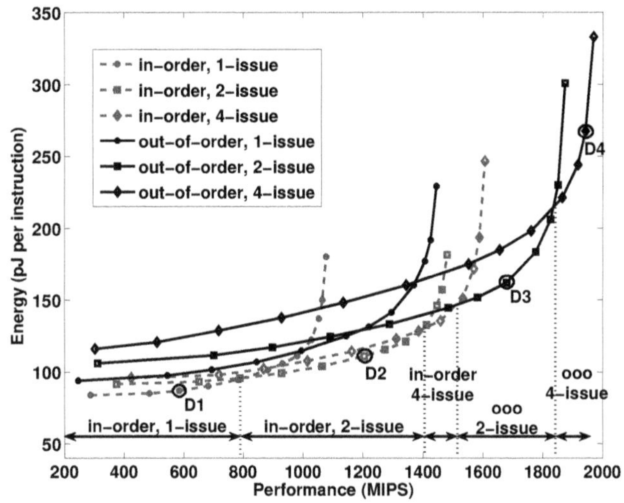

Figure 3: *Overall energy-performance trade-offs of our six macro-architectures for a 90nm CMOS technology, produced by jointly optimizing microarchitectural and circuit parameters. As the performance is pushed, the optimal choice of macro-architecture changes to progressively more aggressive machines. Design details for the circled design points are shown in Table 3.*

4. DESIGN SPACE OPTIMIZATION

We apply the optimization framework to each of our high-level architectures. The resulting energy-performance trade-offs for these architectures are shown in Figure 3. These Pareto-optimal curves show the entire range of trade-offs. As performance is pushed, each architecture uses more aggressive structures and circuits, causing the energy consumed per instruction to increase. Given an energy budget or performance target, a designer can use these curves to identify the most appropriate design.

We note that these Pareto-optimal trade-off curves between performance and energy are more general than commonly used metrics like ED or ED^2. ED^n metrics essentially set an exchange ratio between energy and performance, with higher powers of n favoring more performance; in this sense, they can be somewhat arbitrary. Graphically, ED^n metrics define a set of iso-cost contours in the energy-performance space. For example, in a log/log energy-performance plot ED would correspond to slope 1 lines, and ED^2 would correspond to slope 2 lines. Minimizing for either metric would produce the point on the Pareto-optimal curve where its slope matches the slope of the chosen metric. Thus, optimizing for ED^n with a particular value of n would correspond to a particular point on the Pareto-optimal curve. Since one generally wants to design for a specific performance target or energy budget, neither of these points is necessarily the desired answer. Representing the results as a trade-off curve between energy per operation and performance provides a more complete picture of the design space to designers.

The overall trade-off space spans approximately 6.5x in performance—from about 300 MIPS to 1950 MIPS—and 4x in energy—from about 80 pJ/op to 320 pJ/op. The various architectures contribute different segments to the overall energy-efficient frontier. As one would expect, the single-

Table 2: *Errors of architectural models generated through statistical inference.*

	1-issue in-order	2-issue in-order	4-issue in-order	1-issue out-of-order	2-issue out-of-order	4-issue out-of-order
bzip2	0.0049	0.0055	0.0041	0.0376	0.0443	0.0466
crafty	0.0618	0.0670	0.0825	0.0656	0.0774	0.0777
eon	0.0393	0.0925	0.0794	0.0637	0.0750	0.0727
gap	0.0110	0.0113	0.0130	0.0458	0.0501	0.0477
gcc	0.0445	0.0231	0.0658	0.0493	0.0630	0.0554
gzip	0.0125	0.0124	0.0625	0.0348	0.0410	0.0424
mcf	0.0233	0.0569	0.0578	0.0583	0.0642	0.0899
parser	0.0063	0.0139	0.0087	0.0341	0.0413	0.0380
perlbmk	0.0337	0.0207	0.0362	0.0562	0.0738	0.0598
twolf	0.0236	0.0340	0.0314	0.0408	0.0597	0.0527
average	**0.0261**	**0.0337**	**0.0442**	**0.0486**	**0.0590**	**0.0583**

Table 3: *Design Configuration Details For Selected Design Points.*

	D1	D2	D3	D4
In-order vs out-of-order	in-order	in-order	out-of-order	out-of-order
Issue width	1-issue	2-issue	2-issue	4-issue
Cycle time (FO4)	27.5	16.9	17.2	16.3
Branch pred size (entries)	264	600	1024	870
BTB size (entries)	64	90	554	1024
I-cache size (KB)	21	32	32	32
D-cache size (KB)	8	11	14	42
Fetch latency	1.0	1.6	2.2	2.1
Decode/Rename latency	1.0	1.7	2.4	3.0
Retire latency	N/A	N/A	2.0	2.2
Integer ALU latency	1.0	1.0	1.0	1.0
FP ALU latency	3.0	4.0	3.9	4.1
L1 D-cache latency	1.0	1.1	1.1	1.1
ROB size	N/A	N/A	22	32
IW size	N/A	N/A	11	9
LSQ size	N/A	N/A	16	16

issue in-order architecture is appropriate for very low energy design points, while the quad-issue out-of-order is only appropriate at very high performance points. In between these two extremes, we find that the dual-issue in-order and out-of-order processors are efficient for large parts of the design space. Thus, the order in which high-level architectural features should be considered from a basic single-issue design is, first, superscalar issue, and then, if more performance is still needed, out-of-order processing. From the perspective of marginal energy per unit performance, the move to a superscalar design is cheaper than investing in out-of-order processing. The quad-issue in-order design is only efficient for a small performance range, not being as energy-efficient as the dual-issue in-order design at lower energy points, and being outmatched at high performance points by the dual-issue out-of-order design. The single-issue out-of-order design is never efficient and does not contribute to the overall efficient frontier. This architecture represents a design that is out of balance. Being able to issue only a single instruction becomes a bottleneck to the out-of-order processor, resulting in wasted effort.

We can also examine how the various underlying parameters are changing throughout the design space. In Table 3, we examine these parameters for design points D1 through D4 as marked on Figure 3. Not surprisingly, as we push for more performance, the frequency and structure sizes generally increase, while latencies generally decrease. Some of the latencies show fractional values which would need to be snapped to discrete values, although techniques such as time borrowing and register retiming can also be used to work with the results. We highlight a few points from these results. First, both the I-cache and D-cache tend to stay away from small sizes, even when targeting lower-performance points. Across the design points, the D-cache reaches a minimum of 8KB even though a 4KB cache is available, and the I-cache never goes below 20KB. Although a smaller cache is less expensive to access, a larger cache potentially saves energy by reducing the number of misses that incur a more expensive access to higher level caches. Thus, for lower power design points, the optimizer determines that the marginal savings it can achieve by reducing misses outweighs the access cost of the larger caches, ultimately finding the right balance and settling on the chosen values. In these results, the I-cache tends to have larger sizes than the D-cache; the I-cache has higher hit rates which means that the marginal cost of increasing its size (per unit performance offered) is lower. Generally, these results show the importance of caches in energy-efficient designs as a way to both save energy and increase performance.

Secondly, we note that the instruction window (IW) is relatively small compared to the maximum available IW of size 32. In this case, a larger IW increases the complexity (and delay) of the instruction dispatch logic. Since, in this machine, the dispatch logic must execute every cycle, the delay of the dispatch circuitry can adversely affect the clock frequency. The optimizer realizes this trade-off and finds the right balance between architectural performance through a higher CPI and pipeline performance through a higher cycle time. Moving from design point D3 to D4, the instruction window size backs off to accommodate frequency scaling. We see a similar effect in the branch predictor size, another structure that needs to execute once per cycle.

Finally, we note that the delays of units such as the integer ALU and the D-cache are critical to resolving data dependencies. It is usually worth the energy cost to ensure these units fit into one clock cycle, so the optimizer always ensures that this is the case. Of course, this is not a surprising fact, and is confirmed by current design practices. It is important to note, however, that the delays of these units are changing with the cycle time, so it is not the case

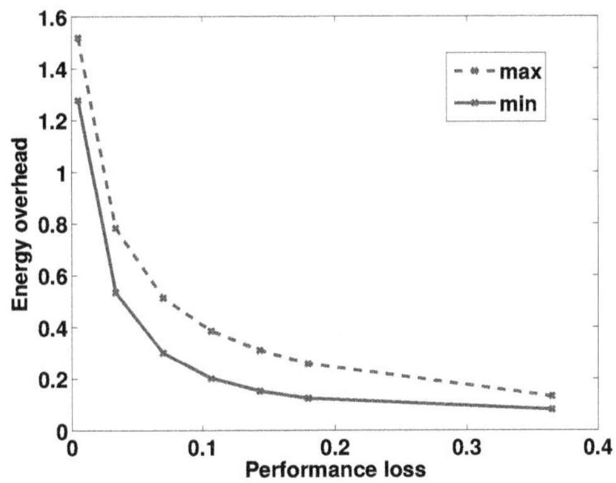

Figure 4: *Plot showing inefficiency caused by using fixed circuit data. Fixed circuit libraries both reduce the achievable peak performance and require more energy than a jointly optimized design. Each fixed library is placed along the x-axis by the performance loss of its fastest solution, so a circuit library at 1% off the minimum delay is located at near 0 performance loss and circuits at 50% off from the minimum delay cause the overall system to slow down 37%. For each library we then find the energy overheads compared to the jointly optimized design. The dotted line is the max overhead throughout the architectural design space, while the solid line is the min overhead. No fixed circuits provide good performance with low energy overhead.*

that the same implementations are being used throughout the design space. Machines with more aggressive cycle times use faster, higher energy versions of these circuits, whereas the lower power design points use lower-energy circuit implementations.

4.1 Circuit Trade-offs

The circuit-aware approach that we use integrates delay and energy information into the optimization, exposing different energy-delay design points to the design space exploration. This improves upon most architectural design space tools and studies which typically use fixed energy costs for each circuit (e.g. Wattch [5], others [26, 17]).

This additional fidelity allows us to trade-off the energy and delay within a circuit to find the optimal circuit operating point. As a result, the optimizer can choose to slow down a circuit to save energy when it does not need to run as fast, or it can allocate more energy to a circuit to speed it up if it finds that circuit to be critical to the system performance. This is an important consideration in the optimization space, especially when we consider that different circuits will be optimal at different performance targets.

To evaluate the advantage of exposing the circuit trade-off space, we compare our approach to a fixed energy cost approach. We restrict our circuit libraries to single energy-delay points, sweeping the fixed points to be at 1, 5, 10, 15, 20, 25 and 50% of the minimum delay. For each of these 'fixed' circuit libraries, we then run a complete architectural optimization, and compare the energy required to the energy consumed in the joint circuit/architecture optimization. Figure 4 shows the resulting inefficiency of using these "fixed" circuit points.

The results show that running all the circuits at near maximum speeds (left-most point, circuits at 1% of their min delay) allows the machine to run at near-peak performance, but comes with significant energy overheads of 130% or more. These large overheads are the result of uniformly running all circuits very fast. Only performance critical units should run at their maximum speed; other units should be slowed down to save energy. If, on the other hand, slower circuits (right-most points) are used in an effort to reduce energy, energy overheads reduce to about 15%, but maximum performance is sacrificed. There is no single circuit design point that can be optimal at both the high performance and low energy points. Circuit energy-delay trade-offs need to be included to yield accurate optimization results.

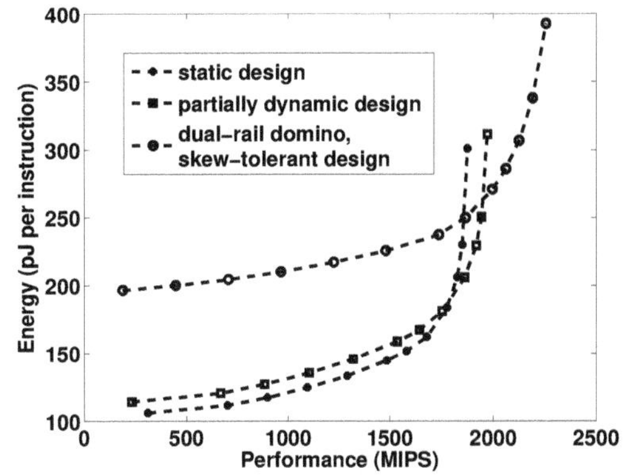

Figure 5: *Trade-offs of dynamic circuits. A partially dynamic design (with a dynamic ALU and issue logic) increases maximum performance by enabling shorter cycle times. A fully dynamic, skew-tolerant design offers even greater performance by removing clocking overheads. Both designs, however, come at significant energy costs which place them on a steep part of the trade-off curve.*

4.2 Dynamic Circuits

Using our optimization framework, we can also explore the effect of using different circuit styles. Our base circuit libraries use static CMOS energy-delay trade-offs which include the space of gate sizings and logic synthesis mappings. Dynamic circuits, however, were once commonly used in high-performance processors and can be significantly faster that static CMOS circuits. However, because of their clock power, dynamic circuits also come at a significant energy cost.

To characterize the performance gains and energy overheads of using dynamic circuits, we compare a dynamic dual-rail domino adder to a static implementation using a circuit optimization tool [21]; these results indicate that the dual-rail domino circuit achieves 0.67x the delay at 4x the energy. Since we do not have a complete dynamic circuit library, we use this adder scaling data as a proxy for all circuits (except memories[3]) to generate dynamic circuit trade-offs.

We examine two dynamic designs using these new libraries. In the first, we use dynamic circuits for certain performance-critical components, speeding up the integer ALU and the out-of-order issue logic. While the ALU does not strictly stand in the way of the cycle time—the ALU is pipelinable—the performance loss of pipelining the ALU due to data de-

[3]Most memories already use some dynamic circuits internally, so we do not change their performance in this experiment.

pendency stalls means it is usually not an energy-efficient design choice. The optimizer generally prefers a 1-cycle ALU with a longer cycle time over a higher frequency design with a multi-cycle ALU. In the case of the issue logic, it cannot be pipelined in our design, and actually limits the use of shorter cycles times.

Dynamic logic has a second potential advantage. Since every dynamic gate already has a clock, it is possible to build an entire system without including any explicit flops or latches. Furthermore, the overall design can be constructed to be tolerant of skew on the clock lines [11, 24]. This type of design essentially removes all clocking overheads that are found in conventional designs. For this method to work, all logic must be a monotonic function of its input (domino logic), so this generally requires one to create dual-rail gates, which compute both true and complement outputs from true and complement inputs. Thus, for our second design, we also explore the performance trade-offs of a complete dual-rail design[4].

Figure 5 shows the results of using these circuit styles on our dual-issue out-of-order architecture. Also shown is the original static version. As expected, both dynamic designs push performance to new limits, but come with some added energy overheads. The partially dynamic design provides more performance because it can now achieve higher cycle times. The faster issue logic now also allows for larger instruction windows of up to 20 entries; this in contrast to the small 8 entry instruction windows we saw in the static design. These performance benefits, of course, come at a somewhat high energy cost: the transition from the static design to the partially dynamic design comes at a marginal cost of 2.3% in energy for 1% in performance. The fully dual-rail, skew-tolerant design offers an even larger performance gain; it virtually eliminates clocking overheads. However, it comes with an even larger energy cost since the entire machine must be implemented in dynamic logic. This design option represents a more expensive choice at about 2.7% in energy for 1% in performance.

While neither of these options are cheap, a designer may be willing to pay the cost if the added performance is truly needed. As we will see in the next section, however, voltage scaling can often offer better marginal costs and should be considered first.

5. VOLTAGE AND MARGINAL COSTS

It is well-known that an important consideration in energy-efficient design is the choice of operating voltage. Figure 6(a) shows the energy and delay scaling characteristics of circuits as a function of voltage as obtained through SPICE simulations. The energy curve follows an expected Vdd^2 profile; the delay shows an inverse relationship proportional to $\frac{1}{Vdd^{3.325}} + 1$ (empirical fit). Composing these two relationships, we get the energy-delay scaling trade-offs of the supply voltage parameter in Figure 6(b).

This data shows that, by itself, voltage tuning from 0.7V to 1.4V provides a range of about 3x in performance and 4x in energy. More importantly, the profile of the energy-performance curve is relatively shallow throughout this entire range. This means that the marginal cost of increasing performance through voltage scaling does not change much as we continue to increase the voltage parameter. At low voltages, the marginal cost is at about 0.80% in energy for 1% in performance; at the high end, this marginal cost reaches 2.3% in energy for 1% in performance.

[4]While the memories would need to be modified to work in this system, the changes would be small and would not cause major changes in memory power or delay.

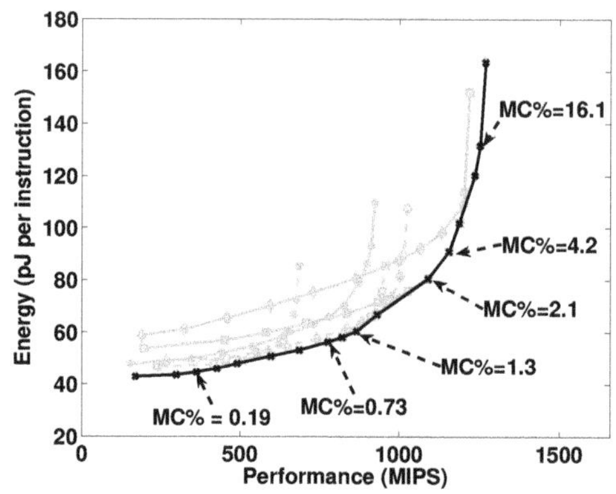

Figure 7: *Marginal costs of the joint architecture and circuit design space. In light are the energy-performance curves of our six architectures. In dark is the overall, composite energy-performance frontier. Data is normalized to 0.9V to allow for comparison to the voltage marginal costs. Marginal costs in the architecture/circuit space vary considerably more than voltage marginal costs. For most practical design objectives the optimal architecture should be selected from the narrow band of designs with a marginal cost of 0.80%-2.3% to match voltage marginal costs.*

We can contrast this marginal cost profile against the marginal cost profile of achieving performance through circuits and architecture, shown in Figure 7. This space shows a much larger range of marginal costs. At the low performance points, the marginal costs are very cheap, while at the high performance points, the marginal costs are very expensive.

We recall that to optimize a design, the marginal costs of all parameters should be equal. If this were not the case, then an arbitrage opportunity would exist, and the more expensive parameters could be exchanged for cheaper parameters: selling the expensive parameter would cause some performance loss, but this performance could be recovered at a lower cost through the cheaper parameter. Comparing the marginal costs of voltage versus architectural parameters, this suggests that, unless we are trying to achieve the very extremes of performance or low power, the optimal set of designs should lie in the range of marginal costs from 0.80% to 2.3% in order to match the marginal costs of voltage scaling. This results in a narrow band of architectural and circuit designs being optimal when the voltage scaling parameter is available.

Figure 8 shows the optimization results when the supply voltage parameter is included in the design space. Confirming the marginal cost analysis, we see that a smaller set of architectures cover a larger part of the energy-efficient frontier. The dual-issue out-of-order processor is energy-efficient for a large part of the design space. At low performance targets, the dual-issue in-order processor takes over, although the dual-issue out-of-order processor is still not overly inefficient. Only at the very extremes, when the voltage knob becomes capped, do the single-issue in-order and quad-issue

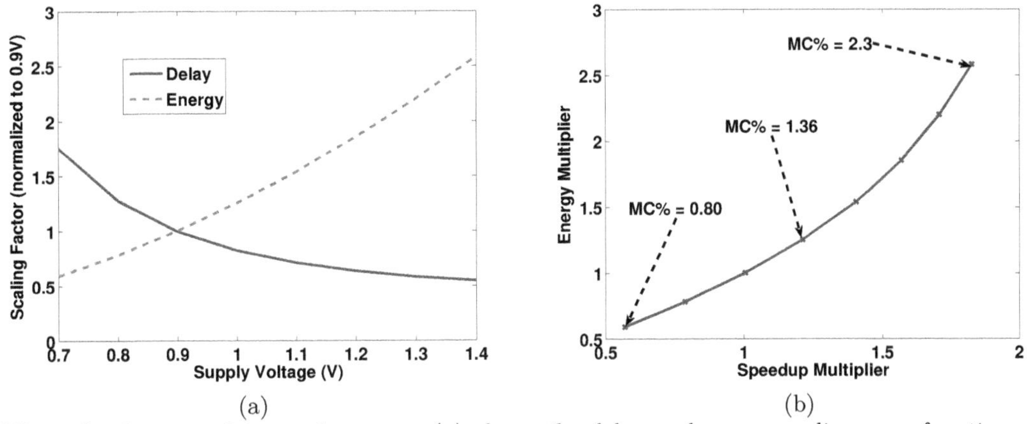

(a) (b)

Figure 6: *Effect of voltage on delay and energy. (a) shows the delay and energy scaling as a function of supply voltage (normalized to 0.9V). (b) shows the corresponding energy-performance trade-off curve. Percentage marginal costs (MC%) is the percentage energy cost required to increase performance by 1%. For a wide range of energy and performance, marginal costs do not change much, making voltage a powerful knob for energy-efficiency.*

out-of-order designs play a role, and these represent designs with very low and very high marginal costs respectively.

This result suggests that a small number of properly tuned designs can cover most of the overall energy-performance frontier at near optimal efficiencies simply by voltage and frequency scaling. We pick one dual-issue in-order processor and one dual-issue out-of-order processor with fixed microarchitectural and circuit parameters, and evaluate these fixed designs under voltage and frequency scaling. Figure 9 shows the energy overheads of scaling these fixed designs as compared to the fully optimized designs which also tune the architecture and circuits. Because design parameters are fixed, we see some inefficiency; the lines deviate from the normalized optimal value of 1. This result is expected because the marginal costs of all parameters in the system are no longer equal. Yet, we see the resulting inefficiency is small—under 3%. Of course, this result requires that we start with the right two designs in the architecture/circuit space sweet spot. Thus, with two carefully selected designs and voltage scaling, we can operate at near optimal energy-efficiencies over a broad performance range.

6. DISCUSSION

Since power has been an issue for many years, there exist a number of tools that help guide architects toward energy-efficient designs. Simulation based tools such as Wattch [5] and PowerTimer [4] have enabled power-performance studies, exploring various aspects of the power-performance space in processor designs. For instance, using these or similar tools people have evaluated power-performance trade-offs in different areas of the design space such as pipeline depth [26, 12, 25]. Applying statistical inference techniques to these tools, Lee and Brooks have evaluated power-performance trade-offs in an even larger microarchitectural design space [19]. Others, like Karkhanis and Smith have used an analytical model to explore trade-offs in the architecture design space [16]. There has even been some work trying to connect circuit and architectural optimization using metrics such as hardware intensity [27, 23].

We extend this prior work in two important ways. First, we integrate circuit trade-offs into the architectural design space analysis and show how it changes the optimization

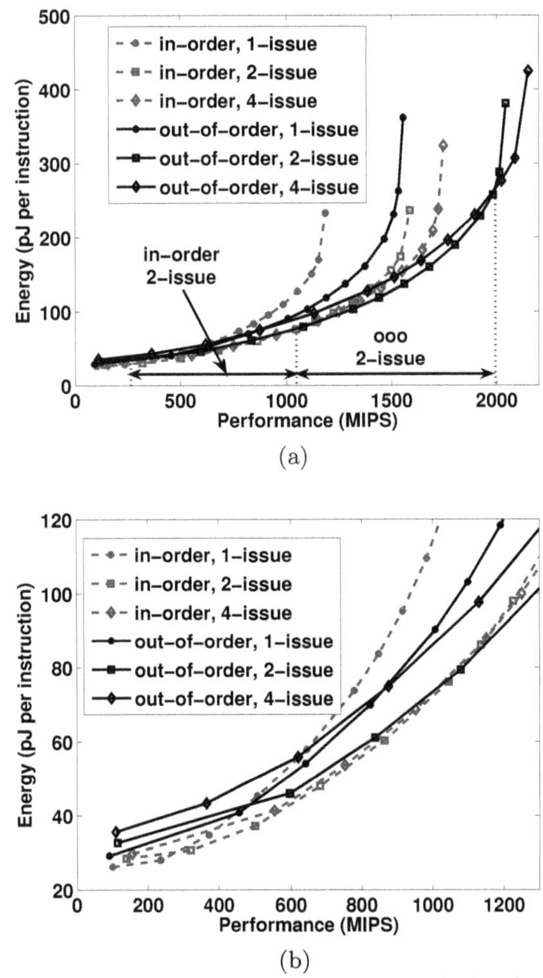

Figure 8: *(a) Energy-performance trade-offs for the processor design space with voltage scaling. The dual-issue out-of-order design now dominates an even larger part of the design space; the dual-issue in-order design is optimal at low energy points. (b) Same results zoomed in on low energy points.*

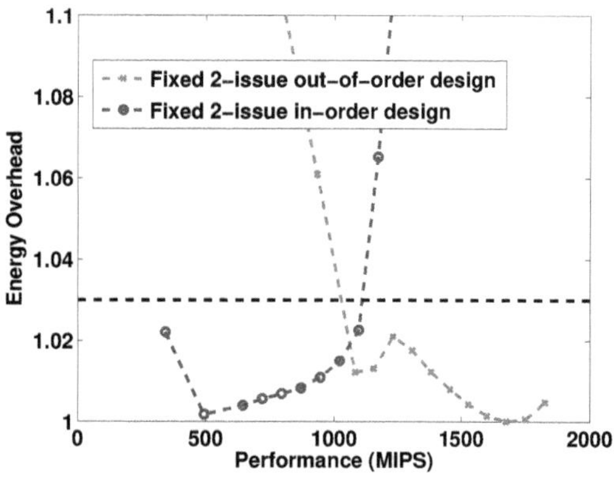

Figure 9: *By using two carefully selected designs—a fixed dual-issue in-order design and a fixed dual-issue out-of-order design—voltage scaling can be used to cover a large performance range within 3% of the optimal energy-efficiency.*

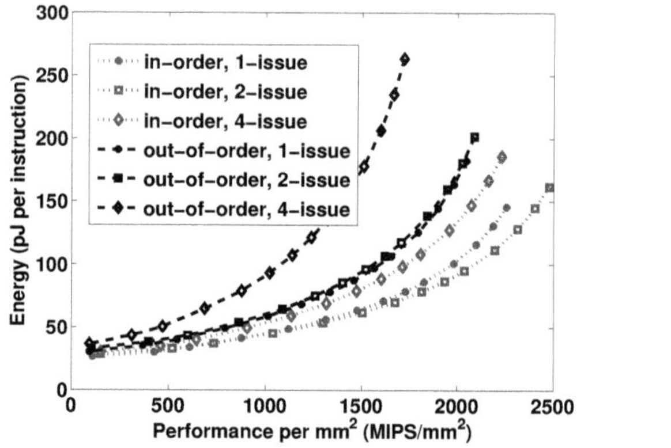

Figure 10: *Energy per op vs performance/mm^2 for a highly parallel workload. The area overheads of out-of-order processing make it a less attractive option.*

results. Second, by using posynomials to model the design space, we can explore the space very quickly—finding an optimal design point in only about 30 seconds. This integration allows us to better understand metrics like hardware intensity (which is simply the relative marginal performance vs. energy cost) and provides a practical framework to optimize this joint design space. Our tool creates the Pareto-optimal curve, which contains the best possible design points for different performance targets or energy budgets, and is not dependent on ED^n metrics.

Using this design framework, we extended the space of prior statistical performance-energy modeling efforts to a wide range of high-level architectures. While this paper has presented the results of optimally tuned processors, the real advantage of this type of design framework is the insight it can give a designer. For example, we initially had each of our macro-architectures fetch instructions according to the width of the machine (e.g. one word for the single-issue machines, etc.). This led to wider machines being more energy efficient than single issue machines even at low performance. Clearly, because of high instruction locality, it makes sense to have all macro-architectures fetch multiple instructions at a time to amortize the cost of going to cache. We are currently looking at our results to see what architectural changes can lead to more efficient cores.

The results presented in this paper have also focused on performance-energy trade-offs, and not considered area (die cost) or what happens for threaded or data parallel applications. It is easy to include these effects using our framework. For example, in the case of multi-core designs for highly parallel workloads, we need to change the performance objective. The number of cores that we can fit on a die is critical to performance, and we must consider both the performance and area of the cores. If we assume infinite parallelism, then we want to optimize the product of the performance per core and the number of cores that will fit in a given area. Thus the performance metric is no longer processor performance, but performance per mm^2. Figure 10 shows optimization results under this new design objective. In this case, the area overheads of implementing out-of-order processors outweigh their performance benefit, and so the dual-issue in-order design is always optimal. To account for workloads with more realistic amounts of parallelism, one just needs to change how the performance scales with the number of cores [13], which will just change the performance/area function that needs to be optimized. In analogous ways we can optimize whole systems that contain SIMD units, external high-power accelerators (i.e. GPUs) or other components that affect energy or performance.

7. CONCLUSION

We have created a general energy-performance optimization tool that will be essential to create the energy efficient designs that the future requires. By constructing a first order circuit library for processors we have been able to rapidly explore a very large processor design space, from a simple single-issue processor, to a wide quad-issue out-of-order machine. While there is clearly more work that can be done using this tool, our initial results have been quite interesting. First, it shows that it is very easy to build a poor machine which is far from the optimal frontier. In fact, hitting the frontier will be very difficult unless you jointly optimize circuits and architecture. More surprising, however, was the marginal cost profile of the optimized performance-energy trade-off space without voltage scaling. While the trade-off spanned a reasonably sized space of 6.5x in performance and 4x in energy, the marginal costs throughout this range were rapidly changing, with very expensive marginal costs for the quad-issue out-of-order design and very low marginal costs for the single-issue in-order design. Since voltage scaling spanned about the same range with smaller changes in marginal performance, we found voltage scaling to be a more effective knob for efficiently trading off energy and performance. With voltage, we found the dual-issue in-order and out-of-order machines were optimal over a large part of the design space. Moreover, by using two machines with the right fixed set of microarchitectural/circuit parameters and only voltage and frequency scaling, we showed that the loss in efficiency compared to the overall optimal machine was only 3%. Thus, by carefully optimizing the circuits and architecture, one can build a machine that can use voltage scaling to efficiently operate at a range performance targets.

In the end, the more important use of this tool will be to generate information and provide insights for the design of new methods that will further reduce the system power. The results can be used to identify both performance and energy limitations of the system, and can direct a designer to focus their attention on these facets of the design. We have already begun to use it in this way, and are starting to apply it to other performance/energy constrained designs.

8. ACKNOWLEDGMENTS

The authors would like to thank the Chip Generator group at Stanford University for their support and feedback. This work was funded in part by the FCRP Focus Center for Circuit & System Solutions (C2S2), under contract 2003-CT-888. This material is also based upon work supported by the National Science Foundation under Grant #0937060 to the Computing Research Association for the CIFellows Project.

9. REFERENCES

[1] O. Azizi, A. Mahesri, J. P. Stevenson, S. Patel, and M. Horowitz. An integrated framework for joint design space exploration of microarchitecture and circuits. In *DATE '10: Proceedings of the conference on Design, automation and test in Europe*, pages 250–255, 2010.

[2] P. Bose and T. M. Conte. Performance analysis and its impact on design. *Computer*, 31(5):41–49, 1998.

[3] S. Boyd and L. Vandenberghe. *Convex Optimization.* Cambridge University Press, March 2004.

[4] D. Brooks, P. Bose, V. Srinivasan, M. K. Gschwind, P. G. Emma, and M. G. Rosenfield. New methodology for early-stage, microarchitecture-level power-performance analysis of microprocessors. *IBM J. Res. Dev.*, 47(5-6):653–670, 2003.

[5] D. Brooks, V. Tiwari, and M. Martonosi. Wattch: a framework for architectural-level power analysis and optimizations. *SIGARCH Comput. Archit. News*, 28(2):83–94, 2000.

[6] A. R. Conn, I. M. Elfadel, J. W. W. Molzen, P. R. O'Brien, P. N. Strenski, C. Visweswariah, and C. B. Whan. Gradient-based optimization of custom circuits using a static-timing formulation. In *DAC '99: Proceedings of the 36th ACM/IEEE conference on Design automation*, pages 452–459, New York, NY, USA, 1999. ACM.

[7] R. Dennard, F. Gaensslen, V. Rideout, E. Bassous, and A. LeBlanc. Design of ion-implanted mosfet's with very small physical dimensions. *Solid-State Circuits, IEEE Journal of*, 9(5):256–268, Oct 1974.

[8] C. Dubach, T. Jones, and M. O'Boyle. Microarchitectural design space exploration using an architecture-centric approach. In *MICRO '07: Proceedings of the 40th Annual IEEE/ACM International Symposium on Microarchitecture*, pages 262–271, Washington, DC, USA, 2007. IEEE Computer Society.

[9] A. N. Eden and T. Mudge. The yags branch prediction scheme. In *MICRO 31: Proceedings of the 31st annual ACM/IEEE international symposium on Microarchitecture*, pages 69–77, Los Alamitos, CA, USA, 1998. IEEE Computer Society Press.

[10] J. P. Fishburn and A. E. Dunlop. Tilos: A posynomial programming approach to transistor sizing. In *IEEE Int. Conf. Computer-Aided Design*, pages 326–328, 1985.

[11] D. Harris. *Skew-tolerant circuit design.* Morgan Kaufmann Publishers Inc., San Francisco, CA, USA, 2001.

[12] A. Hartstein and T. R. Puzak. The optimum pipeline depth considering both power and performance. *ACM Trans. Archit. Code Optim.*, 1(4):369–388, 2004.

[13] M. D. Hill and M. R. Marty. Amdahl's law in the multicore era. *Computer*, 41(7):33–38, 2008.

[14] M. Horowitz, E. Alon, D. Patil, S. Naffziger, R. Kumar, and K. Bernstein. Scaling, power, and the future of cmos. In *Electron Devices Meeting, 2005. IEDM Technical Digest. IEEE International*, pages 7 pp.–15, Dec. 2005.

[15] E. İpek, S. A. McKee, R. Caruana, B. R. de Supinski, and M. Schulz. Efficiently exploring architectural design spaces via predictive modeling. *SIGARCH Comput. Archit. News*, 34(5):195–206, 2006.

[16] T. S. Karkhanis and J. E. Smith. A first-order superscalar processor model. *SIGARCH Comput. Archit. News*, 32(2):338, 2004.

[17] T. S. Karkhanis and J. E. Smith. Automated design of application specific superscalar processors: an analytical approach. In *ISCA '07: Proceedings of the 34th annual international symposium on Computer architecture*, pages 402–411, New York, NY, USA, 2007. ACM.

[18] B. C. Lee and D. M. Brooks. Accurate and efficient regression modeling for microarchitectural performance and power prediction. *SIGARCH Comput. Archit. News*, 34(5):185–194, 2006.

[19] B. C. Lee and D. M. Brooks. Illustrative design space studies with microarchitectural regression models. In *Proceedings of the 13th International Symposium on High Performance Computer Architecture*, 2007.

[20] N. Muralimanohar, R. Balasubramonian, and N. Jouppi. Optimizing NUCA Organizations and Wiring Alternatives for Large Caches With CACTI 6.0. In *Proceedings of the 40th Annual International Symposium on Microarchitecture*, December 2007.

[21] D. Patil, O. Azizi, M. Horowitz, R. Ho, and R. Ananthraman. Robust energy-efficient adder topologies. In *ARITH '07: Proceedings of the 18th IEEE Symposium on Computer Arithmetic*, pages 16–28, Washington, DC, USA, 2007. IEEE Computer Society.

[22] D. Patil, S. J. Kim, and M. Horowitz. Joint supply, threshold voltage and sizing optimization for design of robust digital circuits. Technical report, Department of Electrical Engineering, Stanford University.

[23] Z. J. Qi, M. Ziegler, S. V. Kosonocky, J. M. Rabaey, and M. R. Stan. Multi-dimensional circuit and micro-architecture level optimization. In *ISQED '07: Proceedings of the 8th International Symposium on Quality Electronic Design*, pages 275–280, Washington, DC, USA, 2007. IEEE Computer Society.

[24] J. Silberman, N. Aoki, D. Boerstler, J. Burns, S. Dhong, A. Essbaum, U. Ghoshal, D. Heidel, P. Hofstee, K. T. Lee, D. Meltzer, H. Ngo, K. Nowka, S. Posluszny, O. Takahashi, I. Vo, and B. Zoric. A 1.0-ghz single-issue 64-bit powerpc integer processor. *Solid-State Circuits, IEEE Journal of*, 33(11):1600–1608, Nov 1998.

[25] V. Srinivasan, D. Brooks, M. Gschwind, P. Bose, V. Zyuban, P. N. Strenski, and P. G. Emma. Optimizing pipelines for power and performance. In *MICRO 35: Proceedings of the 35th annual ACM/IEEE international symposium on Microarchitecture*, pages 333–344, Los Alamitos, CA, USA, 2002. IEEE Computer Society Press.

[26] V. Zyuban, D. Brooks, V. Srinivasan, M. Gschwind, P. Bose, P. Strenski, and P. Emma. Integrated analysis of power and performance for pipelined microprocessors. *Computers, IEEE Transactions on*, 53(8):1004–1016, Aug. 2004.

[27] V. Zyuban and P. Strenski. Unified methodology for resolving power-performance tradeoffs at the microarchitectural and circuit levels. In *ISLPED '02: Proceedings of the 2002 international symposium on Low power electronics and design*, pages 166–171, New York, NY, USA, 2002. ACM.

Understanding Sources of Inefficiency in General-Purpose Chips

Rehan Hameed[1], Wajahat Qadeer[1], Megan Wachs[1], Omid Azizi[1], Alex Solomatnikov[2], Benjamin C. Lee[1], Stephen Richardson[1], Christos Kozyrakis[1] and Mark Horowitz[1]

[1]Dept. of Electrical Engineering
Stanford University, Stanford, CA
{rhameed, wqadeer, wachs, oazizi, bcclee, steveri, kozyraki, horowitz}@stanford.edu

[2]Hicamp Systems,
Menlo Park, CA
solomatnikov@gmail.com

ABSTRACT

Due to their high volume, general-purpose processors, and now chip multiprocessors (CMPs), are much more cost effective than ASICs, but lag significantly in terms of performance and energy efficiency. This paper explores the sources of these performance and energy overheads in general-purpose processing systems by quantifying the overheads of a 720p HD H.264 encoder running on a general-purpose CMP system. It then explores methods to eliminate these overheads by transforming the CPU into a specialized system for H.264 encoding. We evaluate the gains from customizations useful to broad classes of algorithms, such as SIMD units, as well as those specific to particular computation, such as customized storage and functional units.

The ASIC is 500x more energy efficient than our original four-processor CMP. Broadly, applicable optimizations improve performance by 10x and energy by 7x. However, the very low energy costs of actual core ops (100s fJ in 90nm) mean that over 90% of the energy used in these solutions is still "overhead". Achieving ASIC-like performance and efficiency requires algorithm-specific optimizations. For each sub-algorithm of H.264, we create a large, specialized functional unit that is capable of executing 100s of operations per instruction. This improves performance and energy by an additional 25x and the final customized CMP matches an ASIC solution's performance within 3x of its energy and within comparable area.

Categories and Subject Descriptors

C.5.4 [**Computer Systems Implementation]:** VLSI Systems – *customization, heterogeneous CMP*; C.1.3 [**Processor Architectures**]: Other Architecture Styles - *Heterogeneous (Hybrid) Systems.*

General Terms

Algorithms, Measurement, Performance, Design, Experimentation.

Keywords

ASIC, H.264, chip multiprocessor, high-performance, energy efficiency, customization, Tensilica.

ISCA'10, June 19–23, 2010, Saint-Malo, France.

1. INTRODUCTION

Most computing systems today are power limited, whether it is the 1W limit of a cell phone, or the 100W limit of a server. Since technology scaling no longer provides the energy savings, it once did [1], designers must turn to other techniques for continued performance improvements and tractable energy costs. One attractive option is to understand and to incorporate sources of ASIC efficiency, since general-purpose processors can be outclassed by three orders of magnitude in both performance and energy efficiency by ASIC designs [5].

The desire to achieve ASIC-like compute efficiencies with microprocessor-like application development cost is pushing designers to explore two new areas. One area aims to create CPU designs with much lower energy per instruction [6], while the other aims to create new design methodologies to reduce the cost of creating customized hardware. Examples of the latter include using higher levels of abstraction (e.g., C-to-RTL [8], [7]), and even full chip generators using extensible processors [2]. A critical first step in all of these approaches is to understand, in quantitative terms, the types and magnitudes of energy overheads in general-purpose processors. Once these are understood, it is then possible to explore ways to eliminate these overheads and assess the feasibility of creating an efficient, general-purpose machine.

This paper quantifies general-purpose overheads, exploring a series of customizations that reduce overheads to achieve ASIC-like efficiency. In particular, we consider three broad strategies: (1) techniques to exploit instruction- and data-level parallelism, such as VLIW and SIMD, (2) techniques to customize instructions by fusing complex, frequently occurring instruction sub-graphs, and (3) techniques to create application-specific data storage with fused functional units. These strategies span a range of general and domain-specific customization, incurring progressively greater design effort.

We evaluate these strategies by transforming a general-purpose, Tensilica-based, extensible CMP system into a highly efficient 720p HD H.264 encoder. We choose H.264 because it demonstrates the large energy advantage of ASIC solutions (500x) and because there exist commercial ASICs that can serve as a benchmark. Moreover, H.264 contains a variety of computational motifs, from highly data parallel algorithms (motion estimation) to control intensive ones (CABAC).

The results are striking. Starting from a 500x energy penalty, adding relatively wide (16x) SIMD execution units improves performance by 10x and energy efficiency by 7x. Since SIMD units are often augmented with special fused instructions to accelerate important applications, we introduce our own custom fused instructions to improve both performance and energy efficiency by an additional 1.4x. Despite these customizations, which collectively improve energy efficiency by 10x, the resulting solution is still 50x less energy efficient than an ASIC.

An examination of the energy breakdown clearly demonstrates why. Since the SIMD unit customizes datapath widths of 8-12bits, functional unit energy comprises less than 10 percent of the total even when performing more than 10 operations per cycle. Thus, to create a truly efficient processor, one needs to construct instructions that aggregate enough computation to offset the energy overheads of flexible instruction and data fetch. Creating such "magic" instructions improves energy efficiency by another 18x and yields a solution within 3x of a full ASIC design.

While identifying the right customizations for a given application takes significant effort, it is hard to achieve ASIC-like efficiencies without them. The inescapable conclusion is that truly efficient designs will require application-specialized hardware. If energy efficiency is going to drive future computing design, then we need frameworks that allow application experts to easily (and at low cost) create customized solutions. The fact that, for our application, we can achieve good efficiency using processor instruction extensions is an encouraging sign.

Since our experiments use an extensible processor, the next section reviews some of the prior work in this area, provides an overview of H.264 encoding, and describes the performance of hardware and software solutions. Section 3 then presents our experimental methodology, describing our baseline, generic H.264 implementation on a Tensilica CMP and outlining our strategies for customizing this system. The performance and efficiency gains are described in Section 4, which also explores the causes of the overheads and different methods for addressing them. Using the insight gained from our results, Section 5 discusses the broader implications for efficient computing and supporting application driven design.

2. BACKGROUND

Since we use an extensible processor for our case study, we first describe prior work on efficient computing, focusing on processor extensions. With this background, we then provide an overview of H.264 encoding and its main compute stages. The section ends by describing hardware and software implementations to demonstrate the performance advantages of an ASIC.

2.1 Related Work in Efficient Computing

General-purpose processors are often customized to improve their efficiency for specific application domains. For example, SIMD architectures achieve higher performance for multimedia and other data-parallel applications, while DSP processors are tailored to perform signal-processing tasks efficiently. More recently, ELM [6] and AnySP [10] have been optimized for embedded and mobile signal processing applications, respectively, by reducing processor overheads. While these strategies are meant to cover a broad spectrum of applications, special instructions are sometimes added to accelerate frequently used or critical operations for specific applications. For example, Intel's SSE4[11][12] includes instructions to accelerate matrix transpose and sum-of-absolute-differences.

Customizable processors allow designers to take the next step, and create instructions tailored to applications. Extensible processors such as Tensilica's Xtensa provide a base design that the designer can extend with custom instructions and datapath units [9]. Extending the ISA for a given application can be done either manually or with automated tools. Tensilica provides an automated ISA extension tool [18], which achieves speedups of 1.2x to 30x for EEMBC benchmarks [17] and signal processing algorithms [16]. Other tools have similarly demonstrated significant gains from automated ISA extension [13][14]. While automatic ISA extensions can be very effective, manually creating ISA extensions gives even larger gains: Tensilica reports speedups of 40x to 300x for kernels such as FFT, AES and DES encryption [19][20][21].

Our work takes customizable processors, which are much less efficient than ASICs, and determines what is required to close that efficiency gap within a flexible framework. While previous studies have demonstrated significant improvements in performance and efficiency, we explore the reasons for these gains, which is essential to determine the nature and degree of customization necessary for future systems. Our approach starts with a generic CMP system, then customizes its memory system and processors to determine the magnitude and sources of overhead eliminated in each step toward achieving a high efficiency 720p HD H.264 encoder.

2.2 H.264 Algorithm and Computational Motifs

To understand how we customize a generic CMP to efficiently implement H.264, we must first understand the basic components of the H.264 algorithm. Five major functions comprise more than 99% of the total execution time in our base CMP implementation:

(i) IME: Integer Motion Estimation

(ii) FME: Fractional Motion Estimation

(iii) IP: Intra Prediction

(iv) DCT/Quant: Transform and Quantization and

(v) CABAC: Context Adaptive Binary Arithmetic Coding.

We implement the H.264 baseline profile at level 3.1; however, we use CABAC in place of CAVLC because CABAC is more complex and more challenging to improve [23][24]. CABAC is also more representative of advanced coding steps in other applications.

IME finds the closest match for an image-block from a previous reference image, and computes a vector to represent the observed motion. While it is one of the most compute intensive parts of the encoder, the basic algorithm lends itself well to data parallel architectures. When run on our base CMP, IME takes up 56% of the total encoder execution time and 52% of total energy.

The next step, FME, refines the initial match from integer motion estimation and finds a match at quarter-pixel resolution. FME is also data parallel, but it has some sequential dependencies and a more complex computation kernel that makes it more challenging to parallelize. FME takes up 36% of the total execution time and 40% of total energy on our base CMP design. Since FME and IME together dominate the computational load of the encoder, optimizing these algorithms is essential for an efficient H.264 system design.

IP then uses previously encoded neighboring image-blocks within the current image to form a prediction for the current image-block. While the algorithm is still dominated by arithmetic operations, the computations are much less regular than the motion estimation algorithms. Additionally, there are sequential dependencies not only within the algorithm but also with the transform and quantization function.

Next, in DCT/Quant, the difference between a current and predicted image block is transformed and quantized to generate quantized coefficients, which then go through the inverse quantization and inverse transform to generate the reconstructed pixels. The basic function is relatively simple and data parallel. However, it is invoked a number of times for each 16x16 image block, which calls for an efficient implementation. For the rest of this paper, we merge these operations into the IP stage. The combined operation accounts for 7% of the total execution time and 6% of total energy.

Finally, CABAC is used to entropy-encode the coefficients and other elements of the bit-stream. Unlike the previous algorithms, CABAC is sequential and control dominated. While it takes only 1.6% of the execution time and 1.7% of total energy on our base design, CABAC often becomes the bottleneck in parallel systems due to its sequential nature. This becomes particularly important because we need to speed up the application by around 250x on a four-processor system. After speedups in the first four functions, CABAC becomes the bottleneck and cannot be ignored.

2.3 Current H.264 Implementations

The computationally intensive H.264 encoding algorithm poses a challenge for general-purpose processors, and is typically implemented as an ASIC. Prior work has demonstrated efficient hardware architectures for various sub-algorithms in H.264 [33][34][35][36]. T.-C. Chen et al. implement a full-system H.264 encoder [4] and demonstrate that real-time HD H.264 encoding is possible in hardware using relatively low power and area cost. Later implementations employ clever algorithmic optimizations which sacrifice some signal-to-noise ratio (SNR) but significantly reduce energy and area [29][30]. While these optimizations are useful, our study works with the basic algorithms similar to those in [4]. Our aim is to understand the mechanisms behind high efficiency of custom hardware, and these insights are not likely to change significantly for a particular algorithmic variant.

There has also been H.264 software optimizations, particularly for motion estimation, which takes most of the encoding time. For example, sparse search techniques along with other algorithmic modifications speed up software performance of IME and FME by up to 10x with negligible loss in SNR [31] [32]. Combining aggressive algorithmic modifications with multiple cores and SSE extensions lead to highly optimized H.264 encoders on Intel processors [3][37].

Despite these optimizations, software implementations of H.264 lag far behind dedicated ASICs. Table 1 compares a software implementation of a 480p SD encoder [3] to a 720p HD ASIC implementation [4]. The software implementation employs a 2.8 GHz Intel Pentium 4 executing highly optimized SSE code. This results in very high-energy consumption and low area efficiency. It is also worth noting that the software implementation relies on various algorithmic simplifications, which drastically reduce the computational complexity to achieve real-time performance, but result in a 20% decrease in compression efficiency for a given SNR [3]. The custom ASIC hardware, on the other hand, consumes over 500x less energy and is far more efficient in its use of silicon area as shown by the area numbers in Table 1. The ASIC makes few algorithmic simplifications and consequently has a negligible drop in compression efficiency [4].

Table 1. Intel's highly optimized, 2.8GHz Pentium 4 implementation of a 480p H.264 encoder versus a 720p HD ASIC. The second row presents Intel's SD data scaled to HD H.264. ASIC numbers have been scaled from 180nm to 90nm.

	Perf. (fps)	Area (mm^2)	Enrgy/frame (mJ)
Intel (720x480 SD)	30	122	742
Intel (1280x720 HD)	11	122	2023
ASIC	30	8	4

3. EXPERIMENTAL METHODOLOGY

Our experiments use a CMP platform based on Tensilica's extensible RISC cores [2][39][40]. This baseline implementation defines the gap we seek to bridge between general-purpose computing and ASIC efficiencies. We use the extensible platform to implement three different classes of customizations, each more application specific than the previous one. We independently customize each processor's datapath using Tensilica's TIE language and optimize memory system parameters. To quickly simulate and evaluate different design options, we created a multiprocessor simulation framework that employs Tensilica's Xtensa Modeling Platform (XTMP) as its base. We use Tensilica's ISA extension framework to specify the number of VLIW slots, the width for the SIMD data paths, the number and size of register files, custom hardware instructions, and custom data storage elements. Tensilica's TIE compiler generates simulation models for different processor configurations and their energy explorer tool [22] estimates the energy and area of the resulting system. Its results are within 30% of the actual energy numbers [25], which is adequate since we are looking for more than two orders of magnitude improvements in energy efficiency.

3.1 Baseline H.264 Implementation

We use H.264 encoder reference code JM 8.6 for our experiments [38]. In the reference implementation, H.264's video encoding path is very long and suffers from sequential dependencies that restrict parallelism. We carefully analyze existing H.264 partitioning techniques and implement algorithmic changes in IME that remove some dependencies and allow mapping of the five major algorithmic blocks to the four-stage macro-block (MB) pipeline shown in Figure 1. This mapping exploits task level parallelism at the macro block level and significantly reduces the inter-processor communication bandwidth requirements by sharing data between pipeline stages.

To build a base system, we map the four-stage macro-block partition of H.264 to a four-processor CMP system where each processor has 16KB 2-way set associative instruction and data caches. Table 2 presents our base system's performance and energy efficiency for the individual 720p HD H.264 sub-algorithms to highlight the large area and energy efficiency gap between our base CMP and the reference ASIC. At approximately 8.6B instructions to process one frame (IME), our base system consumes about 140 pJ/instruction—a reasonable value for a general-purpose system.

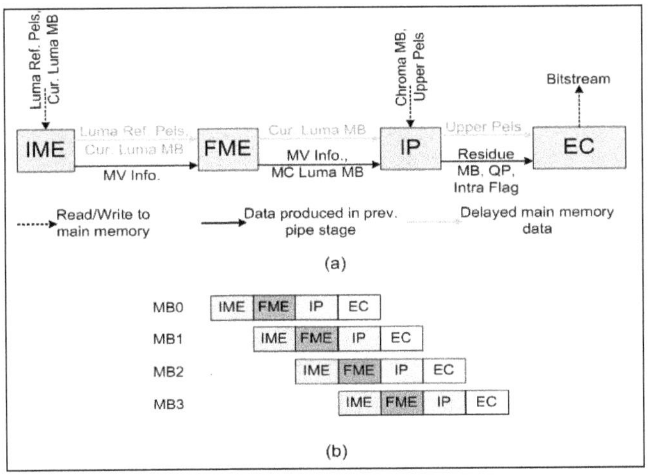

Figure 1. Four stage macroblock partition of H.264. (a) Data flow between different pipeline stages. (b) How the four stage pipeline works on different macro blocks. The IP stage includes DCT+Quant. EC is the CABAC stage.

Table 2. Performance and energy for a generic Tensilica CMP implementation of H.264. Intra combines IP, DCT, and Quant. The gap numbers compare these values to an equivalent ASIC.

	Performance					
	MC/ MB	Frame /sec	Area (mm^2)	Energy/ Frame (mJ)	Perf. Gap	Energy Gap
IME	2.10	0.06	1.04	1179	525.0x	707x
FME	1.36	0.08	1.04	921	342.0x	468x
Intra	0.25	0.48	1.04	137	63.0x	157x
CABAC	0.06	1.82	1.04	39	16.7x	261x

Table 3. Datapath energy breakdown for our base implementation in mJ/frame. IF is instruction fetch/decode (including the I-cache). D-$ is the D-cache. Pip is the pipeline registers, buses, and clocking. Ctl is random control. RF is the register file. FU is the functional elements. Data estimates from processor simulations.

	IF	D-$	Pip	Ctl	RF	FU	Total
IME	410	218	257	113	113	68	1179
FME	286	196	205	90	90	54	921
Intra	54	20	29	13	13	8	137
CABAC	12	2	8	4	4	2	32
Total	762	436	499	220	220	132	2269

We analyze the performance and energy efficiency of this base CMP implementation and compare it to that of the ASIC. We allocate the processor's energy into different functional units as shown in Table 3, which reports the energy consumed by our base four-processor CMP system. As expected, the energy required for each task is related to the time required for that task, since the energy of each instruction is similar. The RISC implementations of IME and FME, which are the major contributors to performance and energy consumption, have a performance gap of 525x and an energy gap of over 700x with respect to the ASIC.

We also note that while IP, DCT, Quant and CABAC are much smaller parts of the total energy/delay, even they need about 100x energy improvements to reach ASIC-level values.

This data makes it clear how far we need to go to approach ASIC efficiency. Clearly, the energy spent in instruction fetch (IF) is an overhead due to the programmable nature of the processors and is absent in a custom hardware state machine, but eliminating all this overhead only increases the energy efficiency by less than 2x. Even if we assume everything but the functional unit energy is overhead, we still end up with energy savings of only 20x—not nearly enough to reach ASIC levels. As the rest of this paper demonstrates, we need to both customize functional units (for correct bit widths, for efficient multi-input or output operations, etc.) and remove almost all other processor overheads (instruction fetches, register file accesses, etc.) to approach ASIC efficiency.

Table 4. Different stages of specialization, and the types of optimizations implemented. Step 1 is very general; step 2 is often done in general-purpose SIMD units for important applications; step 3 builds application specific functional units.

	Step 1	Step 2	Step 3
Inst. decode logic	App. class optimizations e.g. SIMD	App. class optimizations with custom fused instruction sub-graphs	Complex instrs performing multiple independent operations
Register file	App. specific register file size and width. SIMD register file	Consume short-lived intermediate results without sending to register file	App. specific data storage structures and data supply networks
Arithmetic datapath	App. specific precision	Custom fused arithmetic operations	App. specific arithmetic blocks

3.2 Customization Strategies

Table 4 defines three classes of processor customization. At the first stage we restrict ourselves to relatively general purpose datapath extensions such as SIMD and VLIW units; such extensions are frequently found in processor designs today and will be part of future efficient processors.

At the second stage, we add a limited degree of algorithm-specific customization. Operation fusion – the creation of new instructions that combine sequences of existing instructions – produces new functional units. We limit new instructions to operand requirements (i.e., two input operands, one output) that match those for existing instructions; new instructions must fit in existing instruction formats and datapath. This constraint is the same as that of Intel's SSE instructions. These customizations, at least for key functions, are also likely to exist in future processors.

Finally, at the third stage we allow unrestricted tailoring of the datapath according to algorithm needs by introducing arbitrary new compute operations as well as by complementing or even replacing the register files with custom storage structures. The results of these customizations shown in Figures 2, 3 and 4 are described in more detail in the next section.

4. RESULTS

We implement and evaluate the three-customization strategies of Table 4, detailing their effectiveness. For algorithm-specific

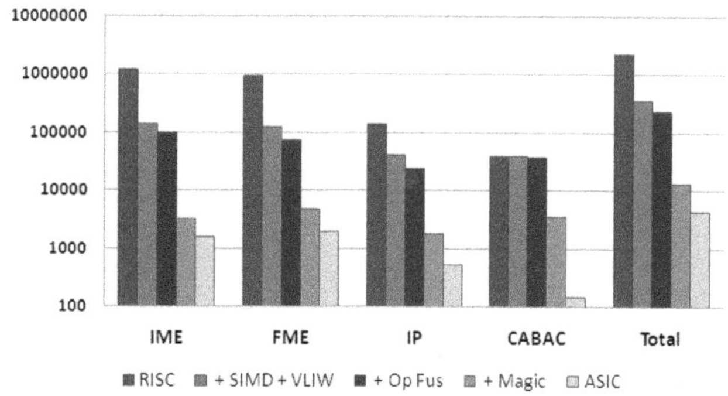

Figure 2. Each set of bar graphs represents energy consumption (μJ) at each stage of optimization for IME, FME, IP and CABAC respectively. Each optimization builds on the ones in the previous stage with the first bar in each set representing RISC energy dissipation followed by generic optimizations such as SIMD and VLIW, operation fusion and ending with "magic" instructions

instructions, we outline strategies for each major phase of computation. Collectively, these results describe how efficiencies improve by 170x over the baseline in Section 3.1.

4.1 SIMD and VLIW Enhancements

Using Tensilica's FLIX (Flexible Length Instruction eXtension) feature, we create processors with 2- and 3-slot VLIW instructions. Using TIE, we add SIMD execution units to the base processor with vector register files of custom depths and widths. As expected, DLP algorithms using SIMD units show a large decrease in processor energy; speedup increases as the number of instructions executed decreases. IME and FME use 16 and 18-way SIMD datapaths and achieve speedups of 10x and 14x. Intra/DCT/Quant using an 8-way SIMD datapath achieves a speedup of 6x. The SIMD units use custom-width functional units instead of standard 32-bit versions to enable more efficient computation, and generally run between 8 and 16 bits. As Figure 4 shows, even performing 16 concurrent operations barely increases the percentage energy used by the functional units, which still comprise around 10% of the total. Even the register file energy decreases by 4-6x using SIMD since we use 8-bit vector elements, and scale down register file depths, so its percentage contribution to the total energy does not increase considerably.

While SIMD only works for data-parallel algorithms, all H.264 sub-algorithms achieve speedups from VLIW instructions, with 2-slot VLIW offering higher energy efficiency than 3 slots. 2-slot VLIW gains up to 1.5x more performance. For CABAC, VLIW instructions increase the code size, and the resulting increase in cache size and cache access energy offsets any energy gains. SIMD and VLIW speed up the application by 10x, decreasing IF energy by 10x, but the percentage of energy going to IF does not change much. IF still consumes more energy than functional units. Furthermore, while CABAC is not initially an issue, its power dissipation is unchanged by these optimizations, and is now a major contributor to overall power dissipation.

4.2 Operation Fusion

The second customization strategy builds on the first and evaluates additional gains offered by the fusion of frequently

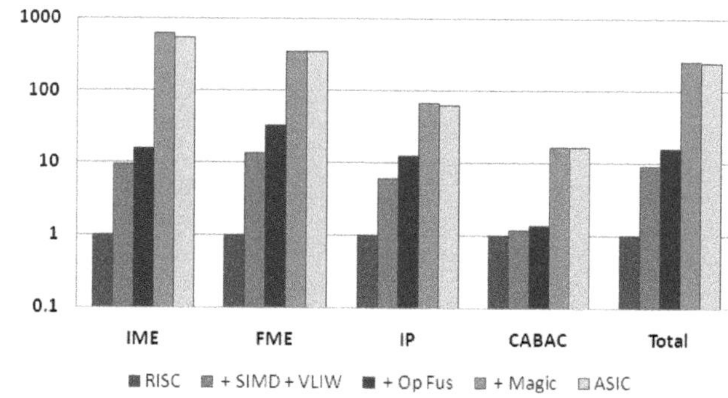

Figure 3. Each set of bar graphs represents speedup at each stage of optimization. Each optimization builds on those of the previous stage with the first bar in each set representing RISC speedup, followed by generic optimizations such as SIMD and VLIW, then operation fusion and finally "magic" instructions

occurring complex instruction subgraphs. Operation fusion is particularly interesting because it can be targeted by a number of automatic tools [22]. Fusion of complex subgraphs is useful because it reduces both instruction count and register file accesses—intermediate results are consumed within the fused operation and do not need to be stored in the register file. An additional benefit is the ability to create more energy efficient hardware implementations of the fused operations. For data parallel algorithms, we fuse together both RISC as well as SIMD operations. We pipeline our functional units to ensure fused operations do not increase clock cycle time.

To illustrate operation fusion, we present a pixel up-sampling example taken from FME:

$$\mathbf{x_n = x_{-2} - 5x_{-1} + 20x_0 + 20x_1 - 5x_2 + x_3}$$

H.264 uses this equation to perform upsampling of pixels in the reference image frame. In the equation $\mathbf{x_n}$ is the newly calculated up-sampled pixel, formed by applying an interpolation filter on pixels $\mathbf{x_{-2}}$ ... $\mathbf{x_3}$ of the reference frame. Upsampling uses a major portion of FME compute time, so we want to enhance its performance and energy efficiency.

Before creating fused instructions, we split the equation into three parts based on computation similarities: $\mathbf{20x_0 + 20x_1}$, $\mathbf{-5x_{-1} - 5x_2}$, and $\mathbf{x_2 + x_3}$. This allows us to keep the number of input operands per fused instruction equal to two and thus we do not increase the number of register file ports. Each instruction fuses addition/subtraction with multiplication, which is implemented using shift and adds. Figure 5 presents the newly created instructions.

Note that the two-input operand restriction is not broken because the accumulator register (acc), internal to the functional unit, is used implicitly. Similarly, the instruction supplies the constant multiplication factor directly, avoiding a register file access. These new instructions improve energy efficiency by reducing register file accesses by forwarding the result of the multiplication directly to an adder and by using an accumulator.

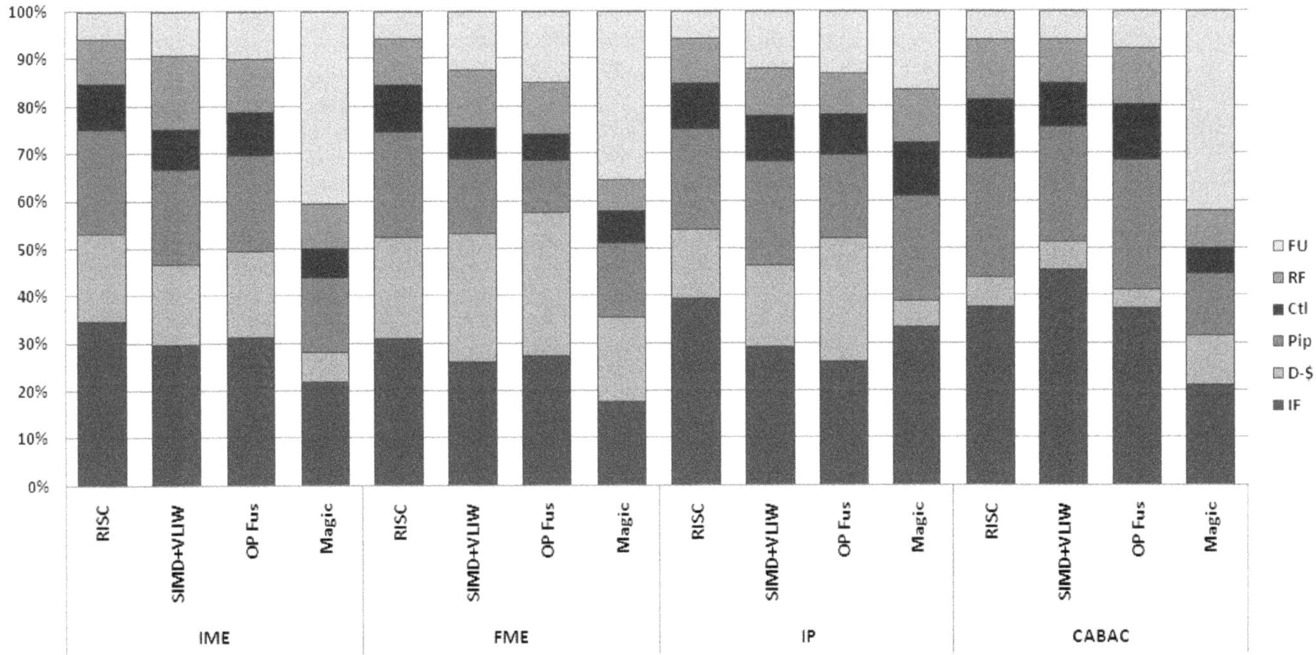

Figure 4. Datapath energy breakdown for H.264. IF is instruction fetch/decode (including the I-cache). D-$ is the D-cache. Pip is the pipeline registers, busses, and clocking. Ctl is random control. RF is the register file. FU is the functional elements. Only the top bar (FU), or perhaps the top two (FU + RF) contribute useful work in the processor. For this application it is hard to achieve much more than 10% of the power in the FU without adding custom hardware units. This data was estimated from processor simulations.

```
acc = 0;
acc = AddShft(acc, x0, x1, 20);
acc = AddShft(acc, x-1, x2, -5);
acc = AddShft(acc, x-2, x3, 1);
xn = Sat(acc);
```

Figure 5. FME upsampling after fusion of two multiplications and two additions. AddShft takes two inputs, multiplies both with the multiplicand and adds the result. Multiplication is performed using shifts and adds. Operation fusion results in 3 instructions instead of the RISC's 5 add/sub and 4 multiplication instructions.

Table 5. Fused operations added to each unit and the resulting performance and energy gains. FME required fusion of large subgraphs to get significant performance improvement.

	# of fused ops	Op Depth	Energy Gain	Perf Gain
IME	4	3-5	1.5	1.6
FME	2	18-34	1.9	2.4
Intra	8	3-7	1.9	2.1
CABAC	5	3-7	1.1	1.1

Table 5 presents the number of fused operations created for each H.264 algorithm, the average size of the fused instruction subgraphs, and the total energy and performance gain achieved through fusion. Interestingly, IME and FME do not share any instructions, though Intra and FME share instructions for the Hadamard transform. DCT transform also implements the same transform instructions. CABAC's fused operations provide negligible performance and energy gains of 1.1x. Fused instructions give the largest advantage for FME, on average doubling the energy/performance advantage of SIMD/VLIW. Employing fused operations in combination with SIMD/VLIW results in an overall performance improvement of 15x for the H.264 encoder, and an energy efficiency gain of almost 10x, but still uses greater than 50x more energy than an ASIC.

The basic problem is clear. For H.264, the basic operations are very simple and low energy. In our base machine we over-estimate the energy consumed by the functional units, since we count the entire 32-wide functional unit energy. When we move to the SIMD machine, we tailor the functional unit to the desired width, which reduces the required energy. However, executing 10s of narrow width operations per instruction still leaves a machine that is spending 90% of its energy on overhead functions, with only 10% going to the functional units.

4.3 Algorithm Specific Instructions

To bridge the remaining gap, we must create instructions that can execute 100s of operations in a single instruction. To achieve this parallelism requires creating instructions that are tightly connected to custom data storage elements with algorithm-specific communication links to supply the large amounts of data required, and thus tend to be very closely tied to the specific algorithmic methods being optimized. These storage elements can then be directly wired to custom designed multiple input and possibly multiple output functional units, directly implementing the required communication for the function in hardware.

Once this hardware is in place, the machine can issue "magic" instructions that can accomplish large amounts of computation at very low costs. This type of structure eliminates almost all the processor overheads for these functions by eliminating most of the communication overhead (register file, bus, and instruction fetch) associated with processors. We call these "magic" instructions, since these operations can have a large effect on both the energy and performance of an application and yet would be difficult to derive directly from the code. They typically require an understanding of the underlying algorithms and the capabilities and limitations of existing hardware resources, thus requiring greater effort on part of the designer. Since the IP stage uses some techniques similar to FME the rest of the section will focus on FME, IME and CABAC.

4.3.1 *FME Strategy*

To illustrate a "magic" instruction, we begin by returning to the pixel upsampling example. In H.264, upsampling uses an FIR filter that requires one new pixel per iteration. Thus after one upsampling step, we can reuse pixels $\mathbf{x}_{-1} \ldots \mathbf{x}_3$, and only need to load $\mathbf{x}_4$. Normal register files require us to do five register transfers for each upsampling step, significantly increasing the energy dissipated in the instruction fetch and decode logic and also in the register file. While some machines have indexing register files that help with this issue [6], we still need to read all the operations from the register file to perform the computation.

To reduce instruction fetches and register file transfers, we augment the processor register file with a custom 8-bit wide, six entry shift register structure which works like a FIFO: every time a new 8-bit value is loaded, all elements are shifted. This eliminates the use of expensive register file accesses for either data shifting or operand fetch, which are now both handled by short local wires. Additionally, since all six entries can now be accessed in parallel we create a six input multiplier/adder which can be implemented much more efficiently (using carry-save addition) than the composition of normal 2 input adders. Finally since we need to perform the upsampling in 2-D, we build a shift register structure that stores the horizontally upsampled data, and feeds its outputs to a number of vertical upsampling units (see **Figure** 6).

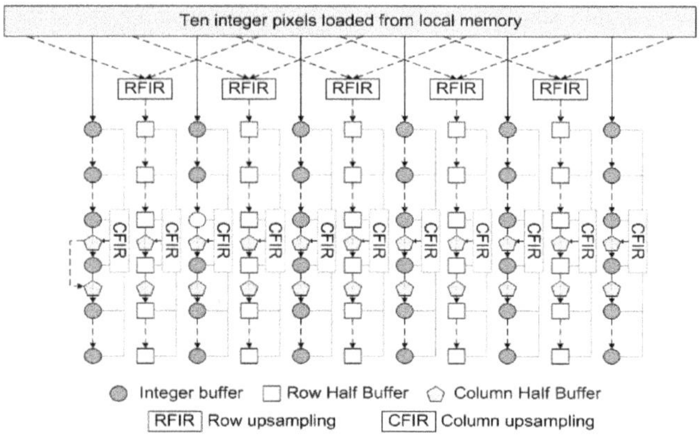

Figure 6. FME upsampling unit, showing merged storage and computation. Customized shift registers directly wired to function logic result in efficient upsampling. Ten integer pixels from local memory are used for row upsampling in RFIR blocks. Half upsampled pixels along with appropriate integer pixels are loaded into shift registers. CFIR accesses six shift registers in each column simultaneously to perform column upsampling.

This transformation yields large savings even beyond the savings in instruction fetch energy. From a pure datapath perspective (register file, pipeline registers, and functional units), this approach dissipates less than 1/30th the energy of a traditional approach.

The FME SIMD code highlights the advantages of this approach over using larger SIMD arrays. The SIMD implementation suffers from code replication and excessive local memory and register file accesses, in addition to not having the most efficient functional units. FME contains seven different sub-block sizes ranging from 16x16 pixel blocks to 4x4 blocks, and not all of them can fully exploit the 18-way SIMD datapath. Additionally, to use the 18-way SIMD datapath, each sub-block requires a slightly different code sequence, which results in code replication and more I-fetch power because of the larger I-cache. Next, FME fits a streaming data flow model where most of the intermediate data has a short life and is consumed by instructions that are only a few cycles behind; by storing such intermediate data in the register file, energy is wasted on unnecessary register file accesses. This intermediate data also leaves less space in the register file for non-intermediate data, resulting in additional loads and stores. Finally, not all computations are able to benefit from fusion because our register files can only supply two operands at a time.

To avoid these issues, our custom hardware upsampler processes 4x4 pixels. This allows us to reuse the same computation loop repeatedly without any code replication, which, in turn, lets us reduce the I-cache from a 16KB 4-way cache to a 2KB direct-mapped cache. Due to the abundance of short-lived data, we remove the vector register files and replace them with custom storage buffers. The magic instruction reduces the instruction cache energy by 54x and processor fetch and decode energy by 14x. Finally, as Figure 4 shows, 35% of the energy is now going into the functional units.

4.3.2 *IME Strategy*

4x4 sum of absolute differences (SAD) calculations are important for IME. Figure 7 shows the custom datapath elements added to the IME processor to accelerate this function. The 16-way SIMD SAD unit of the fusion-optimized processor has been replaced by a 16x16 SAD unit, which can perform 256 SAD operations in one cycle. Since our standard vector register files cannot feed enough data to this unit per cycle, these registers have been replaced by state registers, which allow parallel access to all 16-pixel rows and enable this datapath to perform one 256-pixel computation per cycle. The fetch overhead of SAD operations is thus reduced by roughly 16x. Additionally, this custom storage structure has support for parallel shifts in all four directions, thus allowing much greater data reuse, and drastically reducing the cycles spent on loads, shifts and pointer arithmetic operations as well as data cache accesses. "Magic" instructions and storage elements are also created for other major algorithmic functions in IME to achieve similar gains. More than 65% of total IME cycles are spent in overhead instructions. Thus, by reducing instruction overheads and by amortizing the remaining overheads over larger datapath widths, this strategy improves performance and energy efficiency by 20-30x.

The large number of parallel operations means that this functional unit finally consumes around 40% of the total instruction energy. This would be even higher, but we further reduced energy (approximately 30%) by employing reduced precision arithmetic where only 5 pixel-bits are used in distortion calculations instead of 8. This technique is also employed by our reference ASIC and causes negligible drop in SNR [4]. These optimizations along with a small set of other custom operations enable the IME processor to match ASIC performance and come within 3x of ASIC energy

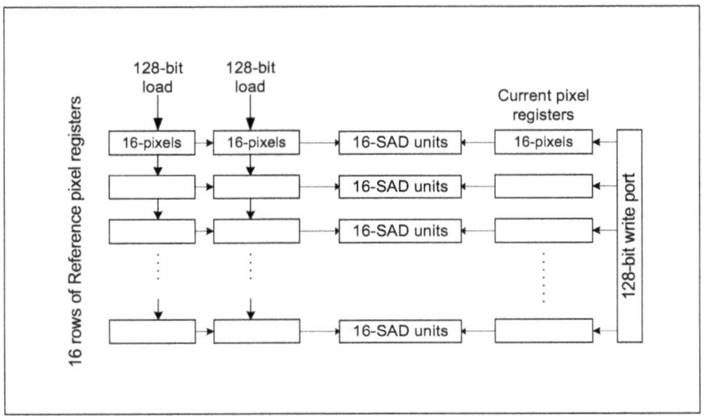

Figure 7. Custom storage and compute blocks for IME's 4x4 SAD calculation. Current and reference-pixel register files allow parallel access to all pixel values to feed the 16x16 SAD array. In addition, the RefPixel Regfile supports operations to shift all pixel rows down by one row or shift all pixel columns right by one pixel location.

4.3.3 *CABAC Strategy*

CABAC originally consumed less than 2% of the total energy. However, after adding "magic" instructions for data parallel components, CABAC dominates the total energy. However, it requires a different set of optimizations because it is highly control oriented and not data parallel. Thus, for CABAC, we are more interested in control fusion than operation fusion.

A critical part of CABAC is the arithmetic encoding stage, which is a highly serialized process with small amounts of computation, but significant control flow. We break arithmetic coding down into a simple pipeline and drastically change it from the reference code implementation, reducing the binary encoding of each symbol to five instructions. While there are several if-then-else conditionals reduced to single instructions (or with several compressed into one), the most significant reduction came in the encoding loop, which is written as a while loop over every bit of the **RANGE** in the reference code as shown in Figure 8. This loop (including the implicit doubly nested loops in **`put_one_bit_plus_outstanding`**) was reduced to a single constant time instruction and a rarely executed small while loop by fundamentally changing the algorithm as shown in Figure 9. Since we now do buffering on a 64-bit basis, **`word1full`** is rarely true, and **`wordsOustanding`** is almost never greater than 0.

The other critical part of CABAC is the conversion of non-binary valued DCT coefficients to binary codes in the binarization stage. To improve the efficiency of this step, we create a 16-entry LIFO structure to store DCT coefficients. To each LIFO entry, we add a single-bit flag to identify zero-valued DCT coefficients. These structures, along with their corresponding logic, reduce register file energy by bringing the most frequently used values out of the register file and into custom storage buffers. Using "magic" instructions we produce Unary and Exponential-Golomb codes using simple operations, which help reduce datapath energy. These modifications are inspired by the ASIC implementation described in [15]. CABAC is optimized to achieve the bit rate required for H.264 level 3.1 at 720p video resolution.

```
while (range < QUARTER) {
  if (low >= HALF) {
    put_one_bit_plus_outstanding(1);
    low -= HALF;
  } else if (low < QUARTER) {
    put_one_bit_plus_outstanding(0);
  } else {
    global_eep.Ebits_to_follow++;
    low -= QUARTER;
  }
  low <<= 1;
  range <<= 1;
}
```

Figure 8. CABAC arithmetic encoding loop in H.264 reference code looping over every bit of the "RANGE."

```
word1full = BIARI_ENCODE_PIPE_5();
if (word1full){
  wordsOutstanding = WRITE_OUT_WORD1();
  while(wordsOutstanding){
    wordsOutstanding =
      WRITE_OUT_UNRESOLVED();
  }
}
```

Figure 9. CABAC arithmetic encoding loop after insertion of "magic" instructions. The loop corresponding to RANGE has been reduced to one single constant time instruction BIARI_ENCODE_PIPE_5.

ASIC-like efficiency required 2-3 special hardware units for each sub-algorithm, which is significant customization work. After this effort, the processors optimized for data-parallel algorithms have a total speedup of up to 600x and an energy reduction of 60-350x compared to our base CMP. For CABAC total performance gain is 17x and energy gain is 8x. Figure 4 provides the final energy breakdowns.

Table 6 - Area and area efficiency at various stages of customization

	Area (mm^2)					Speedup	Area Efficiency (Speedup/ Area)
	IME	FME	IP	CABAC	Total		
RISC	1.39	1.39	1.39	1.39	5.56	1	0.18
RISC with Memory Cust.	0.80	1.39	1.06	1.44	4.69	1	0.21
GP Opt.	1.79	4.12	1.76	1.55	9.22	9.2	1.00
OP Fusion	1.83	3.32	1.63	1.64	8.42	15.7	1.87
Magic	2.10	2.28	1.58	1.1	7.06	256	36.25
ASIC @ 100MHz	2.82	3.33	1.47	0.27	7.89	243	30.81
ASIC @ 435MHz	2.82	3.33	1.47	0.27	7.89	1057	133.97

4.4 Area Efficiency

Table 6 shows area in mm^2 for the evaluated optimization strategies. The last column shows the area efficiency for each step, which is defined as speedup/area. Customizing cache sizes to the requirements of each algorithm results in substantial area savings as depicted by "RISC with Mem Cust". General-purpose optimizations increase the area substantially compared to vanilla RISC versions, but they also help improve the area efficiency for data-parallel algorithms. However, control-intensive CABAC does not benefit from such optimizations. Further customization of datapaths not only improves area efficiency tremendously but also results in a smaller area compared to general-purpose optimizations. Customizations not only reduce the number of instructions, but also substantially improve data reuse inside the processor, which in turn reduces cache sizes. This reduction in memory area helps offset area increases due to addition of custom units.

It might seem that the efficiency of our solution is higher than that of an ASIC, but the ASIC is designed to run at 100MHz in 0.18um while our magic version is designed to run at 435MHz. If we assume that the ASIC in 90nm can run at 435MHz without any modifications, it can achieve 4.35x better performance and thus 4.35x better area efficiency, making it substantially more area efficient than our solution.

4.5 Other Applications

While H.264 is representative of applications with very simple compute operations, other applications, for example floating point (FP) applications, have higher-energy operations. FP arithmetic consumes 10x the energy of integer arithmetic; FP functional units comprise a larger fraction of total instruction energy. Thus, one might think less parallelization is required to amortize instruction overheads for FP applications.

However FP operations comprise only 20% of the dynamic instruction stream for representative applications [26][27]. For this reason, FP energy will likely be a small fraction of total application energy. To match the most efficient H.264 design points, 35% or more of the total application energy should be in the ALU. Thus, with an instruction overhead of approximately 130pJ, functional unit energy will need to be at least 70 pJ, which is equivalent to 7 FP operations, or approximately 35 instructions (given a 20% FP instruction mix). While this level of parallelism might be possible for some applications with SIMD and operation fusion, it seems likely that customizations will be needed to achieve this number of ops/instruction for most applications. This is especially true if some part of the application is control and not data limited.

Finally, some applications are dominated by memory costs. In truly memory-bound applications, computation is not the bottleneck, so data path customizations will have little effect. For these applications, it is the energy efficiency of bringing application data to the core that fundamentally needs to be improved. Co-optimization of the memory system and the application can yield large savings in these situations [28], but the advantages of application customization over a conventional memory design with a few adjustable parameters still needs to be explored.

5. ENERGY EFFICIENT COMPUTERS

It is now easy to see how an ASIC can be 2-3 orders of magnitude lower energy than a processor. For many applications, and most of the ones performed by ASICs, the basic operations being performed are very low energy, using 8-16 bit integers like in H.264. These applications are computation—and not data fetch—limited, so the fundamental energy/operation bound is a couple hundred femtojoules in a 90nm process, which is equivalent to moving one bit less than a mm. All other costs in a processor—instruction fetch, register fetch, data fetch, control, and pipeline registers—are much larger (140pJ) and dominate overall power.

Standard SIMD and simple operation fusion instructions can only go so far to improve the performance and energy efficiency. It is hard to aggregate more than 10-20 operations into an instruction without incurring growing inefficiencies, and with tens of operations per cycle we still have a machine where around 90% of the energy is going into overhead functions. In addition, some of these overhead instructions are just to control or sequence the data (e.g., CABAC).

Thus, the solution is "instructions" that perform hundreds of operations each time they are executed, so the overhead of the instruction is better balanced by the work performed. Unfortunately this is hard to do in a general way, since bandwidth requirements and utilization of a larger SIMD array would be problematic. We solved this problem by building custom storage units tailored to the application, and then directly connecting the necessary functional units to these storage units. These custom storage units greatly amplified the register fetch bandwidth, since data in the storage units are used for many different computations. In addition, since the intra-storage and functional unit communications were fixed and local, they could be managed at ASIC-like energy costs. The efficiencies found in these custom datapaths are impressive, since, in H.264, at least, they take advantage of data sharing patterns and create very efficient multiple input operations. This means that even if researchers are able to a create a processor which decreases the instruction and data fetch parts of a processor by more than 10x, these solutions will not be as efficient as solutions with "magic" instructions.

Of course including these "magic" instructions requires custom hardware, and some might say we are just building an ASIC in our processor. While we agree that creating "magic" instructions requires a thorough understanding of the application as well as hardware, we feel that adding this hardware in an extensible processor framework has many advantages over just designing an ASIC. These advantages come from the constrained processor design environment and the software, compiler, and debugging tools available in this environment.

For example, once the initial effort in understanding the application and its characteristics was done, the extensible processor allowed us to implement and verify the fully customized "magic" configuration for each algorithm in two to three man-months, which would not have been possible with an ASIC flow. Many of the low-level issues, like interface design and pipelining, are automatically handled. In addition, since all hardware is wrapped in a general-purpose processor, the application developer retains enough flexibility in the processor to make future algorithmic modifications. In fact, in this type of design environment, one might be tempted to make the new hardware that supports the "magic" instructions a little more flexible than required, providing some runtime flexibility just to increase the probability of it still being useful if the algorithm changes.

Yet an extensible processor alone is not a sufficient solution, since one still needs to take one or more of these processors and create a working chip system. Designing and validating a chip is an extremely hard and expensive task. If application customization will be needed for efficiency—and our data indicates it will be—we need to start creating systems that will efficiently allow savvy application experts to create these optimized chip level solutions. This will require extending the ideas for extensible processors to extensible full chip systems. We are currently working on this creating this type of system.

6. CONCLUSION

Ideally, we would like ASIC-like energy efficiencies—100x to 1000x more energy efficient than general-purpose CPUs—on our next generation processors. Our data, while not conclusive, indicates that this goal will be hard to achieve. The basic problem is that many applications include extremely simple, low energy operations. Since the energy of these operations is very low, any overhead, from the register fetch to the pipeline registers in a processor, is likely to dominate. The good news is that this large overhead per instruction makes estimating the energy savings easy—you simply look at the performance gains—but the bad news is that adding data parallel hardware like wide SIMD units will still leave you far from an ASIC.

It is encouraging that we were able to achieve ASIC energy levels in a customized processor by creating customized hardware that easily fit inside a processor framework and executed 100s of simple operations per instruction. Extending a processor instead of building an ASIC seems like the correct approach; since it provides a number of software development advantages and the energy cost of this option seems small. The key challenge now is to build a design system that lets application designers create these types of customizations with much greater ease.

7. ACKNOWLEDGMENTS

This work would have not been possible without great support and cooperation from many people at Tensilica including Chris Rowen, Dror Maydan, Bill Huffman, Nenad Nedeljkovic, David Heine, Govind Kamat and others. The authors acknowledge the support of the C2S2 Focus Center, one of six research centers funded under the Focus Center Research Program (FCRP), a Semiconductor Research Corporation subsidiary, and earlier support from DARPA. This material is based upon work partially supported under a Sequoia Capital Stanford Graduate Fellowship. The National Science Foundation under Grant #0937060 to the Computing Research Association also supports this material for the CIFellows Project. Any opinions, findings, and conclusions or recommendations expressed in this material are those of the author(s) and do not necessarily reflect the view of the National Science Foundation or the Computing Research Association.

8. REFERENCES

[1] Horowitz, M., Alon, E., Patil, D., Naffziger, S., Kumar, R., Bernstein, K., "Scaling, Power and the Future of CMOS," 20th Int'l Conference on VLSI Design, 2007, held jointly with 6th Int'l Conference on Embedded Systems, p. 23, 6-10 Jan. 2007.

[2] Solomatnikov, A, Firoozshahian, A., Qadeer,W., Shacham, O., Kelley, K., Asgar, Z., Wachs, M., Hameed, R., Horowitz, M., "Chip Multi-Processor Generator," Proceedings of the 44th Annual Design Automation Conference, 2007, pp. 262–263.

[3] Iverson, V., McVeigh, J., Reese, B., "Real-time H.264/avc Codec on Intel architectures," IEEE Int. Conf. Image Processing (ICIP'04), 2004.

[4] Chen, T.-C., et al., "Analysis and architecture design of an HDTV720p 30 frames/s H.264/AVC encoder," Circuits and Systems for Video Technology, IEEE Transactions on, vol.16, no.6, pp. 673-688, June 2006.

[5] Davis, W.R., Zhang, N., Camera, K., Markovic, D., Smilkstein, T., Ammer, M.J., Yeo, E., Augsburger, S., Nikolic, B., Brodersen, R.W., "A design environment for high-throughput low-power dedicated signal processing systems," Solid-State Circuits, IEEE Journal of, vol.37, no.3, pp.420-431, Mar 2002.

[6] Balfour, J., Dally, W.J., Black-Schaffer, D., Parikh, V., Park, J.S., "An Energy-Efficient Processor Architecture for Embedded Systems," Computer Architecture Letters, vol.7, no.1, pp.29-32, January-June 2007.

[7] McCloud, S., "Catapult C Synthesis-Based Design Flow: Speeding Implementation and Increasing Flexibility," Mentor Graphics Technical Library, http://www.techonline.com/electronics_directory/techpaper/193102520, August 2004.

[8] Kathail,V., "Creating power-efficient application engines for SoC design," Synfora, Inc. SoC Central, Feb 1, 2005.

[9] Rowen, C., Leibson, S., "Flexible architectures for engineering successful SOCs," Design Automation Conf, 2004. Proceedings. 41st , pp. 692-697, 2004.

[10] Woh, M., Seo, S., Mahlke, S., Mudge, T., Chakrabarti, C., and Flautner, K., "AnySP: anytime anywhere anyway signal processing," SIGARCH Comp. Arch. News 37, 3 (Jun. 2009), 128-139.

[11] Intel Corp., "Motion Estimation with Intel® Streaming SIMD Extensions 4 (Intel® SSE4)" [Online]. Available: http://software.intel.com/en-us/articles/motion-estimation-with-intel-streaming-simd-extensions-4-intel-sse4/.

[12] Intel Corp., "Intel SSE4 Programming Reference" [Online]. Available: http://softwarecommunity.intel.com/isn/Downloads/Intel%20SSE4%20Programming%20Reference.pdf.

[13] Clark, N.T., Zhong, H., Mahlke, S.A., "Automated custom instruction generation for domain-specific processor acceleration," Computers, IEEE Transactions on, vol.54, no.10, pp. 1258-1270, Oct. 2005.

[14] Cong, J., Fan, Y., Han, G., and Zhang, Z., "Application-specific instruction generation for configurable processor architectures," Proceedings of the 2004 ACM/SIGDA 12th international Symposium on Field Programmable Gate Arrays (Monterey, California, USA, February 22 - 24, 2004). FPGA '04. ACM, New York, NY, 183-189.

[15] Shojania, H., Sudharsanan, S., "A VLSI Architecture for High-Performance CABAC Encoding," Visual Communications and Image Processing (SPIE), 2005. Proceedings. vol. 5960, June 2005.

[16] Ienne, P., Leupers, R., "Customizable Embedded Processors: Design Technologies and Applications (Systems on Silicon)," Morgan Kaufmann Publishers Inc. 2006.

[17] Tensilica Inc., "Xtensa LX2 Benchmarks" [Online]. Available: http://www.tensilica.com/products/xtensa-customizable/xtensa-lx2/benchmarks.htm.

[18] Tensilica Inc., "The What, Why, and How of Configurable Processors" [Online]. Available: http://www.tensilica.com/products/literature-docs/white-papers/configurable-processors.htm.

[19] Tensilica Inc., "Implementing the Advanced Encryption Standard on Xtensa® Processors", Application note. [Online]. Available: http://www.tensilica.com/products/literature-docs/application-notes/tie-application-notes/advanced-encryption-standard.htm.

[20] Tensilica Inc., "Implementing the Fast Fourier Transform (FFT)", Application note. [Online]. Available: http://www.tensilica.com/products/literature-docs/application-notes/tie-application-notes/fast-fourier-transform-fft.htm.

[21] Tensilica Inc., "Xtensa Processor Extensions for Data Encryption Standard (DES)" Application note. [Online]. Available: http://www.tensilica.com/products/literature-docs/application-notes/tie-application-notes/data-encryption-extensions.htm.

[22] Tensilica Inc., "How to Minimize Energy Consumption while Maximizing ASIC and SOC Performance" White Paper. Available: http://www.tensilica.com/uploads/white_papers/Xenergy_Tensilica.pdf.

[23] Weigand, T., Sullivan, G., Bjontegaard, G., Luthra, A., "Overview of the H.264/AVC Coding Standard," IEEE Transactions on Circuits and Systems for Video Technology, vol 13, no 7, July 2003.

[24] Draft ITU-T Recommendation and Final Draft International Standard of Joint Video Specification, Joint Video Team, ITU-T Recommendation H.264 and ISO/IEC 14496-10 AVC, May 2003.

[25] Tensilica Inc., "Xtensa Energy Estimator (Xenergy) – User's Guide".

[26] Cheveresan, R., Ramsay, M., Feucht, C., Sharapov, I., "Characteristics of workloads used in high performance and technical computing," Proceedings of the 21st annual international conference on Supercomputing, June 17-21, 2007.

[27] Rupnow, K., Rodrigues A., Underwood, K., Compton, K., "Scientific applications vs. SPEC-FP: a comparison of program behavior," Proceedings of the 20th annual international conference on Supercomputing, June 28-July 01, 2006.

[28] Williams, S., Oliker, L., Vuduc, R., Shalf, J., Yelick, K. and Demmel, J., "Optimization of sparse matrix-vector multiplication on emerging multicore platforms", Proceedings of the 2007 ACM/IEEE conference on Supercomputing, ACM New York, NY, USA, 2007.

[29] Lin, Y.-K., Li, D.-W., Lin, C.-C., Kuo, T.-Y., Wu, S.-J., Tai, W.-C., Chang, W.-C. and Chang, T.-S., "A 242mw $10mm^2$ 1080p H.264/AVC high profile encoder chip," Proceedings of the 45th Design Automation Conference, 2008.

[30] Chang, H.-C., Chen, J.-W., Su, C.-L., Yang, Y.-C., Li, Y., Chang, C.-H., Chen, Z.-M., Yang, W.-S., Lin, C.-C., Chen, C.-W., Wang, J.-S. and Guo, J.-I., "A 7mw-to-183mw dynamic quality-scalable h.264 video encoder chip," Proceedings of 2007 IEEE ISSCC Dig. Tech. Papers.

[31] ISO/IEC MPEG & ITU-T VCEG, "Fast Integer Pel and Fractional Pel Motion Estimation for JVT," JVT-F017, 2002.

[32] Yin, P, Tourapis, H.-Y. C., Tourapis, A. M., and Boyce, J., "Fast mode decision and motion estimation for JVT/H.264," Proceedings of IEEE International Conference on Image Processing, 2003.

[33] Chen, C.-Y., Chien, S.-Y., Huang, Y.-W., Chen, T.-C., Wang, T. C. and Chen, L.-Y., "Analysis and Architecture Design of Variable Block-Size Motion Estimation for H.264/AVC," IEEE Transactions on Circuits and Systems, 2006.

[34] Li, S., Wei, X., Ikenaga, T. and Goto, S., "A VLSI architecture design of an edge based fast intra prediction mode decision algorithm for h.264/avc," Proceedings of the 17th ACM Great Lakes Symposium on VLSI.

[35] Chen, T-C., Huang, Y.-W. and Chen, L.-G., "Fully Utilized And Reusable Architecture For Fractional Motion Estimation Of H.264/Avc," Proceedings of IEEE International Conference On Acoustics Speech And Signal Processing, 2004.

[36] Osorio, R. R., Bruguera, J. D., "High-Throughput Architecture for H.264/AVC CABAC Compression System," IEEE Transactions on Circuits and Systems for Video Technology, 2006.

[37] Chen, Y.-K., Li, E. Q., Zhou, X. and Ge, S., "Implementation of H.264 encoder and decoder on personal computers," Journal of Visual Communication and Image Representation, April 2006.

[38] Joint Video Team Reference Software JM8.6, ITU-T.

[39] Firoozshahian, A., Solomatnikov, A., Shacham, O., Asgar, Z., Richardson, S., Kozyrakis, C., Horowitz, M., "A memory system design framework: creating smart memories," Proceedings of the 36th annual international symposium on Computer architecture, 2009.

[40] Solomatnikov, A., Firoozshahian, A. Shacham, O., Asgar, Z., Wachs, M, Qadeer, W, Richardson, S. and Horowitz, M., "Using a Configurable Processor Generator for Computer Architecture Prototyping," Proceedings of the 42nd Annual IEEE/ACM International Symposium on Microarchitecture, 2009.

Translation Caching: Skip, Don't Walk (the Page Table)

Thomas W. Barr, Alan L. Cox, Scott Rixner

Rice University
Houston, TX
{twb, alc, rixner}@rice.edu

ABSTRACT

This paper explores the design space of MMU caches that accelerate virtual-to-physical address translation in processor architectures, such as x86-64, that use a radix tree page table. In particular, these caches accelerate the page table walk that occurs after a miss in the Translation Lookaside Buffer. This paper shows that the most effective MMU caches are *translation caches*, which store partial translations and allow the page walk hardware to skip one or more levels of the page table.

In recent years, both AMD and Intel processors have implemented MMU caches. However, their implementations are quite different and represent distinct points in the design space. This paper introduces three new MMU cache structures that round out the design space and directly compares the effectiveness of all five organizations. This comparison shows that two of the newly introduced structures, both of which are translation cache variants, are better than existing structures in many situations.

Finally, this paper contributes to the age-old discourse concerning the relative effectiveness of different page table organizations. Generally speaking, earlier studies concluded that organizations based on hashing, such as the inverted page table, outperformed organizations based upon radix trees for supporting large virtual address spaces. However, these studies did not take into account the possibility of caching page table entries from the higher levels of the radix tree. This paper shows that any of the five MMU cache structures will reduce radix tree page table DRAM accesses far below an inverted page table.

Categories and Subject Descriptors

C.0 [**General**]: Modelling of computer architecture; C.4 [**Performance of systems**]: Design studies; D.4.2 [**Operating Systems**]: Virtual Memory

General Terms

Performance, Design

Keywords

TLB, Memory Management, Page Walk Caching

1. INTRODUCTION

This paper explores the design space of memory-management unit (MMU) caches for accelerating virtual-to-physical address translation in processor architectures, like x86-64, that implement paged virtual memory using a radix tree for their page table. In particular, these caches accelerate the page table walk that occurs after a miss in the Translation Lookaside Buffer (TLB). In fact, a hit in some of these caches enables the processor to *skip* over one or more levels of the tree and, in the best case, access only the tree's lowest level.

For several generations of x86 processors, from the Intel 80386 to the Pentium, the page table had at most two levels. Consequently, whenever a TLB miss occurred, at most two memory accesses were needed to complete the translation. However, as the physical and virtual address spaces supported by x86 processors have grown in size, the maximum depth of the tree has increased, first to three levels in the Pentium Pro to accommodate a 36-bit physical address within a page table entry, and more recently to four levels in the AMD Opteron to support a 48-bit virtual address space. In fact, with each passing decade since the introduction of the 80386, the depth of the tree has grown by one level.

Recent work has shown the impact of TLB misses on overall system performance ranges from 5-14% for nominally sized applications, even in a non-virtualized environment [9]. As the application's memory footprint increases, TLB misses have a significantly larger impact on performance, approaching 50% in some cases [19]. Although the use of large pages can lessen this impact, with further increases in the memory footprint their effectiveness declines. Therefore, both AMD and Intel have implemented MMU caches for page table entries from the higher levels of the tree [3, 9]. However, their caches have quite different structure. For example, AMD's Page Walk Cache stores page table entries from any level of the tree, whereas Intel implements distinct caches for each level of the tree. Also, AMD's Page Walk Cache is indexed by the physical address of the cached page table entry, whereas Intel's Paging-Structure Caches are indexed by portions of the virtual address being translated. Thus, in this respect, the Page Walk Cache resembles the processor's data cache, whereas the Paging-Structure Caches resemble its TLB.

This paper's primary contribution is that it provides the first comprehensive exploration of the design space occupied by these caches. In total, it discusses five distinct points in this space, including three new designs. Specifically, it presents the first head-to-head comparison of the effectiveness of these designs. In general, the results of this comparison show that the *translation caches*, which store partial translations and allow the page walk hardware to skip one or more levels of the page table, are the best. In addition, the new translation caches that are introduced by this paper are better than the existing caches in many situations and workloads.

Finally, this paper contributes to the age-old discourse concerning the relative effectiveness of different page table organizations. Generally speaking, earlier studies concluded that organizations based on hashing, such as the inverted page table, outperformed organizations based upon radix trees for supporting large virtual address spaces [23, 15]. However, these studies did not take into account the possibility of caching page table entries from the higher levels of the radix tree. This paper shows that radix tables cause up to 20% fewer total memory accesses and up to 400% fewer DRAM accesses than hash-based tables because of the locality in virtual address use.

This paper is organized as follows. The next section provides the background for the rest of the paper. Specifically, it summarizes the relevant aspects of x86/x86-64 virtual-to-physical address translation. Section 3 describes the design space, identifying the essential differences between AMD's Page Walk Cache, Intel's Paging-Structure caches, and the new structures developed in this paper. Section 4 qualitatively compares these structures, and Section 5 describes this paper's methodology for quantitatively comparing them. Section 6 presents quantitative simulation results of their effectiveness as compared to one another, and Section 7 compares the effectiveness of a radix tree page table with these structures to competing page table designs. Additionally, Section 7 examines the interaction between the MMU caches and large pages. Section 8 discusses the related work. Finally, Section 9 summarizes this paper's conclusions.

2. X86 ADDRESS TRANSLATION

All x86 processors since the Intel 80386 have used a radix tree to record the mapping from virtual to physical addresses. Although the depth of this tree has increased, to accommodate larger physical and virtual address spaces, the procedure for translating virtual addresses to physical addresses using this tree is essentially unchanged. A virtual address is split into a page number and a page offset. The page number is further split into a sequence of indices. The first index is used to select an entry from the root of the tree, which may contain a pointer to a node at the next lower level of the tree. If the entry does contain a pointer, the next index is used to select an entry from this node, which may again contain a pointer to a node at the next lower level of the tree. These steps repeat until the selected entry is either invalid (in essence, a NULL pointer indicating there is no valid translation for that portion of the address space) or the entry instead points to a data page using its physical address. In the latter case, the page offset from the virtual address is added to the physical address of this data page to obtain the full physical address. In a simple memory management unit (MMU) design, this procedure requires one memory access per level in the tree.

Figure 1 shows the precise decomposition of a virtual address by x86-64 processors [1]. Standard x86-64 pages are 4KB, so there is a single 12-bit page offset. The remainder of the 48-bit virtual address is divided into four 9-bit indices, which are used to select entries from the four levels of the page table. The four levels of the x86-64 page table are named PML4 (Page Map Level 4), PDP (Page Directory Pointer), PD (Page Directory) and PT (Page Table). In this paper, however, for clarity, we will refer to these levels as L4 (PML4), L3 (PDP), L2 (PD) and L1 (PT). Finally, the 48-bit virtual address is sign extended to 64 bits. As the virtual address space grows, additional index fields (*e.g.*, L5) may be added, reducing the size of the *se* field.

63:48	47:39	38:30	29:21	20:12	11:0
se	L4 idx	L3 idx	L2 idx	L1 idx	*page offset*

Figure 1: Decomposition of the x86-64 virtual address.

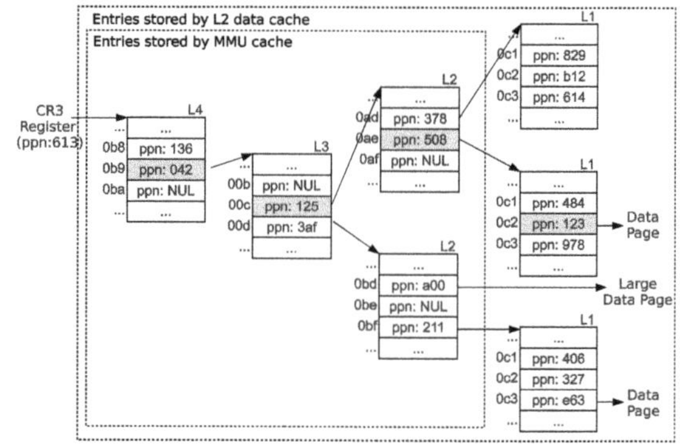

Figure 2: An example page walk for virtual address (`0b9, 00c, 0ae, 0c2, 016`). Each page table entry stores the physical page number for either the next lower level page table page (for L4, L3, and L2) or the data page (for L1). Only 12 bits of the 40-bit physical page number are shown in these figures for simplicity.

An entry in the page table is 8 bytes in size regardless of its level within the tree. Since a 9-bit index is used to select an entry at every level of the tree, the overall size of a node is always 4KB, the same as the page size. Hence, nodes are commonly called page table pages. The tree can be sparsely populated with nodes—if at any level, there are no valid virtual addresses with a particular 9-bit index, the sub-tree beneath that index is not instantiated. For example, if there are no valid virtual addresses with L4 index `0x03a`, that entry in the top level of the page table will indicate so, and the 262,657 page table pages (1 L3 page, 512 L2 pages, and 262,144 L1 pages) beneath that entry in the radix tree page table will not exist. This yields significant memory savings, as large portions of the 256 TB virtual address space are never allocated for typical applications.

Figure 2 illustrates the radix tree page table walk for the virtual address `0x00005c8315cc2016`. For the remainder of the paper, such 64-bit virtual addresses will be denoted as (*L4 index, L3 index, L2 index, L1 index, page offset*) for clarity. In this case, the virtual address being translated is (`0b9, 00c, 0ae, 0c2, 016`). Furthermore, for simplicity of the examples, only 3 hexadecimal digits (12 bits) will be used to indicate the physical page number, which is actually 40 bits in x86-64 processors.

As shown in the figure, the translation process for this address proceeds as follows. First, the page walk hardware must locate the top-level page table page, which stores L4 entries. The physical address of this page is stored in the processor's CR3 register. In order to translate the address, the L4 index field (9 bits) is extracted from the virtual address and appended to the physical page number (40 bits) from the CR3 register. This yields a 49-bit physical address that is used to address the appropriate 8-byte L4 entry (offset `0b9` in the L4 page table page in the figure). The L4 entry may contain the physical page number of an L3 page table page (in this case 042). The process is repeated by extracting the L3 index field from the virtual address and appending it to this physical page number to address the appropriate L3 entry. This process repeats until the selected entry is invalid or specifies the physical page number of the actual data in memory, as shown in the figure. Each page table entry along this path is highlighted in grey in the figure. The page offset from the virtual address is then appended to this physical page number to yield the data's physical address. Note that since page table pages are always aligned on page boundaries, the low order bits of the physical address of the page table pages are not stored in the entries of the page table.

Given this structure, the current 48-bit x86-64 virtual address space requires four memory references to "walk" the page table from top to bottom to translate a virtual address (one for each level of the radix tree page table). As the address space continues to grow, more levels will be added to the page table, further increasing the cost of address translation. A full 64-bit virtual address space will require six levels, leading to six memory accesses per translation.

Alternatively, an L2 entry can directly point to a contiguous and aligned 2MB data page instead of pointing to an L1 page table page. In Figure 2, virtual address (0b9, 00d, 0bd, 123f5d7) is within a large page. This large-page support greatly increases maximum TLB coverage. In addition, it lowers the number of memory accesses to locate one of these pages from four to three. Finally, it greatly reduces the number of total page table entries required since each entry maps a much larger region of memory.

3. CACHING PAGE WALKS

While radix-tree page tables require many accesses to translate a single address, the accesses to the upper level page table entries have significant temporal locality. Walks for two consecutive pages in the virtual address space will usually use the same three upper level entries, since the indices selecting these entries come from high-order bits of the virtual address, which change less frequently.

While the MMU does access the page table through the memory hierarchy, it only has access to the L2 data cache in at least one major commercial x86 design [9]. Since the L2 data cache is relatively slow on modern CPUs, accessing three upper-level page table entries on every page walk will incur a penalty of several tens of cycles per TLB miss, even if all entries are present in the L2 data cache.

Therefore, the x86 processor vendors have developed private, low-latency caches for the MMU that store upper level page table entries [9, 3]. In this section, we describe the design space and provide a nomenclature for the different tagging and partitioning schemes used by these MMU caches.

MMU caches may store elements from the page table tagged by their physical address in memory, as a conventional data cache might. We call such MMU caches *page table caches*. Examples include AMD's *Page Walk Cache* and the L2 data cache, although it is not private to the MMU. Alternatively, MMU caches can be indexed by parts of the virtual address, like a TLB. We call such MMU caches *translation caches*. Intel's *Paging-Structure Caches* are translation caches.

For either of these tagging schemes, elements from different levels of the page table can be mixed in a single cache (a *unified* cache), or placed into separate caches (a *split* cache). Finally, each cache entry can store an entry from one level along the page walk, or it can store an entire path (a *path* cache).

3.1 Page table caches

The simplest example of a page table cache is the processor's L2 data cache. The page walker generates a physical address based upon the page table page to be accessed and an index from the virtual address. This physical address is then fetched from the processor's memory hierarchy starting with the L2 data cache.

Base Location	Index	Next Page
125	0ae	508
042	00c	125
613	0b9	042
...	...	...

Figure 3: An example of the contents of a UPTC. Each entry is tagged with the address of a page table entry, consisting of the 40-bit physical page number of the page table page and a 9-bit index into it. The entry then provides a 40-bit physical page number for the next lower level page table page. (Only 12 bits of the physical page numbers are shown, for simplicity.)

	Base Location	Index	Next Page
L2 entries	125	0ae	508
	...	...	...
L3 entries	042	00c	125
	...	...	...
L4 entries	613	0b9	042
	...	...	...

Figure 4: An example of the contents of a SPTC. Each entry holds the same tag and data as in the UPTC.

Page table caches use this same indexing scheme. Elements are tagged with their physical address in the page table. These tags are the size of the physical page number plus the size of one page table index. L1 entries are not cached in any of the designs presented here (since the TLB itself caches those entries).

3.1.1 Unified Page Table Cache (UPTC)

The simplest design for a dedicated page table cache is a single, high-speed, read-only cache for page table entries, tagged by their physical address in memory. Entries from different levels of the page table are mixed in the same cache, all indexed by their physical address. Such a cache is analogous to a private, read-only L1 data cache for page table entries. However, like a TLB, coherence between this cache and the page table can be maintained by software with little overhead. AMD's Page Walk Cache has this design [9].

Figure 3 shows an example of the Unified Page Table Cache (UPTC) after the MMU walks the page table to translate the virtual address (0b9, 00c, 0ae, 0c2, 016). If the MMU subsequently tries to translate the virtual address (0b9, 00c, 0ae, 0c3, 103), the page walk will begin by looking for the page table entry 0b9 in the L4 page table page (located at 613 and referenced by the CR3 register). Since this page table entry is present in the UPTC, it does not need to be loaded from the memory hierarchy.

This entry indicates that the L3 page table page has physical page number 042. The same process is then repeated to locate the L2 and L1 page table pages. Once the address of the L1 page table page is found, the appropriate entry is loaded from memory to determine the physical page address of the desired data.

Without a page table cache, all four of these accesses to page table entries would have required a memory access, each of which may or may not hit in the L2 data cache. In contrast, with the page table cache, the three top entries hit in the private page table cache, and only one entry (the L1 entry) requires a memory access, which may or may not hit in the L2 data cache.

	L4 index	L3 index	L2 index	Next Page
L2 entries	0b9	00c	0ae	508
	...	...	...	...
L3 entries	0b9	00c		125
	...	...		...
L4 entries	0b9			042
	...			...

Figure 5: An example of the contents of a STC. Each index is 9-bits, and the data holds a 40-bit physical page number of the next page table level. An entry in the L2 cache must match on all three indices, an entry in the L3 must match on two and the L4 on one.

L4 index	L3 index	L2 index	Next Page
0b9	00c	0ae	508
0b9	00c	xx	125
0b9	xx	xx	042
...	...	...	...

Figure 6: An example of the contents of a UTC. An "xx" means "don't care".

3.1.2 Split Page Table Cache (SPTC)

An alternate design for the page table cache separates the page table entries from different levels into separate caches. Figure 4 illustrates a Split Page Table Cache (SPTC). In this design, each individual entry contains the same tag and data as it would in the unified page table cache. The primary difference is that each page table level gets a private cache, and entries from different levels do not compete for common slots.

3.2 Translation caches

As an alternative to tagging cache entries by their physical address, they can be tagged by their indices in the virtual address. An L4 entry will be tagged by the 9 bit L4 index, an L3 entry with the L4 and L3 indices, and an L2 entry with the L4, L3, and L2 indices. We call this device a *translation cache*, because it is storing a partial translation of a virtual address.

With this tagging scheme, data from one entry is not needed to lookup the entry at the next lower level of the page table. All of the lookups can be performed independently of each other. In the end, the MMU will select the entry that matches the longest prefix of the virtual address because it allows the page walk to skip the most levels.

3.2.1 Split Translation Cache (STC)

Like an SPTC, the Split Translation Cache (STC) stores entries from different levels of the page table in separate caches. However, as shown in Figure 5, the STC uses a different way of tagging the entries. The Intel *Paging-Structure Caches* [3] exemplify the STC organization.

The example in Figure 5 shows the split translation cache after the MMU walks the page table to translate the virtual address (0b9, 00c, 0ae, 0c2, 016). If the MMU subsequently starts to translate the virtual address (0b9, 00c, 0dd, 0c3, 929), it will attempt to locate the L1, L2 and L3 page table pages in their corresponding caches using portions of the virtual address. The location of the L3 page table page would be stored in the L4 entry cache and tagged by the L4 index, (0b9). Similarly, the location of the L2 page table page would be stored in the L3 entry cache and tagged by the L4 and L3 indices, (0b9, 00c). Finally, the location of the L1 page table page would be stored in the L2 entry cache and tagged by the L4, L3 and L2 indices, (0b9, 00c, 0dd).

These searches can be performed in any order, and even in parallel. In the above example, the cache can provide the location of the appropriate L3 and L2 page table pages, but not the L1 page table page, as (0b9, 00c, 0dd) is not present in the L2 entry cache. Ultimately, the MMU would use the (0b9, 00c) entry from the L3 entry cache because it allows the page walk to begin further down the tree, at the L2 page table page.

3.2.2 Unified Translation Cache (UTC)

Just as the page table caches can be built with either a split or a unified organization, a Unified Translation Cache (UTC) can also be built. Moreover, just like the UPTC, the UTC mixes elements from all levels of the page table in the same cache.

Figure 6 shows the UTC after the MMU walks the page table to translate the virtual address (0b9, 00c, 0ae, 0c2, 016). If the MMU subsequently starts to translate the virtual address (0b9, 00c, 0dd, 0c3, 929), it will first look in the UTC for the physical page numbers of the L1, L2 and L3 page table pages. As with the previous example that used the STC, the MMU finds two matching entries in the UTC. Ultimately, the MMU decides to use the UTC's second entry, which is an L3 entry that has the L4 and L3 indices (0b9, 00c) as its tag, because this tag matches the longest prefix of the virtual address. Thus, the MMU can skip the L4 and L3 page table pages and start walking from the L2 page table page.

3.3 Translation-Path Cache (TPC)

Note that in the UTC example in Figure 6, the tags for the three entries representing a single path down the page table all have the same content. The L4 and L3 entries use less of the virtual address than the L2 entry does, but the fragments that they do use are the same. Consequently, it is possible to store all three physical page numbers from this example in a single entry. In such a *Translation-Path Cache* (TPC), a single entry represents an entire path, including all of the intermediate entries, for a given walk instead of a single entry along that walk.

L4 index	L3 index	L2 index	L3	L2	L1
0b9	00c	0ae	042	125	508
...	...	...	...	...	...

Figure 7: An example of the contents of the TPC after the virtual address (0b9, 00c, 0ae, 0c2, 016) is walked. The TPC holds three 9 bit indices, as the translation caches do, but all three 40-bit physical page numbers are stored for all three page table levels.

The example in Figure 7 shows the TPC after the MMU walks the page table to translate the virtual address (0b9, 00c, 0ae, 0c2, 016). All data from that walk is stored in one entry. If the MMU subsequently starts to translate the virtual address (0b9, 00c, 0ae, 0c3, 929), the entry referencing the L1 page table page is discovered just as it would have been in the unified translation cache. Specifically, the MMU finds the entry in the cache with the tag (0b9, 00c, 0ae) and reads the physical page number 508 of the L1 page table page from this entry.

If the MMU later starts to translate the virtual address (0b9, 00c, 0de, 0fe, 829), this address shares a partial path (0b9, 00c) with the previously inserted entry. Therefore, the translation-path cache will provide the physical address of the appropriate L2 page table page.

3.4 Design space summary

In summary, the caches described in this section fit into the following two-dimensional design space (annotated with the section number in which each design is described):

	Unified	Split	Path
Page Table Cache	3.1.1	3.1.2	N/A
Translation Cache	3.2.2	3.2.1	3.3

The unified page table cache (UPTC) is the design that appears in modern AMD x86-64 processors. The split translation cache (STC) is the design that appears in modern Intel x86-64 processors. The remaining three designs have been introduced in this paper.

Note that there is no useful page table counterpart to the translation-path cache. This is a direct result of the indexing scheme. While a "path" of physical addresses could be stored as an MMU cache index, it would have to be searched sequentially because the MMU cannot create a path of physical page numbers directly from the virtual address. It must look up each physical page in turn. Therefore, storing complete paths would yield no benefit over the other page table cache designs.

4. DESIGN COMPARISON

All of the designs presented in the previous section are able to accelerate page walks by caching information from the upper levels of the page table. However, these designs have differences in their indexing, partitioning, coverage, and complexity. This section discusses the effects of these differences.

4.1 Indexing

The indexing scheme determines how the cache is searched. Cache indices can be derived from the physical addresses of components of the page table or they can be derived from the virtual address and correspond to the levels of the page table.

Page table caches use the physical addresses of the page table entries as indices. In fact, they operate identically to any physically indexed cache—a UPTC is essentially another data cache in the memory hierarchy dedicated to the page table. The MMU will generate a physical address for the page table entry at each stage of the page walk, and that address will be used as an index into the appropriate page table cache. While this leads to a simple design, it requires the cache lookups to occur in a top-down order. The result of the L4 entry search is required before the L3 entry search can begin, because the L4 entry gives the physical page number of the L3 page table page, which is needed to generate the physical address of the L3 page table entry. Similarly, the L2 search is dependent on the result of the L3 search. In the case where the cache holds all three entries (L4, L3, and L2), the cache must be accessed three times to generate the physical address of the L1 page table entry.

In contrast, translation caches use components of the virtual address as indices. For example, the TLB is an L1 translation cache that uses the virtual page number as its index. In general, for translation caches, the MMU uses a subset of the virtual page number as the index. This allows the translation caches to be searched in any order (L4 first, L2 first, or in parallel). Thus, on a TLB miss, the L2 translation cache can immediately be searched. Upon a hit which yields the L2 translation, the address of the L1 page table entry can be computed immediately. If no L2 translation is available, the L3, then L4, translation caches can be searched. Upon a hit, the page walk would begin at that point in the tree.

4.2 Partitioning

MMU caches can either be unified or partitioned, or they can store complete path information. The partitioning of the cache determines how the entries of the cache are allocated to different levels of the page table. This effectively determines how well the entries from different levels are isolated from each other.

The impact of the partitioning scheme largely depends on whether the application densely or sparsely utilizes its virtual address space. For applications that densely use their virtual memory, a few L4 and L3 entries are heavily utilized and there is significant reuse of the L2 entries. In contrast, for applications that sparsely use their virtual memory, there will be little reuse for L2 entries, but a larger number of L4 and L3 entries will exhibit reuse. The partitioning strategy and replacement policy determine how these entries will compete for slots, which can have a significant impact on the effectiveness of the MMU cache.

For applications that densely use their virtual memory, there will be many more L2 entries than upper level entries in use. However, for a page table cache design, these upper level entries are critical for translation performance. If a random replacement scheme is used in conjunction with a unified cache, these important entries can be frequently replaced, resulting in memory accesses to entries at or near the top of the table. However, if entries from different levels are kept in separate caches, a random replacement policy is less detrimental.

For applications that sparsely use many gigabytes of virtual memory, L2 entries will have very little reuse, and effective caching of L3 entries is critical. In a split entry cache, a static allocation of entries to each level must be made. If this allocation is optimized for small applications, it will have many more L2 entries than L3 entries, harming performance in this situation. Moreover, if an application makes heavy use of large pages and limited use of small pages, the dedicated L2 entries will be of little or no use. In contrast, in a unified cache, the allocation happens dynamically, but recently accessed L2 entries that will not be reused might evict L3 entries that might otherwise be reused. A level-aware replacement policy can help to avoid this.

The Greedy Dual algorithm is a popular content-aware replacement scheme [25]. This algorithm will replace recently used entries early if they are easier to reload into the cache. This scheme can be adapted for MMU caches by preferentially replacing lower-level entries with upper-level entries, thus reducing conflict between entries of high and low reuse. While Greedy Dual is not an algorithm that can easily be implemented in hardware, it is possible to implement a similar algorithm with minimal modification to an LRU cache.

In our modified LRU algorithm, entries from lower levels of the page table are inserted into the LRU queue at a recency position behind the most-recently-used position. If these lower level entries are reused, they are promoted to the most recently used position. However, if they are not reused, the portion of the cache in which lower level entries compete with upper level entries is small. These positions can be fixed, for simplicity, or they can change to adapt to different workloads. We propose a *variable insertion-point LRU replacement policy* whereby entries from lower levels of the cache are inserted into a recency position below the most recently used position that is proportional to the current number of upper level entries stored. For example, if there are two L4 entries and six L3 entries currently in the cache, a new L2 entry is inserted in the ninth most recently used position in the cache.

The path translation cache avoids these partitioning problems, as each slot holds an entry from all levels. This prevents the competition for slots while not requiring a static allocation of slots to

		Unified	Split	Path
Page Table	C	1	$l-1$	N/A
	T	$p-3$	$\{p-3,...,p-3\}$	
	D	$p-12$	$\{p-12,...,p-12\}$	
Translation	C	1	$l-1$	1
	T	$(l-1)\cdot n$	$\{n,...,(l-1)\cdot n\}$	$(l-1)\cdot n$
	D	$p-12$	$\{p-12,...,p-12\}$	$3(p-12)$

Table 1: The number of caches (C), the number of tag bits per entry (T), and the number of data bits per entry (D) for each design.

		Unified	Split	Path
Page Table	C	1	3	N/A
	T	49	$\{49,49,49\}$	
	D	40	$\{40,40,40\}$	
Translation	C	1	3	1
	T	27	$\{9,18,27\}$	27
	D	40	$\{40,40,40\}$	120

Table 2: MMU cache parameters for x86-64 processors. We have used the architectural definition of physical address width, 52 bits [1]. Actual implementations may use fewer bits.

levels. However, since this cache may hold many paths with the same upper level entries, its effective capacity for holding upper level entries is less than three equally sized split entry caches.

4.3 Coverage

Characterizing the coverage of an MMU cache is not straightforward. In particular, the exact meaning of coverage for an MMU cache must first be considered. For example, suppose an address translation hits on an L3 entry in a page table or translation cache but does not hit on an L2 entry. In this case, the translation was accelerated by the MMU cache, but nonetheless required a memory access to fetch the page table's L2 entry. Thus, it is arguable whether or not the MMU cache provided coverage. We take the strict position that coverage means that no memory accesses were required to fetch L4, L3, or L2 page table entries.

In general, with the same number of entries, translation caches are able to cover a larger portion of the address space than page table caches. The reason is that a translation cache can make more efficient use of its entries than a page table cache. For a page table cache to provide coverage it must simultaneously hold an L4, L3, and L2 entry, whereas a translation cache can provide coverage with only an L2 entry. In other words, the translation cache may be able store additional L2 entries in place of the L4 and L3 entries that are required to provide coverage in the page table cache.

When the application is simply too large for the MMU cache to provide full coverage, the unified caches with intelligent replacement policies, the split caches, and the TPC are able to accelerate translations for more of the address space than the unified caches with conventional replacement policies. This is due to the fact that the former caches upper level entries, which provide partial translation for larger regions, are less likely to be evicted in favor of lower level entries. Since these effects are highly dependent on workload, the relative hit rates of the cache designs are studied experimentally in Section 6.

4.4 Complexity

All of the organizations are effectively fully associative caches, which can be implemented by a CAM array to match the tags and a RAM array to store the data entries. However, the different cache organizations have different tag and data widths, and will potentially require differing numbers of entries to achieve similar hit rates. These factors will lead to different implementation complexities for the different organizations.

Table 1 shows the number of caches, tag bits per entry, and data bits per entry that are needed for each organization. These characteristics are parameterized by the number of levels of address translation, l, the number of bits in a physical address, p, and the number of offset bits in a page table index for a particular level, n. In x86-64 processors, $l = 4$, $p = 52$, and $n = 9$, which leads to the values shown in Table 2.

It should be noted that for current architectural parameters, translation caches require significantly smaller tags. This will make a translation cache smaller and more power efficient than an equivalent page table cache, as the CAM array is likely to dominate the cost of the structure.

5. METHODOLOGY

The MMU cache architectures presented in Section 3 were evaluated by running application memory traces through a memory system simulator. The trace-based approach is warranted here for two reasons. First and foremost, the number of memory references required for a page walk is effectively independent of all architectural parameters except for the MMU and the L2 cache organization. A cycle-accurate simulation would have presented a more limited view of the differences for a single point in the processor design space. Second, from a practical standpoint, it would have been nearly impossible to run the types of large memory footprint applications that benefit most from these structures on a slow cycle-accurate simulator.

5.1 Application Memory Traces

The AMD SimNow [8] platform simulator was used to run various benchmarks under FreeBSD 8.0-Release for x86-64. A custom analyzer plugin to SimNow records each virtual memory access made by the simulated system. This trace includes all memory loads and stores made by the tested operating system and processes, but it does not include instruction or page table loads. TLB and MMU invalidations are included in the trace by monitoring the value of the CR3 register, which must change on a context switch. Finally, the plugin counts the total number of instructions executed during the trace.

Virtual memory access traces were captured from these applications, including the SPEC CPU2006 floating-point suite [14], SPECjbb2005 [21], ASCI Sweep3d [2] and HPCC RandomAccess [11]. However, not all of the benchmarks in the SPEC CFP2006 suite could be compiled with the standard tool chain in FreeBSD 8.0, so soplex, calculix and wrf are not included in this study. SPECjbb2005 was run on one warehouse, and Sweep3d was run on a 150x150x150 grid.

5.2 Memory System Simulation

A custom memory system simulator was built to simulate the various MMU cache designs. The simulator includes an MMU that closely resembles the L1 and L2 TLBs in the AMD Opteron [9]. It consists of a 64-entry, fully-associative L1 TLB with random replacement, and a 512-entry, 4-way set associative L2 TLB with LRU replacement. Furthermore, the simulator is able to model all five cache designs described in Section 3. The simulator stores tags (virtual addresses), but not data (physical addresses), to eliminate any operating system dependent behavior from the simulation. This simplifies the design of the simulator and generalizes the results. Unless otherwise specified, the simulator divides all memory into 4KB pages.

A 1MB L2 cache was included in the model, simulated using the Dinero IV cache simulator [12]. Both application data accesses and MMU page table accesses are simulated using a shared L2 cache model. In general, instruction loads are not instrumented are not included in this study. The cache parameters were based on the same AMD Opteron processor that was the basis for the TLB parameters. The L1 cache was not simulated, since the page walk hardware does not use it on the Opteron.

While our simulation environment did not permit us to directly measure power and system performance, the reduction in memory accesses we directly measure here should translate directly into reduced interconnect power consumption and latency. Recall that previous work has shown the uncached system performance impact of unvirtualized TLB misses to be up to 14% for nominally sized applications [9] and up to 50% for large applications [19].

5.3 Synthetic Application Memory Traces

To study the behavior of an application that uses more virtual memory than we can practically trace on our real machines, a trace synthesizer was developed that simulates the memory access pattern of an in-memory database, performing a hash join. Such joins are common, and the performance of large joins is representative of overall database performance [6].

The simulated join is an inner join on two equally sized tables, A and B. The hash join process starts by creating a hash table containing the entries of B, using an open addressing collision resolution scheme. The database then iterates through A, checking to see if each entry is present in the hash table. The result is then placed in an output table [13].

Since the simulation is designed to scale to arbitrary sizes, the simulation works probabilistically rather than operating on a real data set. First, an element is read from the region of memory holding table A. Then, a random element is read from the region of memory storing the hash table, since the hash function will uniformly distribute accesses throughout the table. After the first element is read, a second element is sometimes also read, based on the probability of a hash collision. The collision probability was derived from the expected collision chain length [17]. Finally, an element is written to the result table, and the process repeats itself with the next consecutive element of table A.

6. CACHE DESIGN SIMULATIONS

This section evaluates the five different MMU cache organizations using a wide variety of applications. The TLB miss penalty, structure sizing, and replacement policies are explored. The results show that the unified translation cache with a modified LRU replacement scheme is the best design for the entire range of applications. For the small benchmarks, this cache design is able to reduce the number of memory accesses required per TLB miss from 4 without a dedicated cache to 1.13. It also adapts dynamically to large applications, avoiding the conflicts present in traditional unified caches without the static partitioning required in split caches.

6.1 TLB miss penalty

The purpose of any MMU cache is to lessen the penalty of a TLB miss and the cost of walking the page table. This penalty can be broken down into the number of accesses to the private MMU cache and the number of memory hierarchy accesses required per TLB miss. Without a private cache, there will be four memory hierarchy accesses per walk, one per level. These memory accesses can be further broken down into L2 data cache hits and DRAM accesses, which are far more costly.

6.1.1 *Small Memory Applications*

Even applications that use a modest amount of memory can have frequent TLB misses. Table 3 shows the frequency of TLB misses

Workload	Ins/Walk	Mem/Walk	DRAM accesses/Walk 2MB	1MB	512KB
bwaves	3637.7	2183.8	102.6	104.4	106.2
gamess	37927.8	16905.0	1.1	1.1	1.1
milc	202.3	83.1	3.9	3.9	4.0
zeusmp	3105.2	562.0	77.0	77.8	79.0
gromacs	25399.1	12025.0	42.2	55.4	69.5
cactus	3916.9	2919.4	28.7	30.2	31.9
leslie3d	4185.2	1679.8	67.5	70.5	72.0
namd	49024.9	18498.7	9.0	12.3	16.2
deal	29235.3	10046.7	12.3	14.5	16.9
povray	38328.8	19498.9	1.9	1.9	1.9
Gems	50817.5	19447.8	1.4	1.4	1.4
tonto	30414.8	13711.6	4.5	7.2	28.8
lbm	1844.5	908.1	97.5	101.7	106.7
sphinx3	1858.2	574.4	26.3	28.6	30.2
(avg)	19992.7	8503.2	34.0	36.5	40.4
specjbb	351.0	162.0	2.4	3.4	4.8
Sweep3d	6098.6	3161.3	81.9	83.9	85.4

Table 3: The frequency of TLB misses for each workload, shown as the number of instructions, memory accesses and DRAM accesses between TLB misses. These results are shown for three different L2 data cache sizes and the TLB configuration described in Section 5.2.

for each of the SPEC CFP2006 benchmarks, the SPEC JBB2005 Java server benchmark and the ASCI Sweep3d benchmark. Specifically, the table shows the average number of instructions, program memory accesses and program DRAM accesses (L2 data cache misses) that occur between TLB misses. The number of instructions issued between TLB misses varies from tens of thousands for compute-intensive workloads to hundreds, for data-intensive workloads. For SPECjbb2005, less than five DRAM accesses are made between TLB misses. For data-intensive workloads that may be memory bottlenecked, the DRAM accesses related to page walks are significant.

Table 4 compares the behavior of the different MMU caches. For each kind of MMU cache the table shows how many times the MMU cache, the L2 data cache and DRAM are accessed per TLB miss under each of the benchmarks. All caches are using a least-recently-used replacement policy. In these simulations, the unified and path caches have 24 entries and the split caches have 3×24 entries. While there are some outliers, most of the applications exhibit similar behavior.

As a baseline, Table 4 also presents results with no MMU cache. As expected, with no cache there are four memory accesses per walk. Interestingly, there are only 0.15 DRAM accesses per walk for SPEC CFP2006, meaning that there is a 96% hit rate for page table entries in the L2 data cache. This number varies from application to application, but it never drops below 90%. This demonstrates that page table access for these applications has very high reuse.

Adding any MMU cache drops the average number of memory hierarchy accesses per walk from 4.00 to no more than 1.13 (0.99+0.14) for SPEC CFP2006. Note that DRAM accesses only decrease approximately 7%, from 0.15 to 0.14. This means that most of the avoided memory accesses come out of L2 hits, not DRAM accesses. The decrease in TLB miss latency from a MMU cache with these applications comes from the decreased access latency of an MMU cache as compared to the L2 data cache, not an improved hit rate. For Sweep3d, there is so much locality in virtual address use that memory accesses per TLB miss is further reduced to 1.07.

Since these caches do not store L1 page table entries, this result

	No Cache			UPTC (24 entry)			SPTC (3x24 entry)			UTC (24 entry)			STC (3x24 entry)			TPC (24 path)		
	S	L2	DRAM	S	L2	DRAM	S	L2	DRAM	S	L2	DRAM	S	L2	DRAM	S	L2	DRAM
bwaves	-	3.72	0.28	2.98	0.82	0.25	2.99	0.80	0.24	1.06	0.81	0.26	1.03	0.80	0.24	1.03	0.80	0.23
gamess	-	3.95	0.05	2.94	1.13	0.05	2.94	1.13	0.05	1.15	1.13	0.05	1.15	1.13	0.05	1.15	1.13	0.05
milc	-	3.90	0.10	3.00	0.91	0.10	3.00	0.91	0.09	1.01	0.91	0.09	1.00	0.91	0.09	1.00	0.91	0.09
zeusmp	-	3.81	0.19	2.99	0.85	0.17	2.99	0.85	0.17	1.02	0.85	0.17	1.02	0.85	0.17	1.02	0.85	0.17
gromacs	-	3.80	0.20	2.96	0.91	0.20	2.96	0.91	0.20	1.08	0.90	0.20	1.08	0.91	0.20	1.08	0.91	0.20
cactus	-	3.84	0.16	2.96	1.12	0.16	2.99	0.98	0.15	1.23	1.10	0.15	1.13	0.98	0.15	1.13	0.99	0.15
leslie3d	-	3.79	0.21	2.98	0.88	0.20	2.99	0.85	0.19	1.06	0.88	0.20	1.04	0.85	0.19	1.04	0.86	0.19
namd	-	3.86	0.14	2.88	1.15	0.13	2.88	1.14	0.13	1.23	1.15	0.13	1.23	1.14	0.13	1.23	1.14	0.13
deal	-	3.89	0.11	2.93	1.07	0.11	2.93	1.07	0.11	1.15	1.07	0.11	1.15	1.07	0.11	1.15	1.07	0.11
povray	-	3.92	0.08	2.92	1.10	0.08	2.92	1.10	0.08	1.15	1.10	0.08	1.14	1.10	0.08	1.14	1.10	0.08
Gems	-	3.93	0.07	2.89	1.18	0.07	2.89	1.18	0.07	1.20	1.18	0.07	1.20	1.18	0.07	1.20	1.18	0.07
tonto	-	3.93	0.07	2.94	1.07	0.08	2.94	1.07	0.08	1.12	1.07	0.08	1.12	1.07	0.08	1.12	1.07	0.08
lbm	-	3.79	0.21	2.99	0.83	0.19	2.99	0.83	0.18	1.02	0.83	0.19	1.01	0.83	0.18	1.01	0.83	0.18
sphinx3	-	3.76	0.24	2.99	0.80	0.23	2.99	0.79	0.23	1.02	0.80	0.23	1.02	0.79	0.23	1.02	0.79	0.23
(avg)	-	3.85	0.15	2.95	0.99	0.14	2.96	0.97	0.14	1.11	0.98	0.14	1.09	0.97	0.14	1.09	0.97	0.14
specjbb	-	3.83	0.17	2.98	0.97	0.17	3.00	0.93	0.17	1.14	0.97	0.17	1.11	0.93	0.17	1.11	0.95	0.17
Sweep3d	-	3.77	0.23	2.95	1.01	0.22	2.98	0.87	0.20	1.13	0.94	0.21	1.07	0.87	0.20	1.07	0.88	0.20

Table 4: The number of caching structure accesses (S), L2 data cache hits (L2), and DRAM accesses (DRAM) per TLB miss for the various LRU cache designs over the SPEC CFP2006, SPECjbb2005 and Sweep3d benchmarks.

is very close to the minimum number of memory accesses per TLB miss of 1.00. On these applications, all the caches have similar hit rates. In nearly all TLB misses, all the MMU caches can provide the physical page number of the L1 page table page without having to do any memory accesses. From here, the L2 cache still provides most of the L1 entries at a hit rate of 88% (only 0.14 of the 1.13 memory accesses are DRAM accesses). These hits come from the fact that the L2 cache is much larger than the MMU caches and can store eight entries in a single cache line.

One benchmark, `tonto`, has more DRAM accesses when an MMU cache is used. However, the rounding in Table 4 exaggerates this effect. The actual increase in DRAM accesses is only 0.001 per TLB miss. The MMU cache changes the access pattern to the L2 data cache, so page table entries may be replaced sooner than they would be without an MMU cache, slightly increasing DRAM accesses.

SPECjbb has low address locality at a page and cache line granularity compared to other small memory applications leading to high TLB and cache miss rates. However, there is still enough locality in upper level bits of the address to allow reasonably high MMU cache hit rates. On this workload, 2.87 of the three upper level page table entries are still served by the MMU cache, leaving 0.99 and 0.14 accesses for the L2 data cache and DRAM respectively. These 0.14 DRAM accesses per TLB miss are significant compared to the 3.4 DRAM accesses between TLB misses that come from program execution itself.

Since these caches all provide high hit rates, their primary difference is in the number of accesses to the cache required per walk. Since the translation and path cache search for L2 entries first, they are typically only accessed one time per TLB miss. This reduces both latency and power consumption. The page table caches are accessed an average of three times per walk, since they must walk down the page table. If the size of the virtual address space is expanded by adding an additional level, this penalty will increase.

6.1.2 *Large Memory Applications*

In contrast to the results for small memory applications, the different MMU caches have substantially different hit rates for applications with random access patterns over gigabytes of virtual memory, such as an in-memory database hash join or HPCC RandomAccess. For these applications, the reuse of lower level page table entries is low, and there are many upper level page table entries in use. Consequently, caching as many L3 entries as possible, each of which covers a 1GB region of virtual memory, is critical, but caching L2 entries is of little or no benefit. For a unified cache, a TLB miss that hits on an L3 entry but not an L2 entry will load a new L2 entry into the cache. With LRU replacement, the cache will have about the same number of L2 and L3 entries. The TPC also keeps track of an L2 entry for each L3 entry stored, but it does so in the same associative entry. Therefore, for such applications, a TPC of n paths is roughly equivalent to a UPTC of $2 \cdot n$ entries. When the TPC becomes large, there is the possibility that different stored paths will contain the same L3 entry, reducing hit rate. The split caches do not exhibit this effect, so once the cache is large enough to hold all L3 entries in use, there is a 100% hit rate.

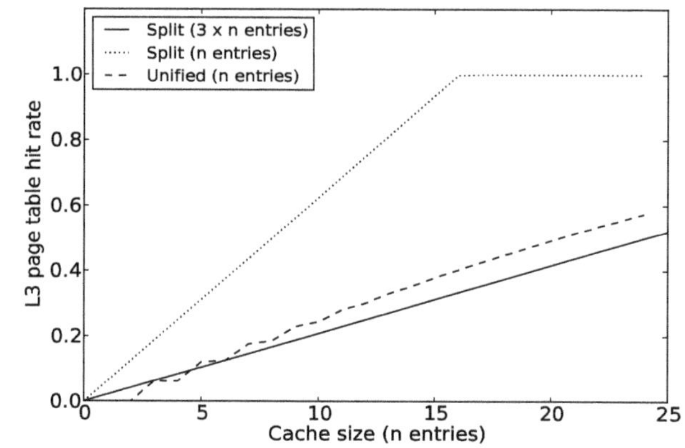

Figure 8: Hit rate compared for the caches with the database join simulation using a 16GB hash table. The different split and unified designs have equivalent coverages.

A database hash join running over a 16GB region (Figure 8) demonstrates this scaling. Here, to have a 50% hit rate on the L3 page table, a 22 entry unified cache is required, while only an 11 path TPC, or a 3×11 entry STC is required.

An application using many terabytes of virtual memory would only have high reuse on L4 page table entries, causing 2/3 of unified cache entries to be wasted, instead of just 1/2 for the 16GB application. This is because for every L4 entry stored, an L3 and an L2 entry are also stored, which are effectively wasted. This causes the TPC to be equivalent to a unified cache of three times the size for such workloads.

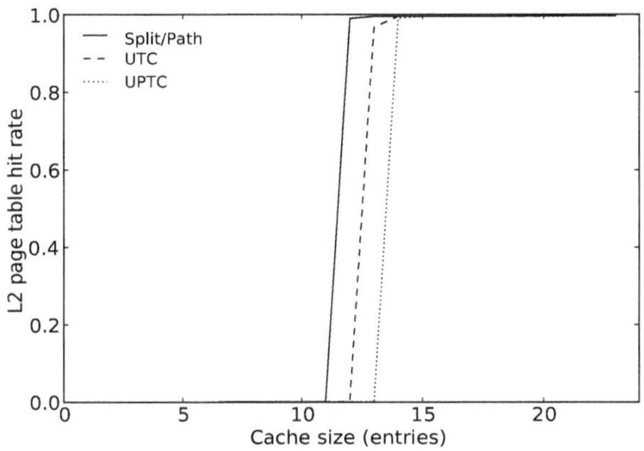

Figure 9: Hit rate for the L2 table for ASCI Sweep3d. This application is very sensitive to sizing. Note that size represents per-level size (all three levels hold n entries) for the split cache included in Figures 9-11.

6.2 Sizing considerations

Appropriate sizing of caches is critical for hit rate in many applications. The ability to not store levels that are skipped in the translation cache allows them to be smaller for a given hit rate. Additionally, the fixed allocation of entries for each level in the split cache designs demands that all levels be large to properly adapt to differing workloads. The TPC and unified caches dynamically allocate entries and adapt well.

ASCI Sweep3d operates on a set of different memory regions. When the first is processed, it moves to the next, and so on. After processing the last region, the program wraps around to the first, and the cycle repeats. If the cache is not large enough to hold all the regions, entries corresponding to earlier regions are pushed out before they are used again, and hit rate is very poor (Figure 9). Since upper levels of the page table are skipped in the translation cache, the UTC can be slightly smaller than the UPTC.

For the small memory applications, there are relatively few upper level page table entries that are in use. As a result, the hit rate of the unified caches holding n entries only slightly trails that of the split caches, which hold a total of $3 \times n$ entries. In this example (Figure 10), a unified page table cache holding 23 entries is equivalent to a split cache holding $3 \times 19 = 57$ entries. Only four entries from the unified cache are stored in upper levels of the split caches. These entries are combined with lower level entries in the TPC, allowing a 19 path TPC to be equivalent to the 23 entry unified cache.

While these applications use more lower level entries than upper level entries, having small upper-level caches in a split cache dramatically reduces hit rate for large applications. If the split cache is reduced in size to 3×8 entries to match the total size of the unified cache, the L3 table hit rate in the database benchmark is reduced from 99% to 44%. Skewing the distribution of entries from higher levels to lower levels will further impact hit rate. Therefore, it is imperative that all levels of a split cache be large, resulting in considerable area overhead.

6.3 Replacement policy

In the unified caches, entries of high reuse (upper level entries) are mixed with entries of lower reuse (lower level entries). This causes the cache to be relatively sensitive to the LRU replacement policy which ensures that frequently accessed components (L4 and L3 entries) are not evicted. In the path and translation caches, these upper level entries are skipped, so they do not need to be protected.

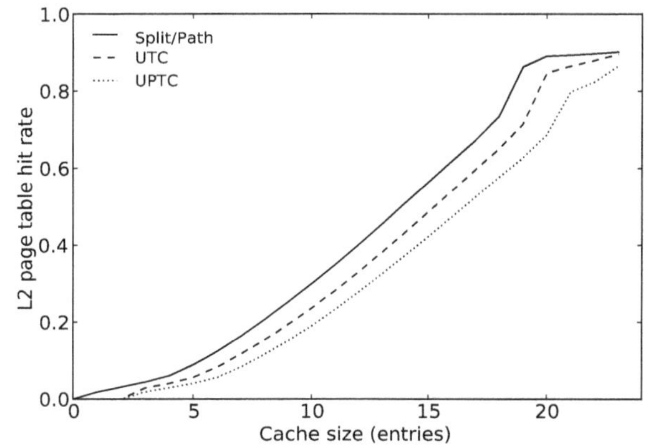

Figure 10: Hit rate for the L2 table alone for the `CactusADM` component of SPEC CPU2006.

Cache	LRU	Random	Increase
UPTC	0.61	1.00	63%
UTC	0.53	0.79	49%
TPC	0.51	0.65	28%
SPTC	0.51	0.64	25%
STC	0.51	0.63	23%

Table 5: The average number of misses per walk for random and LRU replacement, normalized to Random UPTC (lower is better), and the relative increase in misses using random replacement over LRU replacement.

Table 6.3 shows the impact of using a random replacement scheme on the number of MMU cache misses (measured by the number of required memory accesses to locate upper level page table entries). While all structures have a lower hit rate using a random replacement scheme, the unified designs are much more reliant on an LRU replacement scheme.

The primary problem with the unified cache designs for the large applications is that entries with high reuse are evicted to make room for entries of low reuse. For example, in the database join the LRU unified caches hold a relatively useless L2 entry for every useful L3 entry in the cache. If a content-aware replacement scheme is used, this problem can be significantly reduced. If the Greedy Dual algorithm is implemented in the UTC instead of using LRU, the size required for 90% L3 entry hit rate in the 16GB database join is reduced from 52 to 30 entries.

Using our modified LRU replacement scheme (described in Section 4.2) with fixed insertion points, this algorithm actually has a higher hit rate than Greedy Dual for the database benchmark. Only 23 entries are required for 90% hit rate. However, the fixed insertion point for L2 entries reduces hit rate significantly for some other applications, such as Sweep3d. The L2 entries used by Sweep3d, if they are inserted near the least recently used position, are replaced before they are reused resulting in a near zero hit rate.

Using the variable insertion-point LRU scheme solves this. For SPEC CFP2006, SPECjbb2005 and Sweep3d, VI-LRU has a hit rate that is equal to or slightly greater than standard LRU. For the database join, where there are many L2 entries to cache, VI-LRU adapts far better than other replacement schemes. Only 16 entries are required for 90% hit rate in the join benchmark, as opposed to 52 for standard LRU (Figure 11). The VI-LRU cache nearly eliminates the conflict between levels seen in the unified cache, and

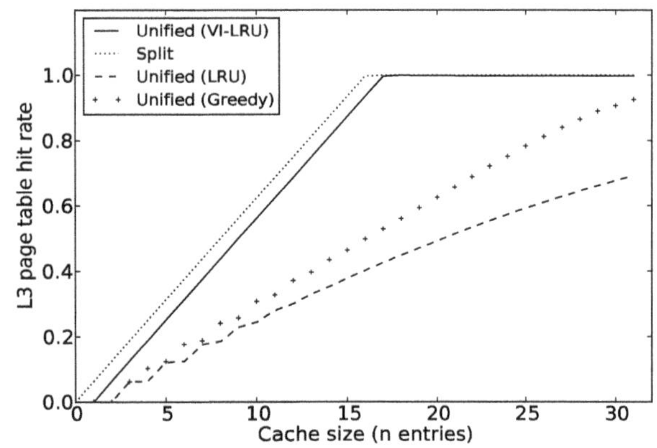

Figure 11: An n entry unified translation-cache with VI-LRU has nearly the same hit rate as a $3 \times n$ split cache.

an n entry VI-LRU UTC has nearly the same hit rate as a $3 \times n$ entry split translation cache.

7. ALTERNATE PAGE TABLE FORMATS

We compared the memory access behavior of the cached page table with its biggest rivals, hash-table based Inverted Page Tables and direct-mapped Translation Storage Buffers. These structures are attractive since they contain only one level, and are therefore insensitive to address space size. However, the unavoidable presence of hash and structural collisions, low access locality and their inability to handle multiple page sizes efficiently cause them to require far more memory accesses than a cached radix table.

7.1 Hashed page tables

We have shown that MMU caches can significantly reduce the overhead of using a radix tree page table, however the possibility remains that the radix tree page table itself should be replaced. The traditional competitor to the radix tree page table is the inverted page table, which uses a hash table to store a large and sparsely used address space efficiently [15]. These designs are usually seen as superior to a multi-level table, because they only need to be referenced once, whereas the radix table requires one access per level. However, hash collisions are unavoidable, so many accesses may require more than one reference to follow a collision chain.

Additionally, we have shown in this paper that MMU caches can reduce the number of memory accesses per walk to nearly one as well. To compare the cached radix table against an inverted page table, a simulator was constructed that maintains and references a hash table storing all the memory locations used during a process' lifetime. The hash table used closely models that used by the Intel Itanium [4]. The number of accesses to this table were counted, as well as the number of such accesses that hit in the L2 data cache.

When the hash table contains twice as many buckets as there are pages to store, the hash table walker references approximately 1.2 locations per TLB miss, *regardless of benchmark or access pattern.* This number comes from the average length of a collision chain, which is a function only of the fullness of the hash table if a sufficiently uniform hash function is used [17]. This number compares poorly to the average number of L2 and memory accesses required per walk of the SPEC CFP2006 applications using page table caching of 1.13. While the hashed page table is insensitive to address space size, it is unable to take advantage of the great locality seen in virtual address space usage like MMU caches can.

	Uncached		TPC	
Page Size	4KB	2MB	4KB	2MB
L2 Hits	2.90	2.92	1.11	1.15
DRAM	1.10	0.06	1.09	0.06

	IPT (1)		IPT (2)		IPT (16)	
Page Size	4KB	2MB	4KB	2MB	4KB	2MB
L2 Hits	0.01	0.00	1.16	1.16	0.55	0.54
DRAM	1.29	1.29	1.14	1.14	1.48	1.49

Table 6: L2 hits and DRAM accesses to the page table per walk for a radix tree page table for the 16GB database join benchmark. Results are shown for an uncached radix tree, a cached radix tree, and a half-full inverted page table with various numbers of clustered translations per tag.

Compounding this issue is the fact that references into the hash table show no spatial locality. Whereas consecutive pages in virtual memory are usually mapped by consecutive entries in the radix table, they are not usually mapped by consecutive entries in a hash table. Since there is usually locality in the access pattern of L1 page table entries in a radix table, these entries are much more effectively cached by the L2 data cache than the entries of the hashed table are. For the SPEC CFP2006 applications examined earlier, only 44% of the 1.2 accesses/walk are served by the L2 data cache. Overall, the inverted page table increases the number of DRAM accesses per walk by *over 400%*.

Spatial locality can be increased by storing multiple adjacent translations with a single tag, as used in *clustered page tables* [23]. This technique also reduces the overhead (virtual address tag and chain pointer) for the hash table. However, for this technique to be effective each virtual tag must be associated with many translations. This means that some translations will need to load multiple cache lines. Additionally, the frequency of hash collisions is not reduced over a standard inverted page table.

Even if the virtual address space is used without locality, as in the database join, the radix tree page table still requires fewer DRAM accesses than a hashed page table. Table 6 shows the memory use per TLB miss for a join using a 16GB hash table. With 4KB pages, the radix tree page table requires fewer DRAM accesses/walk than the inverted page table until a 48GB inverted page table is used.

For this application, clustering does improve L2 cache hit rate since the page table is smaller. However, the tag and data often lie in different cache lines, which requires an increase in the total overall memory references required to perform a translation. Matching the total cluster size to the size of a cache line improves this. However since cache line size may change from implementation to implementation, the appropriate cluster size may change as well.

For larger applications such as this, large page support becomes important. When it comes to supporting the simultaneous use of multiple page sizes, radix trees have an advantage over inverted page tables. With the radix tree, if 2MB pages are used for mapping most of the virtual address space, the entire page table can be cached in the L2 data cache, because the 2MB page mapping takes the place of an L2 entry in the page table and eliminates the need for an entire L1 page table page (see Figure 2). This reduces the number of DRAM accesses per walk dramatically for the radix table designs and also the number of overall memory hierarchy accesses to below that seen in the inverted page table, as shown in Table 6.

In contrast, the simultaneous use of large and small pages does not reduce the size of an inverted page table, and so its memory accesses do not change. In essence, the hash function must take into account the size of the virtual page, but it cannot know the page's size *a priori* if multiple page sizes are in use. Consequently, for a large page, the inverted page table must still have a page table entry corresponding to each of the small pages that make up the large page. Each of these page table entries will, however, designate the mapping as part of a large page, and the TLB will be loaded with a single large page mapping.

7.2 Translation Storage Buffers

The SPARC architecture has traditionally handled TLB misses in software. To accelerate TLB misses, the processor supports a software-managed, direct-mapped cache of translations called the *Translation Storage Buffer* [5]. On a TLB miss, the CPU derives an index from the lower entry bits in the virtual address and checks to see if a corresponding entry is present in the TSB. Although earlier processors performed this TSB lookup in software, some current processors implement it in hardware. Like the inverted page table, a TSB entry stores a tag (a virtual page number) and a translation (a physical page number). Unlike the inverted-page table, there is no chaining. If a translation is not present in the TSB, a software fault occurs.

To compare this design to the radix-tree design, a TSB simulator was also developed. Like the inverted page table simulator, the TSB simulator counts L2 and DRAM accesses per TLB miss. In addition, the TSB simulator also counts software faults that occur when a translation is not present in the cache. Traces are simulated in a two-pass manner. The first pass populates the cache with the translations present in the trace. The second pass actually simulates accesses to the cache, counting hits and misses. This ensures that only conflict misses are counted, providing a lower-bound for cache misses.

Our results show that the TSB uses the L2 data cache poorly as compared to the radix-tree. For example, the `zeusmp` component of the SPEC CFP benchmark generates 0.058 DRAM accesses per TLB miss using the radix-tree with an MMU cache whereas the TSB required 0.078 DRAM accesses per TLB miss. This increase is due solely to the larger size of a TSB entry as compared to a radix tree page table entry. The TSB entry contains a tag and data, whereas the radix-tree only needs to hold data. This increased size reduces the number of entries that will fit in a single L2 cache line from eight to four.

In addition, the TSB also generates 0.024 software faults per TLB miss using the current architectural maximum size of 1 megabyte. These are likely to be extremely expensive, generating not only data cache misses, but also instruction cache misses. While increasing the size of the L2 data cache would reduce the number of L2 cache misses, it would not reduce the number of software faults.

8. RELATED WORK

Some early work on caching page table entries was done before the introduction of AMD and Intel's MMU caches. This work was targeted at accelerating software TLB miss handling. Bala *et al.* introduced a software cache for page table entries [7]. This cache is read by the software page fault handler and manages entries in physical memory to avoid cascading TLB misses that come from reading page table entries in virtual memory space. Wu and Zwanepoel expanded this to a hardware/software design [24]. They propose a single level translation cache to handle only L2 entries. If a translation hits in their structure, the MMU loads the L1 entry directly, as in the caches presented in this paper. If the translation misses, a software fault is triggered.

In a virtualized system using nested paging, both the guest virtual machine and the underlying virtual machine monitor have their own page table. In effect, the virtual machine monitor's page table is used to create a private guest physical address space for the virtual machine. Thus, the guest's page table is used to translate from virtual addresses to guest physical addresses, and the virtual machine monitor's page table is used to translate from guest physical addresses to host physical addresses. Nested paging with radix tree-based page tables leads to a two-dimensional page table walk because every access to the guest's page table during a page walk may result in a page walk on the virtual machine monitor's page table.

Bhargava *et al.* showed that an extended version of AMD's Page Walk Cache could effectively cache most of the upper level page table entries in both the guest's page table and the virtual machine monitor's page table [9]. In addition, they proposed the introduction of a *Nested TLB* (NTLB) that caches guest physical to host physical translations. In effect, a hit in the NTLB allows the two-dimensional page walk to *skip* the page walk on the virtual machine monitor's page table. Thus, if every access to the guest's page table hits in the NTLB, then the number of accesses to the Page Walk Cache and the memory hierarchy is the same as it would be for native execution.

The translation and path caches presented in this paper could also be extended to support nested paging. Moreover, the NTLB is not inextricably tied to the Page Walk Cache or page table caches in general. A NTLB could be beneficially combined with translation and path caches. A NTLB hit allows the two-dimensional page walk to skip the entire page walk on the virtual machine monitor's page table for a single guest page table access, but not the accesses to the upper levels of the guest's page table. This requires a translation or path cache. Moreover, a translation or path cache could accelerate page walks on the virtual machine monitor's page table when a NTLB miss occurs.

Talluri and Hill recognized the importance of efficient use of spatial locality in the page table and developed their clustered and subblock page tables to increase the spatial locality found in inverted page tables [22, 23]. We simulate a similar system in Section 7.1 and compare it to both traditional inverted page tables and cached radix tree tables.

McCurdy *et al.* previously investigated the importance of the L2 data cache in storing page table entries [19]. They show that applications that use large pages can show improved performance even in the face of decreased TLB hit rates. This is due to the shallower, and therefore smaller, page table when using large pages.

Jacob and Mudge [15] show that MMU related memory accesses can cause higher than expected cost due to user program and data being evicted by page table entries. This effect further emphasizes the importance of efficient storage of page table entries.

Saulsbury *et. al.* propose a prefetching scheme for TLBs that preload pages based recently accessed pages [20]. Unlike the techniques presented in this paper, their techniques require page table modification. More recent work [16, 10] has proposed architecturally independent prefectching techniques based on access patterns and inter-core cooperation. These techniques all focus on reducing the frequency of TLB misses while our work focuses on reducing the cost of servicing a TLB miss. Both techniques could easily be combined.

In terms of space, a radix tree-based page table can be an inefficient representation for a large, sparsely-populated virtual address space. Liedtke introduced *Guarded Page Tables* to address this problem [18]. In particular, Guarded Page Tables allow for path compression. If there is only one valid path through multiple levels of the tree, then the entry prior to this path can be configured such that the page walk will skip these levels.

9. CONCLUSION

Since the x86 architecture began using a radix tree page table for address translation in the 80386, the depth of the page table has increased by one level with each passing decade. Unfortunately, without an MMU cache, the page table walk for address translation requires a memory reference for each level of the radix tree. Therefore, MMU caches have become critical components of current and future x86 processors. This paper has presented a quantitative and qualitative comparison of the design space of such MMU caches, including three new designs. While this paper has focused on x86 processors, the results should apply generally to any architecture that uses a radix tree page table.

While AMD and Intel have both developed MMU caches for their microprocessors, this paper has introduced a unified translation cache with a modified LRU replacement scheme that is superior to both existing devices. It adapts well to varying workloads, unlike a split translation cache, as implemented in Intel's Paging Structure Cache. It also prevents conflict between entries of low and high reuse, unlike the LRU unified page table cache, as implemented in AMD's Page Walk Cache.

This paper has also shown that MMU caches dramatically change the trade-offs in page table design for large address spaces. Radix tree page tables make more effective use of the processor's L2 cache than either inverted page tables or translation storage buffers. Radix tree page tables have a smaller page table entry size, because both inverted page tables and translation storage buffers must include a tag in the page table entry. Thus, the L2 cache is able to hold more page table entries from the radix tree, increasing its coverage and reducing DRAM accesses. So, while these alternate structures are superior to the radix tree page table on its own for large address spaces, a well designed MMU cache renders the radix tree organization far superior.

10. REFERENCES

[1] *AMD x86-64 Architecture Programmer's Manual, Volume 2.*

[2] *The ASCI sweep3d Benchmark Code.*

[3] *Intel 64 and IA-32 Architectures Software Developer's Manual Volume 3A: System Programming Guide Part 1.*

[4] *Intel Itanium Architecture Software Developer's Manual - Volume 2: System Architecture, Revision 2.2.*

[5] *UltraSPARC III Cu User's Manual.*

[6] A. Ailamaki, D. J. DeWitt, M. D. Hill, and D. A. Wood. DBMSs on a Modern Processor: Where Does Time Go? In *VLDB '99: Proceedings of the 25th International Conference on Very Large Data Bases*, pages 266–277, San Francisco, CA, USA, 1999. Morgan Kaufmann Publishers Inc.

[7] K. Bala, M. F. Kaashoek, and W. E. Weihl. Software prefetching and caching for translation lookaside buffers. In *OSDI '94: Proceedings of the 1st USENIX conference on Operating Systems Design and Implementation*, page 18, Berkeley, CA, USA, 1994. USENIX Association.

[8] R. Bedicheck. SimNow: Fast platform simulation purely in software. In *Hot Chips 16*, 2004.

[9] R. Bhargava, B. Serebrin, F. Spadini, and S. Manne. Accelerating two-dimensional page walks for virtualized systems. In *ASPLOS XIII: Proceedings of the 13th international conference on Architectural support for programming languages and operating systems*, pages 26–35, New York, NY, USA, 2008. ACM.

[10] A. Bhattacharjee and M. Martonosi. Inter-core cooperative tlb for chip multiprocessors. In *ASPLOS '10: Proceedings of the fifteenth edition of ASPLOS on Architectural support for programming languages and operating systems*, pages 359–370, New York, NY, USA, 2010. ACM.

[11] J. J. Dongarra and P. Luszczek. Introduction to the HPCChallenge Benchmark Suite. Technical Report 05-544, University of Tennessee - Knoxville, http://icl.cs.utk.edu/hpcc/, 2005.

[12] J. Edler and M. D. Hill. Dinero IV Trace-Driven Uniprocessor Cache Simulator, 1998.

[13] H. Garcia-Molina, J. Ullman, and J. Widom. *Database System Implementation.* Prentice Hall, 2000.

[14] J. L. Henning. SPEC CPU2006 benchmark descriptions. *SIGARCH Comput. Archit. News*, 34(4):1–17, 2006.

[15] B. L. Jacob and T. N. Mudge. A look at several memory management units, TLB-refill mechanisms, and page table organizations. In *ASPLOS-VIII: Proceedings of the eighth international conference on Architectural support for programming languages and operating systems*, pages 295–306, New York, NY, USA, 1998. ACM.

[16] G. B. Kandiraju and A. Sivasubramaniam. Going the distance for tlb prefetching: an application-driven study. In *ISCA '02: Proceedings of the 29th annual international symposium on Computer architecture*, pages 195–206, Washington, DC, USA, 2002. IEEE Computer Society.

[17] D. E. Knuth. *The Art of Computer Programming 3. Sorting and Searching: The Classic Work Newly Updated and Revised.* Addison-Wesley Longman, Amsterdam, 2. a. edition, 1998.

[18] J. Liedtke. Address space sparsity and fine granularity. In *EW 6: Proceedings of the 6th workshop on ACM SIGOPS European workshop*, pages 78–81, New York, NY, USA, 1994. ACM.

[19] C. McCurdy, A. L. Cox, and J. Vetter. Investigating the TLB Behavior of High-end Scientific Applications on Commodity Microprocessors. In *ISPASS '08: Proceedings of the ISPASS 2008 - IEEE International Symposium on Performance Analysis of Systems and software*, pages 95–104, Washington, DC, USA, 2008. IEEE Computer Society.

[20] A. Saulsbury, F. Dahlgren, and P. Stenström. Recency-based tlb preloading. In *ISCA '00: Proceedings of the 27th annual international symposium on Computer architecture*, pages 117–127, New York, NY, USA, 2000. ACM.

[21] Standard Performance Evaluation Corporation. The SPEC JBB2005 Benchmark, 2005.

[22] M. Talluri and M. D. Hill. Surpassing the tlb performance of superpages with less operating system support. In *Proceedings of the Sixth International Conference on Architectural Support for Programming Languages and Operating Systems*, 1994.

[23] M. Talluri, M. D. Hill, and Y. A. Khalidi. A new page table for 64-bit address spaces. In *SOSP '95: Proceedings of the fifteenth ACM symposium on Operating systems principles*, pages 184–200, New York, NY, USA, 1995. ACM.

[24] M. Wu and W. Zwaenepoel. Improving tlb miss handling with page table pointer caches. Technical Report TR97-296, Rice University, 1996.

[25] N. Young. On-line caching as cache size varies. In *SODA '91: Proceedings of the second annual ACM-SIAM symposium on Discrete algorithms*, pages 241–250, Philadelphia, PA, USA, 1991. Society for Industrial and Applied Mathematics.

High Performance Cache Replacement Using Re-Reference Interval Prediction (RRIP)

Aamer Jaleel† Kevin B. Theobald‡ Simon C. Steely Jr.† Joel Emer†

†Intel Corporation, VSSAD
Hudson, MA

‡Intel Corporation, MGD
Hillsboro, OR

{aamer.jaleel, kevin.b.theobald, simon.c.steely.jr, joel.emer}@intel.com

ABSTRACT

Practical cache replacement policies attempt to emulate optimal replacement by predicting the re-reference interval of a cache block. The commonly used LRU replacement policy always predicts a near-immediate re-reference interval on cache hits and misses. Applications that exhibit a distant re-reference interval perform badly under LRU. Such applications usually have a working-set larger than the cache or have frequent bursts of references to non-temporal data (called scans). To improve the performance of such workloads, this paper proposes cache replacement using Re-reference Interval Prediction (RRIP). We propose Static RRIP (SRRIP) that is scan-resistant and Dynamic RRIP (DRRIP) that is both scan-resistant and thrash-resistant. Both RRIP policies require only 2-bits per cache block and easily integrate into existing LRU approximations found in modern processors. Our evaluations using PC games, multimedia, server and SPEC CPU2006 workloads on a single-core processor with a 2MB last-level cache (LLC) show that both SRRIP and DRRIP outperform LRU replacement on the throughput metric by an average of 4% and 10% respectively. Our evaluations with over 1000 multi-programmed workloads on a 4-core CMP with an 8MB shared LLC show that SRRIP and DRRIP outperform LRU replacement on the throughput metric by an average of 7% and 9% respectively. We also show that RRIP outperforms LFU, the state-of the art scan-resistant replacement algorithm to-date. For the cache configurations under study, RRIP requires 2X less hardware than LRU and 2.5X less hardware than LFU.

Categories and Subject Descriptors

B.3.2 [Design Styles]: Cache memories, C.1.4 [Parallel architectures]

General Terms

Design, Performance.

Keywords

Replacement, Scan Resistance, Thrashing, Shared Cache

1. INTRODUCTION

An optimal replacement policy makes its replacement decisions using perfect knowledge of the re-reference (or reuse) pattern of each cache block and replaces the block that will be re-referenced furthest in the future. Practical cache replacement policies, on the other hand, can be viewed as basing their replacement decisions on a *prediction* of which block will be re-referenced furthest in the future and pick that block for replacement. Typically, on a miss, replacement policies make a prediction on when the missing block will be re-referenced next. These predictions can be updated when further information about the block is available, for example, on a re-reference.

In the commonly used Least Recently Used (LRU) replacement policy, the LRU chain represents the recency of cache blocks referenced with the MRU position representing a cache block that was most recently used while the LRU position representing a cache block that was least recently used. Recent proposals on cache insertion policies [11, 25, 28, 30] and hit promotion policies [30] have altered the description of the LRU chain. Rather than representing recency, the *LRU chain* can instead be thought of as a *Re-Reference Interval Prediction (RRIP) chain* that represents the order in which blocks are predicted to be re-referenced. The block at the head of the RRIP chain is predicted to have a *near-immediate* re-reference interval while the block at the tail of the RRIP chain is predicted to have a *distant* re-reference interval. A *near-immediate* re-reference interval implies that a cache block will be re-referenced sometime soon while a *distant* re-reference interval implies that a cache block will be re-referenced in the distant future. On a cache miss, the block at the tail of the RRIP chain (i.e., the block predicted to be referenced most far into the future) will be replaced[1].

Using the RRIP framework, LRU replacement predicts that a block filled into the cache has a *near-immediate re-reference* interval and thus places it at the head of the RRIP chain. Upon re-reference to a block, LRU updates its prediction and again anticipates that the block has a *near-immediate* re-reference interval. In effect, LRU predicts that cache blocks are re-referenced in the reverse-order of reference, i.e., LRU predicts that a Most Recently Used (MRU) cache block will be re-referenced much sooner than an LRU cache block.

While LRU provides good performance for workloads with high data locality, LRU limits performance when the prediction of a *near-immediate* re-reference interval is incorrect. Applications whose re-references only occur in the distant future perform badly under LRU. Such applications correspond to situations where the application working set is larger than the available cache or when a burst of references to non-temporal data discards the active working set from the cache. In both scenarios, LRU inefficiently utilizes the cache since newly inserted blocks have no temporal locality after insertion.

The Dynamic Insertion Policy (DIP) [25] improves LRU replacement in situations where the re-reference interval is in the

1. We are viewing the RRIP chain like a "snake" where, for LRU, new cache blocks enter the head and leave at the tail.

$(a_1, a_2, \ldots, a_{k-1}, a_k, a_k, a_{k-1}, \ldots, a_2, a_1)^N$	$(a_1, a_2, \ldots, a_k)^N$	$(a_1, a_2, a_3, a_4, \ldots a_k)$
(a) Recency-friendly Access Pattern (for any *k*)	**(b) Thrashing Access Pattern (*k* > cache size)**	**(c) Streaming Access Pattern (*k* = ∞)**

$$[(a_1, \ldots, a_k, a_k, \ldots, a_1)^A \, P_\varepsilon(a_1, a_2, \ldots, a_k, a_{k+1} \ldots, a_m)]^N$$

$$[(a_1, \ldots, a_k)^A \, P_\varepsilon(b_1, b_2, \ldots, b_m)]^N$$

"scan"

(d) Mixed Access Pattern (*k* < cache size AND *m* > cache size , 0 < ε < 1)

Figure 1: Common Cache Access Patterns.

distant future by dynamically changing the re-reference prediction from a *near-immediate* re-reference interval to a *distant* re-reference interval. At the time of a cache miss, the LRU Insertion Policy (LIP) component of DIP predicts that the cache blocks that already reside in the cache will be re-referenced sooner than the missing cache block. As a result, when the working set is larger than the available cache, LIP preserves part of the working set in the cache by replacing the most recently filled cache block instead of using LRU replacement. DIP dynamically uses LIP for workloads whose working set is larger than the available cache and relies on LRU for all other workloads.

Unfortunately, DIP makes the same predictions for all references of a workload. The LRU component of DIP predicts that *all* re-references to missing cache blocks will be *near-immediate* and inserts them at the head of the RRIP chain. On the other hand, the LIP component of DIP predicts that *all* re-references to missing cache blocks will be in the *distant* future and inserts them at the tail of the RRIP chain. Consequently, when the workload re-reference pattern is mixed, i.e., both *near-immediate* and *distant* re-references occur, neither LRU nor DIP can make accurate predictions. For example, both DIP and LRU limit cache performance when *scans* [5] discard the frequently referenced working-set of an application from the cache. A *scan* is defined as a burst of references to data whose re-reference interval is in the *distant* future. In comparison, accesses that do not belong to the scan have a *near-immediate* re-reference interval. Our studies show that many real world applications suffer from frequent scans in their cache access patterns. Consequently, improving the performance of real world applications require a practical scan-resistant cache replacement policy.

Scans, regardless of their length, do not receive cache hits after their initial reference. This is because the re-reference interval of a scan block is in the *distant* future. The situation may be different for the blocks resident in the cache when the scan first starts. When the data referenced after the scan is different from the data referenced before the scan, replacement decisions during the scan are irrelevant because the references to the new data cause compulsory misses[2]. However, when the data referenced after the scan belongs to the working set prior to the scan, the optimal replacement policy *knows* that a *distant* re-reference interval be applied to cache blocks belonging to the scan and a *near-immediate* re-reference interval be applied to cache blocks belonging to the working set. In doing so, the optimal replacement policy preserves the frequently referenced working set in the cache after the scan completes. Practical replacement policies can potentially accomplish this by using LIP-style replacement during the course of the scan and LRU replacement in the absence of the scan.

In comparison to prior scan-resistant replacement algorithms [5, 13, 17, 22, 27, 29], this paper focuses on designing a high performing scan-resistant replacement policy that requires low hardware overhead, retains the existing cache structure, and most importantly integrates easily into existing hardware approximations of LRU [1, 2]. To that end, we propose a practical replacement policy that uses *Re-reference Interval Prediction (RRIP)*.

RRIP prevents cache blocks with a *distant* re-reference interval (i.e., scan blocks) from evicting blocks that have a *near-immediate* re-reference interval (i.e., non-scan blocks). RRIP accomplishes this by requiring an M-bit register per cache block to store its *Re-reference Prediction Value (RRPV)*. We propose *Static RRIP (SRRIP)* that is scan-resistant and *Dynamic RRIP (DRRIP)* that is both scan-resistant and thrash-resistant. Both SRRIP and DRRIP improve performance over LRU and easily integrate into existing hardware approximations for LRU. In fact, when M=1, SRRIP degenerates to the Not Recently Used (NRU) [2] replacement policy commonly used in modern high performance processors [1, 2].

The rest of this paper is organized as follows, Section 2 motivates the need for a scan-resistant replacement algorithm, Section 3 provides related work, Section 4 introduces RRIP, Section 5 provides the experimental methodology, Section 6 presents results, and finally Section 7 summarizes the paper.

2. MOTIVATION

Efficient last-level cache (LLC) utilization is crucial to avoid long latency cache misses to main memory. Under LRU replacement, many studies have illustrated that the filtering of temporal locality by small caches cause the majority of blocks inserted into the LLC to never be re-referenced [14, 16, 25, 30]. The inefficient cache utilization is because LRU performs poorly for the cache access patterns resulting from the filtered temporal locality.

To better understand when LRU performs poorly, Figure 1 presents several representative cache access patterns commonly found in applications. Let a_i denote the address of a cache line, $(a_1, \ldots, a_k)$ denote a temporal sequence of references to k unique addresses and let $P_\varepsilon(a_1, \ldots, a_k)$ denote a temporal sequence that occurs with some probability ε. A temporal sequence that repeats N times is represented as $(a_1, \ldots, a_k)^N$. The cache access patterns can be classified into the following categories:

- Recency-friendly Access Patterns: Figure 1a presents a typical stack access pattern that repeats N times. In general, recency-friendly access patterns have a *near-immediate* re-reference interval. For any value of k, the access pattern benefits from LRU replacement. Any other replacement policy besides LRU can degrade the performance of these access patterns.
- Thrashing Access Patterns: Figure 1b presents a cyclic access pattern of length k that repeats N times. When k is less than or equal to the number of blocks in the cache, the working set fits into the cache. However, when k is larger than the number of cache blocks, LRU receives zero cache hits due to cache thrashing. For such patterns, LRU provides no cache hits unless

---

2. Compulsory misses cannot be reduced under any replacement policy.

the cache size is increased to hold all k entries of the access pattern. When the available cache is less than k entries, the optimal replacement policy preserves some of the working set in the cache. Unfortunately, LRU is incapable of doing so.

- Streaming Access Patterns: Figure 1c presents a streaming access pattern. When $k = \infty$, the access pattern has no locality in its references. Streaming access patterns can be characterized as workloads that have *infinite re-reference* interval. Consequently, streaming access patterns receive no cache hits under any replacement policy. As a result, LRU is adequate since replacement decisions are irrelevant in the presence of streaming access patterns.
- Mixed Access Patterns: Mixed access patterns can be characterized as workloads where some references have a *near-immediate* re-reference interval while other references have a *distant* re-reference interval. Figure 1d illustrates this using two example access patterns that have scans (highlighted by the grey box in the figure). Both examples include an access pattern of length k that repeats A times followed by a reference to a sequence of length m with probability ε. Both the scan and access pattern repeat N times. The first reference pattern is representative of an application that performs operations on a linked list of m entries. The initial stack reference pattern illustrates operations that have temporal locality to the beginning of the linked list. The scan illustrates a search or update operation that requires traversing the entire list. The second example is representative of an application that operates on a data structure of k entries and then updates a different data structure of m entries. For both access patterns, when $m + k$ is less than the available cache, the total working set fits into the cache and LRU works well. However, when $m + k$ is greater than the available cache, LRU discards the frequently referenced working set from the cache. Consequently, accesses to the frequently referenced working set always misses after the scan. In the absence of scans, mixed access patterns prefer LRU. However, in the presence of scans, the optimal policy preserves the active working set in the cache after the scan completes. Unfortunately, LRU cannot preserve the active working set.

For the access patterns described above, there is room to improve LRU for thrashing and mixed access patterns. DIP [25] addresses the cache thrashing problem by preserving some of the working set in the cache. Unfortunately, DIP only targets workloads that have a working set larger than the available cache and relies on LRU for all other workloads. As a result, DIP limits performance of workloads where frequent scans discard the active working from the cache. To illustrate this problem, Figure 2 compares the cache performance of thrash-resistant DIP to scan-resistant $HYB_{LRU/LFU}$. $HYB_{LRU/LFU}$ is a hybrid cache replacement policy that uses Set Dueling [25] to dynamically choose between the scan-resistant *Least Frequently Used (LFU)*[3] [17] replacement policy and LRU replacement. The study consists of 14 workloads each running on a 2MB LLC. The y-axis presents the average reduction in cache misses compared to LRU while the x-axis presents the applications and their categories. The application categories under study are *PC games*, *multimedia*, *server*, and *SPEC CPU 2006*.

Figure 2 shows that DIP outperforms LFU for two workloads from the SPEC CPU2006 category. However, LFU significantly outperforms DIP for workloads in the PC games and multimedia categories (and the *hmmer* workload in the SPEC CPU2006 category). For example, PC games and multimedia workloads observe no benefit from thrash-resistant DIP but observe up to 20% reduction in cache misses from scan-resistant LFU. The results in Figure 2 motivate the need for a practical cache replacement policy that is not just thrash-resistant but also scan-resistant. Section 4 discusses the design of such a replacement policy.

3. Access frequency is measured by using a 4-bit counter per cache block. All LFU counters in the set are halved whenever any counter saturates.

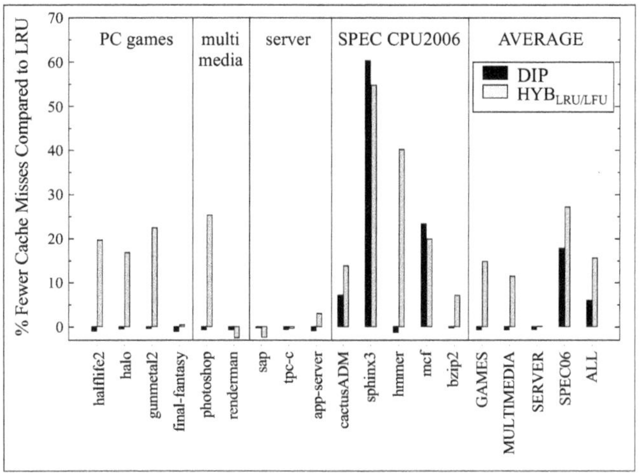

Figure 2: Comparing LRU to Thrash-Resistant DIP and Scan-Resistant LFU.

3. RELATED WORK

Both industry and academia have produced an impressive amount of research work dedicated to improving the performance of replacement policies. While we cannot describe all replacement policies that exist in the literature, we summarize prior art that most closely relates to improving LLC performance by targeting cache blocks that are dead upon cache insertion.

Dead blocks brought in by scans have commonly been addressed by using *access frequency* to predict the re-reference pattern. The proposed *Least Frequently Used (LFU)* [17] replacement policy predicts that blocks that are frequently accessed will be re-referenced in the *near-immediate* future while blocks infrequently accessed will be re-referenced in the *distant* future. LFU accomplishes this by using counters to measure a block's access frequency. While LFU improves the performance of workloads with frequent scans, it significantly degrades the performance of workloads where *recency* is the preferred choice for replacement. Several studies have combined recency and frequency [17, 23, 27] to address the problem but they require several parameters to be tuned on a per-workload basis. Self-tuning adaptive policies [22, 5, 29] exist, however they significantly increase the hardware overhead and complexity. The hardware overhead and complexity can be reduced via hybrid cache replacement [25]. Hybrid cache replacement uses *set dueling* [25] to dynamically choose between multiple replacement policies. While hybrid cache replacement using LRU and LFU can provide scan-resistance, hybrid replacement requires hardware and verification overhead for two *different* cache replacement policies. It would be highly desirable that a single cache replacement policy provide scan resistance and perform well for recency friendly workloads.

Another area of research predicts when the re-reference interval of a cache block becomes *distant*, i.e., a cache block becomes dead [16, 18]. A recent study applied dead block prediction at the LLC [19]. The proposed policy attaches a prediction with each cache block to determine whether or not the block is dead. The proposed policy uses the block's re-reference history to predict *death* after the block moves out of the head of the RRIP chain. The victim selection policy selects dead blocks closer to the tail of the RRIP chain. While dead block prediction improves cache performance, it requires additional hardware overhead for the dead block predictor.

A recent study [25] shows that dead blocks occur when the application working set is larger than the available cache. In such scenarios, the proposed *Dynamic Insertion Policy (DIP)* [25] dynamically changes the insertion policy from always inserting blocks at the head of the RRIP chain to inserting the majority of the blocks at the tail of the RRIP chain. By doing so, DIP preserves some of the working set in the cache. Since DIP makes a single insertion policy decision for *all* references of a workload, DIP only targets workloads whose working set is larger than the available cache. Consequently, in the presence of scans, the LRU component policy of DIP is unable to preserve the active working set in the cache.

Another recent study proposes pseudo-LIFO [8] based replacement policies. The policy proposes cache replacement using a fill stack as opposed to the recency stack. The proposed policy learns the re-reference probabilities of a cache block beyond each fill stack position and finds that evicting blocks from the upper portion of the fill stack improves cache utilization by evicting dead blocks quickly. The proposed policy however requires additional hardware to keep track of a block's fill stack position and also requires a dynamic mechanism to learn the best eviction position on the fill stack.

Various other solutions [6, 13, 20, 26, 31] exist but they either require significant additional hardware or they drastically change the organization of the existing cache. Reuse distance prediction [15] most closely resembles the work presented in this paper. Reuse distance prediction explicitly calculates the reuse distance of a given cache block by using a PC indexed predictor. RRIP does not explicitly calculate reuse distance. Instead, RRIP always predicts that all missing cache block will have the same re-reference interval and updates the prediction when more information is available, for example, on a re-reference. RRIP also differs from prior work in that it proposes a high performing practical scan-resistant cache replacement policy that does not require significant hardware overhead or changes to the existing cache structure.

4. RE-REFERENCE INTERVAL PREDICTION (RRIP)

When workloads have mixed access patterns, LRU replacement and its approximations cannot perfectly distinguish between blocks that have a *distant* re-reference interval from blocks that have a *near-immediate* re-reference interval. Since chain-based LRU replacement is impractical to build in hardware for highly associative caches, we illustrate the problem for mixed access patterns using the *Not Recently Used (NRU)* [1, 2] replacement policy.

4.1. Not Recently Used (NRU) Replacement

The *Not Recently Used (NRU)* replacement policy is an approximation of LRU commonly used in modern high performance processors. NRU uses a single bit per cache block called the *nru*-bit[4]. With only one bit of information, NRU allows two re-reference interval predictions: *near-immediate* re-reference and *distant* re-reference. An nru-bit value of '0' implies that a block was recently used and the block is predicted to be re-referenced in the *near-immediate* future. An nru-bit value of '1' implies that the block was not recently used and the block is predicted to be re-referenced in the *distant* future. On cache fills, NRU always predicts that the missing block will have a *near-immediate* re-reference. Upon re-reference, NRU again anticipates that the block referenced will have a *near-immediate* re-reference. On a cache miss, NRU selects the victim cache block whose predicted re-reference is in the *distant* future, i.e., a block whose nru-bit is '1'. Because multiple blocks may have a *distant* re-reference prediction, a tie-breaker is needed. The NRU victim selection policy always starts the victim search from a fixed location (the left in our studies). In the event that all nru-bits are '0', i.e., all blocks are predicted to be re-referenced in the *near-immediate* future, NRU updates the re-reference predictions of all cache blocks to be in the *distant* future and repeats the victim search. Updating all nru-bits to '1' allows the victim selection policy to make forward progress while also removing stale blocks from the cache.

Figure 3b illustrates the behavior of NRU using a 4-entry cache initialized with invalid blocks 'I'. For reference, Figure 3a also shows the behavior of LRU. The figure also shows the steps taken by the replacement policy on cache hits and cache misses. We use the following bimodal access pattern to illustrate NRU behavior:

$$(a_1, a_2, a_2, a_1)\,(b_1, b_2, b_3, b_4)\,(a_1, a_2, \ldots)$$

Figure 3b shows the four blocks of the cache each with the nru-bit shown in the lower right hand corner. The figure shows that after the scan completes, references to a_1 and a_2 both miss the cache when the optimal replacement policy would have preserved them in the cache.

4.2. Static RRIP (SRRIP)

With only one bit of information, NRU can predict either a *near-immediate* re-reference interval or a *distant* re-reference interval for all blocks filled into the cache. Always predicting a *near-immediate* re-reference interval on all cache insertions limits cache performance for mixed access patterns because scan blocks unnecessarily occupy the cache space without receiving any cache hits. On the other hand, always predicting a *distant* re-reference interval significantly degrades cache performance for access patterns that predominantly have a *near-immediate* re-reference interval. Consequently, without any external information on the re-reference interval for every missing cache block, NRU cannot identify and preserve non-scan blocks in a mixed access pattern.

To address the limitations of NRU, we enhance the granularity of the re-reference prediction stored with each cache block. We propose cache replacement based on *Re-reference Interval Prediction (RRIP)*. RRIP uses M-bits per cache block to store one of 2^M possible *Re-reference Prediction Values (RRPV)*. RRIP dynamically *learns* re-reference information for each block in the cache access pattern. Like NRU, an RRPV of zero implies that a cache block is predicted to be re-referenced in the *near-immediate* future while RRPV of saturation (i.e., 2^M-1) implies that a cache block is predicted to be re-referenced in the *distant* future. Quantitatively, RRIP predicts that blocks with small RRPVs are re-referenced sooner than blocks with large RRPVs. When M=1, RRIP is identical to the NRU replacement policy. When M>1, RRIP enables *intermediate* re-reference intervals that are greater than a *near-immediate* re-reference interval but less than a *distant* re-reference interval.

The primary goal of RRIP is to prevent blocks with a *distant* re-reference interval from polluting the cache. In the absence of any external re-reference information, RRIP statically predicts the block's re-reference interval. Since always predicting a *near-immediate* or a *distant* re-reference interval at cache insertion time is not robust across all access patterns, RRIP always inserts new blocks with a *long* re-reference interval. A *long* re-reference interval is defined as an *intermediate* re-reference interval that is skewed towards a *distant* re-reference interval. We use an RRPV of 2^M-2 to represent a *long* re-reference interval. The intuition behind always predicting a *long* re-reference interval on cache insertion is to prevent cache blocks with re-references in the *distant* future from polluting the cache. Additionally, always predicting a *long* re-reference interval instead of a *distant* re-reference interval allows RRIP more time to learn and improve the re-reference prediction. If the newly inserted cache block has a *near-immediate* re-reference interval, RRIP can then update the re-reference prediction to be shorter than the previous prediction. In effect, RRIP *learns* the block's re-reference interval.

4. This paper describes NRU replacement by inverting the polarity of the bit to represent not-recently used. instead of recently used.

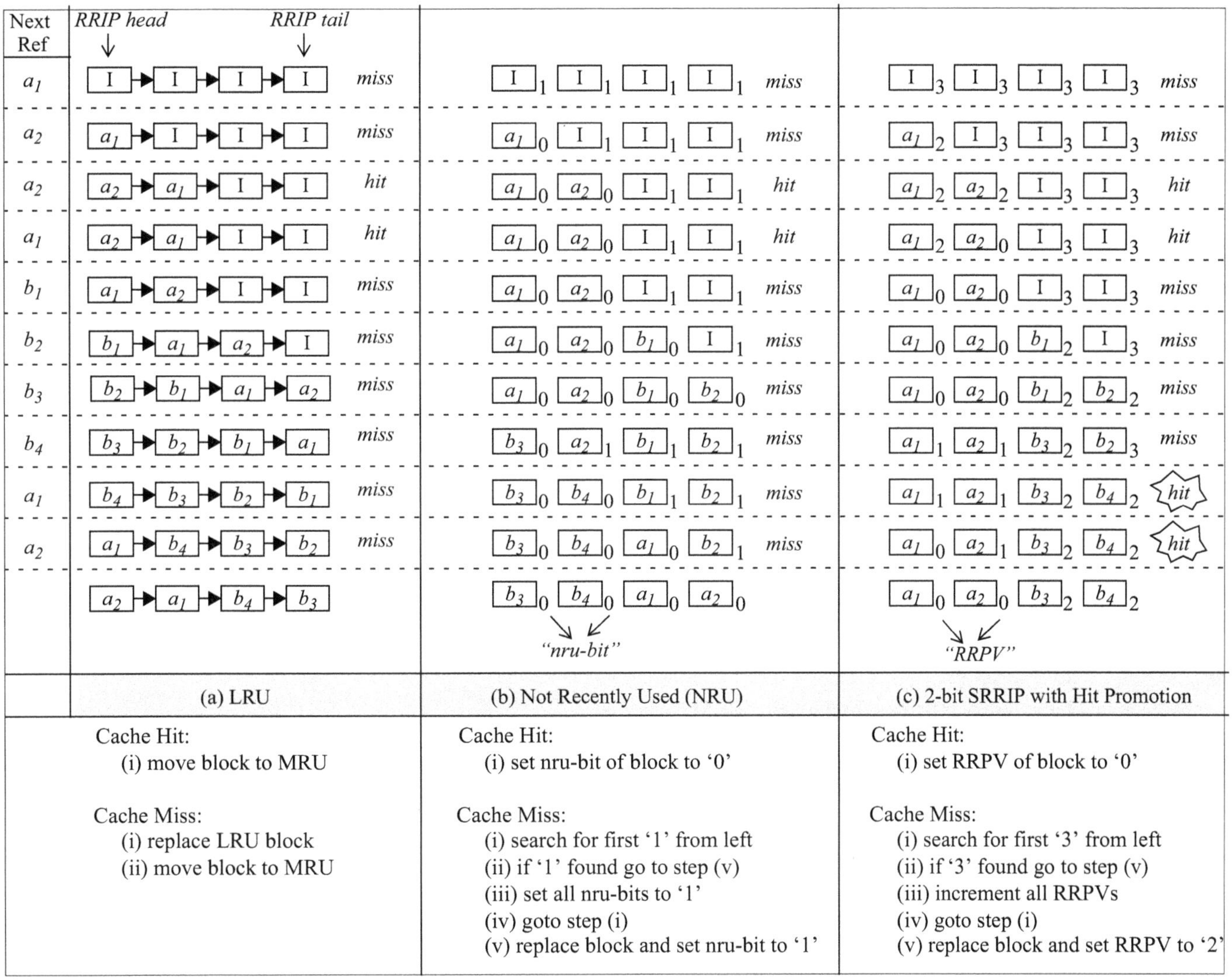

Figure 3: Behavior of LRU, NRU, and SRRIP for a Mixed Access Pattern.

On a cache miss, the RRIP *victim selection policy* selects the victim block by finding the first block that is predicted to be re-referenced in the *distant* future (i.e., the block whose RRPV is 2^M-1). Like NRU, the victim selection policy breaks ties by always starting the victim search from a fixed location (the left in our studies). In the event that RRIP is unable to find a block with a *distant* re-reference interval, RRIP updates the re-reference predictions by incrementing the RRPVs of all blocks in the cache set and repeats the search until a block with a *distant* re-reference interval is found. Updating RRPVs at victim selection time allows RRIP to adapt to changes in the application working set by removing stale blocks from the cache.

A natural opportunity to change the re-reference prediction of a block occurs on a hit to the block. The algorithm for this update of the RRPV register is called the RRIP *hit promotion policy.* The primary purpose of the hit promotion policy is to dynamically improve the accuracy of the predicted re-reference interval of cache blocks. We propose two policies to update the re-reference prediction: *Hit Priority (HP)* and *Frequency Priority (FP)*. The RRIP-HP policy predicts that the block receiving a hit will be re-referenced in the *near-immediate* future and updates the RRPV of the associated block to zero. The goal of the HP policy is to prioritize replacement of blocks that do not receive cache hits over *any* cache block that receives a hit. However, the HP policy can potentially degrade cache performance when a cache block is re-referenced only once after cache insertion. In such situations, the HP policy incorrectly predicts a *near-immediate* re-reference prediction instead of *distant* re-reference prediction for the block and causes the block to occupy valuable cache space without receiving any hits. To address this problem, the RRIP-FP policy uses more information (i.e., cache hits) to update the re-reference prediction. Instead of updating the re-reference prediction to be *near-immediate* on a hit, RRIP-FP updates the predicted re-reference interval to be shorter than the previous re-reference interval each time a block receives a hit. The FP policy accomplishes this by decrementing the RRPV register (unless the RRPV register is already zero) on cache hits. The goal of the FP policy is to prioritize replacement of infrequently re-referenced cache blocks over frequently re-referenced cache blocks.

Since the re-reference predictions made by RRIP are statically determined on cache hits and misses, we refer to this replacement policy as *Static Re-reference Interval Prediction (SRRIP)*. Figure 3c illustrates the behavior of 2-bit SRRIP-HP. The example shows that SRRIP emulates optimal replacement by correctly predicting a *near-immediate* re-reference interval for the actively used cache blocks and a *distant* re-reference interval for the scan blocks.

In general, for associativity A, active working set size w ($w < A$), and scan length S_{len}, M-bit SRRIP is scan-resistant when

$$S_{len} <= (2^{M} - 1) * (A - w) \quad \text{(Eq. 1)}$$

When the condition in Equation 1 does not hold, SRRIP is unable to preserve the active working set in the cache because the RRPVs of the scan blocks and the non-scan blocks become identical due to the aging mechanism of the victim selection policy. In such scenarios, the active working set can be preserved for a longer time by increasing the width of the RRPV register. While large RRPVs can be resistant to long scans, they can result in inefficient cache utilization when a cache block receives its last hit and the RRPV becomes zero. In such situations the effective cache capacity reduces until the victim selection policy updates the re-reference prediction of the dead block to have a *distant* re-reference. Consequently, scan-resistance using RRIP requires that the width of the RRPV register to be appropriately sized to avoid sources of performance degradation.

4.3. Dynamic RRIP (DRRIP)

SRRIP inefficiently utilizes the cache when the re-reference interval of all blocks is larger than the available cache. In such scenarios, SRRIP causes cache thrashing and results in no cache hits. To avoid cache thrashing, we propose *Bimodal RRIP (BRRIP)* that inserts majority of cache blocks with a *distant* re-reference interval prediction (i.e., RRPV of 2^M–1) and infrequently (with low probability) inserts new cache blocks with a *long* re-reference interval prediction (i.e., RRPV of 2^M–2). BRRIP is analogous to the Bimodal Insertion Policy (BIP) [25] component of DIP which helps preserve some of the working set in the cache.

For non-thrashing access patterns, always using BRRIP can significantly degrade cache performance. In order to be robust across all cache access patterns, we propose to dynamically determine whether an application is best suited to scan-resistant SRRIP or thrash-resistant BRRIP. We propose *Dynamic Re-reference Interval Prediction (DRRIP)* that uses *Set Dueling* [25] to identify which replacement policy is best suited for the application. DRRIP dynamically chooses between scan-resistant SRRIP and thrash-resistant BRRIP by using two *Set Dueling Monitors (SDMs)* [11]. An SDM estimates the misses for any given policy by permanently dedicating a few sets[5] of the cache to follow that policy. Set Dueling uses a single policy selection (PSEL) counter to determine the winning policy. DRRIP uses the winning policy of the two SDMs for the remaining sets of the cache.

4.4. Comparing SRRIP to LRU

A natural way of modifying an LRU managed cache to predict the re-reference interval would be by changing the insertion position of blocks on the LRU chain, creating a RRIP chain. The baseline MRU Insertion Policy (MIP) [25] predicts a *near-immediate* re-reference interval by always inserting new blocks at the head of the RRIP chain. The LRU Insertion Policy (LIP) [25] predicts a *distant* re-reference interval by always inserting new blocks at the tail of the RRIP chain. Insertion positions in the middle of the RRIP chain [28, 30] can be used to predict an *intermediate* re-reference interval. While different insertion positions in the RRIP chain can provide scan-resistance, they require tuning on a per-application basis. A static insertion position for all applications can degrade performance when changes in the working set requires an alternate re-reference prediction, i.e., an alternate insertion position on the RRIP chain.

Unlike SRRIP, modified LRU cannot automatically adapt to changes in the application working set size and thus can degrade performance significantly. Set dueling can be used to design a mechanism that dynamically identifies the best insertion position on the RRIP chain suitable to the application (or application phase). Specifically, SDMs can *monitor* the performance of different insertion positions on the RRIP chain and then *apply* the best position to the remainder of the cache. However, using SDMs to identify the best insertion position on the RRIP chain does not scale well with increasing cache associativity. This is because the number of monitor sets required can exceed the total number of sets in the cache. As a result, set dueling controlled policies to identify the best insertion position on the RRIP chain are not considered as a practical solution to provide scan resistance. Nonetheless, we compare SRRIP and DRRIP to an offline profiling mechanism that *knows* the best single insertion location on the RRIP chain on a per application basis. We refer to this scheme as the *Best Offline Insertion Policy (BOIP)*. We do not consider the potentially better and more complex scheme where the insertion position on the RRIP chain dynamically adapts to different phases of an application.

5. Prior work has shown that 32 sets are sufficient to estimate cache performance [11]. Throughout the paper an SDM consists of 32 sets.

4.5. RRIP Extensions to Shared Caches

With the growing number of cores on-chip, shared caches are now very common. Since shared caches receive access patterns from concurrently executing workloads, the combined access stream from the different workloads can also be thought of as a mixed access pattern. Thus, SRRIP naturally extends to shared caches and can minimize cache contention between applications with varying memory demands. For example, using the mixed access pattern terminology, the references to the *active working set* can potentially be described as memory references by an application whose working set is small and fits in the shared LLC and the *scan* can be described as memory references by an application with a very large working set. In such situations, SRRIP reduces cache contention by preserving the small working set in the shared LLC.

Extending DRRIP to shared caches is analogous to the extension of DIP to shared caches. We propose *Thread-Aware DRRIP (TA-DRRIP)* which is similar to the *Thread-Aware Dynamic Insertion Policy (TA-DIP)* [9]. TA-DRRIP uses two SDMs per application to dynamically determine whether the application should use SRRIP or BRRIP in the presence of other applications. Like TA-DIP, TA-DRRIP merely requires a policy selection counter (PSEL) for each hardware thread sharing the LLC.

5. EXPERIMENTAL METHODOLOGY

5.1. Simulator

We use CMP$im [10], a Pin [21] based trace-driven x86 simulator for our performance studies. Our baseline processor is 4-way out-of-order with a 128-entry reorder buffer and a three level cache hierarchy. Only the LLC of the hierarchy enforces inclusion. Our cache hierarchy is roughly comparable to the Intel Core i7 [3]. The L1 instruction and data caches are 4-way 32KB each while the L2 cache is unified 8-way 256KB. The L1 and L2 cache sizes are kept constant in our study. We support two L1 read ports and one L1 write port on the data cache. We evaluate both single-core and 4-core configurations. In the 4-core configuration, the L1 and L2 are private and only the LLC is shared by all four cores. The baseline LLC (L3) is 16-way 2MB in the single-core and 8MB in the 4-core system. All caches in the hierarchy use a 64B line size. For replacement decisions, all caches in the hierarchy use the LRU replacement policy. Only demand references to the cache update the LRU state while non-demand references (e.g., write back references) leave the LRU state unchanged. The load-to-use latencies for the L1, L2, and L3 caches are 1, 10, and 24 cycles respectively. We model a 250 cycle penalty to main memory and support a maximum of 32 outstanding misses to memory.

Table 1: Benchmarks

Category	Workloads
PC Games	final-fantasy, gunmetal2, halflife2, halo
Multimedia	photoshop, renderman
Server	app-server, sap, tpc-c
SPEC CPU2006	bzip2, cactusADM, hmmer, mcf, sphinx3

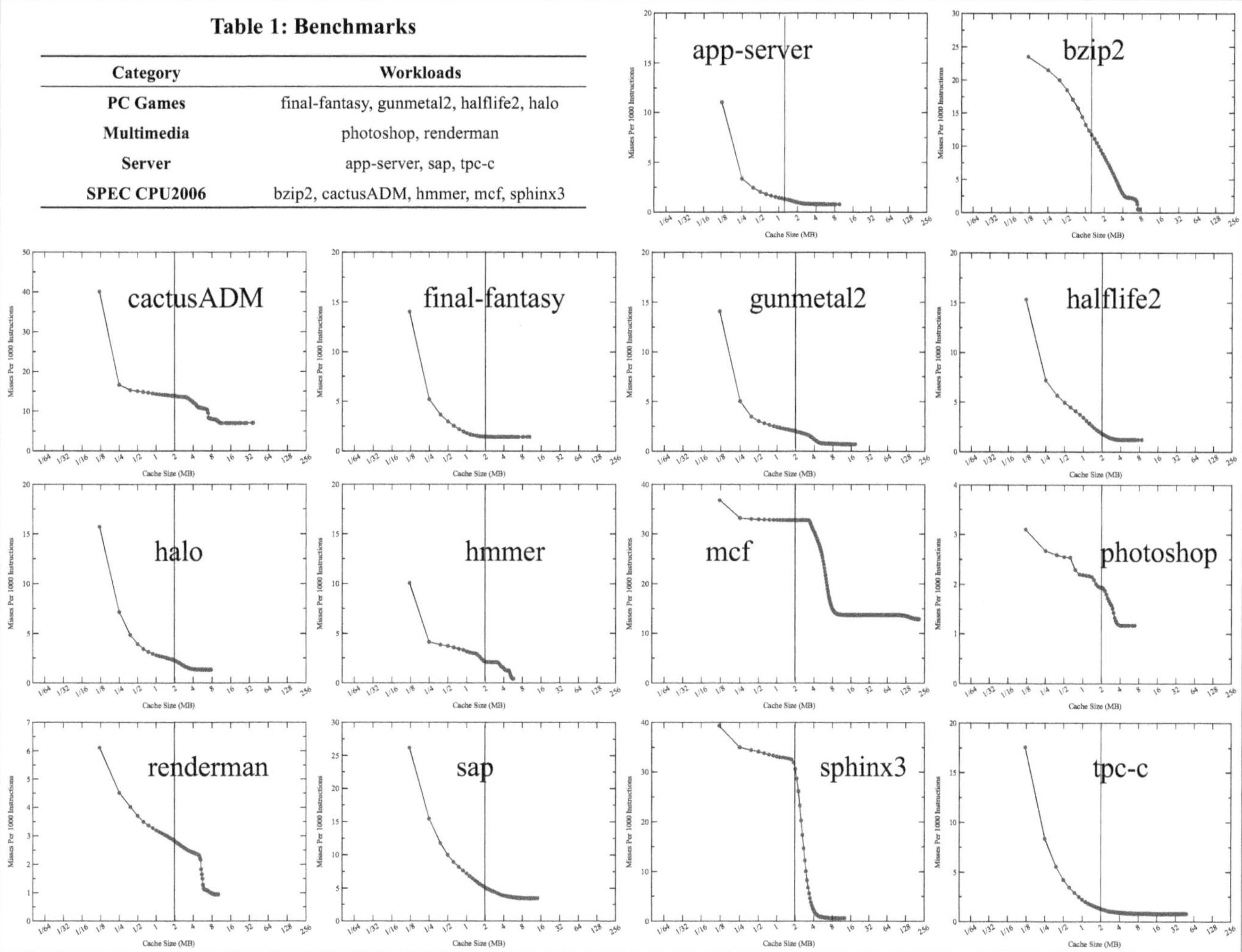

Figure 4: Cache Sensitivity of Workloads Used in this Study.

5.2. Benchmarks

For our single-core studies we use five workloads from the SPEC CPU2006 benchmark suite and nine "real world" workloads from the PC game, multimedia, and server workload segments. These workloads were selected because they are sensitive to memory latency on the baseline processor configuration and there is an opportunity to improve their performance through enhanced replacement decisions. To be thorough, we report results across a broad set of memory intensive and non-memory intensive workloads in the appendix. The SPEC CPU2006 workloads were all collected using PinPoints [24] for the reference input set while the real world workloads were all collected on a hardware tracing platform. The real world workloads include both operating system and user-level activity while the SPEC CPU2006 workloads only include user-level activity. Table 1 lists the workloads used and Figure 4 provides their sensitivity to different cache sizes. The workloads were all run for 250M instructions.

For our multi-core workloads, we created all possible 4-core combinations (14 choose 4 = 1001 workloads). Simulations were run until *all* benchmarks ran 250 million instructions. Statistics for each core were collected only for the first 250 million instructions. If the end of the trace is reached, the model rewinds the trace and restarts from the beginning. The simulation methodology is similar to recent work on shared caches [11, 8, 30, 20].

6. RESULTS AND ANALYSIS

6.1. SRRIP Sensitivity to RRPV on Insertion

Figure 5 shows the sensitivity of SRRIP-HP to the width of the M-bit register and the *Re-reference Prediction Value* on cache insertion when both are changed statically. The y-axis represents the percent reduction in cache misses compared to LRU replacement. For M=1 (NRU), 2, 3, 4, and 5, the x-axis shows all 2^M possible RRPVs for cache insertion. The x-axis labels follow the format "INS=r, M=m" and denotes an m-bit SRRIP configuration where all missing cache blocks are inserted with an RRPV of 'r'. For each SRRIP configuration, the figure also shows the maximum, average, and minimum values for the reduction in cache misses across all workloads. The average is represented by squares while the minimum and maximum values are represented by triangles.

Figure 5 shows that when M>1, always predicting that a missing cache block has a *long* re-reference interval has the best performance. In fact, predicting a *long* re-reference interval consistently outperforms NRU replacement (M=1). This is because RRIP enhances the granularity for predicting the re-reference interval. By always predicting a *long* re-reference interval, cache blocks that do not have temporal locality (i.e., scan blocks) do not pollute the cache for an extended period of time. Always predicting a *distant* re-reference interval has the worst performance because SRRIP does not

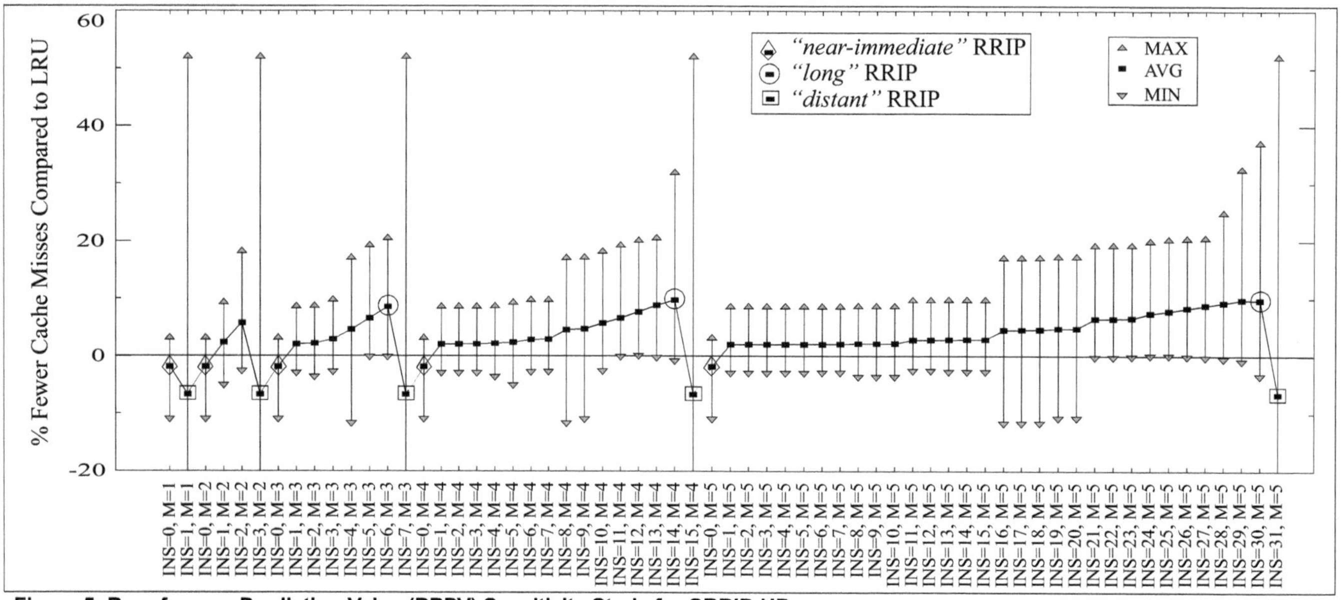

Figure 5: Re-reference Prediction Value (RRPV) Sensitivity Study for SRRIP-HP.

have enough time to improve the blocks re-reference interval. While always predicting *distant* re-reference interval has positive outliers, always predicting a *long* re-reference interval is robust across all workloads and reduces cache misses relative to LRU by 6-10%.

6.2. SRRIP Performance

Figure 6 presents the per-workload behavior for SRRIP-HP and SRRIP-FP for M=1, 2, 3, 4 and 5. Both SRRIP policies always predict a *long* re-reference interval on cache insertion. The x-axis shows the different workloads while the y-axis shows the reduction in cache misses. The x-axis labels GAMES, MULTIMEDIA, SERVER, and SPEC06 represent the average for the workloads in these categories while ALL is the average of all 14 workloads. We use arithmetic mean for cache performance and geometric mean for system performance. Figure 6a shows that SRRIP-FP reduces MPKI by 5-18%. The reductions in MPKI allow SRRIP-FP to outperform

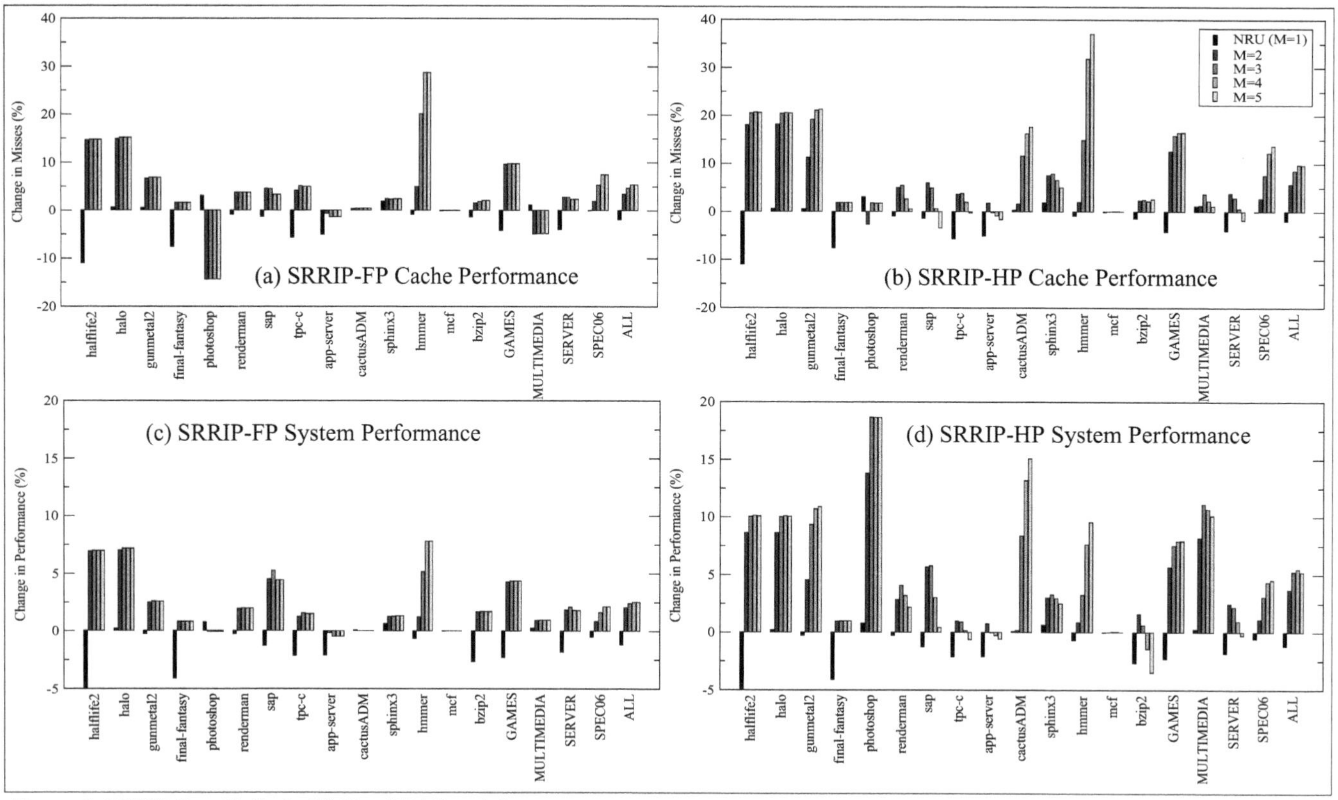

Figure 6: SRRIP Sensitivity to Width of M-bit register.

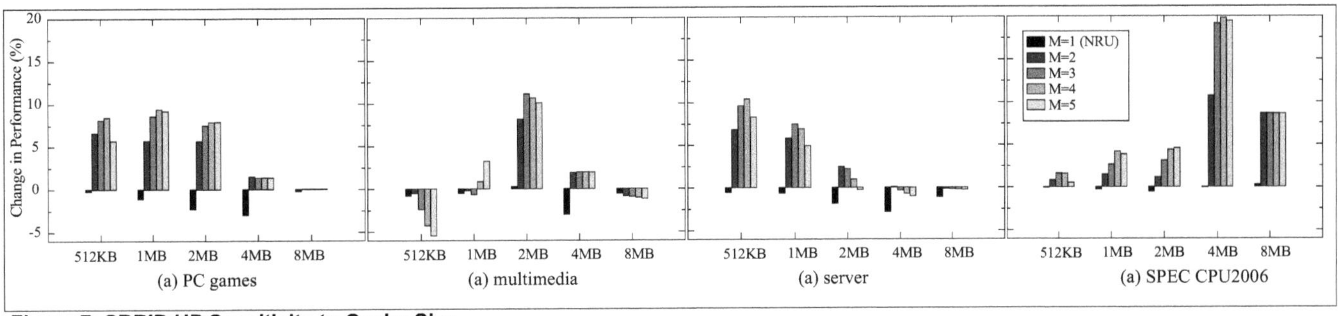

Figure 7: SRRIP-HP Sensitivity to Cache Size.

LRU by an average of 2.5% across all workloads (Figure 6c). PC games receive the most benefit where SRRIP-FP outperforms LRU by 4% on average. On the other hand, SRRIP-HP reduces MPKI by 5-15% for eight of the fourteen workloads (Figure 6b). The reductions in MPKI allow SRRIP-HP to outperform LRU by 5% across all workloads (Figure 6d). PC games and multimedia workloads receive the most benefit over LRU by 8-11%. These results are consistent with Figure 2 where PC games and multimedia workloads benefitted the most from scan-resistance.

On average, SRRIP is insensitive to the width of the RRPV register when M>3. Some workloads experience performance degradation when the width of the RRPV register increases. This is because wider RRPV registers retain stale blocks in the cache for long periods of time (after their last hit) and reduce the effective cache capacity. For the workloads in this study, 2-bit or 3-bit RRPV is sufficient to be scan-resistant.

Finally, both SRRIP-HP and SRRIP-FP outperform LRU. NRU (M=1) almost always performs worse than LRU. Additionally, SRRIP-HP provides twice the performance benefits of SRRIP-FP. This implies that the first order benefit of a scan-resistant replacement algorithm is not from precisely detecting frequently referenced data in the cache but from preserving data that receives cache hits, i.e., the active working set. For the rest of the paper, unless otherwise stated, we only provide results for SRRIP-HP.

6.3. SRRIP Sensitivity to Cache Configuration

Figure 7 presents SRRIP performance for the different workload categories on different LLC sizes: 512KB, 1MB, 2MB, 4MB, and 8MB. All LLCs are 16-way set associative. The y-axis shows the performance relative to LRU replacement of the respective LLC. The figure shows that NRU (M=1) always performs similar to LRU for all cache sizes. However, SRRIP outperforms LRU by 5-20% for various cache sizes. We also conducted a SRRIP sensitivity study by varying the cache associativity from 4-way to 128-way. Our studies yielded results comparable to Figure 6. These results show that SRRIP is scalable to different cache configurations. Since the majority of performance gains is achieved by a 3-bit RRPV register, we focus only on 2-bit and 3-bit SRRIP.

6.4. DRRIP Performance

Figure 8 presents the performance of 2-bit and 3-bit DRRIP[6]. Figure 8a shows that DRRIP significantly improves cache performance for SPEC CPU2006 workloads *sphinx3*, *hmmer*, and *mcf*. These workloads have a *knee* in the working set that is slightly larger than a 2MB cache (see Figure 4). PC games and multimedia workloads also benefit from a reduction in cache misses. Server workloads on the other hand have no *knee* in the working set, hence observe no benefit from DRRIP. Across most workloads, DRRIP has similar or better performance than SRRIP. DRRIP only hurts *photoshop* performance despite the 10% reduction in cache misses. Further analysis showed that *photoshop* is extremely sensitive to a region of memory that is frequently referenced between scans. Since DRRIP optimizes for the cache miss metric and not the throughput metric, DRRIP can degrade performance when the cost of a miss varies in an application. Enhancing DRRIP to optimize for throughput instead of cache misses can address the problem for *photoshop*. Nonetheless, on average, DRRIP improves performance by an additional 5% above SRRIP. Since both 2-bit and 3-bit DRRIP perform similarly, we conclude that 2-bit DRRIP is sufficient for scan-resistance and thrash-resistance. Thus, for the remainder of the paper we only focus on 2-bit RRIP.

6. We use 32-entry SDMs, 10-bit PSEL counter and ε=1/32. [11, 25]

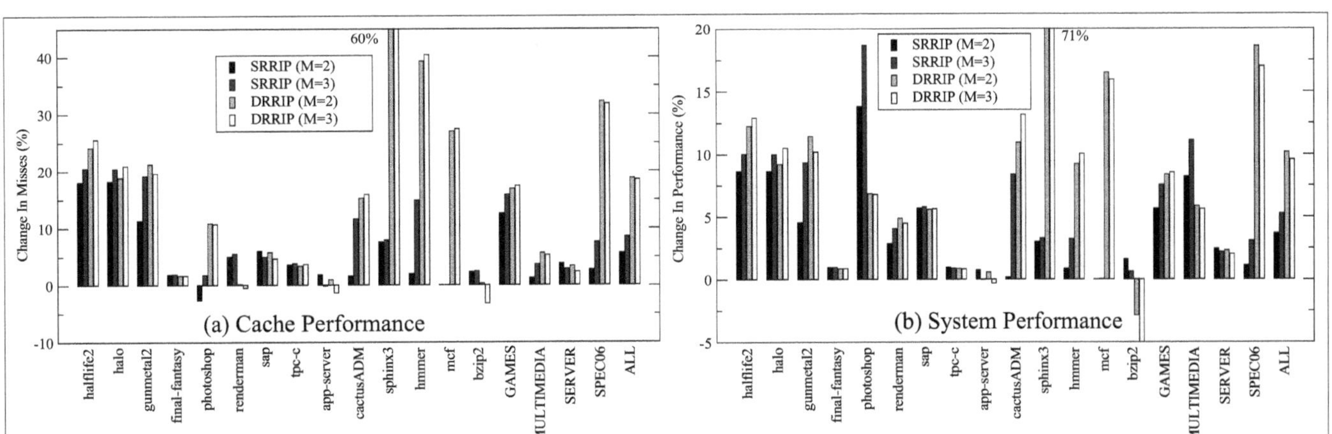

Figure 8: DRRIP Performance.

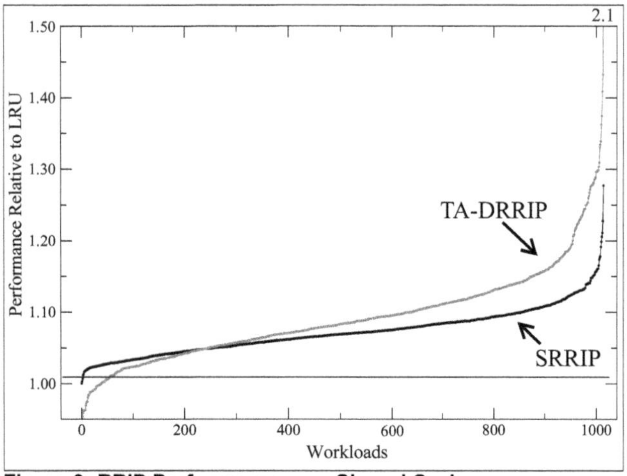

Figure 9: RRIP Performance on a Shared Cache.

6.5. RRIP on Shared Caches

Figure 9 presents the s-curve for the performance of SRRIP and TA-DRRIP compared to LRU for the throughput metric. The x-axis represents all 1001 multi-programmed workloads while the y-axis represents the performance relative to LRU. SRRIP improves performance up to 25% on the 4-core CMP while TA-DRRIP improves performance by as much 2.1X. Across all workloads in the study, SRRIP does not degrade performance for any of the workloads while TA-DRRIP degrades performance by 2-5% for less than 25 workloads due to cost of experimenting with the BRRIP SDMs. On average, across the 1001 multi-programmed workloads, SRRIP improves performance by 7% while TA-DRRIP improves performance by 10%. Thus, these results show that both SRRIP and TA-DRRIP are both robust and high performing.

6.6. RRIP at Different Cache Levels

We compared the performance of SRRIP to LRU when applied at the L1 and L2 caches of our three-level hierarchy. At the L1 cache, SRRIP provides no opportunity to improve performance because the cache size is too small and the temporal locality is too high. At the L2 cache, SRRIP provides no significant performance gains because the L2 cache is small (256KB in our study). SRRIP did not degrade performance of the L1 or L2 caches. To ensure that SRRIP performs well at the LLC, we modified our hierarchy from a 3-level to a 2-level hierarchy by removing the L2 cache. For this 2-level hierarchy, both SRRIP and DRRIP outperform LRU by 4.8% and 10% respectively. Thus, RRIP is most applicable at the LLC where the temporal locality is filtered by smaller levels of the hierarchy[7].

6.7. Hardware Overhead and Design Changes

RRIP requires a 2-bit register per cache block. RRIP integrates into the existing NRU implementation with minor modifications to the victim selection hardware. The NRU victim selection policy searches for the first block with *nru*-bit value of '1'. SRRIP on the other hand searches for the first cache block whose re-reference interval is furthest in the future, i.e., the block whose RRPV is the largest in the set. The search can be implemented by replicating the Find First One (FFO) logic. For 2-bit RRIP, four FFO circuits (with appropriate inputs) are required to find pointers to the first '0', '1', '2', and '3' RRPV registers. A priority MUX chooses the output of the appropriate FFO circuit as the victim. In the event that a block with *distant* RRIP is not found, RRIP also requires additional logic to age the RRPV registers. NRU ages cache blocks by simply inverting all the *nru*-bits in the set. SRRIP requires state machine logic to age all the RRPV registers in the set. DRRIP and TA-DRRIP merely require the per-thread 10-bit policy selection (PSEL) counter and the logic for choosing SDMs. The design changes for SRRIP and DRRIP are not on the critical path and thus do not affect the cache access time.

7. Recent studies [7, 18] have evaluated cache configurations where the linesize of the LLC is larger than the linesize of the L1 and L2 caches. For such configurations, DIP and RRIP require modifications to the hit promotion policy to filter the "false temporal locality" observed by the LLC. For example, re-references to different sectors of the large LLC cache line (due to spatial locality) should not update the LRU state while re-references to the same sector of the line should update the LRU state.

Table 3: Comparison of Replacement Policies on Single Core

Replacement Policy	% Performance Improvement Over LRU	Hardware Overhead[a]
LRU	—	$n \cdot \log_2 n$
NRU	-1.19	n
peLIFO	2.85	$2n \cdot \log_2 n + 2n$
SRRIP	3.69	2n
DIP	5.43	n
$HYB_{NRU/LFU}$	7.57	5n
DRRIP	10.18	2n
BOIP	8.13	N/A

a. Assuming an n-way set associative cache, HW overhead is measured in number of bits required per cache set.

6.8. Comparing RRIP to Other Policies

For the 14 workloads in our study, Table 3 compares the performance of the following replacement policies to LRU replacement: NRU, SRRIP, peLIFO [8], DIP, $HYB_{LRU/LFU}$, DRRIP, and BOIP. Figure 10 presents the performance comparison of these replacement policies on a per application basis. DIP uses set dueling to dynamically select between *near-immediate* and *distant* re-reference interval predictions. Both DIP and peLIFO use NRU replacement as the baseline replacement policy. $HYB_{NRU/LFU}$ also uses set dueling to dynamically choose between NRU and LFU replacement. BOIP uses offline profiling information to determine the best static insertion position on the RRIP chain suitable to the application. peLIFO tracks cache hits on the fill stack to guide cache replacement. SRRIP, a non-adaptive policy, outperforms LRU replacement while DRRIP outperforms the best performing scan-resistant hybrid cache replacement policy ($HYB_{NRU/LFU}$) and also a policy that requires profiling information (BOIP).

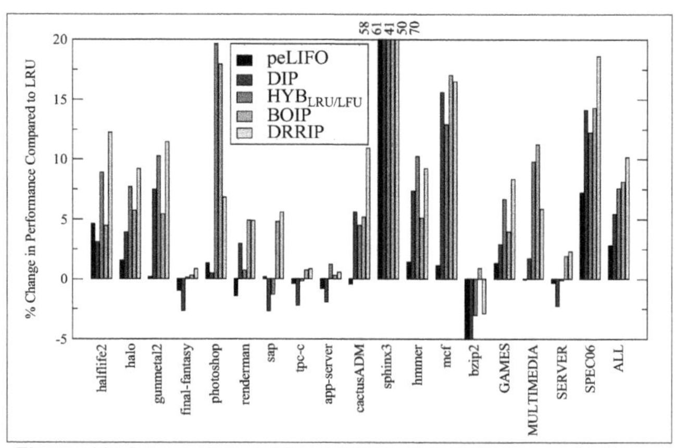

Figure 10: Comparison of Replacement Policies.

We also compared the performance of SRRIP and TA-DRRIP on shared caches to peLIFO and TA-DIP. Both peLIFO and TA-DIP use NRU as the baseline replacement policy. For the 1001 multi-programmed workloads in our study, we found that TA-DIP improved performance relative to LRU by 4% while peLIFO improved performance relative to LRU by 1.5%. SRRIP and TA-DRRIP on the other hand improve performance by 7% and 9% respectively. We believe that our results for peLIFO differ from [8] because we evaluate across a much broader selection of workloads.

RRIP requires less hardware than LRU replacement yet outperforms LRU replacement on average. For an n-way associative cache, LRU replacement requires $n \cdot \log_2 n$ bits per cache set, while RRIP only requires 2n bits per cache set. Compared to $HYB_{NRU/LFU}$, the LFU component policy requires hardware for the frequency counter and the NRU component requires hardware for tracking recency. Assuming four bits for the LFU frequency counter, $HYB_{NRU/LFU}$ requires 5n bits per cache set. In addition, hybrid replacement also requires verification overhead for designing two *different* replacement policies. Comparatively, SRRIP and DRRIP provide scan-resistance and thrash-resistance in a single replacement policy. RRIP requires 2.5X less hardware than $HYB_{NRU/LFU}$.

7. SUMMARY

Practical cache replacement policies attempt to emulate optimal replacement by predicting the re-reference interval of a cache block. The commonly used LRU replacement policy always predicts a *near-immediate* re-reference interval on misses and hits. However, the prediction of *near-immediate* re-reference interval inefficiently utilizes the cache when the actual re-reference interval of the missing block is in the *distant* future. When the re-reference interval of all blocks referenced by an application is in the *distant* future, dynamic insertion policies [25] avoid cache thrashing by preserving some of the blocks in the cache. However, when the re-reference interval of blocks accessed by an application consist of mixed access patterns, dynamic insertion policies cannot preserve blocks with *near-immediate* re-reference interval in the cache. This paper shows that many real world game, server, and multimedia applications exhibit such mixed access patterns. Specifically, such applications experience bursts of references to non-temporal data (called *scans*) that discards their active working set from the cache. This paper improves the performance of such real world applications by making the following contributions:

1. We propose cache replacement using *Re-reference Interval Prediction (RRIP)*. RRIP statically predicts the re-reference interval of all missing cache blocks to be an *intermediate* re-reference interval that is between a *near-immediate* re-reference interval and a *distant* re-reference interval. RRIP updates the re-reference prediction to be shorter than the previous prediction upon a re-reference. We call this policy as *Static RRIP (SRRIP)*. We show that SRRIP is scan-resistant and only requires 2-bits per cache block.
2. We propose two SRRIP policies: *SRRIP-Hit Priority (SRRIP-HP)* and *SRRIP-Frequency Priority (SRRIP-FP)*. SRRIP-HP predicts that any cache block that receives a hit will have a *near-immediate* re-reference and thus should be retained in the cache for an extended period of time. SRRIP-FP on the other hand predicts that frequently referenced cache blocks will have a *near-immediate* re-reference and thus they should be retained in the cache for an extended period of time. We show that SRRIP-HP performs significantly better than SRRIP-FP and conclude that scan-resistance is not from precisely detecting frequently referenced blocks but from preventing blocks that receive hits from getting evicted by blocks that do not receive hits (i.e., *scan* blocks).
3. We propose *Dynamic RRIP (DRRIP)* as an enhancement to SRRIP-HP. DRRIP provides both scan-resistance and thrash-resistance by using set dueling to dynamically select between inserting all missing cache blocks with an *intermediate* re-reference interval or with a *distant* re-reference interval. In addition to the hardware overhead of SRRIP, DRRIP does not require any additional hardware overhead besides a single saturating counter.

We show that SRRIP and DRRIP outperform LRU by an average of 4% and 10% on a single-core processor with a 16-way 2MB LLC. We also show that SRRIP and DRRIP outperform LRU by an average of 7% and 9% on a 4-core CMP with a 16-way 8MB shared LLC. We also show that RRIP outperforms LFU, the state-of the art scan-resistant replacement algorithm to-date, by 2.5%. For the cache configurations under study, RRIP requires 2X less hardware than LRU and 2.5X less hardware than LFU.

In this study, we have applied re-reference interval prediction on cache misses and *learn* the re-reference interval of the missing block without any external information. Re-reference interval prediction on cache hits ideally requires knowledge of when a cache block receives its last hit. RIPP can use such information to update the re-reference prediction of the re-referenced cache block to *intermediate*, *long* or *distant* re-reference interval. Automatically learning the last reference on a cache hit is more challenging without any external information. Predicting re-reference interval on cache hits in the absence of external information or in the presence of dead block and last touch predictors [18, 16] is part of our on-going work.

8. ACKNOWLEDGEMENTS

The authors would like to thank Eric Borch, Malini Bhandaru, Paul Racunas, Krishna Rangan, Samantika Subramaniam and the anonymous reviewers for their feedback in improving this paper.

9. REFERENCES

[1] "Inside the Intel Itanium 2 Processor", HP Technical White Paper, July 2002.

[2] "UltraSPARC T2 supplement to the UltraSPARC architecture 2007", Draft D1.4.3. 2007.

[3] Intel. Intel Core i7 Processor. http://www.intel.com/products/processor/corei7/specifications.htm

[4] H. Al-Zoubi, A. Milenkovic, M. Milenkovic. "Performance evaluation of cache replacement policies for the SPEC CPU2000 benchmark suite." In ACMSE, 2004.

[5] S. Bansal and D. S. Modha. "CAR: Clock with Adaptive Replacement", In FAST, 2004.

[6] A. Basu, N. Kirman, M. Kirman, M. Chaudhuri, J. Martinez. "Scavenger: A New Last Level Cache Architecture with Global Block Priority". In Micro-40, 2007.

[7] L. A. Belady. A study of replacement algorithms for a virtual-storage computer. In IBM Systems journal, pages 78–101, 1966.

[8] M. Chaudhuri. "Pseudo-LIFO: The Foundation of a New Family of Replacement Policies for Last-level Caches". In Micro, 2009.

[9] F. J. Corbat´o, "A paging experiment with the multics system," In Honor of P. M. Morse, pp. 217–228, MIT Press, 1969.

[10] A. Jaleel, R. Cohn, C. K. Luk, B. Jacob. CMP$im: A Pin-Based On-The-Fly Multi-Core Cache Simulator. In MoBS, 2008.

[11] A. Jaleel, W. Hasenplaugh, M. K. Qureshi, S. C. Steely Jr., J. Emer. "Adaptive Insertion Policies for Managing Shared Caches". In PACT, 2008.

[12] S. Jiang and X. Zhang, "LIRS: An efficient low inter-reference recency set replacement policy to improve buffer cache performance," In Proc. ACM SIGMETRICS Conf., 2002.

[13] T. Johnson and D. Shasha, "2Q: A low overhead high performance buffer management replacement algorithm," In VLDB Conf., 1994.

[14] S. Kaxiras, Z. Hu, M. Martonosi. "Cache decay: exploiting generational behavior to reduce cache leakage power." In ISCA-28.

[15] G. Keramidas, P. Petoumenos, S. Kaxiras. "Cache replacement based on reuse-distance prediction". In ICCD, 2007

[16] A. Lai, C. Fide, B. Falsafi. Dead-block prediction & dead-block correlating prefetchers. In ISCA-28, 2001

[17] D. Lee, J. Choi, J. Kim, S. H. Noh, S. Lyul Min, Y. Cho, C. Sang Kim. "LRFU: A spectrum of policies that subsumes the least recently used and least frequently used policies," IEEE Trans. Computers, vol. 50, no. 12, pp. 1352–1360, 2001.

[18] W. Lin and S. K. Reinhardt. "Predicting last-touch references under optimal replacement." Technical Report CSE-TR-447-02, U. of Michigan, 2002.

[19] H. Liu, M. Ferdman, J. Huh, D. Burger. "Cache Bursts: A New Approach for Eliminating Dead Blocks and Increasing Cache Efficiency." In Micro-41, 2008.

[20] G. Loh. "Extending the Effectiveness of 3D-Stacked DRAM Caches with an Adaptive Multi-Queue Policy". In Micro, 2009.

[21] C. Luk, R. Cohn, R. Muth, H. Patil, A. Klauser, G. Lowney, S. Wallace, V. J. Reddi, K. Hazelwood. "Pin: building customized program analysis tools with dynamic instrumentation". In PLDI, pages 190–200, 2005.

[22] N. Megiddo and D. S. Modha, "ARC: A self-tuning, low overhead replacement cache," in FAST, 2003.

[23] E. J. O'Neil, P. E. O'Neil, G. Weikum. "The LRU-K page replacement algorithm for database disk buffering," in Proc. ACM SIGMOD Conf., pp. 297–306, 1993.

[24] H. Patil, R. Cohn, M. Charney, R. Kapoor, A. Sun, A. Karunanidhi. "Pinpointing Representative Portions of Large Intel Itanium Programs with Dynamic Instrumentation". In MICRO-37, 2004.

[25] M. Qureshi, A. Jaleel, Y. Patt, S. Steely, J. Emer. "Adaptive Insertion Policies for High Performance Caching". In ISCA-34, 2007.

[26] K. Rajan and G. Ramaswamy. "Emulating Optimal Replacement with a Shepherd Cache". In Micro-40, 2007.

[27] J. T. Robinson and M. V. Devarakonda, "Data cache management using frequency-based replacement," in SIGMETRICS Conf, 1990.

[28] S. Srinath, O. Mutlu, H. Kim, Y. Patt. "Feedback Directed Prefetching: Improving the Performance and Bandwidth-Efficiency of Hardware Prefetcher". In HPCA-13, 2007.

[29] R. Subramanian, Y. Smaragdakis, G. Loh. "Adaptive caches: Effective shaping of cache behavior to workloads." In MICRO-39, 2006.

[30] Y. Xie and G. Loh. "PIPP: Promotion/Insertion Pseudo-Partitioning of Multi-Core Shared Caches." In ISCA-36, 2009

[31] Y. Zhou and J. F. Philbin, "The multi-queue replacement algorithm for second level buffer caches," in USENIX Annual Tech. Conf, 2001.

10. Appendix

Cache replacement is not a problem for workloads that have a working set that fits in the available cache or for workloads that have a working set that is much larger than the available cache. Nonetheless we conducted a thorough study of SRRIP and DRRIP using a broader set of memory intensive and non-memory intensive workloads for the baseline single-core configuration. The study covers 28 SPEC CPU2006 workloads and 47 workloads from PC games, multimedia, server, and other categories. Table 4 compares the performance and hardware overhead of several replacement policies compared to LRU. Note that the average performance improvement compared to LRU across all workload categories is small (< 2%) because the study also includes workloads that do not benefit from cache replacement. We also compare against two additional hardware LRU approximations: PLRU [4] and CLOCK [5]. DIP provides competitive performance compared to SRRIP for SPEC workloads while SRRIP consistently outperforms LRU, DIP, PLRU, CLOCK, and NRU for PC games, multimedia, and server workloads. This shows the potential pitfalls of using SPEC workloads as a proxy for real world workloads. SRRIP outperforms LRU while requiring 2X less hardware. DRRIP outperforms scan-resistant replacement $HYB_{NRU/LFU}$ with 2.5X less hardware.

Table 4: Hardware Overhead and Performance of Replacement Policies

Replacement Policy	LRU	DIP_{LRU} [25]	PLRU [4]	CLOCK [5]	NRU [1]	DIP_{NRU} [25]	SRRIP	DRRIP	$HYB_{NRU/LFU}$
HW Overhead[a]	$n \cdot \log_2 n$	$n \cdot \log_2 n$	$n-1$	$n+\log_2 n$	n	n	2n	2n	5n
HW for 16-way cache[a]	64	64	15	20	16	16	32	32	80
ALL Workloads[b]	1.0000	1.0081	0.9973	1.0024	0.9952	1.0061	1.0075	1.0172	1.0097
PC Games[b]	1.0000	0.9975	0.9982	1.0101	0.9869	1.0071	1.0294	1.0366	1.0343
Multimedia[b]	1.0000	0.9975	0.9966	1.0037	0.9950	0.9963	1.0287	1.0173	1.0243
Server[b]	1.0000	0.9985	0.9882	1.0069	0.9818	0.9896	1.0153	1.0138	0.9883
CPU2006 - FP[b]	1.0000	1.0325	1.0005	0.9989	0.9989	1.0278	0.9965	1.0320	1.0182
CPU2006 - INT[b]	1.0000	1.0140	0.9939	1.0022	0.9960	1.0141	1.0031	1.0232	1.0127
Other[b]	1.0000	0.9990	0.9990	1.0004	0.9986	0.9949	1.0013	0.9988	0.9953
Max Relative Perf	N/A	1.6589	1.0207	1.0360	1.0079	1.6158	1.1381	1.7112	1.4128
Min Relative Perf	N/A	0.9687	0.9706	0.9806	0.9507	0.9135	0.9853	0.9656	0.9394

a. Assuming an n-way set associative cache, hardware overhead is measured in number of bits required per cache set.

b. Performance is relative to LRU and is reported as geomean across 75 memory intensive and non-memory intensive workloads from server, multimedia, PC games, and the entire SPEC CPU2006 benchmark suite.

The Virtual Write Queue: Coordinating DRAM and Last-Level Cache Policies

Jeffrey Stuecheli[1,2], Dimitris Kaseridis[1], David Daly[3], Hillery C. Hunter[3] & Lizy K. John[1]
[1]ECE Department, The University of Texas at Austin, Austin, TX, USA
[2]IBM Corp., Austin, TX, USA
[3]IBM Thomas J. Watson Research Center, Yorktown Heights, NY, USA
{stuechel, kaseridi}@ece.utexas.edu, {dmdaly, hhunter}@us.ibm.com,
ljohn@ece.utexas.edu

ABSTRACT

In computer architecture, caches have primarily been viewed as a means to hide memory latency from the CPU. Cache policies have focused on anticipating the CPU's data needs, and are mostly oblivious to the main memory. In this paper, we demonstrate that the era of many-core architectures has created new main memory bottlenecks, and mandates a new approach: coordination of cache policy with main memory characteristics. Using the cache for memory optimization purposes, we propose a **Virtual Write Queue** which dramatically expands the memory controller's visibility of processor behavior, at low implementation overhead. Through memory-centric modification of existing policies, such as scheduled writebacks, this paper demonstrates that performance-limiting effects of highly-threaded architectures can be overcome. We show that through awareness of the physical main memory layout and by focusing on writes, both read and write average latency can be shortened, memory power reduced, and overall system performance improved. Through full-system cycle-accurate simulations of SPEC cpu2006, we demonstrate that the proposed **Virtual Write Queue** achieves an average 10.9% system-level throughput improvement on memory-intensive workloads, along with an overall reduction of 8.7% in memory power across the whole suite.

Categories and Subject Descriptors

B.3.1 [**Memory Structures**]: Semiconductor Memories—*Dynamic memory (DRAM)*; B.3.2 [**Memory Structures**]: Design styles—*cache memories, Primary Memories, Shared Memory, Interleaved Memories*

General Terms

Design, Performance

1. INTRODUCTION

It is now well-understood that in the nanometer era, technology scaling will continue to provide transistor density improvements, but that power density and performance improvements will slow. In response, processor designers now target chip-level throughput (instead of raw single-core performance), packing increasing numbers of cores and threads onto a chip. In 2000, virtually all server processors were single-core, single-thread; today we see 16 threads (Intel Nehalem EX), 32 threads (IBM POWER7™), and 128 threads (Sun Rainbow Falls) [3].

ISCA'10, June 19–23, 2010, Saint-Malo, France.

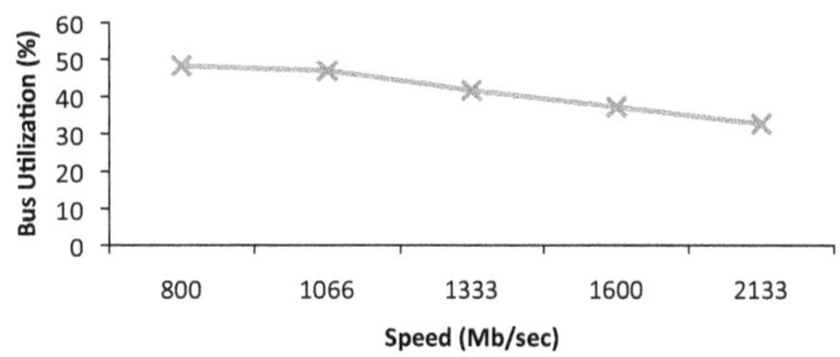

Figure 1: DDR3 single rank bus utilization efficiency, limited by DRAM parameters (tRC, tRRD, tFAW), and bus turnaround time (tWRT)

The processor-memory interface has been particularly challenged by this many-core trend. Technology scaling provides roughly 2x the number of transistors per lithography generation, so when core or thread counts more than double per generation, the result is generally a decrease in the available cache size per core and/or thread. From first principles, a drop in on-chip cache size will result in higher miss rates and higher memory bandwidth demands. Single socket memory demands have thus been rapidly increasing, not only due to core and thread counts, but also from the transition to throughput-type designs, which provide fewer cache bits per thread.

These many-core architectures struggle not only to provide sufficient main memory bandwidth per core/thread, but also to schedule high memory bus utilization efficiency. Server processors generally have one or two main memory controllers per chip, meaning that many cores share a single controller and a memory controller simultaneously sees requests from different work streams. In this context, locality is easily lost, and it becomes difficult to find and schedule spatially sequential accesses. Inefficient scheduling results in performance reductions and consumes unnecessary energy.

Most servers currently use JEDEC-standardized Double-Data-Rate (DDR) memory [2], so a fairly accurate understanding of memory bandwidth scaling can be obtained by looking at DDR trends. In terms of raw IO (Input/Output) speeds, DDR has continued to improve, with peak speeds doubling each generation (400Mbps DDR, 800Mbps DDR2, 1600Mbps DDR3). IO frequencies continue to scale, but other key parameters, such as reading a memory cell or turning a bus around from a write to a read

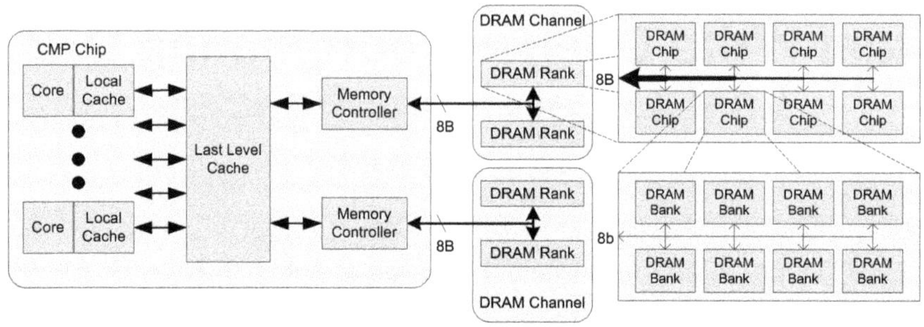

Figure 2: Baseline CMP and memory system

operation, are not scaling at comparable rates. At higher signaling rates, the electrical integrity of busses becomes much more difficult to maintain – both within the DRAM chips and across the main memory path to/from the processor. This results in a complex set of timing parameters which dictate that gaps be inserted when the access stream transitions from a write to a read or vice-versa, significantly degrading effective memory bandwidth. This problem has worsened with each memory generation. For example, tWRT, the Write-to-Read Turnaround delay, has stayed within a range of 5-10ns for DDR through DDR3. Therefore, as DRAM IO frequencies increase, the number of cycles wasted between each access grows. Figure 1, calculated from JEDEC parameters, shows the dramatic impact of these mandatory timing delays on effective bandwidth: even with perfect scheduling, utilization of a single memory rank can be as low as 25-40% for high-frequency DDR. Clearly, this trend cannot continue – in the many-core era, we must find ways to improve not only raw memory bandwidth, but also memory bandwidth efficiency.

Memory efficiency improvements in highly threaded systems have primarily been addressed in the past with various mechanisms to reorder requests received by the memory controller. Work on *Fair Queuing Memory Systems* by Nesbit et al. [18] utilizes *fair queuing* principles at the memory controller, to provide fairness and throughput improvements. *Parallelism-Aware Batch Scheduling* [17] alleviates the same problem by maintaining groups of requests from various threads and issuing them in batches to the controller. While these techniques are useful in improving read scheduling, they do not directly address the memory traffic initiated by write operations. The *Eager writeback* technique [9] takes a step in dealing with write bandwidth to memory, but its approach has minimal communication between the *last-level cache* and the *memory controller*.

Given more write queueing resources, the memory controller can more efficiently determine priorities, pack commands into page mode accesses, and efficiently schedule write requests to the memory bus. The challenge is how to efficiently expand the memory controller's write queueing resources. We propose a *Virtual Write Queue* which leverages the existing last-level cache to expand the memory controller's visibility, allowing improved performance and reduced power consumption. Our proposed scheme uses *Scheduled Writebacks* (writeback operations initiated by the DRAM scheduler) to effectively utilize the available memory bandwidth. This enables significantly longer write bursts that amortize bus turnaround times, and decrease high latency conflicts with read operations.

Based on full-system, cycle-accurate, simulations performed on SIMICS [22] and GEMS [13], *Virtual Write Queue* demonstrates an average 10.9% system throughput improvement on the memory intensive workloads of the SPEC CPU2006 Rate suite [23], when configured using 1 memory rank. In addition, the proposed scheme is able to achieve a memory power reduction of 8.7% across all the SPEC CPU2006 suite. Both throughput and power reductions are demonstrated over a baseline implementation that incorporates a *First-Ready, First-Come-First-Served* (FR_FCFS) [21] memory controller augmented with the *Eager writeback* technique [9] (FR_FCFS+EW). Overall, the *Virtual Write Queue* requires a modest 0.3% hardware overhead by heavily reusing the existing structures and functionality of a typical high performance server design.

To the best of our knowledge this is the first proposed scheme that directly coordinates *memory controller scheduling* with *cache writeback traffic*. While the motivation and evaluations presented in this paper are based on DDR-DRAM, it is important to note that this paper tackles a problem which will only become worse as new memory technologies are incorporated into proposed hybrid and tiered main memory systems. Phase-change memory [19], NOR and NAND Flash, and other non-DRAM storage technologies have noticeably longer write times and larger page sizes (so as to amortize access costs). These factors aggravate existing memory inefficiencies such as *write-to-read* gaps, and make it even more crucial that efficient access opportunities, such as page mode accesses, be made apparent to the memory controller. The techniques in this paper can be extended easily for new technologies, and would be highly effective for improving performance of non-DRAM main memory subsystems.

The rest of the paper is organized as follows. Section 2 describes the typical organization of a DDR DRAM, and in Section 3 we characterize key aspects of memory system behavior. Section 4 elaborates on the proposed *Virtual Write Queue*. Finally, Section 5 includes results and evaluation, followed by a summary of related work in the literature in Section 6.

2. MAIN MEMORY BACKGROUND AND TERMINOLOGY

Figure 2 illustrates our baseline CMP and memory system. To maximize memory bandwidth and memory capacity, server processors have multiple *memory channels* per chip. As Figure 2 shows, each channel is connected to one or more *DIMMs* (memory cards), each containing numerous *DRAM chips*. These DRAM chips are arranged logically into one or more *ranks*. Within a rank, each DRAM chip provides just 4-8 bits of data per data cycle, and a rank of 8-16 DRAM chips works in unison to produce eight bytes per data cycle. The DRAM *burst-length* (BL) specifies an automated number of data beats that are sent out in response to a single command, commonly 8 data beats, to provide 64Bytes of data. From the time of applying an address to the DRAM chips, it takes about 24ns (96 processor clocks at 4GHz) for the first cycle of data, but subsequent data appear at high frequency, closer to 2-3 processor clocks.

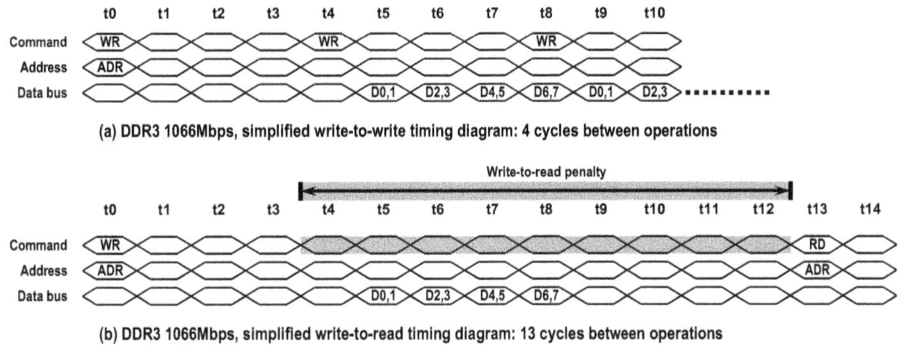

Figure 3: Write-to-read turnaround noticeably worsens command latency and databus utilization. tWPST [2] further worsens turnaround, but has been removed for simplicity

Internally, DRAM chips are partitioned into *banks* that can be accessed independently, and banks are partitioned into *pages*. DRAM *page mode* provides the opportunity to read or write multiple locations within the same DRAM page more efficiently than accessing a new page. Page mode accesses require that the memory controller find requests with adjacent memory addresses, but are executed with fewer timing constraints, and incur lower per-access power than non-page mode accesses.

DRAM chips are optimized for cost, meaning that technology, cell, array, and periphery decisions are made with a high priority on bit-density. This results in devices and circuits which are slower than standard logic, and chips that are more sensitive to noise and voltage drops. A complex set of timing constraints has been developed to mitigate each of these factors for standardized DRAMs, such as outlined in the JEDEC DDR3 standard [2]. These timing constraints result in "dead times" before and after each random access; the processor memory controller's job is to hide these performance-limiting gaps through exploitation of parallelism.

3. CHARACTERIZATION OF MEMORY SYSTEM BEHAVIOR

In order to understand memory system opportunities, we investigated the particular challenges associated with DRAMs in server systems. In our analysis we identified three characteristics as the most important factors in addressing memory interface utilization from the perspective of write memory traffic: a) *bus turnaround penalty*, b) *page mode opportunities*, and c) programs' *bursty behavior*.

3.1 Bus turnaround penalty

As described in the introduction, memory IO frequencies have been improving (resulting in raw bandwidth increases), but timing constraints related to signaling and electrical integrity have, for the most part, remained constant. This is especially well illustrated by tWRT, which defines the minimum delay from the completion of a write to the initiation of a read at the same DRAM rank. tWRT is 7.5ns on DDR3 devices – at 4GHz, this is 30 CPU cycles – a very significant penalty for any reads issued after a write.

Figure 3 conceptually illustrates DDR3 write command timings. Successive writes can be issued back-to-back, realizing 100% data bus utilization (Figure 3.a). On the other hand, when a read follows a write to the same device, the read must not only wait for the write's completion, but also for the bus turnaround time to elapse. This adds noticeable latency to the read operation (Figure 3.b), and results in dismal data bus usage: 31%. For server-class 1066Mbps DDR3, the extra nine DRAM cycles between a write and read amount to a $\approx$66 cycle read penalty at 4GHz.

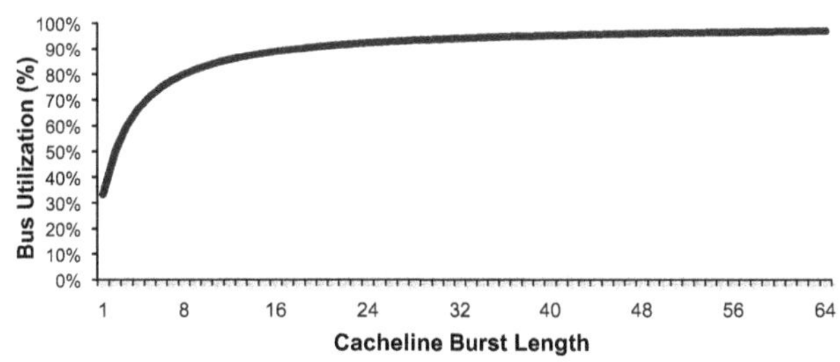

Figure 4: Bus utilization based on cache burst lengths

Memory scheduling efficiency is thus heavily influenced by the mixing of read and write operations. Timing gaps are required when read and write operations are intermingled in a continuous memory access sequence, but with many application streams and limited queuing resources, these turnarounds are generally difficult for the memory controller to avoid. As shown in Figure 4, memory data bus utilization can be greatly improved by significantly increasing the number of consecutive read/write operations the memory controller issues before switching the operation type on the bus. For example, if the scheduler can manage 32 reads/writes per scheduling block, utilization grows to 94%. Throughout the paper, we refer to a stream of consecutive reads or writes as a *cacheline burst* to memory.

3.2 Page mode opportunities

While DRAM devices output only 16-64 bits per request (depending on the DRAM type and burst settings), internally, the devices operate on much larger, $\approx$2Kbit, pages (sometimes referred to as *rows*). Each random access causes all 2Kbits of a page to be read into an internal buffer, followed by a "column" access to the requested sub-block of data. Since the time and power overhead of the page access have already been paid, accessing multiple columns of that page decreases both the latency and power of subsequent accesses. These successive accesses are said to be performed in *page mode*. With page mode, latency is approximately one-half that of accesses to different, random pages. Active power reduction is realized through elimination of extra page reads and extra precharge page writebacks (because DRAM page read is destructive, the data must be restored). Additional details on DRAM architectures can be found in Jacob et al. [5].

Using a DDR3 memory power calculator from Micron Technology [16], we obtained the DRAM chip power characteristics shown in Table 1 for various page mode access rates. We have chosen a server-type configuration, to match the environment used for the class of benchmarks studied in this paper (2Gb DDR3 DRAMs, 1.5V, 1066Mbps, 2:1 read:write ratio, 45% DRAM utilization, multi-rank DIMMs); we also include termination power. Memory power varies widely, depending on the class and capacity of the memory subsystem (frequency and number of ranks, for example). As shown, activation power is greatly reduced with page mode. Total DRAM power can be reduced by 1/3 if operations are executed as four references for each activate.

Table 1: DRAM power estimation based on [16]

% Page Mode	Activate Power (mW)	Total Power (mW)	% DRAM Power Saved
0%	196.9	450.8	Baseline
25%	147.2	401.1	11%
50%	98.1	352.0	22%
75%	49.0	303.9	33%

Page mode DRAM access greatly improves both memory utilization and power characteristics, but the optimization possibilities for read and write operations are significantly different. Reads are visible as the program (or a prefetch engine) generates them; this should enable spatial locality in reference sequences to be executed in page mode. Aligning load references into a page mode sequence often increases latency for critical operations, since they are delayed by younger page hits. Page mode read opportunities are thus commonly limited by conflicts with latency minimization mechanisms [17]. In contrast, write operations (in the common writeback cache policy) are generated as older cache lines are evicted to make room for newly allocated lines. As such, spatial locality at eviction time can be obscured through variation in set usage between allocation and eviction, as shown in Figure 5.

Figure 5 shows the total number of page mode writes possible for various workloads, for a range of memory controller write queue sizes. The workloads and simulation environment for this characterization data are described in Section 5. For practical write queue sizes, such as 32 entries, there is essentially no page mode opportunity (approximately one write possible per page activate). That stated, a large amount of spatial locality is contained within the various cache levels of the system, but today's CPU-centric caches do not give the memory controller visibility into this locality. Significantly larger memory controller write queues, though impractical, would provide the needed visibility and enable significant page mode opportunities.

3.3 Bursty behavior

Most programs exhibit bursty behavior. At the last-level cache, this results in phases when a large number of load misses must be serviced. Common cache allocation/eviction policies compound this effect, as bursts of cache fills create bursts of forced writebacks, thus clustering bursts of reads with bursts of writes.

Figure 6 shows the distribution of time between main memory operations for three workloads. The workloads and analysis are discussed in more detail in Section 5. Note that 20-40% of all memory requests occur with less than ten cycles delay after the previous memory operation, while the median can be in the hundreds of cycles and many requests take significantly longer.

Over-committed multi-threaded systems have always experienced some degree of cache thrashing, as workloads evict one another's data, and threads re-warm their local cache. However,

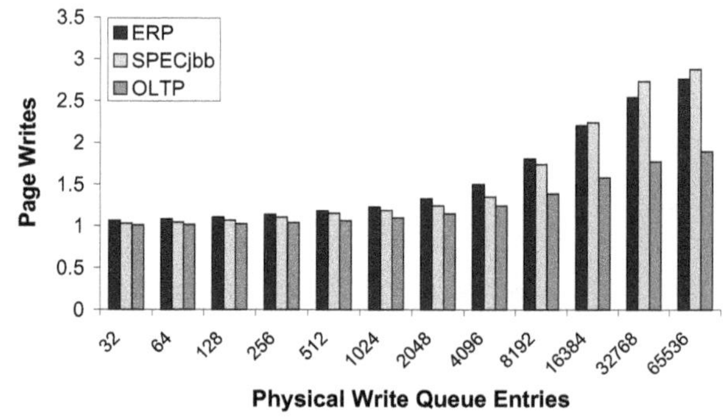

Figure 5: Page writes per activate *vs.* number of Physical Write Queue entries for commercial workloads

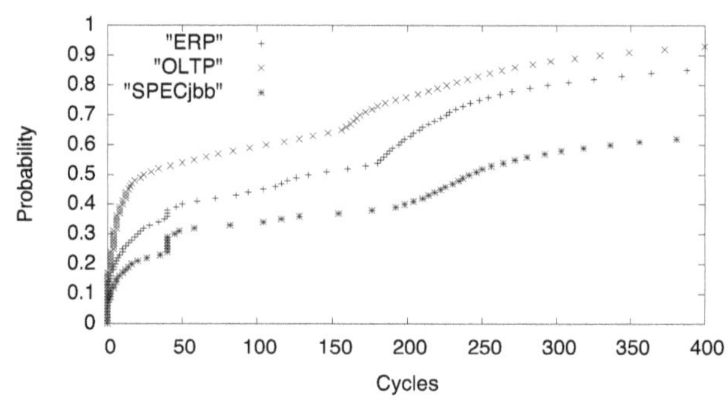

Figure 6: Distribution of time between memory requests for commercial workloads

this is no longer a problem seen only in large-scale SMP systems. Instead, this phenomenon is inherent to today's virtualized computing environments as disparate partitions share a physical CPU. If write operations can be executed early, bursts of read operations execute with lower combined bandwidth demands. Ideally, the memory controller will always have write operations ready to be sent to idle DRAM resources.

4. A COORDINATED CACHE/MEMORY SYSTEM DESIGN

The characteristics identified in the previous section could be addressed if the memory controller were to have increased elasticity and visibility for scheduling write operations to memory. Typical memory controllers contain 10's of queued write operations [7]. Queue structures are costly in terms of area and power, and the size of the write queue is a critical parameter for overall memory performance. In our solution, we propose that the set members close to the LRU position of the last-level cache function as a very large write queue (*e.g.*, 64k effective entries for the lower one-quarter of a 16 MB last-level cache). We refer to the LRU section of the last-level cache as the *Virtual Write Queue*, in that we overload and repurpose the usage of this region. We show that a coordinated cache/memory policy based on direct management from the *Virtual Write Queue* mitigates each of the challenges described in Section 3, increasing the performance of the memory subsystem. Specifically:

1. **Bus turnaround penalty avoidance**: Through a *Scheduled writeback* policy, we efficiently drain more pending write operations, minimizing the probability of interleaved read and write operations, which incur costly scheduling penalties (≈66 processor cycles @ 4GHz).

2. **Harvesting page mode opportunities**: Directed cache lookups, to a broad region of the LRU space, enable harvesting of additional writes to be executed in page mode at higher performance and lower power.

3. **Burst leveling**: With the *Virtual Write Queue*, the ability to buffer ≈1000x more write operations than in a standard memory controller enables significantly greater leveling of memory traffic bursts.

Figure 7(a) shows the *Virtual Write Queue*, which logically consists of some LRU fraction of the last-level cache (1/4 in this example); the *Physical Write Queue* in the memory controller; and the added coordinating control logic and structures. We refer to the structure as virtual because no additional queueing structures are added. The overall area cost is small: ≈0.3% overhead over a typical cache directory implementation (see Section 4.7).

Scheduled Writeback: Traditional writeback cache policies initiate memory writes only when a cache fill replaces an LRU cacheline. We refer to this as *forced writeback*. There are two problems with this policy. First, writes are only sent to the memory controller at the time of cache fills, so idle DRAM cycles cannot be filled with writes. This was addressed with *Eager Writeback* [9], where cachelines are sent to the memory controller when it appears to be idle (an empty write queue is detected). The second problem deals with the mapping of write locations to DRAM resources. Since the memory controller is aware of each DRAM's state, it would ideally decide which writeback operation can be executed most efficiently. With *Eager Writeback*, this selection is made by the cache, without knowledge of what would be best for DRAM scheduling. We introduce *Scheduled Writeback* to solve this problem. With *Scheduled Writeback*, the memory controller can direct the cache to transfer lines that map to specific DRAM resources.

As shown in Figure 7(b), the primary microarchitectural addition over traditional designs is the Cache Cleaner. The Cache Cleaner orchestrates *Scheduled Writebacks* from the last-level cache to the *Physical Write Queue*. While the cache and the *Physical Write Queue* are structurally equivalent to traditional designs (and thus hardware overhead is minimal), the logical behavior is significantly altered. This is reflected in the distribution of *dirty* lines in the system. Specifically, dirty lines have been cleaned from the lower section of the cache, and the *Physical Write Queue* is maintained at a higher level of fullness, with an ideal mix of commands with respect to scheduling DRAM accesses. In addition, typical memory controllers decide write operation priority based on only the *Physical Write Queue*, whereas this system uses the much larger *Virtual Write Queue*. The *Physical Write Queue* becomes a directly managed staging buffer, of the now much larger window of write visibility.

4.1 High Level Description of Coordinated Policies

At steady state, the *Physical Write Queue* is filled to a defined ≈full level with a mix of operations to all DRAM resources. This level is chosen to keep the queue as full as possible, while retaining the capacity to receive cache writebacks. *Scheduled Writebacks* can vary in length, depending on the number of eligible lines found in the same DRAM page; the write queue must maintain capacity to absorb these operations.

The DRAM scheduler executes write operations based on the conditions of the DRAM devices, read queue operations, and the current write priority. Write priority is determined dynamically depending on the fullness of the *Virtual Write Queue*. As write operations are executed to DRAM, the fullness of the *Physical Write Queue* is decreased, so the Cache Cleaner refills the *Physical Write Queue* to the target level. The Cache Cleaner will search the last-level cache *Virtual Write Queue* region for write operations to the desired DRAM resource. This DRAM resource is chosen in two ways: 1) If the memory controller attempts a burst of operations to a specific rank, an operation mapping to that rank will be sent; 2) alternately, if no burst is in progress, the *Physical Write Queue* will be rebalanced by choosing the rank with the fewest operations pending. This maintenance of an even mix of operations to various DRAM resources enables opportunistic write execution, in that a write is always available to any DRAM resource that becomes idle.

As part of the Cache Cleaner function, we harvest additional writes which map to the same DRAM page as the write selected by the Cache Cleaner for writeback. This is accomplished via queries to cache sets which map to the same DRAM page (Section 4.3). In our system, we define groups of such cache sets based on the cache and DRAM address translation algorithms. In our evaluation we found groups of four cache sets to be an ideal size.

Upon completion of the *Scheduled Writebacks*, the *Physical Write Queue* once again contains an ideal mix of operations to be scheduled. While we have described a sequence of operations, in practice, the structure can concurrently operate on all steps, accommodating periods of high utilization.

4.2 Physical Write Queue Allocation

As previously described, the highest barrier to efficient utilization of a main store (whether DRAM or future technologies) is the transition between read and write operations. In addition to write-to-read turnaround, alternating between different ranks on the same bus can introduce wasted bus cycles. To have good efficiency, DRAM banks must additionally be managed such that operations to the same bank, but to different pages, are avoided. These characteristics motivate creation of long bursts of reads or writes to ranks, while avoiding bank conflicts. The *Physical Write Queue* allocation scheme addresses the formation of write bursts.

A key aspect of the *Virtual Write Queue* solution is its two-level design. Since writes can only be *executed* from the *Physical Write Queue*, our *Scheduled Writebacks* must expose parallelism of the *Virtual Write Queue* into the *Physical Write Queue* to achieve the highest value from last-level cache buffering. This is accomplished by maintaining the best possible mix of operations in the *Physical Write Queue*, given what is visible in the entire *Virtual Write Queue* structure.

We accomplish this in two ways. First, we create the capability to opportunistically execute *write operations* to any rank. In this way, we can react to a temporarily idle rank with a burst of writes at any moment. Extending this idea, we must maintain several writes to each rank which can be executed without idle cycles. Ideally, we would maintain many writes to the same DRAM pages. When it is not possible to maintain accesses targeting the same rank and page, we find operations to the same rank, but a different bank. For a write burst to a rank that is longer than what can be stored in the *Physical Write Queue*, we directly generate *Scheduled Writebacks* in concert with execution of writes, such that we can overlap the cache writeback latency with the *Physical Write Queue* transfers to memory. Once the initial latency of the first cache writeback has passed, our cache has the required bandwidth to maintain a busy DRAM bus.

An example timing diagram for this *Virtual Write Queue* function is shown in Figure 8. In this example, the *Physical Write Queue* initially contains four cachelines which map to a target rank

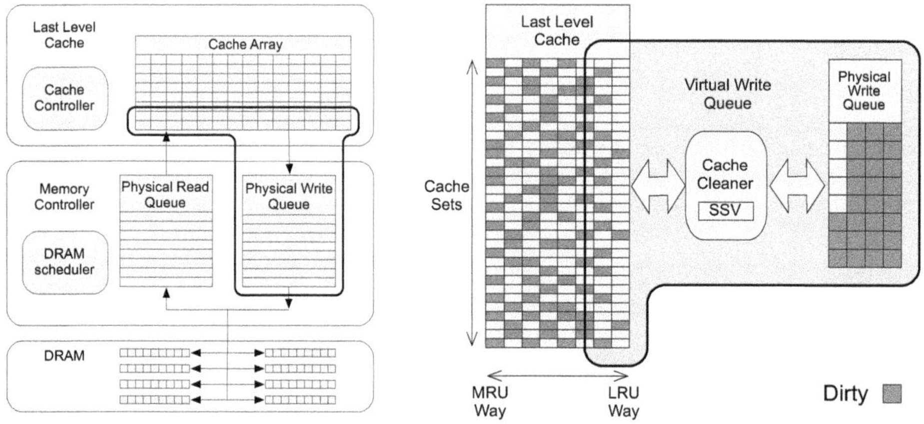

(a) (b)

Figure 7: Memory controller and DRAM for a) a typical system with separate read and write queues, and b) the proposed *Virtual Write Queue*

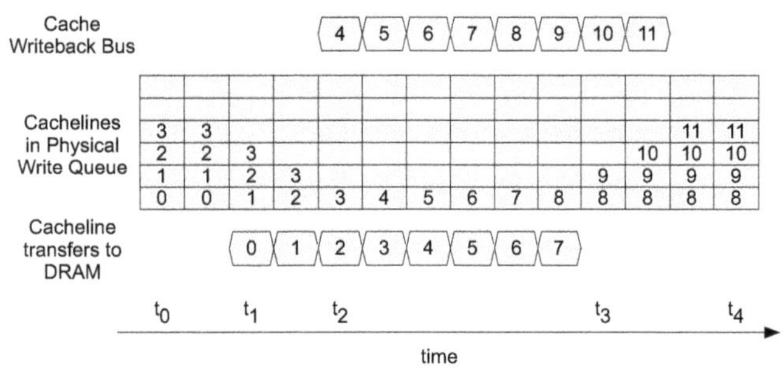

Figure 8: Virtual Write Queue timing diagram of operation

(cachelines 0 to 3 in the first column). At t_0, the scheduler initiates an eight cacheline write burst. While the initial four cachelines of data are available in the write buffer, the remaining lines must be transferred from the last-level cache using the *Scheduled Writeback* mechanism. In this case, a request is made at t_1 to the Cleaner logic coincident with the initiation of the writes to memory. To maintain back-to-back transfers on the DRAM bus, the Cache Cleaner must be able to provide data within the delay of the transfer of data from the *Physical Write Queue* to main memory. For example, in a system using DDR3 1066 memory with a burst length (BL) of 8, each cacheline requires $\approx$8ns to be transferred (*i.e.*, $\approx$32 CPU cycles). Thus the Cleaner must be able to provide a cache line within 32ns, assuming four cachelines stored in the *Physical Write Queue*. Our design analysis shows that this is easily achieved for typical last-level cache latencies (10 ns measured on Intel I7 965 [4]). In the example of Figure 8, we show that the first writeback data, cacheline 4, arrives at time t_2. At this point, the *Physical Write Queue* has been depleted of lines 0-3, and data is streamed from the last-level cache. As the eight-line write burst completes at time t_3, the remaining lines from the last-level cache transfer are used to refill the *Physical Write Queue*. At time t_4, the physical queue is once again full, and ready to execute another write burst.

4.3 The Cache Cleaner

To qualify as an efficient implementation, our scheme must (1) not interfere with the mainline cache controller; (2) be power efficient; and (3) be timely. Specifically, the *Cache Cleaner* must not affect hit rates or cause excessive access to cache directory and data arrays; it must avoid excess reads of cache directory arrays for power efficiency reasons; and cache lines to be cleaned must be located in a timely manner. The Cleaner uses a Set State Vector to accomplish these goals.

4.3.1 The Set State Vector (SSV)

While the cache lines in the *Virtual Write Queue* are contained within the state information of the cache directory itself, direct access is problematic. Specifically, cache directory structures are optimized for efficient CPU-side interaction. This CPU-centric directory organization conflicts with the access requirements of the Cache Cleaner. The Cache Cleaner would like to efficiently search across many sets, in search of *dirty* cache lines to be scheduled for writeback to the DRAM. We enable this efficient search with the addition of the *Set State Vector* (SSV).

At the most basic level, the SSV is used as a structure to decouple the cache cleaner from the actual cache directory for the following reasons. First, the SSV provides a much denser access method. If the actual directory were used, many more bits would need to be read and interpreted, wasting power. This is shown in Figure 9(a), where each 8-way cache set maps to one SSV bit. In addition to the density gains, the organization of the SSV is tailored such that array reads return 64 bits for the specific DRAM resource being targeted (taking advantage of reading entire rows of the storage arrays). This is shown in Figure 9(b), where the set address is remapped to the DRAM rank and bank address. Lastly, the SSV avoids interference between the cache cleaner and the main cache directory pipeline by providing a dedicated read port for the cache cleaner.

The process of calculating the SSV bit is implemented as part of the cache access pipeline where all of the state and LRU information is available as part of the existing cache lookup. While there is additional power in accessing the SSV array, the structures are only a fraction of the size of the actual directory, thus the additional power is not significant.

Each SSV entry contains the *dirty data criticality* of each set. For our system, we define sets with *dirty* data in the oldest $1/4$ of the cache as critical. We derive this criticality from the LRU bits present in the cache pipeline. Our system uses an 8-way true LRU algorithm implemented with 28 bits for each cache set. These 28 bits are used to define pairwise age between every combination of the eight members (7+6+5+4+3+2+1=28 bits). The LRU distance is then calculated by adding the 7 direction bits for each way. If the

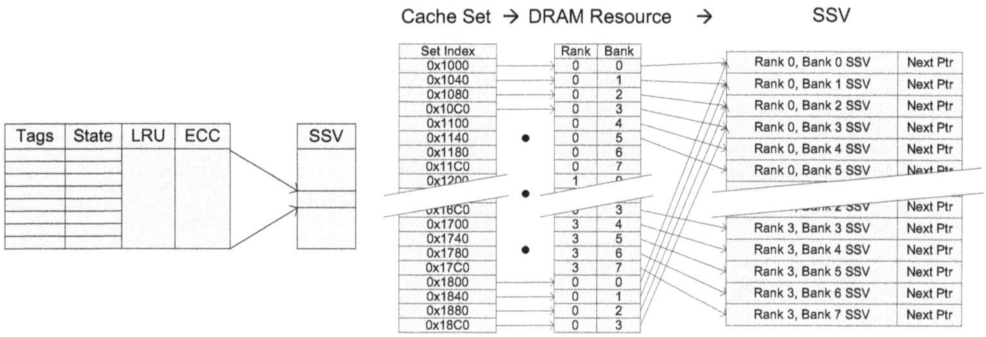

(a) (b)

Figure 9: Set State Vectors (SSVs): a) directory set map to SSV entries, and b) mapping of cache sets to SSVs

distance is greater than the criticality distance (5 in our example), the SSV bit is set. While our system is based around true LRU, this concept can be extended to other replacement algorithms such as pseudo-LRU. For example the relative age in a tree based pseudo-LRU can be estimated by counting the number of pointers towards each way.

4.3.2 Cleaner SSV Traversal

Adjacent entries in the SSV are not necessarily adjacent sets in the cache. The dense packing is based upon the mapping of the system address into the physical mapping on the DRAM's channel/rank/bank resources. Adjacent entries in the SSV all map to the same channel/rank/bank resource.

A mapping example is shown in Figure 9(b). In this example we have a *closed-page* mapping for four ranks, each with 8 banks. In this case, every 32nd cache line maps to the same SSV. In general the mapping logic must be configured to match the DRAM mapping function; this is not a significant constraint, since mappings are known at system boot time. Our scheme requires all bits that feed the DRAM mapping function to be contained within the set selection bits of the cache. This enables not only the SSV mapping function, but also *page mode harvesting*. This restriction does not produce significant negative effects, since all bits above the system page size are effectively random, and large last-level cache sizes have several higher order bits available for more sophisticated mapping functions (which avoid power of two conflicts that are common in simple lower-order bit mappings) [24].

The SSV is then subdivided into regions for each channel / rank / bank configured in the system. The Cache Cleaner maintains a working pointer for each of these configured regions. As the Cache Cleaner receives writeback requests from the memory controller, the associated working pointer reads a section of the SSV (with the matching *Next Ptr* in Figure 9(b)). A set is selected, which will determine the specific set with which a writeback request will be generated. This request is sent to the cache controller to initiate the actual cache cleaning operation.

4.4 Read/write Priority Mechanism

To be most effective, our write queueing system must be able to dynamically adjust the relative priority between *read* and *write* operations. The system must be able to respond to the workload's overall *read*-to-*write* ratio, in addition to being able to handle *bursts* of operations. A well-behaved system will always execute *reads* instead of *writes*, as *writes* only indirectly slow a program as queueing in the system becomes full. Given finite queuing, *writes* must at some point step in front of *reads*. This is an important aspect of our system, in that the *Virtual Write Queue* provides much larger effective buffering capability. To efficiently manage this capacity we must react to the overall fullness of the *Virtual Write Queue*. The behavior of our system as the capacity nears full differs significantly from the previously-proposed *Eager Writeback* technique [9] (which essentially results in no benefits in sustained high bandwidth situations). This is illustrated in the following example.

Some workloads, such as *Stream* [14], require a high level of sustained, regular, bandwidth. *Stream* consumes sequential vectors of data that are not contained within the cache. These vectors are processed within loops with various *read*-to-*write* ratios (e.g., 1:1 R:W for `copy`, 3:1 for `triad`). Despite changes in the *read*-to-*write* ratio, the workloads' memory bandwidth requirement is constant: every instruction executed must read from memory. There is therefore no inherent period of execution in which writes to memory can be hidden. Despite this constraint, memory utilization is significantly reduced if the memory bus is switched between read and write operations at the native requirements of the workload. For workloads with this type of behavior, improving performance requires that we force long write burst lengths, even when no idle bus slots are available. For the `copy` kernel, the native 1:1 ratio yields a memory bus utilization of 31%, while a burst of 32 cachelines can achieve 94% (Figure 4); a 300% improvement in memory efficiency.

Priority Mechanism: We base our *read*-to-*write* priority on a count of the *data criticality* bits set in the SSVs associated with each rank (8, one for each bank). The count is updated as bits are set/reset in the corresponding SSVs. We then utilize *high* and *low water marks* to trigger high priority *writes*. The *high water mark* is chosen such that we do not overflow the LRU of the cache with forced writebacks. In our evaluations we found a value of 4096 to be effective. This represents a half full *Virtual Write Queue*. Larger values resulted in overflow of some cache sets, decreasing the ability to control writebacks. The *low water mark* defines the number of consecutive cachelines to be written. We found a burst of 32 lines to be effective (*low water mark* of 4064 = 4096 - 32).

4.5 Write Page Mode Harvester Logic

The cache eviction mechanism is augmented to query adjacent lines in the directory, such that groups of requests within the same memory page can be detected and sent as a group for batch execution to the DRAM. When a line is pulled out of the cache array, we search the associated sets of the cache that contain possible page mode addresses. If the corresponding page mode addresses are found, these will be sent as a group to the memory controller, to be processed as a burst page-write command sequence. In our evaluation we found that three look-ups associated

Table 2: Core and memory-subsystem parameters used in evaluation section

Core Characteristics	**Clock Frequency**	**Pipeline**	**Reorder Buffer /Scheduler**	**Branch Predictor**
	4 GHz	30 stages / 4-wide fetch / decode	128/64 Entries	Direct YAGS / indirect 256 entries
Memory Subsystem	**L1 Data & Inst. Cache**	**L2 Cache**	**Outstanding Requests**	**Memory Bandwidth**
	64 KB, 2-way associative, 3 cycles access time, 64 Bytes block size, LRU	16 MB, 8 ways associative, 12 cycles bank access, 64 Bytes block size, LRU	16 Requests per Core	16.6 GB/s
	Controller Organization	**DRAM**	**Controller Resources**	**Virtual Write Queue**
	2 Memory Controllers 1, 2, and 4 Ranks per Controller 8 DRAM chips per Rank	8GB DDR3-1066 7-7-7	32 Read Queue & 32 Write Queue Entries	2 LRU ways 4096 High & 4064 Low Watermark

with a block of four cachelines provided significant gains without excessive directory queries.

4.6 Prevention of Extra Memory Writebacks

Since our system speculatively writes dirty data back to memory, there is some chance that extra memory write traffic is introduced. Specifically, if a store occurs to the data after it is cleaned, the cleaning operation is wasted. As a solution to this problem, we add additional cache states to indicate a line was once dirty, but has been cleaned. Lines in *Cleaned* states are excluded from being cleaned a second time. A complete extension to the MOESI protocol would require *Cleaned* version of all four valid states. This presents additional overhead in that the total number of states would reach nine. Since MOESI systems require three state bits of encoding, three unused state encodes are available. To avoid the overhead of adding a fourth state bit, we choose to exclude the *Shared Cleaned* state, maintaining the same state overhead as standard MOESI. Our justification for the exclusion of *Shared Cleaned* is best explained through the state transitions shown in Table 3. In the table, the *Cleaned* states are represented with a lowercase *c*, e.g. *Modified Cleaned* as M_c.

Table 3: Extra coherence protocol transitions introduced to prevent extra memory writebacks

#	Initial State	Event	Next State	Comment
1	M	Clean	E_c	Scheduled Writeback
2	S	Store	M	M If no O_c in system
3	S	Store	M_c	M_c If O_c in system
4	M_c	Snooped Read	O_c	
5	O_c	Store	M_c	
6	O_c	Snooped Read	O_c	
7	E_c	Store	M_c	
8	O	Clean	S	Disallowed due to lack of S_c
9	E_c	Snooped Read	S	Loss of cleaned Information

There are two cases of potential transitions into the *Shared Cleaned* state (S_c). In row 8 of Table 3, we show the case of an *Owned* (O) line that if cleaned would transition to *Shared Cleaned*. In our simulations we do not clean *Owned* lines thus this case is avoided. In row 9 we show the case of a line in *Exclusive Cleaned* state (E_c), where a read operation is snooped. Here the *Exclusive Cleaned* line must transition to an *Shared* state. Since the *Cleaned* modifier is not required for coherence, we simply use the traditional *Shared* state in this case. In our analysis we observed no degradation due to this policy.

4.7 Overall Overhead Analysis of Virtual Write Queue

The actual storage overhead of the proposed *Virtual Write Queue* is limited to the overhead for the SSVs. The rest of the scheme

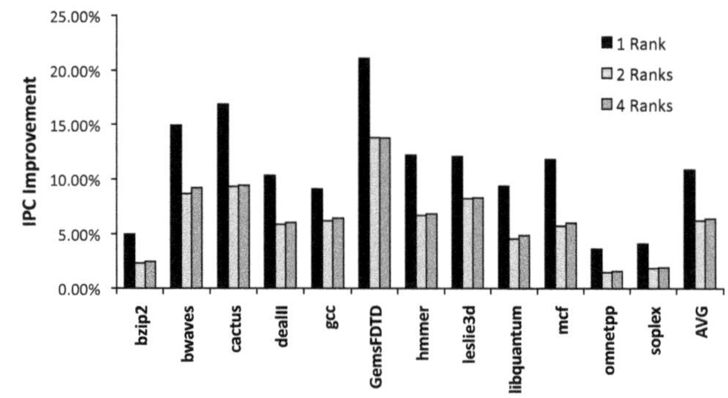

Figure 10: IPC improvements of *Virtual Write Queue* over prior work (FR_FCFS + Eager) [21, 9]

primarily reuses existing structures in the last-level cache and memory controller of a typical CMP system. All of the remaining structures added to the last-level cache controller and memory controller are negligible in size compared to the storage required for the SSVs. We evaluate the overhead of the SSV by comparing it to the cache directory. For a 16MB 8-way associative cache used in our analysis, each cache set requires 346bits (see Figure 9(a): $8 * 32$bits Tag bits, $8 * 3$bits State Bits, 28 LRU bits and 38 ECC bits). Since we add only one SSV bit per cache set, our overhead is approximately 1/346≈0.3% (4Kbytes of storage for the SSV compared to 1384Kbytes for the cache directory).

5. EVALUATION

To evaluate the effectiveness of the proposed *Virtual Write Queue*, we used Simics [22], extended with the Gems toolset [13], to simulate cycle-accurate out-of-order processors and a detailed memory subsystem. We configured our toolset to simulate an 8-core SPARCv9 CMP with 8GB of main memory. The memory subsystem model includes an inter-core last-level cache network that uses a directory-based MOESI cache coherence protocol along with a detailed memory controller. Both the last-level cache and the memory controller were augmented to support a baseline memory controller and the proposed *Virtual Write Queue*. Our baseline implementation simulates a *First-Ready, First-Come-First-Served* (FR_FCFS) [21] memory controller with the addition of *Eager writebacks* [9], referred to as *FR_FCFS+EW* in our evaluation. Enhancements beyond FR_FCFS, such as PAR-BS [17] and Fair-Queueing [18] focus on memory *read* fairness and throughput improvement in heterogeneous environments. In this study we evaluated improvements to the *write* scheduling using homogeneous workloads. System improvements targeting *read* scheduling are non-conflicting and can be used in combination with *Virtual Write Queue*. Therefore a baseline system of FR_FCFS with *eager writebacks* (FR_FCFS+EW) allows us to evaluate our

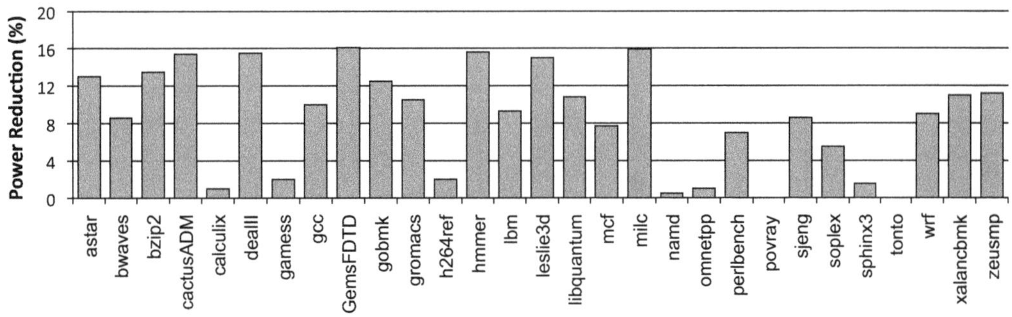

Figure 11: Power reductions achieved by *Virtual Write Queue* for SPEC CPU2006 Rate

proposed scheme. We use the SPEC CPU2006 Rate scientific benchmark suite [23], compiled to the SPARC ISA with full optimizations (peak flags). Each benchmark is fast-forwarded for 4 billion instructions to reach its execution steady-state phase. We then simulate for the next 100M instructions to warm up the last-level cache and our memory controller structures; followed by a final 100M instructions used in our evaluation. Table 2 includes the basic system parameters.

5.1 System Throughput Speedup Analysis

Cycle-accurate simulations of SPEC CPU2006 Rate showed that the *Virtual Write Queue* enables significant throughput gains for workloads with high memory bandwidth requirements. These gains over the baseline FR_FCFS+EW [21, 9] system is shown in Figure 10. We show speedups for three memory bus configurations (1, 2, and 4 DRAM ranks per channel). SPEC workloads not listed in the figure did not show any measurable change in performance. As expected, workloads with high memory utilization showed benefits due to reduction in bus penalties by forming long back-to-back write bursts. The largest speedup is observed on the single rank system. In this case, the controller does not have other ranks to which to send requests, and the "write-to-read-same-rank" penalty is incurred at every bus turnaround. For the 2-rank system, we show smaller gains, since the baseline system is able to schedule around "write-to-read-same-rank" penalties in many cases. In that case, delays due to rank-to-rank transitions become more important. The performance of the 4-rank system is very close to that of the 2-rank since the controller incurs fewer "write-to-read-same-rank" penalties, but generates more frequent rank-to-rank transitions. Overall, the *Virtual Write Queue* achieved average improvements of 10.9% in throughput when configured with 1 rank, while for the cases of 2 and 4 ranks the IPC improvements were found to be 6.4% and 6.7%, respectively.

5.2 Page Mode Analysis

Using the *Virtual Write Queue* we see significant increases in the amount of page mode write operations over the baseline FR_FCFS+EW [21, 9] system. Our full-system simulation shows an average of 3.2 write accesses per page – this contributes to system throughput gains (as observed in Section 5.1) and memory power reduction. While the throughout gains are only observed in high bandwidth workloads, the power reductions are more universal. In Figure 11 we show the DRAM power reduction for each workload estimated using the Micron power estimator [16]. Overall, we observe an average DRAM power reduction of 8.7%. As shown in [20], main memory can be a significant portion of total system power. For *stream*, Rajamani *et al.* indicate that memory power can be 48% of high performance system power, even after accounting for supply losses. The 11-15% power saved for half of

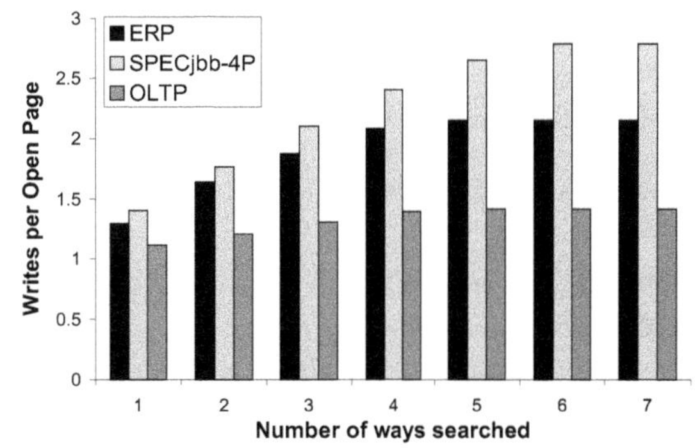

Figure 12: Writes per open-page for varying number of cache ways allocated to the *Virtual Write Queue*. The *Virtual Write Queue* exploits the LRU ways of the last-level cache to virtually expand the write queue.

the workloads through the page mode write scheduling of *Virtual Write Queue* would thus result in a 5-7% system-level savings.

To further evaluate the page mode behavior of the *Virtual Write Queue* we performed a set of simulations using three diverse commercial workloads. Due to the complexity and size of the commercial workloads, a detailed evaluation using a cycle-accurate, full system simulator is prohibitively expensive. As a solution, for commercial workloads we utilize trace-based cache simulations. The first workload is an *On-Line Transaction Processing* (OLTP) workload driven by hundreds of simulated individual clients generating remote transactions against a large database. The second workload represents a typical *Enterprise Resource Planning* (ERP) workload. As with the OLTP workload, the ERP workload was driven by simulated users who sent remote queries and updates to the database. Finally, the third workload is SPECjbb2005 benchmark [23] that targets the performance of a three-tier client/server system with emphasis on the middle tier. We performed the trace-based simulations using an in-house cache simulator augmented to model the *Virtual Write Queue*.

We augmented our cache simulator to monitor the total page mode writes that were possible when varying the number of cache ways that were allocated to the *Virtual Write Queue*. The simulation results are shown in Figure 12. Whenever a dirty line was evicted from the cache, the last N ways of the cache were checked for other dirty lines that mapped to the same DRAM page. As expected, there is a steady increase in page mode opportunity as we increase the number of ways considered, with significant increases in 2 ways, and diminishing returns after considering more than 4 ways, or half the cache. The increased performance from considering more ways of the set must be balanced against the overhead of additional writes introduced by the cleaning. Though

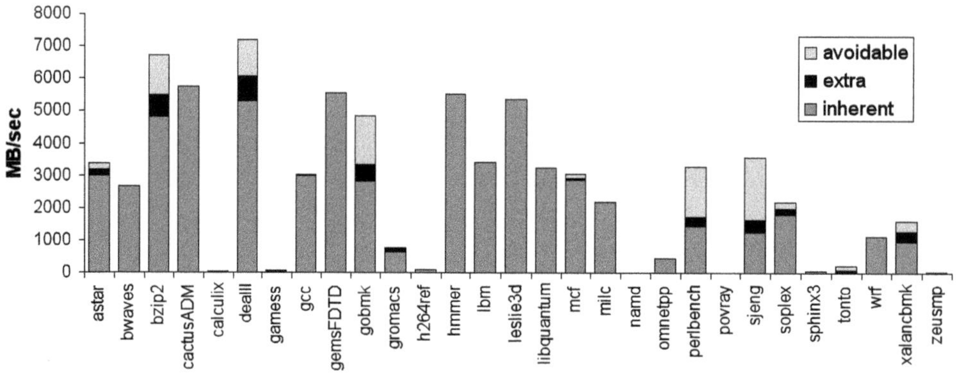

Figure 13: Extra Writeback avoidance for SPEC CPU2006

not shown, it is worth noting the implied difference in performance results across the three workloads. The OLTP workload sees limited benefit, while the ERP and SPECjbb see much larger opportunities.

5.3 Prevention of Extra Memory Writeback Analysis

As described in Section 4.6, the *Virtual Write Queue* mechanisms has the potential to generate additional writeback traffic for cases where a cleaned line is modified after its speculative write-back to the memory. In this section we evaluate the magnitude of the problem, and the solution presented in Section 4.6. Through our cycle-accurate simulations, we classified the writebacks to memory into the following categories: a) *Inherent*: normal bandwidth that is not created by speculative writebacks, b) *Extra*: bandwidth created through speculative writeback that is *not* removed though our cache state enhancements, and c) *Avoidable*: Speculative bandwidth that is avoided with the addition of the proposed cache state enhancements. In Figure 13 we present the total memory bandwidth, in MB/sec, as was collected from our simulations. As shown, certain workloads, such as `sjeng`, see significant extra bandwidth that is eliminated using the cache state enhancements of Section 4.6. Note, our power estimates in Section 5.2 assume these cache state enhancements. In all cases, the power savings achieved at the DRAM using page mode offset the increase from extra traffic (since most of the extra traffic contains no bank activates). In addition, we performed a limited evaluation of commercial workloads to gauge how problematic this behavior is. Again, there are significant differences between the workloads. Using the lower 2-ways of LRU in the *Virtual Write Queue*, SPECjbb showed 1% increase in writebacks compared to an increase of 6% for ERP and 9% for OLTP.

6. RELATED WORK

Multi-threaded aware DRAM schedulers: Multi-threaded aware proposals have primarily addressed mechanisms to reorder requests received by the memory controller. Work on *Fair Queuing Memory Systems* by Nesbit et al. [18] utilizes *fair queuing* network principles on the memory controller to provide fairness and throughput improvements. *Parallelism-Aware Batch Scheduling* [17] alleviates the problem by maintaining groups of requests from the various threads in the system and issuing them in batches to the controller. A suite of work has considered minimizing prefetch impacts on overall memory subsystem performance, some of which consider prioritizing prefetch according to page mode opportunity [10] [11]. As previously described, the *Virtual Write Queue*, which realizes performance and power savings by focusing on writes, is non-conflicting and can be combined with the previous read-oriented memory optimization approaches.

System and DRAM interaction: Proposals to improve interactions between the DRAM controller and other system components have been proposed in the following areas. The *Eager Writeback* technique [9] addresses breaking the connection between cache fills and evictions, but the approach has minimal communication between the last-level cache and the memory controller and thus misses performance and power opportunities which arise through knowledge of logical-to-physical address mapping and troublesome memory timing constraints. In the work evaluating ZettaRAM [25], *Eager Writeback* is shown to work synergistically with the more advanced write characteristics of the described memory technology. This is an example of how future memory technologies can benefit from more sophisticated write-back schemes. We expect the *Virtual Write Queue* to further improve the system characteristics. *SDRAM-aware scheduling* from Jang et al. [6] addresses management of the on-chip network such that requests are ordered with regard to memory efficiency.

DRAM write-read turnaround: For specialized applications, DRAMs have been offered with separated read and write IOs, allowing for high bus utilization, even for mixed read/write access streams [15]. Borkenhagen et al. [1], describe the problem of DRAM *write-to-read* turnaround delay, and recognize the need for cache / memory controller interaction to most effectively alleviate its performance effect. Borkenhagen et al. propose a *read predict* signal, which provides the memory controller early notice that a read may soon arrive at the memory controller. If *read predict* is asserted, the memory controller will not issue pending writes, to avoid incurring a *write-to-read* turnaround delay which would delay the read.

DRAM power management: Several approaches have been proposed for DRAM power management, however most leverage memory sleep states, rather than exploiting page mode power savings. [8] considers the power cost of opening and closing pages, and [12] proposes a *Page Hit Aware Write Buffer* (PHA-WB), a 64-entry structure residing between the memory controller and DRAM, which holds onto writes until their target page is opened by a read. The PHA-WB, however, was evaluated for a write-through cache, for which memory-level access locality will be much more apparent than in a writeback structure. Writeback caches provide significant improvements in available memory bandwidth and power consumption, so are thus a more realistic baseline for many-core server-class systems.

7. CONCLUSIONS

In this work we address the barriers to efficient DRAM operation, which is a key attribute of many-core architectures. We propose a novel approach that coordinates last-level cache and DRAM policies, which significantly improves both system performance and energy characteristics. We modify existing structures and mechanisms in order to allow greater sharing of system state across units, therefore, enabling better scheduling decisions.

Specifically, we expand the memory controller's visibility into the last-level cache, greatly increasing write scheduling opportunities. This enables several improvements in system behavior. We are able to increase page mode writes to DRAM, which both decreases power consumption and increases memory bus efficiency. The longer write bursts achieved through *Scheduled Writebacks* amortize bus turnaround penalties, increasing bus utilization. The larger effective write queue improves read/write priority determination in the DRAM scheduler, enabling burst read operations to proceed uninhibited by write conflicts for longer periods.

We demonstrate through cycle-accurate simulation that the proposed *Virtual Write Queue* scheme is able to achieve significant raw system throughput improvements (10.9%) and power consumption reductions (8.7%) with very low hardware overhead ($\approx$0.3%). Overall, the *Virtual Write Queue* demonstrates that co-optimizations of multiple system components enable low-cost, high-yield improvements over traditional approaches.

Acknowledgements

The authors would like to thank the anonymous reviewers for their suggestions that helped improve the quality of this paper. The authors acknowledge the use of the Archer infrastructure for their simulations, and Kyu-Hyoun Kim for assistance in DRAM bus utilization calculations. This work is sponsored in part by the National Science Foundation under award 0702694 and CRI collaborative awards: 0751112, 0750847, 0750851, 0750852, 0750860, 0750868, 0750884, 0751091, and by IBM. Any opinions, findings, conclusions or recommendations expressed in this material are those of the authors and do not necessarily reflect the views of the National Science Foundation or IBM.

References

[1] J. Borkenhagen, B. Vanderpool & L. Whitley, "Read prediction algorithm to provide low latency reads with SDRAM cache," *US Patent 6801982*, 2004.

[2] DDR3 SDRAM Standard, JEDEC JESD79-3, http://www.jedec.org, June 2007.

[3] P. Glaskowsky, "High-end server chips breaking records," http://news.cnet.com/8301-13512_3-10321740-23.html, Aug. 2009.

[4] J. Hruska, "Nehalem by the numbers: The Ars review," http://arstechnica.com/hardware/reviews/2008/11/nehalem-launch-review.ars/3.

[5] B. Jacob, S. Ng & D. Wang, "Memory systems: Cache, DRAM, disk," *Morgan Kaufmann Publishers Inc.*, USA, 2007.

[6] W. Jang & D. Pan, "An SDRAM-aware router for networks-on-chip," in *Proceedings of the 46th Annual Design Automation Conference*, pp. 800–805, 2009.

[7] R. Kalla, B. Sinharoy & J. M. Tendler,"IBM Power5 chip: A dual-core multithreaded processor," *IEEE Micro, vol. 24, no. 2*, pp. 40–47, 2004.

[8] N. Y. Ker & C. H. Chen, "An effective SDRAM power mode management scheme for performance and energy sensitive embedded systems," in *Proceedings of the Asia and South Pacific Design Automation Conference*, pp. 515–518, 2003.

[9] H. Lee, G. Tyson & M. Farrens, "Eager writeback - a technique for improving bandwidth utilization," in *Proceedings of the International Symposium on Microarchitecture*, pp. 11–21, 2000.

[10] W. Lin, S. Reinhardt & D. Burger, "Reducing DRAM latencies with an integrated memory hierarchy design," in *Proceedings of the International Symposium on High-Performance Computer Architecture*, pp 301–312, 2001.

[11] J. Lin, H. Zheng, Z. Zhu, Z. Zhang & H. David, "DRAM-level prefetching for fully-buffered DIMM: Design, performance and power saving," in *International Symposium on Performance Analysis of Systems & Software*, pp 94–104, 2008.

[12] S. Liu, S. Memik, Y. Zhang & G. Memik, "A power and temperature aware DRAM architecture," in *Proceedings of the 45th Annual Design Automation Conference*, pp 878–883, 2008.

[13] M. Martin *et al.*, "Multifacet's general execution-driven multiprocessor simulator (GEMS) toolset," *Computer Architecture News (CAN)*, September 2005.

[14] J. McCalpin, "Memory bandwidth and machine balance in current high performance computers," *IEEE Computer Society Technical Committee on Computer Architecture (TCCA) Newsletter*, 1995.

[15] Micron Technologies, Inc., "Exploring the RLDRAM II Feature Set," *Technical Report: TN-49-02*, 2004.

[16] Micron Technologies, Inc., DDR3 SDRAM system-power calculator, revision 0.1, Mar. 2007.

[17] O. Mutlu & T. Moscibroda, "Parallelism-aware batch scheduling: Enabling high-performance and fair shared memory controllers," *IEEE Micro vol. 29*, pp. 22–32, 2009.

[18] K. Nesbit, N Aggarwal, J. Laudon & J. Smith, "Fair queuing memory systems," in *Proceedings of the International Symposium on Microarchitecture*, pp. 208–222, 2006.

[19] M. Qureshi, V. Srinivasan & J. Rivers, "Scalable high performance main memory system using phase-change memory technology," in *Proceedings of the International Symposium on Computer Architecture*, pp. 24–33, 2009.

[20] K. Rajamani *et al.*, "Power Management for Computer Systems and Datacenters", tutorial at the *International Symposium on Low Power Electronics and Design (ISLPED)*, 2008.

[21] S. Rixner, W. Dally, U. Kapasi, P. Mattson & J. Owens, "Memory access scheduling," in *Proceedings of International Symposium on Computer Architecture*, pp. 128–138, 2000.

[22] Simics Microarchitect's Toolset, http://www.virtutech.com.

[23] Standard Performance Evaluation Corporation, http://www.spec.org.

[24] M. Valero, T. Lang & E. Ayguadé, "Conflict-free access of vectors with power-of-two strides," in *Proceedings of the International Conference on Supercomputing*, pp. 149–156, 1992.

[25] R. Venkatesan, A. AL-Zawawi & E. Rotenberg, "Tapping ZettaRAM for Low-Power Memory Systems," in *11th International Symposium on High-Performance Computer Architecture*, pp. 83–94, 2005

Reducing Cache Power with Low-Cost, Multi-bit Error-Correcting Codes

Chris Wilkerson, Alaa R. Alameldeen, Zeshan Chishti,
Wei Wu, Dinesh Somasekhar, and Shih-Lien Lu
Intel Labs
Hillsboro, Oregon, USA
{chris.wilkerson, alaa.r.alameldeen, zeshan.a.chishti, wei.a.wu, dinesh.somasekhar, shih-lien.l.lu} @intel.com

ABSTRACT

Technology advancements have enabled the integration of large on-die embedded DRAM (eDRAM) caches. eDRAM is significantly denser than traditional SRAMs, but must be periodically refreshed to retain data. Like SRAM, eDRAM is susceptible to device variations, which play a role in determining refresh time for eDRAM cells. Refresh power potentially represents a large fraction of overall system power, particularly during low-power states when the CPU is idle. Future designs need to reduce cache power without incurring the high cost of flushing cache data when entering low-power states.

In this paper, we show the significant impact of variations on refresh time and cache power consumption for large eDRAM caches. We propose Hi-ECC, a technique that incorporates multi-bit error-correcting codes to significantly reduce refresh rate. Multi-bit error-correcting codes usually have a complex decoder design and high storage cost. Hi-ECC avoids the decoder complexity by using strong ECC codes to identify and disable sections of the cache with multi-bit failures, while providing efficient single-bit error correction for the common case. Hi-ECC includes additional optimizations that allow us to amortize the storage cost of the code over large data words, providing the benefit of multi-bit correction at same storage cost as a single-bit error-correcting (SECDED) code (2% overhead). Our proposal achieves a 93% reduction in refresh power vs. a baseline eDRAM cache without error correcting capability, and a 66% reduction in refresh power vs. a system using SECDED codes.

Categories and Subject Descriptors

B.3.4 [**Memory Structures**]: Reliability, Testing, Fault-Tolerance.

General Terms

Design, Reliability, Power.

Keywords

ECC, Multi-Bit ECC, DRAM, eDRAM, refresh power, Vccmin.

ISCA'10 June 19–23, 2010, Saint-Malo, France.

1. INTRODUCTION

Advances in technology scaling have led to dramatic yearly improvements in on-die cache capacity. New process technologies have also enabled integrating DRAM on a logic process, leading to the use of embedded DRAM (eDRAM) to build on-die caches that are much denser than SRAM-based caches (e.g., IBM Power 7 [14]). However, a side effect of technology scaling is the increasing susceptibility of cache structures to device variations [1, 27], where a few weak cells can constrain the operating range of the whole cache.

In traditional SRAM caches, intrinsic variations force operation at high voltages due to a few weak cells that fail at lower voltages, and impede efforts to reduce power [29, 33]. Likewise, in eDRAM caches, device variations affect the retention time of individual DRAM cells, with a few particularly weak bits determining the refresh time of the whole cache. A high refresh rate significantly increases cache power.

Reducing power consumption is a first-order design constraint for modern processors. In pursuit of improved power and energy efficiency, processors implement a number of idle states to support lower power modes. Reducing the power consumed during idle states is particularly important because the typical CPU spends the vast majority of its time in idle state. Many desktop applications, such as word processors and spreadsheets, spend much of the time waiting for I/O and tend to require the CPU to operate only 10-20% of the time during use. Studies done on the Intel® Core™/Core™ 2 Duo show that an idling processor will consume an average of 0.5W-1.05W [24] depending on the processor and frequency of idle state exits caused by events like OS interrupts. Our analysis projects that a future processor with 128MB of eDRAM cache will consume 926mW just refreshing the eDRAM. Based on these power numbers, we project that the power consumption of large memory structures, like eDRAM caches, will be the biggest contributor to overall idle power.

One popular method to reduce cache power is to power-gate large blocks of memory at the cost of losing its state [6]. But as cache density increases, the performance and power costs of this approach also increase. One of the important goals in implementing idle states is reducing power consumption, while minimizing the transition latency into and out of the idle state. In the Intel® Core™ 2, a transition out of the C4 idle state can take about 100-200us [9]. In contrast, if the state in a 128MB eDRAM cache were sacrificed to save power, it would take 4.2ms to re-fetch the 128MB of lost data assuming full usage of the 30GB/s bandwidth provided by system memory. In future products with denser eDRAM caches, navigating the tradeoffs between idle exit latency and idle power consumption will become increasingly difficult. As the capacity of embedded memory grows, the performance and power cost of flushing this memory also grows. A key challenge for future product designers is to enable flexible memory structures that can operate at very low idle power, without dramatically increasing transition latency to and from the idle power state due to data loss.

In this paper, we evaluate a modern processor with a 128MB eDRAM cache. We show that refresh time plays the key role in determining the eDRAM's power. We first explore the role of variation-related cell failures in determining refresh time. We then evaluate the potential for using error-correcting codes (ECC) to mitigate refresh-related failures. Augmenting eDRAM with error-correcting codes enables reliable cache operation with longer refresh periods, thereby lowering system power.

We propose Hi-ECC, a practical, low-latency, low-cost, error-correcting system that can compensate for high failure rates in eDRAM caches. Hi-ECC implements a strong BCH code with the ability to correct 5 and detect 6 errors (hereafter referred to as a 5EC6ED code). A traditional approach using strong ECC suffers from two prohibitive overheads that limit its applicability. First, building a low-latency decoder for multi-bit ECC codes is extremely costly. Second, the storage overhead of ECC bits is high (around 10% for a 5EC6ED ECC code for a 64 byte line). Hi-ECC proposes architectural solutions to both problems. It uses a simple ECC decoder optimized for the 99.5% of the lines that require little or no correction, and provides a high latency alternative for lines that require complex multi-bit correction. To minimize the performance impact of processing high latency multi-bit corrections, Hi-ECC disables lines with multi-bit failures. Finally, Hi-ECC leverages the natural spatial locality of the data to reduce the cost of ECC storage. We make the following main contributions:

1. We demonstrate that device variations lead to significant increases in cache refresh rates.

2. We propose Hi-ECC, a practical system for using strong error correcting codes that avoids decoder complexity and latency.

3. We show how Hi-ECC can be extended to reduce the storage overhead of the error-correcting codes by amortizing the cost of the code over larger data words. This allows implementing Hi-ECC with a 2% storage overhead, comparable to that of a single error correcting code (SECDED) over 64 byte lines.

4. For a system with a 128 MB eDRAM cache, we show that Hi-ECC can reduce cache refresh power by 93% compared to an eDRAM with no error correction capability, and 66% compared to an eDRAM with SECDED, all for about the same storage overhead as a SECDED code. When accounting for dynamic power, an optimized Hi-ECC reduces total power by 61% relative to SECDED.

The remainder of this paper is organized as follows. In Section 2, we review some of the design tradeoffs for eDRAM caches, including a discussion of retention failures and previous work on mitigating them. Section 3 describes our proposed Hi-ECC architecture, and is followed by a review of the mathematical properties of BCH codes that Hi-ECC relies on in Section 4. We describe our evaluation methodology and results in Section 5 and conclude in Section 6.

2. BACKGROUND

Embedded DRAM technology enables smaller memory cells as compared to SRAM cells, resulting in a three to four times increase in memory density [21]. The higher density of eDRAM makes it a promising candidate to replace SRAM as the last-level on-chip cache in future high performance processors. IBM has recently announced that its upcoming Power7 processor will use a 32 MB on-chip eDRAM cache [14]. As feature sizes continue to decrease, even larger eDRAM caches can be incorporated on chip. In this paper, we model a 128 MB eDRAM cache, two technology generations ahead of IBM Power7's eDRAM cache.

One of the main problems with eDRAM cells is that they lose charge over time due to leakage currents. The retention time of an eDRAM cell is defined as the length of time for which the cell can retain its state. Cell retention time depends on the leakage current, which, in turn, depends on the access device leakage. To preserve the state of stored data, eDRAM cells need to be refreshed on a periodic basis. In order to prevent failures, the refresh period needs to be less than the cell retention time. Because eDRAM uses fast logic transistors with a higher leakage current than conventional DRAM, the refresh time for eDRAM is about a thousand times shorter than conventional DRAM. For example, Barth, et al. [2] report the refresh time of a small eDRAM to be 40us as compared to 64ms refresh time in commodity DRAM [22]. This low refresh time poses serious problems for eDRAM because it not only increases the idle power, but also leads to reduced availability. Previous work has shown that variations in threshold voltage cause retention times of different DRAM cells to vary significantly [8, 10, 11, 18]. These variations are caused predominantly by random dopant fluctuations and manifest themselves as a random distribution of retention times amongst eDRAM cells. We use the data published in [18] to model the retention time distribution in Figure 1.

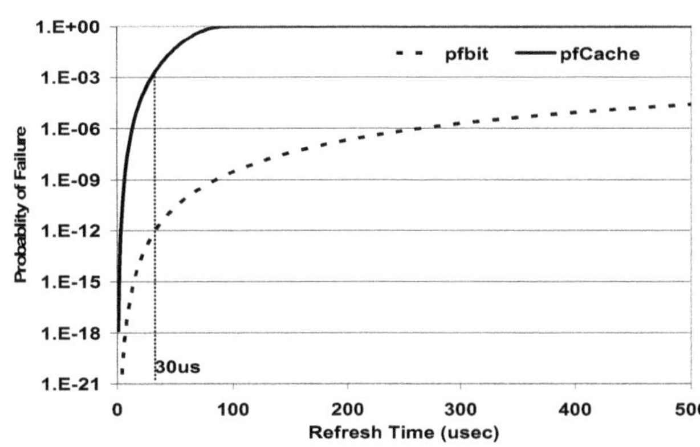

Figure 1: eDRAM retention time distribution

The pfbit curve in Figure 1 represents the probability of a retention failure in a single bit cell (derived from Figure 3 in [18]) and the pfCache curve represents the failure probability of a 128MB eDRAM cache for different refresh times. Our model assumes that bit retention failures are distributed randomly throughout the eDRAM cache, consistent with [18]. A cache containing even a single failure must be discarded. Therefore, the probability of failure for the entire cache is (1 – probability of success), where the probability of success is the probability that each bit in the cache stays failure-free. We assume that the pfCache must be kept at less than 1 out of 1000 to achieve acceptable manufacturing yields [33]. Under these assumptions, data in Figure 1 shows that the refresh time for a baseline 128MB eDRAM cache is 30 microseconds, close to the 40 microseconds refresh time reported in [2] for a 13.5Mbit eDRAM macro.

Refresh mechanisms in eDRAM designs typically use a single worst case refresh period dictated by the cell with the lowest retention time. As eDRAM capacity increases in future generations, eDRAM idle power, dominated by refresh, will grow. Some previous papers have proposed hardware mechanisms to exploit retention time variations by refreshing different DRAM cells at different refresh rates [16, 26]. Venkatesan, et al. [32] proposed a software mechanism that allocates DRAM pages with longer retention time before allocating pages with shorter retention time, and then chooses a refresh period that is determined only by the populated pages instead of the entire DRAM. These approaches require additional storage to track retention times and rely on memory tests to identify marginal bit cells. In [33] Wilkerson et al propose the bit-fix algorithm, another testing-based approach, to address the problem of high failure rates in the context of Vccmin reduction in SRAM caches instead of DRAM refresh time. Since test time grows proportionately with the capacity of the memory being tested, increasing cache capacities may limit the applicability of all testing-based approaches.

Ghosh and Lee [10] recently proposed a SmartRefresh technique to reduce refresh power by adding timeout counters in each DRAM row and avoiding unnecessary refreshes for those rows which were recently read or written. However, SmartRefresh is ineffective during the idle mode when the cache is not being accessed, and therefore does not improve idle power.

Another promising approach to increase DRAM refresh times is the use of error-correcting codes (ECC) to dynamically identify and repair bits that fail [8, 15]. This approach sets refresh time irrespective of the weakest bits, using ECC to compensate for failures. With this approach, a stronger error-correcting code, with the ability to correct multiple bits, implies increased refresh time and reduced power. However, strong ECC codes have a high storage and complexity overhead which limit their applicability. In the following two sections, we propose an architectural mechanism that uses strong ECC codes with a low storage and complexity overhead.

3. STRONG ECC ARCHITECTURE

When designing a large eDRAM cache, a designer strives to minimize eDRAM power consumption in the low-power operating modes without penalizing performance in the normal operating mode. To achieve this objective, we propose Hi-ECC, which implements a multi-bit error-correcting code with very small area, latency, and power overheads.

We propose a system with a large (128MB) eDRAM last level cache. In a baseline configuration with no error correction capability, the time between refreshes for such a cache will be 30 microseconds, leading to a significant amount of power consumed even when the processor is idle. Refresh power can be reduced by flushing and power gating the cache during the low-power operating modes. This, however, causes a significant performance penalty when the processor wakes up from the idle mode since it will need to reload the cache, thereby incurring a large number of cold start misses. Alternatively, we can lower refresh power consumption by decreasing the refresh frequency (i.e., increasing time between refreshes). However, as we show in Figure 1, decreasing refresh frequency implies the need to tolerate a higher number of failures for each cache line. Implementing a strong error-correcting code with the capability to correct multiple errors is necessary to achieve this goal.

At the core of Hi-ECC is a strong 5EC6ED (five bit correction, six bit detection) BCH code. We explain implementation details for BCH codes in Section 4. Traditional implementations of a 5EC6ED BCH code would suffer from two key drawbacks: high storage overhead for the code itself, and high decoder complexity and latency. In this section, we describe how Hi-ECC addresses both of these drawbacks. Since our implementation requires architectural changes that would increase dynamic power, we also propose an architectural optimization to lower the impact on the cache dynamic power.

3.1 Reducing Storage Overhead

The storage required for a 5EC6ED code for a 64B cache line is 51 bits, a 10% overhead. Since the cache occupies a large portion of the die area (50% or higher), augmenting the eDRAM cache with 5EC6ED code will significantly increase the die area and cost. In contrast, a single error correcting, double error detecting (SECDED) code for a 64B line requires 11 bits, an overhead of around 2%. Our goal is to implement the 5EC6ED code with the same storage overhead as the SECDED code.

To achieve this goal, we leverage two important properties. First, the size of an ECC code relative to that of the data word diminishes as the size of the data word grows, as we show in Section 4.3. While a SECDED code for a 64B line has an 11-bit overhead (2%), a SECDED code for a 1KB line has a 15-bit overhead (0.18%). Second, the efficacy of a code only diminishes slightly as the size of the data word increases. In Figure 2, we show the failure probability (i.e., the probability that the line will have more failures than those correctible by ECC) for three different codes: SECDED on a 64B line, SECDED on a 1KB line, and double error correcting, triple error detecting code (DECTED) on a 1KB line. At very low refresh times, failure rates of the SECDED 64B line and the SECDED 1KB line are very close. DECTED-1KB (with only a 29-bit overhead, 0.35%) has a lower failure probability than both SECDED codes, except at high refresh times, such as 500us, where it is very close to the SECDED-64B code. By choosing a stronger code and amortizing the cost of the code over larger cache lines, we can improve our ability to tolerate failures with a very small storage overhead.

Our Hi-ECC design implements a 5EC6ED code on each 1KB line (5EC6ED-1KB), requiring an additional 71 bits (0.87% overhead) for each line to store the code. In Figure 3, we compare the refresh time of a 128MB cache augmented with Hi-ECC to the baseline configuration with no error correction capability as well as a configuration using a SECDED code for each 64B sub-block (SECDED-64B). Like previous work that focused on SRAM [33], we assume that the refresh time will be chosen such that no more than 1E-03 (i.e., 1/1000) of the caches will fail. The baseline configuration with no failure mitigation must operate at the baseline refresh time of 30us. Adding a SECDED code allows a 5X increase in refresh time to 150us. Hi-ECC allows us to increase the refresh time to 440us (almost a 15X reduction in refresh frequency compared to the baseline).

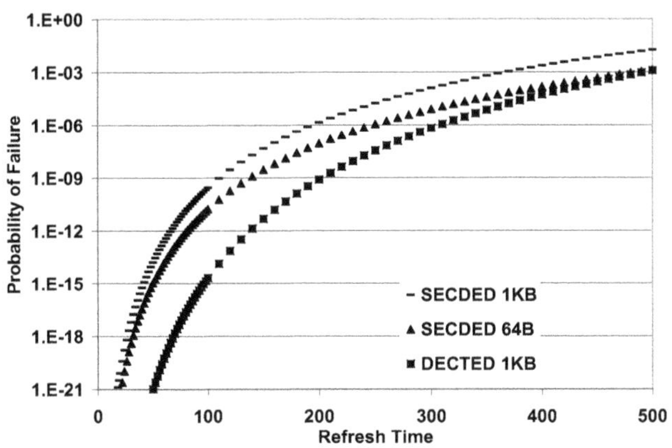

Figure 2. Comparing bit failure probabilities for three code/line size combinations. DECTED on 1KB lines achieves higher refresh time than SECDED on 64B lines

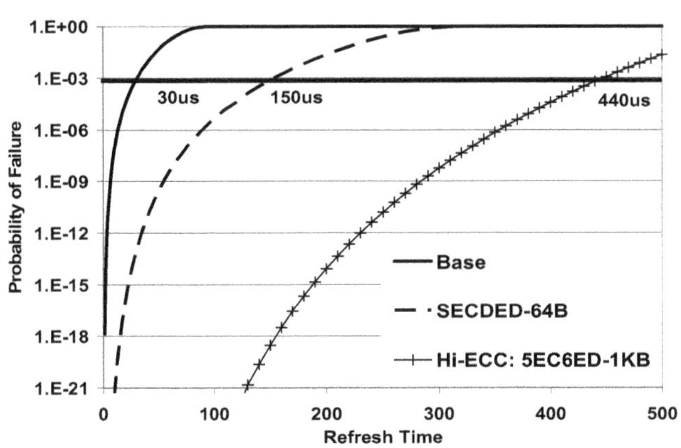

Figure 3. Hi-ECC achieves a higher refresh time than SECDED at the same failure probability

3.2 Reducing Latency

A hardware implementation of a 5EC6ED code is very complex and imposes a long decoding latency penalty, proportional to both the number of error bits corrected and the number of data bits (Section 4.1). If the full strength encoding/decoding was required for every cache access, this could significantly increase cache access latency. However, our proposal leverages the fact that error-prone portions of the cache can be disabled, avoiding the high latency of decode during typical operation.

The Hi-ECC technique relies on a simple, one cycle ECC block to correct a single bit error, and an un-pipelined, high-latency ECC processing block to correct multiple bit failures in a cache line [7, 20]. When a line is read from the cache, a simple decoder generates the syndrome for the line, which includes information on whether it has zero, one, or a higher number of errors (Section 4.2). If the line has zero or one bit failures, the simple ECC decoder can perform the correction in a single cycle. Figure 4 shows a high-level block diagram for Hi-ECC. The block referred to as Quick-ECC contains the syndrome generation logic and the error correction logic for lines with zero or one failures. The Quick-ECC block also classifies lines into two groups based on the syndrome: those that require complex multi-bit error correction and those that have zero or one errors. Lines that require multi-bit error correction are forwarded to a high latency (potentially hundreds of cycles) ECC processing unit that performs error correction using either software or a simple state machine. This allows us to simplify the design at the expense of increased latency for lines with two or more failures. Lines that require one or less error corrections can be immediately corrected and forwarded to the unit requesting the line.

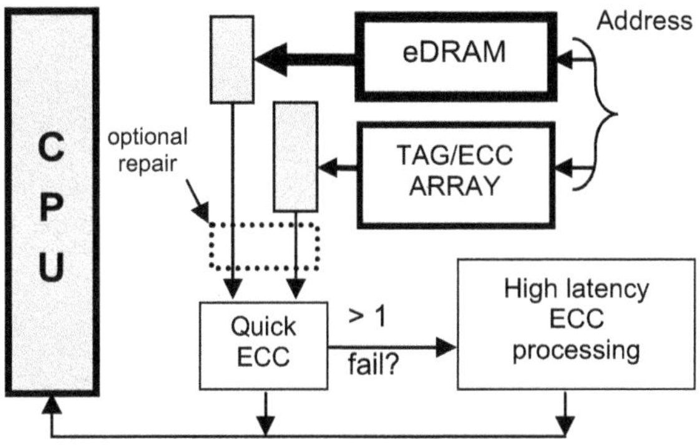

Figure 4: Block diagram for Hi-ECC

The high latency of handling multi-bit failures could significantly reduce performance. To avoid incurring this latency, problematic lines could be completely disabled or a mechanism such as bit-fix [33] could be integrated as shown by the dotted box labeled *optional repair* in Figure 4. This guarantees that the performance penalty of multi-bit decoding is incurred only once, the first time a failure is identified. The frequency of failures plays a role in the disable strategy that we choose. Low multi-bit failure rates motivate a simple approach such as disabling cache lines containing multi-bit failures. On the other hand, cache line disable will result in unacceptable cache capacity loss if multi-bit failure rates are high. In this case, a more complex mechanism such as bit-fix might be used to minimize the capacity lost to disabling.

Figure 5 shows the probability that N (X-axis) or more lines have multi-bit failures for a 128MB eDRAM cache at the refresh time we propose (440us). On average, a 128MB eDRAM will have 750 1KB lines with multi-bit failures that need to be disabled, (0.573% of all lines). As highlighted in the figure, the probability that 900 or more lines (0.7% of all cache lines) will exhibit multi-bit errors is 6.77×10^{-8}. For comparison, Hi-ECC augmented with a simplified version of bit-fix [33] that repairs a single additional bit per cache line requires an additional 13 bits per line (0.13% overhead). However, this 13-bit overhead enables efficient correction of lines with 2-bit errors and reduces the number of lines that need to be disabled. Disabling lines with only 3 or more errors reduces the average number of disabled lines from 750 to 28 (0.02% of all lines), with a probability of 5.95×10^{-8} that 60 or more lines contain three or more errors. Although adding bit-fix reduces wasted cache capacity, the improvement over simple line disable is marginal for the failure rates in our model and doesn't justify the additional latency and complexity. As a result, the rest of this paper will focus on the Hi-ECC approach that relies solely on line disable for lines with multi-bit (two or more) errors.

Due to the implementation of our eDRAM cache, there are restrictions to how many and which lines can be disabled. Since our cache is a 16-way set-associative, and since disabling all lines in a particular cache set could be catastrophic for some workloads, we limit the maximum number of lines that can be disabled in a particular set to 14 of the 16 ways. We also limit the maximum number of failing lines to 900 to quantify overhead. With a refresh time of 440us, the probability of at least one of the lines containing more than 5 failing bits is 6.21×10^{-4} (Figure 3), the probability of more than 900 multi-bit failures (disabled lines) is 6.77×10^{-8} (Figure 5), and the probability of more than 14 multi-bit failures in a single set is 1.12×10^{-61}. This indicates that disabling cache lines with multi-bit failures will have little effect on the overall probability that our cache meets the quality requirements at 440us. The total storage overhead for our approach is 1.58% including a 0.88% overhead for the code and a single per-line disable bit, and a 0.7% overhead for the 900 disabled lines.

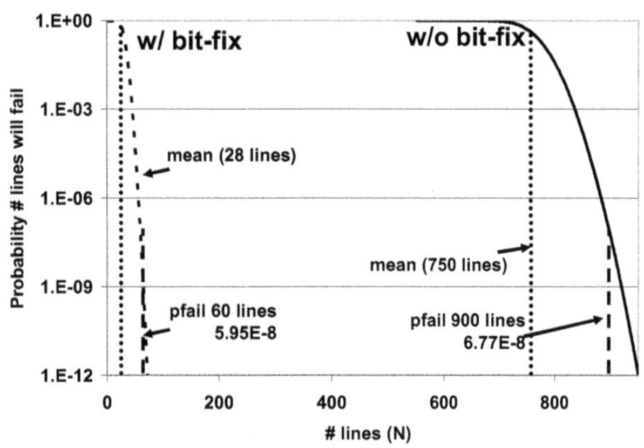

Figure 5. The distribution of failing lines for a 128MB Cache with 1KB lines with (w/) and without (w/o) bit-fix.

3.3 Reducing Dynamic Power

Our Hi-ECC proposal uses larger cache line sizes to reduce the area cost of strong ECC codes. However, larger line sizes introduce some additional challenges. Although 1KB is a reasonable line size for a large embedded memory, our baseline configuration has a much smaller L2 cache with a 64B cache line (referred to as sub-block). Some implementation issues arise when we read from or write to our large L3 eDRAM cache due to the mismatch between its 1KB line size and the 64B sub-blocks used by other caches.

Most writes to the large L3 eDRAM cache will be in the form of smaller 64B sub-blocks generated at lower-level caches or fetched from memory. To modify a 64B sub-block in a 1KB line, we need to perform a read-modify-write operation since we need to compute the ECC code. First, the old 64B block that is being overwritten must be read, along with the ECC code for the entire line. We then use the old data, old ECC, and new data to compute the new ECC for the whole 1KB line. We then write the new 64B sub-block and the new ECC. However, we do not need to read the whole 1KB line to compute the new ECC, as explained later in Section 4.3.

The purpose of most L3 reads will be to provide cache lines for allocation in lower-level caches. Processing any sub-block requires the ECC code to be processed with the entire data word (1KB cache line) that it protects. Since each 64B sub-block must be checked, each reference to a 64B sub-block must be accompanied by a reference to the surrounding 64B sub-blocks. This implies that any L3 read will access all 16 sub-blocks in the 1KB line, as well as the ECC code that they share. As an example, if we need to read eight out of the 16 sub-blocks in one 1KB line, we must read all 16 sub-blocks eight times, for a total of 128 sub-block reads. This large number of additional reads causes a substantial increase in dynamic power consumption and a drastic reduction in the useful bandwidth delivered by the memory.

To address the extra power overhead for L3 reads, we consider the fact that the vast majority of eDRAM failures are retention failures. Since the retention time of our baseline eDRAM is 30us, and each read automatically implies a refresh, we know that retention failures will not occur for 30us after a line has been read. Our proposal leverages this property and also the temporal and spatial locality of the data to minimize the number the superfluous reads. Using a structure we refer to as the *Recently Accessed Lines Table* (RALT), we attempt to track lines that have been referenced in the last 30us.

The first read to a line causes all sub-blocks in the line to be read and checked for failures. The address of the line is then placed in the RALT to indicate that it has recently been checked and will remain free from retention failures for the next 30usec. As long as the address of the line is held in the RALT, any sub-block reads from the line can forgo ECC processing and thus avoid reading the ECC code and other sub-blocks in the line. To operate correctly, the RALT must ensure that none of its entries are more than 30us old. To guarantee this, each 30us is divided into four equal periods (P0, P1, P2, P3). Entries allocated in the RALT during each period are marked with a 2-bit identifier to specify the allocation period. Transitions between periods, P0 to P1 for example, will cause all RALT entries previously allocated in P1 to be invalidated.

Each entry in the RALT consists of the following fields: a line address to identify the line the entry is associated with; a valid bit, a 2-bit period identifier field to indicate in which of the four periods the line was allocated (P0, P1, P2, P3); and a 16-bit parity consisting of one parity bit for each 64B sub-block in the line. The RALT is direct mapped, but supports a CAM invalidate on the 2-bit period field to allow bulk invalidates of RALT entries during period transitions.

Figure 6 compares the implementation of the baseline L3 protection scheme (top) with that of Hi-ECC (bottom). The baseline scheme uses a separate tag for each 1KB line and a separate SECDED code for each 64B sub-block. To read a 64B block, first the ECC and the block itself are read, then the ECC is processed. In our Hi-ECC technique, the first time a sub-block is read the entire ECC code is read along with each sub-block in the 1KB line to allow ECC processing for a single 64B block. We update the RALT with the line address of the referenced line, a 2-bit period ID, and a single parity bit for each sub-block. After the first hit to a line, future accesses to the same 1KB line within the next 30us should hit in the RALT. Figure 7 demonstrates a RALT hit. In most cases, only the requested 64B sub-block is read. Parity for the 64B sub-block is computed and compared to the parity stored in the RALT. If the parity matches, we infer that sub-block is valid and forward it to the requesting cache or processor. A parity mismatch is treated as a RALT miss where the whole 1KB line needs to be read.

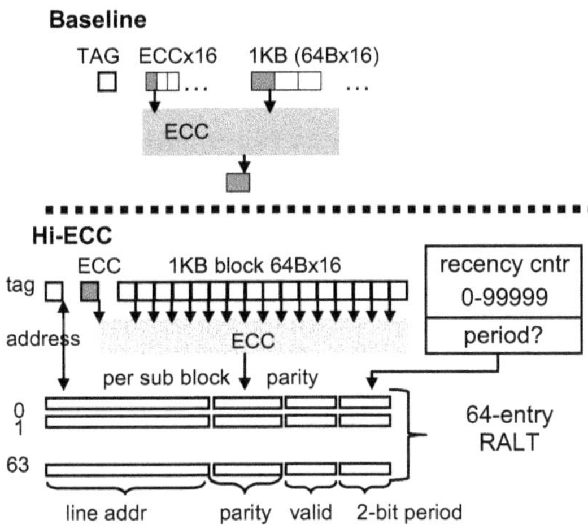

Figure 6: Initial read and update of the Recently Accessed Lines Table (RALT).

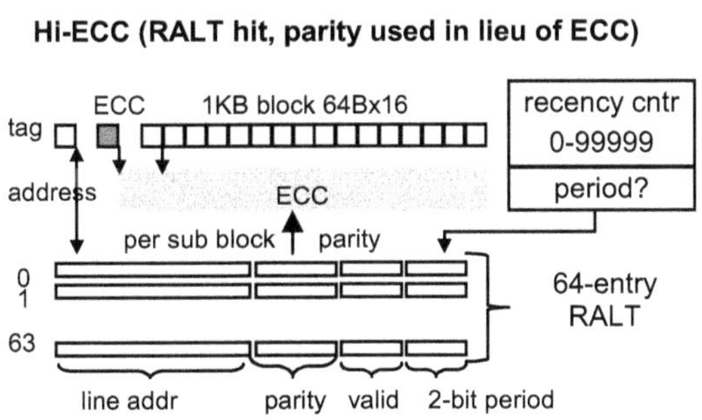

Figure 7: Hits to the Recently Accessed Lines Table (RALT)

3.4 Summary

In this section, we described our L3 cache architecture supporting a strong ECC code. We use a 5-bit correcting code over a 1KB cache line to minimize the area overhead. We check for zero or one-bit errors in the common case to minimize latency and complexity. We use an additional structure, the RALT, to track recently accessed lines so that we avoid reading the whole 1KB line on every cache read, thus minimizing dynamic power. This design allows us to reduce the cache refresh power with minimal area and performance overhead.

4. MULTI-BIT ECC FOR EDRAM CACHES

Error-correcting codes (ECC) have been used extensively in memory and storage devices to tolerate both soft and hard errors. On-chip caches and memory chips typically use simple and fast ECC such as SECDED (single error correction, double error detection) Hamming codes [19], whereas slower devices such as flash memories use multi-bit ECCs with strong error correcting capabilities (e.g., Reed-Solomon codes [19]). The higher decoding latencies of the strong ECC mechanisms do not pose a problem for mass storage devices, because the encoding/decoding latency is insignificant as compared to intrinsic device access time. However, as a result of technology scaling, the on-chip memory arrays are becoming more susceptible to multi-bit errors, and strong ECC codes are becoming desirable for these fast memories as well.

Besides the latency overhead, the storage overhead of more ECC check bits is another obstacle to using strong codes for on-chip caches. In [34], for example, the authors propose to reduce the cost of storing error-correcting codes for the last level cache (LLC) by partitioning the code between the LLC and memory. Many previously proposed techniques have exploited the tradeoff between code complexity and check bit overhead to mitigate the higher latency of multi-bit ECC. These techniques combine simple ECC with bit rearrangement mechanisms such as bit interleaving [28], address skewing [12] or 2-dimensional product codes [5, 17], to correct certain multi-bit error patterns by dispersing multi-bit errors into multiple single-bit errors. While these techniques enable fast correction, they require more check bits and provide insufficient protection from random multi-bit errors [28].

The Hi-ECC architecture, highlighted in the previous section, is a practical, low-latency, low-cost, multi-bit error-correcting system that can compensate for high failure rates in eDRAM caches. Hi-ECC implements a strong BCH code with the ability to correct 5 and detect 6 errors (5EC6ED). In the remainder of this section, we will introduce the multi-bit BCH algorithm, analyze its circuit complexity and latency, and explain in more detail how our selective correction technique mitigates both the high latency and high cost of strong ECC codes.

4.1 Multi-bit BCH Code

BCH codes are a large class of multi-bit error-correcting codes which can correct both highly concentrated and widely scattered errors [28]. In general, each BCH code is a linear block code defined over a finite Galois Field GF(2^m) with a generator polynomial, where 2^m represents the maximum number of code word bits.

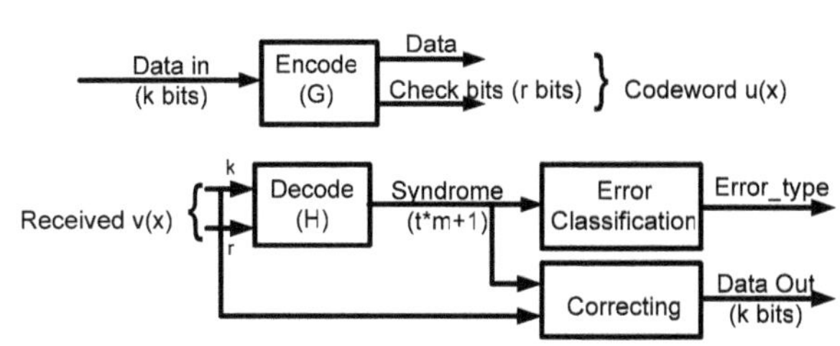

Figure 8. Overview of a BCH-based error-correcting scheme

Figure 8 shows a high-level block diagram for BCH error correction. The ECC logic includes two main components, (i) ECC encoding and (ii) ECC decoding.

(i) ECC encoding: The encoding logic takes the *k*-bit input data word *d* and uses a pre-defined encoder matrix *G* to generate the corresponding code word *u* ($u = d \times G$). Since BCH is a systematic code, the original *k*-bit data is retained in the code word, and is followed by *r* check bits.

(ii) ECC decoding: The decoding logic detects and corrects any errors in the stored code word to recover the original value of data. The decoding logic can be further divided into three components, (a) syndrome generation, (b) error classification and (c) error correction.

(a) Syndrome generation: Let v be a code word with error e, such that $v = u + e$. The decoder first computes a syndrome S by multiplying v with the transpose of a pre-defined H-matrix ($S = v \times H^T$). The detailed derivation of H-matrix is beyond the scope of this paper and can be found in [13, 28]. However, it is relevant to mention that the G and H matrices are constructed in such a way that $G \times H^T = 0$. The general form of H-matrix is as follows:

$$H = \begin{bmatrix} Parity \\ H_1 \\ H_3 \\ \cdots \\ H_{2t-1} \end{bmatrix} = \begin{bmatrix} 1 & 1 & 1 & 1 & \cdots & 1 \\ 1 & \alpha & \alpha^2 & \alpha^3 & \cdots & \alpha^{(n-1)} \\ 1 & \alpha^3 & \alpha^6 & \alpha^9 & \cdots & \alpha^{3(n-1)} \\ \vdots & \vdots & \vdots & \vdots & \cdots & \vdots \\ 1 & \alpha^{(2t-1)} & \alpha^{2*(2t-1)} & \alpha^{3*(2t-1)} & \cdots & \alpha^{(2t-1)*(n-1)} \end{bmatrix} \quad (1)$$

In the finite field GF(2^m), each element α^i can be represented as a polynomial of α with a degree less than m, or simply a vector with m binary coefficients of the polynomial. Therefore, the H matrix can be expanded into a binary matrix with (t*m+1) rows, where t is the maximum number of errors that the code can correct. Since $S = v \times H^T$, S also has t*m+1 bits, which can be divided into multiple components [$Parity$, S_1, S_3, ..., S_{2t-1}].

(b) Error classification: The error classification logic uses the syndrome S to detect if the code word has any errors. Since:

$$S = v \times H^T = (u+e) \times H^T = (d \times G + e) \times H^T = e \times H^T \quad (2)$$

Therefore, in case of zero errors, $S = 0$ and the following equation would hold true:

$$Parity = S_1 = S_3 = \ldots = S_{2t-1} = 0 \quad (3)$$

(c) Error correction: If the above equation is not satisfied then the error correction logic uses the syndrome to pinpoint the locations of corrupted bits. Let the error locations in e be denoted as [j_1, j_2, ... , j_t], then each syndrome component S_i can be specified as:

$$S_i = \alpha^{j1*i} + \alpha^{j2*i} + \ldots + \alpha^{jt*i} \quad (4)$$

The correction logic implements the following three steps:

Step 1: Determine the coefficients of error location polynomial $\sigma(x)$, where $\sigma(x)$ is defined such that the roots of $\sigma(x)$ are given by the inverse of error elements α^{j1}, α^{j2}, ... , α^{jt} respectively,

$$\sigma(x) = 1 + \sigma_1 x + \ldots + \sigma_t x^t = (1 - \alpha^{j1}x)(1 - \alpha^{j2}x)\ldots(1 - \alpha^{jt}x) \quad (5)$$

Step 2: Solve the roots of $\sigma(x)$, which are the error locations. When polynomial $\sigma(x)$ is determined, each field element α^j is substituted into the polynomial. Those elements which make the polynomial equal to zero are the roots.

Step 3: Calculate the correct value for data bits. This is done by simply flipping the bits at error locations.

Previous studies have shown that the decoding procedure of multi-bit BCH is tedious [3, 20] and its complexity grows rapidly with the increase in the number of bit corrections. Error correction is the most complex and time consuming component [31]. Step 1 of error correction is based on a t-step iterative algorithm, where each iteration involves a Galois Field inversion, which alone takes $2m$ operations [4]. The implementation of Step 2 can either take n-cycles with one circuit, or a single cycle with n parallel circuits [7]. Either way, the base circuit is O(t*m^2). Overall, both the decoding latency and area complexity is proportional to (t*m) [31]. Next, we describe a mechanism for lowering the latency and complexity in the common case of zero or one-bit errors.

4.2. Reducing Decoder Overhead

The latency analysis in the previous subsection is based on the worst case scenario of correctable errors, i.e. t-bit errors. However, we observe that for the case of zero or one errors, the detection and correction logic can be a lot simpler and faster:

(i) Detection of zero error: No errors in the code word lead to a syndrome value of zero, as shown in equation (3). This case can be detected by performing a logical OR of all the syndrome bits. This requires $ceil(log_2 tm)$ 2-input gate delays.

(ii) Single-bit error detection and correction: In the case of a single-bit error, the syndrome exactly matches the H-matrix column that corresponds to the error bit. Therefore, one can detect and pinpoint a single-bit error by comparing each column of the H-matrix with the syndrome. Notice that this correction is significantly faster than the general case of t-bit correction (with $t > 1$) because it does not require Step 1 and most of the Step 2 of the error correction logic. In fact, we do not even need to match all the syndrome components with entire H-matrix columns. We just need to compare S_1 to each column in H_1 (defined in equation (1)) and verify that the following equation is satisfied:

$$[(parity{=}1) \,\&\, (S_1^{\,3} == S_3) \,\&\, (S_1^{\,5} == S_5) \,\&\ldots\&\, (S_1^{\,2t-1} == S_{2t-1})] == 1 \quad (6)$$

To minimize latency, we assume that the comparison of S_1 with H_1 and all the comparisons in equation (6) can proceed in parallel.

Based on the above observations, we propose an ECC decoding mechanism that can correct multi-bit errors with a low latency overhead in the common case. The main idea is to differentiate the slow decoding process of multi-bit errors from the case of zero or one errors. In our proposed Hi-ECC mechanism, fast hardware correction is used for the common case of zero or one errors, whereas software or state machine-based correction is used to deal with multi-bit errors, as highlighted in Section 3.2.

4.3 Reducing ECC Storage Overhead

One of the main drawbacks of multi-bit ECC is that correcting more errors requires higher redundancy, which leads to high check bit overhead. To correct t-bit errors in k-bit input data, a BCH code typically requires $r = t * ceil(log_2 k) + 1$ check bits [28]. In order to reduce the check bit overhead, we make the observation that due to the logarithmic relationship between r and k, the number of check bits increases much slower than the size of data. Therefore, we can reduce the ECC check bit overhead by increasing the size of data word, as explained in Section 3.1.

Figure 9 shows the check bit overhead for three types of BCH codes correcting different data sizes. For each data size, we show the total number of check bits (solid lines) and code percentage overhead (dashed lines). The figure shows that the check bit overhead drops significantly with the increase in data size. For example, for 5EC6ED code based on 16B data word, almost 25% of the code word is ECC. However, for a 4KB word, the number of check bits doubles, but the overhead reduces to 0.3%.

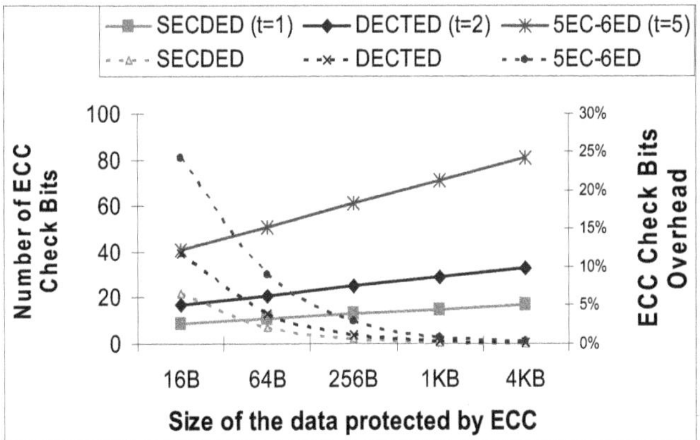

Figure 9. Comparing the storage overhead for check bits for different error-correcting codes. Solid lines represent #check bits (left axis), and dashed lines represent the percentage overhead (right axis).

Using large cache lines introduces another potential problem: writes to sub-blocks within the cache-line may require the entire line to be read every time to regenerate the ECC bits. Fortunately, as a linear code, BCH inherits the additive property of linear systems, which ensures that ECC check bits can be updated using only the information of the modified chunk of data. Let the data word d (representing a cache line) be divided into multiple chunks $[d_{i-1},d_{i-2},\ldots,d_0]$. The G matrix used in ECC encoding can be divided into two parts as $G=[I_k, P]$, where P is the generator for ECC check word C, i.e., $C = d \times P$. If the jth chunk of data d_j is written with a new value d_{j_new}, then the new ECC would be:

$$C_{new} = d_{new} \times P = (d + [0,\ldots,(d_{j\_old} + d_{j\_new}),\ldots,0]) \times P \qquad (7)$$
$$= C + [0,\ldots,(d_{j\_old} + d_{j\_new}),\ldots,0] \times P$$

The above equation shows that the generation of new check bits requires only the old value of check bits, and the old and new values of the sub-block being modified.

4.4 Logic Overhead

In Section 3, we show that the area overhead for storing the multi-bit error-correcting code is 71 bits for every 1KB line. We estimate the total gate count for the error detection and correction based on Strukov's analysis [31]. Each 64B L3 read requires about 290 XOR gates for each of the 71 check bits for a total of 21k XOR gates. The ECC encoding process requires another 21k XOR gates. The one-cycle single error correction logic consists of three components: 1) error detection (70 ORs), 2) error classification (1k XORs and 1k ANDs) and 3) 1-bit correction (7k XORs and 7k ORs). The logic to handle multi-bit errors integrates the BM algorithm [20] with Chien's search algorithm [7] and uses ~ 47 registers, 28 GF additions, 28 GF multiplications and tens of logic gates, equivalent to fewer than 14k XOR gates but needs many cycles to perform the correction. Overall, the logic uses fewer than 100k XOR gates. Assuming each gate is equal in area to six eDRAM cells, the total logic overhead is similar to that of 600k bits, or less than 0.1% of the total area for a 128MB cache.

5. EVALUATION

In this section we evaluate the impact of our Hi-ECC proposal on cache power and system performance. We demonstrate that Hi-ECC has almost no impact on performance, while significantly reducing refresh and total power. We first describe our simulation framework, benchmarks, and methodology. We then compare the performance and power of Hi-ECC and other alternatives.

5.1 Simulation Framework

Baseline simulation configuration. We use a cycle-accurate, execution-driven simulator running IA32 binaries. The simulator is micro-operation (uOp) based, executes both user and kernel instructions, and models a detailed memory subsystem. As a baseline, we model an out-of-order superscalar processor that is similar to the Intel® Core™ i7 processor with the addition of a large 128MB eDRAM last-level (L3) cache instead of a traditional SRAM cache. Our memory system includes a 32KB, 8-way set-associative L1 instruction cache, a 32KB, 8-way set-associative L1 data cache, a 256KB, 16-way set-associative unified L2 cache, and a 128MB eDRAM 16-way set-associative L3 (last-level) cache. L1 and L2 caches use 64-byte lines, and the baseline L3 cache uses 1KB lines with no error correction capability. Our processor runs at 2 GHz, and we assume a 40-cycle latency for an L3 hit.

Benchmarks. In our experiments, we simulate nine categories of benchmarks. For each individual benchmark, we select multiple sample traces that well represent the benchmark behavior. Table 1 lists the number of traces and example benchmarks included in each category. We use instructions per cycle (IPC) as the performance metric. We calculate IPC of each category as the geometric mean of IPCs for all traces within that category. We normalize the IPC of each category to the baseline to show relative performance. We use activity factors for different cache structures as inputs to our power model to estimate power consumption. When modeling power consumption, we model a 16-core system running multi-program benchmarks.

Simulated configurations. We model four different configurations, starting with the baseline configuration (BASE) with 1KB L3 cache lines and a 40-cycle L3 hit latency. The second configuration (SD) models an eDRAM augmented with a single error correcting, double error detecting (SECDED) ECC code, and has an additional 2-cycle latency for each L3 hit to model ECC checking, i.e., a 42-cycle total latency. The last two configurations are variations on our Hi-ECC mechanism with and without a RALT. Recall that Hi-ECC uses the multi-bit ECC code to identify and remove lines with high failure rates. Consequently, the latency of multi-bit error processing only impacts processor initialization latency and doesn't impact runtime performance. Furthermore, the 1% reduction in cache capacity (line disable) has a negligible performance impact. As a result, in our performance analysis we focus on the impact of increased L3 latency introduced by Hi-ECC. The Hi-ECC configuration without the RALT (HE) suffers a small penalty for each write (since it must be preceded with a read) and large 32-cycle additional latency penalty for each read (since each 2-cycle 64B read is accompanied by reads to the other 15 sub-blocks in the line to allow for ECC processing). The Hi-ECC including the RALT (HER) configuration attempts to avoid the additional read latency penalty. With the RALT, the 32-cycle additional penalty typically only applies to the first read in a 1KB line. Subsequent references to other sub-blocks in the line that hit in the RALT will check the sub-block against the parity stored in the RALT. We assume the RALT will be accessed in parallel to the eDRAM to minimize additional latency, but we model the parity check as additional 2-cycle penalty, similar to the SECDED ECC check.

Table 1. Evaluation benchmarks

Category	# traces	Example benchmarks
Digital home (DH)	46	H264 decode/encode, flash
SPECINT2006 (ISPEC)	12	www.spec.org
SPECFP2006 (FSPEC)	22	www.spec.org
Games (GM)	10	Doom, quake
Multimedia (MM)	49	Photoshop, raytracer
Office (OFF)	38	Spreadsheet/word processing
Productivity (PROD)	34	File compression, Winstone
Server (SERV)	15	SQL, TPC-C
Workstation (WS)	24	CAD, bioinformatics
ALL	250	

5.2 Results

Performance. We compare the performance of four configurations with different L3 hit latencies across all nine benchmark categories. On average, the SECDED configuration loses less than 0.1% of its performance compared to our baseline with no error correction. With no RALT, Hi-ECC configuration loses 0.48% of the baseline performance. When we add a RALT with 64 entries, performance loss goes down to 0.35%. With a 512-entry RALT, performance loss is below 0.1%, the same as that of the SECDED configuration. We do not show detailed performance results since they are almost indistinguishable from the baseline. These results show that Hi-ECC can achieve performance comparable to the baseline configuration.

Power modeling. We compared the refresh power, dynamic power, and total power for our four configurations. We used an analytical model for power that uses activity factors from our simulation experiments (e.g., number of L3 reads/writes and number of RALT hits/misses per second) to obtain different power components. We assume a 16-core system for power modeling, since the dynamic power consumed by a single core is almost insignificant compared to refresh power. We provide more details on our power model in Appendix A. We estimate that the baseline refresh power is approximately 926mW. We also estimate that the dynamic power is 421mW per L3 sub-block read, 425mW per L3 sub-block write, 22mW per RALT access, and 5152mW for reading an entire 1K line with 16 sub-blocks.

Refresh power. We scale the refresh time from 30us for the baseline to 150us and 440us for SECDED and Hi-ECC, respectively. This scaling leads to a similar scaling for refresh power, from 926mW for the baseline to 185 and 63mW for SECDED and Hi-ECC, respectively. SECDED achieves a 5X reduction in refresh power compared to our baseline, and Hi-ECC achieves almost a 3X reduction compared to SECDED (almost 15X compared to the baseline).

Dynamic power. The additional activities due to extra reads, writes and ECC checks cause the dynamic power of the SECDED and Hi-ECC configurations to increase. Figure 10 shows the refresh power, dynamic (read and write) power, and total power across all benchmark categories for our four configurations. The figure demonstrates that SECDED has a marginal increase in dynamic power over our baseline due to ECC checks. However, the Hi-ECC configuration with no RALT (HE) incurs a significant increase in dynamic power due to reading the whole 1K cache line with 16 sub-blocks on every L3 read. If only refresh power is considered, Hi-ECC will consume 34% of the power consumed by SECDED. However, the increase in Hi-ECC's dynamic power pushes its total power to 58% of SECDED's total power. On the other hand, using a 512-entry RALT (HER) decreases the number of 1KB line accesses significantly, and the total power for Hi-ECC with RALT becomes 39% of the total power of SECDED (including the extra power due to RALT accesses).

6. CONCLUSIONS

In this paper, we have argued that a significant portion of idle power in future systems will be used to refresh eDRAM. To address this, we have developed Hi-ECC, a practical system for tolerating refresh-related failures in eDRAM-based caches. Hi-ECC reduces the cache refresh power by 93%, compared to an eDRAM with no error correction, and by 66% compared to an eDRAM with a single error-correcting code (SECDED). We accomplish this with only 2% storage overhead and without the loss of any cache state.

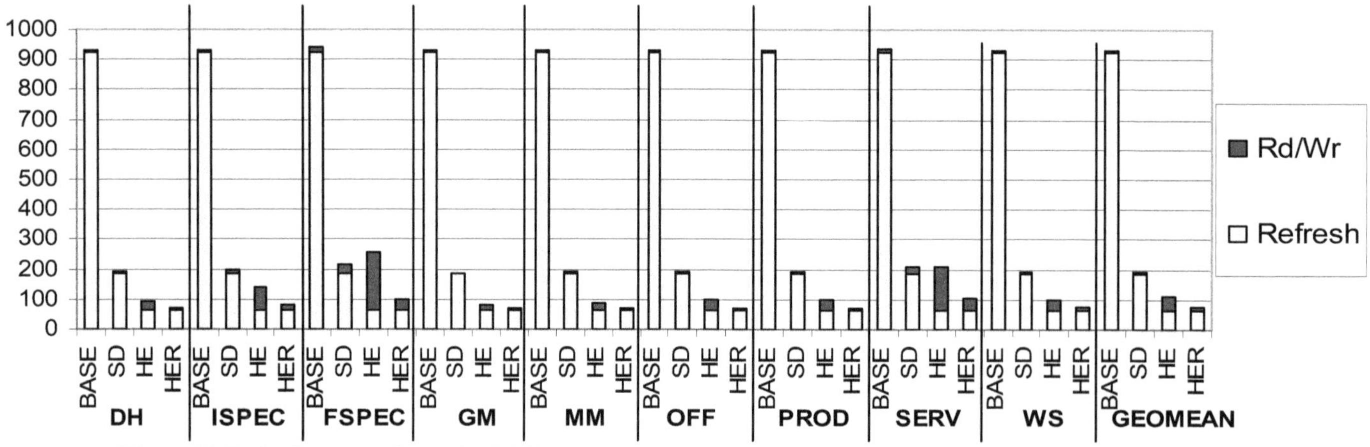

Figure 10. Refresh power, dynamic (Rd/Wr) power and total power in mW for different benchmark categories across all four configurations on 16 cores.

By employing a strong error-correcting code and augmenting it with other failure mitigation mechanisms, such as bit-fix, Hi-ECC offers a highly scalable solution for addressing very high failure rates. Furthermore, although this paper's evaluation focuses on eDRAM, elements of Hi-ECC are applicable to many different memory technologies and failure types, including Vccmin related SRAM failures. In addition, Hi-ECC's reliance on strong error-correcting codes instead of memory tests to identify bit failures makes it applicable to high capacity memories, such as bulk DRAM and phase change memories.

7. ACKNOWLEDGMENTS

We would like to thank Ilya Wagner, Greg Taylor and the anonymous reviewers for their feedback and suggestions.

8. REFERENCES

[1] A. Agarwal, et al., "Process variation in embedded memories: failure analysis and variation aware architecture," *IEEE Journal of Solid-state Circuits*, vol. 40, no. 9, pp. 1804-1814, Sep., 2005.

[2] J. Barth, et al., "A 500 MHz random cycle, 1.5 ns latency, SOI embedded DRAM macro featuring a three-transistor micro sense amplifier", *IEEE Journal of Solid State Circuits*, vol. 43, no. 1, pp. 86–95, Jan. 2008.

[3] E. R. Berlekamp, Algebraic coding theory, New York: McGraw-Hill, chapter 7, 1968.

[4] H. Brunner, A. Curiger and M. Hofstetter, "On computing multiplicative inverses in GF(2^m)," *IEEE Transactions on Computers*, vol. 42, pp. 1010-1015, Aug. 1993.

[5] H. O. Burton and E. J.Weldon, Jr., "Cyclic product codes," *IEEE Transactions on Information Theory*, vol. 11, no. 3, pp. 433–439, Jul. 1965.

[6] J. Chang, et al., "The 65-nm 16-MB shared on-die L3 cache for the dual-Core Intel® Xeon processor 7100 series," *IEEE Journal of Solid-state Circuits*, vol. 42, no. 4, pp. 846-852, Apr. 2007.

[7] R. T. Chien, "Cyclic decoding procedures for Bose-Chaudhuri-Hocquenghem codes," *IEEE Transactions on Information Theory*, vol. 10, no. 4, pp. 357-363, Oct. 1964.

[8] P. Emma, W. Reohr and M. Meterelliyoz, "Rethinking refresh: Increasing availability and reducing power in DRAM for cache applications," *IEEE Micro*, vol. 28, no. 6, pp. 47-56, Nov 2008.

[9] V. George, "45nm next generation Intel Core microarchitecture (Penryn)," Hot Chips 19, Stanford, CA, Aug. 2007.

[10] M. Ghosh and H. Lee, "Smart refresh: An enhanced memory controller design for reducing energy in conventional and 3D die-stacked DRAMs," in *Proceedings of the 40th International Symposium on Microarchitecture*, pp. 134–145, Dec. 2007.

[11] T. Hamamoto, S. Sugiura and S, Sawada, "On the retention time distribution of dynamic random access memory (DRAM)," *IEEE Transactions on Electron Devices*, vol. 45, no. 6, pp. 1300-1309, Jun. 1998.

[12] Mu Y. Hsiao, Douglas C. Bossen, "Orthogonal latin square configuration for LSI memory yield and reliability enhancement," *IEEE Transactions on Computers*, vol. 24, no. 5, pp. 512-516, May 1975.

[13] H. Imai and Y. Kamiyanagi, "A construction method for double error correcting codes for application to main memories," *Transactions of the IECE Japan*, vol. J60-D, pp. 861-868, Oct. 1977.

[14] R. Kalla, "Power7: IBM's next generation POWER microprocessor," Presentation at Hot Chips 21, Stanford, CA, Aug. 2009.

[15] J. Kim and M. Papaefthymiou, "Dynamic memory design for low data-retention power," in *Proceedings of the 10th International Workshop on Integrated Circuit Design, Power and Timing Modeling, Optimization and Simulation*, pp. 207-216, Sep. 2000.

[16] J. Kim, M. Papaefthymiou, "Block-based multiperiod dynamic memory design for low data-retention power," *IEEE Transactions on Very Large Scale Integration (VLSI) Systems*, vol. 11, no. 6, pp.1006-1018, Dec. 2003.

[17] J. Kim, et al., "Multi-bit error tolerant caches using two-dimensional error coding," in *Proceedings of the 40th Annual International Symposium on Microarchitecture (MICRO)*, pp. 197-209, Dec. 2007.

[18] W. Kong, et al., "Analysis of retention time distribution of embedded DRAM - A new method to characterize across-chip threshold voltage variation," in *Proceedings of IEEE International Test Conference (ITC 2008)*, pp. 1-7, Oct. 2008.

[19] S. Lin and D. J. Costello. Error control coding, Second Edition. Prentice-Hall, Inc., Upper Saddle River, NJ, USA, 2004.

[20] J. L. Massey, "Step-by-step decoding of the Bose-Chaudhuri-Hocquenghem codes," *IEEE Transactions on Information Theory*, vol. 11, no. 4, pp. 580–585, Apr. 1965.

[21] R. Matick and S. Schuster, "Logic based eDRAM: origins and rationale for use," *IBM Journal of Research and Development*, vol. 49, no. 1, pp. 145 – 165, Jan. 2005.

[22] Micron Technology, Inc. "TN-41-01 : Calculating memory system power for DDR3", http://download.micron.com/pdf/technotes/ddr3/TN41_01DDR3%20Power.pdf

[23] K.Mistry, et al., "A 45nm logic technology with high-k+metal gate transistors, strained silicon, 9 Cu interconnect layers, 193nm dry patterning, and 100% Pb-free packaging," in *Proceedings of IEDM* 2007, pp. 247–250, Dec. 2007.

[24] A. Naveh, et al., "Power and thermal management in the Intel® Core® Duo processor," *Intel Technology Journal*, vol. 10, no. 2, May 2006.

[25] S. Natarajan, et.al., "A 32nm logic technology featuring 2nd-generation high-k + metal-gate transistors, enhanced channel strain and 0.171um^2 SRAM cell size in a 291Mb array," in *Proceedings of IEDM* 2008, pp. 1-3, Dec. 2008.

[26] T. Ohsawa, K. Kai and K. Murakami, "Optimizing the DRAM refresh count for merged DRAM/Logic LSIs," in *Proceedings of the 1998 International Symposium on Low Power Electronics and Design (ISLPED)*, pp. 82-87, August 1998.

[27] S. Ozdemir, et. al., "Yield-aware cache architectures," in *Proceedings of the 39th Annual International Symposium on Microarchitecture (MICRO)*, pp. 15-25, Dec, 2006.

[28] T. Rao, E. Fujiwara, "Error-control coding for computer systems," Prentice-Hall, Inc., Upper Saddle River, NJ, 1989.

[29] D. Roberts, N. Kim and T. Mudge, "On-chip cache device scaling limits and effective fault repair techniques in future nanoscale technology," in *Proceedings of 10th Euromicro Conference on Digital System Design Architectures, Methods and Tools*, pp. 570-578, Aug. 2007.

[30] D. Somasekhar, et al., "Multi-phase 1GHz voltage doubler charge-pump in 32nm logic process," in *Proceedings of 2009 Symposium on VLSI Circuits*, pp. 196-197, Jun. 2009.

[31] D. Strukov, "The area and latency tradeoffs of binary bit-parallel BCH decoders for prospective nanoelectronic memories," in *Proceedings of 2006 Asilomar Conference on Signals Systems and Computers*, pp. 1183-1187, Oct. 2006.

[32] R. Venkatesan, S. Herr and E. Rotenberg, "Retention aware placement in DRAM (RAPID): Software methods for quasi-non-volatile DRAM," in *Proceedings of 12th International Symposium on High Performance Computer Architecture (HPCA)*, pp. 155-165, Feb. 2006.

[33] C.Wilkerson, et. al, "Trading off cache capacity for reliability to enable low voltage operation," in *Proceedings of 35th International Symposium on Computer Architecture (ISCA-35)*, pp. 203-214, Jun. 2008.

[34] D. H. Yoon and M. Erez, "Memory Mapped ECC: Low-Cost Error Protection for Last Level Caches", in *Proceedings of the 36th International Symposium on Computer Architecture (ISCA-36)*, pp. 116-127, June, 2009.

APPENDIX A: EDRAM POWER MODEL

Figure 11 shows the topology of the bit-cell and the array organization for the 128MB cache used in this study. This cache is organized with 128x32 sub-arrays. Each sub-array is made out of 67 I/O columns. A pair of "data-in data-out" (16 cells) is referred to as an I/O column. Each I/O column has 16 columns and 256 rows. This array organization allows data to move out of the cache in multiple cycles. To deliver the 64B data word, 8 sub-arrays are activated at a time.

In order to account for all capacitance for power calculation, we need to estimate the silicon area. Area is calculated with a conservative cell size of $16F^2$ where F is ½ of the minimum pitch of the process technology cell. Note that [2] quotes cell sizes smaller than this study. Table 2 illustrates the scaling of the technology parameters to a projected 22nm node. VccE is the voltage of the stored cell, while Vcc is the supply voltage for logic circuits. Array area calculation is performed based on a sense-amplifier structure efficiency loss of 35%, a wordline decoder loss of 25% and an overall assembly loss of 90% in each of the X and Y dimensions.

In calculating the power consumption, we use the I/O column structure and the key technology metrics depicted in Figure 12. Note that the voltage swing on the word line is higher (1.8 V [2]) and is assumed to be generated by a 60% efficient charge pump [30]. Other design parameters include the usage of a small-signal sense amplifier with half-Vcc precharge, I/O column structure and a design with strobed data in the sense-amplifier which is pulled out using column selection (YSEL devices) to a final CMOS driver. Dynamic power of the nets is estimated by first computing an effective switched capacitance *Cdyn* and then putting it into the equation: $Pdyn = ActivityFactor \times Cdyn \times Vcc2 \times F$. *Cdyn* accounts for global nets, clock circuit and repeater buffers. With this organization refreshing 8 sub-arrays requires only 256 refresh cycles each *Trc* clocks long and occurs at the retention rate. Thus, the amortized refresh power for 128MB over a retention period of 30 microseconds is 926 mW.

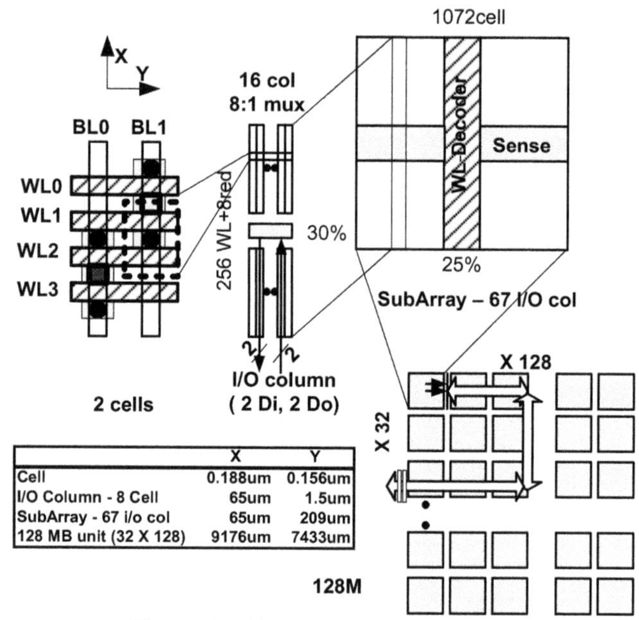

Figure 11. 32MB eDRAM organization

Node	Met Pitch	BL Pitch	Gate Pitch	Min Device	Sense Dev	VccE	Vcc
45 nm	160nm	320nm	192nm	135nm	3600nm	1V	1V
32 nm	112nm	224nm	134nm	96nm	2560nm	1V	0.9V
22 nm projected	**78nm**	**156nm**	**94nm**	**66nm**	**1760nm**	**1V**	**0.8V**

Table 2. Process technology parameters [23, 25]

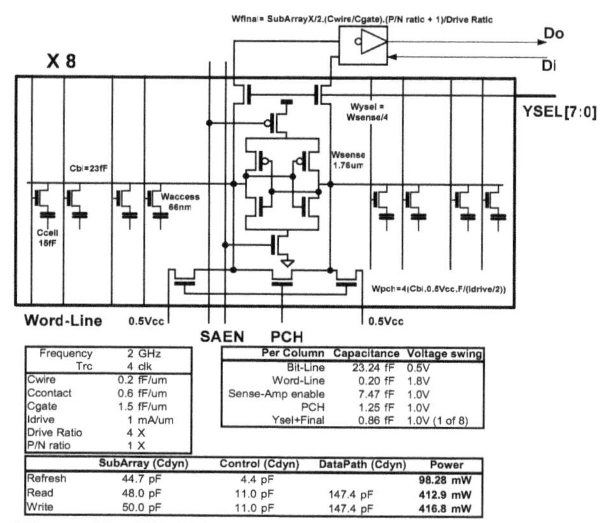

Figure 12. I/O Column structure and technology metrics for power modeling

An Intra-Chip Free-Space Optical Interconnect*

Jing Xue, Alok Garg, Berkehan Ciftcioglu, Jianyun Hu, Shang Wang
Ioannis Savidis, Manish Jain†, Rebecca Berman†, Peng Liu
Michael Huang, Hui Wu, Eby Friedman, Gary Wicks†, Duncan Moore†
Dept. Electrical & Computer Engineering and †Institute of Optics
University of Rochester, Rochester, NY 14627, USA

ABSTRACT

Continued device scaling enables microprocessors and other systems-on-chip (SoCs) to increase their performance, functionality, and hence, complexity. Simultaneously, relentless scaling, if uncompensated, degrades the performance and signal integrity of on-chip metal interconnects. These systems have therefore become increasingly communications-limited. The communications-centric nature of future high performance computing devices demands a fundamental change in intra- and inter-chip interconnect technologies.

Optical interconnect is a promising long term solution. However, while significant progress in optical *signaling* has been made in recent years, *networking* issues for on-chip optical interconnect still require much investigation. Taking the underlying optical signaling systems as a drop-in replacement for conventional electrical signaling while maintaining conventional packet-switching architectures is unlikely to realize the full potential of optical interconnects. In this paper, we propose and study the design of a fully distributed interconnect architecture based on free-space optics. The architecture leverages a suite of newly-developed or emerging devices, circuits, and optics technologies. The interconnect avoids packet relay altogether, offers an ultra-low transmission latency and scalable bandwidth, and provides fresh opportunities for coherency substrate designs and optimizations.

Categories and Subject Descriptors: C.1.4 [Processor Architecture]: Parallel Architecture C.2.1 [Computer-communication Networks]: Network Architecture and Design

General Terms: Design, Performance

Keywords: 3D, intra-chip, free-space optical interconnect

1. INTRODUCTION

Continued device scaling enables microprocessors and other systems-on-chip (SoC) to increase their performance, functionality, and complexity, which is evident in the recent technology trend toward multi-core systems [1]. Simultaneously, uncompensated scaling degrades wire performance and signal integrity. Conventional copper interconnects are facing significant challenges to meet the increasingly stringent design requirements on bandwidth, delay, power, and noise, especially for on-chip global interconnects.

Optical interconnects have fundamental advantages compared to metal interconnects, particularly in delay and potential bandwidth [2,3], and significant progress in the technology has been made in recent years [4]. However, while *signaling* issues have received a lot of attention [5], *networking* issues in the general-purpose domain remain under-explored. The latter cannot be neglected as conventional packet-switched interconnects are ill-suited for optics: Without major breakthroughs, storing packets optically remains impractical. Hence packet switching would require repeated optoelectronic (O/E) and electro-optic (E/O) conversions that significantly diminish the advantages of optical signaling. The alternative topologies such as buses or rings [6,7] avoid packet switching by sharing the transmission media (optical waveguides), and rely on wavelength division multiplexing (WDM) to achieve large bandwidth. Purely relying on WDM, however, poses rather stringent challenges to the design and implementation of on-chip E/O modulators, *e.g.*, requiring precise wavelength alignment and extremely low insertion loss. Furthermore, on-chip interconnect poses different constraints and challenges from off-chip interconnect, and offers a new set of opportunities. Hence architecting on-chip interconnect's for future microprocessors requires novel holistic solutions and deserves more attention.

In this paper, we propose to leverage a suite of newly-developed or emerging device, circuits, and optics technologies to build a relay-free interconnect architecture:

- Signaling: VCSELs (vertical cavity surface emitting lasers) provide light emission without the need of external laser sources and routing the "optical power supply" all over the chip. VCSELs, photodetectors (PDs) and supporting micro-optic components can be implemented in GaAs technologies and 3-D integrated with the silicon chip – the latter includes CMOS digital electronics as well as the transmitters and receivers.
- Propagation medium: Free-space optics using integrated micro-optic components provides an economic medium allowing speed-of-light signal propagation with low loss and low dispersion.
- Networking: Direct communications through dedicated

*This work is supported by NSF under grant 0829915 and also in part by grants 0747324 and 0901701.

ISCA'10, June 19–23, 2010, Saint-Malo, France.

VCSELs, PDs, and micro-mirrors (in small-scale systems) or via phase array beam-steering (in large-scale systems) allows a quasi-crossbar structure that avoids packet switching, offers ultra-low communication latency in the common case, and provides scalable bandwidth thanks to the fully distributed nature of the interconnect.

The rest of the paper is organized as follows: Section 2 discusses the background of on-chip optical interconnect; Section 3 introduces our free-space optical interconnect and the array of enabling technologies; Section 4 and 5 discuss the architectural design issues and optimizations; Section 6 presents the quantitative analysis; Section 7 discusses related work; and Section 8 concludes.

2. CHALLENGES FOR ON-CHIP OPTICAL INTERCONNECT

First, it is worth noting that on-chip electrical interconnects have made tremendous progress in recent years, driven by continuous device scaling, reverse scaling of top metal layers, and the adoption of low-k inter-layer dielectric. The bandwidth density is projected to reach 100 Gbps/μm with 20-ps/mm delay at the 22-nm technology node by 2016 [8]. Assisted by advanced signal processing techniques such as equalization, echo/crosstalk cancellation, and error correction coding, the performance of electrical interconnects is expected to continue advancing at a steady pace. Therefore, on-chip optical interconnects can only justify the replacement of its electrical counterpart by offering significantly higher aggregated bandwidth with lower power dissipation and without significant complexity overhead.

Current optical interconnect research efforts focus on using planar optical waveguides, which will be integrated onto the same chip as CMOS electronics. This *in-plane waveguide* approach, however, presents some significant challenges. First, all-optical switching and storage devices in silicon technologies remain far from practical. Without these capabilities, routing and flow control in a packet-switched network, as typically envisioned for an on-chip optical interconnect system, require repeated O/E and E/O conversions, which can significantly increase signal delay, circuit complexity, and energy consumption. Simultaneously, efficient silicon E/O modulators remain challenging due to the inherently poor nonlinear optical properties of silicon [9]. Hence the modulator design requires a long optical length, which results in large device size, *e.g.*, typically in centimeters for a Mach-Zehnder interferometer (MZI) device [10]. Resonant devices such as micro-ring resonators (*e.g.*, [11]) can effectively slow the light and hence reduce the required device size. These high-Q resonant devices, however, have relatively small bandwidth and need to achieve very stringent spectral and loss requirements, which translates into extremely fine device geometries and little tolerance for fabrication variability. Fine-resolution processing technologies such as electron beam lithography are needed for device fabrication, which poses cost and yield challenges that are even greater than integrating non-silicon components at present. Further, accurate wavelength tuning is required at runtime, especially when facing the large process and temperature variations and hostile thermal environment on-chip. Typical wavelength tuning using resistive thermal bias [12] substantially increases the system complexity and static energy consumption [13].

Further, there is a fundamental bandwidth density challenge for the in-plane waveguided approach: the mode diameter of optical waveguides, which determines the minimum distance required between optical waveguides to avoid crosstalk, is significantly larger than metal wire pitch in electrical interconnect in nanoscale CMOS technologies, and will deteriorate with scaling [8]. Wavelength division multiplexing (WDM), proven in long distance fiber-optic communications, has been proposed to solve the problem and achieve the bandwidth-density goal. WDM, however, is much more challenging for an intra-chip environment due to a whole array of issues. First, wavelength multiplexing devices such as micro-ring based wavelength add-drop filters [11] require fine wavelength resolution and superior wavelength stability, which exacerbates the device fabrication and thermal tuning challenges. Second, these multiplexers introduce insertion loss (on the orders of 0.01-0.1 dB per device) to the optical signals on the shared optical waveguide. Using multiple wavelengths exponentially amplifies the losses, and significantly degrades the link performance. This problem would be almost prohibitive in a bus or ring topology with a large number of nodes. Lastly, a multi-wavelength light source (laser array, supercontinuum generation, or spectrum slicing) is needed, which is more complex and expensive than a single-wavelength laser.

Another challenge facing the in-plane waveguide approach is the optical loss and crosstalk from the large number of waveguide crossings [14], which severely limit the topology of the interconnect system [13] and hence the total aggregated system bandwidth. Placing waveguides onto a dedicated optics plane with multiple levels would require multiple silicon-on-insulator (SOI) layers, increasing the process complexity, and the performance gain is not scalable.

In summary, we believe that (a) it is critical to achieve the highest possible data rate in each optic channel at a fixed wavelength in an on-chip optical interconnect system in order to replace the electrical interconnects; (b) using WDM and in-plane optical waveguides may not be the best solution to achieve the bandwidth goal and certainly should not be the sole focus of our effort; and (c) electronics and photonics have different physics, follow different scaling rules, and probably should be fabricated separately.

3. OVERVIEW

To address the challenges of building high-performance on-chip optical interconnects, we seek to use free-space optics and supporting device, circuit, and architecture techniques to create a high performance, complexity-effective interconnect system. We envision a system where a free-space optical communication layer, consisting of arrays of lasers, photodetectors, and micro-optics devices such as micro-mirrors and micro-lenses, is superimposed on top of the CMOS electronics layer via 3-D chip integration. This *free-space optical interconnect* (FSOI) system provides all-to-all direct communication links between processor cores, regardless of their topological distance. As shown in Figure 1, in a particular link, digital data streams modulate an array of lasers; each modulated light beam emitted by a laser is collimated by a micro-lens, guided by a series of micro-mirrors, focused by another micro-lens, and then detected by a photodetector (PD); the received electrical signals are finally converted to digital data. Note that the optical links are running at multiples of the core clock speed.

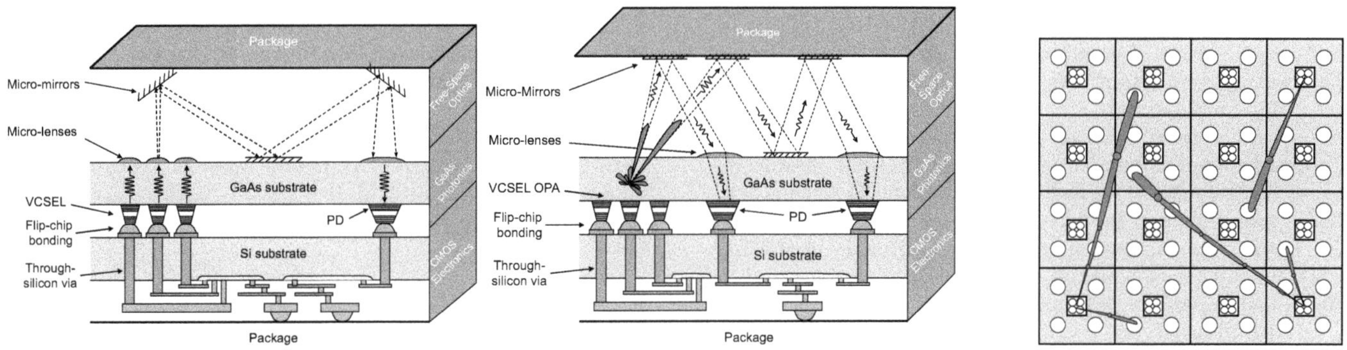

(a) Side view (mirror-guided only) (b) Side view (with phase array beamforming) (c) Top view

Figure 1: Illustration of the overall interconnect structure and 3-D integrated chip stack. (a) and (b) also show two different optics configuration. In the top view (c), the VCSEL arrays are in the center and the photodetectors are on the periphery within each core.

Without packet switching, this design eliminates the intermediate routing and buffering delays and makes the signal propagation delay approach the ultimate lower bound, *i.e.*, the speed of light. These links can operate at a much higher speed than core logic, making it easy to provide high throughput. On the energy efficiency front, bypassing packet relaying clearly keeps energy cost low. As compared to waveguided optical interconnect, FSOI also avoids the loss and cross-talk associated with modulators and waveguide crossings. In the future, by utilizing the beamsteering capability of an optical phase array (OPA) of lasers, the number of lasers and photodetectors in each node can be constant, providing crucial scalability.

3.1 Lasers and Photodetectors

The lasers used in this FSOI system are vertical-cavity surface-emitting lasers (VCSELs) [15]. A VCSEL is a nanoscale heterostructure, consisting of an InGaAs quantum well active region, a resonant cavity constructed with top and bottom dielectric mirrors (distributed Bragg reflectors), and a pn junction structure for carrier injection. They are fabricated on a GaAs substrate using molecular beam epitaxy (MBE) or metal-organic chemical vapor deposition (MOCVD). A VCSEL is typically a mesa structure with several microns in diameter and height. A large 2-D array with millions of VCSELs can be fabricated on the same GaAs chip. The light can be emitted from the top of the VCSEL mesa. Alternatively, at the optical wavelength of 980-nm and shorter when the GaAs substrate is transparent, the VCSELs can also be made to emit from the back side and then through the GaAs substrate. A VCSEL's optical output can be directly modulated by its current, and the modulation speed can reach tens of Gbps [16, 17].

The photodetectors can be either integrated on the CMOS chip as silicon p-i-n photodiodes [18], or fabricated on the same GaAs chip using the VCSELs as resonant cavity photodiodes [19, 20]. In the latter case, an InGaAs active region is enhanced by the resonant cavity similar to a VCSEL, and the devices offer a larger bandwidth and are well suited for this FSOI system.

3.2 Micro-lenses and Micro-mirrors

In the free-space optical interconnect, passive micro-optics devices such as micro-lenses and micro-mirrors collimate, guide, and focus the light beams in free space. Collimating and focusing allow smaller size VCSELs and PDs to be used, which reduces their parasitic capacitance and improve their bandwidth. Micro-lenses can be fabricated either on top of VCSELs when the latter are top emitting [21, 22], or on the backside of the GaAs substrate for substrate-emitting VCSELs [23, 24].

Micro-mirrors will be fabricated on silicon or polymer by micro-molding techniques [25, 26]. Note that commercial micro-mirror arrays (*e.g.*, Digital Micromirror Device chips from Texas Instrument) have mirrors that can turn on and off thousands of times per second and are in full HD density (millions of pixels). Our application requires only fixed mirrors at the scale of at most n^2 (n is the number of nodes).

3.3 3-D Integration and Thermal Issues

In this FSOI system, 3-D integration technologies are applied to electrically connect the free space and photonics layers with the electronics layer, forming an electro-optical system-in-package (SiP). For example, the GaAs chip is flip-chip bonded to the back side of the silicon chip, and connected to the transceiver circuits there using through-silicon-vias (TSVs). Note that the silicon chip is flip-chip bonded to the package in a normal fashion. In general, such electro-optical SiP reduces the latency and power consumption of the global signaling through optical interconnect, while permitting the microprocessors to be implemented using standard CMOS technologies. Significant work has explored merging various analog, digital, and memory technologies in a 3-D stack. Adding an optical layer to the 3-D stack is the next logical step to improve overall system performance.

Thermal problems have long been a major issue in 2-D integrated circuits degrading both maximum achievable speed and reliability [27]. By introducing a layer of free space, our proposed design further adds to the challenge of air cooling. However, even without this free space layer, continued scaling and the trend towards 3-D integration are already making air cooling increasingly insufficient as demonstrated by researchers that explored alternative heat removal techniques for stacked 3-D systems [28–30].

One such technique delivers liquid coolants to microchannel heat sinks on the back side of each chip in the 3-D stack using fluidic TSVs [28]. Fluidic pipes [29] are used to propagate heat produced by the devices to the microchannel heat sinks. The heat is further dissipated through external fluidic tubes that can be located on either side of the 3-D stack.

A second technique exploits the advanced thermal conductive properties of emerging materials. Materials such as diamond, carbon nanotubes, and graphene have been proposed for heat removal. The thermal conductivity of diamond ranges from 1000 to 2200 W per meter per kelvin. Carbon nanotubes have an even higher thermal conductivity of 3000 to 3500 W/m·K, and graphene is better [30]. These materials can be used to produce high heat conductive paths from the heat sources to the periphery of the 3-D stack through both thermal vias (vertical direction) and in plane heat spreaders (lateral direction).

In both alternatives, thermal pipes are guided to the side of the 3-D stack, allowing placement of the free space optical system. Finally, we note that replacing air cooling in high-end chips is perhaps not only inevitable but also desirable. For instance, researchers from IBM showed that liquid cooling allows the reuse of the heat, reducing the overall carbon footprint of a facility [31, 32].

4. ARCHITECTURAL DESIGN

4.1 Overall Interconnect Structure

As illustrated in Figure 1, in an FSOI link, a single light beam is analogous to a single wire and similarly, an array of VCSELs can form essentially a multi-bit bus which we call a *lane*. An interesting feature of using free-space optics is that signaling is not confined to fixed, prearranged waveguides and the optical path can change relatively easily. For instance, we can use a group of VCSELs to form a phase-array [33] – essentially a single tunable-direction laser as shown in Figure 1(b). This feature makes an all-to-all network topology much easier to implement.

For small- and medium-scaled chip-multiprocessors, fixed-direction lasers should be used for simplicity: each outgoing lane can be implemented by a dedicated array of VCSELs. In a system with N processors, each having a total of k bits in all lanes, $N * (N - 1) * k$ VCSELs are needed for transmission. Note that even though the number scales with N^2, the actual hardware requirement is far from overwhelming. For a rough sense of scale, for $N = 16$, $k = 9$ (our default configuration for evaluation), we need approximately 2000 VCSELs. Existing VCSELs are about $20\mu m$x$20\mu m$ in dimension [16, 17]. Assuming, conservatively, $30\mu m$ spacing, 2000 VCSELs occupy a total area of about $5mm^2$. Note that on the receiving side, we do not use dedicated receivers. Instead, multiple light beams from different nodes share the same receiver. We do not try to arbitrate the shared receivers but simply allow packet collisions to happen. As will be discussed in more detail later, at the expense of having packet collisions, this strategy simplifies a number of other design issues.

4.2 Optical Links

To facilitate the architectural evaluation, a single-bit FSOI link is constructed (Figure 2) and the link performance is estimated for the most challenging scenario: communication across the chip diagonally. Note that the transceiver here is based on a conventional architecture, and can be simplified for lower power dissipation. Since the whole chip is synchronous (*e.g.*, using optical clock distribution), no clock recovery circuit is needed.[1] The optical wavelength is chosen as 980 nm, which is a good compromise between VCSEL and PD performance. The serialized transmitted data is fed to the laser driver driving a VCSEL. The light from the back-emitting VCSEL is collimated through a microlens on the backside of the 430-μm thick GaAs substrate. Using a device simulator, DAVINCI, and 2007 ITRS device parameters for the 45-nm CMOS technology, the performance and energy parameters of the optical link are calculated and detailed in Table 1.

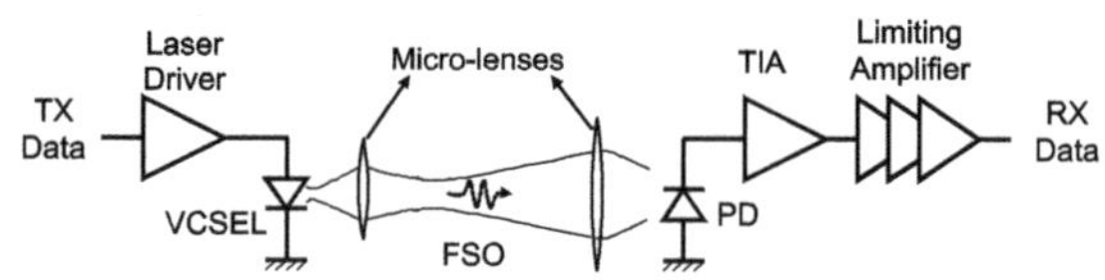

Figure 2: Intra-chip FSOI link calculation.

Our transmitter is much less power hungry than a commercial one because (a) more advanced technology (45-nm CMOS) is used; (b) the load is smaller (the integrated VCSEL exhibits a resistance of over 200 Ω, as compared to typically 25 Ω when driving an external laser or modulator); and (c) signal swing is much smaller (the VCSEL voltage swing is about 100 mV instead of several hundred mV). Further, the transmitter goes into standby when not transmitting to save power: the VCSEL is biased below threshold, and the laser driver is turned off. The receiver is kept on all the time. Note that the power dissipation of the serializer in the transmitter and deserializer in the receiver is much smaller compared to that of the laser driver and TIA, and hence is not included in the estimate.

Free-Space Optics	
Trans. distance	2 cm
Optical wavelength	980 nm
Optical path loss	2.6 dB
Microlens aperture	90 μm @ transmitter 190 μm @ receiver
Transmitter & Receiver	
Laser driver	bandwidth=43 GHz
VCSEL	aperture=5 μm parasitic=235 Ω, 90 fF threshold=0.14 mA extinction ratio=11:1
PD	responsivity=0.5 A/W capacitance=100 fF
TIA & Limiting amp	bandwidth=36 GHz, gain=15000 V/A
Link	
Data rate	40 Gbps
Signal-to-noise ratio	7.5 dB
Bit-error-rate (BER)	10^{-10}
Cycle-to-cycle jitter	1.7 ps
Power Consumption	
Laser driver	6.3 mW
VCSEL	0.96 mW (0.48 mA@2V)
Transmitter (standby)	0.43 mW
Receiver	4.2 mW

Table 1: Optical link parameters.

4.3 Network Design

4.3.1 Tradeoff to Allow Collision

In our system, optical communication channels are built directly between communicating nodes within the network in a totally distributed fashion, without arbitration. An important consequence is that packets destined for the same receiver at the same time will collide. Such collisions require

[1]There will be delay differences between different optical paths, which can be up to tens of picoseconds, or equivalent to about 3 communication cycles. To maintain chip-wide synchronous operation, we delay the faster paths by padding extra bits in the serializer, and fine tuning the delay using digital delay lines in the transmitter.

detection, retransmission, and extra bandwidth margin to prevent them from becoming a significant issue. However, for this one disadvantage, our design allows a number of other significant advantages (and later we will show that no significant over-provisioning is necessary):

- Compared to a conventional crossbar design, we do not need a centralized arbitration system. This makes the design scalable and reduces unnecessary arbitration latency for the common cases.
- Compared to a packet-switched interconnect, this design
  1. Avoids relaying and thus repeated O/E and E/O conversions in an optical network;
  2. Guarantees the absence of network deadlocks;[2]
  3. Provides point-to-point message ordering in a straightforward fashion and thus allows simplification in coherence protocol designs;
  4. Reduces the circuit needs for each node to just drivers, receivers, and their control circuit. Significant amount of logic specific to packet relaying and switching is avoided (*e.g.*, virtual channel allocation, switch allocators, and credit management for flow control).
- The design allows errors and collisions to be handled by the same mechanism essentially requiring no extra support than needed to handle errors, which is necessary in any system. Furthermore, once we accept collisions (with a probability on the orders of about 10^{-2}), the bit error rates of the signaling chain can be relaxed significantly (from 10^{-10} to, say, 10^{-5}) without any tangible impact on performance. This provides important engineering margins for practical implementations and further opportunities for energy optimization on the entire signaling chain.

4.3.2 Collision Handling

Collision detection:.
Since we use the simple on-off keying (OOK), when multiple light beams from different source nodes collide at the same receiver node, the received light pulse becomes the logical "OR" of the multiple underlying pulses. The detection of the collision is simple, thanks to the synchrony of the entire interconnect. In the packet header, we encode both the sender node ID (PID) and its complement ($\overline{PID}$). When more than one packet arrives at the same receiver array, then at least one bit of the IDs (say PID_i) would differ. Because of the effective "OR" operation, the received PID_i and $\overline{PID_i}$ would both be 1, indicating a collision.

Structuring:.
We take a few straightforward structuring steps to reduce the probability of collision.

1. Multiple receivers: It is beneficial to have a few receivers at each node so that different transmitter nodes target different receivers within the same node and reduce the probability of a collision. The effect can be better understood with some simple theoretical analysis. Using a simplified transmission model assuming equal probability of transmission and random destination, the probability of a collision in a cycle in any node can be described as $1-[(1-\frac{p}{N-1})^n+\binom{n}{1}\frac{p}{N-1}(1-\frac{p}{N-1})^{n-1}]^R$,where N is the number of nodes; p is the transmission probability of a node; R is the number of receivers (evenly divided among the $N-1$ potential transmitters); and $n=\frac{N-1}{R}$ is the number of nodes sharing the same receiver.

Numerical results are shown visually in Figure 3. It is worth noting that the simplifying assumptions do not distort the reality significantly. As can be seen from the plot, experimental results agree well with the trend of theoretical calculations.

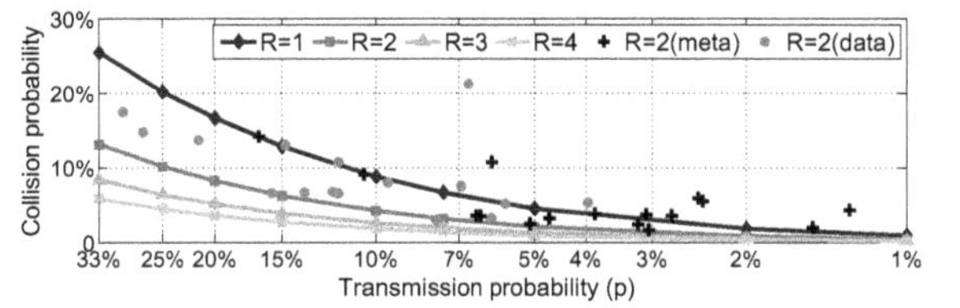

Figure 3: Collision probability (normalized to packet transmission probability) as a function of transmission probability p and the number of receivers per node (R). The result has an extremely weak dependency on the number of nodes in a system (N) as long as it is not too small. The plot shown is drawn with $N=16$. To see that this simplified theoretical analysis is meaningful, we show experimental data points using two receivers (R=2). We separate the channels ("meta" and "data" channels as explained later).

To a first-order approximation, collision frequency is inversely proportional to the number of receivers. Therefore, having a few (*e.g.*, 2-3) receivers per node is a good option. Further increasing the number will lead to diminishing returns.

2. Slotting and lane separation: In a non-arbitrated shared medium, when a packet takes multiple cycles to transmit, it is well known that "slotting" reduces collision probability [35]. For instance, suppose data packets take 5 processor cycles to transmit, then they can only start at the beginning of a 5-cycle slot. In our system, we define two packet lengths, one for *meta* packets (*e.g.*, requests and acknowledgments) and one for data packets (which is about 5 times the former). Each type will thus have a different slot length. In that case, slotting only reduces the chance of collision between two packets of the same length (and thus the same slot length). Furthermore, the different packet lengths (especially because one is much longer than the other) also make the retransmission difficult to manage. One option to deal with both problems is to separate the packets into their own lanes and manage each lane differently.

3. Bandwidth allocation: Given a fixed bandwidth, we need to determine how to allocate the bandwidth between the two lanes for optimal performance. Even though a precise analytical expression between bandwidth allocation and performance is difficult to obtain, some approximate analysis can still be derived: each packet has an expected total latency of $L+P_c*L_r$, where L, P_c, and L_r are basic transmission latency, probability of collision, and collision resolution latency, respectively. L, P_c, and L_r are inversely proportional to the bandwidth allocated to a lane.[3] The overall latency can be expressed as $\frac{C_1}{B_M}+\frac{C_2}{B_M^2}+\frac{C_3}{1-B_M}+\frac{C_4}{(1-B_M)^2}$,

[2] Note that *fetch deadlock* is an independent issue that is not caused by the interconnect design itself. It has to be either prevented with multiple virtual networks, which is very resource intensive, or probabilistically avoided using NACKs [34]. We use the latter approach in all configurations.

[3] P_c is not exactly inversely proportional to bandwidth [9].

where B_M is the portion of total bandwidth allocated to the meta packets, the constants ($C_1..C_4$) are a function of statistics related to application behavior and parameters that can be calculated analytically.[4] In our setup, the optimal latency value occurs at $B_M = 0.285$: about 30% of the bandwidth should be allocated to transmit meta packets. In our system, we use 3 VCSELs for the meta lane and 6 for the data lane, with a serialization latency of 2 (processor) cycles for a (72-bit) meta packet and 5 cycles for a (360-bit) data packet. Because we are using 2 separate receivers to reduce collisions, the receiving bandwidth is twice the transmitting bandwidth. For comparison, we use a baseline mesh network where the meta and data packets have a serialization latency of 1 and 5 cycles, respectively.

Confirmation:.
Because a packet can get corrupted due to collision, some mechanism is needed to infer or to explicitly communicate the transmission status. For instance, a requester can time out and retry. However, solely relying on timeouts is not enough as certain packets (*e.g.*, acknowledgments) generate no response and the transmitter thus has no basis to infer whether the transmission was successful.

A simple hardware mechanism can be devised to confirm uncorrupted transmissions. We dedicate a single-VCSEL lane per node just to transmit a beam for confirmation: Upon receiving an uncorrupted packet, the receiver node activates the confirmation VCSEL and sends the confirmation to the sender. Note that by design, the confirmation beam will never collide with one another: when a packet is received in cycle n, the confirmation is sent after a fixed delay (in our case, in cycle $n+2$, after a cycle for any delay in decoding and error-checking). Since at any cycle n, only one packet (per lane) will be transmitted by any node, only one confirmation (per lane) will be received by that node in cycle $n+2$. Other than confirming successful packet receipt, the confirmation can also piggy-back limited information as we show later.

Retransmission:.
Once packets are involved in a collision, the senders retry. In a straightforward way, the packet is retransmitted in a random slot within a window of W slots after the detection of the collision. The chance of further collision depends on W. A large W results in a smaller probability of secondary collisions, but a longer average delay in retransmission. Furthermore, as the retry continues, other packets may arrive and make collisions even more likely, greatly increasing the delay and energy waste. If we simply retry using the same window size, in the pathological case when too many packets arrive in a concentrated period, they can reach a critical mass such that it is more likely to have a new packet from a different node join the existing set of competing senders than to have one successfully transmitted and leave the competition. This leads to a virtual live lock that we have to guard against.

Thus, we adopt an exponential back-off heuristic and set the window size to grow as the number of retries increases.

[4]For example, the composition of packets (requests, data replies, forwarded requests, memory fetches, etc), the percentage of meta and data packets that are on the critical path, the average number of expected retries in a back-off algorithm.

Specifically, the window size for the rth retry W_r is set to $W \times B^{r-1}$, where B is the base of the exponential function. While doubling the window size is a classic approach [36], we believe setting B to 2 is an over-correction, since the pathological case is a very remote possibility. Note that B need not be an integer. To estimate the optimal values of W and B without blindly relying on expensive simulations, we use a simplified analytical model of the network to derive the expression of the average collision resolution delay given W and B, taking into account the confirmation laser delay (2 cycles). Although the calculation does not lead to a simple closed-form expression, numerical computation using packet transmission probability measured in our system leads to the results shown in Figure 4.

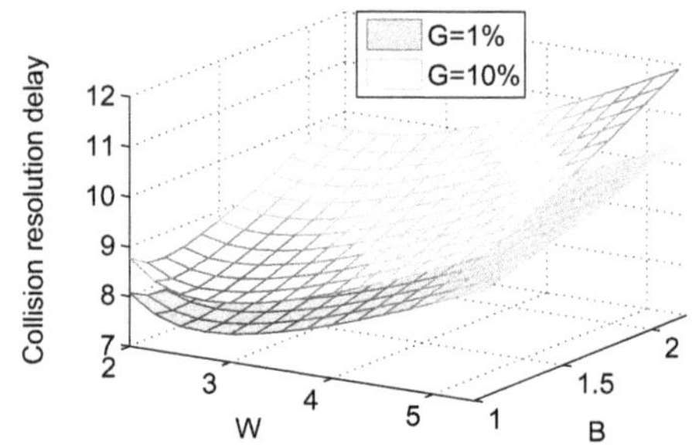

Figure 4: Average collision resolution delay for meta packets as a function of starting window size and back-off speed. While retransmission is attempted, other nodes continue regular transmission. This "background" transmission rate (G=1% and 10% shown) has a negligible impact on the optimal values of W and B.

The minimum collision resolution delay occurs at $W = 2.7, B = 1.1$. We selected a few data points on the curve and verified that the theoretical computation agrees with execution-driven simulation rather well. For instance, for $W = 2.7, B = 1.1$, the computed delay is 7.26 cycles and the simulated result is between 6.8 and 9.6 with an average of 7.4 cycles. The graph clearly shows that $B = 1.1$ produces a decidedly lower resolution delay in the common case than when $B = 2$. This does not come at the expense of unacceptable delay in the pathological case. For example, in a 64-node system, when all other nodes send one packet to a particular node at about the same time, it takes an average of about 26 retries (for a total of 416 cycles) to get one packet to come through. In contrast, with a fixed window size of 3, it would take 8.2×10^{10} number of retries. Setting B to 2, shortens this to about 5 retries (199 cycles).

4.4 Protocol Considerations

The delivery-order property of the interconnect can impact the complexity of the coherence protocol [34]. Our system does not rely on relaying and thus it is easy to enforce point-to-point message ordering. We delay the transmission of another message about a cache line until a previous message about that line has been confirmed. This serialization reduces the number of transient states the coherence protocol has to handle. We summarize the stable and transient states transitions in [9].

5. OPTIMIZATIONS

While a basic design described above can already support the coherency substrate and provide low-latency communication, a perhaps more interesting aspect of using optical interconnect is to explore new communication or protocol opportunities. Below, we describe a few optimizations that we have explored in the proposed interconnect architecture.

5.1 Leveraging Confirmation Signals

In a cache coherence system, we often send a message where the whole point is to convey *timing*, such as the release of a barrier or lock. In these cases, the information content of the payload is extremely low and yet carrying out synchronization accounts for about a quarter of total traffic in our simulated 64-node mesh-based chip-multiprocessor. Since usually the receiver is anticipating such a message, and it is often latency-sensitive, we can quickly convey such timing information using the confirmation laser. Compared to sending a full-blown packet, we can achieve even lower latency and higher energy efficiency, while reducing traffic and thus collisions on the regular channels.

Take invalidation acknowledgments for example. They are needed to determine write completion, so as to help ensure *write atomicity* and determine when memory barriers can finish in a relaxed consistency model [34]. In our system, we can eliminate the need for acknowledgment altogether by using the confirmation (of receiving the request) as a *commitment* of carrying out the invalidation [34]. This commitment logically serializes the invalidation before any subsequent externally visible transaction.[5]

Now let us consider typical implementation of locks using load-linked (`ll`) and store-conditional (`sc`) instructions and barriers. Both can involve spinning on boolean values, which incurs a number of invalidations, confirmations, and reloading requests when the value changes. We choose to (a) transmit certain boolean values over the confirmation channel and (b) use an update protocol for boolean synchronization variables when feasible.

When a `ll` or `sc` misses in the L1 cache, we send a special request to the directory indicating reserved timing slots on the confirmation channel. Recall that each CPU cycle contains multiple communication cycles, or mini-cycles. If, for example, mini-cycle i is reserved, the directory can use that mini-cycle in any cycle to respond the value or state of store-conditional directly. In other words, the information is encoded in the relative position of the mini-cycle.

Using such a mechanism over the confirmation channel, a requester can receive single-bit replies for `ll` requests. The value received is then recorded in the link register, essentially forming a special cache line with just one single-bit word. Such a "line" lends itself to an update protocol. Nodes holding these single bits can be thought of as having *subscribed* to the word location and will continue to receive updates via the same mini-cycle reserved on the confirmation lane earlier. The directory, on the other hand, uses one or more registers to track the subscriptions. When a node issues a `sc` with a boolean value, it sends the value directly through the request (rather than just seeking write permission of the entire line). The directory can thus perform updates to subscribers. Note that our design does not assume any specific implementation of lock or barrier. It merely implements the semantics of `ll` and `sc` differently when feasible, which expedites the dissemination of single-bit values. Also, this change has little impact on regular coherence handling. A normal store request to the line containing subscribed words simply invalidates all subscribers.

[5]For instance, in a sequentially consistent system, any load (to the invalidated cache line) following that externally visible transaction need to reflect the effect of the invalidation and replay if it is speculatively executed out of order. For practical implementation, we freeze the retirement of any memory instructions until we have applied all pending invalidations in the input packet queue and performed necessary replays [37].

5.2 Ameliorating data packet collisions

Since data packets are longer than meta packets, their collisions cause more damage and take longer to resolve. Fortunately, data packets have unique properties that can be leveraged in managing collisions: they are often the result of earlier requests. This has two implications. First, the receiver has some control over the timing of their arrival and can use that control to reduce the probability of a collision to begin with. Second, the receiver also has a general idea which nodes may be involved in the collision and can play a role coordinating retransmissions.

Request spacing:.

When a request results in a data packet reply, the most likely slot into which the reply falls can be calculated. The overall latency includes queuing delays for both the request and the reply, the collision resolution time for the request, and the memory access latency. All these components can be analyzed as independent discreet random variables. Figure 5 shows an example of the distribution of the overall latency of a read-miss request averaged over all application runs in our environment for illustration. As we can see, the probability is heavily concentrated in a few choices. Accordingly, we can reserve slots on the receiver. If a slot is already reserved, a request gets delayed to minimize the chance of collision.

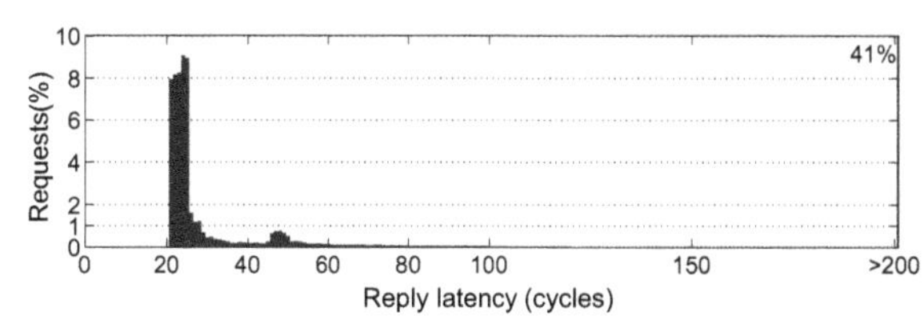

Figure 5: Probability distribution of the overall latency of a request resulting in a data reply.

Hints in collision resolution:.

When packets collide, each sender retries with the exponential back-off algorithm that tries to balance the wait time and the probability of secondary collisions (Section 4.3.2). However, the design of the algorithm assumes no coordination among the senders. Indeed, the senders do not even know the packet is involved in a collision until cycles after the fact nor do they know the identities of the other parties involved.

In the case of the data packet lane, the receiver knows of the collision early, immediately after receiving the header that encodes PID and $\overline{PID}$. It can thus send a no-collision notification to the sender before the slot is over. The absence of this notification is an indication that a collision has occurred. Moreover, even though in a collision the PID and $\overline{PID}$ are corrupted due to the collision and only indicate a super-set of potential transmitters,[6] the receiver has

[6]Clearly, for small-scale networks, one could use a bit vector

the benefit of additional knowledge of the potential candidates – those nodes that are expected to send a data packet reply. Based on this knowledge, the receiver can select one transmitting node as the winner for the right to re-transmit immediately in the next slot. This selection is beamed back through a notification signal (via the confirmation laser) to the winner only. All other nodes that have not received this notification will avoid the next slot and start the re-transmission with back-off process from the slot after the next. This way, the winning node suffers a minimal extra delay and the remaining nodes will have less retransmission contention. Note that, this whole process is probabilistic and the notification is only used as a hint.

Finally, we note that packet collisions are ultimately infrequent. So a scheduling-based approach that avoid all possible collisions does not seem beneficial, unless the scheduling overhead is extremely low.

6. EXPERIMENTAL ANALYSIS

The proposed intra-chip free-space optical interconnect has many different design tradeoffs compared with a conventional wire-based interconnect or newer proposals of optical versions. Some of these tradeoffs can not be easily expressed in quantitative terms, and are discussed in the architectural design and later in the related work section. Here, we attempt to demonstrate that the proposed design offers ultra-low latency, excellent scalability, and superior energy efficiency. We also show that accepting collisions does not necessitate drastic bandwidth over-provisioning.

6.1 Experimental Setup

We use an execution-driven simulator to model in great detail the coherence substrate, the processor microarchitecture, the communication substrate, and the power consumption of both a 16-way and a 64-way chip-multiprocessor (CMP). We leave the details of the simulator in [9] and only show the system configuration in Table 2.

Processor core	
Fetch/Decode/Commit	4 / 4 / 4
ROB	64
Functional units	INT 1+1 mul/div, FP 2+1 mul/div
Issue Q/Reg. (int,fp)	(16, 16) / (64, 64)
LSQ(LQ,SQ)	32 (16,16) 2 search ports
Branch predictor	Bimodal + Gshare
- Gshare	8K entries, 13 bit history
- Bimodal/Meta/BTB	4K/8K/4K (4-way) entries
Br. mispred. penalty	at least 7 cycles
Process specifications	Feature size: 45nm, Freq: 3.3 GHz, V_d: 1 V
Memory hierarchy	
L1 D cache (private)	8KB [38], 2-way, 32B line, 2 cycles, 2 ports, dual tags
L1 I cache (private)	32KB, 2-way, 64B line, 2 cycle
L2 cache (shared)	64KB slice/node, 64B line, 15 cycles, 2 ports
Dir. request queue	64 entries
Memory channel	52.8GB/s bandwidth, memory latency 200 cycles
Number of channels	4 in 16-node system, 8 in 64-node system
Prefetch logic	stream prefetcher
Network packets	Flit size: 72-bit, data packet: 5 flits, meta packet: 1 flit
Wired interconnect	4 VCs, latency: router 4 cycles, link 1 cycle, buffer: 5x12 flits
Optical interconnect (each node)	
VCSEL	40 GHz, 12 bits per CPU cycle
Array	Dedicated (16-node), phase-array w/ 1 cycle setup delay (64-node).
Lane widths	6/3/1 bit(s) for data/meta/confirmation lane
Receivers	2 data (6b), 2 meta (3b), 1 for confirmation (1b)
Outgoing queue	8 packets each for data and meta lanes.

Table 2: System configuration.

Evaluation is performed using a suite of parallel applications [9] including SPLASH2 benchmark suite [38], a program to solve electromagnetic problem in 3 dimensions (*em3d*), a parallel genetic linkage analysis program (*ilink*), a program to iteratively solve partial differential equations (*jacobi*), a 3-dimensional particle simulator (*mp3d*), a shallow water benchmark from the National Center for Atmospheric Research to solve differential equations on a two-dimensional grid for weather prediction (*shallow*), and a branch-and-bound based implementation of the non-polynomial (NP) traveling salesman problem (*tsp*). We follow the observations in [38] to scale down the L1 cache to mimic realistic cache miss rates.[7]

encoding of PID and thus allow the receiver to definitively identify the colliding parties all the time.

6.2 Performance Analysis

We start our evaluation with the performance analysis of the proposed interconnect. We model a number of conventional interconnect configurations for comparison. To normalize performance, we use a baseline system with canonical 4-cycle routers. Note that while the principles of conventional routers and even newer designs with shorter pipelines are well understood, practical designs require careful consideration of flow control, deadlock avoidance, QoS, and load-balancing and are by no means simple and easy to implement. For instance, the router in Alpha 21364 has hundreds of packet buffers and occupies a chip area equal to 20% of the combined area of the core and 128KB of L1 caches. The processing by the router itself adds 7 cycles of latency [39]. Nevertheless, we provide comparison with conventional interconnects with aggressive latency assumptions.

In Figure 6-(a), we show the average latency of transferring a packet in our free-space optical interconnect and in the baseline mesh interconnect. Latency in the optical interconnect is further broken down into queuing delay, intentionally scheduled delay to minimize collision, the actual network delay, and collision resolution delay. Clearly, even with the overhead of collision and its prevention, the overall delay of 7.5 cycles is very low.

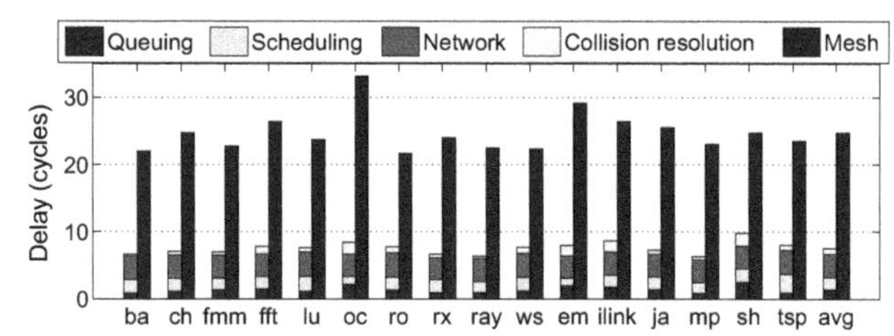

(a) Latency

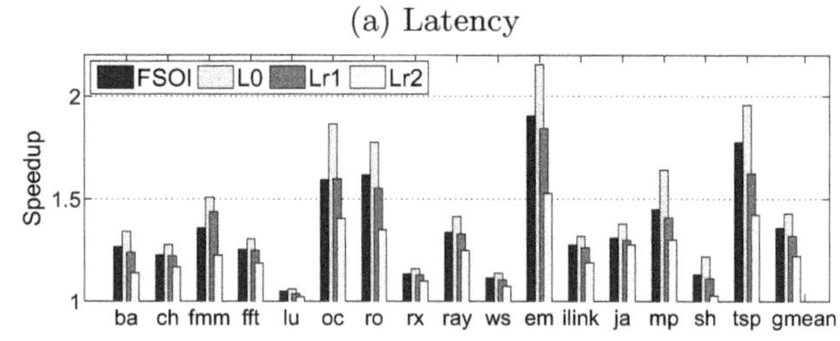

(b) Speedup

Figure 6: Performance of 16-node systems. **(a)** Total packet latency in the free-space optical interconnect (left) broken down into 4 components (queuing delay, scheduling delay, network latency, and collision resolution delay) and the conventional mesh (right). **(b)** Speedups of free-space optical interconnect (FSOI) and various configurations of conventional mesh relative to the baseline.

[7]Our studies also show that not scaling down the cache size only affects the quantitative results marginally [9].

The application speedups are shown in Figure 6-(b). We use the ultimate execution time[8] of the applications to compute speedups against the baseline using a conventional mesh interconnect. For relative comparison, we model a number of conventional configurations: L_O, L_{r1}, and L_{r2}. In L_O, the transmission latency is idealized to 0 and only the throughput is modeled. In other words, the only delay a packet experiences is the serialization delay (1 cycle for meta packets and 5 cycles for data packets) and any queuing delay at the source node. L_O is essentially an idealized interconnect. L_{r1} and L_{r2} represent the cases where the overall latency accounts for the number of hops traveled: each hop consumes 1 cycle for link traversal and 1 or 2 cycles respectively for router processing. Like in L_O, we do *not* model any contentions or delays inside the network. Thus, they only serve to illustrate (loose) performance upper-bounds when aggressively designed routers are used.

While the performance gain varies from application to application, our design tracks the ideal L_O configuration well, achieving a geometric mean of 1.36 speedup versus the ideal's 1.43. It also outperforms the aggressive L_{r1} (1.32) and L_{r2} (1.22) configurations.

Although a mesh interconnect is scalable in terms of aggregate bandwidth provided, latency worsens as the network scales up. In comparison, our design offers a direct-communication system that is scalable while maintaining low latency. The simulation results of 64-node CMP are shown in Figure 7.

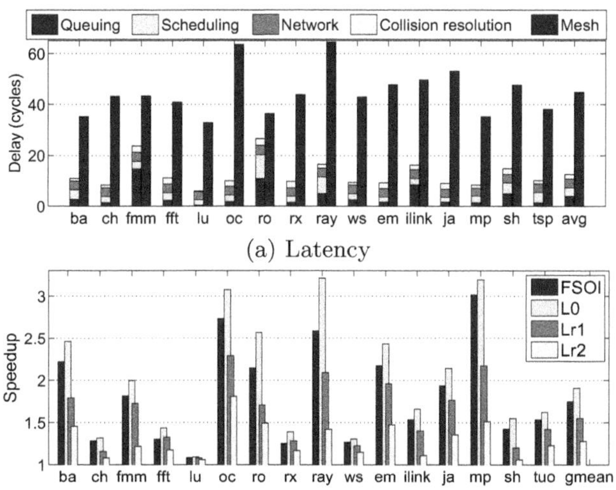

(a) Latency

(b) Speedup

Figure 7: Performance of 64-node systems.

As expected, latency in mesh interconnect increases significantly. The latency does increase in our network too, from 7.5 cycles (16-node) system to 12.6 cycles. However, in addition to the 1 cycle phase array setup delay, much of this increase is due to an increase of 2.7 cycles (from 1.4 to 4.1 cycles) in queuing delays on average. In certain applications (*e.g.*, *raytrace*), the increase is significant. This increase in queuing delays is not a result of interconnect scalability bottleneck, but rather a result of how the interconnect is *used* in applications with a larger number of threads. For example, having more sharers means more invalidations that cause large temporary queuing delays. Indeed, the queuing delay of 4.1 cycles in our system is only marginally higher than the 3.1 cycles in the ideal L_O configuration.

[8]For applications too long to finish, we measure the same workload, *e.g.*, between a fixed number of barrier instances.

Understandably, the better scalability led to wider performance gaps between our optical interconnect and the non-ideal mesh configurations. The speedup of our FSOI continues to track that of the ideal L_O configuration (with a geometric mean of 1.75 vs 1.91), and pulls further ahead of those of L_{r1} (1.55) and L_{r2} (1.29). Not surprisingly, interconnect-bound applications show more significant benefits. If we take the eight applications that experience above average performance gain from the ideal L_O, the geometric mean of their speedup in FSOI is 2.30, compared to L_O's 2.59 and L_{r1}'s 1.92.

To summarize, the proposed interconnect offers an ultra-low communication latency and maintains a low latency as the system scales up. The system outperforms aggressively configured packet-switched interconnect and the performance gap is wider for larger-scale systems and for applications whose performance has a higher dependence on the interconnect.

6.3 Energy Consumption Analysis

We have also performed a preliminary analysis of the energy characteristics of the proposed interconnect. Figure 8 shows the total energy consumption of the 16-node system normalized to the baseline configuration using mesh. Our direct communication substrate avoids the inherent inefficiency in repeated buffering and processing in a packet-switched network. Thanks to the integrated VCSELs, we can keep them powered off when not in use. This leads to an insignificant 1.8W of average power consumption in the optical interconnect subsystem. The overall energy consumption in the interconnect is 20X smaller than that in a mesh-based system. The faster execution also saves energy overhead elsewhere. On average, our system achieves a 40.6% energy savings. The reduction in energy savings outstrips the reduction in execution time, resulting in a 22% reduction in average power: 156W for conventional system and 121W for our design. The energy-delay product of FSOI is 2.7X (geometric mean) better than baseline in the 16-node system and 4.4X better in the 64-node system.

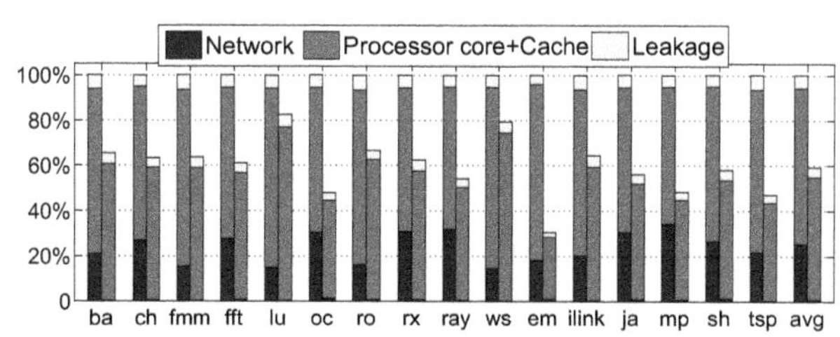

Figure 8: Energy relative to baseline mesh interconnect.

6.4 Analysis of Optimization Effectiveness

Meta packet collision reduction:.

Our design does not rely on any arbiter to coordinate the distributed communication, making the system truly scalable. The tradeoff is the presence of occasional packet collisions. Several mechanisms are used to reduce the collision probability. The most straightforward of these mechanisms is using more receivers. We use 2 receivers per lane. Our detailed simulations show that this indeed roughly reduces collisions by half in both cases as predicted by the simplified theoretical calculation and Monte Carlo simulations. This partly validates the use of simpler analytical means to make early design decisions.

Leveraging confirmation signals:.

Using the confirmation of successful invalidation delivery as a substitute for an explicit acknowledgment packet is a particularly effective approach to further reduce unnecessary traffic and collisions. Figure 9 shows the impact of this optimization. The figure represents each application by a pair of points. The coordinates show the packet transmission probability and the collision rate of the meta packet lane.

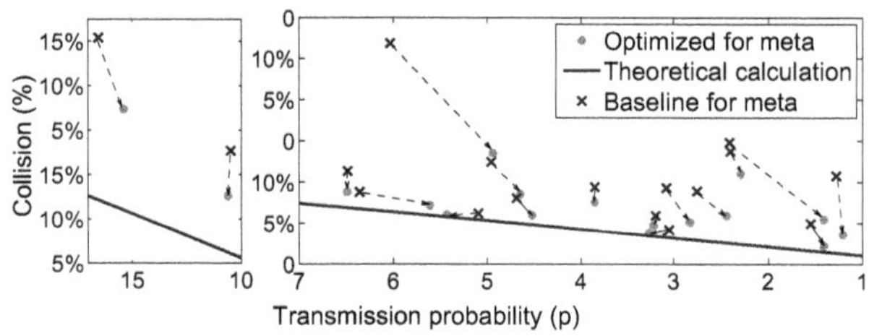

Figure 9: Change in packet transmission probability and collision rate with and without the optimization of using confirmation signal to substitute acknowledgment. For clarity, the applications are separated into two distinctive regions.

In general, as we reduce the number of packets (acknowledgments), we reduce the transmission probability and naturally the collision rate. However, if reduction of the transmission probability is the only factor in reducing collisions, the movement of the points would follow the slope of the curve which shows the theoretical collision rate given a transmission probability. Clearly, the reduction in collision is much sharper than simply due to the reduction of packets. This is because the burst of the invalidation messages sent leads to acknowledgments coming back at approximately the same time and much more likely to collide than predicted by theory assuming independent messages. Indeed, after eliminating these "quasi-synchronized" packets, the points move much closer to the theoretical predictions. Clearly, avoiding these acknowledgments is particularly helpful. Note that, because of this optimization, some applications speed up and the per-cycle transmission probability actually increases. Overall, this optimization reduces traffic by only 5.1% but eliminates about 31.5% of meta packet collisions.

Confirmation can also be used to speed up the dissemination of boolean variables used in load-linked and store-conditional. Other than latency reduction, we also cut down the packets transmitted over regular channels. Clearly, the impact of this optimization depends on synchronization intensity of the application. Some of our codes have virtually no locks or barriers in the simulated window. Seven applications have non-trivial synchronization activities in the 64-way system. For these applications, the optimization reduces data and meta packets sent by an average of 8% and 11%, respectively, and achieves a speedup of 1.07 (geometric mean). Note that the benefit comes from the combination of fast optical signaling and leveraging the confirmation mechanism that is already in place. A similar optimization in a conventional network still requires sending full-blown packets, resulting in negligible impacts.

Data packet collision reduction:.

We also looked at a few ways to reduce collisions in the data lane. These techniques include probabilistically scheduling the receiver for the incoming replies, applying split transactions for writebacks to minimize unexpected data packets, and using hints to coordinate retransmissions (Section 5.2). Figure 10 shows the breakdown of the type of collisions in the data packet lane with and without these optimizations. The result shows the general effectiveness of the techniques: about 38% of all collisions are avoided.

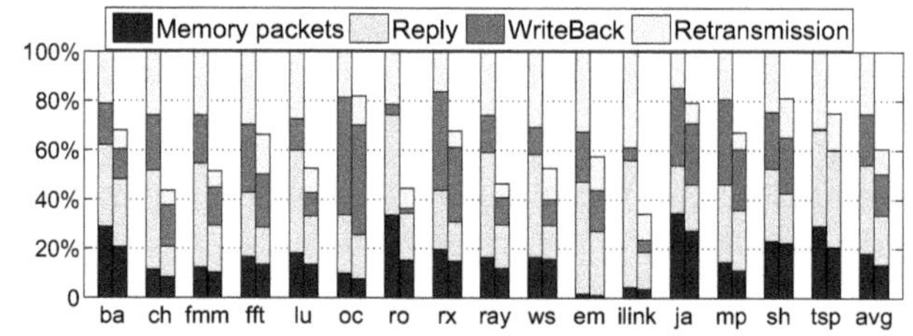

Figure 10: Breakdown of data packet collisions by type: involving memory packets (Memory packets), between replies (Reply), involving writebacks (Writeback), and involving re-transmitted packets (Retransmission). The left and the right bars show the result without and with the optimizations, respectively. The collision rate for data packets ranges from 3.0% to 21.2%, with an average of 9.4%. After optimization, the collision rate is between 1.2% and 12.2% with an average of 5.8%.

Data packet collision resolution hint:.

As discussed in Section 5.2, when a data lane collision happens we can guess the identities of the senders involved. From the simulations, we can see that based on the information of potential senders and the corrupted pattern of PID and $\overline{PID}$, we can correctly identify a colliding sender 94% of the time. Even for the rest of the time when we mis-identify the sender, it is usually harmless: If the mis-identified node is not sending any data packet at the time, it simply ignores the hint. Overall, the hints are quite accurate and on average, only 2.3% of the hints cause a node to wrongly believe it is selected as a winner to re-transmit. As a result, the hint improves the collision resolution latency from an average of 41 cycles to about 29 cycles.

Finally, note that all these measures that reduce collisions may not lead to significant performance gain when the collision probability is low. Nevertheless, these measures lower the probability of collisions when traffic is high and thus improve the resource utilization and the performance robustness of the system.

6.5 Sensitivity Analysis

As discussed before, we need to over-provision the network capacity to avoid excessive collisions in our design. However, such over-provisioning is not unique to our design. Packet-switched interconnects also need capacity margins to avoid excessive queuing delays, increased chance of network deadlocks, etc. In our comparison so far, the aggregate bandwidth of the conventional network and of our design are comparable: the configuration in the optical network design has about half the transmitting bandwidth and roughly the same receiving bandwidth as the baseline conventional mesh. To understand the sensitivity of the system performance to the communication bandwidth provided, we progressively reduce the bandwidth until it is halved. For our design, this involves reducing the number of VCSELs, rearranging them between the two lanes, and adjusting the cycle-slotting as the serialization latency for packets increases.[9] Figure 11 shows the overall performance impact. Each network's result is normalized to that of its full-bandwidth configuration. For brevity, only the average slowdown of all applications is shown.

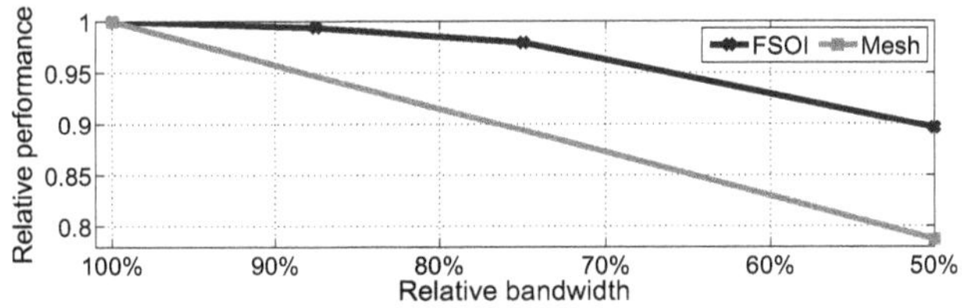

Figure 11: Performance impact due to reduction in bandwidth.

We see that both interconnects demonstrate noticeable performance sensitivity to the communication bandwidth provided. In fact, our system shows *less* sensitivity. In other words, both interconnects need to over-provision bandwidth to achieve low latency and high execution speed. The issue that higher traffic leads to higher collision rate in our proposed system is no more significant than factors such as queuing delays in a packet-relaying interconnect; it does not demand drastic over-provisioning. In the configuration space that we are likely to operate in, collisions are reasonably infrequent and accepting them is a worthwhile tradeoff. Finally, thanks to the superior energy efficiency for the integrated optical signaling chain, bandwidth provisioning is rather affordable energy-wise.

7. RELATED WORK

The effort to leverage optics for on-chip communication spans multiple disciplines and there is a vast body of related work, especially on the physics side. Our main focus in this paper is to address the challenge in building a scalable interconnect for general-purpose chip-multiprocessors, and doing so without relying on repeated O/E and E/O conversions or future breakthroughs that enable efficient pure-optical packet switching. In this regards, the most closely related design that we are aware of is [4].

In [4], packets do not need any buffering (and thus conversions) at switches within the Omega network because when a conflict occurs at any switch, one of the contenders is dropped. Even though this design addresses part of the challenge of optical packet switching by removing the need to buffer a packet, it still needs high-speed optical switches to decode the header of the packet in a just-in-time fashion in order to allow the rest of the packet to be switched correctly to the next stage. In a related design [40], a circuit-switched photonic network relies on an electrical interconnect to route special circuit setup requests. Only when an optical route is completely set up can the actual transfer take place. Clearly, only bulk transfers can amortize the delay of the setup effort. In contrast to both designs, our solution does not rely on any optical switch component.

Among the enabling technologies of our proposed design, free-space optics have been discussed in general terms in [3, 41]. There are also discussions of how free-space optics can serve as a part of the global backbone of a packet-switched interconnect [42] or as an inter-chip communication mechanism (*e.g.*, [43]). On the integration side, leveraging 3D integration to build on-chip optoelectronic circuit has also been mentioned as an elegant solution to address various integration issues [6].

Many proposals exist that use a globally shared medium for the optical network and use multiple wavelengths available in an optical medium to compensate for the network topology's non-scalable nature. [44] discussed dividing the channels and using some for coherence broadcasts. [7] also uses broadcasts on the shared bus for coherence. A recent design from HP [13,45] uses a microring-based EO modulator to allow fast token-ring arbitration to arbitrate the access to the shared medium. A separate channel broadcast is also reserved for broadcast. Such wavelength division multiplexing (WDM) schemes have been proven highly effective in long-haul fiber-optic communications and inter-chip interconnects [46, 47]. However, as discussed in Section 2 there are several critical challenges to adopt these WDM systems for intra-chip interconnects: the need for stringent device geometry and runtime condition control; practical limits on the number of devices that can be allowed on a single waveguide before the insertion loss becomes prohibitive; and the large hidden cost of external multi-wavelength laser.

In summary, while nano-photonic devices provide tremendous possibilities, integrating them into microprocessors at scale is not straightforward. Network and system level solutions and optimizations are a necessary venue to relax the demands on devices.

8. CONCLUSION

While optics are believed to be a promising long-term solution to address the worsening processor interconnect problem as technology scales, significant technical challenges remain to allow scalable optical interconnect using conventional packet switching technology. In this paper, we have proposed a scalable, fully-distributed interconnect based on free-space optics. The design leverages a suite of maturing technologies to build an architecture that supports a direct communication mechanism between nodes and does not rely on any packet switching functionality and thus sidesteps the challenges involved in implementing efficient optical switches. The tradeoff is the occasional packet collisions from uncoordinated packet transmissions. The negative impact of collisions is minimized by careful architecting of the interconnect and novel optimizations in the communication and coherence substrates of the multiprocessor.

Based on parameters extracted from device and circuit simulations, we have performed faithful architectural simulations with detailed modeling of the microarchitecture, the memory subsystems, the communication substrate, and the coherence substrates to study the performance and energy metrics of the design. The study shows that compared to conventional electrical interconnect, our design provides good performance (superior than even the most aggressively configured mesh interconnect), better scalability, and a far better energy efficiency. With the proposed architectural

[9]For easier configuration of the optical network, we use a slightly different base configuration for normalization. In this configuration, both data and meta lanes have 6 VCSELs and as a result, the serialization latency for a meta packet and a data packet is 1 and 5 cycles respectively – the same as in the mesh networks.

optimizations to minimize the negative consequences of collisions, the design is also shown to be rather insensitive to bandwidth capacity. Overall, we believe the proposed ideas point to promising design spaces for further exploration.

REFERENCES

[1] SIA. International Technology Roadmap for Semiconductors. Technical report, 2008.

[2] J. Goodman et al. Optical Interconnections for VLSI Systems. *Proc. IEEE*, 72:850–866, Jul. 1984.

[3] D. Miller. Optical Interconnects to Silicon. *IEEE J. of Selected Topics in Quantum Electronics*, 6(6):1312–1317, Nov/Dec 2000.

[4] A. Shacham and K. Bergman. Building Ultralow-Latency Interconnection Networks Using Photonic Integration. *IEEE Micro*, 27(4):6–20, July/August 2007.

[5] Y. Vlasov, W. Green, and F. Xia. High-Throughput Silicon Nanophotonic Wavelength-Insensitive Switch for On-Chip Optical Networks. *Nature Photonics*, (2):242–246, March 2008.

[6] R. Beausoleil et al. Nanoelectronic and Nanophotonic Interconnect. *Proceedings of the IEEE*, February 2008.

[7] N. Kirman et al. Leveraging Optical Technology in Future Bus-based Chip Multiprocessors. In *Proc. Int'l Symp. on Microarch.*, pages 492–503, December 2006.

[8] M. Haurylau et al. On-Chip Optical Interconnect Roadmap: Challenges and Critical Directions. *IEEE J. Sel. Quantum Electronics*, (6):1699–1705, 2006.

[9] J. Xue et al. An Intra-Chip Free-Space Optical Interconnect: Extended Technical Report. Technical report, Dept. Electrical & Computer Engineering, Univ. of Rochester, April 2010. `http://www.ece.rocehster.edu/~mihuang/`.

[10] L. Liao et al. High Speed Silicon Mach-Zehnder Modulator. *Opt. Express*, 13(8):3129–3135, 2005.

[11] Q. Xu et al. Micrometre-scale Silicon Electro-optic Modulator. *Nature*, 435(7040):325–327, May. 2005.

[12] S. Manipatruni et al. Wide Temperature Range Operation of Micrometer-scale Silicon Electro-Optic Modulators. *Opt. Lett.*, 33(19):2185–2187, 2008.

[13] R. Beausoleil et al. A Nanophotonic Interconnect for High-Performance Many-Core Computation. *IEEE LEOS Newsletter*, June 2008.

[14] W. Bogaerts et al. Low-loss, Low-cross-talk Crossings for Silicon-on-insulator Nanophotonic Waveguides. *Opt. Lett.*, 32(19):2801–2803, 2007.

[15] R. Michalzik and K. Ebeling. *Vertical-Cavity Surface-Emitting Laser Devices*, chapter 3, pages 53–98. Springer, 2003.

[16] K. Yashiki et al. 1.1-um-Range Tunnel Junction VCSELs with 27-GHz Relaxation Oscillation Frequency. In *Proc. Optical Fiber Communications Conf.*, pages 1–3, 2007.

[17] Y. Chang, C. Wang, and L. Coldren. High-efficiency, High-speed VCSELs with 35 Gbit/s Error-free Operation. *Elec. Lett.*, 43(19):1022–1023, 2007.

[18] B. Ciftcioglu et al. 3-GHz Silicon Photodiodes Integrated in a 0.18-mum CMOS Technology. *IEEE Photonics Tech. Lett.*, 20(24):2069–2071, Dec.15 2008.

[19] A. Chin and T. Chang. Enhancement of Quantum Efficiency in Thin Photodiodes through Absorptive Resonance. *J. Vac. Sci. and Tech.*, (339), 1991.

[20] G. Ortiz et al. Monolithic Integration of $In_{0.2}Ga_{0.8}As$ Vertical-cavity Surface-emitting Lasers with Resonance-enhanced Quantumwell Photodetectors. *Elec. Lett.*, (1205), 1996.

[21] S. Park et al. Microlensed Vertical-cavity Surface-emitting Laser for Stable Single Fundamental Mode Operation. *Applied Physics Lett.*, 80(2):183–185, 2002.

[22] K. Chang, Y. Song, and Y. Lee. Self-Aligned Microlens-Integrated Vertical-Cavity Surface-Emitting Lasers. *IEEE Photonics Tech. Lett.*, 18(21):2203–2205, Nov.1 2006.

[23] E. Strzelecka et al. Monolithic Integration of Vertical-cavity Laser Diodes with Refractive GaAs Microlenses. *Electronics Lett.*, 31(9):724–725, Apr. 1995.

[24] D. Louderback et al. Modulation and Free-space Link Characteristics of Monolithically Integrated Vertical-cavity Lasers and Photodetectors with Microlenses . *IEEE J. of Selected Topics in Quantum Electronics*, 5(2):157–165, Mar/Apr 1999.

[25] S. Chou et al. Sub-10 nm Imprint Lithography and Applications. *J. Vac. Sci. Tech. B.*, 15:2897–2904, 1997.

[26] M. Austin et al. Fabrication of 5 nm Linewidth and 14 nm Pitch Features by Nanoimprint Lithography. *Appl. Phys. Lett.*, 84:5299–5301, 2004.

[27] K. Banerjee et al. On Thermal Effects in Deep Sub-Micron VLSI Interconnects. *Proc. of the IEEE/ACM Design Automation Conf.*, pages 885–890, Jun. 1999.

[28] D. Tuckerman and R. Pease. High Performance Heat Sinking for VLSI. *IEEE Electron Device Lett.*, 2(5):126–129, May 1981.

[29] B. Dang. *Integrated Input/Output Interconnection and Packaging for GSI*. PhD thesis, Georgia Inst. of Tech., 2006.

[30] A. Balandin. Chill out. *IEEE Spec.*, 46(10):34–39, Oct. 2009.

[31] C. Hammerschmidt. IBM Brings Back Water Cooling Concepts. *EE Times*, June 2009. `http://www.eetimes.com/showArticle.jhtml?articleID=218000152`.

[32] C. Hammerschmidt. IBM, ETH Zurich Save Energy with Water-Cooled Supercomputer. *EE Times*, June 2009. `http://eetimes.eu/showArticle.jhtml?articleID=218100798`.

[33] P. McManamon et al. Optical Phased Array Technology. *Proc. of the IEEE*, 84(2):268–298, Feb. 1996.

[34] D. Culler and J. Singh. *Parallel Computer Architecture: a Hardware/Software Approach*. Morgan Kaufmann, 1999.

[35] L. Roberts. ALOHA Packet System With and Without Slots and Capture. *ACM SIGCOMM Computer Communication Review*, 5(2):28–42, April 1975.

[36] R. Metcalfe and D. Boggs. Ethernet: Distributed Packet Switching for Local Computer Networks. *Communications of the ACM*, 26(1):90–95, January 1983.

[37] K. Yeager. The MIPS R10000 Superscalar Microprocessor. *IEEE Micro*, 16(2):28–40, April 1996.

[38] S. Woo, M. Ohara, E. Torrie, J. Singh, and A. Gupta. The SPLASH-2 Programs: Characterization and Methodological Considerations. In *Proc. Int'l Symp. on Comp. Arch.*, pages 24–36, June 1995.

[39] S. Mukherjee, P. Bannon, S. Lang, A. Spink, and D Webb. The ALpha 21364 Network Architecture. *IEEE Micro*, 22(1):26–35, January 2002.

[40] A. Shacham, K. Bergman, and L. Carloni. On the Design of a Photonic Network-on-Chip. In *First Proc. Int'l Symp. on Networks-on-Chip*, pages 53–64, May 2007.

[41] A. Krishnamoorthy and D. Miller. Firehose Architectures for Free-Space Optically Interconnected VLSI Circuits. *Journal of Parallel and Distributed Computing*, 41:109–114, 1997.

[42] P. Marchand et al. Optically Augmented 3-D Computer: System Technology and Architecture. *Journal of Parallel and Distributed Computing*, 41:20–35, 1997.

[43] A. Walker et al. Optoelectronic Systems Based on InGaAs Complementary-Metal-Oxide-Semiconductor Smart-Pixel Arrays and Free-Space Optical Interconnects. *Applied Optics*, 37(14):2822–2830, May 1998.

[44] J. Ha and T. Pinkston. SPEED DMON: Cache Coherence on an Optical Multichannel Interconnect Architecture. *Journal of Parallel and Distributed Computing*, 41:78–91, 1997.

[45] D. Vantrease et al. Corona: System Implications of Emerging Nanophotonic Technology. In *Proc. Int'l Symp. on Comp. Arch.*, June 2008.

[46] E. de Souza et al. Wavelength-division Multiplexing with Femtosecond Pulses. *Opt. Lett.*, 20(10):1166, 1995.

[47] B. Nelson et al. Wavelength Division Multiplexed Optical Interconnect Using Short Pulses. *IEEE J. of Selected Topics in Quantum Electronics*, 9(2):486–491, Mar/Apr 2003.

Aérgia: Exploiting Packet Latency Slack in On-Chip Networks

Reetuparna Das§ Onur Mutlu† Thomas Moscibroda‡ Chita R. Das§
§Pennsylvania State University †Carnegie Mellon University ‡Microsoft Research
{rdas,das}@cse.psu.edu onur@cmu.edu moscitho@microsoft.com

Abstract

Traditional Network-on-Chips (NoCs) employ simple arbitration strategies, such as round-robin or oldest-first, to decide which packets should be prioritized in the network. This is suboptimal since different packets can have very different effects on system performance due to, e.g., different level of memory-level parallelism (MLP) of applications. Certain packets may be performance-critical because they cause the processor to stall, whereas others may be delayed for a number of cycles with no effect on application-level performance as their latencies are hidden by other outstanding packets' latencies. In this paper, we define slack *as a key measure that characterizes the relative importance of a packet. Specifically, the slack of a packet is the number of cycles the packet can be delayed in the network with no effect on execution time. This paper proposes new router prioritization policies that exploit the available slack of interfering packets in order to accelerate performance-critical packets and thus improve overall system performance. When two packets interfere with each other in a router, the packet with the lower slack value is prioritized. We describe mechanisms to estimate slack, prevent starvation, and combine slack-based prioritization with other recently proposed application-aware prioritization mechanisms.*

We evaluate slack-based prioritization policies on a 64-core CMP with an 8x8 mesh NoC using a suite of 35 diverse applications. For a representative set of case studies, our proposed policy increases average system throughput *by 21.0% over the commonly-used round-robin policy. Averaged over 56 randomly-generated multiprogrammed workload mixes, the proposed policy improves system throughput by 10.3%, while also reducing application-level unfairness by 30.8%.*

Categories and Subject Descriptors

C.1.2 [**Computer Systems Organization**]: Multiprocessors; Interconnection architectures; C.1.4 [**Parallel Architectures**]: Distributed architectures

General Terms

Design, Algorithms, Performance

Keywords

On-chip networks, multi-core, arbitration, prioritization, memory systems, packet scheduling, slack, criticality

ISCA'10, June 19–23, 2010, Saint-Malo, France.

1. Introduction

Network-on-Chips (NoCs) are widely viewed as the de facto solution for integrating a large number of components future microprocessors will consist of. In contrast to ad-hoc point-to-point global wiring, shared buses or monolithic crossbars, NoCs are scalable and have well-controlled and highly predictable electrical properties. It is thus foreseeable that on-chip networks will become one of the most critical shared resources in many-core systems, and that the performance of such systems will heavily depend on the resource sharing policies employed in the on-chip networks. Therefore, devising efficient and fair scheduling strategies is particularly important (but also challenging) when the network is shared by diverse applications, with potentially different requirements.

Managing shared resources in a highly parallel system is one of the most fundamental challenges that we face. While interference of applications is relatively well understood for many important shared resources, such as shared last-level caches [18, 30, 5, 4, 11] or memory bandwidth [26, 23, 24, 19], less is known about the interference behavior of applications in NoCs, and the impact of this interference on applications' execution times. One reason why analyzing and managing multiple applications in a shared NoC is challenging is that application interactions in a distributed system can be complex and chaotic, with numerous first- and second-order effects (queueing delays, different memory-level parallelism (MLP), burstiness, impact of the spatial location of cache banks, etc.) and hard-to-predict interference patterns that can have a significant impact on application-level performance.

A major algorithmic question that governs application interactions in the network is the NoC router's *arbitration policy*, i.e., which packet to prioritize if two or more packets arrive at the same time, and they want to take the same output port. Traditionally, arbitration policies used in on-chip networks have been very simple heuristics, including round-robin (RR) and age-based arbitration (oldest-first). These arbitration policies treat all packets equally, irrespective of source applications' characteristics. In other words, these policies arbitrate between packets as if each packet had exactly the same impact on application-level performance. In reality, however, applications can be diverse with unique and dynamic characteristics/demands. Different packets can have a vastly different importance to their respective application's performance. In the presence of memory level parallelism (MLP) [16, 22], although there might be multiple outstanding load misses in the system, not every load miss is a *bottleneck-causing (i.e. critical)* miss [14]. Assume, for example, that an application issues two concurrent network requests, one after another, first to a remote node in the network, and second to a closeby node. Clearly, the packet going to the closeby node is less critical, because even if it is delayed for several cycles in the network, its latency will be hidden from the application by the packet going to the distant node, which takes more time. Thus, the delay tolerance of each packet with regard to its impact on its application's performance can be different.

In this paper, we exploit this diversity of packets to design higher-performance and more application-fair NoCs. We do so by differ-

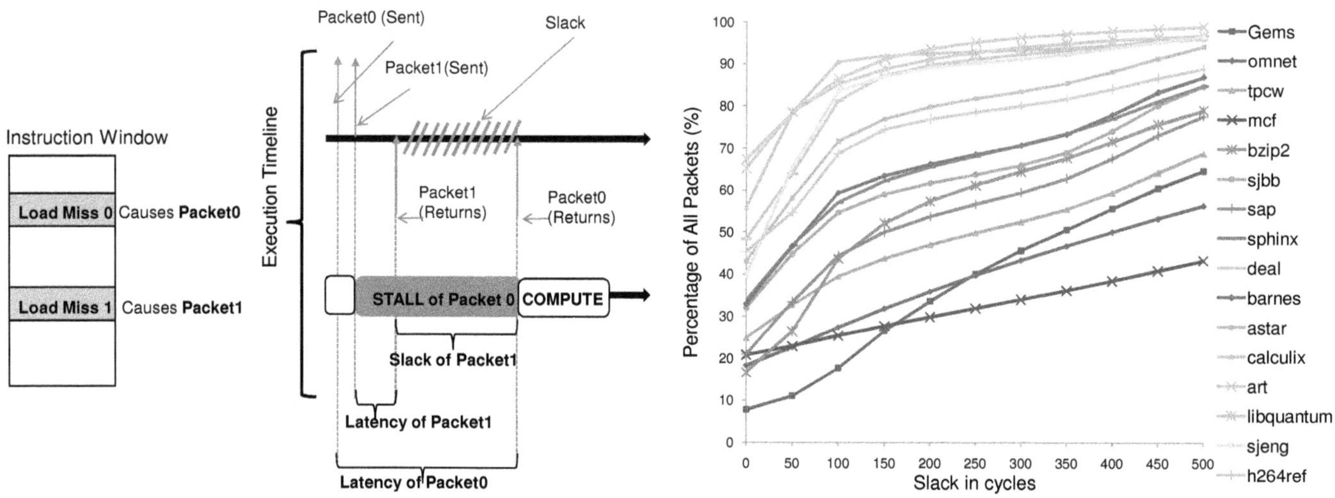

Figure 1: (a) The concept of slack, (b) Packet distribution of applications based on slack cycles

entiating packets based on their *slack*, a measure that captures the packet's importance to its application's performance. Particularly, we define the slack of a packet to be the number of cycles the packet can be delayed in the network without having an effect on the application's execution time. Hence, a packet is relatively non-critical until the time it spends in the network exceeds the packet's available slack. In comparison, increasing the latency of packets with no available slack (by de-prioritizing them during arbitration in NoC routers) will cause the application to stall.

We describe *Aérgia*[1], a new NoC architecture that contains new router prioritization mechanisms to accelerate the critical packets with low slack values by prioritizing them over packets with larger slack values. To this end, we devise techniques to efficiently estimate the slack of a packet dynamically. Prior to injection into the network, each packet is tagged with a priority that depends on the estimated slack of the packet. We propose extensions to routers to prioritize packets with lower slack at the contention points within the router (i.e., buffer allocation and switch arbitration). Finally, to ensure forward progress and starvation freedom from prioritization, *Aérgia* groups packets into batches, and ensures that all the packets from an earlier batch are serviced before packets from a later batch. Experimental evaluations on a cycle-accurate simulator show that our proposal effectively increases overall system throughput and application-level fairness in the NoC. To summarize, the main **contributions** of this paper are the following:

- We observe that the packets in the network have varying degree of slack, and analyze the correlation of slack to application characteristics, such as the application's MLP. We observe that existing arbitration policies schedule packets regardless of their slack, and that state-of-the-art global application-aware prioritization (STC) mechanisms proposed in [8] can sometimes lead to unfairness because they treat packets of an application equally.
- We propose novel, slack-aware prioritization mechanisms (online slack estimation, and slack-aware arbitration) to improve application-level system throughput and application-level fairness in NoCs. Our key idea is to dynamically estimate the available slack of each network packet and prioritize critical packets with lower available slack in the network.
- We qualitatively and quantitatively compare our proposal to previous local and global arbitration policies, GSF [21], and STC [8]. We show that our proposal provides the highest *overall system throughput* as well as the best *application-level fairness* (10.3% improvement in weighted speedup and 30.8% reduction in unfairness over the baseline round-robin policy across 56 diverse multiprogrammed workloads).
- We show that Aérgia is a fine-grained prioritization mechanism that can be used as a *complementary technique with any other prioritization substrate* to improve performance and fairness. Thus, using Aérgia within the STC framework improves both system performance and fairness, respectively by 6.7% and 18.1% compared to STC over 56 diverse multiprogrammed workloads.

[1] Aérgia is the female spirit of laziness in Greek mythology. Inspired from the observation that packets in Network-on-Chip can afford to slack (off), we name our architecture Aérgia.

2. Motivation

2.1 Concept of Slack

Modern microprocessors employ several memory latency tolerance techniques (e.g., out-of-order execution [35] and runahead execution [10, 25, 22]) to hide the penalty of load misses. These techniques exploit *Memory Level Parallelism* (MLP) [16] by issuing several memory requests in parallel with the hope of overlapping future load misses with current load misses [22]. In the presence of MLP in an on-chip network, the existence of multiple outstanding packets leads to overlap of packets' latencies, which introduces slack cycles. Intuitively, the *slack of a packet* is the number of cycles the packet can be delayed without affecting the overall execution time. For example, consider the processor execution time-line shown in Figure 1 (a). In the instruction window, the first load miss causes a packet (*Packet0*) to be sent into the network to service the load miss, and the second load miss generates the next packet (*Packet1*). In the execution time-line of Figure 1 (a), *Packet1* has lower network latency than *Packet0*, and returns to the source earlier. Nonetheless, the processor cannot commit *Load0* and stalls until *Packet0* returns. Thus, *Packet0 is the bottleneck packet*, which *allows the earlier-returning Packet1 some slack cycles* as shown in the figure. *Packet1* could be delayed for the slack cycles without causing significant application-level performance loss.

2.2 Advantages of Exploiting Slack

In this paper, we show that a network-on-chip architecture that is aware of slack can lead to better system performance and fairness. The number of slack cycles a packet has is an indication of the importance or criticality of that packet to the processor core. If the NoC were aware of the remaining slack of a packet, it could take arbitration decisions that would accelerate packets with a small slack, which would improve the overall performance of the system.

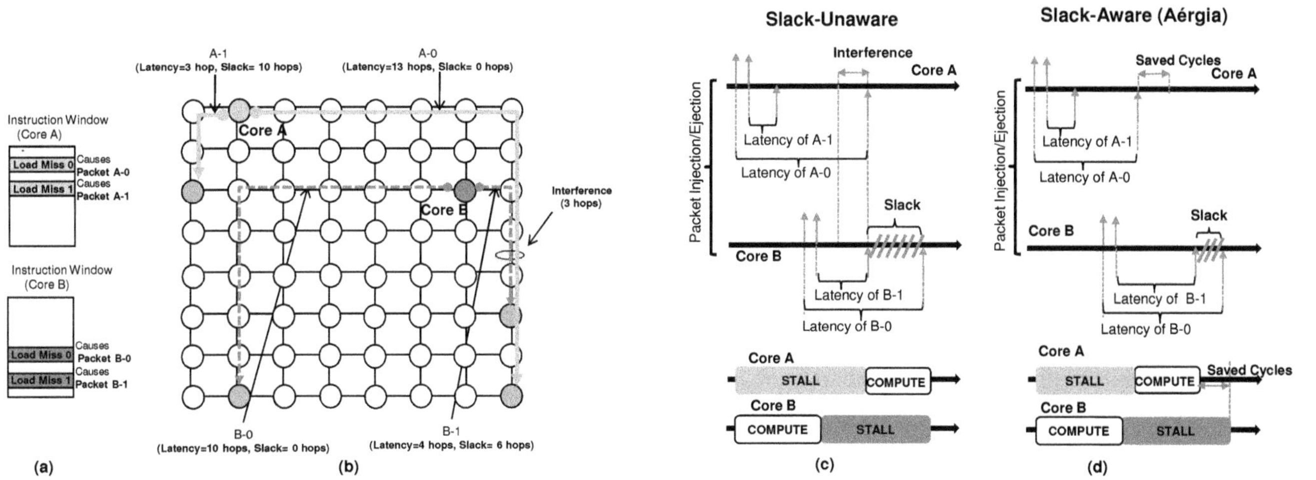

Figure 2: Conceptual example showing the advantage of incorporating slack into prioritization decisions in the NoC

Figure 2 shows a motivating example. Figure 2(a) shows the instruction window of two processor cores (Core A at node (1,2) and Core B at node (3,7)). The network consists of an 8x8 mesh as shown in Figure 2(b). Core A generates two packets (*A-0* and *A-1*). The first packet (*A-0*) is not preceded by any other packet and is sent to node (8,8), hence it has a latency of 13 hops and a slack of 0 hops. In the next cycle, the second packet (*A-1*) is injected towards node (3,1). This packet has a latency of 3 hops, and since it is preceded (and thus overlapped) by the 13-hop packet (*A-0*), it has a slack of at least 10 hops (13 hops - 3 hops). Core B also generates two packets, (*B-0* and *B-1*). The latency and slack of Core B's packets can be calculated similarly. *B-0* has a latency of 10 hops and slack of 0 hops. *B-1* has a latency of 4 hops and slack of 6 hops.

The concept of slack can be exploited when there is interference between packets with different slack values. In Figure 2(b), for example, packets *A-0* and *B-1* interfere. The critical question is, which of the two packets should be prioritized by the router, and which one should be queued/delayed?

Figure 2(c) shows the execution time-line of the cores with the baseline slack-unaware prioritization policy that prioritizes packet *B-1*, thereby delaying packet *A-0*. In contrast, if the routers were aware of the slack of packets, they would prioritize packet *A-0* over *B-1* because the former has smaller slack, as shown in Figure 2(d). Doing so would reduce the stall time of Core A *without significantly increasing* the stall time of Core B, thereby improving overall system throughput, as Figure 2 shows. The critical observation is that delaying a packet with a higher slack value can improve overall system performance by allowing a packet with a lower slack value to stall its core less.

2.3 Diversity in Slack and Its Analysis

The necessary condition to exploit slack is that there should be sufficient diversity in slack cycles of interfering packets. In other words, it is only possible to benefit from prioritizing low-slack packets if the network contains a good mix of both high- and low-slack packets at any time. Fortunately, we find that there exists sufficient slack diversity in realistic systems and applications.

Let us define the term *predecessor packets*, or simply *predecessors* for a given packet P as all packets that are i) still outstanding and ii) have been injected into the network earlier than P. Conversely, we call subsequent packets to be successor packets (or *successors*). The number of slack cycles for each packet varies within application phases as well as between different applications. This is primarily due to variations in 1) *latency of predecessors* and 2) *number of predecessors* for a given packet. Specifically, a packet is likely to have high slack if it has high-latency predecessors or if it has a large number of predecessors, since in both cases, the likelihood of its latency to be overlapped (i.e. its slack to be high) is higher.

The *latency of a predecessor* varies depending on whether it is an L2 cache hit or miss. An L2 miss has very high latency due to off-chip DRAM access, and therefore, causes very high slack to its successor packets (unless the successors are also L2 misses). Also, as demonstrated in the above example, predecessor latency varies depending on the distance or number of hops the predecessor packet has to traverse in the network. The *number of predecessor packets* is determined by the injection rate of packets (i.e., L1 cache miss rates) as well as the burstiness of packet generation of a source application running on a particular node.

Figure 1(b) shows a cumulative distribution function of the diversity in slack cycles for different applications.[2] The X-axis shows the number of slack cycles per packet.[3] The Y-axis shows the fraction of total packets that have *at least* as many slack cycles per packet as indicated by the X-axis. Two trends are visible. First, most applications have a good spread of packets with respect to number of slack cycles, indicating sufficient *slack diversity within an application*. For example, 17.6% of `Gems`' packets have at most 100 slack cycles, but 50.4% of them have more than 350 slack cycles. Second, different applications have different slack characteristics. For example, the packets of `art` and `libquantum` have much lower slack in general than `tpcw` and `omnetpp`.

3. Characterization and Online Estimation of Slack

The premise of this work is to identify critical packets with low slack and accelerate them by de-prioritizing packets with high slack cycles. In this section, (i) we formally define slack (ii) since slack itself cannot be directly measured, we perform detailed characterization of slack to find indirect metrics that correlate with slack (iii) we then show how these metrics can be quantized into specific priority levels and (iv) finally, we describe on-line techniques to dynamically approximate the indirect metrics (and hence slack) in an NoC.

[2] Although our final performance evaluation spans a suite of 35 applications, in all our characterization plots we show a subset of 16 applications for clarity. These 16 applications represent equally, heavy, medium, light utilization and network sensitive applications. We collected these statistics over 56 randomly generated workloads (See Section 6 for system configuration).

[3] The value on the X axis (slack cycles per packet) is proportional to end-to-end predecessor packet latency (which includes DRAM access latency and all network-on-chip transactions). Hence, we characterize slack up to the potentially maximum memory access latency of 1700 cycles.

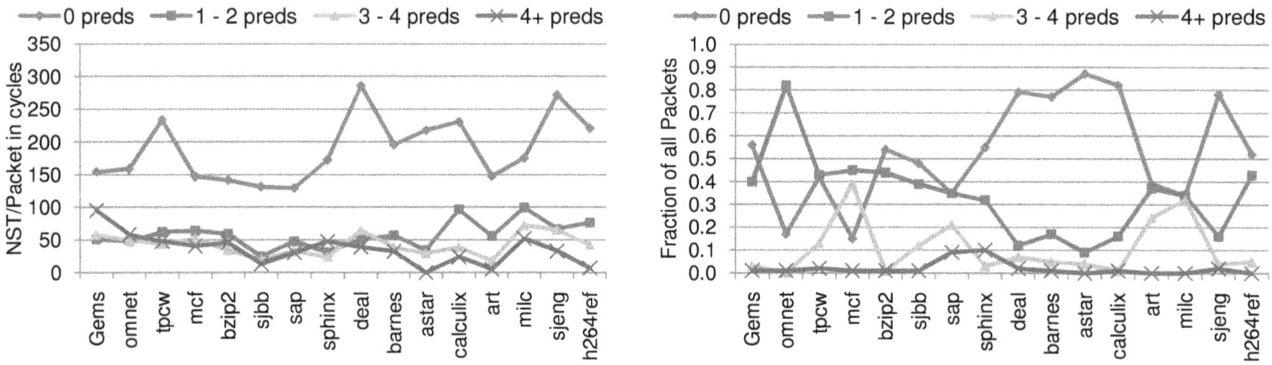

Figure 3: (a) Packet criticality based on number of miss-predecessors, (b) Distribution of packets based on number of miss-predecessors

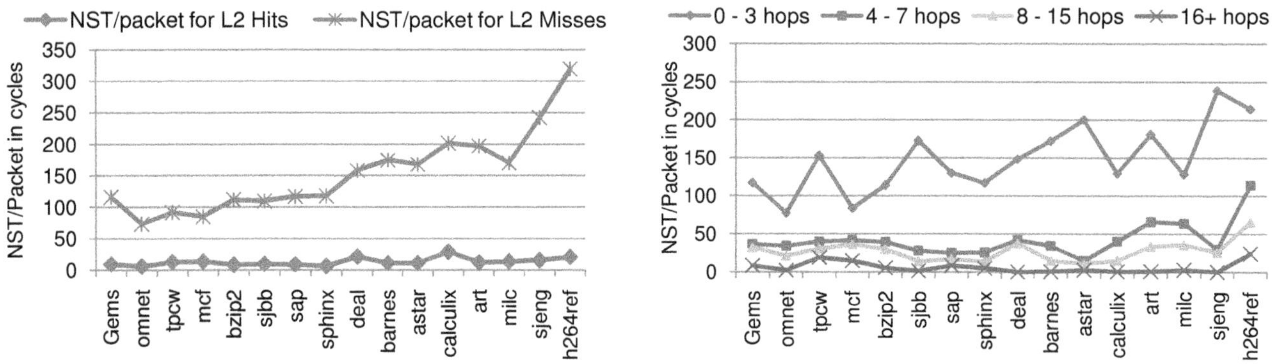

Figure 4: Packet criticality based on (a) L2 cache hit vs. miss (b) slack in terms of hops

3.1 Slack Definition

Slack can be defined locally or globally [13]. Local slack is the number of cycles a packet can be delayed without delaying *any subsequent instruction.* Global slack is the number of cycles a packet can be delayed without delaying the *last instruction in the program.* The computation of a packet's global slack requires critical path analysis of the entire program, rendering it impractical in our context. Hence, we focus on local slack. The ideal local slack of a packet could depend on instruction-level dependencies, which are hard to capture in the NoC. Hence, in order to keep the implementation in the NoC simple, we conservatively consider slack only with respect to outstanding network transactions. We formally define the available *local network slack* (or in this paper simply *slack*) of a packet to be the difference between the maximum latency of its predecessor packets (i.e., any *outstanding* packet that was injected into the network earlier than this packet) and its own latency:

$$Slack(Packet_i) = \max_k Latency(Packet_{k\ \forall\ k=0\ to\ NumberofPredecessors}) - Latency(Packet_i) \quad (1)$$

The key challenge in estimating slack is to accurately predict latencies of predecessor packets and the current packet being injected. Unfortunately, it is *difficult to predict network latency exactly in a realistic system.* Our solution is that instead of predicting the exact slack in terms of cycles, we aim to categorize/quantize slack into different priority levels, based on *indirect metrics* that *correlate with the latency of predecessors and the packet being injected.* To accomplish this, we characterize slack as it relates to various indirect metrics.

3.2 Slack Characterization

To characterize slack, we measured criticality of packets in *network stall cycles per packet*, i.e. NST/packet, which is the average number of cycles an application stalls due to an outstanding network packet. We found that the three most important factors impacting packet criticality (hence, slack) are 1) the number of predecessors that are L2 cache misses, 2) whether the injected packet is an L2 cache hit or miss, and 3) the number of a packet's extraneous hops in the network (compared to its predecessors).

Number of miss-predecessors: We define a packet's *miss predecessors* as its predecessors that are L2 cache misses. We found that the number of miss-predecessors of a packet correlates with the criticality of the packet. This is intuitive as the number of miss predecessors tries to capture the *first term of the slack equation*, i.e. Equation (1). Figure 3(a) shows the criticality (NST/packet) of packets with different number of miss-predecessors. Packets with zero miss-predecessors have the highest criticality (NST/packet) and likely the lowest slack because their latencies are unlikely to be overlapped by those of predecessors. Indeed, the difference in significant: packets with zero predecessors have much higher criticality than packets with one or more predecessors.

Figure 3(b) shows the fraction of packets that have a certain number of predecessors. The fraction of packets with more than four predecessors is very low. Thus, a mechanism that uses levels of priority based on the number of miss-predecessors need not contain many levels. Note that, since the number of miss-predecessors captures only the first term of slack equation and ignores the second term (latency of the injected packet), the correlation between it and packet criticality is imperfect; for example, in `Gems`, packets with 4+ miss-predecessors appear to have higher criticality than packets with 0 miss-predecessors. Therefore, we use two additional indirect metrics to take into account the latency of a newly injected packet.

L2 cache hit/miss status: We observe that whether a packet is an L2 cache hit or miss correlates with how critical the packet is, and hence the packet's slack. If the packet is an L2 miss, it likely has high latency due to DRAM access and extra NoC transactions to/from memory controllers. The packet therefore likely has smaller slack as its long latency is less likely to be overlapped by other packets.

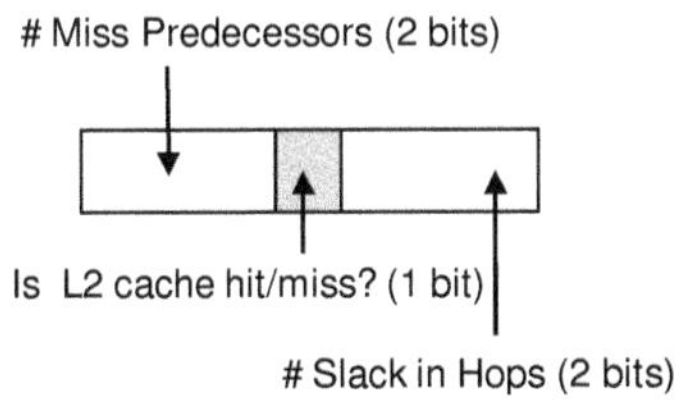

Figure 5: Priority structure for estimating slack of a packet. A lower priority level corresponds to a lower slack value.

Figure 4(a) quantifies the criticality (NST/packet) of packets based on their L2 hit/miss status. Across all applications, L2-miss packets have at least ten times higher NST/packet than L2-hit packets. Note that two priority levels suffice to designate a packet as cache hit or miss.

Slack in terms of number of hops: Our third metric captures both terms of the slack equation, and is based on the *distance* traversed in the network. This metric was illustrated in our motivating example in Section 2.2, where we approximated latency and slack as the number of hops between a source and destination. Specifically:

$$Slack_{hops}(Packet_i) = \max_k Hops(Packet_{k\ \forall k=0\ to\ Number of Predecessors}) - Hops(Packet_i) \quad (2)$$

Figure 4(b) shows that such hop-based slack indeed correlates with the criticality of packets (NST/packet). Packets with a smaller hop-based slack (0-3 hops) have significantly higher criticality than packets with a larger hop-based slack in almost all applications. For this reason, we use hop-based slack as the third component for determining the slack priority level of a packet.

3.3 Slack Priority Levels

Our analysis shows the above three metrics correlate with slack. We combine these metrics to form the *slack priority level* of a packet in Aérgia. When a packet is being injected, the above three metrics are computed and *quantized* to form a three-tier priority, shown in Figure 5. The head flit of the packet is tagged with these priority bits. (i) We use 2 bits for the first tier, which is assigned based on the number of miss-predecessors. (ii) We use a single bit for the second tier to indicate if the packet being injected is (predicted to be) an L2 hit or miss. (iii) We use 2 bits for the third tier to indicate the hop-based slack of a packet. The combined slack-based priority level is then used to prioritize between packets in routers (see Section 4).

3.4 Slack Estimation

In Aérgia, assignment of a slack priority level to a packet requires the estimation of the above-described three metrics when the packet is injected.

3.4.1 Estimating the number of miss-predecessors

Every core maintains a list of the outstanding L1 load misses (predecessor list). Note that the size of this list is bounded by the size of the miss status handling registers (MSHRs) [20]. Each of these L1 misses is associated with a corresponding *L2-miss-status* bit. At the time a packet is injected into the NoC, its actual L2 hit/miss status is unknown because the shared L2 cache is distributed across the nodes. Therefore, an L2 hit/miss predictor is consulted (as described below) and the *L2-miss-status* bit is set accordingly. The miss-predecessor slack priority level is computed as the number of outstanding L1 misses in the predecessor list whose *L2-miss-status* bits are set (to indicate a predicted or actual L2 miss). Our implementation keeps track of L1 misses issued in the last 32 cycles and sets the maximum number of miss-predecessors to 8.

In case of an error in prediction, the *L2-miss-status* bit is updated to the correct value when the data response packet returns to the core. In addition, if a packet that is predicted to be an L2 hit actually results in an L2 miss, the corresponding L2 cache bank notifies the requesting core that the packet actually resulted in an L2 miss so that the requesting core updates the corresponding *L2-miss-status* bit accordingly. To reduce control packet overhead, the L2 bank piggy-backs this information to another packet traveling through the requesting core as an intermediate node.

3.4.2 Estimating whether a packet will be L2 cache hit or miss

At the time a packet is injected, it is not known whether or not it will hit in the remote L2 cache bank it accesses. We use an L2 hit/miss predictor in each core to guess the cache hit/miss status of each injected packet, and set the second-tier priority bit accordingly in the packet header. If the packet is predicted to be an L2 miss, its L2 miss priority bit is set to 0, otherwise it is set to 1. Note that this priority bit within the packet header is corrected when the actual L2 miss status is known when the packet accesses the L2.

We develop two types of L2 miss predictors. The first is based on the *global branch predictor* [36]. A shift register records the hit/miss values for the last "M" L1 load misses. This register is then used to index into a pattern history table (PHT) containing two-bit saturating counters. The accessed counter indicates whether or not the prediction for that particular pattern history is a hit or a miss. The counter is updated when the hit/miss status of a packet is known. The second predictor, called the *threshold predictor*, uses the insight that misses occur in bursts. This predictor updates a counter if the access is a known L2 miss. The counter is reset after every "M" L1 misses. If the number of known L2 misses in the last "M" L1 misses exceeds a threshold ("T"), then the next L1 miss is predicted to be an L2 miss. The global predictor requires more storage bits (PHT) and has marginally higher design complexity than the threshold predictor. Note that, for correct updates, both predictors require an extra bit in the response packet indicating whether or not the transaction was an L2 miss.

3.4.3 Estimating hop-based slack

The hops per packet for any packet is calculated by adding the X and Y distance between source and destination. The hop-based slack of a packet is then calculated using Equation (2).

4. Aérgia Network-on-Chip Architecture

4.1 Aérgia Routers

We propose a new network-on-chip architecture, *Aérgia*, that utilizes the described slack priority levels arbitration. In this section, we describe the proposed architecture, starting ground-up from the baseline. We also address some design challenges that come along with prioritization mechanisms: i) mitigating priority inversion (using multiple network interface queues) and ii) starvation avoidance (using batching).

4.1.1 Baseline

A generic NoC router architecture is illustrated in Figure 6 (see also [7]). The router has P input and P output channels/ports; typically $P = 5$ for a 2D mesh, one from each direction and one from the network interface (NI). The Routing Computation unit, RC, is responsible for determining the next router and the virtual channel within the next router for each packet. Dimension Ordered Routing (DOR) is the most commonly used routing policy for its low complexity and deadlock freedom. Our baseline assumes XY DOR, where packets are first routed in X direction followed by Y direction. The Virtual channel Arbitration unit (VA) arbitrates amongst all packets requesting access to the same output VC in the downstream router and decides on winners. The Switch Arbitration unit (SA) arbitrates amongst all input VCs requesting access to the crossbar and grants permission to the winning packets/flits. The winners are then able to traverse the crossbar and are placed on the output links. Current routers use simple, local arbitration policies (round-robin, oldest-first) to decide which packet should be scheduled next (i.e., which packet wins arbitration). Our baseline NoC uses the round-robin policy.

4.1.2 Arbitration

Slack Priority Levels: In Aérgia, the Virtual channel Arbitration (VA) and Switch Arbitration (SA) units prioritize packets with lower slack priority levels. Thus, low-slack packets get the first preference for buffers as well as the crossbar, and hence, are accelerated in the network. Since in wormhole switching, only the head flit arbitrates for and reserves the VC, the slack priority value is carried by the head flit only. This header information is utilized during VA for priority arbitration. In addition to the state maintained by the baseline architecture, each virtual channel has one additional priority field, which is updated with the slack priority level of the head flit when the head flit reserves the virtual channel. This field is utilized by the body flits during SA for priority arbitration.

Batching: Without adequate counter-measures, prioritization mechanisms can easily lead to starvation in the network. In order to prevent starvation, we combine our slack-based prioritization with a "batching" mechanism similar to [8]. Time is divided into intervals of T cycles, called *batching intervals*. Packets inserted into the network during the same interval belong to the same batch, i.e. have the same *batch priority* value. Packets belonging to older batches are prioritized over those from younger batches. Only if two packets belong to the same batch, they are prioritized based on their available slack, i.e. the slack priority levels. Each head flit carries a 5-bit slack priority value and a 3-bit batch number/priority, as shown in Figure 7. We use adder delays in [27] to estimate the delay of an 8-bit priority arbiter (P=5,V=6) to be 138.9 picoseconds and a 16-bit priority arbiter to be 186.9 picoseconds at 45nm technology.

4.1.3 Network Interface

For effectiveness, prioritization is necessary not only within the routers but also at the network interfaces. We split the monolithic injection queue at a network interface into a small number of equal-length queues. Each queue buffers packets with slack priority levels within a different programmable range. Packets are guided into a particular queue based on their slack priority levels. Queues belonging to higher priority packets are prioritized over those of lower priority packets. Such prioritization reduces priority inversion and is especially needed at memory controllers where packets from all applications buffered together at the network interface, and thus, monolithic queues can cause severe priority inversion.

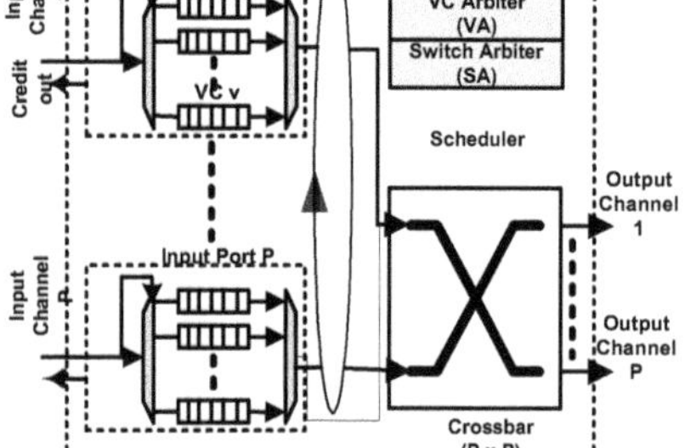

Figure 6: Baseline router microarchitecture

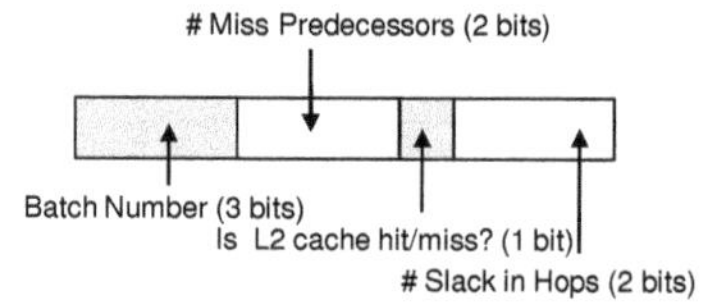

Figure 7: Final Aérgia priority structure

5. Qualitative Comparison to Application Aware Scheduling and Fairness Policies

Application-Aware Prioritization Mechanism (STC): Das et al. [8] proposed an application-aware coordinated arbitration policy (called STC) to accelerate network-sensitive applications. The key idea is to rank applications at regular intervals based on their network intensity (L1 miss rate per instruction, L1-MPI), and prioritize *all packets* of a non-intensive application over *all packets* of an intensive application. Within applications belonging to the same rank, packets are prioritized using the baseline round-robin order in a slack-unaware manner. Packet batching is used for starvation avoidance. The concept of STC and slack are complementary. There are several important differences between Aérgia and STC:

• Aérgia exploits slack at the fine granularity of *individual packets*. In contrast, STC is a coarse-grained approach that identifies critical applications (from the NoC perspective) and prioritizes them over non-critical ones. An application as a whole might be less critical than another, but even within an application there could be packets that impact its performance more than others. By focusing on application-level intensity, STC cannot capture this fine grained packet-level criticality that is exploited by a slack-aware mechanism like Aérgia.

• STC uses the L1-MPI of each application to differentiate between applications over a long ranking interval. This coarse-grained metric of application intensity does not capture finer-grained distinctions between applications/packets in both time and space. For example, this heuristic does not distinguish between applications that traverse a large vs. small number of hops. Two applications might have the same L1 miss rate but one of them might have higher intensity in the network because it either traverses longer distances or has much smaller L2 miss rate, thereby putting more pressure on the network. STC is unable to distinguish between such applications whereas Aérgia's packet based slack estimation takes into account these factors, thereby prioritizing applications/packets based on different aspects of criticality.

Note that STC and Aérgia are complementary and can be combined to take advantage of both algorithms' strengths. In this paper, we propose and evaluate such a combination. The combined architecture prioritizes higher ranked applications over lower ranked applications as STC does. Within the same ranking class, however, it uses slack-based prioritization, as Aérgia does. Our results show that the combination provides better performance and fairness than STC and Aérgia alone.

Globally Synchronized Frames (GSF): Since any prioritization mechanism is likely to impact the fairness of the system, we quantitatively compare Aérgia to a state-of-art fairness scheme, Globally Synchronized Frames (GSF) [21]. GSF provides prioritization mechanisms within the network to ensure 1) guarantees on minimum bandwidth and minimum network delay each application experiences, and 2) that each application achieves equal network throughput. To accomplish this, GSF employs the notion of frames, which

Processor Pipeline	2 GHz processor, 128-entry instruction window
Fetch/Exec/Commit width	2 instructions per cycle in each core; only 1 can be a memory operation
L1 Caches	32 KB per-core (private), 4-way set associative, 128B block size, 2-cycle latency, write-back, split I/D caches, 32 MSHRs
L2 Caches	1MB banks, shared, 16-way set associative, 128B block size, 6-cycle bank latency, 32 MSHRs
Main Memory	4GB DRAM, up to 16 outstanding requests for each processor, 260 cycle access, 4 on-chip Memory Controllers (one in each corner node).
Network Router	2-stage wormhole switched, virtual channel flow control, 6 VC's per Port, 5 flit buffer depth, 8 flits per Data Packet, 1 flit per address packet.
Network Topology	8x8 mesh, each node has a router, processor, private L1 cache, shared L2 cache bank (all nodes) 128-bit bi-directional links.

Table 1: Baseline Processor, Cache, Memory, and Network Configuration

#	Benchmark	NST/packet	Inj Rate	Load	NSTP	Bursty	#	Benchmark	NST/packet	Inj Rate	Load	NSTP	Bursty
1	wrf	7.75	0.07%	low	low	low	19	sjbb	8.92	2.20%	high	high	high
2	applu	16.30	0.09%	low	high	low	20	libquantum	12.35	2.49%	high	high	low
3	perlbench	8.54	0.09%	low	high	low	21	bzip2	5.00	3.28%	high	low	high
4	dealII	5.31	0.31%	low	low	high	22	sphinx3	8.02	3.64%	high	high	high
5	sjeng	8.35	0.37%	low	high	low	23	milc	14.73	3.73%	high	high	low
6	namd	4.59	0.65%	low	low	high	24	sap	4.84	4.09%	high	low	high
7	gromacs	5.19	0.67%	low	low	high	25	sjas	5.15	4.18%	high	low	high
8	calculix	7.10	0.73%	low	low	low	26	xalancbmk	15.72	4.83%	high	high	low
9	gcc	2.14	0.89%	low	low	high	27	lbm	8.71	5.18%	high	high	high
10	h264ref	12.41	0.96%	low	high	high	28	tpcw	5.64	5.62%	high	low	high
11	povray	2.07	1.06%	low	low	high	29	leslie3d	5.78	5.66%	high	low	low
12	tonto	3.35	1.18%	low	low	high	30	omnetpp	2.92	5.72%	high	low	low
13	barnes	7.58	1.24%	low	low	high	31	swim	10.13	6.06%	high	high	low
14	art	42.26	1.58%	low	high	low	32	cactusADM	8.30	6.28%	high	high	low
15	gobmk	4.97	1.62%	low	low	high	33	soplex	8.66	6.33%	high	high	low
16	astar	6.73	2.01%	low	low	low	34	GemsFDTD	4.82	11.95%	high	low	low
17	ocean	9.21	2.03%	low	high	high	35	mcf	5.53	19.08%	high	low	low
18	hmmer	6.54	2.12%	high	low	high							

Table 2: Application Characteristics. NST/packet (NSTP): Average network stall-time per packet, Inj Rate: Average packets per 100 Instructions, Load: low/high depending on injection rate, NSTP: high/low, Bursty: high/low.

is similar to our concept of batches. Within a frame, GSF does not distinguish between different applications; in fact, it does not specify a prioritization policy. In contrast, Aérgia employs a slack-aware prioritization policy within packets of the same batch. As a result, Aérgia provides better system-level throughput by prioritizing those packets that would benefit more from network service (as shown in our evaluation). Note that the goals of GSF and Aérgia are different: GSF aims to provide network-level QoS, whereas Aérgia optimizes system throughput by exploiting the notion of packet slack.

6. Methodology

6.1 Experimental Setup

We evaluate our techniques using a trace-driven, cycle-level x86 CMP simulator. Table 1 provides the configuration of our baseline, which contains 64 cores in a 2D, 8x8 Mesh NoC. The memory hierarchy uses a two-level directory-based MESI cache coherence protocol. Each core has a private write-back L1 cache. The network connects the cores, L2 cache banks, and memory controllers. Each router uses a state-of-the-art two-stage microarchitecture. We use the deterministic X-Y routing algorithm, finite input buffering, wormhole switching, and virtual-channel flow control. We faithfully model all implementation details of the proposed prioritization framework (Aérgia) as well as previously proposed STC and GSF. The parameters used for GSF are: 1) active window size $W = 6$, 2) synchronization penalty $S = 16$ cycles, 3) frame size $F = 1000$ flits. The default parameters used for STC are: 1) ranking levels $R = 8$, 2) batching levels $B = 8$, 3) ranking interval = 350,000 cycles, 4) batching interval = 16,000 packets. We use the threshold predictor for Aérgia with M=4 and T=2.

6.2 Evaluation Metrics

We evaluate our proposal using several metrics. We measure **application-level system performance** in terms of weighted and harmonic speedup [12], two commonly used multi-program performance metrics based on comparing the IPC of an application when it is run alone versus when it is run together with others. Hmean-speedup balances performance and fairness.

$$W.\ Speedup = \sum_i \frac{IPC_i^{shared}}{IPC_i^{alone}},\ H.\ Speedup = \frac{NumThreads}{\sum_i \frac{1}{IPC_i^{shared}/IPC_i^{alone}}}$$

Network stall cycles (NST) is the number of cycles the processor stalls waiting for a network packet [8]. To isolate effects of only the on-chip network, NST *does not include* the stall cycles due to off-chip DRAM access or on-chip cache access. We define **network-related slowdown** of an application as the network-stall time when running in a shared environment (NST^{shared}), divided by, network-stall time when running alone (NST^{alone}) on the same system. The application-level **network unfairness** of the system is the maximum network-related slowdown observed in the system:

$$NetSlowdown_i = \frac{NST_i^{shared}}{NST_i^{alone}},\quad Unfairness = \max_i NetSlowdown_i$$

6.3 Application Categories and Characteristics

We use a diverse set of multiprogrammed application workloads comprising scientific, commercial, and desktop applications. In total, we study 35 applications, including SPEC CPU2006 benchmarks, applications from SPLASH-2 and SpecOMP benchmark suites, and four commercial workloads traces (`sap`, `tpcw`, `sjbb`, `sjas`). We choose representative execution phases using [28] for all our workloads excluding commercial traces, which were collected over Intel servers. To have tractable simulation time, we choose a smaller

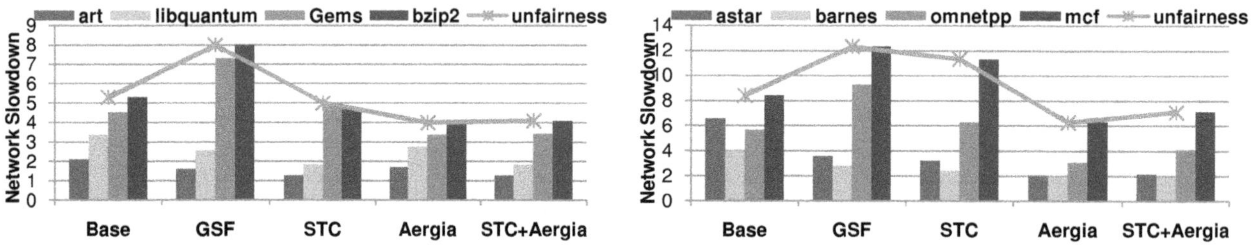

Figure 8: Network Slowdowns for (a) Case Study I on the left (b) Case Study II on the right

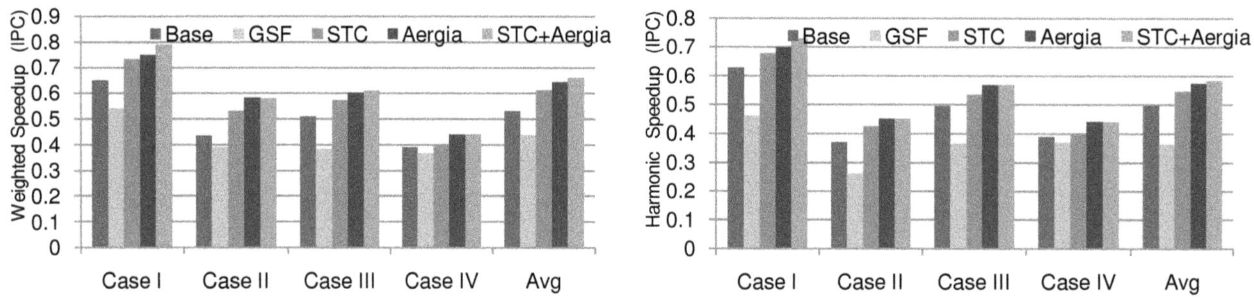

Figure 9: (a) Weighted Speedup for all Case Studies (b) Harmonic Speedup for all Case Studies

representative window of instructions (5 million per application), obtained by profiling each application. All our experiments study multi-programmed workloads, where each core runs a separate application. We simulate at least 320 million instructions across 64 processors. Table 2 characterizes our applications. The reported parameters are for the applications *running alone* on the baseline CMP system without any interference. We categorize applications into three groups based on their network characteristics: applications with 1) high/low *load* are called *heavy/light*, 2) high Network Stall Cycles per Request Packet (NSTP) are called *sensitive*, and 3) bursty injection patterns are called *bursty*. Our aggregate results are based on 56 different workload combinations.

7. Performance Evaluation

We first compare Aérgia to the baseline, GSF, and STC, using four case studies to provide insight into the behavior of each scheme with different types of workloads. Figures 8 and 10 show the network slowdowns (the lower the better) of the individual applications. Figure 9 shows system performance (weighted speedup[4] and harmonic speedups) of the different schemes for all case studies. Section 7.5 reports aggregate results averaged over 56 different workloads, showing that the benefits of our scheme hold over a wide variety of workloads. Finally, Section 7.6 examines the effect of L2 miss predictor accuracy on system performance.

7.1 Case Study I: Heterogenous mix of heavy latency-tolerant and network-sensitive applications

We mix 16 copies each of two heavy applications (`GemsFDTD` and `bzip2`) and two network-sensitive applications (`libquantum` and `art`); and compare Aérgia to baseline, GSF and STC. We make several observations:

- Figure 8 (a) shows the network slowdowns of applications. The baseline algorithm slows down applications in hard-to-predict ways as local round-robin arbitration is application-oblivious. `bzip2` has the highest slowdown (and hence determines the unfairness index) due to heavy demand from the network and high L2 cache miss rate.
- GSF unfairly penalizes the heavy applications because they quickly run out of frames and stop injecting. Thus, the network slowdowns of `GemsFDTD` and `bzip2` increase by 1.6X and 1.5X over baseline. Since GSF guarantees minimum bandwidth to all applications, it improves the network slowdown of network-sensitive applications over the baseline (by 21% for `libquantum` and 26% for `art`) by ensuring that heavier applications do not deny service to the lighter applications. However, GSF does not prioritize any application within a frame, thus there is scope for further reduction of network-sensitive applications' slowdowns. Overall, GSF degrades system throughput by 16.6% and application-level fairness by 50.9% because it unfairly penalizes the heavy applications.
- STC prioritizes the network-sensitive applications using ranking, and ensures, using batching, that heavy applications are not overly penalized. The result is that it significantly reduces the slowdown of network-sensitive applications (by 1.9X for `libquantum` and 1.6X for `art`). Heavy applications suffer marginally from lower ranking because 1) of batching 2) they are latency tolerant, i.e. have sufficient slack to tolerate de-prioritization in the network (See Figure 1 (b)), and 3) sensitive applications are light and hence negatively affect a small fraction of packets of heavy applications. STC improves weighted speedup by 12.6% over baseline.
- Aérgia exploits slack and criticality at the fine granularity of individual packets and thus optimizes for instantaneous behavior of applications. Unlike STC, which improves only network-sensitive applications, **Aérgia improves the network slowdowns of all applications** (by 24% for `libquantum`, 21% for `art`, 26% for `GemsFDTD` and 35% for `bzip2` over the baseline). *This leads to a weighted speedup improvement of 15.1% over the baseline. By improving all applications, Aérgia reduces the maximum network slowdown, and thus has the best network fairness (32% over baseline and 25% over STC).* The best improvements are seen for `bzip2` for two reasons. First, although a heavy application, at least 30% `bzip2`'s packets are critical with fewer than 50 slack cycles. These critical packets are deprioritized by STC as well as the baseline because neither is aware of the slack of these packets and they both delay bzip2 simply because it is heavy. Second, `bzip2` has better performance than `GemsFDTD` because it has a higher fraction of critical packets than `GemsFDTD`, which are prioritized by using the available slack in all applications.
- As discussed in Section 5, Aérgia and STC are complementary techniques that exploit slack and criticality at different granularity. Thus, we evaluate a combination of both architectures (referred to as STC+Aérgia in figures). While STC prioritizes the light, network-

[4] Weighted speedup is divided by number of cores (=64) in results charts for clarity.

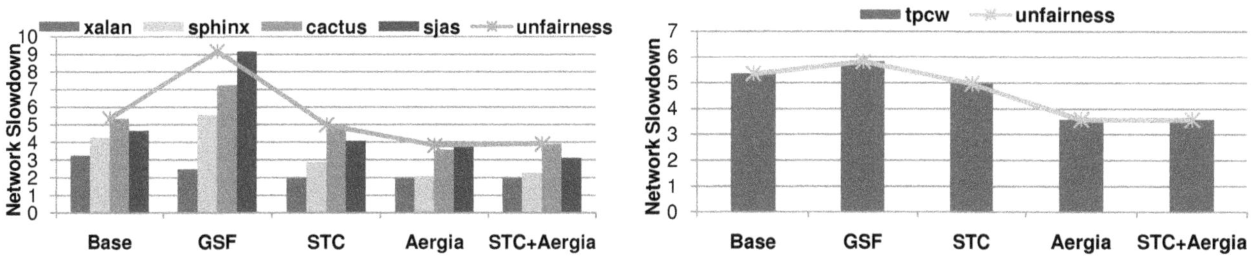

Figure 10: Network Slowdowns for (a) Case Study III on the left (b) Case Study IV on the right

sensitive applications effectively, Aérgia can exploit the differential slack within the packets of an application to improve the performance of heavy applications as well as light ones. As a result, the combination of both techniques provides the best performance (21.5% over baseline, 5.6% over Aérgia and 7.7% over STC) and almost similar fairness to Aérgia (23% and 19% better fairness over baseline and STC).

7.2 Case Study II: Heterogenous mix of heavy critical applications and light applications

We mix 16 copies each of two heavy applications (`omnetpp` and `mcf`) and two light applications (`astar` and `barnes`). The case study shows a scenario in which fairness is a problem with STC, while Aérgia is effective at prioritizing light applications that have high-slack packets. The following observations are in order:

• The baseline and GSF have similar trends as discussed in Case Study I. Although STC still provides 21.9% speedup by prioritizing the light applications (network slowdown of `astar`/`barnes` improves 2.0X/1.6X over baseline in STC), it degrades the fairness of the system by penalizing the heavy applications in this case study (STC increases unfairness by 1.35X over baseline). Some packets of these applications have high criticality (i.e. low slack), but STC deprioritizes all such packets because the applications they belong to are network-intensive.

These heavy applications have high criticality due to their high L2 miss rates, but STC deprioritizes them because they are network-intensive.

• As opposed to Case Study I, in this case study, Aérgia is more effective than STC in prioritizing light applications.[5] This result shows that to prioritize a light application, it is not necessary to prioritize *all* packets of that application as STC does. A prioritization mechanism that prioritizes only the critical/low-slack packets (like Aérgia) can provide even better speedups for a light application than a prioritization mechanism that prioritizes all packets of that light application over packets of other applications (like STC). This is because a finer-grained packet based prioritization mechanism can actually prioritize critical packets over the non-critical ones *within* the light application. `astar` and `barnes` have a small fraction of critical packets, which are prioritized over others with Aérgia but not distinguished from non-critical ones with STC. Aérgia also reduces slowdown of heavy applications because it can prioritize critical packets of such applications over non-critical packets. As a result, Aérgia improves weighted speedup by 33.6% and 9.4% over the baseline and STC, respectively.

• STC+Aérgia solves the fairness problem in STC because it reduces the network slowdown of heavy applications by prioritizing the important packets of such applications over less important packets of the same applications. Hence, it reduces the penalty the heavy applications have to pay for prioritizing the light applications in the original STC scheme. Overall STC+Aérgia provides 33.2% speedup over baseline, while reducing unfairness by 1.6X over STC (1.2X over baseline).

7.3 Case Study III: Heterogenous mix of heavy applications

In [8], authors demonstrate a case study to show the dynamic behavior of STC: applications may have similar average behavior (e.g., all are heavy), but if their transient behaviors are sufficiently different, STC can still provide high performance gains. We run 16 copies each of four heavy applications (`xalan`, `sphinx`, `cactus`, and `sjas`) to demonstrate a similar scenario. Figure 10 (a) shows the network slowdowns for this case study. Aérgia provides better performance than all schemes for such workloads (18.1% weighted speedup over baseline), while providing the best fairness (26% over baseline). Aérgia is more effective in reducing the slowdowns of `sphinx` and `cactus` than STC by exploiting criticality of packets at much finer levels. Since Aérgia prioritizes based on the slack at the packet level, it can easily distinguish between the packets of different applications and prioritize the critical ones even though the intensities of applications are similar.

7.4 Case Study IV: Homogeneous mix with multiple copies of the same application

The purpose of this homogenous case study is to demonstrate effectiveness of Aérgia in a scenario when STC can provide minimal performance gains. We run *a copy of the same application,* `tpcw` *on all 64 nodes.* Figure 10 (b) shows the network slowdowns. STC treats all cores the same, i.e. at the same priority level, because the L1-MPIs of the cores are similar. Batching framework of STC provides 2.8% higher weighted speedup over baseline by reducing starvation that occurs in the baseline. In contrast, Aérgia can provide attractive performance gains (13.7% weighted speedup over baseline) even for such homogenous workloads. This is because, even though applications and their network intensities are the same, individual packet criticality is different. Hence, Aérgia takes advantage of the disparity in packet criticality within the same application class to provide better performance and fairness.

7.5 Overall Results Across 56 Multi-Programmed Workloads

Figures 11 (a) and (b) compare all the schemes averaged across 56 workload mixes. The mixes consist of 12 homogenous workloads and 48 heterogenous workloads with applications picked randomly from different categories (See Table 2). The aggregate results are consistent with the observations made in the three case studies. Aérgia improves average system throughput by 10.3%/11.6% (weighted/ harmonic) compared to the baseline, while also improving network fairness by 30.8%. Aérgia combined with STC improves average system throughput by 6.5%/5.2% (weighted/ harmonic) compared to STC alone while also improving network fairness by 18.1%. We conclude that Aérgia provides the best system performance and network fairness over a very wide variety of work-

[5]Network slowdown of `astar`/`barnes` improves 3.2X/2.0X over baseline in Aérgia.

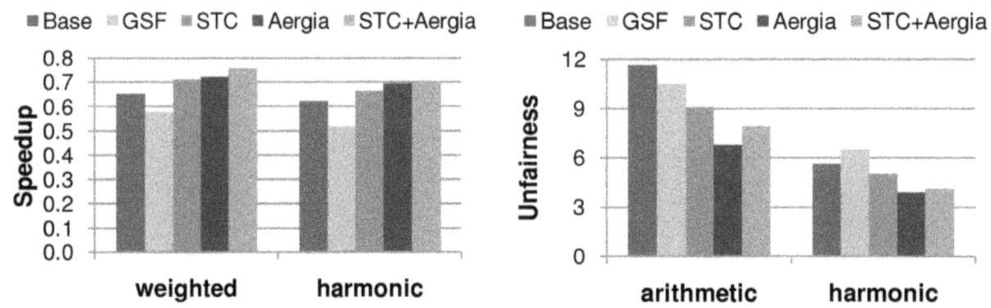

Figure 11: Aggregate results across 56 workloads (a) System Speedup (b) Network Unfairness

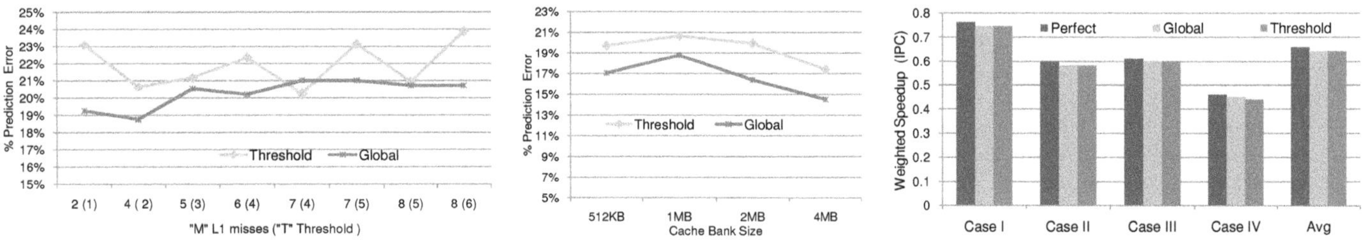

Figure 12: Analysis of L2 miss predictors: (a) error with parameters, (b) error with cache size, (c) effect of perfect prediction

loads whether used independently or in conjunction with application-aware prioritization techniques.

7.6 Effect of L2 Cache Miss Predictor

Figure 12 (a) shows the sensitivity of prediction accuracy to the parameters of the two predictors we developed: M (number of accesses in history) and T (threshold value, which is used only for the threshold predictor). Figure 12 (b) shows the sensitivity of prediction accuracy to size of cache banks for both predictors. Averaged over 56 workloads for 1MB L2 cache banks, the global predictor has an error of 18.7% (M=4) and the threshold predictor has an error of 20.7% (M=4, T=2). Figure 12 (c) shows the performance difference between perfect miss prediction, the global predictor, and the threshold predictor. Results show that only 2.4% performance improvement is possible if the predictor were perfect. This is mainly because the negative impact of a misprediction is limited because we update the L2 cache hit/miss priority field of a packet once the miss status is known after L2 access.[6] We conclude that the miss predictors we develop provide sufficient accuracy for slack estimation purposes.

8. Related Work

To our knowledge, no previous work characterized slack in packet latency and proposed mechanisms to exploit it for on-chip network arbitration. We briefly describe the most closely related previous work.

Instruction Criticality and Memory Level Parallelism: A large amount of research has been done to predict criticality/slack of instructions [32, 14, 13, 33] and prioritize critical instructions in the processor core and caches. MLP-aware cache replacement exploits cache miss criticality differences due to memory-level parallelism [29]. Parallelism-aware memory scheduling [24] and other rank-based memory scheduling algorithms [19] reduce application stall-time by improving bank-level parallelism of each thread. These works are related to ours only in the sense that we also exploit criticality to improve system performance. However, our methods (for computing slack) and mechanisms (for exploiting it) are very different due to the distributed nature of on-chip networks.

Prioritization in On-Chip and Multiprocessor Networks: We have already compared our approach extensively, both to state-of-the-art local arbitration, QoS-oriented prioritization (GSF [21]), and application-aware prioritization (STC [8]) policies in NoCs. Bolotin et al. [3] propose prioritizing control packets over data packets in the NoC, but do not distinguish packets based on available slack. Frameworks for QoS [2, 31, 17] on NoCs were proposed, which can possibly be combined with our approach. Arbitration policies [37, 6, 15, 1, 9, 38] have also been proposed in multi-chip multiprocessor networks and long-haul networks. Their goal is to provide guaranteed service or fairness, while ours is to exploit slack in packet latency to improve system performance. In addition, most of the above previous mechanisms *statically assign priorities/bandwidth* to different flows in off-chip networks to satisfy real-time performance and QoS guarantees. In contrast, our proposal *dynamically computes and assigns priorities to packets* based on slack.

Batching: We use packet batching in NoC for starvation avoidance, similarly to [8]. The idea of batching/frames has been used in disk scheduling [34], memory scheduling [24], and QoS-aware packet scheduling [21, 17] to prevent starvation and provide fairness.

9. Conclusion

The network-on-chip is a critical shared resource likely to be shared by diverse applications with varying characteristics and service demands. Thus, characterizing, understanding, and optimizing the interference behavior of applications in the NoC is an important problem for enhancing system performance and fairness. Towards this end, we propose fine-grained prioritization mechanisms to improve the performance and fairness of NoCs. We introduce the concept of *packet slack* and characterize it in the context of on-chip networks. In order to exploit packet slack, we propose and evaluate a novel architecture, called Aérgia, which identifies and prioritizes low-slack (critical) packets. The key components of the proposed architecture are techniques for online estimation of slack in packet latency and slack-aware arbitration policies. Averaged over 56 randomly-generated multiprogrammed workload mixes on a 64-core 8x8-mesh CMP, Aérgia improves overall system throughput by 10.3% and network fairness by 30.8% on average. Our results show that Aérgia outperforms three state-of-the-art NoC scheduling/prioritization/fairness techniques. We conclude that the proposed network architecture is effective at improving overall system throughput as well as reducing application-level network unfairness.

Acknowledgments

This research is supported in part by NSF grant CCF 0702519, CMU CyLab, and GSRC. We thank Satish Narayanasamy, Soumya Eachempati and the anonymous reviewers for discussions and suggestions.

[6]Thus, the priority is corrected for data response packets, which have much higher latency than request packets. Also, request packets to on-chip DRAM controller have the corrected priority.

References

[1] N. J. Boden, D. Cohen, R. E. Felderman, A. E. Kulawik, C. L. Seitz, J. N. Seizovic, and W. king Su. Myrinet - A Gigabit-per-Second Local-Area Network. *IEEE Micro*, 1995.

[2] E. Bolotin, I. Cidon, R. Ginosar, and A. Kolodny. QNoC: QoS architecture and design process for network on chip. *Journal of Systems Arch.*, 2004.

[3] E. Bolotin, Z. Guz, I. Cidon, R. Ginosar, and A. Kolodny. The Power of Priority: NoC Based Distributed Cache Coherency. In *NOCS'07*, 2007.

[4] D. Chandra, F. Guo, S. Kim, and Y. Solihin. Predicting inter-thread cache contention on a chip multi-processor architecture. In *HPCA-11*, 2005.

[5] J. Chang and G. S. Sohi. Cooperative cache partitioning for chip multiprocessors. In *ICS-21*, 2007.

[6] A. A. Chien and J. H. Kim. Rotating Combined Queueing (RCQ): Bandwidth and Latency Guarantees in Low-Cost, High-Performance Networks. *ISCA-23*, 1996.

[7] W. J. Dally and B. Towles. *Principles and Practices of Interconnection Networks*. Morgan Kaufmann, 2003.

[8] R. Das, O. Mutlu, T. Moscibroda, and C. Das. Application-Aware Prioritization Mechanisms for On-Chip Networks. In *MICRO-42*, 2009.

[9] A. Demers, S. Keshav, and S. Shenker. Analysis and simulation of a fair queueing algorithm. In *SIGCOMM*, 1989.

[10] J. Dundas and T. Mudge. Improving data cache performance by pre-executing instructions under a cache miss. In *ICS-11*, 1997.

[11] E. Ebrahimi, C. J. Lee, O. Mutlu, and Y. N. Patt. Fairness via Source Throttling: A Configurable and High-Performance Fairness Substrate for Multi-Core Memory Systems. In *ASPLOS-XV*, 2010.

[12] S. Eyerman and L. Eeckhout. System-level performance metrics for multiprogram workloads. *IEEE Micro*, May-June 2008.

[13] B. Fields, R. Bodík, and M. Hill. Slack: Maximizing performance under technological constraints. In *ISCA-29*, 2002.

[14] B. Fields, S. Rubin, and R. Bodík. Focusing processor policies via critical-path prediction. In *ISCA-28*, 2001.

[15] D. Garcia and W. Watson. Servernet II. *Parallel Computing, Routing, and Communication Workshop*, June 1997.

[16] A. Glew. MLP Yes! ILP No! Memory Level Parallelism, or, Why I No Longer Worry About IPC. In *ASPLOS Wild and Crazy Ideas Session*, 1998.

[17] B. Grot, S. W. Keckler, and O. Mutlu. Preemptive Virtual Clock: A Flexible, Efficient, and Cost-effective QOS Scheme for Networks-on-Chip. In *MICRO-42*, 2009.

[18] L. R. Hsu, S. K. Reinhardt, R. Iyer, and S. Makineni. Communist, utilitarian, and capitalist cache policies on cmps: caches as a shared resource. In *PACT-15*, 2006.

[19] Y. Kim, D. Han, O. Mutlu, and M. Harchol-Balter. ATLAS: A Scalable and High-Performance Scheduling Algorithm for Multiple Memory Controllers. In *HPCA-16*, 2010.

[20] D. Kroft. Lockup-free instruction fetch/prefetch cache organization. In *ISCA-8*, 1981.

[21] J. W. Lee, M. C. Ng, and K. Asanovic. Globally-Synchronized Frames for Guaranteed Quality-of-Service in On-Chip Networks. In *ISCA-35*, 2008.

[22] O. Mutlu, H. Kim, and Y. N. Patt. Efficient runahead execution: Power-efficient memory latency tolerance. *IEEE Micro*, 2006.

[23] O. Mutlu and T. Moscibroda. Stall-time fair memory access scheduling for chip multiprocessors. In *MICRO-40*, 2007.

[24] O. Mutlu and T. Moscibroda. Parallelism-Aware Batch Scheduling: Enhancing both Performance and Fairness of Shared DRAM Systems. In *ISCA-35*, 2008.

[25] O. Mutlu, J. Stark, C. Wilkerson, and Y. Patt. Runahead execution: an alternative to very large instruction windows for out-of-order processors. In *HPCA-9*, 2003.

[26] K. J. Nesbit, N. Aggarwal, J. Laudon, and J. E. Smith. Fair queuing memory systems. In *MICRO-39*, 2006.

[27] V. G. Oklobdzija and R. K. Krishnamurthy. *Energy-Delay Characteristics of CMOS Adders, High-Performance Energy-Efficient Microprocessor Design*, chapter 6. Springer US, 2006.

[28] H. Patil, R. Cohn, M. Charney, R. Kapoor, A. Sun, and A. Karunanidhi. Pinpointing Representative Portions of Large Intel Itanium Programs with Dynamic Instrumentation. In *MICRO-37*, 2004.

[29] M. Qureshi, D. Lynch, O. Mutlu, and Y. Patt. A Case for MLP-Aware Cache Replacement. In *ISCA-33*, 2006.

[30] M. Qureshi and Y. Patt. Utility-Based Cache Partitioning: A Low-Overhead, High-Performance, Runtime Mechanism to Partition Shared Caches. In *MICRO-39*, 2006.

[31] E. Rijpkema, K. Goossens, A. Radulescu, J. Dielissen, J. van Meerbergen, P. Wielage, and E. Waterlander. Trade-offs in the design of a router with both guaranteed and best-effort services for networks on chip. *DATE*, 2003.

[32] S. T. Srinivasan and A. R. Lebeck. Load latency tolerance in dynamically scheduled processors. In *MICRO-31*, 1998.

[33] S. Subramaniam, A. Bracy, H. Wang, and G. Loh. Criticality-based optimizations for efficient load processing. In *HPCA-15*, 2009.

[34] T. J. Teorey and T. B. Pinkerton. A comparative analysis of disk scheduling policies. *Communications of the ACM*, 1972.

[35] R. M. Tomasulo. An efficient algorithm for exploiting multiple arithmetic units. *IBM Journal of Research and Development*, 1967.

[36] T. Y. Yeh and Y. N. Patt. Two-level adaptive training branch prediction. In *MICRO-24*, 1991.

[37] K. H. Yum, E. J. Kim, and C. Das. QoS provisioning in clusters: an investigation of router and NIC design. In *ISCA-28*, 2001.

[38] L. Zhang. Virtual clock: a new traffic control algorithm for packet switching networks. *SIGCOMM*, 1990.

Silicon-Photonic Network Architectures for Scalable, Power-Efficient Multi-Chip Systems

Pranay Koka
Sun Labs, Oracle
pranay.koka@oracle.com

Michael O. McCracken
Sun Labs, Oracle
michael.mccracken@oracle.com

Herb Schwetman
Sun Labs, Oracle
herb.schwetman@oracle.com

Xuezhe Zheng
Sun Labs, Oracle
xuezhe.zheng@oracle.com

Ron Ho
Sun Labs, Oracle
ron.ho@oracle.com

Ashok V. Krishnamoorthy
Sun Labs, Oracle
ashok.krishnamoorthy@oracle.com

ABSTRACT

Scaling trends of logic, memories, and interconnect networks lead towards dense many-core chips. Unfortunately, process yields and reticle sizes limit the scalability of large single-chip systems. Multi-chip systems break free of these areal limits, but in turn require enormous chip-to-chip bandwidth. The "macrochip" concept presented here integrates multiple many-core processor chips in a single package with silicon-photonic interconnects. This design enables a multi-chip system to approach the performance of a single large die.

In this paper we propose three silicon-photonic network designs that provide low-power, high-bandwidth inter-die communication: a static wavelength-routed point-to-point network, a "two-phase" arbitrated network, and a limited-connectivity point-to-point network. We also adapt two existing intra-chip silicon-photonic interconnects: a token-ring-based crossbar and a circuit-switched torus.

We simulate a 64-die, 512-core cache-coherent macrochip using all of the above networks with synthetic kernels, and kernels from Splash-2 and PARSEC. We evaluate the networks on performance, optical power and complexity. Despite a narrow data-path width compared to the token-ring or torus, the point-to-point performs 3.3× and 3.9× better respectively. We show that the point-to-point is over 10× more power-efficient than the other networks. We also show that, contrary to electronic network designs, a point-to-point network has the lowest design complexity for an inter-chip silicon-photonic network.

Categories and Subject Descriptors

B.4.3 [**Hardware**]: Interconnections—*Topology*
; C.1.2 [**Computer Systems Organization**]: Multiprocessors—*Interconnection architectures*

General Terms

Design, Performance

Keywords

Interconnection Networks, Nanophotonics

1. INTRODUCTION AND MOTIVATION

Today, state-of-the art processors feature multiple cores, such as processors with 4 to 8 cores along with the concomitant cache and memory controllers all on one die [17, 32]. Projections for the next decade indicate tens to hundreds of cores on a die [2,4,39]. As the number of chips and memories grow, the need for efficient on-chip interconnect networks becomes even greater, especially as chip power becomes dominated not by processor cores but by the need to transport data between processors and to memory [23]. Over the years, many electronic technologies [8,18] and on-chip network and router architectures [11, 21, 26] have been proposed to meet the need for increasing on-chip communications. For this communication, on-chip wires can provide suitably high-bandwidth and low-power interconnect [15, 16, 20, 29].

The trend to larger numbers of cores coupled with recent memory and on-chip communications technologies leads to dense, powerful compute blocks–a single many-processor chip. Unfortunately, the scalability of this single processor-chip approach is limited by the low process yields of large chips [31, 38]. One way to overcome this area constraint is to aggregate together several chips in a package, breaking free of the "reticle limit" of a single chip by using many individual smaller chips. Such a strategy requires enormous chip-to-chip bandwidth for these separate chips to perform as a contiguous piece of silicon, as well as the ancillary packaging, power delivery, and heat removal technologies for the aggregated chips. A popular strategy for such integration is to use vertical "3D" stacking of chips, connected using through-silicon-vias [5]. However, limits on delivering power to–and removing heat from–chips placed squarely atop one another means that vertical stacking is best employed for low-power applications such as DRAM integration. By contrast, high-performance and high-power processors are ideally spread out as an array of chips in a larger package, allowing power delivery to the chips' fronts and heat removal from their backs. Interconnecting such an array of chips presents a challenge: the density of off-chip I/O and package routes dramatically lags that of on-chip wires [36], forcing the use of overclocked and high-power serial links. Newer approaches using coupled data communication [12, 19] bypass soldered I/O and package routing and instead employ silicon "bridge" chips between processors, thus carrying all data over dense on-chip wires [30]. While these systems enable modest arrays of chips, their scalability is limited by the low speed of on-chip wires, especially over distances longer than 10mm.

Silicon photonics is an emerging technology that may help to fill this need for high bandwidth, low power-per-bit channels essential for the deployment of multi-chip systems based on these many-core processors [3, 14, 23, 37, 40, 43]. On-chip optical channels paired seamlessly with inter-chip optical waveguides can provide up to 20 Gb/sec per wavelength of light. The ability to multiplex many wavelengths onto a single waveguide promises very high bandwidth density. Optical links are expected to provide latencies of 0.1 ns/cm at an energy cost of 160 femto-joules/bit (fJ/bit) using coupling structures to silicon waveguides of under 20 micron pitch [24, 25]. At such a low area, energy, and latency cost–especially relative to electrical interconnects–these optical links dramatically reduce the incremental cost of chip-to-chip bandwidth and open up entirely new areas of system exploration.

One such direction might be to widely separate discrete processor chips and interconnect them using fibers, thus using optical links to create physically large but logically dense systems. This would offer simpler packaging, power, and heat requirements yet seemingly provide the bandwidth advantages of wavelength multiplexing. However, chips connect to fibers at a relatively large 250 μm core pitch, not the 20 μm pitch of optical proximity couplers, so chip-to-chip bandwidth over fibers would not be much improved over area solder balls connected to package routes. To truly exploit the bandwidth advantages of silicon photonics, a high-performance system should instead employ dense silicon waveguides with fine-pitch connectors and tightly packed processors.

We introduce the macrochip, which is a technology platform for building a large processor node by integrating multiple processor die with a silicon-photonic interconnection network. The network is embedded in a Silicon-on-Insulator (SOI) substrate, and the processor die are connected to the network using optical proximity communication, which together make inter-die and intra-die communication bandwidths nearly equivalent. This approach provides a single-package compute block much larger than a single processor, but requiring neither large chips with low yield nor large numbers of input/output pins, which are expensive in area and power. The macrochip can thus be viewed as a silicon-photonic-based large scale shared memory multi-processor or a "cluster on a chip." In this paper we have attempted to provide all architecturally-relevant information about the Silicon-photonic technology used. Full details about specific devices can be found in [25]. Fundamental to such a system, however, is the silicon photonic network that connects together the individual chips.

Prior work in silicon-photonic networks has introduced network topologies such as an optical crossbar with tokenring arbitration [40] and a torus [37] in the context of single-die systems. In this paper, we propose the architecture and design of three silicon photonic networks for macrochip-like architectures: a statically-routed wavelength division multiplexed (WDM) point-to-point network that requires minimum optical complexity and no arbitration or switching; a limited point-to-point network that requires no more than one electronic router-hop per message; and a shared row data network with two-phase arbitration that provides

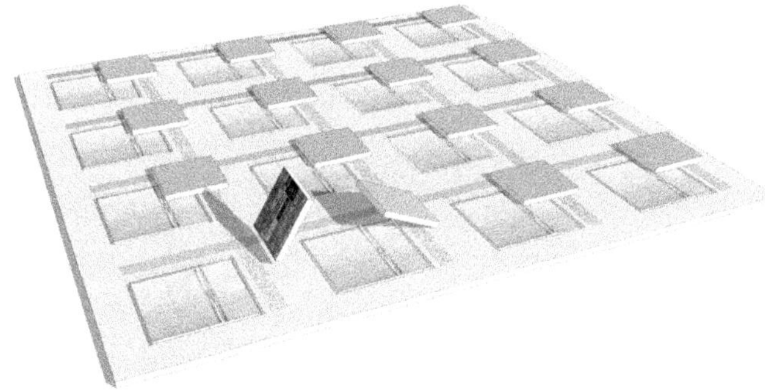

Figure 1: Physical Layout of a 4×4 Macrochip. Two Face-Down CPU Die Are Shown At An Angle.

greater die-to-die bandwidth but uses optical switches. We also evaluate the performance, power, and complexity of these networks in a macrochip-like architecture.

Because no prior work has focused on a macrochip-like shared memory multiprocessor, we adapt two promising silicon photonic intra-chip network architectures to the macrochip layout and technology as a point of comparison. We perform a thorough simulation-based performance evaluation of all five network architectures on two of the SPLASH-2 shared-memory benchmarks [42], three of the PARSEC benchmarks [6], and four synthetic benchmarks.

The contributions of this paper include:

- An architectural introduction to the macrochip, a technology platform for a computing system embodying a silicon-photonic intra-die interconnection network with high peak aggregate bandwidth, low latency and low power.
- A classification of optical on-chip networks.
- Three interconnection network topologies designed for the macrochip, two previously unpublished. One network is optimized for all-to-all communications patterns and the other two offer improved link bandwidths.
- A thorough performance, power and complexity evaluation of all network architectures.

The rest of the paper is organized as follows. In section 2, we describe the enabling silicon-photonic technology with regards to the various optical components used including their power, bandwidth and latencies. In section 3, we present a brief description of the macrochip architecture and give some of its advantages. In section 4, we describe the architecture and design of the three proposed network architectures along with the adapted reference architectures. In sections 5 and 6, we describe our evaluation methodology and analyze our results. Finally we survey the background work in related areas in section 7 and conclude in section 8.

2. SILICON-PHOTONIC TECHNOLOGY

In this section, we give a brief overview of the silicon-photonic components used in a macrochip. A macrochip consists of a large silicon routing substrate containing optical waveguides. This routing layer has chip-sized openings etched into its surface, and in each opening (called a site) is a processor chip with several cores and caches, and a memory

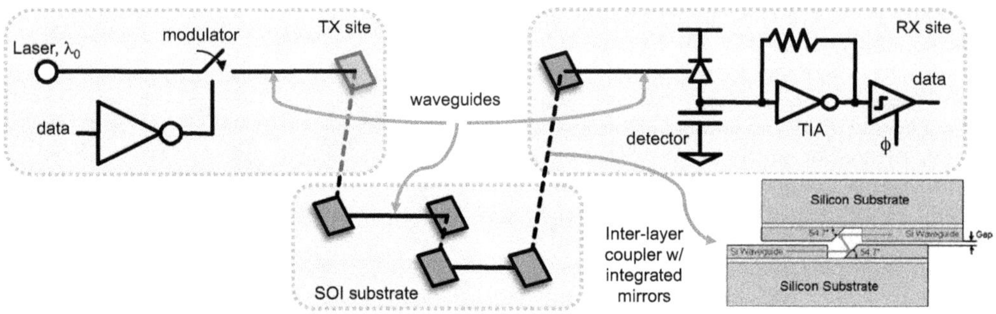

Figure 2: A Single Photonic Link. Not Shown Are Mux/Demux Devices for WDM.

	Energy	Signal Loss
Modulator	35 fJ/bit (dynamic)	4 dB
OPxC	*negligible*	1.2 dB
Waveguide	*negligible*	0.5 dB/cm
Drop Filter	*negligible*	0.1 dB or 1.5 dB
Receiver	65 fJ/bit (dynamic)	N/A
Switch	*negligible*	1 dB
Laser	50 fJ/bit (static)	N/A

Table 1: Optical Component Properties

chip. Site-to-site communication uses the optical waveguides in the routing layer; the silicon routing layer contains nothing but these passive optical waveguides, making its yield reasonable (see [25, 43] for details).

Figure 2 shows a canonical representation of a site-to-site photonic link. Fiber arrays bring off-chip continuous wave laser sources into the macrochip. At each source site, a single-wavelength laser light is modulated by an electronic digital data signal using an electro-optic (EO) modulator. The resulting optical data signal couples to a waveguide on the silicon photonic routing layer through low-loss optical proximity communication (OPxC) [43]. As shown in figure 2, in which two chips placed face-to-face transfer light from waveguide to waveguide through a pair of matching and aligned reflective mirrors [9]. On the silicon-photonic routing layer, the optical data signal travels along waveguides to the destination, where it couples via OPxC up to the destination site. There, a photodetector and electronic amplifier convert the optical data signal into an electronic digital stream.

Wavelength division multiplexing (WDM) in the network increases bandwidth density by reducing the number of routing waveguides and enabling multiple data channels per waveguide. With WDM, several modulated data streams at different wavelengths (from different source lasers) share a single waveguide.

Next, we discuss technology options for each of the major optical components and describe their performance characteristics. The component parameters are based on extensive, on-going device development and reasoned extrapolations to the 2014–2015 time frame. Table 1 presents a summary of the component energy and signal loss characteristics.

Off-chip **laser sources** connect to the macrochip via optical fiber array cables using either edge coupling or surface normal coupling enabled by grating couplers. A commercially available WDM-compatible distributed feedback laser can source a single wavelength at 10 mW of optical power. Optical power sharing can then reduce the total number of laser sources required.

Modulators convert an electronic data stream into an optical data stream. One of the most promising candidate technologies is a silicon CMOS modulator consisting of a reverse-biased, carrier-depletion ring resonator [44]. For such rings running at 20 Gb/sec we envision the modulator power to be 0.7 mW, and have a resonator Q of about 12,000. During operation, ring modulators introduce considerable optical loss; we target a total loss of 4 dB. When disabled, ring loss is significantly smaller at 0.1 dB.

A **multiplexer** combines multiple channels on separate wavelengths into a single waveguide. One way to implement a compact multiplexer is to use cascaded silicon CMOS ring resonators [46]. The primary challenge for using such rings is efficiently tuning them to overcome fabrication tolerances and ambient temperature variations of the ring filter; we target 0.1 mW per wavelength tuning power. We target worst-case channel insertion loss of 2.5 dB.

Optical proximity communication (OPxC) couples an optical data signal from a waveguide on one chip to a waveguide on another, if the chips are placed face-to-face. The coupling is broadband with a targeted insertion loss of 1.2 dB per coupling. One way to accomplish this is to use mutually aligned waveguide gratings on two chips [28, 41]. Another approach employs a pair of mutually aligned reflecting mirrors [24, 43].

Waveguides route optical signals from their source site to their destination site. The macrochip employs two types of waveguides: short local waveguides on a thinned SOI substrate with less than 0.5 dB/cm loss, and global waveguides on a 3 μm thick SOI routing layer with less than 0.1 dB/cm loss. The low-loss global waveguides have a pitch of 10 μm. Across the largest envisioned macrochip, the worst case waveguide loss for site-to-site transmission is 6 dB.

A **drop-filter** demultiplexes a single wavelength from a shared multi-wavelength waveguide. A filter has two outputs: one output carries the optical data stream at the selected wavelength, and the other carries the remaining wavelength channels. Silicon CMOS ring resonators are a promising candidate for implementing compact, low-power drop filters. As with multiplexers, the power required to tune the drop-filter is targeted to be 0.1 mW per wavelength. The insertion loss is 0.1 dB for each wavelength that passes through the device and 1.5 dB for the selected drop wavelength.

A **receiver** consists of a waveguide photodetector and

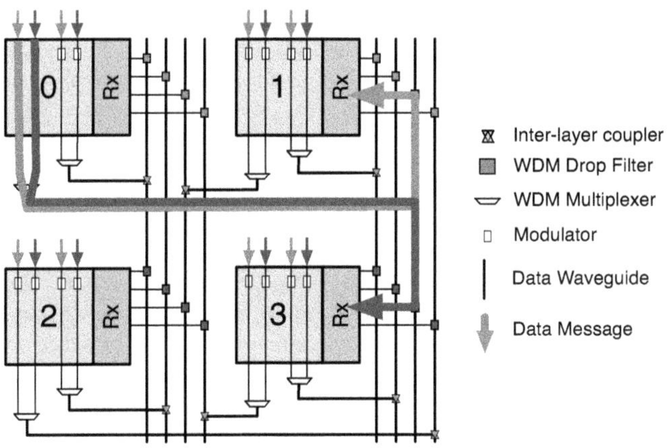

Figure 3: 2×2 Static-WDM Point to Point Network Routing

electronic amplifiers, and converts a single-wavelength optical signal into an electronic digital signal [45]. We target operation at 20 Gb/sec with a sensitivity of -21 dBm, and consume 1.3 mW.

A **broadband optical switch** can be implemented using waveguide Mach-Zehnder interferometers [13], although at large area cost. A compact quasi-broadband optical switch can be created using the periodic resonances of a ring resonator of an appropriate size [27]. Such a switch can direct input light to one of two output channels over a 30 nm wavelength range. With aggressive development, we target the maximum insertion loss for the switch to be under 1 dB, with a power consumption of 0.5 mW.

With these envisioned components, the optical link loss for an un-switched link is 17 dB. If a laser launches 0 dBm power at the modulator, a receiver sensitivity of -21 dBm provides 4 dB margin, which should be sufficient for reliable link operation.

Silicon photonic interconnection networks are being actively researched because of at least two important properties. First, they promise high-speed, low-latency data transmission, at about 0.3c in SOI waveguides. Second, optics potentially provides low energy data transmission, projected to be significantly less than 1 picojoule/bit [25]. Achieving such energy targets involves many optics and circuits challenges, including high efficiency resonator tuning, efficient WDM lasers, ultra-low power modulator and receiver circuits, precision chip alignment, low cost packaging, seamless fiber-optic off-chip communications, and many more. While these issues are beyond the scope of this paper, they are discussed in many of the references, including [25].

3. THE MACROCHIP

The macrochip architecture integrates multiple conventional die, each about 225 mm^2 in size, using silicon photonics to achieve performance similar to that of an equivalent 64x225 mm^2 single die. This design bypasses die size limits imposed by technology yields and makes possible dramatically more cores on a virtual "chip." The macrochip can be viewed as a large scale shared-memory multiprocessor or a cluster, whose performance is not restricted by the limited pin counts on processor die because all cores are interconnected through dense silicon photonics.

The macrochip achieves multi-die integration through a large SOI substrate supporting an array of physically separate CMOS die, called sites. The substrate contains two layers of silicon optical waveguides; the layers run in orthogonal directions much like on-chip electrical wiring, with via-like connections between the layers built using low-loss OPxC connectors. By using two optical routing layers, orthogonal waveguides avoid physically intersecting and suffering signal crosstalk. The substrate layers are SOI because the silicon waveguides require a buried oxide for light confinement [25], although photonics-enabled bulk silicon may in the future eliminate the need for SOI [33].

The macrochip shown in figure 1 is an 8×8 array of sites, where each site contains both processor and memory die. The memory can be conventional DRAM or other technology, and occupies up to 225 mm^2 in area. It sits face-up in a cutout in the SOI routing substrate. A smaller 125 mm^2 processor die sits face-down, partly overlapping the memory and the SOI substrate and spanning the two. The processor and memory die are connected using electrical proximity [12]. Additional memory can be located off the macrochip and accessed via optical fibers. The processor is a multi-core die with memory controllers, a cache hierarchy, and an intra-die interconnect network [10]. The details of the processor die are beyond the scope of this paper. The processor and memory die connect using electrical proximity communication [12]. The processor die also includes optical transmitters, receivers, and waveguides positioned to overlap the SOI routing substrate, and uses OPxC to connect its waveguides to those in the SOI routing substrate [24]. Power is delivered to each site from a top plate and connected using solderless spring contacts that allow chip replaceability for higher system yield [30].

An Oracle Niagara 2 [32] processor scaled for low-power operation in 2015 can operate at 5 GHz, in a 16 nm technology with 64 single-issue cores in 125 mm^2. This chip will require 1 W/core or 64 W/site, including the processor, the optical interfaces, memory controller and caches. This means that a 64-site macrochip will dissipate about 4 kW of power. Cooling such a package, while challenging, can be done using liquid and direct-bonded copper cold plates with microchannels to directly shunt cold water to each chip site. Today, vendors sell plates for a few hundred dollars that can cool 3 kW over a 5 cm x 5 cm area [1], so cooling 4 kW over a much larger macrochip area can be done with a similar design.

The inter-site interconnection network is designed to offer 2.56 TB/sec bandwidth into a site and 2.56 TB/sec from a site, by employing 1024 transmitters and 1024 receivers, each running at 20 Gb/sec (2.5 GB/sec). This gives a total peak aggregate bandwidth of 160 TB/sec. The waveguides each carry 16 wavelengths.

The lasers used for the silicon photonic interconnect will be located off-macrochip and brought in using optical fibers to edge connectors on the macrochip. We assume lasers capable of generating eight discrete wavelengths will be available in 2015, and each wavelength can be split to drive eight channels using power sharing. Thus, 1024 lasers will be needed to drive the entire interconnection network. Because a macrochip can support up to 2000 edge fiber connections, the optical bandwidth will be sufficient for inter-site communications, off-macrochip memory accesses, and I/O connections.

The macrochip architecture as described enables building a large-scale shared-memory multiprocessor in a single logical chip made up of 64 die. The remainder of this paper is devoted to describing five different network designs for connecting these die and, for each design, evaluating performance, power and complexity.

4. NETWORK ARCHITECTURES

Section 3 described a target system for the 2015 time frame. However, simulating such a large system is currently intractable. Therefore, in the following sections we describe and analyze a scaled-down system where both the compute power and network bandwidth are reduced by a factor of eight. Therefore, each site has 128 transmitters and 128 receivers, the total peak network bandwidth is 20 TB/sec, and there are 8 wavelengths per waveguide and 8 cores per site. These are detailed in tables 4 and 6.

4.1 Classification of Optical Network Architectures

Implementing electronic dynamic packet switching is relatively straightforward. Therefore, designers of conventional on-chip networks can choose from a wide range of multi-hop network topologies [10]. However, optical dynamic packet switching is much more difficult. A switched optical network is either circuit switched, using dynamically set optical switches; or requires multiple optical-electrical conversions and routing in the electronic domain. The goal of this paper is to propose and evaluate optical network architectures of various types for the macrochip. Based on the switching or routing architecture used by the network, we classify optical network topologies into the four broad categories below.

Optical Networks Without Switching or Routing. The only network that falls under this category is a fully connected optical point-to-point network. A fully connected electronic point-to-point network is difficult to implement due to the quadratic growth in the number of wires and connections. In the optical domain, however, we exploit WDM in silicon waveguides to reduce waveguide area and routing complexity. We show in section 6.4 that a point-to-point network is less complex than other, switch-based architectures. A point-to-point networks has almost no overhead for data transmission, but is limited to low-bandwidth and narrow datapath site-to-site optical channels.

Circuit Switched Networks. These architectures use a network of waveguides and optical switches with multiple host access points to interconnect compute nodes. Each compute node sets up a series of optical switches, using an independent optical/electrical path-setup network, to connect the node to the destination. No explicit arbitration among senders is required for data transmission. Depending on the topology and complexity, these networks are either blocking or non-blocking. A non-blocking network implies that a circuit established between any pair of nodes 'A' and 'B' will not block a circuit between any other pair of nodes 'C' and 'D'. We adapt the architecture of the optical circuit-switch torus proposed in [35] to the macrochip technology.

Arbitration-Based Switched Optical Networks. Arbitrated networks are fundamentally circuit switched networks but differ in the way the optical circuit is established. All sources contending for a shared data channel arbitrate for data slots prior to data transmission. The arbitration mechanism also sets up the appropriate switches for data transmission. These networks usually require a separate arbitration network for control. One proposed optical crossbar architecture uses optical token ring arbitration to access the network [40]. We adapt this network topology to the macrochip architecture. Based on our power analysis we find the crossbar architecture has high power consumption when adapted to the macrochip. We propose a two-phase arbitration-based network that has lower power requirements at the expense of lower site-to-site bandwidth than the network in [40].

Optical Networks with Electronic Routing. These networks use multiple hops between the source and destination nodes; however at each hop, the optical packets are converted to the electronic domain, packet switched to the appropriate output port, and then converted back to the optical domain. We modify the point-to-point network (above) to limit the number of direct connections and use a maximum of one electronic switching hop in order to provide full connectivity in the network. This facilitates higher bandwidth site-to-site optical channels compared to the point-to-point network.

The five networks chosen for the macrochip have remarkably different properties. The point-to-point network has the least overhead but is limited by low-bandwidth narrow-datapath site-to-site channels whereas the switched networks have higher bandwidth wider-data-path data channels but with higher overhead in the form of arbitration, path setup or electronic routing.

4.2 Statically-Routed Point-to-Point Network

In the static WDM-routed point-to-point network, each site has a dedicated optical data path to every other site. Figure 3 shows a 2×2 point-to-point network. The figure shows a packet transfer from site 0 to sites 1 and 3. Site 0 uses the same horizontal and vertical waveguide for both transfers, but uses a different wavelength for each destination, blue for site 3 and red for site 1.

The network layout consists of horizontal waveguides between the rows of the macrochip and vertical waveguides between the columns of the macrochip. The horizontal and vertical waveguides are laid on the bottom and top layers, respectively, of the SOI routing substrate, and horizontal waveguides connect to vertical waveguides using inter-layer couplers. Each vertical waveguide drops one wavelength at each site in the column. A transmitting site can communicate with any receiving site S by choosing the waveguides leading to the column of site S and the wavelength that is then dropped at site S.

In the 8×8 macrochip configuration, each site sources 16 horizontal waveguides, each carrying 8 wavelengths of light, for a total of 128 wavelengths. At a bit-rate of 20 Gb/sec (2.5 GB/sec) per wavelength, and with 64 sites, the network has a total peak bandwidth of 20 TB/sec. Each point-to-point data channel uses two wavelengths for 5 GB/sec. The network uses 8192 total horizontal and twice as many vertical waveguides, because each vertical channel consists of two waveguides for communicating both up and down. A more detailed component count is presented in table 6.

The statically routed point-to-point network has no switching or arbitration overheads. However, the narrow 2-bit site-

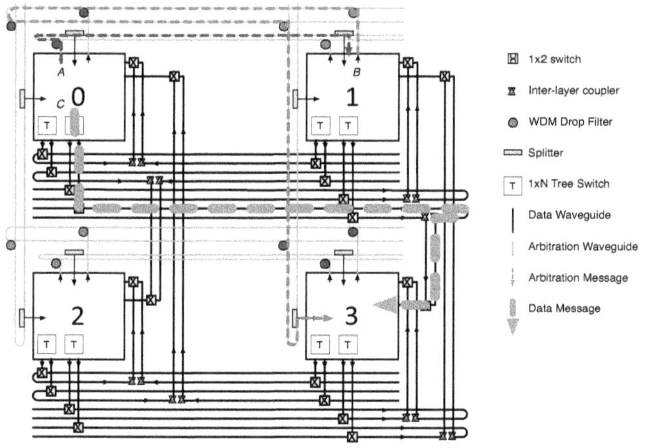

Site 0 sends to S3. First, S0 sends an arb. request in blue along its row. An arb. slot is assigned to the request. Then S1 sends the switch request in red along the column. S3 sets the input switch. Finally, S0 sends using the data waveguide going to S3.

Figure 4: Two-Phase Arbitrated Network

to-site data-path is a potential performance limiter. This observation motivates the investigation of other types of networks with higher point-to-point bandwidth.

4.3 Two-Phase Arbitration-Based Switched Optical Network

Data Network Topology. This architecture uses shared data channels between sites to increase the bandwidth per site-to-site logical connection. Figure 4 shows a small 2×2 version of the macrochip with this network. All sites in a row of the macrochip share an optical data channel to one other site. Thus, an 8×8 macrochip has 512 shared channels. Sites that share a channel are said to belong to the same arbitration domain. Each site connects to 64 shared horizontal channels, each comprised of two waveguides with 8 wavelengths per waveguide. Each of the waveguides in a row is coupled to a vertical waveguide using an inter-layer coupler, and this vertical waveguide is connected to one destination site. Each shared channel is 40 GB/sec and 16 bits wide. Due to the physical restriction that only one transmitter at a time can feed directly into a waveguide, a shared waveguide is implemented using broadband switches at the feeding points. Each switch hop along the path of an optical signal causes 1 dB loss. To minimize the optical loss through the switches, each waveguide is implemented as two parallel waveguide segments. We refer to the pair of segments that form a logical waveguide as simply waveguides in this section.

In order to minimize the number of transmitters in the network, each site is limited to transmitting to only one site in any column and hence can sustain, at most, 8 simultaneous 40 GB/sec transmissions to different columns. Each site uses a tree of broadband switches per column, shown as "T" in figure 4, to choose a destination in that column. This results in a maximum of 7 switch hops between any source and destination and hence only a 7 dB loss. The use of switch trees to minimize the number of switches on a path can result in contention when a site has multiple packets to send to a single column. An alternate version of this network uses twice the amount of laser power and double the number of switch trees, to reduce the potential for contention. This alternative, called "2-phase Arb ALT" in the remainder of the paper, is evaluated along with the base design in section 6.

Arbitration Network Topology. Figure 4 illustrates the topology and operation of the arbitration network. Due to the mesochronous properties of the macrochip [25], we can employ a completely distributed arbitration mechanism to reduce the arbitration overheads. Each node in an arbitration domain makes the same decision for every arbitration request as made by all of the sites in that domain, at the same time.

Data transmission from any site 'A' to any site 'B' requires contention resolution among the sites in the arbitration domain and a control operation to set the appropriate switches for data transmission. The arbitration network consists of a request waveguide for each row for contention resolution, and a notification waveguide for each column to set the appropriate destination switches. Each site can transmit on the request and the notification waveguides using pre-assigned wavelengths. In addition, each site is a column manager of its column in its arbitration domain. The arbitration wavelengths are assigned in cyclic fashion as shown in figure 4, to enable WDM and reduce the number of arbitration waveguides. The request waveguides are snooped by all sites in the corresponding row, and the notification waveguides are snooped by the all sites in the corresponding column. Snooping requires higher input power proportional to the number of sites snooping the waveguide. In this case the arbitration waveguides need to be sourced with $7\times$ more laser power. Since the arbitration network uses a small number of lasers (in comparison to the data network), the increase in power is negligible. The increase in area due to arbitration is also small, because it adds only 16 horizontal and 8 vertical waveguides to the data network.

Arbitration Mechanism. Sites arbitrate for access to a destination in arbitration slots. Each arbitration slot is about 0.4 ns, enough to transmit an arbitration request. Multiple arbitration requests are pipelined to improve bandwidth utilization on the optical data channels. The data channels are are also time-slotted. The size of each slot is variable but an integral multiple of a basic slot size. Data transmission for every packet requires the following steps:

Phase 1:

1) All requests during an arbitration interval are posted to the request network.

2) Each site in the arbitration domain sees the request after the propagation time.

3) Each site maintains a round-robin counter for every destination node. The counter specifies the order of assignment of successive slots to the requesters. All sites in the arbitration domain assign the same slot T_r to a requester.

Phase 2:

1) At arbitration slot T_a, $T_a < T_r$, the column manager for the destination column sends a switch request on the notification waveguide in the pre-assigned wavelength.

2) Prior to slot T_r, all the row sites in the arbitration domain set their respective broadband switches, the destination site sets its input-select switch, and the source site transmits the data over the optical circuit to the destination.

The switch request notification is timed to accommodate

the switch delay. When an optical switch is set, it remains in that position until another switch request notification changes it.

This network provides a wider 16-bit 40 GB/sec data path but incurs arbitration and switch-delay overheads. A detailed component count for the data and arbitration networks is given in table 6.

4.4 Token-Ring-Based Optical Crossbar

The Corona architecture is an optical crossbar with token-ring arbitration, using a ring topology with no waveguide crossings [40]. Each site or cluster in the Corona architecture has a dedicated waveguide bundle shared by all sites transmitting data to that site. Access to the shared bundle is arbitrated using a token ring. One token for each destination is propagated on a token bus by that site. A site that needs to transmit data to the destination diverts the token by tuning its receiver on the token channel to the correct wavelength. On completing data transmission, the site releases the token by re-injecting a light pulse into the token bus. We adapted the Corona network to the macrochip by using the bottom substrate to route both the token and data waveguides and the modulators.

The Corona network architecture uses 64-way WDM and hence each wavelength of light passes by 4,096 modulator rings. Each modulator when tuned off-resonance causes a 0.1 dB loss to the signal causing a 409.6 dB loss along the path. Even a WDM factor of 8 as used by the macrochip, causes a 51.2 dB loss. In order to limit the power loss due to the rings to 12.8 dB, we reduced the WDM factor to 2 and increased the number of waveguides by a factor of 4.

The macrochip dimensions are 10× the dimensions of the chip proposed for Corona. We scaled the 8 cycle round-trip token latency specified in [40] based on dimension. In our adaptation, it takes 80 cycles for a token to complete a round-trip.

4.5 Circuit Switched Network

A circuit switched network requires a path setup procedure to set the appropriate optical switches along the path from the source to the destination. The circuit-switched-style network in [35] uses an electronic torus overlaying an optical torus. The optical torus uses a 4×4 optical switch at each switching point. This optical torus network enables non-blocking operation. The electronic network is a low-bandwidth packet-switched network and is used to set up an optical path from the source to the destination. Each switching point in the electronic network is attached to the 4×4 optical switch that it controls. To establish an optical circuit, a source node initiates a path-setup packet on the electronic network from its gateway; this setup packet is routed through multiple switch points to the destination. At each switch point the router sets the corresponding optical switch and routes the packet towards the destination site. Similarly, a post-communication path-breakdown procedure is followed to tear down the optical circuit.

We adapted the network topology and architecture in [35] for the macrochip. Adding an inter-site electronic network for path setup on the macrochip would require an active substrate with long running wires/lines, complicating the design of the macrochip. Therefore, in our adaptation, we used a low bandwidth optical network for path setup instead of an electronic network.

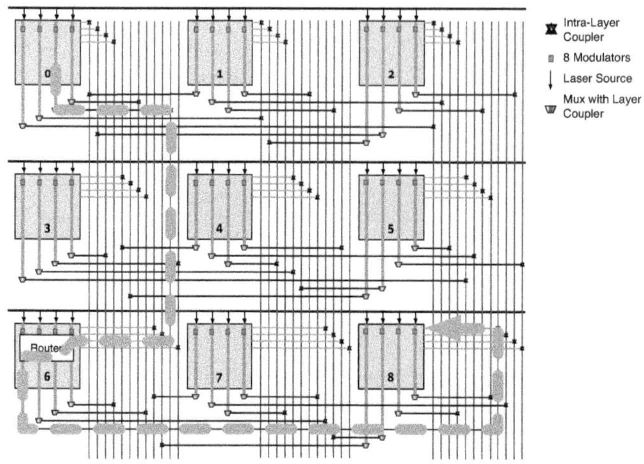

S0 sends to S8, forwarded through S6. S0 transmits in all wavelengths in the marked channel. S6 receives, converts, routes electronically, then re-sends the packet as an optical signal to S8.

Figure 5: 3×3 Limited Point to Point Network Topology

We perform the path setup, acknowledgment and path tear-down using the optical control network. We added the the additional routers required for non-blocking operation to the macrochip sites. The optical torus adapted to the macrochip is similar to that in [35] and is completely routed in the lower substrate to reduce the coupler loses. Each macrochip site sources 16 waveguides with 8 wavelengths per waveguide. This requires 64 waveguide loops between each row of sites in the macrochip, resulting in 50% fewer waveguides compared to the WDM point-to-point network.

This network however has two major drawbacks. First, it requires a large number of waveguide crossings. Waveguide crossings induce significant crosstalk into a waveguide, especially when one waveguide is crossed at multiple points [7]. Because we do not know the crosstalk loss assumptions used in [35], we assume negligible crosstalk at waveguide crossings for the macrochip adaptation of this network. Second, there are similar questions about the power loss due to broadband switches. As shown in Table 1, we project that a broadband 1×2 switch will cause a 1 dB power loss. For the adaptation of the circuit-switched network, we use a more aggressive power loss assumption of 0.5 dB loss per 4×4 optical switch. The worst case path in the network requires 31 optical switch hops causing approximately 15 dB loss to the input signal, requiring an approximate 30x increase in the laser power. More detailed component counts and power estimates are shown in tables 6 and 5.

4.6 Limited Point-to-Point Network with Electronic Routing

Figure 5 shows a 3×3 version of the limited point-to-point network. The topology of this network is similar to that of the point-to-point network. Each site has direct optical connectivity using a separate waveguide to every site in its row and its column, called row-peers and column-peers respectively. This provides a 20 GB/sec direct optical channel to each of its row and column peers and a total of 20 TB/sec peak network bandwidth. In this arrangement, there are no direct optical channels to the other sites - the sites that are not in the row or column of the source site. Electronic routing is used to extend the connectivity of a site to the remaining sites. This routing is implemented by adding two 7×7 electronic routers on each site: one for forwarding packets from row peers to column peers and one for forwarding from column peers to row peers. Communication between non-peer sites requires that a data packet be first forwarded to a site that is a peer to both the source and the destination. At the forwarding site, the data packet is converted to the electronic domain, forwarded to the appropriate output port, and then converted back to the optical domain to reach the destination. By the use of this configuration, each transmission requires a maximum of one intermediate O-E/E-O conversion. Table 6 gives the component count for this network architecture. The routers used in the sites are assumed to have a latency of one cycle.

5. SIMULATION METHODOLOGY

We performed a detailed evaluation of the five network architectures for the macrochip using two kinds of workloads: application kernels and synthetic benchmarks. We used five shared memory application benchmarks, two from the SPLASH-2 suite and three from the PARSEC suite. The benchmarks and the data sets used are listed in Table 2. The SPLASH-2 benchmarks were compiled with the Sun Studio 12 compiler suite with `-fast` optimization and the PARSEC benchmarks were compiled using g++ version 3.4.3 with `-O3` optimization for the UltraSparc T2+ processor.

The four synthetic benchmarks were chosen to represent a range of traffic patterns. In the butterfly and transpose pattern, each site only sends to one unique destination, whereas in the nearest-neighbor pattern, each site communicates with four neighbors. Table 3 lists and describes the synthetic benchmarks. These benchmarks were driven by two types of coherence mixes: Less Sharing (LS) and More Sharing (MS). In the LS mix, 90% of coherence requests have no sharers for the cache block, while in the MS mix, 40% of requests have three sharers. All of the synthetic benchmarks are driven at a rate equivalent to an L2 cache miss rate of 4% per instruction.

Table 4 shows the simulated macrochip configuration. We reduced the number of cores per site from 64, in the configuration proposed in section 3, to 8 to make the simulation more tractable. Accordingly we reduced the total network bandwidth by 8 times, to a peak of 20 TB/sec for all the networks. We also used a 256 KB cache, shared by all cores on the site, to suit the data set sizes of the applications. The optical-fiber-connected main memory is not modeled in detail. We leave the study of effect of main memory technologies on performance to future work.

Our simulation infrastructure consists of two parts. The macrochip CPU simulator is an instruction-trace driven multiprocessor core/cache simulator that models an MOESI coherence protocol. The CPU simulator generates L2 miss traffic along with detailed coherence information for all 512 cores. The network simulator models all five network architectures and is driven using the coherence traffic generated by the CPU simulator. The network model simulates all necessary network messages required by the coherence protocol to satisfy a coherence request. We model finite MSHRs, network I/O buffers and virtual channels for cache coherence operations. To keep simulation time manageable, we do not model the intricate details of the cache coherency protocol.

Benchmark	Size	Suite
Radix	32 M integers	Splash-2
Barnes	16 K particles	Splash-2
Blackscholes	simlarge	PARSEC
Fluidanimate (forces)	simlarge	PARSEC
Fluidanimate (densities)	simlarge	PARSEC
Swaptions	simlarge	PARSEC

Table 2: Benchmarks Used

Pattern	Destination ID
Uniform	Random for every packet
Transpose	First half of the bits in source site-id are swapped to second half
Butterfly	Swap LSB and MSB of source site-id
Neighbor	Source (x,y) randomly selects from (x,y-1), (x,y+1), (x-1,y), (x+1,y)

Table 3: Synthetic Patterns

6. EVALUATION

6.1 Latency and Throughput Analysis

We performed tests with 64-byte raw data packets to determine the maximum throughput of each network. In these tests, we compared the five networks using the synthetic patterns listed in table 3. The input driver for these simulations probabilistically generates data packets in a specific communication pattern. Each data packet is 64 bytes, to represent a cache line transfer. We measured the latency per packet, defined as the time elapsed from when the packet was generated to when the packet was received by the destination site. The bandwidth per site and the total peak bandwidth used for each network are as shown in table 4. Figure 6 shows the latency response for all the networks on the synthetic patterns. The latency per packet increases with load. The vertical asymptote of the latency response curve shows the maximum sustainable bandwidth for that network.

The point-to-point network performs best on the uniform random pattern, shown in figure 6, because it has no arbitration or path setup overheads. The sustained bandwidth scales well up to 95% of peak. The token-ring network is limited by token arbitration overheads, and so scales only to 40% of peak. The limited point-to-point network sustains up to 47% of the peak bandwidth. This is because 75% of the traffic is forwarded through another site. This causes each packet to use two point-to-point links, reducing the effective bandwidth by about 50%. The circuit-switched network has high path setup overhead at this message size and has the lowest sustained bandwidth, only 2.5% of peak. The original two-phase arbitration network wastes bandwidth due to

Number of sites	64
Shared L2 Cache per site	256 KB
Bandwidth per site	320 GB/sec
Total peak bandwidth	20 TB/sec
Cores per site	8
Threads per core	1
FPU per core	1

Table 4: Simulated Macrochip Configuration

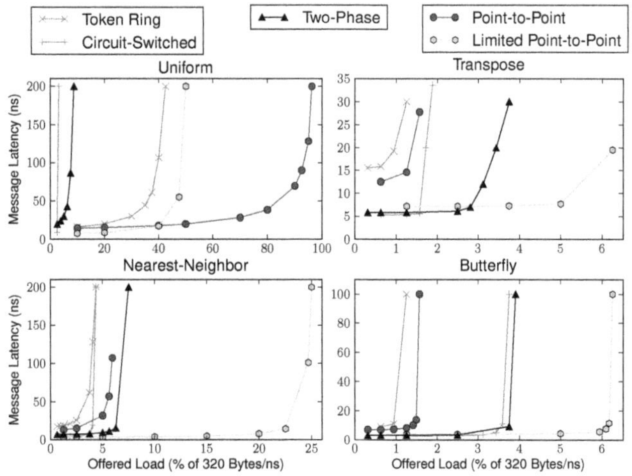

Figure 6: Latency vs. Offered Load for Four Message Patterns

switch tree contention, resulting in a sustained bandwidth of 7.5% of peak. As discussed in section 4.3, this contention can be resolved by either increasing the number of transmitters or by using a more logic-intensive arbitration protocol that provides an efficient assignment of data slots. One such alternate configuration is evaluated further in section 6.2.

In the butterfly and transpose traffic patterns, each site communicates with only one other site. These patterns limit the throughput of the point-to-point network to 5 GB/sec because they use only one of the available 64 links. The token-ring network throughput on these patterns reaches a maximum below 1% of peak. It takes only one cycle to transmit a 64-byte packet, but requires 80 cycles to reacquire the token. Because the communication pattern is one-to-one, the token latency reduces the bandwidth utilization.

In the nearest-neighbor pattern, each site communicates with four other sites at a time. This pattern maps well to the row/column connectivity of the limited point-to-point network. No packet requires any intermediate router hops. Each site uses four of its 20 GB/sec point-to-point links with no contention or overheads and the network achieves a sustained bandwidth of up to 25% of the peak.

6.2 Benchmark Performance Analysis

Figure 7 shows the speedup of each network relative to the circuit-switched network, which had the lowest performance. The five columns on the right show results for the synthetic benchmarks shown in table 3, and the six on the left show results for the application benchmarks in table 2. Figure 8 shows corresponding data for average latency per coherence operation.

In figure 7 we see that the networks that require arbitration perform poorly on the transpose and butterfly patterns. In these patterns, each site only sends to one other site. As discussed above, the token-ring network's token latency results in low bandwidth utilization. In comparison, the point-to-point network has lower data-path width, but avoids this setup overhead, providing a higher overall speedup and a reduction in latency. There is a relatively small variation in speedup on the butterfly pattern because 50% of the communication is intra-node, and we have modeled intra-node traffic as a single cycle loop-back link.

Network Type	Power Loss Factor	Laser Power (W)
Token-Ring	19×	155
Point-to-Point	1×	8
Circuit-Switched	30×	245
Limited Pt.-to-Pt.	1×	8
Two-Phase:		
Data	5×	41
Data (ALT)	4×	65.5
Arbitration	8×	1

Table 5: Network Optical Power

The "MS" sharing mix consists of a large number of invalidate and acknowledgment packets which are small in size, and so the arbitration overhead dominates performance. Due to this, the point-to-point network performance on this mix, regardless of message pattern, is at least 4.5× better than the arbitrated networks. Therefore, the figures show results for only one pattern with the "MS" mix.

The two-phase arbitration network has lower overhead than the token-ring and circuit-switched networks, and thus provides a speedup of at least 1.6× compared to these networks. For the reasons discussed in section 6.1, the limited point-to-point network performs better than any other network on the nearest-neighbor pattern and has a speedup of 5× compared to the circuit-switched network. The all-to-all pattern causes the maximum network load of all the synthetic benchmarks and causes more contention for the input switch tree in the two-phase arbitration network. The "Two-phase (ALT)" alternate design discussed above improves performance by 1.4× by reducing this contention.

The left six bars in figure 7 show results for the application benchmark kernels normalized to the circuit-switched network. The point-to-point network consistently outperforms the other networks on the application benchmarks, with a maximum speedup of 8.3× over the circuit-switched network and 3× over the token-ring network on the swaptions benchmark. This follows from the latency per coherence operation shown in figure 8. The point-to-point network has a maximum latency of only 54 nanoseconds for the application benchmarks and 100 nanoseconds on the synthetic benchmarks.

Despite relatively low data-path width per link, the point-to-point network is a better choice for the small, latency-sensitive messages in cache coherence traffic. This is due to the absence of arbitration or path setup overhead.

The token-ring and circuit-switched torus networks have been shown to provide good performance when used as an intra-chip network, but when scaled to the dimensions of the macrochip, token propagation and path-setup latency hurt performance on the class of applications we evaluated.

The Barnes benchmark shows relatively low speedups. This benchmark does not stress any of the networks, due to a relatively low L2 cache miss rate.

6.3 Power Analysis

In this section, we discuss power estimates for each network. The static power consumed by the networks, shown in table 5, is calculated using the component counts shown

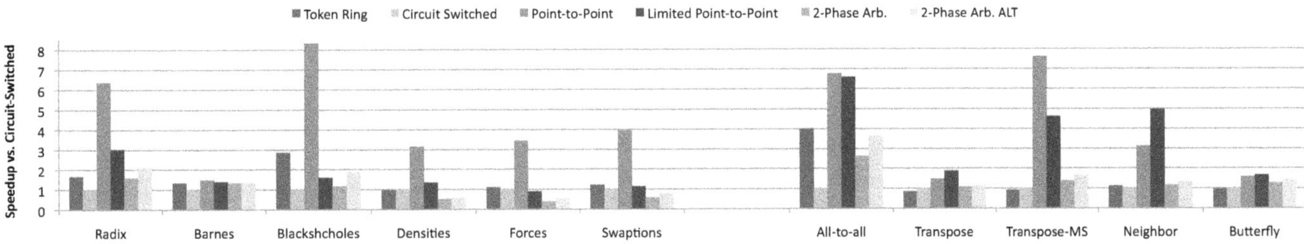

Figure 7: Speedup For Benchmarks and Synthetic Message Patterns, Normalized to Circuit-Switched Network

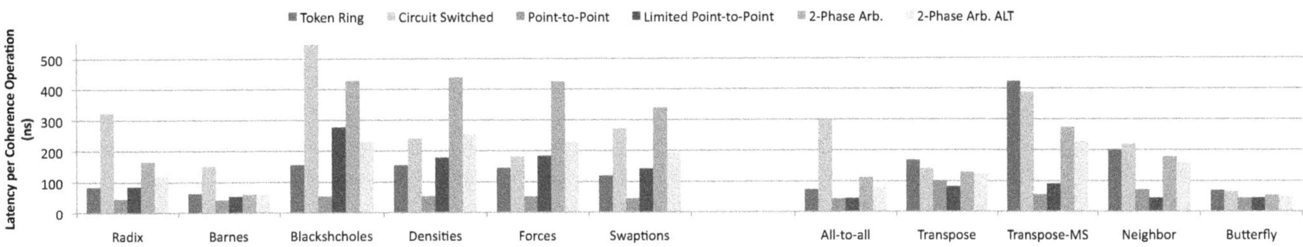

Figure 8: Latency per Coherence Operation

in table 6 and the per-component static energy from table 1. The dynamic power is calculated from the transmitter and receiver energies shown in table 1.

When the optical signal passes through switches, non-resonant modulators, or is split into two waveguides, it suffers signal loss. The total loss is listed as the power loss factor in table 5. To compensate for this signal loss, the laser power must be increased by the loss factor. The basic laser power is assumed to be 1 mW per wavelength. For example, in the token-ring network, which has two wavelengths per waveguide, each wavelength passes through 128 modulators, which have an off-resonance coupling loss of 0.1 dB. This causes a total signal loss of 12.8 dB, or a 19× power loss factor.

The power estimates for the limited point-to-point network include dynamic router power. The energy required by the routers to switch a single byte was conservatively assumed to be 60 picojoules [34]. Figure 9 shows the energy consumed by the routers for each workload as a percentage of total energy. The energy consumed by routers was a maximum of 17% for the synthetic benchmarks, and a maximum of 10.4% for the application benchmarks.

Figure 10 shows the energy-delay product (EDP) for each network on each workload. This graph is normalized to the point-to-point network, which has the lowest power requirements. On all but one of the application benchmarks, the point-to-point network has more than 100× lower EDP than the arbitrated or circuit-switched networks. The point-to-point network also has up to 26× lower EDP than the limited point-to-point network. The alternate configuration of the two-phase arbitration network is an improvement on four of the six application benchmarks. On the Blackscholes kernel, it has an EDP 62% of the base two-phase configuration, but on the Barnes kernel, it has an EDP of 160% of the base. The point-to-point network not only performs well, but has superior EDP when compared to the other networks.

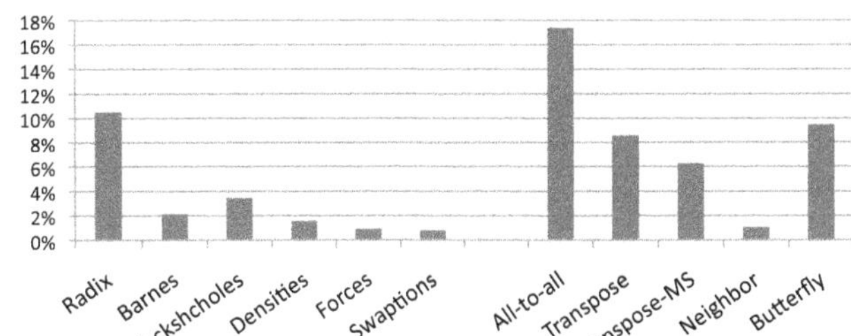

Figure 9: Energy Used By Routers in Limited Point-to-Point Network as a Percentage of Total

6.4 Complexity Analysis

An important factor to be considered in evaluating silicon-photonic network architectures is scalability in terms of the number and types of the individual components. In this section we make a qualitative assessment of network complexity based on those factors.

Table 6 shows total component counts for each of the six networks. The number of physical waveguides used by the token ring network is only 8192. However, since every waveguide is routed along every row, it adds to the total area for waveguides and hence is shown as 32 K waveguides in Table 6. The waveguide counts for the point-to-point, limited point-to-point and the two phase arbitration networks include both the vertical and horizontal waveguides.

As the number of wavelengths per waveguide increases with improvements in technology, the peak bandwidth for a point-to-point network can increase without increasing the number of waveguides. This is contrary to the case of electronic point-to-point networks where scalability is limited by the quadratic increase in the number of wires. The other networks analyzed in this paper require additional compo-

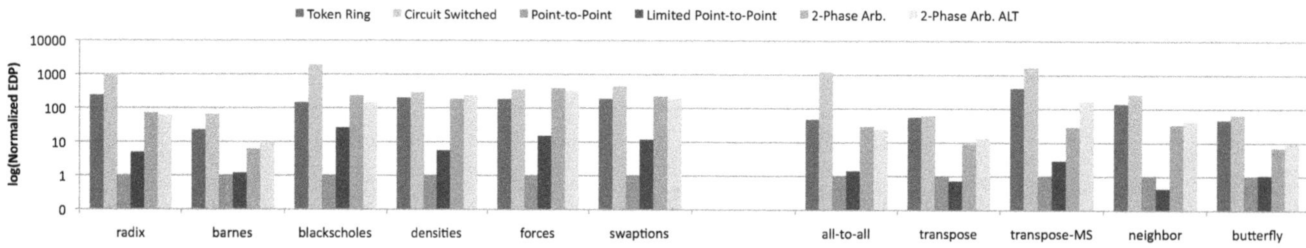

Figure 10: Log Plot of Energy-Delay Product, Normalized to the Point-to-Point Network

Network Type	Tx	Rx	Wgds	Switches
Token-Ring	512K	8192	32K	0
Point-to-Point	8192	8192	3072	0
Circuit-Switched	8192	8192	2048	16K[a]
Limited Point-to-Point	8192	8192	3072	128[b]
Two-Phase:				
Data	8192	8192	4096	16K
Data (ALT)	16384	8192	4096	15K
Arbitration	128	1024	24	0

Table 6: Total Optical Component Counts

[a] 4×4 switches
[b] 7×7 electronic routers

nents, such as switches and arbitration/control networks, which increases contention and limits the scalability of these networks.

7. RELATED WORK

In recent years, a variety of architectures have been proposed using Silicon-photonic technology to build on-chip networks for single-die multicore systems.

The Corona architecture uses a high-speed optical crossbar with token-ring arbitration, interconnecting 64 cores on a single die [40]. Because the links on a single die are short, the token propagation latency is very low. In a multi-die system with link distances an order of magnitude larger, this propagation latency becomes a significant performance issue.

The non-blocking torus proposed in [35,37] uses a packet-switched electronic network to setup an end-to-end optical circuit in the companion optical network. This is also an on-chip network for a single-die multicore chip. The path-setup latency in such a network causes significant delays for small transfers such as cache lines.

The Firefly network is a hierarchical network for a single die that uses an electronic network for messages local to a cluster of cores and an optical crossbar between clusters [34]. The optical crossbar is similar to that used in the Corona architecture, and will suffer the same token latency problems when scaled to a large multi-die system.

A detailed investigation of a silicon-photonic cache-coherent bus for a single multicore die is presented in [22]. The authors demonstrate that the use of silicon-photonics can offer improvements in performance, power and area over a similar all-electric bus for the shared-memory workloads they analyzed.

In contrast to the above papers, our work focuses on design and evaluation of silicon-photonic networks for large, multi-die systems. We have proposed three optical networks that have low power requirements for a multi-die system. When evaluated on a large multi-die system, the performance and power characteristics of the previously proposed intra-die designs change considerably. We show that a low-complexity point-to-point network performs better than other solutions in the context of the evaluated shared-memory workloads on a multi-die system.

8. CONCLUSIONS

In this paper, we describe the macrochip technology platform, which uses a silicon-photonic interconnection network to enable building a large, high-performance single logical chip with very high core counts.

To achieve high-bandwidth, low-power communication on the macrochip, we proposed three silicon-photonic network designs and adapted two promising designs from previous work on intra-chip silicon-photonic interconnects. The networks covered in this paper vary widely in communication overheads, power consumption, complexity and data-path width.

We simulated the performance of all the networks on five synthetic benchmarks and five application kernels, two from the SPLASH-2 benchmark suite and three from the PARSEC benchmark suite. We also performed a detailed power and complexity estimation for each of the networks. Based on our evaluation, we find that the static WDM point-to-point network, despite having 1/64th the per-link data-path width of some of the other networks, performs between 3 to 8 times better than other networks that have wider data-paths but larger communication overheads. Due to its simplicity, the energy-delay product of the point-to-point network is between 10 and 100 times lower than the wider data-path networks on some of the benchmarks. We have also shown that, contrary to the case in electronic networks, a silicon-photonic point-to-point network has the lowest design complexity and a high degree of scalability. Future work will evaluate network architectures for message passing workloads and the performance impacts of different memory technologies and site architectures on the macrochip.

Acknowledgment

We would like to thank the ISCA reviewers, in particular Al Davis, for comments that improved the quality of the final paper.

This material is based upon work supported, in part, by DARPA under Agreement No. HR0011-08-09-0001. The authors thank Dr. Jag Shah of DARPA MTO for his inspiration and support of this program. The views, opinions, and/or findings contained in this paper are those of the authors and should not be interpreted as representing the official views or policies, either expressed or implied, of the Defense Advanced Research Projects Agency or the Department of Defense. Approved for public release, distribution unlimited.

9. REFERENCES

[1] High performance coolers. http://www.electrovac.com/sprache2/n160352/i229935.html.
[2] K. Asanovic, R. Bodik, et al. The landscape of parallel computing research: A view from Berkeley. Technical Report UCB/EECS-2006-183, EECS, UC Berkeley, 2006.
[3] R. Beausoleil, J. Ahn, et al. A nanophotonic interconnect for high-performance many-core computation. In *HOTI*, Aug. 2008.
[4] S. Bell, B. Edwards, et al. Tile64 - processor: A 64-core SoC with mesh interconnect. In *ISSCC*, 2008.
[5] K. Bernstein, P. Andry, et al. Interconnects in the third dimension: design challenges for 3D ICs. In *DAC*, 2007.
[6] C. Bienia, S. Kumar, et al. The PARSEC benchmark suite: Characterization and architectural implications. In *PACT*, 2008.
[7] W. Bogaerts, P. Dumon, et al. Low-loss, low-cross-talk crossings for silicon-on-insulator nanophotonic waveguides. *Opt. Lett.*, 32(19), 2007.
[8] M. Chang, J. Cong, et al. CMP network-on-chip overlaid with multi-band RF-interconnect. In *HPCA*, 2008.
[9] J. Cunningham, X. Zheng, et al. Optical proximity communication in packaged SiPhotonics. In *IEEE Group IV Photonics*, 2008.
[10] W. Dally, B. Towles, et al. *Principles and Practices of Interconnection Networks.* Morgan Kaufman, 2004.
[11] R. Das, S. Eachempati, et al. Design and evaluation of a hierarchical on-chip interconnect for next-generation cmps. In *HPCA*, Feb. 2009.
[12] R. Drost, R. Hopkins, et al. Proximity communication. *JSSC*, 2004.
[13] R. Espinola, M. Tsai, et al. Fast and low-power thermooptic switch on thin silicon-on-insulator. *Photonics Technology Letters, IEEE*, 2003.
[14] R. Ho, J. Lexau, et al. Circuits for silicon photonics on a "macrochip". In *ASSCC*, Nov. 2009.
[15] R. Ho, K. Mai, et al. The future of wires. *Proceedings of the IEEE*, 89(4), Apr 2001.
[16] R. Ho, I. Ono, et al. High-speed and low-energy capacitively-driven on-chip wires. In *ISSCC*, Feb. 2007.
[17] Intel. First tick, now tock: Next generation Intel microarchitecture. techreport, http://intel.com/, 2009.
[18] A. Jose, K. Shepard, et al. Distributed loss-compensation techniques for energy-efficient low-latency on-chip communication. *JSSC*, 2007.
[19] K. Kanda, D. Antono, et al. 1.27Gb/s/pin 3mW/pin wireless superconnect (WSC) interface scheme. In *ISSCC*, 2003.
[20] B. Kim, V. Stojanovic, et al. A 4Gb/s/ch 356 fJ/b 10mm equalized on-chip interconnect with nonlinear charge-injecting transmit filter and transimpedance receiver in 90nm CMOS. In *ISSCC*, 2009.
[21] J. Kim, W. Dally, et al. Microarchitecture of a high-radix router. In *ISCA*, 2005.
[22] N. Kırman, M. Kırman, et al. Leveraging optical technology in future bus-based chip multiprocessors. In *MICRO*, 2006.
[23] P. Kogge, K. Bergman, et al. Exascale computing study: Technology challenges in achieving exascale systems, 2008.
[24] A. V. Krishnamoorthy, J. E. Cunningham, et al. Optical proximity communication with passively aligned silicon photonic chips. *J. Quant. Elec.*, 45(4), 2009.
[25] A. V. Krishnamoorthy, R. Ho, et al. Computer systems based on silicon photonic interconnects. *Proc. IEEE*, 97(7), 2009.
[26] R. Kumar, V. Zyuban, et al. Interconnections in multi-core architectures: understanding mechanisms, overheads and scaling. In *ISCA*, 2005.
[27] B. Lee, A. Biberman, et al. All-optical comb switch for multiwavelength message routing in silicon photonic networks. *IEEE Photon. Technol. Lett*, 20(10):767–769, 2008.
[28] G. Masanovic, V. Passaro, et al. Coupling to nanophotonic waveguides using a dual grating-assisted directional coupler. *IEEE Proc. Optoelectronics*, 152(1), 2005.
[29] E. Mensink, D. Schinkel, et al. A 0.28pJ/b 2Gb/s/ch transceiver in 90nm CMOS for 10mm on-chip interconnects. In *ISSCC*, 2007.
[30] J. Mitchell, J. Cunningham, et al. Integrating novel packaging technologies for large scale computer systems. In *InterPACK*. ASME, July 2009.
[31] B. Murphy. Cost-size optima of monolithic integrated circuits. *Proc. IEEE*, 52(12), 1964.
[32] U. Nawathe, M. Hassan, et al. An 8-core 64-thread 64b power-efficient SPARC SoC. In *ISSCC*, Feb. 2007.
[33] J. Orcutt, A. Khilo, et al. Demonstration of an electronic photonic integrated circuit in a commercial scaled bulk cmos process. In *Conf. on Lasers and Electro-Optics*, 2008.
[34] Y. Pan, P. Kumar, et al. Firefly: illuminating future network-on-chip with nanophotonics. *ISCA*, 2009.
[35] M. Petracca, B. G. Lee, et al. Design exploration of optical interconnection networks for chip multiprocessors. In *HOTI*, 2008.
[36] Semiconductor Industries Association. International technology roadmap for semiconductors. webpage, 2008. http://www.itrs.net/Links/2008ITRS/Home2008.htm.
[37] A. Shacham, B. Lee, et al. Photonic NoC for DMA communications in chip multiprocessors. In *HOTI*, 2007.
[38] C. Stapper. On murphy's yield integral. *IEEE Trans. Semiconductor Manufacturing*, 4(4), 1991.
[39] S. Vangal, J. Howard, et al. An 80-tile sub-100-W TeraFLOPS processor in 65-nm CMOS. *JSSC*, 2008.
[40] D. Vantrease, R. Schreiber, et al. Corona: System implications of emerging nanophotonic technology. In *ISCA*, June 2008.
[41] L. Vivien, G. Maire, et al. A high efficiency silicon nitride grating coupler. In *IEEE Group IV Photonics*, pages 1–3, Sept. 2007.
[42] S. Woo, M. Ohara, et al. The SPLASH-2 programs: Characterization and methodological considerations. In *ISCA*, 1995.
[43] X. Zheng, P. Koka, et al. Silicon photonic WDM point-to-point network for multi-chip processor interconnects. In *IEEE Group IV Photonics*, 2008.
[44] X. Zheng, J. Lexau, et al. Ultra-low energy all-CMOS modulator integrated with driver. *Optics Express*, 18(3):3059–3070, 2010.
[45] X. Zheng, F. Liu, et al. An sub-picojoule-per-bit CMOS photonic receiver for densely integrated systems. *Optics Express*, 18(1):204–211, 2010.
[46] X. Zheng, I. Shubin, et al. A tunable 1×4 silicon CMOS photonic wavelength multiplexer/demultiplexer for dense optical interconnects. *Optics Express*, 18(5):5151–5160, 2010.

Re-Architecting DRAM Memory Systems with Monolithically Integrated Silicon Photonics

Scott Beamer,[†] Chen Sun,[‡] Yong-Jin Kwon,[†]
Ajay Joshi,[§] Christopher Batten,[¶] Vladimir Stojanović,[‡] Krste Asanović[†]

[†] Dept. Of EECS
University of California
Berkeley, CA
{sbeamer,kwon,krste}
@berkeley.edu

[‡] Dept. of EECS
Massachusetts Institute of Technology
Cambridge, MA
{sunchen,vlada}
@mit.edu

[§] Dept. of ECE
Boston University
Boston, MA
joshi
@bu.edu

[¶] School of ECE
Cornell University
Ithaca, NY
cbatten
@cornell.edu

ABSTRACT

The performance of future manycore processors will only scale with the number of integrated cores if there is a corresponding increase in memory bandwidth. Projected scaling of electrical DRAM architectures appears unlikely to suffice, being constrained by processor and DRAM pin-bandwidth density and by total DRAM chip power, including off-chip signaling, cross-chip interconnect, and bank access energy. In this work, we redesign the DRAM main-memory system using a proposed monolithically integrated silicon-photonic technology and show that our photonically interconnected DRAM (PIDRAM) provides a promising solution to all of these issues. Photonics can provide high aggregate pin-bandwidth density through dense wavelength-division multiplexing. Photonic signaling provides energy-efficient communication, which we exploit to not only reduce chip-to-chip interconnect power but to also reduce cross-chip interconnect power by extending the photonic links deep into the actual PIDRAM chips. To complement these large improvements in interconnect bandwidth and power, we decrease the number of bits activated per bank to improve the energy efficiency of the PIDRAM banks themselves. Our most promising design point yields approximately a 10× power reduction for a single-chip PIDRAM channel with similar throughput and area as a projected future electrical-only DRAM. Finally, we propose optical power guiding as a new technique that allows a single PIDRAM chip design to be used efficiently in several multi-chip configurations that provide either increased aggregate capacity or bandwidth.

Categories and Subject Descriptors

B.3.1 [**Memory Structures**]: Semiconductor Memories—*DRAM*; B.4.3 [**Input/Output and Data Communications**]: Interconnections—*fiber optics, physical structures, topology*

General Terms

Design

1. INTRODUCTION

The move to parallel microprocessors would appear to continue to allow Moore's Law gains in transistor density to be converted to gains in processing performance. Unfortunately, off-chip memory bandwidths are unlikely to scale in the same way and could ultimately constrain achievable system performance. Area and power overheads of high-speed transceivers and package interconnect limit the number of pins. Improved per-pin signaling rates are possible but only at a significant cost in energy efficiency and therefore will not necessarily improve aggregate off-chip bandwidth in a power-constrained system. It seems unlikely that pin bandwidth will increase dramatically without a disruptive technology. Even if we remove pin-bandwidth limitations, memory system performance could be constrained by the energy consumption of other components in current DRAM architectures. Apart from the I/O energy required to send a bit from the processor to the DRAM chip, considerable energy is expended traversing the intra-chip interconnect from the DRAM chip I/O to the desired bank and then accessing the actual storage cell.

In this paper, we propose photonically interconnected DRAM (PIDRAM) which uses a monolithically integrated silicon-photonic technology to tackle all of these challenges. Dense wavelength-division multiplexing (DWDM) allows multiple links (wavelengths) to share the same media (fiber or waveguide) yielding two orders of magnitude greater bandwidth density than electrical technology. Silicon photonics also demonstrates significantly better energy efficiency, supporting far larger off-chip bandwidths at a reasonable power budget. Monolithic integration allows energy-efficient photonic links to not only replace electrical I/O in DRAM chips, but to also extend across the DRAM chip to greatly reduce intra-chip interconnect energy. By redesigning DRAM banks to provide greater bandwidth from an individual array core, we can supply the bandwidth demands with much smaller pages thereby reducing bank activation energy. Our results show a promising design for a single-chip PIDRAM memory channel that provides a 10× improvement in throughput at similar power. Surprisingly, this does not incur an area penalty as higher bandwidth from each array core means fewer larger array blocks are required.

DRAMs are commodity parts, and ideally a single mass-produced part should be usable in a wide variety of system configurations. We propose optical power guiding as a technique to enable greater scalability of PIDRAM configurations, where we use guided photonic buses to direct optical power only to the PIDRAM chips that are actually accessed on a channel. Optical power guiding grace-

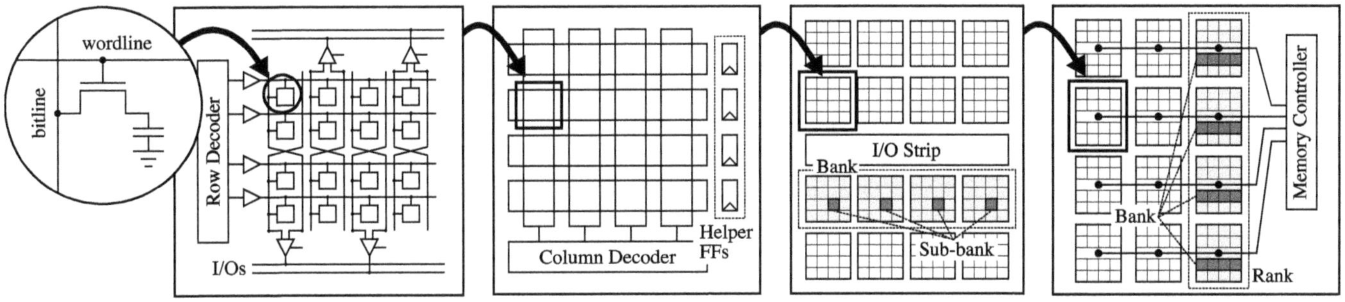

(a) Array Core (b) Array Block (c) Bank and Chip (d) Channel

Figure 1: DRAM Memory System – Each inset shows detail for a different level of current electrical DRAM memory systems.

fully scales the requirements for optical loss and power delivery, and allows a flexible tradeoff between optical power, capacity, and bandwidth, while using the same PIDRAM part and only customizing the memory controller. Our results show optical power guiding scales significantly better than shared and split photonic bus implementations.

2. DRAM TECHNOLOGY

Figure 1 shows the structure of modern DRAMs, which employ multiple levels of hierarchy to provide fast, energy-efficient access to billions of storage cells. At the lowest level, each *cell* contains a transistor and a capacitor and holds one bit of storage.

Cells are packed into 2D arrays and combined with the periphery circuitry to form an *array core* (Figure 1(a)). Each row shares a wordline with peripheral wordline drivers, and each column shares a bitline with peripheral sense-amplifiers. Differential sense-amplifiers are used to amplify and latch low-swing signals when reading from the bitlines and to regenerate full-rail voltages to refresh the cell or write new values into the cell. The array core is sized for maximum cell density for a reasonable delay and energy per activation or refresh. In this paper, we model a folded bitline DRAM, which provides better common-mode noise rejection for the sense amp [12]. However, our general assumptions are also valid for the open bitline architecture which is making a comeback due to better scalability and area efficiency. Array cores are limited to a modest size that grows very slowly with respect to technology scaling due to intrinsic capacitances, so we assume a typical array core size of 512 wordlines by 1024 bitlines. Even though on any activation of an array core every cell in the activated row is read, only a few bits will be transferred over the array core I/O lines during a column access. A few row hits are possible for some workloads, but most of the other bits read from a row are never accessed before a different row is activated.

An *array block* is a group of array cores that share circuitry such that only one of the array cores is active at a time (Figure 1(b)). Each array core shares its sense-amplifiers and I/O lines with the array cores physically located above and below it, and the array block provides its cores with a global predecoder and shared helper flip-flops for latching data signals entering or leaving the array block. As a result, the access width of an array block is equivalent to the number of I/O lines from a single array core.

A *bank* is an independently controllable unit that is made up of several array blocks working together in lockstep (Figure 1(c)). The number of array blocks per bank sets the bank's access width. Array blocks from the same bank do not need to be placed near each other, and they are often striped across the chip to ease interfacing with the chip I/O pins. When a bank is accessed, all of its array blocks are activated, each of which activates one array core, each of which activates one row. The set of activated array cores within a bank is the *sub-bank* and the set of all activated rows is the *page*.

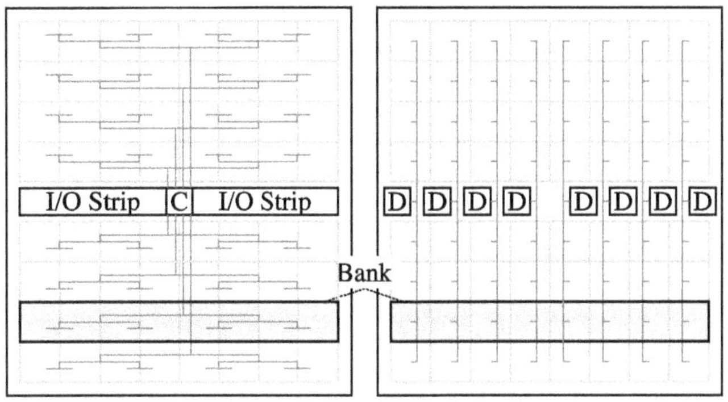

(a) Command Bus (b) Read- & Write-Data Buses

Figure 2: DRAM Chip Organization – Example chip with eight banks and eight array blocks per bank: (a) command bus is often implemented with an H-tree to broadcast control bits from the command I/O pins to all array blocks on the chip, (b) the read- and write-data buses and array blocks are bit-sliced across the chip to match the data I/O pins. (C = off-chip command I/O pins, D = off-chip data I/O pins, on-chip electrical buses shown in red)

A *chip* includes multiple banks that share the chip's I/O pins to reduce overheads and help hide bank busy times (Figure 1(c)). Figure 2 shows how the I/O strip for the off-chip pads and drivers connects to the array blocks in each bank. The DRAM command bus must be available to every array block in the chip, so a gated hierarchical H-tree bus is used to distribute control and address information from the centralized command pins in the middle of the I/O strip (Figure 2(a)). The read- and write-data buses are striped across the chip such that all array blocks in a column are connected to the same data bus pin in the I/O strip (Figure 2(b)).

A *channel* uses a memory controller to manage a collection of banks distributed across one or more DRAM chips (Figure 1(d)). The channel includes three logical buses: the command bus, the read-data bus, and the write-data bus. To increase bandwidth, multiple DRAM chips are often ganged in parallel as a *rank*, with a slice of each bank present on each chip. To further scale bandwidth, the system can have multiple memory channels. To increase capacity, multiple ranks can be placed on the same channel, but with only one accessed at a time.

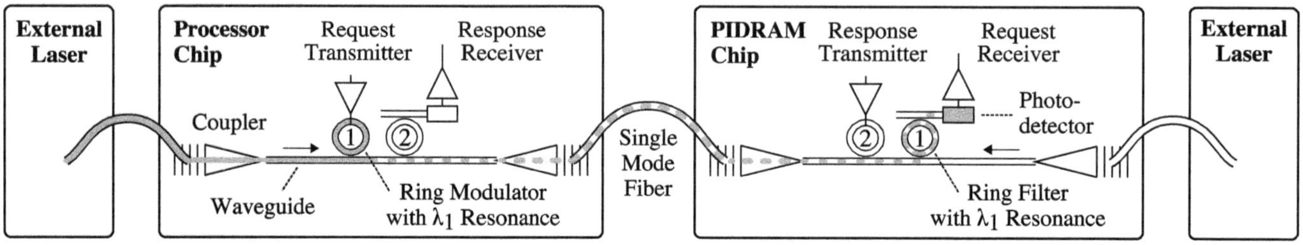

Figure 3: PIDRAM Link – Two DWDM links in opposite directions between a memory controller in a processor chip and a bank in a PIDRAM chip. λ_1 is used for the request and λ_2 is used for the response in the opposite direction on the same waveguides and fiber.

	Transmitter Energy (fJ/bt)			Receiver Energy (fJ/bt)		
I/O Technology	Data Dependent	Fixed	Thermal Tuning	Data Dependent	Fixed	Thermal Tuning
Electrical	1050	1450	n/a	1050	1450	n/a
Photonic (aggressive)	40	5	16	20	10	16
Photonic (conservative)	100	20	32	50	30	32

Table 1: Projected Electrical and Photonic I/O Energy – fJ/bt = average energy per bit-time assuming 50% bit transition probability, fixed energy includes clock and leakage, thermal tuning energy assumes 20 K temperature range. Electrical I/O projected from an 8 pJ/bt at 16 Gb/s design in a 40 nm DRAM process [14], to a 5 pJ/bt at 20 Gb/s design in a 32 nm DRAM process. Photonic I/O runs at 10 Gb/s/wavelength. Photonic projections based on our own preliminary test chips and ongoing circuit designs.

3. SILICON PHOTONIC TECHNOLOGY

Monolithically integrated silicon photonics is a promising new technology for chip-level interconnects. Photonics offers improved energy efficiency and bandwidth density compared to electrical interconnect for intra-chip and especially inter-chip links (e.g. memory channels). In this section, we first describe our assumed photonic technology and then discuss the various costs involved in implementing a unified on-chip/off-chip PIDRAM link.

The various components in a PIDRAM link are shown in Figure 3. For a command or write data, light from an external broadband laser source is coupled into a photonic waveguide on the processor chip. The light passes along a series of ring resonators in the memory controller that each modulate a unique wavelength. The modulated light is then transmitted to the PIDRAM chip on a single-mode fiber. At the receiver side, the light is filtered by the tuned ring filters and dropped onto the photodetector. The photodetector converts light into electrical current which is sensed by the electrical receiver. For the read data, light is sent in the reverse direction on the same waveguides and fiber from the PIDRAM chip back to the processor chip. In this example, two wavelengths are multiplexed onto the same waveguide, but the real potential of silicon photonics lies in its ability to support dense wavelength-division multiplexing (DWDM) with dozens of wavelengths per waveguide. There are times when it is advantageous to filter a set of wavelengths at a time, and this can be accomplished using a bank of small single-wavelength rings or multi-wavelength comb filters. These ring filter banks can be either passively tuned to a fixed frequency or actively tuned to enable optical switching.

Both 3D and monolithic integration of photonic devices have been proposed in the past few years to implement processor-to-memory photonic networks. With 3D integration, the processor chips, memory chips, and a separate photonic chip are stacked in a variety of configurations. The photonic devices can be implemented in monocrystalline silicon-on-insulator (SoI) dies with thick layer of buried oxide (BOX) [6], or in a separate layer of silicon nitride (SiN) deposited on top of the metal stack [2]. Since the photonic devices are on a separate layer, engineers can employ customized processing steps to improve photonic device performance (e.g. like introducing ridge waveguides or epitaxial Ge for photodetectors).

Photonic Device Parameter	Value
Optical fiber loss	0.5e-5 dB/cm
Coupler loss	0.5–1 dB
Splitter loss	0.2 dB
Non-linearity loss at 30 mW	1 dB
Modulator insertion loss	1 dB
Waveguide loss	2–4 dB/cm
Waveguide crossing loss	0.05 dB
Filter through loss	1e-4–1e-3 dB
Filter drop loss	1 dB
Photodetector loss	1 dB
Laser efficiency	30–50%
Receiver sensitivity	-20 dBm

Table 2: Projected Photonic Device Parameters – Based on coupler designs in [21], waveguide losses from [6], filter designs in [19] as well as our preliminary photonic transceiver test chips and ongoing device work.

In this work, we assume monolithic integration, where photonic devices have to be designed using the existing process layers of a standard logic and DRAM process. The photonic devices can be implemented in polysilicon on top of the shallow-trench isolation (STI) in a standard bulk CMOS process [8, 19] or in monocrystalline silicon with advanced thin BOX SoI. Photodetectors can be implemented using the silicon-germanium that is already present in the majority of sub-65 nm processes (and proposed for future DRAM processes [10]). Although monolithic integration may require some post-processing, its manufacturing cost should be much lower than 3D integration. Monolithic integration decreases the area and energy required to interface electrical and photonic devices, but it requires active area for waveguides and other photonic devices. It also requires an additional step in a DRAM process to

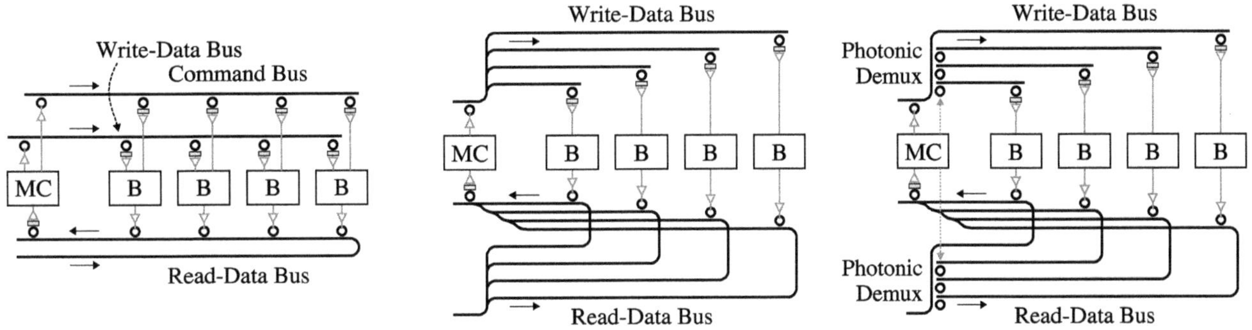

(a) Shared Photonic Buses (b) Split Photonic Buses (c) Guided Photonic Buses

Figure 4: Photonic Implementations of Command, Write-Data, and Read-Data Buses – (a) *shared photonic buses* where optical power is broadcast to all banks along a shared physical medium, (b) *split photonic buses* where optical power is split between multiple direct connections to each bank, and (c) *guided photonic buses* where optical power is actively guided to a single bank. For clarity, command bus is not shown in (b,c), but it can be implemented in a similar fashion as the corresponding write-data bus. (MC = memory controller, B = bank)

deposit undoped polysilicon, since, unlike in a logic process, all polysilicon layers in a DRAM process are deposited heavily doped to minimize fabrication cost and resistivity of polysilicon interconnect.

A photonic link consumes several types of power: laser power, data-dependent and fixed power in the electrical transmitter and receiver circuits (where fixed power includes clock and static power), and thermal tuning power which is required to stabilize the frequency response of the thermally sensitive ring resonators. Table 1 shows our predictions based on current ongoing designs for the data-dependent and fixed power spent in the electrical circuits and in the in-plane heaters for thermal tuning. The laser power depends on the amount of optical loss that any given wavelength experiences as it travels from the laser, through various optical components, and eventually to the receiver (see Table 2). Some optical losses, such as non-linearity, photodetector loss, and filter drop loss, are independent of the main-memory bandwidth and layout. We will primarily focus on losses (waveguide loss, through-ring loss, and coupler loss) affected by the required main-memory bandwidth and layout of the photonic interconnect. These components contribute significantly to the total optical path loss and set the required optical laser power and correspondingly the electrical laser power.

For our photonic links, we assume that with double-ring filters and a 4 THz free-spectral range, up to 128 wavelengths modulated at 10 Gb/s can be placed on each waveguide (64 λ in each direction, interleaved to alleviate filter roll-off requirements and crosstalk). A non-linearity limit of 30 mW at 1 dB loss is assumed for the waveguides. The waveguides are single mode and a pitch of 4 μm minimizes the crosstalk between neighboring waveguides. The diameters of a regular modulator/filter ring is $\approx$10 μm and that of a comb filter ring is $\approx$40 μm. In the following photonic layouts, we conservatively assume that these photonic components can fit in a 50 μm STI trench around each waveguide, when monolithically integrated. We also project from our ongoing circuit designs that the area of the photonic E/O transceiver circuit is around 0.01 mm^2 for modulator driver, data, and clock receivers and associated SerDes datapaths. From [14] we assume that area for an electrical I/O transceiver will be mostly bump-pitch limited at around 0.25 mm^2. While chip-to-chip links with energy as low as 1 pJ/bt at rates of 10-20 Gb/s have been demonstrated to date in advanced logic process nodes [5, 18], they operate over very mild channels with roughly -10 dB loss using weak forms of equalization. At 20 Gb/s, memory channels typically have roughly -20 dB of loss, which in combination with slower transistors on the DRAM chip makes it difficult to preserve such low energy while increasing the amount of equalization and transmit-swing or receiver gain necessary to operate at this higher loss. Hence, in our analysis we use the results from an emulated DRAM transceiver chip [14], scaled optimistically to both lower energy per bit and higher data rate per pin.

4. PIDRAM CHANNEL ORGANIZATION

As described in Section 2, a DRAM memory channel uses a memory controller to manage a set of DRAM banks that are distributed across one or more DRAM chips. The memory system includes three logical buses: a command bus, a write-data bus, and a read-data bus. Figure 4 illustrates three ways to implement these buses using the photonic components discussed in the previous section. For now we assume that a PIDRAM bank never needs to be distributed across multiple chips, and later in this section we will revisit this assumption.

Figure 4(a) shows a *shared photonic bus*, which is similar to several photonic DRAM proposals in the literature [7, 24] and logically works like a standard electrical bus. In this implementation, the memory controller first broadcasts a command to all of the banks and each bank determines if it is the target bank for the command. For a PIDRAM write command, just the target bank will then tune-in its photonic receiver on the write-data bus. The memory controller places the write data on this bus; the target bank will receive the data and then perform the corresponding write operation. The interaction of the command and write-data bus resembles the single-writer multiple-reader buses described in other nanophotonic networks [13, 26]. For a PIDRAM read command, just the target bank will perform the read operation and then use its modulator on the read-data bus to send the data back to the memory controller. The read-data bus resembles the multiple-writer single-reader buses described in other nanophotonic networks [24], except that the memory controller schedules the read-data bus to avoid any need for global arbitration.

At first glance, the shared photonic bus seems attractive since, when the bus is active, all of the optical laser power is fully utilized. Unfortunately, each bus is shared and the losses multiply together making the optical laser power an *exponential* function of the number of banks. If all of the banks are on the same PIDRAM chip, then the losses can be manageable. However, to scale to larger capacities, we will need to "daisy-chain" the shared photonic bus through multiple PIDRAM chips. Each PIDRAM chip adds two coupler losses, waveguide losses, and extra ring losses. The coupler losses are particularly difficult to mitigate, since even with optimized designs and process steps, the coupler loss is usually more than 0.5 dB [21]. Large coupler losses and the exponential scaling of laser power combine to make the shared photonic bus feasible only for connecting banks within a PIDRAM chip as opposed to connecting banks across PIDRAM chips.

Figure 4(b) shows an alternative implementation that we call a *split photonic bus*, which divides the long shared bus into multiple branches. In the command and write-data bus, modulated laser power is still sent to all receivers, and in the read-data bus, laser power is still sent to all modulators. The split nature of the bus, however, means that the total laser power is roughly a *linear* function of the number of banks. If each bank was on its own PIDRAM chip, then we would use a couple of fibers per chip (one for modulated data and one for laser power) to connect the memory controller to each of the PIDRAM chips. Each optical path in the write-data bus would only traverse one optical coupler to leave the processor chip and one optical coupler to enter the PIDRAM chip regardless of the total number of banks. This implementation reduces the extra optical laser power as compared to a shared photonic bus at the cost of additional splitter and combiner losses in the memory controller. It also reduces the effective bandwidth density of the photonic bus, by increasing the number of fibers for the same effective bandwidth. In this example with four banks per bus, we will need to use four waveguides/fibers where we only needed one in the shared photonic bus. The significant bandwidth density of our photonic technology can potentially make this a reasonable tradeoff.

To further reduce the required optical power, we introduce the the concept of a *guided photonic bus*, shown in Figure 4(c), which uses optical power guiding in the form of photonic demultiplexers to actively direct power to just the target bank. Each photonic demultiplexer uses an array of either ring or comb filters, and these filters are actively tuned by the memory controller to guide the light down the desired branch, leaving the unused branches dark. For the command and write-data bus, the photonic demultiplexer is placed after the modulator to direct the modulated light to the target bank. For the read-data bus, the photonic demultiplexer is placed before the modulators to allow the memory controller to manage when to guide the light to the target bank for modulation. Since the optical power is always guided down a single branch, the total laser power is roughly *constant* and independent of the number of banks. The optical loss overhead due to the photonic demultiplexers and the reduced bandwidth density due to the branching make a guided photonic bus most attractive when working with relatively large per-bank optical losses.

Figure 5 illustrates in more detail our proposed PIDRAM memory system. The figure shows a processor chip with multiple independent PIDRAM memory channels; each memory channel includes a memory controller and a PIDRAM DIMM, which in turn includes a set of PIDRAM chips. To prevent the on-chip processor network from becoming a bottleneck, the multiple PIDRAM channels could be distributed around the processor chip and connected to the cores with one of the recently proposed on-chip photonic networks [9, 13, 24, 26]. In the rest of this paper, we will focus on the implementation of a single PIDRAM memory channel.

Each PIDRAM chip contains a set of banks, and each bank is completely contained within a single PIDRAM chip. We use a hybrid approach to implement each of the three logical buses. The memory scheduler within the memory controller orchestrates access to each bus to avoid conflicts. The command bus is implemented with a single wavelength on a guided photonic bus. The

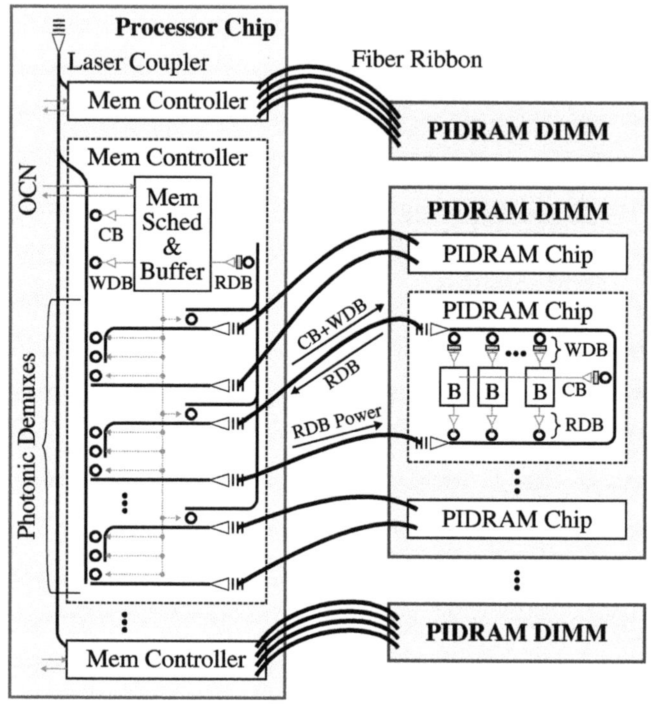

Figure 5: PIDRAM Memory System – Each PIDRAM memory channel connects to a PIDRAM DIMM via a fiber ribbon. The memory controller manages the command bus (CB), write-data bus (WDB), and read-data bus (RDB), which are wavelength division multiplexed onto the same fiber. Photonic demuxes guide power to only the active PIDRAM chip. (OCN = on-chip network, B = PIDRAM bank, each ring represents multiple rings for multi-wavelength buses, on-chip electrical wiring shown in red)

command wavelength is actively guided to the PIDRAM chip containing the target bank. Once on the PIDRAM chip, a single receiver converts the command into the electrical domain and then electrically broadcasts the command to all banks in the chip. Preliminary analysis suggested that an electrical broadcast will require significantly less energy than optically broadcasting the command wavelength to all banks. Very high bandwidth channels supporting many banks may require a second command wavelength to ensure sufficient command bandwidth. Both the write-data and read-data buses are implemented with a guided photonic bus to actively guide optical power to a single PIDRAM chip within a PIDRAM DIMM, and then they are implemented with a shared photonic bus to distribute the data within the PIDRAM chip. Section 5 will describe the exact floorplan for the PIDRAM chip, and Section 6 will provide more detail on the PIDRAM bank design.

Providing one laser per PIDRAM chip is not economical, so a handful of large but efficient lasers are used with their optical power brought on to the processor chip and subsequently divided among the memory channels and guided to the PIDRAM chips. This approach places fibers destined for the same PIDRAM chip in physical proximity, allowing them to be grouped into a fiber ribbon to ease assembly. For economic and packaging reasons, we assume each PIDRAM chip will only have two fibers: one for the three buses and one for the unmodulated read-data optical power. Figure 5 illustrates how the command, write-data, and read-data buses are wavelength division multiplexed onto the same fiber. Routing the read-data optical power through the processor chip also en-

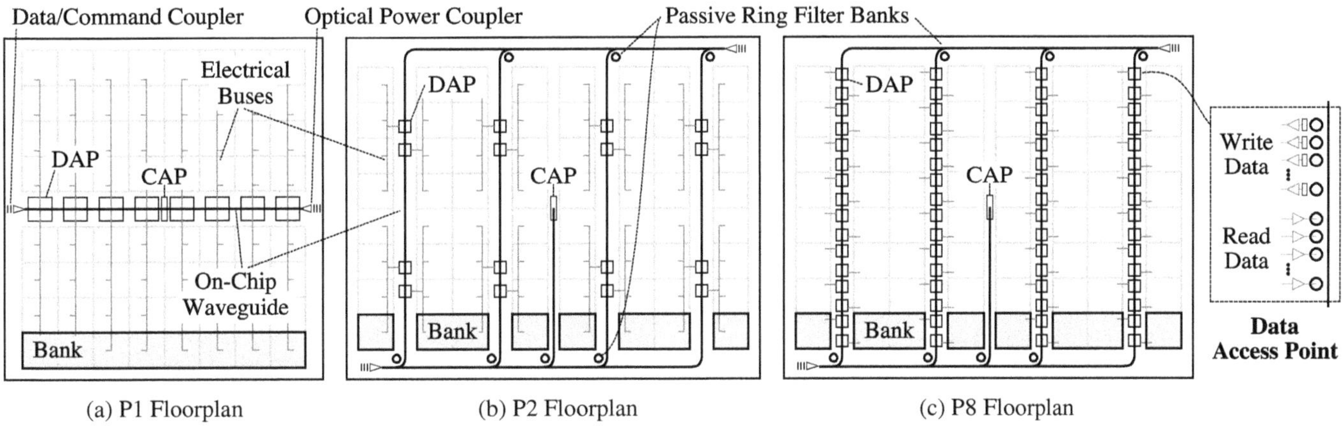

Figure 6: PIDRAM Chip Floorplans – Three floorplans are shown for an example PIDRAM chip with eight banks and eight array blocks per bank. For all floorplans, the photonic command bus ends at the command access point (CAP), and an electrical H-tree implementation efficiently broadcasts control bits from the command access point to all array blocks. For clarity, the on-chip electrical command bus is not shown, but it is similar to that shown in Figure 2(a). The data buses shown in the floorplans gradually extend the photonics deeper into the PIDRAM chip: (a) *P1* uses photonic chip I/O for the data buses but fully electrical on-chip data bus implementations, (b) *P2* uses seamless on-chip/off-chip photonics to distribute the data bus to a group of four banks, and (c) *P8* uses photonics all the way to each bank. (CAP = command access point, DAP = data access point, on-chip electrical buses shown in red)

ables a guided photonic bus implementation, since the corresponding photonic demultiplexer can be positioned within the appropriate memory controller.

So far in this section we have assumed that a bank is completely contained within a single PIDRAM chip, but this is in contrast to traditional electrical DRAM memory systems where banks are almost always distributed across multiple chips. Electrical DRAM chips are usually pin-bandwidth limited to a few bits per bus clock cycle. For example, to obtain all 512 bits needed for a 64-byte cache line, a bank might be striped across eight different chips and each access activates all chips in parallel. Unfortunately, this leads to large page sizes and wasted energy as most of the activated page is unused. Alternatively, electrical DRAM memory systems could activate just a single chip and wait for the entire cache line to stream out. Unfortunately, the limited pin bandwidth per chip will significantly increase serialization latency. A PIDRAM memory channel supports much higher bandwidth to each PIDRAM chip. A single data fiber can provide 80 GB/s in each direction, enabling an entire cache line to be stored in a single chip without incurring additional serialization latency. By locating a bank (and a cache-line access) on a single PIDRAM chip, the page size can be reduced by a factor of eight or more resulting in significant activation energy savings. Of course there are additional chip-level and bank-level considerations with providing this amount of memory bandwidth that will be discussed in the next two sections.

5. PIDRAM CHIP ORGANIZATION

In the previous section we motivated using guided photonic buses to implement the inter-chip portion of the command, write-data, and read-data buses while using shared photonic buses for the intra-chip portion of these buses. There is an important design trade-off in terms of how much of the on-chip portion of these buses should be implemented photonically versus electrically. This design choice is primarily driven by trade-offs in area and power.

Figure 6(a) illustrates the approach labeled *P1*, where the electrical I/O strip in Figure 2 is replaced with a horizontal waveguide and multiple *photonic access points*. Each photonic access point converts the corresponding bus between the optical and electrical domains. The on-chip electrical H-tree command bus and vertical electrical data buses remain as in traditional electrical DRAM shown in Figure 2.

Figures 6(b) and 6(c) illustrate our approach for implementing more of the on-chip portion of the data buses with photonics to improve cross-chip energy-efficiency. We use a *waterfall floorplan*, where the waveguides are distributed across the chip. The horizontal waveguides contain all of the wavelengths, and the optically passive ring filter banks at the bottom and top of the waterfall ensure that each of these vertical waveguides only contains a subset of the channel's wavelengths. Each of these vertical waveguides is analogous to the electrical vertical buses in *P1*, so a bank can still be striped across the chip horizontally to allow easy access to the on-chip photonic interconnect. Various waterfall floorplans are possible that correspond to more or less photonic access points. For a *Pn* floorplan, *n* indicates the number of partitions along each vertical electrical data bus. All of the photonic circuits have to be replicated at each data access point for each bus partition. This increases the fixed link power due to link transceiver circuits and ring heaters. It can also potentially lead to higher optical losses, due to the increased number of rings on the optical path. In Section 7 we further evaluate these trade-offs. Our photonic floorplans all use the same on-chip command bus implementation as traditional electrical DRAM: a command access point is positioned in the middle of the chip and an electrical H-tree command bus broadcasts the control and address information to all array blocks.

6. PIDRAM BANK ORGANIZATION

After redesigning the DRAM memory channel and DRAM chip to use an energy-efficient photonic interconnect, the next limiting factor is the power consumed within the banks themselves. During a bank access, every constituent array block activates an array core, which activates an entire array core row, of which only a handful of bits are used. The energy spent activating the other bits is wasted, and this waste dominates bank energy consumption. Reducing wasted accesses while keeping the bank access size constant requires either decreasing the array core row size or increasing the number of I/Os per array core and using fewer array cores in parallel. Reducing the array core row size results in a greater area penalty due to less amortization of fixed area overheads, so we propose increasing the number of array core I/Os to improve access efficiency. Increasing the number of I/Os per array core, while keeping the bank size and access width constant, will have the effect of decreasing the number of array blocks per bank. Currently there is little incentive to make this change because the energy savings within the bank are small compared to the electrical inter-chip and intra-chip interconnect energy. Even if there were energy savings, current designs are also pin-bandwidth limited, so there would be no benefit to supporting such a wide bank access width, since that would increase serialization latency. The improvements in bandwidth density and energy efficiency realized through photonic bus implementations are key enablers for increasing the number of array core I/Os and thus reducing the bank activation energy.

With increased bandwidth, it also becomes advantageous to have more banks per chip, to hide bank busy times by interleaving between multiple parallel banks. Currently, however, rapid bank interleaving puts strain on the power delivery network of a DRAM chip because activates draw significant instantaneous current. To reduce the cost of the power delivery network, modern DRAM standards include two new timing constraints, t_{RRD} and t_{FAW}, which mandate minimum intervals between activate commands [16]. These constraints are the result of aggressive cost-cutting, and could potentially handicap any benefits from additional banks by limiting the number of activates per unit time. Recent industry focus on improving DRAM core efficiency have yielded designs that reduce t_{RRD} and t_{FAW} significantly [17]. Furthermore, implementing inter-chip communication with photonics frees up a number of pins, which can be used as power pins to improve power delivery. We can also reduce instantaneous power draw by decreasing the number of bits activated. Increasing the number of I/Os per array core reduces the number of array blocks activated, which reduces the total number of bits activated. But increasing chip access width forces each chip to activate more bits. Since we scaled access width up to an entire 512-bit cache line per chip, the number of I/Os per array core must also scale proportionally if we want to keep the number of activated bits constant.

7. EVALUATION OF SINGLE-CHIP PIDRAM MEMORY CHANNEL

In this section, we compare various PIDRAM configurations and floorplans to a baseline electrical DRAM implementation with the same capacity. This baseline design is labeled *E1* and is similar to that described in Section 2. In this section, we limit our study to a single-chip PIDRAM memory channel, and we ignore bandwidth-density constraints for the electrical baseline. In the next section, we will explore scaling to multi-chip PIDRAM memory channels.

7.1 Methodology

To evaluate the energy efficiency and area tradeoffs of the proposed DRAM architectures, we use a heavily modified version of the Cacti-D DRAM modeling tool [22]. Though we were able to use some of Cacti-D's original models for details such as decoder sizing, gate area calculations and technology parameter scaling, the design space we explored required a complete overhaul of Cacti-D's assumed DRAM organization and hierarchy. To this end, we built our own architectural models for the DRAM core, from circuit-level changes at the array core level, to the array block level and higher bank organization levels as shown in Figure 1, while relying on Cacti-D's original circuit models to handle most of the low-level circuit and process technology details. To validate our electrical models, we tested them against known points for a range of processes and configurations. In addition to covering the baseline electrical DRAM design, we accounted for the overhead of each relevant photonic design in our models and developed a comprehensive methodology for calculating the power and area overheads of off-chip I/O for both the electrical and photonic cases of interest. Since silicon photonics is an emerging technology, we also explore the space of possible results with both aggressive and conservative projections for photonic devices and photonic link circuits. All energy and area calculations presented are for a 32 nm DRAM process. For all of our designs the photonic command-bus power was a small enough fraction of the data-bus power that we ignore it for the purposes of our evaluation.

To quantify the performance of each DRAM design, we use a detailed cycle-level microarchitectural C++ simulator. We use synthetic traffic patterns to issue loads and stores at a rate capped by the number of in–flight messages. The memory controller converts requests into DRAM commands which are issued based on a round-robin arbitration scheme and various timing constraints based on contemporary timing parameters found in the Micron DDR3 SDRAM data sheet [16]. These timing parameters are also in agreement with our modified CACTI-D models. We simulate a range of different designs by varying: floorplan, number of I/Os per array core, number of banks, and the channel bandwidth. We use the events and statistics from the simulator to animate our DRAM and photonic device models to compute the energy per bit.

We find that for random traffic, a bank with a 512-bit access width has a bi-directional data bandwidth of approximately 10 Gb/s independent of system size, which matches our analytical model. Since each wavelength (λ) has a uni-directional bandwidth of 10 Gb/s, this translates to an equivalent bandwidth of 1/2 λ in each direction under balanced read and write workloads. Accordingly, we find the knee in the curve of sustained random bandwidth versus number of banks occurs when the number of λ per direction is half the number of banks.

For streaming traffic the effective bank bandwidth is higher, however, we believe random traffic is more representative of expected system traffic in future systems. In the manycore era, even if every core has locality in its access stream, there will be so many of them, that from the point of view of any memory controller, accesses will appear random. An intelligent memory controller could reorder the accesses to re-extract some of the locality, but this is unlikely to scale to many cores. Consequently, we perform most of our design and analysis assuming random traffic.

Latency is not an important figure of merit for this work because we do not expect PIDRAM to affect it significantly. We do not change the array core internals, which sets many of the inherent latencies for accessing DRAM. Moreover, our bank bandwidths are sufficiently sized such that the serialization latency is not significant, especially for random traffic, when compared to the inherent DRAM latencies. As to be expected, as the channel approaches peak utilization, the latency does rise dramatically due to queuing delays.

Although we evaluate hundreds of design points with our methodology, we will limit the rest of this section to the three configurations shown in Table 3. These configurations are either optimal or representative for their given parameters. The *b64-io4* configuration and the *b64-io32* configuration represent high-bandwidth PIDRAM chips (we include both to demonstrate the tradeoffs for changing the number of array core I/Os) and the *b8-io32* configuration represents low-bandwidth PIDRAM chips. All of our configurations are for a capacity of 8 Gb, which yields a reasonably sized chip given the 32 nm DRAM process technology. The DRAM-chip

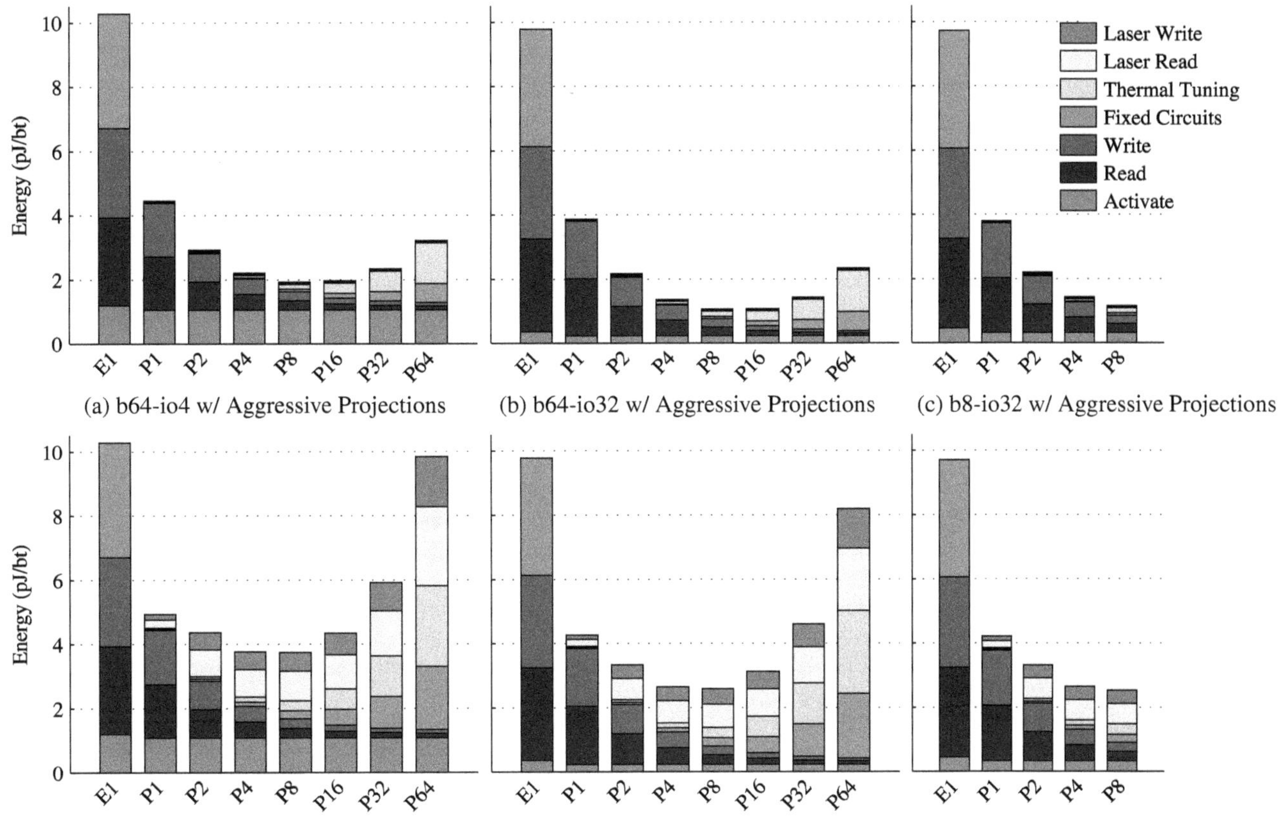

(a) b64-io4 w/ Aggressive Projections (b) b64-io32 w/ Aggressive Projections (c) b8-io32 w/ Aggressive Projections

(d) b64-io4 w/ Conservative Projections (e) b64-io32 w/ Conservative Projections (f) b8-io32 w/ Conservative Projections

Figure 7: Energy Breakdown for Various DRAM Designs – (a–c) assume aggressive projections for photonic devices, while (d–f) assume more conservative projections as discussed in Section 3. Results for (a,b,d,e) are at a peak bandwidth of ≈500 Gb/s and (c,f) are at a peak bandwidth of ≈60 Gb/s with random traffic. Thermal tuning energy assumes 20 K temperature range, and fixed circuits energy includes clock and leakage. Read energy includes chip I/O read, cross-chip read, and bank read energy. Write energy includes chip I/O write, cross-chip write, and bank write energy. Activate energy includes chip I/O command, cross-chip row address energy, and bank activate energy.

access width (bits per request) is 512 bits, which is scaled up from the 64 bits in contemporary DRAM. This is to enable the transfer of a 64-byte cache line from a single chip with a single request.

7.2 Energy Breakdown

Figure 7 shows the energy-efficiency breakdown for various floorplans implementing our three representative PIDRAM configurations. Each design is subjected to a random traffic pattern at peak utilization and the results are shown for the aggressive and conservative photonic technology projections. Across all designs it is clear that replacing the off-chip links with photonics is advantageous, as *E1* towers above the rest of the designs. How far photonics is taken on chip, however, is a much richer design space. To achieve the optimal energy efficiency requires balancing both the data-dependent and data-independent components of the overall energy. For Figure 7, the data-independent energy includes: electrical laser power for the write bus, electrical laser power for the read bus, fixed circuit energy including clock and leakage, and thermal tuning energy. As shown in Figure 7(a), *P1* spends the majority of the energy on intra-chip communication (write and read energy) because the data must traverse long global wires to get to each bank. Taking photonics all the way to each array block with *P64* minimizes the cross-chip energy, but results in a large number of photonic access points (since the photonic access points in *P1* are replicated 64 times in the case of *P64*), contributing to the large data-independent component of the total energy. This is due to the fixed energy cost of photonic transceiver circuits and the energy spent on ring thermal tuning. By sharing the photonic access points across eight banks, the optimal design is *P8*. This design balances the data-dependent savings of using intra-chip photonics with the data-independent overheads due to electrical laser power, fixed circuit power, and thermal tuning power.

Once the off-chip and cross-chip energies have been reduced (as in the *P8* floorplan for the *b64-io4* configuration), the activation energy becomes dominant. Figure 7(b) shows the results for the *b64-io32* configuration which increases the number of bits we read or write from each array core to 32. This further reduces the activate energy cost, and overall this optimized design is 10× more en-

Parameter	b64-io4	b64-io32	b8-io32
Banks	64	64	8
Bandwidth (λ / direction)	32	32	4
I/Os per Array Core	4	32	32

Table 3: Representative Configurations – We explored designs consisting of 8, 16, 32, and 64 banks, each with 4, 8, 16, 32 and 64 λ/dir, and 4, 8, 16, and 32 I/Os per array core. All configurations were evaluated for all floorplans possible with that configuration.

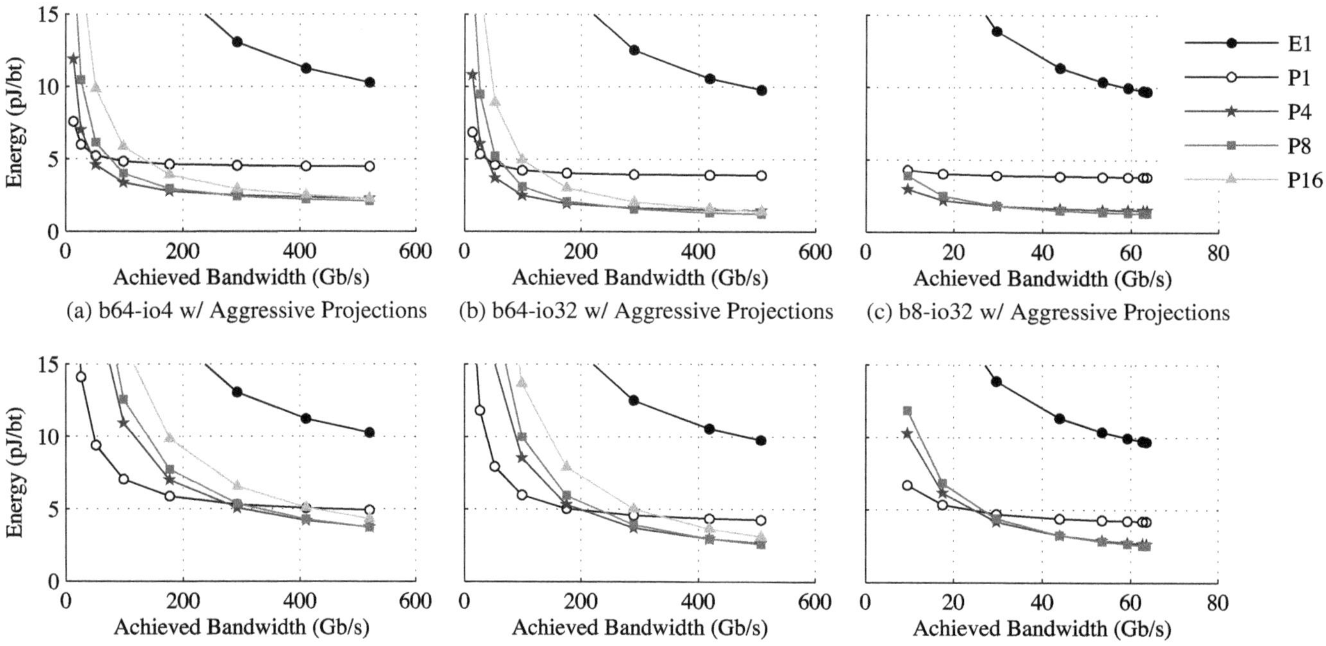

(a) b64-io4 w/ Aggressive Projections (b) b64-io32 w/ Aggressive Projections (c) b8-io32 w/ Aggressive Projections

(d) b64-io4 w/ Conservative Projections (e) b64-io32 w/ Conservative Projections (f) b8-io32 w/ Conservative Projections

Figure 8: Energy vs. Utilization – (a–c) assume aggressive projections for photonic devices, while (d–f) assume more conservative projections as discussed in Section 3. To reduce clutter, we only plot the three most energy efficient waterfall floorplans (*P4*, *P8*, *P16*). *P16* is not shown for (c,f) since *b8-io32* only has eight banks.

ergy efficient than the baseline electrical design. Figure 7(c) shows similar tradeoffs for the low-bandwidth *b8-io32* configuration.

Figure 7(d–f) shows the same designs as Figure 7(a–c), but for conservative silicon-photonic technology assumptions. Replacing the off-chip links with silicon photonics still helps significantly, but bringing photonics across the chip closer to the array blocks is less of an improvement. This is a consequence of the lossier components which require more laser power. The optimal floorplan still appears to be *P8*, but it has a smaller margin over *P1*. Changing the number of I/Os per array core still proves to be beneficial, but this improvement is diluted.

7.3 Energy vs. Utilization

Although low power at peak throughput is important, a system designer is often just as concerned about energy efficiency at low utilization. For a given design, we scale back the utilization by reducing the number of messages that can be in flight, and the results are shown in Figure 8(a–c). As expected, the energy per bit increases as utilization goes down due to the data-independent power components. Although there are laser power, fixed circuit, and thermal tuning overheads for our PIDRAM designs, the fixed circuit overheads for the electrical baseline are significant enough to result in poor energy-efficiency regardless of utilization.

Systems with higher data-independent power will have a steeper slope, and this tradeoff can clearly be shown when comparing *P8* and *P16* to *P1*. The higher numbered *Pn* floorplans do better for the high-utilization cases because the global electrical wires connecting the array blocks to the photonic access points are shorter. However, they do worse than the *P1* floorplan for low utilization because the data-independent power of their rings and idle photonic circuits adds up. Essentially, this is a trade-off between the data-dependent and data-independent power components, and the target system utilization will determine the appropriate design.

Figure 8(d–f) shows the effects of less capable photonic devices, which result in a relatively large penalty for low utilization of high-bandwidth systems. This most notably affects the *P4*, *P8*, and *P16* floorplans.

7.4 Area

Figure 9 shows the total area breakdown of each design. Increasing the number of I/Os per array core results in significant area savings for all floorplans (less intra-bank and inter-bank overhead for *b64-io32* vs. *b64-io4*) because each array block has fixed area overheads. Recall from Section 6, increasing the number of I/Os per array block reduces the number of array blocks when keeping the access width constant.

Replacing the off-chip links with photonics results in significant area savings (*E1* vs. *P1*) due to the large size of bump-pitch limited electrical off-chip I/Os. Taking photonics deeper on-chip results in the jump in I/O overhead area between the *P1* and *P2* floorplans which can be explained by the move from the single photonic strip in *P1* to the waterfall in *P2* and above. Since we assume a very conservative 50 µm width for each photonic trench in the area calculations, the vertical trenches needed by the waterfall present a noticeable area increase. Interestingly, the losses in the conservative case require the laser power per wavelength to be so high that only 8 wavelengths can be supported per waveguide to stay within the 30 mW nonlinearity limit. This requires 16 waveguides instead of one in *P1* and two per column instead of one for the waterfall of *P2* and above. This however results in less than 1 mm^2 additional area overhead due to the compact waveguide pitch in each trench.

Much of the area savings is from increasing the number of I/Os per array core, but the most energy efficient design (*b64-io32-P8*) has slightly smaller area than the electrical baseline (*b64-io32-E1*). Additionally, the electrical baseline I/O area is mostly bump-pitch limited and unlikely to scale much in more advanced process nodes,

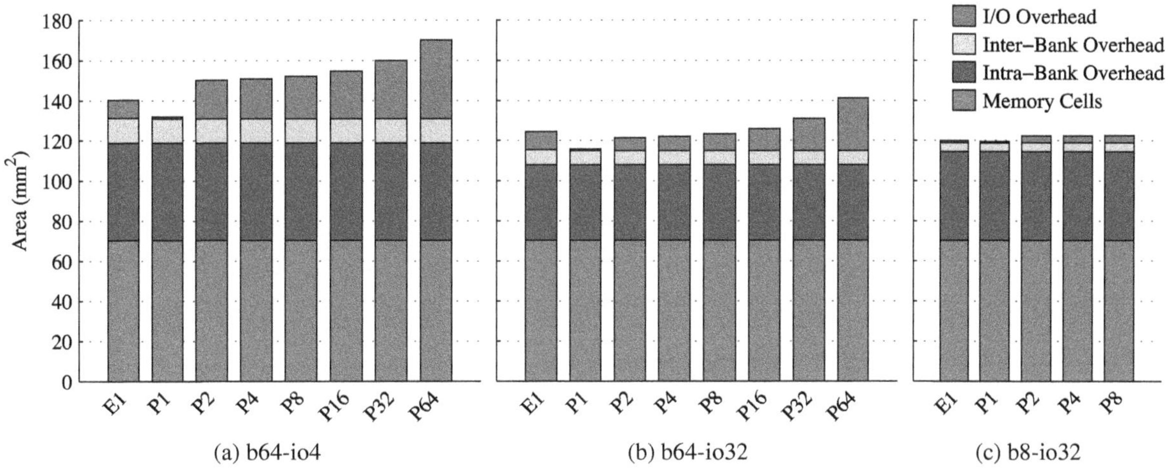

Figure 9: Area Breakdown for Various DRAM Designs with Aggressive Photonic Projections – The I/O overhead includes the area costs of circuits that form the access points as well as the area overhead of the waveguides. The inter-bank overhead is the area cost of wires and buffers used to bring bits from the banks to the photonic access points. The intra-bank overhead refers to the area taken up by the peripheral circuitry of each bank (e.g., decoders and sense-amplifiers). The memory cell area is the area taken up by the actual DRAM cells.

setting the upper bound on memory area efficiency for a required I/O bandwidth. Photonic access points, on the other hand, are relatively small both in size and number of vertical couplers. They are allowed to scale due to dense wavelength division multiplexing and continue to shrink with the scaling of electrical back-end circuits.

8. SCALING TO MULTI-CHIP PIDRAM MEMORY CHANNELS

When the number of PIDRAM chips per channel is scaled to increase capacity, the primary concern is the amount of laser power needed to overcome the extra losses that result from the overhead of adding more chips. In this section, we first quantitatively examine the laser power trade-offs between the shared, split, and guided photonic bus approaches, before qualitatively discussing 3D integration as a complementary technique for further capacity scaling.

8.1 Optical Power Guiding

For our -20 dBm receiver sensitivity and 30% laser efficiency, an optical path loss in the range of roughly 15–25 dB is needed to keep the background laser power below the link energy cost. With a daisy-chained shared bus approach, the optical loss grows exponentially by the loss through a PIDRAM chip (3.5–7 dB aggressive or 7–13 dB conservative, depending on the floorplan) for each additional chip on the channel. With 5.5 dB (aggressive) to 10 dB (conservative) already lost in the memory controller waveguides, couplers, and rings, this approach becomes impractical beyond one or two chips. With 32 *b64-io32-P8* chips sitting on a channel implemented as a shared bus, the optical loss grows to 213 dB and 407 dB for the aggressive and conservative projections, respectively.

The split bus approach fares significantly better than shared bus as the required laser power grows roughly linearly with the number of chips per channel. For a single *b64-io32-P8* chip channel, the optical loss is 12 dB aggressive and 22 dB conservative, and grows to 27 dB and 37 dB when 32 *b64-io32-P8* chips are attached the channel for the aggressive and conservative projections, respectively.

With a guided bus, the laser power is sent only to the necessary chip. The fixed loss in the memory controller increases by 2–3 dB due to the extra power guiding ring and the need to also couple the read path laser in and out of the memory controller. A second increase in the memory controller loss results from the power guiding rings added to the memory controller with each additional chip. More rings along the path means more ring through loss and longer waveguides within the memory controller, amounting to an extra 0.1 dB to 0.3 dB loss for each additional chip. A guided bus channel with 32 *b64-io32-P8* chips has an optical loss of 17 dB and 33 dB for the aggressive and conservative projections, respectively.

Figure 10 shows how much the laser power contributes to the overall energy/bit for several floorplans of the *b64-io32* configuration. We can see that the guided bus designs have much more room to scale, as the shared and split bus approaches quickly become infeasible after only a few chips. As expected, designs that do not go as far into the PIDRAM chip consume less power, which makes sense since the PIDRAM chips themselves contribute less loss to the optical critical path. Interestingly, with conservative components, the split bus in Figure 10(b) can outperform the guided bus for smaller number of chips per channel, because the loss-overhead of guiding on the memory controller side is bigger than the linear increase in power required for the split bus.

8.2 3D Integration

Three dimensional stacking is a complementary technology to photonics. This technology can be used to increase the capacity of PIDRAM memory channels without additional fiber wiring and packaging overhead. We introduce the concept of a PIDRAM cube, which is a collection of stacked PIDRAM dies (e.g., as in [11]), connected electrically by through-silicon vias and optically by vertical coupling in through-silicon via holes.

Stacking can be especially useful for high-capacity systems, where a significant fraction of the fibers would be unused with optical power guiding. By stacking these chips in a PIDRAM cube and adding a second stage of power guiding within the stack, we can reduce the number of packages and fibers in the system while maintaining the same capacity and bandwidth. The first stage of

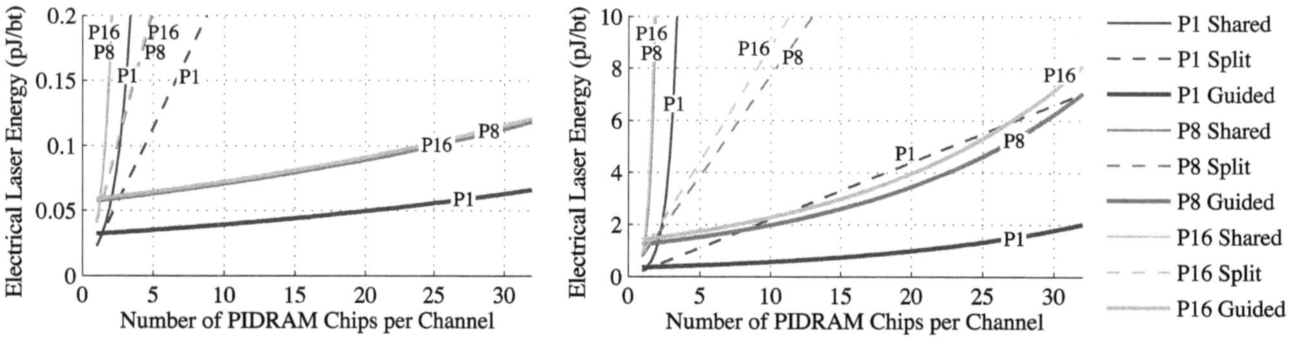

(a) b64-io32 w/ Aggressive Projections

(b) b64-io32 w/ Conservative Projections

Figure 10: Electrical Laser Power Scaling for Multi-Chip PIDRAM Memory Channels – Laser power increases more slowly with the proposed guided photonic bus implementation versus either the shared or the split photonic bus implementations.

power guiding determines which PIDRAM cube gets the channel, while the second stage determines which die in the cube gets the channel.

With our photonic design, all of the dies in the stack after the base die will be the same, which greatly reduces the manufacturing costs. For example, for a stack of eight die, the generic die needs a total of 16 couplers. Only one in each direction will be active in any given die, and the others will be drilled-out by the TSV holes. Although stacking DRAM chips on top of the CPU die may increase the DRAM chip temperature (and hence refresh power), stacking PIDRAM chips in a cube away from the CPU should have minimal temperature effects on PIDRAM leakage and photonic components as overall PIDRAM chip power dissipation is relatively small.

9. RELATED WORK

Microthreading [25] and multicore DIMMs [1] are techniques to reduce the effective page size in current electrical memory modules by partitioning a wide multichip DRAM interface into multiple narrow DRAM interfaces each with fewer chips. Since both approaches use commodity electrical DRAM chips, they result in either smaller access sizes or longer serialization latencies. Architectural modifications to commodity DRAM, such as single subarray access and selective bitline access [23], also trade-off number of activated bits with serialization latency and area. Although our approach also reduces the ratio of activated to accessed bits, the energy-efficiency and bandwidth-density advantages of silicon photonics allows us to maintain the original access size and access latency while in addition reducing on-chip and off-chip interconnect energy.

Several researchers have proposed leveraging alternative technologies such as 3D stacking [11, 15, 20] and proximity communication [4] to address the manycore memory bandwidth challenge. Both technologies would offer either local DRAM physically packaged with the processor chip, or a tightly integrated multichip memory module connected to the processors via standard electrical interconnect. 3D stacking relies on through-silicon vias (TSVs) to communicate between layers, but monolithically integrated silicon photonics can also use the TSV holes for free-space optical communication. An optical scheme would have significantly higher bandwidth density than recently demonstrated stacked DRAM [11], requiring fewer TSVs while improving yield, as metal is not required to fill the TSV. Even a more advanced TSV technology with a 10 µm pitch at 20 Gb/s per via, would offer 5–10× lower bandwidth-density compared to an integrated optical vertical coupler. Furthermore, 3D stacking does not improve the horizontal communication required to connect any processing core to any memory bank. Although tight integration of a few DRAM chips and compute logic in a single package can serve some markets well, other systems demand much larger ratios of DRAM to compute logic. Stacked memory modules improve DRAM capacity but are connected to the processor chip through energy-inefficient and comparatively low-bandwidth electrical interconnect. In contrast, PIDRAM provides a flexible and scalable way to support different system configurations with high bandwidth density and energy efficiency.

Previous studies have illustrated the advantages of using an optical channel between on-chip memory controllers and a *buffer chip* positioned near a rank of DRAM chips. These schemes used either shared buses with arbitration at the memory controller [7] or point-to-point links with arbitration at the buffer chip [3]. Our work examines the channel-level, chip-level, and bank-level implications of fully integrating photonics into the actual DRAM chip, and our analysis shows the importance of considering all of these aspects to realize significant energy-efficiency gains. The Corona system briefly mentions a photonic memory-controller to buffer-chip channel, but then proposes using 3D stacked DRAM to mitigate the buffer chip to DRAM energy [24]. Although this mitigates some of the disadvantages of 3D stacking mentioned earlier, the Corona scheme relies on daisy-chained memory modules to increase capacity. We have found that this channel-level organization places stringent constraints on the device optical loss parameters, especially waveguide and coupler loss. In this work, we have proposed optical power guiding as a new way to increase capacity with less aggressive devices. The Corona work assumed a single DRAM organization, but our studies have shown that the advantages of photonics vary widely depending on the channel-level, chip-level, and bank-level configurations.

10. CONCLUSION

Photonic technology continues to improve rapidly, and could well form an essential ingredient in future multiprocessor performance scaling by improving interconnect performance. We have developed new photonically integrated DRAM architectures, and while photonics is a clear win for chip-to-chip communication, leveraging this new technology on the PIDRAM chip itself requires a careful balance between fixed and dynamic power. Background power is as important as active power, and should be addressed in future photonic device development, e.g., by providing fine-grain control of laser power to give better energy-efficiency at low to zero utilization. Surprisingly, despite the need to increase the number of array core I/O lines to obtain greater energy savings, PIDRAM area does not necessarily grow thanks to the high bandwidth density. High performance, low cost, and energy efficiency at the chip level are not sufficient for PIDRAMs to become successful high-volume commodity parts, they must also support a wide range of multi-chip configurations with different capacity and bandwidth tradeoffs. Our new laser power guiding technique can be used to construct a scalable high-capacity memory system with low background power by only illuminating active paths in the memory system.

ACKNOWLEDGEMENTS

This work was supported in part by Intel Corporation and DARPA awards W911NF-08-1-0134, W911NF-08-1-0139, and W911NF-09-1-0342. Research also supported in part by Microsoft (Award #024263) and Intel (Award #024894) funding and by matching funding by U.C. Discovery (Award #DIG07-10227).

We would like to acknowledge the MIT photonic team, including J. Orcutt, A. Khilo, M. Popovic, C. Holzwarth, B. Moss, H. Li, M. Georgas, J. Leu, J. Sun, C. Sorace, F. Kaertner, J. Hoyt, R. Ram, and H. Smith. We would also like to thank David Patterson and members of the Berkeley Par Lab for feedback.

11. REFERENCES

[1] J. Ahn et al. Multicore DIMM: An energy-efficient memory module with independently controlled DRAMs. *Computer Architecture Letters*, 8(1):5–8, Jan/Jun 2009.

[2] T. Barwicz et al. Silicon photonics for compact, energy-efficient interconnects. *Journal of Optical Networking*, 6(1):63–73, Jan 2007.

[3] C. Batten et al. Building manycore processor-to-DRAM networks with monolithic CMOS silicon photonics. *IEEE Micro*, 29(4):8–21, Jul/Aug 2009.

[4] R. Drost et al. Challenges in building a flat-bandwidth memory hierarchy for a large scale computer with proximity communication. *Int'l Symp. on High-Performance Interconnects*, Aug 2005.

[5] K. Fukuda et al. A 12.3 mW 12.5 Gb/s complete transceiver in 65 nm CMOS. *Int'l Solid-State Circuits Conf.*, Feb 2010.

[6] C. Gunn. CMOS photonics for high-speed interconnects. *IEEE Micro*, 26(2):58–66, Mar/Apr 2006.

[7] A. Hadke et al. OCDIMM: Scaling the DRAM memory wall using WDM based optical interconnects. *Int'l Symp. on High-Performance Interconnects*, Aug 2008.

[8] C. Holzwarth et al. Localized substrate removal technique enabling strong-confinement microphotonics in bulk Si CMOS processes. *Conf. on Lasers and Electro-Optics*, May 2008.

[9] A. Joshi et al. Silicon-photonic Clos networks for global on-chip communication. *Int'l Symp. on Networks-on-Chip*, May 2009.

[10] I. Jung et al. Performance boosting of peripheral transistor for high density 4 Gb DRAM technologies by SiGe selective epitaxial growth technique. *Int'l SiGe Technology and Device Mtg.*, 2006.

[11] U. Kang et al. 8 Gb 3D DDR3 DRAM using through-silicon-via technology. *Int'l Solid-State Circuits Conf.*, Feb 2009.

[12] B. Keeth et al. *DRAM Circuit Design: Fundamental and High-Speed Topics*. Wiley-IEEE Press, 2008.

[13] N. Kırman et al. Leveraging optical technology in future bus-based chip multiprocessors. *MICRO*, Dec 2006.

[14] H. Lee et al. A 16 Gb/s/link, 64 GB/s bidirectional asymmetric memory interface. *IEEE Journal of Solid-State Circuits*, 44(4):1235–1247, Apr 2009.

[15] G. Loh. 3D-stacked memory architectures for multi-core processors. *ISCA*, June 2008.

[16] Micron DDR SDRAM products. Online Datasheet, `http://www.micron.com/products/dram/ddr3`.

[17] T.-Y. Oh et al. A 7 Gb/s/pin GDDR5 SDRAM with 2.5 ns bank-to-bank active time and no bank-group restriction. *Int'l Solid-State Circuits Conf.*, Feb 2010.

[18] F. O'Mahony et al. A 47x10 Gb/s 1.4 mW/(Gb/s) parallel interface in 45 nm CMOS. *Int'l Solid-State Circuits Conf.*, Feb 2010.

[19] J. Orcutt et al. Demonstration of an electronic photonic integrated circuit in a commercial scaled bulk CMOS process. *Conf. on Lasers and Electro-Optics*, May 2008.

[20] H. Sun et al. 3D DRAM design and application to 3D multicore systems. *IEEE Design and Test of Computers*, 26(5):36–47, Sep/Oct 2009.

[21] D. Taillaert, P. Bienstman, and R. Baets. Compact efficient broadband grating coupler for silicon-on-insulator waveguides. *Optics Letters*, 29(23):2749–2751, Dec 2004.

[22] S. Thoziyoor et al. A comprehensive memory modeling tool and its application to the design and analysis of future memory hierarchies. *ISCA*, June 2008.

[23] A. Udipi et al. Rethinking DRAM design and organization for energy-constrained multi-cores. *ISCA*, June 2010.

[24] D. Vantrease et al. Corona: System implications of emerging nanophotonic technology. *ISCA*, June 2008.

[25] F. Ware and C. Hampel. Improving power and data efficiency with threaded memory modules. *Int'l Conf. on Computer Design*, Oct 2007.

[26] P. Yan et al. Firefly: Illuminating on-chip networks with nanophotonics. *ISCA*, June 2009.

Use ECP, not ECC, for Hard Failures in Resistive Memories

Stuart Schechter, Gabriel H. Loh†, Karin Strauss, Doug Burger
Microsoft Research, Redmond, WA
†Georgia Institute of Technology, Atlanta, GA
{stus,kstrauss,dburger}@microsoft.com, loh@cc.gatech.edu

ABSTRACT

As leakage and other charge storage limitations begin to impair the scalability of DRAM, non-volatile resistive memories are being developed as a potential replacement. Unfortunately, current error-correction techniques are poorly suited to this emerging class of memory technologies. Unlike DRAM, PCM and other resistive memories have wear lifetimes, measured in writes, that are sufficiently short to make cell failures common during a system's lifetime. However, resistive memories are much less susceptible to transient faults than DRAM. The Hamming-based ECC codes used in DRAM are designed to handle transient faults with no effective lifetime limits, but ECC codes applied to resistive memories would wear out faster than the cells they are designed to repair. This paper proposes *Error-Correcting Pointers* (ECP), a new approach to error correction optimized for memories in which errors are the result of permanent cell failures that occur, and are immediately detectable, at write time. ECP corrects errors by permanently encoding the locations of failed cells into a table and assigning cells to replace them. ECP provides longer lifetimes than previously proposed solutions with equivalent overhead. Furthermore, as the variance in cell lifetimes increases – a likely consequence of further process scaling – ECP's margin of improvement over existing schemes also increases.

Categories and Subject Descriptors

B.3.4 [**Hardware**]: Memory Structures—*Reliability, Testing, Fault-Tolerance, Error-Checking*

General Terms

Reliability

Keywords

Memory, Error Correction, Hard Failures, Resistive Memories, Phase-Change Memory

1. INTRODUCTION

The scaling of DRAM technology to smaller feature sizes is in jeopardy, as physical limitations – particularly limited charge – may prevent DRAM scaling beyond 30nm [1, 12]. The small number of electrons that can be stored on these shrinking capacitors, particularly in the presence of sub-threshold leakage, may limit further scaling. Resistive memories, which arrange atoms within a cell and then measure the resistive drop through the atomic arrangement, are promising as a potentially more scalable replacement for DRAM and Flash. These technologies include spin-torque-transfer magnetoresistive memory (STT-MRAM), ferroelectric memory (FRAM), memristors, and phase-change memories (PCM). Of these emerging technologies, PCM has received the most research attention in the architecture literature [7, 11, 21, 22, 26, 27, 28], as it is closest to commercialization [18, 24].

Instead of representing information as the presence or absence of electrical charge, PCM encodes bits in different physical states of a chalcogenide material [2, 3, 4, 10, 14, 18, 20, 23]. Through the application of different programming currents, the phase of the material can be melted and then re-solidified into either a crystalline or amorphous state, each with a distinct electrical resistance.

Since the state of the material is effectively a static configuration of atoms, the material, once programmed, retains its state for long periods of time. This characteristic obviates the need for leakage control and refresh operations. PCM technology is predicted to scale well to smaller feature sizes, with 9nm devices having been demonstrated. While PCM is slower than DRAM to read (two to three times) and considerably slower and more power intensive to write [13], the write latency and power shrinks as PCM cells scale down, since the total volume of phase-change material per cell also decreases. Memory architectures have been proposed to address PCM's latency and power issues to make PCM competitive with DRAM [13, 22, 28].

The major limitation of PCM as a DRAM replacement is its limited write endurance. Next-generation PCM designs can only endure 10^7 to 10^9 writes before the cell permanently fails [1, 8]. In contrast, DRAM cells can be written up to 10^{15} times before failure, which is effectively unlimited. Additionally, the failure mode of PCM cells more closely resembles Flash than DRAM. The heating and cooling process required to write a cell, and the expansion and contraction that results, eventually cause the heating element to detach from the chalcogenide. Detachment of the heating element results in a "stuck-at" hard fault that can be subsequently read but not rewritten. Unlike charge-based DRAM, the material state of PCM cells is not susceptible to particle-induced soft errors [15, 17, 29]. While resistive drift, resulting from gradual atomic motion at high temperatures, can eventually lead to soft errors, PCM cells are expected to hold their state for years at typical operating temperatures.

Making PCM technology a viable DRAM replacement will require mitigating wear-related failures through architectural enhancements such as write buffers [13, 22], compression schemes [26], wear-leveling mechanisms [21, 22, 26, 27, 28], error-correcting codes [27], or operating system page remapping [11, 27, 28]. These techniques will reduce the total write traffic, spread the writes more uniformly over the memory cells, and cope with failures after they occur. An additional, highly effective technique that can both alleviate wear and quickly detect failures is a "read-write-read" pattern for write operations. Initially, a read is performed from the row buffers or the PCM array to access the prior value of the memory, which is bitwise compared to the write data. The write is then performed, with only the changed bits being written to the array. Subsequently, a final read checks to ensure that the data were correctly written. If the checking read returns an incorrect result, the write operation may be reissued, or a correction action must be taken.

The standard ECC implementations used in DRAM are less than ideal given these three aspects of resistive memories: the strong need to reduce writes, the dominance of hard failures, and the ability to identify failures at the time of the write. Hamming-based ECC codes modify the error-correction bits whenever any data in the protected block change, resulting in high entropy that increases wear. These codes face an unappealing choice when selecting the region size; protecting a larger region induces more wear, as the codes must be rewritten when any data in that region are changed. Protecting finer-grain regions reduces the ECC bits' wear but makes each page fail when enough cells fail within any of the small protected regions. This early failure problem can be exacerbated by cell lifetime variation. Many of the previously proposed techniques assume that all of the PCM memory cells have the same write endurance, with each cell failing after exactly W writes. In real systems, however, parametric variations in the manufacturing process create a non-uniform distribution of cell characteristics [5, 6, 19, 26]. As resistive memories are scaled to smaller dimensions, lifetime variability may become more pronounced, making it crucial for error-correcting schemes to handle numerous early cell failures gracefully.

This paper proposes *Error-Correcting Pointers* (ECP) that work to minimize write wear, handle permanent faults rather than soft errors, and improve overall memory lifetime in the presence of high parametric variation and corresponding early cell failures. Whereas error-correcting codes associate a number of coded bits with each block of data bits, ECP encodes and stores the addresses of failed cells and allocates additional cells to replace them. This ECP encoding scheme can also correct failures in the correction cells themselves without additional error-correcting schemes or cells.

ECP is also complementary to previously proposed approaches that reduce the number of writes to the PCM (*e.g.*, write combining), enabling those approaches to be composed with ECP for additional longevity. As resistive memories scale to smaller geometries, and the parametric variations within them likely increase, ECP will better tolerate clustered errors without exacerbating wear-out, and may be necessary to permit further device scaling.

As designers increase ECP entries, at some point the extended lifetime obtained from additional ECP entries reaches diminishing returns, since the rate of cell failures grows over time. This paper evaluates two additional approaches to extend lifetime further. First, a layered ECP approach provides small pointers for each row and a row of larger pointers per page, balancing both the number of pointers using a given overhead and the reach of each pointer. Layered ECP is able to reduce lifetime over the best-performing ECP organization with equivalent overhead. Second, we observe that both ECP and layered ECP eventually reach a point where adding more pointers provides less lifetime benefit than simply adding more pages. We show how to obtain that point, and, thus for a given correction scheme, demonstrate how to compute the minimum storage needed to allow a memory size M to be available for W writes, assuming a lifetime coefficient of variance V. This result will permit memory vendors to reason about the overhead and cost of supporting higher variances for target capacities and lifetimes as resistive memories are scaled to near-atomic dimensions.

2. BACKGROUND

2.1 Phase-Change Memory Failure Model

While the longer access latencies and write power pose some challenges, the limited write endurance of PCM may prove to be the greatest obstacle to widespread adoption of PCM as a DRAM replacement. Writing PCM requires elevating the temperature of the phase-change material to 650 degrees Celsius. After enough write cycles (on the order of 10^8), the mechanical stresses of repeated thermal expansion and contraction cause the heating element to separate from the phase-change material, rendering the cell unmodifiable. Without any additional protection or enhancements, this limited write endurance can render a PCM memory useless in less than one month of operation [13]. The useful lifetime of PCM must be extended to many years for it to be a practical main memory technology. Because of good thermal insulation between cells, we expect that cell failures will be independent and identically distributed, and that cell lifetimes will follow a normal distribution in keeping with other sorts of parametric variation. Finally, while PCM cells' values can decay (due to atomic motion), resulting in soft errors, the refresh period at typical operating temperatures is measured in years. System designers must ensure that the ambient PCM temperatures do not exceed a sustained level that will result in soft errors not caught by an occasional (daily?) refresh operation.

2.2 Error Correction

Error-correcting codes have been studied and applied in a variety of contexts for decades. Single-error-correcting (SEC) Hamming codes [9], which include commonly used dual-error-detecting SECDED varieties, are best known for providing error protection for DRAM as well as on-chip structures such as caches [16]. Error codes are specified as "(n,k)" where k bits of actual data are encoded into $n > k$ bits of redundant/protected data. For example, Hamming introduced a (7,4) code that can correct a single error and detect (but not correct) up to two errors by appending the k=4 original data bits with three additional error-correcting bits. The coding is generalizable to larger blocks of data, such as the (72,64) code used to provide SECDED protection on 64-bit DRAM data.

To provide multiple-bit error correction in PCMs, more complex coding schemes may be considered. Polynomial-based codes, such as Reed-Solomon, and Bose, Ray-Chaudhuri, Hocquenghem (BCH) have already been employed in Flash storage devices and optical media to deal with multiple bit failures within a block. BCH has also been proposed for correcting for PCM bit failures [27].

The Hamming Bound provides a theoretical lower limit on the space overhead s in bits required to enable up to n errors to be corrected while encoding d data bits.

$$S_{min} \geq \left\lceil \log_2 \sum_{e=0}^{n} \binom{d+n}{e} \right\rceil$$

3. ERROR-CORRECTING POINTERS

Traditional Error-Correcting Codes (ECC) store sufficient information to derive the source of errors in locations undetermined at encoding time, allowing them to correct soft errors discovered when a block of data is read. Conversely, Error-Correcting Pointers (ECP) directly store the address of memory cells determined to have permanently failed during the verification of a memory write. ECP operates within each memory chip at the row level.

The ECP_n scheme uses n *correction pointers* to specify the addresses of failed cells, and pairs each pointer with a replacement memory cell. Together, the pointer and replacement cell form a *correction entry.*

Figure 1a illustrates the simplest ECP implementation, ECP_1, where a single correction entry corrects up to one bit. The example uses a row with 512 data bits. When no errors are present in the data, the correction pointer is empty, the full bit is set to 0 (false). This indicates the entry is *inactive* as there are no errors to correct. When a bit fails, for example bit 2 in Figure 1a, the correction entry is marked full (or *active*), the correction pointer is set to point to bit 2, and the replacement cell now stores the value that belongs in bit 2. Henceforth, when the row is written, the value to be written to the failed cell identified by the correction pointer is instead written to the replacement cell. When the row is read, the value in the replacement cell supersedes the value read from the defective cell.

Generalizing ECP_1 to n entries (ECP_n) is illustrated in Figure 1b, using ECP_5 as an example. The full bit is now set only when *all* error-correction entries are in use. Otherwise, the full bit is set to 0 and the bits of the last correction entry ($n-1$=4) contain a unary-encoded counter denoting how many of the other $n-1$ correction entries (entry 0 to $n-2$=3) are active. In the illustration, the full bit is set to false (0) and the two lowest order bits in entry 4 are set, indicating that correction entries 0 and 1 are active. As before, the first bit to fail (bit 2) is replaced by correction entry 0. The availability of a second correction entry (entry 1) enables us to correct a second failure (bit 509).

Errors in replacement cells are less likely to occur than errors in the original data cells, as they do not begin to wear until they are put into use to replace a failed cell. ECP can still correct these errors. When two correction entries point to the same cell, the correction entry at the higher index takes precedence over the one with the lower index, just as the correction entry at the lower-index takes precedence over the failed bit in the data array. For example in Figure 1c, the replacement cell in correction entry 0 has failed. To compensate for this, we activate correction entry 1 and have it point to the same failed cell. The replacement cell in entry 1 supplants both the original failed cell and the failed replacement cell in entry 0.

Precedence rules also make possible the correction of errors in correction pointers. Such errors are even less likely than errors in replacement cells, as these are written to at most once (twice for the cells in entry $n-1$ that are also used to activate other cells). Almost all errors in the pointers themselves will be cells that failed upon manufacture. An error in a correction pointer, as illustrated in Figure 1d, effectively replaces a working cell with a working replacement cell, doing no harm but also failing to repair the failure for which it was allocated (bit 2). We thus allocate an additional correction entry to correct the original failure of bit 2. Overall, two bits have failed and two error-correction entries have been consumed.

ECP can correct errors both in data cells and in its own data structures, while allocating only enough bits per correction pointer to address data bits. ECP_n can correct *any* n cell failures, regardless of whether they are in data cells or correction entries.[1] Because the scheme works at the cell level, it is equally effective for use in multi-level cell (MLC) memories that store more than one bit per cell.

ECP requires 1 full bit, n replacement bits, and n pointers large enough to address the original data bits. Thus the fractional space overhead $S(\text{ECP}_n)$ for a row with $d = 512$ data bits is:

$$S(\text{ECP}_n) = \frac{1+n+n\cdot\lceil\log_2 d\rceil}{d} = \frac{1+n\cdot(1+\lceil\log_2 512\rceil)}{512}$$

$$S(\text{ECP}_6) = \frac{1+6\cdot 10}{512} = \frac{61}{512} = 11.9\%$$

4. EXPERIMENTS

Memory failure simulation presents special challenges, as it is impractical to perfectly simulate the real operation of a memory over a full lifetime or to simulate all possible wear patterns. We make a number of simplifying assumptions in our simulation. First, we assume that existing wear-leveling techniques (*e.g.*, stop-gap [21], fine-grained wear leveling [22]) already spread writes evenly over the memory. Second, we assume that memory chips store data in 512-bit rows, and that each contiguous block of memory is spread over eight chips. Third, we assume that writes modify a single region of bits randomly located within the page. When evaluating competing schemes that divide memory rows into smaller blocks, we assume that writes that are narrower than a block touch only one block – maximizing the endurance of the competing schemes. Each bit within the region modified by the write is assumed to change value with probability 0.5.

For each scheme, our simulator lays out a full page of memory and allocates a cell for each bit, including both data bits and meta-data structures such as correction en-

[1]The one extraordinarily rare exception to this rule occurs when a failure activates a high-precedence correction entry, its replacement cell fails, and no higher-precedence correction entry is available to repair it. For example, such a failure could be caused if the full bit is manufactured stuck at 1 (activating all correction entries) and the replacement bit in the highest-precedence correction entry fails.

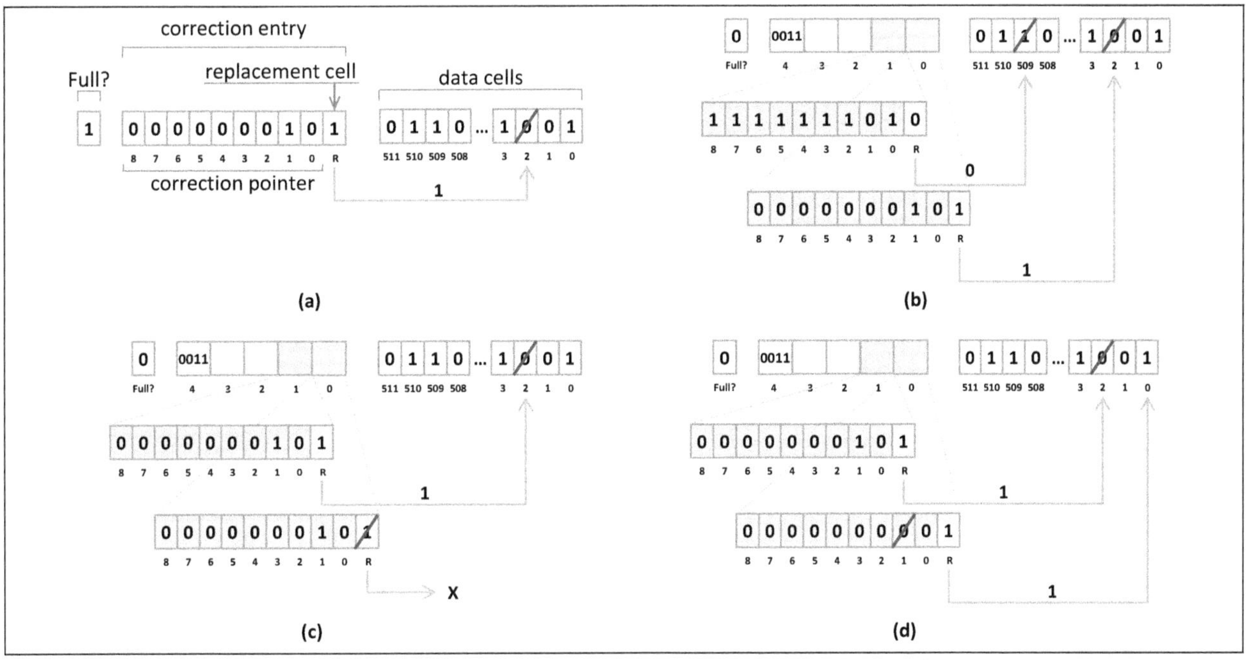

Figure 1: Correction entries enable permanent replacement of failed memory cells. (a) A simple ECP_1 scheme that corrects up to a single bit error. The correction pointer specifies the location of a dead cell to be supplanted by the replacement cell. (b) The ECP_5 scheme that corrects up to five failed cells. (c) A failure in the replacement cell can be handled by allocating an overriding correction entry at the same address, and similarly (d) a rare cell fault within a correction pointer can harmlessly cause a still-operational cell to be replaced by another working cell, requiring an additional correction entry to be allocated to replace the data cell that the faulty correction entry was intended to replace.

tries. Wear-rates are then assigned to each cell based on the calculated expected bit changes per page write. For example, for a write modification width of 2 bytes to the 4096 byte page, the expected wear on each data bit would be $0.5 \cdot \frac{2}{4096}$. The initial wear-rate for an unused replacement bit would initially be set to 0.

Next, for each simulation run, the simulator assigns a random lifetime to each cell using a normal distribution with a mean of 10^8 bit-writes-until-fail and a variance of 0.25 (unless specified otherwise). Each cell's expected remaining lifetime in page-writes-until-fail is calculated by dividing the remaining bit-writes-until-fail by the cell's wear rate. The next bit to fail is identified by finding the bit with the lowest page-writes-until-fail.

When a bit fails, the model determines whether the failure is terminal to the page and, if it isn't, simulates the action taken within the page to correct it. For example, when a cell dies in the ECP_n design, the cell that replaces it begins to encounter wear.

We assume a memory architecture in which 4KB logical pages are mapped to 4KB physical pages. When a physical page encounters an uncorrectable error, the page dies and is mapped out by the OS. Each page death reduces the size of the physical memory, which increases wear on the remaining pages. In other words, when a physical page dies there is one fewer page over which to spread the wear placed on the logical memory. The surviving pages will collectively absorb the wear that had previously been incurred by the newly deceased page. We assume each surviving page absorbs an equal amount of this increased wear. We simulate the impact of dying pages by, upon each page death, decreasing each of the survivors' remaining lifetimes by the fraction of the additional wear that each will now incur.

Page size	4KB	(32768 bits)
Row size	32B	(512 bits)
Rank	1	
Chips per rank	8	
Bit lines per chip	x8	
Mean cell lifetime	10^8	
Lifetime variance	0.25	

Table 1: Default architectural assumptions.

We use the architectural parameters shown in Table 1. For each configuration we simulate at least 2,000 physical page lifetimes. We present results using the metric of mean-writes-per-page.

5. COMPARISON TO EXISTING SCHEMES

Today's DRAM memories use single-error-correction (SEC) Hamming codes. Eight memory chips with eight data lines, providing a total of 64 data bits per bus cycle, are paired with a ninth chip. SEC requires 7 additional bits to correct 64 data bits, and so the eighth bit on the spare chip allows for detection, but not correction, of a second error (SECDED). As we assume all errors are detectable following a write, the additional detection is of no value.

We assume that our schemes should have at most 12.5% space overhead so that they, like SEC, fit in a ninth memory chip (for schemes that correct blocks spanning chips) or in the equivalent overhead (for ECP and other row-based schemes that operate on rows within a chip).

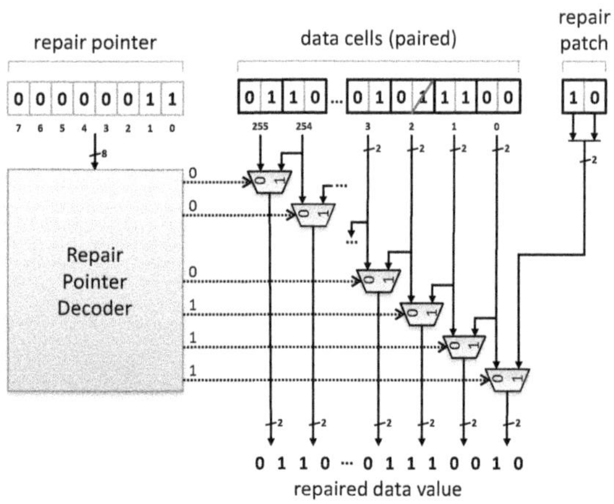

Figure 2: The "bit-fix" scheme proposed by Wilkerson *et al.*

5.1 Schemes Compared

SEC_{64}

SEC_{64} simulates the correction scheme in today's DRAM. It chunks memory into 64-bit blocks, each divided evenly over eight chips, and corrects for up to one error in each block. A second error within a block is terminal. For all schemes, we assume that memory is deallocated at the page level, and so a second error within a block will cause the entire page to be deallocated. We simulate SEC_{64} by assuming that each SEC bit within a block will change with probability 0.5 any time one or more data bits are written to the block. The space overhead of SEC_{64} is 7 bits per 64-bit block, or 10.9%.

$Wilkerson_4$

The most closely related error-correcting scheme to ECP was introduced by Wilkerson *et al.* for use in caches in which certain cells may fail to operate correctly at desired voltages [25]. Wilkerson's "bit-fix" scheme, illustrated in Figure 2, pairs up cells and provides an extra replacement pair, called a repair patch. Whereas ECP directly substitutes failed cells with replacement cells, Wilkerson's scheme locates replacement cells on the logical edge of the data line, shifting as much of the row as necessary to fill vacancies left by the failed cells. This seemingly small architectural difference makes it difficult for Wilkerson's scheme to create entries that correct failures in other correction entries – the replacement cells are not themselves addressable. Instead, each 10-bit correction entry (an 8-bit pointer to select one of the 256 bit pairs, and the 2-bit replacement pair) in the bit-fix scheme requires five dedicated SECDED bits (not shown in the figure). In addition to this 50% space overhead, these SECDED bits are a potential source of wear failure, as their values change whenever the replacement bit in the correction entry changes.

To be an appropriate comparison with ECP, we extended Wilkerson's scheme to target a PCM implementation of main memory, using state stored within each memory row. Specifically, we optimized Wilkerson's scheme for PCM by using 4-bit SEC within correction entries instead of 5-bit SECDED; write-time error detection obviates the need for the double-error detection. Although the SEC code covers the entire 10-bit repair entry, it is only the repair bits that will experience frequent modifications, and so we strategically place these two bits within the 10-bit entry so that the minimum number of SEC bits toggle on updates to the repair patch.

In our implementation, Wilkerson's scheme requires 1 full bit, and contains n entries each with 2 replacement bits, 8 address bits, and 4 SEC bits. The 40% overhead that SEC bits add to each entry limits Wilkerson to four error-correction entries (Wilkerson_4) within our 12.5% overhead constraint.

$$S(\text{Wilkerson}_n) = \frac{1 + n \cdot (2 + 8 + 4)}{512}$$

$$S(\text{Wilkerson}_4) = \frac{1 + 4 \cdot 14}{512} = \frac{57}{512} = 11.1\%$$

$Pairing_8$

Ipek *et al.* recently introduced a hardware/software hybrid scheme to tolerate block failures within a page [11]. Their scheme assigns a parity bit to every 8-bit block, though the scheme generalizes to blocks of arbitrary size (Pairing_n). A block dies when any bit within it, or its parity bit, fails. Dead blocks are recognizable by their non-matching parity bit. In the rare event that a second bit failure occurs at the same time as the first, any non-dead bit within the block (including the parity bit) may be flipped to ensure a parity failure continues to be detectable. One parity bit per eight data bits results in an overhead of exactly 12.5%.

When the first failed bit within a 4KB page causes a block to die, the page is then *paired* with another page that is selected to ensure that the set of failed block indices do not intersect. In other words, if a block at index i is dead in one page, it must not be dead in the other page. If future failures cause this invariant to be violated, the affected pages must be taken offline until new matches can be identified for them. Ipek *et al.* show that the Pairing_8 scheme is viable for up to 160 block failures in each page. We treat the 161st block failure as terminal.

$Perfect\_Code_9$

To address the primary limitation of SEC_{64} – the failure of a page should two errors happen to fall within the same 64-bit block – we also evaluated a multi-bit scheme that corrects errors over a larger block. Specifically, we consider correction of multiple errors within a 512-bit block. Rather than test a specific multi-error-correction scheme, we test against the theoretical limit: a perfect n-error-correcting code over the entire block. The number of code bits $S(\text{Perfect\_Code}_n)$ required is dictated by the Hamming Bound:

$$S(\text{Perfect\_Code}_n) = \frac{\lceil \log_2 \sum_{e=0}^{n} \binom{512+n}{e} \rceil}{512}$$

$$S(\text{Perfect\_Code}_9) = \frac{\lceil \log_2 \sum_{e=0}^{9} \binom{512+9}{e} \rceil}{512} = \frac{64}{512} = 12.5\%$$

To simulate Perfect_Code_9 we allocate 64 error-correcting bits per 512-bit row, each of which changes value with probability 0.5 any time one or more data bits are written to the line. We simulate Perfect_Code_9 not because it is realistic, but because it provides a theoretical limit on traditional error-correcting schemes. In reality, decoding multi-bit error-correction schemes is expensive and correcting errors at the granularity of an entire block prevents any critical-word-first optimization, as reads cannot complete until the full line is read and errors decoded. The alternative to off-memory-chip correction is to apply the multi-bit error-correcting codes at the row level on the memory chip, but doing so results in disproportionately high, lifetime-limiting wear to the error-correcting bits.

5.2 Results

Table 2 summarizes the error-correction schemes evaluated in this paper.

	overhead	failure unit	failures survivable per unit
SEC_{64}	10.9%	64b block	1
$Pairing_8$	12.5%	4KB page	160
$Wilkerson_4$	11.1%	512b row	4
$Perfect\_Code_9$	12.5%	512b block	9
ECP_6	11.9%	512b row	6

Table 2: Overheads for error-correction schemes in this paper. Blocks span memory chips while rows are contiguous bits within a single chip.

Figure 3 shows the fraction of pages that survive a given number of page writes with a coefficient of variation of 0.25 in the mean cell lifetime and modified region widths of 128, 256 and 512 bits (equal to one physical row). Figure 4 fixes the modified region width to 512 bits and presents these page-survival fractions for coefficients of variance of 0.2, 0.25, and 0.3 (Figure 3c and Figure 4b are the same). Employing no correction results in the worst lifetimes. Almost all pages see one early fault and so this scheme's lifetime curve drops quite early and very sharply.

The relative endurance of $Perfect\_Code_9$ is worst for small modifications, as is illustrated in Figure 3a, and best for wider modifications that cover the entire block (Figure 3c). When modification widths are small, error-correction bits receive more wear than data bits and so the first bits to fail are likely to be the error-correction bits themselves. The same effect would be seen in SEC_{64} for writes that modify regions smaller than 64 bits within a 64-bit block, such as might occur when manipulating strings. One might even see this effect in $Pairing_8$ for writes that modify regions smaller than eight bits of an 8-bit block, such as those from writes to a Bloom filter.

In the middle of the endurance curves are the SEC_{64} and $Pairing_8$ schemes. As pages in the $Pairing_8$ scheme encounter their first bit error, they are paired with other pages and so once all pages have encountered their first bit error the number of available pages is cut in half. This capacity reduction doubles the effective wear on each page as there are half as many physical pages to spread the wear placed on the logical memory space. The SEC_{64} scheme suffers because the first occurrence of two errors within a 64-bit block is fatal.

The results for SEC_{64} differ from the SECDED results reported in Ipek *et al.* [11]. Like us, they implement $Pairing_8$ under the assumption that writes are followed by a verifying read. However, they compare to standard SECDED, which must deallocate a page after the first error is detected and corrected, since standard SECDED does not assume writes are re-read and verified. As a result, Ipek *et al.*'s standard implementation of SECDED with no verifying reads performs closer to our simulations of no error-correcting codes with verifying reads. When we extend SECDED to model a verifying read after each write, enabling deallocation only after the second error in a region, SEC_{64} outperforms $Pairing_8$ for lower coefficients of variance. As the variance grows, the lifetime of $Pairing_8$ improves relative to SEC_{64}, eventually exceeding it.

Wilkerson *et al.*'s scheme differs from ECP primarily in its use of a single-error-correction (SEC) Hamming code, instead of precedence rules, to correct errors in its own correction entries. Since the precedence rules incur no bit storage overhead there is no reason not to implement both. We thus enhance the $Wilkerson_4$ scheme with ECP's precedence rules. We find that the benefits of these Hamming codes over precedence rules alone are undetectable: when we graphed ECP_6 and $Wilkerson_6$ (not shown), their curves always overlapped completely; any difference in lifetime was so small as to be undetectable. Yet, Wilkerson *et al.*'s scheme can store only four correction entries within the 12.5% storage overhead constraint, whereas ECP can store six. ECP_6 outperforms the $Wilkerson_4$ scheme with similar storage overhead.

The ECP_6 scheme corrects two thirds of the errors possible with a perfect multi-error-correction Hamming code ($Perfect\_Code_9$) under the same space constraint. When the region of bits modified during a write is significantly smaller than 512 bits, pages using ECP_6 actually outlive those using a perfect multi-error-correction Hamming code. This advantage relative to a "perfect code" is possible because these write-modification widths cause Hamming codes to suffer more wear than the bits they are intended to correct (smaller average writes show larger relative wear on ECC bits). In contrast, ECP's correction pointers suffer near-zero wear and ECP's replacement bits suffer only as much wear as the data bits they replace.

6. INTRA-ROW WEAR LEVELING

The endurance of $Perfect\_Code_9$ suffers when writes to a block contain regions that are unmodified, as the correction bits suffer heavier wear than data bits and may fail first. We could compensate for this shortcoming by leveling wear throughout the block's data and correction cells. While throughout this paper we assume that writes are already wear-leveled across rows and pages, external wear-leveling mechanisms can only level wear within externally visible data cells; they cannot spread wear among the internal meta-data cells used for error-correction structures.

To address uneven wear between correction and data cells, we could architect rows (or blocks) to periodically rotate the positions of the logical row by a random offset to place them into different physical cells. This rotation would spread the impact of wear on the logical error-correction bits over all of the physical cells, presumably making $Perfect\_Code_9$ more competitive with ECP for write modification widths that do not span a full block.

In the next experiment, we introduce such a rotating wear leveler into $Perfect\_Code_9$ and ECP_6. The wear leveler rotates all logical structures (except its own) around random positions over a single set of physical cells, as shown in Figure 5a. We do not track the number of writes since the last rotation as doing so would incur additional space overhead and wear; we instead assume a scheme initiates rotations at random intervals with a uniform probability at each write.

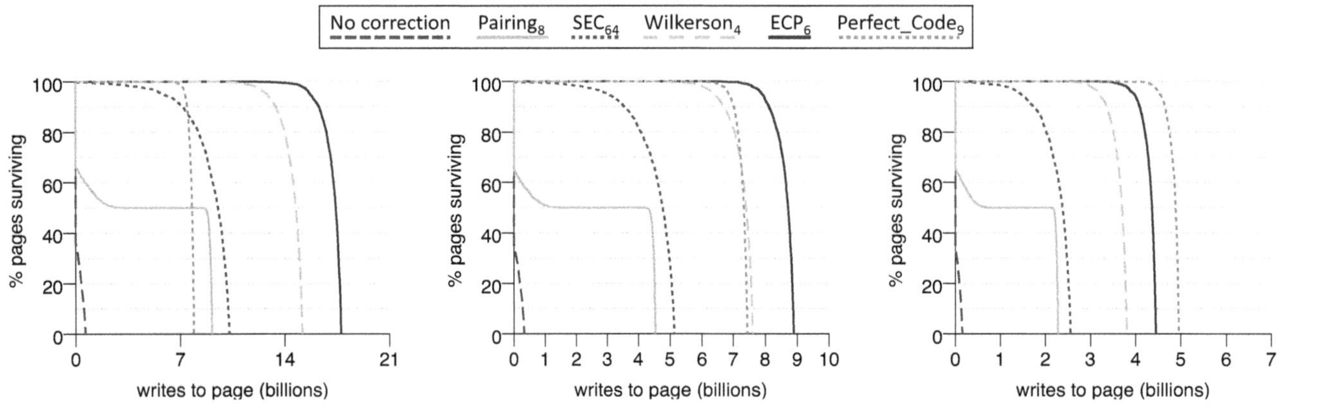

(a) 128 bits (b) 256 bits (c) 512 bits

Figure 3: Page lifetimes in writes-per-page. A write of a 512-bit row may only modify a subset of the bits. The graphs assume writes that span (a) 128, (b) 256, and (c) 512 bits. Each bit within the span of modification changes value with probability 0.5.

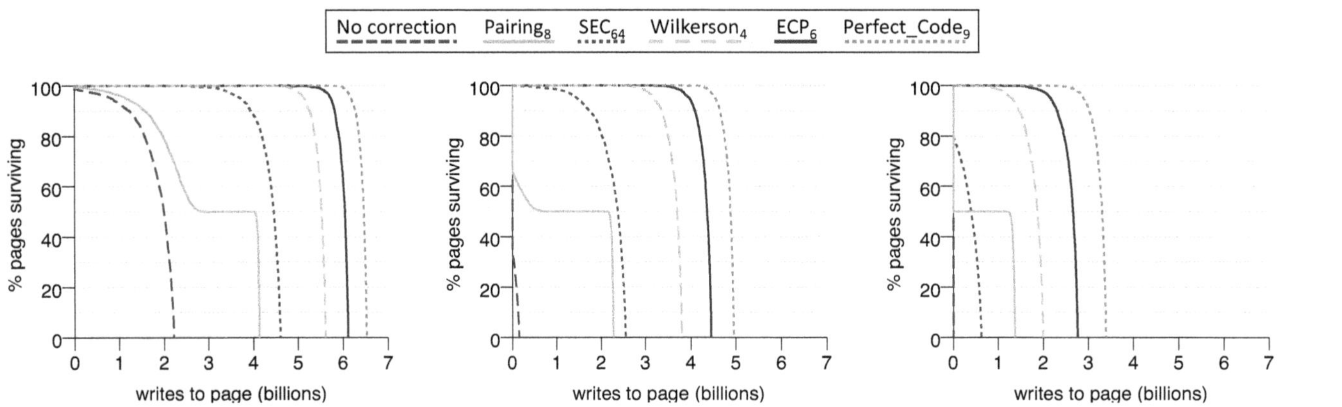

(a) Cell lifetime variance = 0.2 (b) Cell lifetime variance = 0.25 (c) Cell lifetime variance = 0.3

Figure 4: Page lifetimes for various error-correction schemes for a row with 512 data bits, write width of 512 bits and various variances: (a) 0.2, (b) 0.25, and (c) 0.3.

For a mean cell lifetime of 10^8 bits, we select a rotation probability of 10^{-4}. Since the probability that a given bit will change during a rotation is 0.5, the expected wear induced by the wear-leveling on each bit is $0.5 \cdot 10^{-4}$ bit-writes per write to the row. While infrequent enough to minimize the probability of wear-failure within this structure, the rotator is expected to visit each possible rotation approximately twenty times over a period of 10^8 writes to a 512-bit row.

For a row of m data and repair bits, the rotating wear leveler requires $\lceil log_2 m \rceil$ bits to represent the rotation position. ECP_6 and $Perfect\_Code_9$ use rows/blocks of 512 data bits and have overhead of at most 64 bits (12.5%), and so 10 bits will be required to store the rotation position. The very low frequency of wear-leveling ensures that cell failures within the wear leveler itself are extremely rare. Rather than correct for these outliers, we simply accept that a negligible fraction of pages will reach the end of their lifetime as the result of a cell failure within a wear leveler, and not after n failures within a row. This assumption will not affect the experimental comparison, as the same wear leveler is used for all architectures and so a failure within the wear leveler is equally improbable for each of them.

In addition to using the rotating wear leveler to spread wear, we add an additional physical data cell to the space that the wear leveler can address. Thus, at any given time one cell is rotated out of use. This extra cell enables the scheme to repair one additional failed cell. Figure 5b shows a line using ECP_5 where all five correction entries have already been used up and a sixth error has been detected. By rotating this final error out of use, this scheme tolerates up to $n+1$ failures per block, though after the final failure the wear leveler will be stuck in a single position until the terminal failure occurs. This cessation of rotation is likely to hasten the arrival of the terminal failure, as pointer bits may no longer absorb their share of wear, but it provides additional lifetime at the cost of only one extra bit.

Following a rotation, ECP implementations may need to re-discover failed bits that had been located in a correction pointer in the previous rotation, as ECP does not need to store these locations explicitly to correct them.

In Figure 6 we present the comparative page lifetimes for $Perfect\_Code_9$ and ECP_6, both equipped with rotating wear levelers. While wear-leveling significantly improves the relative endurance of $Perfect\_Code_9$ for smaller write-

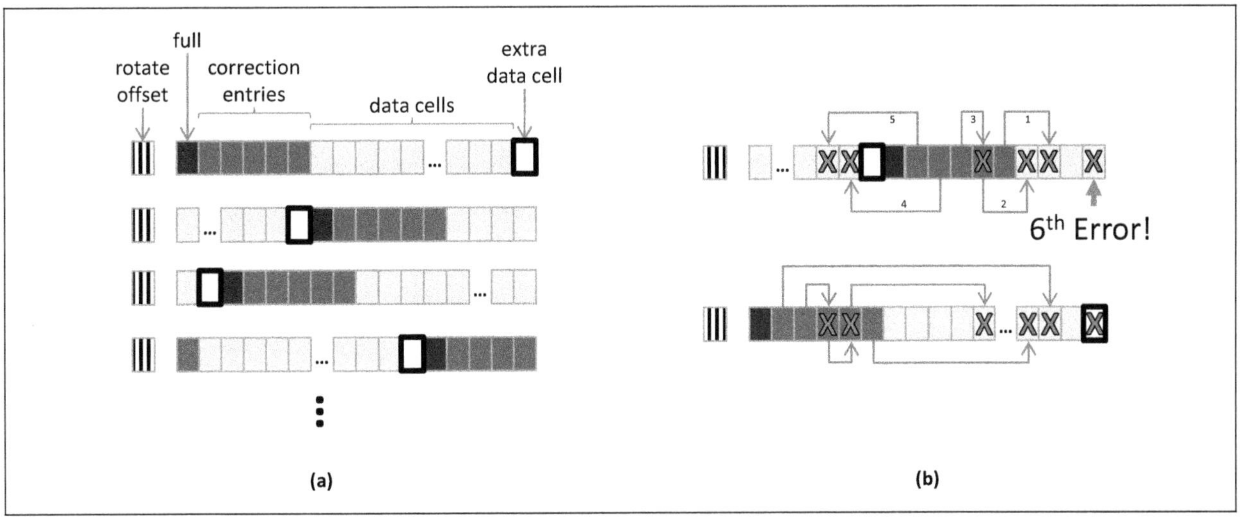

Figure 5: (a) The rotating wear leveler periodically rotates the entire PCM row including data and correction bits by a random offset. (b) The inclusion of one extra data cell provides a slight increase in expected lifetime and enables the tolerance of one additional bit failure. For ECP_n, the first n failures are handled by the correction entries, and the $n{+}1^{st}$ is covered by rotating the row such that the extra data bit aligns with the failed cell, although this comes at the cost that the wear leveler can no longer be used.

modification regions, ECP dominates Perfect_Code_9 whenever the region of modified bits within a write does not span the full block; even when the extra error-correct-ing-code wear can be spread out, the wear has a significant impact on the overall block. ECP's relative endurance actually improves when writes modify the whole block, as wear to the data and replacement bits is now spread to the address bits.

7. COMPARISON TO OPTIMAL ECP

A space-optimal version of ECP could store the locations of failed cells using a more compact representation than ECP. ECP does contain redundancy; for example, a two-pointer ECP organization could correct bit 4 in entry 0 and bit 5 in entry 1, or vice versa, resulting in two encodings to correct the same two bit failures. Ignoring precedence rules, ECP_n has $n!$ different representations of the same n data bit failures (permutation of n error pointers).

An optimal replacement-cell scheme would ignore the unlikely event of failures in the low-wear error-locating mechanism, which is written to at most n times, and only correct failures of data and replacement bits. The optimal encoding only needs to identify failures in the $d{+}n{-}1$ repairable cells experiencing wear: the d data cells and the first $n-1$ replacement cells (pointing to a defect in the nth replacement cell would serve no purpose as there are no cells to replace it). The number of combinations of 0 to n error locations in these $d+n-1$ cells is:

$$\sum_{e=0}^{n} \binom{d+n-1}{e}$$

For a row size of 512 data bits ($d = 512$), a perfect replacement-cell scheme using the smallest possible representation of the failed bit locations would thus require sufficient space to represent the error location combinations above and to store the n replacement cells:

$$S(\text{Perfect\_Replacement}_n) = \frac{n + \lceil \log_2 \sum_{e=0}^{n} \binom{512+n-1}{e} \rceil}{512}$$

Decoding such a scheme would require significantly more overhead than decoding ECP; a naive approach would require multiple divisions. Since this scheme represents the most storage-efficient pointing mechanism possible, it provides an important point of comparison to illustrate the room for improvement in compressing ECP. Table 3 shows the comparative storage overheads for schemes to correct one to ten errors. The relative overhead of ECP increases with the number of errors, since the number of redundant representations grows as $n!$. The overhead is acceptably small for most practical values of n.

8. LAYERING ECP

In the final experiment, we explore a multi-level ECP scheme, which attempts to provide the best of having many small restricted pointers and larger pointers that can correct any fault in a region. The small *row-level* pointers correct errors within a row, and the larger pointers can correct errors throughout a 4KB page. This extension allocates an extra row of 15-bit correction entries for each page – wide enough to correct any error in the page. These *page-level* correction entries would be allocated for errors within those rows that have exhausted their row-level correction entries.

We call this scheme $\text{Layered\_ECP}_{n,m}$, which has n row-level correction entries and m page-level correction entries. Since the page-level correction entries consume one row of physical memory cells, and the row width is a function of the number of row-level correction entries, m is a function of n. Figure 7 shows the organization of the original data rows (with per-row ECP) along with the additional page-level ECP entries (bottom row in the figure). Each row contains one extra bit that indicates whether any page-level entries have been allocated to correct errors in this row (*i.e.*, all of the row-level entries have already been activated and more errors need to be fixed). Reading/writing of the row storing the page-level correction entries is only needed when this bit is set.

Table 4 compares the endurance and space overhead of ECP_x with $\text{Layered\_ECP}_{x-1,y}$ (which includes the extra

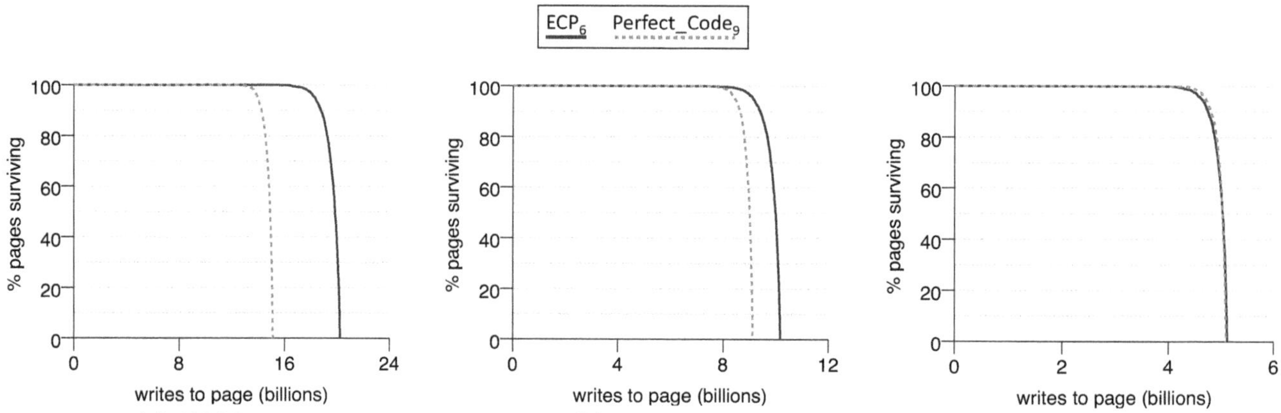

(a) 128 bits (b) 256 bits (c) 512 bits

Figure 6: The comparative endurance of Perfect_Code$_9$ and ECP$_6$, using rotating wear leveling to spread wear evenly over both data bits and correction structures. The graphs assume writes that span (a) 128, (b) 256, (c) 512 bits.

Percentage space overhead for correction of n errors										
Errors correctable (n)	1	2	3	4	5	6	7	8	9	10
ECP$_n$	2.1%	4.1%	6.0%	8.0%	10.0%	11.9%	13.9%	15.8%	17.8%	19.7%
Perfect_Replacement$_n$	2.1%	3.9%	5.5%	7.0%	8.6%	10.0%	11.3%	12.7%	14.1%	15.4%

Table 3: Space overheads to correct 1 to 10 errors, comparing ECP with a storage-optimal replacement-cell encoding.

row for page-level correction entries). At similar overheads, Layered_ECP$_{x-1,y}$ has better relative endurance than ECP$_x$. However, the endurance gap narrows as the number of entries grow, and Layered_ECP$_{x-1,y}$ is more complex to implement and may incur additional performance and power overheads when accessing rows that require page-level correction.

9. OPTIMIZING MEMORY FOR CORRECTION

As resistive memories scale down to smaller geometries, and frequent faults become more prevalent with higher variation, it will be useful to determine how much overhead, for a specified lifetime variance, will be required to provide a desired capacity for a predetermined lifetime (measured in writes). This capability will allow architects to reason about cost and overheads for different failure rates. We next formulate the problem and walk the reader through the process of solving it.

Stated formally, we wish to build the smallest possible physical memory to store M bits of data (the *effective memory*) while withstanding W writes to the memory system (the *effective lifetime*).

The next step is to determine the *survival function* $s_n(w)$ for ECP$_n$: the fraction of memory with variation V surviving after w total writes, which can be done with simulations like those presented in this paper. Starting from m bits of physical storage, the fraction of physical memory available to store data after w writes, the *fractional effective memory*, is the product of the data fraction times the survival function.

$$f_n(m, w) = d_n \cdot s_n(w)$$

Figure 8 shows this fractional effective memory function plotted for ECP$_5$ with variance 0.3.

The *effective memory*, the portion of the memory used to store data bits and that has survived w writes, is simply m times the fractional effective memory $e_n(m, w)$:

$$e_n(m, w) = m \cdot f_n(m, w) = m \cdot d_n \cdot s_n(w)$$

Architects have two tools with which to scale up the effective memory and lifetime to meet the target goals. They can increase n, which increases the survival function but also increases the ECP overhead, reducing the fraction of memory used to store data. They can also increase the size of the physical memory by a multiplier k (to a total of km), for which we might wish to calculate the effective memory $e_n(km, W)$. This has two effects. First, the total amount memory is increased to km and so whatever fractional memory remains after page deaths is increased by a factor of k. Second, increasing the memory size by a factor of k spreads wear over k times as much memory, effectively dividing the wear by k. Thus, for a choice of n and k, the effective memory at lifetime W, $e_n(km, W)$, is equal to:

$$e_n(km, W) = km \cdot f_n(m, \frac{W}{k}) = k \cdot e_n(m, \frac{W}{k})$$

The optimal configuration is thus the one that results from finding the pair (n, k) with the smallest possible k that meets our constraint $M \leq e_n(km, W)$.

10. DISCUSSION

10.1 Hardware Implementation

The implementation of ECP (and the derivative schemes) can introduce additional delay in reading and writing the PCM. For ECP$_1$, the read operation needs the equivalent of a 9-to-512 bit row-decoder (for a 512-bit data block) to align the replacement bit with the dead cell being corrected. Figure 9a illustrates the logic for ECP$_1$. Instead of explicitly

ECP											
Number of errors tolerated	0	1	2	3	4	5	6	7	8	9	10
Space overhead	0	2.1%	4.1%	6.0%	8.0%	10.0%	11.9%	13.9%	15.8%	17.8%	19.7%
Writes before 5% capacity drop (10^9)	0	0.6	1.9	2.6	3.2	3.6	3.9	4.2	4.4	4.7	4.9
Writes before 50% capacity drop (10^9)	0	1.6	2.6	3.2	3.7	4.1	4.4	4.6	4.8	5.0	5.2
ECPL											
Number of errors tolerated (row)		0	1	2	3	4	5	6	7	8	9
Number of errors tolerated (page)		32	32	33	33	34	35	35	36	37	37
Space overhead	-	1.8%	3.7%	5.7%	7.7%	9.7%	11.7%	13.6%	15.6%	17.6%	19.6%
Writes before 5% capacity drop (10^9)	-	2.6	3.5	4.1	4.4	4.8	5.0	5.2	5.4	5.6	5.7
Writes before 50% capacity drop (10^9)	-	2.8	3.7	4.2	4.6	4.9	5.1	5.3	5.5	5.7	5.8

Table 4: Space-overhead-equivalent comparison of ECP and layered ECP (ECPL).

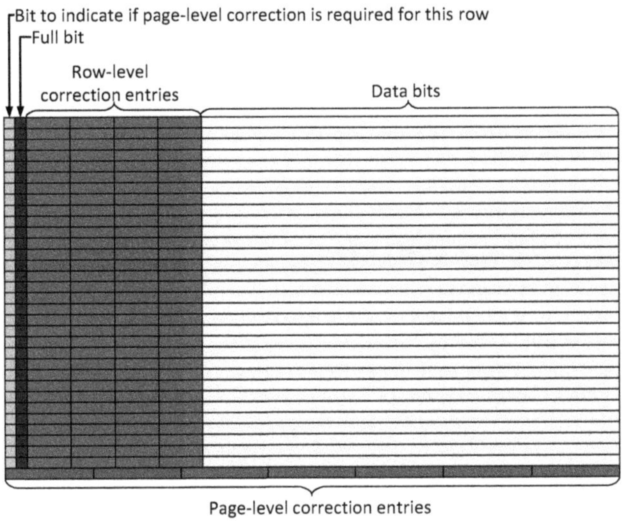

Figure 7: Hardware organization for layered ECP including both row-level ECP and page-level ECP. Row-level correction entries are applied after all reads. If the leftmost bit of the row-to-be-read is set, a second row containing page-level correction entries must also be read and will contain at least one entry that points within the row-to-be-read. All entries pointing within the row-to-be-read must be applied.

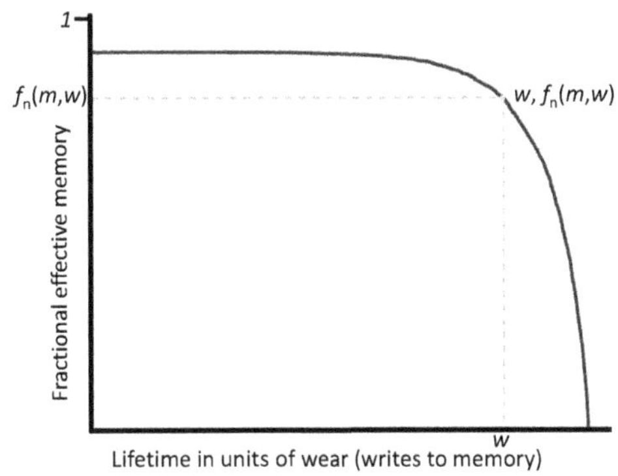

Figure 8: The fractional effective memory function plotted for ECP_5 with coefficient of variance 0.3.

storing the replacement value, we use a differential encoding where the replacement bit conditionally inverts the failed bit. If the failed bit is stuck at the wrong value, then the replacement bit performs a correction by inverting the bad data value. The row decoder also requires an "enable" input such that all outputs are zero when the corresponding ECP has not yet been allocated.

A 512-way decoder has a reasonably small latency; consider that modern processors have branch prediction tables with thousands of entries that need to be accessed in a single cycle and that these row-decoders only account for a fraction of their overall access latencies. Furthermore, the access latency of the PCM array itself is already slow enough that the addition of some extra combinatorial logic will only have a minor effect on the final PCM access latency as well as on overall system performance.

Figure 9b shows the hardware organization for ECP_5; the logic in the shaded box is detailed in Figure 9c. One decoder per ECP entry is required. The chain of OR gates computes a prefix operation indicating whether any ECP entries to the left (*i.e.*, higher precedence) have been activated for this row. If a higher precedence entry exists, then the multiplexer will pass the corresponding replacement bit through to the right. At the end of the logic chain, if any ECP entry was activated for this row, the OR chain will evaluate to true and allow the highest-precedence replacement bit to pass through. If none of the row decoders are activated for this row, then the final AND gate outputs a zero; the differential encoding interprets this to not invert the corresponding data bit. Without the differential encoding, all of the XOR gates in the right portion of Figure 9b would have to be replaced by muxes and additional routing would be needed for the mux control inputs.

Although Figure 9c shows a linear chain of logic, for large n, the circuits can be replaced with a log-depth parallel prefix circuit. The total gate delay overhead would then be $O(\log d)$ for a d-way row decoder, $O(\log n)$ for a log-depth version of the logic illustrated in Figure 9c, and another $O(1)$ for the final AND and XOR gates. The total overhead is $O(\log n + \log d)$ which scales gracefully for both the number of ECP entries used and the width of a data block covered by each entry.

10.2 Orthogonality and Composability

The ECP scheme provides resilience to PCM cell failures within a memory row, allowing many more writes before

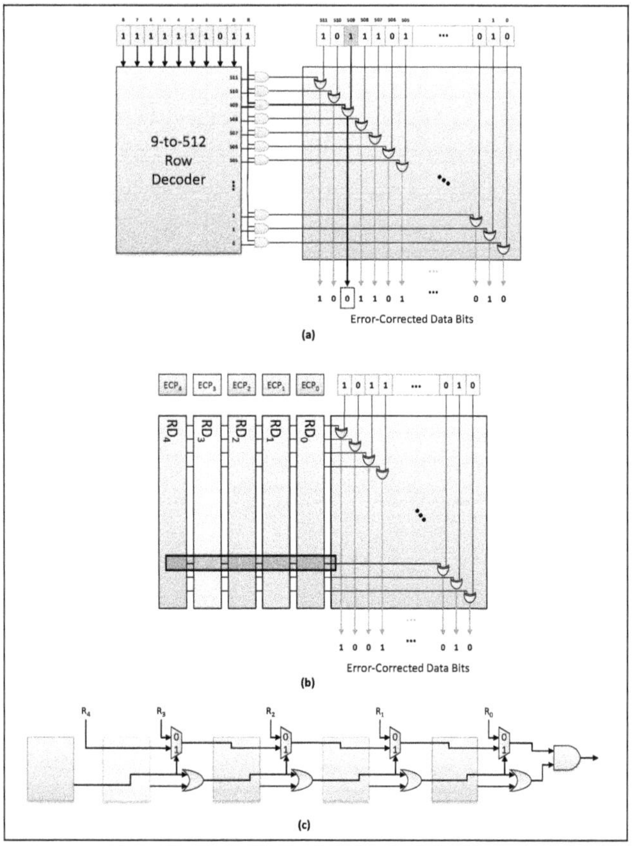

Figure 9: Hardware implementation for (a) ECP_1, (b) ECP_5, and (c) a close-up of one row of logic for ECP_5.

the row is forcibly decommissioned. There have been several other recent proposals that can extend the lifetime of phase-change memories. Qureshi *et al.* proposed a hybrid DRAM/PCM organization where a write-tolerant DRAM buffer can act as a large write combining buffer (among other optimizations) to condense many write commands from the processor into a single bulk write operation to the PCM [22]. The proposed ECP correction scheme does not come into play until the final write operations are presented to the PCM chips themselves, therefore techniques that reduce external write traffic before reaching the PCM can be directly composed with ECP to further extend the expected lifetime of PCM. These schemes do not compete with ECP but rather they complement each other.

Existing PCM wear-leveling schemes modify the mapping of rows within memory [21, 22, 28] so that the writes destined for frequently written rows are spread out over time across all of the available rows. In this fashion, no single row receives a disproportionately higher amount of the write traffic. Although the writes are now uniformly distributed across rows, the writes within a row may still be clustered. In the worst case, *all* of the writes may be destined for only a single bit (*e.g.*, a Boolean variable placed in memory using cache line padding to prevent false sharing). Each of the ECP and derivative schemes can be applied in conjunction with any memory-wide wear leveling scheme so that non-uniform write patterns are both *evenly distributed* across rows and *tolerated* within rows.

10.3 Transient Errors

The ECP approach assumes that soft errors are not a problem for phase-change memories; PCM cells are expected to reliably maintain their state for years under typical operating conditions. If transient faults occur with any reasonable probability (*e.g.*, operation in a high-temperature environment or multi-level cells that are much more sensitive to thermal drift), additional error correction beyond ECP will be required, which brings back all of the problems associated with traditional ECC codes.

If transient errors are not spatially located, one way to address them would be to layer a traditional error correction scheme (*e.g.* SEC_{64}) on top of ECP, using wear leveling to distribute the additional wear. The lower-level ECP would do the heavy lifting of correcting for multiple wear-induced failures while the SEC_{64} would correct for up to one transient error. SEC_{64} adds a 7 bit modification region (3.5 bit values are expected to flip) for each 64 bit block that is modified. If each modification spans all 64 bits of a modified block (32 bits are expected to flip), then adding SEC_{64} will result in an 11% increase in wear, spread over an additional 11% increase in storage bits.

11. CONCLUSIONS

The traditional approach for handling faults in main memories (SECDED ECC) works well for correcting rare transient faults, seen in DRAM, but not for correcting multiple wear-induced cell failures. ECC codes over small blocks cannot correct for multiple errors with reasonable space overhead. Using multiple-error correction Hamming codes over a larger block size reduces space overhead but, when data is written in small chunks, writing the large error correction codes can become a source of wear–inducing more errors.

Error-Correcting Pointers (ECP) function much better than Hamming codes for correcting multiple wear-induced hard faults. Like Hamming codes, ECP is able to efficiently correct errors in both data and in the correction structures themselves. Whereas Hamming codes must be updated each time a block of data is written, causing additional wear, ECP adds wear only in the rare case in which a new cell failure must be accounted for. The results show that ECP provides close to ideal correction capabilities and improved lifetime over previously proposed solutions at equivalent overheads. What's more, we provide with ECP the mathematical tools with which optimally allocate precious storage space between error-correction entries and spare memory when building a memory system to meet constraints of effective memory size, wear lifetime, and cell lifetime variance.

Acknowledgments

We are indebted to David Molnar and Thomas Moscibroda for their help in brainstorming and in providing feedback. Ed Nightingale was invaluable in helping us to understand prior work. We especially appreciate the insights of our anonymous reviewers, whose comments inspired numerous improvements. We are also thankful to Sean Eilert from Numonyx for providing us information about PCM architecture and failure models.

References

[1] Emerging research devices. In *International Technology Roadmap for Semiconductors*, 2007.

[2] S. J. Ahn, Y. J. Song, C. W. Jeong, J. M. Shin, Y. Fai, Y. N. Hwang, S. H. Lee, K. C. Ryoo, S. T. Lee, J. H. Park, H. Horii, Y. H. Ha, J. H. Yi, B. J. Kuh, G. H. Koh, G. T. Jeong, H. S. Jeong, K. Kim, and B. I. Ryu. Highly manufacturable high density phase change memory of 64Mb and beyond. In *International Electron Devices Meeting*, 2004.

[3] G. Atwood and R. Bez. Current status of chalcogenide phase change memory. In *Device Research Conference*, 2005.

[4] F. Bedeschi, R. Fackenthal, C. Resta, E. M. Donze, M. Jagasivamani, E. C. Buda, F. Pellizzer, D. W. Chow, A. Cabrini, G. Calvi, R. Faravelli, A. Fantini, G. Torelli, D. Mills, R. Gastaldi, and G. Casagrande. A multi-level-cell bipolar-selected phase-change memory. In *International Solid-State Circuits Conference*, 2008.

[5] A. J. Bhavnagarwala, X. Tang, and J. D. Meindl. The impact of intrinsic device fluctuations on CMOS SRAM cell stability. *IEEE Journal of Solid-State Circuits*, 36(4), Apr. 2001.

[6] S. Borkar, T. Karnik, S. Narendra, J. Tschanz, A. Keshavarzi, and V. De. Parameter variation and impact on circuits and microarchitecture. In *Proceedings of 40th Design Automation Conference*, June 2003.

[7] G. Dhiman, R. Ayoub, and T. Rosing. PDRAM: A hybrid PRAM and DRAM main memory system. In *Proceedings of 47th Design Automation Conference*, June 2009.

[8] R. Freitas and W. Wickle. Storage-class memory: The next storage system technology. *IBM Journal of Research and Development*, 52(4/5):439–447, 2008.

[9] R. Hamming. Error detecting and error correcting codes. *Bell System Technical Journal*, 29(2), April 1950.

[10] H. Horii, J. H. Yi, J. H. Park, Y. H. Ha, I. H. Baek, S. O. Park, Y. N. Hwang, S. H. Lee, Y. T. Kim, K. H. Lee, U.-I. Chung, and J. T. Moon. A novel cell technology using N-doped GeSbTe films for phase change RAM. In *Symposium on VLSI Technology*, 2003.

[11] E. Ipek, J. Condit, E. Nightingale, D. Burger, and T. Moscibroda. Dynamically replicated memory: Building resilient systems from unreliable nanoscale memories. In *To appear at The Fifteenth International Conference on Architectural Support for Programming Languages and Operating Systems (ASPLOS 2010)*, Mar. 2010.

[12] K. Kim. Technology for sub-50nm DRAM and NAND flash manufacturing. In *International Electron Devices Meeting*, 2005.

[13] B. Lee, E. Ipek, O. Mutlu, and D. Burger. Architecting phase-change memory as a scalable DRAM alternative. In *International Symposium on Computer Architecture*, June 2009.

[14] K.-J. Lee, B.-H. Cho, W.-Y. Cho, S. Kang, B.-G. Choi, H.-R. Oh, C.-S. Lee, H.-J. Kim, J.-M. Park, Q. Wang, M.-H. Park, Y.-H. Ro, J.-Y. Choi, K.-S. Kim, Y.-R. Kim, I.-C. Shin, K.-W. Lim, H.-K. Cho, C.-H. Choi, W.-R. Chung, D.-E. Kim, Y.-J. Yoon, K.-S. Yi, G.-T. Jeong, H.-S. Jeong, C.-K. Kwak, C.-H. Kim, and K. Kim. A 90nm 1.8V 512Mb diode-switch PRAM with 266 MB/s read throughput. *Journal of Solid-State Circuits*, 43(1), January 2008.

[15] T. May and W. Woods. Alpha-particle-induced soft errors in dynamic memories. *IEEE Transactions on Electronic Devices*, 26(2):2–9, 1979.

[16] C. McNairy and R. Bhatia. Montecito: A dual-core, dual-thread itanium processor. *IEEE Micro Magazine*, 25(2):10–20, March/April 2005.

[17] S. S. Mukherjee, J. Emer, and S. K. Reinhardt. The soft error problem: An architectural perspective. In *Proceedings of 11th International Symposium on High-Performance Computer Architecture*, pages 243–247, San Francisco, CA, USA, February 2005.

[18] Numonyx. The basics of phase change memory technology. In *Numonyx White Paper*, 2007.

[19] M. Orshansky, L. Milor, P. Chen, K. Keutzer, and C. Hu. Impact of spatial intrachip gate length variability on the performance of high-speed digital circuits. *IEEE Transactions on Computer-Aided Design of Integrated Circuits and Systems*, 21(5), May 2002.

[20] F. Pellizzer, A. Benvenuti, B. Gleixner, Y. Kim, B. Johnson, M. Magistretti, T. Marangon, A. Pirovano, R. Bez, and G. Atwood. A 90nm phase change memory technology for stand-alone non-volatile memory applications. In *Symposium on VLSI Circuits*, 2006.

[21] M. K. Qureshi, M. Fraceschini, V. Srinivasan, L. Lastras, B. Abali, and J. Karidis. Enhancing lifetime and security of phase change memories via start-gap wear leveling. In *International Symposium on Microarchitecture*, December 2009.

[22] M. K. Qureshi, V. Srinivasan, and J. A. Rivers. Scalable high performance main memory system using phase-change memory technology. In *International Symposium on Computer Architecture*, June 2009.

[23] S. Raoux, G. W. Burr, M. J. Breitwisch, C. T. Rettner, Y.-C. Chen, R. M. Shelby, M. Salinga, D. Krebs, S.-H. Chen, H.-L. Lung, and C. H. Lam. Phase-change random access memory: A scalable technology. *IBM Journal of Research and Development*, 52(4/5), Jul/Sept 2008.

[24] Samsung. Samsung introduces the next generation of nonvolatile memory - pram. In *Samsung News Release*, Sept. 2006.

[25] C. Wilkerson, H. Gao, A. R. Alameldeen, Z. Chishti, M. Khellah, and S.-L. Lu. Trading off cache capacity for reliability to enable low voltage operation. In *The 35th Annual International Symposium on Computer Architecture*, June 2008.

[26] W. Zhang and T. Li. Characterizing and mitigating the impact of process variations on phase change memory systems. In *International Symposium on Microarchitecture*, December 2009.

[27] W. Zhang and T. Li. Exploring phase change memory and 3d die-stacking for power/thermal friendly, fast and durable memory architectures. In *International Conference on Parallel Architectures and Compilation Techniques*, Sept. 2009.

[28] P. Zhouand, B. Zhao, J. Yang, and Y. Zhang. A durable and energy efficient main memory using phase change memory technology. In *International Symposium on Computer Architecture*, June 2009.

[29] J. F. Ziegler and G. R. Srinivasan. Terrestrial cosmic rays and soft errors. *IBM Journal of Research and Development*, 40(1), 1996.

Morphable Memory System: A Robust Architecture for Exploiting Multi-Level Phase Change Memories

Moinuddin K. Qureshi   Michele M. Franceschini   Luis A. Lastras-Montaño   John P. Karidis
IBM T. J. Watson Research Center, Yorktown Heights NY
{moinqureshi, franceschini, lastrasl, karidis}@us.ibm.com

ABSTRACT

Phase Change Memory (PCM) is emerging as a scalable and power-efficient technology to architect future main memory systems. The scalability of PCM is enhanced by the property that PCM devices can store multiple bits per cell. While such Multi-Level Cell (MLC) devices can offer high density, this benefit comes at the expense of increased read latency, which can cause significant performance degradation. This paper proposes *Morphable Memory System (MMS)*, a robust architecture for efficiently incorporating MLC PCM devices in main memory. MMS is based on observation that memory requirement varies between workloads, and systems are typically over-provisioned in terms of memory capacity. So, during a phase of low memory usage, some of the MLC devices can be operated at fewer bits per cell to obtain lower latency. When the workload requires full memory capacity, these devices can be restored to high density MLC operation to have full main-memory capacity. We provide the runtime monitors, the hardware-OS interface, and the detailed mechanism for implementing MMS. Our evaluations on an 8-core 8GB MLC PCM-based system show that MMS provides, on average, low latency access for 95% of all memory requests, thereby improving overall system performance by 40%.

Categories and Subject Descriptors:
B.3.1 [Semiconductor Memories]: Phase Change Memory

General Terms: Design, Performance

Keywords: Phase Change Memory, Multi-Level Cell, Morphable Memory, Memory Monitor.

1. INTRODUCTION

As DRAM-based memory systems get limited by power wall and scalability challenges, architects are turning their attention towards exploiting emerging memory technologies for building future memory systems. Phase Change Memory (PCM) has emerged as one of the most promising technologies to incorporate into main memories. PCM devices are expected to scale better than DRAM and prototypes with feature size as small as 3nm have been fabricated [17]. Recently, several studies [8][25][14] have advocated for PCM-based memory systems, given the scalability and density advantages of PCM.

PCM devices exploit the property of chalcogenide glass to switch between two states, amorphous and crystalline, with the application of heat using electrical pulses. The phase change material can be switched from one phase to another a large number of times reliably. Data is stored in PCM devices in the form of resistance – the amorphous phase has high electrical resistivity and the crystalline phase has low resistance. The difference in resistance between the two states is typically 3 orders of magnitude. To achieve high density PCM memories are expected to exploit this high resistance range to store multiple bits in a single cell, forming what is known as Multi-Level Cell or MLC devices [1][4]. The density advantage of PCM is, in part, dependent on storing more and more bits in the MLC devices.

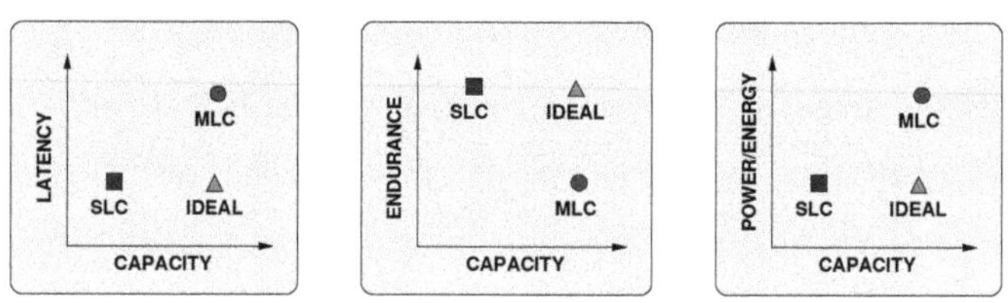

Figure 1: Comparison of SLC vs. MLC (Figure not to scale).

While MLC devices offer more density than devices that store one bit per cell (also called as SLC devices), this advantage comes at a significant price. MLC devices require precise reading of the resistance value. The number of levels in the MLC device increases exponentially with the number of bits stored, which implies that the resistance region assigned to each data value decreases significantly. For example, in a 4-bit per cell device the resistance range is divided so as to encode sixteen levels, and reading the data stored in the cell requires accurately differentiating between the 16 resistance ranges. The read latency of MLC devices, depending with the sensing amplifier technology, can increase linearly or exponentially with the number of bits. Furthermore, when programming (writing) an MLC device, it is likely that attaining a resistance value that is within the desired range will require the use of iterative write algorithms [13][15]. These algorithms contain several steps of read-verify-write operations that increase the write energy and further negatively impact the limited lifetime of PCM memories. Figure 1 captures this trade-off between MLC and SLC. Ideally we would like to have PCM memories with the capacity of MLC devices at the latency, energy, and lifetime of SLC devices.

ISCA'10, June 19–23, 2010, Saint-Malo, France.

Architecting a main memory system with MLC devices is thus a challenge as the density advantage of MLC can be useful only if the associated drawbacks are handled carefully. The objective of our paper is design a memory architecture that can obtain the latency, lifetime, and energy of fewer bit per cell devices in the common case while still having the ability to provide the high memory capacity enabled by MLC.

We base our solution on the observation that memory capacity requirements vary widely between different applications as well as within the execution of the same application, and the system is typically provisioned with enough memory capacity to be able to efficiently execute the worst-case workload of interest. In current DRAM-based systems, increasing the main memory capacity does not significantly change the memory latency. However, in case the memory system is based on MLC devices, the capacity boost comes at the expense of increased latency. If the workload does not use all the capacity, then it is beneficial to convert the excess main memory capacity to store fewer bits per cell (from MLC to SLC, for example). Especially given that it is fairly easy to restrict the number of levels used in a MLC device to emulate a fewer bits per cell device. To this end, we propose *Morphable Memory System (MMS)*, that dynamically regulates the number of bits per cell in memory system depending on the workload requirement.

Conceptually, MMS divides the main memory into two regions. First, a high-density high-latency region that contains pages in MLC mode. We denote such a memory region as *High-Density PCM or HDPCM* region. Second, a low-latency low-density region that contains the PCM devices in half the number of bits per cell than in the HDPCM region. We denote such a memory region as *Low-Latency PCM or LLPCM* region. As the percentage of total memory pages that are in LLPCM mode increases, the likelihood of an access being satisfied by the LLPCM region increases, but at the expense of reduction in overall memory capacity. Thus, the key decision in MMS is to determine what fraction of all memory pages must be in LLPCM mode to optimally balance this latency and capacity trade-off.

MMS contains a Memory Monitoring circuit (MMON) that tracks the workload memory requirement at runtime to determine the best partition between LLPCM and HDPCM regions. MMON performs the well-known Stack Distance Histogram (SDH) analysis [12] [21] [16], at runtime for a few sampled pages to estimate the page miss ratio curve [24]. This information along with the estimated benefit from accessing pages in LLPCM region is used to determine the best partition. MMS periodically consults MMON to obtain the estimate for the best partition and accordingly varies the number of pages in LLPCM region.

If a memory access occurs to a page in the HDPCM region, that page can be upgraded to the LLPCM region for reduced latency on subsequent accesses. MMS allows such transfers between the HDPCM and LLPCM regions in order to automatically provide lower latency to frequently accessed pages. Such a transfer between HDPCM and LLPCM region is handled transparently by the MMS hardware, without any involvement of software or the OS. A separate hardware structure, called the *Page Redirection Table (PRT)*, keeps track of the physical location of each page and is consulted on each memory access.

Unlike conventional memory system, the total memory capacity (in terms of number of pages) that are available to the OS can vary at runtime in a system that implements MMS. We provide a hardware-OS interface to facilitate this communication. This allows the OS to evict some of the allocated pages to make them available to the MMS hardware, if the number of pages in the LLPCM region is to be increased. When the demand for memory capacity increases the hardware transfers pages from the LLPCM region to HDPCM region, and the pages thus freed up can be reclaimed by the OS to accommodate another page.

We evaluate the MMS proposal on a 8GB PCM-based system consisting of MLC devices. Our evaluations with 10 workloads show that for workloads with low capacity requirement MMS performs similar to a memory system with fewer bits per cell, whereas for workloads that are capacity constrained MMS offers the full memory capacity. On average, MMS services 95% of all read requests and 90% of writebacks from the LLPCM region. MMS improves overall system performance by 40% on average. Satisfying most of the accesses in LLPCM region also has the associated benefits of saving energy and improving lifetime.

2. BACKGROUND ON MULTI-LEVEL PCM

PCM is emerging as a promising technology to build main memory systems in a power-efficient and scalable manner. One of the important ways in which PCM devices are expected to scale in terms of bits per unit area is by storing multiple bits per cell. As this is one of the first architecture papers on efficiently exploiting such Multi Level Cell (MLC) PCM devices, this section first provides the basic operation of MLC, then the trade-offs with MLC devices, and finally the design of a morphable PCM cell.

2.1 What is MLC and Why MLC?

PCM is a memory technology that stores data by programming and reading the resistance of the memory elements. Although earlier research on PCM was focused on single bit operation, recently, the focus of PCM research has been moving towards MLC operation, mainly to keep up with the increasing demand for low cost memory. Figure 2 shows the concept of MLC devices that can store 2 bits/cell and 4 bits/cell. The resistance range of each level decreases exponentially as the number of bits per cell increases. The maximum number of bits that can be stored in a given MLC device is a function of precision in reading technology, device data integrity, and precision in writing. As technology improves, the number of bits in MLC devices is expected to increase. The ITRS roadmap [1] projects that PCM cells will have 4 bits/cell by 2012.

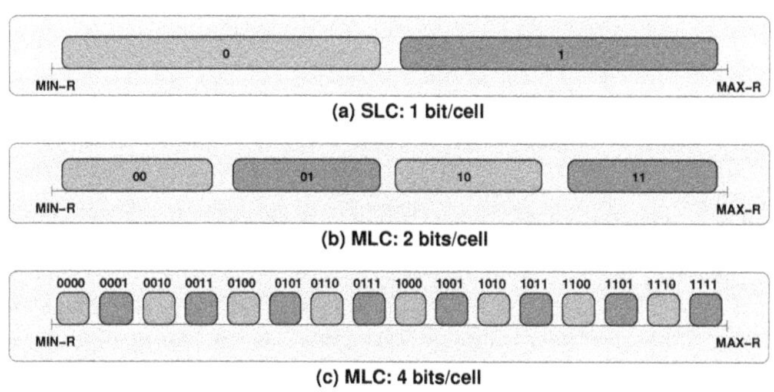

Figure 2: Concept of Multi-Level PCM (Figure not to scale)

2.2 Reading Techniques for MLC

Reading a data value from MLC device requires distinguishing precisely between different resistance levels that are spaced closely. The reading operation is performed by selecting, biasing, and sensing the given PCM device. Although, to the best of our knowledge, there is no published material on sensing devices for MLC PCM, from an high level perspective, possible solutions are limited to the most area efficient ADCs. We will discuss two ADC technologies that are scalable to more than 2 bits per cell.

2.2.1 *Integrating ADC Model*

An integrating ADC (e.g., *charge run-down ADC*) [3] uses a counter to measure the discharge time of a capacitor through the PCM element. An example of this scheme is shown in Figure 3. To represent n bits, the counter must be able to count 2^n different values, thus implying that the number of clock steps is exponential in the number of bits stored in the device. The difference in sensing time between the lowest data value and the highest data value grows exponentially, indicating doubling of sensing time from SLC to 2 bits/cell, and quadrupling from 2 bits/cell to 4 bits/cell.

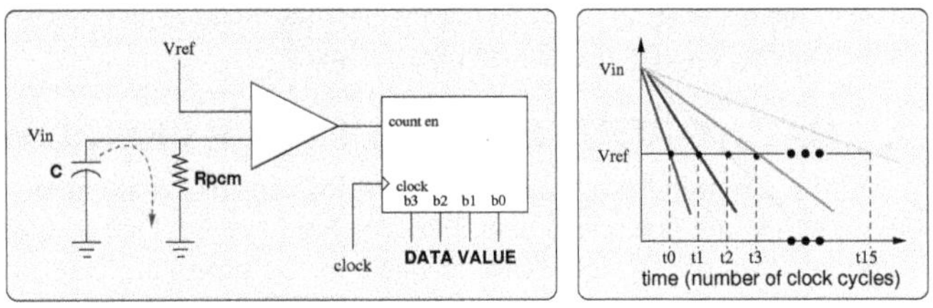

Figure 3: Example of integrating ADC: structure and working.

2.2.2 *Successive Approximation ADC Model*

Figure 4 shows an example of a successive approximation ADC [18, 3]. The conversion is performed in steps, at each step the hardware is reused to obtain an additional bit. The sensing time with this approach increases linearly with the number of bits stored in the MLC devices, thus increasing by a factor of two with each doubling of the number of bits per cell.

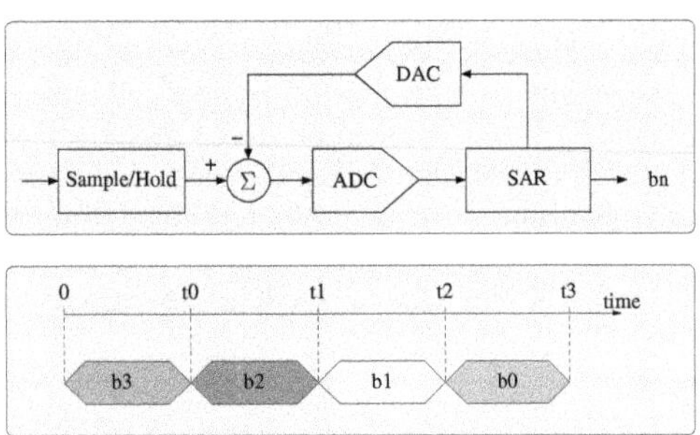

Figure 4: Example of successive approximation ADC.

2.3 Writing Technique for MLC

In MLC devices, each data value is assigned a limited resistance range, which means the writing process must be accurate enough to program that narrow range of resistance. The increased programming precision is obtained by means of iterative write algorithms that contains several steps of write-and-verify operations [15]. The number of iterations required for writing increases (almost exponentially) with the number of bits per cell [13]. Thus, with more bits per cell, these algorithms will consume increasingly more write energy, and exacerbate the limited lifetime of PCM memories.

2.4 A Morphable PCM Device

While MLC devices offer more density, this advantage comes at significant price of increased read latency, increased energy consumption, and reduced lifetime. Ideally, we want a PCM cell that offers the density of MLC but the latency, energy, and lifetime of fewer bits/cell devices. While this may not be practical, it is possible to program the MLC device to store restricted data values and emulate the functionality (and performance) of a lower density device. Examples of such flexible devices can be already found in Flash [5][7], and will conceivably be available in PCM.

PCM is fundamentally an analog medium that stores data in terms of resistance. For changing the number of bits per cell in a PCM cell, one need not change the device itself but just make minor changes to the sensing circuit. For example, a normalized resistance (R) value of 0.6 would indicate a "1" ($R > 0.5$) in SLC mode and a "10" ($0.5 < R < 0.75$) in 2 bits per cell MLC mode. Similarly, a cell that stores 4 bits per cell can also be used to store 2 bits per cell by simply regulating the resistance range in which data values get stored and providing a control signal that specifies the bits/cell associated with the device. For example, in integrating ADC model, a subset of the levels can be used and the *Vref* value can be increased to reduce the reading time. Whereas, in case of successive approximation ADC, only the most significant bits can be retrieved, which improves the reading time linearly.

We refer to such a MLC PCM cell that can be programmed to two different cell density as a *Morphable PCM Cell*. The Morphable PCM cell can be operated in two modes: First, high-density high-latency *(HDPCM)*, which stores as many bits per cell as permitted by the technology. Second, low-density low-latency *(LLPCM)*, which stores half the number of bits per cell but with low latency access.[1] Throughout this paper we assume that such a morphable PCM device is feasible and can be used in memory system.

3. MOTIVATION

MLC PCM is expected to be a cost effective means of providing a large main memory. However, architecting a main memory system with MLC devices is a challenge as the density advantage of MLC can be useful only if the associated drawbacks are handled carefully. We base our solution on the observation that memory capacity requirement varies widely across applications, and the system is typically provisioned with enough memory capacity to be able to efficiently execute the worst-case workload of interest. For example, consider the benchmarks in the SPEC CPU 2006 suite. There are 29 benchmarks in the suite, some with multiple (reference) input sets, for a total of 55 unique benchmark-inputset pairs. SPEC specifies that the machine on which these benchmarks are evaluated must have at-least 1GB of main memory [20], and the worst-case workload indeed requires close to 1GB of memory.

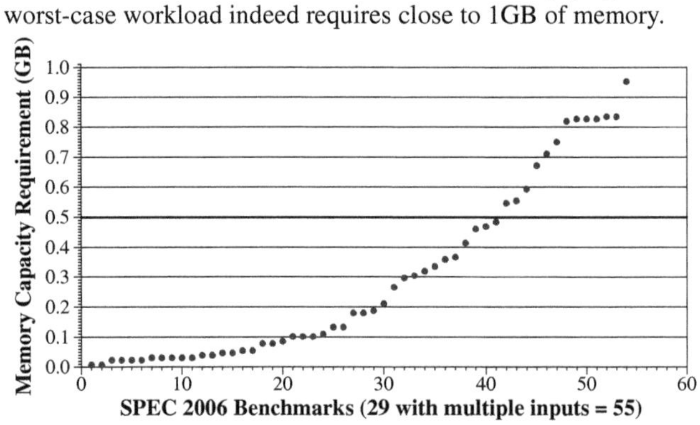

Figure 5: Variation in memory capacity requirement of different applications. Each dot in the graph represents one benchmark-inputset pair from the SPEC CPU 2006 suite.

[1]The density vs. latency trade-off is present not only in MLC and SLC but also within MLC devices of different densities. For example, HDPCM may denote 4 bits/cell MLC and LLPCM can denote 2 bits/cell MLC, and MMS can try to obtain the density of 4 bits/cell at the latency of 2 bits/cell. Therefore, we use the terms HDPCM and LLPCM instead of MLC and SLC.

Figure 5 shows the memory requirement curves for these 55 benchmarks.[2] While the worst-case requirement is close to 1GB, most of the applications require much less than 0.5GB of memory capacity. However, the system must be provisioned with enough capacity to run the worst-case benchmark in the suite. Otherwise, such benchmarks would experience significantly degraded execution time because of memory thrashing, given that page faults require two to four orders of magnitude more latency to service than memory accesses.

It is common to over-provision memory and often applications do not use all the memory throughout the execution. When applications do not use all the memory capacity, it would be appealing to avoid paying the penalties associated with high density MLC when a smaller, less dense memory would have provided better performance. If we can morph the memory on-the-fly, then it is possible to get the benefit of low density PCM in common case, and still retain capacity for applications that need all the memory capacity. To this end, we propose *Morphable Memory System (MMS)*, a memory architecture than can dynamically regulate the bits/cell in MLC devices depending on the workload requirement.

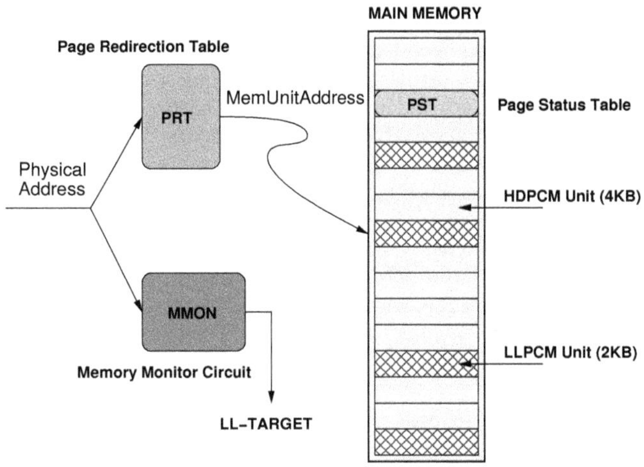

Figure 6: Architecture of Morphable Memory System (Figure not to scale)

4. MORPHABLE MEMORY SYSTEM

MMS uses a memory consisting of MLC devices that can be morphed between LLPCM and HDPCM modes. For applications that are not capacity constrained, it is beneficial to have most of the memory in LLPCM mode. Whereas, for capacity-intensive workloads it is better to have most (or all) of the memory in the HDPCM mode. MMS achieves these goals. The next subsections describe the architecture and working of MMS.

4.1 Architecture

Figure 6 shows the architecture of MMS. Main memory is arranged in terms of pages[3] (4KB each) and physical memory units (fixed number of PCM cells storing either 2KB or 4KB). Each page can be in one of two states: HDPCM (occupying one 4KB memory unit) or in LLPCM (occupying two 2KB memory units). The OS sees a addressable memory size as if each page occupies one memory unit, i.e., all pages in HDPCM mode. In this way, there is a one to one relation between addressable pages and memory units.

Conceptually, MMS divides the main memory into two regions. First, a high density high latency region (HDPCM region). Second, a low latency, low density region (LLPCM region). A key decision in MMS is to determine what fraction of all memory pages must be in LLPCM mode to optimally balance the latency and capacity trade-off. A memory monitoring (MMON) circuit observes the traffic received by main memory to estimate the capacity requirement of the workload. Periodically, the MMON is consulted to determine the number of pages that must be in LLPCM mode for best overall performance. This number of pages is termed as the *LL-Target*.

When a page is accessed in HDPCM mode, it can be upgraded to LLPCM mode for lower latency. Such an upgraded page occupies two memory units (2KB each). The first half of the page is resident in its corresponding memory unit. A separate hardware structure, *Page Redirection Table (PRT)*, provides the physical location of the second half of the pages that are in LLPCM mode.

Given that some of the pages in memory can be in LLPCM mode, the number of pages usable by the OS reduces. Furthermore, for correctness reasons, the OS must ensure that it does not allocate a memory unit that is storing the second half of another page in LLPCM mode. This hardware-OS interface is accomplished by a memory mapped table, called the *Page Status Table (PST)*. The PST contains information about which units are usable by OS, and which units can be used as placeholders for the second halves of LLPCM pages. In the next subsections we will describe each structure of MMS.

4.2 Memory Monitoring (MMON)

The heart of the MMS is the memory monitoring circuit (MMON), which tracks the memory reference stream. The role of MMON is to estimate the statistics of the memory usage and to set a target for the fraction of LLPCM pages (LL-Target). To estimate the memory requirement of the system, we use the classical stack distance histogram (SDH) analysis [12] that has been widely used in literature for page miss rate curve [24] and cache requirement [21][16] studies. Using the SDH analysis it is possible to estimate the hit-rate for various capacity using a single pass. Figure 7(a) shows an example of SDH analysis for a memory containing four pages. Four counters, one each per recency position, count the number of hits obtained for that recency position. As shown in the example of Figure 7(b) given the counter values, it is possible to compute the miss rate when memory contained only one, two, three or four pages.

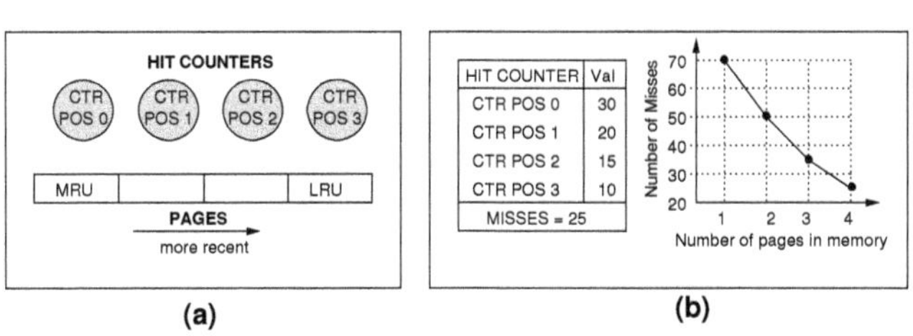

Figure 7: Stack distance analysis for memory with four pages

[2]This data was generated by full run execution of each benchmark-inputset pair using an instrumentation tool. The memory size at which page misses increase by more than 1% compared to unlimited memory size is deemed the memory requirement of the benchmark. We do not use specrand in our studies.

[3]We use the term pages for a region of memory 4KB in size for convenience as it is the commonly used pagesize in OS. If the OS has a pagesize larger than 4KB, then MMS can manage the memory at a sub-page granularity of 4KB. This also allows MMS to automatically handle heterogeneous page sizes, as long as each pagesize is a multiple of 4KB.

A typical memory system contains millions of pages, so it is impractical to measure the exact recency information using a stack algorithm for a fully associative structure of this size. Therefore, we conceptually divide the memory into rows of 64 columns each, and perform a recency analysis using the ordering of pages only within each row. Thus, the SDH information will be discretized to 64 values, much like this information would be present in a 64-way cache. Figure 8(a) shows how such a MMON circuit would work by accruing global counts of hits in each recency position of any row. Note that each row only contains ordering information for all the columns in that row and does not contain any tag (all pages have a corresponding entry) or data values. The number of global counters equals the number of columns (64).

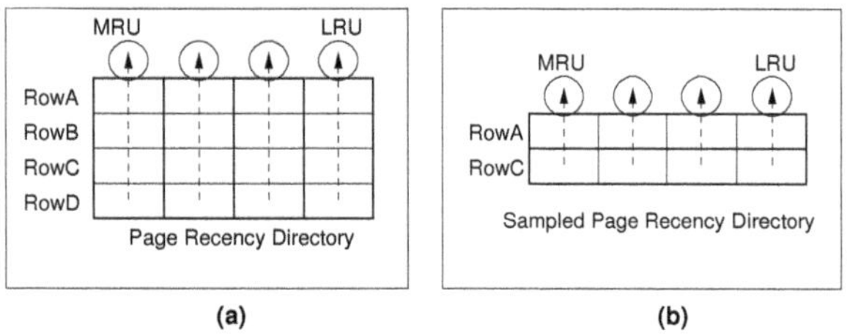

Figure 8: Memory monitor concept and implementation

Obtaining recency ordering for each row requires $64 \cdot \log_2 64 =$ 384 bits = 48B per row. A typical memory system would contain several hundred thousand rows. We reduce the monitoring hardware by using the well understood concept of set sampling [23][16]. We use only 64 rows in MMON to estimate the memory hit rate. This means only $64 * 64 = 4096$ pages ($< 1\%$ of all pages) participate in monitoring. A sampled MMON has accuracy similar to having all rows participate and incurs a storage overhead of less than 4KB. The proposed MMON is shown in Figure 8(b). The counts of the sampled MMON are scaled by a factor that is equal to **NumTotalRows/NumSampledRows** to estimate the global hit counts.

```
BestOffCols = 0, MaxCols = 64, BestCycleSaving =0
for OffCols = 1 to MaxCols/2 do
    PageFaultIncrease = SDHCounters [MaxCols-1] + ... + SDHCounters[MaxCols-OffCols]
    LowLatencyHits = SDHCounters [0] + ... + SDHCounters[OffCols-1]
    CyclesSaved = LowLatencyHits * (HDPCM Hit Latency - LLPCM Hit Latency)
    CyclesIncrease = PageFaultIncrease * AveragePageFaultLatency
    if CyclesSaved-CyclesIncrease > BestCycleSaving then
        BestOffCols = OffCols
        BestCycleSaving = CyclesSaved - CyclesIncrease
    end if
end for
Return LL-Target = (BestOffCols/MaxCols)*NumTotalPages (END)
```

Figure 9: Algorithm to estimate LL Target.

Periodically the counters in MMON are read to estimate the increase in page fault and the benefit from LLPCM hits. This is done by using the algorithm described in Figure 9. For a 64 column MMON, there are 33 possible values for LL-Target in terms of columns (0-32). The algorithm estimates for each such point the increase in execution time due to increased page-fault rate and reduction in execution time due to low latency LLPCM hits. The point that minimizes the expected execution time is selected as the LL-Target. We invoke this algorithm once every 250ms. At each invocation, the counters in MMON are multiplied by 0.9 to account for changing phase behavior, similar to as done in [21].

4.3 Changing Effective Memory Size via Ballooning and Page Status Table

The MMON estimates of LL-Target is periodically read by the OS. If the number of LLPCM pages in the system is less than LL-Target, the OS evicts some HDPCM pages so that the memory units associated with those pages can be used for LLPCM operation. To enable this, we use the concept of *Ballooning* which is an effective way of reclaiming idle pages in the system [23]. The concept of Balloon is described in Figure 10. A balloon process is a dummy process which can take away physical memory pages from running processes. When the OS wants to reduce the available pages, it inflates the balloon and vice versa.

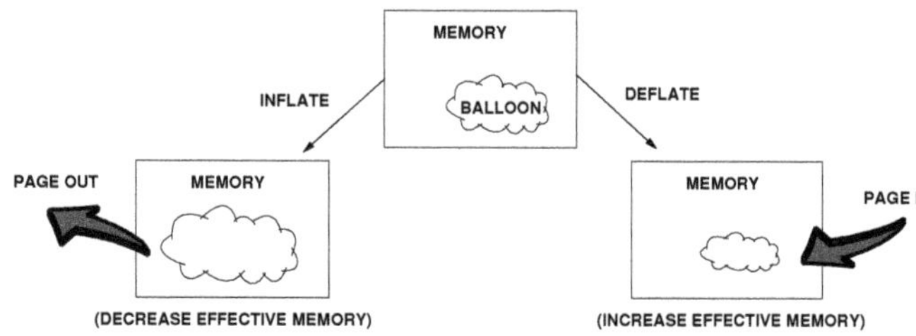

Figure 10: Concept of Balloon process for stealing pages [23]

In MMS, the memory units associated with the pages claimed by the balloon process, are marked by the OS to be free for storing second halves of LLPCM pages. This information is communicated to the hardware using a memory mapped table, called the *Page Status Table (PST)*. Each page can be in one of the four states: a normal OS page (`Normal`), a monitor page used by MMON (`Monitor`), a balloon page that is available to be used in LLPCM mode (`BalloonFree`), and a balloon page that is currently being used in LLPCM mode (`BalloonUsed`). The PST contains a two bit status field for each page (which means PST occupies $<$ 0.01% of main memory). The OS uses it to specify a balloon page, and to reclaim a `BalloonFree` page in case it wants to increase memory capacity. The PST avoids the scenario where OS can victimize a `BalloonUsed` page for allocating another page during page fault. The PST is kept coherent by disallowing any updates to PST from the hardware when the OS is operating on it.

When **NumBalloonPages** $<$ **LLTarget**, the OS converts some `Normal` pages into `BalloonFree` pages using its own replacement algorithm, ensuring that a `Monitor` page is not converted into `BalloonFree`. The hardware can then use these pages for LLPCM operation. When the **NumBalloonPages** $>$ **LLTarget**, the OS converts `BalloonFree` pages into `Normal` pages. If there are not enough `BalloonFree` pages, the hardware is instructed to actively convert some of the `BalloonUsed` pages into `BalloonFree` pages. The LL-Target thus set by MMON is enforced lazily by adjusting the number of balloon pages.

4.4 Redirection, Upgrades, and Downgrades

For pages that are stored in LLPCM mode, the actual physical location of the pages may be different from the physical address specified by the OS. MMS contains a hardware table called the *Page Redirection Table (PRT)*, which is responsible for the translation from a physical address to the PCM memory address. Each page has a corresponding entry in the PRT, which contains a valid bit, a ref bit, and a pointer. For pages in HDPCM mode, the associated PRT entry is invalid. For pages in the LLPCM mode, the associated entry has a pointer which stores the address of the physical memory unit that stores the second half of the page. The first half of such a page is always stored in place, albeit in LLPCM mode. We now describe the process of accessing memory in MMS, and converting pages between HDPCM and LLPCM modes.

4.4.1 Memory Access

The incoming line address is applied to the PRT. If the associated page has an invalid PRT entry then the page is a HDPCM page and the physical location corresponds with the incoming address. That location is accessed in HDPCM mode. If the PRT entry is valid, and the line address corresponds to the first half of the page, then the physical location still corresponds with the incoming address, except that location is accessed in LLPCM mode. Whereas, if the second half of the page is accessed then the pointer in the PRT entry specifies which physical location must be accessed. That location is accessed in LLPCM mode.

4.4.2 Upgrades

When there is a miss in the PRT, the HDPCM page may be converted into LLPCM page for lower latency. We call this process a *Page Upgrade*. This process is performed as follows. First, a victim unit is found either from one of the `BalloonFree` units or from one of the units that is already in LLPCM mode. If the victim is a `BalloonFree`, then it's status is changed to `BalloonUsed` in the PST. The contents of the original page are read out and stored in LLPCM mode for the first half, and the second half is stored in the victim unit, again in the LLPCM mode. The PRT entry for the page is upgraded to be valid, and the pointer field is set to the victim unit. If the victim unit was already in LLPCM mode, then the upgraded page resident in that location must be downgraded first, which we describe next.

4.4.3 Downgrades

We use the term *Page Downgrade* to denote the process of converting a page from LLPCM mode to HDPCM mode. A page downgrade can happen either when the page is being victimized to upgrade another page, or if the LL-Target is much smaller than the number of balloon pages, so the hardware is trying to convert `BalloonUsed` pages to `BalloonFree` pages. The process of downgrade is performed as follows: The data is read out from both memory units occupied by the LLPCM page and is stored in HDPCM format in the original location. The corresponding entry in PRT is invalidated. The PST entry is updated to change the status of the freed unit from `BalloonUsed` to `BalloonFree`.

4.5 OS Support

MMS requires the OS to support the dynamically changing memory capacity. First, the page replacement algorithm is updated to check PST and not victimize Balloon pages. Second, an OS process must periodically check (e.g., every 250ms) to ensure that the target set by MMON is close to number of balloon pages. If the target is higher, then the OS inflates the balloon to create more balloon pages. If the target is lower, then the OS deflates the balloon and converts `BalloonFree` pages into `Normal` pages.

5. CASE STUDY

We now analyze the effectiveness of MMS using a simple kernel *RandStep* as a case study to provide insights. Detailed evaluations with standard benchmarks will be presented in Section 7. RandStep randomly accesses one of the lines in its working set once every 100 instructions. The working set size changes once every 20 Billion instructions, as described in Figure 11. It has three modes: small working set (30% memory), medium working set (60% memory), and large working set (90% memory).

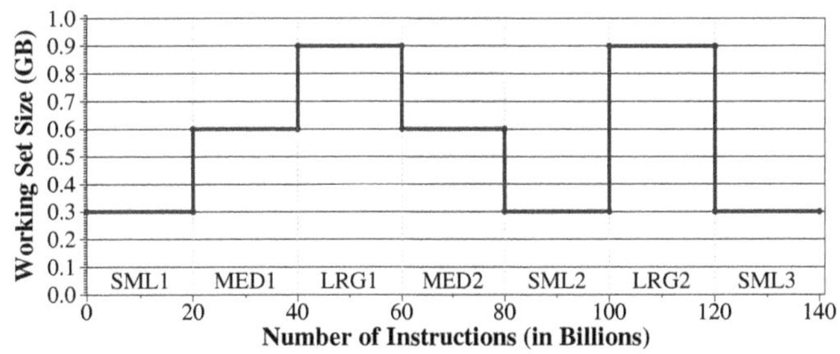

Figure 11: RandStep Kernel: Accesses random memory line in working set once every 100 instructions

Ideally the system should have almost all the memory in LLPCM mode for SML1, SML2, and SML3 phases. For LRG1 and LRG2 almost all the memory should be in HDPCM mode to accommodate the working set. We execute this kernel on a single-core system with 1GB of memory with MMS enabled (other parameters shown in Table 1). We sampled the system once every billion instructions to measure various statistics. Figure 12 shows the effective memory capacity visible to the OS for different phases of the kernel.

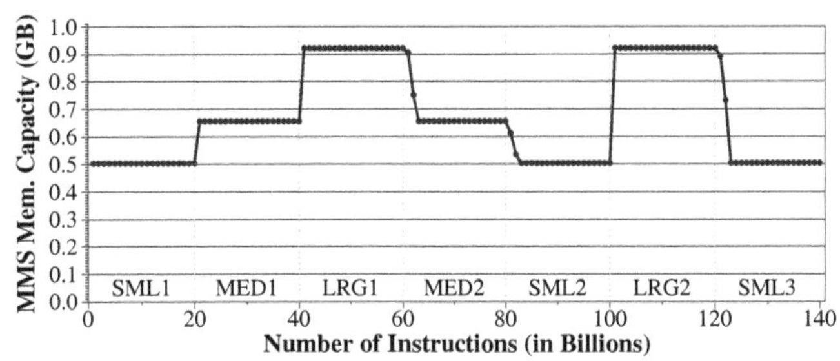

Figure 12: Effective memory capacity usable by OS with MMS

During the SML phases the effective capacity is halved which means almost all pages in memory can be in LLPCM mode. The effective capacity of the system increases as the demand for capacity increases. These results also show the need for dynamic adaptation to different phases as a static partition of memory between LLPCM and HDPCM regions causes thrashing in phases LRG1 and LRG2.

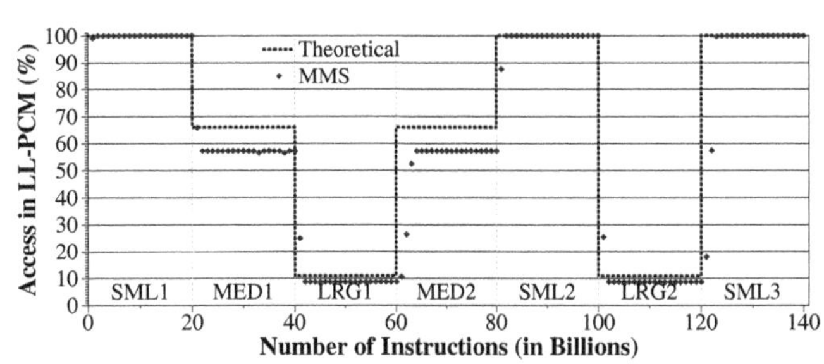

Figure 13: Percentage of memory accesses in LLPCM mode: Expected and with MMS

We also measured the number of accesses that occur in the LLPCM mode. Given that RandStep accesses memory randomly, we can compute the expected percentage of accesses in LLPCM mode for a theoretical system. For SML phases, all the memory accesses can happen in LLPCM mode. For MED phases, 40% of the memory pages are available for optimizing 60% of memory capacity, which means two-thirds of the accesses can be in LLPCM mode. And, for LRG phases, about 10%/0.9=11% of the accesses can happen in LLPCM mode. Figure 13 shows the percentage of all memory accesses that occur in the LLPCM region, both the expected theoretical bounds and the measured statistics with MMS. The two results match well and MMS comes close to the theoretical possible improvement.

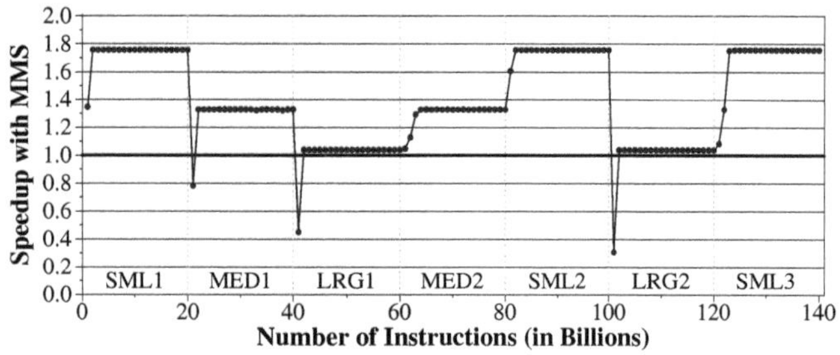

Figure 14: Normalized performance of MMS over HDPCM

Figure 14 shows the performance of MMS normalized with respect to the baseline system, which has all the pages in HDPCM mode, measured over periods of executing one billion instructions each. For SML and MED phases, MMS provides significant performance improvement. However, when the phases changes such that the working set increases instantly MMS takes more time than baseline to accommodate this working set, hence the drop in performance for phase transitions from SML to MED, MED to LRG, and SML to LRG. But once the working set gets accommodated MMS has similar or significantly better performance. MMS reduces overall execution time for this kernel by 22%, providing an effective speedup of 1.28x.

6. EXPERIMENTAL METHODOLOGY

6.1 Configuration

We use an in-house system simulator for our studies. The baseline system is shown in Figure 15 with the parameters given in Table 1. The system contains an eight core CMP. We use a simple in-order processor model so that we can evaluate our proposal for several hundred billion instructions. The baseline also contains a 256MB write-back DRAM cache organized as a 32MB per-core private cache. The DRAM cache uses a linesize of 128B. Write requests arrive at main memory only on DRAM cache evictions.

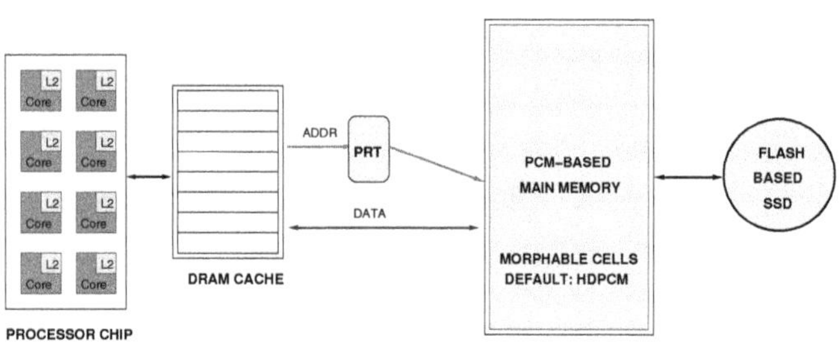

Figure 15: Simulated System (Figure not to scale)

The 8GB PCM-based main memory consists of morphable PCM cells that are defaulted to HDPCM mode in the baseline. We assume that the baseline memory system is sufficiently banked such that the contention between requests is negligible. Memory is assumed to have a read latency of 1000 cycles if the page is in HDPCM mode and 500 cycles if the page is in LLPCM mode.

A page size of 4KB is assumed. Virtual to physical address translation is performed using a page table built in our simulator. A clock style algorithm is used to perform page replacements. Page misses are serviced by a Flash based solid state disk (SSD), which has a latency of 100K cycles.

For the MMS enabled system, we incorporate an EDRAM-based PRT of 6MB (2M pages * 3 byte per entry).[4] To model the latency overhead of PRT-based indirection, we assume that each memory access in MMS incurs extra latency of 5ns (20 cycles). This latency overhead is not present in non-MMS systems.

Table 1: Baseline Configuration

System	8-core CMP, 4GHz single-issue in-order core private-L1
L2 cache (private)	2MB, 4-way, LRU, 128B linesize
DRAM cache (private)	32MB, 8-way, 128B linesize 25 ns (100 cycle) access, writeback policy
Main memory	8GB PCM, consisting of morphable PCM cells that are in HDPCM mode
PCM read latency	HDPCM : 250ns (1000 cycles) LLPCM : 125 ns (500 cycles)
Flash-Based SSD	unlimited size, read latency 25 micro seconds (100K cycles)

6.2 Workloads

We use eight benchmarks from the SPEC CPU 2006 suite: BWaves, CactusADM, GemsFDTD, lbm, mcf, leslie3d, milc, and zeusmp. These benchmarks were chosen because they have at least 1 memory access per 1000 instructions out of the 32MB cache (for workloads that fit in the cache, the proposed scheme neither helps nor hurts performance). We skip the first 50 billion instructions for each benchmark and then execute the next 50 billion instructions. Table 2 shows the main-memory read accesses per 1000 instructions, write backs per 1000 instructions, on average for a 1-core 1GB system. It also shows the page faults at 0.5GB, 0.6GB, and 0.75GB memory normalized to the page fault rate with 1GB memory. The first four benchmarks need less than half of the allocated 1GB capacity, milc needs slightly more than 0.5GB, and the next three benchmarks need more than 0.75GB.

Table 2: Benchmark Characteristics (PF denotes Relative Page Fault Rate with respect to 1GB Memory Size).

Name	Reads PKI	Writes PKI	PF 0.5GB	PF 0.6GB	PF 0.75GB
CactusADM	1.32	0.43	1.00x	1.00x	1.00x
lbm	6.42	3.22	1.00x	1.00x	1.00x
leslie3d	3.15	1.65	1.00x	1.00x	1.00x
zeusmp	1.68	0.69	1.00x	1.00x	1.00x
milc	10.8	4.08	1.35x	1.00x	1.00x
BWaves	6.4	0.86	5.08x	4.15x	2.75x
mcf	3.7	0.04	27.1x	26.1x	13.4x
GemsFDTD	6.6	3.36	70.4x	22.9x	7.00x

[4]The storage of PRT can be reduced by restricting both halves of LLPCM pages to be within 256 pages from each other. This would decrease the storage overhead of PRT to approximately 2MB. It is also possible to have a memory mapped PRT and cache the PRT entries in a smaller structure based on demand. We do not consider such optimizations in this paper.

To form multiprogrammed workloads, we run these benchmarks in a rate mode, where each processor executes the same benchmark in a separate virtual space. We also created two heterogeneous workloads: mix_1 consisting of two copies each of milc, Bwaves, mcf, and GemsFDTD. And mix_2 consisting of four copies each of mcf and GemsFDTD. The workloads used in our study are described in Table 3. We execute one benchmark per core. The simulation continues till each core has executed 50 billion instructions. Execution time of the workload is determined by the time when simulation terminates.

Table 3: Workload Summary.

Name	Description
cactus_r	8 copies of CactusADM
lbm_r	8 copies of lbm
leslie_r	8 copies of leslie3d
zeusmp_r	8 copies of zeusmp
milc_r	8 copies of milc
bwaves_r	8 copies of BWaves
mcf_r	8 copies of mcf
gems_r	8 copies of GemsFDTD
mix_1	2 copies of milc , BWaves , mcf , and GemsFDTD
mix_2	4 copies each of mcf and GemsFDTD

7. RESULTS AND ANALYSIS

7.1 Performance

Figure 16 shows the speedup (normalized to baseline) for four systems: the baseline 8GB system with all memory in HDPCM mode, an iso-area system that has 4GB memory all in LLPCM mode, the proposed MMS system with 8GB morphable memory, and a system that has 8GB all in LLPCM mode. Note that the 8GB LLPCM system requires 2x the area as the other three systems and it serves as an upper bound on the speedup possible with MMS. The bar labeled *Gmean* is the geometric mean over all the workloads.

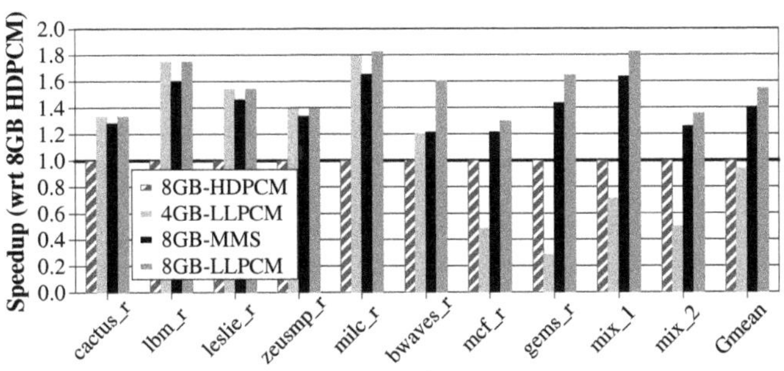

Figure 16: Speedup of MMS with respect to other systems

Neither 8GB HDPCM nor 4GB LLPCM works well across all workloads. For the first five workloads, latency is more important than capacity, hence they show significant improvement with the 4GB LLPCM system. BWaves has phases where sometimes it is latency sensitive and sometimes capacity sensitive. Four workloads, mcf_r, gems_r, mix_1, and mix_2, are capacity intensive and see significant degradation in performance with 4GB LLPCM system. Thus, simply using HDPCM memory instead of LLPCM memory does not provide significant overall improvement. MMS dynamically changes memory mode between LLPCM and HDPCM depending on application demand and provides an average speedup of 1.4x, which is significantly compared to the 1.54x possible with the upper-bound system.[5]

7.2 Memory Accesses from LLPCM

MMS divides memory into LLPCM and HDPCM regions. Ideally we would like to have almost all the accesses satisfied from the LLPCM region, as that mode of operation has lower latency and is expected to have better endurance and energy-efficiency. Figure 17 shows the percentage of hits serviced in the LLPCM mode with MMS. The data is separated in terms of read accesses, write backs from DRAM cache, and overall accesses. The bar labeled *Amean* represents the arithmetic mean measured over all workloads.

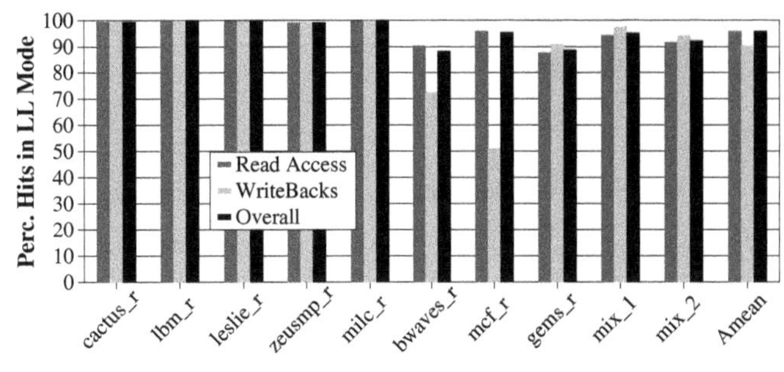

Figure 17: Percentage of accesses serviced from LLPCM

The first five workloads are not capacity sensitive and almost all of the read and write requests are satisfied in LLPCM mode. For capacity sensitive workloads (next five) almost 90% of the accesses are satisfied in LLPCM mode. The writeback stream in mcf_r has poor locality hence only half of the write-backs hit in LLPCM mode. However, mcf has negligible writeback traffic ($\approx$1% of all accesses). Overall, on average, 90% of the writebacks and 95% of read requests are satisfied in LLPCM mode. These benefits come at a small overhead of $<$ 4 transfers between HDPCM and LLPCM, every 1000 memory accesses.

Energy Implications: Satisfying more than 90% of the accesses in LLPCM mode also means that energy consumption of the MMS system would be much closer to LLPCM rather than HDPCM. The exact energy savings between the two modes is a function of bits/cell in each mode and the ADC technology.

Lifetime Implications: Studies in Flash domain have shown MLC devices to have 10x lower endurance than SLC devices [22], indicating significant room for lifetime improvement. MMS enhances lifetime significantly compared to naively using MLC-PCM. For example, if SLC-PCM has endurance of 10^8 writes and MLC-PCM has lifetime of 10^7 writes , then the effective endurance with MMS would be approximately $0.9 \cdot 10^8$ writes, if 90% of the writes were satisfied in SLC-PCM mode.

Write Bandwidth Implications: MLC PCM is expected to suffer from poor write bandwidth. MMS fundamentally solves this problem by satisfying 90% of the writes in LLPCM (SLC) mode (no iterative writes). Since MMS satisfies most of the writes from SLC, the effective write bandwidth is much closer to SLC. For example, if SLC write bandwidth = 5 units, and MLC=1 units, then with MMS the write bandwidth is approximately equal to 4.6 $(0.9 \cdot 5 + 0.1 \cdot 1)$ units.

[5] We also evaluated the overall performance improvement on other metrics as well and got similar results. MMS obtained an average improvement of 38.4% on weighted speedup metric [19] compared to 53.5% possible with upper-bound system. MMS obtained an average improvement of 38% on hmean-fairness metric [11] compared to 53% possible with upper-bound system.

7.3 Dynamic Memory Capacity with MMS

Figure 18 shows the effective memory capacity when MMS is enabled, averaged over the entire execution. The first five workloads have close to 50% capacity, meaning almost all memory is in LLPCM mode. For the other five workloads, memory capacity gets extended to fit the working set each of the workload.

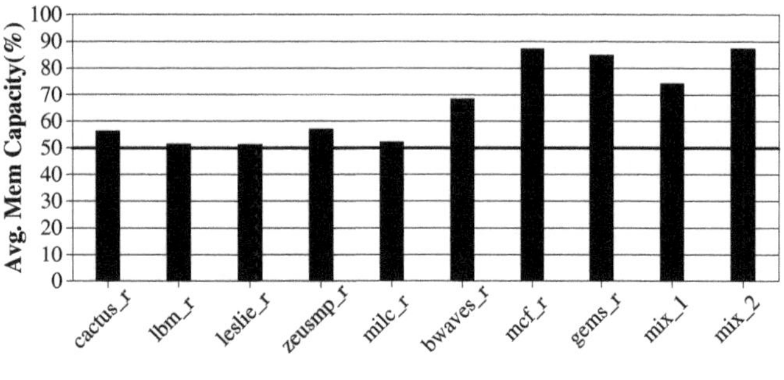

Figure 18: Average memory capacity with MMS

The average capacity statistics do not capture the dynamic variation in memory demand of workloads. Figure 19 shows the dynamic capacity with MMS, for bwaves_r and mcf_r. The data is obtained by sampling the system once every one billion instructions. BWaves has phases of execution where the working set increases close to full capacity, and MMS responds to this demand by increasing the available memory capacity. Other workloads, such as mcf_r, have a regular demand for memory capacity and hence a constant memory capacity with MMS, after the initial period.

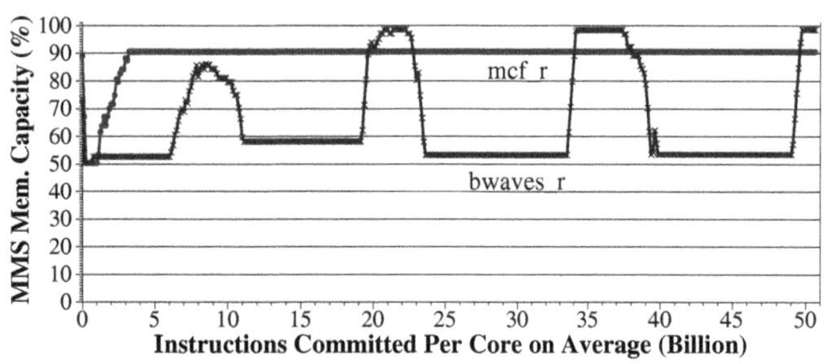

Figure 19: Phase behavior of bwaves_r and mcf_r with MMS

We also evaluated equal cell-capacity Static Memory System (SMS) that statically partitions between LLPCM and HDPCM. However, our baseline already has a relatively large (3.25% of memory-capacity) DRAM cache so a small partition of LLPCM does not help. If LLPCM partition is made large (25%) then it hurts workloads which need more (>75%) memory capacity. As MMS can adapt to variation in memory capacity demand, MMS is much more robust and effective than SMS.

7.4 Page Fault Rate

MMS tries to modulate the capacity of the system in response to the workload. If the workload gets less capacity than required, it would result in increased page fault rate. Figure 20 shows the page faults of 4GB LLPCM system and 8GB MMS system normalized to 8GB HDPCM baseline. For gems_r and mcf_r, the 4GB system has significantly increased page fault at 4GB, whereas MMS has page fault similar to baseline. For bwaves_r, the transitions in demand causes page fault rate to increase with MMS when capacity increases from 50% to 90%. Whereas, the 8GB baseline could accommodate the entire working set of bwaves_r at all times. On average, the number of page faults with MMS (1.3x) is much closer to the 8GB baseline system, as compared to the 4GB system (4.6x).

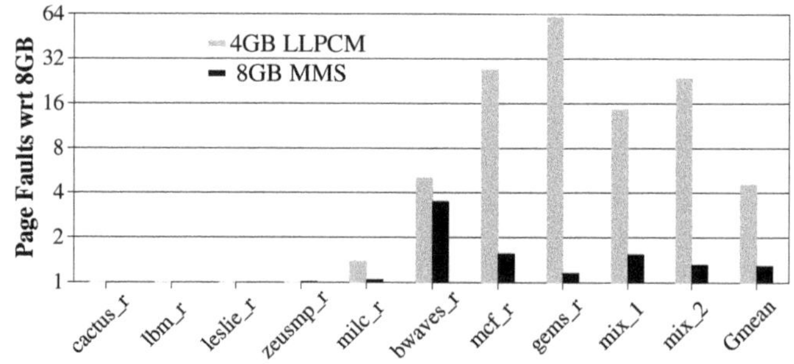

Figure 20: Normalized Page Fault Rate (Y axis in log scale)

8. RELATED WORK

In our work, we have exploited the observation that memory capacity demand varies at runtime. Therefore, a transient excess memory capacity can be used to improve performance by converting the memory from high-density mode to low-latency mode. Lim et al. [6] also showed that memory demand can vary even within the same application for workloads such as TPCC-H and proposed using memory blades to efficiently share capacity between multiple blade systems. Note that the overall capacity of the entire system still remains constant in their solution, and their solution is not geared towards improving hit latency of memory.

Kgil et al. [7] proposed dynamically downgrading MLC pages to SLC pages for Flash-based disk cache when the page nears its lifetime, thereby increasing the overall lifetime of the system. The concept of dynamically choosing between single level cells and multi-level cells for Flash storage was proposed in [9]. Note that managing storage vs. managing main memory are fundamentally different in that data from storage cannot be evicted by controller just to improve performance, whereas in main memory unused resident pages can be evicted to improve overall performance. FlexFS [9] leverages only unused portion (that does not store any data) of Flash storage for improving latency. It typically takes users several months or years to fill up an SSD, so leveraging unused portions for latency optimizations is acceptable in that domain. However, in our case, main memory typically fills up in minutes, so relying only on unused portion is not a viable option. Furthermore, FlexFS does not need to the estimate dynamically varying capacity demand. Whereas, the demand for main memory capacity changes frequently, and hence requires a dynamic mechanism to determine the optimal partition between fast region and high density region.

MMS tries to reduce memory latency by trading off memory capacity. A converse approach is to exploit redundancy in data stored in memory to increase capacity, albeit at higher latency. Both memory compression and MMS require similar support from OS to handle the dynamically changing memory capacity and to reduce or increase balloon pages [2] to control effective memory size. However, these two approaches are fundamentally different in that compression is dependent on data values and not on demand. It cannot be used to reduce the latency for memory hits. These two approaches are orthogonal and can be combined.

We have proposed a hardware managed MMS, where the hardware regulates which pages are in LLPCM mode and which pages are in HDPCM mode. MMS can also be implemented completely as a software module within the OS. In such a case, the OS can divide memory into two regions, and use dynamic page remapping [10] to upgrade frequently accessed page from HDPCM region to LLPCM region. Such a technique obviates the PRT-based indirection of MMS, but requires monitoring usage of each page and performing the upgrades and downgrades in software, which incurs significant performance overhead.

9. SUMMARY

The demand for main memory capacity and the scaling challenges of DRAM call for architects to look towards exploiting other emerging technologies that are expected to be more scalable. Phase Change Memory (PCM) has emerged as a promising technology that has better scalability than DRAM. One of the ways PCM devices are expected to improve density is by packing multiple bits per cell. While such Multi-Level Cells (MLC) have better density they have much higher read latency, reduced lifetime, and higher energy compared to cells that store one bit. Ideally we would like to have the capacity of MLC while having the latency, lifetime, and energy of SLC devices. To this end, our paper exploits the fact that typical applications do not use all the available memory capacity, and makes the following contributions:

1. We propose an adaptive infrastructure, *Morphable Memory System (MMS)* that can dynamically partition the memory into high-density pages and low-latency pages. MMS leverages morphable PCM cells that can be programmed to be in either high-density mode or low-latency mode.
2. We propose a cost-effective runtime mechanism to determine the best partition between high-density region and low-latency region in MMS. This mechanism uses stack distance histogram analysis and sampling to estimate the best partition, while incurring a total storage overhead of less than 4KB.
3. We provide the hardware-software interface for the OS to handle dynamically varying memory capacity. The OS uses the information from the monitoring circuit to regulate memory capacity in order to free up a given number of pages for low latency access.

We evaluate the MMS system using a kernel as well as ten workloads on a system with 8GB of main memory consisting of MLC PCM cells. Our evaluations show that on average MMS satisfies 95% of the read requests and 90% of the writebacks from the low latency region, while keeping the overall page fault rate close to the 8GB system. On average, MMS provides a performance improvement of 40%, bridging three-fourth of the performance difference between SLC and MLC PCM devices.

We believe an architecture such as MMS will be crucial in incorporating technologies that present a trade-off between density and latency, and can be morphed dynamically. In this work, we restricted morphing to two levels, in which one of the level has half the density of the other. A more generalized structure that allows any number of levels without restrictions can also be architected. In our proposal we optimized the partition based on performance, other partitioning algorithms better suited to optimize lifetime or energy can also be investigated. Furthermore, wear leveling algorithms better suited to morphable memory structures can be developed. Exploring such extensions is a part of our future work.

Acknowledgments

We thank Bulent Abali, Basil Smith, and Vijayalakshmi Srinivasan for discussions and feedback during this work.

10. REFERENCES

[1] *International Technology Roadmap for Semiconductors, ITRS 2008 Update*. http://www.itrs.net/Links/2008ITRS/Home2008.htm.

[2] B. Abali et al. Hardware compressed main memory: Operating system support and performance evaluation. *IEEE Trans. Comput.*, 50(11):1219–1233, 2001.

[3] Analog Devices Inc. *Data Conversion Handbook*.

[4] F. Bedeschi et al. A bipolar-selected phase change memory featuring multi-level cell storage. *IEEE Journal of Solid-State Circuits*, 44(1):217–227, 2009.

[5] T. Cho et al. A dual-mode NAND flash memory: 1-Gb multilevel and high-performance 512-Mb single-level modes. *IEEE Journal of Solid-State Circuits*, 36(11), 2001.

[6] L. Kevin et al. Disaggregated memory for expansion and sharing in blade servers. In *ISCA-36*, pages 267–278, 2009.

[7] T. Kgil, D. Roberts, and T. Mudge. Improving nand flash based disk caches. In *ISCA-35*, 2008.

[8] B. Lee et al. Architecting Phase Change Memory as a Scalable DRAM Alternative. In *ISCA-36*, 2009.

[9] S. Lee et al. FlexFS: A Flexible Flash File System for MLC NAND Flash Memory. In *USENIX '09*, 2009.

[10] J. Lin et al. Gaining insights into multicore cache partitioning: Bridging the gap between simulation and real systems. In *HPCA-14*, 2008.

[11] K. Luo et al. Balancing throughput and fairness in SMT processors. In *ISPASS-2001*.

[12] R. L. Mattson et al. Evaluation techniques in storage hierarchies. *IBM Journal of Research and Development*, 9(2):78–117, 1970.

[13] T. Nirschl et al. Write strategies for 2 and 4-bit multi-level phase-change memory. In *Proceedings of the IEEE International Electron Devices Meeting*, 2007.

[14] M. Qureshi et al. Scalable high performance main memory system using phase-change memory technology. In *ISCA-36*, 2009.

[15] M. K. Qureshi et al. Improving read performance of phase change memories via write cancellation and write pausing. In *HPCA-16*, 2010.

[16] M. K. Qureshi and Y. N. Patt. Utility-based cache partitioning: A low-overhead, high-performance, runtime mechanism to partition shared caches. In *MICRO-39*, 2006.

[17] S. Raoux et al. Phase-change random access memory: A scalable technology. *IBM Journal of R. and D.*, 52(4/5):465–479, 2008.

[18] B. Razavi. *Principles of data conversion system design*. Wiley-IEEE Press., New York, 1995.

[19] A. Snavely, D. M. Tullsen, and G. Voelker. Symbiotic jobscheduling with priorities for a simultaneous multithreading processor. In *SIGMETRICS-2002*.

[20] The Standard Performance Evaluation Corporation. *Requirements of SPEC CPU 2006*. http://www.spec.org/cpu2006/Docs/system-requirements.html.

[21] G. E. Suh et al. A new memory monitoring scheme for memory-aware scheduling and partitioning. In *HPCA-8*, 2002.

[22] J. Thatcher et al. Nand flash solid state storage for the enterprise: An in-depth look at reliability. Solid State Storage Initiative (SNIA), 2009.

[23] C. A. Waldspurger. Memory resource management in VMware ESX server. *SIGOPS Oper. Syst. Rev.*, 36(SI):181–194, 2002.

[24] P. Zhou et al. Dynamic tracking of page miss ratio curve for memory management. In *ASPLOS-XI*, 2004.

[25] P. Zhou, B. Zhao, J. Yang, and Y. Zhang. A durable and energy efficient main memory using phase change memory technology. In *ISCA-36*, 2009.

SieveStore: A Highly-Selective, Ensemble-level Disk Cache for Cost-Performance

Timothy Pritchett
School of Electrical and Computer Engineering
Purdue University
tpritche@purdue.edu

Mithuna Thottethodi
School of Electrical and Computer Engineering
Purdue University
mithuna@purdue.edu

ABSTRACT

Emerging solid-state storage media can significantly improve storage performance and energy. However, the high cost-per-byte of solid-state media has hindered wide-spread adoption in servers. This paper proposes a new, cost-effective architecture – SieveStore– which enables the use of solid-state media to significantly filter access to storage ensembles. Our paper makes three key contributions. First, we make a case for highly-selective, storage-ensemble-level disk-block caching based on the highly-skewed block popularity distribution and based on the dynamic nature of the popular block set. Second, we identify the problem of *allocation-writes* and show that selective cache allocation to reduce allocation-writes – *sieving* – is fundamental to enable efficient ensemble-level disk-caching. Third, we propose two practical variants of SieveStore. Based on week-long block-access traces from a storage ensemble of 13 servers, we find that the two components (sieving and ensemble-level caching) each contribute to SieveStore's cost-effectiveness. Compared to unsieved, ensemble-level disk-caches, SieveStore achieves significantly higher hit ratios (35%-50% more, on average) while using only $1/7^{th}$ the number of SSD drives. Further, ensemble-level caching is strictly better in cost-performance compared to per-server caching.

Categories and Subject Descriptors

D.4.2 [**Operating Systems**]: Storage Management—Storage hierarchies

General Terms

Design, Performance

1. INTRODUCTION

The storage layer is a significant factor in the capital cost, operating cost (energy), and performance of servers and data-centers. Emerging high-performance, low-energy, non-volatile, solid-state storage media (e.g., flash-based memory, phase-change memory) show enormous promise to solve two of the three problems (storage performance and energy); but cost remains a concern. Recent work has examined several ways to use flash-based solid-state media; as a buffer-cache [11, 10], as swap space for virtual memory [19], and as the storage component of custom-architectures [3]. Further, there has also been research on the organization of solid-state drives (SSDs) for improved performance [4, 7]. However, in spite of the many advances and significantly higher performance of solid-state drives (SSDs), the high cost-per-byte of solid-state media has hindered wide-spread adoption in servers. Per-server SSD deployment incurs excessive cost for modest performance improvements. To enable servers to benefit from high-performance SSDs, we propose a highly-selective, ensemble-level disk cache – SieveStore– which represents a superior cost-performance point. SieveStore enables the use of a small amount of solid-state media (~16GB-32GB, thus reducing cost) to serve a significant fraction of accesses (thus improving performance) to larger storage ensembles that support several servers (e.g., 10+ servers, 5-10 TB total capacity, 1.5TB-2.5TB daily accesses).

SieveStore's architecture is based on the following two key observations from analysis of storage access traces of an ensemble of 13 servers over a week [14, 15].

(O1) A very small fraction (~1%) of "popular" blocks accessed each day account for a significant fraction of accesses (between 14%-53%). Beyond the top 1% of blocks, the number of accesses per block diminishes rapidly. For example, 99% of all blocks accessed in a day see 10 or fewer accesses. The least popular 97% of all blocks accessed in a day see 4 or fewer accesses. This is not surprising because the buffer caches in memory filter out most reuse leaving very little reuse at the block device layer.

(O2) Though the degree of skew for the ensemble as a whole remains invariant (i.e., not much reuse beyond the top 1% popular blocks), the distribution of the popular blocks varies across servers, across storage volumes of the same server and over time.

Per-server disk-caches incur high cost, and may also perform poorly because the disk-cache capacity associated with servers that have few hot blocks cannot be shared by the hot blocks of other servers. In contrast, a small, shared, ensemble-level disk-cache of the popular blocks would be better because (1) the combination of small and shared capacity keeps costs low and (2) the cache would capture the popular blocks (via temporal locality) as well as the dynamic changes in the popular block set (by dynamically sharing cache space).

However, while the costs of a small, shared disk-cache are indeed low, achieving high performance is challenging

ISCA'10, June 19–23, 2010, Saint-Malo, France.

because conventional disk-cache allocation policies such as *allocate-on-demand (AOD)*, which allocates on a miss, and *write-no-allocate (WMNA)*, which allocates only on read misses, will result in poor performance because of three problems. First, because a large number of blocks have little reuse (O1), a large fraction of accesses will be misses, each of which will allocate and write a block in the cache (*allocation-writes*). Because the cache uses write-asymmetric storage media like flash-based SSDs, where writes are significantly slower than reads, such allocation-writes can have a significant impact on performance. Second, the large number of low-reuse blocks can cause cache pollution, reducing the hit ratio. Third, aggregating the hot blocks of several servers in a single disk cache may create a bandwidth bottleneck.

To avoid the cost of allocation-writes (the first problem), SieveStore uses selective cache allocation policies that aim to reduce allocation writes while improving the hit-ratio – *sieving*. One may think that sieving is simply an alternate way to perform the same function as the replacement policy (i.e., modulate the contents of the cache). However, while they may both be used to control the contents of the cache (and hence the hit-ratios), only sieving can limit allocation-writes caused by misses to low-reuse data. We show in Section 3.1 that, in the absence of sieving, even an ideal (oracle) replacement policy will not achieve significant performance improvement. We also show that using selective allocation to maximize hits does not necessarily minimize allocation-writes.

Sieving, if done accurately to capture the popular blocks, avoids the problem of cache pollution (the second problem). However, correctly identifying popular blocks poses a challenge that conventional caches do not face. Conventional caches that use unsieved allocation (i.e., AOD or WMNA) maintain metastate for only those blocks that are present in the cache because the allocation decision depends only on the current state of the cache (hit/miss) and the type of the request (read/write). In contrast, sieving fundamentally requires us to maintain state for many blocks that are *not* present in the cache. We propose two practical sieving variants that differ in how they identify popular blocks and in how they maintain metastate.

The first approach is an offline, discrete-allocation variant – SieveStore-D – which enforces selectivity using an *access-count based discrete batch-allocation (ADBA)* mechanism. SieveStore-D maintains precise metastate, by logging each access, and periodically combines the metastate in an offline pass. Blocks are allocated a frame only if their access count in an epoch exceeds a threshold. The second approach is an online, continuous allocation variant – SieveStore-C – which sieves accesses using a *hysteresis-based, lazy cache allocation* mechanism wherein disk blocks are allocated a frame on the nth (for some threshold n) miss over a recent time window. To minimize the metastate of uncached blocks, SieveStore-C uses a two-tier structure; a preliminary tier that sieves with imprecise (potentially aliased) metastate, followed by an accurate tier to maintain quality of sieving.

Finally, in spite of aggregating the hot blocks of several servers in a single cache, SieveStore can handle the increased traffic, partly because SSDs that are currently in the market offer significantly higher I/O throughput (IOPS), and partly because correlated I/O bursts across independent servers in the ensemble are rare [14]. Both variants of SieveStore can handle the increased traffic with only one enterprise-class SSD over 99.9% of the time and with two SSDs 100% of the time. Further, without any special effort on the part of SieveStore to limit writes, there are no SSD wearout/lifetime problems even though SieveStore caches write-hot blocks as well.

	Sieved	Unsieved
Ensemble-Level	SieveStore-C SieveStore-D	II
Per-Server	III	IV

Figure 1: Design space

Implementation and Overheads: A SieveStore implementation can be realized as a transparent appliance (with processor, memory, SSD drives) that plugs in to existing storage ensembles at a data-center. The minimal cost of the one additional box for a small data-center has to be weighed against the benefit of significant reduction in accesses to the storage ensemble.

In summary, the major contributions of this paper are:

- Driven by our observations of (1) extreme popularity skew in real storage traces, and (2) dynamic changes in the popular block sets, we propose SieveStore – a highly-selective, ensemble-level disk-cache.
- We identify *sieving* – selective cache-allocation to reduce allocation-writes while improving the hit ratio – as a fundamental mechanism to enable cost-effective, ensemble-level disk-caching.
- We propose two variants of SieveStore – one with discrete sieving (SieveStore-D), and another with continuous sieving (SieveStore-C).

The two key ideas proposed in this paper – ensemble-level disk caching and sieving – can be applied independently of each other. Consider the quadrants in the design space, as shown in Figure 1. To show that SieveStore, which combines both the ideas (i.e., quadrant *I* in Figure 1), is a superior cost-performance design point, we evaluate SieveStore against other quadrants using traces of a storage-ensemble of 13 servers over a week. Our key results are:

- SieveStore-D and SieveStore-C, which lie in quadrant *I*, capture 35% and 50%, respectively, more accesses than the best unsieved ensemble-level disk-cache (quadrant *II*) while requiring $(1/7)^{th}$ the number of SSD drives.
- Both variants of SieveStore, due to to their ensemble-level caching approach, capture more accesses at the same cost (and the same number of accesses at lower cost) than an ideal per-server cache (quadrants *III* and *IV*), which is not surprising given the dynamic nature of popular blocks (O2).

The rest of the paper is organized as follows. Section 2 analyzes the traces to support our observations. Section 3 describes the two SieveStore variants. Section 4 describes our evaluation methodology. Section 5 discusses experimental results. Related work is described in Section 6. Section 7 briefly discusses some forward-looking issues on scaling and tuning. Finally, Section 8 concludes this paper.

Table 1: Trace Summary (from [14, 15])

Key	Name	Vol-umes	Spindles	Size (GB)
Usr	User home dirs	3	16	1367
Proj	Project dirs	5	44	2094
Prn	Print server	2	6	452
Hm	Hardware monitor	2	6	39
Rsrch	Research projects	3	24	277
Prxy	Web proxy	2	4	89
Src1	Source control	3	12	555
Src2	Source control	3	14	355
Stg	Web staging	2	6	113
Ts	Terminal server	1	2	22
Web	Web/SQL server	4	17	441
Mds	Media server	2	16	509
Wdev	Test web server	4	12	136
	Total	36	179	6449

2. STORAGE ENSEMBLE ACCESS CHARACTERISTICS

We analyze storage ensemble behavior using traces from [14]. The traces capture requests to block devices below the buffer cache, and are typical of small/medium datacenters. Table 1 reproduces the key trace characteristics (reproduced from [14]). The traces span eight calendar days for each server although the trace length is for seven days because trace collection started at 5:00pm GMT on the first day. We analyze all traces on a calendar day basis, so we treat it as an 8-day trace.

Popularity Skew.

For each day of the trace, we sort the blocks in descending order of popularity and group them into 10,000 bins such that each bin contains 0.01% ($=1/10,000$) of all blocks accessed on that day. Figure 2(a) plots the average access count of each bin (Y-axis, log-scale) against the percentile rank of the bin (X-axis, log-scale) with one curve for each day. For example, the vertical line at 1% corresponds to the 100th bin of blocks which is at the top first percentile in popularity. Though the most popular 0.01th percentile bin of blocks have an average of over 1000 accesses on each day, the bin at the top 1st percentile, averages fewer than 10 accesses per day. Further, because the averages at the top 1st percentile do not hide any large variations within the bin, the maximum number of accesses (not shown) is also 10 on all days except on day 2 when it is 11. Similarly, when we exclude the top 3%, blocks have fewer than 4 accesses on average. Below the 50th percentile, blocks that are accessed are never reused.

To illustrate the fraction of accesses the popular blocks account for Figure 2(b) plots for each bin (shown in ranked percentile order on the X-axis), the cumulative fraction of accesses (Y-axis) for all bins that are at higher percentiles. Because the knee of the curve occurs close to the very top 1st percentile, we show a zoomed in graph of the same data but limit the X-axis to the top 5% most popular blocks in Figure 2(c). The knee-of the curve occurs at less than 1% of blocks accessed on any given day. Though the amount of data accessed in a day varies from a minimum of 335 GB to a maximum of 1190 GB (685GB/day, on average) for the ensemble, the most popular 1% of blocks is significantly smaller (at most 11.9GB) and would fit comfortably within a modest 16-32GB SSD with room to spare.

Note, day 1's accesses are an outlier because of our decision to use traces partitioned by calendar days.

Popularity Skew Variation.

While the above analysis considered the trace of the entire storage ensemble, it is important to understand whether the observed popularity skew is truly a property that emerges at the ensemble-level even though that behavior may not be uniformly present in the traces of individual servers, or if the same behavior is also observable at the individual server level. If each server's accesses exhibits the same skewed behavior, then the per-server caching approach (quadrants III and IV from Figure 1) might be attractive (ignoring minimum drive sizes). If, on the other hand, there is significant variation in behavior at the individual server level, then an ensemble-level approach (quadrants I and II) may be well-motivated.

Our trace analysis (Figure 3) reveals that the popularity skew behavior exhibits significant variation across servers, across storage volumes of the same server and across time for the same server. Figure 3(a), which plots the cumulative access distribution (Y-axis) for block bins (in sorted, descending order of access count on the X-axis) from the proxy server (Prxy) and the source control server (Src1), illustrates server-to-server variation in popularity skew. The proxy server exhibits popularity skew with a small fraction of blocks accounting for nearly all of the days accesses. On the other hand, the source control server's near-linear cumulative access count shows that the popularity skew is minimal. Figure 3(b) uses similar axes with curves for individual storage volumes within a single server (Web, volumes 0 and 1) to compare the access characteristics of storage volumes within a server. While both volumes exhibit some degree of skew for the most popular blocks, volume-0 exhibits significantly more skew than volume-1. Even within the same server the popularity skew may vary in time as shown in Figure 3(c). For the web staging server (Stg), day 5 exhibits significant popularity skew, but day 3 does not.

Finally, returning to the ensemble trace, Figure 3(d) plots the composition of the most popular 1% of blocks in the ensemble in terms of what fraction is contributed by each server (Y-axis) for each day of the trace (X-axis). The variation in contribution from each server demonstrates time-varying behavior that no statically (potentially unequally) partitioned per-server cache can capture.

Summary.

Trace analysis reveals that there is significant variation in popularity skew across servers, within servers across storage volumes, and in time for the same server. Despite such variation, the aggregate trace of the whole ensemble exhibits stable emergent behavior wherein the most-accessed 1% of blocks account for a large fraction of total accesses. The next section examines how this observation may be exploited to improve storage.

3. SieveStore

The goal of SieveStore is to capture the top 1% most popular blocks of the storage ensemble in an SSD cache to achieve cost-effective storage acceleration. There are two ways to modulate the contents of a cache to ensure that it holds the desirable blocks; either by controlling who gets in (allocation

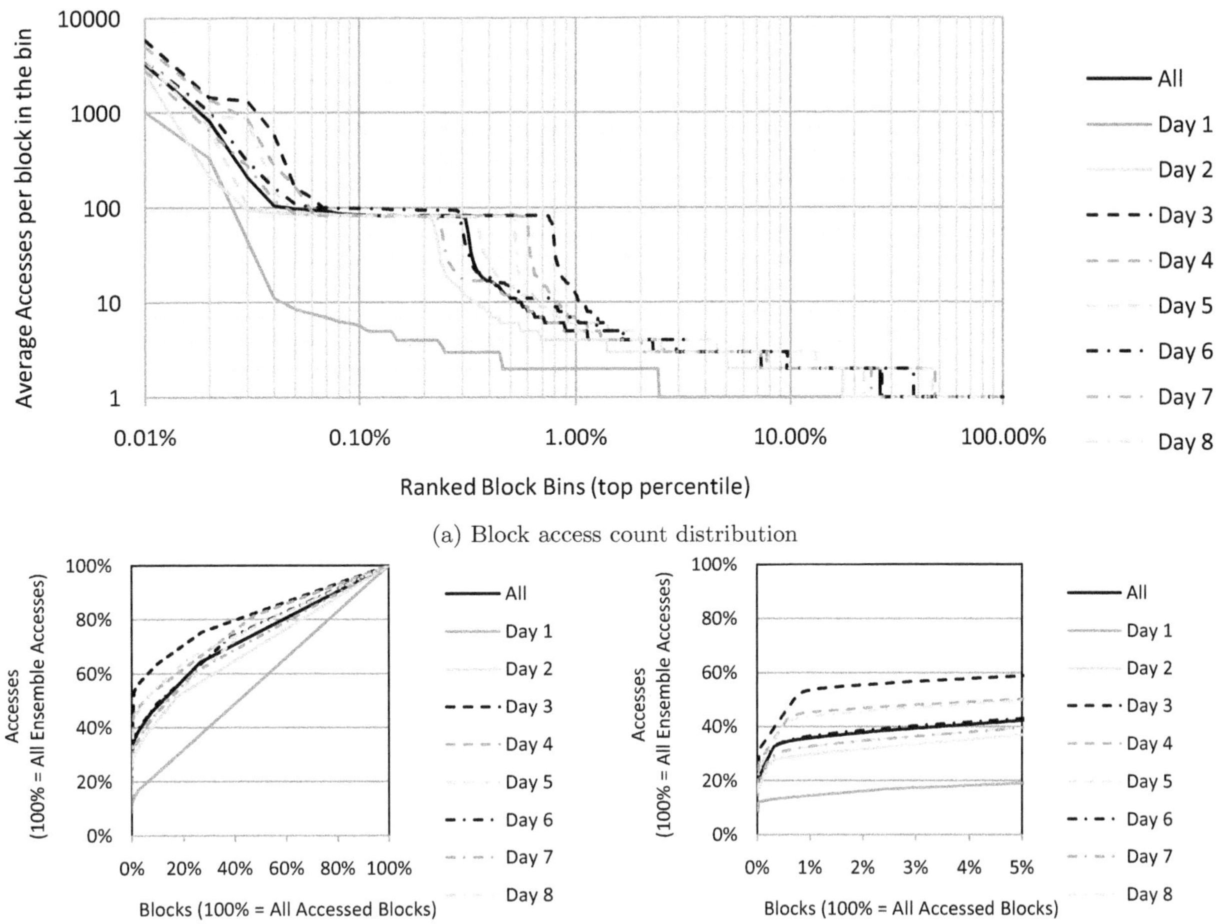

(a) Block access count distribution

(b) Block popularity (CDF)

(c) Zoomed-in CDF for Top 5th percentile

Figure 2: Popularity Skew Characterization

policy) or by controlling who gets evicted (replacement policy). One of the claims in this paper is that disk-caching at the ensemble-level fundamentally requires selective cache allocation to prevent low-reuse blocks from entering the cache. Section 3.1 uses a thought-experiment to justify the above claim by showing that (1) in the absence of sieving, even an ideal (oracle) replacement policy will not achieve significant performance improvement and (2) an ideal (but impractical) sieve offers significant benefits. We also show that performing selective allocation solely to maximize hits is inadequate to control the number of allocation-writes. Section 3.2 and Section 3.3 describe our two practical sieve implementations that capture most of the benefits of the ideal (impractical) sieve.

3.1 The case for sieving

Consider an oracle-replacement algorithm that magically evicts only those blocks that are not in the top 1% frequently accessed blocks on each day. Narayanan *et.al.* consider a similar oracle-replacement algorithm called LTR (Long-term Random; a policy that retains frequently accessed blocks over the long-term) at the per-server level [15]. (Note, the above oracle policy is not the same Belady's MIN/OPT oracle replacement algorithm [2] which replaces the block which is accessed farthest out in the future. We discuss MIN briefly at the end of this section.)

To isolate the cost of allocation-writes from that of misses, we conservatively assume that using the above-defined ideal (oracle) replacement policies can ensure that the top 1% of blocks are always cache-resident for both on-demand allocation (AOD) and the write-miss no-allocate (WMNA) allocation policies. We can now compare the number of allocation writes for each of the allocation policies, as compared to an ideal selective allocation policy (distinct from the ideal replacement policy). For AOD, each access (hit or miss) causes an SSD operation with a (slow) allocation-write operation for each miss. Table 2 computes the number of writes assuming a hit rate of 35% (the approximate average hit-rate for the ideal-allocation scheme over all eight calendar days), and assuming a 3:1 ratio of reads and writes in both hits and misses. The mechanism will cause 73.75% of all ensemble accesses to initiate writes to a single SSD (see first row, Table 2). The number of SSD operations increase from 35% (hits only) to 100% (all accesses), a large fraction of which are slow writes (73.75%).

With the WMNA allocation policy and the oracle replacement policy (second row of Table 2), while the hit-ratio remains unchanged, allocation-writes are avoided on write misses. (Note, changing allocation policies does affect the

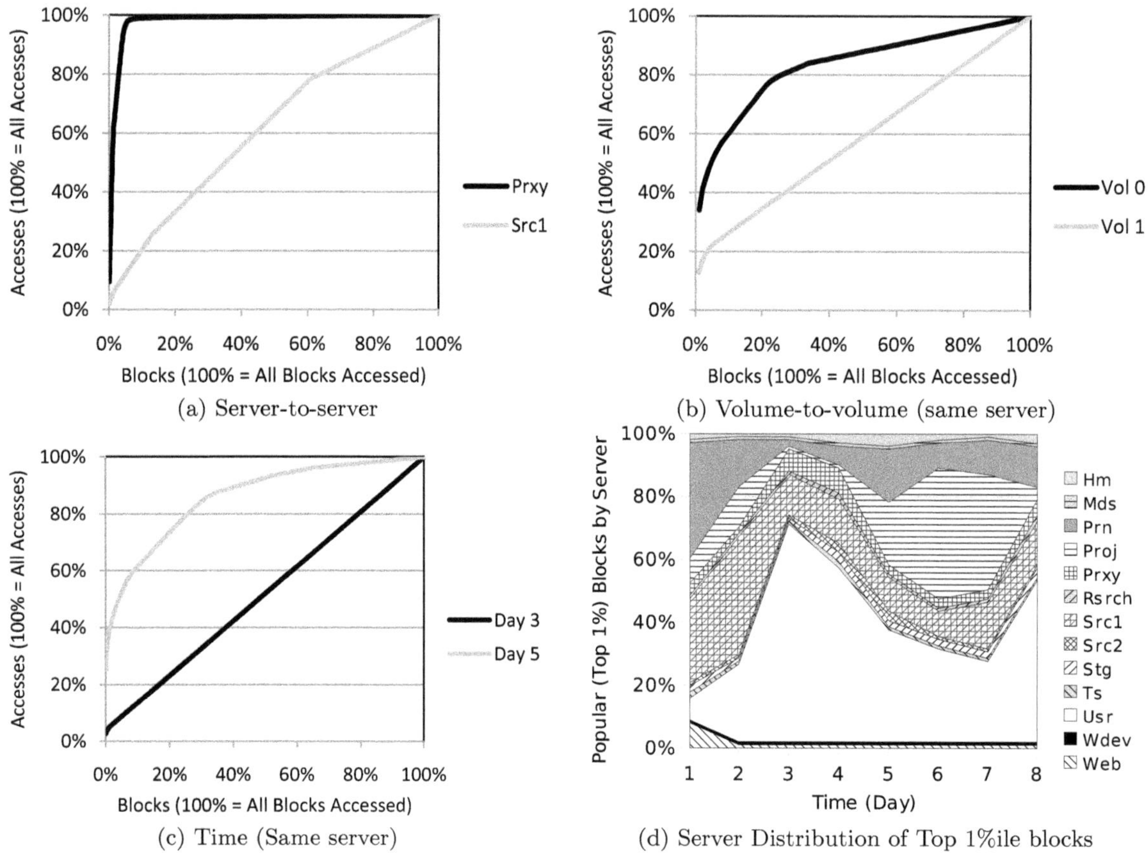

(a) Server-to-server
(b) Volume-to-volume (same server)
(c) Time (Same server)
(d) Server Distribution of Top 1%ile blocks

Figure 3: Popularity skew variation

hit-ratio. However, because of our assumption that the oracle policy ensures that the most popular 1% of blocks always remains cache-resident, we conservatively assume the same hit rate.) Allocation writes will account for 48.75% (read misses $= (1 - 35\%) \times 3/4$) of all the accesses, which results in (1) more than doubling the number of SSD operations (2.4X), and (2) increasing the number of SSD writes by a factor of 5.6X. In contrast, the ideal allocation cache causes exactly 1% of accessed blocks to result in allocation-writes to bring in the top 1% of blocks. Note, the number of allocation-writes is 1% of the number of unique blocks accessed which is smaller than 1% of the accesses (and hence written as ϵ% in the last row of Table 2).

To extend the analysis to Belady's MIN algorithm, (assuming AOD allocation, as in the original paper) we attain bounds on the number of allocation-writes in terms of number of unique blocks (as opposed to number of accesses used in Table 2). Recall from Figure 2(a) that 50% of the blocks have at most 1 access and that the next 47% of blocks have 4 or fewer accesses, which implies that 97% of blocks will incur a minimum of 50% + 47%/4 = 61.75% compulsory misses, and hence allocation-writes. Note, in comparison that ideal sieving requires only 1% of blocks to be allocated.

Finally, we show that extending Belady's replacement algorithm to do selective allocation does not necessarily minimize allocation-writes. Such an extension would allocate a block only if the block's next use is earlier than the next use of at least one of the blocks in the cache. However, while such an extension will maximize the number of hits, it is not guaranteed to minimize allocation-writes. A simple example can be constructed using a 1-entry cache and the address stream `a,a,b,b,a,a,c,c,a,a,d,d,a,a,e,e,...` and so on. Belady's selective allocation would allocate blocks in `a,b,a,c,a,d,a,e,...` order with the long term hit ratio converging to 50%. Effectively, each miss causes an allocation because the block has an immediate use after that miss, resulting in 50% of accesses causing allocation-writes. In contrast, using a fixed allocation for the address `a` captures nearly the same number of hits in the long-term (nearly 50%) while also minimizing the allocation-writes to exactly 1.

While the above discussion proved that ideal sieving is effective in reducing the number of SSD write operations, ideal sieving is impractical. In the next two sections, we present two practical variants of SieveStore.

3.2 Discrete SieveStore (SieveStore-D)

SieveStore-D employs a discrete caching model wherein allocation and replacement occur in batches at discrete epoch boundaries. All blocks selected by SieveStore-D's sieving mechanism at the end of the ith epoch are batch-allocated to the cache where they remain (i.e., no replacement) till the end of the $(i+1)^{th}$ epoch. Logically, each resident block is replaced at the end of the epoch and is replaced by the newly allocated blocks. In practice, if a block that is to be replaced at the end of an epoch is found to be allocated for the next epoch, the replacement and allocation cancel each other to eliminate unnecessary block moves.

SieveStore-D uses access counts to sieve cache allocation in the following way. All blocks whose access-count in the

Table 2: Impact of Allocation Policies (assuming oracle replacement policy)

Allocation Policy	Hits	Misses	Alloc.-writes	SSD operations	
				Read hits	Write hits + Alloc.-writes
Allocate-on-demand (AOD)	35%	65%	65%	26.25%	73.75% (=8.75% + 65%)
Write-no-allocate (WMNA)	35%	65%	48.75%	26.25%	57.5% (=8.75%+48.75%)
Ideal-selective-allocate (ISA)	35%	65%	ϵ%	26.25%	<9.75% (=8.75%+ϵ%)

i^{th} epoch exceeds a threshold (t) are selected for allocation at the end of the ith epoch. Our design choice of access-count-based sieving in general, and the choices of the epoch as one day and the threshold $t = 10$ in particular, flow directly from our observation (O1) that 99% of blocks have low (fewer than 10/day) access counts. One may think there is a tension between our claim that the top 1% popular block set is dynamic from day-to-day and SieveStore-D's strategy of using one day's access counts to identify the hot set for the next day (which implies persistence of the hot-set). There is no real contradiction between those claims; while popular sets do drift from day-to-day (with the hot set drifting significantly with increasing time separation), there is significant overlap in successive days.

There are two potential problems that sieving must address. First, SieveStore-D must maintain access-counts for all blocks – even the blocks that are not cache resident. SieveStore-D logs all accesses for offline analysis. The analysis requires simple, per-key reductions to gather counts of all the addresses that are logged to SieveStore-D node's local storage (not the SSD-based disk-cache). Such per-key-reduction can be efficiently implemented by using a map-reduction-like structure where (1) each access is logged as a $< address, 1 >$ tuple to one of R files where the file is selected by a hash-function on the address, and (2) each of the R files are sorted, and (3) contiguous n-long "runs" of the same address are counted and emitted as a $< address, n >$ tuple. Further, such per-key reductions may be periodically performed in an incremental way to reduce the size of the logs. At the end of the epoch, tuples with n value greater than the threshold, are allocated for the next epoch.

Second, because the blocks are allocated at the end of each discrete epoch, the bulk data movement required at the end of each epoch could be a bottleneck. In practice, the movement of allocated data can be staggered by moving data when the periodic analysis of access logs identify the high-access count blocks. We show later in Section 5 that the number of blocks moved is insignificant compared to the number of accesses ($\leq 0.5\%$), and that there are significant periods of slack bandwidth in the SSD where such moves may be scheduled. Consequently, SieveStore-D moves can avoid creating a burst of heavy traffic.

3.3 Continuous SieveStore (SieveStore-C)

SieveStore-D's discrete allocation model limits the rate at which the system can adapt to changes in the hot set. To address that problem, we develop another variant called SieveStore-C. SieveStore-C's sieving is performed in an online fashion where each access is first checked if it is a hit or a miss. If it is a miss, it is further checked if it qualifies for allocation (i.e., sieving). If it does, the block is allocated. If not, the block is accessed directly from the underlying storage ensemble.

SieveStore-C uses hysteresis-based lazy allocation to ensure that only the nth miss of a block in a recent window of time (W) results in an allocation. Such lazy allocation fundamentally requires us to maintain metastate for blocks that are accessed even if the block is not resident in the cache because block-miss-counts must be maintained. Unlike in SieveStore-D's case where the metastate was maintained in files and was never on any access critical path, SieveStore-C's continuous allocation model poses another key challenge: the metastate must be looked up on each miss to determine if the block is to be allocated. Thus the metastate must be memory resident. Unfortunately, because of the large number of unique blocks that are accessed, even assuming a small amount of state per accessed block results in state explosion that makes perfect state tracking infeasible (at least in a cost-effective way).

To address the state explosion problem, SieveStore-C uses a two-tier sieve where the first tier maintains imprecise (potentially aliased) miss-counts and the second tier maintains accurate miss-counts. At the first tier, SieveStore-C uses an *imprecise miss count table (IMCT)* of fixed size. Because the space of block addresses is significantly larger than the size of the IMCT table, the mapping from blocks to entries in the table is many-to-one. Such many-to-one mapping may be prone to aliasing, which results in access counts being inaccurate. Indeed, we found aliasing to be a significant problem because too many blocks with low-reuse were found to be piggy-backing on the miss-counts of more popular blocks and receiving undeserved cache allocations. Such cache allocations cause pollution, and allocation-writes; symptoms that single-tier sieving was not effective.

To address ineffective sieving at the imprecise layer, we employ an additional perfect Miss Count Table (MCT) which is implemented as a hash-table. With the IMCT/MCT two-tier sieve, only blocks that see a minimum number of misses in the IMCT (say threshold t_1) make it past the IMCT to the MCT. However, because IMCT is prone to aliasing, SieveStore-C further requires each block that satisfies the IMCT threshold to undergo a precise MCT threshold check. As part of the MCT check, the block has to further see an additional minimum number of misses (say threshold t_2). The two tier approach worked well in practice because the IMCT reduced the amount of perfect metastate that must be tracked and the MCT reduced the number of low-reuse blocks that are allocated cache space. We experimentally tuned t_1 and t_2 to be 9 and 4, respectively. For the traces, our implementation of IMCT and MCT occupied about 8GB of memory.

One note on the implementation of IMCT and MCT. Logically, the IMCT and MCT track the number of misses over the past W time units (say hours). However, since keeping miss counts for every time slice is impractical, we discretize the time window into k subwindows of W/k hours each. The implementation uses k counters to track the misses in each subwindow and a counter to track the last time the counters were updated. If during a miss, the current time window is larger than the last-updated counter by k or more, then

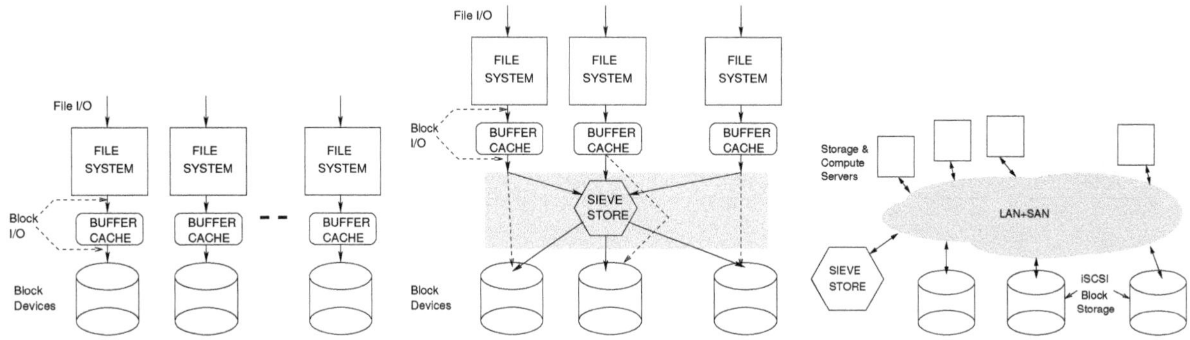

(a) Base storage-ensemble (b) Logical organization (c) Physical organization

Figure 4: SieveStore Organization

all counters are inferred to be stale and zeroed out. Periodically we prune the MCT to eliminate stale blocks. We experimentally tuned the parameters to set W to 8 hours, with k set to 4 (i.e., four subwindows of 2 hours each).

Implementation.

Both SieveStore variants may be implemented as a transparent caching appliance that can easily be deployed in existing storage-area-networks to cover a larger storage ensemble. Though the logical organization corresponds to the illustration shown in Figure 4(b) (a central cache with bypass paths), the physical realization is shown in Figure 4(c). Figure 4 assumes iSCSI block protocol and hence shows a common LAN/SAN for illustration purposes only. In practice, any connection fabric (Fibre Channel) or protocol may be used. Even if iSCSI-over-Ethernet is used, the network may use dedicated links/switches for performance.

One concern that SieveStore must address is the issue of the entire ensemble's I/O funneling through the SieveStore node. The issue may be subdivided into four different activities that are aggregated in SieveStore. First, requests are aggregated at the SieveStore node. Request processing is not a significant concern because (1) request processing is entirely in memory (e.g., cache-hit determination and sieving) except for hits and allocation-writes, and (2) the entire week's request traffic amounts to approximately 434 million multi-block requests, which is dwarfed by the amount of traffic that hits in the disk-cache. Second, the issue of handling the I/O requests that require SSD operations (hits and allocation-writes) is discussed later in Section 5.2. Third, the issue of SSD-wearout because SieveStore aggregates write-hot blocks in the SSD is also shown not to be a significant concern later in Section 5.1. Fourth, there is concern that the SieveStore node could become a network bottleneck. There are two sources of network traffic; SSD hits wherein blocks are served *from* the SieveStore node and the allocated-misses wherein blocks are copied *to* the SieveStore node. A simple worst case analysis reveals that servicing hits is well within the network bandwidth of a reasonably configured node with four Gigabit Ethernet links. Even the maximum SSD access throughput (100% sequential reads, 250MB/s) accounts for approximately 50% of the network bandwidth. In practice, the SSD accesses are neither sequential nor all-writes. Further, the SSD load is considerably lower than 100% of an SSD's bandwidth, as we show later in Section 5.2. The second source of network traffic (allocation data) is negligible because sieving is effective in reducing the number of allocation writes, as shown later in Section 5.1.

4. EXPERIMENTAL METHODOLOGY

Trace analysis, as well as analysis of the ideal case and SieveStore-D involved access-counting and was performed using simple scripts and mapreductions. (Recall, there is no need for cache-simulation for SieveStore-D because allocation/deallocation are only at epoch boundaries.) For SieveStore-C, we developed a trace-based simulator that includes the data-structures for sieving (IMCT and MCT) and for the metastate of a fully-associative, 16GB cache with LRU replacement (tags, LRU stack information). Note, LRU replacement was common for all the continuous configurations (i.e., SieveStore-C, AOD, and WMNA; but not SieveStore-D) irrespective of allocation policies.

The cache simulations operate on the trace and faithfully model the cache operation including allocation-writes. Because allocation requests can occur only after the data has been fetched from the underlying storage, each allocation request to a block was assumed to start at the time that the corresponding request in the original trace completed (as reported in the trace). We used linear interpolation to infer completion times for individual blocks in cases of large, multi-block requests.

Because SieveStore funnels all of the ensemble's hot blocks to a single node, it is important to ascertain that the IOPS and bandwidth requirements can both be satisfied at that node. At a high-level, the increased IOPS/bandwidth requirements of SieveStore is helped by the high IOPS and high bandwidth provided by SSDs. However, there may be peak bursts where the requests of 13 individual servers saturate even the high I/O throughput of the SSD, thus requiring more SSDs for parallelism. To catch such peaks, if any, our cache simulator exports the required IOPS and required bandwidth (MB/s) (separately for reads and writes) in each minute of the trace.

We assume SieveStore uses an SSD for caching blocks. The SSD's parameters are modeled after Intel's X25-E Extreme SATA SSD [8], which achieves 35,000 random read IOPS, 3300 random write IOPS, 250MB/s sustained sequential read bandwidth and 170MB/s sustained sequential write bandwidth, assuming 4KB pages. The random bandwidth (computed from random IOPS for 4KB transfers) is 140MB/s and 13.2 MB/s which is a tighter constraint than sequential bandwidth. So we evaluate the drives needed under the tighter IOPS constraint.

To assess cost, we compute the drives needed to satisfy the IOPS requirements of our workloads. To that end, we compute a *Drive IOPS occupancy* metric for each minute in the trace. We assume that each 4KB read I/O occu-

Table 3: Allocation policies

Key	Allocation Policy	When is a block allocated?
AOD	Allocate-on-demand	On a miss
WMNA	Write-no-allocate	On a read-miss
SieveStore-D	Access count-based, discrete batch-allocation with threshold=n	Blocks that are accessed at least n times in an epoch enter the cache at the end of that epoch
SieveStore-C	Lazy allocation, threshold=n, window=W	On the nth miss in the previous time window.

pies the drive for $1/35000^{th}$ of a second (because read IOPS is 35000/s) and each 4KB write I/O occupies the drive for $1/3300^{th}$ of a second (because write IOPS is 3300/s). This is a rather simple model that ignores queueing. However, we will show that, with SieveStore variants, the drives are typically operating at a significantly lower load point than supported by the SSD. Consequently, queueing is unlikely to be a significant problem. The number of drives needed each minute is computed as the ceiling of the drive occupancy of all requests for that minute. Because the SSD performance parameters are specified for 4KB units, we assumed 4KB accesses. However, because there were a small number (6%) of accesses that were not 4KB-aligned, we conservatively assessed the same cost for a sub-4KB I/O as that of a 4KB I/O. (We use this conservative approximation only for assessing drive-needs. All other numbers count I/O blocks/accesses assuming 512-byte blocks for accuracy.)

Finally, we arrive at the required number of drives for the whole trace under various coverage assumptions. For 100% coverage, the number of drives needed is the maximum of the number of drives for each minute of the trace, which is a worst-case design. We also consider reducing coverage in cases where a large decrease in the number of drives may be obtained by sacrificing a little coverage.

5. RESULTS

There are three primary conclusions from our experiments.

1. We show that sieving fundamentally enables ensemble-level caching to achieve higher performance. SieveStore-D (SieveStore-C) improves the number of hits by 35% (50%) over the best unsieved ensemble-level caching, while also reducing the number of allocation-writes by over two orders of magnitude. (Section 5.1.)

2. With a single SSD, SieveStore-D (SieveStore-C) can satisfy the IOPS and bandwidth requirement of the ensemble with 100% (99.9%) time coverage. (Section 5.2.)

3. SieveStore's approach of ensemble-level caching is a superior cost-performance point compared to ideal private (per-server) caching because it can achieve higher performance at the same cost OR lower cost for the same performance. (Section 5.3.)

5.1 Sieved vs. Unsieved Ensemble-level caches

We compare the two SieveStore variants with the unsieved allocation policies for ensemble-level caches (quadrant *I* vs. quadrant *II* in Figure 1). Figure 5 plots the total number of accesses captured by ensemble-level caches (normalized to the total number of accesses, Y-axis) allocated on each day of the trace (X-axis) by each allocation technique (bars in each group). The accesses caught by the ideal SieveStore that captures the top 1% of blocks each day is the left-most bar. In addition to the ideal case, we include the sieve-based techniques SieveStore-C and SieveStore-D as well as two randomized allocation policies (RandSeive-BlkD and RandSieve-C) to illustrate the fact that SieveStore truly identifies and captures hot blocks (beyond what random sampling would achieve). The RandSieve-BlkD variant allocates a randomly chosen 1% of the *blocks* accessed each day and batch-allocates them to the cache for the next day. RandSieve-C is a continuous variant that randomly allocates 1% of all misses. We also include the two unsieved allocation policies (AOD, WMNA). For the unsieved ensemble caches, we also compare against a cache that is twice the size (32GB) of the SieveStore variants to account for the possibility that the additional hits from sieving may be captured by using the additional DRAM/storage needed to hold the sieve data-structures/logs. Like the 16GB cache, the 32GB cache is also fully-associative with LRU replacement. The accesses of the non-ideal allocation mechanisms also show the breakdown of reads and writes.

On average, SieveStore-D and SieveStore-C[1] are within 14% and 4% of the ideal case. Both SieveStore variants are, at worst, within 16.7% and 6.6% of the ideal case, with the exception of SieveStore-D on days 1 and 2. On average, SieveStore-D and SieveStore-C capture 35% and 50% more accesses (hits) than the best of AOD and WMNA.

SieveStore-D shows zero accesses on day 1 because it needs one day's access logs to bootstrap its sieve. Consequently, the average excludes the first day. The exceptional behavior of SieveStore-D on day 2 is because block popularity on day 1 is significantly more skewed than the remainder of the days because of our calendar-day-based analysis (Section 2); only 0.04% of accessed blocks have 10 or more accesses (Figure 2(a)). Consequently, SieveStore-D which allocates blocks only if their access count exceeds 10, allocates a significantly smaller set of blocks at the end of day 1. In spite of the smaller number of blocks, SieveStore-D captures more than half of accesses on day 2. In contrast, SieveStore-C can react on a continuous basis and achieves a significantly higher hit-ratio on day 2. On days 3 , 4 and 8, SieveStore-C achieves a marginally higher hit-ratio than the (day-by-day) ideal case.

Neither of the two random sieving variants (bars A and D in Figure 5) performs well, achieving only marginally higher hitrates than the unsieved allocation policies. The extremely poor hit ratio of RandSieve-BlkD is to be expected because of the low likelihood of randomly selecting the hot blocks. However, the poor performance of RandSieve-C requires some explanation. One may think that RandSieve-C should work well in principle because popular blocks occur

[1]The ideal configuration uses day-by-day discrete allocation, and hence is an upper-bound for SieveStore-D, but not for SieveStore-C because SieveStore-C can continuously change the blocks it holds.

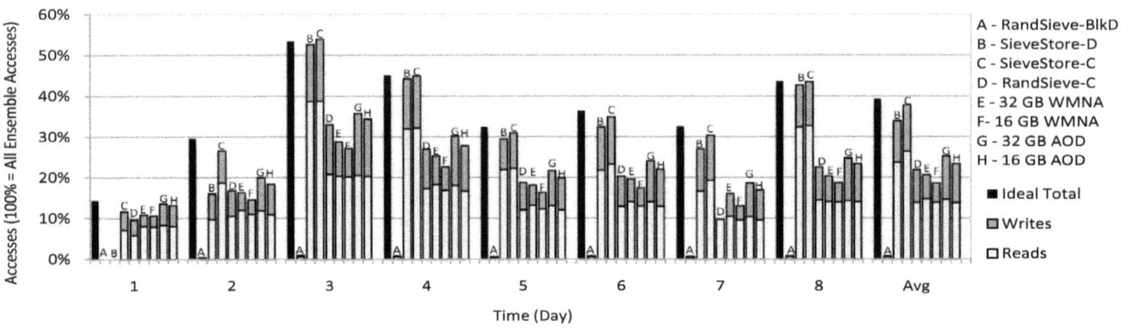

Figure 5: Sieving Effectiveness: Accesses Captured

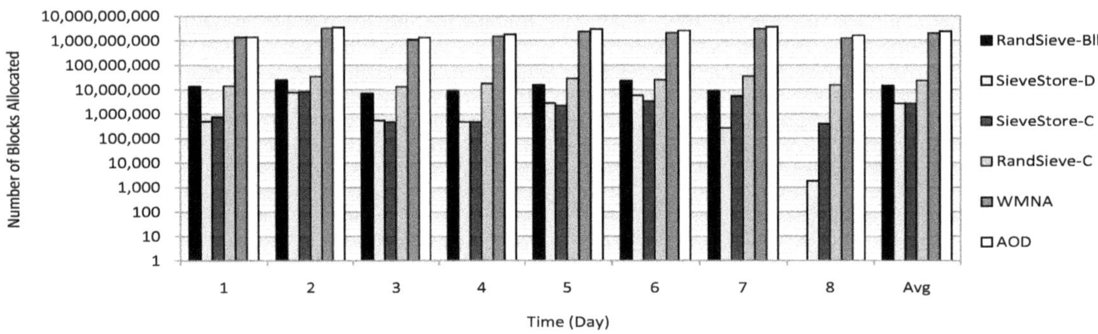

Figure 6: Sieving Effectiveness: Allocation Writes

repeatedly in the miss-stream and are thus more likely to be sampled. However, because the fraction of accesses that come from low-reuse blocks is significant (approximately 60%, on average), random sieving will result in 60% of allocations being those of low-reuse blocks. Such spurious allocations explain the lower hit ratio.

Finally, while larger disk-caches help the unsieved ensemble caches (bars labeled E,F in Figure 5), there remains a significant gap between the hit ratios of SieveStore variants and AOD/WMNA. In the rest of the paper, we use the 32GB variant of AOD/WMNA as they offer better hit ratios.

Allocation writes.

Figure 6 plots the number of allocation-writes (Y-axis, log-scale) for each day of the trace (X-axis) for our allocation mechanisms (bars). The number of allocation-writes required by SieveStore-D and SieveStore-C is a more than two orders of magnitude smaller than those of AOD and WMNA. (Though not shown in Figure 6 the number of allocation-writes for 16GB caches with AOD and WMNA were qualitatively similar.) The random sampling sieves do reduce the number of allocation writes significantly compared to AOD and WMNA. However, they are almost an order of magnitude (8.5X) worse than the SieveStore variants, on average.

SSD accesses.

In order to account for the total number of accesses to the SSD, and also to put the magnitude of the allocation-writes in the context of other accesses, Figure 7 combines the information from both Figure 5 and Figure 6. The Y-axis shows all SSD operations (at 512-byte block granularity). Each bar has three components: reads (hits), writes (hits) and allocation-writes. Three key observations can be made from Figure 7.

First, the allocation-writes bar reveals the importance of sieving. Without sieving, the allocation-writes constitute the dominant fraction of all SSD accesses. Combined with the fact that writes are slower in SSDs, such allocation-writes can have a crippling impact. For SieveStore-C and SieveStore-D, the bars for the *allocation-writes are included* as a thin (nearly-invisible at scale) bar.

Recall, from Section 1 that we do not differentiate between reads and writes in SieveStore. One may think that caching write-hot blocks can (1) reduce lifetime for SSDs and (2) impose an opportunity cost by preventing other read-hot blocks which can benefit from significantly higher IOPS. However, because the number of writes for SieveStore (= write hits + allocation-writes) never exceeds 500 million writes of 512 bytes each on any given day, and because the X25-E SSD drive can endure 1 petabyte (10^{15}B) of writes [8], the disk's endurance is over 10 years = $(10^{15}/(5 \times 10^8 \times 512 \times 365))$. Further, there is no opportunity cost in the sense that write-hot blocks preclude read-hot blocks because a 16GB disk can contain all the top 1% popular blocks with room to spare. Finally, there is the "pull" factor that makes it attractive to cache write-hot blocks; SSD write IOPS is an order of magnitude higher than the write IOPs of enterprise HDDs.

Sensitivity.

Due to lack of space, we briefly summarize the results of sensitivity analysis without providing detailed results. We

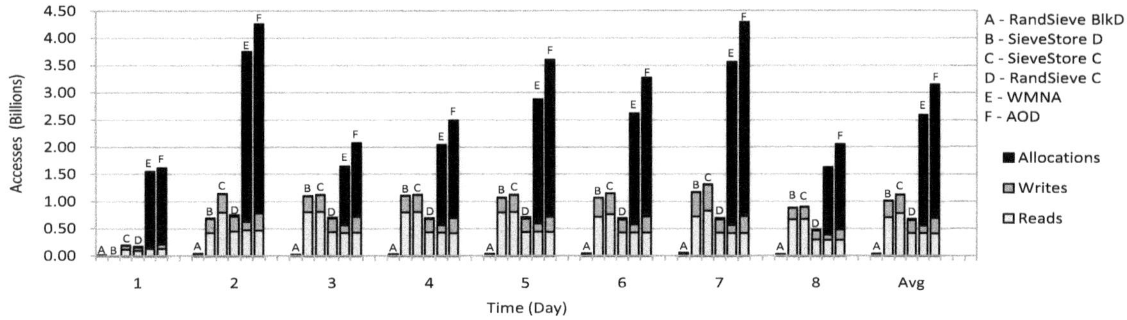

Figure 7: Total SSD Accesses

found that SieveStore is sensitive to variations in the threshold in only one direction. If the threshold is too low (e.g., below 8 for SieveStore-D), we have inadequate sieving and poor performance. But if the threshold is varied in the high range (e.g., 8-20 for SieveStore-D), the hit-rate does not vary significantly. Similarly, SieveStore was relatively insensitive to significant variations in epoch/window lengths although we observed that lengths shorter than 8 hours caused some performance degradation.

5.2 Assessing costs of SieveStore

Recall, the methodology for computing the number of drives uses IOPS rating of the Intel X25-E SSD drive and compares that to the IOPS requirement in each of the 10080 ($=7 \times 24 \times 60$) minutes of the trace.

Figure 8 plots two graphs showing the drive IOPS occupancy (Y-axis) against each minute in the trace (X-axis, in chronological order). Individually, Figure 8(a) and Figure 8(b) compare WMNA allocation policy with SieveStore-D and SieveStore-C, respectively. AOD is omitted because it is strictly worse than WMNA. The cost of the large number of allocation-writes of the WMNA policy is manifested in the regions where drive IOPS occupancy peaks (gray curve in both Figure 8(a) and Figure 8(b)). In contrast, the occupancy of SieveStore variants is significantly lower and mostly under 1. SieveStore-D never requires more than one disk with the caveat that SieveStore-D assumes that batch allocation can be done during periods of low disk activity. Note, the assumption is reasonable because there is significant downtime in SSD activity. SieveStore-C, which explicitly accounts for all allocation-writes, maintains its drive IOPS occupancy under 1 more than 99.9% of the time. The requirement goes up to two drives for only 9 minutes out of a total of 10080 minutes of the trace.

Figure 9 plots the number of drives needed (Y-axis) for each minute (X-axis) of the trace for each allocation policy (curves in the figure). The Y-axis values in Figure 9 are simply the values of the curves in Figure 8 rounded up to the next integer (i.e., ceiling function). Note, the minutes are not in chronological order but in increasing order of drive-requirements. Note the small peak at the right for SieveStore-C that represents the 9 minutes where we need two drives. The WMNA policy would require 7 drives for 99.9% coverage. Even after diluting the coverage requirement to 90% WMNA would require 4 drives.

At a higher level, the result that a large fraction of the ensemble's accesses can be satisfied comfortably by a single SSD in 99.9% of the cases is not surprising because (1) the

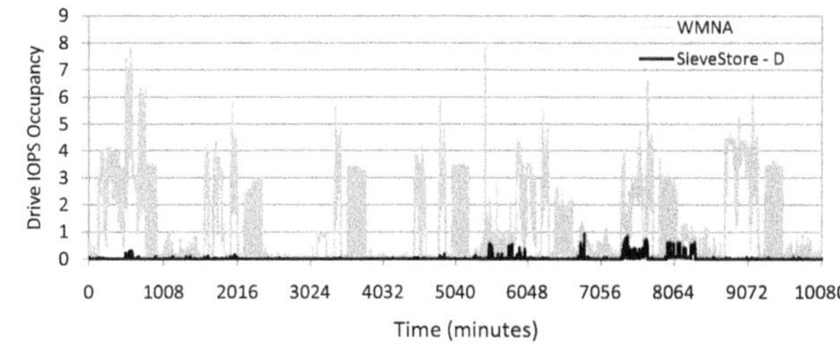

(a) SieveStore-D vs. WMNA

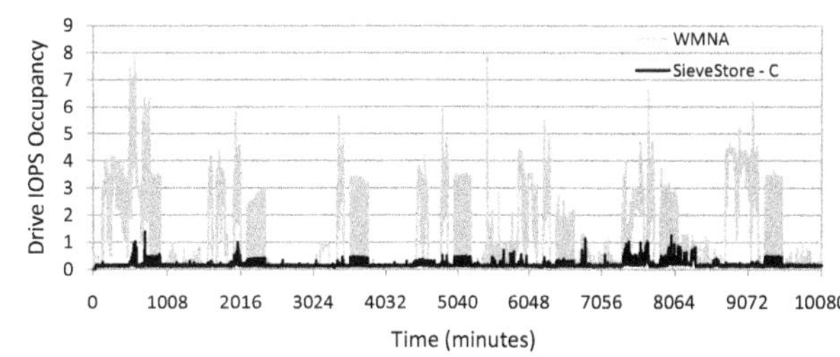

(b) SieveStore-C vs. WMNA

Figure 8: Drive IOPS occupancy

IOPS offered by the SSD is two orders of magnitude higher for reads and one order of magnitude higher for writes when compared to HDDs, and (2) the probability that a large number of servers across the ensemble will experience a correlated burst of disk activity at the same time is low [14].

5.3 Ensemble vs. per-server caching

In this section, we extend the comparison to include per-server disk-caches (quadrant III and quadrant IV in Figure 1). To strengthen our argument that ensemble-level caching, in general, and SieveStore, in particular, are superior in cost-performance, we compare the cost/performance of SieveStore-C and SieveStore-D to that of two ideal per-server caching configurations. First, under the unreasonable, but conservative, assumption that SSD capacity is elastic (i.e., arbitrarily small SSDs can be built without changing the cost per byte), we compare against a per-server configuration in which each server caches the top 1% of its accessed blocks. Such a configuration is effectively an iso-capacity (and hence iso-cost, by our elasticity assumption) config-

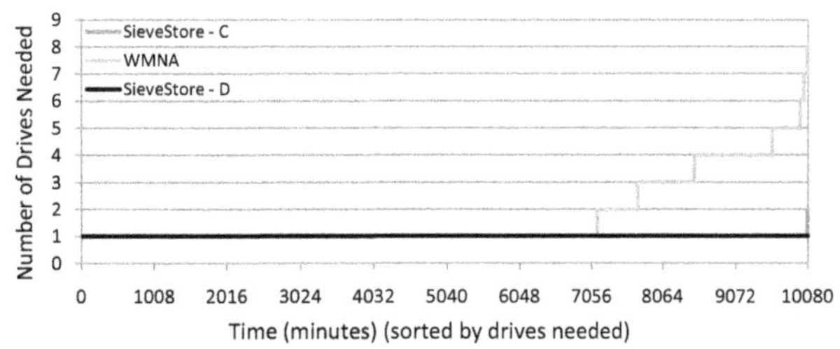

Figure 9: Number of drives needed

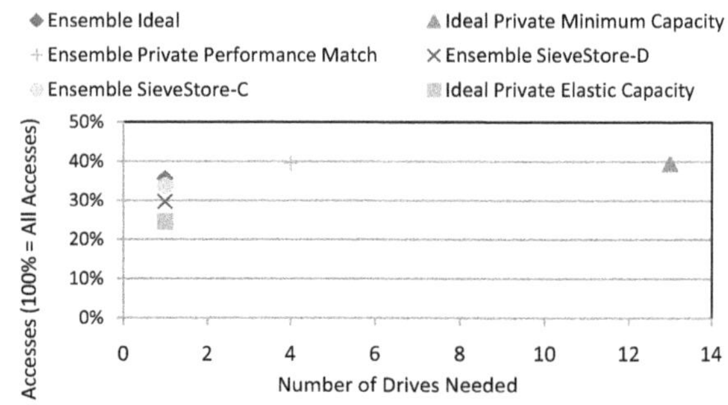

Figure 10: Cost-Performance Tradeoffs

uration with a proportional, static partition of the cache capacity among servers.

Second, under a more reasonable assumption that there is a minimum size for SSDs (i.e., non-elastic drives, we assume 16GB), the per-server caching incurs the cost of 13 SSDs. On the other hand, each server is now able to cache more data. Again, we conservatively assume that the per-server caches are filled with as many of the most popular blocks as the capacity allows.

Figure 10 compares the cost-benefit tradeoffs for the various ensemble caching configurations (ideal and SieveStore) and the two ideal per-server caching configurations. We use the number of SSDs (X-axis) as a proxy for cost and the fraction of ensemble accesses (Y-axis) that hit in the disk cache as a measure of performance.

First, focusing purely on the ideal cases with elastic SSDs, we observe that the Ideal ensemble version which caches the top 1% of blocks is significantly better than the Ideal-private configuration with elastic drives which caches the top 1% of blocks of each server. Even though the cost of the two configurations are the same, the ensemble version captures 45% more accesses than the per-server version.

Second, we compare the ideal ensemble version with ideal per-server configuration with non-elastic drives. In that case, we assume that each server has the capacity to cache as much as 1% of the entire ensemble's data, which will be a larger fraction of the server's data. This configuration increases the cost by a factor of 13X (1300%) since it needs one SSD drive per server. However, the accesses captured goes up by only 11%. This is not surprising because the benefits of increasing cache capacity beyond the 1% most popular blocks are minimal because of low-reuse (Section 2). To emphasize this point, we include an ensemble-level ideal configuration that captures the same number of accesses as the per-server configuration (labeled as Iso-performance in Figure 10). Such an ensemble configuration requires fewer SSD drives than the per-server approach (i.e., lower cost for the same benefit). More importantly, it illustrates the fact that caching more data beyond the top 1% is not cost-effective even at the ensemble-level because the cost increase (4X) is not commensurate with the benefits (11%).

Finally, SieveStore-D and SieveStore-C which are both practical, capture 21% and 37% more accesses than the ideal (impractical) iso-cost, per-server caching configuration. Thus *practical* variants of our ensemble-level caching perform better than an *ideal version* of the per-server caching technique at the same cost.

6. RELATED WORK

The advantage of dynamically sharing resources in the specific context of data-center ensembles have been widely-studied. Various researchers have described the benefits of managing power at the ensemble level [16, 5]. More recently, Lim *et.al.* proposed using a shared pool of memory that could be dynamically allocated to computers in an ensemble to alleviate the reducing memory-capacity per core [13]. Narayanan *et.al.* have shown that treating storage bandwidth of an ensemble as a pooled resource enables efficient handling of peak throughput bursts [14]. SieveStore applies similiar ensemble-level management in another context. Note, the ensemble-level approach cannot blindly be applied to other resources. Just as the observation that not all nodes in the ensemble were operating at peak power (or utilizing large amounts of memory, or placing peak demand for I/O bandwidth) at the same time was central to motivating the ensemble-level power-management (or memory-pooling, or storage-bandwidth pooling) techniques, our observations that there is extreme dynamic popularity skew in storage-ensemble block-access traces, and that sieving can filter allocation-writes, led to the SieveStore design.

There is a large body of work on replacement algorithms that achieve better hit ratios than LRU replacement by handling special cases (e.g., loop/streaming accesses) separately [6, 17], and by considering frequency in addition to recency [12]). As shown in Section 3.1, our sieving is fundamentally different in its ability to reduce allocation-writes. In the context of microprocessor caches, various static and dynamic bypassing policies have been proposed to avoid allocating cache blocks that have little reuse/value [20, 9, 18]. Because the allocation-write problem is not significant in microarchitectural SRAM caches, such bypass techniques have focused on improving hits without aiming to minimize allocation writes. In contrast, our policies aim to minimize allocation writes (while also improving hits). As shown in Section 3.1, maximizing hits need not necessarily reduce allocation writes, even when using selective allocation. Finally, Behar *et.al.* use a sampling-based selective allocation for improved tracecache performance [1]. As discussed earlier in Section 5, applying randomized sampling in ensemble-level disk caches performs poorly compared to SieveStore variants.

Prior work has examined the use of flash-based memories as extensions of the VM system (a fast swap space) [19], and in customized architectures [3]. Our work is orthogonal. We emphasize that though our work uses SSD as one possible caching mechanism, our primary contribution is the use of ensemble-level disk caching based on sieving and is independent of underlying storage medium. Indeed the storage medium could be phase-change memory. Battery-backed

DRAM could also be used. Although DRAM write-accesses are as fast as reads, sieving is still valuable because of other benefits such as improved memory bandwidth (by avoiding allocation writes) and network bandwidth (by avoiding allocation traffic). Kgil *et.al.* have proposed a flash-based per-server buffer cache [11, 10]. Recall from Section 5.3, sieve-based, ensemble-level disk-caches are superior to per-server disk-caches in cost and performance.

7. DISCUSSION: SCALING AND TUNING

While our results showed that a 16GB SieveStore was adequate for the ensemble of 13 servers, the more general question of provisioning SieveStore for larger ensembles with different capacity, IOPS, and bandwidth requirements must also be considered. If SieveStore's limited capacity is inadequate to hold all the blocks that make it past the sieve (an indicator of underprovisioning), the glut of blocks being allocated to the cache could result in cache pollution and/or degraded performance. The above problem has two possible solutions. First, multiple SieveStore nodes may be added by exploiting parallelism (1) across groups of servers, wherein smaller ensembles would each be assigned a SieveStore node, or (2) across block addresses, wherein block addresses would be striped/partitioned across the two SieveStore nodes. Second, if adding SieveStore nodes is not an option, adaptively raising the thresholds in SieveStore-D and SieveStore-C may increase selectivity and gracefully handle SieveStore underprovisioning. We leave a study of scaling and adaptive threshold tuning for future work.

8. CONCLUSIONS

The adoption of SSDs to accelerate/filter accesses to traditional magnetic hard disk-drive based storage is attractive from a power/performance point of view. But cost-effectiveness remains a serious impediment because of the high cost-per-byte of SSD capacity [15]. We propose SieveStore – a highly selective, ensemble-level, disk-cache that filters a significant fraction of disk accesses of a server ensemble with a small, shared SSD. SieveStore is driven by the observations that (1) there is extreme popularity skew among blocks that are accessed, and (2) that the popular set is dynamic. While the above observations directly make the case for ensemble-level caching, conventional cache allocation policies incur a high overhead because of a large number of allocation-writes caused by misses. We show that selective allocation to avoid such overhead – sieving – is necessary. We describe two practical SieveStore variants – SieveStore-D and SieveStore-C. Trace-based evaluations reveal that SieveStore's twin strategies of ensemble-level disk-caching with sieving is a superior cost-performance point compared to per-server caches and unsieved ensemble-level caches.

Acknowledgments.

We thank the anonymous reviewers for their feedback. We thank T. N. Vijaykumar for comments on an early draft of this paper. This work is supported in part by National Science Foundation (Grant no. CCF-0621457).

9. REFERENCES

[1] M. Behar, A. Mendelson, and A. Kolodny. Trace cache sampling filter. In *Proc. of the 14th International Conference on Parallel Architectures and Compilation Techniques*, pages 255–266, 2005.

[2] L. A. Belady. A study of replacement algorithms for a virtual-storage computer. *IBM Systems Journal*, 5(2):78–101, 1966.

[3] A. M. Caulfield, L. M. Grupp, and S. Swanson. Gordon: using flash memory to build fast, power-efficient clusters for data-intensive applications. *SIGPLAN Not.*, 44(3):217–228, 2009.

[4] C. Dirik and B. Jacob. The performance of pc solid-state disks (ssds) as a function of bandwidth, concurrency, device architecture, and system organization. In *ISCA '09: Proc. of the 36th annual international symposium on Computer architecture*, pages 279–289, 2009.

[5] X. Fan, W.-D. Weber, and L. A. Barroso. Power provisioning for a warehouse-sized computer. In *ISCA '07: Proc. of the 34th annual international symposium on Computer architecture*, pages 13–23, 2007.

[6] G. Glass and P. Cao. Adaptive page replacement based on memory reference behavior. In *Proc. of the 1997 ACM SIGMETRICS international conference on Measurement and modeling of computer systems*, pages 115–126, 1997.

[7] A. Gupta, Y. Kim, and B. Urgaonkar. Dftl: a flash translation layer employing demand-based selective caching of page-level address mappings. In *ASPLOS '09: Proc. of the 14th intl. conference on Architectural support for programming languages and operating systems*, pages 229–240, 2009.

[8] Intel. *Intel X25-E SATA Solid State Drive Datasheet*. http://download.intel.com/design/flash/nand/extreme/319984.pdf.

[9] T. L. Johnson and W.-m. W. Hwu. Run-time adaptive cache hierarchy management via reference analysis. In *Proc. of the 24th annual International Symposium on Computer architecture (ISCA '97)*, pages 315–326, 1997.

[10] T. Kgil and T. Mudge. Flashcache: a nand flash memory file cache for low power web servers. In *Proc. of the 2006 international conference on Compilers, architecture and synthesis for embedded systems*, pages 103–112, 2006.

[11] T. Kgil, D. Roberts, and T. Mudge. Improving nand flash based disk caches. In *Proc. of the 35th International Symposium on Computer Architecture*, pages 327–338, 2008.

[12] D. Lee, J. Choi, J. H. Kim, S. H. Noh, S. L. Min, Y. Cho, and C. S. Kim. Lrfu: A spectrum of policies that subsumes the least recently used and least frequently used policies. *IEEE Trans. Comput.*, 50(12):1352–1361, 2001.

[13] K. Lim, J. Chang, T. Mudge, P. Ranganathan, S. K. Reinhardt, and T. F. Wenisch. Disaggregated memory for expansion and sharing in blade servers. *SIGARCH Comput. Archit. News*, 37(3):267–278, 2009.

[14] D. Narayanan, A. Donnelly, E. Thereska, S. Elnikety, and A. I. T. Rowstron. Everest: Scaling down peak loads through i/o off-loading. In *OSDI*, pages 15–28, 2008.

[15] D. Narayanan, E. Thereska, A. Donnelly, S. Elnikety, and A. Rowstron. Migrating server storage to ssds: analysis of tradeoffs. In *EuroSys '09: Proc. of the 4th ACM European conference on Computer systems*, pages 145–158, 2009.

[16] P. Ranganathan, P. Leech, D. Irwin, and J. Chase. Ensemble-level power management for dense blade servers. *SIGARCH Comput. Archit. News*, 34(2):66–77, 2006.

[17] Y. Smaragdakis, S. Kaplan, and P. Wilson. Eelru: simple and effective adaptive page replacement. *SIGMETRICS Perform. Eval. Rev.*, 27(1):122–133, 1999.

[18] E. S. Tam, J. A. Rivers, V. Srinivasan, G. S. Tyson, and E. S. Davidson. Active management of data caches by exploiting reuse information. *IEEE Trans. Comput.*, 48(11):1244–1259, 1999.

[19] H.-W. Tseng, H.-L. Li, and C.-L. Yang. An energy-efficient virtual memory system with flash memory as the secondary storage. In *ISLPED*, pages 418–423, 2006.

[20] G. Tyson, M. Farrens, J. Matthews, and A. R. Pleszkun. A modified approach to data cache management. In *MICRO 28: Proc. of the 28th annual international symposium on Microarchitecture*, pages 93–103, 1995.

Rethinking DRAM Design and Organization for Energy-Constrained Multi-Cores

Aniruddha N. Udipi
University of Utah
Salt Lake City, UT
udipi@cs.utah.edu

Naveen Muralimanohar
Hewlett-Packard Laboratories
Palo Alto, CA
naveen.murali@hp.com

Niladrish Chatterjee
University of Utah
Salt Lake City, UT
nil@cs.utah.edu

Rajeev Balasubramonian
University of Utah
Salt Lake City, UT
rajeev@cs.utah.edu

Al Davis
University of Utah
Salt Lake City, UT
ald@cs.utah.edu

Norman P. Jouppi
Hewlett-Packard Laboratories
Palo Alto, CA
norm.jouppi@hp.com

ABSTRACT

DRAM vendors have traditionally optimized the cost-per-bit metric, often making design decisions that incur energy penalties. A prime example is the overfetch feature in DRAM, where a single request activates thousands of bitlines in many DRAM chips, only to return a single cache line to the CPU. The focus on cost-per-bit is questionable in modern-day servers where operating costs can easily exceed the purchase cost. Modern technology trends are also placing very different demands on the memory system: (i) queuing delays are a significant component of memory access time, (ii) there is a high energy premium for the level of reliability expected for business-critical computing, and (iii) the memory access stream emerging from multi-core systems exhibits limited locality. All of these trends necessitate an overhaul of DRAM architecture, even if it means a slight compromise in the cost-per-bit metric.

This paper examines three primary innovations. The first is a modification to DRAM chip microarchitecture that retains the traditional DDRx SDRAM interface. Selective Bitline Activation (SBA) waits for both RAS (row address) and CAS (column address) signals to arrive before activating exactly those bitlines that provide the requested cache line. SBA reduces energy consumption while incurring slight area and performance penalties. The second innovation, Single Subarray Access (SSA), fundamentally re-organizes the layout of DRAM arrays and the mapping of data to these arrays so that an entire cache line is fetched from a single subarray. It requires a different interface to the memory controller, reduces dynamic and background energy (by about 6X and 5X), incurs a slight area penalty (4%), and can even lead to performance improvements (54% on average) by reducing queuing delays. The third innovation further penalizes the cost-per-bit metric by adding a checksum feature to each cache line. This checksum error-detection feature can then be used to build stronger RAID-like fault tolerance, including chipkill-level reliability. Such a technique is especially crucial for the SSA architecture where the entire cache line is localized to a single chip. This DRAM chip microarchitectural change leads to a dramatic reduction in the energy and storage overheads for reliability. The proposed architectures will also apply to other emerging memory technologies (such as resistive memories) and will be less disruptive to standards, interfaces, and the design flow if they can be incorporated into first-generation designs.

Categories and Subject Descriptors

B.3.1 [**Memory Structures**]: Semiconductor Memories—*Dynamic memory (DRAM)*; B.3.2 [**Memory Structures**]: Design Styles—*Primary memory*; B.8.1 [**Performance and Reliability**]: Reliability, Testing and Fault-Tolerance; C.5.5 [**Computer System Implementation**]: Servers

General Terms

Design, Performance, Reliability

Keywords

DRAM Architecture, Energy-efficiency, Locality, Chipkill, Subarrays

1. INTRODUCTION

The computing landscape is undergoing a major change, primarily enabled by ubiquitous wireless networks and the rapid increase in the usage of mobile devices which access the web-based information infrastructure. It is expected that most CPU-intensive computing may either happen in servers housed in large datacenters, *e.g.*, cloud computing and other web services, or in many-core high-performance computing (HPC) platforms in scientific labs. In both situations, it is expected that the memory system will be problematic in terms of performance, reliability, and power consumption.

The memory wall is not new: long DRAM memory latencies have always been a problem. Given that little can be done about the latency problem, DRAM vendors have chosen to optimize their designs for improved bandwidth, increased density, and minimum cost-per-bit. With these objectives in mind, a few DRAM architectures, standards, and

ISCA'10, June 19–23, 2010, Saint-Malo, France.

interfaces were instituted in the 1990s and have persisted since then. However, the objectives in datacenter servers and HPC platforms of the future will be very different than those that are reasonable for personal computers, such as desktop machines. As a result, traditional DRAM architectures are highly inefficient from a future system perspective, and are in need of a major revamp. Consider the following technological trends that place very different demands on future DRAM architectures:

- *Energy:* While energy was never a first-order design constraint in prior DRAM systems, it has certainly emerged as the primary constraint today, especially in datacenters. Energy efficiency in datacenters has already been highlighted as a national priority [50]. Many studies attribute 25-40% of total datacenter power to the DRAM system [11, 33, 34, 37]. Modern DRAM architectures are ill-suited for energy-efficient operation because they are designed to fetch much more data than required. This *overfetch* wastes dynamic energy. Today's DRAMs employ coarse-grained power-down tactics to reduce area and cost, but finer grained approaches can further reduce background energy.
- *Reduced locality:* Single-core workloads typically exhibit high locality. Consequently, current DRAMs fetch many kilobytes of data on every access and keep them in open row buffers so that subsequent requests to neighboring data elements can be serviced quickly. The high degree of multi-threading in future multi-cores [42] implies that memory requests from multiple access streams get multiplexed at the memory controller, thus destroying a large fraction of the available locality. The severity of this problem will increase with increased core and memory controller counts that are expected for future microprocessor chips. This trend is exacerbated by the increased use of aggregated memory pools ("memory blades" that are comprised of many commodity DIMMs) that serve several CPU sockets in an effort to increase resource utilization [34]. This mandates that future DRAM architectures place a lower priority on locality and a higher priority on parallelism.
- *Queuing Delays:* For several years, queuing delays at the memory controller were relatively small because a single core typically had relatively few pending memory operations and DRAM systems were able to steeply increase peak memory bandwidth every year [20]. In the future, the number of pins per chip is expected to grow very slowly. The 2007 ITRS Road-map [26] expects a 1.47x increase in the number of pins over an 8-year time-frame – over the same period, Moore's Law dictates at least a 16x increase in the number of cores. This implies that requests from many cores will be competing to utilize the limited pin bandwidth. Several studies have already highlighted the emergence of queuing delay as a major bottleneck [24, 31, 40, 41, 44, 56]. A DRAM architecture that is geared towards higher parallelism will likely be able to de-queue requests faster and better utilize the available limited data bandwidth.
- *Efficient Reliability:* Recent studies have highlighted the need for DRAM architectures that are resilient to single faults or even failure within an entire DRAM chip [8, 46], especially in datacenter platforms. Because these fault-tolerant solutions are built upon commodity DRAM chips, they incur very high overheads in terms of energy and cost. New DRAM architectures can provide much more efficient reliability if fault-tolerant features are integrated into the DRAM chip microarchitecture at design time.
- *Lower relevance of DRAM chip area:* DRAM vendors have long optimized the cost-per-bit metric. However, given that datacenters consume several billion kilowatt hours of energy every year [50], it has been shown that the 3-year operating energy costs of today's datacenters equal the capital acquisition costs [33]. Therefore, it may now be acceptable to incur a slightly higher cost-per-bit when purchasing DRAM as long as it leads to significantly lower energy footprints during operation.

The design of DRAM devices specifically addressing these trends has, to the best of our knowledge, not been previously studied and is now more compelling than ever. We attempt to fundamentally rethink DRAM microarchitecture and organization to achieve highly reliable, high performance operation with extremely low energy footprints, all within acceptable area bounds. In this work, we propose two independent designs, both attempting to activate the minimum circuitry required to read a single cache line.

We make the following three significant contributions:

- We introduce and evaluate *Posted RAS* in combination with a *Selective Bitline Activation (SBA)* scheme. This entails a relatively simple change to DRAM microarchitecture, with only a minor change to the DRAM interface, to provide significant dynamic energy savings.
- We propose and evaluate a reorganization of DRAM chips and their interface, so that cache lines can be read via a *Single Subarray Access (SSA)* in a single DRAM chip. This approach trades off higher data transfer times for greater (dynamic and background) energy savings.
- In order to provide chipkill-level reliability [18, 35] even though we are reading a cache line out of a single DRAM device, we propose adding a checksum to each cache line in the SSA DRAM to provide error detection. We then evaluate the use of RAID techniques to reconstruct cache lines in the event of a chip failure.

While this study focuses on DRAM as an evaluation vehicle, the proposed architectures will likely apply just as well to other emerging storage technologies, such as phase change memory (PCM) and spin torque transfer RAM (STT-RAM).

2. BACKGROUND AND MOTIVATION

2.1 DRAM Basics and Baseline Organization

We first describe the typical modern DRAM architecture [27]. For most of the paper, our discussion will focus on the dominant DRAM architecture today: JEDEC-style DDRx SDRAM, an example is shown in Figure 1.

Modern processors [45, 48, 54] often integrate memory controllers on the processor die. Each memory controller is connected to one or two dedicated off-chip memory channels. For JEDEC standard DRAM, the channel typically has a 64-bit data bus, a 17-bit row/column address bus, and an 8-bit command bus [38]. Multiple dual in-line memory modules (*DIMMs*) can be accessed via a single memory channel and memory controller. Each DIMM typically comprises multiple *ranks*, each rank consisting of a set of DRAM

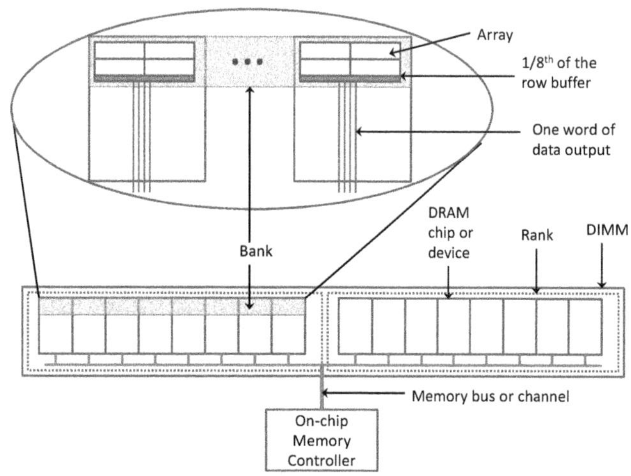

Figure 1: An example DDRx SDRAM architecture with 1 DIMM, 2 ranks, and 8 x4 DRAM chips per rank.

chips. We will call this a *rank-set*. Exactly one *rank-set* is activated on every memory operation and this is the smallest number of chips that need to be activated to complete a read or write operation. Delays on the order of a few cycles are introduced when the memory controller switches between ranks to support electrical bus termination requirements. The proposed DRAM architecture is entirely focused on the DRAM chips, and has neither a positive or negative effect on rank issues. Figure 1 shows an example DIMM with 16 total DRAM chips forming two rank-sets.

Each DRAM chip has an intrinsic *word size* which corresponds to the number of data I/O pins on the chip. An xN DRAM chip has a word size of N, where N refers to the number of bits going in/out of the chip on each clock tick. For a 64-bit data bus and x8 chips, a rank-set would require 8 DRAM chips (Figure 1 only shows 8 x4 chips per rank-set to simplify the figure). If the DIMM supports ECC, the data bus expands to 72-bits and the rank-set would consist of 9 x8 DRAM chips. When a rank is selected, all DRAM chips in the rank-set receive address and command signals from the memory controller on the corresponding shared buses. Each DRAM chip is connected to a subset of the data bus; of the 64-bit data packet being communicated on the bus on a clock edge, each x8 chip reads/writes an 8-bit subset.

A rank is itself partitioned into multiple *banks*, typically 4-16. Each bank can be concurrently processing a different memory request, thus affording a limited amount of memory parallelism. Each bank is distributed across the DRAM chips in a rank; the portion of a bank in each chip will be referred to as a *sub-bank*. The organization of a sub-bank will be described in the next paragraph. When the memory controller issues a request for a cache line, all the DRAM chips in the rank are activated and each sub-bank contributes a portion of the requested cache line. By striping a cache line across multiple DRAM chips, the available pin and channel bandwidth for the cache line transfer can be enhanced. If the data bus width is 64 bits and a cache line is 64 bytes, the cache line transfer happens in an *burst* of 8 data transfers.

If a chip is an xN part, each sub-bank is itself partitioned into N *arrays* (see Figure 1). Each array contributes a single bit to the N-bit transfer on the data I/O pins for that chip on a clock edge. An array has several rows and columns of single-bit DRAM cells. A cache line request starts with a RAS command that carries the subset of address bits that identify the bank and the row within that bank. Each array within that bank now reads out an entire row. The bits read out are saved in latches, referred to as the *row buffer*. The row is now considered *opened*. The *page size* or *row buffer size* is defined as the number of bits read out of all arrays involved in a bank access (usually 4-16 KB). Of these, only a cache line worth of data (identified by the CAS command and its associated subset of address bits) is communicated on the memory channel for each CPU request.

Each bank has its own row buffer, so there can potentially be 4-16 open rows at any time. The banks can be accessed in parallel, but the data transfers have to be serialized over the shared data bus. If the requested data is present in an open row (a *row buffer hit*), the memory controller is aware of this, and data can be returned much faster. If the requested data is not present in the bank's row buffer (a *row buffer miss*), the currently open row (if one exists) has to first be closed before opening the new row. To prevent the closing of the row from being on the critical path for the next row buffer miss, the controller may adopt a *close-page policy* that closes the row right after returning the requested cache line. Alternatively, an *open-page policy* keeps a row open until the bank receives a request for a different row.

As an example system, consider a 4 GB system, with two 2 GB ranks, each consisting of eight 256 MB x8, 4-bank devices, serving an L2 with a 64 byte cache line size. On every request from the L2 cache, each device has to provide 8 bytes of data. Each of the 4 banks in a 256 MB device is split into 8 arrays of 8 MB each. If there are 65,536 rows of 1024 columns of bits in each array, a row access brings down 1024 bits per array into the row buffer, giving a total row buffer size of 65,536 bits across 8 chips of 8 arrays each. The page size is therefore 65,536 bits (8 KBytes) and of these, only 64 Bytes are finally returned to the processor, with each of the eight chips being responsible for 64 bits of the cache line. Such a baseline system usually significantly under-utilizes the bits it reads out (in the above example, only about 0.8% of the row buffer bits are utilized for a single cache line access) and ends up unnecessarily activating various circuits across the rank-set.

2.2 Motivational Data

Recent studies have indicated the high energy needs of datacenters [50] and that memory contributes up to 40% of total server power consumption [11, 33, 37]. We start with a workload characterization on our simulation infrastructure (methodology details in Section 4.1). Figure 2 shows the trend of steeply dropping row-buffer hit rates as the number of threads simultaneously accessing memory goes up. We see average rates drop from over 60% for a 1 core system to 35% for a 16 core system. We also see that whenever a row is fetched into the row-buffer, the number of times it is used before being closed due to a conflict is often just one or two (Figure 3). This indicates that even on benchmarks with high locality and good average row buffer hit rates (for example, *cg*), a large number of pages still don't have much reuse in the row-buffer. These trends have also been observed in prior work on Micro-Pages [47]. This means that the energy costs of activating an entire 8 KB row is amortized over very few accesses, wasting significant energy.

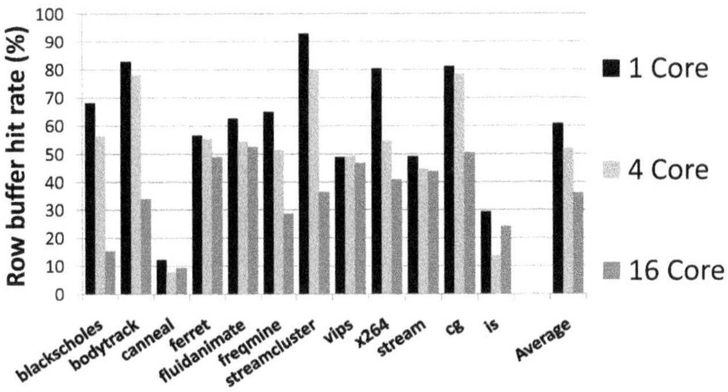

Figure 2: **Row buffer hit rate trend**

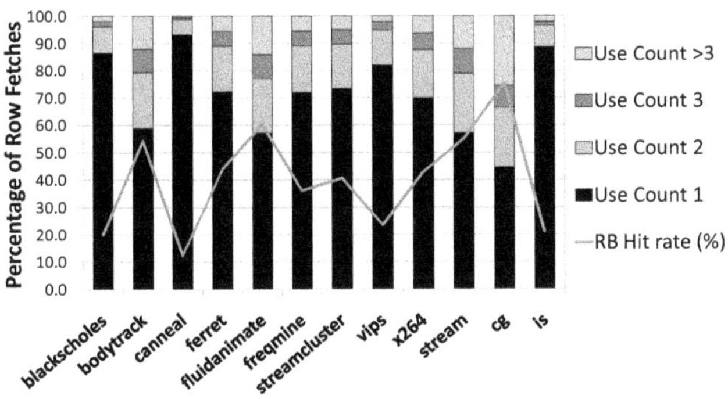

Figure 3: **Row use count for 8 cores**

3. PROPOSED ARCHITECTURE

We start with the premise that the traditional row-buffer locality assumption is no longer valid, and try to find an energy-optimal DRAM design with minimal impacts on area and latency. Our first novel design (Selective Bitline Activation, Section 3.1) requires minor changes to DRAM chip microarchitecture, but is compatible with existing DRAM standards and interfaces. The second novel design (Single Subarray Access, Section 3.2) requires non-trivial changes to DRAM chip microarchitecture and its interface to the memory controller. Section 3.3 describes our novel chipkill solution for the proposed architecture.

3.1 Selective Bitline Activation (SBA)

In an effort to mitigate the overfetch problem with minimal disruption to existing designs and standards, we propose the following two simple modifications: (i) we activate a much smaller segment of the wordline and (ii) we activate only those bitlines corresponding to the requested cache line. Note that we will still need a wire spanning the array to identify the exact segment of wordline that needs to be activated but this is very lightly loaded and therefore has low delay and energy. Thus, we are not changing the way data gets laid out across DRAM chip arrays, but every access only brings down the relevant cache line into the row buffer. As a result, the notion of an open-page policy is now meaningless. After every access, the cache line is immediately written back. Most of the performance difference from this innovation is because of the shift to a close-page policy: for workloads with little locality, this can actually result in performance improvements as the page precharge after write-back is taken off the critical path of the subsequent row buffer miss. Next, we discuss the microarchitectural modifications in more detail.

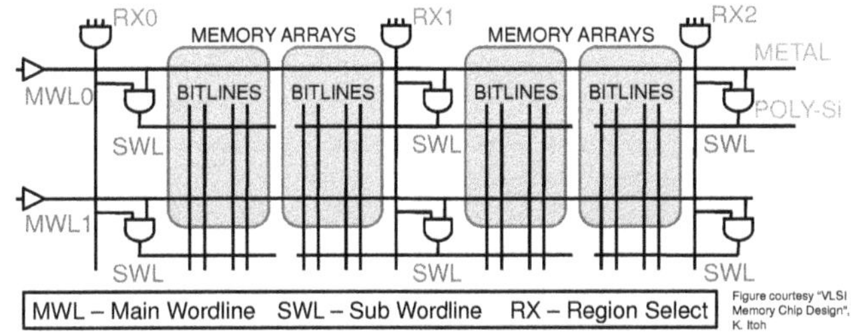

Figure 4: **Hierarchical wordline with region select.**

Memory systems have traditionally multiplexed RAS and CAS commands on the same I/O lines due to pin count limitations. This situation is unlikely to change due to technological limitations [26] and is a hard constraint for DRAM optimization. In a traditional design, once the RAS arrives, enough information is available to activate the appropriate wordline within the array. The cells in that row place their data on the corresponding bitlines. Once the row's data is latched into the row buffer, the CAS signal is used to return some fraction of the many bits read from that array. In our proposed design, instead of letting the RAS immediately activate the entire row and all the bitlines, we wait until the CAS has arrived to begin the array access. The CAS bits identify the subset of the row that needs to be activated and the wordline is only driven in that section. Correspondingly, only those bitlines place data in the row buffer, saving the activation energy of the remaining bits. Therefore, we need the RAS and the CAS before starting the array access. Since the RAS arrives early, it must be stored in a register until the CAS arrives. We refer to this process as *Posted-RAS*[1]. Because we are now waiting for the CAS to begin the array access, some additional cycles (on the order of 10 CPU cycles) are added to the DRAM latency. We expect this impact (quantified in Section 4) to be relatively minor because of the hundreds of cycles already incurred on every DRAM access. Note again that this change is compatible with existing JEDEC standards: the memory controller issues the same set of commands, we simply save the RAS in a register until the CAS arrives before beginning the array access.

The selective bitline activation is made possible by only activating a small segment of the wordline. We employ hierarchical wordlines to facilitate this, at some area cost. Each wordline consists of a Main Wordline (MWL), typically run in first-level metal, controlling Sub-Wordlines (SWL), typically run in poly, which actually connect to the memory cells (see Figure 4). The MWL is loaded only by a few "AND" gates that enable the sub-wordlines, significantly reducing its capacitance, and therefore its delay. "Region Select (RX)" signals control activation of specific SWLs.

Hierarchical wordlines have been previously proposed for DRAMs [25] to reduce delay (rather than energy). Until now, other techniques (metal shunted wordlines [28], for instance) partially achieved what has been perceived as the

[1]Many memory controllers introduce a gap between the issue of the RAS and CAS so that the CAS arrives just as the row buffer is being populated and the device's T_{rcd} constraint is satisfied [27]. Some memory systems send the CAS immediately after the RAS. The CAS is then saved in a register at the DRAM chip until the row buffer is ready. This is referred to as Posted-CAS [29]. We refer to our scheme as Posted-RAS because the RAS is saved in a register until the arrival of the CAS.

advantage of hierarchical wordlines: significant reductions in wordline delay. In a shunted wordline, a metal wordline is stitched to the low-pitch poly wordline at regular intervals by metal-poly contacts. This reduces the wordline delay by limiting the high resistance poly to a small distance while saving area by having only a few metal-poly contacts. The increased area costs of hierarchical wordlines have therefore not been justifiable thus far. Now, with the increasing importance of energy considerations, we believe that using hierarchical wordlines is not only acceptable, but actually necessary. Note that wordlines do not contribute as much to overall DRAM energy, so this feature is important not for its wordline energy savings, but because it *enables* selective bitline activation. In our proposed design, a subset of the CAS address is used to trigger the RX signal, reducing the activation area and wordline/bitline energy. Note that since the MWL is not directly connected to the memory cells, the activation of the MWL across the array does not result in destruction of data, since only the small subset of cells connected to the active SWL read their data out.

We incorporated an analytical model for hierarchical wordlines into CACTI 6.5 [39, 49] (more details in Section 4.1) to quantify the area overhead. For the specific DRAM part described in Section 4.1, we observed that an area overhead of 100% was incurred when enough SWLs were introduced to activate exactly one cache line in a bank. This is because of the high area overhead introduced by the AND gate and RX signals for a few memory cells. While this results in activating a minimum number of bitlines, the cost may be prohibitive. However, we can trade-off energy for lower cost by not being as selective. If we were to instead read out 16 cache lines, the SWLs become 16 times longer. This still leads to high energy savings over the baseline, and a more acceptable area overhead of 12%. Most of our results in Section 4 pertain to this model. Even though we are reading out 16 cache lines, we continue to use the close-page policy.

In summary, the SBA mechanism (i) reduces bitline and wordline dynamic energy by reading out a limited number of cache lines from the arrays (to significantly reduce overfetch), (ii) impacts performance (negatively or positively) by using a close-page policy, (iii) negatively impacts performance by waiting for CAS before starting array access, (iv) increases area and cost by requiring hierarchical wordlines, and finally (v) does not impact the DRAM interface. As we will discuss subsequently, this mechanism does not impact any chipkill solutions for the DRAM system because the data organization across the chips has not been changed.

3.2 Single Subarray Access (SSA)

While the SBA design can eliminate overfetch, it is still an attempt to shoehorn in energy optimizations in a manner that conforms to modern-day DRAM interfaces and data layouts. Given that we have reached an inflection point, a major rethink of DRAM design is called for. An energy-efficient architecture will also be relevant for other emerging storage technologies. This sub-section defines an energy-optimized architecture (SSA) that is not encumbered by existing standards.

Many features in current DRAMs have contributed to better locality handling and low cost-per-bit, but also to high energy overhead. Arrays are designed to be large structures so that the peripheral circuitry is better amortized. While DRAMs can allow low-power sleep modes for arrays, the

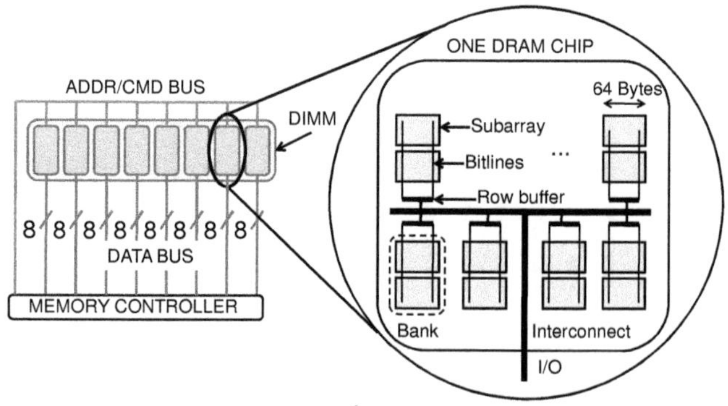

Figure 5: SSA DRAM Architecture.

large size of each array implies that the power-down granularity is rather coarse, offering fewer power-saving opportunities. Since each DRAM chip has limited pin bandwidth, a cache line is striped across all the DRAM chips on a DIMM to reduce the data transfer time (and also to improve reliability). As a result, a single access activates multiple chips, and multiple large arrays within each chip.

Overview: To overcome the above drawbacks and minimize energy, we move to an extreme model where an entire cache line is read out of a single small array in a single DRAM chip. This small array is henceforth referred to as a *"subarray"*. Figure 5 shows the entire memory channel and how various sub-components are organized. The subarray is as wide as a cache line. Similar to SBA, we see a dramatic reduction in dynamic energy by only activating enough bitlines to read out a single cache line. Further, remaining inactive subarrays can be placed in low-power sleep modes, saving background energy. The area overhead of SSA is lower than that of SBA since we divide the DRAM array at a much coarser granularity.

If the DRAM chip is an x8 part, we either need to provide 8 wires from each subarray to the I/O pins or provide a single wire and serialize the transfer. We adopt the former option and as shown in Figure 5, the subarrays place their data on a shared 8-bit bus. In addition, since the entire cache line is being returned via the limited pins on a single chip, it takes many more cycles to effect the data transfer to the CPU. Thus, the new design clearly incurs a higher DRAM latency because of slow data transfer rates. It also only supports a close-page policy, which can impact performance either positively or negatively. On the other hand, the design has much higher concurrency, as each DRAM chip can be simultaneously servicing a different cache line. Since each chip can implement several independent subarrays, there can also be much higher intra-chip or bank-level concurrency. We next examine our new design in greater detail.

Memory Controller Interface: Just as in the baseline, a single address/command bus is used to communicate with all DRAM chips on the DIMM. The address is provided in two transfers because of pin limitations on each DRAM chip. This is similar to RAS and CAS in a conventional DRAM, except that they need not be called as such (there isn't a column-select in our design). The address bits from both transfers identify a unique subarray and row (cache line) within that subarray. Part of the address now identifies the DRAM chip that has the cache line (not required in conventional DRAM because all chips are activated). The entire address is required before the subarray can be identified or accessed. Similar to the SBA technique, a few more cycles are added to the DRAM access latency. An additional requirement is that every device has to be capable of latching commands as they are received to enable the command bus to then move on to operating a different device. This can easily be achieved by having a set of registers (each capable of signaling one device) connected to a demultiplexer which reads commands off the command bus and redirects them appropriately. The data bus is physically no different than the conventional design: for an xN DRAM chip, N data bits are communicated between the DRAM chip and the memory controller every bus cycle. Logically, the N bits from every DRAM chip on a DIMM rank were part of the same cache line in the conventional design; now they are completely independent and deal with different cache lines. Therefore, it is almost as if there are eight independent narrow channels to this DIMM, with the caveat that they all share a single address/command bus.

Subarray Organization: The height of each subarray (i.e. the number of cache lines in a given subarray) directly determines the delay/energy per access within the subarray. Many small subarrays also increase the potential for parallelism and low-power modes. However, a large number of subarrays implies a more complex on-die network and more energy and delay within this network. It also entails greater overhead from peripheral circuitry (decoders, drivers, senseamps, etc.) per subarray which directly impacts area and cost-per-bit. These are basic trade-offs considered during DRAM design and even incorporated into analytical cache models such as CACTI 6.5 [39, 49]. Figure 5 shows how a number of subarrays in a column share a row buffer that feeds the shared bus. The subarrays sharing a row buffer are referred to as a bank, and similar to the conventional model, a single bank can only be dealing with one access at a time. Our SSA implementation models hierarchical bitlines in which data read from a subarray are sent to the row buffer through second level bitlines. To distribute load and maximize concurrency, data is interleaved such that consecutive cache lines are first placed in different DRAM chips and then in different banks of the same chip. To limit the impact on area and interconnect overheads, if we assume the same number of banks per DRAM chip as the baseline, we still end up with a much higher number of total banks on the DIMM. This is because in the baseline organization, the physical banks on all the chips are simply parts of larger logical banks. In the SSA design, each physical bank is independent and a much higher degree of concurrency is offered. Our analysis with a heavily extended version of CACTI 6.5 showed that the area overhead of SSA is only 4%.

Since subarray widths are only 64 bytes, sequential refresh at this granularity will be more time-consuming. However, it is fairly easy to refresh multiple banks simultaneously, *i.e.*, they simply act as one large bank for refresh purposes. In addition, there exist simple techniques to perform refresh that keep the DRAM cell's access transistor on long enough to recharge the storage capacitor immediately after a destructive read, without involving the row-buffer [27].

Power-Down modes: In the SSA architecture, a cache line request is serviced by a single bank in a single DRAM chip, and only a single subarray within that bank is activated. Since the activation "footprint" of the access is much smaller in the SSA design than in the baseline, there is the opportunity to power-down a large portion of the remaining area that may enjoy longer spells of inactivity. Datasheets from Micron [38] indicate that modern chips already support multiple power-down modes that disable various circuitry like the input and output buffers or even freeze the DLL. These modes do not destroy the data on the chip and the chip can be reactivated with a latency penalty proportional to the amount of circuitry that has been turned off and the depth of the power-down state. We adopt a simple strategy for power-down: if a subarray has been *Idle* for I cycles, it goes into a power-down mode that consumes P times less background power than the active mode. When a request is later sent to this subarray, a W cycle latency penalty is incurred for wake-up. The results section quantifies the performance and power impact for various values of I, P, and W.

Impact Summary: In summary, the proposed organization targets dynamic energy reduction by only activating a single chip and a single subarray (with short wordlines and exactly the required number of bitlines) when accessing a cache line. Area overhead is increased, compared to conventional DRAM, because each small subarray incurs the overhead of peripheral circuitry and because a slightly more complex on-die interconnect is required. Background energy can be reduced because a large fraction of the on-chip real estate is inactive at any point and can be placed in low-power modes. The interface between the memory controller and DRAM chips has been changed by effectively splitting the channel into multiple smaller width channels. The impact on reliability is discussed in the next sub-section. Performance is impacted favorably by having many more banks per DIMM and higher concurrency. Similar to the baseline, if we assume that each chip has eight banks, the entire DIMM now has 64 banks. Performance may be impacted positively or negatively by adopting a close-page policy. Performance is negatively impacted because the cache line is returned to the memory controller via several serialized data transfers (an x8 part will take 64 transfers to return a 64 byte cache line). A negative impact is also incurred because the subarray access can begin only after the entire address is received.

We believe that SSA is superior to SBA, although it requires a larger re-design investment from the DRAM community. Firstly, in order to limit the area overhead of hierarchical wordlines, SBA is forced to fetch multiple cache lines, thus not completely eliminating overfetch. SSA therefore yields higher dynamic energy savings. By moving from large arrays in SBA to small subarrays in SSA, SSA also finds many more opportunities to place subarrays in low-power states and save leakage energy. In terms of performance, SSA is hurt by the long data transfer time, and will outdo SBA in workloads that have a high potential for bank-level concurrency.

3.3 Chipkill

Recent studies have shown that DRAMs are often plagued with errors and can lead to significant server downtime in datacenters [46]. Therefore, a low-power DRAM design targeted at datacenters must be amenable to an architecture that provides a high standard of reliability. A common expectation of business-critical server DRAM systems is that they are able to withstand a single DRAM chip failure. Just as an entire family of error-resilient schemes can be built for bit failures (for example, Single Error Correction Double Error Detection, SECDED), a family of error-resilient schemes can also be built for chip failure (for example, Single Chip error Correction Double Chip error Detection, SCCDCD), and these are referred to as *Chipkill* [18, 35]. We now focus on the design of an SCCDCD chipkill scheme; the technique can be easily generalized to produce stronger flavors of error-resilience.

First, consider a conventional design where each word (say 64 bits) has been appended with an 8-bit ECC code, to provide SECDED. For a chipkill scheme, each DRAM chip can only contribute one bit out of the 72-bit word. If a chip were to contribute any more, chip failure would mean multi-bit corruption within the 72-bit word, an error that a SECDED code cannot recover from. Therefore, each 72-bit word must be striped across 72 DRAM chips. When a 64-byte cache line is requested, 72 bytes are read out of the 72 DRAM chips, making sure that each 72-bit word obtains only a single bit from each DRAM chip. Such an organization was adopted in the Dell Poweredge 6400/6450 servers [35]. This provides some of the rationale for current DRAM systems that stripe a cache line across several DRAM chips. This is clearly energy inefficient as 72 DRAM chips are activated and a very small fraction of the read bits are returned to the CPU. It is possible to reduce the number of DRAM chips activated per access if we attach ECC codes to smaller words as has been done in the IBM Netfinity systems [18]. This will have high storage overhead, but greater energy efficiency. For example, in a design attaching an ECC word to 8 bits, say, one may need five extra DRAM chips per eight DRAM chips on a single DIMM. ECC gets progressively more efficient as the granularity at which it is attached is increased.

In the SSA design, we intend to get the entire cache line from a single DRAM chip access. If this DRAM chip were to produce corrupted data, there must be a way to re-construct it. This is a problem formulation almost exactly the same as that for reliable disks. We therefore adopt a solution very similar to that of the well-studied RAID [20] solution for disks, but that has never been previously employed within a DIMM. Note that some current server systems do employ RAID-like schemes across DIMMs [2, 6]; within a DIMM, conventional ECC with an extra DRAM chip is employed. These suffer from high energy overheads due to the large number of chips accessed on every read or write. Our approach is distinct and more energy-efficient. In an example RAID design, a single disk serves as the "parity" disk to eight other data disks. On a disk access (specifically in RAID-4 and RAID-5), only a single disk is read. A checksum associated with the read block (and stored with the data block on the disk) lets the RAID controller know if the read is correct or not. If there is an error, the RAID controller re-constructs the corrupted block by reading the other seven data disks and the parity disk. In the common error-free case, only one disk needs to be accessed because the checksum enables self-contained error detection. It is not fool-proof because the block+checksum may be corrupted, and the checksum may coincidentally be correct (the larger the checksum, the lower the probability of such a silent data corruption). Also, the parity overhead can be made arbitrarily low by having one parity disk for many data disks. This is still good enough for error detection and recovery because the checksum has already played the role of detecting and identifying the corrupted bits. The catch is that writes are more expensive as every write requires a read of the old data block, a read of the old parity block, a write to the data block, and a write to the parity block. RAID-5 ensures that the parity blocks are distributed among all nine disks so that no one disk emerges as a write bottleneck.

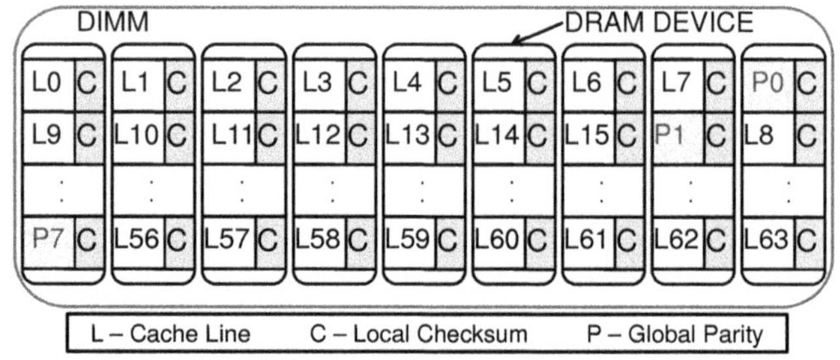

Figure 6: Chipkill support in SSA (only shown for 64 cache lines).

We adopt the same RAID-5 approach in our DRAM SSA design (Fig. 6). The DRAM array microarchitecture must now be modified to not only accommodate a cache line, but also its associated checksum. We assume an eight bit checksum, resulting in a storage overhead of 1.625% for a 64-byte cache line. The checksum function uses bit inversion so that stuck-at-zero faults do not go undetected. The checksum is returned to the CPU after the cache line return and the verification happens in the memory controller (a larger burst length is required, not additional DRAM pins). We cannot allow the verification to happen at the DRAM chip because a corrupted chip may simply flag all accesses as successfully passing the checksum test. The DIMM will now have one extra DRAM chip, a storage overhead of 12.5% for our evaluated platform. Most reads only require that one DRAM chip be accessed. A write requires that two DRAM chips be read and then written. This is the primary performance overhead of this scheme as it increases bank contention (note that an increase in write latency does not impact performance because of read-bypassing at intermediate buffers at the memory controller). We quantify this effect in the results section. This also increases energy consumption, but it is still far less than the energy of reliable or non-reliable conventional DRAM systems.

Most chipkill-level reliability solutions have a higher storage overhead than our technique. As described above, the energy-efficient solutions can have as high as 62.5% overhead, the Dell Poweredge solution has a 12.5% overhead (but requires simultaneous access to 72 DRAM chips), and the rank-sub-setting DRAM model of Ahn et al. [8] has a 37.5% overhead. The key to our higher efficiency is the localization of an entire cache line to a single DRAM chip and the use of checksum for self-contained error detection at modest overhead (1.625%) plus a parity chip (12.5% for 8-way parity). Even on writes, when four DRAM accesses are required, we touch fewer DRAM chips and read only a single cache line in each, compared to any of the prior solutions for chipkill [8, 18, 35]. Therefore, our proposed SSA architecture with chipkill functionality is better than other solutions in terms of area cost and energy. As we show in Section 4, the performance impact of write contention is also low because of the high degree of bank concurrency afforded by SSA.

Processor	8-Core OOO, 2GHz
L1 cache	Fully Private, 3 cycle 2-way, 32 KB each I and D
L2 cache	Fully shared, 10 cycle 8-way, 2 MB, 64B Cache lines
Row-buffer size	8 KB
DRAM Frequency	400 MHz
DRAM Part	256MB, x8
Chips per DIMM	16
Channels	1
Ranks	2
Banks	4
T-rcd, T-cas, T-rp	5 DRAM cyc

Table 1: **General parameters**

4. RESULTS

4.1 Methodology

We model a baseline, 8-core, out-of-order processor with private L1 caches and a shared L2 cache. We assume a main memory capacity of 4 GB organized as shown in Table 1. Our simulation infrastructure uses Virtutech's SIMICS [5] full-system simulator, with out-of-order timing supported by Simics' *'ooo-micro-arch'* module. The *'trans-staller'* module was heavily modified to accurately capture DRAM device timing information including multiple channels, ranks, banks and open rows in each bank. Both open- and close-row page management policies with first-come-first-serve (FCFS) and first-ready-first-come-first-serve (FR-FCFS) scheduling with appropriate queuing delays are accurately modeled. We also model overlapped processing of commands by the memory controller to hide precharge and activation delays when possible. We also include accurate bus models for data transfer between the memory controller and the DIMMs. Address mapping policies were adopted from the DRAMSim [52] framework and from [27]. DRAM timing information was obtained from Micron datasheets [38].

Area, latency and energy numbers for DRAM banks were obtained from CACTI 6.5 [1], heavily modified to include accurate models for commodity DRAM, both for the baseline design and with hierarchical wordlines. By default, CACTI divides a large DRAM array into a number of mats with an H-tree to connect the mats. Such an organization incurs low latency but requires large area. However, traditional DRAM banks are heavily optimized for area to reduce cost and employ very large arrays with minimal peripheral circuitry overhead. Read or write operations are typically done using long multi-level hierarchical bitlines spanning the array instead of using an H-tree interconnect. We modified CACTI to reflect such a commodity DRAM implementation. Note that with a hierarchical bitline implementation, there is a potential opportunity to trade-off bitline energy for area by only using hierarchical wordlines at the higher-level bitline and leaving the first-level bitlines untouched. In this work, we do not explore this trade-off. Instead, we focus on the maximum energy reduction possible. The DRAM energy parameters used in our evaluation are listed in Table 2. We evaluate our proposals on subsets of the multi-threaded PARSEC [13], NAS [9] and STREAM [4] benchmark suites. We run every application for 2 million DRAM accesses (corresponding to many hundreds of millions of instructions) and report total energy consumption and IPC.

Component	**Dynamic Energy(nJ)**
Decoder + Wordline + Senseamps - Baseline	1.429
Decoder + Wordline + Senseamps - SBA	0.024
Decoder + Wordline + Senseamps - SSA	0.013
Bitlines - Baseline	19.282
Bitlines - SBA/SSA	0.151
Termination Resistors Baseline/SBA/SSA	7.323
Output Drivers	2.185
Global Interconnect Baseline/SBA/SSA	1.143
Low-power mode	**Background Power (mW)**
Active	104.5
Power Down (3 mem. cyc)	19.0
Self Refresh (200 mem. cyc)	10.8

Table 2: **Energy parameters**

4.2 Results

We first discuss the energy advantage of the SBA and SSA schemes. We then evaluate the performance characteristics and area overheads of the proposed schemes relative to the baseline organization.

4.2.1 Energy Characteristics

Figure 7 shows the energy consumption of the close-page baseline, SBA, and SSA, normalized to the open-page baseline. The close-page baseline is clearly worse in terms of energy consumption than the open-page baseline simply due to the fact that even accesses that were potentially row-buffer hits (thus not incurring the energy of activating the entire row again) now need to go through the entire activate-read-precharge cycle. We see an average increase in energy consumption by 73% on average, with individual benchmark behavior varying based on their respective row-buffer hit rates. We see from Figure 8 (an average across all benchmarks) that in the baseline organizations (both open and close row), the total energy consumption in the device is dominated by energy in the bitlines. This is because every access to a new row results in a large number of bitlines getting activated *twice*, once to read data out of the cells into the row-buffer and once to precharge the array.

Moving to the SBA or SSA schemes eliminates a huge portion of this energy component. By waiting for the CAS signal and only activating/precharging the exact cache line that we need, bitline energy goes down by a factor of 128. This results in a dramatic energy reduction on every access. However, as discussed previously, prohibitive area overheads necessitate coarser grained selection in SBA, leading to slightly larger energy consumption compared to SSA. Compared to a baseline open-page system, we see average dynamic memory energy savings of *3X* in SBA and *over 6.4X* in SSA. Note that the proposed optimizations result in energy reduction only in the bitlines. The energy overhead due to other components such as decoder, pre-decoder, inter-bank bus, bus termination, etc. remains the same. Hence, their contribution to the total energy increases as bitline energy goes down. Localizing and managing DRAM accesses at

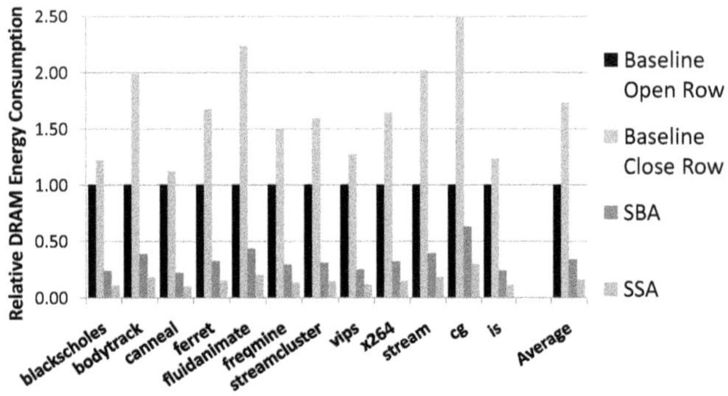

Figure 7: **DRAM dynamic energy consumption**

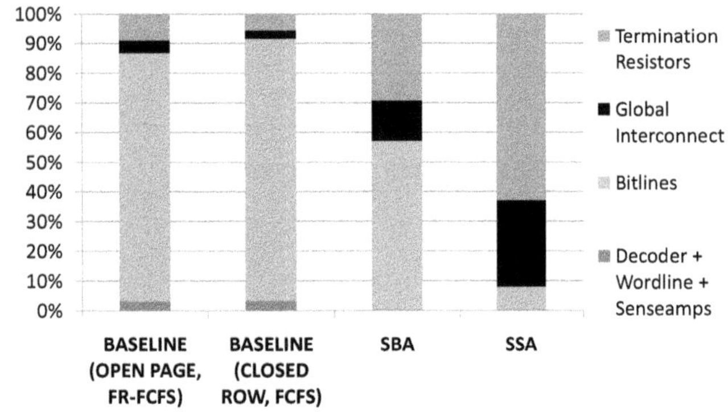

Figure 8: **Contributors to DRAM dynamic energy**

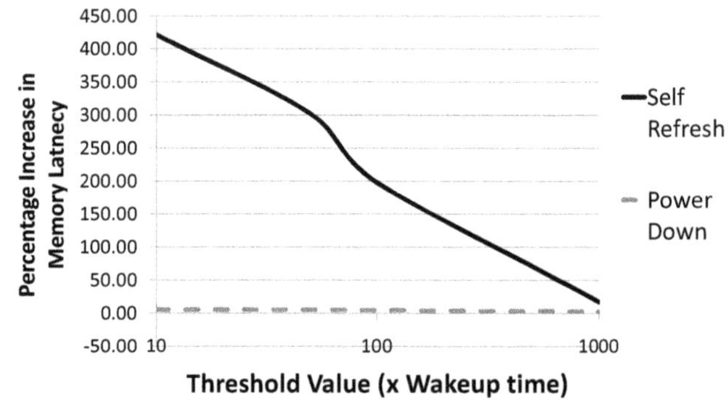

Figure 9: **Memory latency impact of using low-power states**

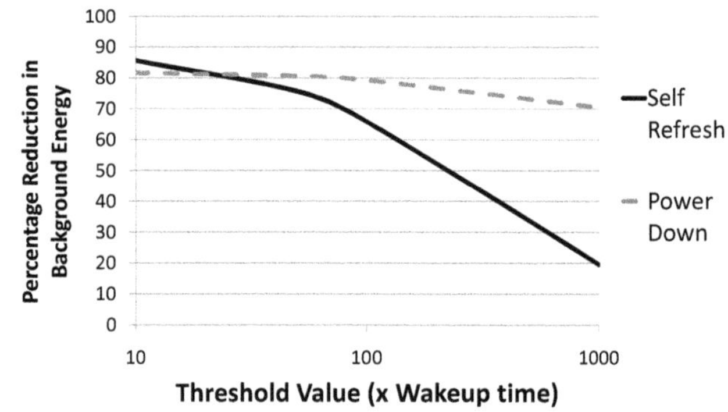

Figure 10: **Energy reduction using low-power states**

a granularity as fine as a subarray allows more opportunity to put larger parts of the DRAM into low-power states. Current DRAM devices support multiple levels of power-down, with different levels of circuitry being turned off, and correspondingly larger wake-up penalties. We evaluate two simple low-power modes with P (Power savings factor) and W (Wakeup) values calculated based on numbers shown in Table 2, obtained from the Micron datasheet and power system calculator [3, 38]. In the deepest sleep mode, *Self Refresh*, P is 10 and W is 200 memory cycles. A less deep sleep mode is *Power Down*, where P is 5.5, but W is just 3 memory cycles. We vary I (Idle cycle threshold) as multiples of the wake-up time W. Figures 9 and 10 show the impact of these low-power states on performance and energy consumption in the SSA organization. We see that the more expensive *Self Refresh* low-power mode actually buys us much lower energy savings compared to the more efficient *Power Down* mode. As we become less aggressive in transitioning to low-power states (increase I), the average memory latency penalty goes down, from just over 5% to just over 2% for the "Power-down" mode. The percentage of time we can put subarrays in low-power mode correspondingly changes from almost 99% to about 86% with energy savings between 81% and 70%. The performance impacts are much larger for the expensive *Self-Refresh* mode, going from over 400% at a very aggressive I to under 20% in the least aggressive case. Correspondingly, banks can be put in this state between 95% and 20% of the time, with energy savings ranging from 85% to 20%. Naturally, these power down modes can be applied to the baseline architecture as well. However, the granularity at which this can be done is much coarser, a DIMM bank at best. This means that there are fewer opportunities to move into low-power states. As a comparison, we study the application of the low-overhead "Power Down" state to the baseline. We find that on average, even with an aggressive sleep threshold, banks can only be put in this mode about 80% of the time, while incurring a penalty of 16% in terms of added memory latency. Being less aggressive dramatically impacts the ability to power down the baseline, with banks going into sleep mode only 17% of the time with a minimal 3% latency penalty. As another comparison point, we consider the percentage of time subarrays or banks can be put in the deepest sleep Self Refresh mode in SSA vs. the baseline, for a constant 10% latency overhead. We find that subarrays in SSA can go into deep sleep nearly 18% of the time whereas banks in the baseline can only go into deep sleep about 5% of the time.

4.2.2 *Performance Characteristics*

Employing either the SBA or SSA schemes impacts memory access latency (positively or negatively) as shown in Figure 11. Figure 12 then breaks this latency down into the average contributions of the various components. One of the primary factors affecting this latency is the page management policy. Moving to a close-page policy from an open-page baseline actually results in a drop in average memory latency by about 17% for a majority (10 of 12) of our benchmarks. This has favorable implications for SBA and SSA which must use a close-page policy. The remaining benchmarks see an increase in memory latency by about 28% on average when moving to close-page. Employing the "Posted-RAS" scheme in the SBA model causes an additional small latency of just over 10% on average (neglecting two outliers).

As seen in Figure 12, for these three models, the queuing delay is the dominant contributor to total memory access latency. Prior work [15] has also shown this to be true in

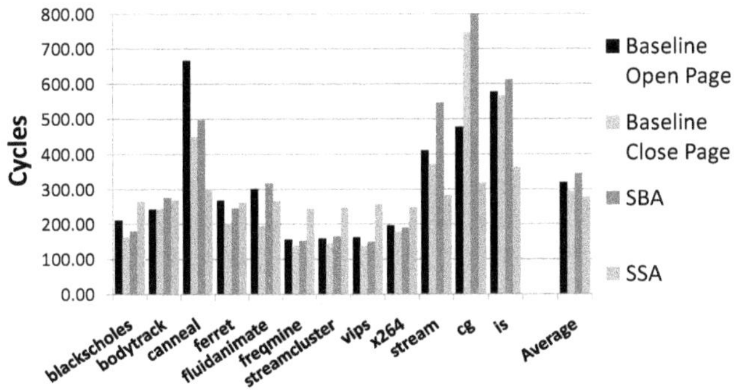

Figure 11: Average main memory latency

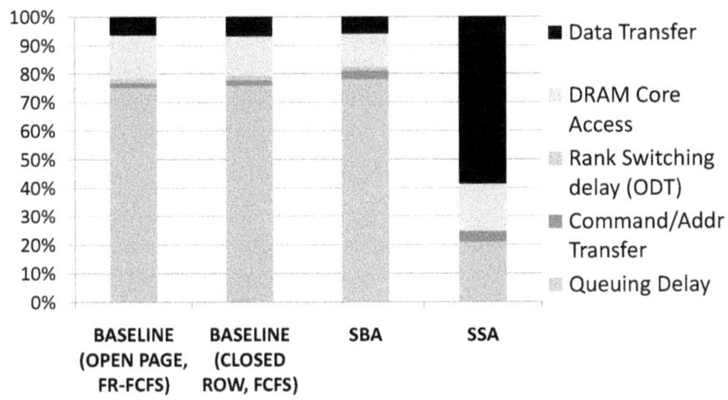

Figure 12: Contributors to total memory latency

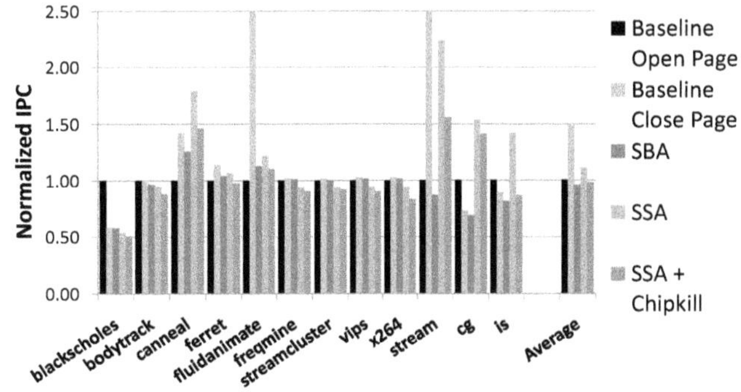

Figure 13: Normalized IPCs of various organizations

many DRAM systems. We therefore see that the additional latency introduced by the "Posted-RAS" does not significantly change average memory access latency.

The SSA scheme, however, has an entirely different bottleneck. Every cache line return is now serialized over just 8 links to the memory controller. This data transfer delay now becomes the dominant factor in the total access time. However, this is offset to some extent by a large increase in parallelism in the system. Each of the 8 devices can now be servicing independent sets of requests, significantly reducing the queuing delay. As a result, we do not see a greatly increased memory latency. On half of our benchmarks, we see latency increases of just under 40%. The other benchmarks are actually able to exploit the parallelism much better, and this more than compensates for the serialization latency, with average access time going down by about 30%. These are also the applications with the highest memory latencies. As a result, overall, SSA in fact outperforms all other models.

Figure 13 shows the relative IPCs of the various schemes under consideration. Like we saw for the memory latency numbers, a majority of our benchmarks perform better with a close-row policy than with an open-row policy. We see performance improvements of just under 10% on average (neglecting two outliers) for 9 of our 12 benchmarks. The other three suffered degradations of about 26% on average. These were the benchmarks with relatively higher last-level cache miss rates (on the order of 10 every 1000 instructions). Employing the "Posted RAS" results in a marginal IPC degradation over close-row baseline, about 4% on average, neglecting two outlier benchmarks.

The SSA scheme sees a performance degradation of 13% on average compared to the open-page baseline on the six benchmarks that saw a memory latency increase. The other 6 benchmarks with a decreased memory access latency see performance gains of 54% on average. These high numbers are observed because these applications are clearly limited by bank contention and SSA addresses this bottleneck. To summarize, in addition to significantly lowered DRAM access energies, SSA occasionally can boost performance, while yielding minor performance slowdowns for others. We expect SSA to yield even higher improvements in the future as ever more cores exert higher queuing pressures on memory controllers. Figure 13 shows the IPC degradation caused when we augment SSA with our chipkill solution. Note that this is entirely because of the increased bank contention during writes. On average, the increase in memory latency is a little over 70%, resulting in a 12% degradation in IPC. Compared to the non-chipkill SSA, there is also additional energy consumption on every write, resulting in a 2.2X increase in dynamic energy to provide chipkill-level reliability, which is still significantly lower than a baseline organization.

4.2.3 System Level Characteristics

To evaluate the system level impact of our schemes, we use a simple model where the DRAM subsystem consumes 40% of total system power (32% dynamic and 8% background). Changes in performance are assumed to linearly impact the power consumption in the rest of the system, both background and dynamic. Having taken these into account, on average, we see 18% and 36% reductions in system power with SBA and SSA respectively.

5. RELATED WORK

The significant contribution of DRAM to overall system power consumption has been documented in several studies [10, 32, 37]. A majority of techniques aimed at conserving DRAM energy try to transition inactive DRAM chips to low power states [30] as effectively as possible to decrease the background power. Researchers have investigated prediction models for DRAM activity [19], adaptive memory controller policies [23], compiler-directed hardware-assisted data layout [16], management of DMA and CPU generated request streams to increase DRAM idle periods [22, 43] as well as managing the virtual memory footprint and physical memory allocation schemes [14, 17, 21] to transition idle DRAM devices to low power modes.

The theme of the other major volume of work aimed at DRAM power reduction has involved rank-subsetting. In addition to exploiting low-power states, these techniques attempt to reduce the dynamic energy component of an access. Zheng et al. suggest the subdivision of a conventional

DRAM rank into mini-ranks [56] comprising of a subset of DRAM devices. Ahn et al. [7, 8] propose a scheme where each DRAM device can be controlled individually via a demux register per channel that is responsible for routing all command signals to the appropriate chip. In their multicore DIMM proposal, multiple DRAM devices on a DIMM can be combined to form a Virtual Memory Device (VMD) and a cache line is supplied by one such VMD. They further extend their work with a comprehensive analytical model to estimate the implications of rank-subsetting on performance and power. They also identify the need to have mechanisms that would ensure chipkill level reliability and extend their designs with SCCDCD mechanisms. A similar approach was proposed by Ware et al. by employing high-speed signals to send chip selects separately to parts of a DIMM in order to achieve dual/quad threaded DIMMs [53]. On the other hand, Sudan et al. [47] attempt to improve row-buffer utilization by packing heavily used cache lines into "Micro-Pages".

Other DRAM-related work includes design for 3-D architectures (Loh [36]), and design for systems with photonic interconnects (Vantrease et al. [51] and Beamer et al. [12]). Yoon and Erez [55] outline efficient chipkill-level reliability mechanisms for DRAM systems but work with existing microarchitectures and data layouts.

However, to the best of our knowledge, our work is the first to attempt fundamental microarchitectural changes to the DRAM system specifically targeting reduced energy consumption. Our SBA mechanism with Posted-RAS is a novel way to reduce activation and can eliminate overfetch. The SSA mechanism re-organizes the layout of a DRAM chip to support small subarrays and the mapping of data to only activate a single subarray. Our chipkill solution that uses checksum-based detection and RAID-like correction has not been previous considered and is more effective than those used for prior DRAM chipkill solutions [8, 18, 35].

6. CONCLUSIONS

We propose two novel techniques to eliminate overfetch in DRAM systems by activating only the necessary bitlines (SBA) and then going as far as to isolate an entire cache line to a single small subarray on a single DRAM chip (SSA). Our solutions will require non-trivial initial design effort on the part of DRAM vendors and will incur minor area/cost increases. A similar architecture will likely also be suitable for emerging memory technologies such as PCM and STT-RAM. The memory energy reductions from our techniques are substantial for both dynamic (6X) and background (5X) components. We observe that fetching exactly a cache line with SSA can improve performance in some cases (over 50% on average) due to its close-page policy and also because it helps alleviate bank contention in some memory-sensitive applications. In other applications that are not as constrained by bank contention, the SSA policy can cause performance degradations (13% on average) because of long cache line data transfer times out of a single DRAM chip.

Any approach that reduces the number of chips used to store a cache line also increases the probability of correlated errors. With SSA, we read an entire cache line out of a single DRAM array, so the potential for correlated errors is increased. In order to provide chipkill-level reliability in concert with SSA, we introduced checksums stored for each cache line in the DRAM, similar to that provided in hard drives. Using the checksum we can provide robust error detection capabilities, and provide chipkill-level reliability through RAID techniques (however in our case, we use a Redundant Array of Inexpensive DRAMs). We show that this approach is more effective in terms of area and energy than prior chipkill approaches, and only incurs a 12% performance penalty compared to an SSA memory system without chipkill.

7. ACKNOWLEDGMENTS

This work was supported in parts by NSF grants CCF-0430063, CCF-0811249, CCF-0916436, NSF CAREER award CCF-0545959, SRC grant 1847.001, and the University of Utah. The authors would also like to thank Utah Arch group members Kshitij Sudan, Manu Awasthi, and David Nellans for help with the baseline DRAM simulator.

8. REFERENCES

[1] CACTI: An Integrated Cache and Memory Access Time, Cycle Time, Area, Leakage, and Dynamic Power Model. http://www.hpl.hp.com/research/cacti/.

[2] HP Advanced Memory Protection Technologies - Technology Brief. http://www.hp.com.

[3] Micron System Power Calculator. http://www.micron.com/support/part info/powercalc.

[4] STREAM - Sustainable Memory Bandwidth in High Performance Computers. http://www.cs.virginia.edu/stream/.

[5] Virtutech Simics Full System Simulator. http://www.virtutech.com.

[6] M. Abbott et al. Durable Memory RS/6000 System Design. In *Proceedings of International Symposium on Fault-Tolerant Computing*, 1994.

[7] J. Ahn, J. Leverich, R. S. Schreiber, and N. Jouppi. Multicore DIMM: an Energy Efficient Memory Module with Independently Controlled DRAMs. *IEEE Computer Architecture Letters*, vol.7(1), 2008.

[8] J. H. Ahn, N. P. Jouppi, C. Kozyrakis, J. Leverich, and R. S. Schreiber. Future Scaling of Processor-Memory Interfaces. In *Proceedings of SC*, 2009.

[9] D. Bailey et al. The NAS Parallel Benchmarks. *International Journal of Supercomputer Applications*, 5(3):63–73, Fall 1991.

[10] L. Barroso. The Price of Performance. *Queue*, 3(7):48–53, 2005.

[11] L. Barroso and U. Holzle. *The Datacenter as a Computer: An Introduction to the Design of Warehouse-Scale Machines*. Morgan & Claypool, 2009.

[12] S. Beamer et al. Re-Architecting DRAM Memory Systems with Monolithically Integrated Silicon Photonics. In *Proceedings of ISCA*, 2010.

[13] C. Benia, S. Kumar, J. P. Singh, and K. Li. The PARSEC Benchmark Suite: Characterization and Architectural Implications. Technical report, Department of Computer Science, Princeton University, 2008.

[14] P. Burns et al. Dynamic Tracking of Page Miss Ratio Curve for Memory Management. In *Proceedings of ASPLOS*, 2004.

[15] V. Cuppu and B. Jacob. Concurrency, Latency, or System Overhead: Which Has the Largest Impact on Uniprocessor DRAM-System Performance. In *Proceedings of ISCA*, 2001.

[16] V. Delaluz et al. DRAM Energy Management Using Software and Hardware Directed Power Mode Control. In *Proceedings of HPCA*, 2001.

[17] V. Delaluz et al. Scheduler-based DRAM Energy Management. In *Proceedings of DAC*, 2002.

[18] T. J. Dell. A Whitepaper on the Benefits of Chipkill-Correct ECC for PC Server Main Memory. Technical report, IBM Microelectronics Division, 1997.

[19] X. Fan, H. Zeng, and C. Ellis. Memory Controller Policies for DRAM Power Management. In *Proceedings of ISLPED*, 2001.

[20] J. L. Hennessy and D. A. Patterson. *Computer Architecture: A Quantitative Approach*. Elsevier, 4th edition, 2007.

[21] H. Huang, P. Pillai, and K. G. Shin. Design And Implementation Of Power-Aware Virtual Memory. In *Proceedings Of The Annual Conference On Usenix Annual Technical Conference*, 2003.

[22] H. Huang, K. Shin, C. Lefurgy, and T. Keller. Improving Energy Efficiency by Making DRAM Less Randomly Accessed. In *Proceedings of ISLPED*, 2005.

[23] I. Hur and C. Lin. A Comprehensive Approach to DRAM Power Management. In *Proceedings of HPCA*, 2008.

[24] E. Ipek, O. Mutlu, J. Martinez, and R. Caruana. Self Optimizing Memory Controllers: A Reinforcement Learning Approach. In *Proceedings of ISCA*, 2008.

[25] K. Itoh. *VLSI Memory Chip Design*. Springer, 2001.

[26] ITRS. International Technology Roadmap for Semiconductors, 2007 Edition. http://www.itrs.net/Links/2007ITRS/Home2007.htm.

[27] B. Jacob, S. W. Ng, and D. T. Wang. *Memory Systems - Cache, DRAM, Disk*. Elsevier, 2008.

[28] M. Kumanoya et al. An Optimized Design for High-Performance Megabit DRAMs. *Electronics and Communications in Japan*, 72(8), 2007.

[29] O. La. SDRAM having posted CAS function of JEDEC standard, 2002. United States Patent, Number 6483769.

[30] A. Lebeck, X. Fan, H. Zeng, and C. Ellis. Power Aware Page Allocation. In *Proceedings of ASPLOS*, 2000.

[31] C. Lee, O. Mutlu, V. Narasiman, and Y. Patt. Prefetch-Aware DRAM Controllers. In *Proceedings of MICRO*, 2008.

[32] C. Lefurgy et al. Energy management for commercial servers. *IEEE Computer*, 36(2):39–48, 2003.

[33] K. Lim et al. Understanding and Designing New Server Architectures for Emerging Warehouse-Computing Environments. In *Proceedings of ISCA*, 2008.

[34] K. Lim et al. Disaggregated Memory for Expansion and Sharing in Blade Servers. In *Proceedings of ISCA*, 2009.

[35] D. Locklear. Chipkill Correct Memory Architecture. Technical report, Dell, 2000.

[36] G. Loh. 3D-Stacked Memory Architectures for Multi-Core Processors. In *Proceedings of ISCA*, 2008.

[37] D. Meisner, B. Gold, and T. Wenisch. PowerNap: Eliminating Server Idle Power. In *Proceedings of ASPLOS*, 2009.

[38] Micron Technology Inc. *Micron DDR2 SDRAM Part MT47H256M8*, 2006.

[39] N. Muralimanohar, R. Balasubramonian, and N. Jouppi. Optimizing NUCA Organizations and Wiring Alternatives for Large Caches with CACTI 6.0. In *Proceedings of MICRO*, 2007.

[40] O. Mutlu and T. Moscibroda. Stall-Time Fair Memory Access Scheduling for Chip Multiprocessors. In *Proceedings of MICRO*, 2007.

[41] O. Mutlu and T. Moscibroda. Parallelism-Aware Batch Scheduling: Enhancing Both Performance and Fairness of Shared DRAM Systems. In *Proceedings of ISCA*, 2008.

[42] U. Nawathe et al. An 8-Core 64-Thread 64b Power-Efficient SPARC SoC. In *Proceedings of ISSCC*, 2007.

[43] V. Pandey, W. Jiang, Y. Zhou, and R. Bianchini. DMA-Aware Memory Energy Management. In *Proceedings of HPCA*, 2006.

[44] B. Rogers et al. Scaling the Bandwidth Wall: Challenges in and Avenues for CMP Scaling. In *Proceedings of ISCA*, 2009.

[45] V. Romanchenko. Quad-Core Opteron: Architecture and Roadmaps. http://www.digital-daily.com/cpu/quad_core_opteron.

[46] B. Schroeder, E. Pinheiro, and W. Weber. DRAM Errors in the Wild: A Large-Scale Field Study. In *Proceedings of SIGMETRICS*, 2009.

[47] K. Sudan, N. Chatterjee, D. Nellans, M. Awasthi, R. Balasubramonian, and A. Davis. Micro-Pages: Increasing DRAM Efficiency with Locality-Aware Data Placement. In *Proceedings of ASPLOS-XV*, 2010.

[48] R. Swinburne. Intel Core i7 - Nehalem Architecture Dive. http://www.bit-tech.net/hardware/2008/11/03/intel-core-i7-nehalem-architecture-dive/.

[49] S. Thoziyoor, N. Muralimanohar, and N. Jouppi. CACTI 5.0. Technical report, HP Laboratories, 2007.

[50] U.S. Environmental Protection Agency - Energy Star Program. *Report To Congress on Server and Data Center Energy Efficiency - Public Law 109-431*, 2007.

[51] D. Vantrease et al. Corona: System Implications of Emerging Nanophotonic Technology. In *Proceedings of ISCA*, 2008.

[52] D. Wang et al. DRAMsim: A Memory-System Simulator. In *SIGARCH Computer Architecture News*, volume 33, September 2005.

[53] F. A. Ware and C. Hampel. Improving Power and Data Efficiency with Threaded Memory Modules. In *Proceedings of ICCD*, 2006.

[54] D. Wentzlaff et al. On-Chip Interconnection Architecture of the Tile Processor. In *IEEE Micro*, volume 22, 2007.

[55] D. Yoon and M. Erez. Virtualized and Flexible ECC for Main Memory. In *Proceedings of ASPLOS*, 2010.

[56] H. Zheng et al. Mini-Rank: Adaptive DRAM Architecture For Improving Memory Power Efficiency. In *Proceedings of MICRO*, 2008.

LReplay: A Pending Period Based Deterministic Replay Scheme

Yunji Chen[†‡], Weiwu Hu[†‡*], Tianshi Chen[§†], Ruiyang Wu[†‡]

† Key Laboratory of Computer System and Architecture,
Institute of Computing Technology, Chinese Academy of Sciences
‡ Loongson Technologies Corporation Limited
§ School of Computer Science and Technology, University of Science and Technology of China

ABSTRACT

Debugging parallel program is a well-known difficult problem. A promising method to facilitate debugging parallel program is using hardware support to achieve deterministic replay. A hardware-assisted deterministic replay scheme should have a small log size, as well as low design cost, to be feasible for adopting by industrial processors. To achieve the goals, we propose a novel and succinct hardware-assisted deterministic replay scheme named LReplay. The key innovation of LReplay is that instead of recording the logical time orders between instructions or instruction blocks as previous investigations, LReplay is built upon recording the pending period information [6]. According to the experimental results on Godson-3, the overall log size of LReplay is about 0.55B/K-Inst (byte per k-instruction) for sequential consistency, and 0.85B/K-Inst for Godson-3 consistency. The log size is smaller in an order of magnitude than state-of-art deterministic replay schemes incuring no performance loss. Furthermore, LReplay only consumes about 1.3% area of Godson-3, since it requires only trivial modifications to the existing components of Godson-3. The above features of LReplay demonstrate the potential of integrating hardware-assisted deterministic replay into future industrial processors.

Categories and Subject Descriptors

F.1.2 [**Modes of Computation**]: Parallelism and concurrency; D.2.5 [**Testing and Debugging**]: Distributed debugging

General Terms

Reliability, Design, Performance

*Corresponding Author: Weiwu Hu (hww@ict.ac.cn), P.O. Box 2704-25, Beijing 100190, P. R. China. This work is partially supported by the National Natural Science Foundation of China under Grants No.60736012, No.60921002, the National Grand Fundamental Research 973 Program of China under Grant No.2005CB321600, and the National High Technology Development 863 Program of China under Grants No.2008AA110901.

ISCA'10, June 19–23, 2010, Saint-Malo, France.

Keywords

Pending period, deterministic replay, multi-core processor, DFD, global clock, physical time order

1. INTRODUCTION

1.1 Motivation

Nowadays, Multi-Core Processor (MCP) has become the mainstream of general-purpose processor. To fully exploit the computational ability of MCP, parallel programming is one of the reasonable solutions. However, debugging parallel program is a well-known difficult problem. For example, the non-determinism of parallel programming may introduce some "Heisen bugs" of which exhibit an erroneous behavior under certain conditions but disappear when in probing or attempting to isolate it. A promising method to tackle the above non-determinism is called the deterministic replay. Such a scheme continuously records the non-deterministic factors in the original execution (production-run) of a parallel program as logs, and utilizes the logs to force another execution (replay-run) exhibiting the same logical behavior as the production-run. During the last two decades, deterministic replay has been employed not only debugging parallel programs [4] but also many other applications, such as fault tolerance [16], performance prediction [40], and intrusion detection [9]. Due to the broad applications, deterministic replay has received intensive investigations in the architecture society.

In general, deterministic replay schemes mainly focus on dealing with the uncertainty of memory races, i.e., the execution order between a pair of successive conflicting memory instructions accessing the same memory location. In production-run, they dynamically identify and record the logical time order between instructions (or instruction blocks), which is the transitive closure of program and execution orders; in replay-run, they use the execution orders inferred from the recorded logical time orders to constrain the execution of parallel program. According to the current methodology of implementing deterministic replay, there are mainly two categories of schemes: the software-only schemes and the hardware-assisted schemes.

To deal with execution order, the software-only schemes purely rely on the supports of specific system software environments, such as operating system, virtual machine, and library [25, 2, 15, 39]. However, these schemes impose many restrictions on system software. Therefore, they have to suffer remarkable performance losses. Furthermore, although software-only schemes can guarantee the replay-run to behave the same as to the production-run, given the same specific software environment, they cannot guarantee that a bug happened in a normal software environment is reproducible in the specific software environment. Such reproducibility problem may limit the usage of software-only schemes.

Unlike software-only schemes, which impose many restrictions on system software, the hardware-assisted deterministic replay schemes pursue dedicated hardware support to efficiently record and replay [4, 37, 38, 28, 29, 26, 16, 8, 27], and do not require specific software environments in most cases. Hence, hardware-assisted schemes have relatively less performance loss in production-run in comparison with the software-only ones, and meanwhile, can avoid the reproducibility problem resulted from different software environments.

The previous studies on hardware-assisted deterministic replay scheme have made significant academic contributions. Nevertheless, implementing them may still encounter some practicality problems, such as large log size, design complexity, and relatively high area impacts. A potential way to overcome these difficulties is to design a hardware-assisted deterministic replay scheme complying the following typical industrial guidelines of Design-For-Debug (DFD) [20, 34, 22, 19, 1, 17, 7, 41, 11]: DFD functionality should affect the performance in production-run as little as possible; DFD functionality should be decoupled from the normal functionality of design to avoid introducing extra design cost; the area consumption of DFD should be low; the log size of DFD should be small enough to fit the limited bandwidth of debug I/O. The rest of the paper will focus on designing such a hardware-assisted scheme that can potentially be integrated as a DFD feature.

1.2 Our Idea and Contributions

By taking the guidelines of DFD into account, we propose a novel hardware-assisted deterministic replay scheme named LReplay to bridge the gap between the academia and industry. The key innovation of LReplay is that it considers the existence of a global clock, records the pending period information [6] in production-run, and cost-effectively stores them. Most execution orders can be inferred from the recorded pending period information, only the non-inferable execution orders are directly recorded by LReplay. To be specific, the pending period of an instruction is a time interval on the global clock in which the instruction starts (or begins) and finishes (or ends) [5, 6]. Meanwhile, in multiprocessor systems providing store atomicity[1], the *perform time* of an instruction, which is the time when a memory instruction is observed by all processors, must be in its pending period. Hence, two instructions with disjoint pending periods can be naturally ordered by the sequence of their perform times. Chen *et al.* called the above order the *physical time order*. It can be proved that the execution orders cannot violate the physical time orders, implying that many execution orders can be inferred from the physical time orders. Intuitively, consider a load instruction l getting its value stored by a store instruction s. If s ends before l starts, then the execution order $s \xrightarrow{E} l$ can be inferred by the existing physical time order $s \xrightarrow{T} l$.

An example of inferring execution orders from the physical time orders is illustrated in Figure 1. Two processors, P_1 and P_2, execute instructions u and v (with subscripts) respectively. All the instructions in the upper block finish before the time 200, and all the instructions in the lower block start after the time 220. According to the definition of physical time order, any instruction in the upper block must precede any instruction in the lower block in physical time order. Consequently, among the execution orders represented by the arrows in Figure 1, most of them are inferable from physical time orders, except the execution order $u_{126} \xrightarrow{E} v_{212}$ (the bold arrow in Figure 1). Hence, to replay all the execution orders illustrated in Figure 1, one needs to only record the end time of the instructions in the upper block, the start time of the instructions in the lower block, and the only non-inferable execution order $u_{126} \xrightarrow{E} v_{212}$ in the production-run.

[1]Most modern multi-core processors support store atomicity [3]. In this paper we only consider store atomic multiprocessor systems.

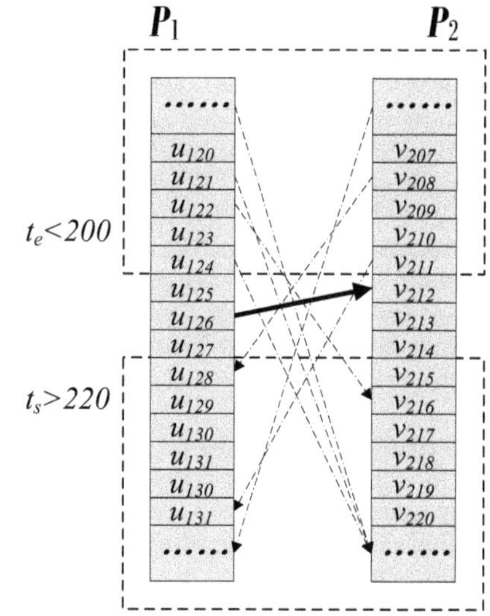

Figure 1: Example of "recovering" execution order from physical time order. The arrows represent execution orders. Among these execution orders, only $u_{126} \xrightarrow{E} v_{212}$ (the bold arrow from u_{126} to v_{212}) is non-inferable from physical time order.

To record pending period, LReplay periodically samples the memory instruction counter of each processor, and records an approximate increment between the values of the memory instruction counter in two successive samplings. With such a lossy compression technique, the pending period log (PPL) of LReplay costs only 1 bit per sample period (typically 256 cycles). For the non-inferable execution orders, LReplay identifies them by comparing the address of each memory instruction missing in L1 dcache with the addresses of the most recent store instructions. To be specific, if the former address hits one of the latter addresses, the corresponding execution order is identified to be non-inferable, and then recorded in the non-inferable execution order log (NEL). Furthermore, to support relaxed memory consistency models such as processor consistency [14] and Godson-3 consistency [5], LReplay can record the load instructions violating sequential consistency in the memory consistency log (MCL), which is a log dedicated to record the additional information for relaxed memory consistency models.

To evaluate LReplay empirically, we implemented it on the RTL design of a commercial multi-core processor Godson-3 [18]. The implementation of LReplay on Godson-3 requires only adding few registers for observing the state of the core, while keeping most components of the multi-core processor such as L2 cache, memory controller, cache coherence protocol and network-on-chip unmodified. Such trivial modification incurs no performance penalties. The experimental results on Godson-3 show that LReplay needs only about 0.41Byte per Kilo-Instruction (B/K-Inst) to record the pending period information in PPL. For the SPLASH-2 benchmarks, the resultant physical time order of PPL can infer more than 99% execution orders in average. Only the residual non-inferable execution orders (less than 1% in average), those between instructions without physical time order, are directly recorded in

NEL with 0.14B/K-Inst. Moreover, the log size of NEL can be further reduced if adopting transitive reduction technique as Regulated Transitive Reduction (RTR) [38]. On the other hand, to support relaxed memory consistency models such as Godson-3 consistency, LReplay requires additional 0.30B/K-inst to record MCL. In summary, the overall log size of LReplay is only 0.55B/K-Inst for sequential consistency, and 0.85B/K-Inst for Godson-3 consistency; with the fact that a small log can be dynamically transferred to outside with JTAG, which compiles to common technique of debug I/O in the industry. To our best knowledge, this is the first time that a hardware-assisted deterministic replay scheme is implemented and evaluated on a system with a relaxed memory consistency model.

The main contributions of LReplay can be summarized as the following. First, it is the first time that a pending period based deterministic replay scheme is proposed. The pending period, which is a novel and fundamental concept proposed for multiprocessor systems with global clock [6], is easy to record in multi-core processors. Moreover, it can be employed to infer most execution orders. Secondly, to our best knowledge, LReplay has the smallest log size among all deterministic replay schemes incuring no performance loss in production-run. Thirdly, LReplay is an open scheme which can be incorporated with other logical time order based schemes to further reduce the cost on recording non-inferable execution orders. Last but not least, LReplay meets most industrial DFD requirements. The above notable feature, together with the promising performance of LReplay in the context of the relaxed memory consistency models, shows the potential of integrating hardware-assisted deterministic replay into future industrial processors.

Rest of the paper introduces the theoretical basis of LReplay, including pending period, physical time order; presents the implementation details of LReplay; empirically evaluates LReplay via analyzing the corresponding experimental results; briefly reviews some related work; discusses some issues about LReplay; and concludes the paper.

2. THEORETICAL BASIS OF LREPLAY

The logical clock was proposed by Lamport to order events in distributed systems without physical global clocks [23]. Over the past decades, multiprocessor systems were often treated as variations of distributed systems, and thus inherited Lamport's logical lock and logical time order for distributed systems. Admittedly, when the logical time order information is perfect, the logical behavior of a multiprocessor system can be determined. However, under many circumstances, it is both hard and ineffective to directly observe and record all the logical time orders, while conjecturing and inferring the unrecorded logical time orders may face high time complexities. As a result, many important problems about multiprocessor systems, which include memory consistency verification [13], event ordering [30], and data race detection [38], were considered to be essentially hard when relying purely on logical clock and logical time orders.

Fortunately, due to the improvement of manufacturing process, the physical distances between processor cores in multiprocessor systems are continuously scaling down. Hence, it has become feasible to overcome the primary obstacle of adopting physical global clock. To be specific, the physical distance between different processors in a modern multiprocessor system is short enough to allow the existence of a physical global clock with tolerable inaccuracy. Once a global clock is given, it is a natural idea to order memory instructions by their perform times on the global clock. However, the precise perform time of an instruction is not only hard to observe (the global performing of an instruction may involved many processors), but also difficult to record (there may be billions of instructions performed in one second). To make global clock practical for ordering events in multiprocessor systems, Chen *et al.* relaxed the precise perform time to a time interval named the pending period which contains the perform time [6]. Consequently, two instructions with disjoint pending periods can be ordered by the sequence of their perform times. Such an order is called *physical time order.* Based on the above concepts, a series of techniques, which were named pending period analysis as a whole, were proposed to analyze multiprocessor systems with global clocks [6]. So far these techniques have significantly reduced the time complexity of memory consistency verification, which is another problem widely concerned by both academia and industry [32, 5].

In the rest part of this paper, we assume that a global clock does exist in a multi-core processor. Later, we will briefly introduce the concepts of pending period and physical time order. Then, the relationship between physical time order and execution order, which is the theoretical basis of LReplay, is presented.

2.1 Pending Period and Physical Time Order

Generally speaking, the prototype of pending period is the instruction window, which is a common architecture concept. Before an instruction enters the instruction window of the corresponding processor, it cannot affect any other instruction; if an instruction retired from the instruction window of the corresponding processor, it must have been viewed by all the processors in the system. Hence, an instruction is globally performed when it is in the instruction window of the corresponding processor. Based on the above facts of instruction window, we can assign a start time and an end time on the global clock as the relaxation of perform time for each instruction.

DEFINITION 1 (START AND END TIME OF INSTRUCTION). [2] *Consider an instruction u executed on a processor P. The start time $t_s(u)$ of u is a time point on the global clock, which is no later than the time point when u enters the instruction window of P. The end time $t_e(u)$ of u is a time point on the global clock, which is no earlier than the time point when u retires from the instruction window of P. The perform time $t_p(u)$ of u is in the time interval between $t_s(u)$ and $t_e(u)$, i.e., $t_s(u) \leq t_p(u) \leq t_e(u)$.*

Based on the above concept of start time and end time, Chen *et al.* provided a definition of pending period:

DEFINITION 2 (PENDING PERIOD [6]). *The pending period of u is the period from its start time $t_s(u)$ to its end time $t_e(u)$.*

Pending period information can be used to order instructions in many cases. Considering two instructions u and v with disjoint pending periods, and the pending period of u is earlier than the pending period of v, i.e., $t_e(u) < t_s(v)$ holds. Since $t_p(u) \leq t_e(u)$ and $t_s(v) \leq t_p(v)$, it can be concluded that $t_p(u) < t_p(v)$ holds. Thus instruction u is globally performed earlier than v. Such kind of partial order determined by the sequence of pending period is called physical time order by Chen *et al.* in [6]:

DEFINITION 3 (PHYSICAL TIME ORDER [6]). *Given two instructions u and v, if the end time of instruction u is before the start time of instruction v, then we say that u is before v in physical time order. Formally,*

$$(t_e(u) < t_s(v)) \leftrightarrow (u \xrightarrow{T} v) \tag{1}$$

[2]It is worth noting that the definitions of start time and end time are flexible to facilitate observing and recording them in concrete applications.

2.2 Relationship between Physical Time Order and Execution Order

In this subsection, we investigate the relationship between physical time order and execution order. Before that, we need to briefly introduce the concept of execution order. Execution order is a type of logical time order which exists between two successive conflicting memory instructions. Here, we say that "two memory instructions are conflicting" if two instructions access the same memory location and at least one of them is a store instruction. The concrete definition of execution order is as below.

DEFINITION 4 (EXECUTION ORDER). *We say that a store instruction w is before instruction u in execution order if and only if w is the latest store instruction before u that accesses the same location as u. We denote this as $w \xrightarrow{E} u$. We say that a store instruction w is after instruction u in execution order if and only if w is the consecutive store instruction after u that accesses the same location as u. We denote this as $u \xrightarrow{E} w$.*

The execution order is an important type of logical time order, since it can totaly determine the logical behavior of a multiprocessor system: two executions of one parallel program with identical execution orders have the identical results. Therefore, the basic idea of traditional deterministic replay schemes is to record sufficient logical time order information in production-run, so that they can infer all the execution orders in replay-run.

When concerning the relationship between execution order and physical time order, one would note that they are based on distinct types of clocks, i.e., logical clock and physical global clock. Chen *et al.* proved that the orders on the two types of clocks are consistent [6]. As a corollary of their result, we have the following theorem.

THEOREM 1 (INFERRING EXECUTION ORDER THEOREM). *If u and v are successive conflicting instructions, and u is before v in physical time order, then u is before v in execution order. Formally,*

$$(succ\_conflict(u, v) \wedge (u \xrightarrow{T} v)) \rightarrow (u \xrightarrow{E} v) \qquad (2)$$

Proof. According to the definition of physical time order, $t_e(u) < t_s(v)$ holds. Since $t_p(u) \leq t_e(u)$ and $t_s(v) \leq t_p(v)$, $t_p(u) < t_p(v)$ holds. If v is before u in execution order, then $t_p(v) < t_p(u)$ holds, which contradicts with $t_p(u) < t_p(v)$. Therefore, u is before v in execution order. □

Theorem 1 is the theoretical basis of our work. According to Theorem 1, the physical time order resulted from the pending period information recorded in the production-run can be employed to impose restriction on many execution orders in the replay-run. Consequently, these execution orders in replay-run must be identical with the corresponding execution orders in production-run, otherwise Theorem 1 is violated. Hence, only the residual execution orders, which are non-inferable from the physical time order, require to be recorded directly in the production-run.

3. IMPLEMENTATION OF LREPLAY

In this section, we introduce the implementation of LReplay in detail. LReplay is implemented based on the RTL design of a commercial multi-core processor Godson-3 [18]. Its main features are listed in Table 1. The key innovation of LReplay is that it records the pending period information of instruction blocks[3], and partitions the execution orders into two categories: the most execution orders which are inferable from the physical time orders infused by the pending period information, and the residual non-inferable execution orders. LReplay adopts different policies to deal with these two categories. For the first category of inferable execution orders, LReplay does not directly record them in production-run, since they can be inferred from the recorded pending period information. For the second category of non-inferable execution orders, LReplay directly records them in production-run and replays them in replay-run, which is similar to other deterministic replay schemes.

In the rest of the section, we first manage to effectively record pending period information, which is sufficient to infer most execution orders. After that, we introduce a conservative way of dealing with the residual non-inferable execution orders. Then, we introduce the way of recording the additional log for the relaxed memory consistency models (such as processor consistency [14] and Godson-3 consistency [5]). In addition, we introduce how to replay with the log recorded by LReplay. Finally, we present the hardware supports of LReplay.

3.1 Recording Pending Period

LReplay is a deterministic replay scheme based on pending period information. In this subsection, the tangible way of recording the pending period information is presented.

3.1.1 Intuitive Idea: A Pending-period-tight Approach

An intuitive idea is to record as tight as possible pending period of each memory instruction, which can infer almost all execution orders. However, such idea is far from perfect, because it needs to record the pending period of each instruction respectively. As we know, a modern multi-core processor can execute (more than) 10^{10} instructions per second. If it requires 8B (bytes) to record the start time and end time of each instruction, the bandwidth needed for recording pending periods is 80GB per second, which is quite a challenge for modern multi-core processors.

As discussed above, the cost would be the main shortcoming of the pending-period-tight approach. Noting that obtaining pending periods is only an intermediate instrument to guarantee the identity between the execution orders in production-run and replay-run, we should find some cost-effective way of recording the pending period information.

3.1.2 Practical Method: Relaxation of Pending Period

To reduce the log size of recording pending period information, LReplay records the pending period of each *instruction block* instead of each *individual instruction.* A way of obtaining the pending period of instruction block is to sample the precise value of memory instruction counter periodically. For example, considering a sequential consistent system, we sample the memory instruction counter of a processor every 100 cycles. If the sampled value of memory instruction counter is 50 at the time 100 and 120 at the time 200, the pending period of the instruction block from memory instruction 50 to memory instruction 120 can be assigned to the time interval [100, 200]. However, such a way is still inefficient since it consumes several byte per sample period. In fact, we can periodically record the approximate increment of memory instruction counter, and thus further reduce the log size for pending period information, as long as the deviation between the obtained information and the actual value of memory instruction counter is bounded.

LReplay adopts the above idea to record pending period infor-

[3]The pending period of an instruction block is the time interval between the start time of the first start instruction in the block, and the end time of the last end instruction in the block.

Table 1: Features of Godson-3.

Core Number	$4-16$ cores
Frequency	$1.0-1.5$ GHz
Network	Crossbar+Mesh
Pipeline	Four-issue, nine-stage, out-of-order
Instruction Window	64 instructions including at most 16 memory instructions
Functional Unit	Two 64-bit fix-point units, two 256-bit vector/ft units, one 128-bit memory unit
L1 dcache	Private, 4 way, 32KB, writeback, 32B per line, non-blocking, random replacement, ECC protected, load-to-use 3(fix)/4(ft) cycles
L1 icache	Private, 4 way, 64KB, 32B per line, random replacement, parity protected
L2 Cache	Unified address, Share, 4-16 bank, 512K-1MB per bank, 4 way, 32B per line, random replacement, ECC protected, 30-35 cycles latency, 32 bit directory per line corresponding to all L1 caches
Memory	1-4 DDR2/3 controller, $>$ 1GB per controller, 333MHz frequency, ECC protected, $\sim$ 120 cycles latency
Cache Coherence	Directory-based MSI protocol
Memory Consistency	Godson-3 consistency: store instruction cannot precede prior memory instructions in program order

Algorithm 1: Recording Pending Period in the PPL log.

```
module pending_period_sampler(i, j);
begin
    reg [63:0] mem_inst_cnt;
    reg [54:0] mem_cnt_div, pre_mem_cnt_div;
    always@(every clock) begin
        if (cmt_mem_inst) then
            mem_inst_cnt ⇐ mem_inst_cnt + 1'b1;
        end
    end
    always@(every sample_period clock) begin
        pre_mem_cnt_div ⇐ mem_cnt_div;
        mem_cnt_div ⇐
        ⌊mem_inst_cnt/sample_period⌋;
    end
    log(PPL_{i,j}, (pre_mem_cnt_div ≠ mem_cnt_div)?1 :
    0);
end
```

mation. As shown in Algorithm 1, the responsibility of the pending_period_sampler module is to record $PPL_{i,j}$, which is the pending period log for processor P_i at the jth sampling. Register *mem_inst_cnt* is the memory instruction counter of P_i, which is updated every clock cycle by increasing 1 if a memory instruction commits in the last clock cycle. Register *mem_cnt_div* is sampled every *sample_period* cycles to record the quotient of *mem_inst_cnt* divided by *sample_period*. If *mem_cnt_div* is the same with *pre_mem_cnt_div* which holds the value of *mem_cnt_div* in the previous $(j-1)^{th}$ sampling, then the approximate increment is 0, and LReplay records 0 in $PPL_{i,j}$. Otherwise, LReplay records 1 in $PPL_{i,j}$ to represent that the approximate increment is *sample_period* since at most *sample_period* memory instructions can be executed in one sample period[4]. With this method, only 1 bit per processor is needed for each sample period to record the pending period information, which is relatively tiny when the sample period is long enough. To match with the precision of the information recorded in PPL, the number of memory instructions in each instruction block should be the same to the length of sample period for sequential consistency.

With the help of PPL, LReplay can estimate $mem\_inst\_cnt_{i,j}$, which is the value of memory instruction counter on P_i at the jth sampling:

$$mem\_inst\_cnt_{i,j} \sim \big[sample\_period\sum_{k=1}^{j} PPL_{i,k},\ sample\_period(\sum_{k=1}^{j} PPL_{i,k}+1)-1\big]. \quad (3)$$

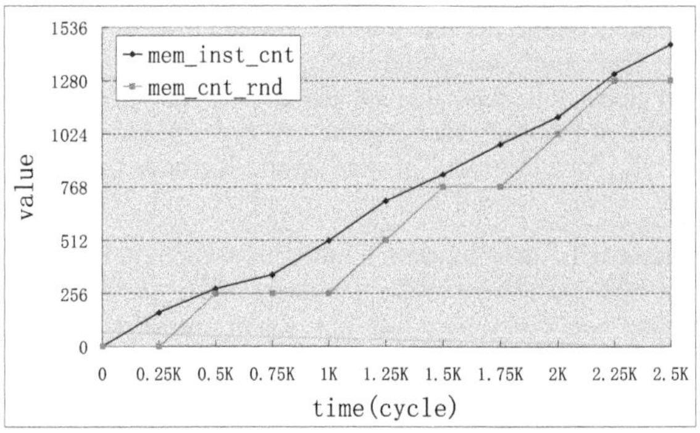

Figure 2: An example of sampling the approximate increment of memory instruction counter. The sample period is 256. The horizontal axis is the sample time, and vertical axis represents either *mem_inst_cnt* or *mem_cnt_rnd* (rounding *mem_inst_cnt* downward by 256).

An example of recording the approximate increment of memory instruction counter is illustrated in Figure 2, where the memory instruction counter is sampled every 256 cycles for 10 times, i.e., there are 256 memory instructions in each instruction block. The values of memory integer counter (*mem_inst_cnt* in the figure) are 165, 278, 345, 510, 700, 828, 974, 1105, 1312 and 1453 for the 10 samplings respectively, while the values of memory integer counter rounded downward by 256 (*mem_cnt_rnd* in the figure) are 0, 256, 256, 256, 512, 768, 768, 1024, 1280 and 1280 for the 10 samplings respectively. Therefore, we only need to record a log of 0100110110 for the 10 samplings. Moreover, recovering an approximate memory instruction counter from the log is rather straightforward. For example, the *mem_inst_cnt* for the 7th sampling should be in the interval $[256(0+1+0+0+1+1+0), 256(0+1+0+0+1+1)+255]$, i.e., $[768, 1023]$; The *mem_inst_cnt* for the 9th sampling should be in the interval of $[256(0+1+0+0+1+1+0+1+1), 256(0+1+0+0+1+1+0+1+1)+255]$, i.e., $[1280, 1535]$. Hence, memory instruction 1024 does not start

[4]Most processor cores can execute at most one memory instruction per clock cycle. We assume this point in the rest of paper.

at the 7th sampling, and memory instruction 1279 has ended before the 9th sampling. Thus it can be concluded that the instruction block from memory instruction 1024 to memory instruction 1279 is in the pending period of $[1792, 2303]$ which is the time interval from the 7th sampling to the 9th sampling.

The remaining problem is to choose an appropriate length for each sample period. A shorter sample period leads to a larger log size of PPL, while a longer sample period results in a larger amount of non-inferable execution orders. Specifically, the latter fact is due to the further relaxation of pending period because of the longer sample period. Furthermore, a longer sample period requires more hardware costs to identify the non-inferable execution orders, which will be discussed in Section 3.5. Through the experiments in Section 4.1, we find that 256 is a promising choice for the length of the sample period, because in such a case, the log size of PPL is only about 0.41B/K-Inst, while $> 99\%$ execution orders are inferable. Furthermore, when the sample period is 256 cycles, the area cost of LReplay is only 1.3% of the chip.

3.2 Recording Non-inferable Execution Orders

Although we have mentioned that $> 99\%$ execution orders can be inferred from physical time order, there are still some non-inferable execution orders existing between pairs of instructions without physical time order. To achieve deterministic replay, it is crucial for LReplay to identify and record directly these non-inferable execution orders in production-run. However, there are still three problems to cope with.

First, *when should LReplay identify the non-inferable execution orders*? LReplay identifies whether an execution order is inferable when a memory instruction misses in L1 dcache. Consider a memory instruction u missing in L1 dcache, there must be a corresponding conflicting store instruction w which sources its value to u, thus there is an execution order $w \xrightarrow{E} u$. At that time, LReplay can identify whether a read-after-write (RAW) or write-after-write (WAW) style execution order can be inferable from physical time order. It is worth noting that for sequential consistency, LReplay does not consider the write-after-read (WAR) style execution orders like most deterministic replay schemes, since they can be inferred from WAW and RAW style execution orders.

Secondly, *how to identify the non-inferable execution orders*? Let us consider a memory instruction u missing in L1 dcache. There must be some store instruction w which sources its value to w. Therefore, there is an execution order $w \xrightarrow{E} u$. LReplay identifies its infer-ability with one CAM for each processor, which records the memory addresses of the most recent 512 (twice as the length of sample period) memory instructions of the processor. *If the memory address of u does not hit any address of recent store instruction recorded in the CAMs of other processors*, it means that w happens at least one sample period before u. Therefore, the end time of the instruction block containing w must be precede the end time of the instruction block containing u. Section 3.4 will introduce that in replay-run. LReplay always selects the instruction block with the earliest end time to execute when no instruction block has been selected to execute, hence the instruction block containing w must be selected to execute before the instruction block containing u. Therefore $w \xrightarrow{E} u$ is inferable from the recorded information, it does not need to be directly recorded. *If the address of u hits the address of a recent store instruction in the CAM of some other processor*, w must happen recently. In such a case, $w \xrightarrow{E} u$ is identified as a non-inferable order from physical time order, and needs to be recorded directly.

Finally, *how to record the non-inferable execution orders*? If an execution order $w \xrightarrow{E} u$ has been identified to be non-inferable, LReplay records it through logging the exact processor number and memory instruction counter of w and u in NEL, which is the dedicated log for non-inferable execution order. To further reduce the log size of NEL, LReplay adopts a simple no-lost compression technique to reduce the size of memory instruction counter, which uses one additional bit to show how many bits are required to record the increment of memory instruction counter as in Algorithm 2.

Algorithm 2: Recording Memory Instruction Counter in the NEL log.

```
module IC_log();
begin
    reg [31:0] instruction_count_now;
    reg [31:0] instruction_count_last;
    reg [31:0] increment =
    instruction_count_now − instruction_count_last;
    always@(An instruction count need to log) begin
        if (increment[31:16] == 16'b0) then
        |  log(NEL.ic,{1'b0,increment[15:0]});
        end
        else
        |  log(NEL.ic,{1'b1,increment});
        end
    end
end
```

3.3 Tackling Relaxed Memory Consistency Models

LReplay can support various memory consistency models, including sequential consistency [33], processor consistency [14], and Godson-3 consistency [5]. For the relaxed memory consistency models, the instruction block size of LReplay should be reduced, and each load instruction that causes the violation with sequential consistency should be identified and recorded in a dedicated log named MCL.

The contained memory instructions of each instruction block should be reduced from $sample\_period$ to $sample\_period - 2 * memory\_inst\_window\_size$, where $memory\_inst\_window\_size$ is the size of memory instruction window. For the corresponding reasons, let us recall the example given at the beginning of Section 3.1.2. We have mentioned that the memory instruction counter of a processor is 50 at the time 100 and 120 at the time 200. For sequential consistency, the pending period of the instruction block from memory instruction 50 to memory instruction 120 is the time interval of $[100, 200]$. However, for relaxed memory consistency models such as processor consistency and Godson-3 consistency, the time interval of $[100, 200]$ is the pending period of the instruction block from memory instruction $50 + 16$ to memory instruction $120 - 16$. The reason is that, although load instructions may precede memory instructions in program order of processor consistency and Godson-3 consistency; the instruction window of Godson-3 only tolerates 16 outstanding memory instructions, preventing a load instruction from preceding any memory instruction that is no less than 16 memory instructions. Therefore, any instruction that is no earlier than memory instruction $50 + 16$ starts after time 100, and any instruction that is no later than memory instruction $120 - 16$ has ended before time 200.

On the other hand, LReplay identifies whether a load instruction may cause a violation of sequential consistency, which is similar to RTR [38]. Concretely, when a store instruction w misses in L1 dcache, LReplay compares its address with the addresses of the recent load instructions recorded in the aforementioned CAMs.

If a recorded load instruction r has the same address with w, it may cause a violation of sequential consistency; therefore, we can record the processor number, memory instruction counter and value of r in the MCL log. To reduce the log size of MCL, we use a compression technique that is similar to Algorithm 2.

3.4 Replaying with PPL, NEL, and MCL Log

Algorithm 3: Replaying the log recorded by LReplay.

```
int ISS_replayer();
begin
    while (1) do
        /*select an unexecuted block based on PPL*/
        B = select_block();
        replay_block(proc(B), B, end_of_block(B));
    end
end
int replay_block(P, B, u');
begin
    for (u = first_unexc_inst(B); u <= u'; u++) do
        if (in_NEL(v -E-> u)) then
            replay_block(proc(block(v)), block(v), v);
        end
        execute_inst(P, B, u);
        if (in_MCL(u)) then
            set_result(u, MCL);
        end
        set_first_unexc_inst(B, u + 1);
    end
end
```

To verify the mechanism of LReplay, we have developed an Instruction Set Simulator (ISS) Replayer to replay the recorded PPL (the log for pending period), NEL (the log for non-inferable execution order) and MCL (the additional log for relaxed memory consistency models). It replays the recorded instructions in a block manner, where each instruction block contains 256 consecutive memory instructions in a same processor for sequential consistency, or 224 (i.e., $256 - 2 \times 16$) memory instructions for relaxed consistency models.

The main idea of the ISS Replayer is to replay instruction blocks with disjoint pending periods in physical time order, and instruction blocks with overlapped pending periods in execution order. As shown in Algorithm 3, the ISS Replayer starts by selecting an unexecuted instruction block B, which has the earliest end time based on the PPL log, with the $select\_block()$ function. Then, the ISS Replayer calls the $replay\_block()$ function to replay block B. In $replay\_block()$, the instructions in B are consecutively processed. If an instruction u in block B is after some unexecuted memory instruction v in another instruction block in execution order ($v \xrightarrow{E} u$), according to the NEL log, the ISS Replayer will call $replay\_block(proc(block(v)), block(v), v)$ to switch to replay the block containing v. Once v has been executed, the ISS replayer should switch back to execute u in block B. To replay the execution in relaxed memory consistency models, the ISS Replayer adopts a method similar to RTR [38]: if u is recorded in MCL for possibly causing the violation of sequential consistency, the result of u is directly given by the corresponding value recorded in MCL. Once all instructions in block B have been executed, the ISS Replayer will select another unexecuted instruction to continue.

An example of the process of replaying is as shown in Figure 3. The instruction block B_1 and instruction block B_2 are on processor P_1, while the instruction block B_3, instruction block B_4, and instruction block B_5 are on processor P_2. Instruction block B_1 is before instruction block B_4 and instruction block B_5 in physical time order, instruction block B_2 is before instruction block B_3 in physical time order. The dashed arrows in the figure represent inferable execution orders from physical time orders, and the bold arrows represent non-inferable execution orders. It is worth noting that the execution order from "sb t0, 0x83(t2)" to "sd s4,0x788(t5)" is also inferable, since the Replayer will replay block B_4 before block B_2. It can be guaranteed that "sb t0, 0x83(t2)" is always replayed before "sd s4,0x788(t5)" in replay-run.

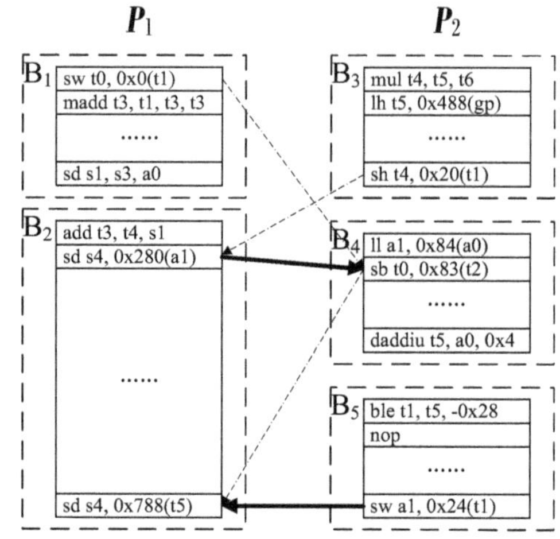

Figure 3: Example of replaying. The dashed arrows represent inferable execution orders, and the bold arrows represent non-inferable execution orders.

To be specific, the procedures of replaying are as follows: First the ISS replayer selects block B_1 to execute, since B_1 has the earliest end time among all unexecuted instruction blocks. When block B_1 has been executed, block B_3 is selected to execute since it has the earliest end time among all the unexecuted instruction blocks. After that, block B_4 is selected to execute. However, before "sb t0, 0x83(t2)" in B_4 is executed, the ISS Replayer should switch to execute block B_2 since instruction "sb t0, 0x83(t2)" in B_4 depends on instruction "sd s4, 0x280(a1)" in block B_2. When the ISS Replayer has executed "sd s4, 0x280(a1)" in B_2, it will switch back to execute block B_4. Then, the ISS Replayer will execute block B_4, block B_5 and block B_2 one after another. It is obvious that in such a replay-run, both inferable and non-inferable execution orders are identical with those in production-run.

3.5 Hardware Support of LReplay

In this subsection, we introduce the modification on Godson-3 RTL for implementing LReplay. For the existing components of Godson-3, LReplay only adds few registers in processor core to facilitate the observability of the memory instruction information, while keeps most components such as L2 cache, memory controller, cache coherence protocol, and switch+mesh interconnection unmodified. The major modification required by LReplay is adding a log processing unit (LPU), the backbone of the hardware supports for LReplay. LPU collects the memory instruction information through a dedicated and simple network with star topology.[5] The gathered information is processed in LPU to generate the log

[5]Adopting a dedicated yet simple network for debug is common in DFD since it can avoid to modify existing components of the design [1].

of which can be shifted out through JTAG, the well known DFD port in industry.

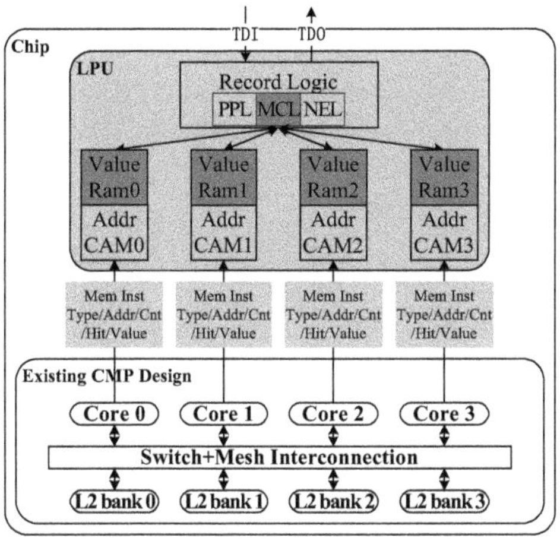

Figure 4: Hardware support is needed by LReplay. The white blocks represent the existing components, the grey blocks represent the hardware supports of deterministic replay for sequential consistency, and the green blocks represent the additional hardware supports of deterministic replay for a relaxed memory consistent model. The information of the recent executed memory instructions of each processor is saved in the corresponding CAM and RAM.

The detailed structure of LPU is illustrated in Figure 4. LPU contains several grey and green blocks, where the grey blocks are to support deterministic replay in sequential consistent system, and the grey blocks together with green blocks can support deterministic replay in a system with a relaxed memory consistency model. In addition, there is a CAM for each processor core to record the information of recent memory instructions including their type, address, counter, and cache hit information. For relaxed memory consistency models, the value of each load instruction is also gathered and saved in the corresponding RAM. There are 512 entries in each CAM/RAM, which is twice as the length of the sample period for pending period. Both CAM and RAM adopt a first-in-first-out (FIFO) scheme: When a new memory instruction needs to be registered, the oldest entry in the CAM (or RAM) is discarded to leave room for the new memory instruction.

LPU samples the memory instruction counter of each core at every sample period, and processes the values of memory instruction counters by the method of Algorithm 1 to generate the PPL log. On the other hand, LPU compares the address of each instruction miss in L1 dcache with the addresses of the store operations recorded in the CAMs of other processors to identify whether there is a non-inferable execution order. The non-inferable execution order is recorded in the NEL log. LPU compares the address of each store instruction missing in L1 dcache with the addresses of the load operations recorded in the CAMs of other processors, to identify whether there is some load operation possibly violating sequential consistency. The processor number, memory instruction counter and value of each load instruction violating sequential consistency are recorded in the MCL log.

4. EVALUATION

In this section, the log size and design cost of LReplay are discussed. The empirical evaluation of LReplay is carried out on the RTL design of the 8-core Godson-3. The experiment platform is an Xtreme-III simulation accelerator [36], which consists of 240 FPGA to achieve at 400KHz simulation top speed. The benchmarks used to evaluate LReplay are the core applications of SPLASH-2 [35].

4.1 Log Size of LReplay

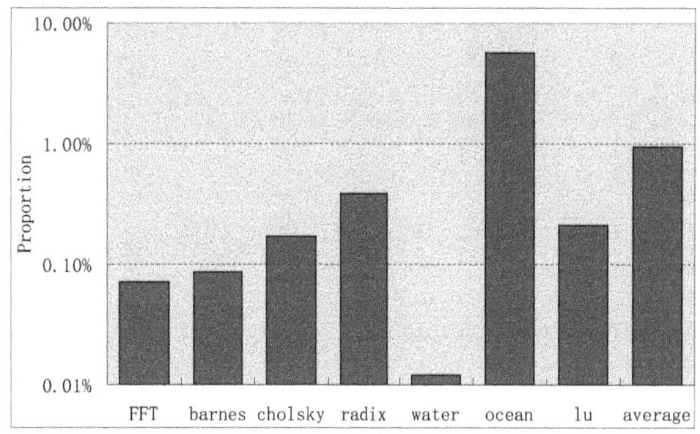

Figure 5: Proportion of non-inferable execution orders when the sample period is 256 cycles.

As mentioned, LReplay divides execution orders into two types, the inferable and non-inferable. The proportion of the non-inferable execution orders in all execution orders is critical to the log size of LReplay. As shown in Figure 5, on the SPLASH-2 benchmarks, the average of non-inferable proportion of execution order is 0.91% when the sample period is at 256 cycles. Specifically, the non-inferable proportions on most benchmarks are around 0.1%, and the smallest of them (the benchmark "water") is just 0.01%. The only exception is the benchmark "ocean" the non-inferable proportion of execution order is 5.66% with 256-cycle sample period. A potential explanation to the above experimental results is that a processor seldom uses the data modified by other processors immediately except lock, semaphore or barrier.

With 256-cycle sample period, Figure 6.a shows the log size of LReplay for sequential consistency. Over our benchmarks, the overall log size of LReplay is 0.55B/K-Inst in average. Meanwhile, the average log sizes of PPL and NEL are 0.41B/K-Inst and 0.14B/K-Inst respectively. Except the benchmark "ocean", the log size of NEL for most benchmarks is less than 0.01B/K-Inst, while the log size of NEL for the benchmark "ocean" is 0.55B/K-Inst actually the log size of NEL for non-inferable execution orders can be further reduced with transitive reduction technique [31]. On the other hand, the log size of PPL is relatively stable over our benchmarks, since the log size of PPL is $0.5/IPC$ B/K-Inst due to that PPL is 1 bit per 256 cycles, where the IPC on these benchmarks is between $1.04 - 1.35$. Therefore, PPL is the main constituent of the overall log for most benchmarks. Figure 6.b shows the log size of LReplay for Godson-3 consistency, which is a relaxed memory consistency model allowing load instruction to precede memory instructions in program order. To support Godson-3, LReplay needs to record MCL in addition to PPL and NEL. Over our benchmarks, MCL requires a log size of 0.30B/K-Inst in average. As a consequence, the overall log size of LReplay for Godson-3 consistency is only 0.85B/K-Inst. Thus, the log of LReplay is small enough to be transferred to outside through JTAG, whose bandwidth is less than 10MB per second.

It is worth to mention that previous hardware-assisted deterministic replay schemes are not directly involved in our experiments due to the difficulty of implementing them in an industrial RTL

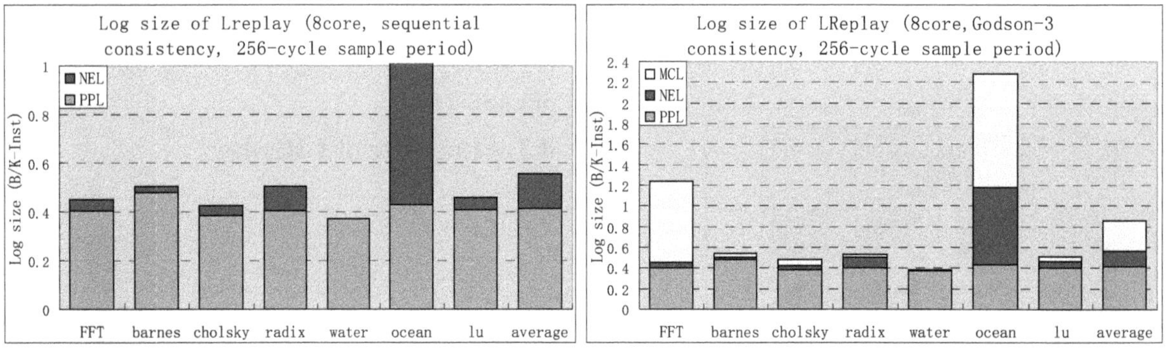

(a) (b)

Figure 6: Log size of LReplay: (a) Log size of LReplay for sequential consistency; (b) log size of LReplay for Godson-3 consistency. PPL is the log for pending period, NEL is the log for non-inferable execution order, and MCL is the additional log for relaxed memory consistency models.

design adopting a relaxed memory consistency model. However, as a reference, Rerun, which is a state-of-art deterministic replay scheme, has a log size of about 4B/K-Inst for sequential consistency [16], which is remarkably larger than the log size of LReplay 0.55K/B-Inst.

4.2 Design Cost of LReplay

The design cost of LReplay can be analyzed from the following aspects.

Logical Design: Implementing LReplay on Godson-3 needs to implement a LPU, trivially modify the processor core to facilitate observing about 200 internal signals of the memory functional unit by LPU, connects LPU to the processor core and to the JTAG TAP controller through a simple network-on-chip. The above procedures require no modification to other components of Godson-3.

Physical Design: LReplay mainly requires a LPU, and a dedicated network-on-chip with about 2000 wires. For 8-core Godson-3, the LPU mainly includes eight 512×27 CAM and eight 512×32 RAM. To synthesize the LPU with STMicro 65nm GP/LP mixed process, we utilized Synopsys's Design Compiler. The report shows that the LPU's area consumption is about 3.6 square millimeter. If only needs to support sequential consistency, the area of LPU will be about 2.5 square millimeter, since the eight 512×32 RAM are not needed. Moreover, both placing and routing 2000 wires are trivial for the physical design of a commercial processor considering that the crossbar of Godson-3 has hundreds of thousands of wires. Noting that the overall area of the 8-core Godson-3 is about 300 square millimeter, conclusively that the area consumption of LReplay is only about 1.3% of the chip.

Verification: The existing components of Godson-3 are almost unmodified, their functionalities are not affected by LReplay. No re-verification is required for Godson-3.

Performance: There is no performance loss since LReplay does not have any impact on the normal functionality of Godson-3.

According to the above, it can be concluded that LReplay has very low design cost, which should be acceptable in industry: LReplay does not affect the performance in production-run; LReplay is decoupled from the normal functionality of the multi-core processor; the area consumption of LReplay is only 1.3% of the multi-core processor; the log size of LReplay is small enough to fit the limited debug I/O bandwidth.

5. RELATED WORK

Debugging parallel program is a well-known difficult problem due to the intrinsic non-determinism of execution orders in parallel systems. To solve this problem, LeBlanc and Mellor-Crummey proposed the first deterministic replay scheme, InstantReplay [25]. The key idea of InstantReplay is to record all execution orders by software, i.e., InstantReplay can be categorized as a software-only scheme. Since then, a number of software-only schemes have been proposed for deterministic replay. With the penalty of the large amount of memory races, even the state-of-art software-only schemes would bring remarkable slowdown in production-run [2, 15, 39].

To improve the effectiveness of deterministic replay, hardware-assisted deterministic replay schemes were proposed. Bacon and Goldstein proposed the first hardware-assisted deterministic replay scheme [4], which requires to record the cache coherence messages on the snooping bus of multiprocessor system. Yet the log size of this pioneer approach is quite large. Later, some hardware-assisted deterministic replay schemes adopt the transitivity reduction technique proposed by Netzer [31] in order to reduce the number of logical time orders between individual instructions required to record. Flight Data Recorder (FDR), proposed by Xu *et al.* [37], is the first one of these schemes. BugNet [28] further improves FDR by adopting hardware-based dictionary to record the outputs of load instructions. In 2006, an enhanced version of FDR and RTR was proposed [38]. The main improvement of RTR is that RTR records the logical time orders between memory instructions while FDR records merely the execution orders, which enables a more aggressive transitivity reduction technique.

Recently, some hardware-assisted deterministic replay schemes manage to record the logical time orders between instruction blocks rather than individual instructions. Strata [29] partitions the whole execution into many stratums. Before any processor issues a second inter-process communication, a stratum is stored. Each stratum is a vector of counters recording the number of memory instructions issued by each processor after the last stratum has been stored. Rerun [16] records the length of each episode, which refers to an instruction block without inter-process communication by Hower and Hill, and the execution orders between episodes. Furthermore, some instruction block based schemes restrict the possible interleaving between blocks to achieve tiny even zero log size [26, 27, 8]. However, these schemes must pay remarkable cost of performance loss and need significant modifications on existing processors.

Substantially different from the previous schemes which directly record the logical time order between instructions or instruction blocks, LReplay makes use of global clock to record pending period information. Benefited from the global clock, LReplay can use loss compression technique to inaccurately record position and relation of instruction blocks with only 1bit per sample period. In contrast, without a global clock, previous block based schemes have to record instruction block information accurately. LReplay also uses a fixed size for instruction block, which further reduces the log size of LReplay. As a result, LReplay can achieve the log size of 0.55B/K-Inst, which is significantly smaller than previous deterministic replay schemes that incurs no performance loss in production-run [37, 28, 38, 29, 16].

Another advantage of LReplay is that it aims at meeting the requirements of designing an industrial processor. Different from the most (if not all) previous hardware-assisted deterministic replay schemes which entangles themselves with many existing components of a multi-core processor - LReplay can be decoupled from normal functionality to reduce its modification to the existing components of the multi-core processor. Furthermore, to our best knowledge LReplay is the first hardware-assisted deterministic replay scheme has been implemented and evaluated on relaxed memory consistency model that is widely adopted in industry.

6. DISCUSSION

In this section, some additional issues about LReplay are discussed.

Global clock: Global clock is the foundation of LReplay. One may concern whether a future many core processor can provide a global clock. Actually, any on-chip clock can be treated as a global clock if we use it to measure on-chip events. Admittedly, the main burden of global clock is the inaccuracy, which is mainly determined by how long the clock signal can traverse the diagonal line of the chip. However, the inaccuracy would be less than 50ns even for future many core processors: A signal can travel 20mm/1ns under STMicro 65nm process, while it is hard to imagine a chip with $>$ 1000mm diagonal line considering that the diagonal line of 16-core Godson-3 is $<$ 40mm. Such an inaccuracy is not a problem by LReplay, with the loss compression technique that can tolerate the inaccuracy of hundreds of cycles.

DFD guideline: The current industrial DFD guidelines are hard to be fulfilled by previous hardware-assisted deterministic replay schemes. To push industrial acceptance of deterministic replay, LReplay is designed to comply with these stringent guidelines. However, we totally agree that these DFD guidelines should be relaxed for debugging parallel program in future industrial practices due to the ever increasing demand of parallel programming/debugging convenience. Actually, when an architect estimates a DFD technique for debugging parallel program, it should be taken into account that the importance of debugging capability may be as important as the performance for a multi-core processor.

I/O log: In a multiprocessor system, I/O is also an important source of non-determinism as well as memory races. Therefore, LReplay also provides support for logging I/O. However, I/O logging has been known as a matured technique, thus we only focus on introducing memory race logging as [16, 26].

Replaying: The replayer of LReplay (the ISS Replayer) is more complicated than the replayers of previous hardware-assisted schemes. Its main difficulty is to deal with both physical and logical time orders. Besides, the ISS Replayer can only replay in a single-thread manner, which may cause significant slow-down of replay-run. Improving the performance of replayer will be left as our future work.

7. CONCLUSION

Hardware-assisted deterministic replay is a promising solution for debugging parallel program, and has attracted broad interests from the academia and industry. To bridge the gap between academic and industrial fields, LReplay is proposed as the first attempt to combine the cutting-edge academic investigation (i.e., global clock and pending period of multi-core processor) with the industrial requirements of DFD. The low cost and high efficiency of LReplay on the RTL design of a commercial processor can possibly alleviate the hesitations of industry about the risk brought by adding the hardware supports for deterministic replay.

Acknowledgments

We are grateful to Douglas M. Carmean, Min-Cheng Lo, Yungang Bao, and the anonymous reviewers for their helpful comments and insightful suggestions to the paper. We also appreciate the colleagues in Godson (Loongson) project for their kind helps.

8. REFERENCES

[1] M. Abramovici, K. Goossens, B. Vermeulen, J. Greenbaum, N. Stollon, and A. Donlin. "You Can Catch More Bugs with Transaction Level Honey". In *Proceedings of the 6th International Conference on Hardware/Software Codesign and System Synthesis (CODES+ISSS'08)*, 2008.

[2] G. Altekar and I. Stoica. "ODR: Output-Deterministic Replay for Multicore Debugging". In *Proceedings of the 22nd ACM Symposium on Operating Systems Principles (SOSP'09)*, 2009.

[3] Arvind and J. Maessen. "Memory Model = Instruction Reordering + Store Atomicity". In *Proceedings of the 33rd International Symposium on Computer Architecture (ISCA'06)*, 2006.

[4] D. Bacon and S. Goldstein. "Hardware-assisted Replay of Multiprocessor Programs". In *Proceedings of the Workshop on Parallel and Distributed Debugging*, 1991.

[5] Y. Chen, Y. Lv, W. Hu, T. Chen, H. Shen, P. Wang, and H. Pan. "Fast Complete Memory Consistency Verification". In *Proceedings of the 15th International Symposium on High-Performance Computer Architecture (HPCA'09)*, 2009.

[6] Y. Chen, T. Chen, and W. Hu. "Global Clock, Physical Time Order and Pending Period Analysis in Multiprocessor Systems". CoRR abs/0903.4961, 2009. (http://arxiv.org/pdf/0903.4961)

[7] CoreSight Program Flow Trace Architecture Specification. http://infocenter.arm.com/help/topic/com.arm.doc.ihi0035a/ index.html

[8] J. Devietti, B. Lucia, L. Ceze, and M. Oskin. "DMP: Deterministic Shared Memory Multiprocessing". In *Proceedings of the 14th International Conference on Architectural Support for Programming Languages and Operating Systems (ASPLOS'09)*, 2009.

[9] G. Dunlap, S. King, S. Cinar, M. Basrai, and P. Chen. "ReVirt: Enabling Intrusion Analysis Through Virtual-Machine Logging and Replay". In *Proceedings of the 5th USENIX Symposium on Operating System Design and Implementation (OSDI'02)*, 2002.

[10] M. Dubois, C. Scheurich, and F. Briggs. "Memory Access Buffering in Multiprocessors". In *Proceedings of the 13rd International Symposium on Computer Architecture (ISCA'86)*, 1986.

[11] T. Foster, D. Lastor, and P. Singh. "First Silicon Functional Validation and Debug of Multicore Microprocessors". *IEEE Transaction on VLSI System*, Vol. 15, No. 5, 2007.

[12] K. Gharachorloo, D. Lenoski, J. Laudon, P. Gibbons, A. Gupta, and J. Hennessy. "Memory Consistency and Event Ordering in Scalable Shared-Memory Multi Processors". In *Proceedings of the 17th International Symposium on Computer Architecture (ISCA'90)*, 1990.

[13] P. Gibbons and E. Korach. "On Testing Cache-Coherent Shared Memories". In *Proceedings of the 6th ACM Symposium on Parallel Algorithms and Architectures (SPAA'94)*, 1994.

[14] J. Goodman. "Cache Consistency And Sequential Consistency ". *Technical Report No. 61*, SCI committee, 1989.

[15] Z. Guo, X.Wang, J. Tang, X. Liu, Z. Xu, M.Wu, M. F. Kaashoek, and Z. Zhang. "R2: An Application-Level Kernel for Record and Replay". In *Proceedings of the 8th USENIX Symposium on Operating System Design and Implementation (OSDI'08)*, 2008.

[16] D. Hower and M. Hill. "Rerun: Exploiting Episodes for Lightweight Memory Race Recording". In *Proceedings of the 35th International Symposium on Computer Architecture (ISCA'08)*, 2008.

[17] M. Hsieh and C. Huang. "An Embedded Infrastructure of Debug and Trace Interface for the DSP Platform". In *Proceedings of the 45th Design Automation Conference (DAC'08)*, 2008.

[18] W. Hu, J. Wang, X. Gao, Y. Chen, Q. Liu, and G. Li. "Godson-3: A Scalable Multicore RISC Processor with x86 Emulation". *IEEE Micro*, Vol. 29, No. 2, 2009.

[19] W. Huott, M. McManus, D. Knebel, S. Steen, D. Manzer, P. Sanda, S. Wilson, Y. Chan, A. Pelella, and S. Polonsky. "The Attack of the "Holey Shmoos": A Case Study of Advanced DFD and Picosecond Imaging Circuit Analysis (PICA)". In *Proceedings of the International Test Conference (ITC'99)*, 1999.

[20] D. Josephson. "The Good, the Bad, and the Ugly of Silicon Debug". In *Proceedings of the 43rd Design Automation Conference (DAC'06)*, 2006.

[21] IEEE Std. 1149.1-1990. IEEE Standard Test Access Port and Boundary-Scan Architecture-Description.

[22] C. Kao, I. Huang , and C. Lin. "An Embedded Multi-resolution AMBA Trace Analyzer for Microprocessor-based SoC Integration". In *Proceedings of the 44th Design Automation Conference (DAC'07)*, 2007.

[23] L. Lamport. "Time, Clocks, and the Ordering of Events in a Distributed System". *Communications of the ACM*, Vol. 21, No. 7, 1978.

[24] L. Lamport. "How to Make a Multiprocessor Computer That Correctly Executes Multiprocess Programs". *IEEE Transactions on Computers*, Vol. 28, No. 9, 1979.

[25] T. LeBlanc and J. Mellor-Crummey. "Debugging Parallel Programs with Instant Replay". *IEEE Transactions on Computers*, Vol. 36, No. 4, 1987.

[26] P. Montesinos, L. Ceze, and J. Torrellas. "DeLorean: Recording and Deterministically Replaying Shared-Memory Multiprocessor Execution Effciently". In *Proceedings of the 35th International Symposium on Computer Architecture (ISCA'08)*, 2008.

[27] P. Montesinos, M. Hicks, S. King, and J. Torrellas. "Capo: Abstraction and Software-hardware Interface for Hardware-assited Deterministic Multiprocessor Replay". In *Proceedings of the 14th International Conference on Architectural Support for Programming Languages and Operating Systems (ASPLOS'09)*, 2009.

[28] S. Narayanasamy, G. Pokam, and B. Calder. "BugNet: Continuously Recording Program Execution for Deterministic Replay Debugging". In *Proceedings of the 31st International Symposium on Computer Architecture (ISCA'05)*, 2005.

[29] S. Narayanasamy, C. Pereira, and B. Calder. "Recording Shared Memory Dependencies Using Strata". In *Proceedings of the 12nd International Conference on Architectural Support for Programming Languages and Operating Systems (ASPLOS'06)*, 2006.

[30] R. Netzer and B. Miller. "On the Complexity of Event Ordering for Shared-Memory Parallel Program Executions". In *Proceedings of the International Conference on Parallel Processing (ICPP'90)*, 1990.

[31] R. Netzer. "Optimal Tracing and Replay for Debugging Shared-Memory Parallel Programs". In *Proceedings of the Workshop on Parallel and Distributed Debugging*, 1993.

[32] A. Roy, S. Zeisset, C. Fleckenstein, and J. Huang. "Fast and Generalized Polynomial Time Memory Consistency Verification". In *Proceedings of the 18th International Conference on Computer Aided Verification (CAV'06)*, 2006.

[33] C. Scheurich and M. Dubois. "Correct Memory Operation of Cached-Based Multiprocessors". In *Proceedings of the 14th International Symposium on Computer Architecture (ISCA'87)*, 1987.

[34] I. Silas, I. Frumkin, E. Hazan, E. Mor, and G. Zobin. "System-Level Validation of the Intel Pentium M Processor". *Intel Technical Journal*, Vol. 7, No. 2, 2003.

[35] S. Woo, M. Ohara, E. Torrie, J. Singh, and A. Gupta. "The SPLASH-2 Programs: Characterization and Methodological Considerations". In *Proceedings of the 22nd International Symposium on Computer Architecture (ISCA'95)*, 1995.

[36] Incisive Xtreme Series Datasheet. http://www.cadence.com/rl/Resources/datasheets/Cadence_6569_DS_R2.pdf.

[37] M. Xu, R. Bodik, and M. Hill. "A "Flight Data Recorder" for Enabling Full-System Multiprocessor Deterministic Replay". In *Proceedings of the 30th International Symposium on Computer Architecture (ISCA'03)*, 2003.

[38] M. Xu, M. Hill, and R. Bodik. "A Regulated Transitive Reduction (RTR) for Longer Memory Race Recording". In *Proceedings of the 12nd International Conference on Architectural Support for Programming Languages and Operating Systems (ASPLOS'06)*, 2006.

[39] R. Xue, X. Liu, M. Wu, Z. Guo, W. Chen, W. Zheng, Z. Zhang, G. Voelker. "MPIWiz: Subgroup Reproducible Replay of MPI Applications". In *Proceedings of the 14th Annual Symposium on Principles and Practice of Parallel Programming (PPoPP'09)*, 2009.

[40] J. Zhai, W. Chen, and W. Zheng. "Phantom: Predicting Performance of Parallel Applications on Large-Scale Parallel Machines Using a Single Node". In *Proceedings of the 15th Annual Symposium on Principles and Practice of Parallel Programming (PPoPP'10)*, 2010.

[41] M. Zilmer. "Non-intrusive On-chip Debug Hardware Accelerates Development for MIPS RISC Processors". http://cms.mips.com/media/files/white-papers/ejtag _debug_eetimes.pdf

Timetraveler: Exploiting Acyclic Races for Optimizing Memory Race Recording

Gwendolyn Voskuilen*, Faraz Ahmad* and T. N. Vijaykumar (* both primary student authors)
School of Electrical and Computer Engineering, Purdue University
{geinfeld,fahmad,vijay}@ecn.purdue.edu

ABSTRACT

As chip multiprocessors emerge as the prevalent microprocessor architecture, support for debugging shared-memory parallel programs becomes important. A key difficulty is the programs' non-deterministic semantics due to which replay runs of a buggy program may not reproduce the bug. The non-determinism stems from memory races where accesses from two threads, at least one of which is a write, go to the same memory location. Previous hardware schemes for memory race recording log the predecessor-successor thread ordering at memory races and enforce the same orderings in the replay run to achieve deterministic replay. To reduce the log size, the schemes exploit transitivity in the orderings to avoid recording redundant orderings. To reduce the log size further while requiring minimal hardware, we propose *Timetraveler* which for the first time exploits acyclicity of races based on the key observation that an acyclic race need not be recorded even if the race is not covered already by transitivity. Timetraveler employs a novel and elegant mechanism called *post-dating* which both ensures that acyclic races, including those through the L2, are eventually ordered correctly, and identifies cyclic races. To address false cycles through the L2, Timetraveler employs another novel mechanism called *time-delay buffer* which delays the advancement of the L2 banks' timestamps and thereby reduces the false cycles. Using simulations, we show that Timetraveler reduces the log size for commercial workloads by 88% over the best previous approach while using only a 696-byte time-delay buffer.

Categories and Subject Descriptors

C.4 [**Computer Systems Organization**]: Performance of Systems - *Measurement Techniques*; D.2.5 [**Software Engineering**]: Testing and Debugging - *Debugging Aids*;

General Terms

Algorithms, Measurement, Reliability.

Keywords

Race Recording, Debugging, Determinism, Replay.

1. INTRODUCTION

Chip multiprocessors (CMPs) are emerging as a better alternative to uniprocessors in terms of power dissipation and performance. However, CMPs run shared-memory parallel programs which are significantly harder to debug than sequential programs due to the programs' non-deterministic semantics. That is, multiple runs of a buggy shared-memory program may result in the bug not manifesting. The reason for the non-deterministic semantics is that *memory races* among threads via shared memory — i.e., accesses to a memory location at least one of which must be a write — change based on the interleaving of the threads. If the interleaving changes due to variations in thread scheduling or access latencies (e.g., due to differences in cache behavior induced by changes in thread-core mappings), then the memory races change resulting in a different program outcome (e.g., lack of bug manifestation).

One approach to address this problem is to provide system support for deterministic replay which achieves the same memory race order, and hence produces the same (buggy) execution as the original run. System support for such replay handles two aspects: (1) a checkpoint state of the program from which a replay may start (to aid in debugging, this checkpoint should capture the state before the bug); and (2) additional state to capture the *predecessor-successor ordering* of the threads involved in each memory race (i.e., a load from one thread occurs before or after a store from another thread). While the former aspect is well-studied (e.g., [4,25,28]), the latter aspect has recently been receiving attention. Because such memory races always involve a write to shared memory and because cache coherence generates global events for such memory races (i.e., write invalidations and read misses), hardware support leverages cache coherence to capture the ordering. Because the hardware treats alike all memory races — synchronization accesses and data races, such schemes are applicable to programs with and without data races.

While previous work has proposed both centralized [16,18] and distributed schemes [30,31], we explore a distributed scheme due to its scalability (see Section 2). In distributed schemes, the hardware records the predecessor-successor ordering among the racing accesses by implementing Lamport's clocks [13]. A per-thread *log* in the program's memory records the races (i.e., no special hardware structure). The schemes incur two significant overheads: (1) large log sizes and (2) hardware overhead of the per-block instruction count in the L1 cache. Reducing the log size enables longer debugging traces and reducing hardware overhead facilitates widespread adoption.

Targeting the first overhead, previous work [20,30] exploits transitivity in the ordering among threads to avoid logging redundant orderings (e.g., if thread *A* is already ordered after thread *B* by an earlier recorded race, then another memory race that implies the same ordering need not be recorded). Other transitivity-based optimizations have also been proposed [31]. Targeting the second overhead, a recent distributed scheme, *Rerun* [12], builds on Strata [18] to eliminate the per-block instruction count in the L1 caches. Rerun partitions a thread's dynamic instruction stream into *episodes*, each of which is an atomic sequence of instructions that ends at a *current-race*. We call a memory race a *past-race* if the race is between previously-ended predecessor episode(s) and a currently-live successor episode, and a *current-race* if the race is among currently-live predecessor and successor episodes. Rerun exploits the fact that past-races are covered by transitivity and need not be recorded, whereas current-races are not covered. Accordingly, Rerun's episodes may include several past-races. While previous schemes use a full-blown timestamp per L1 block to establish thread ordering, Rerun needs only to distinguish whether the block was accessed in a previously-ended episode (for a past-race) or in a currently-live episode (for a current-race), and need not know the exact access time of the block. Rerun combines this distinction with a single timestamp per thread to order the episodes. Rerun's *binary* distinction requires significantly less hardware than the previous schemes (e.g., read/write bits per block or Bloom filters).

We propose *Timetraveler* to achieve smaller logs than Rerun while requiring minimal hardware by exploiting, for the first time, *acyclicity* of races. Bringing this completely new property to bear on the problem of memory race recording is the key intellectual novelty of this paper. Timetraveler addresses three key limitations of Rerun via two novel mechanisms. The first limitation is that the predecessor episode ends *immediately* upon a current-race to address the potential threat that the predecessor's timestamp will later advance past the successor's timestamp. Such ending prevents longer episodes and hence increases the log size. Instead, we make the key observation that episodes may include multiple current-races as long as (1) the predecessor and successor episodes involved in every such race can *eventually* be ordered properly, and (2) the predecessor-successor ordering imposed by the current-races on currently-live episodes is not cyclic (e.g., episode *B* is ordered after episode *A*, and *A* needs to be ordered after *B*). Clearly, cyclicity would make predecessor-successor order ill-defined. Accordingly, Timetraveler partitions a thread's dynamic instruction stream into *chapters*, each of which ends only when the threads appear to be involved in a cyclic, current-race. Thus, a chapter is an atomic sequence of instructions that may include several acyclic, current-races. While previous schemes benefit from transitivity because current-races are rarer than past-races, we observe that cyclic current-races are even rarer, enabling Timetraveler to achieve longer chapters, and hence smaller log.

Timetraveler's first novel and elegant mechanism, called *post-dating*, satisfies both the constraints of our observation. For the first constraint, the predecessor chapter provides a *post-dated* timestamp to the successor chapter with the guarantee that in the future the predecessor chapter's timestamp will not advance beyond the post-dated timestamp; essentially, post-dating creates some "breathing room" for the predecessor chapter. The successor chapter advances its own timestamp beyond the predecessor's post-dated timestamp, guaranteeing that the successor is ordered after the predecessor and neither needs to end its chapter. Cyclic ordering would imply that a chapter has to advance beyond its own post-dated timestamp. Thus, post-dating easily detects when the second constraint is about to be violated and forces the offending chapter to end. Post-dating's elegance stems from achieving the above functionality while adding merely one post-dated timestamp register per core and not any complicated cycle-detection hardware as one might expect. While post-dating handles memory races via L1-resident blocks, the chapters would be shortened by Rerun's second limitation of ending an episode upon the eviction of an L1 block accessed by the episode. Rerun conservatively ends the episode because current-races via the block may go undetected in the shared L2 due to lack of coherence (if the L2 employs coherence then this problem would occur at memory). We again employ post-dating to overcome this limitation. Upon evicting a current-block, a chapter does not end and instead sends its post-dated timestamp to the L2 bank, guaranteeing that any successor is ordered after the predecessor (evicting thread).

Although post-dating handles races via both L1-resident blocks and L1-evicted blocks, L1 evictions cause another problem which is Rerun's third limitation. To ensure correct ordering of races via the L2 while avoiding the overhead of per-block timestamps, Rerun employs a single timestamp for each L2 bank which inherits the latest timestamp among the in-coming, evicted L1 blocks. If Timetraveler were to employ this scheme, a chapter that hits in an L2 bank would advance its timestamp beyond the bank's timestamp to ensure proper ordering with whichever previous chapter had last accessed the block. Unfortunately, L1 eviction of a single recently-accessed block would force the *entire* L2 bank to advance to the evicted block's timestamp, even if all the other blocks in the bank were accessed at much older timestamps. Such advancement would often cause the bank's timestamp to exceed a chapter's post-dated timestamp, inducing false cycles upon L2 hits and forcing the chapter to end. We make the key observation that if L1 evictions are delayed from advancing the L2 bank's timestamp, the current chapters' post-dated timestamps would not be exceeded and the false cycles would be prevented. To this end, we propose a per-L2-bank *time-delay buffer*, Timetraveler's second novel mechanism, to delay the advancement of the L2 bank's timestamp by holding a few recent L1 evictions.

Timetraveler's key contributions are:

- While previous schemes exploit transitivity to reduce the log size, Timetraveler is the first to exploit acyclicity of races.
- Timetraveler proposes two novel and elegant mechanisms, post-dating and delay buffers, which achieve reduction in the log size while incurring *minimal* hardware overhead;
- Using simulations, we show that Timetraveler reduces the log size compared to Rerun by 88% and 99% for commercial and scientific benchmarks, respectively, while adding over Rerun only a 696-byte time-delay buffer and two 32-bit registers for post-dated timestamp and past timestamp per core.

The rest of the paper is organized as follows. We discuss related work in Section 2. We describe Timetraveler and its mechanisms, post-dating and time-delay buffer, in Section 3. Section 4 describes our experimental methodology. We show our results in Section 5, and conclude in Section 6.

2. RELATED WORK

Bacon and Goldstein [6] pioneered the idea of recording memory races in hardware. They record races by logging coherence messages on the snoopy bus. Recent schemes exploit Netzer's transitivity [20] to reduce the log size by avoiding recording memory races whose ordering is implied by transitivity. These schemes include centralized and distributed implementations. Strata [18] proposes the key idea of exploiting race-free instruction sequences which are captured in *strata*, each of which contains the memory-access count of *all* the threads between the last and the current-race. Strata uses a centralized monitor to log each stratum. Unfortunately, Strata's log size is large and does not scale well with thread count [12]. DeLorean [16] proposes a novel chunk-based scheme where a *chunk* is a memory-race-free sequence of instructions in a thread (similar to episodes in Rerun). DeLorean's basic version records the chunk size and the ordering of the chunks in a race, achieving log sizes similar to Rerun. DeLorean employs two optimizations, *OrderOnly* and *PicoLog*, where, respectively, the chunk size is pre-defined but the thread ordering is logged, and both the chunk size and thread ordering are pre-defined. In OrderOnly, any memory race before the pre-defined chunk size is reached, causes one of the threads to roll back. In PicoLog, because even the thread ordering in a race is pre-defined, any race involving a different order causes a rollback. By not recording chunk sizes and thread ordering, these optimizations produce much smaller logs than Rerun. However, DeLorean commits the chunks via a centralized arbiter which cannot scale to a large number of threads, and the rollbacks require substantial hardware support for memory speculation (via BulkSC [8]) which does not exist in conventional CMPs.

The distributed schemes, on the other hand, are more scalable as each thread locally logs the thread ordering for its memory races using Lamport clocks [13]. However, to determine the ordering, FDR-1 [30] and FDR-2 [31] incur significant overhead in the L1 caches. Each cache block has an instruction count of the time of the thread's last access to the block. FDR-1 and FDR-2 log the following upon a memory race at a block: (a) the predecessor thread's instruction count at the time of its access to the block as recorded in its L1 cache, (b) the predecessor thread's identifier, and (c) the current instruction count of the successor thread. This information is sufficient to enforce race ordering in a replay run. Rerun [12] improves upon FDR-1 and FDR-2 to produce comparable log sizes while significantly reducing the hardware overhead — i.e., the per-block instruction counts in the L1 cache. We contrast to Rerun throughout the paper.

BugNet [19] is a software development tool to replay user code and shared libraries and uses FDR-1's hardware. CORD [21], a race recording and detection scheme, uses the concept of scalar clocks to improve performance and race detection accuracy over previous schemes. ReEnact [22], a memory race detector, leverages thread level speculation to rollback and reexecute upon data race detection. ReEnact explores the interesting idea where subsequent re-executions use a library of race signatures to characterize or even eliminate the detected race. Unfortunately, in addition to needing considerable hardware support, this approach requires programmers to identify data races, and incurs performance overhead even during race-free execution.

3. TIMETRAVELER

Recall from Section 1 that Timetraveler exploits, for the first time, acyclicity of races to address Rerun's three key limitations and reduce the log size. To this end, Timetraveler introduces *chapters*, each of which is an atomic instruction sequence that ends at a

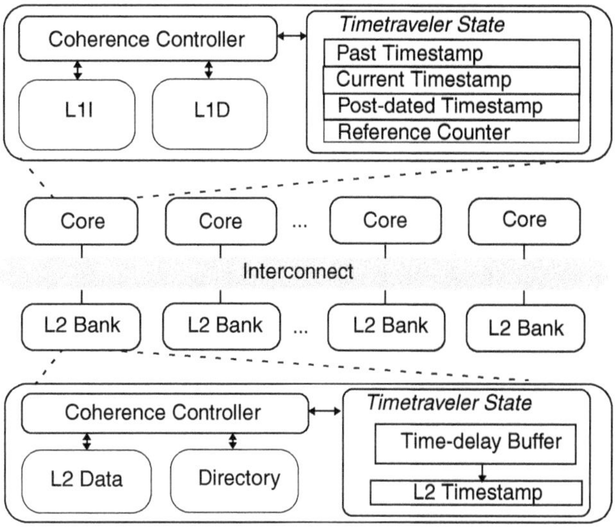

Figure 1. Timetraveler architecture

cyclic, *current* memory race. We call a memory race a *past-race* if the race is between previously-ended predecessor chapters and a currently-live successor chapter, and a *current-race* if the race is among currently-live predecessor and successor chapters. Current-races are called *cyclic* if the predecessor-successor ordering imposed by the races on currently-live chapters is cyclic (e.g., chapter *B* is ordered after chapter *A*, and *A* needs to be ordered after *B*). While Timetraveler's chapters do not end on past-races similar to Rerun's episodes, a chapter may include several, acyclic current-races, unlike Rerun's episodes which end at a current-race.

We describe Timetraveler's implementation as an extension of Rerun's implementation while pinpointing the similarities and differences. We emphasize that Timetraveler is amenable to be implemented as a simple extension of Rerun even though Timetraveler exploits the completely new property of acyclicity of races, illustrating the elegance of Timetraveler's key mechanisms, post-dating and time-delay buffer.

Like Rerun, each thread has a timestamp which is incremented upon the end of a chapter; a chapter's timestamp may also advance as the chapter proceeds, as we see below. Timetraveler logs the chapter's length and final timestamp which represents the chapter's start time in a replay run so that at replay, a chapter starts after the chapters with lower timestamps from *all* the threads have ended. Each log entry corresponds to a chapter and is of the form *<TS, REFS>* where *TS* is the chapter's timestamp and *REFS* encodes the chapter's length as the memory-reference count in the chapter. Because non-memory instructions are purely functional in nature (i.e., deterministically repeat the same behavior in any execution as long as their inputs are the same), non-memory instructions need not be counted in the chapter length. This observation reduces *REFS* and hence the log size.

Figure 1 presents Timetraveler's architecture which we describe via its two novel mechanisms: post-dating and time-delay buffer. Our discussions assume sequential consistency where all memory accesses occur atomically and in program order, so that replay runs also make accesses in the same order. We leave applying Timetraveler to weaker consistency models for future work.

3.1 Post-dating

There are three kinds of races relevant to Timetraveler: past, acyclically current, and cyclically current. Because Timetraveler ends its chapters upon only the third kind and not the first two kinds, we need a way to distinguish among them. As Rerun also does not end its episodes upon past-races, we borrow Rerun's method of distinguishing between past- and current-races.

3.1.1 Post-dating: Overview

Rerun deems a race via a block to be a past-race or current-race depending on whether the *predecessor thread* (that accessed the block first) accessed the block, respectively, in a *previous* episode or in the *current* episode. In the former case of a past-race, because the predecessor thread's previous episode has *already* ended, the successor thread's episode can ensure proper ordering by advancing its timestamp beyond the predecessor thread's *current* timestamp. Because the predecessor thread's current timestamp is guaranteed to be ordered after *its own* previous episode, transitivity guarantees that the successor thread's episode is ordered after the predecessor thread's previous episode. Not ending the successor threads' episodes in such cases enables Rerun to achieve long episodes, and hence small logs. We take the same approach for past-races with one small modification: The successor advances its timestamp beyond the predecessor's *previous* chapter's timestamp instead of the predecessor's current timestamp. Because the above transitivity guarantee still holds, the correct ordering is captured. To this end, Timetraveler keeps two timestamps per thread, a *current timestamp* for the current chapter's timestamp and a *past timestamp* for the last completed chapter's timestamp.

In the latter case of current-races, Rerun ends the predecessor episode (the first limitation discussed in Section 1) so that the predecessor's timestamp does not advance beyond the successor's timestamp, ensuring proper predecessor-successor ordering. Not ending the predecessor would allow the predecessor's timestamp to advance due to other memory races which may violate the ordering. Timetraveler does not end a chapter on a current-race and addresses this problem via *post-dating* based on the key observation that chapters may include multiple current-races as long as (1) the predecessor and the successor chapters involved in every such race can *eventually* be ordered properly, and (2) the predecessor-successor ordering imposed by the current-races on the currently-live chapters is not cyclic.

For the first constraint, the predecessor chapter provides a *post-dated* timestamp to the successor chapter with the guarantee that in the future the predecessor chapter's timestamp will not advance beyond the post-dated timestamp. The post-dated timestamp is a fixed offset, called the *post-dating offset*, from the chapter's current timestamp (there is a corner case where the offsetting is different for optimization purposes, as we explain in Section 3.1.3). The successor chapter advances its own timestamp beyond the predecessor's post-dated timestamp, guaranteeing that it will always be ordered after the predecessor chapter. Cyclic ordering would require the chapter to advance beyond its own post-dated timestamp. Post-dating easily detects this condition and forces the offending chapter to end. All threads which do not have any post-dated timestamp (threads with no memory race and successor-only threads) do not have any constraints on their timestamps and they can continue execution without ending their chapters. In case a

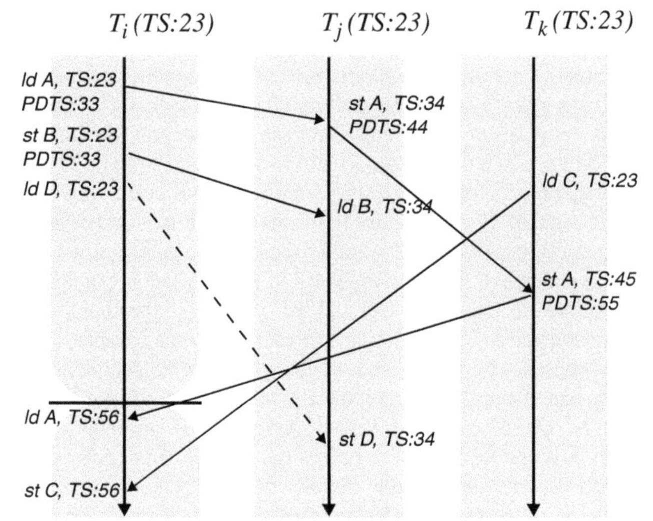

Figure 2. Timetraveler's chapters

memory race requires a successor to increase its timestamp beyond the post-dated timestamp, the successor will end its current chapter, log it, clear the post-dating and start a new chapter. Because cyclic current-races are rarer than acyclic current-races, Timetraveler achieves longer chapters than Rerun, resulting in reduced log size.

To distinguish between past- and current-races, Rerun tracks whether a block has been accessed by a currently-live predecessor episode (i.e., a *current-block)*, or by a previously-ended predecessor episode (i.e., a *past-block*). This binary information requires significantly less hardware (e.g., bit per block or Bloom filters), compared to the exact instruction count of the access in the L1 as done in [30,31]. Rerun employs a pair of Bloom filters per thread to track the current-blocks as the set of blocks read and written by the thread's current episode. While races always involve a write, tracking reads and writes together in one set would misidentify multiple episodes reading the same block as being involved in a race. Therefore, reads and writes are tracked separately. Instead of Bloom filters, Timetraveler uses read/write bits in the cache tags (Section 3.1.4).

3.1.2 Post-dating: Example

To illustrate post-dating, Figure 2 shows an example of Timetraveler chapters for three threads T_i, T_j and T_k, each with the initial timestamp of $TS = 23$. Time progresses downward; the arrows represent races and the ordering between the racing threads. At the time of each racing reference, we show the local timestamp. We omit the memory references that do not cause races (e.g., L1 cache hits). Each grey box represents a chapter and a horizontal line marks the end of a chapter. For the current-race between T_i and T_j via current-block *A*, T_i provides a post-dated timestamp (*PDTS*) of 33 to T_j (the *post-dating offset* is 10). As a result, T_j advances its timestamp (*TS*) to 34 and provides a *PDTS* of 44 to T_k for the current-race via current-block *A*. Accordingly, T_k advances its *TS* to 45. Another current-race between T_i and T_j via current-block *B* causes T_i to provide its already-established *PDTS* of 33 to T_j. However, because T_j's *TS* is already 34 (i.e., T_i and T_j are ordered correctly already), this race does not change T_j's *TS*. For the current-

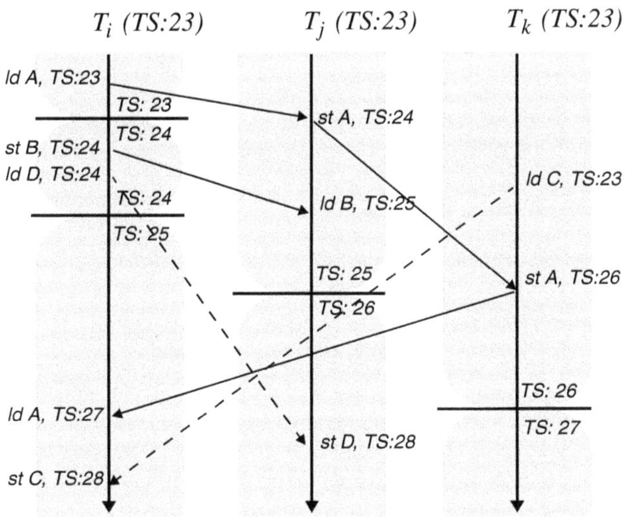

Figure 3. Rerun's episodes

race between T_i and T_k via current-block A, T_k provides a PDTS of 55 to T_i. Advancing T_i's TS to 56 would cause T_i to exceed its PDTS of 33, indicating a cyclic race. Consequently, T_i ends its chapter before the offending instruction, and starts a new chapter with a TS of 56. For the current-race between T_i and T_k via block C, T_k provides a PDTS of 55 to T_i whose TS is already 56, and hence results in no change. Finally, the race between T_i and T_j via block D is a past-race because the thread T_i has ended the chapter in which it last accessed the block. The thread T_j does not change its timestamp because the thread T_i's past timestamp is lower than the thread T_j' current timestamp. At the time of replay, the chapters are ordered as follows: T_i's first chapter (TS = 23),T_j's chapter (34 <= TS <= 44), T_k's chapter (45 <= TS <= 55), and T_i's second chapter (TS >= 56). There is a corner case where the predecessor's PDTS is different than the value determined by the post-dating offset, as we explain in Section 3.1.3.

In the case of Rerun, this example shows two past-races and four current-races, resulting in four episodes as shown in Figure 3. T_i's first episode ends at TS = 23 because it is the predecessor in the current-race with T_j via block A. T_i's second episode starts at TS = 24 and ends at TS = 24 because it is the predecessor in the current-race with T_j via block B. For each of these races, the figure shows how T_j's TS advances from 23 to 24 and then to 25. The dotted arrows show past-races, e.g., block C is a past-block for T_k at the time of T_i's access because T_k accesses C in its first episode which ends before T_i's access. Being a past-race, this race does not cause T_k's second episode to end and simply causes T_i's TS to advance to 28. We see that there are a total of four current-races which result in four episodes. At the time of replay. the episodes would be ordered as follows: T_i first episode (TS = 23), T_i second episode (TS = 24), T_j first episode (TS = 25), and T_k first episode (TS = 26).

3.1.3 Post-dating: Operation

To track the memory blocks accessed in a current chapter, a thread increments its REFS counter for the current chapter and sets the read/write bits for the accessed blocks upon commit of a memory operation (see Figure 4, lines 1-3). In the absence of cache misses, a thread executes without ending its current chapter and its timestamp remains unchanged. In the case of a miss, races are detected

```
[1] On commit of a mem op
[2] REFS++
[3] set read/write bit based on load/store

[4] On sending request for block A
[5] REQUEST (A, PDTS)

[6] At predecessor (On data/ack send for block A)
[7] If the access is a memory race
[8]     If A is a past-block
[9]         SEND (A, PTS)
[10]    else                // current-block
[11]        if rec_PDTS is unset,
[12]            if my_PDTS unset then my_PDTS = CTS + D_PDTS
[13]        else if CTS ≥ rec_PDTS // successor ends, cycle detected
[14]            if my_PDTS unset then my_PDTS = CTS + D_PDTS
[15]        else // successor also has PDTS, try half-way
[16]            my_PDTS = min (my_PDTS, (CTS + (rec_PDTS - CTS) /2))
[17]        SEND (A, my_PDTS)
[18] If the access is not a memory race
[19]    If A is a past-block
[20]        SEND (A, PTS)
[21]    else
[22]        SEND (A, CTS)

[23] At successor (On data receive, RECEIVE (A, rec_TS))
[24] If rec_TS ≥ my_PDTS // limit reached, end chapter
[25]        LOG (REFS, CTS)
[26]        clear read/write bits and REFS
[27]        clear PDTS
[28]        PTS = CTS
[29]        CTS = rec_TS + 1
[30] else // increment my timestamp without ending chapter
[31]        CTS = max (rec_TS + 1, CTS )
```

Abbreviations:	
PDTS = Post-dated timestamp	REFS = Memory references count
CTS = Current timestamp	rec_PDTS = Received timestamp
PTS = Past timestamp	rec_TS = Received timestamp
D_PDTS = Post-dating offset	

Figure 4. Post-dating algorithm

through coherence actions as done in previous schemes — e.g., a successor thread's read miss satisfied by a remote predecessor's dirty block. The successor thread sends its post-dated timestamp along with the coherence request message for a block (see Figure 4, lines 4-5). The predecessor thread(s) check the read/write bits in the L1 to determine whether a race exists and if so, whether it is a past- or a current-race (i.e., the requested block is a past-block or a current-block for the predecessor respectively). We discuss the cases of a past-race and a current-race first and then the case of the absence of a race.

In the case of a past-race (via a past-block), the predecessor threads send their last-completed chapters' timestamps piggy-backed on the coherence reply payload (data or acknowledgement, as appropriate) to the successor thread (see Figure 4, lines 8-9).

This action is similar to Rerun's action (Section 3.1.1). The successor thread advances its timestamp one more than the largest of the predecessors' past timestamps. Neither the predecessor nor the successor threads end their chapters.

In the case of a current-race (via a current-block), Timetraveler's actions are different from Rerun's (Section 3.1.1). There are three cases based on the successor's PDTS, which is sent in the coherence request payload. (i) If the successor's PDTS is not set, then the predecessor sends its PDTS (if the predecessor's PDTS was not set, then it is set to be the current timestamp added to the post-dating offset) (see Figure 4, lines 11-12). (ii) If the predecessor's current timestamp already exceeds the successor's PDTS, the predecessor sends its PDTS and the successor ends its chapter, clears its read/write bits, REFS, and PDTS, and starts a new chapter which is ordered correctly after the predecessor's PDTS (see Figure 4, lines 13-14, 24-29). (iii) If the successor's PDTS is set, the successor's *TS* is already limited by its *PDTS*; therefore, if the predecessor blindly sends its PDTS to the successor, then this computed value may exceed the successor's PDTS causing the successor's chapter to end. Instead, the predecessor *tries* to change its own PDTS to half-way between the successor's PDTS and the predecessor's current timestamp, so that the successor has some room and its chapter need not end (see Figure 5). If this half-way point exceeds the predecessor's current PDTS, the predecessor's PDTS does not change (because a predecessor cannot increment its PDTS once assigned) and the successor chapter ends like the second case. If the half-way point does not exceed the predecessor's current PDTS then the predecessor's PDTS would retreat in time so that the predecessor's other successors are still ordered correctly. Therefore this change occurs only if the halfway point does not exceed the predecessor's current PDTS (see Figure 4, lines 15-16). The half-way computation is approximate and done by simply dropping the least-order bit instead of expensive, accurate dividing. This third case is the corner case mentioned in Section 3.1.2.

For both past- and current-races, the successor always advances its current timestamp by incrementing beyond the received timestamp if the received timestamp is greater than its timestamp (see Figure 4, lines 29,31). If there are multiple predecessors, then all the predecessors take the above actions and the successor advances beyond the largest received timestamp.

So far, we have covered the cases when a predecessor detects a past- or a current-race. Now we discuss the case of a predecessor detecting the absence of a race (i.e., a read miss encounters a clean, shared block). The read miss must still be ordered after the last write to the block. The issue is that the block may have changed coherence state after the last write due to either reads from other cores (e.g., Modified to Shared downgrade) or evictions (we cover L1 evictions later in Section 3.1.4). As such, the state changes hide the fact that a write has occurred. However, ordering the read miss after the entity that has the block (another thread or L2) would ensure that the read is ordered after the write (that entity would have been ordered after the write). Accordingly, the reader advances its own timestamp to one more than the received timestamp. If the sending entity is another thread, then depending upon whether the block is past or current with respect to the thread's current chapter, the thread sends its last-completed chapter's timestamp or the current timestamp (see Figure 4, lines 18-22).

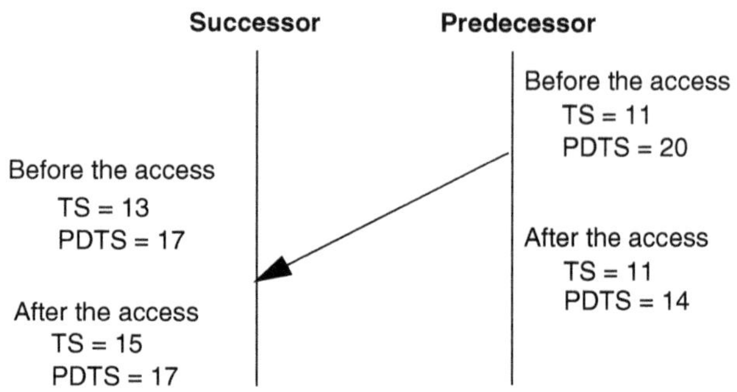

Figure 5. Half-way example

Following Rerun, we send the timestamps as part of coherence message payloads, incurring minimal latency and bandwidth overheads (we report our overhead in Section 5.1). In addition to the obvious impact of the overheads on performance and hence adoption of the scheme, support for deterministic replay should not perturb execution such that turning on the support introduces non-determinism in the observability of bugs. Because the higher the overheads the higher the perturbance, achieving minimal latency/ bandwidth overhead is important. We note that the additional hardware needed for post-dating is minimal: one post-date timestamp register per core.

3.1.4 L1 evictions and L2

The remaining issues with post-dating are L1 evictions and modified-to-shared downgrades. If a block accessed by a currently-live chapter (i.e., a *current-block*, as defined in Section 3.1.1) is evicted or downgraded from the L1 then a current-race via the block may go undetected in the shared L2. To avoid this problem, Rerun conservatively ends the episode upon a current-block eviction or downgrade (the second limitation discussed in Section 1), essentially converting potential future current-races into past-races by forcing all evicted or downgraded blocks to be past-blocks. As in the case of current-races via L1-resident blocks, not ending the predecessor would allow the predecessor's timestamp to advance which may violate the predecessor-successor ordering.

Even though the episode is ended upon current-block evictions and downgrades, the ended episode's timestamp is needed to advance the successor's timestamp and properly order the successor episode. We first explain how Rerun addresses this problem before explaining how Timetraveler addresses L1 evictions and downgrades. In Rerun, L1 evictions and downgrades send their timestamps to L2 which maintains a coarse-grain, per-bank timestamp to avoid the overhead of per-block timestamps (because races through the L2 are less frequent than those through the L1). The per-bank timestamp is updated whenever the L1 timestamp is larger than the per-bank timestamp. Silent replacements (i.e., replacements of a clean, shared copy), a key optimization of directory coherence, also end the episodes like non-silent replacements on current-block evictions but do not generate any traffic to the directory and hence do not update the L2 timestamp. However, the directory forwards requests to the L1 cache for silently-replaced blocks due to lack of knowledge of the replacements. The L1 replies to the requests with the current timestamp, so that the successor is guaranteed to be ordered after the current timestamp, and hence by transitivity, after the episode-ending silent L1 eviction, which occurred in the past.

Because ending the chapters upon L1 evictions and downgrades would shorten the chapters, Timetraveler instead employs post-dating to address this limitation. Upon evicting or downgrading a current-block, a chapter sends its post-dated timestamp to the L2 bank, without ending the chapter. The post-dated timestamp guarantees that any successor accessing the block in the L2 is ordered after the predecessor (evicting thread). For past-block evictions or downgrades, a chapter sends its past timestamp to the L2 bank. While we employ post-dating for non-silent replacements, we perform an additional optimization for silent replacements. Blindly post-dating upon silent replacements of current-blocks would unnecessarily shorten chapters, which cannot advance past the post-dated timestamp in the common case where there are no future requests for the silently-replaced current-block. Instead, we employ a single bit per cache set indicating that a current-block in the set has been replaced silently. Later coherence requests to such silently-replaced blocks are guaranteed to be forwarded to the L1 by the directory. Such requests would miss in the cache but would map to a set with the bit turned on. Accordingly, we post-date the chapter under the conservative assumption that a current-race is about to occur via the replaced block. This bit per set is similar to FDR-2's per-set timestamp for replaced blocks.

Finally, Rerun's Bloom filters decouple the timestamp state from the cache so that the cache is not complicated by the timestamp state, and the filters and the cache can be sized independently. While such decoupling was proposed first in FDR-2 which has full-blown timestamps per block, Rerun has only two bits per block which is not so large as to complicate the cache. Further, though 512-bit and 1024-bit filters suffice so that the state held by the filters is small (64-128 bytes) [12], each bit in the 512-bit filter needs to be addressed requiring a 9-to-512 decoder which incurs a large area overhead [24]. Reducing the area overhead via smaller filters causes false positives which force Rerun's episodes to end. Consequently, we advocate using read/write bits in the cache tags like many speculative memory schemes [9,10,26] and hardware transactional memory schemes [11,17]. Unlike many of these schemes, Timetraveler's bits do not interact with or change coherence actions in any way (i.e., no nacks or wait states which may cause deadlocks or livelocks), and hence do not add any complexity to coherence. Though one may think that updating the read bits on a read access requires an extra write upon a read access, reads already update replacement information (e.g., LRU) which could be extended to update the Timetraveler read bits.

3.2 Time-delay Buffer

In Rerun, the L2 bank inherits the evicted or downgraded blocks' normal or post-dated timestamps based on whether the block is past or current. However, eviction or downgrade of a single recently-accessed block forces the *entire* L2 bank to advance to the block's (normal or post-dated) timestamp, even if all the other blocks in the bank were accessed at much older timestamps (the third limitation discussed in Section 1). If Timetraveler were to employ this inheritance, a current chapter that hits in an L2 bank would advance its timestamp beyond the bank's timestamp and hence ensure correct ordering with respect to the chapters that last accessed the block. If the bank's timestamp were to exceed the chapter's post-dated timestamp upon an L2 hit, the requester would have to end its chapter even if the access is made to an unrelated L2 block — that is, even if it is a false cycle. To address this problem, we make the key observation that if L1 evictions are delayed from advancing the L2 bank's timestamp, the current chapters' post-dated timestamps would not be exceeded and false cycles would be prevented. To this end, we propose a per-L2-bank *time-delay buffer*, Timetraveler's second novel mechanism, which holds the timestamps of a few recent evictions (Figure 1).

If an L1 writeback's timestamp is greater than the L2 bank's timestamp, the L1 writeback checks the buffer for address matches. In the absence of a match, the writeback address and timestamp are placed in the buffer — the writeback data is sent to the L2 and not held in the buffer; upon a match, the matching entry's timestamp is updated if the writeback timestamp is larger. L1 misses also check the buffer for address matches and upon a match, the matching entry's timestamp is returned. In the case of an exclusive access, the entry is removed from the buffer. This removal occurs because a matching L1 miss implies that the block has now moved into an L1 with a more recent timestamp than that in the entry, so that races via the block would be caught by coherence and hence the entry in the buffer is obsolete.

The buffer is organized as a FIFO which empties its entries into the L2 bank. Each dequeued entry from the buffer updates the L2 bank's timestamp if the entry's timestamp is larger. Emptying the buffer as per timestamp order instead of arrival order does not reduce the impact of the L2 bank's timestamp on chapter ending enough to justify complex timestamp-ordering circuitry.

We optimize the time-delay buffer to avoid false self-cycles. Blocks that are written back by a chapter may be accessed later by the same chapter and the chapter may have to end because of its own post-dating. To avoid this problem, we include the core identifier in the buffer entry so that the entry's timestamp is ignored upon a core identifier match (i.e., the chapter's timestamp is not changed when a block is re-accessed). One complication that arises is that when the block is moved back into the L1 from the buffer after a previous L1 eviction within the same chapter, the block loses the read/write bits from before the eviction. If the block was written prior to the eviction and read after the eviction, then the block read/write bits would reflect only the read and not the write. Thus, Timetraveler may miss some conflicts via such blocks. Thus we keep read/write bits in the buffer as well to propagate the block state from the delay-buffer to L1. If the block is dequeued from the buffer and sent to the L2 before being re-accessed, the re-access would result in a self-race causing the chapter to end (this case may shorten chapters but occurs only when the buffer capacity is exceeded). We observe that this case is infrequent.

We summarize the hardware requirements for Rerun and Timetraveler in Table 1. While Timetraveler's time-delay buffer is extra, the buffer holds only addresses and timestamps, but not data. We find that a modest-sized buffer suffices (e.g., 8 entries per bank).

For OS events such as context switches and thread migrations, we end chapters, like Rerun. There is one minor interaction between thread migration and the core identifiers in the time-delay buffer entries. The buffer may incorrectly consider a newly-migrated thread on a core, with the same core identifier as the previous thread on the core, to be the previous evictor of a block, assume a self-cycle, and ignore the block's timestamp. Such ignoring may cause Timetraveler to miss some current-races between the previous and newly-migrated threads. To address this problem, a newly-

Table 1. Hardware requirement

Hardware	Rerun	Timetraveler
Per Core	-Episode length counter -One timestamp register -Read and write Bloom filters	-Chapter length counter -Three timestamp registers for current, past, and post-dated timestamps -One read and one write bit per L1 cache block and one bit per L1 set
Per L2 Bank	-One timestamp register	-One timestamp register -Time-delay buffer where each entry holds a block address, R/W bits, core id, and a timestamp.

migrated thread's timestamp starts by advancing one more than the larger of (1) the thread's starting timestamp for its next chapter and (2) the previous thread's post-dated timestamp. This advancing ensures that the previous thread's blocks held in the time-delay buffer are in the past of the newly-migrated thread and hence cannot cause current-races.

3.3 Discussion

While most often chapters end due to cyclic, current-races, Timetraveler may prematurely end a chapter due to the following false reasons: (1) an acyclic race where the successor's post-dated timestamp happens, by chance, to be smaller than the predecessor's timestamp (Section 3.1.3); (2) exceeding the post-dated timestamp due to past-races (Section 3.1.3), (3) exhaustion of the post-dated timestamp due to half-way division (Section 3.1.3), (4) unnecessary post-dating due to L1-evicted current-blocks that are not accessed by any other thread; (5) false cycles through the L2 upon exceeding the Time-delay buffer's capacity (Section 3.2); and (6) exhaustion of the memory reference counter (i.e., REFS in Section 3). We found that in practice these cases are uncommon.

Finally, because post-dating advances the timestamps by the post-dating offset, Timetraveler's timestamps may advance much faster than Rerun's timestamps and may exhaust the timestamp space sooner (e.g., 32 bits). Upon such exhaustion, all the threads' chapters end, and the time-delay buffer and L2 banks' timestamps are reset. However, because a thread's successive chapters' timestamps differ only by small amounts (e.g., 256), we can employ well-known log compression [23] to record only the differences between successive timestamps instead of the entire timestamp. This compression scheme allows a larger timestamp space without increasing the log size; only the timestamp registers in the core and the time-delay buffer need to be wider.

4. METHODOLOGY

We simulate Timetraveler using Wisconsin GEMS-2.1 [15] built on top of Simics, a full-system simulator[14]. We simulate a SPARC-based multicore system running Solaris 10. The hardware parameters are given in Table 2. We use three commercial workloads and three scientific applications from Splash-2 suite [29], as described in Table 3. To account for statistical variations, we use enough randomly-perturbed runs to achieve 95% confidence [5]. We compare Timetraveler with Rerun, the best previous distributed scheme. We simulate Rerun using Bloom filters of the same size as in [12] — i.e., 256 bits for the write filter and 1024 bits for the read filter. Timetraveler uses two read/write bits per L1 cache block, one bit per L1 set for silent replacements (Section 3.1.4), post-dating offset of 10, and a 696-byte, 8-entry time-delay buffer per L2 bank, where each entry holds an address, a timestamp, core identifier, and R/W bits. For both Timetraveler and Rerun, we assume 32-bit timestamps and a 16-bit memory reference counter. While log compression via timestamp differences is possible (as mentioned in Section 3.3), we assume uncompressed logs for both Timetraveler and Rerun.

Table 2. Base system configuration

Cores	8, in-order
L1 Caches	Split I&D, Private, 32K 4-way set associative, write-back, 64B cache block, LRU replacement, 3 cycle hit
L2 Cache	Unified, Shared, Inclusive, 8M 8-way set associative, write-back, 8 banks, LRU replacement, 37 cycle hit
Directory	Full bit vector in the L2
Memory	8 GB, 300 cycles
Coherence	MESI Directory, silent replacements

5. EXPERIMENTAL RESULTS

We start by comparing the log sizes of Timetraveler against those of Rerun, followed by a dissection of the chapters and an analysis of the various reasons due to which the chapters end (either due to true or false cycles, as discussed in Section 3.3). Next, we isolate

Table 3. Benchmarks

Commercial (com)
Apache is a web server. We use Apache 2.2.11 [27] and SURGE v1.3 [7] with http 1.1 capability to generate web requests from a repository of 20,000 files (~500MB). We simulate 3200 clients, each with 25ms think time between requests, and warm up for ~1,500,000 transactions before measuring 600 transactions.
Online Transaction Processing (OLTP) models the database for a wholesale supplier, with many users performing concurrent transactions. We use PostgreSQL v8.3.7 [2] database server and Open Source Development Labs Test Suite DBT-2 v0.40[1] for modeling users based on TPC-C specifications. We use a 5 GB database with 25,000 warehouses. We simulate 128 users with 0 think time, and warm up the database for ~100,000 transactions before taking measurements for 200 transactions.
SPECjbb2005 is a java-based server workload v1.07[3] for online transaction processing in middle ware. We use Sun J2SE v1.5.0 JVM. We simulate 1.5 warehouses per processor with 0 think time, warm up for 350,000 transactions and take measurement for 10,000 transactions.
Scientific (sci)
SPLASH-2: We use *ocean*, *raytrace*, and *water-nsquared* from SPLASH-2[29]. We run these applications to completion using default parameters. For raytrace, we render the "car" object as provided by the SPLASH-2 suite.

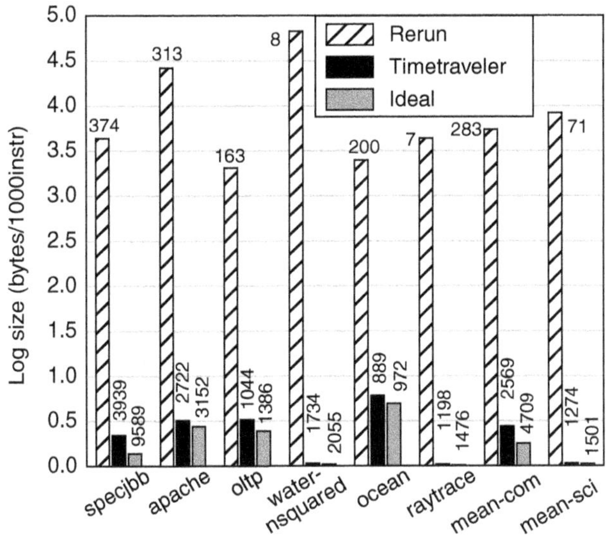

Figure 6. Log size

the contributions of post-dating and time-delay buffer. Then, we present Timetraveler's sensitivity to its various parameters (e.g., time-delay buffer size). We conclude this section by showing the scalability of Timetraveler with the number of cores.

5.1 Timetraveler's Log Size

We compare Timetraveler with Rerun in terms of the log size. The *Ideal* bar represents true cyclic, current-races which we identify using a race table by recording in a graph the races among the threads' live chapters via all (L1-resident and L1-evicted) blocks, and detecting true cycles using a depth-first-search of the graph without using post-dating. Figure 6 shows the log size of the schemes in bytes per thousand instructions executed (Y-axis, lower is better) for each benchmark (X-axis). The two rightmost clusters show the mean for the commercial benchmarks (*mean-com*) and scientific benchmarks (*mean-sci*). Because the commercial and scientific benchmarks behave quite differently, we separate their means. The numbers on top of the bars are the average lengths in number of memory references of Timetraveler's chapters and Rerun's episodes. Rerun's log sizes for the commercial benchmarks as obtained by us are in line with the original paper (which does not show scientific benchmarks).

Timetraveler achieves lower log growth rate (i.e., smaller log) than Rerun for all benchmarks providing 91%, 89%, and 84% reductions for *specjbb*, *apache*, and *oltp*, respectively, and 99%, 77%, and 99% reductions for *water-nsquared*, *ocean*, and *raytrace*, respectively, with mean reductions of 88% and 99% for the commercial and scientific benchmarks, respectively. Timetraveler's log size on average is 0.44 and 0.03 bytes per 1000 instructions for the commercial and scientific benchmarks, respectively, which are close to Ideal's log size of 0.25 and 0.02 bytes per 1000 instructions. Because the scientific benchmarks have much less data sharing and synchronization, and hence significantly fewer cyclic races than the commercial benchmarks, Timetraveler achieves greater log size reduction over Rerun in the scientific benchmarks than the commercial benchmarks.

To put these reductions in perspective, for an 8-core multicore using aggressive 2-GHz, 1-cycle-per-instruction cores, Timetraveler's log grows as 950 KB/s and 59 KB/s for the commercial and scientific benchmarks, respectively, as compared to Rerun's rate of 8 MB/s and 7.3MB/s. Timetraveler's mean chapter lengths are 2569 and 1274 memory references for the commercial and scientific benchmarks, respectively, as compared to Rerun's episode length of 283 and 71 memory references, and Ideal's chapter lengths of 4709 and 1501 memory references. Due to rampant replacements which force Rerun to end its episodes, *water-nsquared* and *raytrace* have unusually short episodes in Rerun. The log reductions show the benefit of Timetraveler's approach of exploiting both past- and acyclic, current-races over Rerun's approach of exploiting only past-races. This improvement requires Timetraveler's time-delay buffer which is extra hardware but the overhead is only 696 bytes for an 8-core CMP. The overhead due to piggybacking timestamps on coherence messages and writing the log increases Timetraveler's total chip bandwidth by nearly 11% which is close to Rerun's 10% increase.

We now turn to DeLorean [16], the latest centralized scheme. In addition to being more scalable and using less hardware, Timetraveler achieves a log size of 0.05 bits per core/1000 instructions compared to DeLorean's 0.3 bits per core/1000 instruction for PicoLog without compression, as reported in [16]. We present this comparison with the caveat that the numbers are from different systems using different hardware parameters and benchmarks.

5.2 Chapter Analysis

In this subsection, we first present a dissection of the chapters and later we analyze the reasons contributing to the ending of a chapter

5.2.1 Chapter Dissection

Table 4 shows the events occurring inside a chapter. *Current-races* (A) are the total number of current-races per chapter. *Current-block replacements* are divided into two categories; those that would have resulted in current-races had they not been replaced and had the chapter not ended (B), and those that do not lead to races (C). Column (D) shows the total number of current-races within a chapter which is the sum of (A) and (B). Columns (A), (B), and (C) represent the cases where Rerun ends its episodes. However, the numbers in the table do not directly relate to Timetraveler's improvements over Rerun because Timetraveler's chapters are longer than Rerun's episodes, and hence may have more current-block replacements compared to Rerun's episodes. Also, some of the past-races in Rerun may turn into current-races for Timetraveler, and vice versa. From the table, we see that a chapter covers 6.8 and 6.4 current-races, on average, for the commercial and scientific benchmarks, respectively. *Timestamp sent from buffer* (E) shows the number of times the time-delay buffer, and not the L2, sends the timestamp for an L1 miss. This count shows the number of times a chapter may avoid potential false cycles through the L2.

5.2.2 Reasons for Ending Chapters

We analyze the reasons — false ones listed below and the true one of cyclic, current-races — for Timetraveler to end a chapter and show that the majority of chapters end on true cycles. In Figure 7, the Y-axis represents the fraction of chapters ended due to each of the reasons (normalized to 100%), and the X-axis shows the benchmarks. *True cycles* represent cyclic, current-races as mentioned in Section 5.1. We list the false reasons as follows

Table 4. Chapter dissection

Benchmarks	Current-races (A)	Current-block replacements: Current-races (B)	Current-block replacements: Non-races (C)	Total current-races/ chapter (D)	Timestamp sent from buffer (E)
specjbb	0.6	1.1	21.0	1.7	0.79
apache	1.5	8.0	26.1	9.5	3.02
oltp	3.4	5.8	12.2	9.3	1.95
water-nsquared	2.3	6.4	228.2	8.7	6.41
ocean	1.8	2.4	5.1	4.1	1.47
raytrace	2.4	3.9	197.8	6.3	3.26
mean-com	1.8	4.9	19.8	6.8	1.92
mean-sci	2.1	4.2	143.7	6.4	3.71

(Section 3.3). *False cycles through L1* represents the chapters ending due to acyclic races via L1-resident blocks where the successor's post-dated timestamp happens, by chance, to be greater than the predecessor's timestamp. *False cycles through L2* represents the chapters ending due to one of two cases: (1) L1 misses which also miss in the time-delay buffer and the L2 bank's timestamp is greater than the requesting thread's post-dated timestamp though the L2 block's real timestamp would be smaller than the post-dated timestamp. (2) unnecessary post-dating for L1-evicted current-blocks that are not accessed by any other thread. *Past-races* represent the chapters ending on past-races when a successor exceeds its post-dated timestamp. Other false reasons discussed in Section 3.3 — half-way division and memory reference counter exhaustion — contribute less than 1% and hence are not shown.

From the graph, we see that the false reasons contribute to nearly 28% of chapter endings most of which are false cycles through the L1 and L2. While false cycles through the L1 occur by chance and may be hard to remove, false cycles through the L2 can be reduced by increasing the time-delay buffer's size (see Section 5.4). Because *specjbb* exerts higher capacity pressure on the L1 than the other workloads, *specjbb* has many more false cycles through the L2. As we show in Section 5.4, *specjbb*'s false cycles can be reduced by increasing the time-delay buffer size.

5.3 Impact of Timetraveler's Mechanisms

We isolate the contributions of Timetraveler's mechanisms — bit-per-set optimization for silent replacements (Section 3.1.4), time-delay buffer and post-dating — by showing three variants of Timetraveler. The first variant, called *Timetraveler-no-bit-per-set* is Timetraveler without the per-cache-set bits. The second variant, called *Timetraveler-no-tdb,* is Timetraveler without the time-delay buffer, where all replacements directly update the L2 bank's timestamp. We also present Rerun, which is equivalent to Timetraveler excluding the bit-per-set optimization, time delay buffer, and post-dating.

Figure 8 shows the average chapter length in terms of total number of memory references on the Y-axis for each variant (higher is better).

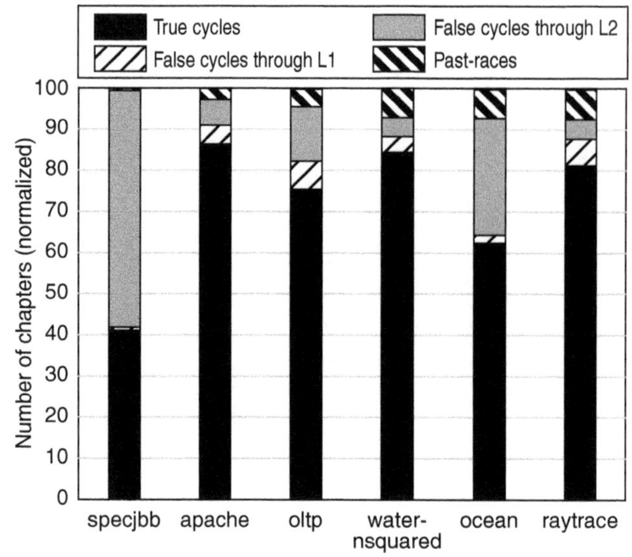

Figure 7. Reasons for ending chapters

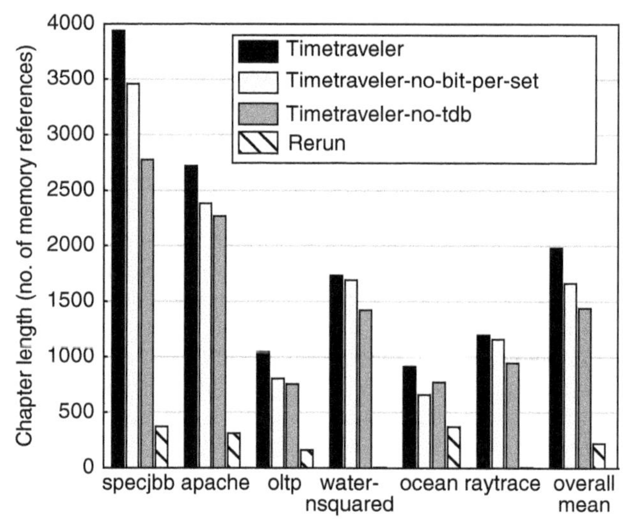

Figure 8. Impact of Timetraveler's mechanisms

The mean chapter length of Timetraveler at 1921 is significantly better than that of *Timetraveler-no-bit-per-set* at 1698, and *Timetraveler-no-tdb* at 1488, showing the effectiveness of employing, respectively, bit-per-set optimization, and the time-delay buffer which delays advancement of the L2 banks' timestamps. *Timetraveler-no-tdb*'s mean chapter length is 1488 as compared to Rerun's 238. This difference highlights the impact of post-dating for current-races and current-block replacements. Overall, we see that all of Timetraveler's mechanisms have significant impact on the log size.

5.4 Sensitivity to Post-dating Offset and Time-delay Buffer Size

Figure 9 shows Timetraveler's sensitivity to two of its design parameters — post-dating offset and time-delay buffer size. The Y-axis shows chapter length in number of memory references. *Tt-default* represents Timetraveler with the default parameters (post-dating offset of 10 and per-bank time-delay buffer of 8 entries). For all the other bars in the figure, one specific parameter is changed

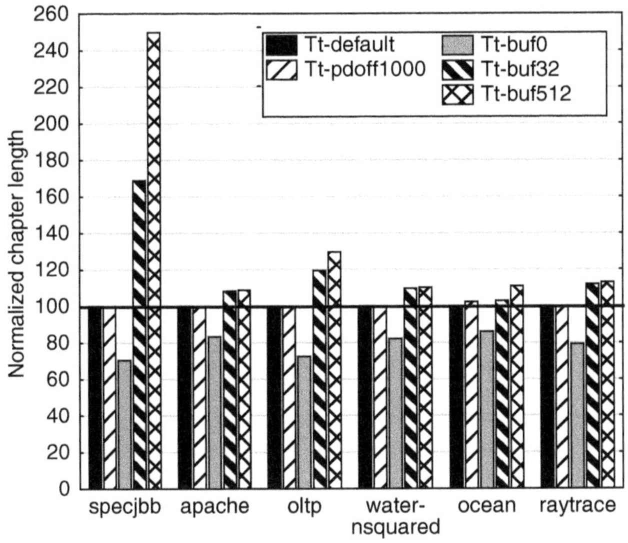

Figure 9. Timetraveler sensitivity

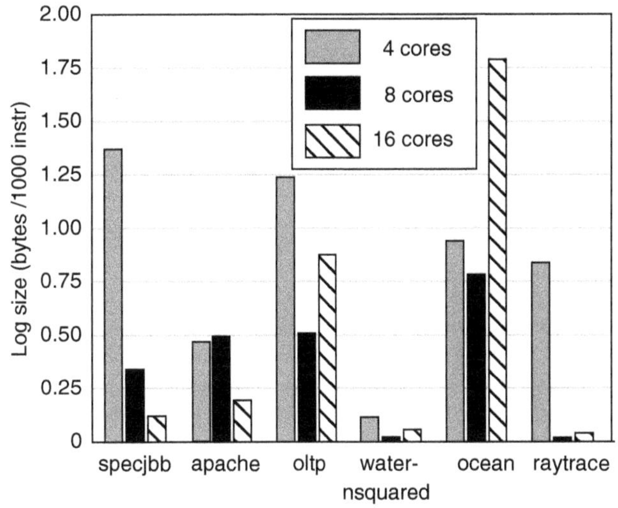

Figure 10. Scaling with number of cores

and the rest are kept the same as that of *Tt-default*. *Tt-pdoff1000* represents Timetraveler with a post-dating offset of 1000. We observe that the chapter length does not vary much as we increase the post-dating offset from 10 (*Tt-default*) to 1000. This lack of variation is because most of the chapters do not exceed the post-dated timestamp before encountering a current cycle which causes the chapters to end naturally (i.e., cases such as the repeated half-way division, which increase the chances of exceeding the post-dated timestamps, are rare). We also observed that decreasing the post-dating offset below 10 (default) deteriorates the chapter length (not shown). Though post-dating offsets of 10 and 1000 produce similar results, we choose 10 as our default because a smaller offset causes timestamps to advance less rapidly and the timestamp space to be exhausted less often.

The next set of bars vary the buffer size. *Tt-buf0* does not have a time-delay buffer and is the same as *Timetraveler-no-tdb* (Section 5.3). *Tt-buf32* and *Tt-buf512* use 32- and 512-entry time-delay buffers per L2 bank, respectively. The graph shows that the chapter length increases as we increase the buffer size. *specjbb,* with its higher capacity pressure, is more sensitive to buffer size as compared to the other benchmarks. This is because *specjbb* has a lot more capacity misses than the other two workloads which require larger buffer size to accommodate the misses. Consequently, the time-delay buffer's fine-grained timestamps have a higher impact on *specjbb* than on the others.

5.5 Scaling the Number of Cores

In Figure 10, we show the scaling trend of Timetraveler's log sizes as we increase the number of cores. The Y-axis shows the log size in bytes per thousand instructions whereas the X-axis represents our workloads. From the graph, we see that the log growth rate scales well as we add more cores though the trend across the benchmarks is not consistent.

6. CONCLUSION

Our goals were to achieve smaller logs for recording memory races than currently achieved by exploiting transitivity of races and to require minimal hardware to do so. To these ends, we proposed *Timetraveler* which for the first time exploits acyclicity of races based on the key observation that an acyclic race need not be recorded even if the race is not covered already by transitivity. Timetraveler employs a novel and elelgant mechanism called *post-dating* which both ensures that acyclic races, including those through the L2, are eventually ordered correctly, and identifies cyclic races. To address the problem of false cycles through the L2, Timetraveler employs another novel mechanism called *time-delay buffers* which delay the advancement of the L2 banks' timestamps and thereby reduce the false cycles. Using simulations, we showed that Timetraveler reduces the log size by 88% and 99% over Rerun for commercial and scientific benchmarks, respectively, while using only a 696-byte time-delay buffer.

The elegance of post-dating and time-delay buffers ensures that Timetraveler requires minimal additional hardware over a conventional chip multiprocessor (CMP) despite exploiting the completely new property of acyclicity of races. By achieving significant reduction in log size while requiring minimal hardware, Timetraveler lowers the barrier for adoption of hardware support for memory-race recording in commercial CMPs. While we assumed sequential consistency in this paper, we will extend Timetraveler to other consistency models in our future work.

REFERENCES

[1] Open Source Development Labs Database Test Suite 2 v0.40 http://osdldbt.sourceforge.net/.

[2] PostgreSQL. v8.3.7. http://www.postgresql.org/.

[3] The standard performance evaluation corporation. SPECjbb2005 suite. http://www.spec.org/jbb2005/.

[4] R. Ahmed, R. Frazier, and P. Marinos. Cache-aided rollback error recovery (CARER) algorithm for shared-memory multiprocessor systems. In *20th International Symposium on Fault-Tolerant Computing, 1990 (FTCS-20) Digest of Papers.,* pages 82–88, 1990.

[5] A. R. Alameldeen and D. A. Wood. Variability in architectural simulations of multi-threaded workloads. In *Proceedings of the 9th International Symposium on High-Performance Computer Architecture*, page 7, 2003.

[6] D. F. Bacon and S. C. Goldstein. Hardware-assisted replay

of multiprocessor programs. In *Proceedings of the 1991 ACM/ONR workshop on Parallel and Distributed Debugging (PADD)*, 1991.

[7] P. Barford and M. Crovella. Generating representative web workloads for network and server performance evaluation. In *Proceedings of ACM Sigmetrics International Conference on Measurement and Modeling of Computer Systems*, 1998.

[8] L. Ceze, J. Tuck, P. Montesinos, and J. Torrellas. BulkSC: Bulk enforcement of sequential consistency. In *ISCA '07: Proceedings of the 34th Annual International Symposium on Computer Architecture*, pages 278–289, 2007.

[9] M. Cintra, J. F. Martinez, and J. Torrellas. Architectural support for scalable speculative parallelization in shared-memory multiprocessors. In *ISCA '00: Proceedings of the 27th Annual International Symposium on Computer Architecture*, pages 13–24, 2000.

[10] S. Gopal, T. Vijaykumar, J. Smith, and G. Sohi. Speculative versioning cache. In *Fourth International Symposium on High-Performance Computer Architecture,* page 195, 1998.

[11] L. Hammond, V. Wong, M. Chen, B. D. Carlstrom, J. D. Davis, B. Hertzberg, M. K. Prabhu, H. Wijaya, C. Kozyrakis, and K. Olukotun. Transactional memory coherence and consistency. In *Proceedings of the 31st Annual International Symposium on Computer Architecture*, page 102, 2004.

[12] D. R. Hower and M. D. Hill. Rerun: Exploiting episodes for lightweight memory race recording. In *ISCA '08: Proceedings of the 35th International Symposium on Computer Architecture*, pages 265–276, 2008.

[13] L. Lamport. Time, clocks, and the ordering of events in a distributed system. *Commun. ACM*, 21(7):558–565, 1978.

[14] P. Magnusson, M. Christensson, J. Eskilson, D. Forsgren, G. Hallberg, J. Hogberg, F. Larsson, A. Moestedt, and B. Werner. Simics: A full system simulation platform. *Computer*, v. 35 pages 50-58, 2002.

[15] M. M. K. Martin, D. J. Sorin, B. M. Beckmann, M. R. Marty, M. Xu, A. R. Alameldeen, K. E. Moore, M. D. Hill, and D. A. Wood. Multifacet's general execution-driven multiprocessor simulator (GEMS) toolset. *SIGARCH Comput. Archit. News*, 33(4):92–99, 2005.

[16] P. Montesinos, L. Ceze, and J. Torrellas. Delorean: Recording and deterministically replaying shared-memory multiprocessor execution efficiently. In *ISCA '08: Proceedings of the 35th International Symposium on Computer Architecture*, pages 289–300, 2008.

[17] K. Moore, J. Bobba, M. Moravan, M. Hill, and D. Wood. LogTM: Log-based transactional memory. In *The Twelfth International Symposium on High-Performance Computer Architecture*, pages 254–265, 2006.

[18] S. Narayanasamy, C. Pereira, and B. Calder. Recording shared memory dependencies using strata. In *ASPLOS-XII: Proceedings of the 12th International Conference on Architectural Support for Programming Languages and Operating Systems*, pages 229–240, 2006.

[19] S. Narayanasamy, G. Pokam, and B. Calder. Bugnet: Continuously recording program execution for deterministic replay debugging. In *ISCA '05: Proceedings of the 32nd Annual International Symposium on Computer Architecture*, pages 284–295, 2005.

[20] R. H. B. Netzer. Optimal tracing and replay for debugging shared-memory parallel programs. In *PADD '93: Proceedings of the 1993 ACM/ONR workshop on Parallel and Distributed Debugging*, 1993.

[21] M. Prvulovic. Cord: cost-effective (and nearly overhead-free) order-recording and data race detection. In *The Twelfth International Symposium on High-Performance Computer Architecture*, pages 232–243, 2006.

[22] M. Prvulovic and J. Torrellas. ReEnact: using thread-level speculation mechanisms to debug data races in multithreaded codes. In *ISCA '03: Proceedings of the 30th Annual International Symposium on Computer Architecture*, pages 110–121, 2003.

[23] M. Ronsse, L. Levrouw, and K. Bastiaens. Efficient coding of execution-traces of parallel programs. In *ProRISC & IEEE-Benelux workshop on Circuits, Systems, and Signal Processing*, pages 251–258, 1995.

[24] D. Sanchez, L. Yen, M. D. Hill, and K. Sankaralingam. Implementing signatures for transactional memory. In *MICRO '07: Proceedings of the 40th Annual IEEE/ACM International Symposium on Microarchitecture*, pages 123–133, 2007.

[25] D. J. Sorin, M. M. K. Martin, M. D. Hill, and D. A. Wood. SafetyNet: improving the availability of shared memory multiprocessors with global checkpoint/recovery. In *ISCA '02: Proceedings of the 29th Annual International Symposium on Computer Architecture*, pages 123–134, 2002.

[26] J. G. Steffan, C. B. Colohan, A. Zhai, and T. C. Mowry. A scalable approach to thread-level speculation. In *ISCA '00: Proceedings of the 27th Annual International Symposium on Computer Architecture*, pages 1–12, 2000.

[27] Apache http Server. v2.2.11. The apache software foundation. http://httpd.apache.org/.

[28] Y.-M. Wang, Y. Huang, K.-P. Vo, P.-Y. Chung, and C. Kintala. Checkpointing and its applications, In *Proceedings of the 25th International Symposium on Fault-tolerant Computing,* page 22, 1995.

[29] S. C. Woo, M. Ohara, E. Torrie, J. P. Singh, and A. Gupta. The splash-2 programs: characterization and methodological considerations. In *ISCA '95: Proceedings of the 22nd Annual International Symposium on Computer Architecture*, pages 24–36, 1995.

[30] M. Xu, R. Bodik, and M. D. Hill. A "flight data recorder" for enabling full-system multiprocessor deterministic replay. In *ISCA '03: Proceedings of the 30th Annual International Symposium on Computer Architecture*, pages 122–135, 2003.

[31] M. Xu, M. D. Hill, and R. Bodik. A regulated transitive reduction (RTR) for longer memory race recording. In *ASPLOS-XII: Proceedings of the 12th International Conference on Architectural Support for Programming Languages and Operating Systems*, pages 49–60, 2006.

Conflict Exceptions: Simplifying Concurrent Language Semantics with Precise Hardware Exceptions for Data-Races

Brandon Lucia† Luis Ceze† Karin Strauss‡† Shaz Qadeer‡† Hans-J. Boehm§

†University of Washington
http://sampa.cs.washington.edu

‡Microsoft Research
http://research.microsoft.com

§HP Labs
http://hpl.hp.com

{blucia0a,luisceze}@cs.washington.edu {kstrauss,qadeer}@microsoft.com hans.boehm@hp.com

ABSTRACT

We argue in this paper that concurrency errors should be treated as exceptions, *i.e.*, have fail-stop behavior and precise semantics. We propose an exception model based on conflict of synchronization-free regions, which precisely detects a broad class of data-races. We show that our exceptions provide enough guarantees to simplify high-level programming language semantics and debugging, but are significantly cheaper to enforce than traditional data-race detection. To make the performance cost of enforcement negligible, we propose architecture support for accurately detecting and precisely delivering these exceptions. We evaluate the suitability of our model as well as the behavior of our architectural mechanisms using the PARSEC benchmark suite and commercial applications. Our results show that the exception model largely reflects how programmers are already writing code and that the main memory, traffic and performance overheads of the enforcement mechanisms we propose are very low.

Categories and Subject Descriptors

C.1.2 [**Processor Architectures**]: Multiple Data Stream Architectures (Multiprocessors); D.1.3 [**Programming Techniques**]: Concurrent Programming; D.3.3 [**Programming Languages**]: Language Constructs and Features

General Terms

Design, Languages, Reliability

Keywords

multicores, memory consistency models, threads, data-races, bug detection

1. INTRODUCTION

As multicores become pervasive, there is a growing need to simplify the process of developing shared memory parallel programs. The nondeterministic nature of shared memory multiprocessing, and data-races in particular, make it very hard to debug and test parallel programs. Moreover, when data-races or similar concurrency bugs manifest themselves, they normally lead to either data corruption or crashes well past the point were the buggy code is actually executed. Finally, data-races have major implications in programming language specifications [2, 12, 27, 37]. Collectively, these issues lead to severe software reliability issues.

We address all these problems with the following approach to data-races: *make them fail-stop and deliver an exception before the race manifests itself* — *i.e.*, before the code with a race is allowed to execute. Treating data-races as exceptions has major implications in debuggability because execution can stop exactly at the point where the race happened. It also improves safety, because the exception will either exit the program and avoid delayed ill-effects or could trigger a recovery action that prevents misbehavior. Most importantly, supporting fail-stop behavior for data-races has major implications in the specification of programming languages [2, 12], as it avoids having to define semantics of data-races and thus eliminates the need for the most complex and least satisfactory piece of, for example, the Java memory model specification [8, 27, 37].

The requirements for supporting data-races as exceptions are: (1) the detection mechanism *cannot* have false positives; (2) exception-free executions must have strong and precisely defined properties; (3) performance degradation needs to be negligible for "always-on" use; and (4) exception delivery needs to be precise, *i.e.*, the instruction that triggered the exception cannot execute and all prior instructions must have completed. We believe hardware support is instrumental in achieving negligible performance cost.

Several past proposals on hardware support for concurrency bug detection have taken a best-effort approach, enabling cheaper implementations at the cost of inaccuracies [25, 33, 42], or more accurate detection with higher state overhead and performance cost [31]. Unfortunately, these approaches are unsuitable for us because we require precise semantics and very low performance cost. On the other hand, implementing precise happens-before race detection [16, 17] (vector clocks) is expensive. We address this issue by proposing an exception model that, while still being fully precise, does not incur the high cost of happens-before race detection. The fundamental observation is that some races are sufficiently distant in the execution and therefore can not directly affect it. We leverage that observation by proposing a new property, *conflict-freedom of synchronization-free regions*: if all regions separated by synchronization operations of an execution do not interact with other concurrently executing regions, then the execution either did not have any races or the racy accesses were sufficiently distant from one another. Detecting this property is much cheaper than full happens-before data-race detection because it associates additional access information primarily with cached data, adding reasonable overhead to cache area, and with negligible main memory overhead.

We make the following contributions: (1) we present the case for fail-stop behavior for data-races and argue that hardware support is an enabler; (2) we propose an exception model that provides most of the benefits of full happens-before race detection but without its prohibitive cost; (3) we propose a reference architecture implementation based on extensions to a standard coherence protocol and caches; and (4) we evaluate the proposed architecture support, as well as the suitability of our exception model.

In the remainder of the paper, we further explain the problem and provide more background (Section 2). We describe our exception model, discuss its properties, and then formally specify its guarantees (Section 3 and Appendix A). We then describe our architecture support (Section 4) and provide a detailed evaluation of our model and hardware mechanisms (Section 5). Finally, we discuss related work (Section 6), and then conclude (Section 7).

2. BACKGROUND AND MOTIVATION

Memory models from the language down to the architecture. The memory consistency model of a programming language defines the values retrieved by shared memory accesses. It must be obeyed across the entire system stack, including the compiler, runtime system, and hardware.

The simplest memory model is sequential consistency [23], in which execution behaves as if there were some global interleaving of the per-thread memory instructions. Although sequential consistency is simple to define, it leaves little room for the compiler and hardware to perform optimizations. For example, reordering-based compiler transformations designed for single-threaded applications are allowable only under very special conditions.

The restrictions sequential consistency imposes have given rise to a variety of work on "relaxed memory models". Until relatively recently, this was concentrated primarily in the hardware community (*e.g.*, [3]) with an occasional, and largely disconnected, effort on the programming languages side (*e.g.*, in Ada 83 [39]). In the last decade, as multiprocessing became more pervasive, relaxed memory models started to receive more attention from the programming languages community, and brought to light a number of problems with prior approaches [13, 27, 34]. In many cases these reflected the historical disconnect between hardware and programming language efforts.

Sequential consistency for data-race-free programs. The treatment of shared memory in most programming languages is converging on what is normally termed "sequential consistency for data-race-free programs" [4, 13, 21, 27]. This approach divides memory operations into two categories: *synchronization* operations (*e.g.*, locks, Java `volatile` or C++0x `atomic` variables), and *data* operations. As usual, we define two operations to *conflict* if they access the same memory location and at least one of them is a write. A data-race is defined as two conflicting concurrent accesses, where at least one is a data access.[1] So long as the programmer prevents data-races, the language implementation guarantees sequential consistency. This applies, for example, to the often used core specification of Java and C++0x [13, 22], the next C++ standard.

[1] At the programming language level, each variable or scalar object field is usually viewed as its own memory location. Simultaneous accesses to adjacent byte fields do not constitute a data-race [32].

Unlike full sequential consistency, this approach allows both hardware *and compiler* to reorder memory accesses in code sections with no synchronization operations. This is possible only because data-race freedom guarantees that the execution of synchronization-free code sections appears indivisible. An obvious benefit of this model is to re-enable single-threaded compiler optimizations.

For example, a loop nest with no cross-thread synchronization can be optimized largely as in the single-threaded case. A less obvious benefit of indivisibility is that the execution of a program is not affected by the granularity of data memory accesses (*e.g.*, byte vs. double word), or by intermediate values produced when executing a purely sequential library call. For example, if a synchronization-free library routine stores a password in a global variable and then overwrites it, no other thread in a data-race-free program can observe the password.

Dealing with data-races. While data-race freedom as a contract between the programmer and the system is easy to understand, it is very difficult to enforce statically. Even in spite of the explicit prohibition of data-races[2], programming errors resulting in races are common. If a programming language leaves the semantics of data-races completely undefined, as in C++0x, we have no way to bound the damage caused by untrusted code containing data-races, and this makes it difficult to debug the race. While this is somewhat acceptable for C++, languages like Java must guarantee security properties, which would be violated if untrusted, sand-boxed code could somehow conjure up a reference to an object, *e.g.,* representing a password, "out-of-thin-air". Undefined behavior, as in C++0x, does not prevent "out-of-thin-air" values. On the other hand, successful attempts to preclude them have been elusive, since many seemingly unimportant cases are surprisingly difficult to distinguish from real, and important, compiler transformations [8, 37].

There are three ways to deal with these implications of data-races: (1) Attempt to define semantics for programs that actually execute data-races — Java takes this route, but the result is not entirely satisfactory, in that it is overly complicated, and has surprising, ill-understood, and unfortunate implications on compiler optimization [8, 37]; (2) Design the programming language to statically preclude races — over the past 35 years, a variety of static type and effect systems [1, 11, 19] have been proposed to ensure data-race freedom, but these systems have not yet been widely adopted for mainstream applications; and (3) Continuously monitor and dynamically detect that a "problematic" data-race is about to execute and raise an exception, instead of executing the data-race. Since programs are designed to be data-race-free, it is safe to treat any of these as an error that should be reported to the programmer. This greatly simplifies the programmer's job, as subtle failures from accidental data-races are reported directly at the point of occurrence and produce easily describable outcomes. This last alternative (3) is what we explore in this paper.

The problem with happens-before race detection. The major obstacle to treating data-races as exceptions is implementation difficulty. We know how to report data-races precisely, even without hardware support [16, 17], but unfortunately at a time and space cost prohibitive for always-on use. Race checks are frequent (potentially on every memory access) and a large amount of state is

[2] [21] POSIX standard, Base definitions, 4.10: "Applications shall ensure that access to any memory location by more than one thread of control (threads or processes) is restricted such that no thread of control can read or modify a memory location while another thread of control may be modifying it."

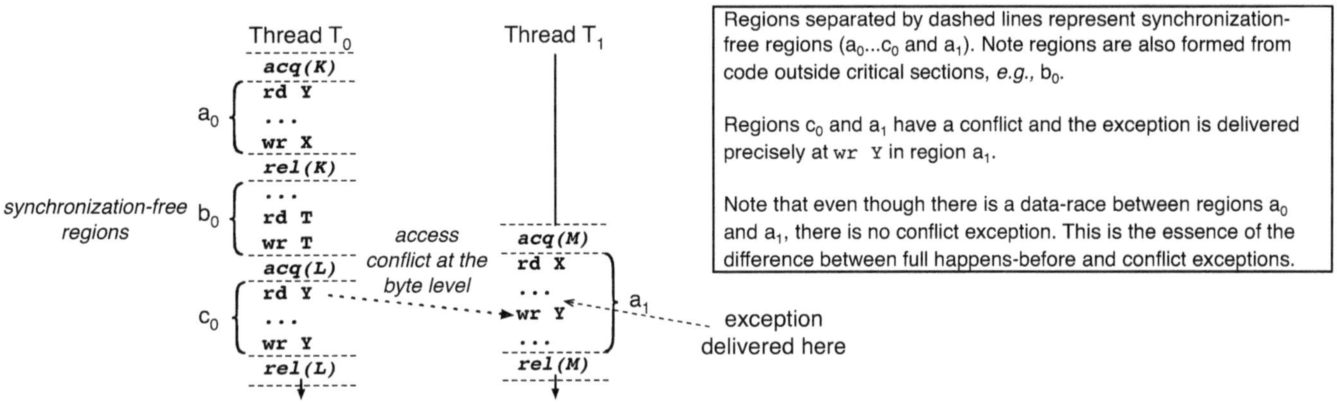

Figure 1: Example of conflict exception.

associated with each object. With vector clock algorithms, we potentially need to remember the time each object was last read by each thread, so that we can determine whether a write was properly ordered with respect to each of those reads. Since objects can be as small as a byte, each byte may require as many time stamps as there are threads in the process, possibly hundreds or thousands. And in a system in which not every pair of threads interacts regularly (think of a background thread that fails to synchronize with other threads for a long time, a case often found in real large systems), this information may need to be maintained essentially indefinitely. While optimizations have been proposed [17], they still do not result in a system that can be mandated by a language specification and used for always-on data-race detection.

To enforce data-race freedom with runtime exceptions *we need a precise detection mechanism that has near-zero time cost and low space overhead.* This is the gap we fill. We propose an exception model and implementation that preserves the utility of precise race detection at a fraction of the cost of prior approaches.

3. CONFLICT EXCEPTIONS

We propose a new property to enforce data-race freedom with runtime exceptions: *conflict-freedom for synchronization-free regions*. Synchronization-free regions of a thread are sections of an execution demarcated by synchronization operations. If a synchronization-free region has a conflict, it means that the region interacted with some other code that was executing concurrently, which *must* have been the result of a data-race. If all synchronization-free regions are free of conflicts, the execution *may* still have data-races, but the conflicting operations must have been separated by some potentially unrelated synchronization operation in that particular execution of the program. A *conflict exception* is delivered right at the point in the execution where the conflict happened (more precisely, right before the instruction that caused the conflict is committed). Figure 1 shows an example. Thread T_0 has three synchronization-free regions, a_0, b_0 and c_0, and Thread T_1 has one, a_1. Note that b_0 is formed of code *outside* a critical section and that synchronization-free regions by construction never nest. c_0 and a_1 have a conflict in memory location `Y`, and the exception is delivered right before `wr Y` in T_1. Also note that `wr X` in T_0 races with `rd X` in T_1 but that does not generate an exception because the regions do not execute concurrently. That illustrates the key difference between conflict exceptions and happens-before data-race detection.

Conflict exceptions provide most of the benefits of data-race detection. We articulate these benefits below.

Simpler programming language semantics. Conflict exceptions provide the following nice properties: (1) The compiler or hardware can reorder memory accesses and eliminate redundant loads or stores within a synchronization-free region, without affecting the semantics of the program; (2) Synchronization-free regions always appear atomic, and thus the semantics of the program are independent of the granularity of memory accesses. Moreover, the semantics of synchronization-free library routines do not depend on the ordering of memory accesses inside those routines; (3) An exception-free execution is guaranteed to be sequentially consistent[3] even in the presence of compiler and hardware optimizations; (4) The fundamental programming rules are unchanged: The programmer needs to avoid data-races, but does *not* need to understand memory ordering issues. Data-race-free programs exhibit sequential consistency as before. This largely abstracts the complexity of relaxed memory models; (5) Programs with data-races exhibit much more well defined behavior than with the current Java or C++0x definitions. Even malicious sandboxed code that is trying to exploit data-races to introduce a security hole cannot violate atomicity of synchronization-free regions. We expect this will facilitate reasoning about security properties. Similarly, code with accidental data-races cannot violate this property, and cannot expose compiler transformations that might otherwise produce very unexpected results under the manifestation of the race. As a result, it enables more natural reasoning about buggy programs and makes them easier to debug; (6) The need for Java's complex and problematic "causality" rules [2, 27, 37] is eliminated, since only sequentially consistent executions are ever produced — we no longer need to choose between comprehensible specifications and security properties.

Note that having the hardware enforce sequential consistency [15, 18, 41] is not sufficient to offer many of the nice properties of conflict exceptions, such as (1), (2) and (5). Compiler transformations (1) are often critical for performance, and granularity independence (2) is very important for programmability.

Appendix A formally articulates the guarantees that conflict exceptions provide from a programming language perspective.

Most debugging benefits of full data-race detection. Executions free of conflict exceptions ensure that no synchronization-free code segment interacts in any way with concurrently executed code. Equivalently, every synchronization-free code section behaves as though it were executed indivisibly, *i.e.*, it is isolated. This main-

[3] We prove this statement in Appendix A.

tains a significant fraction of the debugging utility of full race detection. Any data access that observes or interferes with the effect of a concurrently executing synchronization-free region will lead to a conflict exception, which is likely to cover a large fraction of the observable manifestation of data-races.

Although a data-race can no longer directly interfere with a synchronization-free region, it is possible that conflict exceptions will miss races, as discussed earlier. However, for every data-race we miss, there exists a schedule that would lead to a conflict exception.

Note that full dynamic data-race detection can also miss races from the programmer's perspective due to coincidental intervening synchronization of other kinds (e.g., malloc() calls in both threads[4]). The key difference between full data-race detection and conflict exceptions is that full data-race detection can be fooled in this manner only if both threads perform *matching* coincidental synchronization, *e.g.,*, by acquiring or releasing the same lock. Conflict exceptions can fail to detect a conflict even as a result of *unmatched* coincidental synchronization, *e.g.,* as a result of acquiring or releasing different locks. In all cases, though, the same race would be detected in some different schedule of execution.

Recovery action support. Although exceptions indicate a data-race, and thus a violation of the programming rules, it might be reasonable to continue execution. It may be possible to shut down only the offending sub-system. Since exceptions are raised only for visible data-races, it may even be feasible to simply retry the access and continue after logging the error.

4. ARCHITECTURAL SUPPORT FOR CONFLICT EXCEPTIONS

Our support for conflict exceptions has three components: (1) hardware/software interface; (2) recording memory accesses inside a region at the granularity of individual bytes; and (3) monitoring for byte-level conflicts (*write-after-write*, *read-after-write*, and *write-after-read*) in concurrent regions, and delivering a precise exception when one occurs.

A natural implementation of (2) and (3) above is to extend cache lines with meta-data that keeps access information, and to leverage existing cache coherence protocols to perform the monitoring. This resembles conflict detection mechanisms in hardware transactional memory systems [6, 30, 35]. However, we cannot afford to monitor and record access at the granularity of lines — this would lead to false, spurious exceptions, which is unacceptable. This is one of the major challenges we face in our design.

4.1 Hardware/Software Interface

Our system divides the execution of threads into *regions* demarcated by special instructions, `beginR` and `endR`, which, in the intended usage scenario, exactly encapsulate a synchronization-free region (*i.e.*, the code executed between any two synchronization operations in a thread). For code outside regions, each instruction is a *singleton region* (*e.g.*, the code between a_0 and b_0 in Figure 1). Synchronization operations are implemented with singleton regions.[5] The execution of regions and singleton regions within a given thread preserves program order, *i.e.*, they are never reordered with respect to each other. We say a region is active if it has begun but not ended yet. An access a raises a conflict exception if and only if: (1) a is a *write* and some other active region has performed a *read* or *write* operation in the same byte address; *or* (2) a is a *read* and some other active region has performed a *write* operation in the same byte address. The exception is delivered precisely *before* a is actually committed, and after all previous instructions in the same thread have committed. Instructions inside singleton regions do not raise exceptions unless they conflict with explicit regions.

4.2 Protocol State and Invariants

Without loss of generality, we describe our protocol as an extension to a baseline directory-based MOESI protocol that maintains cache coherence within private L1 caches.

State. Each cache line is associated with four bit vectors, *access bits*, each containing as many bits as bytes in the cache line. Access bits keep track of bytes read/written within the active region of the local thread, as well as active regions of remote threads. As Table 1 describes, local bits are set as the local processor accesses data. Remote bits are set by piggy-backing on coherence messages: responses to coherence requests carry the local bits of suppliers and other caches that have access bits set for the line.

Name	What it records	Set on	Cleared on
Local read bits	Bytes read by the local thread during active region	Local read access (hit/miss)	End of region in local thread
Local write bits	Bytes written by the local thread during active region	Local write access (hit/miss)	
Remote read bits	Bytes read by other threads in their active regions	Local read or write miss	End of region in remote thread that originally set the bit
Remote write bits	Bytes written by other threads in their active regions	Local read or write miss	

Table 1: Access bit vectors associated to a cache line and their purposes.

High-level description of protocol operation. The protocol will be explained in more detail in Sections 4.3.1 and 4.3.2, but a basic description follows. When a region starts, all local bits are clear. On any access performed within a region, a local bit is set accordingly. A cache that suffers a miss receives the local bits of other threads and accumulates them into the corresponding remote bits with a logical OR operation. When a region ends, the local cache sends a message to other caches that might have access information in their remote bits, so that they can be cleared accordingly. The local cache then clears its local access bits. Regions do not nest, so there can only be one active region per thread. Before performing any access, the cache checks for exception conditions. An exception is thrown when a cache detects a byte-level conflict between a local access and a remote active region, *e.g.*, a local read accesses a byte with the remote write bit set. The exception is thrown precisely before the operation is performed. Table 2 enumerates all possible conflicts and how they are detected using access bits.

Conflict type	Local access	Remote access	Condition 1	Condition 2
RAW	Read	Write	Thread is about to read byte	Remote write bit set and local write bit clear
WAW	Write	Write	Thread is about to write byte	Remote write bit set and local write bit clear
WAR	Write	Read	Thread is about to write byte	Remote read bit set

Table 2: Conflict conditions and how to detect them (both conditions must be true for an exception to be thrown).

[4]For example: T_1 reads x and later writes to x (which should have been atomic); and T_2 updates x between the T_1's operations. Also, both threads repeatedly call `malloc()`, which acquires and releases a lock. The synchronization operations inside `malloc()` may impose happens-before orderings between T_1 and T_2 and consequently prevent the race in a particular thread schedule, but without hiding the resulting atomicity violation.

[5]This includes lock-free data-structures routines. Note this represents the desired behavior: singleton regions have sequentially consistent behavior and do not lead to exceptions if facing conflicting accesses from other singleton regions.

#	State	Type of bit set	Invariant
1	Any	Local read bits	A local read bit is set if and only if the local thread has read the corresponding byte within its active region.
2	Any	Local write bits	A local write bit is set if and only if the local thread has written the corresponding byte within its active region.
3	M or E	Remote read bits	A remote read bit is set in a cache if and only if at least one thread other than the local one has read the corresponding byte within its active region.
4	O or S	Remote read bits	A remote read bit is set in a cache *only if* at least one thread other than the local one has read the corresponding byte within its active region.
5	Any	Remote write bits	A remote write bit is set in a cache if and only if at least one thread other than the local one has written the corresponding byte within its active region.

Table 3: Invariants guaranteed by our extended protocol.

Invariants. Table 3 shows the invariants guaranteed by our protocol. Each invariant concerns a particular combination of coherence state and access bits. The second column shows the local state of the cache line, the third column indicates to which type of access bit set the invariant applies, and the last column states the invariant. For example, consider invariant 3: when a cache line is in state Modified or Exclusive, a remote read bit is set *if and only if* at least one thread other than the local one has read the corresponding byte within its active region. Invariant 3 says that, when a write access is about to complete (requires Modified or Exclusive state), the cache's remote read bits reflect exactly which bytes were read by other threads within their active regions. This guarantees that these remote read bits are up-to-date at the time an exception check is performed for this write access. In Section 4.4 we explain in detail why these invariants hold.

4.3 Adding Support to the Coherence Protocol

In addition to access bits, we add a *supplied bit* to each cache line, which indicates whether the line was supplied to any other cache during the active region. We also add three other bits to each cache: (1) an *in-region bit* to indicate whether the local thread is currently in an active region; (2) a *cache-level supplied bit*, used to summarize whether any cache line accessed within the active region was supplied to another cache; and (3) an *out-of-cache bit*, used to indicate whether any line with non-null access bits was evicted.

All the state used to record information about cache lines is stored into a separate state table that has the same basic geometry (same number of sets and ways) as the cache itself, as shown in Figure 2. This table is backed by main memory, as will be explained in Section 4.3.2.

4.3.1 Basic In-Cache Operation

We now explain the protocol assuming in-cache operation, *i.e.*, there is no eviction of line with access bits set and misses are always serviced by a peer cache. We cover out-of-cache operation in Section 4.3.2. We have written a model of the in-cache operation of our protocol and checked that the invariants introduced in Section 4.2 indeed hold. We provide more detail on how we checked it in Section 5.1.

Starting a region. When a processor executes a `beginR` instruction, it sets the in-region bit. The `beginR` instruction has the effect of a full fence instruction.

Exception check. Before any memory access within an active region is allowed to proceed, the cache performs an exception check. The exception conditions are described in Table 2.

Cache hits. After the exception check, the cache sets the corresponding local (read or write) bit.

Cache misses. When a miss is serviced and the line arrives in the local cache, the access bits of the incoming line are accumulated into the remote access bits with a bitwise OR. The only exception is when an incoming write bit is set and the corresponding local write bit is also set, in which case the remote access bit is not set[6]. This is necessary to keep invariant 5 in Table 3. On global read misses, if any other cache indicates it has local read bits set for the requested line, the line is brought from memory in shared state, instead of exclusive. This is necessary to keep invariant 3 in Table 3.

Servicing a remote read miss request. When a cache supplies data for a read miss, it appends to the reply message: one bit indicating whether the line has any local read bit set and the local write bits OR-combined with the remote write bits. The line-level and cache-level supplied bits are then set.

Servicing a remote write or invalidate miss request. When a cache receives a write or invalidate request, it sends both its local read and write bits to the requester (if they are set), even if the line is in invalid state, and independent of being able to supply the data. Then, the cache sets its line-level and cache-level supplied bits and invalidates its cache line, but preserves the supplied and access bits associated with the cache line.

Ending a region. When the `endR` instruction is executed and the cache-level supplied bit is clear, the in-region bit is cleared together with each of the line-level supplied bits and local access bits[7]. If the cache-level supplied bit is set, the cache iterates over the line-level supplied bits, appending the following to an *end-of-region message*: the line address; and the corresponding local read and write bits of cache lines for which the supplied bit is set. The message is then sent to other caches that may have received access bits from the ending region.[8] When all acknowledgments are received, the bits are cleared as above. The `endR` instruction acts as a full fence.

Processing an incoming end-of-region message. When a cache receives an end-of-region message, it checks for the presence of access bits for each address in the message. If a remote bit is present and set, the cache checks if the corresponding bit in the message is also set. If so, the cache clears its remote bit. In addition, if the cleared bit is a remote read bit, and the cache line is in a state that allows a write hit (M or E), this line is downgraded to a state that disallows it (O or S). This is necessary to guarantee remote read

[6] If both incoming write bit and the corresponding local write bit are set, this indicates that the cache suffering the miss was the original writer of that byte. If this were not the case, a conflict exception would have been thrown earlier by the supplier cache.

[7] This can be done efficiently with gang-clearing [29].

[8] One way of doing this distribution is to leverage the directory. Instead of indicating sharers of the data, the directory could indicate which caches share the data *or* have been supplied with any access bits that have not been cleared yet. Clearing directory bits can be done lazily at invalidates in which no caches respond with access bits to avoid extra complexity.

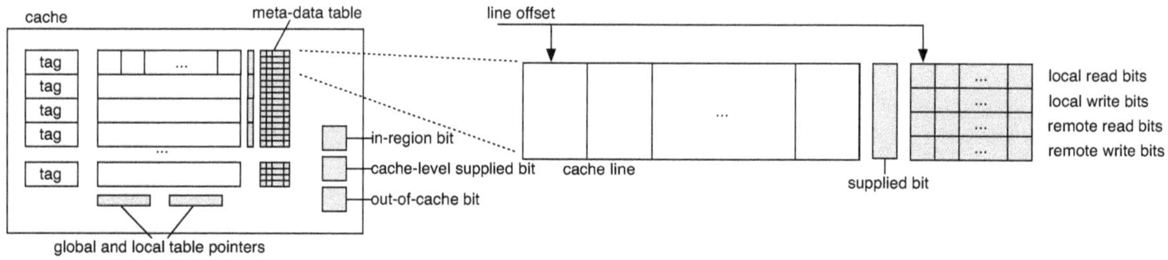

Figure 2: Cache modifications for conflict exception detection. New structures are shown in grey.

bits are refetched when the processor is about to write the cache line and avoid problems when multiple processors read the same byte within active regions (invariant 3 in Table 3).

Singleton regions. Memory accesses in singleton regions do not set access bits. Therefore, conflicts between accesses of two singleton regions do not lead to exceptions. However, if a singleton region conflicts with an explicit region, an exception is delivered to the instruction in the singleton region.

4.3.2 *Out-of-Cache Operation*

In-cache operation is the common case, but caches may have to occasionally evict cache lines with access bits set. When a line is evicted, if any supplied or local access bits are set, they need to be saved. They will be used in three situations: (1) when the cache that evicted the line suffers another miss on the line; (2) when the cache that evicted the line ends its region, and (3) when another cache suffers a cache miss on the line.

We chose to save evicted state in two distinct structures in memory. The *local table* is a per-thread table that stores a list of addresses accessed and evicted within the active region, used in cases (1) and (2). The *global table* is a per-process table that individually saves supplied and local bits for all threads that had to evict them, used in all three cases above. The global table is organized hierarchically (like page tables) and is indexed using the physical address of a line. We augment each cache with two memory pointers, one for each table (see Figure 2). We also augment the directory state for each cache line with an *in-memory bit* that indicates whether any thread has saved access bits for that line in memory. We extend the in-cache operation described earlier to save, search and restore access and supplied bits, as explained below.

Cache evictions. If a cache line being evicted has a supplied or local bit set, the line address is saved in the local table and local access/supplied bits are saved in the global table. The out-of-cache bit is then set and the directory is notified to set the in-memory bit for the corresponding line.

Cache misses. During a miss, if the in-memory bit in the directory is set, other threads' local bits are retrieved from memory by accessing the global table and the corresponding supplied bit is set. The bits retrieved from memory are OR-combined into the remote bits, together with local bits received from other caches (if any). If the out-of-cache bit is set, the cache also searches the global table for its supplied, local read and local write bits in case they have been previously evicted, and restores them.

Ending a region. If the out-of-cache bit is set, even if the cache-level supplied bit is not set, the cache retrieves evicted line addresses from its local table and supplied and local bits from the global table, and appends to the end-of-region message those that have their supplied bit set. The cache clears its in-memory local table in the process, as well as the corresponding entries in the global table.

4.3.3 *Examples*

Figure 3(a) shows an example of in-cache operation. For simplicity, all operations involve the same cache line x (2 bytes long) and all caches are in an active region. Initially, cache A writes byte 0 and sets local write bit 0 (1). Then, cache B suffers a miss when attempting to write byte 1 and sends an invalidation to cache A (2), which invalidates its line and sends data, its local read bits and OR-combined local and remote write bits to cache B (3). Cache B then OR-combines the received bits into its remote read and write bits, performs an exception check (no exception is thrown because it is attempting to write byte 1), and completes the write operation by setting local write bit 1. Later, cache C attempts to read byte 0, suffers a miss and sends a read request to cache B (4). B responds with the data, a single bit indicating that all its read bits are clear and its OR-combined local and remote write bits (5). Finally, cache C receives the response from B. It ignores the read bit because it is transitioning to a shared state, OR-combines the received write bits into its remote write bits and is ready to perform an exception check (6). An exception is thrown because cache C is attempting to read byte 0, but it finds its remote write bit 0 set, indicating that another cache has written this byte in an active region.

Figure 3(b) shows another example. A reads byte 0 and sets its local read bit 0 (1). C then reads byte 0 and sets its local read bit 0 (2). Next, B writes byte 1 (3), collects local read bits from A and C, and sets its remote read bit 0 (4). C then ends its region and sends an end-of-region message (5). When the message arrives at cache B (6), B clears its remote read bit 0 and downgrades the line. When B suffers a write miss for byte 0 (7), it sends invalidates, collects A's local read bit, sets its remote read bit 0, and finally throws an exception (8). Note that if the line had not been downgraded, B would not have detected the conflict.

Figure 3(c) shows an out-of-cache operation example. Again, for simplicity, assume a single cache line x and all caches are in active regions. First, cache A writes byte 0 and sets its local write bit 0 (1). Then, cache A evicts line x by sending its supplied, local read and local write bits to memory (2). At this point, the directory sets the in-memory bit for the corresponding line. Later, cache B suffers a write miss when attempting to write byte 1 and sends a write request to the directory (3), which responds notifying B that another cache has local bits in memory (4). B then performs a global table walk to retrieve those local bits and set the corresponding supplied bit in memory (5). B then OR-combines the local bits it retrieved into its remote bits, checks for exceptions and continues (6). Notice that, had B attempted to write byte 0, it would have correctly thrown an exception because it would have its remote write bit 0 set, even though it did not retrieve this information directly from cache A, but from the in-memory global table.

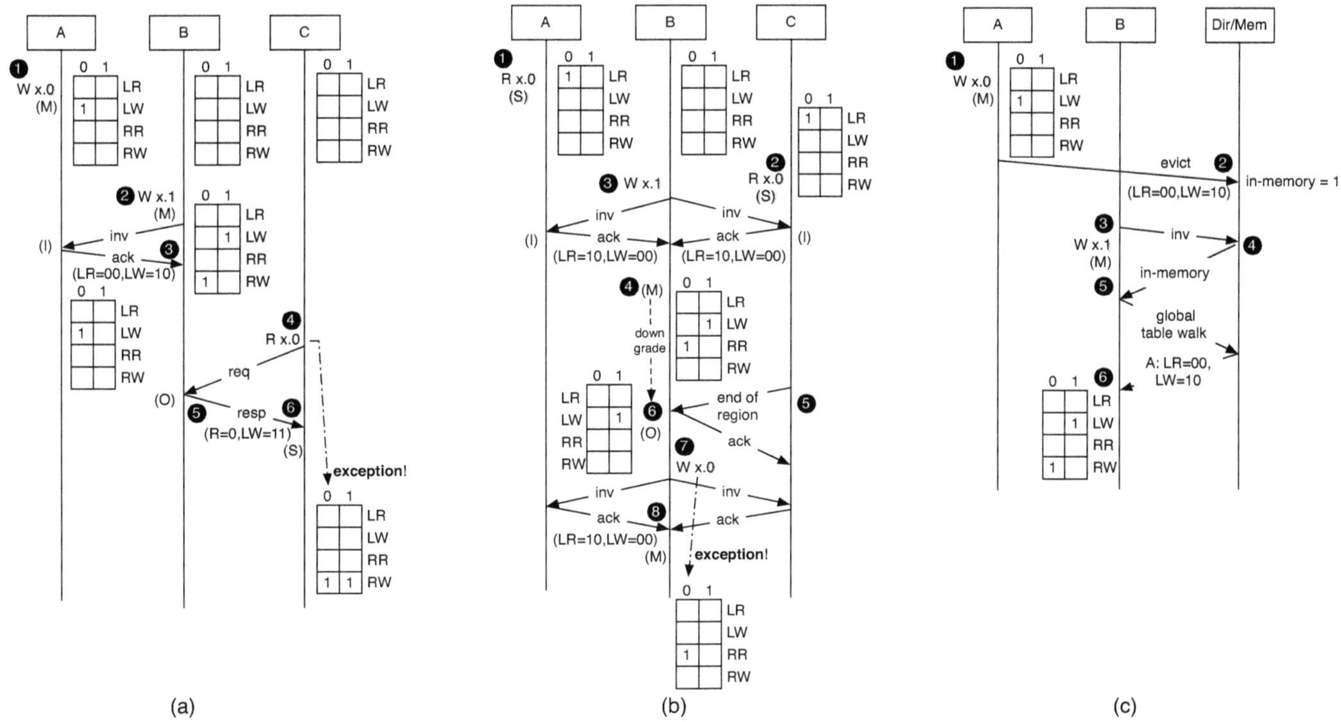

Figure 3: Examples: (a) In-cache operation; (b) In-cache operation with downgrade; and (c) Out-of-cache operation. Caches A, B and C access the same cache line x, which consists of two bytes. Letters in parenthesis show the MOESI coherence state.

4.4 Why Invariants Hold

We now justify why the proposed invariants hold and why they are sufficient to guarantee our exception specification. Exception checks are done when a memory operation is about to complete. For a memory operation to reach this point, the cache controller must have already performed all related coherence actions, so the line must be in a stable state (any valid state for a read, M or E states for a write). The invariants guarantee that the remote bits needed at exception check time accurately reflect whether any other thread has touched that line within their currently active region.

Table 4 shows the invariants and the protocol mechanisms that guarantee them. First, consider invariants 1-2: both local read bits and local write bits are set and cleared only based on local events, so those invariants follow directly from the local cache operation. Next, consider invariants 3-5 (Column 4): they say that a remote read bit set for a thread implies that some other thread has accessed the corresponding byte within its (still active) region. This is guaranteed by our protocol because remote bits are always OR-combinations of local bits of other threads, and the protocol guarantees they are cleared when the region in which they were set ends. Now, consider invariant 3 (Column 5). It says that, if the state of a line is Modified or Exclusive, remote read bits accurately represent read accesses of other threads within active regions. The protocol guarantees this invariant by collecting all local read bits from other threads on write misses and by only transitioning to Exclusive state if no other thread has any local read bit set. Notice that invariant 4 does not guarantee an access within an active region in one thread implies a set remote read bit for another thread when the cache line state is owned or shared. This is not an issue because these states do not allow write hits, and read-read conflicts do not throw exceptions.

Finally, consider the last column of invariant 5. This invariant concerns remote write bits and says that they accurately represent in-region write accesses of other threads. The protocol guarantees this invariant because it enforces exclusiveness and serialization of write operations to the same cache line (coherence) and ensures that all write bits set within active regions are communicated to caches being supplied with the cache line by OR-combining its local write bits and its remote write bits. This guarantees that any writer has the most up-to-date set of remote write bits for the line and propagates those to any subsequent readers.

4.5 System Issues

Exception cleanup. When an exception is raised, the system still leaves the current region active. To support this, the access bits need to be kept throughout the execution of the handler, however support must be provided to prevent the handler code from affecting the access bits.

Virtualization. Access bits are associated with a specific thread and not with a physical cache, therefore, architecture resources need to be virtualized. Context switches are done by extending the thread context to contain the local and global table pointers, the cache-level supplied bit, the in-region bit, and the out-of-cache bit, which are all saved when a thread is switched out. Moreover, all cached lines that have non-null access bits need to be sent to the in-memory log and the access bits are reset — note that this potential cost can be mitigated if context switches tend to happen at synchronization points, which is often the case.

When memory is paged out to disk, the OS needs to associate the corresponding access bits in the local and global tables (if any) with the virtual address of the page being sent to disk. When the page is brought back, the OS need to remap the old entries to the new physical address.

#	State	Type of bit set	Reason why a set bit implies an access within an active region	Reason why an access within an active region implies a bit is set
1	Any	Local read bits	Follows directly from local access actions. Bits are set on access and cleared when a region ends.	
2		Local write bits		
3	M or E	Remote read bits	Remote bits are a combination of local bits from other threads. end-of-region message clears all remote bits previously set by data supplied to other caches, including the local cache.	Read misses can only result in exclusive state if no local read bits for the line are set for other threads. Transitions to M state require acknowledgments with local read and write bits from other threads.
4	O or S			Not enforced.
5	Any	Remote write bits		If an access happens after an in-region remote write, it will be satisfied with data supplied by the cache that wrote that byte or by a cache that wrote it later. The combination of local and remote write bits guarantees they are properly propagated.

Table 4: Reasons why invariants hold on exception checks.

Speculative Loads. Compilers will have to avoid "control speculative" loads, *i.e.*, performing loads that might not be requested by the programmer on that control path. These can introduce data-races. These issues did not appear in our experiments. Moreover, they can typically be replaced by prefetch instructions.

5. EVALUATION

The goals of this evaluation are to: (1) understand the costly events in the protocol; (2) assess space and traffic overhead of access bits storage and transfers; (3) assess the suitability of our exception model.

5.1 Experimental Setup

Model checking. We ensured the correctness of the protocol with model-checking of its in-cache operation using Zing [7]. We used configurations with at most three caches and two bytes per cache line, and executions of at most four requests. We could not check larger configurations due to the space explosion problem inherent to model checking, but we believe the largest configuration we successfully checked is sufficient to show the invariants indeed hold.

Simulation. We evaluate performance using a simulator based on Pin [26] and SESC [36]. The simulator faithfully models the exception detection and the cache coherence protocol, including cache-to-cache and off-cache operation. Given that our goal is to understand the protocol itself, the simulator does not include a timing model. We model a multiprocessor with 8 cores, with 8-way 32KB L1 caches and 32-byte lines.

Benchmarks. There are no programs written from scratch assuming our exception model yet. Nevertheless, the model is intuitive enough that legacy programs tend to conform to the model. We leverage this fact and use existing parallel C/C++ programs to evaluate our architecture support. Sections of execution between calls to pthreads are considered synchronization-free regions — *i.e.*, between the *return* from any pthread function call and the next *call* to a pthread function. This includes code outside critical sections. Instructions inside the pthreads library are considered singleton regions. We used the PARSEC benchmark suite [9] (`simsmall` input set), MySQL (sysbench OLTP benchmark), and Apache (apache-bench utility).

5.2 Performance

Table 5 characterizes dynamic region count and size (Columns 2 and 3) and false sharing between active regions (Columns 4-6). There is a large variance of region size among applications. For example, `fluidanimate` has many (3M) small regions (< 1K memory operations), whereas `freqmine` has very few (96) large regions (>50M memory operations). False sharing also varies significantly among applications.

The most significant events for performance evaluation purposes are end-of-region messages and access bit lookups in memory that occur on cache misses. We characterize end-of-region messages in Columns 7-9 of Table 5. First, note that less than 2% of regions send end-of-region messages for most benchmarks, many times close to zero (Column 7). Moreover, end-of-region messages typically contain access bits for just a handful of lines (Column 8), many times a single line (*e.g.,*`vips`). However, they often must get this information from memory (Column 9). We find a couple of outliers, both in terms of percentage of regions with end-of-region messages (`freqmine` and `swaptions`) and in terms of average number of lines per end-of-region message (`freqmine` and `facesim`). Even then, the fraction of regions with messages is no higher than 9% and at worst, messages contain fewer than 300 lines. Note that the size of regions for these benchmarks is large enough to amortize the cost of end-of-region messages. As expected, benchmarks with more false sharing also have more end-of-region messages, and they tend to be larger. This shows an opportunity to reorganize the code and reduce false sharing, potentially eliminating end-of-region messages and reducing the number of lines in an end-of-region message, among other desirable performance benefits. Overall, end-of-region messages are unlikely to be a performance issue.

We now analyze the other main source of overheads, the lookup of access bits in memory. Columns 10 and 11 in Table 5 show the frequency of lookups. Remote access bit lookups (Column 10) happen when a thread needs to fetch access bits from remote threads. Generally, costly remote bit lookups are infrequent (never more than 7 per million memory operations, which is very low). In `swaptions`, the benchmark with highest cost, frequent false sharing and evictions lead to an increase in remote bit lookups. Local bit lookups (Column 11) occur whenever a line with access bits is evicted and accessed again in the same region. We observe they are correlated with cache miss rates. The rate of local bit lookups is modest — from less than 10 every 100K memory operations (`fluidanimate`) to around 1 every 100 (`streamcluster`, which has high cache miss rates). Note that both remote and local access bit lookups only happen on cache misses, and only on a fraction of them, so they are also unlikely to lead to significant performance degradation. They can also be reduced with an "access bit victim buffer", which we do not explore in this work.

App.	Regions		False Sharing / 1B Mem. Ops			EOR Messages			Mem. M-D Lkup / 100K Mem. Ops		Mem. Ovhd	Traffic Ovhd (B/MB)			
	Total #	Mem. Ops / Region	WaW	WaR	RaW	% Reg. w/ Msg.	Avg. # Lines	% to Mem.	Rem. Bits	Loc. Bits	(% Ftpt)	Rd Reply	Inv Ack	EOR Msgs	Evic.
blackscholes	50	12M	0.0	0.0	11.5	2.00	1	100	0.01	70.81	0.42	2.55	0.00	1.00	60K
bodytrack	37K	70K	8.0	3.4	15.6	0.02	3	100	0.01	58.41	2.29	0.63	0.46	0.87	31K
facesim	35K	2M	487.0	0.1	2251.5	0.05	297	100	0.14	285.09	8.58	62.49	13.52	3.60	58K
ferret	87K	30K	0.0	0.0	0.0	0.00	0	0	0.00	769.20	27.36	0.00	0.00	0.00	66K
fluidanimate	3M	996	0.0	0.0	1.4	0.00	1	100	0.01	9.60	1.58	0.23	0.00	0.13	30K
freqmine	96	54M	9.7	0.8	1048.0	5.21	112	100	0.05	213.29	17.09	63.89	0.64	11.47	64K
swaptions	96	20M	112.2	31.1	460.4	8.33	21	100	0.67	492.53	0.46	27.76	8.64	9.29	69K
vips	17K	252K	2.1	0.7	2.3	0.09	1	100	0.00	163.78	1.32	0.06	0.07	0.28	59K
x264	1K	1M	0.0	0.0	0.0	0.00	0	0	0.00	474.93	6.89	0.00	0.00	0.00	69K
canneal	118	39M	1.5	0.0	2.8	1.69	7	100	0.00	683.44	5.09	0.06	0.03	0.11	60K
dedup	18K	204K	68.8	28.7	96.5	1.92	1	100	0.07	104.96	1.01	3.63	3.67	11.85	49K
streamcluster	1K	1M	0.0	0.0	2.8	0.08	2	100	0.01	1465.45	7.10	0.03	0.00	0.02	53K
MySQL	1M	7K	0.0	0.0	0.1	0.00	1	100	0.00	24.15	0.24	0.01	0.00	0.02	50K
Apache	62K	27K	5.9	0.6	2.3	0.01	1	100	0.01	153.86	6.13	0.07	0.20	0.45	17K
Mean	304K	9M	49.7	4.7	278.2	1.39	32	86	0.07	354.96	6.11	11.53	1.95	2.79	52K

Table 5: Protocol events in detecting conflict exceptions. "Mem. Ops" refer to issued load and store instructions.

5.3 Overheads: Space, Traffic

Columns 12-16 in Table 5 characterize storage and traffic overheads. We report the maximum memory overhead to keep the local and global tables of access bits as a fraction of the maximum application footprint (Column 12). The memory overhead is less than 2.5% for most benchmarks and often less than 1% (`blackscholes`, `MySQL`). `freqmine` and `ferret` have the highest overhead, due to frequent eviction of lines with access bits, and in the case of `freqmine`, extremely long regions.

There are three sources of traffic overhead: the addition of access bits to coherence messages (Columns 13 and 14), sending end-of-region messages (Column 15), and the cost of preserving access bits in memory on evictions (Column 16). The dominant source of traffic overhead is sending access bits to memory when a line is evicted. Across benchmarks, this overhead is between 1.7% and 6.9%. This number tends to be high in two cases: when bad locality leads to frequent evictions (*e.g.*,`ferret`); and when regions are long, because longer regions likely leads to more evictions (*e.g.*, `blackscholes`). The working sets of our benchmarks are much larger than the capacity of our L1 caches [9], resulting in relatively frequent evictions, moreover, regions are relatively long on average (9M Mem. Ops). The other sources of traffic overhead are much less significant, and are a function of false sharing. Applications with higher false sharing have higher overheads. This is most apparent in `freqmine` and `facesim`, with higher overheads deriving from these causes, but still low overall (<< 1%).

5.4 Suitability Analysis

It is important that programmers using a system with support for conflict exceptions can write programs in a familiar way. We show that with few or no changes, our benchmarks can be run with no exceptions. In Table 6, we show the code size for each benchmark (Column 2) and the fraction of regions experiencing exceptions (Column 3), as well as the number of unique instructions (Column 4), lines of code (Column 5), and functions (Column 6) involved in exceptions. Several benchmarks (*e.g.*, `blackscholes`) run unchanged with no exceptions at all. For most applications experiencing exceptions, the exceptions involve under 50 lines of code. Typically, these lines are co-located in just a few functions (13.4, on average). The grouping of code with exceptions suggests that making changes to eliminate these data-races would not be hard.

Examining code that led to exceptions, we found that handcrafted synchronization was a common culprit. `streamcluster`, for instance, uses a flag variable in the master thread to coordinate

App.	KLOC	% Vio. Regions	# Vio PCs	# Vio Lines	# Vio Fns
blackscholes	0.5	0	0	0	0
bodytrack	5.9	5.6	161	22	16
facesim	22.6	6.8	101	21	13
ferret	9.2	1.4	1080	248	50
ferret†	9.2	0	0	0	0
fluidanimate	0.9	0	0	0	0
freqmine	2.7	0	0	0	0
swaptions	1.3	0	0	0	0
vips	109.3	2.6	234	133	41
x264	40.4	7.3	6	6	4
canneal	3.4	4.5	1	1	1
dedup	3.7	35.6	104	58	12
streamcluster	1.3	44.4	147	52	6
MySQL	1600.0	0.05	92	76	41
Apache	602.0	30.1	68	54	17
Mean	160.8	9.2	132.9	44.7	13.4

Table 6: Number of exceptions in our benchmarks and their distribution throughout the code.

workers. In `canneal`, a similar mechanism is used to communicate a loop termination condition between threads. Both cases implemented synchronization incorrectly, using a non-atomic data variable. We eliminated the exceptions thrown in `canneal` by synchronizing around accesses to the flag. Changes affected only 3 lines, and were straightforward.

In `ferret`, there were many exceptions. These were thrown because `ferret` employs pipeline parallelism, and pipeline stages' task queue operations were not properly synchronized. Doing so eliminated all exceptions thrown (see `ferret`† in Table 6). In `MySQL`, exceptions were caused by true data-race errors. These races had no ill effect on our experimental executions, but could result in unexpected behavior. In this case, exceptions aid in debugging by guiding developers to racy code. Note that although POSIX is not completely clear on certain aspects of data-races, the races we found are clearly disallowed. C++0x and Java provide alternative facilities to correctly write such code enabling automatic insertion of `beginR` and `endR`, eliminating the exceptions.

6. RELATED WORK

We discussed accurate software race detection in Section 2. In addition, the desire for fail-stop behavior of data-races has been discussed recently in informal forums [12, 14], but this is the first concrete proposal.

Adve et al. [5] addressed the problem of whether a race detected during a weakly-consistent execution necessarily reflects a possible race in a sequentially-consistent execution, and hence represents a programmer-meaningful race.

High-performance enforcement of sequential consistency (SC) has been actively investigated [15, 18, 40, 41]. SC at the hardware level is definitely valuable but does not provide many crucial guarantees for debugging and simple language semantics, *e.g.*, precise race detection, atomicity for synchronization-free regions and memory access granularity independence. Compiler-based techniques for enforcing sequential consistency [24, 38] share similar properties with the hardware approaches.

Conflict exceptions fundamentally solve a different problem than Transactional Memory (TM), namely providing fail-stop behavior for concurrency errors that result from missing or incorrect synchronization, as opposed to providing a better synchronization primitive, but they are related in several ways. The two features may prove to be synergistic. Our precise byte-level conflict detection mechanism could be used in TM systems, as several current proposals [10, 35] provide only block-level conflict detection, which can result in spurious transaction aborts. Also, data-races are as much a problem in emerging transactional memory specifications [20] as they are in lock-based systems. The detailed implementation considerations and language semantics for such a combined system are beyond the scope of this paper.

One could argue that synchronization-free regions could be converted into transactions and the guarantees would be similar to conflict exceptions. Although conceptually correct, this provides inferior functionality at substantially increased cost. Using transactions in this way could mask some errors, but not all. For example, consider an identity function `id` that happens to acquire and release a lock unrelated to `x`; if we forget a lock around `x=id(x+1)`, we do not atomically increment `x` in either approach. Putting transactions around synchronization-free regions would eliminate any hope of detection while still producing incorrect output. Conflict exceptions would correctly identify the problem of missing synchronization. Also, the cost of the TM approach is higher because transactions formed out of regions can be expected to be quite long and would have to buffer a significant amount of data. Moreover, conflict require neither checkpointing nor memory versioning support.

Concurrently with our work, Marino et al. [28] have proposed *memory model exceptions* to address the same programming language semantics issues that we address here. As in our approach, all programs either contain a data-race and raise an exception, or guarantee a sequentially consistent execution. Unlike our work, they guarantee atomicity for bounded, short compiler-selected regions, not full synchronization-free regions. Thus they provide weaker guarantees to the programmer, and disallow some common compiler optimizations, especially for unbounded loops. In return, they can bound the additional state that needs to be maintained to detect conflicts. They further detect conflicts lazily rather than at the point of conflicting access, and therefore do not provide precise exception delivery.

7. CONCLUSIONS

In this paper we argued that data-races should have fail-stop behavior. However, providing precise race detection at a low enough cost to be always-on is challenging. We address this challenge with conflict exceptions, which provide enough guarantees to significantly improve debugging and enable the design of simple parallel language semantics. Our evaluation showed that conflict exceptions can be enforced at a low cost. Our suitability study showed that the exception model in fact largely reflects how programmers have already been writing multithreaded programs, which supports the intuitiveness of our model.

Going forward, we advocate that hardware resources should be spent to improve the programmability of multiprocessor systems. We believe that not only hardware should help with debugging, but should also provide enough *guarantees* such that even programming languages can rely on it.

Acknowledgements

We thank the anonymous reviewers for their helpful feedback. We thank the SAMPA group at the University of Washington for their invaluable feedback on the manuscript and insightful discussions. Special thanks go to Dan Grossman, Tom Bergan and Joe Devietti. This work was supported in part by NSF CAREER grant CCF-0846004 and a Microsoft Research Faculty Fellowship.

8. REFERENCES

[1] M. Abadi, C. Flanagan, and S. Freund. Types for Safe Locking: Static Race Detection for Java. *ACM Transactions on Programming Languages and Systems (TOPLAS)*, 2006.

[2] S. V. Adve and H.-J. Boehm. Memory Models: A Case for Rethinking Parallel Languages and Hardware. to appear, CACM; authors' preliminary version at `http://rsim.cs.uiuc.edu/Pubs/10-cacm-memory-models.pdf`.

[3] S. V. Adve and K. Gharachorloo. Shared Memory Consistency Models: A Tutorial. *IEEE Computer*, 29(12), 1996.

[4] S. V. Adve and M. D. Hill. Weak Ordering—A New Definition. In *International Symposium on Computer Architecture (ISCA)*, 1990.

[5] S. V. Adve, M. D. Hill, B. P. Miller, and R. H. B. Netzer. Detecting Data Races on Weak Memory Systems. In *International Symposium on Computer Architecture (ISCA)*, 1991.

[6] C. S. Ananian, Krste Asanovic, B. C. Kuszmaul, C. E. Leiserson, and S. Lie. Unbounded Transactional Memory. In *International Symposium on High-Performance Computer Architecture (HPCA)*, February 2005.

[7] T. Andrews, S. Qadeer, S. K. Rajamani, J. Rehof, and Y. Xie. Zing: Exploiting Program Structure for Model Checking Concurrent Software. In *CONCUR*, 2003.

[8] D. Aspinall and J. Sevcik. Java Memory Model Examples: Good, Bad, and Ugly. In *VAMP*, 2007.

[9] C. Bienia, S. Kumar, J. P. Singh, and K. Li. The PARSEC Benchmark Suite: Characterization and Architectural Implications. In *International Conference on Parallel Architectures and Compilation Techniques (PACT)*, 2008.

[10] J. Bobba, N. Goyal M. D. Hill, M. M. Swift, and D. A. Wood. TokenTM: Efficient Execution of Large Transactions with Hardware Transactional Memory. In *International Symposium on Computer Architecture (ISCA)*, 2008.

[11] R. Bocchino, V. Adve, D. Dig, S. Adve, S. Heumann, R. Komuravelli, J. Overbey, P. Simmons, H. Sung, and M. Vakilian. A type and effect system for deterministic parallel Java. In *Conference on Object-Oriented Programming Systems, Languages and Applications (OOPSLA)*, October 2009.

[12] H. Boehm. Simple Thread Semantics Require Race Detection. PLDI FIT, 2009.

[13] H.-J. Boehm and S. V. Adve. Foundations of the C++ Concurrency Memory Model. In *Conference on Programming Language Design and Implementation (PLDI)*, 2008.
[14] L. Ceze, J. Devietti, B. Lucia, and S. Qadeer. A Case for System Support for Concurrency Exceptions. In *USENIX HotPar*, 2009.
[15] L. Ceze, J. Tuck, P. Montesinos, and J. Torrellas. BulkSC: Bulk Enforcement of Sequential Consistency. In *International Symposium on Computer Architecture (ISCA)*, 2007.
[16] T. Elmas, S. Qadeer, and S. Tasiran. Goldilocks: a Race and Transaction-aware Java Runtime. In *Conference on Programming Language Design and Implementation (PLDI)*, 2007.
[17] C. Flanagan and S. Freund. FastTrack: Efficient and Precise Dynamic Race Detection. In *Conference on Programming Language Design and Implementation (PLDI)*, 2009.
[18] C. Gniady, B. Falsafi, and T. N. Vijaykumar. Is SC + ILP = RC? In *International Symposium on Computer Architecture (ISCA)*, May 1999.
[19] P. B. Hansen. The programming language Concurrent Pascal. *IEEE Transactions on Software Engineering*, June 1975.
[20] IBM, Intel, and Sun. Draft specification of transactional language constructs for C++, version 1.0. http://software.intel.com/file/21569, August 2009.
[21] IEEE and The Open Group. *IEEE Standard 1003.1-2001*, 2001.
[22] ISO/IEC JTC1/SC22/WG21. ISO/IEC 14882, Programming Language - C++ (Final Committee Draft). `http://www.open-std.org/jtc1/sc22/wg21/docs/papers/2010/n3092.pdf`, March 2010.
[23] L. Lamport. How to Make a Multiprocessor Computer That Correctly Executes Multiprocess Programs. *IEEE Transactions on Computers*, 1979.
[24] J. Lee and D. Padua. Hiding Relaxed Memory Consistency with Compilers. In *International Conference on Parallel Architectures and Compilation Techniques (PACT)*, 2000.
[25] S. Lu, J. Tucek, F. Qin, and Y. Zhou. AVIO: Detecting Atomicity Violations via Access Interleaving Invariants. In *International Conference on Architectural Support for Programming Languages and Operating Systems (ASPLOS)*, 2006.
[26] C. K. Luk, R. S. Cohn, R. Muth, H. Patil, A. Klauser, P. G. Lowney, S. Wallace, V. J. Reddi, and K. M. Hazelwood. PIN: Building Customized Program Analysis Tools with Dynamic Instrumentation. In *Conference on Programming Language Design and Implementation (PLDI)*, 2005.
[27] J. Manson, W. Pugh, and S. Adve. The Java Memory Model. In *Symposium on Principles of Programming Languages (POPL)*, 2005.
[28] D. Marino, A. Singh, T. Millstein, M. Musuvathi, and S. Narayanasamy. DRFx: A Simple and Efficient Memory Model for Concurrent Programming Languages. In *Conference on Programming Language Design and Implementation (PLDI)*, 2010.
[29] J. F. Martínez, J. Renau, M.C. Huang, M. Prvulovic, and J. Torrellas. Cherry: Checkpointed Early Resource Recycling in Out-of-order Microprocessors. In *International Symposium on Microarchitecture (MICRO)*, November 2002.
[30] K. Moore, K. E. Moore, J. Bobba, M. J. Moravan, M. D. Hill, and D. A. Wood. LogTM: Log-based Transactional Memory. In *International Symposium on High-Performance Computer Architecture (HPCA)*, 2006.
[31] A. Muzahid, D. Suarez, S. Qi, and J. Torrellas. SigRace: Signature-Based Data Race Detection. In *International Symposium on Computer Architecture (ISCA)*, 2009.
[32] C. Nelson and H.-J. Boehm. Concurrency Memory Model (final revision). C++ standards committee paper WG21/N2429=J16/07-0299, `http://www.open-std.org/JTC1/SC22/WG21/docs/papers/2007/n2429.htm`, October 2007.
[33] M. Prvulovic and J. Torrellas. ReEnact: Using Thread-Level Speculation Mechanisms to Debug Data Races in Multithreaded Codes. In *International Symposium on Computer Architecture (ISCA)*, 2003.
[34] W. Pugh. The Java Memory Model is Fatally Flawed. *Concurrency - Practice and Experience*, 12(6), 2000.
[35] R. Rajwar, M. Herlihy, and K. Lai. Virtualizing Transactional Memory. In *International Symposium on Computer Architecture (ISCA)*, 2005.
[36] J. Renau, B. Fraguela, J. Tuck, W. Liu, M. Prvulovic, L. Ceze, S. Sarangi, P. Sack, K. Strauss, and P. Montesinos. SESC Simulator, January 2005. http://sesc.sourceforge.net.
[37] J. Sevcik and D. Aspinall. On Validity of Program Transformations in the Java Memory Model. In *European Conference on Object-Oriented Programming (ECOOP)*, 2008.
[38] D. Shasha and M. Snir. Efficient and correct execution of parallel programs that share memory. *ACM Transactions on Programming Languages and Systems (TOPLAS)*, April 1988.
[39] United States Department of Defense. *Reference Manual for the Ada Programming Language: ANSI/MIL-STD-1815A-1983 Standard 1003.1-2001*, 1983. Springer.
[40] E. Vallejo, M. Galluzzi, A. Cristal, F. Vallejo, R. Beivide, P. Stenstrom, J. E. Smith, and M. Valero. Implementing Kilo-Instruction Multiprocessors. In *International Conference on Pervasive Services (ICPS)*, 2005.
[41] T. F. Wenisch, A. Ailamaki, B. Falsafi, and A. Moshovos. Mechanisms for Store-wait-free Multiprocessors. In *International Symposium on Computer Architecture (ISCA)*, 2007.
[42] P. Zhou, R. Teodorescu, and Y. Zhou. HARD: Hardware-Assisted Lockset-based Race Detection. In *International Symposium on High-Performance Computer Architecture (HPCA)*, 2007.

APPENDIX

A. FORMAL SPECIFICATION OF CONFLICT EXCEPTIONS

Each thread execution consists of a sequence of $Events$. The function Op categorizes these events into different kinds of operations:

$$\begin{array}{rcl} SyncOps & & \\ LoadOps & = & \{Load\} \times ByteAddrs \\ StoreOps & = & \{Store\} \times ByteAddrs \\ DataOps & = & LoadOps \cup StoreOps \\ Ops & = & SyncOps \cup DataOps \\ Tid & \in & Events \rightarrow ThreadIds \\ Op & \in & Events \rightarrow Ops \end{array}$$

We assume that $SyncOps$ and $DataOps$ are disjoint sets.

The following identifiers range over the corresponding sets:

$$\begin{array}{rcl} e, f, r, w & \in & \mathit{Events} \\ E & \in & 2^{\mathit{Events}} \\ t & \in & \mathit{ThreadIds} \\ a & \in & \mathit{ByteAddrs} \end{array}$$

We define the following subsets of a set of events E:
$\mathit{SyncEvents}(E)$ is the subset of synchronization events in E;
$\mathit{ThreadEvents}(E, t)$ is the subset of events by thread t;
$\mathit{LoadEvents}(E, a)$ is the subset of load events to address a;
$\mathit{AllLoadEvents}(E)$ is the subset of all load events;
$\mathit{StoreEvents}(E, a)$ is the subset of store events to address a; and
$\mathit{AllStoreEvents}(E)$ is the subset of all store events.

An execution $(E, \mathit{SyncOrder}, \mathit{ThreadOrder}, \mathit{StoreOrder}, \mathit{Source})$ is a tuple satisfying the following conditions: (1) E is a set of events. (2) $\mathit{SyncOrder}$ is a partial order on $\mathit{SyncEvents}(E)$. Hence, synchronization events are independent of all other events. (3) $\mathit{ThreadOrder}$ maps each $t \in \mathit{ThreadIds}$ to a total order $\mathit{ThreadOrder}(t)$ on $\mathit{ThreadEvents}(E, t)$. We overload $\mathit{ThreadOrder}$ to refer to the partial order $\bigcup_{t \in \mathit{ThreadIds}} \mathit{ThreadOrder}(t)$. (4) $\mathit{StoreOrder}$ maps each $a \in \mathit{ByteAddrs}$ to a total order $\mathit{StoreOrder}(t)$ on $\mathit{StoreEvents}(E, a)$. We overload $\mathit{StoreOrder}$ to refer to the partial order $\bigcup_{a \in \mathit{ByteAddrs}} \mathit{StoreOrder}(a)$. (5) Source is a map from $\mathit{AllLoadEvents}(E)$ to $\mathit{AllStoreEvents}(E)$. For all $a \in \mathit{ByteAddrs}$, if $e \in \mathit{LoadEvents}(E, a)$ then $\mathit{Source}(e) \in \mathit{StoreEvents}(E, a)$. Thus, Source provides for each load event the corresponding store event that supplied the data for it.

Given an execution, we define two relations on the set of events E. The causal relation Causal orders a store event w before every load event r that sees the value written by w. The anti-causal relation $\mathit{AntiCausal}$ orders a load event r before every store event w that comes later than the source of r according to $\mathit{StoreOrder}$.

$$(w, r) \in \mathit{Causal} \stackrel{def}{=} w = \mathit{Source}(r)$$

$$(r, w) \in \mathit{AntiCausal} \stackrel{def}{=} \begin{array}{l} r \in \mathit{AllLoadEvents}(E) \wedge \\ w \in \mathit{AllStoreEvents}(E) \wedge \\ (\mathit{Source}(r), w) \in \mathit{StoreOrder} \end{array}$$

An execution has a *data-race* on address a if and only if there are two events $e, f \in E$ such that: (1) e and f are unordered by the transitive closure of $\mathit{ThreadOrder} \cup \mathit{SyncOrder}$; (2) $\mathit{Op}(e) = (\mathit{Store}, a)$; and (3) $\mathit{Op}(f) = (\mathit{Store}, a)$ or $\mathit{Op}(f) = (\mathit{Load}, a)$.

The set of events in an execution can be partitioned into a collection of regions, each being one of three kinds: (1) the set of all data events in a thread before its first synchronization event; (2) the set of all data events in a thread between two synchronization events; (3) the set of all data events in a thread after its last synchronization event.

Let $\mathit{ThreadOrder}'$ be the projection of $\mathit{ThreadOrder}$ onto the set $E \setminus \mathit{SyncEvents}(E)$. The constraint graph of an execution is a graph (R, N), where R is the set of regions in the execution and N is the set of edges defined as follows: $(p, q) \in N$ iff p is different from q and there exists $e \in p$ and $f \in q$ such that e is ordered before f by the transitive closure of $\mathit{ThreadOrder}' \cup \mathit{StoreOrder} \cup \mathit{Causal} \cup \mathit{AntiCausal}$. An execution is *isolated* iff its constraint graph is acyclic.

Our exception mechanism provides the following two guarantees: (1) If an execution is exception-free, then it is isolated. (2) If an execution throws an exception, then it has a data-race. Further, the definition of isolation also guarantees that in the absence of an exception the execution (projected onto the data events) is sequentially consistent. We present a proof of this guarantee below.

These guarantees translate directly to programming language specifications: We can define data-races as we do now and specify that the program is *always* executed as an interleaving of regions, with the one simple adjustment that the second of two accesses that race in the execution may raise an exception.

LEMMA 1. *An isolated execution projected on to data events is sequentially consistent.*

PROOF. The constraint graph of an isolated execution is acyclic. Therefore, it must be the case that the transitive closure of $\mathit{ThreadOrder}' \cup \mathit{StoreOrder} \cup \mathit{Causal} \cup \mathit{AntiCausal}$ is also acyclic and hence a partial order. Let l be a linearization of this partial order. Since $\mathit{ThreadOrder}' \subseteq l$, the total order l clearly respects the order of instructions performed in each thread. Since $\mathit{StoreOrder} \cup \mathit{Causal} \cup \mathit{AntiCausal} \subseteq l$, the total order l respects all dependencies between stores and loads — every load event e to an address a returns the value written by the last (according to l) store event f to a prior to e. Therefore, the total order l is a witness to the sequential consistency of the isolated execution. □

ColorSafe: Architectural Support for Debugging and Dynamically Avoiding Multi-variable Atomicity Violations

Brandon Lucia† Luis Ceze† Karin Strauss†‡

†University of Washington
http://sampa.cs.washington.edu

‡Microsoft Research
http://research.microsoft.com

{blucia0a,luisceze}@cs.washington.edu kstrauss@microsoft.com

ABSTRACT

In this paper, we propose ColorSafe, an architecture that detects and dynamically avoids single- and multi-variable atomicity violation bugs. The key idea is to group related data into colors and then monitor access interleavings in the "color space". This enables detection of atomicity violations involving any data of the same color. We leverage support for meta-data to maintain color information, and signatures to efficiently keep recent color access histories. ColorSafe dynamically avoids atomicity violations by inserting ephemeral transactions that prevent erroneous interleavings. ColorSafe has two modes of operation: (1) *debugging mode* makes detection more precise, producing fewer false positives and collecting more information; and, (2) *deployment mode* provides robust, efficient dynamic bug avoidance with less precise detection. This makes ColorSafe useful throughout the lifetime of programs, not just during development. Our results show that, in deployment mode, ColorSafe is able to successfully avoid the majority of multi-variable atomicity violations in bug kernels, as well as in large applications (Apache and MySQL). In debugging mode, ColorSafe detects bugs with few false positives.

Categories and Subject Descriptors

C.1.2 [**Processor Architectures**]: Multiple Data Stream Architectures (Multiprocessors); D.1.3 [**Programming Techniques**]: Concurrent Programming; D.2.5 [**Software Engineering**]: Testing and Debugging

General Terms

Design, Reliability, Languages

Keywords

Debugging, Bug Avoidance, Atomicity Violations, Concurrency Errors, Multi-variable, Data Coloring

ISCA'10, June 19–23, 2010, Saint-Malo, France.

1. INTRODUCTION

Concurrency bugs are easy to create but very difficult to fix. In addition, nondeterminism in multiprocessor systems makes bugs difficult to reproduce, complicating testing and debugging. Nevertheless, the ubiquity of multicores is adding pressure to write multithreaded code that takes advantage of the increased parallelism. This trend has spurred significant interest in concurrency bug detection tools.

Many software-only tools were proposed to detect bugs such as data-races [22], locking discipline violations [24], and atomicity violations [11]. However, the overhead these techniques incur is very high. This motivated the proposal of architectural support for debugging [11, 14, 15, 19, 30, 33]. Unfortunately, even with sophisticated tools and thorough testing [18], hard bugs still make it to deployment. For this reason, recent research has also proposed improving the reliability of multithreaded execution with dynamic concurrency bug avoidance [14, 20, 21] by decreasing the probability that concurrency bugs will actually manifest in the field.

Most past work on architectural support for concurrency debugging has dealt with bugs involving a single variable, making them fundamentally limited in helping with a wide variety of defects. The likely reason is that the complexity (*i.e.*, state required and number of cases to be considered) of concurrency bug detection grows very quickly with the number of variables involved. Also, until not long ago, the belief was that multi-variable bugs were rare. However, recent work [12, 13] shows that multi-variable concurrency bugs are much more common than expected.

What we need, then, are general solutions for both single- and multi-variable concurrency bugs that use a single set of simple architectural mechanisms. Moreover, to justify architecture support, these mechanisms must be useful for the system's lifetime, from development to deployment. This is the gap this paper fills.

Our work focuses on atomicity violations, which are an especially challenging and pervasive category of concurrency errors. They occur when programmers overlook the need for atomicity of a set of memory accesses and fail to enclose them inside the same critical section. This allows interleavings of remote operations that lead to wrong behavior. What makes them tricky is that they can occur even in programs free of data-races. According to a recent study by Lu *et al.* [13], atomicity violations account for about 66% of non-deadlocking concurrency errors. This study also shows that a significant fraction of atomicity violation errors (33%) involve multiple variables. However, prior work such as AVIO [11] and Atom-Aid [14] address only single-variable atomicity violations or a subset of multi-variable atomicity violations (SVD [30]), and therefore miss a significant fraction of important concurrency bugs.

In this paper, we make the observation that combining variables

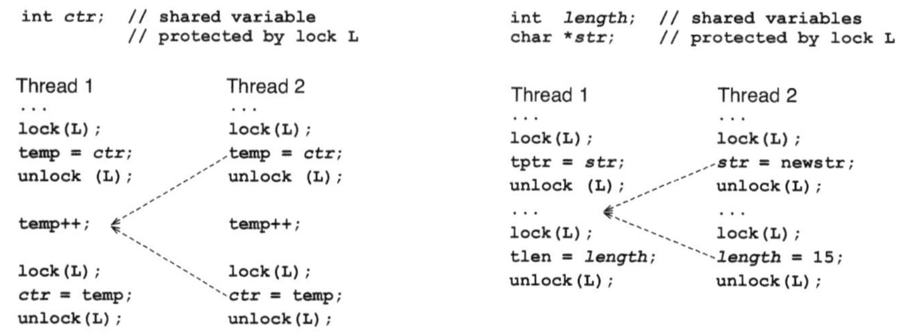

(a)
Single-variable atomicity violation. Concurrent increments to **ctr** might lose an update.

(b)
Multivariable atomicity violation.
Thread 1 reads inconsistent **str/length**.

Figure 1: Examples of a single-variable (a) and a multi-variable (b) atomicity violation. The example in (b) was distilled from https://bugzilla.mozilla.org/show_bug.cgi?id=73291.

into sets (or colors) and then performing serializability checks on colors rather than on individual variables allows us to detect and avoid single- and multi-variable atomicity violations. We leverage the insight of assigning colors to variables from data-centric synchronization [4, 26] and combine it with serializability analysis for bug detection [11, 30] and avoidance techniques [14]. We propose to combine these techniques in a novel way. By grouping variables into colors, our detection mechanism can treat a set of variables as a single unit. Detecting erroneous interleavings of accesses to same-colored data fundamentally enables us to detect both single- and multi-variable atomicity violations. The result is ColorSafe. ColorSafe provides dynamic bug avoidance using ephemeral transactions to prevent unintended interleavings. This is different from prior work on avoidance [14] because it doesn't require the architectural complexity of transactions-all-the-time and avoids a more general class of bugs.

ColorSafe has two modes of operation: (1) *debugging mode* collects more information and makes detection more strict to reduce false positives; and, (2) *deployment mode* provides robust, efficient dynamic bug avoidance by making detection less strict but more proactive in detecting potential bugs. This makes ColorSafe useful throughout the lifetime of programs, not just for development, and therefore more compelling to processor manufacturers. Moreover, the mechanisms used in both modes are almost exactly the same.

In the rest of this paper, Section 2 provides background information on atomicity violations and contrasts single- and multi-variable bug categories. Section 3 describes ColorSafe and provides a high-level description of how it works. In Section 4, we provide a more detailed description of ColorSafe and its architectural components. Section 5 discusses our debugging framework based on ColorSafe. In Section 6, we present an evaluation of ColorSafe in debugging and deployment mode. Section 7 discusses related work and Section 8 concludes.

2. BACKGROUND: ATOMICITY VIOLATIONS AND SERIALIZABILITY

Consider the example shown in Figure 1(a). The shared variable `ctr` is being incremented by two threads simultaneously. The read and the write of `ctr` are inside critical sections, so the program is data-race free. However, it is still incorrect: the write from Thread 2 can interleave with the read and write from Thread 1 and cause a counter increment to be lost. In this example, what is missing is *atomicity* [7], since both the read and write of `ctr` should have been atomic and isolated[1] to avoid unwanted interleaving of accesses to `ctr` from other threads. This is an example of a single-variable *atomicity violation*, since it only involves accesses to `ctr`. Additionally, such an interleaving is said to be *unserializable*, as there is no un-interleaved execution of the accesses that results in the same final state as the interleaved execution. Lu *et al.* [11] provide a list of unserializable memory operations to a single variable.

In contrast, consider the example in Figure 1(b), which is a classic example of a *multi-variable* atomicity violation. Two shared variables, `str` and `length`, are used to express related properties of a string. Just after Thread 1 reads the `str` pointer, Thread 2 updates both variables, causing Thread 1 to read a value of `length` inconsistent with the value of `str` that it read. This could later result in a crash or, even worse, silent data corruption. Note that, if accesses to each individual variable are considered separately (*e.g.*, read and write of `str`), they do *not* characterize an atomicity violation. Conversely, we make the observation that, if `str` and `length` are considered together as a unit, the atomicity violation is clear: two reads of the unit by Thread 1 are interleaved by writes to the same unit by Thread 2. Moreover, these accesses are unserializable with respect to the unit, since there are no un-interleaved executions that would produce the same result as the interleaved one. To ensure the examples in Figure 1 behave as intended, the programmer needs to enclose both memory operations inside the same critical section, instead of each in its own critical section or in none whatsoever. Vaziri *et al.* [26] provide a serializability analysis of accesses involving two variables.

In this work, we employ the idea of detecting unserializable interleavings not only to detect single-variable atomicity violations, but also to detect and avoid multi-variable atomicity violations, which are fundamentally harder and more elusive. The next section explains how.

3. COLORSAFE: DETECTING AND AVOIDING MULTI-VARIABLE ATOMICITY VIOLATIONS

We now explain how grouping variables into colors enables detection of multi-variable atomicity violations. We focus on describing the conceptual mechanisms ColorSafe uses to detect and dynamically avoid atomicity violations. Section 4 describes the actual architecture extensions and their implementation.

[1] In this paper, when we refer to atomicity, we also imply isolation.

3.1 Leveraging Data Coloring

Detecting multi-variable atomicity violations is uniquely challenging because code may contain no violations of atomicity with respect to a single variable. Recall the example in Figure 1(b). In this example, we only see the atomicity violation when we consider `str` and `length` as a single unit of data. This concept of considering groups of variables together, instead of single variables alone, is the cornerstone of ColorSafe.

We propose to associate *colors* with shared variables, giving related variables the same color. ColorSafe then monitors interleavings of accesses to colors to determine whether they are serializable. This contrasts with past proposals such as AVIO [11] and Atom-Aid [14], which monitor interleavings of accesses to individual addresses. For example, in Figure 1(b), `str` and `length` would be given the same color since they are semantically correlated. In the color space, this example consists of two reads interleaved by at least one remote write to the same color, which is unserializable.

In Table 1, we discuss each type of multi-variable unserializable interleaving. Note that Cases 1-4 are unserializable from a single-variable point of view as well. Case 5, however, is only unserializable if multiple variables are involved. To understand Case 5, consider the example in Figure 2. The writes from Thread 2 interleaved with the writes from Thread 1, leaving the consistency between `length` and `str` compromised: `str` may point to `ptr2` but `length` will have value 10. Note that, if `str` and `length` are given the same color, the color access interleaving just described is not serializable.

Case	Interleaving	Description
1	R, R ←W	The interleaving write makes the second read see inconsistent data.
2	R, W ←W	The second write writes data based on stale or inconsistent data.
3	W, R ←W	The read gets data from the interleaving write which is inconsistent.
4	W, W ←R	The interleaving read gets inconsistent data.
5	W, W ←W	The interleaving write leaves the data inconsistent (Figure 2).

Table 1: Unserializable access interleavings to colors.

Grouping correlated variables into colors and performing atomicity violation detection based on accesses to colors, as opposed to memory addresses, greatly simplifies the detection of multi-variable atomicity violations. One can think of it as reducing the high complexity of detecting multi-variable atomicity violations [12, 26] to the complexity of detecting single-color (or single-variable) atomicity violations.

```
int  length;  // shared
char *str;    // variables

Thread 1              Thread 2
...                   ...
lock(L);              lock(L);
str = ptr1;           str = ptr2;
unlock (L);           unlock(L);
...                   ...
lock(L);              lock(L);
length = 10;          length = 15;
unlock(L);            unlock(L);
```

Figure 2: Example of Case 5 in Table 1. `str` and `length` are left mutually inconsistent.

Coloring Data. Program data structures can be colored either manually or automatically. On one hand, if programmers manually color data, they encode precise information about the relationships between the data. Automatic coloring, on the other hand, does not require programmer effort, but may yield less accurate correlation information.

The main use of manual coloring is in debugging. Manual coloring requires source code annotations, by which the programmer expresses the semantic relationship between variables. It is reasonable to expect a programmer to manually color data correctly. During debugging, the programmer is likely starting from a bug report, and can identify which data are involved in a bug from the symptoms described. Furthermore, grouping related data manually has been used in past work to simplify the specification of synchronization constraints of data (*e.g.*, atomic sets [26], coloring [4], and locking discipline [17]). This past work showed that expressing which data should be grouped is not excessively difficult, since it requires only reasoning about the data at the point of its declaration. In contrast, correctly implementing synchronization (writing bug-free code) requires complex global reasoning at every access.

Automatic coloring is primarily useful for bug avoidance. It is better suited to this task than manual coloring because it doesn't require the programmer to anticipate all potential bugs, and color the involved data. Instead, data are colored according to a heuristic. There are many ways to automatically color data. For example, we could assign the same color to all fields of a `struct`, to all blocks of memory allocated by the same `malloc()` call, or even entire object instances if using object-oriented languages. Exhaustively exploring different coloring techniques is beyond the scope of the paper. We do, however, explore both manual coloring and automatic coloring to give the reader a flavor of the differences. We evaluate one automatic coloring technique by giving the same color to data allocated together (malloc-coloring). Past work has addressed ways of finding correlations between variables [12], but it did not thoroughly address atomicity violations. Such work is complementary to ColorSafe, as we can use its correlations to color data.

3.2 Detecting Unserializable Color-Access Interleavings

In this section we explain how ColorSafe detects actual unserializable interleavings in debugging mode. The next section explains its differences from deployment mode. The atomicity violation detection mechanism used by ColorSafe consists of three conceptual components: (1) a history of accesses performed by the local processor (*local history*); (2) a history of accesses performed by remote processors (*remote history*); and, (3) a set of rules that determine whether the interleaving of accesses in the history is serializable.

It is important to note that unserializable interleavings are not necessarily manifestations of atomicity violations. However, for an atomicity violation to manifest itself, it is necessary that an unserializable interleaving happens. Moreover, unserializable interleavings, especially in a short window, are strong indicators of atomicity violation bugs [11, 14]. Hence, we identify likely bugs by detecting unserializable interleavings.

Since our goal is to detect whether accesses to colors are serializable, ColorSafe's access histories are kept in terms of colors. This means the data addresses of memory accesses need to be translated to colors before being inserted in the history. Local accesses are inserted into the local history as the local processor performs them. Remote access histories are built from coherence protocol events; read and invalidate requests are inserted into the remote history as

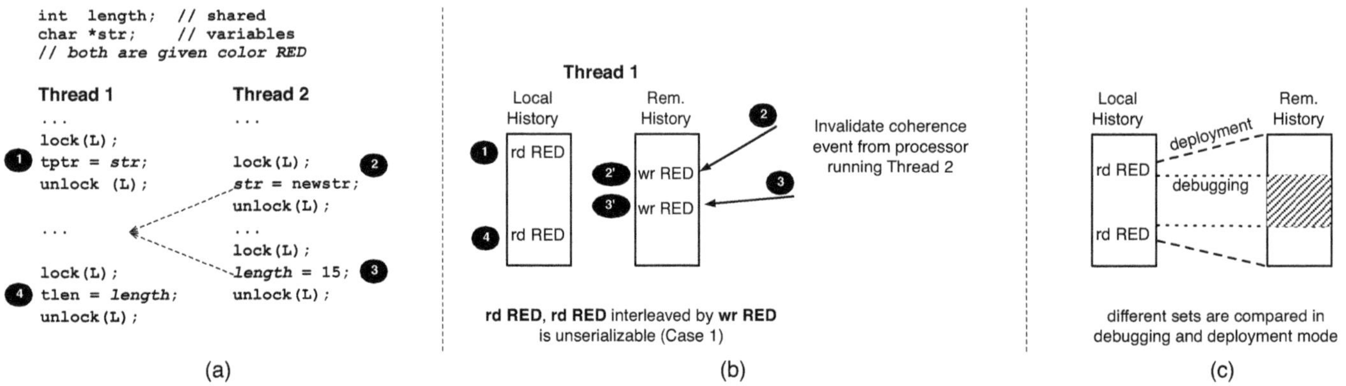

Figure 3: Overview of how ColorSafe detects multi-variable atomicity violations. The numbers in the dark circles denote the order of events happening in (a) and (b).

the processor receives those requests. Local and remote histories are kept separately and ColorSafe retains some information about the relative order of groups of local and remote accesses.

To detect atomicity violations, ColorSafe determines whether any unserializable interleaving from Table 1 exists between the local and remote histories. Figure 3 shows an example of this process using the same code from Figure 1(b), which is reproduced in Figure 3(a), and contains a multi-variable atomicity violation involving two variables. Variables `str` and `length` are both colored *RED*. The numbers in the dark circles denote the order of accesses. The accesses are inserted into their corresponding history as they happen (Figure 3(b)). Accesses 2 and 3 performed by thread 2 generate invalidate coherence messages and are inserted as writes into thread 1's remote history (2' and 3'). As soon as access 4 is performed, ColorSafe detects that the accesses in the history are unserializable, matching Case 1 in Table 1 (two reads interleaved by a write).

One might wonder how long a history we need to capture the majority of unserializable interleavings that indicate bugs. Recent work [13, 14] shows that, for many known bugs, this window is fairly small, on the order of tens of thousands of instructions at most. This is intuitive because the longer the distance between operations that should have been atomic, the higher the chance that the bug manifests itself during testing. Therefore, hard bugs tend to be the ones that occur in a short window.

3.3 Debugging vs. Deployment Mode

The previous section described what we call *debugging mode*, as it detects only interleavings that are actually unserializable. In *deployment mode*, ColorSafe attempts to dynamically avoid atomicity violations by (1) detecting when an atomicity violation is likely to happen, and (2) dynamically starting a special form of transaction — an ephemeral transaction — to prevent an unserializable interleaving from happening.

In deployment mode, we aim to detect *potentially* unserializable interleavings that are related to atomicity violations. The avoidance mechanism can then be triggered before an unserializable interleaving actually happens, to prevent it from happening. We relax the criterion used to detect unserializable interleavings in debugging mode such that it covers interleavings that could potentially happen. More precisely, we define a *potentially unserializable interleaving* as a pair of memory accesses in the local history that, if interleaved by any access in the remote history, would have been unserializable according to Table 1. For example, consider the scenario in Figure 3: if the remote writes to *RED* had happened anywhere in the remote history window, even if they did not actually interleave with the reads from *RED* in the local history, this would be detected as a potentially unserializable interleaving. Figure 3(c) illustrates the difference between debugging and deployment mode.

The intuition behind this definition of a potentially unserializable interleaving is that, because ColorSafe observed an unserializable interleaving that almost happened, it could observe the actual interleaving at a future point in the execution. This could result in an atomicity violation manifesting itself, which is what ColorSafe is trying to avoid. It is possible that potentially unserializable interleavings are, in fact, just benign accesses. In this case, the only effect is that ColorSafe initiates unnecessary bug avoidance actions[2].

Once a potentially unserializable interleaving is detected, the color of the data accessed is inserted into a set called the *HazardColorSet*. From then on, all accesses to data whose color is in the HazardColorSet trigger an ephemeral transaction of a finite size. The ephemeral transaction will make the short period of the execution beginning with these accesses appear to execute atomically and in isolation, effectively preventing any unwanted interleaving with remote accesses from happening in the meantime. The goal is that this ephemeral transaction will begin with the first instruction of an atomicity violation and be long enough to cover all local memory accesses involved in the violation, consequently preventing its manifestation.

Ephemeral transactions are transactions dynamically inferred by ColorSafe and do not correspond to any program annotation. It is important to point out that the ephemeral transactions inserted by ColorSafe cannot, in any way, break the semantics of the program, since the resulting interleaving of accesses with ephemeral transactions is still a valid interleaving with respect to the program semantics. Section 4.4 provides more details.

4. ARCHITECTURAL SUPPORT

ColorSafe needs four basic architectural mechanisms: support for data coloring (Section 4.1); histories of recent memory accesses, in terms of colors (Section 4.2); a means of detecting unserializable interleavings based on the access histories (Section 4.3); and, for bug avoidance, a way of maintaining the set of colors involved in unserializable interleavings together with support for ephemeral transactions (Section 4.4).

[2]While this is not a correctness problem and typically not a performance problem either, the system provides hooks to the programmer to disable avoidance actions in performance sensitive parts of the code.

4.1 Support for Data Coloring

ColorSafe represents the color of data items as meta-data (memory tags). There have been several proposals to support memory tagging for various purposes, such as security and information flow tracking [6, 32] and as support for new programming models [4]. To support ColorSafe, we chose a design similar to Colorama [4], which is based on the Mondrian Memory Protection scheme [29]. Mondrian provides an efficient way to associate protection information with arbitrary regions of memory by using a hierarchical multilevel permissions table. ColorSafe uses the same structure but stores ColorIDs instead of permission information. We call this table the Multilevel Color Table. Based on the number of colors required in the applications used in our experiments, we used a 12-bit ColorID field.

The Multilevel Color Table resides in memory and is accessible by all processors. Its ranges of addresses are expanded to keep the ColorID information at the desired granularity (word, line, page, etc.). The Color Lookaside Buffer (CLB) directly caches coloring information from the Color Table to provide fast lookup. To look up an address, the processor checks the CLB. In case of a miss, the processor fetches the entry from the Multilevel Color Table in memory. Software can update color information in user-mode by writing to the Multilevel Color Table. When the color table is written, the CLB needs to eventually be updated, but not immediately. ColorSafe can tolerate this transient color information incoherence, since this will not affect program semantics in any way.

Note that there are other alternatives to providing support for data coloring. For example, Loki [32] proposes a multi-granular tagging mechanism, in which tags can be associated with whole pages and, only when necessary, expanded to individual words to provide fine-grain tagging. Such a scheme would also be adequate for our purposes. Yet another alternative would be to add a ColorID field on a per cache line basis. We opted not to do this for three reasons: (1) we want to allow arbitrary coloring without forcing the user to adjust data layout; (2) the Multilevel Color Table is more space efficient; and, (3) we did not want to touch sensitive structures in the memory hierarchy.

4.2 Color Access Histories

In ColorSafe, each processor stores information about the recent history of color accesses in a *history buffer*. A history buffer holds four types of histories: (1) local read, (2) local write, (3) remote read, and (4) remote write.

ColorSafe keeps tens of thousands of instructions worth of history. Therefore it needs a resource-efficient way of keeping them, as we cannot use a searchable FIFO with tens of thousands of items. We chose to encode the color of accesses in bloom-filter-based signatures [2]. This way, each of the four history types is a *signature file* organized as a FIFO queue, in which each signature is a superset hash-encoding of ColorIDs of memory accesses for an arbitrary number of dynamic instructions. Since only colors, instead of individual addresses, are recorded into signatures, the amount of imprecision (aliasing) in the signatures is low. Figure 4(a) shows a color access signature file.

ColorSafe divides the execution of a program into *epochs*, arbitrary length sequences of consecutive dynamic instructions (*e.g.*, 400). A *history item* is a set of four signatures (one of each history type) that contains color accesses collected during an epoch. Figure 4(b) shows a complete history buffer, which is a set of history items that covers the last n epochs of execution. When an epoch ends, both local and remote accesses start being encoded in the next history item. In summary, a history item H_i consists of a Local Read signature $LocR_i$, a Local Write signature $LocW_i$,

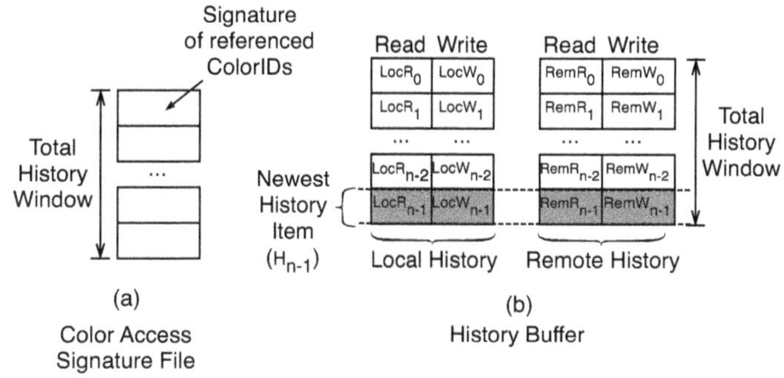

Figure 4: Keeping color access history.

a Remote Read signature $RemR_i$, and a Remote Write signature $RemW_i$.

Note that ColorSafe sacrifices information about the relative order of operations within a history item. Information about the relative order across history items is preserved, though. The trade-off in determining the history item granularity (assuming fixed total history window) is one of precision versus cost. Smaller history items (finer-grain) improve precision by preserving more relative order information and suffer from less signature aliasing. Larger (coarser-grain) history items use less storage and comparison logic, since fewer history items are necessary and consequently fewer intersection operations need to be performed.

Collecting Local Access Information. Local access information can be easily obtained. ColorSafe uses the mechanism described in Section 4.1 to look up the ColorID for each load and store issued locally. The resulting ColorID is then encoded in the appropriate local read and write signatures for the current history item. When an epoch completes, accesses start being inserted in the next history item.

Collecting Remote Access Information. Recording remote color accesses requires minimal additional cache coherence protocol support. To collect color information for remote accesses, we augment coherence requests without affecting coherence protocol functionality in any way. On a read miss, the processors retrieve the color information of the data being accessed (actual referenced address, as opposed to block address) and append it to the coherence request sent to potential sharers. When a processor receives a read request from a remote processor, it adds the ColorID in the request to its current remote read signature. Likewise, an invalidate request generated by a write miss or a write on shared miss is augmented with a ColorID. Receiving processors add the ColorID to their current remote write signature. ColorSafe only needs color information for accesses that cause inter-processor communication, and so it is sufficient to piggyback on coherence protocol messages.

4.3 Detecting Unserializable Interleavings

ColorSafe detects unserializable interleavings by intersecting signatures in the history buffer. A signature intersection is a simple bit-wise *AND*. For example, suppose we want to detect whether Case 1 in Table 1 happened in the history buffer. Using the symbols in Figure 4(b), ColorSafe computes $LocR_i \cap LocR_j \cap RemW_k$, for all i and j, where $i \neq j$, and for values of k that depend on whether ColorSafe is in debugging mode or deployment mode (Figure 5), which we discuss shortly. If the resulting signature is not empty, then it is likely that the execution contains an unserializable interleaving involving the color(s) in the resulting set. Testing for the

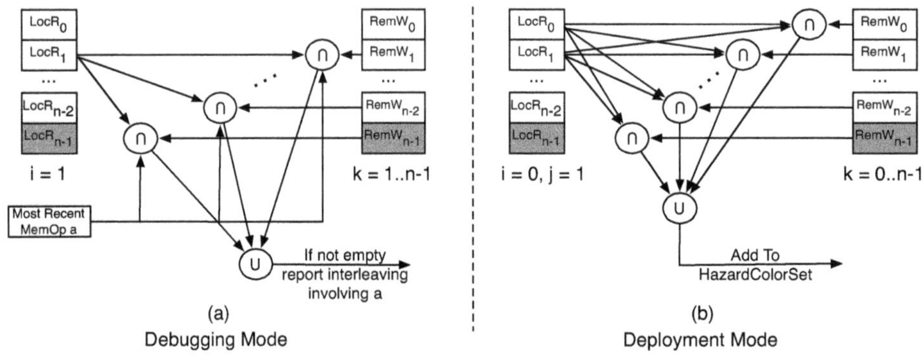

Figure 5: Detecting unserializable interleavings in (a) debugging mode and (b) deployment mode. In (a), only actual interleavings are being considered for the serializability test: the current access to a, the local history item i and the remote history items with $k \geq i$. In (b), all items in the remote history are being considered for the serializability test: local history item i, followed by local history item j, and all possible remote history items ($k = 0, ..., n-1$).

remaining cases in Table 1 is analogous, except signatures of the applicable type are intersected.

Two issues remain: (1) determining when to evaluate the detection expression and (2) choosing values of k. These choices depend on whether ColorSafe is in debugging mode or in deployment mode.

Debugging mode. In debugging mode, we want ColorSafe to detect only unserializable interleavings that actually occur. We also want to know the instruction address of the memory operation that led to the interleaving. Therefore we choose k such that $i \leq k$ and we use a set containing only the most recent memory operation issued locally as the second local set in the intersection (instead of all possible H_j). This implies that only history items that actually interleave history item H_i and the most recent memory operation are considered. Figure 5(a) illustrates this process. If the resulting set is not empty, then an unserializable interleaving involving the just-issued memory instruction is reported. This includes both the instruction address and the type of interleaving (cases in Table 1). Note that for efficiency, the set of all intersections need not be evaluated from scratch at every memory operation, because the partial intersection between local and remote history items can be reused until the corresponding history items are pushed out of the history buffer.

Deployment mode. In deployment mode, we want ColorSafe to detect *potentially* unserializable interleavings. Hence, ColorSafe performs 3-way intersections consisting of all pairs of distinct local signatures and each remote signature, regardless of whether the history items actually interleave (*i.e.,* $k = 0...n-1$), shown in Figure 5(b). When the result set is not empty, it is added to the HazardColorSet. Also, we do not need to know the instruction that led to a potential atomicity violation — we need only the colors to enable dynamic avoidance. This allows us to perform detection only at the end of an epoch instead of at each memory access, which significantly decreases the frequency of intersection operations.

4.4 Support for Dynamic Avoidance of Multi-variable Atomicity Violations

Whenever a potentially unserializable interleaving happens in deployment mode, ColorSafe adds the color involved to the HazardColorSet. Each ColorSafe processor has its own HazardColorSet. This set is also encoded as a signature. Insertions are a bit-wise *OR* operation between the detection intersections' results and the HazardColorSet itself. Upon a memory access, the processor checks whether the access's ColorID is in the HazardColorSet. If so, it starts an ephemeral transaction to prevent a potentially unserializable interleaving. If there is an ephemeral transaction already in progress, the event is ignored, *i.e.*, transactions do not nest.

Implementing Ephemeral Transactions. From a mechanism perspective, ephemeral transactions are just like typical memory transactions [9]. Unlike regular transactions, though, ephemeral transactions are implicit, as they do not rely on code markers. As such, they do not guarantee that a set of dynamic instructions will always execute atomically and in isolation. Ephemeral transactions provide strong atomicity, since they must roll back in the event of conflicts with any remote accesses and attempt to execute again. To guarantee forward progress, ColorSafe provides a mechanism for recognizing repeated rollbacks. ColorSafe then reduces the size of the ephemeral transaction until it is able to commit or falls back to non-transactional execution.

4.5 Discussion on Hardware Complexity

Although ColorSafe requires additional hardware support, we argue that its cost is reasonable and leverages well understood technology. Mechanisms to keep track of sets of addresses and memory tagging have been proposed before (*e.g.,* Mondrian Memory Protection [29] and Loki [32], IBM 801 [5]). Mondrian and Loki use hierarchical data structures to map memory regions to tags, keeping storage overheads manageable. The buffers and logic required to handle history items are very simple, since they are based on address signatures [2, 23]. The additional support in the coherence protocol involves only an extra field in request messages and does not change any protocol state machine. Finally, support for transactional memory is being considered for actual off-the-shelf processors [1].

5. DEBUGGING WITH COLORSAFE

We have developed a debugging methodology for ColorSafe's debugging mode. The key idea is to reduce the rate of false-positives by focusing on detections most likely to indicate bugs.

Invariant-based reduction of false positives. We assume a mode in which developers run the program multiple times and classify

Type	Name	Description	% Bug Ex.	Intlv. Type
Kernel	nsText	Mozilla-0.9: During update of string buffer offset and length, inconsistent data can be read.	0.19%	WRW
	NetIO	Mozilla-0.9: Read of flag and conditional write can be interleaved, invalidating data.	0.14%	RWW
	jsStr	Mozilla-0.9: Between update to string buffer and length, inconsistent data can be read by remote read.	0.22%	WRW
	interp	Mozilla-0.8: Between table update and flag update, interleaving can make table inconsistent.	2.8%	WWW
	msgPane	Mozilla-0.8: Interleaving read of flag indicates content loaded in msg. pane before content is loaded.	0.22%	WRW
Full	Ap2.0	Apache-2.0.48: Character buffer and string length made inconsistent by concurrent accesses.	0.91%	WRW
	AGet	AGet-0.4: During update of log contents/length, inconsistent data can be read by signal handler.	0.47%	WRW
	MySQL	MySQL-3.23.57: Accesses can be logged out of order by highly concurrent access to replay log.	33.21%	WWW

Table 2: Bugs used to evaluate ColorSafe.

each execution as buggy or non-buggy by observing its outcome (crashes, data corruptions, etc). For each execution, we collect ColorSafe's output and produce a set of *detection identifiers*, which are composed of the instruction address where an unserializable interleaving was detected, and the type of interleaving (Table 1). The detection identifiers from buggy runs are added to the *buggyDetSet*, and those from non-buggy execution are added to *nonBuggyDetSet*. We then set-subtract *nonBuggyDetSet* from *buggyDetSet*, producing the *vioSet*. This set contains the detection identifiers for interleavings that occurred only during the buggy runs. These are the points in the code on which a developer should focus to locate the bug. In Section 6.4, we show that this simple technique actually prunes most false positives.

6. EVALUATION

Our goals in evaluating ColorSafe are to assess how well deployment mode dynamically avoids atomicity violations (Section 6.2) and at what performance cost (Section 6.2.1), to understand design trade-offs (Section 6.2.2 and Section 6.2.3), to understand metadata usage (Section 6.3), and to assess how accurately debugging mode locates bugs in the code (Section 6.4).

6.1 Experimental Setup

We developed a ColorSafe simulator using the PIN binary instrumentation framework [16]. The simulator models all ColorSafe structures, including the Multilevel Color Table, translation of data addresses to colors, the history buffer, unserializable interleaving detection using signature operations on history items, the HazardColorSet and ET support. The simulator models both debugging and deployment mode. In debugging mode, it produces the unserializable interleaving detection output that is used by our invariant-based debugging framework. In deployment mode, the simulator determines how often atomicity violations were avoided by determining whether the violation executed entirely within an ET. To assess performance impact, we model ET conflicts.

We use a variety of benchmarks consisting of "bug kernels" and full applications. Table 2 provides a description of each kernel and application, along with the portion of the dynamic execution spent in buggy code (Column 4) and the interleaving pattern that causes the bug (Column 5). The bug kernels are segments of buggy code extracted from full applications. We extracted five kernels from various versions of the Mozilla Project, all previously discussed in the literature [12, 13]. We paid special attention to maintaining the original data structure hierarchies and the layout of the code surrounding the bug. As our full applications workloads, we use the AGet parallel download accelerator, the Apache httpd webserver and the MySQL database server. To exercise the buggy regions of Apache, we used scripts to repeatedly launch 100 concurrent requests. We exercised the MySQL bug using a version of the sqlbench benchmark modified to execute many concurrent requests. The bug in AGet involves a signal handler, so to exercise the buggy code, we fetched a file from a network resource, and interrupted the transmission with a Unix signal.

We experiment with both manual coloring and malloc-coloring, as described in Section 3.1. To perform manual coloring, we added explicit annotations to the code to associate colors with data. For malloc-coloring, our simulator monitors calls to memory allocation functions and assigns a new color to the allocated region.

6.2 Deployment Mode: Bug Avoidance

We start by showing that ColorSafe is able to avoid most instances of atomicity violations in bug kernels and applications. All experiments had epochs of 400 instructions, a total history window of 12,000 instructions (*i.e.,* 30 history items), and 3,000-instruction ETs. Table 3 shows the number of violation instances avoided.

App.	% Avoided	
	Manual	Malloc
nsText	99.95	99.95
NetIO	99.95	99.95
jsStr	100	100
interp	99.95	0
MsgPane	99.95	0
Ap2.0	98.72	94.18
AGet	99.28	0
MySQL †	77.0	71.4

Table 3: Violations avoided in bug kernels and full applications using manual and malloc data coloring. †We used a different system configuration for MySQL. We explain the details below (Difficulties with MySQL).

For bug kernels, ColorSafe avoids nearly 100% of the violation instances using manual coloring. Malloc-coloring is capable of avoiding almost all atomicity violations in most kernels, but it is not effective for all kernels. The bugs in *interp* and *msgPane* each involve accesses to one global variable, and one dynamically allocated variable. They are not allocated together, so using malloc-coloring does not capture their correlation. As a result ColorSafe is unable to avoid these bugs.

Table 3 shows that ColorSafe avoids nearly all violation instances in our full application benchmarks. In runs of Ap2.0, ColorSafe avoids virtually all instances of the violation, using both manual and malloc-coloring. Malloc-coloring has a slightly lower rate of avoidance. This is because ETs triggered by accesses to data unrelated to the violation end up preventing useful ETs from proceeding. In runs of AGet, ColorSafe avoids more than 99% of instances of the violation using manual coloring. The bug in AGet involves a dynamically allocated variable and a global variable, so unfortunately malloc-coloring is unable to identify their correlation.

Difficulties with MySQL. ColorSafe was unable to avoid violation instances in MySQL using our standard configuration. This is because the violation is nearly 20,000 instructions long, and cannot execute entirely within an ET of 3,000 instructions. We re-ran MySQL using 64,000-instruction ETs, 1,000-instruction epochs, and a total history window of 30,000 instructions. With this configuration, ColorSafe avoids 77% of the violations using manual coloring, and 71.4% of violations using malloc-coloring. ColorSafe's avoidance is lower using this configuration because longer ETs triggered in response to false positive detections prevent useful ETs from beginning over a much longer window.

Could Avoidance Happen by Chance? A Comparison with Random Ephemeral Transactions. One may wonder whether the bug avoidance achieved by ColorSafe would be possible simply by starting ETs at random points. Here we show empirically that this is not the case. Consider an experiment using AGet. Using 3,000-instruction ETs and at random starting about 5 ETs per 100,000 dynamic instructions (the rate of transaction starts for AGet using standard ColorSafe) avoids 1.8% of all violations. ColorSafe is able to avoid 99.28% of all violations using the same configuration. Performing the same experiment with Ap2.0, we see that random ETs avoid only 6.97% of violations. ColorSafe avoids 98.72% of violations. Results were similar for other benchmarks. This stark contrast shows that ColorSafe's avoidance performs significantly better than chance.

6.2.1 Overheads

ColorSafe in deployment mode imposes modest impact on performance. We now discuss and quantify the key sources of overheads, which are coloring support and ETs. ColorSafe leverages existing cache coherence support to handle the exchange of color information between processors. As a result, communicating color information imposes negligible runtime overhead. The interconnect traffic overhead associated with communicating colorIDs is not likely to be problematic because the meta-data is small, and is only communicated between processors on a subset of cache misses. Color information lookup depends on the meta-data scheme underlying ColorSafe. While a lookup is not free, the cost is minimized using caches for meta-data information. Moreover, color information is mostly read-only (*i.e.,* written only at allocation time). This means that any additional overhead associated with meta-data writes is unlikely to affect performance. Finally, regarding energy, the structures used to store color information are similar to TLBs, and like TLBs, amount to a small fraction of total power consumption.

The main sources of performance degradation are ETs. Namely, they are bookkeeping overhead and re-execution due to conflicts. In Table 4, we report the percentage of dynamic instructions that triggered an ET (% ET Start), the number of ETs that were useful in preventing an atomicity violation (% Useful ETs), and the percentage of useless ETs that experienced a conflict (% Useless Conflicts). We report the number of ET starts as a fraction of the total number of dynamic instructions to quantify how often the overhead of starting an ET is incurred. The fraction of useful ETs is a measure of how often the cost of an ET was worthwhile, because it prevented a violation. The fraction of conflicting useless ETs is an approximation of the amount of work wasted in ETs that served no purpose and still had to be re-executed. In Table 4 we also show the fraction of total dynamic instructions that executed inside ETs (% in ETs), that executed in useful ETs (% in Useful ETs), and that executed in useless ETs that had conflicts (% in Useless ETs w/ Conflicts). We report data only for full applications, as kernels execute in tight loops around buggy code, making them unsuitable for this analysis.

There are two important results in these data. First, for all applications, the rate at which ETs are triggered is very low: 3 ETs per 100,000 instructions for MySQL, 5 per 100,000 for AGet, and

App.	% ET Start	% in ETs	% Useful ETs	% in Useful ETs	% Useless Conflicts	% in Useless ETs w/ Conflicts
Ap2.0	0.02	38.4	7.4	5.8	4.1	3.2
AGet	0.005	12.8	63.8	10.7	6.4	1.1
MySQL	0.003	24.7	9.0	20.2	0.5	1.2

Table 4: The rate of ET starts, % of useful ETs, and % of conflicting useless ETs for full applications in deployment mode. Ap2.0 and MySQL were run using malloc coloring, and AGet, manual coloring. MySQL was run with the same modified configuration as above (Difficulties with MySQL).

20 per 100,000 for Ap2.0. The low frequency of ET starts indicates that the cost of starting, ending and verifying ETs will have little effect on performance. We also see a relatively small fraction (12–38%) of the execution is executed transactionally.

Second, very little computation is wasted by re-executing useless ETs. The data show that the fraction of useful ETs ranges from 7.4% (Ap2.0) to 63.8% (AGet). At first glance this may suggest that useless ETs are frequent, and hence problematic. However, the rate of aborts for useless ETs is very low — just 0.5% for MySQL, and at most 6.4% in AGet. The work wasted in these useless, aborted ETs amounts to just a small fraction of dynamic instructions, from 1.1% to 3.2%. Thus, if an ET is useless, it rarely experiences a conflict, so very little work is wasted. If an ET is useful, it is more likely to abort, but we consider it profitable to sacrifice this small amount of performance in exchange for prevention of buggy behavior. Additionally, only a small fraction of the execution (5.8%–20.2%) executes in useful ETs, and incurs the higher likelihood of abort.

6.2.2 Sensitivity to Ephemeral Transaction Length

Table 5 shows avoidance for each application as the size of ETs is varied between 3,000 and 15,000. For all the bugs we considered — except the very long MySQL bug — ColorSafe's avoidance is stable, for the sizes shown, and all sizes within this range. This insensitivity to ET size shows two things: (1) large ETs do not inhibit the avoidance capability of ColorSafe; and (2) there is flexibility in the selection of this design parameter. We chose a default ET size of 3,000 instructions; any smaller, and we risk being unable to avoid modestly large violations; any larger and we increase the chances of unnecessary abort.

App.	% Violations Avoided			
	3,000 Inst ET	5,000 Inst ET	10,000 Inst ET	15,000 Inst ET
nsText	99.95	99.95	99.95	99.95
NetIO	99.95	99.95	99.95	99.95
jsStr	100.0	100.0	100.0	100.0
interp^m	99.95	99.95	99.95	99.95
msgPane^m	99.95	99.90	99.90	99.95
AGet^m	99.28	97.93	99.10	99.18
Ap2.0	94.18	90.55	98.64	94.16

Table 5: Stable bug avoidance for a variety of ET sizes. Applications marked with a ^{m} were run using manual coloring, because their bugs involve global and heap variables; All others were run with malloc-coloring.

6.2.3 Sensitivity to History Buffer Configuration

The history buffer configuration determines which interleavings are observable by ColorSafe and affects which unserializable interleavings can be detected. We now evaluate the effect of varying the granularity of the history items in the history buffer. We do this by injecting "noise" into a bug kernel to simulate high-frequency concurrent access to shared data. We add noise by allocating an array of random integers unrelated to the bug in the kernel. Randomly, 1% of the elements in the array are given the same color as the data in the bug. We add five extra threads to the program that spin in a loop, repeatedly accessing noise data. Each iteration, they make a random number of accesses between 1 and 10 and determine whether each is a read or a write by "flipping a coin." The noise level parameter is the inverse of the size of the array of noise data: The higher the noise level, the smaller the array. At higher noise levels, there is a higher probability that a random access into the array will access an element colored the same as the data involved in the bug.

Figure 6 shows avoidance in the presence of noise, with a fixed total instruction history (12,000 instr.) and using both coarse-grain (1,200 instr.) and fine-grain (400 instr.) history items. These data show that as the noise level decreases, avoidance improves. Note though, that avoidance is still effective even at the highest noise level. We see the improvement because as noise decreases, the number of ETs triggered by accesses unrelated to the bug decreases, permitting useful ETs to proceed (recall ETs don't nest).

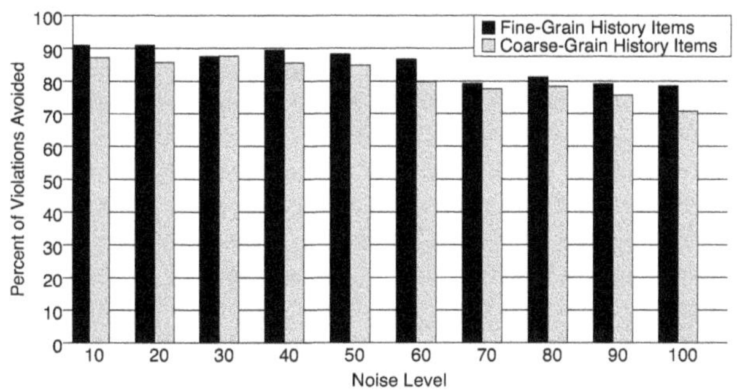

Figure 6: Atomicity violations avoided in kernel NetIO under synthetic noise for fine- and coarse-grain history items with a constant history window.

This figure also shows that using fine- rather than coarse-grain history items improves avoidance. The reason is that fine-grain history items encode the relative order of memory accesses more precisely. Using coarse history items, more accesses occur within the same history item and are considered simultaneous. This prevents ColorSafe from seeing an interleaving of these accesses. When fine-grain history items are used, ColorSafe is able to observe these interleavings, enabling earlier detection of buggy interleavings.

Figure 7 shows the proportion of useful ETs in these experiments. There is an inverse relationship between the noise level and the fraction of useful ETs. This relationship corroborates our above conclusion that avoidance is slightly impeded by the presence of noise because more useless ETs occur. The data also show that using fine-grain history items results in a larger fraction of useful ETs. This is in agreement with our findings from Figure 6, that fine-grain history items lead to more precise detection.

6.3 Characterizing Meta-Data Requirements

The size of the color meta-data in ColorSafe is derived from the total number of necessary colors. In our experiments using malloc-coloring, we saw as few as 265 colors in Ap2.0, around 900 colors in MySQL and as many as 4,015 colors (in jsStr). Using manual coloring, we saw just a single color in most cases (kernels, AGet, MySQL), and at most 5 colors in Ap2.0. These numbers represent

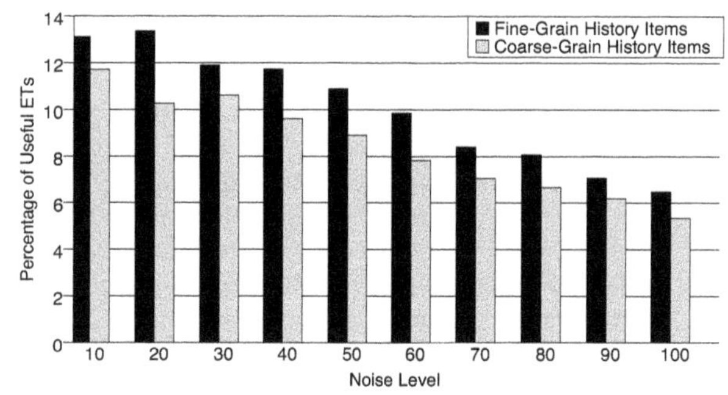

Figure 7: Percentage of useful ETs in NetIO with synthetic noise, 12,000-instruction total history length, and varied history item granularities.

the total number of coloring events (*e.g.*, allocations) in the execution.

We chose to use 12 bits of meta-data to represent colors in ColorSafe. For manual coloring, 12 bits provides ample space, according to our experimental results. Using malloc-coloring, capacity will be an issue for applications that frequently allocate memory. One way of handling this is to recycle colors when their associated memory is deallocated. Also, at additional cost, ColorSafe could be implemented with wider meta-data fields.

6.4 Debugging Mode: Locating Bugs in the Code

We focus on full applications for our debugging experiments. We collect the report of unserializable interleavings generated by ColorSafe using both manual coloring and malloc-coloring (when possible). We present a comparison of the detection capability in deployment mode versus debugging mode to show the effect of a stricter detection policy. We quantify the report in terms of code points — *i.e.*, lines of code to inspect.

Using malloc-coloring in debugging mode, ColorSafe reported a large number of detection code points — 1,493 for Ap2.0. By applying invariant-based processing, we saw a marked reduction in detections to just 58. This much smaller set of detections would lead a programmer directly to a bug, or short of that, would help a programmer decide how to manually color data.

We foresee ColorSafe being more useful for debugging if data structures that are suspected to be related to a bug are manually colored by a developer. We consider it reasonable to assume a programmer would be able to do this, given a standard bug report, output from ColorSafe using malloc-coloring, and knowledge about the data structures in the program. It is realistic to assume that the programmer can manually color data because it requires only local reasoning, when the data is declared (or allocated). Reasoning of this sort is the basis of prior proposals focusing on data-centric synchronization models [4, 10, 26].

Table 6 shows the number of code points produced by ColorSafe using manual coloring. We show results for deployment mode (Column 2), debugging mode (Column 3) and using our invariant approach described in Section 5 (Column 4). Most notably, ColorSafe is able to detect the bug in Ap2.0, with only 2 false positives (3 code points) in deployment mode, and just 1 false positive (2 code points) in debugging mode. ColorSafe detects the bug in AGet with just a handful of false positives as well, in both deployment mode, and debugging mode.

Two other facts stand out amongst these data. First, there is a decrease in detections from deployment mode to debugging mode. This is because debugging mode has a stricter policy for determining that an interleaving is unserializable (Section 3.2). There is a reduction of approximately 21% (256 code points) in the number of code points reported for MySQL, and 17% (4 code points) for AGet. However, further improvement is still desirable — even necessary — with hundreds of code points left to sift through for MySQL. This brings us to our second result: The reduction in reports resulting from applying invariant-based processing is dramatic. Invariant-based pruning eliminates hundreds of false positives for MySQL, leaving 40 code points to be analyzed in a software package of over a million lines. For AGet, we reduce the number of code points reported to just 8.

This shows that ColorSafe debugging, coupled with manual coloring and our invariant-based approach, leads to very few false positives, or virtually none. The reason that the invariant based approach works so well is that there are many similarities between non-buggy runs and buggy runs in terms of the unserializable interleavings. These similarities are filtered by our invariant-based approach, leaving only relevant detections.

App.	# Detections		
	Deployment	Debugging	Post-Processed
Ap2.0	3	2	2
AGet	24	20	8
MySQL	821	677	40

Table 6: Number of code points reported by ColorSafe using deployment mode, debugging mode, and debugging mode with invariant post-processing.

7. RELATED WORK

There are several major differences between ColorSafe and prior work on architectural support for concurrency bug detection. First, ColorSafe provides a general solution to support for atomicity violation detection (single-variable and multi-variable). Second, ColorSafe not only detects but also dynamically avoids multi-variable atomicity violations in the field. Finally, the same set of mechanisms are used for debugging and deployment, making ColorSafe useful throughout the lifetime of a system.

Atom-Aid [14] leverages the observation that architectures that execute programs as a continuum of implicit transactions [3, 9, 25, 28] can decrease the amount of interleaving of memory accesses between threads and potentially avoid atomicity violations. Atom-Aid detects single-variable atomicity violations and manipulates the boundaries of implicit transactions to avoid them. ColorSafe addresses the more general problem of multi-variable atomicity violations (not detected by Atom-Aid) and does *not* rely on continuous implicit transactions, but rather on ephemeral transactions, which are simpler and less costly. In addition, ColorSafe has drastically fewer false positives.

AVIO [11] was one of the first proposals of architectural support for atomicity violation detection. AVIO is only useful for debugging. AVIO monitors interleaving by extending the caches, so it is inherently limited to single-variable atomicity violations. In contrast, ColorSafe uses a history buffer of color accesses decoupled from caches. AVIO uses training runs to extract interleaving invariants and then checks if these invariants hold in future runs. This was the inspiration for our invariant-based debugging framework. MUVI [12] proposes static analysis to detect data correlations, but does not address atomicity violations.

ToleRace [21] and ISOLATOR [20] avoid concurrency errors that happen when one thread correctly follows a locking discipline but other threads do not. ToleRace detects such conditions by determining if the atomicity of a critical section was violated via single-variable serializability analysis, similarly to AVIO and Atom-Aid. ISOLATOR detects such scenarios by having the programmer annotate the code to declare the locking discipline. The avoidance mechanism used by these systems is based on keeping shadow copies of data that are speculatively updated and committed at the end of critical sections.

Serializability Violation Detector (SVD) [30] heuristically infers atomic sections based on control and data dependencies. SVD then detects single-variable atomicity violations and some multi-variable atomicity violations in these inferred sections. The authors briefly mention that their technique could use hardware support and avoid bugs via global checkpoint and restart. ColorSafe detects and avoids a broader class of bugs because of its more inclusive serializability analysis and its data correlation information. ColorSafe also differs from SVD in that it does *proactive* avoidance, preventing potential bugs, and without costly global checkpointing.

The Interleaving Constrained Shared Memory MultiProcessor [31] is a bug avoidance technique based on building invariants during testing and then using architecture support to enforce these invariants at run time. The invariants are encoded in sets of happens-before relationships between static memory instructions (PSets). PSets cannot be used to avoid multi-variable bugs because PSets do not encode correlation between memory locations (which is the cornerstone of ColorSafe). PSets requires a training phase to enable avoidance, whereas ColorSafe does not. Moreover, it requires checking whether memory accesses are allowed to proceed, which the authors claim that can be done with online binary rewriting and hardware support. Finally, PSets focuses on avoidance, so it is unclear whether the false positives would be tolerable for debugging.

Object Race Detection [27] is a software-only technique for dynamic race detection that tracks accesses at the level of objects in Java. While Object Race Detection does not detect violations of atomicity, it is related to ColorSafe because it tracks whole objects as units, similarly to ColorSafe's use of colors. Data coloring in ColorSafe, however, is more general, as it does not need to follow object boundaries and is not tied to a specific category of languages.

Colorama [4] is an architecture that supports a programming model based on data coloring, in which the programmer groups related data-structures into colors and the system automatically infers critical sections dynamically. Vaziri [26] *et al.* proposed a software implementation of such a model for object oriented languages, in which programmers group data into atomic sets and a compiler infers critical sections. These two pieces of work are related to ColorSafe in that they use data grouping to convey information about data-consistency, but none of them uses this information for debugging or bug avoidance. More recently and concurrently with our work, Hammer *et al.* [8] used atomic sets for serializability violation detection in Java programs. The required annotations go beyond grouping objects in atomic sets: it also requires programmers to annotate the expected atomicity of some methods ("units of work"). ColorSafe detects this automatically with high accuracy.

8. CONCLUSIONS

Shared memory parallel programming is a challenge for software developers. We believe it is extremely important to provide support for debugging such programs. It is still very likely that bugs will elude developers, making bug avoidance in the field appealing. We advocate that mechanisms to support bug detection should also enable dynamic bug avoidance post-deployment, making them useful throughout the lifetime of systems.

We propose ColorSafe, an architecture that provides both precise detection and dynamic bug avoidance. It is general, covering both single- and multi-variable atomicity violations and could be extended to support other forms of bugs. The key idea is to group correlated variables into colors and then to monitor access interleavings in the color space. This enables detection of bugs involving a set of variables, not just a single variable.

ColorSafe has two modes of operation: debugging mode produces detailed information about how and where atomicity violations may have happened; deployment mode performs less strict detection, but automatically starts ephemeral transactions to avoid erroneous interleavings, without affecting the semantics of the program. Our results show that ColorSafe in deployment mode is able to avoid virtually all violations in bug kernels and the vast majority of violations in full applications, such as Apache and MySQL, and imposes little performance overhead. In addition, ColorSafe in debugging mode yields very few false positives using a simple post-processing technique to prune spurious reports.

Acknowledgements

We thank the anonymous reviewers for their helpful feedback. We thank the SAMPA group at the University of Washington for their invaluable feedback on the manuscript and insightful discussions. This work was supported in part by NSF under grants CNS-0720593, a Microsoft Research Faculty Fellowship, and gifts from Microsoft Research and Intel.

9. REFERENCES

[1] Advanced Synchronization Facility: Proposed Architectural Specification. `http://developer.amd.com/assets/45432-ASF_Spec_2.1.pdf`, March 2009.

[2] L. Ceze, J. Tuck, C. Cascaval, and J. Torrellas. Bulk Disambiguation of Speculative Threads in Multiprocessors. In *International Symposium on Computer Architecture*, 2006.

[3] L. Ceze, J. Tuck, P. Montesinos, and J. Torrellas. BulkSC: Bulk Enforcement of Sequential Consistency. In *International Symposium on Computer Architecture*, 2007.

[4] L. Ceze, P. Montesinos, C. von Praun, and J. Torrellas. Colorama: Architectural Support for Data-Centric Synchronization. In *International Symposium on High-Performance Computer Architecture*, 2007.

[5] A. Chang and M. Mergen. 801 Storage: Architecture and Programming. *ACM Transactions Computer Systems*, February 1988.

[6] M. Dalton, H. Kannan, and C. Kozyrakis. Raksha: A Flexible Information Flow Architecture for Software Security. In *International Symposium on Computer Architecture*, 2007.

[7] C. Flanagan and S. Qadeer. A Type and Effect System for Atomicity. In *Conference on Programming Language Design and Implementation*, 2003.

[8] C. Hammer, J. Dolby, M. Vaziri, and F. Tip. Dynamic Detection of Atomic-Set-Serializability Violations. In *International Conference on Software Engineering*, 2008.

[9] L. Hammond, V. Wong, M. Chen, B. Carlstrom, J. Davis, B. Hertzberg, M. Prabhu, H. Wijaya, C. Kozyrakis, and K. Olukotun. Transactional Memory Coherence and Consistency. In *International Symposium on Computer Architecture*, 2004.

[10] C. Hoare. Monitors - An Operating System Structuring Concept. *Communications of the ACM*, 1974.

[11] S. Lu, J. Tucek, F. Qin, and Y. Zhou. AVIO: Detecting Atomicity Violations via Access Interleaving Invariants. In *International Conference on Architectural Support for Programming Languages and Operating Systems*, 2006.

[12] S. Lu, S. Park, C. Hu, X. Ma, W. Jiang, Z. Li, R. Popa, and Y. Zhou. MUVI: Automatically Inferring Multi-variable Access Correlations and Detecting Related Semantic and Concurrency Bugs. In *Symposium on Operating System Principles*, 2007.

[13] S. Lu, S. Park, E. Seo, and Y. Zhou. Learning from Mistakes-A Comprehensive Study on Real World Concurrency Bug Characteristics. In *International Conference on Architectural Support for Programming Languages and Operating Systems*, 2008.

[14] B. Lucia, J. Devietti, K. Strauss, and L. Ceze. Atom-Aid: Detecting and Surviving Atomicity Violations. In *International Symposium on Computer Architecture*, 2008.

[15] B. Lucia and L. Ceze. Finding Concurrency Bugs With Context-Aware Communication Graphs. In *International Symposium on Microarchitecture*, 2009.

[16] C. Luk, R. Cohn, R. Muth, H. Patil, A. Klauser, G. Lowney, S. Wallace, V. Reddi, and K. Hazelwood. PIN: Building Customized Program Analysis Tools with Dynamic Instrumentation. In *Conference on Programming Language Design and Implementation*, 2005.

[17] B. McCloskey, F. Zhou, D. Gay, and E. Brewer. Autolocker: Synchronization Inference for Atomic Sections. In *Symposium on Principles of Programming Languages*, 2006.

[18] M. Musuvathi and S. Qadeer. CHESS: Systematic Stress Testing of Concurrent Software. In *International Symposium on Logic-based Program Synthesis and Transformation*, 2006.

[19] M. Prvulovic and J. Torrellas. ReEnact: Using Thread-Level Speculation Mechanisms to Debug Data Races in Multithreaded Codes. In *International Symposium on Computer Architecture*, 2003.

[20] S. Rajamani, G. Ramalingam, V. Ranganath, and K. Vaswani. ISOLATOR: Dynamically Ensuring Isolation in Concurrent Programs. In *International Conference on Architectural Support for Programming Languages and Operating Systems*, 2009.

[21] P. Ratanaworabhan, M. Burtscher, D. Kirovski, B. Zorn, R. Nagpal, and K. Pattabiraman. Detecting and Tolerating Asymmetric Races. In *Annual Symposium on Principles and Practice of Parallel Programming*, 2009.

[22] M. Ronsee and K. De Bosschere. RecPlay: A Fully Integrated Practical Record/Replay System. *Transactions on Computer Systems*, 1999.

[23] D. Sanchez, L. Yen, M. Hill, and K. Sankaralingam. Implementing Signatures for Transactional Memory. In *International Symposium on Microarchitecture*, 2007.

[24] S. Savage, M. Burrows, G. Nelson, P. Sobalvarro, and T. Anderson. Eraser: A Dynamic Data Race Detector for Multi-Threaded Programs. *Transactions on Computer Systems*, 1997.

[25] E. Vallejo, M. Galluzzi, A. Cristal, F. Vallejo, R. Beivide, P. Stenstrom, J. Smith, and M. Valero. Implementing Kilo-Instruction Multiprocessors. In *International Conference on Pervasive Services*, 2005.

[26] M. Vaziri, F. Tip, and J. Dolby. Associating Synchronization Constraints with Data in an Object-Oriented Language. In *Symposium on Principles of Programming Languages*, 2006.

[27] C. von Praun and T. Gross. Object Race Detection. In

Conference on Object-Oriented Programming Systems, Languages and Applications, 2001.

[28] T. Wenisch, A. Ailamaki, B. Falsafi, and A. Moshovos. Mechanisms for Store-wait-free Multiprocessors. In *International Symposium on Computer Architecture*, 2007.

[29] E. Witchel, J. Cates, and K. Asanovic. Mondrian Memory Protection. In *International Conference on Architectural Support for Programming Languages and Operating Systems*, 2002.

[30] M. Xu, R. Bodik, and M. Hill. A Serializability Violation Detector for Shared-Memory Server Programs. In *Conference on Programming Language Design and Implementation*, 2005.

[31] J. Yu and S. Narayanasamy. A Case for an Interleaving Constrained Shared-Memory Multi-Processor. In *International Symposium on Computer Architecture*, 2009.

[32] N. Zeldovich, H. Kannan, M. Dalton, and C. Kozyrakis. Hardware Enforcement of Application Security Policies Using Tagged Memory. In *Symposium on Operating Systems Design and Implementation*, 2008.

[33] P. Zhou, R. Teodorescu, and Y. Zhou. HARD: Hardware-Assisted Lockset-based Race Detection. In *International Symposium on High-Performance Computer Architecture*, 2007.

Shared Caches in Multicores: The Good, The Bad, and The Ugly

Mary Jane Irwin
Pennsylvania State University

Abstract: As we transition from clock-frequency performance scaling to performance scaling with multicores, the pressure on the memory hierarchy is increasing dramatically. Many different on-chip cache topologies have been proposed/implemented; effective management of these shared caches is crucial to multicore performance.

This talk will begin with a description of a cache miss classification scheme for multicores (compulsory, inter-core misses, intra-core misses) that gives insight into the interactions between memory transactions of the different cores on a chip sharing a cache. Ways to improve the on-chip cache performance with architectural enhancements, compiler enhancements, and runtime system enhancements will then be discussed. If the application thread mapping and the on-chip topology is static (i.e., does not change during runtime), then compiler enhancements that support cache topology aware code optimization can be used to significantly improve an application's performance. Results from such an augmented compiler, where the topology is exposed to the compiler and where the compiler also does thread-to-core mapping assignments, will be presented. If the application thread mapping or the on-chip topology is dynamic, then other alternatives exist. For example, a thread scheduler, or allocator, can make decisions about moving threads to different cores during runtime in the hopes of improving overall cache performance. Initial experiments with the REEact system being developed by researchers at Penn State-UPittsburgh-UVirginia that "reacts" to hardware conditions (such as cache miss rates, hot-spots, etc.) by reallocating threads at runtime will be outlined. Finally, if the on-chip cache topology itself is dynamic (i.e., is designed to be reconfigurable at runtime), large performance benefits might be obtained. However, both hardware and software design challenges to realizing such a dynamic system abound. Some of these challenges will be briefly discussed.

Categories & Subject Descriptors: C.0 Computer Systems Organization; General.

General Term: Design.

ISCA'10, June 19–23, 2010, Saint-Malo, France.
ACM 978-1-4503-0053-7/10/06.

Dynamic Warp Subdivision for Integrated Branch and Memory Divergence Tolerance

Jiayuan Meng
Department of Computer Science
University of Virginia
jm6dg@virginia.edu

David Tarjan*
Department of Computer Science
University of Virginia
dtarjan@cs.virginia.edu

Kevin Skadron
Department of Computer Science
University of Virginia
skadron@cs.virginia.edu

ABSTRACT

SIMD organizations amortize the area and power of fetch, decode, and issue logic across multiple processing units in order to maximize throughput for a given area and power budget. However, throughput is reduced when a set of threads operating in lockstep (a warp) are stalled due to long latency memory accesses. The resulting idle cycles are extremely costly. Multi-threading can hide latencies by interleaving the execution of multiple warps, but deep multi-threading using many warps dramatically increases the cost of the register files (multi-threading depth × SIMD width), and cache contention can make performance worse. Instead, intra-warp latency hiding should first be exploited. This allows threads that are ready but stalled by SIMD restrictions to use these idle cycles and reduces the need for multi-threading among warps. This paper introduces *dynamic warp subdivision* (DWS), which allows a single warp to occupy more than one slot in the scheduler without requiring extra register file space. Independent scheduling entities allow divergent branch paths to interleave their execution, and allow threads that hit to run ahead. The result is improved latency hiding and memory level parallelism (MLP). We evaluate the technique on a coherent cache hierarchy with private L1 caches and a shared L2 cache. With an area overhead of less than 1%, experiments with eight data-parallel benchmarks show our technique improves performance on average by 1.7X.

Categories and Subject Descriptors: C.1.2 PROCESSOR ARCHITECTURES: Multiple Data Stream Architectures (Multiprocessors)

General Terms: Design, Performance

Keywords: SIMD, Branch Divergence, Latency Hiding, Memory Divergence, Warp

1. INTRODUCTION

Single instruction, multiple data (SIMD) organizations use a single instruction sequencer to operate multiple datapaths or "lanes" in lockstep. SIMD is generally more efficient than *multiple instruction, multiple data* (MIMD) in exploiting data parallelism, because it allows greater throughput within a given area and power budget by amortizing the cost of the instruction sequencing over multiple datapaths. This observation is becoming important, both because data parallelism is common across a wide range of applications; and because data-parallel throughput is increasingly important for high performance as single-thread performance improvement slows.

SIMD lockstep operation of multiple datapaths can be implemented with vector units, where the SIMD operation is explicit in the instruction set and a single thread operates on wide vector registers. SIMD lockstep can also be *implicit*, where each lane executes distinct threads that operate on scalar registers, but the threads progress in lockstep. The latter is also referred to by NVIDIA as *single instruction multiple threads* (SIMT). For purpose of generality in this paper, we refer to the set of operations happening in lockstep as a *warp* and the application of an instruction sequence to a single lane as a *thread*. We refer to a set of hardware units under SIMD control as a *warp processing unit* or WPU.[1] SIMD organizations of both types are increasingly common in architectures for high throughput computing, exemplified today in STI's Cell Broadband Engine (CBE) [11], Clearspeed's CSX600 [20], Intel's Larrabee [27], Cray [26], and Tarantula [9]. Graphics processors (GPUs), including NVIDIA's Tesla [8] and Fermi [1], and AMD/ATI's recent architectures [2] also employ SIMD organizations and are increasingly used for general-purpose computing. Academic researchers have also proposed stream architectures that employ SIMD organizations [13, 25], and in fact this history goes back to the Illiac project [21]. For both productivity and performance purposes, an increasing number of SIMD organizations support *gather and scatter*, where each lane can load from or store to unrelated addresses. (Vector architectures implement this by loading or storing a vector of data from or to a vector of addresses [7, 8, 27].) This introduces the possibility of "divergent" memory access latency, because a SIMD gather or scatter may access a set of data that is not fully in a particular level of the cache.

As in other throughput-oriented organizations that try to maximize thread concurrency and hence do not waste area on discovering instruction level parallelism, WPUs typically employ in-order pipelines that have limited ability to execute past L1 cache misses or other long latency events. To hide memory latencies, WPUs instead time-multiplex among multiple concurrent warps, each with their own PCs and registers. However, the multi-threading depth (i.e., number of warps) is limited because adding more warps multiplies the area overhead in register files, and may increase cache contention as well. As a result of this limited multi-threading depth, the WPU may run out of work. This can occur even when there are runnable threads that are stalled *only* due to SIMD lockstep restrictions. For example, some threads in a

*Now with NVIDIA Research

[1]We invent a new term here to distinguish it from "cores", "lanes" or "PEs," terms which are sometimes used to refer to individual scalar pipelines that constitutes the WPU.

ISCA'10, June 19–23, 2010, Saint-Malo, France.

warp may be ready while others are still stalled on a cache miss.

This paper observes that when a WPU does not have enough warps with all threads ready to execute, some individual threads may still be able to proceed. This occurs in two cases:

- Branch divergence: Branch divergence occurs when threads in the same warp take different paths upon a conditional branch. In current organizations, the WPU can only execute one path of the branch at a time for a given warp, with some threads masked off if they took the branch in the alternate direction. In array organizations, this is handled in hardware by a re-convergence stack [10] or conditional streams [12]; in vector organizations, this is handled in software by using the branch outcomes as a set of predicates [15, 28, 29]. In either case, allowing both paths to run creates problems in re-converging the warp.
- Memory latency divergence: Memory latency divergence occurs when threads from a single warp experience different memory-reference latencies caused by cache misses or accessing different DRAM banks. In current organizations, the entire warp must wait until the last thread has its reference satisfied. This occurs in both array and vector organizations (if the vector instruction set allows gather/scatter).

We propose *dynamic warp subdivision* (DWS) to utilize *both* thread categories. Warps are selectively subdivided into *warp-splits*. Each has fewer threads than the available SIMD width, but can be *individually regarded as an additional scheduling entity* to hide latency and can both be active:

- Upon branch divergence, a warp can be divided into two *active* warp-splits, each representing threads that fall into one of the branch paths. The WPU can then interleave the computation of different branch paths to hide memory latency.
- Upon memory latency divergence, a warp can be divided into two warp-splits as well: one represents threads whose memory operations have completed, the other represents threads that are still stalled (e.g., on a cache miss). The former warp-split need not suspend; it can run ahead non-speculatively and in the process touch and potentially prefetch cache lines that may also be needed by threads that fell behind.

In both cases, stall cycles are reduced, latency hiding is improved, and the ability to overlap more outgoing memory requests increases memory level parallelism (MLP). The challenge is to manage this process without reducing overall throughput: aggressive subdivision may result in performance degradation because it may lead to a large number of narrow warp-splits that only exploit a fraction of the SIMD computation resources. A dynamic mechanism is needed because the divergence pattern depends on run-time dynamics such as cache misses and may vary across applications, phases of execution, and even different inputs.

We evaluate several strategies for dynamic warp subdivision based upon eight distinct data-parallel benchmarks. Experiments are conducted by simulating WPUs operating over a two-level cache hierarchy that has private L1 caches sharing an inclusive, on-chip L2. The results show that our technique improves the average performance across a diverse set of parallel benchmarks by 1.7X. It is robust and shows no performance degradation on the benchmarks that were tested. We estimate that dynamic warp subdivision adds less than 1% area overhead to a WPU.

2. IMPACT OF MEMORY LATENCY DIVERGENCE

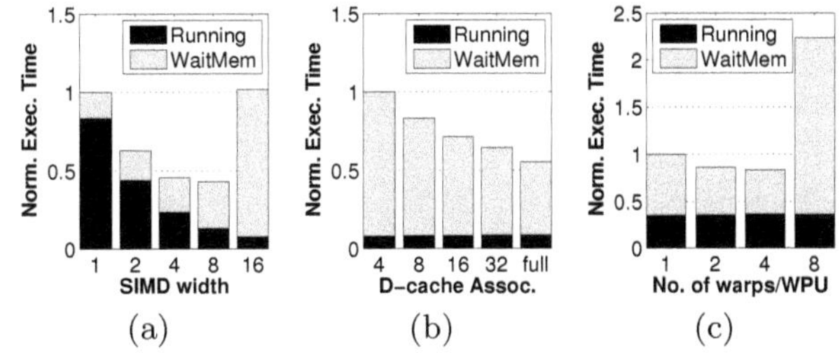

Figure 1: (a) A wider SIMD organization does not always improve performance due to increased time spent waiting for memory. The number of warps is fixed at four. (b) 16-wide WPUs with 4 warps even suffer from highly associative D-caches. (c) A few 8-wide warps can beneficially hide latency, but too many warps eventually exacerbates cache contention and increases the time spent waiting for memory. Results are harmonic means across the benchmarks listed in Table 2 on the system configuration in Table 3.

As SIMD width increases, the likelihood that at least one thread will stall the entire warp increases. However, *inter*-warp latency tolerance (*i.e.*, deeper multi-threading via more warps) is not sufficient to hide these latencies. The number of threads whose state fits in an L1 cache is limited. That is why *intra*-warp latency tolerance is needed. Intra-warp latency also provides opportunities for memory-level parallelism (MLP) that conventional SIMD organizations do not.

In order to illustrate the impact of memory latency divergence, the limitations on warp count, and the need for intra-warp latency tolerance, Figure 1a shows the performance scaling when varying the SIMD width from 1 to 16 with four warps sharing a 32 KB L1 D-cache. As the SIMD width grows, the overall execution time first improves (thanks to greater throughput) but eventually starts to get worse even though this experiment is increasing the total computation resources; although the time spent in SIMD computation keeps decreasing, the time spent waiting for memory drastically increases and eventually dominates. The reasons for this trend are two-fold: first, a wider SIMD organization incorporates more threads, which increase D-cache contention; second, wider warps are more likely to incur memory divergence and suspend due to individual cache misses. The overall effect is fewer active warps but more latency to hide. Figure 1c shows that adding more warps does exacerbate L1 contention. This is a capacity limitation, not just an associativity problem, as shown in Figure 1b, where time waiting on memory is still significant even with full associativity.[2] These results are all averages across the benchmarks described in Section 3.2 and obtained with the configuration described in Section 3.

Intra-warp latency tolerance hides latencies without requiring extra threads. However, intra-warp latency tolerance is only beneficial when threads within the same warp

[2]It is true that current GPU architectures such as Tesla [8] and Fermi [1] have much higher warp counts because they reference global memory frequently (no L2 for Tesla and L2 is only a victim cache in Fermi), and have very long WPU latencies to issue back to back instructions from the same thread. If we increase L1 miss latency to 300 cycles (similar to having no L2), our architecture's optimal warp count also jumps to 8 or 16; the extra cache contention is now justified by the dramatic need for extra latency hiding. Intra-warp latency hiding is still beneficial in this case, of course.

	FFT	Filter	HotSpot	LU	Merge	Short	KMeans	SVM
Avg. instruction count between branches	59	12	16	53	9	19	10	12
Percentage of divergent branches	3.4%	0%	1.4%	4.3%	13.1%	22.0%	2.0%	4.3%
Avg. instruction count between misses	7	27	7	5	45	6	47	11
Avg. instruction count between div. misses	10	30	10	6	75	8	57	17
Percentage of divergent memory accesses	69%	88%	77%	81%	60%	79%	83%	62%

Table 1: Characterization of the frequency of branch divergence and SIMD cache misses.

exhibit divergent behavior. Table 1 shows that many benchmarks exhibit frequent memory divergence. A further advantage of intra-warp latency tolerance is that the same mechanisms also improve throughput in the presence of branch divergence.

In summary, scaling SIMD width is not always beneficial in systems with limited on-chip storage capacity. In order to host wider SIMD organizations and further improve throughput, it is necessary to hide such latency without additional threads. Section 4 and Section 5 show how DWS can address both branch and memory divergence. DWS is the first technique that can address both sources of divergence using the same hardware mechanism.

3. METHODOLOGY

3.1 Overall Architecture

Branch and memory-latency divergence can affect a variety of architectures. In order to draw more general conclusions, this paper models a general system that blends important aspects of modern CPU and GPU architectures: general-purpose ISAs (represented here by the Alpha ISA), SIMD organization, multi-threading, and a cache-coherent memory hierarchy. We model implicit, array-style SIMD instead of a vector architecture because this places fewer burdens on software. While there are simulators available for vector architectures, traditional CPUs, and GPUs, we are not aware of any that combine these aspects. We therefore developed MV5 [17] to simulate WPUs. MV5 is a cycle-accurate, event-driven simulator based on M5 [3]. Because existing thread schedulers do not directly support the management of SIMD threads, applications are simulated in system emulation mode with a set of primitives to create and schedule threads on SIMD resources.

The simulated applications are programmed in an OpenMP-style API implemented in MV5, where data parallelism is expressed in `parallel for` loops. Applications are cross-compiled to the Alpha ISA using G++ 4.1.0, with new instructions recognized by MV5 inserted to signal SIMD thread management to the simulator. The code for a thread is compiled as a scalar code, and the programming model then launches multiple copies for SIMD execution. Neighboring tasks are assigned to threads in the same warp in a way that exploits both spatial and temporal data locality [16].

3.2 Benchmarks

We simulate a set of benchmarks shown in Table 2. The benchmarks are selected from several benchmark suites including MineBench [19], Splash2 [32], and Rodinia [4]. No consideration of SIMD divergence was present in selecting the benchmarks. The benchmarks are the same as those used to study thread scheduling when many threads share a cache [16]. These benchmarks are common, data-parallel kernels and applications. They cover the application domains of scientific computing, image processing, physics simulation, machine learning and data mining. They demonstrate varied data access and communication patterns. We increase the input sizes from the original benchmarks so that

	Benchmark Description
FFT	Fast Fourier Transform (Splash2 [32]). Spectral methods. Butterfly computation Input: a 1-D array of 65,536 (2^{16}) numbers
Filter	Edge Detection of an Input Image. Convolution. Gathering a 3-by-3 neighborhood Input: a gray scale image of size 500 × 500
HotSpot	Thermal Simulation (Rodinia [4]). Iterative partial differential equation solver Input: a 300 × 300 2-D grid, 100 iterations
LU	LU Decomposition (Splash2 [32]). Dense linear algebra. Alternating row-major and column-major computation Input: a 300 × 300 matrix
Merge	Merge Sort. Element aggregation and reordering Input: a 1-D array of 300,000 integers
Short	Winning Path Search for Chess. Dynamic programming. Neighborhood calculation based on the the previous row Input: 6 steps each with 150,000 choices
KMeans	Unsupervised Classification (MineBench [19]). Distance aggregation using Map-Reduce. Input: 10,000 points in a 20-D space
SVM	Supervised Learning (MineBench [19]). Support vector machine's kernel computation. Input: 100,000 vectors with a 20-D space

Table 2: Simulated benchmarks with descriptions and input sizes.

we have reasonable simulation times of within six hours. All means reported in this paper are harmonic means.

3.3 Architecture Details

The baseline SIMD architecture used in this study is illustrated in Figure 2. The system has a two level coherent cache hierarchy. Each WPU has private I- and D-caches which interact with an on-chip, shared, last-level cache (LLC). Only the LLC communicates with the off-chip memory. Examples of SIMD organizations that use cache hierarchies include Larrabee [27] and Fermi [1], both of which support general purpose computation. (Fermi's caches, however, are not cache-coherent). WPUs are simulated with up to 64 thread contexts and 16 lanes. The experiments in this paper are limited to four WPUs because this provide reasonable simulation time.

A WPU groups scalar threads into warps. A fetched instruction is executed by threads within the same (active portion of a) warp simultaneously. Each thread's register state resides in a particular lane and the thread must execute in the corresponding lane. The register file is highly banked, with banks corresponding to lanes, so that multiple threads can access their operands at the same time without requiring deep multi-porting. Branch divergence is enabled by a re-convergence stack [10] — using a bit mask, threads that do not fall into the current control path are not executed. The mechanism is described in more detail in Section 4.1. Due to the lack of compiler support, we manually instrument the application code with post-dominators to signal control flow re-convergence after branches.

For the WPU lanes, we model in-order issue of one instruction per cycle. All instructions have latency of one except for memory references, which are modeled faithfully through the memory hierarchy (although we do not model memory controller reordering effects). The 4-way 16 KB L1

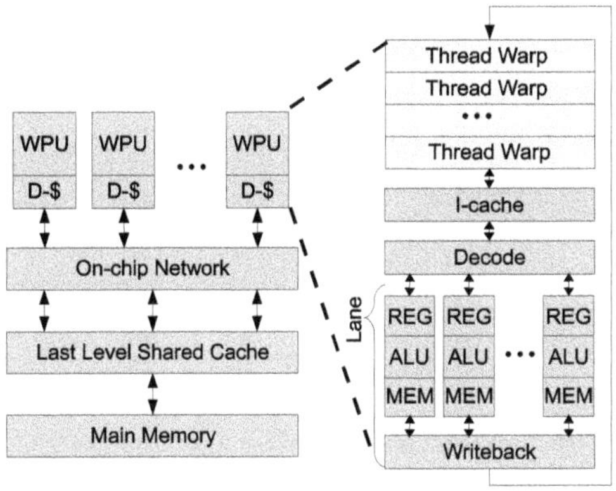

Figure 2: The baseline SIMD architecture groups scalar threads into warps and executes them using the same instruction sequencer. A thread operates over a scalar pipeline or lane that consists of register files, ALUs, and memory units.

I-cache has a 1-cycle latency, while the baseline 8-way, 32 KB, L1 D-cache has a 3-cycle latency. Both caches use 128-byte lines. To hide latency on cache misses, a WPU switches to execute a different warp when the current warp accesses the cache. Switching warps takes no extra latency; the next warp is scheduled while the current warp issues.

This study does not model non-blocking loads whose benefits are limited with in-order issue. The hardware overhead is also considerable as the number of threads (SIMD width × multi-threading depth) goes up. DWS would further increase the state for tracking non-blocking loads by the number of warp-splits allowed. These considerations are interesting areas for future work.

Each WPU has a private I-cache and D-cache. I-caches are not banked because only one instruction is fetched every cycle and distributed across all lanes. D-caches are always banked according to the number of lanes to cater to the high bandwidth demand of memory accesses. We assume there is a crossbar connecting the lanes with the D-cache banks. If bank conflicts occur, these memory requests are serialized and a small queuing overhead (one cycle) is charged. The queuing overhead can be smaller than the hit latency because we assume requests can be pipelined. Each cache bank performs its own tag match to support gather and scatter. All caches are physically indexed and physically tagged and use an LRU replacement policy. Memory coalescing is performed at the L1. All requests from a warp to the same cache line are coalesced in the MSHR. Otherwise, requests to the L2 are serialized. Each MSHR hosts a cache line and can track as many requests to that line as the SIMD width requires. Because the WPU supports gather/scatter, the TLB is multi-ported according to the number of lanes. The L1 caches connect to L2 banks through a crossbar. Coherence uses a directory-based MESI protocol.

Table 3 summarizes the main architectural parameters. Note that the aggregate L2 access latency is broken down into L1 lookup latency, crossbar latency, and the L2 tag and data lookup. The L2 then connects to the main memory through a 266 MHz memory bus with a bandwidth of 16 GB/s. The latency in accessing the main memory is assumed to be 100 cycles, and the memory controller is able to pipeline the requests.

4. DYNAMIC WARP SUBDIVISION UPON BRANCH DIVERGENCE

To hide more latency in the case of insufficient warps, we identify two categories of threads that may be unnecessarily suspended and can actually continue to execute. In this section, we discuss threads suspended due to branch divergence. Section 5 discusses threads suspended due to memory divergence.

Tech. Node	65 nm
WPU	1 GHz, 0.9 V Vdd, Alpha ISA, in-order 64 hardware thread contexts 4 warps with a SIMD width of 16 SIMD threads translate addresses simultaneously
I-Cache	16 KB, 4-way associative, 128 B line size 1 cycle hit latency, 4 MSHRs, LRU, write-back physically tagged, physically indexed
D-Cache	32 KB, 8-way associative, 128 B line size MESI directory-based coherence 3 cycle hit latency, LRU, write-back 32 MSHRs each hosts up to 8 requests physically tagged, physically indexed
L2 Cache	4096 KB, 16-way associative, 128 B line size 30 cycle hit latency, LRU, write-back 256 MSHRs each hosts up to 8 requests
Crossbar	300 MHz, 57 Gbytes/s
Memory	100 cycles access latency

Table 3: Parameters for the two-level coherent cache hierarchy.

4.1 Branch Divergence, Memory Latency and MLP

Figure 3 illustrates the conventional mechanism presented by Fung *et al.* [10] to handle divergent branches. Assume that a warp with a SIMD width of eight encounters a conditional branch at the end of code block A. Six of the threads branch to code block B (indicated by bit mask 11111001 in Figure 3), while the other two threads branch to code block C (indicated by bit mask 00000110 in Figure 3). The WPU first chooses to execute code block B. It then pushes the warp's re-convergence stack with the above two sets of bit masks, with the one that corresponds to code block B on the top of the stack (TOS). The first PC in code block D becomes the *immediate post-dominator* of B. Not until this post-dominator is reached can the re-convergence stack pop and switch to activate threads executing the alternate path (code block C) — in this way, the re-convergence stack is able to handle potentially nested branches within code block B. Eventually code block C re-converges at the same post-dominator into code block D.

The fact that the re-convergence stack can only activate one branch path at a time may limit a WPU's ability to hide latency and leverage MLP. Figure 4 illustrates this scenario. If threads executing code block B miss the cache and all other warps are waiting for memory as well, the WPU has to stall even though the threads that branched into code block C do not suffer from cache misses; these threads could actually continue to execute if it were not for the re-convergence mechanism.

The post-dominator based re-convergence may also undermine MLP when threads that have reached their post-dominator have to wait for those that have not. As shown in Figure 5, if threads executing code block C miss the cache and all other warps are waiting for memory as well, the WPU has to stall even though the threads that finished code block B do not suffer from cache misses. If re-convergence can be relaxed, these threads can make progress themselves, getting their own memory requests issued earlier, as well as prefetching for the others.

It is important to note that DWS upon branch divergence can hide latency and improve MLP *with or without the presence of memory divergence.* As we will discuss in Section 5, DWS upon branch divergence and DWS upon memory divergence are independent, complementary techniques, but DWS allows them to be integrated using the same hard-

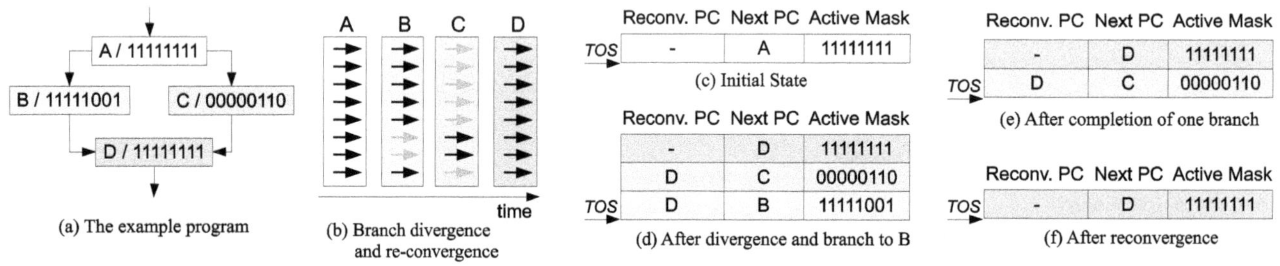

Figure 3: Conventional mechanism to handle branch divergence and re-convergence for a SIMD organization. (a) An example program; (b) the execution trace of diverged threads; (c)-(f) the state of the re-convergence stack. This is adapted from a figure by Fung *et al.* [10].

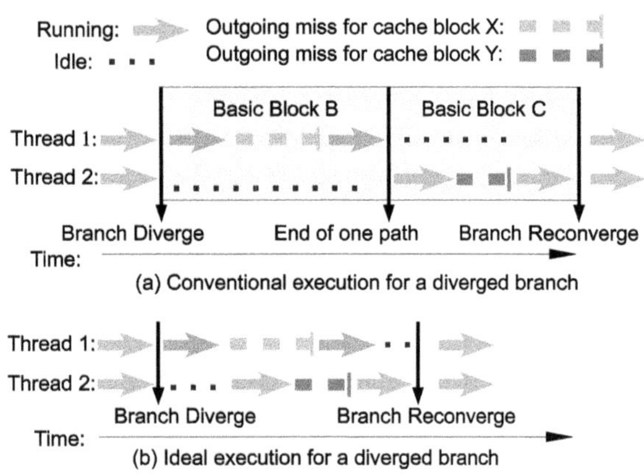

Figure 4: (a) The conventional mechanism serializes the execution of different branch paths. (b) By allowing threads that take different paths to interleave their execution, more latency can be hidden and memory level parallelism can be improved.

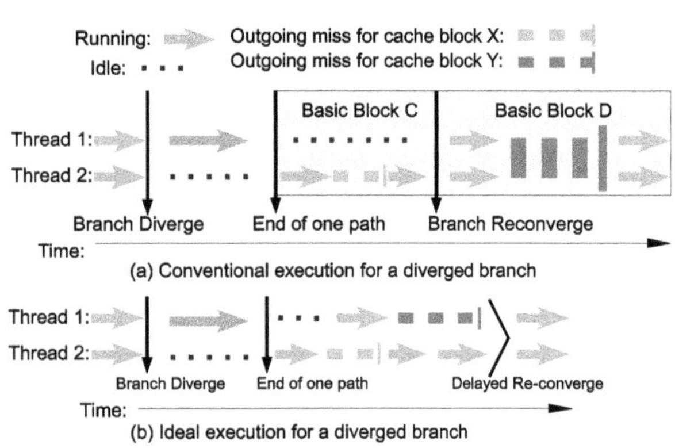

Figure 5: (a) The conventional mechanism forces diverged threads to re-converge at the post-dominator. (b) By allowing threads that reach the post-dominator first to run ahead, they can issue more outgoing requests to leverage memory level parallelism.

ware mechanisms and re-convergence policies. In order to isolate the role of branch divergence, results in this section disable the ability to perform DWS on memory divergence (i.e., warps cannot proceed until all threads' memory operations have completed).

4.2 Relaxing the Re-convergence Stack for Memory Throughput

We propose to subdivide a warp into two warp-splits upon branch divergence. Warp-splits are *independent scheduling entities* and are treated equally as warps by the scheduler. A warp-split can conceivably be recursively subdivided in future divergence events until it consists of only one thread. A full warp can be viewed as a *root warp-split* with full SIMD width. We use the term *SIMD groups* to refer to both full warps and warp-splits in the rest of the paper.

After a divergent branch subdivides a warp, the resulting warp-splits can interleave their computation to hide latency and improve memory level parallelism. This is demonstrated by an example in Figure 6. After a divergent branch in code block B, the conventional approach uses the re-convergence stack to serialize different branch paths (Figure 6b). Alternatively, dynamic warp subdivision uses a warp-split table described in Section 4.4 so that a warp can progress like a binary tree with simultaneously active warp-splits (Figure 6d).

4.3 Over-subdivision

Warps may not benefit from subdivision upon *every* divergent branch — such aggressive subdivision may lead to a large number of narrow warp-splits, which can otherwise run altogether in a wider SIMD group. This phenomenon is referred to in the rest of the paper as *over-subdivision*. Due to the potential for over-subdivision, we subdivide warps conditionally upon selected branches.

A static approach is used to select which branches are allowed to subdivide warps. As a side effect of subdivision, SIMD resources may be under-utilized if warp-splits are not re-converged in time. This occurs when two warp-splits have both passed their common post-dominator, but are not able to re-converge. This is illustrated in Figure 6 when the execution reaches time T2. We therefore use the heuristic that warps only subdivide upon branches whose associate post-dominator is followed up by a short basic block (F in the example of Figure 6) of no more than 50 instructions. This value was chosen because it takes roughly the same time to execute that many instructions as to handle an L1 miss, so run-ahead threads resulting from subdivision can hide some latency and initiate some further memory requests without running too far ahead and potentially inhibiting re-convergence. We manually instrumented the code to identify branches that subdivide warps, but in practice this process would be automated by the compiler.

4.4 Unrelenting Subdivision

When warp-splits independently execute the same instruction sequence while there is not much latency to hide, SIMD resources are under-utilized for little benefit. This scenario

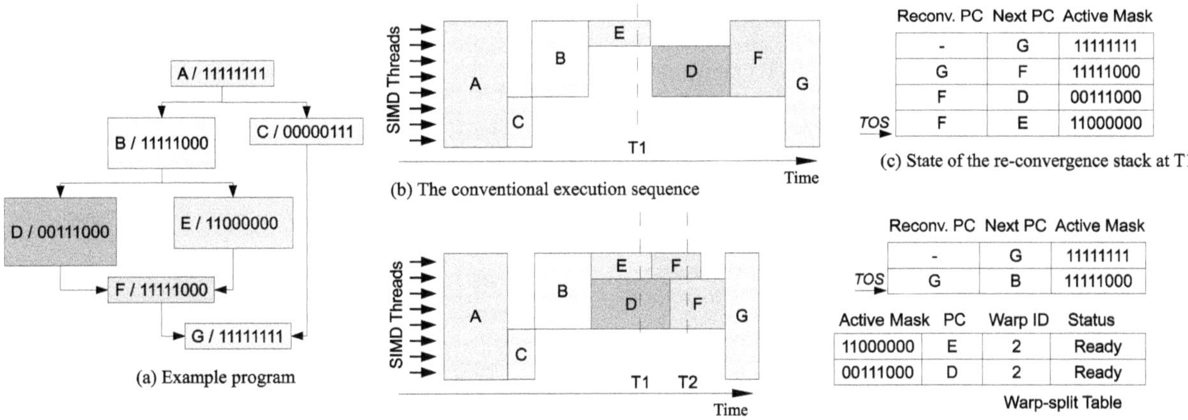

(a) Example program

(b) The conventional execution sequence

(c) State of the re-convergence stack at T1

(d) The execution sequence using dynamic warp subdivision. E and D are simultaneously active and their execution can be interleaved.

(e) State of the re-convergence stack and the warp-split table at T1

Figure 6: An example of dynamic warp subdivision upon branch divergence. Conventionally, different branch paths in the example program (a) are pushed to different layers in the re-convergence stack (c) and the execution of different paths is serialized (b). With dynamic warp subdivision, branch paths create entries in the warp-split table instead (e), denoting SIMD thread groups that can be simultaneously active. Their immediate post-dominator is ignored as well and no longer enforces re-convergence. As a result, diverged threads can interleave their execution (d), and they no longer have to re-converge at the beginning of code block F. Therefore, F is executed twice by different warp-splits; this may improve MLP but it also risks pipeline under-utilization.

is referred to in the rest of the paper as *unrelenting subdivision*. Under such circumstances, it may be better to re-converge the warp-splits as soon as possible so they can execute together as a wider SIMD group. Therefore it is important *both* to create warp-splits and to re-converge them appropriately.

To meet such requirement, a warp-split table (WST) is introduced *in addition to* the re-convergence stack to keep track of subdivision while preserving the re-convergence mechanism. Each entry in the WST corresponds to a warp-split. It records the warp-split's parent warp, the current PC, and the active mask that indicates the associated threads. Figure 6 illustrates an example of warp subdivision. Upon a divergent branch at the end of code block B, the warp can choose to push the re-convergence stack to serialize code blocks E and D (Figure 6b, c), or it can choose to be subdivided according to the branch outcome so that code blocks E and D can be interleaved (Figure 6d, e). If a warp is subdivided, two additional entries are created in the warp-split table. The re-convergence stack remains intact to avoid imposing a particular execution order of the paths; it can therefore no longer keep track of this and future branches nested within the branch registered on its TOS. As a result, future nested branches as well as their post-dominators are ignored by the re-convergence stack; warp-splits continue executing asynchronously and keep being subdivided upon future divergent branches until they reach the post-dominator associated with the top of the re-convergence stack. At this point, the warp-split stalls waiting to be re-united with other warp-splits once they reach the same post-dominator. The re-convergence is performed by the re-convergence stack in the conventional manner. We name this scheme *stack-based re-convergence*.

4.5 PC-based Re-convergence

Using stack-based re-convergence, warp-splits can eventually re-converge; however, they can re-converge earlier when they happen to execute the same instruction. For example, at time T2 in Figure 6d, both warp-splits are asynchronously executing the same code block and they *might* arrive at the same PC. In such cases, the two warp-splits can be re-united naturally without stalling any of them.

By recording the PC of each warp-split in the warp-split table, the WPU can identify and re-unite warp-splits belonging to the *same* warp that are *ready* to execute and share the same PC. We name this scheme *PC-based re-convergence*. Note that stack-based re-convergence is still used if PC-based re-convergence does not occur. A similar principle has been used in Fung et al.'s dynamic warp formation, although it was used to group *any* threads from *different* warps that execute the same branch path [10].

While comparing multiple PCs may take three to four cycles, such PC-based re-convergence does not have to be checked every cycle, and the latency can usually be hidden. Because the scheduler only switches SIMD groups upon cache accesses, resumed warp-splits from the ready queue always start with memory instructions. As a result, PCs need only be compared when the running warp-split executes a memory instruction. Furthermore, because re-convergence takes place only when there are one or more SIMD groups in the ready queue, the WPU can immediately switch to execute another SIMD group, preferably from a different warp, to hide the latency PC comparisons.

4.6 Results

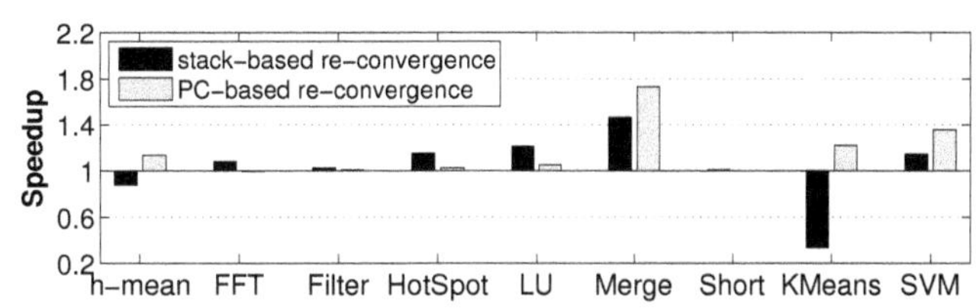

Figure 7: Performance gained by dynamic warp subdivision upon branch divergence. Speedups are normalized to that of the equivalent WPUs without DWS. Compared to stack-based re-convergence, PC-based re-convergence reduces unrelenting subdivision and improves performance significantly without ever making performance worse.

Dynamic warp subdivision upon branch divergence is evaluated with both stack-based re-convergence and PC-based re-convergence. Figure 7 compares their speedups over a conventional architecture with no DWS. While stack-based re-convergence demonstrates performance gains for some applications, it penalizes the performance of KMeans significantly due to over-subdivision and unrelenting subdivision — the average SIMD width for executed instructions are reduced to 4 for 16-wide WPUs. By introducing PC-based re-convergence, the average SIMD width for executed instructions increases to 9. This drastically reduces the under-utilization of SIMD resources. However, without memory divergence handling, warp-splits re-converged upon the same PC are not able to split again upon cache misses to hide intra-warp latency. As a result, for some applications, stack-based re-convergence performs slightly better than PC-based re-convergence. Overall, PC-based re-convergence outperforms stack-based re-convergence and it generates an average speedup of 1.13X.

Not all benchmarks are sensitive to branch divergence. Table 1 shows that the benchmarks benefiting from DWS frequently encounter conditional branches and the branch outcomes exhibit a significant fraction of divergence. Besides the occurrence of divergent branches, the benefit of DWS is also affected by other run-time dynamics. In the case of KMeans and Merge, memory divergence occurs frequently and there are usually ample instructions for latency hiding between cache misses. Therefore, they benefit significantly from having more warp-splits to hide latency.

5. DYNAMIC WARP SUBDIVISION UPON MEMORY DIVERGENCE

In conventional SIMD implementations, memory divergence stalls an entire warp. We propose to dynamically subdivide warps upon memory divergence so threads that hit can continue execution to hide latency for the threads that missed. This also offers the possibility for run-ahead threads to bring in cache lines that the fall-behind threads will also need. Warp-splits can be subdivided recursively upon future memory divergence.

5.1 Improve Performance upon Memory Divergence

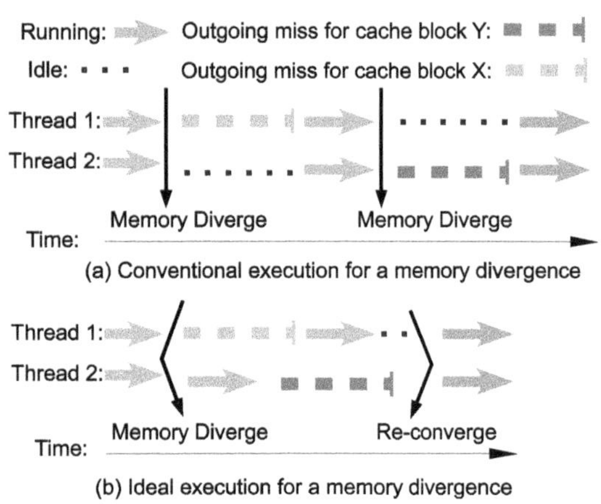

Figure 8: Dynamic warp subdivision upon memory divergence can reduce pipeline stalls and improve MLP. For illustration purposes, the SIMD width is shown as two but similar scenarios exist for wider SIMD organizations as well.

Figures 8 and 9 compare conventional SIMD execution with dynamic warp subdivision upon memory divergence.

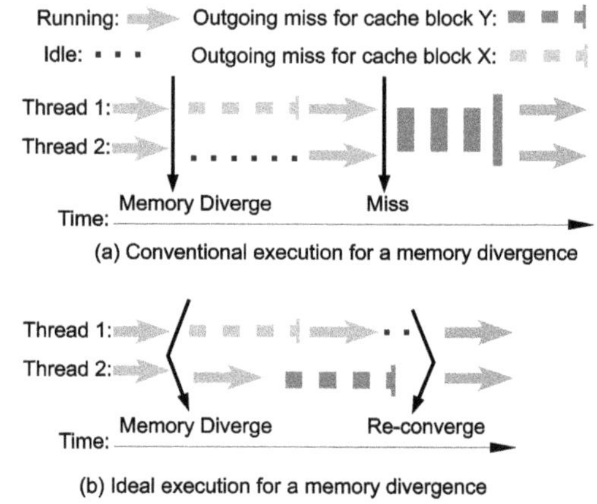

Figure 9: Dynamic warp subdivision upon memory divergence allows run-ahead threads to prefetch cache blocks for the fall-behind.

Consider a warp with two memory instructions (not necessarily consecutive). Assuming all other warps have been suspended already, DWS can reduce pipeline stalls and leverage MLP in two scenarios:

- Threads that miss upon the former instruction hit the cache with the latter instruction, while threads that hit first later miss the cache. In this case, DWS allows run-ahead threads to initiate their misses earlier (Figure 8).
- Some threads hit and some miss on the first instruction, but all threads miss on the same cache block with the latter instruction. In this case, the run-ahead warp-splits in DWS not only initiate their misses earlier; they also prefetch data for the fall-behind warp-split (Figure 9). In contrast to speculative precomputation [6] or run-ahead simultaneous threads [23], the run-ahead warp-split always performs *useful* computation and threads' states are saved right away, requiring no ROB or dependency analysis that would otherwise complicate the design of the simple, in-order WPU.

The above scenario is applicable to both array and vector organizations if they support gather loads or scatter stores. Using the same principle as DWS in array organizations, a WPU can use a set of bit masks to mark out vector components that hit the cache so that they can continue their execution and issue more memory requests. The PC upon which the memory divergence occurs can be stored in a table so that those vector components that miss can resume later at the recorded PC afterwards.

However, DWS may not improve performance if the same subset of threads keep missing the cache and requesting disparate addresses. If other SIMD groups are not able to hide sufficient memory latency, the computation *and* the memory latency incurred by those fall-behind threads become the critical path of the execution. As a result, the overall execution time would stay the same even if DWS allows other threads to run ahead.

Similar to branch divergence, unconstrained warp subdivision may lead to over-subdivision. Therefore, we investigate several methods in Section 5.2 to selectively subdivide warps upon memory divergence. On the other hand, to reduce unrelenting subdivision, we exploit different mechanisms in Section 5.3.1 to re-converge warp-splits. Finally, it is important to handle branch divergence correctly even with the introduction of warp subdivision upon memory divergence. This is ensured by re-convergence techniques described in Section 5.3.1.

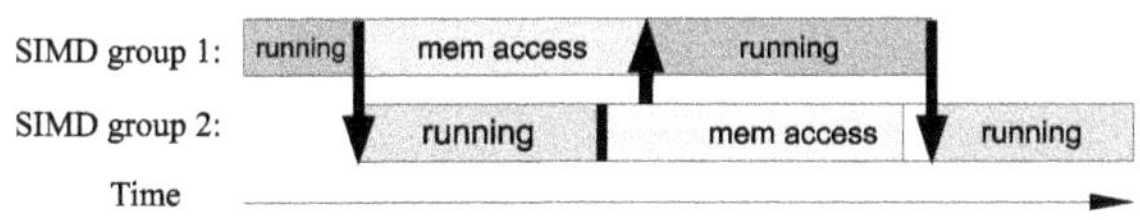

(a) Example case for conventional SIMT execution

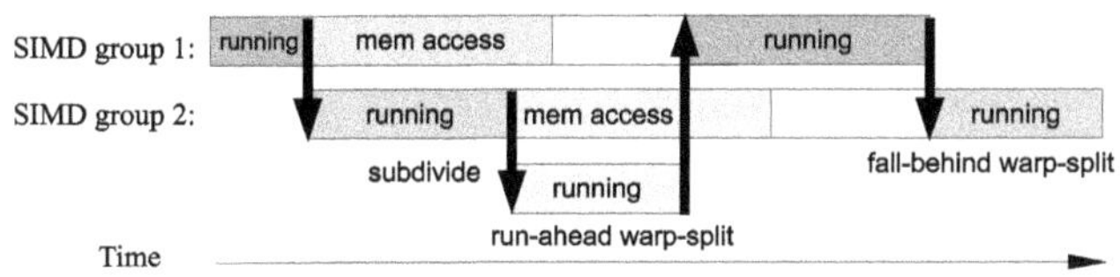

(b) Subdivision upon misses may lead to performance degradation

Figure 10: Performance may degrade if the run-ahead warp-split does not generate long latency memory requests before any outgoing request completes. Such case may take place with LazySplit and ReviveSplit. We demonstrate the case with two warps with arrows pointing to the warp-split that the WPU executes.

5.2 Preventing Over-subdivision

Warp subdivision is not likely to provide benefits when there are already sufficient active warps to hide latency. Aggressively subdividing warps upon every memory divergence regardless of the existence of other active SIMD groups may unnecessarily generate many narrow warp-splits which under-utilize SIMD resources. This brute force subdivision scheme is referred to in the rest of the paper as *AggressSplit*.

To lower the chance of unnecessary warp subdivision, the WPU can create more warp-splits only when there are no other SIMD groups to hide latency. Upon memory divergence, the WPU checks whether all other SIMD groups are waiting for memory. If so, the WPU subdivides the current active warp or warp-split to allow threads that hit to run ahead. This subdivision scheme is referred to as *LazySplit*.

However, LazySplit risks the inability to effectively subdivide warps. If the last active SIMD group has all its threads miss the cache, LazySplit has to stall the WPU's pipeline even though there may be other SIMD groups that have previously incurred memory divergence but were not subdivided and are waiting for memory. We therefore extend LazySplit by allowing it to look for those suspended SIMD groups that are eligible for subdivision when the pipeline is stalled. To avoid over-subdivision, only one SIMD group is subdivided at a time. We name this subdivision scheme *ReviveSplit*.

While ReviveSplit can leverage all SIMD groups that can be subdivided upon memory divergence, its performance may still be suboptimal. Since ReviveSplit attempts to subdivide warps whenever the pipeline is stalled, performance may degrade if the resulting run-ahead warp-split is not able to issue subsequent long latency memory requests in time (*i.e.*, before a suspended SIMD group is resumed by a completed request), as illustrated in Figure 10. In this case, the run-ahead warp-split may occupy the pipeline, keeping those resumed warp-splits from making progress while exploiting no more MLP. Afterwards, the same instruction stream will be executed again by the fall-behind warp-split, increasing the number of executed cycles. However, to make an optimal decision to subdivide warps, foreknowledge or speculation is required to estimate how soon a run-ahead warp-split will encounter another cache miss and how soon outgoing requests will complete and resume awaiting SIMD groups. Compiler analysis, dynamic optimization, or prediction hardware may be able to provide such information, and this is an interesting area for future work.

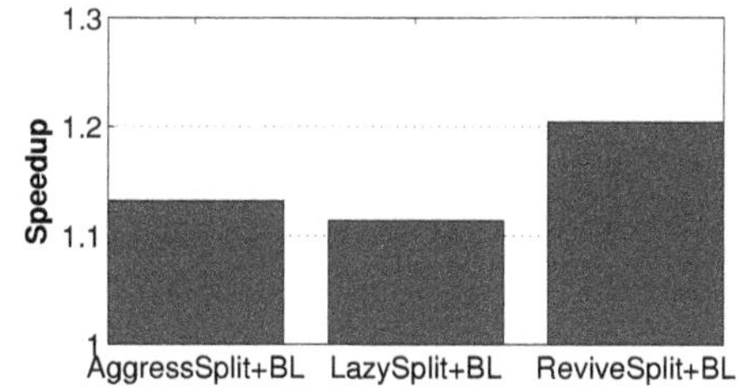

Figure 11: Harmonic means of speedups across all benchmarks. Dynamic warp subdivision upon memory divergence alone has limited benefits due to frequent branches. The BranchLimited re-convergence (specified by *BL*) results in little performance gains for all subdivision schemes, including AggressSplit, LazySplit, and ReviveSplit.

5.3 To Re-converge or To Run Ahead

If warp-splits are not re-converged, they will individually execute the same instruction sequence that could otherwise be run together in a wider warp. If such overhead outweighs the benefits of latency hiding and MLP brought by warp-slits, warp subdivision may penalize performance. On the other hand, if re-convergence is enforced too early, the run-ahead warp-split is likely to stall waiting for the fall-behind warp-split before it can beneficially issue another memory request to overlap outgoing requests. Nevertheless, PC-based re-convergence introduced in Section 4.5 allows multiple warp-splits to run together as a wider SIMD group without the cost of stalling any warp-split. Therefore it is always used in DWS upon memory divergence. However, since PC-based re-convergence does not force a run-ahead warp-split to wait for the fall-behind, it alone may still lead to unrelenting subdivision.

Similar to the process of subdivision, determining the optimal timing to enforce re-converge requires foreknowledge about whether future cache misses can occur in time to overlap with outgoing requests. In this paper, we exploit several heuristics to effectively address re-convergence; some natural places to force warp-splits to re-converge are branches and post-dominators, as discussed below.

5.3.1 *Branch Handling after Memory Divergence*

Branches may interfere with the re-convergence process of warp-splits that divided upon memory divergence. Upon branches or post-dominators, the re-convergence stack acts implicitly as a barrier for the subdivided warp-splits to re-converge; when warp-splits are synchronized and re-converged, the re-convergence stack can be pushed or popped in a conventional manner. Afterwards, the warp can be subdivided again upon future memory divergence. In other words, only those threads masked on the TOS are subdivided into warp-splits. Since this re-convergence scheme limits a warp-split's lifespan between branches and post-dominators, we name it *BranchLimited re-convergence*.

Although BranchLimited re-convergence allows DWS upon memory divergence while preserving the structure of the re-convergence stack, characterizations show it is likely to limit the benefit in latency hiding and MLP. As shown in Table 1, most benchmarks experience frequent branch instructions with only tens of instructions in between. Given such small basic blocks, a run-ahead warp-split is likely to reach the end of the basic block immediately and stall waiting for the fall-behind warp-split before beneficially issuing further memory requests. As a result, the performance gains from BranchLimited re-convergence are limited, as shown in Figure 11.

5.3.2 *Run Ahead Beyond Branches and Loops*

If run-ahead warp-splits can proceed beyond branches, they would have a better chance of issuing and overlapping further memory requests with the stall experienced by the fall-behind threads. Fortunately, we have already discussed in Section 4.2 how to use DWS to relax the re-convergence stack for branch divergence. Upon a future divergent branch, the run-ahead warp-split is subdivided into two warp-splits. As a result, the status of the re-convergence stack remains intact while more entries are added to the warp-split table. These warp-splits re-converge when their PCs met. Otherwise, they are forced to wait for others to re-converge once they hit the post-dominator denoted by the re-convergence stack's TOS. We name this re-convergence scheme *BranchBypass*. Note that with BranchBypass, warps can be subdivided upon both memory divergence *and* branch divergence.

By allowing run-ahead warp-splits to proceed beyond branches, it may appear harder for the fall-behind warp-split to catch up with the run-ahead. However, it is important to note that the ability to bypass branches naturally entitles the run-ahead warp-split to bypass loop boundaries into the next iteration. In such cases, the fall-behind warp-split may not have to execute the same number of instructions as the run-ahead to get re-united with it, especially if the loop body is short (*i.e.*, contains only a few instructions). In such a scenario, the run-ahead warp-split may frequently revisit the PC at which the fall-behind warp-split stopped. Once this PC is revisited and the run-ahead warp-split finds the fall-behind split is ready to execute, it re-unites with the fall-behind split immediately, despite potentially being a few iterations ahead of the fall-behind. In contrast to adaptive slip [30], which exploits this same opportunity, DWS warp-splits do not rely on short loops to re-converge: the fall-behind warp-split always resumes itself upon completion of data requests so that it can catch up with the run-ahead split in the case of a large loop body.

5.4 Implementation

Dynamic warp subdivision upon memory divergence is handled *in the same way* as DWS for branch divergence, except that the branch outcome that is used to divide threads is replaced by a *hit mask* that marks threads that hit the cache. Figure 12 illustrates the process. After memory divergence, two warp-splits are created: one with threads that hit and are ready to execute; another with threads that miss and are waiting for memory. Note that after subdivision, the entry of the obsolete parent warp-split is overwritten by one of the resulting child warp-splits so that *the WST only records existing warp-splits*. Moreover, creating a new scheduling entity does not require any other new state. Warp-splits still share the same register file resources, etc. Once the two warp-splits re-unite, their WST entries are merged into one by taking an "or" operation on their active masks. The hardware overhead is discussed in more detail in Section 5.6. There is no need to differentiate warp-splits resulting from memory divergence with those resulting from branch divergence. *Any* warp-split can be further subdivided upon either branch or memory divergence.

Divergence does not break synchronization or communication semantics if programming models do not implicitly *guarantee* threads in a warp to operate in lockstep. Otherwise, DWS is not compatible because it allows warp-splits to proceed asynchronously for variable periods of time. With DWS, inter-thread synchronization or communication is only guaranteed through the use of explicit synchronization primitives, upon which warp-splits simply re-converge. Of course, frequent synchronization will limit intra-warp latency tolerance.

Compared to the baseline architecture, warp-splits merely change the ordering of execution for threads within the same warp. This does not affect memory exceptions. It only affects consistency for threads within the same warp. However, most SIMD programming models do not impose such sequential consistency. Finally, precise traps can still be handled for each individual warp-split.

5.5 Results

In Figure 13, we compare variations of dynamic warp subdivision and characterize the benefits of individual optimizations. DWS upon branch divergence (*DWS.BranchOnly*) alone reaches a speedup of 1.13X. DWS upon memory divergence alone using ReviveSplit (*DWS.ReviveSplit.MemOnly*) achieves a speedup of 1.20X. While DWS for branch and memory divergence are complementary and can be integrated, the overall benefit of DWS is sensitive to the combination of specific subdivision and re-convergence schemes. For example, *DWS.AggressSplit* and *DWS.LazySplit* combine BranchBypass with AggressSplit and LazySplit respectively, and they both lead to performance degradation. Nevertheless, the combination of the best subdivision scheme (ReviveSplit) and re-convergence scheme (BranchBypass) does not harm performance in any case and it achieves an overall speedup of 1.71X (*DWS.ReviveSplit*). On average, *DWS.ReviveSplit* reduces the percentage of time in which WPUs stall waiting for memory from 76% to 36%; in the mean time, the average SIMD width per instruction drops from 14 to 4.

Different benchmarks exhibit different responses to dynamic warp subdivision. Merge benefits mainly from DWS upon branch divergence. KMeans, HotSpot, LU, and Filter benefit mainly from DWS upon memory divergence. FFT and SVM, on the other hand, have many cache misses but a large portion of these misses are not divergent, therefore warp subdivision occurs less often compared to other benchmarks. It is also observed that memory divergence may not be uniformly distributed across SIMD threads due to runtime dynamics. In fact, the pattern varies across benchmarks or even phases of execution. It is therefore difficult to statically pinpoint threads or lanes for warp subdivision.

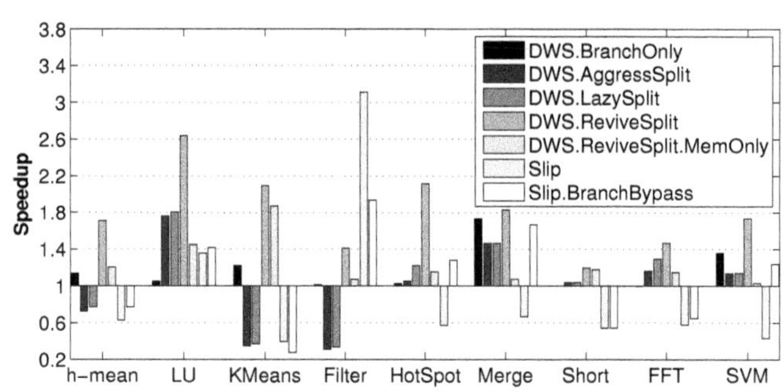

Figure 13: Comparing various DWS schemes. Speedups are normalized to that of equivalent baseline WPUs without DWS. Modest speedups are achieved when DWS applies to branch divergence alone (*DWS.BranchOnly*) or memory divergence alone (*DWS.ReviveSplit.MemOnly*). However, the combination of the two achieves a speedup of 1.71X (*DWS.ReviveSplit*). Slip only outperforms DWS in Filter and it is often subject to performance degradation, even after being modified to bypass branches (*Slip.BranchBypass*). The harmonic mean of the speedups for all benchmarks is shown as `h-mean`.

5.6 Hardware Overhead

Because DWS does not increase the demand for tags and TLB ports, the hardware cost only lies in the WST and the scheduler. For a given WPU, the maximum number of warp-splits may become as large as the number of threads if each warp-split consists of a single thread. With a large number

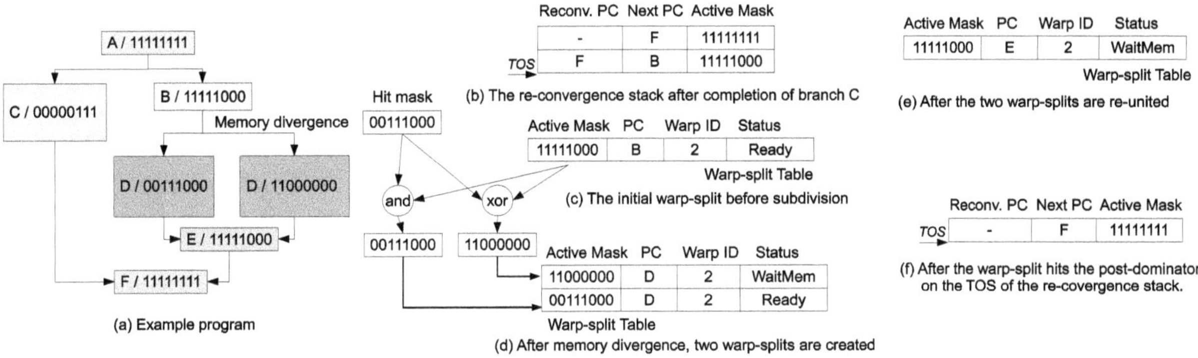

Figure 12: An example of dynamic warp subdivision upon memory divergence. While divergent branches can still be handled using the re-convergence stack (b, f), the warp-split table can be used to create warp-splits using the *hit mask* that marks threads that hit the cache (c-e).

of threads per WPU, this may drastically increase the complexity of the hardware scheduler (*e.g.*, a priority encoder) in order to identify the next ready SIMD group in one cycle. We therefore model a scheduler that only doubles the number of entries in a conventional setting. This approximately doubles the cost of any scheduling structure, but can accommodate more scheduling entities resulting from DWS. In case there are more warp-splits than scheduling slots, the extra warp-splits sit idle until a scheduling slot is available. We also limit the number of WST entries to 16 to reduce its storage cost; warps are not able to be subdivided when the WST is already full. Sensitivity study shows that the above limitations only cost less than 1% of the overall performance.

To estimate area overhead, we measure the realistic sizes for the different units of a core according to a publicly available die photo of the AMD Opteron processor in 130nm technology. We scale the functional unit areas to 65nm, assuming a 0.7 scaling factor per generation. We assume each SIMD lane has a 32 bit data path (adjacent lanes are combined if 64 bit results are needed). We also measure the cache area per 1 KB of capacity and scale that according to the cache capacity. If the WPU has four warps with a SIMD width of 16, each entry needs 16 bits for the active mask, 2 bits for the warp ID, 64 bits for the PC, and 2 bits for the warp status. The resulting size for each WST entry is then 84 bits or 11B. With up to 16 WST entries, the WST state consumes less than 1% of the storage area in a WPU, assuming the WPU has a 32 KB D-cache and a 16 KB I-cache.

5.7 Comparison with Adaptive Slip

Tarjan *et al.* [30] proposed *adaptive slip*, which allows a subset of threads to continue while other threads in the same warp are waiting for memory. Those threads that wait for memory stay suspended until the run-ahead threads in that warp revisit the same memory instruction again, presuming memory divergence mainly occurs within iterative short loops. Their approach presumes aggressive predication so that run-ahead threads can always "slip" into the next iteration regardless of branch divergence.

We compare the performance of DWS to that of adaptive slip without aggressive branch predication, which we refer to in Figure 13 as *Slip*. To adaptively find out the maximum allowed thread divergence for adaptive slip, an interval of 100,000 cycles is used for dynamic profiling. The maximum allowed thread divergence is incremented if the WPU spends more than 70% of the time waiting for memory, and it is decremented if the pipeline actively executes for more than 50% of the time. These thresholds are obtained by experimenting with various combinations and selecting the combination that yields the best performance.

While adaptive slip leads to significant speedup for Filter, it results in performance degradation for many other benchmarks. The reasons are three-fold:

- Without aggressive predication, the run-ahead threads have to stall waiting for the fall-behind upon a conditional branch. This is because the re-convergence stack needs to generate the branch outcome for all threads masked by the TOS. As a result, adaptive slip is hardly effective when the main computation involves frequent conditional branches inside loops. Such is the case with HotSpot, Merge and Short.
- A diverged warp may not be re-united in time. This can be caused by long loops (*i.e.*, loops with a large section of code in each iteration) where slipping into the next iteration may take a long time (*e.g.*, FFT). The same situation may also occur in the case of nested loops where memory divergence takes place inside the outer loop but outside of the inner loop; the fall-behind threads cannot be resumed until the run-ahead threads jump out of the inner loop (*e.g.*, KMeans).
- The appropriate thresholds to increase or decrease the maximum allowed thread divergence vary across benchmarks and hardware configurations. The same thresholds may work well for Filter while penalizing the performances of SVM.

We also attempt to combine adaptive slip with DWS upon branch divergence so that run-ahead threads can continue beyond branches to "slip" into subsequent iterations. This scheme is referred to in Figure 13 as *Slip.BranchBypass*. While this scheme significantly improves performance for many benchmarks, it does not address all the issues with adaptive slip and still harms performance for KMeans, Short, and FFT. Moreover, if memory divergence occurs within a branch path that is rarely visited and the run-ahead threads proceed to the next iteration, it may take a long time before the run-ahead can branch into the same path and re-converge with the fall-behind threads. In this case, this scheme can even perform worse than adaptive slip, as can be observed from KMeans.

6. SENSITIVITY ANALYSIS

The benefit of dynamic warp subdivision in latency hiding and memory level parallelism depends on various factors: the frequency of branch and memory divergence, the length of memory latencies, and the WPU's ability to hide latency with existing warps. We study its sensitivity to various architectural factors. We show that DWS can bring performance gains in a wide range of configurations. In this section, we use the configuration *DWS.ReviveSplit* to represent the performance of DWS which can subdivide warps upon both branch and memory divergence. We refer to the conventional architecture without DWS as *Conv*. Further sensitivity analysis results appear in an extended, technical report version of this paper [18].

6.1 Cache Misses and Memory divergence

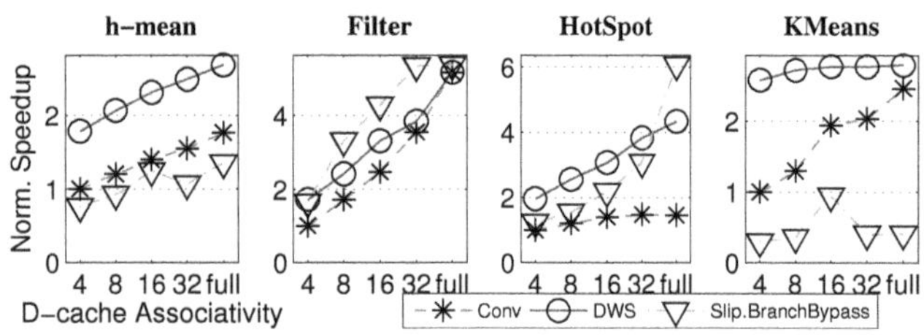

Figure 14: Speedup vs. D-cache associativity. DWS refers to *DWS.ReviveSplit* in Figure 13. Systems are configured according to Table 3. Performance is normalized to each benchmark's execution time under *Conv*. The harmonic mean for the normalized speedup of all benchmarks is shown as `h-mean`. Several individual applications with diverse behavior are also shown.

With larger D-cache associativity, both cache miss rate and memory divergence tend to decrease, and hence there is less latency to hide and less memory level parallelism to exploit. As a result, DWS may occur less often and its benefit may decrease. Figure 14 demonstrates this trend when the D-cache associativity is varied from four to fully-associative.

It can also be observed from Figure 14 that the benefit from DWS does not always increase with smaller D-cache associativity. Because small D-cache associativity leads to more cache misses, threads in a SIMD group are more likely to miss the cache simultaneously, and therefore the the occurrence of divergent memory accesses may decrease. As a result, DWS upon memory divergence is less likely to take effect — in benchmarks such HotSpot, performance of DWS drops more than that of the conventional architecture when the D-cache associativity decreases to four.

6.2 Miss Latency

The amount of latency to hide also affects the effectiveness of DWS. The D-cache miss latency is largely dependent on the memory hierarchy. While most of the evaluation in this paper is based upon a shared L2 cache as the last-level cache, there are various alternatives. Some architectures use private L2 caches while others do not have L2 caches at all and L1 misses are sent directly to the main memory [8]. The L1 miss latency can therefore vary from a few cycles to hundreds of cycles.

We study the sensitivity of the L1 miss latency by varying the L2 lookup latency from 10 cycles to 300 cycles. Results in Figure 15 shows that while DWS also suffers from longer miss latency, its speedup compared to the equivalent conventional architecture *increases*. This is not surprising because more SIMD groups are needed to hide longer latency; DWS achieves this by generating more warp-splits on demand.

7. RELATED WORK

Fung *et al.* [10] addressed the under-utilization of the SIMD resources due to branch divergence. They proposed dynamic warp formation (DWF) in which diverged threads that happen to arrive at the same PC, *even though they belong to different warps*, can be grouped and run together as a wider SIMD group. However, if a subset of threads in a warp miss the cache and stall, there is still no way to allow the threads that hit to continue: this behavior is not compatible with the active mask on top of the re-convergence stack. As Table 1 has shown, divergent memory accesses can be more common than divergent branches in some applications. Furthermore, dynamic warp formation only occurs when multiple warps arrive at the same PC; if such condition is not met, the conventional re-convergence stack still prevents threads in the same warp from hiding each other's latency upon branch divergence. Our approach instead creates separate scheduling entities so that each warp-split can execute independently. This means that even after a divergent branch, threads on both paths are able to make progress and hide each others' latency. By creating new scheduling entities after each branch or miss divergence, our approach fully integrates branch and miss handling.

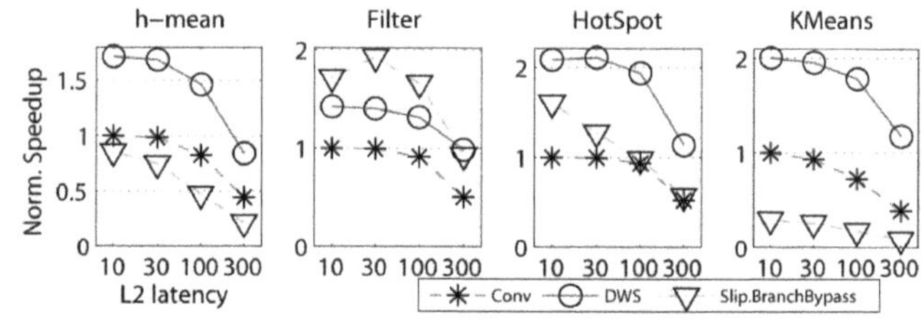

Figure 15: Speedup vs. L2 lookup latency. DWS refers to *DWS.ReviveSplit* in Figure 13. The speedup of DWS compared to *Conv* increases with longer L2 latency. Systems are configured according to Table 3. Performance is normalized to each benchmark's execution time under *Conv* with an L2 lookup latency of 10 cycles. The harmonic mean for the normalized speedup of all benchmarks is shown as `h-mean`.

Similar to dynamic warp formation, stream processors such as Imagine can split streams conditionally according to branch outcomes [12], and each resulting stream follows the same control flow. Although conditional streams reduce unnecessarily predicated computation and communication, they do not address latency hiding. In fact, latency hiding is not necessary for stream processors; data is always available through the stream register file. For this reason, memory divergence never occurs as well.

Our technique is complementary to Vector Lane Threading (VLT) [24] and the Vector-Thread (VT) Architecture [14]. VLT assigns groups of lanes to different user-level threads; lanes belonging to the same user-level thread execute in SIMD, but they do not need to execute in lockstep with lanes in other groups. However, lanes belonging to the same SIMD group may still stall unnecessarily due to branch and memory divergence. VT is a MIMD implementation of vector semantics, where each lane has the autonomy and overhead of its own fetch/decode/scoreboard logic. It is therefore not a strict SIMD organization and not subject to the divergence phenomena addressed in this paper. Nevertheless, the principles of DWS may also apply to VT when it executes data-parallel applications.

Adaptive slip [30] addresses memory divergence to improve latency hiding for SIMD organizations. It employs a mechanism that is similar to a re-convergence stack, by simply using the cache access outcome instead of branch outcome so that threads that hit can continue. Similar to using the re-convergence stack, threads exhibiting divergent behavior cannot interleave their execution to hide latency, which limits benefits. It also assumes aggressive branch predication to avoid forced re-convergence at conditional branches within a loop body. Section 5.7 compares adaptive slip with DWS in more detail.

Existing techniques that address long latency memory accesses in the context of simultaneous multi-threading (SMT) do not help in the case of SIMD because SMT threads share a single datapath. With SMT, the problem is resource contention and reduced instruction level parallelism (ILP), since a stalled thread occupies expensive issue queues, rename-registers, and reorder-buffer entries, which limits ILP discovery for the other thread. Techniques for SMT resource distribution [5, 31] do not apply to in-order SIMD organizations, since SIMD threads operating on different lanes do not compete for pipeline resources. Instead, the main problem raised by long latency memory accesses is the risk of stall cycles due to inadequate latency hiding. Pre-computation using speculative threads [6] or runahead threads [23] improves MLP. However, these speculative approaches require run-time dependency analysis among instructions as well as the ability for out-of-order execution and commit. These requirements are usually not met with simple, in-order SIMD hardware. We provide a solution designed specifically for SIMD hardware that allows it to exploit more MLP without speculative execution.

We have not considered the effect of prefetching or non-blocking loads. Nevertheless, DWS is complementary to both. It helps even in cases where the access pattern is not easily prefetched. Moreover, prefetching may increase contention for cache and bandwidth, especially when contention among many threads is severe. On the other hand, non-blocking loads employed by Tesla [8] and Fermi [1] are still in-order issue so they improve MLP but provide minimal latency hiding benefit. In both cases, memory divergence still occurs if threads in a warp are not all runnable at the same time.

Dynamic warp subdivision is also complementary to MLP-aware cache replacement [22]. While DWS creates additional scheduling entities to hide latency and issue more over-lapping requests, MLP-aware cache replacement smartly prioritizes these outgoing requests to reduce their aggregate latency.

8. CONCLUSIONS & FUTURE WORK

This paper proposes dynamic warp subdivision to create warp-splits in the case that the SIMD processor does not have sufficient warps to hide latency and leverage MLP. Warp-splits are simply extra schedulable entities that do not require extra register file state. They can be generated upon branch divergence or memory divergence. The conventional re-convergence stack is amended with a warp-split table to relax the serialization of different branch paths and it allows threads in the same warp to interleave their execution in an asynchronous manner.

We evaluate the technique using a general purpose multicore processor with four 16-wide WPUs, each with four warps operating over a coherent cache hierarchy. Using a two level cache hierarchy, DWS generates an average speedup of 1.7X. We further study the sensitivity of DWS to various architectural parameters and demonstrate that the performance of DWS is robust and it does not degrade performance on any of the benchmarks tested.

One opportunity for future work is to integrate DWS with dynamic warp formation [10]. It may further improve performance by speculating cache miss frequency and miss latencies in order to better decide when to subdivide warps. Finally, it would be interesting to study applications quantitatively to identify those that would benefit from particular SIMD architectures according to their degree of divergence.

9. ACKNOWLEDGEMENTS

This work was supported in part by SRC grant no. 1607, NSF grant nos. IIS-0612049 and CNS-0615277, a grant from Intel Research, a professor partnership award from NVIDIA Research, and an NVIDIA Ph.D. fellowship (Meng). We would like to thank Michael Boyer, Mario D. Marino, and Gregory Faust for their suggestions. We would also like to thank the anonymous reviewers for their helpful comments.

10. REFERENCES

[1] NVIDIA's next generation CUDA compute architecture: Fermi. *NVIDIA Corporation*, 2009.
[2] ATI. Radeon 9700 Pro. http://mirror.ati.com/products/pc/radeon9700pro, 2002.
[3] N. L. Binkert, R. G. Dreslinski, L. R. Hsu, K. T. Lim, A. G. Saidi, and S. K. Reinhardt. The M5 simulator: Modeling networked systems. *IEEE Micro*, 26(4), 2006.
[4] S. Che, M. Boyer, J. Meng, D. Tarjan, J. W. Sheaffer, and K. Skadron. A performance study of general purpose applications on graphics processors using CUDA. *JPDC*, 2008.
[5] S. Choi and D. Yeung. Learning-based SMT processor resource distribution via hill-climbing. In *ISCA*, 2006.
[6] J. D. Collins, D. M. Tullsen, H. Wang, and J. P. Shen. Dynamic speculative precomputation. In *MICRO 34*, 2001.
[7] Intel Corporation. Intel AVX: New frontiers in performance improvements and energy efficiency, 2009.
[8] NVIDIA Corporation. GeForce GTX 280 specifications. 2008.
[9] R. Espasa, F. Ardanaz, J. Emer, S. Felix, J. Gago, R. Gramunt, I. Hern, T. Juan, G. Lowney, M Mattina, and A. Seznec. Tarantula: A vector extension to the Alpha architecture. In *ISCA*, 2002.
[10] W. W. L. Fung, I. Sham, G. Yuan, and T. M. Aamodt. Dynamic warp formation and scheduling for efficient GPU control flow. In *MICRO*, 2007.
[11] M. Gschwind. Chip multiprocessing and the Cell Broadband Engine. In *CF*, 2006.
[12] U. J. Kapasi, J. Dally, W, S. Rixner, P. R. Mattson, J. D. Owens, and B. Khailany. Efficient conditional operations for data-parallel architectures. In *MICRO 33*, 2000.
[13] C. Kozyrakis. A media-enhanced vector architecture for embedded memory systems. Technical report, University of California, Berkeley, 1999.
[14] R. Krashinsky, C. Batten, M. Hampton, S. Gerding, B. Pharris, J. Casper, and K. Asanovic. The Vector-Thread architecture. In *ISCA*, 2004.
[15] R. A. Lorie and H. R. Strong. Method for conditional branch execution in SIMD vector processors. *US Patent 4,435,758*, 1984.
[16] J. Meng, J. W. Sheaffer, and K. Skadron. Exploiting inter-thread temporal locality for chip multithreading. In *IPDPS*, 2010.
[17] J. Meng and K. Skadron. Avoiding cache thrashing due to private data placement in last-level cache for manycore scaling. In *ICCD*, 2007.
[18] J. Meng, D. Tarjan, and K. Skadron. Dynamic warp subdivision for integrated branch and memory divergence tolerance: Extended results. *U.Va. Tech. Report CS-2010-5*, 2010.
[19] R. Narayanan, B. Ozisikyilmaz, J. Zambreno, G. Memik, and A. Choudhary. Minebench: A benchmark suite for data mining workloads. *IISWC*, 2006.
[20] Y. Nishikawa, M. Koibuchi, M. Yoshimi, K. Miura, and H. Amano. Performance improvement methodology for ClearSpeed's CSX600. In *ICPP*, 2007.
[21] S. E. Orcutt. Implementation of permutation functions in illiac iv-type computers. *IEEE Trans. Comput.*, 25(9), 1976.
[22] M. K. Qureshi, D. N. Lynch, O. Mutlu, and Y. N. Patt. A case for MLP-aware cache replacement. In *ISCA*, 2006.
[23] T. Ramirez, A. Pajuelo, O.J. Santana, and M. Valero. Runahead threads to improve SMT performance. *HPCA*, 2008.
[24] S. Rivoire, R. Schultz, T. Okuda, and C. Kozyrakis. Vector lane threading. In *ICPP*, 2006.
[25] S. Rixner, W. J. Dally, U. J. Kapasi, B. Khailany, A. López-Lagunas, P. R. Mattson, and J. D. Owens. A bandwidth-efficient architecture for media processing. In *MICRO 31*, 1998.
[26] R. M. Russell. The CRAY-1 computer system. *Commun. ACM*, 21(1), 1978.
[27] L. Seiler, D. Carmean, E. Sprangle, T. Forsyth, M. Abrash, P. Dubey, S. Junkins, A. Lake, J. Sugerman, R. Cavin, R. Espasa, E. Grochowski, T. Juan, and P. Hanrahan. Larrabee: a many-core x86 architecture for visual computing. *ACM Trans. Graph.*, 27(3), 2008.
[28] Y. Takahashi. A mechanism for SIMD execution of SPMD programs. In *HPC-ASIA*, 1997.
[29] D. Talla and L. K. John. Cost-effective hardware acceleration of multimedia applications. In *ICCD*, 2001.
[30] D. Tarjan, J. Meng, and K. Skadron. Increasing memory miss tolerance for SIMD cores. In *SC*, 2009.
[31] D. M. Tullsen and J. A. Brown. Handling long-latency loads in a simultaneous multithreading processor. In *MICRO 34*, 2001.
[32] S. C. Woo, M. Ohara, E. Torrie, J. P. Singh, and A. Gupta. The SPLASH-2 programs: Characterization and methodological considerations. *ISCA*, 1995.

A Dynamically Configurable Coprocessor for Convolutional Neural Networks

Srimat Chakradhar, Murugan Sankaradas, Venkata Jakkula and Srihari Cadambi
NEC Laboratories America, Inc.
4 Independence Way, Princeton NJ 08540.
{chak, murugs, jakkula, cadambi}@nec-labs.com

ABSTRACT

Convolutional neural networks (CNN) applications range from recognition and reasoning (such as handwriting recognition, facial expression recognition and video surveillance) to intelligent text applications such as semantic text analysis and natural language processing applications. Two key observations drive the design of a new architecture for CNN. First, CNN workloads exhibit a *widely varying mix of three types of parallelism*: parallelism within a convolution operation, intra-output parallelism where multiple input sources (features) are combined to create a single output, and inter-output parallelism where multiple, independent outputs (features) are computed simultaneously. Workloads differ significantly across different CNN applications, and across different layers of a CNN. Second, the number of processing elements in an architecture continues to scale (as per Moore's law) much faster than off-chip memory bandwidth (or pin-count) of chips. Based on these two observations, we show that for a given number of processing elements and off-chip memory bandwidth, a new CNN hardware architecture that dynamically configures the hardware on-the-fly to match the specific mix of parallelism in a given workload gives the best throughput performance. Our CNN compiler automatically translates high abstraction network specification into a parallel microprogram (a sequence of low-level VLIW instructions) that is mapped, scheduled and executed by the coprocessor. Compared to a 2.3 GHz quad-core, dual socket Intel Xeon, 1.35 GHz C870 GPU, and a 200 MHz FPGA implementation, our 120 MHz dynamically configurable architecture is 4x to 8x faster. This is the *first CNN architecture to achieve real-time video stream processing* (25 to 30 frames per second) on a wide range of object detection and recognition tasks.

Categories and Subject Descriptors

C.1.3 [Other Architecture Styles]: Adaptable architectures, Neural nets, pipeline processors.

General Terms

Design, Experimentation, Performance.

Keywords

Convolutional Neural Networks, Dynamic Reconfiguration, Parallel Computer Architecture.

1. INTRODUCTION

Feed-forward multilayer neural networks [12] are computational models that are widely used in diverse domains such as video and image processing [22], medical diagnosis systems [14] and financial forecasting [15]. These computation models serve one of two roles: pattern recognition to provide a meaningful categorization of input patterns, or functional approximation where the models find a smooth function that approximates the actual mapping between input and output patterns. A vast majority of these computational models are still implemented in software on general-purpose and embedded processors. However, these processors do not fully exploit the parallelism inherent in these computational models. Numerous custom hardware implementations have also been proposed to parlay the abundant parallelism inherent in these computational models into significantly higher performance [21].

Traditional pattern recognition systems use two distinct steps to recognize individual patterns. First, a feature extractor transforms the input patterns into short strings of symbols (low-dimensional vectors) that can be easily matched or compared. These features are relatively invariant with respect to transformations and distortions that do not change the inherent nature of the patterns. The feature extractor is usually rather specific to the task. It is also the focus of most design effort, because it is entirely hand-crafted. Second, a classifier categorizes the feature vectors into a few classes. The classifier is usually general-purpose, and a standard, fully-connected multi-layer neural network can be automatically trained to do the classification. However, recognition accuracy is largely determined by the ability of the designer to extract an appropriate set of features. Feed-forward, multi-layer artificial neural networks like the Convolutional Neural Networks (CNN) [2][11][13][16][17][20][23] have found increasing use in several new applications because they have the potential to process vast amounts of labeled data to *automatically* learn and extract complex features. CNNs are especially attractive because they can recognize visual patterns directly from pixel images with very minimal preprocessing of the image. CNNs can easily recognize patterns with extreme variability (such as handwritten characters). Also, their recognition ability is not impaired by distortions or simple geometric transformations (for example, translation or rotation) of the image.

Neural networks have multiple layers of neurons (an input layer, an output layer and one or more hidden layers). Every connection between an input and a neuron is assigned a value called *weight*. Each neuron computes a weighted sum of all its inputs, followed by a non-linear or sigmoid function to restrict its output value within a reasonable range. Neurons in the hidden layers are also called the *hidden* units. As an example, consider one layer of a multi-layer neural network and the task of connecting 1024 inputs to 784 hidden units to produce a set of 784 output values. The 1024 inputs can be the 1024 pixel values in a 32 x 32 image. The 784 hidden units produce 784 output values (also called as a *feature map*) which can be interpreted as pixels in a 28 x 28 output image. A fully-connected neural network connects every input to every hidden unit, resulting in a network that has 1024*784 = 802,816 different weights (free parameters). Learning these weights will require a very large number of training instances. Furthermore, a fully-connected architecture ignores the topology of the input image because input values can be presented in any order without affecting the outcome of the training. On the contrary, images have strong two-dimensional local structure where pixels that are spatially nearby are highly correlated. Therefore, each hidden unit in a CNN is connected to only on a small number of inputs, say 25 inputs. These 25 inputs, also called as the *receptive field* of the hidden unit, correspond to a 5 x 5 pixel area in the input image. Only 25 weights are now necessary to connect the inputs to a hidden unit. Since such an elementary feature detector is likely to be useful across other 5 x 5 pixel areas in the input image, many different hidden units are used to cover the entire image. Receptive fields of these hidden units can overlap, and the degree of overlap can be pre-specified. Hidden units, whose receptive fields are located at different places on the image, can be forced to detect the same elementary feature by reusing the same 25 weights. Hidden units that share the same set of weights form a *plane*, and outputs of units in a plane constitute the feature map. Hidden units in a plane can together extract visual features like edges, corners etc. If we represent the 25 distinct weights as a 5 x 5 matrix (also called as the *kernel* matrix), then outputs of all the 784 hidden units can be computed as the convolution of the 32 x 32 input image with the 5 x 5 kernel matrix [1].

After the convolution step, we have a 28 x 28 image in which a feature of interest has been detected, and the exact location of the feature becomes less important. The value of every hidden unit is also subjected to a squashing function (non-linearity). A simple way to reduce the precision with which the distinctive features are encoded in the image is to reduce the spatial resolution of the image by using sub-sampling. This also reduces the sensitivity of the outputs to shifts or distortions. A typical CNN has multiple layers of hidden units (with multiple feature maps per layer) to perform complex object recognition tasks.

Evaluating a trained CNN involves performing a huge number of convolutions with considerable data movement. Convolution computation is a performance bottleneck, but reducing overheads of data movement is also necessary to accelerate the performance of a CNN. Consider a simple object (face) recognition application that is used on relatively high resolution streaming images. With a 320x240 (QVGA) image, a CNN network that can be used to identify faces within all possible 32x32 windows in the image runs at approximately 6.5 frames per second on a 2.5GHz Intel Xeon processor when optimized using BLAS (Intel MKL v11). Multi-threading this to 4 and 8 cores on quad-core and dual quad-core machines only improves the speed by a little over 2x due to synchronization overheads, and the fact that different threads share common inputs. Therefore, the most optimized software implementation on state-of-the-art processors struggles to achieve about 8 to 10 frames per second when we analyze VGA (640x480 pixels) images. VGA (or larger) images are more realistic in practical use-case scenarios such as security cameras. Can the abundant parallelism in CNN workloads be leveraged by custom architectures to improve the feed-forward processing speeds to be close to real-time (25 to 30 frames per second)? To answer this question, we investigate a dynamically reconfigurable architecture in which the hardware parallelism can be tailored to suit the parallelism offered by the specific application workload.

1.1 Related Work

Implementation of the convolution operation in hardware has been studied extensively. Both FPGA and LSI implementations have been proposed. Digital media processors with a large number of high-speed multiply-and-accumulate (MAC) units have been used to implement the convolution operation [18]. LSI architectures using a mixed analog-digital approach [20] as well as several FPGA-based implementations have also been proposed [3][4][5][6][7][19][24].

Fast implementations of a 2D convolution core are necessary but not sufficient to accelerate the CNN workload. A host processor can carve out the convolution operations from the CNN workload and off-load the convolutions to the hardware implementation. For each off-load, the host processor provides the image and weight values, and retrieves the convolved output image from the accelerator. Some optimizations are possible to store kernel values or some intermediate data on the accelerator. However, for CNNs used in practice, the data dependencies within a layer (sub-sampling and non-linearity operations) and across multiple network layers of the CNN, the management of significant amount of intermediate data over a slow host to hardware accelerator link, and the detailed orchestration of complex control and data flows by the host processor quickly offset performance gains obtained by using a fast hardware core only for 2D convolutions. There are no reported LSI implementations of CNNs but several software implementations on GPUs exist [8][25]. However, none of the prior implementations are able to process video feeds (640 x 480 pixel VGA frame) in *real-time* (about 25 to 30 frames per second).

An FPGA implementation of CNN was reported recently [9]. This architecture uses one hardware convolver for data processing, and a general-purpose soft-processor for control, all implemented on a Virtex 4 FPGA from Xilinx. The self-contained unit was developed for video processing in mobile robot applications. In contrast, we use a very different approach. We employ a configurable bank of hardware convolvers, a hardwired controller (to manage complex data movement patterns), and configurability hardware that dynamically configures HW resources on-the-fly to match the precise type and mix of parallelism in the CNN workload. In [9], no attempt is made to alter the hardware computing paths to match type or extent of parallelism in the workload.

1.2 Our Contribution

While several earlier efforts have implemented convolutions and neural networks in hardware, to our knowledge, this is the first effort to create a co-processor architecture that automatically analyzes workloads and dynamically configures its hardware and software components to match the exact mix of different types of parallelism in the workload. Our most novel contribution is dynamic configurability and a method to quickly match HW (on-the-fly) to workload characteristics. For the first time, we achieve a 'tipping point' (sustained real-time recognition). We enable new, real-time on-line classification applications that were not possible before.

A high abstraction-level software API, along with a run-time software component allows domain-experts to easily specify and execute arbitrary convolutional neural network workloads. Unlike prior work, our co-processor architecture is forward-scalable. As we scale the number of processing elements, and the available off-chip memory bandwidth, CNN applications continue to automatically improve in performance. Domain-experts do not have to re-write the application. Instead, a software run-time component determines the optimal configuration of processing elements (and memory architecture) for each layer of the CNN workload, and the coprocessor architecture is dynamically configured to match the workload characteristics. This allows the throughput and performance of the coprocessor architecture to be very close to the peak throughput of the individual processing elements. Dynamic configurability in hardware is fast (single-cycle instruction), and it is under the control of software. Our coprocessor (with different functional units) can easily implement different feed-forward neural networks and classifiers such as HMAX [17][27], DBN [29][30]and HoG methods [28].

The rest of this document is organized as follows. In Section 2, we provide a background for CNNs. In Section 3, we discuss the parallelism in CNN workloads. In Section 4, we present a motivating example that illustrates the benefits of a dynamically reconfigurable architecture. In Section 5, we describe the coprocessor architecture and Section 6 describes dynamic configurability. We present architectural evaluation results in Section 7, and conclude in Section 8.

2. CNN: A COMPUTE PERSPECTIVE

We briefly review the forward propagation phase of a CNN. In this paper, we do not consider the learning phase of the CNN that determines the kernel values that will be used in each layer. Rather, we assume that a trained CNN is available and focus on forward propagation. Tasks performed by end-users (to classify images, for instance) involve forward propagation on trained CNNs. There are often stringent real-time performance and power constraints and hardware acceleration is necessary to achieve these goals. Forward propagation is also a core computation in the back-propagation based learning algorithm, and our solution can also accelerate the learning phase.

We provide a computational perspective of the forward propagation phase of a CNN. Figure 1 shows one layer of a typical CNN. Several such layers are cascaded to create a feed-forward neural network where each layer (except the last layer) feeds only the next layer and receives inputs only from the immediately preceding layer. Every CNN layer is a cascade of two distinct computations or sub-layers: convolution, and sub-sampling. Hardware implementations must also consider issues of numerical precision and dynamic range of values computed by the network.

2.1 Convolution Sub-layer

A convolution sub-layer accepts n images $Y_1 ... Y_n$ as inputs and produces m intermediate outputs $O_1 ... O_m$. To produce the intermediate output image O_i, the images $Y_1 ... Y_n$ are first individually convolved with kernels K_{1i} ... K_{ni}. Then, the individual convolution results from each input image are summed, or *aggregated*. A "bias" value is added to each pixel in the aggregated output, and a suitable non-linear function (for example, *tanh*) is used to limit the pixel value to be within a reasonable range. The intermediate output image O_i is roughly the same size as the input images. All kernels used in the convolution

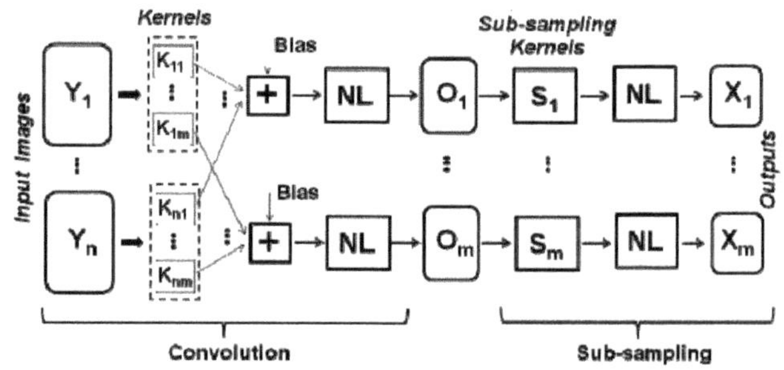

Figure 1: Typical structure of one layer of a CNN.

sub-layer of the CNN are of the same size (rows and columns). However, kernel sizes and the number of input and output images can vary from one CNN layer to another. Mathematically, output image O_i in a convolution sub-layer is as follows:

$$O_i = \tanh\left(bias + \sum_{j=1}^{n} Y_j * K_{ji} \right)$$

Here, $Y_j * K_{ji}$ represents the convolution operation between image Y_j and kernel K_{ji}, and tanh is the non-linear function. Since $m*n$ image-kernel convolutions are performed per CNN layer, from a computational point of view, these convolutions are the most compute intensive portion of a CNN. If the kernels are of size 1, then the CNN degenerates into a regular neural network [1].

For convolving an image with I_r rows and I_c columns with a kernel with W_r rows and W_c columns, the computation workload is $(I_r - W_r) * (I_c - W_c) * W_r * W_c$ multiply-accumulates (MACs). For a CNN layer, we perform $n * m$ convolutions. For each convolution, it is also easy to see that the computation ratio to memory IO ratio is $W_r * W_c$ since for every pixel fetched from memory we perform $W_r * W_c$ MACs. Therefore, CNNs are compute-intensive, especially as the kernel sizes get larger.

2.2 Sub-sampling and non-linearity

In Figure 1, the convolution sub-layer output O_i is sub-sampled. In the simplest case, sub-sampling averages four neighboring elements in O_i to produce a single element in the output image X_i. The output image X_i will have approximately half the number of rows and columns as compared with O_i. In general, O_i can be sub-sampled by using a suitable sub-sampling kernel S_i. After sub-sampling, each element in the output can be subjected to a non-linear operation to produce one pixel of the output X_i. A sub-sampled output image X_i is given by: $X_i = \tanh(O_i \,.\, S_i)$, where tanh is the non-linear function, and the operation $(O_i \,.\, S_i)$ represents sub-sampling of image O_i according to kernel S_i. Compared to the convolution sub-layer, sub-sampling is less compute intensive since it requires, on average, only one MAC operation per input pixel.

3. PARALLELISM IN CNN WORKLOADS

The CNN forward propagation task can be parallelized in several ways. In a multi-layer CNN, due to the feed-forward nature of forward propagation, the data dependencies between successive layers preclude parallel execution of all layers of the CNN. Therefore, task-parallelism across layers is limited and it is also more difficult to exploit.

Operator-level (fine-grained) parallelism: Consider one image-kernel convolution that convolves an image with Ir rows and Ic columns and a kernel with Wr rows and Wc columns. Each

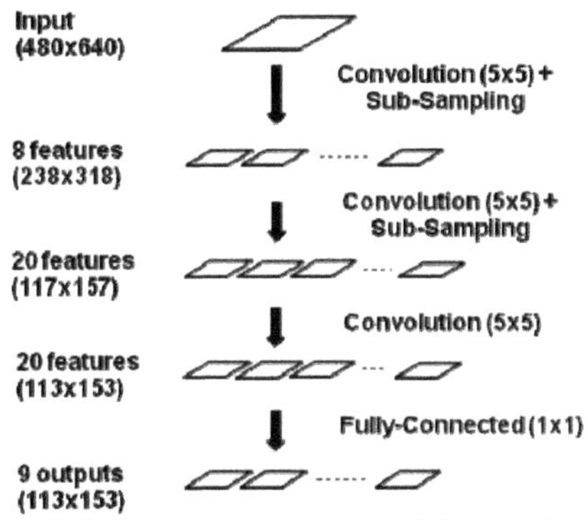

Figure 2: CNN for face recognition (with angle/pose detection).

output pixel requires $Wr*Wc$ multiply-accumulations all of which can be performed in parallel. The output pixels themselves are all independent. Numerous 2D-convolver designs exist that exploit the parallelism inherent in the image-kernel convolution, and we employ a standard systolic design. Practical considerations like available memory bandwidth, hardware computation resources, and power considerations do limit the amount of fine-grained parallelism we can exploit in hardware. For example, it is not practical to simultaneously perform all the sub-convolutions in parallel due to the excessive memory bandwidth that will be necessary to bring in almost the entire image in one cycle.

Coarse-grain parallelism: If a CNN layer has n input images and m outputs, then all $m*n$ image-kernel convolutions can, in theory, be performed in parallel. However, for typical m and n, provisioning enough memory bandwidth to keep $m*n$ convolvers busy is impractical. With a smaller number of convolvers, we can extract parallelism in two ways: inter-output and intra-output. We can parallelize the computation of a single output image since it is the sum of n input-kernel convolutions. We refer to this as *intra-output parallelism.* Also, multiple output images can be computed in parallel, and we refer to this as *inter-output parallelism.* The key observation is that different layers in a CNN network exhibit vastly different amount of intra-output and inter-output parallelism. As explained in Section 4, due to this variability, fixed hardware architectures have worse performance than an adaptive, configurable architecture.

4. A MOTIVATING EXAMPLE

In this section, we motivate the case for a dynamically configurable CNN coprocessor. We show that CNN workload characteristics change dramatically not only from one application to another, but also across different layers of a single CNN. We designed several hardware architectures and observed the performance of a variety of CNN workloads on each of these architectures. Specifically, we designed a hardware architecture expressly tailored to accelerate workload in a particular layer of the CNN, and evaluated the performance of workloads in other layers of the CNN (and even other applications) on this hardware architecture. We observed that for any given hardware architecture, the CNN layer workload for which the hardware architecture was designed for does exhibit good performance, but a majority of other CNN layer workloads exhibit poor performance. Our study attributes the poor performance of most CNN layer workloads to a mismatch of the computing architecture and the workload characteristics of various CNN layers.

Figure 2 shows a CNN network we use in video applications to detect faces (and their angle and pose). The resolution of the input image is VGA (640x480). The network has 4 layers. The first two layers employ both convolutions as well as sub-sampling (the figure leaves out non-linearity and bias for simplicity). The third layer is only a convolutional layer while the last is a traditional fully-connected layer where all inputs are connected to all outputs. The convolutional kernels (2D array of weights) are of size 5x5 in the entire network. The 9 outputs encode the face, its angle and pose (each output is a 113x153 image).

Our architectural template for the CNN coprocessor consists of an array of convolver primitives connected to external memory. Each convolver primitive can convolve one image with one kernel. The number of convolver primitives, the number of memory ports and the port width are pre-specified for an architecture. The hardware also has no internal storage and requires that all convolver primitives are fed data continuously in a streaming manner. For hidden layers, the values of the hidden units are the intermediate outputs. If the computing architecture has fewer than n convolvers per output then accesses to off-chip memory are required to store intermediate data. This is because the computing architecture has no internal storage for intermediate data.

Given this architectural template, there are different ways of organizing the convolver primitives within the memory port (and port width) constraints. We show that the best performance is achieved when the layers use different organizations. We first note that all layers have fine-grained parallelism within a convolution operation. However, a software implementation of a CNN when run on a processor cannot effectively leverage that parallelism due to thread synchronization. Our convolution primitives exploit the parallelism inherent in a convolution using well-known systolic architectures.

Of more interest are the inter-output and intra-output parallelisms. The first layer, which produces 8 outputs from a single input image, exhibits inter-output parallelism, while the second layer exhibits intra-output parallelism. Let us assume the hardware has 8 convolver primitives, 2 memory ports of width 8 pixels (i.e., the ability to transfer 8 pixels per port each cycle). Consider the first layer. It has 1 input image and 8 outputs. If we organize the 8 available convolver primitives so that we have a single broadcast of the input image and the computation of the 8 outputs in parallel, then the computing architecture executes the first layer with maximum performance. However the same arrangement will work poorly for the second layer which has 8 input images and 20 output images. With a single broadcast input and 8 convolvers, we can only process one input at a time, but compute 8 partial outputs in parallel. With no intermediate storage, the 8 partially computed outputs must be written out to off-chip memory resulting in an increase in intermediate data memory traffic. Furthermore, each input image, which participates in producing 20 outputs, will have to be read three times from the off-chip memory in order to generate and write out all the 20 outputs. The execution time is roughly the same as the time it takes to read one of the images 24 times.

On the other hand, assume that the second layer had a different arrangement of the 8 convolver primitives where the 8 convolvers simultaneously process 8 different input images, but the results of the 8 convolutions are combined to produce a single output. With 8 convolvers processing eight different input images,

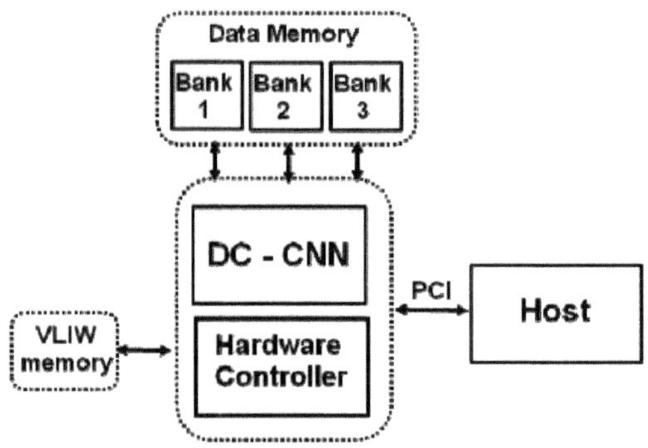

Figure 3: System Overview.

we are computing each of the 20 outputs in a serial fashion. However, each output is being computed in parallel (8 images are being processed in parallel to produce an output). Note that there is no intermediate data to be written off-chip since no partial outputs are computed. This is intra-output parallelism. The execution time for the second layer is roughly the same as the time it takes to read an image, about 20 times. Clearly, the execution time for the second layer is much shorter than the case where the 8 convolvers are processing the same image but producing 8 different (partial) outputs. As shown in the experimental results section, the performance improvement could be as much as 3X for CNN layers in several real-world CNN applications.

5. CNN COPROCESSOR ARCHITECTURE

Our architectural template primarily consists of a processing core and a memory sub-system. The processing core itself is stateless, and we require that input, intermediate and output data are continuously streamed between the processing core and the memory sub-system.

5.1 System Overview

As shown in Figure 3, the processing core DC-CNN communicates with a separate processor ("Host") that executes the main application. The host off-loads the entire CNN computation to the co-processor. In particular, the host transfers the input images and the detailed CNN network structure to the co-processor (number of layers, kernels used in each layer, bias values, sampling kernels, non-linearity etc.). The coprocessor has access to 3 external memory banks (Data Memory) to store input images, kernels and intermediate data.

We have developed a CNN compiler (it executes on the host platform) that automatically translates high abstraction network specification written by domain experts into a parallel microprogram (a sequence of low-level VLIW instructions) that is mapped, scheduled and executed by the coprocessor (hardware controller in Figure 3). Instructions to facilitate dynamic configurability, complex control and data flows, as well as on-the-fly packing of intermediate data to minimize off-chip memory transfers, are also natively supported by the coprocessor.

The co-processor performs forward propagation across all the network layers and returns the output of the last layer back to the host. We chose a high-level of abstraction for the host interface since implementing only the convolution task on the co-processor will require the host to co-ordinate complex control and data flows, and this will severely degrade the performance. Also, significant amounts of intermediate data are generated within and across layers of the CNN. Moving the intermediate data across the slow host-coprocessor interface will negate any advantage we get from performing fast convolutions on the co-processor.

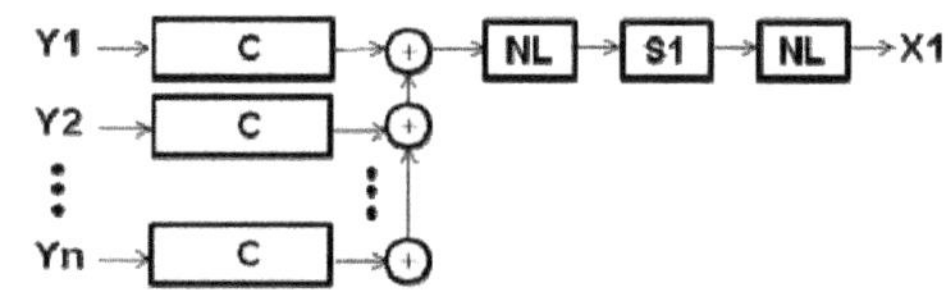

Figure 4: Basic computational element: hardware pipeline of convolvers (C), non-linearity (NL) and sub-sampling (S1).

5.2 The Processing Core

Each layer of the CNN reads one or more images as input, and computes one or more images as output. Our basic computational element, shown in Figure 4, is designed to compute one output image at a time. This computational element is architected to take advantage of intra-output parallelism. The basic computation primitive is the 2D convolver that can store a kernel internally. We use a bank of 2D convolvers whose outputs are aggregated. The computation element also has a specialized hardware pipeline to compute non-linearity (NL) and sub-sampling (S1). If more than ***n*** images have to be combined to realize an output, then the aggregated output from the convolver bank may only be a partial output (i.e. intermediate data) that must be stored in off-chip memory. Partial outputs are not subjected to non-linearity or sub-sampling.

If the coprocessor reads one pixel every cycle, then the time taken for reading the input is the same as the total number of pixels in the input images. If the memory architecture is designed so that the co-processor can input multiple pixels in one cycle, then the time taken for reading the input information will reduce proportionally. Either way, every pixel in every input image has to be examined at least once to compute an output image. Fetching data from off-chip memory consumes significantly more power than typical operations performed within the processor. Therefore, minimizing memory transfers has a significant effect on power consumption. One of our key design goals is to read each input pixel exactly once, and compute the output image within a few (fixed number of) cycles after the last input pixel is read. By computing the output image in approximately the same time it takes to read input data, the basic computational element is optimal with respect to a given off-chip memory bandwidth, power consumption, and throughput.

If we use multiple computational elements, each input image can be simultaneously used to compute more than one output image. Since the same image is used to compute different output images, we can fetch the input image only once. Figure 5 shows

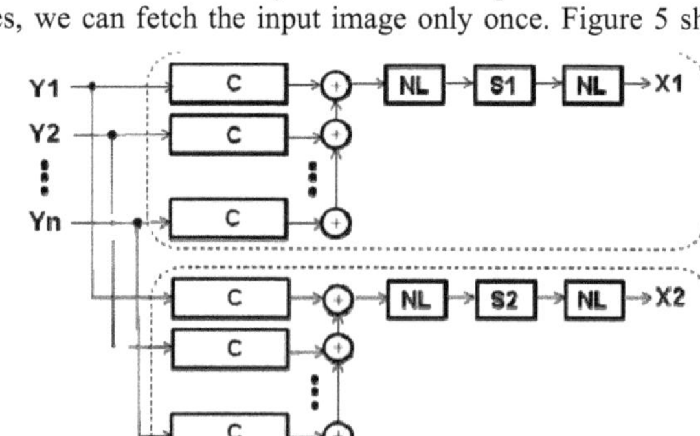

Figure 5: Processing core with two computational elements.

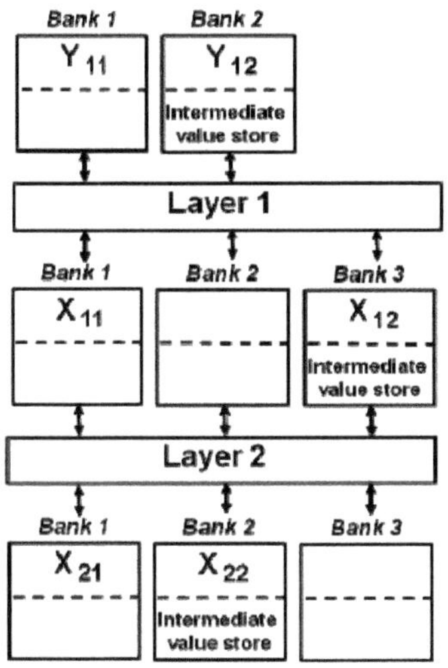

Figure 6: Use of three memory banks.

an array of two computational elements (X_1 and X_2) where the inputs of the first computational element are also broadcast to the second element. With such a configuration, we can leverage inter-output parallelism, since we can now compute two outputs simultaneously.

By varying the number of convolvers in a computational element (Y), as well as the total number of computational elements (X), we can control the extent to which the two different parallelisms are parlayed to match the exact computational workload of any layer of a CNN. Note that by replacing the convolver primitive with a different functional unit, we can easily implement different feed-forward neural networks and classifiers such as HMAX [17][27], Deep Belief Networks [29][30] and HoG methods [28].

5.3 The Memory Sub-system

Design of the memory subsystem has a big impact on the performance of CNNs as well as other artificial neural networks. Since our processing core is stateless, multiple banks that can be simultaneously read from and written to are necessary. A banked memory subsystem is indispensible for CNNs rather than a single memory with the same or higher aggregate bandwidth and storage. For the discussion in this section, we assume that the memory subsystem consists of one or more banks, and each bank has exactly one single-ported memory. However, basic ideas described in this section can be easily adapted to multi-port memories. If Y, the number of convolvers in a computational element, is less than I_n, then we need multiple passes to compute each output, thereby resulting in intermediate data values. We assume that each memory bank has the necessary port width to either read Y input pixels (and if necessary, X intermediate data values for the X output images being computed simultaneously) and write X output pixels (or X intermediate data values), every cycle.

In this section, we show that three independent memory banks suffice to ensure uninterrupted data flow for the stateless CNN architecture. Consider Figure 6. Layer 1 of a CNN produces 2 outputs (X_{11} and X_{12}) from 2 input images (Y_{11} and Y_{12}). Also, assume that we choose a co-processor architecture that has $Y = 1$ and $X = 1$ (i.e. one 2D convolver, and one NL-SS-NL pipeline). Since $Y = 1$, we process one image at a time. Every cycle, we read a pixel from an input image. We either generate an intermediate value or we compute a pixel of one of the output images, but not both.

To compute the output image X11, we first read pixels of image Y_{11} that is stored in Bank 1. Processing of every pixel in Y_{11} generates one intermediate value. Since we are reading a pixel from Bank 1 in every cycle, we cannot also write the intermediate value to Bank 1 in the same cycle. Furthermore, while reading pixels of image Y_{12}, we must also read the intermediate values. Therefore, intermediate values and pixels of Y_{12} are laid out in the same memory bank (Bank 2). Convolution of image Y_{12} will not result in intermediate values since this is the last image. Since X_{11} cannot be written to Bank 2, we store X_{11} in Bank 1. After we compute X_{12}, where do we store X_{12}? Like Layer 1 where the two input images Y_{11} and Y_{12} were in different banks, Layer 2 processing dictates that X_{11} and X_{12} be stored in different memory banks. Therefore, we store the output X_{12} in a new bank (Bank 3). Clearly, three memory banks are necessary and sufficient to support stateless processing. Output images of Layer 1 are the input images for Layer 2, and we can argue similarly to determine the location of Layer 2's output images (X_{21} and X_{22}).

6. DYNAMIC CONFIGURATION

In order to make the core adapt to the different types of parallelism across CNN layers, we introduce an input switch as shown in Figure 7. The switch allows the convolvers to be grouped in different ways by varying Y and X. The maximum values of Y and X are determined by the memory bandwidth and the area budget of the chip. Assuming a 3-bank architecture, if the memory bandwidth per bank is P bits per cycle, the input pixel width is I_b bits, intermediate data width T_b and output pixel width O_b, then the maximum value of Y, given by Y_{max} is $\left\lfloor \min\left(\frac{P}{Ib}, \frac{P}{Tb}\right) \right\rfloor$. Similarly, the maximum value of X (X_{max}) is $\left\lfloor \min\left(\frac{P}{Ob}, \frac{P}{Tb}\right) \right\rfloor$.

Note that every computational element has to sum the Y convolutions prior to non-linearity and sub-sampling. Since Y can change in the configurable architecture, this summation is achieved by using a sea of adders each statically designed to add Y_{max} values. Specifically, we need X_{max} adders, each with Y_{max} inputs. The output switch appropriately routes the $Y * X$ convolver outputs to appropriate inputs of these adders. The routing is done in a block-wise fashion, i.e., groups of Y outputs from the convolvers are routed to a single adder with Y_{max}-inputs.

6.1 Input Switch and Output Switch

Figure 8 shows the details of the input and output switch for a design where $Y_{max} = 6$ ***and*** $X_{max} = 2$. The input switch is constructed from a simple selector (multiplexor). The selector has three inputs (one select signal and two input values, one of which is 0). Depending on the value of the 'Select' signal, the selector either produces a 0 value as output or it forwards the input value. Each selector is connected to exactly one convolver. We achieve dynamic configurability as follows. For a CNN layer with 3 input images (Y_1, Y_2 and Y_3), and one output image X_1, we generate select signals so that the first three selectors of computational element X_1 (selectors M_1, M_2 and M_3) are enabled to forward their inputs (images Y_1, Y_2 and Y_3) to their convolvers. Selectors M_4, M_5 and M_6 are configured to forward a value of 0. So, these selectors are effectively *disabled.* Please note that the 2D convolvers are also designed to perform no computations if their corresponding selector is disabled (this is not required for correctness of the result, but it saves the power that would otherwise be consumed by the convolver). Similarly, the first three selectors of

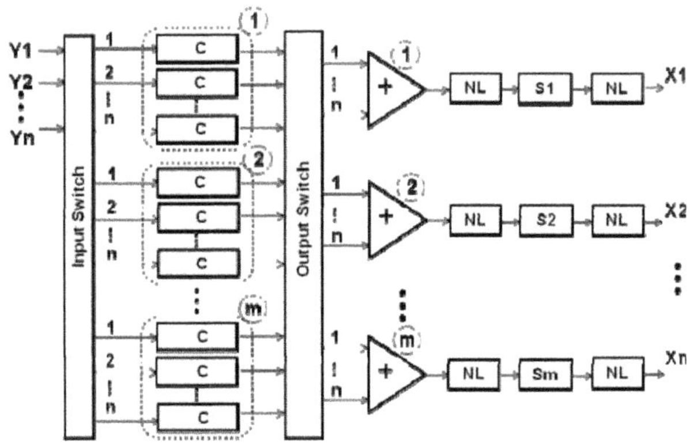

Figure 7: Dynamically configurable CNN architecture.

computational element X_2 (M_{19}, M_{20} and M_{21}) are configured to forward images Y_1, Y_2 and Y_3 to their convolvers. Selectors M_{22}, M_{23} and M_{24} are disabled.

In a simple implementation of the output switch, we chain the convolvers in a computational element to realize the pipelined summation of the convolver outputs. For example, selectors M_1, M_2 and M_3 are set to forward input images Y_1, Y_2 and Y_3 to their convolvers. Outputs of the three convolvers are aggregated over time as shown in Figure 8. The aggregated value is then processed by the non-linearity and sub-sampling units.

6.2 Exploring Architectural Configurations

Scaling the number of processing elements in a chip is easier than scaling off-chip memory bandwidth. Therefore, in practice, finding the optimal values of Y and X for a CNN layer boils down to finding a judicious mix of intra-output and inter-output parallelism that saturates the available off-chip bandwidth.

We first examine constraints on Y and X, assuming a 3-bank memory subsystem where each bank transfers **P** bits per cycle. Again, assume that the input pixel width is $\mathbf{I_b}$, the intermediate data width is $\mathbf{T_b}$, the output pixel width is $\mathbf{O_b}$ and that there are **C** convolvers in the hardware. The product of Y and X *must* be less than or equal to the total hardware available which means $X*Y \leq C$. Several constraints are due to the memory sub-system. Specifically, it is straightforward to see that:

$X * I_B \leq P$ (if X is used to write intermediate data)

$X * O_B \leq P$ (if X is used to write final outputs)

$Y * T_B \leq P$ (if Y is used to read intermediate data)

$Y * I_B \leq P$ (if Y is used to read first layer inputs)

When computing a CNN layer, if we only read primary inputs (and no temporary intermediate result), the number of memory bits read per cycle is $Y * I_B$. If there are temporary results, there are $(Y * I_B) + (X * T_B)$ bits read per cycle. Similarly, the number of memory bits written per cycle is $X * T_B$ or $X * O_B$ depending on whether we store intermediate or final outputs. Read requests per cycle or write requests per cycle cannot exceed P bits per cycle.

For a CNN layer with n inputs and m outputs, the number of passes required for completion is $(n/Y)*(m/X)$. The time for completing one pass is simply the time required to fetch the image from memory one pixel at a time (since we have a stateless streaming architecture): $I_r * I_c$ where I_r is the number of image rows, and I_c the number of image columns. Therefore, the execution time for completing the entire layer is $(I_r * I_c) * n/Y * m/X$. This is the cost function that we want to minimize subject to the memory sub-system constraints, and total hardware available (number of convolvers). From a system point of view, a run-time software component analyzes the CNN workload, and determines the best (Y,X) for each layer. The CNN architecture is then dynamically configured for each layer by using a special instruction in the instruction set of the coprocessor.

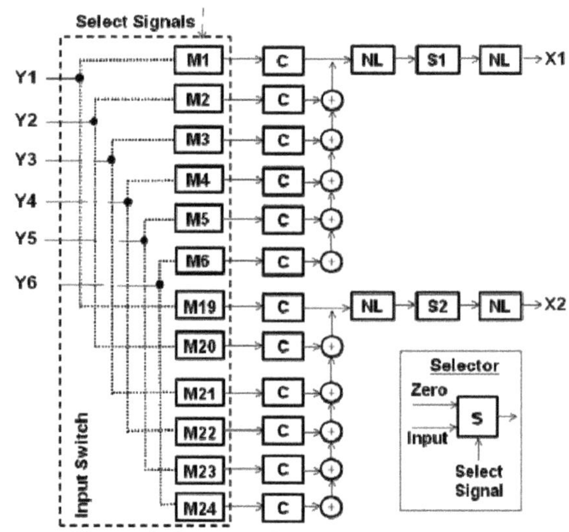

Figure 8: Input and output switches.

The algorithm for choosing the best (Y, X) for each layer uses integer factorization techniques to identify different candidate integer values of Y and X so that $X*Y \leq C$. For each value of Y and X, we evaluate the memory sub-system constraints to determine if the specific combination of Y and X is a feasible solution. We compute the cost function for every feasible solution, and select the feasible solution that minimizes the cost function (execution time for processing the entire layer). Although no efficient integer factorization algorithm is known for factoring very large numbers (with 100 to 200 digits), there are several reasons why this approach works well in practice. First, the largest number of hardware convolvers (C) we considered is 40. Even if C increases by two or three orders of magnitude (very unlikely due to power and hardware constraints), fortunately, integer factorization for small numbers is fast [10]. Second, by using dynamic programming, we are able to quickly prune many combinations of Y and X. For example, consider the case of C = 40 convolvers, and a memory port-width of 128 bits of data per cycle. To determine the best configuration for Layer 3 of the Video Surveillance workload, only a small number (14) of feasible combinations, shown in Figure 9, had to be considered.

7. EXPERIMENTAL RESULTS

In this section, we first compare the performance of a fixed coprocessor and a dynamically reconfigurable coprocessor using several real CNN workloads. We then examine the scalability of the new architecture with respect to scaling (increase) in number of processing elements, as well as memory bandwidth, and show that dynamic configurability has a consistent, first-order effect on performance. Finally, we compare the performance of our dynamically configurable CNN coprocessor with leading CNN workload implementations reported recently on several other computing platforms.

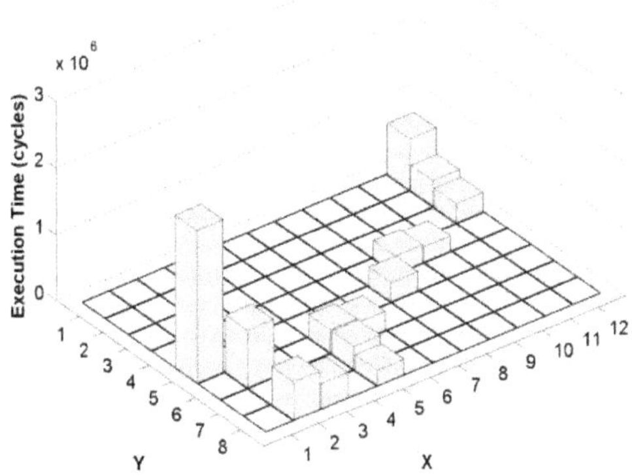

Figure 9: Feasible architectural configurations for Layer 3 of the Video Surveillance workload.

We estimated performance and scalability using a simulator that provides cycle-accurate execution time estimates of the architectural components. In the simulator, ***Y*** and ***X*** could be parameterized per layer or they can be fixed for the entire CNN workload. Our architectural simulator uses an emulation of a 20-convolver, 3-memory bank (128 bits of data per cycle per port per bank), dynamically configurable CNN architecture (including the hardware learning engine controller) on a Virtex 5 SX240T FPGA platform (1024 multiply-accumulate units) to more accurately estimate execution cycles. The RTL (Verilog) for the 20-convolver design was mapped to the FPGA by using design tools from Synplicity. In all CNN workloads, an input or output value is represented using 16 bits, and an intermediate data value is represented using 48 bits. All CNN workloads are specified by using a simple, high abstraction level software programming API. A CNN compiler (running on the host processor) automatically translates the entire high abstraction network specification into a parallel micro-program (a sequence of low-level VLIW instructions) that is mapped, scheduled and executed on the coprocessor FPGA implementation. Instructions to facilitate complex control and data flows, as well as on-the-fly packing of intermediate data to minimize off-chip memory transfers, are also natively supported by the coprocessor.

7.1 Workloads

Table 1 shows the five different CNN workloads we considered. In the "Video Surveillance" workload that was developed internally, the CNN is used to identify human activity within a video frame and to recognize specific physical characteristics such as age, gender and race. The "Face Recognition" workload is obtained from [26]. The "Automotive Safety" workload is a vision, range and motion sensing network, used in automotive safety applications, to process video-feeds from vehicle-mounted cameras. This application was developed internally for a major Japanese automobile manufacturer. The "Mobile Robot Vision" workload is obtained from [9]. Here, a CNN is used for learning long-range vision (on-vehicle Robot) for autonomous, off-road driving. The "Face Detection" workload is obtained from [25]. As shown in Table 1, the CNNs used in these applications have a wide range of inputs and outputs across different layers. All examples use VGA frames (640 x 480 pixels per frame).

7.2 Advantage of Dynamic Configurability

Table 2 compares the dynamically configurable architecture with the best fixed-architecture, in terms of execution cycles. The fixed architecture has the same **(*Y, X*)** for all three layers, while the dynamically configurable architecture adapts to each layer of the CNN. For all workloads, the hardware constraint is 20 convolvers, and the memory port-width is 128 bits of data per cycle. The column "Best Fixed Architecture" reports the values of ***Y*** and ***X*** that were chosen, and the total execution cycles for each of the workloads. Note that the ***Y*** and ***X*** values are fixed for all three layers of a CNN. The column "Dynamically configurable" reports (a) the values of ***Y*** and ***X*** that were chosen for each layer of a CNN workload, and (b) the total execution cycles for all three layers of a CNN workload. The last column reports the speedup of the dynamically configurable version as compared with the fixed architecture case. Our results show that a dynamically configurable architecture consistently outperforms a fixed architecture. Depending on the CNN workload, speedup factors range from 1.5x to 2.3x.

To understand the scalability of the new architecture with respect to scaling (increase) in number of processing elements, as well as increase in memory bandwidth, we considered four CNN coprocessor architectures with 10, 20, 30 and 40 convolvers. In addition, we considered three different memory port widths (64 bits per cycle, 128 bits per cycle and 256 bits per cycle) for each of the four CNN architectures. For all architectures, we used 3 independent memory ports. Figure 10, Figure 11 and Figure 12 show the speedup obtained for three different CNN workloads, as a function of the number of convolvers and memory port width (due to space constraints, we are not able to include data for all experiments). For example, consider the case of the "Automotive Safety" workload. We designed the best possible fixed architecture, assuming a hardware constraint of 10 convolvers, and a memory port width of 64 bits of data per cycle. In order to obtain the best fixed architecture, we examine all possible valid combinations of ***Y*** and ***X***, and select the best one for a fair comparison. Then, we designed a dynamically configurable architecture under the same hardware and memory constraints. From the figures, we observe that the dynamically configurable version is about 2.2x faster than the best fixed-architecture version (for 10-convolvers, and 64-bit memory port width). Similar

Table 1 : CNN workload characteristics.

	Video Surveillance		Face Recognition		Automotive Safety		Mobile Robot Vision		Face detection	
	Inputs	Outputs	Inputs	Outputs	Inputs	Outputs	Inputs	Output	Inputs	Outputs
Layer 1	5	6	1	20	1	8	1	6	1	6
Layer 2	6	16	20	25	8	20	6	16	6	16
Layer 3	16	120	25	40	8	20	16	80	16	100

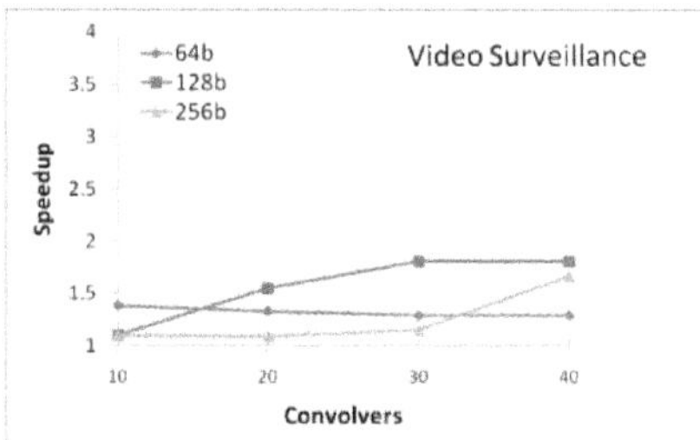

Figure 11: Speedup for Video Surveillance.

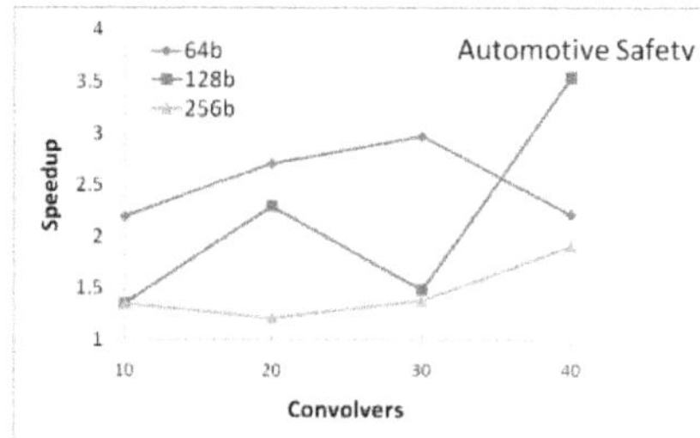

Figure 10: Speedup for Automotive Safety.

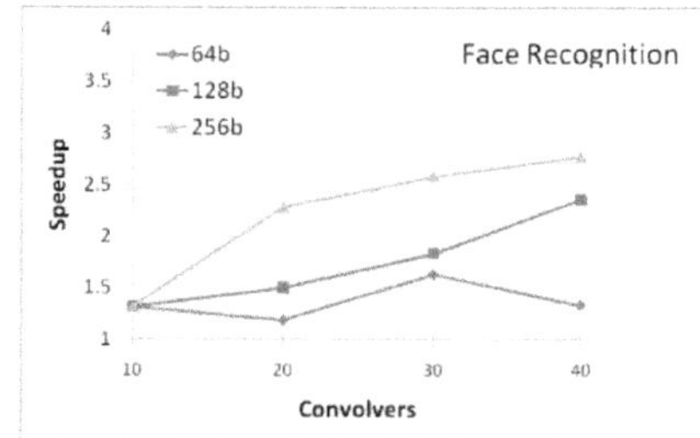

Figure 12: Speedup for Face Recognition.

experiments were conducted to obtain data for all the four architectures and three different memory port widths per architecture.

We note three interesting trends from the data. First, irrespective of the number of convolvers or the memory port width, the dynamically configurable version is consistently faster (speedups range from 1.2x to 3.4x) than the corresponding, best fixed-architecture version. Second, increasing the number of convolvers (for a given memory port width) usually results in higher speedups. However, in some cases the best fixed architecture also happens to be a reasonably good match for the given workload, resulting in an occasional low speedup factor for the dynamically configurable version. For example, consider the 128-bit memory port width case for the "Automotive Safety" workload. With 30 convolvers, the dynamic version is only 1.5x faster than the best fixed architecture (for a 20-convolver design, the dynamic version is 2.3x faster than the best fixed architecture for the same workload). Third, increasing the memory port width (for a given number of convolvers) may or may not result in higher speedups. It does improve both designs (fixed or dynamically configurable) but the amount of improvement can be very different. For some workloads like the "Face Recognition" workload, with large amount of intermediate data across the three layers, the advantage of dynamic configurability is more pronounced at wider memory port widths. We see the exact opposite effect for the "Automotive Safety" workload, where higher speedups are usually achieved for smaller memory port widths. The absolute performance of fixed or dynamically configurable architecture always improves with higher memory port widths, and so does the power consumption. In all cases, the utilization factor of the hardware convolvers or the available memory bandwidth is close to 100%.

7.3 Comparison with Other Implementations

We also compared the performance of our dynamically configurable CNN coprocessor (20 convolvers, 128-bit memory port width) with leading CNN workload implementations reported recently on several platforms: (a) 128-core, 1.35GHz NVIDIA's GPU with 1.5GB RAM, and a fast PCI Express connection to the x86 host [26] (b) an internal software implementation on an dual-socket, quad-core, 2.33 GHz Intel Xeon (Intel Multicore with eight 2.33 GHz cores), and (c) a 200 MHz, fixed architecture CNN co-processor called CNP that was implemented on a Virtex 4 FPGA part from Xilinx [9].

Results for the Intel Xeon (8-processor) multicore (column "Multicore" in Table 3) were obtained by using an internal software implementation of CNN on the multicore. This implementation uses the latest BLAS library that has been specially optimized for dense linear algebra operations. The performance of the multicore implementation is quite competitive with the GPU implementations. GPU results reported in [26] used an older, 600 MHz NVIDIA GPU. They report a processing time of 210 ms per frame for the "Face Detection" workload. Their frame has less pixels than our VGA frame. On a faster GPU (1.35GHz), we achieve a processing time of 105 ms per VGA frame. If we factor in the difference in clock speeds, the two GPU implementations are comparable. We use our GPU implementation to generate results for all the other workloads.

Performance of software CNN implementations on embedded processors is poor. For example, processing times per frame on the Intel Atom processor were 1.67 s (Automotive Safety), 2.05s (Video Surveillance), 1.95s (Face Recognition), 1.23 s (Mobile Robot Vision), and 0.97s (Face Detection). We see a clear 10X pullback from software implementations on the Xeon.

Results for the 200 MHz CNP (column "CNP" in Table 3) were taken from [9]. They report a processing time of 100 ms per frame for the "Mobile Robot Vision" workload. Since they do not use a separate host processor, there is no need to transfer the video feed from the host. Also, we do not have access to their hardware, and we are unable to report results for the remaining workloads on their platform.

Results for the proposed dynamically configurable CNN coprocessor (column "DC-CNN" in Table 3) were obtained using

Table 2 : Comparison of fixed and dynamically configurable, 20-convolver, 128-bit memory port width.

CNN workload	Best Fixed Architecture		Dynamically configurable		Speedup
	Y,X	Performance Cycles	*Y,X*	Performance Cycles	
Automotive Safety	***7,2***	3,340,800	L 1: ***1,8*** L 2: ***8,2*** L 3: ***10,2***	1,518,545	2.2x
Video Surveillance	***7,2***	4,972,000	L 1: ***5,4*** L 2: ***4,5*** L 3: ***10,2***	3,225,600	1.5x
Face Recognition	***8,2***	7,603,200	L 1: ***1,8*** L 2: ***8,2*** L 3: ***10,2***	5,068,800	1.5x
Mobile Robot Vision	***10,2***	3,072,000	L 1: ***1,6*** L 2: ***10,2*** L 3: ***10,2***	2,457,600	1.3x
Face Detection	***8,2***	3,456,000	L 1: ***1,6*** L 2: ***8,2*** L 3: ***10,2***	2,841,600	1.2x

Table 3: Comparison with other CNN implementations.

CNN (640 x 480 pixels input image)	**Multicore** (Xeon @ 2.33 Ghz, 8 Cores, 16 GB) BLAS	**GPU** (C870 @ 1.35 Ghz, 1.5 GB RAM) PCIe	**CNP** (FPGA @200 MHz)	**DC-CNN** @ 120 Mhz 20 conv., 128-bit port width, PCI		**Speedup** of DC-CNN		
				Compute time	Transfer time	Over 2.3 GHz, 8-core	Over 1.35 GHz, 128-core GPU	Over CNP
Automotive Safety	110 ms	85 ms	-	13 ms	11 ms	8.5x	6.5x	-
Video Surveillance	212 ms	163 ms	-	27 ms	34 ms	7.8x	6.0x	-
Face Recognition	217 ms	167 ms	-	42 ms	11 ms	5.2x	4.0x	-
Mobile Robot Vision	147 ms	114 ms	100 ms	21 ms	11 ms	7.0x	5.4x	4.8x
Face Detection	136 ms	105 ms	-	24 ms	11 ms	5.7x	4.4x	-

a 120 MHz FPGA implementation of our dynamically configurable co-processor, with 20 convolvers and 128-bit memory port width. We report separately the time taken to transfer the images (from the x86 host to the coprocessor) and output the results (from coprocessor to the host). In our implementation, transfer of images or output results overlaps with the CNN computation. Therefore, the total processing time for any CNN workload is the maximum of the execution time of the coprocessor and the data transfer time. For example, consider the case of the "Face Recognition" workload. It takes 11 ms to transfer the input image data to the co-processor, and it takes 42 ms to perform the processing for all three Layers in the CNN workload. However, processing of a Layer begins as soon as portions of images are available on the coprocessor.

Similarly, some of the output results computed by the coprocessor are transferred to the host while other outputs are still being computed by the co-processor. Therefore, due to the overlap, the total time required to process the frame was only 42 ms. Column "Speedup" in Table 3 shows the performance advantage of the dynamically configurable architecture over the multicore, GPU and CNP. We observe that the dynamically configurable architecture is 4x to 8x faster. More importantly, the additional speedup of the dynamically configurable architecture now enables an important tipping point. *By easily processing 25 to 30 frames per second, the proposed dynamically configurable co-processor is the first CNN architecture to enable real-time video stream processing on a wide range of object detection and recognition tasks.* Due to clock frequencies in the GHz range, the GPU and the Intel Multicore implementations consume more than 150 Watts. The 200 MHz Virtex4 implementation consumes 15 Watts [9]. In comparison, our 120MHz dynamically configurable co-processor prototype on a Virtex 5 FPGA consumes less than 14 watts of power (for all components on the FPGA board, including memory banks).

8. CONCLUSIONS

We presented a dynamically reconfigurable architecture for feed-forward neural networks used in recognition, analysis and reasoning applications. The design of the architecture is driven by two key observations. The first is based on the fact that CNNs exhibit "inter-output" and "intra-output" parallelism. Inter-output parallelism is where different outputs can be computed independently, and in parallel. Intra-output parallelism exploits parallelism within a single output computation. We showed that different CNN workloads exhibit a widely varying mix of these two types of parallelism within a single network. That is, different layers of a network must be parallelized in different ways. We therefore argued that the architecture itself must adapt to the way a particular layer of a network needs to be parallelized. This adaptive architecture is achieved by allocating an array of convolver primitives and dynamically configuring their organization at run-time to achieve optimal performance. The second observation is based on the fact that CNNs have large intermediate data which cannot be stored on-chip. Therefore, we designed a streaming architecture with multiple memory ports where input data, intermediate data and output data are continuously flowing between the processor and off-chip memory. We showed that a dynamically configurable architecture can provide speedups ranging from 1.2x to 3.5x over a similar fixed custom architecture with the best possible fixed configuration of the convolver primitives.

REFERENCES

[1] LeCun, Y., Bottou, L., Bengio, Y., & Haffner, P. (1998). Gradient-based learning applied to document recognition. Proceedings of the IEEE, (pp. 1-46).

[2] Collobert, R.; Weston, J., "A unified architecture for natural language processing: deep neural networks with multitask learning," *Proceedings of the 25th International Conference on Machine Learning (ICML 2008)*, vol. 307, pp.160-167, Jul 2008.

[3] Benkrid, K.; Belkacemi, S., "Design and implementation of a 2D convolution core for video applications on FPGAs," *Digital and Computational Video, 2002. DCV 2002. Proceedings. Third International Workshop on*, pp. 85-92, 14-15 Nov. 2002.

[4] Cardells-Tormo, F.; Molinet, P.-L., "Area-efficient 2-D shift-variant convolvers for FPGA-based digital image processing," *Circuits and Systems II: Express Briefs, IEEE Transactions on*, vol.53, no.2, pp. 105-109, Feb. 2006.

[5] Hui Zhang; Mingxin Xia; Guangshu Hu, "A Multiwindow Partial Buffering Scheme for FPGA-Based 2-D Convolvers," *Circuits and Systems II: Express Briefs, IEEE Transactions on*, vol.54, no.2, pp.200-204, Feb. 2007.

[6] Savich, A.W.; Moussa, M.; Areibi, S., "The Impact of Arithmetic Representation on Implementing MLP-BP on

FPGAs: A Study," *Neural Networks, IEEE Transactions on*, vol.18, no.1, pp.240-252, Jan. 2007.

[7] Gironés, R. G.; Palero, R. C.; Boluda, J. C.; Cortés, A. S., "FPGA Implementation of a Pipelined On-Line Backpropagation," *J. VLSI Signal Process. Syst.*, vol. 40, no. 2, pp.189-213., Jun 2005.

[8] Catanzaro, B.; Sundaram, N.; Keutzer, K., "Fast Support Vector Training and Classification on Graphics Processors," *Machine Learning, 25th International Conference on, (ICML 2008)*, Jul. 2008.

[9] C. Farabet, C. Poulet, J. Y. Han, and Y. LeCun, "CNP: An FPGA-based Processor for Convolutional Networks", in *Proc. International Conference on Field Programmable Logic and Applications (FPL'09)*, IEEE, Prague, 2009.

[10] Dixon, J. D. (1981). Asymptotically fast factorization of integers. *Math. Comput.*, *36*, 255-260.

[11] Hadsell, R. e. (2009). Learning long-range vision for Autonomous off-road Driving. *Journal of Field Robotics*, *26* (2), 120-144.

[12] Haykin, S. (2008). *Neural networks and learning machines.* Prentice Hall.

[13] Korekado, K., Morie, T., Nomura, O., Nakano, T., Matsugu, M., & Iwata, A. (2005). An Image Filtering Processor for Face/Object Recognition using Merged Analog-digital architecture. *Symposium on VLSI Circuits*, (pp. 220-223).

[14] Lisboa, P., Ifeachor, E., & Szczepaniak, P. (2009). *Artificial neural networks in Biomedicine.* Springer

[15] McNelis, P. D. (2005). *Neural Networks in Finance: Gaining Predictive Edge in the Market.* Academic Press.

[16] Mirowski, P. e. (2008). Comparing SVM and Convolutional networks for Epileptic Seizure Prediction from Intracranial EEG. *Proceedings of Machine Learning and Signal Processing*, (pp. 244-249).

[17] Mutch, J., & Lowe, D. (2006). Multiclass object recognition with sparse, localized features. *International Conference on Computer Vision and Pattern Recognition*, (pp. 11-18).

[18] Nakajima, M., & al., e. (2006). A 40GOPS 250mw massively parallel processor based on matrix architecture. *International Solid-state Circuits Conference*, (pp. 410-411).

[19] Nichols, K., Moussa, M., & Areibi, S. (2002). Feasibility of floating-point arithmetic in FPGA based artificial neural networks. *Proceedings of the 15th International Conference on Computer Applications in Industry and Engineering.* San Diego, California

[20] Nomura, O., & Morie, T. (2007). Projection-Field-Type VLSI Convolutional Neural Networks Using Merged/Mixed Analog-Digital approach. *International Conference on Neural Information Processing* (pp. 1081-1090). Springer-Verlag.

[21] Omondi, A., & Rajapakse, J. (2006). *FPGA Implementations of Neural Networks.* Springer.

[22] Prasad, B., & Prasanna, S. (2008). *Speech, Audio, Image and Biomedical Signal Processing using Neural Networks.* Springer.

[23] Sermanet, P. e. (2009). Multi-range architecture for collision-free off-road Robot Navigation. *Journal of Field Robotics*, *26* (1), 58-87.

[24] Wolf, D. F., Romero, R. A., & Marques, E. (2001). Using embedded processors in hardware models of artificial neural networks. *Proceedings of SBAI - Simposio Brasileiro de Automao Inteligente*, (pp. 78-83).

[25] Steve Lawrence, C. Lee Giles, Ah Chung Tsoi, Andrew D. Back, Face Recognition: A Convolutional Neural Network Approach. IEEE Transactions on Neural Networks 1997.

[26] Nasse, F., et al , "Face Detection using GPU-based Convolutional Neural Network", CAIP 2009, LNCS pp 83-90, Springer Verlag

[27] Serre, T. et al "Object recognition with features inspired by the visual cortex", Proceedings of Computer Vision and Pattern Recognition 2006.

[28] Dalal, N. et al, "Histograms of oriented gradients for human detection", Proceedings of Computer Vision and Pattern Recognition, 2005

[29] Raina, R. et al, "Large-scale Deep Unsupervised Learning using Graphics Procesors", Proceedings of International Conference on Machine Learning, 2009 (pp. 873-880).

[30] Lee, H. et al, "Convolutional Deep Belief Networks for Scalable Unsupervised Learning of Hierarchical Representations", Proceedings of International Conference on Machine Learning, 2009 (pp. 873-880).

RETCON: Transactional Repair without Replay

Colin Blundell
University of Pennsylvania
blundell@cis.upenn.edu

Arun Raghavan
University of Pennsylvania
arraghav@cis.upenn.edu

Milo M. K. Martin
University of Pennsylvania
milom@cis.upenn.edu

Abstract

Over the past decade there has been a surge of academic and industrial interest in optimistic concurrency, *i.e.* the speculative parallel execution of code regions that have the semantics of isolation. This work analyzes scalability bottlenecks of workloads that use optimistic concurrency. We find that one common bottleneck is updates to auxiliary program data in otherwise non-conflicting operations, *e.g.* reference count updates and hashtable occupancy field increments.

To eliminate the performance impact of conflicts on such auxiliary data, this work proposes RETCON, a hardware mechanism that tracks the relationship between input and output values symbolically and uses this symbolic information to transparently repair the output state of a transaction at commit. RETCON is inspired by instruction replay-based mechanisms but exploits simplifying properties of the nature of computations on auxiliary data to perform repair *without* replay. Our experiments show that RETCON provides significant speedups for workloads that exhibit conflicts on auxiliary data, including transforming a transactionalized version of the Python interpreter from a workload that exhibits no scaling to one that exhibits near-linear scaling on 32 cores.

Categories and Subject Descriptors

C.1.4 Computer Systems Organization [*Processor Architectures*]: Parallel Architectures

General Terms

Design, Languages, Performance

Keywords

Transactional Memory, Parallel Programming

1. Introduction

The past decade has seen a great deal of academic and industrial interest in the area of speculative synchronization, both in the form of hardware transactional memory (HTM) [16] and in the form of speculative parallel execution of traditional lock-based critical sections [21, 29]. Speculation allows code regions with the semantics of isolation to execute in parallel by detecting conflicting accesses to the same data and rolling back when a conflict occurs. Speculation thus makes the degree of concurrency dependent on the amount of data sharing rather than the granularity of locking, potentially easing the task of writing high-performance parallel programs. In spite of much research, however, the impact of such speculation on workload performance is not clear.

ISCA'10, June 19–23, 2010, Saint-Malo, France.

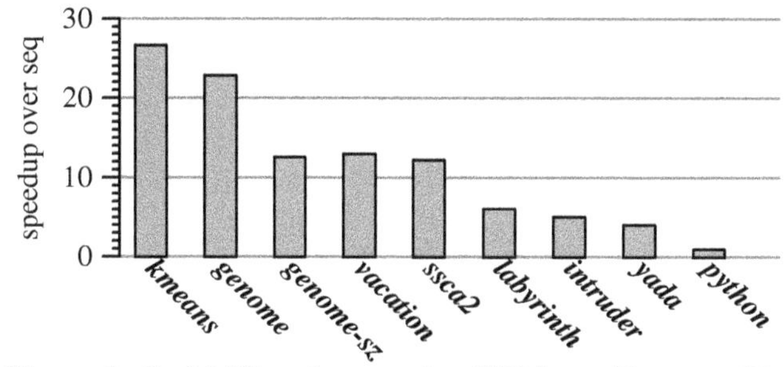

Figure 1. Scalability of aggressive HTM on 32 cores. The HTM is configured to eliminate cache overflows and has a robust timestamp-based contention management policy.

This paper undertakes a study of the potential impact of speculative concurrency on the scalability of parallel programs. To drive our study we intentionally choose benchmarks that would be challenging for speculation (described in Section 3). Our baseline system is a state-of-the-art hardware transactional memory system with reasonable contention management policies that is configured to avoid cache overflows. Nonetheless, Figure 1 shows that the performance of these workloads is mixed: although some workloads achieve near-linear speedup, nearly half of the workloads obtain a speedup of less than 10x on 32 cores.

As Section 3 describes, the dominant bottleneck to scalability is serialization arising from conflicts. We find that many sources of conflicts can be eliminated via simple software restructurings. After performing these restructurings, however, a common pattern remains of conflicts on *auxiliary data*, that is, data such as reference counters and hashtable occupancy fields that is not related to the main computation of the program itself. These conflicts cause significant performance loss on several of our workloads, for example completely serializing execution on a transactionalized version of the Python interpreter. This result is especially troubling because the operations in these workloads are conceptually non-conflicting, *e.g.*, simultaneous reads of a reference-counted shared object.

Others have reported similar patterns on a variety of workloads. Carlstrom *et al.* [7] found that a shared global identifier variable in a transactional version of SPECjbb was a bottleneck to an otherwise-scalable workload. An Azul Systems engineer analyzed the performance of Azul Systems' speculative lock elision on its clients' Java workloads and reported that programmers and library writers do not naturally write "TM-friendly code" and that counters such

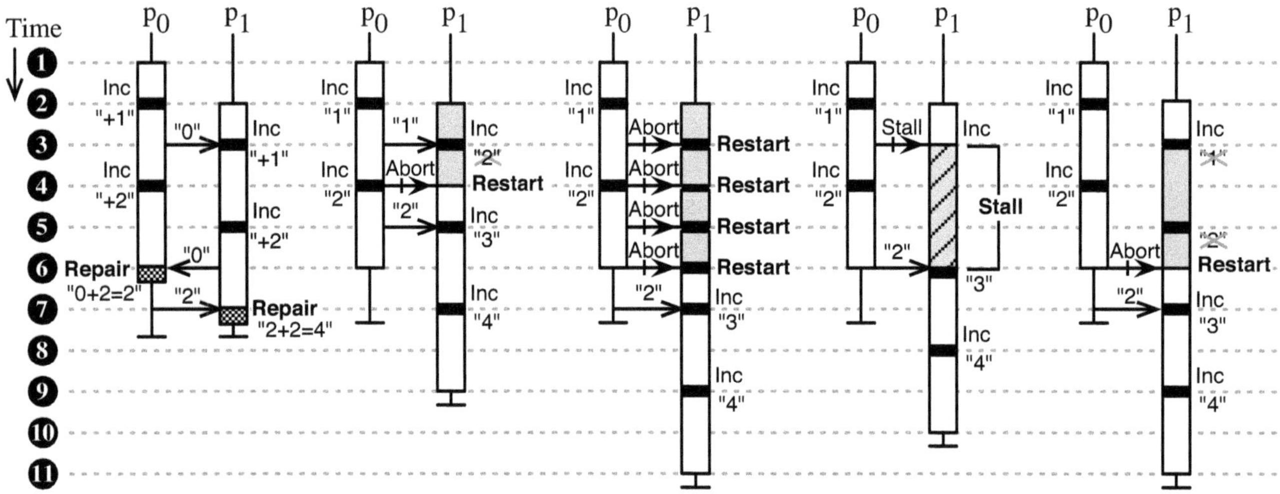

(a) RETCON (b) DATM (c) Eager TM (d) Eager TM - Stall (e) Lazy TM

Figure 2. Comparison of RETCON to other approaches. P_0 and P_1 begin transactions at times ❶ and ❷ respectively. Each transaction performs two increments to a shared counter variable that is initialized to zero. *(a)* RETCON symbolically tracks the counter address and repairs its value at commit by adding the computed increment. *(b)* DATM [30] forwards the speculatively incremented counter variable at time ❸, but must abort a transaction when the second increment introduces a cyclic dependence at time ❹. *(c)* In EagerTM, P_1 suffers repeated aborts until P_0 commits at time ❻. *(d)* EagerTM-Stall stalls P_1's first increment until P_0 commits at time ❻. *(e)* In LazyTM, P_1 performs both its speculative increments but then aborts when it detects a conflict on the commit of P_0 at time ❻.

as hashtable occupancy fields lead to "a general pattern of updates to peripheral shared values" that significantly impact performance due to "presenting a true data conflict" [10].

As the second part of this work, therefore, we seek to provide hardware support for minimizing the performance impact of such patterns. We observe that auxiliary data is usually accessed by short, simple computations that do not affect the larger transaction.[1] This property suggests a hardware-based approach of reacquiring lost data at commit and using the current values of this data to repair local state as necessary. Such a repair-based approach was proposed by ReSlice [32] to lessen the impact of conflicts in thread-level speculation, and similar slicing has been employed in other contexts as well [8, 17, 35]. These proposals use instruction-based repair by saving the dependent instructions of a conflicting load to later re-execute these instructions with the updated value of the load (either in a special-purpose core or by re-using the resources of the processor itself).

Guided by the nature of this auxiliary data, we propose a different approach. As the processor executes a transaction, it also tracks the relationship between input values and output values symbolically. Conditionals form constraints on the acceptable range of values that an input can take when reacquired at commit. At commit time, all inputs that have been lost are reacquired, constraints are checked, and symbolic computation is reapplied to these values (see Figure 2).

Our instantiation of this approach, RETCON,[2] is tailored to fit the needs of the auxiliary data present in our workloads. RETCON tracks an input symbolically through a sequence of loads, simple arithmetic operations, branches, and stores, with more complex computation creating a constraint that the input value be the same at commit. To track symbolic information, RETCON adds a buffer to hold the initial values of symbolically-tracked blocks, a buffer to hold constraints, and a buffer to hold symbolically-tracked stores. Our data shows that these structures can be small–*e.g.*, eight entries.

Although RETCON's focus is on repairing remotely changed values, its mechanisms have the secondary benefit of reducing conflicts in other ways. RETCON's resolution of conflicts at commit implicitly provides selective lazy conflict detection [6, 33, 39]. In addition, by performing conflict detection based on values [25, 37], RETCON also avoids conflicts due to false sharing [19], silent sharing, and temporally silent sharing [20].

We quantitatively evaluate RETCON and find that it has a significant impact on the performance of our workloads. RETCON's selective laziness and value-based conflict detection contribute to this performance impact, but it is RETCON's ability to repair true conflicts on auxiliary data that provides most of the benefit. Altogether, RETCON provides a speedup of more than 40% on several workloads and in one case transforms a workload that exhibited no scaling to instead exhibit near-linear scaling.

2. Hardware Transactional Memory Baseline

Supporting speculative concurrency in hardware entails several tasks. First, the hardware must be able to detect conflicting requests between two speculative regions (conflict detection). Second, it must employ a policy to resolve conflicts by stalling or aborting one of the conflicting speculative regions (contention management). Third, it must be able to roll back to pre-speculative state on an abort (version management). Below, we describe how our baseline hardware supports these tasks.

Conflict detection. Our baseline system detects conflicts through the cache coherence protocol by adding a "speculatively-read" bit and a "speculatively-written" bit to each block in the primary data cache. As the processor accesses blocks within a speculative region, it sets the read/written bits for those blocks. External requests snoop these bits to determine conflicts, where a

[1] Throughout this paper we will generally refer to speculative regions as transactions for convenience, but they could equally well be speculative lock-based critical sections.

[2] Retcon, short for *retroactive continuity*, refers to soap operas' and comic books' practice of revising past events as necessary to match current reality.

Workload	Description and Input Parameters
genome	From STAMP, gene sequencing program, *g1024 s48 n65536*
genome-sz	Variant of genome with resizable hashtable
intruder	From STAMP, network packet intrusion detection program, *a10 l4 n2038 s1*
intruder_opt	Variant of intruder optimized with fixed-size hashtable and thread-private queues
intruder_opt-sz	Variant of intruder optimized with resizable hashtable and thread-private queues
kmeans	From STAMP, partition-based clustering program, *m15 n15 t0.05 irandom-n2048-d16-c16.txt*
labyrinth	From STAMP, shortest-distance path routing, *irandom-x32-y32-z3-n96.txt*
ssca2	From STAMP, graph kernels, *s13 i1.0 u1.0 l3 p3*
vacation	From STAMP, travel reservation system, *n4 q60 u90 r16384 t4096*
vacation_opt	Variant of vacation optimized with fixed-size hashtable
vacation_opt-sz	Variant of vacation optimized with resizable hashtable
yada	From STAMP, Delaunay mesh refinement, *a20 i633.2*
python	Python interpreter, *bm_threading.py (from Google's Unladen-Swallow [2] suite)*
python_opt	Variant of python with interpreter optimizations

Table 1. Workloads used to drive our study.

conflict is defined as an external write request to a block that has been speculatively read or any external request to a speculatively-written block. Such conflicts invoke the contention management policy, described below. This work uses OneTM [4] as a backing mechanism for transactions that overflow the local cache hierarchy. Our baseline also includes a read-only permissions-only cache [4] to reduce the frequency with which overflows occur. On the workloads analyzed in this work, the permissions-only cache essentially eliminates cache overflows entirely.

Contention management. When a conflict occurs, the processor either: (1) aborts the local speculation, (2) aborts the remote speculation, or (3) stalls the remote speculation, taking care to ensure that such stalling will not cause deadlock. Our baseline uses the "oldest transaction wins" timestamp-based conflict resolution policy. Prior studies [6, 33] and our own experimental reconfirmation have found that this policy generally performs the same or better than other policies, ensures timely forward progress, and is fairly robust across a range of workloads.

Version management. To support rollback of speculation to pre-speculative state, the baseline system uses a "clean-to-L2" approach similar to that used in prior work (*e.g.*, [5, 21]). On the first speculative write to a non-speculatively dirty block, the old value of the block is first written back ("cleaned") to the second-level (L2) cache. On an abort, the system flash-invalidates all speculatively-written blocks. The pre-speculative values of such blocks will be refetched from the lower levels of the memory hierarchy as needed via ordinary cache misses.

3. Remaining HTM Performance Challenges

We evaluate the performance of the baseline system on a variety of workloads that stress the performance of speculation (the details of these workloads are given in Table 1). The STAMP benchmark suite [22] is a set of transactional memory benchmarks that for the most part use coarse-grained transactions, with the intent of simulating the practices of naive programmers. We run all workloads in the suite except `bayes`, from which we could not extract useful conclusions due to high runtime variability. The benchmark `labyrinth` includes a code snippet wherein a large shared grid is copied privately within a transaction and then released early from conflict detection, as the algorithm itself detects conflicts on the grid at the semantic level. To achieve the same behavior without early release (a mechanism that our system does not provide), we modified the code to perform the grid copy before entering the transaction.

STAMP includes a hashtable that defaults to be non-resizable. For all workloads that use this hashtable we also run a second variant in which the hashtable is configured via STAMP's compile-time flags to automatically resize as needed. The resizable variants reflect the performance of using standard library implementations of hashtables in Java and C++, which are generally resizable by default. These variants have "`-sz`" appended to their names.

In addition to analyzing STAMP, we created a transactionalized version of the standard Python interpreter implementation, `python`. This workload is a challenging case for speculation: although the interpreter supports threading, this threading is explicitly designed for responsive graphical user interfaces and I/O events—not for supporting parallel execution on multicores. In fact, threads synchronize using a global interpreter lock (GIL). Although threads may perform selected system calls without holding the GIL, threads may interpret bytecodes only while holding the GIL. Thus, in the absence of speculation, bytecode interpretation is completely serialized by the GIL. By applying speculative lock elision to the GIL, we are attempting to extract parallelism from this complex workload that was written assuming sequential execution.

Figure 3 shows that the performance of the baseline system on the above-described workloads varies significantly. (The workload variants with "`_opt`" suffixes are described below.) As the execution breakdown presented in Figure 4 indicates, the primary bottleneck to scalability on many workloads is conflicts.[3] The goal of this section is to (1) quantify the impact that straightforward software restructurings can have on reducing these conflicts and (2) characterize the conflicts that remain after such restructurings.

Opportunities for software restructurings. We find several opportunities for straightforward software restructurings. First, `python` contains global variables that are conceptually thread-private but were not made so due to the assumption that only one thread would be operating on them at a time. We trivially made these variables thread-private using the C "`__thread`" variable annotation supported by GCC and other compilers. Second, `intruder` dequeues work from one highly contended queue and enqueues work onto another highly contended queue; we split these queues to be thread-private. Third, both `intruder` and `vacation` have aborts due to rebalancing operations of a red-black tree used to implement a map interface. We replaced the tree implementation with STAMP's hashtable implementation. The conflicts in `yada` are due to irregular traversals of a shared mesh; we have not found a way to reduce these conflicts short of restructuring the algorithm, which is beyond the scope of straightforward software restructuring.

On the graphs, the `_opt` variants of the above workloads have the above software restructurings applied. An examination of the

[3] Exceptions are `labyrinth`, in which the algorithm induces load imbalance, and `ssca2`, which has poor caching behavior.

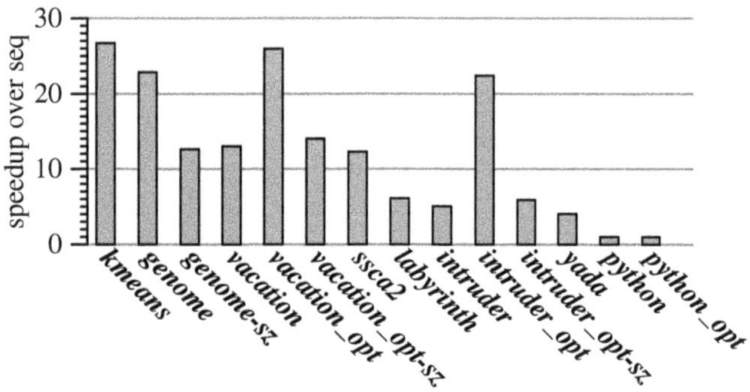

Figure 3. Scalability of workloads on baseline system before and after applying software optimizations. The optimizations performed to obtain the variant workloads are detailed in Table 1.

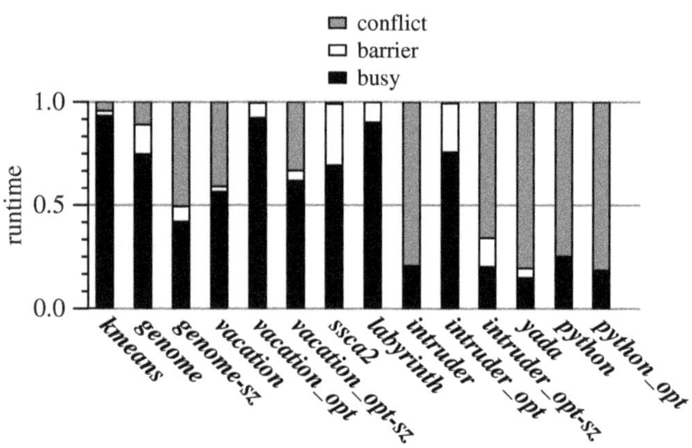

Figure 4. Time breakdown of workloads on the baseline system before and after applying software optimizations. The "busy" segment represents all time spent not stalled on synchronization. The "barrier" segment represents time stalled at a barrier, an indicator of load imbalance. The "conflict" segment represents time spent either stalled by another processor or doing work in a transaction that is ultimately aborted.

scalability of these variants (Figure 3) shows first that these simple changes have a dramatic effect on the behavior of `intruder_opt` and `vacation_opt`, increasing scalability from 5x and 13x respectively to over 20x in both cases. For the other variants, however, the picture is less rosy: the software changes do not improve scalability, and Figure 4 indicates that these workloads remain abort-bound even after elimination of the most obvious sources of conflicts.

Characterizing remaining conflicts. The `python_opt` workload conflicts on reference counts of shared objects; `vacation_opt-sz`, `intruder_opt-sz`, and `genome-sz` conflict on the occupancy field that the resizable hashtable increments on every insert to determine when to resize; and as mentioned above, `yada` conflicts on mesh operations. We note that except for `yada`, all of the remaining conflicts occur on operations that are auxiliary to the main computation of the workload. Unfortunately, these conflicts are less amenable to straightforward software restructuring (for example, distributing reference counts per-thread would result in high storage and performance overheads). Instead of exploring more sophisticated software modifications, we next explore extending hardware to transparently eliminate the performance impact of such conflicts.

4. Repair via Symbolic Tracking

Our approach to the problem of eliminating conflicts on auxiliary data exploits a few key properties of the operations on such data. First, the control flow in which this data is involved is often highly biased in one direction and relatively insensitive to the exact value of the data (for example, most hashtable inserts do not cause resizes in a well-configured hashtable). This fact implies that remote updates to auxiliary data will often leave the control flow of a transaction unaffected, changing only the output values of that transaction that are dependent on the variable in question. Second, the amount of computation performed on auxiliary data is often small relative to the computation of the transaction as a whole, *i.e.* the dependent slice of the data is much smaller than the dataflow graph of the entire transaction.

Together, these facts suggest an approach that eschews rollback in favor of a lighter-weight *selective repair*. By maintaining a record of the computation performed on auxiliary data, a transaction can allow conflicts to occur on this data without rolling back. As part of the commit process, the transaction repairs output state by atomically reacquiring all locations that have been lost and reperforming the computation dependent on those locations using current architectural values as input. As long as changes in values do not result in control flow changes, the output thus produced will be the same as if the transaction had executed using those input values in the first place.

Hardware support for such selective repair has been proposed in various contexts in the form of *instruction-based replay* [8, 11, 17, 18, 32, 35]. The proposal most relevant in our context is ReSlice [32]. Within the context of thread-level speculation, ReSlice tracks the slice of instructions dependent on a load that is likely to result in a conflict, recording this slice in an instruction buffer. At commit, ReSlice sequentially re-executes the dependent slice of all loads whose input value has changed. As long as all branch outcomes are the same (*i.e.*, control flow is unchanged) and no memory dependences have changed, such replay can successfully repair speculation, allowing it to commit. Such instruction-based replay has additionally been used for latency-tolerant checkpoint-based micro-architectures [17, 35], and some schemes are able to repair limited control-flow changes as well [3, 18].

We build upon this prior work, but we take an alternative approach to repair that is based on *symbolic tracking*. Rather than maintaining the dependent instruction slice of a conflicting load directly, our proposal tracks the symbolic relationships between inputs and outputs. As transactions execute, values are tagged with a symbolic representation of the computation that produced that value. For example, if the processor loads a value and then increments it twice, the processor tracks information indicating that it can calculate the final value by adding two to whatever value the load eventually takes. Such *symbolic values* propagate through registers and memory, while conditional operations result in constraints that the symbolic value must satisfy at the time of commit. If computation that is too complex to track symbolically occurs on a given input, the system constrains that input to remain equal to its original value when reacquired. In this case, our approach still provides performance gains due to an implicit use of lazy [6, 33, 39] and value-based [25, 37] conflict detection, as discussed in Section 5.3. Figure 2(a) gives a high-level example of symbolic tracking.

One appealing aspect of this approach is that the processor collapses the computation necessary to transform inputs to outputs during execution. The degree to which computation can be collapsed and the complexity of doing so, however, is dependent on the nature of computation being tracked. By choosing what types of computation to symbolically track, a system designer can make an informed tradeoff between complexity and generality. The next section presents RetCon, an instantiation of symbolic tracking tailored to fit the needs of auxilary data that we have observed.

5. RetCon

This section describes RetCon, an instantiation of symbolic tracking that optimizes for design simplicity by restricting the type of computation that it can track symbolically. RetCon restricts operations to have at most one symbolic input and tracks only data (not memory addresses) symbolically. These restrictions allow RetCon to maintain symbolic information efficiently and admit a streamlined commit process. We describe the high-level RetCon algorithm below, followed by a discussion of operational details, implementation optimizations, and benefits that RetCon provides beyond the ability to repair conflicts on auxiliary data.

Key to RetCon are the concepts of *symbolic locations*, *symbolic values*, and *symbolic constraints*. A symbolic location is a memory address that RetCon decides to track symbolically (determined via a predictor trained by past history of conflicts). The symbolic value of a register or memory location is a representation of the computation that was performed to calculate the concrete value of that location. As an example, the symbolic value of the register output of the first load to symbolic location *A* would be "[*A*]". Finally, symbolic constraints are a combination of a symbolic value, a boolean operator, and a constant. An *equality constraint* is a special type of constraint that simply specifies that a given symbolic location must be equal to the value first read for that location by the transaction.

Initiating symbolic tracking. During transaction execution, loads and stores not involved with symbolic repair use the conflict detection mechanism of the underlying TM system. A *symbolic load*, a load that reads from a symbolic location, initiates symbolic tracking of dependent operations by associating a symbolic value with the load's output register (recorded in the symbolic register file, described in Figure 5). The value written to the register file by a symbolic load is the processor's best-guess value for the location (*i.e.*, the architectural value at the time or a value prediction [26, 27, 37]) and execution continues based on that concrete value. The first load to a symbolic location also records the *initial concrete value* of the location (recorded in the *initial value buffer*, described in Figure 5). A load to a symbolic location does *not* set the read bit in the cache, thus allowing the block to be stolen away without triggering a conflict.

Execution with symbolic tracking. Transaction execution is determined entirely by the concrete values, but symbolic values are tracked and propagated from instruction to instruction. If an instruction's specific operation is one that can be tracked symbolically, the symbolic input is propagated to the symbolic value output. The processor performs as much computation as it can during this propagation. As an example, if a register with concrete value 5 and symbolic value "[*A*]+7" is used as input to an increment instruction, the output register's concrete value would be 6 and its symbolic value would be "[*A*]+8".

Symbolic tracking through memory. When writing a register with a symbolic value to memory, both the concrete and symbolic values are recorded and propagated to subsequent loads (using the *symbolic store buffer*, described in Figure 5). Correspondingly, all loads check the symbolic store buffer (as well as the initial value buffer, as described above) in parallel with the data cache. When a load forwards from a store that has a symbolic value, it copies that symbolic value (rather than initializing its symbolic value to the

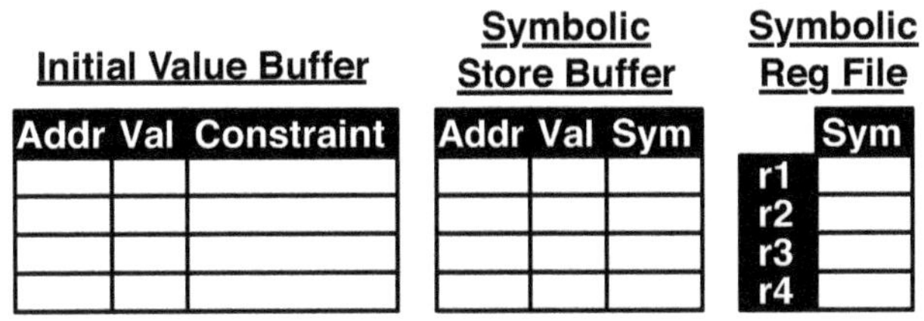

Figure 5. RetCon structures. The **initial value buffer** is a cache-like structure indexed by data address. Each entry contains the address tag bits, the initial concrete value of the symbolic memory location, and the symbolic constraints associated with that memory location (if any). The **symbolic store buffer** records symbolically-tracked stores. It is indexed by data address and accessed like a conventional cache-like unordered store buffer. Each entry contains the address tag bits, the store's concrete value, and the store's symbolic value (if any). The **symbolic register file** records the current symbolic value (if any) for each register. The value recorded in the traditional register file is the concrete value of each register, which is used to guide execution.

address of the store). In essence, RetCon collapses all store-load forwarding during execution. Figure 6 contains a flowchart of the operation of loads and stores in RetCon.

Symbolic control-flow constraints. If the source register of a branch has a symbolic value, RetCon adds a symbolic constraint to capture the necessary condition to ensure consistent control flow. For example, a taken branch based on a register with symbolic value "[*A*]+1" is greater than 5 would generate the constraint: "[*A*]+1>5" or, simplified, "[*A*]>4". Non-taken branches record the negation of the branch condition ("[*A*]<=4" in this case). The constraint is recorded in the initial value buffer entry corresponding to the root memory location of the symbolic value.

Equality constraints. An equality constraint is set whenever a symbolic input is used in a way that cannot be tracked symbolically, thus ensuring that any difference in the initial value and final value will result in an abort. Equality constraints are introduced when symbolic values are supplied as inputs to (1) complicated arithmetic operations the implementation has chosen not to track symbolically (*e.g.*, integer divide) or (2) the address calculation of loads or stores (but, critically, not the data input of store instructions). In addition, if an operation has multiple symbolic values as inputs, equality constraints are set on all but one to maintain the invariant that all operations have at most one symbolic input.

Pre-commit repair. As part of the commit process, the system enforces symbolic constraints by re-loading the *final concrete value* for each symbolic location. Symbolic constraints are evaluated using this final concrete value to ensure that the control flow remains valid. Next, RetCon generates the final concrete values for each symbolic register value and symbolic memory value (*i.e.*, stores with symbolic data input register values). This involves updating the concrete value in the register file and writing concrete values into the data cache. To ensure atomicity during the repair process, all loads and stores set the read/written bits in the cache and conflict detection reverts to that of the baseline system (described in Section 2). Once repair has completed, the normal baseline transaction commit commences. Figure 7 describes the repair algorithm in detail, and Figure 8 presents a step-by-step example of RetCon's operation.

5.1 Operational Details

The above text assumes word-granularity aligned memory operations and conditionals that operate directly on register values. However, RetCon must handle features from real-world architectures

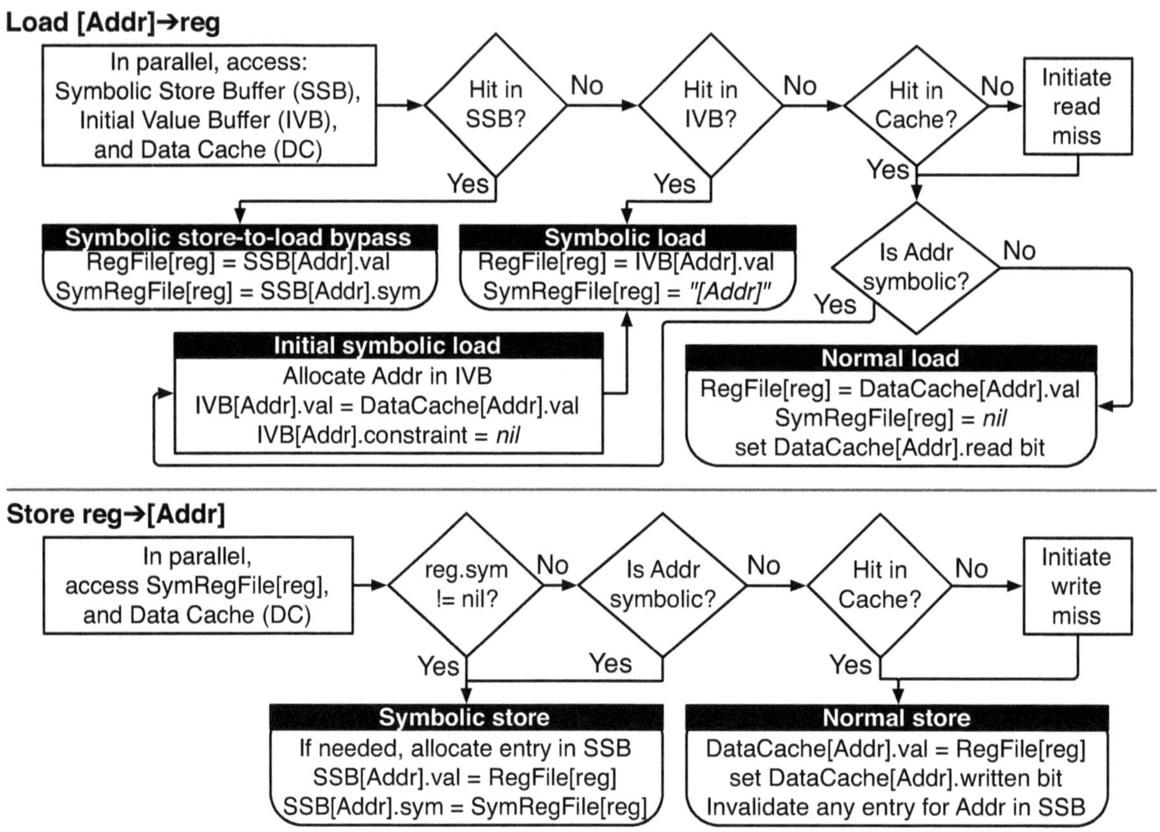

Figure 6. RetCon memory operation flowchart.

RetCon Pre-Commit Process

Step #1. Reacquire all lost blocks to obtain final concrete values, record them in the initial value buffer, and check that all control-flow constraints are satisfied by the current values of the blocks:

```
foreach Address A in Initial Value Buffer (IVB):
  if not already in cache, obtain read permission to A
  set DataCache[A].read bit
  IVB[A].value <- DataCache[A].value
  if new value does not satisfy IVB[A].constraint:
    abort
```

Step #2. Update memory and register state based on the values in the initial value buffer (which as of step #1 above, now contains the final concrete values):

```
foreach Address A in Symbolic Store Buffer (SSB):
  if not already in cache, obtain write permission to A
  set DataCache[A].written bit
  if SSB[A].sym == nil:
    DataCache[A].value <- SSB[A].value
  else:
    DataCache[A].value <- SSB[A].sym evaluated with value from Initial Value Buffer (IVB)

foreach Register R in Symbolic Register File (SRF):
  if SRF[R].sym != nil:
      RF[R].value <- SRF[R].sym evaluated with value from Initial Value Buffer (IVB)
```

Figure 7. RetCon pre-commit repair algorithm. To ensure atomicity of the commit process, the speculatively read/written bits are set when reacquiring lost blocks and before writing values into the data cache. If a conflict occurs during this pre-commit process, the baseline conflict management logic is invoked. Once the above repair has completed, the normal baseline transactional commit commences.

Figure 8. Example of RETCON operation. This diagram shows the symbolic execution and commit operations of a processor due to block A that gets stolen away mid-transaction. The load to register r1 at time ❶ initiates symbolic execution, populates the initial value buffer and the symbolic and concrete register files for r1; note that the read bit in the cache is not set. The symbolic data flows to r2 via the register file at time ❷, which in turn introduces a constraint for A at time ❸. At time ❹, r2 is stored in address B, causing it to be tracked in the symbolic store buffer. The load from B at ❺ forwards from the symbolic store buffer. Also at this time, A is removed from the cache due to a remote request; no conflict is triggered because A's read bit was not set. At time ❻, register r1 is overwritten with a new offset. The branch at time ❼ updates the initial value buffer with an additional constraint on A. At time ❽, the symbolic store to the symbolically tracked address A introduces another store buffer entry. The store to block B at time ❾ is non-symbolic, hence B's entry is invalidated in the symbolic store buffer and the store value is written speculatively into the cache. The commit process begins at time ❿ by fetching A into the cache speculatively, verifying that the new value of A (6) still satisfies the constraint and computing the new value to be stored to A in the symbolic store buffer. In the final step of the commit process, r1's concrete value is written back into the register file and store to A is drained from the store buffer to the cache, and any speculative bits in the cache are flash-cleared.

Parameter	Value
Processor	32 in-order x86 cores, 1 IPC
L1 cache	64 KB, 4-way set associative, 64B blocks, 1-cycle hit latency
L2 cache	Private, 1MB, 4-way set associative, 64B blocks, 10-cycle hit latency
Memory	100-cycle DRAM lookup latency
Permissions-only cache	4KB, 4-way set associative, read-only
Coherence	Directory-based protocol, 20-cycle hop latency
RETCON structures	8-entry initial value buffer, 8-entry constraint buffer, 32-entry symbolic store buffer
RETCON predictor	512-entry table, 8-bit saturating counters, 1:100 up/down training ratio

Table 2. Simulated machine configuration.

such as condition codes, sub-word memory operations and unaligned memory operations. Furthermore, RETCON must prevent transactions operating on potentially-inconsistent data from raising spurious exceptions or entering infinite loops.

To handle condition codes, each condition code register is extended with a symbolic constraint field. When an arithmetic operation with a symbolically-tracked input updates a condition code register, the symbolic constraint of the condition code is updated to reflect the constraint required for that condition code to retain the same value. The form of the constraint depends on the semantics of the condition code. For example, for the "equal-to-zero" condition code, the constraint operator is one of equality if the condition code is set to true and one of inequality if the condition code is set false. When a conditional operation is performed on a condition code being tracked symbolically, the condition code's constraint is added as a constraint on its root address.

To handle sub-word operations, RETCON adds a size field to symbolic values. If store-load communication becomes too complex (*e.g.*, an 8-byte load forwards from two 4-byte stores or a 4-byte store partially overwrites an 8-byte symbolic load), RETCON sets equality constraints on the relevant inputs. Similarly, RETCON treats unaligned memory operations as computation that cannot be tracked symbolically, adding equality constraints to the input word(s) of the operation.

RETCON's approach to the inconsistent data problem is similar to that taken by prior proposals [30]. When a transaction that has lost a block raises an exception, the hardware restarts the transaction with RETCON disabled. To prevent transactions from entering infinite loops due to inconsistent data, RETCON periodically reacquires stolen blocks and validates constraints.

5.2 Implementation Optimizations

The basic structures and operations described above admit several optimizations, which we describe below.

Maintenance of initial value buffer entries at cache-block granularity. To avoid reacquiring a stolen block each time a byte in the block is accessed for the first time, the initial value buffer maintains entries at cache-block granularity. A symbolic load starts symbolic tracking of the entire block. Constraints are maintained by a separate address-indexed and word-granularity buffer.

Compressed representation of equality constraints. RETCON represents equality constraints using per-byte "equality bits" added to entries in the initial value buffer. This optimization works synergistically with the previous one as it reduces pressure on the constraint buffer.

Avoidance of upgrade misses during pre-commit. As described thus far, during the commit process RETCON issues two misses for blocks that it has symbolically read and written (first to acquire the block via a read to check constraints followed by an upgrade miss when writing the block into the cache). To avoid this second miss, RETCON includes per-block written bits on initial value buffer entries. If the written bit is set, the block is acquired with write permission during the initial precommit phase.

Efficient representation of symbolic computation. Limiting the type of computation that can be symbolically tracked to be only additions and subtractions allows optimization of symbolic representations [28]. RETCON (1) tracks symbolic values succintly as "`(input_address, increment)`" pairs, (2) collapses all arithmetic computation on symbolic values to cumulative increments, and (3) represents constraints by succinct intervals. RETCON precisely represents any number of constraints $(\leq, <, =, >, \geq)$ by the *most restrictive interval* bounding the symbolic value. Similarly, RETCON compactly represents any number of not-equal-to constraints—at the cost of some loss of precision—by tracking the interval in which the value cannot reside.

5.3 Other Benefits of RETCON

Although the purpose of RETCON is to enable recovery from remotely-changed inputs, its potential benefits extend further. First, RETCON's property of selectively delaying conflict resolution until transaction commit provides a form of lazy conflict detection [12, 23]; prior work [33, 38, 39] has shown that this strategy can enhance concurrency by allowing readers to commit before a conflicting writer. Second, RETCON's value-based detection of conflicts at a sub-block granularity eliminates conflicts due to false sharing [19] and silent sharing [20] in a similar manner to prior proposals on value-based conflict detection [25, 37]. We analyze the impact of these benefits in Section 6.2.

Researchers have also proposed the usage of speculative values in order to avoid conflicts on true sharing, for example by forwarding values from in-progress transanctions [30] or by predicting values [9, 26, 27, 36]. RETCON does not currently incorporate speculative value forwarding, but it is well-suited to do so. By generating constraints throughout execution and checking that the current architectural value satisfies all generated constraints at commit, RETCON ensures correctness regardless of the source of the value used during execution (*e.g.*, the current architectural value, a forwarded value from an in-progress transaction, or a predicted value).

6. Experimental Evaluation

Our experimental evaluation demonstrates RETCON's ability to eliminate the performance impact of conflicts due to auxiliary data and analyzes the resulting workload scalability improvements. We further examine the amount of state required by RETCON to achieve these results and explore the nature of conflicts that RETCON is unable to repair to give insight on future directions.

6.1 Methodology

As discussed in Section 5.3, RETCON provides multiple benefits over the baseline HTM system described in Section 2 (denoted as *eager* on the graphs): in addition to admitting transaction commits wherein a value read has been changed remotely, RETCON can

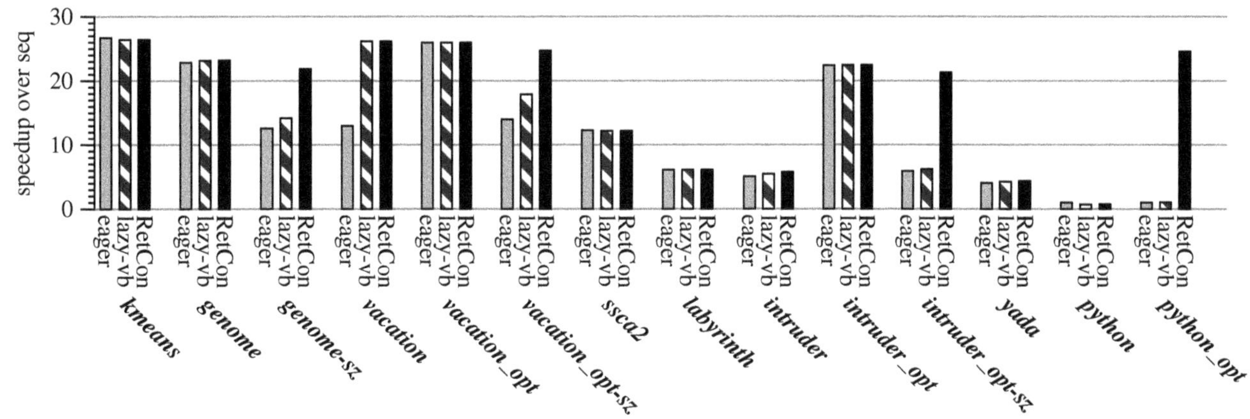

Figure 9. Scalability over sequential execution.

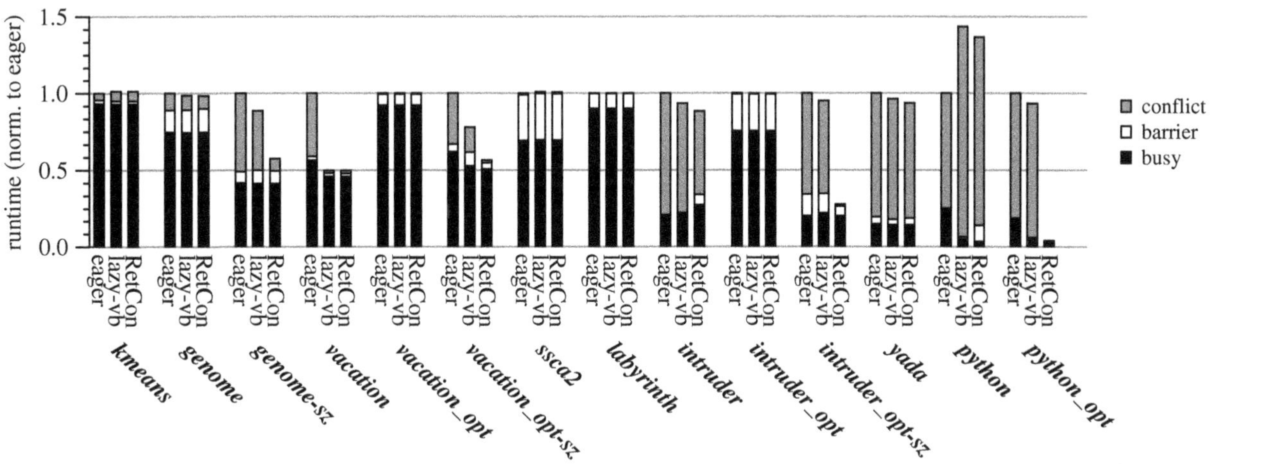

Figure 10. Breakdown of execution time.

reduce conflicts versus the baseline system due to its selective use of laziness and value-based conflict detection. To provide insight into the sources of RETCON's performance gains, we also evaluate a limited variant of RETCON in which values read are not allowed to change: instead, all reads are checked to have the same value at commit (at a precise byte granularity). This RETCON variant, which we refer to as *lazy-vb*, captures commits due to laziness and false/silent sharing but does not allow commits where a value read has been changed remotely.

We model RETCON and our baseline transactional memory implementation (Section 2) using a full-system simulator based on the publicly-available FeS_2 simulator [1], but with further modifications. Our simulator models a 32-processor x86-64 multiprocessor with memory system parameters set to approximate a modern multicore (Table 2). All of our simulated configurations use the "clean-to-L2" version management scheme described in Section 2. The version of RETCON that we evaluate employs the optimizations discussed in Section 5.2. We limit RETCON to support tracking at most eight cache blocks symbolically and maintaining constraints on up to eight word-granularity addresses. Vagaries of our simulator prevented us from easily bounding the size of the word-granularity symbolic store buffer; we analyze this number below, finding that a 32-entry buffer would be sufficient. We configure RETCON's commit-time repair process to reacquire all lost blocks in parallel and reperform stores serially after all blocks have been reacquired; Section 6.3 analyzes the impact of an alternative configuration in which blocks are reacquired serially.

RETCON uses a predictor to determine which data blocks invoke value-based and symbolic tracking. This predictor is an untagged table of 512 eight-bit saturating counters indexed by nine low-order bits of the data block address. The predictor learns based on observed conflicts. To avoid elongating the amount of time that is spent in transactions that will eventually abort, a violated constraint causes the predictor to train down aggressively, requiring the observation of 100 conflicts on that block before attempting symbolic tracking on that block again.

6.2 Impact of RETCON on Performance

Figure 9 presents workload scalability over sequential execution when run under the three configurations. In several cases, the ability of RETCON to repair conflicts changes the qualitative behavior of the workload. Most significantly, RETCON tranforms `python_opt` from a workload that has no scaling for the *lazy-vb* configuration to one that has near-linear scaling (25x on 32 cores) by eliminating the performance impact of reference counter updates. Similarly, RETCON's ability to resolve conflicts on hashtable occupancy field updates without rollbacks changes the characteristics of `genome-sz` (50% speedup over *lazy-vb* by converting a 14x speedup over the baseline into a 21x speedup), `intruder_opt-sz` (243% speedup over *lazy-vb* by converting a 6x speedup into a 21x speedup), and `vacation_opt-sz` (38% speedup over *lazy-vb* by converting a 18x

Application	blocks lost	blocks tracked	symbolic registers	private stores	constr. addrs.	commit cycles	commit stall %	input changed %	slice size
kmeans	0.1 (2.0)	0.6 (3.0)	0.0 (1.0)	1.0 (17.0)	0.0 (0.0)	10.6	2.5	0.0	0.0 (0.0)
genome	0.0 (5.0)	2.9 (8.0)	0.2 (3.0)	0.2 (19.0)	1.2 (8.0)	2.6	0.1	0.9	3.0 (3.0)
genome-sz	0.0 (7.0)	3.9 (8.0)	0.4 (2.0)	0.3 (22.0)	1.8 (8.0)	28.4	0.9	1.2	8.8 (60.0)
vacation	0.7 (3.0)	3.3 (8.0)	0.0 (2.0)	0.2 (7.0)	3.6 (8.0)	52.9	0.7	0.0	6.0 (9.0)
vacation_opt	0.0 (0.0)	0.0 (1.0)	0.0 (1.0)	0.0 (0.0)	0.0 (1.0)	1.0	0.1	0.0	0.0 (0.0)
vacation_opt-sz	0.6 (3.0)	1.7 (5.0)	0.9 (1.0)	0.1 (3.0)	0.1 (6.0)	40.8	2.1	2.2	6.2 (15.0)
labyrinth	0.0 (1.0)	0.1 (1.0)	0.0 (0.0)	0.0 (1.0)	0.0 (3.0)	1.2	0.1	0.0	0.0 (0.0)
intruder	0.3 (6.0)	2.9 (8.0)	0.2 (2.0)	0.6 (15.0)	1.6 (8.0)	29.0	1.5	3.6	3.3 (5.0)
intruder_opt	0.0 (1.0)	0.2 (3.0)	0.0 (1.0)	0.0 (6.0)	0.0 (5.0)	1.1	0.2	0.0	0.0 (0.0)
intruder_opt-sz	0.2 (1.0)	0.4 (3.0)	0.2 (2.0)	0.2 (6.0)	0.2 (6.0)	22.1	3.2	16.6	5.0 (5.0)
yada	0.2 (6.0)	2.2 (8.0)	0.3 (2.0)	1.3 (35.0)	1.1 (8.0)	53.3	0.3	0.1	11.5 (30.0)
python	5.6 (8.0)	8.0 (8.0)	0.0 (1.0)	7.6 (12.0)	7.9 (8.0)	99.2	0.2	42.9	127.5 (230.0)
python_opt	5.1 (8.0)	5.4 (8.0)	0.0 (0.0)	5.9 (10.0)	7.2 (8.0)	319.5	0.8	89.8	199.3 (230.0)

Table 3. RETCON structure utilization and pre-commit runtime overhead. The columns, in order, show the average and maximum (in parentheses) number of *(a)* 64B blocks stolen away during a transaction, *(b)* initial value buffer entries, *(c)* symbolic registers repaired at commit, *(d)* symbolic stores performed at commit, *(e)* symbolic constraints to be checked at commit, *(f)* stall cycles during the pre-commit repair process, *(g)* percentage of transaction execution that is spent in pre-commit repair, *(h)* percentage of committed transactions that had a remotely-changed input, and *(i)* instructions in a dependent slice (*i.e.*, the number of instructions that would need to be buffered and replayed in an instruction replay-based scheme).

speedup into a 25x speedup). Whereas without RETCON the performance of these workloads is significantly worse than the corresponding variants with a fixed-size hashtable, the addition of RETCON makes them insensitive to whether the hashtable is fixed-size or resizable.

To provide insight into the performance improvements of RETCON, Figure 10 presents a breakdown of execution time. We observe that RETCON is able to completely eliminate time spent in conflicts on several workloads that are abort-bound on the baseline system. RETCON can also have secondary effects of reducing load imbalance (*e.g.*, `intruder_opt-sz`) and/or reducing contention in the memory system (the source of the reduction in busy time in `vacation_opt-sz` and `python_opt`).

Analysis of the relative performance of RETCON and *lazy-vb* shows that in most cases RETCON's performance gains come from its ability to repair remotely-changed inputs rather than its usage of lazy value-based conflict detection and false/silent sharing. One exception is `vacation`; further investigation revealed that the increase in performance on this workload is due to laziness. To test RETCON's ability to eliminate conflicts due to false sharing we ran an experiment on `raytrace`, a benchmark from the SPLASH2 suite [40] with a well-known instance of false sharing [23]; RETCON increased speedup over sequential execution from 14x to 21x on 32 cores. These results point to RETCON's ability to provide performance benefits beyond eliminating the negative impact of auxiliary data conflicts.

6.3 RETCON Implementation Considerations

State required by RETCON. Table 3 shows that the amount of state that RETCON tracks symbolically is relatively small. In fact, the initial value buffer ("blocks tracked" column) and constraint buffers ("const. addrs." column) fill on only half the workloads. In addition, the "private stores" column indicates that a 32-entry symbolic store buffer would be sufficient to hold virtually all the private stores of these workloads. We performed experiments with larger buffers (not shown), and all but one of our workloads (`python_opt`) were insensitive to increased buffering. With 16-entry initial value buffer and constraint buffers, the speedup obtained on `python_opt` increased marginally from 25x to 26x, and remained at this value even with 1024-entry buffers. Even with such large buffers the average number of blocks lost remained below 8 in all workloads except for the unmodified `python`, which averaged 11 blocks lost.

RETCON pre-commit process. The "blocks lost" column of Table 3 shows that the number of blocks lost during execution of a transaction is in general quite small on our workloads. In fact, only `python` and `python_opt` lose more than one block per transaction on average. The characteristics of the number of stores that must be reperformed prior to commit (the "private stores" column) are qualitatively similar. As a result, the average number of cycles that a transaction spends in the pre-commit process is quite small (the "commit cycles" column). In fact, the time spent in the pre-commit process is under 1% of total transaction execution time on all but four of our workloads and under 4% on all workloads (the "commit stall %" column). To study the sensitivity of this result to bandwidth with which lost blocks are reacquired, we ran a configuration that conservatively reacquired lost blocks serially (not shown). The only change was a decrease in the performance of `python_opt` from 25x to 20x.

6.4 Analyzing the Limitations of RETCON

As Figure 9 and Figure 10 show, there are three workloads with significant conflicts that RETCON does not greatly affect: the unmodified variants of `intruder`, `yada`, and `python`. The nominal reason that RETCON cannot help on these workloads is that each of these workloads experiences conflicts due to multiple threads simultaneously enqueueing and dequeueing from shared lists. As the variables on which there is contention are used to index into memory (*e.g.*, the pointer to the list head), RETCON is not able to repair these conflicts.

However, these workloads also serve as examples that a repair-based approach is not always the right one to take. In each of these cases, the data elements being operated on are central to the dataflow of the entire transaction. Therefore, a repair that involves selecting a different list element at commit than one previously selected during execution would likely involve redoing most of the work of the transaction, resulting in little savings over a full abort. In such cases, an approach based on forwarding speculative values (*e.g.*, the pointer to the head of the queue in `intruder`) such as dependence-aware transactional memory (DATM) [30] may be more useful. As discussed in Section 5.3, integrating techniques based on communication of speculative values into RETCON is a potential area of future work.

7. Related Work

Several proposals have focused on mitigating the performance limitations caused by conflicts in optimistic concurrency mechanisms such as transactional memory [16], speculative locking [21, 29], or thread-level speculation [9, 13, 34, 36]. Bobba *et al.* [6] examine the performance pathologies present in conflict resolution schemes, including eager or lazy conflict detection [12, 23, 33], and recent work proposes mixed eager/lazy strategies [33, 38, 39]. Value-based conflict detection has been used in the context of transactional memory for avoiding conflicts due to false sharing [37] as well as for compatibility with library code [25].

Researchers have proposed the use of speculative values to avoid conflicts due to true sharing. Dependence-aware transactional memory (DATM) [30] forwards speculatively written data between transactions. A globally enforced commit order guarantees atomicity and forward progress. DATM prevents aborts due to conflicts when transactions access shared data acyclically (such as incrementing a shared counter once), but aborts when there are repeated accesses to shared data between transactions (see Figure 2). Other proposals have explored value prediction in the context of thread-level speculation and transactional memory [9, 26, 27, 36].

Proposals such as open nested transactions [7, 12, 24], abstract nested transactions [14], and transactional boosting [15] seek to increase concurrency by providing programming abstractions. RETCON differs from these proposals by trading off generality for programmer transparency.

RETCON is inspired by proposals for repair via selective instruction replay [8, 11, 17, 18, 32, 35]. The tradeoffs in symbolic tracking versus instruction slicing are efficiency of representation vs. generality of recomputation. On the side of efficiency, a long transaction might, for example, perform many hashtable inserts or reference count updates; RetCon would perform a constant amount of recomputation vs. the linear amount of state tracked and computation reperformed by an instruction replay-based scheme. In contrast, an instruction replay-based scheme can support replay of more complex types of computation (*e.g.*, ReSlice allows memory addresses to change in re-execution as long as the new address does not change the dataflow of the slice).

Finally, Riley and Zilles [31] explore software restructuring and observe aborts due to false conflicts when studying the behavior of the `PyPy` python interpreter with transactional memory. One key difference in the tasks of parallelizing `PyPy` and parallelizing standard `python` is that `PyPy` uses a conservative garbage collector and thus does not raise the problem of conflicts on reference counts.

8. Conclusions

This work proposes RETCON, a mechanism for hardware transactional memory that allows transactions to lose data during execution and transparently repairs the effects of remote modifications at commit. RETCON uses symbolic tracking of the relationships between inputs and outputs to achieve repair without replay. Our quantitative results indicate that RETCON is able to eliminate the performance impact of conflicts on auxiliary data. When combined with simple software restructurings, this elimination of auxiliary data as a source of performance loss results in speedups of 40% or more on several workloads including a 25x speedup on `python`, a complex program that was never intended to be run in parallel. In the future we plan to investigate the integration of RETCON with mechanisms that use speculative value forwarding such as transactional value prediction and dependence-aware transactional memory to broaden the scope of conflicts that RETCON eliminates.

References

[1] The FeS2 simulator. URL `http://fes2.cs.uiuc.edu/acknowledgements.html`.

[2] The Unladen-Swallow Benchmark Suite. URL `http://code.google.com/p/unladen-swallow/wiki/Benchmarks`.

[3] A. S. Al-Zawawi, V. K. Reddy, E. Rotenberg, and H. H. Akkary. Transparent Control Independence (TCI). In *Proceedings of the 34th Annual International Symposium on Computer Architecture*, June 2007.

[4] C. Blundell, J. Devietti, E. C. Lewis, and M. M. K. Martin. Making the Fast Case Common and the Uncommon Case Simple in Unbounded Transactional Memory. In *Proceedings of the 34th Annual International Symposium on Computer Architecture*, June 2007.

[5] C. Blundell, M. M. K. Martin, and T. Wenisch. InvisiFence: Performance-Transparent Memory Ordering in Conventional Multiprocessors. In *Proceedings of the 36th Annual International Symposium on Computer Architecture*, June 2009.

[6] J. Bobba, K. E. Moore, H. Volos, L. Yen, M. D. Hill, M. M. Swift, and D. A. Wood. Performance Pathologies in Hardware Transactional Memory. In *Proceedings of the 34th Annual International Symposium on Computer Architecture*, June 2007.

[7] B. D. Carlstrom, A. MacDonald, H. Chafi, J. Chung, C. C. Minh, C. Kozyrakis, and K. Olukotun. The Atomos Transactional Programming Language. In *Proceedings of the SIGPLAN 2006 Conference on Programming Language Design and Implementation*, June 2006.

[8] S. Chaudhry, R. Cypher, M. Ekman, M. Karlsson, A. Landin, S. Yip, H. Zeffer, and M. Tremblay. Simultaneous Speculative Threading: A Novel Pipeline Architecture Implemented in Sun's ROCK Processor. In *Proceedings of the 36th Annual International Symposium on Computer Architecture*, June 2009.

[9] M. Cintra and J. Torellas. Eliminating Squashes Through Learning Cross-Thread Violations in Speculative Parallelization for Multiprocessors. In *Proceedings of the Eighth Symposium on High-Performance Computer Architecture*, Feb. 2002.

[10] C. Click, Feb. 2009. URL `http://blogs.azulsystems.com/cliff/2009/02/and-now-some-hardware-transactional-memory-comments.html`.

[11] R. Desikan, S. Sethumadhavan, D. Burger, and S. W. Keckler. Scalable Selective Re-execution for EDGE Architectures. In *Proceedings of the 11th International Conference on Architectural Support for Programming Languages and Operating Systems*, Oct. 2004.

[12] L. Hammond, B. D. Carlstrom, V. Wong, B. Hertzberg, M. Chen, C. Kozyrakis, and K. Olukotun. Programming with Transactional Coherence and Consistency (TCC). In *Proceedings of the 11th International Conference on Architectural Support for Programming Languages and Operating Systems*, Oct. 2004.

[13] L. Hammond, M. Willey, and K. Olukotun. Data Speculation Support for a Chip Multiprocessor. In *Proceedings of the 8th International Conference on Architectural Support for Programming Languages and Operating Systems*, Oct. 1998.

[14] T. Harris and S. Stipic. Abstract Nested Transactions. In *Proceedings of the Second ACM SIGPLAN Workshop on Transactional Computing*, Aug. 2007.

[15] M. Herlihy and E. Koskinen. Transactional Boosting: A Methodology for Highly-Concurrent Transactional Objects. In *Proceedings of the 13th ACM SIGPLAN Symposium on Principles and Practice of Parallel Programming (PPOPP)*, 2008.

[16] M. Herlihy and J. E. B. Moss. Transactional Memory: Architectural Support for Lock-Free Data Structures. In *Proceedings of the 20th Annual International Symposium on Computer Architecture*, May 1993.

[17] A. D. Hilton, S. Nagarakatte, and A. Roth. iCFP: Tolerating All-Level Cache Misses in In-Order Processors. In *Proceedings of the 14th Symposium on High-Performance Computer Architecture*, Feb. 2008.

[18] A. D. Hilton and A. Roth. Ginger: Control Independence Using Tag Rewriting. In *Proceedings of the 34th Annual International Symposium on Computer Architecture*, June 2007.

[19] J. Huh, J. Chang, D. Burger, and G. S. Sohi. Coherence Decoupling: Making Use of Incoherence. In *Proceedings of the 11th International Conference on Architectural Support for Programming Languages and Operating Systems*, Oct. 2004.

[20] K. M. Lepak and M. H. Lipasti. Temporally Silent Stores. In *Proceedings of the 10th International Conference on Architectural Support for Programming Languages and Operating Systems*, Oct. 2002.

[21] J. F. Martinez and J. Torrellas. Speculative Synchronization: Applying Thread-Level Speculation to Explicitly Parallel Applications. In *Proceedings of the 10th International Conference on Architectural Support for Programming Languages and Operating Systems*, Oct. 2002.

[22] C. C. Minh, J. Chung, C. Kozyrakis, and K. Olukotun. STAMP: Stanford Transactional Applications for Multi-Processing. In *Proceedings of the IEEE International Symposium on Workload Characterization*, 2008.

[23] K. E. Moore, J. Bobba, M. J. Moravan, M. D. Hill, and D. A. Wood. LogTM: Log-based Transactional Memory. In *Proceedings of the 12th Symposium on High-Performance Computer Architecture*, Feb. 2006.

[24] M. J. Moravan, J. Bobba, K. E. Moore, L. Yen, M. D. Hill, B. Liblit, M. M. Swift, and D. A. Wood. Supporting Nested Transactional Memory in LogTM. In *Proceedings of the 12th International Conference on Architectural Support for Programming Languages and Operating Systems*, Oct. 2006.

[25] M. Olszewski, J. Cutler, and J. G. Steffan. JudoSTM: A Dynamic Binary Rewriting Approach to Software Transactional Memory. In *Proceedings of the International Conference on Parallel Architectures and Compilation Techniques*, 2007.

[26] S. M. Pant and G. T. Byrd. Limited Early Value Communication to Improve Performance of Transactional Memory. In *Proceedings of the 23rd International Conference on Supercomputing*, June 2009.

[27] S. M. Pant and G. T. Byrd. A Study of Conflicting Data in TM Programs and Methods to Increase Concurrency Using Value Prediction. In *Proceedings of the Sixth ACM Conference on Computing Frontiers*, May 2009.

[28] V. Petric, T. Sha, and A. Roth. RENO: A Rename-Based Instruction Optimizer. In *Proceedings of the 32nd Annual International Symposium on Computer Architecture*, June 2005.

[29] R. Rajwar and J. R. Goodman. Speculative Lock Elision: Enabling Highly Concurrent Multithreaded Execution. In *Proceedings of the 34th Annual IEEE/ACM International Symposium on Microarchitecture*, Dec. 2001.

[30] H. E. Ramadan, C. J. Rossbach, and E. Witchel. Dependence-Aware Transactional Memory for Increased Concurrency. In *Proceedings of the 41st Annual IEEE/ACM International Symposium on Microarchitecture*, Nov. 2008.

[31] N. Riley and C. Zilles. Hardware Transactional Memory Support for Lightweight Dynamic Language Evolution. In *Proceedings of the 21st SIGPLAN Conference on Object-Oriented Programming, Systems, Languages and Application (OOPSLA)*, Oct. 2006.

[32] S. R. Sarangi, W. Liu, J. Torrellas, and Y. Zhou. ReSlice: Selective Re-Execution of Long-Retired Misspeculated Instructions Using Forward Slicing. In *Proceedings of the 38th Annual IEEE/ACM International Symposium on Microarchitecture*, Nov. 2005.

[33] A. Shriraman and S. Dwarkadas. Refereeing Conflicts in Hardware Transactional Memory Systems. In *Proceedings of the 23rd International Conference on Supercomputing*, June 2009.

[34] G. Sohi, S. Breach, and T. Vijaykumar. Multiscalar Processors. In *Proceedings of the 22nd Annual International Symposium on Computer Architecture*, June 1995.

[35] S. T. Srinivasan, R. Rajwar, H. Akkary, A. Gandhi, and M. Upton. Continual Flow Pipelines. In *Proceedings of the 11th International Conference on Architectural Support for Programming Languages and Operating Systems*, Oct. 2004.

[36] J. G. Steffan, C. B. Colohan, A. Zhai, and T. C. Mowry. Improving Value Communication for Thread-Level Speculation. In *Proceedings of the Eighth Symposium on High-Performance Computer Architecture*, Feb. 2002.

[37] F. Tabba, A. W. Hay, and J. R. Goodman. Transactional Value Prediction. In *Proceedings of the Fourth ACM SIGPLAN Workshop on Transactional Computing*, Feb. 2009.

[38] R. Titos, M. E. Acacio, and J. M. Garcia. Speculation-Based Conflict Resolution in Hardware Transactional Memory. In *Proceedings of the International Parallel and Distributed Processing Symposium Symposium*, May 2009.

[39] S. Tomić, C. Perfumo, C. Kulkarni, A. Armejach, A. Cristal, O. Unsal, T. Harris, and M. Valero. EazyHTM: Eager-Lazy Hardware Transactional Memory. In *Proceedings of the 42nd Annual IEEE/ACM International Symposium on Microarchitecture*, Nov. 2009.

[40] S. C. Woo, M. Ohara, E. Torrie, J. P. Singh, and A. Gupta. The SPLASH-2 Programs: Characterization and Methodological Considerations. In *Proceedings of the 22nd Annual International Symposium on Computer Architecture*, June 1995.

Thread Tailor: Dynamically Weaving Threads Together for Efficient, Adaptive Parallel Applications

Janghaeng Lee, Haicheng Wu, Madhumitha Ravichandran, and Nathan Clark
College of Computing
Georgia Institute of Technology
Atlanta, GA, USA
{janghaeng, hwu36, madhumitha, nate.clark}@gatech.edu

ABSTRACT

Extracting performance from modern parallel architectures requires that applications be divided into many different threads of execution. Unfortunately selecting the appropriate number of threads for an application is a daunting task. Having too many threads can quickly saturate shared resources, such as cache capacity or memory bandwidth, thus degrading performance. On the other hand, having too few threads makes inefficient use of the resources available. Beyond static resource assignment, the program inputs and dynamic system state (e.g., what other applications are executing in the system) can have a significant impact on the right number of threads to use for a particular application.

To address this problem we present the Thread Tailor, a dynamic system that automatically adjusts the number of threads in an application to optimize system efficiency. The Thread Tailor leverages offline analysis to estimate what type of threads will exist at runtime and the communication patterns between them. Using this information Thread Tailor dynamically combines threads to better suit the needs of the target system. Thread Tailor adjusts not only to the architecture, but also other applications in the system, and this paper demonstrates that this type of adjustment can lead to significantly better use of thread-level parallelism in real-world architectures.

Categories and Subject Descriptors

C.0 [**Computer Systems Organization**]: System architectures; D.3.3 [**Programming Languages**]: Language Constructs and Features—*Dynamic storage management*; D.3.4 [**Programming Languages**]: Processors—*Run-time environments*

General Terms

Experimentation, Performance

1. INTRODUCTION

Chip-multiprocessors (CMPs) have become the industry standard method for scaling performance in recent years. Instead of providing a single high-capability processor, CMPs provide multiple less-capable processors on a single chip, yielding more aggregate performance for a given power envelope [25]. The implication of this trend is that applications must exploit thread-level parallelism (TLP) in order to realize performance benefits from CMPs.

ISCA'10 June 19–23, 2010, Saint-Malo, France.

Increasingly applications are rising to meet this challenge. There are many mature programming methodologies, such as MPI and OpenMP [6], enabling developers to leverage TLP, and many new programming paradigms, such as NVidia's CUDA [24], Intel's Ct [10], and the Galois Project [15], are emerging to make this even easier. By leveraging these programming models developers are often able to effectively divide their application into many independent threads of computation.

One increasingly important problem, for both programmers and programming models, is deciding exactly how many threads of computation to use. Selecting too few threads can grossly under utilize the resources provided by the CMP, yielding an inefficient application. On the other hand, too many threads will likewise create an inefficient application, as certain system resources quickly become saturated. Several researchers have already demonstrated that dividing an application into too many threads ends up making the application run *slower* as contention in shared resources such as memory bandwidth and cache space increases [23, 29].

To address the problem of selecting the appropriate number of threads, previous work has proposed techniques that statically profile an application and choose an appropriate number of threads offline [16]. Unfortunately, static solutions are very likely to be lacking for several reasons:

- *Inputs Change:* Many applications have varying degrees of parallelism based on their inputs. For example, the H.264 video codec has very different behavior based on the size and quality of the video being decoded [28]. Statically determining how to partition this application into threads will poorly utilize system resources for any inputs that were not represented in static profiling runs.
- *The System Changes:* In many computer systems, the application must share the system resources with many other processes that it has no control over. Determining the number of threads to use statically for the application cannot be done effectively without knowing what resources are available. For example if application X is currently using half of the cache space, then application Y should not have threads whose aggregate working set consume the entire cache. A thread partitioning like that for application Y would degrade performance of the entire system. Beyond shared resources like cache space, thermal throttling of resources is another example of dynamic system behavior that static thread allocation simply cannot account for.
- *Hardware Changes:* The hardware running the applications will necessarily evolve. The proper selection of threads for today's architecture is almost certain to be suboptimal on tomorrow's platforms. A static selection of how to divide threads will either create inefficient applications, or require costly application re-engineering whenever the architecture changes.

For all of these reasons static thread selection leaves much room for improvement. In this work we propose a different approach: instead of statically choosing the number of threads, the static software tool chain creates as many threads as can potentially be used by an architecture, and a dynamic compiler will stitch them together when needed. That is, the dynamic compiler will generate sequential code semantically equivalent to the running the two threads simultaneously, but with lower resource utilization and synchronization. By stitching the threads together, the dynamic compiler, or *Thread Tailor*, utilizes traditional compiler analysis to remove any unnecessary overheads introduced by splitting the application into threads statically. For example, if only two threads access a shared variable, and the runtime determines that they should be combined, the Thread Tailor will remove the unnecessary synchronization between them. Combining threads will likewise naturally reduce the amount of communication on CMP interconnection networks and contention in shared resources.

The challenge for dynamically combining threads is twofold: identifying what threads should be combined (if any), and performing the optimizations to remove thread overheads. To address the first issue, this paper makes a new contribution: the *communication graph*. The communication graph is a statically constructed graph, where nodes represent threads and edges represent the amount of data passed between threads (both data communication and synchronization traffic). This graph is very helpful in determining which threads to combine, as merging nodes (thus removing edges) reflects that non-local communication and synchronization has been reduced in the application. Once the Thread Tailor leverages the communication graph to decide which threads to combine, standard compiler analysis is used to remove unnecessary overheads between threads that are combined. While a static communication graph does not account for input variation, it does represent an important step in creating truly adaptable parallel programs.

This paper demonstrates the effectiveness of the Thread Tailor by evaluating several parallel applications with significantly varying available system resources. The Thread Tailor has negligible dynamic overhead to the parallel application, and at the same time intelligently combines threads creating a more efficient and adaptive multicore system.

2. RELATED WORK

Determining how to allocate system resources in an environment with many different computation threads is one of the classic problems in operating systems research. With the mainstream adoption of CMPs, this problem has received renewed interest in the field with the added complications of asymmetric cores and reducing power consumption as an optimization criteria [4, 17, 18, 19, 30]. Most previous work from the scheduling perspective looked at doing the best job of ordering the threads using various types of performance prediction. That is, these techniques typically work with the threads provided and do not consider the possibility of changing the threads themselves.

Another significant limitation of most OS-based thread scheduling work is that it typically does not recognize communication and synchronization patterns that provide valuable hints as to where and when threads should execute. For example, if two threads had a producer-consumer relationship, it may make sense to run them consecutively on the same core to leverage temporal data locality. However, most OS scheduling techniques (including thread pool libraries) would not be able to recognize this opportunity, as it requires dataflow analysis on the code within the threads. It's important to note that the inefficiency created by ignoring relationships between threads will be exacerbated as core count increases and the odds of the OS accidentally making good scheduling decisions decrease.

Wu et al. noted the advantages of using code-conscious techniques to dynamically optimize the voltage and frequency settings for single-threaded applications [32]. In that work they note, "hardware or OS techniques may not be able to infer enough about the application code attributes and find the most effective adaptation points." Similarly, when determining how many threads an application should leverage, the OS and hardware likely cannot infer enough information about the application to make effective choices, thus motivating the use of dynamic compilation.

Strictly looking at work related to dynamically adjusting the number of threads, several researchers have observed that more threads is not always a good thing. For example, Suleman et al. used simulations to demonstrate that many applications can improve performance and/or power consumption by taking memory bandwidth and synchronization into account [29]. Nieplocha et al. demonstrate this trend on real hardware as well, showing that some applications saturate shared resources in the Sun Niagara processor with as few as 8 threads, even though the chip has hardware support for 32 simultaneous threads [23].

Jung et al. [12] and Suleman et al. [29] describe two similar approaches for dynamically altering the number of threads used by an application. Both papers propose monitoring the execution and use similar models for predicting the appropriate number of threads given the system state. Jung's work relies on the OpenMP library to automatically adjust the thread decomposition. Suleman's approach requires the static compiler to augment parallelizable loops such that the profiling code can later adjust how the threads are divided just by dynamically setting a small number of variables (i.e., it does no code generation online, just sets a parameter used to partition the work). There are a couple advantages of our technique over these works: first, Jung's and Suleman's works were only effective on data-parallel loops, as they did not take inter-iteration dependencies into consideration. Neither previous work combined threads from different loop bodies, either. The approach in this paper does not suffer these limitations. Additionally, both of these previous works required some type of static support: Jung's approach only worked on OpenMP programs and Suleman's approach leveraged help from the static compiler. The Thread Tailor requires no external support and works on legacy applications, provided the dynamic compiler is cognizant of the semantics of the threading/synchronization mechanisms (e.g., pthreads or MPI) used in the application.

Three other related works are also similar to what is accomplished in this paper [5, 7, 21]. These papers can handle legacy executables and dynamically adjust the number of threads based both on performance and power optimization. There are three primary differences between these three previous works and this paper. First, similar to Jung and Suleman, these prior works required that the application be written in a framework, such as OpenMP, where the thread partitioning is adjustable simply by specifying the desired number of threads. Thread Tailor does not have this limitation. Second, Thread Tailor uses dataflow and memory dependence analysis to drive the thread grouping process. By taking inter-thread communication and synchronization into account the Thread Tailor can do a more effective job of optimizing system goals. Lastly, this paper leverages dynamic code generation to optimize away unnecessary synchronization after combining threads. To our knowledge, these features are fundamentally different from all previous work in the area.

The contributions of this paper include:

```
⊠⊠⊠oi⊠⊠⊠o⊠p⊠te⊠ensities⊠⊠(int i)⊠
⊠⊠⊠⊠⊠or(int i⊠ ⊠⊠⊠ri⊠s⊠i⊠⊠s⊠⊠⊠i⊠ ⊠⊠⊠ri⊠s⊠i⊠⊠e⊠⊠⊠⊠⊠i⊠)
⊠⊠⊠⊠⊠⊠⊠or(int i⊠ ⊠⊠⊠ri⊠s⊠i⊠⊠s⊠⊠⊠i⊠ ⊠⊠⊠ri⊠s⊠i⊠⊠e⊠⊠⊠⊠⊠i⊠)
⊠⊠⊠⊠⊠⊠⊠⊠⊠or(int ix⊠⊠⊠⊠ri⊠s⊠i⊠⊠sx⊠⊠ix⊠⊠⊠⊠ri⊠s⊠i⊠⊠ex⊠⊠⊠⊠ix)
⊠⊠⊠⊠⊠⊠⊠⊠⊠⊠⊠or(int ⊠⊠⊠⊠⊠⊠⊠⊠⊠⊠⊠np⊠⊠⊠⊠⊠)
⊠⊠⊠⊠⊠⊠⊠⊠⊠⊠⊠⊠⊠or(int inc⊠⊠⊠⊠⊠⊠inc⊠⊠⊠n⊠⊠⊠ei⊠⊠⊠e⊠⊠s⊠⊠⊠⊠inc)⊠
⊠⊠⊠⊠⊠⊠⊠⊠⊠⊠⊠⊠⊠⊠⊠⊠⊠co⊠p⊠tation⊠⊠ere⊠⊠⊠
8               if(border[index]){
⊠⊠⊠⊠⊠⊠⊠⊠⊠⊠⊠⊠⊠⊠⊠⊠⊠pt⊠rea⊠_⊠⊠tex_⊠oc⊠(&⊠⊠tex⊠in⊠ex⊠⊠⊠⊠)⊠
⊠⊠⊠⊠⊠⊠⊠⊠⊠⊠⊠⊠⊠⊠⊠⊠⊠ce⊠⊠⊠⊠ensit⊠⊠⊠⊠⊠⊠⊠⊠tc⊠
⊠⊠⊠⊠⊠⊠⊠⊠⊠⊠⊠⊠⊠⊠⊠⊠⊠pt⊠rea⊠_⊠⊠tex_⊠n⊠oc⊠(&⊠⊠tex⊠in⊠ex⊠⊠⊠⊠)⊠
⊠⊠⊠⊠⊠⊠⊠⊠⊠⊠⊠⊠⊠⊠⊠⊠⊠e⊠se⊠⊠
⊠⊠⊠⊠⊠⊠⊠⊠⊠⊠⊠⊠⊠⊠⊠⊠⊠ce⊠⊠⊠⊠ensit⊠⊠⊠⊠⊠⊠⊠⊠tc⊠
⊠⊠⊠⊠⊠⊠⊠⊠⊠⊠⊠⊠⊠⊠⊠⊠⊠
15              if(border[indexNeigh]){
⊠⊠⊠⊠⊠⊠⊠⊠⊠⊠⊠⊠⊠⊠⊠⊠⊠pt⊠rea⊠_⊠⊠tex_⊠oc⊠(&⊠⊠tex⊠in⊠ex⊠⊠ipar⊠ei⊠⊠⊠)⊠
⊠⊠⊠⊠⊠⊠⊠⊠⊠⊠⊠⊠⊠⊠⊠⊠⊠nei⊠⊠⊠⊠ensit⊠⊠⊠⊠⊠⊠⊠⊠tc⊠
⊠⊠⊠⊠⊠⊠⊠⊠⊠⊠⊠⊠⊠⊠⊠⊠⊠pt⊠rea⊠_⊠⊠tex_⊠n⊠oc⊠(&⊠⊠tex⊠in⊠ex⊠⊠ipar⊠ei⊠⊠⊠)⊠
⊠⊠⊠⊠⊠⊠⊠⊠⊠⊠⊠⊠⊠⊠⊠⊠⊠e⊠se⊠⊠
⊠⊠⊠⊠⊠⊠⊠⊠⊠⊠⊠⊠⊠⊠⊠⊠⊠nei⊠n⊠⊠ensit⊠⊠⊠⊠⊠⊠⊠⊠tc⊠
⊠⊠⊠⊠⊠⊠⊠⊠⊠⊠⊠⊠⊠⊠⊠⊠⊠
⊠⊠⊠⊠⊠⊠⊠⊠⊠⊠⊠⊠⊠⊠⊠
⊠⊠
⊠⊠⊠⊠
```

Figure 1: Portion of fluidanimate benchmark illustrating communication and synchronization overheads

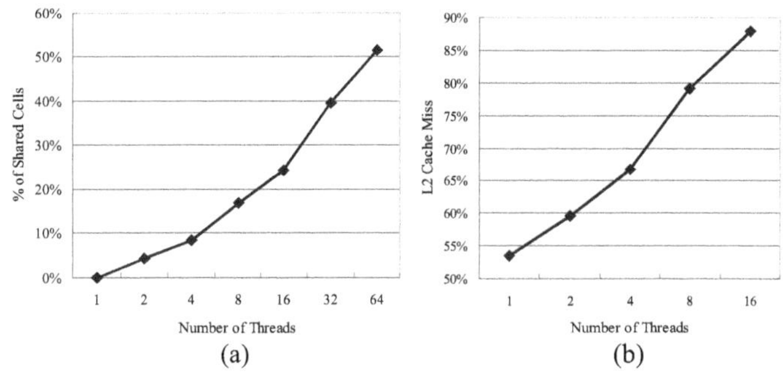

Figure 2: Number of threads in `fluidanimate` showing impacts on (a) shared data and (b) L2 cache misses

- A novel graph representation of thread interaction to facilitate partitioning and combining threads in multi-threaded applications.
- A partitioning algorithm and code generation methodology that quickly and effectively selects the appropriate number of threads an application should be using and generates new threads without unnecessary synchronization or communication overheads. This system does not require any support from the compiler toolchain and is effective on legacy applications.
- Evidence that leveraging dataflow analysis can sometimes yield significantly better system behavior than techniques which do not utilize this analysis.
- A demonstration of a complete dynamic compiler that has very low runtime overhead and yet does a very effective job at managing memory and bandwidth resources for several benchmark applications.

3. MOTIVATION AND DESIGN OF THREAD TAILOR

Most parallel applications set the number of threads created statically to match the number of cores on the target system [29]. This leaves room for improvement as the optimal number of threads can only be known at execution-time, because of different input, system status, and underlying hardware. Poorly selecting the number of threads wastes system power and can exacerbate performance problems.

The primary reasons why more threads is not necessarily better is that (1) too many threads can saturate a shared resource, such as memory bandwidth, and (2) additional threads can increase synchronization overheads. Figure 1 shows a critical code sequence from fluidanimate, part of the Parsec benchmark suite [2], which demonstrates these trends. Fluidanimate performs a computation on a large grid by decomposing the work into several subgrids based on the user-defined number of threads. Whenever work is performed on the borders of a subgrid, the program must acquire a mutex lock to read and update the cells. As the number of threads increases, so does the fraction of time working on subgrid borders, which means there will be an increasing amount of synchronization and shared data.

Figure 2(a) shows the fraction of time spent performing computation on subgrid boundaries growing as the number of threads increases in fluidanimate. With 64 threads almost half of cells are located in borders, which can have a significant affect on performance. Increased shared data not only increases lock overhead, but also aggravates cache miss rates because of both false and true sharing. More threads is not a clear win. Additionally, blindly combining threads does not necessarily lead to benefits, either. Combining threads without understanding the subgrid relationship will not reduce the locking overhead at all.

Figure 2(b) demonstrates how having too many threads can also saturate shared system resources in fluidanimate. The chart here shows the shared L2 cache miss-rate increases very quickly as the number of threads in fluidanimate increases. Each thread carries some overhead with it, and once the total working set of the threads exceeds the shared L2 capacity, additional threads only exacerbate the problem. Shared resources can take many forms, from caches, to memory bandwidth, to the single FPU shared on the Niagara [22], and exceeding their capacity with additional threads can significantly impact system throughput. Since Thread Tailor cannot possibly monitor all-possible shared resources, the remainder of the paper will only considers the most commonly saturating shared resources that we observed: off-chip memory bandwidth, on-chip cache traffic, and cache utilization.

On this particular system, fluidanimate performed best with four threads (12% better than eight threads, and 75% better than two threads), where the parallelism was balanced against synchronization and cache misses. The fluidanimate example motivates why selecting the number of threads dynamically, considering both synchronization and shared-resources, is essential for efficient systems. Figure 3 shows the overview of the proposed Thread Tailor design to accomplish this. First, developers create a binary that uses a high number of threads. That binary is profiled offline to collect statistics on the number of threads created, and the communication and synchronization patterns between them. This forms a communication graph, which is stored offline as metadata and used by the dynamic compiler when the application runs. The communication graph can be formed using legacy binaries, and does not require source code access for a recompile.

At runtime, the dynamic compiler will take a quick snapshot of the system state to determine how many free resources are available (e.g., number of available cores or available cache space), and run a partitioning algorithm on the communication graph. Partitioning tries to balance the work among available cores while minimizing the amount of communication and synchronization between

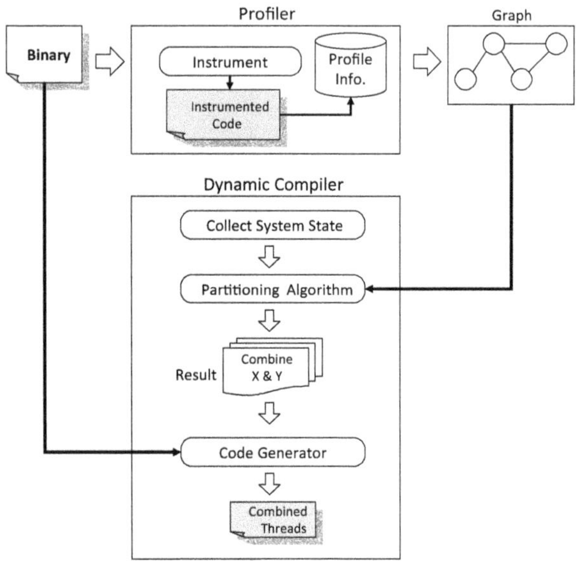

Figure 3: Thread Tailor system overview

Thread 1

Address	LD Count	ST Count
...	...	...
0x00001234	5	10
0x00001338	4	9
...	...	...
0x00004000	7	7
...	...	...

Thread 2

Address	LD Count	ST Count
...	...	...
0x00001234	0	7
0x00002000	4	4
...	...	...
0x00004000	3	8
...	...	...

(a)

```
0x00001234: MIN(5, 7) + MIN(10, 0) + MIN(10, 7) = 12
0x00004000: MIN(7, 8) + MIN( 7, 3) + MIN( 7, 8) = 17

Total Communication Cost: 12 + 17 = 29
```

(b)

Figure 4: (a) memory access table for threads, and (b) computing an estimate of communication cost

threads. Threads within a partition are then merged, removing any unnecessary synchronization or communication overhead (in the case of programming models with explicit communication, such as MPI) when possible[1]. After generating code for the new threads, the dynamic compiler intercepts future calls to thread creations, and redirects them to the combined threads. Details of graph construction, thread partitioning, and code generation by dynamic compiler are discussed in the following subsections.

3.1 Constructing the Communication Graph

The ultimate goal of the Thread Tailor is to dynamically adjust the number of threads an application uses to increase system efficiency. In order to accomplish this the Thread Tailor needs a heuristic to estimate the quality of a particular grouping of threads. The approach advocated in this work is to construct a graph representing the application threads and partition it. The graph vertices represent computation threads, and have weights that correspond to the estimated cycles of computation ($Cycle_i$), the working set size ($Workset_i$), and the amount of off-chip memory bandwidth needed (BW_i). Edges in the graph represent communication or synchronization traffic between threads. The graph can then be dynamically partitioned to balance the number of cycles allocated to each available processor, while limiting the amount of communication between thread-partitions, and keeping the partitions from over-saturating shared caches or memory bandwidth. This heuristic approach allows us to leverages the vast amount of related work on graph partitioning and also effectively incorporates all of the first-order design considerations in deciding which threads to combine. The challenge now becomes how to construct this graph.

The first design decision is whether to generate this graph information online, as the application is running, or offline as a profiling run. Online profiling could be advantageous, as the information would be input-specific and it could handle situations where the number threads generated varies based on dynamic properties. However, there is considerable overhead in collecting the necessary data dynamically, and there are currently no simple performance counters to collect information such as working set size. For these reasons, this paper proposes the use of offline profiling. A representative input is fed into the system, and performance counters are used to track properties such as cycle count for each thread. Properties such as working set size, which cannot be collected by performance counters, are generated using code instrumentation. After the data is aggregated the graph is appended to the binary as metadata, and later used by the dynamic compiler. While this does not allow for adjusting based on input-specific behavior, it does make applications adaptable based on hardware and system-level changes.

One drawback of this type of profiling is that it requires the same number of threads to be created during each execution, and for those threads to be created in the same order. In order to overcome this restriction we propose appending the profiling information not to individual threads, but instead to thread creation sites. The intuition behind this decision is that applications that create a variable number of threads based on input, typically do this by breaking the input data into fixed-size chunks. Thus, every thread originating from a particular creation-site typically has the same working set size, communication properties, etc. Identifying where the thread creation sites exist in a binary is a straight forward process that leverages the symbol table in libraries (e.g., Thread Tailor can identify calls to `pthread_create()` by using the symbol table). This is one of the reasons Thread Tailor must be cognizant of the thread creation semantics used in the application.

Given this profiling strategy, the data must be collected to construct the graph. Hardware performance counters are sufficient to generate the number of cycles and memory bandwidth utilized in each thread. However, the profiler still must determine the working set size, and the communication traffic and synchronization traffic between threads. In applications where communication is explicit, it is very easy to compute the total amount of communication between threads, however in shared-memory programs this is significantly more challenging. To estimate communication traffic, the original binary is instrumented to count memory accesses for each address per thread.

An example of this is shown in the Figure 4(a). Intuitively, communication between two threads takes place when one thread accesses a block address where another thread writes during its life time. Therefore, the amount of communication can be estimated as the minimum of access count for overlapped block addresses between two threads. For instance, in the Figure 4(a) thread 1 reads

[1]The runtime must be able to prove that synchronization/communication is in fact unnecessary. This process is discussed in Section 3.3

address 0x1234 five times and thread 2 writes that address seven times, meaning there could be five cache-blocks worth of communication. This accounts only for load-store traffic; factoring in store-load and store-store is also done, as shown in Figure 4(b). Together the sum of communication weights for all addresses accessed by threads becomes one edge in the graph. Load-load relations can be ignored, because generally they do not generate communication in coherence protocols, but in practice combining threads with load-load relations may reduce cold- and capacity-misses. These misses were negligible in the applications used in the experimentation. Clearly adding all memory interactions is an overestimation of the amount of communication that actually occurs in the application, however it does capture the relative amount of communication between threads. Empirically speaking, this fidelity was sufficiently accurate to guide the graph partitioner toward making the correct decisions.

The working set size of each thread is also estimated using the memory access table in Figure 4(a). For each thread, all addresses are sorted based on the number of times they are accessed within that thread. Thread Tailor then determines how many unique block addresses are needed to comprise 90% of total accesses and considers that to be the working set.

The last profiling statistic needed is thread synchronization. To collect this data, the dynamic compiler instruments the original binary to check the amount of waiting time needed for synchronization. For example, a counter checks the time before and after each call to `pthread_cond_wait()` and records how many cycles were needed spent waiting and which thread signals the waiting completion. This is one of the reasons that Thread Tailor must be aware of the semantics of the threading library. Without knowing what code segments signify the start and end of synchronization, it is impossible to measure the benefit that will be achieved by serializing the threads. As it stands, this profile weight will not consider synchronization overheads that are done outside of libraries, e.g., polling on a shared variable.

Once all statistics are collected, the communication graph is constructed. Each node has a three node weights for execution cycles, memory bandwidth, and working set size. For edges in the graph, the profiler converts the communication measurements into approximate cycle equivalents. The reason for this conversion is that it simplifies graph partitioning, and will become clearer in the next section. To estimate the number of cycles it takes to communicate between two threads, we assumed a non-uniform cache architecture with 2D-mesh network and directory-based coherence protocol (this could easily be substituted with another analytical model based on the target architecture). If we assume threads are randomly assigned to cores, then the average communication latency will be $3 * \sqrt{Cores * L}$, where L is the latency to the lowest-level shared cache, $\sqrt{Cores}$ is the average distance between two cores in a grid, and three is for messages (1) from the requester to the directory, (2) from the directory to the owner, and (3) from the owner back to the requester. Again, this is a very rough estimate, and better estimates are certainly possible using more refined architecture information. However, this graph does account for the first-order design parameters needed to make effective grouping decisions and we found this heuristic to work well for the applications in Section 4.

3.2 Thread Partitioning Algorithm

Now that a graph is created, the goal of the Thread Tailor is to partition that graph, creating groups of threads where execution time of the application is minimized. This optimization problem is modeled using as a graph partitioning problem, where work is balanced across available cores, while minimizing communication and synchronization between partitions and not over-utilizing shared resources such as memory bandwidth and shared cache space. Again, this decision must be made dynamically because the number of cores, free cache space, etc. all change based on what else is happening in the system, and the dynamic compiler has information the operating system does not have that is needed to make appropriate decisions.

Before partitioning begins, the Thread Tailor takes a snapshot of the system to determine the available resources. Current processor utilization can be retrieved from common utilities, such as `mpstat` in Linux, and recent memory bandwidth utilization can be determined from on-chip performance counters. Cache utilization is a much more difficult property. Thread Tailor will group threads so as not to exceed a certain cache utilization, but it is not clear how much cache space the application can occupy without significantly affecting other applications. Indeed, determining how to allocate shared cache space is very much an open research question [26, 33]. Thread Tailor makes the simplifying assumption that shared cache should be allocated equally amongst all threads, although this assumption could easily be altered if better solutions are discovered.

If the partitioner decides to combine two threads, Thread Tailor needs a method to estimate the weights of the combined threads. We assume that $Workset_i$ and BW_i do not overlap between threads, thus the summation of these weights represents the working set and bandwidth of the threads when combined. This assumption makes intuitive sense, because if two threads shared significant amounts of read/write data in the working set, then there would be significant communication between the threads, which hinders parallelism.

Estimating cycles is slightly more complicated than working set size or bandwidth, as combining threads reduces the amount of communication and synchronization that must be done in the application. By maintaining edge weights that represent how many cycles threads spend communicating and synchronizing between each other, the partitioner can get an estimate on the total execution time of the combined threads. Take Figure 5(a) as an example. If threads A and B were combined into one partition, the synchronization and communication latency, 60, between these threads could be removed. Thus the estimated performance of the combined A-B threads is (100 + 100 - 60) = 140 cycles. Generalizing, the execution cycles of combined threads is estimated to be $Cycles_P = \sum_{i \in P} Cycles_i - \sum_{i \in P, j \in P} Cycles_{E_{i,j}}$. Edge weights are updated as the sum of previous edge weights, e.g., the A-B partition would have an edge weighted 120 to node C because $Cycles_{E_{A,C}}$ = 60 and $Cycles_{E_{B,C}}$ = 60 prior to the combining.

Given these estimates for partition execution time, the goal of the current partitioner is to minimize execution time[2]. Since all the partitions run in parallel, the number of cycles in the slowest partition is the time needed to execute the program. The partitioning algorithm is constrained so that it does not exceed total memory bandwidth allocated to the system or the application's fair share of cache space, i.e., $Workset_{P_n} \leq CacheAllocation$ and $BW_{P_n} \leq MemBW$ for all partitions.

The partitioning algorithm must determine both the proper number of partitions and which threads should be combined. This is an extension of the NP-Hard bin packing problem [9] and a common problem in load balancing parallel systems [3]. Many heuristics could potentially be used, however, one significant limitation is that Thread Tailor is performing this partitioning dynamically, thus the algorithm runtime must be very fast so as not to overwhelm potential benefits from dynamic adjustment. This restriction rules out ex-

[2]Although this could easily be changed to minimizing energy, or some combination of factors.

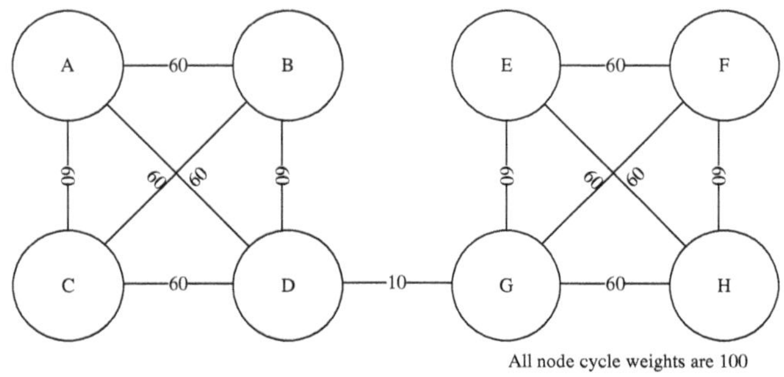

(a)

Partition 1	Partition 2	Partition 1 Cycle Estimation	Partition 2 Cycle Estimation	Move From	Move Node
B C D G	A E F H	210	220	2	A
A B C D G	E F H	130	120	1	G
A B C D	E F G H	40	40	1	D

(b)

Figure 5: Partitioning example: (a) graph to be partitioned and (b) the first 3 steps of partitioning

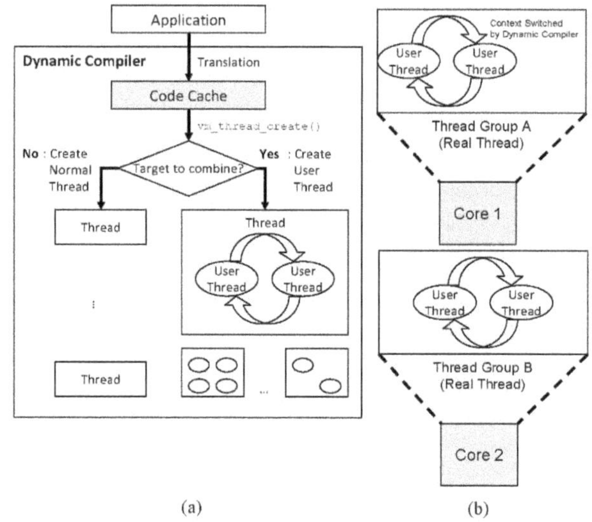

Figure 6: (a) thread combining system overview, and (b) combined threads running on cores

act partitioning strategies, such as integer-linear programming solutions [14].

In the current design, Thread Tailor utilizes the Kernighan-Lin (KL) graph partitioning heuristic to reach these goals [13]. The KL algorithm has found significant use in many important problems [27], and prior work has shown that it runs in linear time with the size of the graph [8]. The KL algorithm requires knowing the target number of partitions a priori, and so Thread Tailor runs it several times, starting with the number of partitions equal to half the number of threads in the application then using binary search to discover the best solution.

The basic idea of KL algorithm is to start with some number of partitions, then repeatedly identify the node that will reduce the total weight of cut edges the most, and move it to another partition. Figure 5 shows a high-level example of the algorithm using two partitions (assume the cache utilization and memory bandwidth constraints are satisfied at all times). If the whole graph were combined into one partition, the estimated runtime is $(100 \times 8) \quad (60 \times 12) \quad 10 = 70$ cycles. Initially, Thread Tailor divides the graph into two random partitions, {C, B, D, G} and {A, E, H, F}. Figure 5(b) shows the first three moves the algorithm would perform. Again, the node to move is selected by determining which node would reduce the weight of cut edges the most. After the third move, the algorithm arrives at the optimal solution for two partitions. The algorithm can be repeatedly run to generate three, four, or as many as eight different solutions, but in this example two partitions has the minimal estimated execution time.

Note that KL algorithm is greedy, and may stop at a local minima. Moreover, the methods for estimating combined thread performance do not account for many interactions between threads, and thus may be inaccurate. Despite these potential drawbacks, our experiments show that the proposed approach is very fast, a critical design criteria, and the partitioning results perform better than previously proposed thread-combining techniques for the benchmarks evaluated.

3.3 Code Generation for Combined Threads

Now that the Thread Tailor understands what threads should be combined, the next step is actually combining them. The current implementation is a user-level virtual machine that takes an application as input, translates functions on-demand, and then places a copy into an internally managed code cache. If the implementation were system-level, as opposed to user-level, then it could optimize for several different applications simultaneously thus making better decisions on how to partition shared resources, but the same general architecture applies in both situations.

When the compiler detects any calls to thread creation, communication, or synchronization functions, they are automatically replaced with a function wrapper, enabling the Thread Tailor to take control of the process. These wrappers also enable the Thread Tailor to work with any parallelization primitives (pthreads, MPI, etc.) as long as the semantics of the library are understood by Thread Tailor and the appropriate wrapper functions exist.

Figure 6(a) illustrates an example how this function combines the threads. When a function calls the wrapper, `vm_thread_create`, if the thread does not need to be combined, a thread is created just as it normally would be. If the function is part of a group and this is the first member of the group to call the creation wrapper, then a new thread is created and the current thread's context is saved into an array. Subsequent threads in the group will not create a thread, but merely add their contexts into the array. These contexts are created using one of many user-thread libraries, which exist outside control of the OS scheduler. The real thread can then use OS hooks to guarantee which processor it is run on and use the array of contexts to honor the partitioning, dynamically switching amongst the combined threads. This scenario is shown in Figure 6(b).

One challenge in dealing with explicit serialization of these threads is correctly handling synchronization. For example, consider a barrier synchronization that occurs half-way through each combined thread. The translated application, with its combination of user-threads and kernel-threads must still honor the semantics that each thread must reach the barrier before proceeding, shown in Figure 7(a). To guarantee correctness, the virtual machine uses function wrappers for synchronization primitives. For example, Figure 7(b) shows the functionality of the wrapper for a barrier. Whenever the `barrier_wait` wrapper is called from a group of user threads, it must keep track of which user threads have actually reached the barrier, and switch to another context until all user threads have satisfied the condition. Only then can the actual barrier be executed, signaling threads in other partitions.

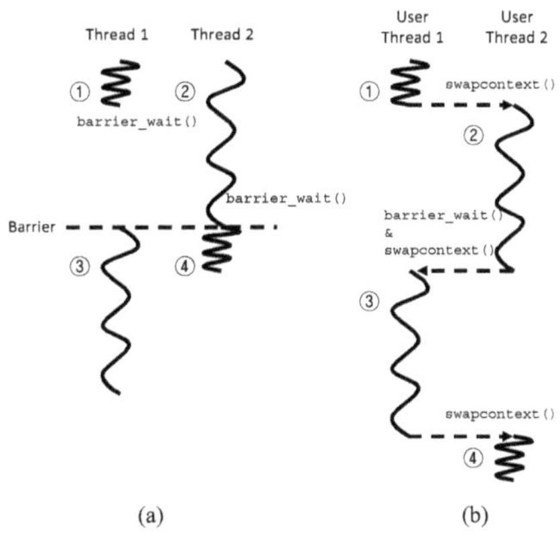

Figure 7: Example showing barrier synchronization (a) before thread combining and (b) after thread combining

Point-to-point synchronization (e.g., `thread_cond_wait()`, which atomically unlocks mutex variables and waits for the condition), does not require any special handling, although optimizations are possible. For example, if the virtual machine knows which thread will signal the wake up and it happens to be in the same kernel-thread, it can use that information to better schedule the user threads. Threads that do not use semantically well defined synchronization primitives, e.g., polling on a shared variable, will also be executed without modification.

As discussed earlier, one of the benefits of serializing multithreaded applications is optimizing away unnecessary synchronization and communication between threads. Communication can be removed whenever it can be proven that the source and destination(s) are within the same kernel thread, since the data will be local after combining. In programming models with explicit communication this is straightforward, as the source/destination(s) are encoded in the program. At thread creation time, if the source/destination of explicit communication are determinable via dataflow analysis, a special buffer is allocated for each communication. The calls to functions such as `MPI_Send` and `MPI_Recv` are then converted to into reads and writes to the buffer allocated for that particular communication. By writing into a buffer instead of calling those functions the communication is kept local to the user threads.

In programs with implicit communication, there is no reason to remove communication, as the underlying environment will remove it automatically. E.g., in shared memory programs, the combined threads will naturally keep communication local to the shared core through the memory coherence protocol.

Removing synchronization is more difficult than communication. Mutual exclusion can be removed if it can be proven that the combined threads are the only ones that access the memory comprising the lock, and the Thread Tailor runtime guarantees that the threads will not be interrupted in the mutually exclusive region. The latter is easily enforced by the runtime, but the problem of determining what threads can access a particular lock reduces to memory dependence analysis, i.e., determining which loads can read from which stores in each of the threads.

Memory dependence analysis in dynamic environments has been well studied [11], and taking a cue from this prior work, Thread Tailor utilizes a customized version of Andersen's analysis [1] to determine points-to relationships in the target application. Using Andersen's algorithm in conduction with detaflow analysis gives Thread Tailor a conservative view of all load-store dependences between threads, and thus it may identify a superset of threads that access a particular mutex lock. That is, Thread Tailor will very likely remove most unnecessary synchronization, but is not guaranteed to remove all of it. Better memory dependence analysis could improve the amount of synchronization removed, but we leave this for future work.

Using program analysis and dynamic code generation to remove communication and synchronization is one aspect of Thread Tailor that is novel in comparison to prior approaches.

4. EXPERIMENTAL EVALUATION

The Thread Tailor was prototyped using the Low-Level Virtual Machine (LLVM) toolset [20]. LLVM includes a static compiler, link-time optimizer, and just-in-time (JIT) compiler that converts the compiler IR into native assembly code. While LLVM does not operate on legacy binaries, its bytecode is very close to assembly code, and LLVM is much easier to modify and faster than other open source dynamic compilers. Thread Tailor uses no features of the IR (e.g., type information) that are not readily available in legacy binaries.

The applications used are from assorted benchmark suites: blackscholes, fluidanimate, and swaptions from the Parsec suite [2]; two bus-limited applications used in prior work by Suleman et al. [29] (transpose, and twister); and one from SPLASH2 [31] (water_n^2). All the benchmarks were statically compiled to use 128 threads, using parameters already in the applications. That is, the work in the applications was partitioned by the programmer, not by us. Benchmarks from these suites omitted from the results were due to limitations in the current implementation (e.g., LLVM currently does not handle inline assembly code well, and the JIT has difficulty linking some dynamic libraries) or because they did not demonstrate any behavior not exhibited in the other benchmarks. Applications were not omitted because of any limitations of the Thread Tailor approach or to skew the results.

Each of the applications was run through the LLVM static compiler to generate bytecode, and the bytecode was run through the JIT once to generate the communication graph using a training data set. After the graph is appended to the bytecode, the application executes in the JIT again to dynamically combine and execute thread groups with reference inputs. We tested Thread Tailor on three systems: a dual-core 2.4 GHz Intel Core 2 6600 with 4 MB L2 and 2 GB of RAM, a quad-core 2.4 GHz Intel Core 2 Q6600 with 8 MB L2 and 4 GB of RAM, and a dual quad-core (i.e., 8-cores total in 2 packages) 2.26 GHz Intel Xeon E5520 with SMT enabled, 8 MB L2, and 24 GB of RAM. Each system used Linux kernel 2.6.28 and each experiment was run five times using the largest available input with the median result reported below.

4.1 Results

When designing scalable applications, programmers typically use the same number of threads as processors in the system. This provides one comparison point for the Thread Tailor approach, which instead advocates creating many threads and dynamically reducing that number. Again, the number of threads used in each application was adjusted using a programmer supplied variable, i.e., the benchmark developer provided a suitable work partitioning; we did not intentionally choose a poor baseline.

As a second point of comparison to Thread Tailor, we also evaluate the FDT technique proposed by Suleman et al. [29], which dynamically adjusts the number of threads used, but only works on data parallel loops and only considers synchronization and bandwidth when deciding how many threads to use. The FDT algorithm used for these experiments was modified to optimize for minimizing runtime, as the original work optimized for energy-delay prod-

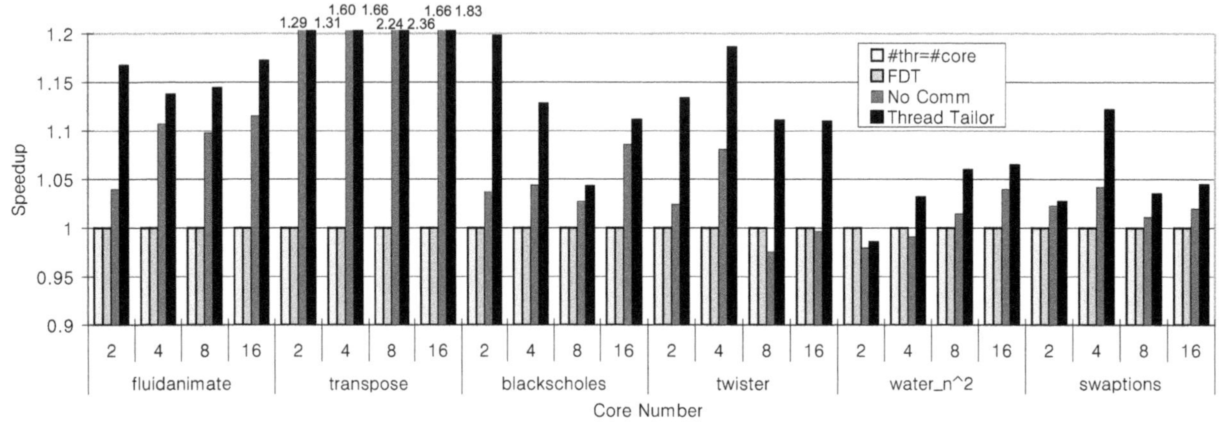

Figure 8: Relative performance of benchmarks

uct. This provides a fair comparison against Thread Tailor, which currently ignores energy in its optimization criteria. A third comparison point is a version of Thread Tailor that operates exactly as presented in Section 3 but without considering communication and synchronization. This third point is intended to somewhat mimic prior works that do not leverage code analysis to understand inter-thread relationships [5, 7, 12, 21]. Note that this is not an exact comparison, as these prior techniques did not perform any dynamic code generation.

Figure 8 shows the performance results for the three dynamically adjusting systems compared to the baseline, where applications use a statically declared number of threads equal to the number of cores on the system. For example, the left-most set of bars in this figure show the performance of statically creating two threads for fluidanimate and running it on our two core machine, compared to an application that creates 128 threads statically and dynamically combines them using three strategies: FDT, Thread Tailor, and Thread Tailor when ignoring communication and synchronization. The second set of bars compares against 4 threads statically created and run on a 4 core machine. The bars listed corresponding to 16 cores were generated running on the dual-quad core machine listed above with hyper-threading enabled, thus making the operating system believe there were more cores than actually existed.

It is important to keep in mind that the applications executed in each bar perform the same computation but are not identical. For example, the Thread Tailor applications are statically compiled to target a large number of threads, whereas the "#thr = #core" are statically compiled targeting a much smaller number, thus having less thread spawning, synchronization, etc. In fact, the Thread Tailor version executes 1-4% more dynamic instructions in each application. Similarly, the FDT programs all have a small preloop that is used to dynamically alter the number of threads to be utilized, which is different from either of the other strategies. Even if FDT and Thread Tailor decide to create the same number of threads, the actual threads they execute are likely to be very different.

Several interesting trends are illustrated in Figure 8. Most prominently, Thread Tailor outperforms "#thr = #core" in virtually every application. In most cases, Thread Tailor actually creates the same number of threads as there are cores, however the Thread Tailor version does a more effective job of balancing shared resources, especially in the transpose benchmark. Transpose is a simple benchmark that transposes an m by n matrix and stores it in a new location as an n by m matrix. This benchmark is dominated by memory accesses, half of which load the input matrix and half store the

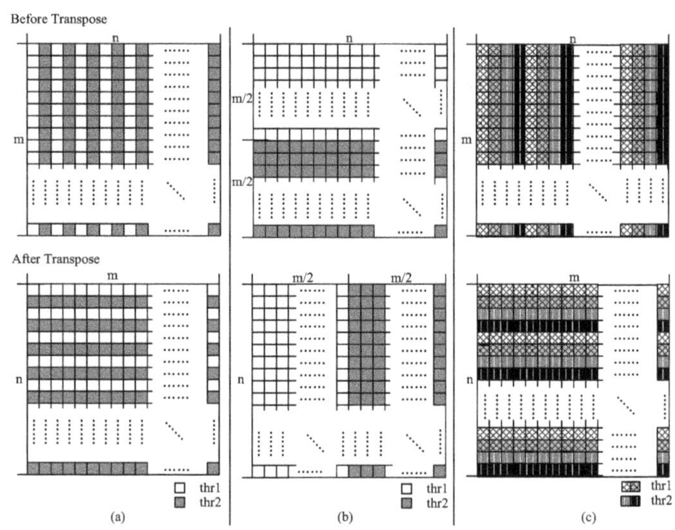

Figure 9: Comparison between how (a) "#thr = #core", (b) FDT, and (c) Thread Tailor partitioning of transpose

result. To better understand exactly why Thread Tailor performs better than other techniques, we investigated the combined threads, shown in Figure 9.

Figure 9(a) shows how "#thr=#core" partitions the work statically into two threads. If we assume cache blocks are aligned in rows and data is read first by rows before columns, then the loading threads will only have at best 50% cache utilization (and potential problems with false sharing) because the data they are accessing lies in alternating columns. The storing threads will have issues, too, because each write will be to a different cache block as elements are written in column order, and temporal locality will only help if the cache can hold $n/2$ blocks. Said another way, this partitioning creates threads with large working sets. Figure 9(b) shows the FDT partitioning, which divides the matrix into two halves. Here the loading thread has twice the spatial locality, but the storing thread will only get to the same cache line after n accesses, again causing problems because of a large working set. These misses balanced out between the two techniques in the end.

Figure 9(c) shows how Thread Tailor combines 4 threads down to 2 (the different colors in Figure 9(c) represent different static threads). Thread Tailor combines the first two as a group and the

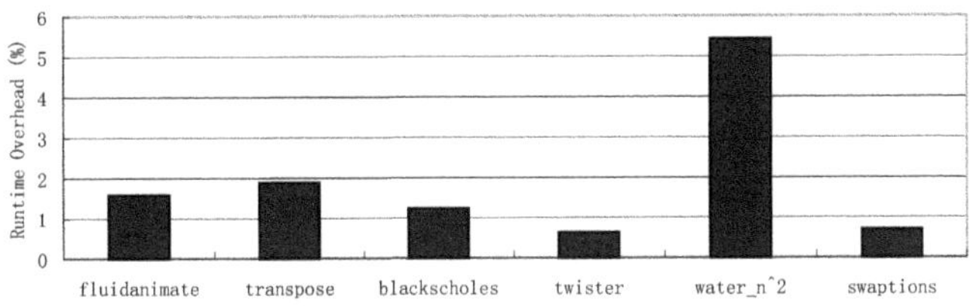

Figure 10: Dynamic overhead from Thread Tailor

last two as the other group. Thread 1 of Thread Tailor's grouping would traverse the first, fifth, ninth, etc. columns initially, which transposes every fourth element in the matrix. After that, thread 1 will transpose the second, sixth, etc. columns. Loading elements in this order has less temporal locality than FDT's partitioning, but as long as the cache can hold $n/4$ blocks, then the second, sixth, etc. columns will be hits. Similarly, the Thread Tailor store pattern has smaller working set size, writing to the same cache block every $n/4$ stores, as opposed to every n stores for FDT and every $n/2$ stores for "#thr = #core". Essentially, by taking working set size into consideration, Thread Tailor did a better job blocking the memory accesses than other techniques.

Turning back to Figure 8, comparing Thread Tailor with "No Comm" shows the relative importance of leveraging communication and synchronization patterns to group threads. Simply combining threads that ignore thread communication and synchronization patterns, the system does 6% worse on average. The communication agnostic strategy tries to balance computation and working set size across threads, and does remove unnecessary communication and synchronization, however it does not proactively try to group threads to improve the amount of code removed. The "No Comm" strategy generally performs better than FDT because it can combine threads from different loops and was conscious of working set size. Note that transpose still performed well without considering communication and synchronization, because most of the benefit for that application resulted from constraining the working set size. Benchmarks with a significant difference between "No Comm" and "Thread Tailor" bars indicate that the benefit resulted from considering synchronization and bandwidth limitations. For example, fluidanimate showed reduced synchronization overhead of 70.4% on 2 cores, 27.0% on 4 cores, 19.2% on 8 cores, and 15.2% on 16 cores due to removing unnecessary boundary locking described in Section 3.

A last interesting trend to take from Figure 8 is that "FDT" is virtually identical to "#thr = #core" for the applications. This result stems from the fact that none of these applications is currently bandwidth or synchronization bound on the systems we experimented with. This is a direct result of the experimental setup, and in no way an indictment of the FDT technique. Indeed, as the number of cores increases the FDT technique becomes more and more useful, and we expect the gap between FDT and Thread Tailor will narrow.

As a last result, Figure 10 shows the dynamic runtime overhead from running the Thread Tailor system. That is, the percent difference between executing a native binary with many threads versus executing the bytecode compiled with many threads and performing all the thread partitioning code but without any combining. This chart essentially shows the overhead of running the application in a JIT combined with the overhead of dynamic thread partitioning and code analysis. Sources of overhead include time to translate the bytecode to native code, time for program analysis to detect what synchronization can be removed, graph partitioning time, and overhead from the wrapper function calls that intercept control to/from the threading library.

The important point to take from Figure 10 is that the Thread Tailor typically has very low overheads (less than 2% of application time). Figure 8 demonstrates that Thread Tailor cannot always overcome this overhead: water_n^2, which has relatively high overhead and little resource saturation for small numbers of processors, shows a slowdown when using Thread Tailor. The reason for this is the relatively small input sets available for this application; water_n^2 comes from SPLASH2, an older benchmark suite, thus the costs of dynamic translation were not amortized over a longer execution time. In the majority of benchmarks Thread Tailor's benefit far outweighs the overheads, though.

5. SUMMARY

Modern applications are increasingly making use of thread-level parallelism (TLP) to extract more performance out of CMPs. A critical problem in leveraging TLP is selecting the appropriate number of threads: too few threads will under-utilize on chip resources and too many will quickly saturate the processor, hurting overall system throughput. To address this problem, this paper presents the Thread Tailor, a dynamic compilation system that can automatically stitch threads together based on the architecture, dynamic system state, and communication and synchronization relationships between threads.

The Thread Tailor enables a developer to create a single application that will effectively adjust online, thus performing better on today's systems and providing a likelihood of performing well on future systems as well. This paper demonstrates that the Thread Tailor is a low-overhead layer of indirection capable of effectively utilizing shared system resources, such as cache space, while not significantly hurting performance when the application does an effective job of resource management. This paper also demonstrates that using program analysis to detect communication and synchronization patterns is critical for effective thread management in many applications, and reports a geometric mean performance benefit of 19% on real hardware.

6. ACKNOWLEDGEMENTS

We sincerely wish to thank Aater Suleman, Moin Qureshi, and Yale Patt for reviewing a draft of this work and helping us understand the workings of FDT. Discussions with Gregory Diamos, Sudha Yalamanchili, and tips from the anonymous referees also greatly helped shape this paper. Portions of this work were made possible through financial support from Google and LogicBlox.

7. REFERENCES

[1] L. O. Andersen. Program analysis and specialization for the c programming language. Technical report, University of Copenhagen, 1994.

[2] C. Bienia, S. Kumar, J. P. Singh, and K. Li. The PARSEC Benchmark Suite: Characterization and Architectural Implications. In *Proceedings of the 17th International Conference on Parallel Architectures and Compilation Techniques*, Oct. 2008.

[3] M. Chu, R. Ravindran, and S. Mahlke. Data Access Partitioning for Fine-grain Parallelism on Multicore Architectures. In *Proc. of the 40th Annual International Symposium on Microarchitecture*, pages 369–378, 2007.

[4] J. Corbalan, X. Martorell, and J. Labarta. Performance-driven processor allocation. In *Proc. of the 2000 International*

Symposium on on Operating Systems Design and Implementation, pages 255–266, 2008.

[5] M. Curtis-Maury, J. Dzierwa, C. D. Antonopoulos, and D. S. Nikolopoulos. Online power-performance adaptation of multithreaded programs using hardware event-based prediction. In *Proc. of the 2006 International Conference on Supercomputing*, pages 157–166, 2006.

[6] L. Dagum and R. Menon. OpenMP: an industry standard API for shared-memory programming. *IEEE Computer Science and Engineering*, 5(1):46–55, 1998.

[7] Y. Ding, M. Kandemir, P. Raghavan, and M. Irwin. A helper thread based edp reduction scheme for adapting application execution in cmps. In *Proc. of the 2008 IEEE Symposium on on Parallel and Distributed Processing*, pages 1–14, 2008.

[8] C. Fiduccia and R. Mattheyses. A linear time heuristic for improving network partitions. In *Proc. of the 19th Design Automation Conference*, pages 175–181, 1982.

[9] M. R. Garey and D. S. Johnson. *Computers and Intractability: A Guide to the Theory of NP-Completeness*. W. H. Freeman & Co., 1979.

[10] A. Ghuloum. Ct: C for throughput computing (whitepaper), 2009. http://techresearch.intel.com/articles/Tera-Scale/1514.htm.

[11] M. Hirzel, D. von Dincklage, A. Diwan, and M. Hind. Fast online pointer analysis. *ACM Transactions on Programming Languages and Systems*, 29(2):11, Apr. 2007.

[12] C. Jung, D. Lim, J. Lee, and S. Han. Adaptive execution techniques for SMT multiprocessor architectures. In *Proc. of the 10th ACM SIGPLAN Symposium on Principles and Practice of Parallel Programming*, pages 236–246, 2005.

[13] B. Kernighan and S. Lin. An efficient heuristic procedure for partitioning graphs. *The Bell System Technical Journal*, 49(2):291–207, Feb. 1970.

[14] M. Kudlur and S. Mahlke. Orchestrating the execution of stream programs on multicore platforms. In *Proc. of the SIGPLAN '08 Conference on Programming Language Design and Implementation*, pages 114–124, June 2008.

[15] M. Kulkarni et al. Optimistic Parallelism Requires Abstractions. In *Proc. of the SIGPLAN '07 Conference on Programming Language Design and Implementation*, pages 211 – 222, June 2007.

[16] R. Kumar, G. Agrawal, and G. Gao. Compiling several classes of communication patterns on a multithreaded architecture. In *Proc. of the 2002 IEEE Symposium on on Parallel and Distributed Processing*, pages 18–23, 2002.

[17] R. Kumar et al. Single-ISA Heterogeneous Multi-Core Architectures for Multithreaded Workload Performance. In *Proc. of the 31st Annual International Symposium on Computer Architecture*, 2004.

[18] R. Kumar, K. I. Farkas, N. P. Jouppi, P. Ranganathan, and D. M. Tullsen. Single-ISA Heterogeneous Multi-Core Architectures: The Potential for Processor Power Reduction. In *Proc. of the 36th Annual International Symposium on Microarchitecture*, pages 81–92, Dec. 2003.

[19] N. Lakshiminarayana, S. Rao, and H. Kim. Asymmetricity Aware Scheduling Algorithms for Asymmetric Processors. In *Workshop on the Interaction between Operating Systems and Computer Architecture*, 2009.

[20] C. Lattner and V. Adve. LLVM: A Compilation Framework for Lifelong Program Analysis and Transformation. In *Proc. of the 2004 International Symposium on Code Generation and Optimization*, pages 75–86, 2004.

[21] J. Li and J. Martinez. Dynamic power-performance adaptation of parallel computation on chip multiprocessors. In *Proc. of the 12th International Symposium on High-Performance Computer Architecture*, pages 77–87, 2006.

[22] U. Nawathe et al. An 8-core, 64-thread, 64-bit, power efficient SPARC SoC (Niagara2), Feb. 2007. In *Proc. of ISSCC*.

[23] J. Nieplocha et al. Evaluating the potential of multithreaded platforms for irregular scientific computations. In *Proc. of the 2007 ACM Conference on Computing Frontiers*, pages 47–58, 2007.

[24] Nvidia. *CUDA Programming Guide*, June 2007. http://developer.download.nvidia.com/compute/cuda.

[25] K. Olukotun et al. The case for a single chip multiprocessor. In *Seventh International Conference on Architectural Support for Programming Languages and Operating Systems*, pages 2–11, 1996.

[26] M. Qureshi and Y. Patt. Partitioning: A low-overhead, high-performance, runtime mechanism to partition shared caches. In *Proc. of the 39th Annual International Symposium on Microarchitecture*, pages 423–432, 2006.

[27] R. Ravindran, R. Senger, E. Marsman, G. Dasika, M. Guthaus, S. Mahlke, and R. Brown. Increasing the Number of Effective Registers in a Low-Power Processor Using a Windowed Register File. In *Proc. of the 2003 International Conference on Compilers, Architecture, and Synthesis for Embedded Systems*, pages 125–136, 2003.

[28] H. Schwartz, D. Marpe, and T. Wiegand. Overview of the scalable video coding extension of the h.264/avc standard. *IEEE Transactions on Circuits and Systems for Video Technology*, 17(9):1103 – 1120, Sept. 2007.

[29] M. A. Suleman, M. Qureshi, and Y. Patt. Feedback Driven Threading: Power-Efficient and High-Performance Execution of Multithreaded Workloads on CMPs. In *16th International Conference on Architectural Support for Programming Languages and Operating Systems*, pages 277–286, 2008.

[30] P. Wang et al. EXOCHI: architecture and programming environment for a heterogeneous multi-core multithreaded system. In *Proc. of the SIGPLAN '07 Conference on Programming Language Design and Implementation*, pages 156 – 166, 2007.

[31] S. Woo, M. Ohara, E. Torrie, J. Singh, and A. Gupta. The SPLASH-2 programs: Characterization and methodological considerations. In *Proceedings of the 22nd annual international symposium on Computer architecture*, pages 24–36, 1995.

[32] Q. Wu et al. A dynamic compilation framework for controlling microprocessor energy and performance. In *Proc. of the 38th Annual International Symposium on Microarchitecture*, pages 271–282, 2005.

[33] Y. Xie and G. H. Loh. PIPP: Promotion/Insertion Pseudo-Partitioning of Multi-Core Shared Caches. In *Proc. of the 36th Annual International Symposium on Computer Architecture*, pages 174–183, 2009.

An Integrated GPU Power and Performance Model

Sunpyo Hong
Electrical and Computer Engineering
Georgia Institute of Technology
shong9@gatech.edu

Hyesoon Kim
School of Computer Science
Georgia Institute of Technology
hyesoon@cc.gatech.edu

ABSTRACT

GPU architectures are increasingly important in the multi-core era due to their high number of parallel processors. Performance optimization for multi-core processors has been a challenge for programmers. Furthermore, optimizing for power consumption is even more difficult. Unfortunately, as a result of the high number of processors, the power consumption of many-core processors such as GPUs has increased significantly.

Hence, in this paper, we propose an integrated power and performance (IPP) prediction model for a GPU architecture to predict the optimal number of active processors for a given application. The basic intuition is that when an application reaches the peak memory bandwidth, using more cores does not result in performance improvement.

We develop an empirical power model for the GPU. Unlike most previous models, which require measured execution times, hardware performance counters, or architectural simulations, IPP predicts execution times to calculate dynamic power events. We then use the outcome of IPP to control the number of running cores. We also model the increases in power consumption that resulted from the increases in temperature.

With the predicted optimal number of active cores, we show that we can save up to 22.09% of runtime GPU energy consumption and on average 10.99% of that for the five memory bandwidth-limited benchmarks.

Categories and Subject Descriptors

C.1.4 [**Processor Architectures**]: Parallel Architectures;
C.4 [**Performance of Systems**]: Modeling techniques;
C.5.3 [**Computer System Implementation**]: Microcomputers

General Terms

Measurement, Performance

Keywords

Analytical model, CUDA, GPU architecture, Performance, Power estimation, Energy

1. INTRODUCTION

The increasing computing power of GPUs gives them a considerably higher throughput than that of CPUs. As a result, many programmers try to use GPUs for more than just graphics applications. However, optimizing GPU kernels to achieve high performance is still a challenge. Furthermore, optimizing an application to achieve a better power efficiency is even more difficult.

The number of cores inside a chip, especially in GPUs, is increasing dramatically. For example, NVIDIA's GTX280 [2] has 30 streaming multiprocessors (SMs) with 240 CUDA cores, and the next generation GPU will have 512 CUDA cores [3]. Even though GPU applications are highly throughput-oriented, not all applications require all available cores to achieve the best performance.

In this study, we aim to answer the following important questions: Do we need *all cores* to achieve the highest performance? Can we save power and energy by using *fewer cores*?

Figure 1 shows performance, power consumption, and efficiency (performance per watt) as we vary the number of active cores.[1] The power consumption increases as we increase the number of cores. Depending on the circuit design (power gating, clock gating, etc.), the gradient of an increase in power consumption also varies. Figure 1(left) shows the performances of two different types of applications. In Type 1, the performance increases linearly, because applications can utilize the computing powers in all the cores. However, in Type 2, the performance is saturated after a certain number of cores due to bandwidth limitations [22, 23]. Once the number of memory requests from cores exceeds the peak memory bandwidth, increasing the number of active cores does not lead to a better performance. Figure 1(right) shows performance per watt. In this paper, the number of cores that shows the highest performance per watt is called the optimal number of cores.

In Type 2, since the performance does not increase linearly, using all the cores consumes more energy than using the optimal number of cores. However, for application Type 1, utilizing all the cores would consume the least amount of energy because of a reduction in execution time. The optimal number of cores for Type 1 is the maximum number of available cores but that of Type 2 is less than the maximum value. Hence, if we can predict the optimal number of cores at static time, either the compiler (or the programmer) can configure the number of threads/blocks[2] to utilize fewer cores, or hardware or a dynamic thread manager can use fewer cores.

To achieve this goal, we propose an integrated power and performance prediction system, which we call *IPP*. Figure 2 shows an overview of IPP. It takes a GPU kernel as an input and predicts both power consumption and performance together, whereas previ-

[1] Active cores mean the cores that are executing a program.
[2] The term, *block*, is defined in the CUDA programming model.

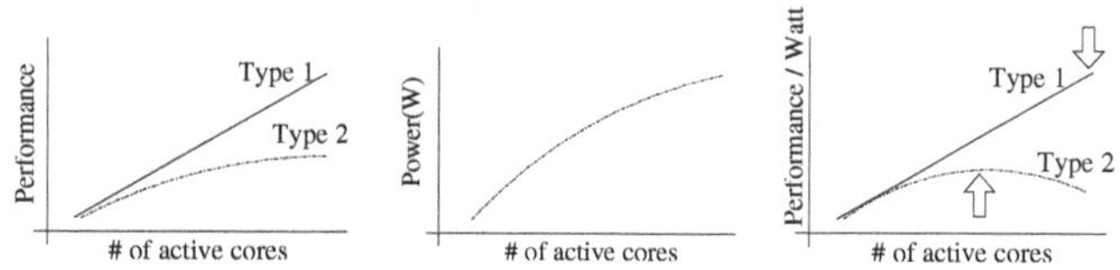

Figure 1: Performance, power, and efficiency vs. # of active cores (left: performance, middle: power, right: performance per watt)

ous analytical models predict only execution time or power. More importantly, unlike previous power models, IPP does not require architectural timing simulations or hardware performance counters; instead it uses outcomes of a timing model.

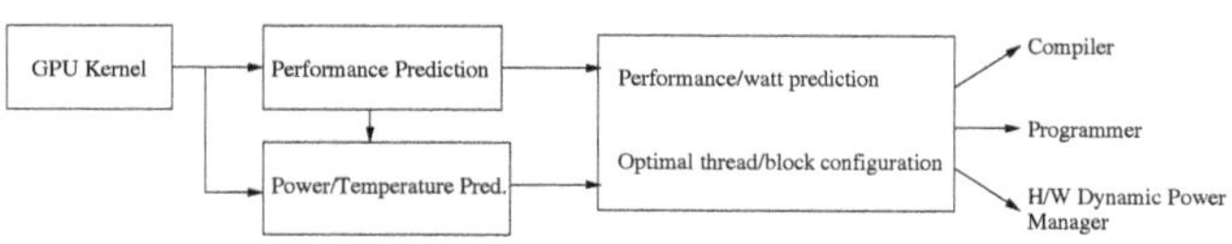

Figure 2: Overview of the IPP System

Using the power and performance outcomes, IPP predicts the optimal number of cores that results in the highest performance per watt. We evaluate the IPP system and demonstrate energy savings in a real GPU system. The results show that by using fewer cores based on the IPP prediction, we can save up to 22.09% and on average 10.99% of runtime energy consumption for the five memory bandwidth-limited benchmarks. We also estimate the amount of energy savings for GPUs that employ a power gating mechanism. Our evaluation shows that with power gating, the IPP can save on average 25.85% of the total GPU power for the five bandwidth-limited benchmarks.

In summary, our work makes the following contributions:

1. We propose what, to the best of our knowledge, is the first analytical model to predict performance, power and efficiency (performance/watt) of GPGPU applications on a GPU architecture.
2. We develop an empirical runtime power prediction model for a GPU. In addition, we also model the increases in runtime power consumption that resulted from the increases in temperature.
3. We propose the IPP system that predicts the optimal number of active cores to save energy.
4. We successfully demonstrate energy savings in a real system by activating fewer cores based on the outcome of IPP.

2. BACKGROUND ON POWER

Power consumption can be divided into two parts: dynamic power and static power, as shown in Equation (1).

$$Power = Dynamic\_power + Static\_power \quad (1)$$

Dynamic power is the switching overhead in transistors, so it is determined by runtime events. Static power is mainly determined by circuit technology, chip layout and operating temperature.

2.1 Building a Power Model Using an Empirical Method

Isci and Martonosi [12] proposed an empirical method to building a power model. They measured and modeled the Intel Pentium 4 processor.

$$Power = \sum_{i=0}^{n}(AccessRate(C_i) \times ArchitecturalScaling(C_i) \quad (2)$$
$$\times MaxPower(C_i) + NonGatedClockPower(C_i)) + IdlePower$$

Equation (2) shows the basic power model discussed in [12]. It consists of the idle power plus the dynamic power for each hardware component, where the $MaxPower$ and $ArchitecturalScaling$ terms are heuristically determined. For example, $MaxPower$ is empirically determined by running several training benchmarks that stress fewer architectural components. Access rates are obtained from performance counters. They indicate how often an architectural unit is accessed per unit of time, where one is the maximum value.

2.2 Static Power

As the technology is scaled, static power consumption is increased [4]. To understand static power consumption and temperature effects, we briefly describe static power models.

Butts and Sohi [6] presented the following simplified leakage power model for an architecture-level study.

$$P_{static} = V_{cc} \cdot N \cdot K_{design} \cdot \hat{I}_{leak} \quad (3)$$

V_{CC} is the supply voltage, N is the number of transistors in the design, and K_{design} is a constant factor that represents the technology characteristics. $\hat{I}_{leak}$ is a normalized leakage current for a single transistor that depends on V_{th}, which is the threshold voltage. Later, Zhang et al. [24] improved this static power model to consider temperature effects and operating voltages in *HotLeakage*, a software tool. In their model, K_{design} is no longer constant and depends on temperature, where $\hat{I}_{leak}$ is a function of temperature and supply voltage. The leakage current can be expressed as shown in Equation (4).

$$\hat{I}_{leak} = \mu_0 \cdot C_{OX} \cdot \frac{W}{L} \cdot e^{b(V_{dd}-V_{dd0})} \cdot v_t^2 \cdot (1 - e^{\frac{-V_{dd}}{v_t}}) \cdot e^{\frac{-|V_{th}|-V_{off}}{n \cdot v_t}} \quad (4)$$

v_t is the thermal voltage that is represented by kT/q, and it depends on temperature. The threshold voltage, V_{th}, is also a function of temperature. Since v_t^2 is the dominant temperature-dependent factor in Equation (4), the leakage power quadratically increases with temperature. However, in a normal operating temperature range, the leakage power can be simplified as a linear model [21].

3. POWER AND TEMPERATURE MODELS

3.1 Overall Model

GPU power consumption (GPU_power) is modeled similar to Equation (2) [12] in Section 2. The GPU_power term consists of $Runtime\_power$ and $IdlePower$ terms, as shown in Equation (5). The $NonGatedClockPower$ term is not used in this model, because the evaluated GPUs do not employ clock gating. $IdlePower$ is the power consumption when a GPU is on but no application is running. $Runtime\_power$ is the additional power consumption required to execute programs on a GPU. It is the sum of runtime-powers from all SMs(RP_SMs) and GDDR memory (RP_Memory).

Table 1: List of instructions that access each architectural unit

PTX Instruction	Architectural Unit	Variable Name
add_int sub_int addc_int subc_int sad_int div_int rem_int abs_int mul_int mad_int mul24_int mad24_int min_int neg_int	Int. arithmetic unit	RP_Int
add_fp sub_fp mul_fp fma_fp neg_fp min_fp lg2_fp ex2_fp mad_fp div_fp abs_fp	Floating point unit	RP_Fp
sin_fp cos_fp rcp_fp sqrt_fp rsqrt_fp	SFU	RP_Sfu
xor cnot shl shr mov cvt set setp selp slct and or	ALU	RP_Alu
st_global ld.global	Global memory	RP_GlobalMem
st_local ld.local	Local memory	RP_LocalMem
tex	Texture cache	RP_Texture_Cache
ld_const	Constant cache	RP_Const_Cache
ld_shared st_shared	Shared memory	RP_Shared
setp selp slct and or xor shr mov cvt st_global ld_global ld_const add mad24 sad div rem abs neg shl min sin cos rcp sqrt rsqrt set mul24 sub addc subc mul mad cnot ld_shared st_local ld_local tex	Register file	RP_Reg
All instructions	FDS (Fetch/Dec/Sch)	RP_FDS

$$GPU\_power = Runtime\_power + IdlePower \tag{5}$$

$$Runtime\_power = \sum_{i=0}^{n} RP\_Component_i \tag{6}$$
$$= RP\_SMs + RP\_Memory$$

3.2 Modeling Power Consumption from Streaming Multiprocessors

In order to model the runtime power of SMs, we decompose the SM into several physical components, as shown in Equation (7) and Table 1. The texture and constant caches are included in the $SM\_Component$ term, because they are shared between multiple SMs in the evaluated GPU system. One texture cache is shared by three SMs, and each SM has its own constant cache. RP_Const_SM is a constant runtime power component for each active SM. It models power consumption from several units, including I-cache, and the frame buffer, which always consume relatively constant amount of power when a core is active.

$$\sum_{i=0}^{n} SM\_Component_i = RP\_Int + RP\_Fp + RP\_Sfu \tag{7}$$
$$+ RP\_Alu + RP\_Texture\_Cache + RP\_Const\_Cache$$
$$+ RP\_Shared + RP\_Reg + RP\_FDS + RP\_Const\_SM$$

$$RP\_SMs = Num\_SMs \times \sum_{i=0}^{n} SM\_Component_i \tag{8}$$

Num_SMs: Total number of SMs in a GPU

Table 1 summarizes the modeled architectural components used by each instruction type and the corresponding variable names in Equation (7). All instructions access the FDS unit (Fetch/Dec/Sch). For the register unit, we assume that all instructions accessing the register file have the same number of register operands per instruction to simplify the model. The exact number of register accesses per instruction depends on the instruction type and the number of operands, but we found that the power consumption difference due to the number of register operands is negligible.

Access Rate: As Equation 2 shows, dynamic power consumption is dependent on access rate of each hardware component. Isci and Martonosi used a combination of hardware performance counters to measure access rates [12]. Since GPUs do not have any speculative execution, we can estimate hardware access rates based on the dynamic number of instructions and execution times without hardware performance counters.

Equation (9) shows how to calculate the runtime power for each component ($RPcomp$) such as RP_Reg. $RPcomp$ is the multiplication of $AccessRate_{comp}$ and $MaxPower_{comp}$. $MaxPower_{comp}$ is described in Table 2 and will be discussed in Section 3.4. Note that RP_Const_SM is not dependent on $AccessRate_{comp}$.

Equation (10) shows how to calculate the access rate for each component, $AccessRate_{comp}$. The dynamic number of instructions per component ($DAC\_per\_th_{comp}$) is the sum of instructions that access an architectural component. $Warps\_per\_SM$ indicates how many warps[3] are executed in one SM. We divide execution cycles by four because one instruction is fetched, scheduled, and executed every four cycles. This normalization also makes the maximum value of the $AccessRate_{comp}$ term be one.

$$RP_{comp} = MaxPower_{comp} \times AccessRate_{comp} \tag{9}$$

$$AccessRate_{comp} = \frac{DAC\_per\_th_{comp} \times Warps\_per\_SM}{Exec\_cycles/4} \tag{10}$$

$$DAC\_per\_th_{comp} = \sum_{i=0}^{n} Number\_Inst\_per\_warps_i(comp) \tag{11}$$

$$Warps\_per\_SM = \left(\frac{\#Threads\_per\_block}{\#Threads\_per\_warp} \times \frac{\#Blocks}{\#Active\_SMs}\right) \tag{12}$$

3.3 Modeling Memory Power

The evaluated GPU system has five different memory spaces: global, shared, local, texture, and constant. The shared memory space uses a software managed cache that is inside an SM. The texture and constant memories are located in the GDDR memory, but they mainly use caches inside an SM. The global memory and the local memory are sharing the same physical GDDR memory, hence RP_Memory considers both. Shared, constant, and texture memory spaces are modeled separately as SM components.

$$RP\_Memory = \sum_{i=0}^{n} Memory\_component_i \tag{13}$$
$$= RP\_GlobalMem + RP\_LocalMem$$

3.4 Power Model Parameters

To obtain the power model parameters, we design a set of synthetic microbenchmarks that stress different architectural components in the GPU. Each microbenchmark has a loop that repeats a certain set of instructions. For example, the microbenchmark that stresses FP units contains a high ratio of FP instructions.

The optimum set of $MaxPower_{comp}$ values in Equation (9) that minimize the error between the measured power and the outcome of the equation is searched. However, to avoid searching through a large space of values, the initial seed value for each architecture unit is estimated based on the relative physical die sizes of the unit [12]. Table 2 shows the parameters used for $MaxPower_{comp}$. Eight

[3]Warp is a group of threads that are fetched/executed together inside the GPU architecture.

power components require a special piecewise linear approach [12]: an initial increase from idle to relatively low access rate causes a large granularity of increase in power consumption while a further increase causes a smaller increase. Spec.Linear column indicates whether the $AccessRate_{comp}$ term in Equation (9) needs to be replaced with the special piecewise linear access rate based on the following simple conversion; $0.1365 * ln(AccessRate_{comp}) + 1.001375$. The parameters in this conversion are empirically determined to have a piecewise linear function.

Table 2: Empirical power parameters

Units	MaxPower	OnChip	Spec.Linear
FP	0.2	Yes	Yes
REG	0.3	Yes	Yes
ALU	0.2	Yes	No
SFU	0.5	Yes	No
INT	0.25	Yes	Yes
FDS (Fetch/Dec/Sch)	0.5	Yes	Yes
Shared memory	1	Yes	No
Texture cache	0.9	Yes	Yes
Constant cache	0.4	Yes	Yes
Const_SM	0.813	Yes	No
Global memory	52	No	Yes
Local memory	52	No	Yes

Figure 3 shows how the overall power is distributed among the individual architectural components for all the evaluated benchmarks (Section 5 presents the detailed benchmark descriptions and the evaluation methodology). On average, the memory, idle power, and RP_Const_SM consume more than 60% of the total GPU power. REG and FDS also consume relatively higher power than other components because almost all instructions access these units.

3.5 Active SMs vs. Power Consumption

To measure the power consumption of each SM, we design another set of microbenchmarks to control the number of active SMs. These microbenchmarks are designed such that only one block can be executed in each SM, thus as we vary the number of blocks, the number of active SMs varies as well. Even though the evaluated GPU does not employ power gating, idle SMs do not consume as much power as active SMs do because of low-activity factors [18] (i.e., idle SMs do not change values in circuits as often as active SMs). Hence, there are still significant differences in the total power consumption depending on the number of active SMs in a GPU.

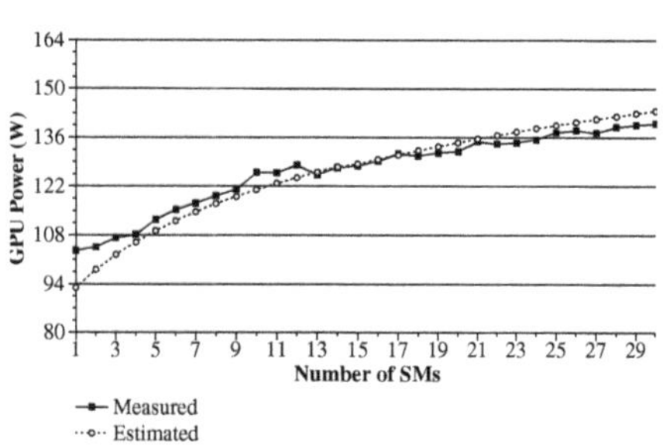

Figure 4: Power consumption vs. active SMs

Figure 4 shows an increase in power consumption as we increase the number of active SMs. The maximum power delta between using only one SM versus all SMs is 37W. Since there is no power gating, the power consumption does not increase linearly as we increase the number of SMs. We use a log-based model instead of a linear curve, as shown in Equation (14). We also model the memory power consumption following the exact same log-based trend although it is not directly dependent on the number of active SMs. Finally, runtime power can be modeled by taking the number of active SMs as shown in Equation (16)

$$RP\_SMs = Max\_SM \times log_{10}(\alpha \times Active\_SMs + \beta) \quad (14)$$

$$Max\_SM = (Num\_SMs \times \sum_{i=0}^{n} SM\_Component_i) \quad (15)$$

$$\alpha = (10 - \beta)/Num\_SMs, \beta = 1.1$$

$$Runtime\_power = (Max\_SM + RP\_Memory) \times log_{10}(\alpha \times Active\_SMs + \beta) \quad (16)$$

$Active\_SMs$: Number of active SMs in the GPU

3.6 Temperature Model

CPU Temperature models are typically represented by an RC model [20]. We determine the model parameters empirically by using a step function experiment. Equation (17) models the rising temperature, and Equation (18) models the decaying temperature.

$$Temperature_{rise}(t) = Idle\_temp + \delta\left(1 - e^{-t/RC\_Rise}\right) \quad (17)$$

$$Temperature_{decay}(t) = Idle\_temp + \gamma\left(e^{-t/RC\_Decay}\right) \quad (18)$$

$$\delta = Max\_temp - Idle\_temp, \gamma = Decay\_temp - Idle\_temp$$

$Idle\_temp$: Idle operating chip temperature
Max_temp: Maximum temperature, which depends on runtime power
$Decay\_temp$: Chip temperature right before decay

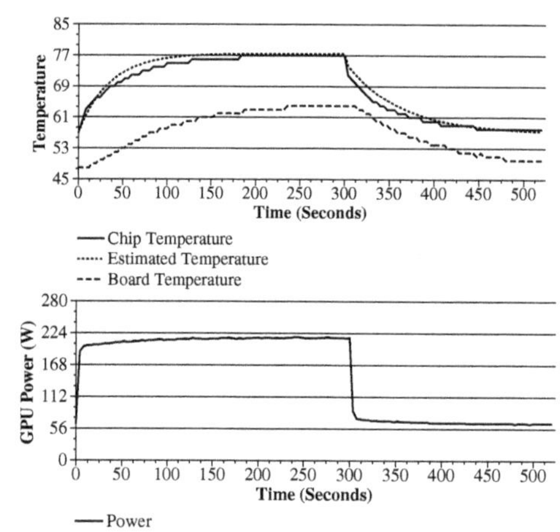

Figure 5: Temperature effects from power, (top): Measured and estimated temperature, (bottom): Measured power

Figure 5 shows estimated and measured temperature variations. Both the chip temperature and the board temperature are measured with the built-in sensors in the GPU. Max_temp is a function of runtime power, which depends on application characteristics. We discovered that the chip temperature is strongly affected by the rate of GDDR memory accesses, not only runtime power consumption. Hence, the maximum temperature is modeled with a combination of them as shown in Equation (19). The model parameters are described in Table 3. Note that $Memory\_Insts$ includes global and local memory instructions.

$$Max\_temp(Runtime\_Power) = (\mu \times Runtime\_Power) + \lambda + \rho \times MemAccess\_intensity \quad (19)$$

$$MemAccess\_intensity = \frac{Memory\_Insts}{NonMemory\_Insts} \quad (20)$$

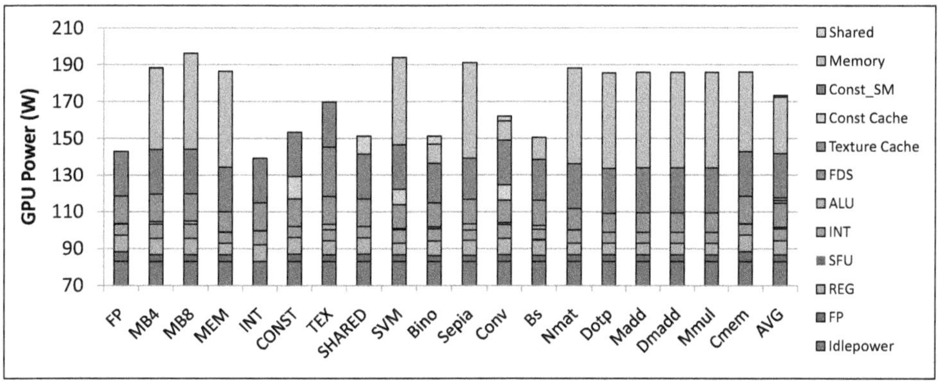

Figure 3: Power breakdown graph for all the evaluated benchmarks

Table 3: Parameters for GTX280

Parameter	Value
μ	0.120
λ	5.5
ρ	21.505
RC_Rise	35
RC_Decay	60

3.7 Modeling Increases in Static Power Consumption

Section 2.2 discussed the impact of temperature on static power consumption. Because of the high number of processors in the GPU chip, we observe an increase in runtime power consumption as the chip temperature increases, as shown in Figure 6. To consider increases in static power consumption, we include the temperature model (Equations (17) and (18)) into the runtime power consumption model. We use a linear model to represent increases in static power as discussed in Section 2.2. Since we cannot control the operating voltage of the evaluated GPUs at runtime, we only consider operating temperature effects.

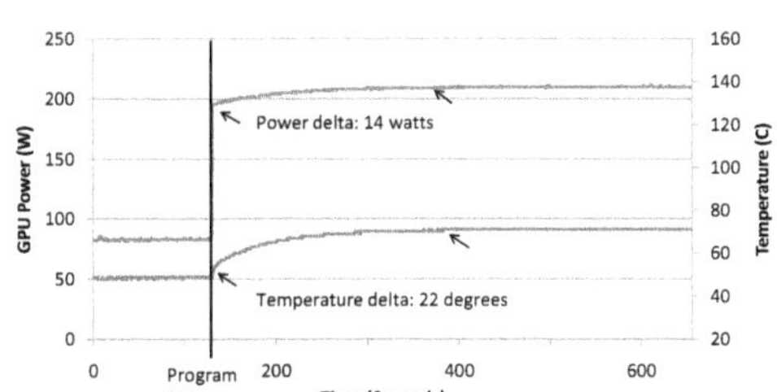

Figure 6: Static power effects

Figure 6 shows that power consumption increases gradually over time after an application starts,[4] and the delta is 14 watts. This delta could be caused by increases in static power consumption or additional fan power. By manually controlling the fan speed from lowest to highest, we measure that the additional fan power consumption is only 4W. Hence, the remaining 10 watts of the power consumption increase is modeled as the additional static power increase that resulted from the increases in temperature. Equation (21) shows the comprehensive power equation over time that includes the increased static power consumption, which depends on σ (the ratio of power delta over temperature delta (σ = 10 / 22)). Note that $Runtime\_power_0$ is an initial power consumption obtained from (16), and the model assumes a cold start (i.e., the system is in the idle state). $Temperature(t)$ in (23) is obtained from (17) or (18).

$$GPU\_power(t) = Runtime\_power(t) + IdlePower \quad (21)$$
$$Runtime\_power(t) = Runtime\_power_0 + \sigma \times Delta\_temp(t) \quad (22)$$
$$Delta\_temp(t) = Temperature(t) - Idle\_temp \quad (23)$$

4. IPP: INTEGRATED POWER AND PERFORMANCE MODEL

In this section, we describe the integrated power and performance model to predict performance per watt and the optimal number of active cores. The integrated power and performance model (IPP) uses predicted execution times to predict power consumption instead of measured execution times.

4.1 Execution Time and Access Rate Prediction

In Section 3, we developed the power model that computes access rates by using measured execution time information. Predicting power at static time requires access rates in advance. In other words, we also need to predict the execution time of an application to predict power. We used a recently developed GPU analytical timing model [9] to predict the execution time. The model is briefly explained in this section. Please refer to the analytical timing model paper [9] for the detailed descriptions.

In the timing model, the total execution time of a GPGPU application is calculated with one of Equations (24), (25), and (26) based on the number of running threads, MWP, and CWP in the application. MWP represents the number of memory requests that can be serviced concurrently and CWP represents the number of warps that can finish one computational period during one memory access period. N is the number of running warps. Mem_L is the average memory latency (430 cycles for the evaluated GPU architecture). Mem_cycles is the processor waiting cycles for memory operations. $Comp\_cycles$ is the execution time of all instructions. $Repw$ is the number of times that each SM needs to repeat the same set of computation.

[4]The initial jump of power consumption exists when an application starts.

Case1: If (MWP is N warps per SM) and (CWP is N warps per SM)

$$(Mem\_cycles + Comp\_cycles + \frac{Comp\_cycles}{\#Mem\_insts} \times (MWP - 1))(\#Repw) \quad (24)$$

Case2: If (CWP >= MWP) or (Comp_cycles > Mem_cycles)

$$(Mem\_cycles \times \frac{N}{MWP} + \frac{Comp\_cycles}{\#Mem\_insts} \times (MWP - 1))(\#Repw) \quad (25)$$

Case3: If (MWP > CWP)

$$(Mem\_L + Comp\_cycles \times N)(\#Repw) \quad (26)$$

IPP calculates the AccessRate using Equation (27), where the predicted execution cycles ($Predicted\_Exec\_Cycles$) are calculated with one of the Equations (24),(25), and (26).

$$AccessRate_{comp} = \frac{DAC\_per\_th_{comp} \times Warps\_per\_SM}{Predicted\_Exec\_Cycles/4} \quad (27)$$

4.2 Optimal Number of Cores for Highest Performance/Watt

IPP predicts the optimal number of SMs that would achieve the highest performance/watt. As we showed in Figure 1, the performance of an application either increases linearly (in this case, the optimal number of SMs is always the maximum number of cores) or non-linearly (the optimal number of SMs is less than the maximum number of cores). Performance per watt can be calculated by using Equation (28).

$$perf.\ per\ watt(cores) = \frac{(work/execution\ time(\#\ of\ cores)}{(power(\#\ of\ cores))} \quad (28)$$

Equations (24),(25), and (26) calculate execution times. Among the three cases, only Case 2 has a memory bandwidth limited case. Case 1 is used when there are not enough number of running threads in the system, and Case 3 models when an application is computationally intensive. So both Cases 1 and 3 would never reach the peak memory bandwidth. To understand the memory bandwidth limited case, let's look at MWP more carefully. The following equations show the steps in calculating MWP. MWP is the number of memory requests that can be serviced concurrently. As shown in Equation(29), MWP is the minimum of $MWP\_Without\_BW$, MWP_peak_BW, and N. N is the number of running warps. If there are not enough warps, MWP is limited by the number of running warps. If an application is limited by memory bandwidth, MWP is determined by MWP_peak_BW, which is a function of a memory bandwidth and the number of active SMs. Note that $Departure\_delay$ represents the pipeline delay between two consecutive memory accesses, and it is dependent on both the memory system and the memory access types (coalesced or uncoalesced) in applications.

$$MWP = MIN(MWP\_Without\_BW, MWP\_peak\_BW, N) \quad (29)$$

$$MWP\_peak\_BW = \frac{Mem\_Bandwidth}{BW\_per\_warp \times \#ActiveSM} \quad (30)$$

$$BW\_per\_warp = \frac{Freq \times Load\_bytes\_per\_warp}{Mem\_L} \quad (31)$$

$$MWP\_Without\_BW\_full = Mem\_L/Departure\_delay \quad (32)$$

$$MWP\_Without\_BW = MIN(MWP\_Without\_BW\_full, N) \quad (33)$$

We could calculate $\frac{d(perf.\ per\ watt(\#\ of\ active\ cores)}{d(\#\ of\ active\ cores)} = 0$ to find the optimal number of cores. However, we observed that once MWP_peak_BW reaches N, the application usually reaches the peak bandwidth. Hence, based on Equation (30), we conclude that the optimal number of cores can be calculated using the following equations to simplify the calculation.

if (1) (MWP == N) or (CWP == N) or (34)
(2) MWP > CWP or
(3) MWP < MWP_peak_BW

$$Optimal\ \#\ of\ cores = Maximum\ available\ \#\ of\ cores$$

else

$$Optimal\ \#\ of\ cores = \frac{Mem\_Bandwidth}{(BW\_per\_warp) \times N}$$

4.3 Limitations of IPP

IPP requires both power and timing models thereby inheriting the limitations from them. Some examples of limitations include the following: control flow intensive applications, asymmetric applications, and texture cache intensive applications.

IPP also requires an instruction information. However, IPP does not require an actual number of total instructions. It calculates only access rates that can be easily normalized with an input data size. Nonetheless, if an application shows a significantly different behavior depending on input sizes, IPP needs to consider the input size effects, which will be addressed in our future work.

4.4 Using Results of IPP

In this paper, we constrain the number of active cores based on an output of IPP by only limiting the number of blocks inside an application, since we cannot change the hardware or the thread scheduler. If the number of active cores can be directly controlled by hardware or by a runtime thread scheduler, compilers or programmers do not have to change their applications to utilize fewer cores. Instead, IPP only passes the information of the number of optimal cores to the runtime system, and either the hardware or runtime thread scheduler enables only the required number of cores to save energy.

5. METHODOLOGY

5.1 Power and Temperature Measurement

The NVIDIA GTX280 GPU, which has 30 SMs and uses a 65nm technology, is used in this work. We use the Extech 380801 AC/DC Power Analyzer [1] to measure the overall system power consumption. The raw power data is sent to a data-log machine every 0.5 second. Each microbenchmark executes for an average of 10 seconds.

Since we measure the input power to the entire system, we have to subtract $Idlepower\_System$ (159W) from the total system input power to obtain GPU_Power.[5] The $Idle\_Power$ value for the evaluated GPU is 83W. The GPU temperature is measured with the *nvclock* utility [16]. The command "nvclock -i" outputs board and chip temperatures. Temperature is measured every second.

[5] IdlePower_System is obtained by measuring system power with another GPU card whose idle power is known

5.2 Benchmarks

To test the accuracy of our IPP system, we use the Merge benchmarks [15, 9], five additional memory bandwidth-limited benchmarks (Nmat, Dotp, Madd, Dmadd, and Mmul), and one computational intensive (i.e., non-memory bandwidth limited) benchmark (Cmem). Table 4 describes each benchmark and summarizes the characteristics of them.

To calculate the number of dynamic instructions, we use a GPU PTX emulator, Ocelot [13]. It also classifies instruction types.

6. RESULTS

6.1 Evaluation of Runtime Power Model

Figure 7 compares the predicted power consumption with the measured power value for the microbenchmarks. According to Figure 3, the global memory consumes the most amount of power. MB4, MB8, and MEM benchmarks consume much greater power than the FP benchmark, which consists of mainly floating point instructions. Surprisingly, the benchmarks that use texture cache or constant cache also consume high power. This is because both the texture cache and the constant cache have higher $MaxPower$ than that of the FP unit. The geometric mean of the error in the power prediction for microbenchmark is 2.5%. Figure 8 shows the access rates for each microbenchmark. When an application does not have many memory operations such as the FP benchmark, dynamic access rates for FP or REG can be very close to one. FDS is one when an application reaches the peak performance of the machine.

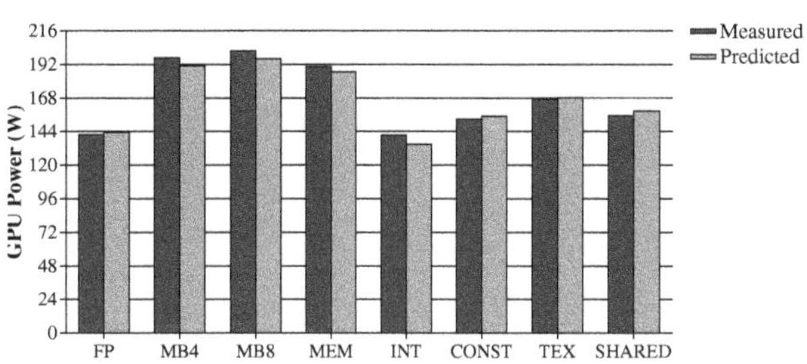

Figure 7: Comparison of measured and predicted GPU power consumption for the microbenchmarks

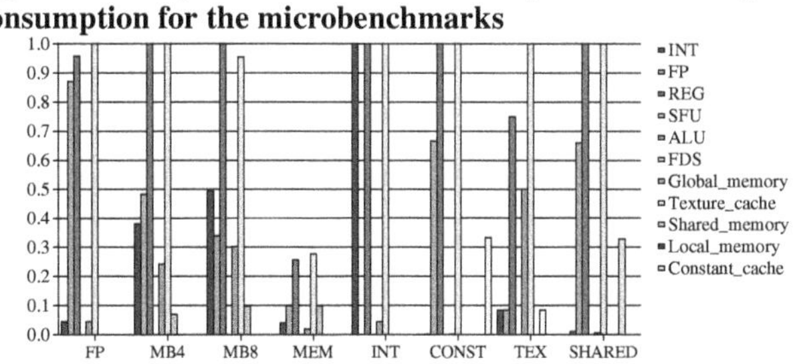

Figure 8: Dynamic access rate of the microbenchmarks

Figure 9 compares the predicted power and the measured power consumptions for the evaluated GPGPU kernels. The geometric mean of the power prediction error is 9.18% for the GPGPU kernels. Figure 10 shows the dynamic access rates. The complete breakdown of the GPU power consumption is shown in Figure 3. Bino and Conv have lower global memory access rates than others, which results in less power consumption than others. Sepia and Bs are high performance applications. This explains why they have high REG and FDS values. All the memory bandwidth-limited benchmarks have higher power consumption even though they have relatively lower FP/REG/FDS access rates.

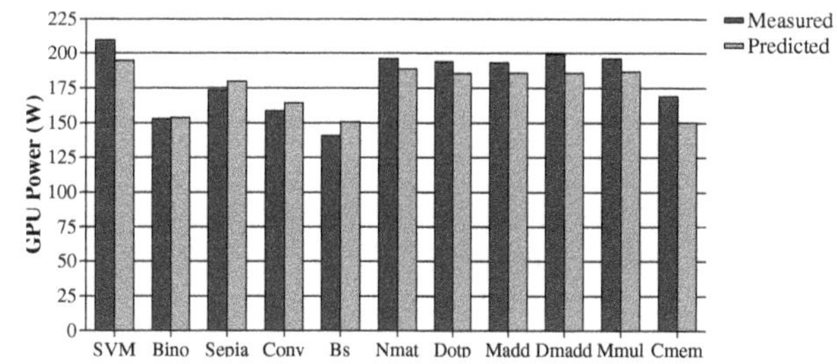

Figure 9: Comparison of measured and predicted GPU power consumption for the GPGPU kernels

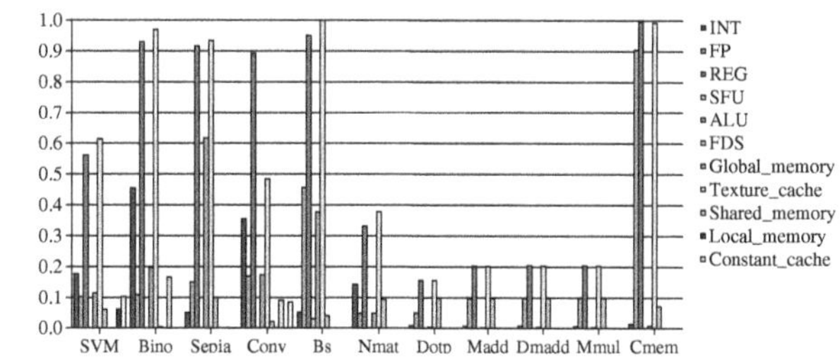

Figure 10: Dynamic access rate of the GPGPU kernels

6.2 Temperature Model

Figure 11 displays the predicted chip temperature over time for all the evaluated benchmarks. The initial temperature is 57°C, the typical GPU cold state temperature in our evaluated system. The temperature is saturated after around 600 secs. The peak temperature depends on the peak run-time power consumption, and it varies from 68°C (the INT benchmark) to 78°C (SVM). Based on Equation (22), we can predict that the runtime power of SVM would increase by 10W after 600 seconds. However, for the INT benchmark, it would increase by only 5W after 600 seconds.

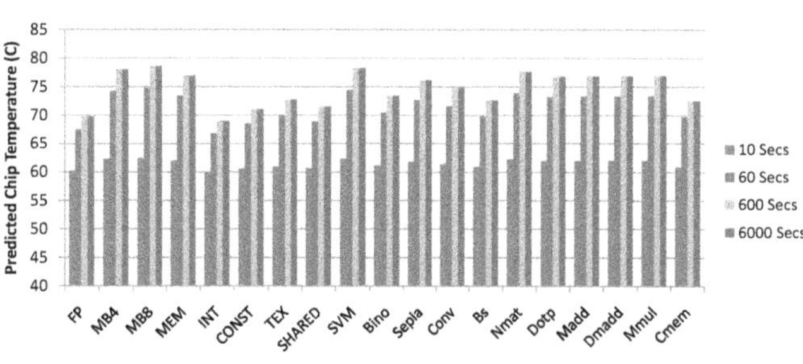

Figure 11: Peak temperature prediction for the benchmarks. Initial temperature: 57°C

6.3 Power Prediction Using IPP

Figure 12 shows the power prediction of IPP for both the microbenchmarks and the GPGPU kernels. These are equivalent to the experiments in Section 6.1. The main difference is that Section 6.1 requires measured execution times while IPP uses predicted times using the equations in Section 4. Using predicted times could have increased the error in prediction of power values, but since the error of timing model is not high, the overall error of the IPP system is not significantly increased. The geometric mean of the power prediction of IPP is 8.94% for the GPGPU kernels and 2.7% for the microbenchmarks, which are similar to using real execution time measurements.

Table 4: Characteristics of the Evaluated Benchmarks (AI means arithmetic intensity.)

Benchmark	Description	Peak Bandwidth (GB/s)	MWP	CWP	AI
SVM [15]	Kernel from a SVM-based algorithm	54.679 (non-bandwidth limited)	5.875	11.226	11.489
Binomial(Bino) [15]	American option pricing	3.689 (non-bandwidth limited)	14.737	1.345	314.306
Sepia [15]	Filter for artificially aging images	12.012 (non-bandwidth limited)	12	12	8.334
Convolve(Conv) [15]	2D Separable image convolution	16.208 (non-bandwidth limited)	10.982	3.511	43.923
Blackscholes(Bs) [17]	European option pricing	51.033 (non-bandwidth limited)	3	5.472	24.258
Matrixmul(Nmat)	Naive version of matrix multiplication	123.33 (bandwidth limited)	10.764	32	3.011
Dotp	Matrix dotproduct	111.313 (bandwidth limited)	10.802	16	0.574
Madd	Matrix multiply-add	115.058 (bandwidth limited)	10.802	16	1.049
Dmadd	Matrix double memory multiply add	109.996 (bandwidth limited)	10.802	16	1.0718
Mmul	Matrix single multiply	114.997 (bandwidth limited)	10.802	16	1.060
Cmem	Matrix add FP operations	64.617 (non-bandwidth limited)	10.802	9.356	12.983

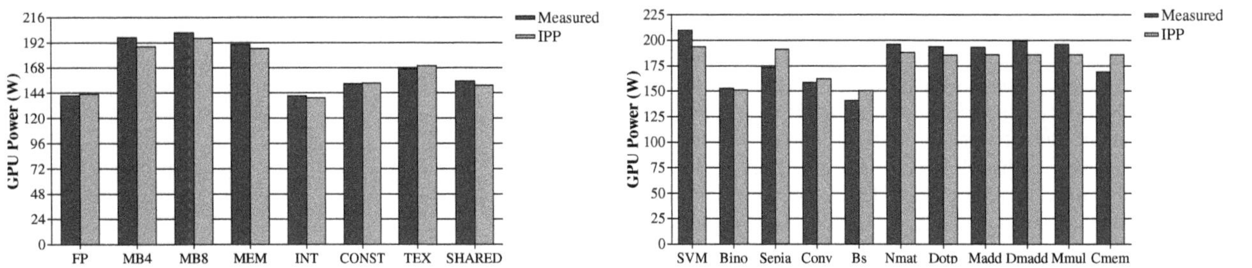

Figure 12: Comparison of measured and IPP predicted GPU power comparison (Left:Microbenchmarks, Right:GPGPU kernels)

6.4 Performance and Power Efficiency Prediction Using IPP

Based on the conditions in Equation (34), we identify the benchmarks that reach the peak memory bandwidth. The five merge benchmarks do not reach the peak memory bandwidth as shown in Table 4. CWP values in Bino, Sepia and Conv are equal to or less than the MWP values of them, so these benchmarks cannot reach the peak memory bandwidth. Both SVM's MWP (5.878) and Bs's MWP (3) are less than MWP_peak_BW (10.8). Thus they cannot reach the peak memory bandwidth also.

To further evaluate our IPP system, we use the benchmarks that reach the peak memory bandwidth (the 3rd column in Table 4 shows the average memory bandwidth of each application). We also include one non-bandwidth limited benchmark (Cmem) for a comparison. In this experiment, we vary the number of active cores by varying the number of blocks in the CUDA applications. We design the applications such that one SM executes only one block. Note that, all different configurations (in this section) of one application have the exact same amount work. So, as we use fewer cores (i.e., fewer blocks), each core (or block) executes more number of instructions. We use Giga Instructions Per Sec (GIPS)[6] instead of Gflops/s for a metric.

Figure 13 shows how GIPS varies with the number of active cores for both the actual measured data and the predictions of IPP. Only Cmem has a linear performance improvement in both the measured data and the predicted values. The rest of the benchmarks show a nearly saturated performance as we increase the number of active cores. IPP still predicts GIPS values accurately except for Cmem. Although the predicted performance of Cmem does not exactly match the actual performance, IPP still correctly predicts the trend. Nmat shows higher performance than other bandwidth limited benchmarks, because it has a higher arithmetic intensity.

Figure 14 shows the actual bandwidth consumption of the experiment in Figure 13. Cmem shows a linear correlation between its bandwidth consumption and the number of active cores, but it still cannot reach the peak memory bandwidth. The memory bandwidths of the remaining benchmarks are saturated when the number of active cores is around 19. This explains why the performance of these benchmarks is not improved significantly after approximately 19 active cores.

Figure 15 shows GIPS/W for the same experiment. The results show both the actual GIPS/W and the predicted GIPS/W using IPP. Nmat shows a salient peak point, but for the rest of benchmarks,

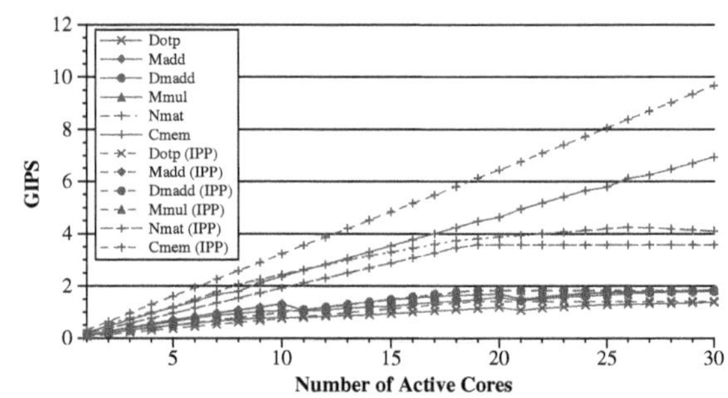

Figure 13: GIPS vs. Active Cores

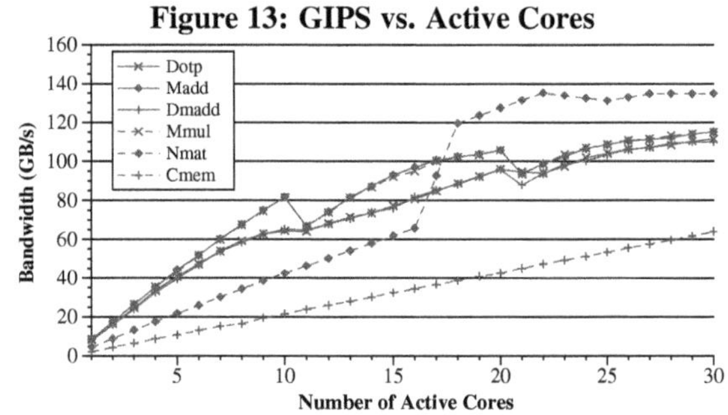

Figure 14: Average measured bandwidth consumption vs. # of active cores

[6] We decide to use GIPS instead of Gflop/s because the performance efficiency should include non-floating point instructions.

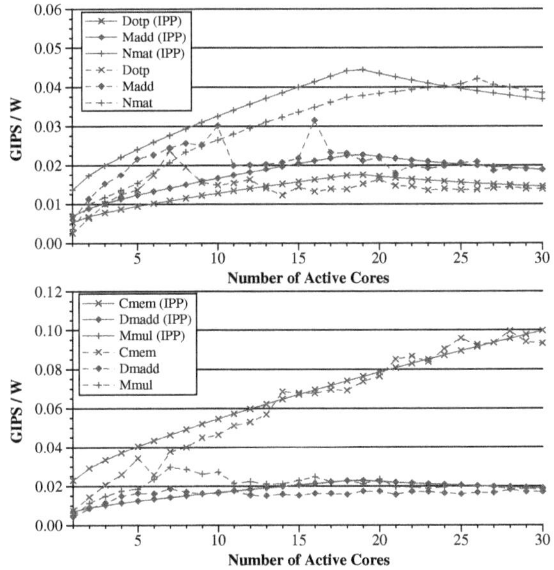

Figure 15: Performance per watt variation vs. # of active cores for measured and the predicted values

the efficiency (GIPS/W) has a very smooth curve. As we have expected, only GIPS/W of Cmem increases linearly in both the measured data and the predicted data.

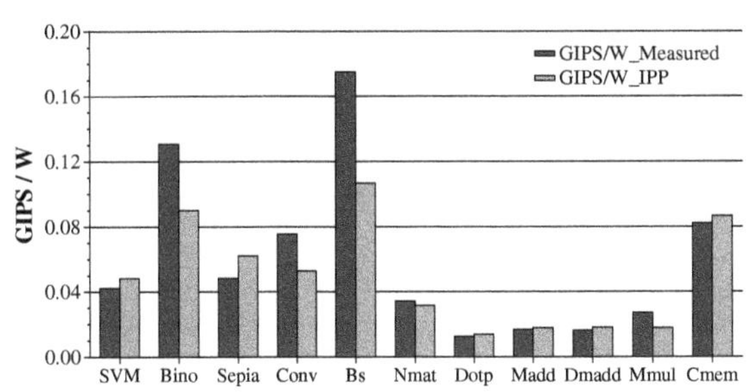

Figure 16: GIPS/W for the GPGPU kernels

Figure 16 shows GIPS/W for all the GPGPU kernels running on 30 active cores. The GIPS/W values of the non-bandwidth limited benchmarks are much higher than those of the bandwidth limited benchmarks. GIPS/W values can vary significantly from application to application depending on their performance. The results also include the predicted GIPS/W using IPP. Except for Bino and Bs, IPP predicts GIPS/W values fairly accurately. The errors in the predicted GIPS/W values of Bino and Bs are attributed to the differences between their predicted and measured runtime performance.

6.4.1 *Energy Savings by Using the Optimal Number of Cores Based on IPP*

Based on Equation (34), IPP calculates the optimal number of cores for a given application. This is a simple way of choosing the highest GIPS/W point among different number of cores. IPP returns 20 for all the evaluated memory bandwidth limited benchmarks and 30 for Cmem.

Figure 17 shows the difference in energy savings between the use of the optimal number of cores and the maximum number (30) of cores. *Runtime+Idle* shows the energy savings when the total GPU power is used in the calculation. *Runtime* shows the energy savings when only the runtime power from the equation (5) is used. *Powergating* is the predicted energy savings if power gating is applied. The average energy savings for *Runtime* cases is 10.99%.

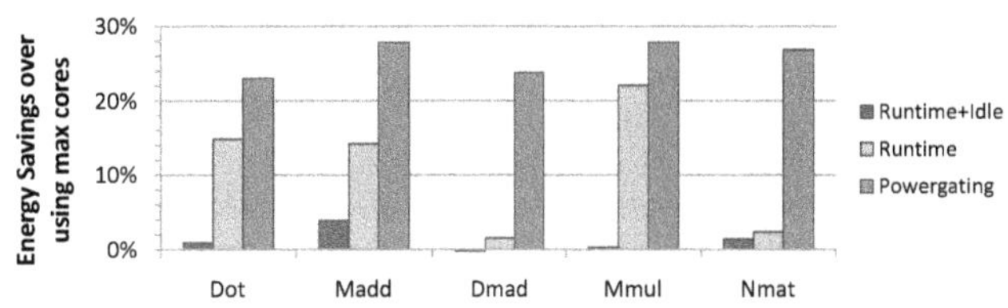

Figure 17: Energy savings using the optimal number of cores based on the IPP system (NVIDIA GTX 280 and power gating GPUs)

6.4.2 *Energy Savings in Power Gating GPUs*

The current NVIDIA GPUs do not employ any per-core power gating mechanism. However, future GPU architectures could employ power gating mechanisms as a result of the growth in the number of cores. As a concrete example, CPUs have already made use of per-core power gating [11].

To evaluate the energy savings in power gating processors, we predict the GPU power consumption as a linear function of the number of active cores. For example, if 30 SMs consume total 120W for an application, we assume that each core consumes 4W when per-core power gating is used. There is no reason to differentiate between Runtime+Idle and Runtime power since the power gating mechanism eliminates idle power consumption from in-active cores. Figure 17 shows the predicted amount of energy savings for the GPU cores that employ power gating. Since power consumption of each individual core is much smaller in a power-gating system, the amount of energy savings is much higher than in the current NVIDIA GTX280 processors. When power gating is applied, the average energy savings is 25.85%. Hence, utilizing only fewer cores based on the outcomes of IPP will be more beneficial in future per-core power-gating processors.

7. RELATED WORK

7.1 Power Modeling

Isci and Martonosi proposed power modeling using empirical data [12]. There have been follow-up studies that use similar techniques for other architectures [7]. Wattch [5] has been widely used to model dynamic power consumption using event counters from architectural simulations. HotLeakage models leakage current and power based on circuit modeling and dynamic events [24]. Skadron et al. proposed temperature aware microarchitecture modeling [20] and also released a software, *HotSpot*. Both HotLeakage and HotSpot require architectural simulators to model dynamic power consumption. All these studies were done only for CPUs.

Sheaffer et al. studied a thermal management for GPUs [19]. In their work, the GPU was a fixed graphics hardware. Fu et al. presented experimental data of a GPU system and evaluated the efficiency of energy and power [8].

Our work is also based on empirical CPU power modeling. The biggest contribution of our GPU model over the previous CPU models is that we propose a GPU power model that does not require performance measurements. By integrating an analytical timing model and an empirical power model, we are able to predict the power consumption of GPGPU workloads with only the instruction mixture information. We also extend the GPU power model to model increases in the leakage power consumption over time, which is becoming a critical component in many-core processors.

7.2 Using Fewer Number of Cores

Huang et al. evaluated the energy efficiency of GPUs for scientific computing [10]. Their work demonstrated the efficiency for only one benchmark and concluded that using all the cores provides the best efficiency. They did not consider any bandwidth limitation effects.

Li and Martinez studied power and performance considerations for CMPs [14]. They also analytically evaluated the optimal number of processors for best power/energy/EDP. However, their work was focused on CMP and presented heuristics to reduce design space search using power and performance models.

Suleman et al. proposed a feedback driven threading mechanism [22]. By monitoring the bandwidth consumption using a hardware counter, their feedback system decides how many threads (cores) can be run without degrading performance. Unlike our work, it requires runtime profiling to know the minimum number of threads to reach the peak bandwidth. Furthermore, they demonstrate power savings through simulation without a detailed power model. The IPP system predicts the number of cores that reaches the peak bandwidth at static time, thereby allowing the compiler or thread scheduler to use that information without any runtime profiling. Furthermore, we demonstrate the power savings by using both the detailed power model and the real system.

8. CONCLUSIONS

In this paper, we proposed an integrated power and performance modeling system (IPP) for the GPU architecture and the GPGPU kernels. IPP extends the empirical CPU modeling mechanism to model the GPU power and also considers the increases in leakage power consumption that resulted from the increases in temperature. Using the proposed power model and the newly-developed timing model, IPP predicts performance per watt and also the optimal number of cores to achieve energy savings.

The power model using IPP predicts the power consumption and the execution time with an average of 8.94% error for the evaluated GPGPU kernels. IPP predicts the performance per watt and the optimal number of cores for the five evaluated bandwidth limited GPGPU kernels. Based on IPP, the system can save on average 10.99% of runtime energy consumption for the bandwidth limited applications by using fewer cores. We demonstrated the power savings in the real machine. We also calculated the power savings if a per-core power gating mechanism is employed, and the result shows an average of 25.85% in energy reduction.

The proposed IPP system can be used by a thread scheduler (power management system) as we have discussed in the paper. It can be also used by compilers or programmers to optimize program configurations as we have demonstrated in the paper. In our future work, we will incorporate dynamic voltage and frequency control systems in the power and performance model.

Acknowledgments

Special thanks to Gregory Diamos, Andrew Kerr, and Sudhakar Yalamanchili for Ocelot support. We thank the anonymous reviewers for their comments. We also thank Mike O'Connor, Alex Merritt, Tom Dewey, David Tarjan, Dilan Manatunga, Nagesh Lakshminarayana, Richard Vuduc, Chi-keung Luk, and HParch members for their feedback on improving the paper. We gratefully acknowledge the support of NSF CCF0903447, NSF/SRC task 1981, 2009 Georgia Tech Innovation Grant, Intel Corporation, Microsoft Research, and the equipment donations from NVIDIA.

9. REFERENCES

[1] Extech 380801. `http://www.extech.com/instrument/products/310_399/380801.html`.
[2] NVIDIA GeForce series GTX280, 8800GTX, 8800GT. http://www.nvidia.com/geforce.
[3] Nvidia's next generation cuda compute architecture. http://www.nvidia.com/fermi.
[4] S. Borkar. Design challenges of technology scaling. *IEEE Micro*, 19(4):23–29, 1999.
[5] D. Brooks, V. Tiwari, and M. Martonosi. Wattch: a framework for architectural-level power analysis and optimizations. In *ISCA-27*, 2000.
[6] J. A. Butts and G. S. Sohi. A static power model for architects. *Microarchitecture*, 0:191–201, 2000.
[7] G. Contreras and M. Martonosi. Power prediction for intel xscale processors using performance monitoring unit events. In *ISLPED*, 2005.
[8] R. Fu, A. Zhai, P.-C. Yew, W.-C. Hsu, and J. Lu. Reducing queuing stalls caused by data prefetching. In *INTERACT-11*, 2007.
[9] S. Hong and H. Kim. An analytical model for a gpu architecture with memory-level and thread-level parallelism awareness. In *ISCA*, 2009.
[10] S. Huang, S. Xiao, and W. Feng. On the energy efficiency of graphics processing units for scientific computing. In *IPDPS*, 2009.
[11] Intel. Intel®Nehalem Microarchitecture. http://www.intel.com/technology/architecture-silicon/next-gen/.
[12] C. Isci and M. Martonosi. Runtime power monitoring in high-end processors: Methodology and empirical data. In *MICRO*, 2003.
[13] A. Kerr, G. Diamos, and S. Yalamanchili. A characterization and analysis of ptx kernels. In *IISWC*, 2009.
[14] J. Li and J. F. Martínez. Power-performance considerations of parallel computing on chip multiprocessors. *ACM Trans. Archit. Code Optim.*, 2(4):397–422, 2005.
[15] M. D. Linderman, J. D. Collins, H. Wang, and T. H. Meng. Merge: a programming model for heterogeneous multi-core systems. In *ASPLOS XIII*, 2008.
[16] NVClock. Nvidia overclocking on Linux. http://www.linuxhardware.org/nvclock/.
[17] NVIDIA Corporation. *CUDA Programming Guide, V3.0*.
[18] K. Roy, S. Mukhopadhyay, and H. Mahmoodi-Meimand. Leakage current mechanisms and leakage reduction techniques in deep-submicrometer cmos circuits. *Proceedings of the IEEE*, 91(2):305–327, Feb 2003.
[19] J. W. Sheaffer, D. Luebke, and K. Skadron. A flexible simulation framework for graphics architectures. In *HWWS*, 2004.
[20] K. Skadron, M. R. Stan, K. Sankaranarayanan, W. Huang, S. Velusamy, and D. Tarjan. Temperature-aware microarchitecture: Modeling and implementation. *ACM Trans. Archit. Code Optim.*, 1(1):94–125, 2004.
[21] H. Su, F. Liu, A. Devgan, E. Acar, and S. Nassif. Full chip leakage estimation considering power supply and temperature variations. In *ISLPED*, 2003.
[22] M. A. Suleman, M. K. Qureshi, and Y. N. Patt. Feedback driven threading: Power-efficient and high-performance execution of multithreaded workloads on cmps. In *ASPLOS-XIII*, 2008.
[23] S. Williams, A. Waterman, and D. Patterson. Roofline: an insightful visual performance model for multicore architectures. *Commun. ACM*, 52(4):65–76, 2009.
[24] Y. Zhang, D. Parikh, K. Sankaranarayanan, K. Skadron, and M. Stan. Hotleakage: A temperature-aware model of subthreshold and gate leakage for architects. Technical report, University of Virginia, 2003.

A Case for FAME: FPGA Architecture Model Execution

Zhangxi Tan, Andrew Waterman, Henry Cook, Sarah Bird, Krste Asanović, David Patterson

The Parallel Computing Laboratory
CS Division, EECS Department, University of California, Berkeley

{xtan,waterman,hcook,slbird,krste,pattrsn}@eecs.berkeley.edu

ABSTRACT

Given the multicore microprocessor revolution, we argue that the architecture research community needs a dramatic increase in simulation capacity. We believe FPGA Architecture Model Execution (FAME) simulators can increase the number of useful architecture research experiments per day by two orders of magnitude over Software Architecture Model Execution (SAME) simulators. To clear up misconceptions about FPGA-based simulation methodologies, we propose a FAME taxonomy to distinguish the cost-performance of variations on these ideas. We demonstrate our simulation speedup claim with a case study wherein we employ a prototype FAME simulator, RAMP Gold, to research the interaction between hardware partitioning mechanisms and operating system scheduling policy. The study demonstrates FAME's capabilities: we run a modern parallel benchmark suite on a research operating system, simulate 64-core target architectures with multi-level memory hierarchy timing models, and add experimental hardware mechanisms to the target machine. The simulation speedup achieved by our adoption of FAME—250×—enables experiments with more realistic time scales and data set sizes than are possible with SAME.

Categories and Subject Descriptors

C.5.3 [**Computer System Implementation**]: Microprocessors; I.6.8 [**Simulation and Modeling**]: Discrete Event

General Terms

Design, Performance, Experimentation

1. INTRODUCTION

Computer architects have long used software simulators to explore instruction set architectures, microarchitectures, and approaches to implementation. Compared to hardware prototyping, their low capital cost, relatively low cost of implementation, and ease of change have made them the ideal choice for the early stages of research exploration. In addition, when uniprocessor performance was doubling every 18 months, simulation speed correspondingly doubled every 18 months without any special programming effort.

The recent abrupt transition to multicore architectures [5, 19], however, has both increased the complexity of the systems architects want to simulate and removed the straightforward path to simulator performance scaling. Parallel applications exhibit more complex behaviors than sequential ones, including timing-dependent non-deterministic execution, cache coherence traffic, and operating system scheduler interactions. Applications now also commonly have dynamically generated code, including code that is automatically tuned to the underlying hardware platform. Although it is generally well understood how to model these phenomena, accurate models require detailed cycle-level simulation. Unfortunately, detailed cycle-level simulation is notoriously difficult to parallelize due to the need for regular cycle-by-cycle synchronization, and hence sequential software simulators have fallen far behind the performance required to support the new wave of parallel systems research.

This paper argues that architecture research now faces a crisis in simulation because of the new requirements and the consequences of the move to multicore processors. Indeed, we found that the median instructions simulated per benchmark was similar in ISCA papers in 1998 and 2008. In recent papers, however, those instructions were simulated across an average of 16 times as many processors, so the number of instructions per processor significantly decreased over that decade. To tackle this *simulation gap*, several research groups, including those in the RAMP Project [41], have been exploring the use of FPGAs to build various forms of FPGA-accelerated architecture simulators. In this paper, we use the terms *Software Architecture Model Execution (SAME)* or *FPGA (Field-Programmable Gate Array) Architecture Model Execution (FAME)* to label the two approaches to multicore simulation. Due to the rapid progress made by the whole FAME community over the last few years, there appears to be considerable confusion about the structure and capabilities of FAME simulators in the broader architecture community. This paper proposes a four-level taxonomy of increasingly sophisticated FAME levels to help explain the capabilities and limitations of various FPGA simulation approaches.

We then present the detailed design of the RAMP Gold simulator, a very efficient architectural simulator for early-stage design exploration. We describe how RAMP Gold supports various forms of architecture experimentation and

ISCA'10, June 19–23, 2010, Saint-Malo, France.

how modifications could be made to support others. The following section presents a case study to illustrate the effectiveness of RAMP Gold in modern systems research. We also provide a quantitative evaluation of the RAMP Gold simulator against Simics+GEMS [24, 25], a popular SAME simulator. We compare simulation speeds for the PARSEC benchmark suite [7]. We show that while pure functional simulations of a few cores run at about the same speed, RAMP Gold runs detailed models on 64 cores on average 263× faster than Simics+GEMS, with a maximum speedup of 806×. Not only does this provide a dramatic increase in simulation capacity, it also markedly reduces simulation latency thereby improving experimenter productivity.

2. MULTIPROCESSOR SIMULATION

A modern processor running an application workload is difficult to model analytically, yet building a prototype for each design point is prohibitively expensive. Software simulators have therefore become the primary method used to evaluate architectural design choices. In this paper, we refer to the machine being simulated as the *target* and the machine on which the simulation runs the *host*.

Simulating parallel target machines is much more difficult than simulating uniprocessors. Part of the added complexity is simply that the target hardware is more complex, with multiple cores and a cache-coherent shared memory hierarchy. Also, a parallel software runtime must be present to support multithreading or multiprogramming across the multiple cores of the simulated target, which adds additional complexity. For multiprocessor research, trace-driven simulation is still often used despite the inability of traces to capture the effects of timing-dependent execution interleaving, as developing a full system environment capable of running large workloads is difficult.

As with uniprocessor simulators, many parallel simulators only model user-level activity of a single application. One popular early example was RSIM [29], which provided detailed models of out-of-order superscalar processors connected via coherent shared memory but without support for an operating system. The SimOS project demonstrated how to run an operating system on top of a fast software simulator [34]. SimOS supported multiple levels of simulation detail, with the fastest version of SimOS using dynamic binary translation to speed target instruction emulation while emulating cache hierarchies in some detail [44]. A similar technique was incorporated into the commercial product Simics, which allows researchers to study large application programs and the operating system running together. Although the architecture research community is not a large market, Simics offers an interface that allows researchers to plug in their own detailed execution-driven performance model to evaluate detailed portions of the computer [24]. Augmented with detailed performance models developed by other researchers [25], Simics has become a popular tool in the architecture community; we provide a detailed evaluation of its performance in Section 5.

Sadly, parallelizing detailed multiprocessor simulations to run efficiently on parallel host machines is difficult. The need for cycle-by-cycle interaction between components limits the parallel speedup due to the high cost of software synchronization. If this cycle-by-cycle synchronization is relaxed, parallelized software simulators can attain some speedup but at the cost of needing to validate that the missing interactions do not affect the experiment's results [26, 33].

As with uniprocessors, researchers have considered using sampling to reduce multiprocessor simulation time. Alas, mixed-mode simulation and sampling do not work well in general for multiprocessor simulations [6]. For uniprocessors, the program execution should be the same independent of the underlying microarchitecture, and so the architectural state of the processor is correct at the beginning of any sample point for any target microarchitecture. Such is not the case for multiprocessors because software thread interleavings change depending on the behavior of the microarchitecture in each core. For example, an experiment exploring the impact of relaxed consistency models on multithreaded programs might never encounter the interesting events if the functional simulation used sequential consistency to obtain sample start points. Sampling can give representative results for multiprogrammed workloads, since processes running on different cores generally do not interact via shared memory. Others have argued that transaction-oriented applications such as databases are also amenable to sample-based simulation, since any sample is representative of some legal overlap of independent transactions [43].

Implicit in many techniques used to reduce simulation time is the assumption that software is compiled statically, changes slowly, and is independent of the target architecture. Architects have generally treated benchmark programs as static artifacts to be measured without understanding the problems being solved or the algorithms and data structures being used. Thus, collections of old software like SPEC were considered reasonable benchmarks for future architectures, as long as the SPEC suite changed every five years to reduce gamesmanship. In fact, many architectural studies have just used precompiled binaries distributed with a shared simulator infrastructure. New applications, new programming models, and new programming languages have been largely ignored. The move to ubiquitous parallel processing is such a disruptive change that this *laissez faire* approach will no longer work, since by definition we need new programs, models, and languages. Moreover, as mentioned above, modern software dynamically adapts to the hardware microarchitecture by generating and measuring code at runtime. Existing simulation time shortcuts are not likely to be useful, and simulation latency is now at least as important as simulation throughput.

3. FPGA-BASED SIMULATION

FPGAs have become a promising vehicle for architecture experiments, providing a highly parallel programmable execution substrate that can run simulations several orders of magnitude faster than software [41]. Previously, FPGA processor models were hampered by the need to partition a processor across multiple FPGAs, which increases hardware costs, reduces performance, and significantly increases development effort. But FPGA capacity has been scaling with Moore's Law and so now, depending on complexity, multiple processors can fit on a single FPGA. Furthermore, future scaling should allow FPGA capability to continue to track simulation demands as the number of cores in target systems grows. Due to high volumes, FPGA boards have also become relatively inexpensive; the RAMP Gold design, for example, uses a $750 commercial board.

Multiple groups have now developed working FPGA-based systems [11, 14, 28, 21, 12], but using perhaps an even greater variety of techniques than software simulators, and correspondingly a wider range of tradeoffs between simulator performance, accuracy, and flexibility. Consequently, we have heard much confusion in our discussions with other architects about how FAME relates to prior work using FPGAs for architecture prototyping and chip simulation, and what can and cannot be done using FAME.

In this section, we first present three binary dimensions within which we can categorize FAME approaches. Next, inspired by the five-level RAID classification, we present four levels of FAME that capture the most important design points in this space. Our hope is these FAME levels will help explain FPGA-based emulation approaches to the broader architecture community.

3.1 FAME Implementation Techniques

We use the following three binary dimensions to characterize FAME implementation approaches.

3.1.1 Direct vs. Decoupled

The *Direct* approach is characterized by the direct mapping of a target machine's RTL description into FPGA gates, where a single target clock cycle is executed in a single host clock cycle. An advantage of the direct approach is that, in theory, a re-synthesis of the target RTL for the FPGA provides a guaranteed cycle-accurate model of the target processor. The direct approach has been popular in chip verification; one of the first uses of FPGAs was emulating a new chip design to catch logic bugs before tapeout. Quickturn [16] was an early example, where boxes packed with FPGAs running at about 1–2 MHz could run much larger test programs than feasible with software ECAD logic simulators. Direct emulation is also often used by intellectual property (IP) developers to supply a new core design to potential customers for evaluation and software porting before committing to an ASIC. Direct emulation has become much easier as the growth in FPGA capacity reduces the need to partition monolithic RTL blocks, such as CPUs, across FPGAs, but large system designs may still require many FPGAs. The inefficiency of FPGAs at emulating common logic structures—such as multiported register files, wide muxes, and CAMs—exacerbates capacity problems.

A more powerful FAME option, which improves efficiency and enables other more advanced options, is to adopt a *Decoupled* design, where a single target clock cycle can be implemented with multiple or even a variable number of host clock cycles [18]. For example, direct mapping of a multi-ported register file is inefficient on FPGAs because discrete FPGA flip-flops are used to implement each register state bit with large combinational circuits used to provide the read ports. A more efficient decoupled model would implement a target multi-ported register file by time-multiplexing a single-ported FPGA RAM over multiple FPGA clock cycles. The drawback of a decoupled design is that models have to use additional host logic to model target time correctly, and a protocol is needed to exchange target timing information at module boundaries if modules have different target to host clock cycle ratios [18, 31].

3.1.2 Full RTL vs. Abstracted Machine

When the full RTL of a target machine is used to build a FAME model, it ensures precise cycle-accurate timing. However, the desired RTL design is usually not known during early-stage architecture exploration, and even if the intended RTL design is known, it can require considerable effort to implement a working version including all corner cases. Even if full correct RTL is available, it may be too unwieldy to map directly to an FPGA.

Alternatively, we can use a higher-level description of the design to construct a FAME model. Abstraction can reduce both model construction effort and FPGA resource needs. The primary drawback is that an abstract model needs validation to ensure accuracy, usually by comparing against RTL or another known good model. If the mechanism is novel, an RTL prototyping exercise might be required to provide confidence in the abstraction. Once validated, however, an abstract component can be reused in multiple designs.

HAsim [30] was an early example of the *Abstract* FAME option, where the processor model was divided into separate functional and timing models that do not correspond to structural components in the target machine. Split functional and timing models provide similar benefits as when used in SAME simulators. Only the timing model needs to change to experiment with different microarchitectures, and the timing model can include parameters such as cache size and associativity that can be set at runtime without resynthesizing the design, dramatically increasing the number of architecture experiments that can be performed per day.

3.1.3 Single-Threaded vs. Multi-Threaded

A cycle-accurate FAME model synchronizes all model components on every target clock cycle. Some complex components might experience long host latencies, for example, to communicate with off-chip memory or other FPGAs, reducing simulator performance. For processors, a standard approach to tolerate latencies and obtain greater performance is to switch threads every clock cycle so that all dependencies are resolved by the next time a thread is executed [3]. The same approach can be applied when implementing FAME models in a technique we call *host multithreading*, and is particularly applicable to models of parallel target machines.

When the target system contains multiple instances of the same component, such as cores in a manycore design, the host model can be designed so that one physical FPGA pipeline can model multiple target components by interleaving the component models' execution using multithreading. For example, a single FPGA processor pipeline might model 64 target cores or a single FPGA router pipeline might model 16 on-chip routers.

Host multithreading greatly improves utilization of FPGA resources by hiding host communication latencies. For example, while one processor target model makes a request to a memory module, we can interleave the activity of 63 other target processor models. Provided modeling of the memory access takes fewer than 64 FPGA clock cycles, the emulation will not stall. Multithreaded emulation adds additional design complexity but can provide a significant improvement in emulator throughput. ProtoFlex is an example of a FAME simulator that host-multithreads its functional model [12]. The same concept has also been used in SAME simulators, *e.g.*, later versions of the Wisconsin Wind Tunnel were also host multithreaded [27].

3.2 FAME Levels

A combination of these FAME implementation techniques

Level	*Name*	*Example*	*Strength*	*Experiments per Day*	*Experiments per Day per $1000*
000	Direct FAME	Quickturn, Palladium	Debugging logical design	1	0.001
001	Decoupled FAME	Green Flash	Higher clock rate; lower cost	24	0.667
011	Abstract FAME	HAsim	Simpler, parameterizable design; faster synthesis; lower cost	40	40.000
111	Multi-threaded FAME	RAMP Gold	Lower cost; higher clock rate	128	170.000

Table 1: Summary of four FAME Levels, including examples.

often makes sense. The next four sections present a four-level taxonomy of FAME that improves in cost, performance, or flexibility. The four levels are distinguished by their choices from the three options above, so we can number the levels with a three-bit binary number, where the least-significant bit represents Direct (0) vs. Decoupled (1) and the most-significant bit represents Single-Threaded (0) vs. Multi-Threaded (1). Table 1 summarizes the levels and gives examples and the strengths of each level. Each new FAME level lowers cost and usually improves performance over the previous level, while moving further away from the concrete RTL design of the target.

To quantify the cost-performance difference of the four FAME levels, we propose as a performance measure the number of simulation experiments that can be performed per day. Given the complex dynamics of manycore processors, operating systems, and workloads, we believe the minimum useful experiment is simulating 1 second of target execution time at the finest level of detail for 16 cores at a clock rate of 2 GHz with shared memory and cache coherence. We employ this as an approximate unit to measure an experiment. The same experiment but running for 10 target seconds is 10 units, the same experiment but running for 1 second at 64 cores is 4 units, and so on. Note that in addition to host simulation time, experiment setup time (*e.g.* design synthesis time) must also be included. To obtain a cost-performance metric, we simply divide the number of experiments per day by the cost of that FAME system. To keep the numbers from getting too small, we calculate experiments per day per $1000 of the cost of the FAME system. The last column of Table 1 estimates this metric for 2010 prices.

3.2.1 Direct FAME (Level 000): (e.g., Quickturn)

The common characteristic of Direct FAME emulation systems, such as Quickturn, is that they are designed to model a single chip down to the gate level with a one-to-one mapping of target cycles to host cycles.

Let's assume we could simulate the gates of 16 cores on a $1 million Direct FAME system at 2 MHz. Each run would then take 2 GHz/2 MHz =1000 seconds or 17 minutes. Because the model is not parameterized, we have to rerun the CAD tool chain for each experiment to resynthesize the design. Given the large number of FPGAs and larger and more complicated description of a hardware-ready RTL design, it can take up to 30 hours to set up a new design [39]. If Direct FAME can do 1 experiment per day, the number of experiments per day per $1000 is 0.001.

In addition to high simulation turnaround time, Direct FAME requires great design effort to change the RTL for each experimental machine, unlike some of the later FAME levels. Although helpful in the later stages of debugging the design of a real microprocessor intended for fabrication, Direct FAME is too expensive and time consuming to use for early-stage architectural investigations.

Newer gate-level emulation products, such as Cadence Palladium and MentorGraphics Veloce, are no longer based on commercial FPGAs but instead use custom-designed logic simulation engines. However, they still have relatively low target clock rates [1] and cost millions of dollars, though the tools are superior to FPGA tools for this purpose.

3.2.2 Decoupled FAME (Level 001): (e.g., Green Flash memory system)

Programmable logic is slow compared to hardwired logic, and some ASIC features, such as multiported register files, map poorly to FPGAs, consuming resources and cycle time. For example, Green Flash [42] can fit two Tensilica cores with floating-point units per medium-sized FPGA, but it runs at only 50 MHz [35]. The memory system uses off-chip DRAM, however, which runs much faster than the logic (200 MHz) and so decoupling is used in the memory system to match the intended target machine DRAM timing.

Performing a 16-core experiment needs 2 BEE3 [15] boards, which cost academics about $15,000 per board, plus the FPGAs and DRAMs, which cost about $3000 per board, or $36,000 total. It takes 8 hours to synthesize and place and route the design and about 40 seconds (2 GHz/50 MHz) to run an experiment. Since this level has a few timing parameters, such as DRAM latency and bandwidth, Green Flash can run about 24 experiments per synthesis [35]. Alas, the state of FPGA CAD tools means FPGA synthesis is a human-intensive task; only one synthesis can be run per workday. Thus, the number of experiments per day per $1000 is 24/$36K or 0.667. Decoupled FAME (Level 001) improves the cost-performance over Direct FAME (Level 000) by a factor of almost 700×. This speedup is mostly due to processor cores fitting on a single FPGA, thus avoiding the off-chip communication that slows Direct FAME systems; also, Decoupled FAME uses a simple timing model to avoid resynthesis for multiple memory system experiments.

It is both a strength and a weakness of Decoupled FAME that the full target RTL is modeled. The strength is that the model is guaranteed to be cycle accurate. Also, the same RTL design can be pushed through a VLSI flow to obtain reasonable area, power and timing numbers from actual chip layout [37]. The weakness is that designing the full RTL for a system is labor-intensive and rerunning the tools is slow. This makes Decoupled FAME less suitable for early-stage architecture exploration, where the designer is not ready to commit to a full RTL design. Decoupled FAME thus takes a great deal of effort to perform a wide range of experiments compared to Abstract and Multithreaded FAME. These higher levels, however, require decoupling to implement their timing models, and hence we assume that all the following levels are Decoupled (or odd-numbered in our enumeration).

3.2.3 Abstract FAME (Level 011): (e.g., HAsim)

Abstract FAME allows high-level descriptions for early-stage exploration, which simplifies the design and thereby reduces the synthesis time to under 1 hour. More importantly, it allows the exploration of many design parameters without having to resynthesize at all, which dramatically improves cost-performance.

Let's assume we need 1 BEE3 board for 16 cores, so the cost is $18,000. To simulate cache coherency, the simulator will take several host cycles per target cycle for every load or store to snoop on the addresses. Let's assume a clock frequency of 65 MHz, as with HAsim [32], and an average number of host cycles per target cycle of 4. The time for one experiment is then $4 \times 2\,\mathrm{GHz}/65\,\mathrm{MHz} = 123$ seconds. Since human intervention isn't needed to program the FPGAs, the number of experiments per day is 24 hours/123 seconds = 702. The number of experiments per day per $1000 is then 702/$18K or about 40. Abstract FAME (Level 011) makes a dramatic improvement in this metric over lower FAME levels: by a factor of almost 60 over Decoupled FAME (Level 001) and a factor of 40,000 over Direct FAME (Level 000).

In addition to the improvement in cost-performance, Abstract FAME allows many people to perform architecture experiments without having to modify the RTL, which both greatly lowers the effort for experiments and greatly increases the number of potential experimenters. Once again, the advantages of abstract designs and decoupled designs are so great that we assume any subsequent level is both Abstract and Decoupled.

3.2.4 Multithreaded FAME (Level 111): (e.g., RAMP Gold)

The main cost of Multithreaded FAME is more RAM to hold copies of the state of each thread, but RAM is one of the strengths of FPGAs — a single programmable logic unit can be exchanged for 64-bits of RAM in a Virtex-5 FPGA. Hence, Multithreaded FAME increases the number of cores that can be simulated efficiently per FPGA. Multithreading can also increase the clock rate of the host simulator by removing items on the critical path, such as bypass paths.

Since we are time-multiplexing the FPGA models, a much less expensive XUP board ($750) suffices. Multithreading reduces RAMP Gold's host cycles per target core-cycle to 1.90 (measured) and enables a clock rate of 90 MHz. Since the simulator is threaded, the time for a 16-core simulation is $16 \times 2\,\mathrm{GHz}/90\,\mathrm{MHz} \times 1.9 = 675$ seconds. The number of experiments per day is 24 hours / 675 seconds = 128. The number of experiments per day per $1000 is then 128/$0.75K or about 170. Multithreaded FAME (Level 111) improves this metric by more than a factor of 4 over Abstract FAME (Level 011), by a factor of about 250 over Decoupled FAME (Level 001), and by a factor of 170,000 over Direct FAME (Level 000). We expect that Version 2 of RAMP Gold will fit three pipelines on a single FPGA and run at 100 MHz, allowing over 550 experiments per day per $1000.

In addition, Multithreaded FAME lowers the cost of entry by a factor of 24–48 versus Abstract or Decoupled FAME, making it possible for many more researchers to use FAME for parallel architecture research.

3.2.5 Other Possible FAME Levels

By definition, direct mapping cannot be combined with abstract models or multithreading. An RTL design can be multithreaded, however, whereby every target register is replicated for each threaded instance but combinational logic is shared by time multiplexing. We ignored this Multithreaded RTL combination (101) as a FAME level because, although plausible, we have not seen instances of this combination in practice.

3.2.6 Hybrid FAME Simulators

Although we present levels as completely separate approaches for pedagogic reasons, real systems will often combine modules at different levels, or even use hybrid designs partly in FPGA and the rest in software. For example, System-on-a-Chip IP providers will often use a mixed design to provide a fast *in situ* emulation of their IP blocks for customers. The IP block is modeled by mapping the final ASIC RTL to the FPGA (Direct FAME, Level 000), but the enclosing system is described at an abstract level (Abstract FAME, Level 011). FAST [11] is an example of a hybrid FAME/SAME system, where the functional model is in software and the timing model is in hardware.

3.2.7 FPGA Computers

Another use of FPGAs is to build *FPGA computers*, where FPGAs are the final target technology. For example, FPGAs are used to build computers to run real production compute workloads (e.g., Xilinx Microblaze [2], Convey HC-1 [9]). Research processors can also be prototyped using FPGAs at much lower cost, risk, and design effort compared to a custom chip implementation [36, 28, 21, 40]. Although an FPGA research prototype bears little resemblance to a custom chip in terms of cycle time, area, or power, it can yield valuable insights into the detailed implementation of a new architectural mechanism, as well as provide a fast platform to evaluate software interactions with the new mechanisms.

Although often confused with Direct FAME (level 000), FPGA computers are not intended to model a target machine; rather, they *are* the target machine. As such, we do not include FPGA computers in the FAME taxonomy.

4. THE RAMP GOLD SIMULATOR

RAMP Gold [1] is a Multithreaded FAME (Level 111) simulator deployed on a single $750 Xilinx Virtex-5 FPGA board. In this section, we describe the design of RAMP Gold and how it attains high efficiency by tailoring the design to the FPGA environment.

The current RAMP Gold simulated target is a tiled, shared-memory manycore system with up to 64 single-issue, in-order SPARC V8 cores. RAMP Gold is a full-system simulator, which boots the Linux 2.6 kernel, as well as ROS [20, 23], our manycore research operating system. RAMP Gold's target machine is highly parameterized and most simulation options are runtime configurable: Without resynthesizing a new FPGA configuration, we can vary the number of target cores, cache parameters (size, associativity, line size, latency, banking), and DRAM configuration (latency, bandwidth, number of channels). This extensive runtime parameterization accelerates design space exploration and comes

[1] RAMP Gold source code is available at http://ramp.eecs.berkeley.edu/gold

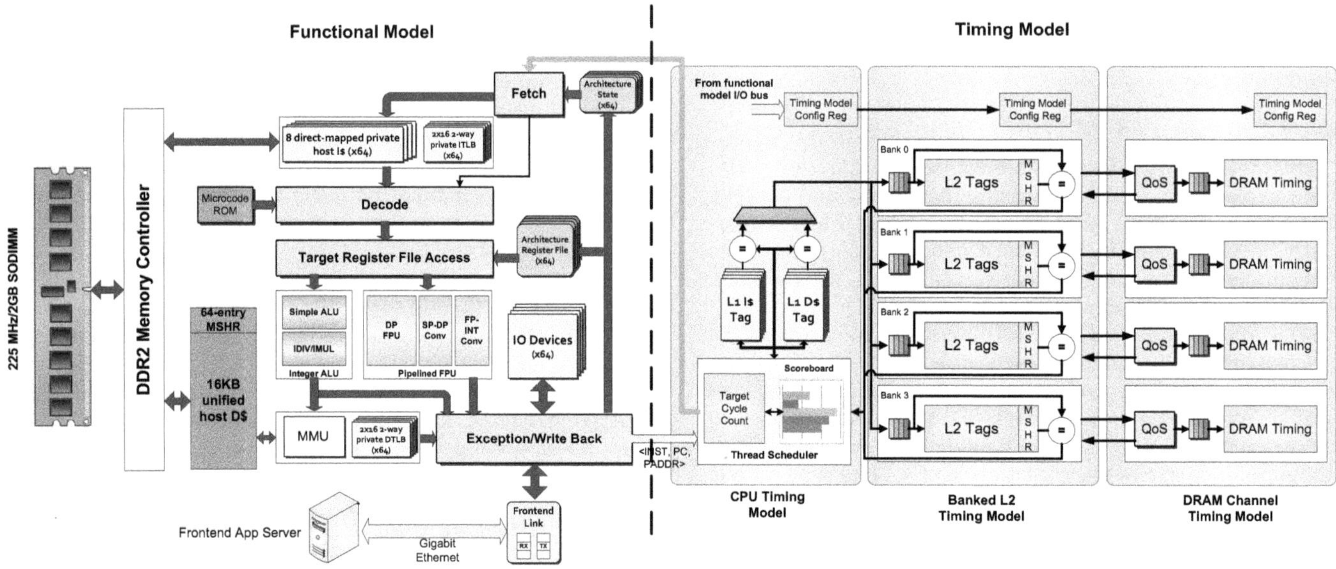

Figure 1: RAMP Gold Microarchitecture

at little cost to simulator performance: with a detailed memory system timing model, we can simulate over 40 million target core-cycles per second.

4.1 RAMP Gold Microarchitecture

Figure 1 shows the microarchitecture of RAMP Gold. The simulator decouples timing from function. The functional model faithfully executes the SPARC V8 ISA and maintains architected state, while the timing model determines instruction execution time in the target machine. Both models reside in one FPGA to minimize synchronization costs, and both are host-multithreaded to achieve high utilization of FPGA resources.

The functional model implements the full SPARC V8 ISA in hardware, including floating-point and precise exceptions. It also provides sufficient hardware to run an operating system, including MMUs, timers, and interprocessor interrupts. The functional model is deeply pipelined, and avoids features such as highly ported register files and wide bypass muxes that map poorly to FPGAs. The functional model carefully exploits Virtex-5 features, for example, double-clocking block RAMs and mapping target ALU instructions to hardwired DSP blocks. The single in-order issue functional pipeline is 64-way multithreaded, enabling functional simulation of 64 target cores. Each thread's private state includes a 7-window register file, a 32-entry instruction TLB and 32-entry data TLB, a 256-byte direct-mapped instruction cache, and the various processor state registers. Although 64 copies of this state seems large, trading state for increased pipeline utilization is attractive in the FPGA fabric, wherein storage is cheap relative to computation.

The threaded functional pipeline has a single, shared, lockup-free host data cache. It is 16 KB, direct-mapped, and supports up to 64 outstanding misses. Sharing a very small host cache between 64 threads is a design point peculiar to the FPGA fabric: the low latency to the host DRAM, approximately 20 cycles in the worst case, is covered easily by multithreading. Thus, the lower miss rate of a large, associative host cache offers little simulation performance advantage. Indeed, across a subset of the PARSEC benchmarks, the small host cache incurs at most a 3.8% performance penalty compared to a perfect cache. (The tiny 256-byte instruction caches have even less of an impact on performance—at most 2.3% worse than a perfect cache.)

The timing model tracks the performance of a target 64-core tiled manycore system. The target core is currently a single-issue, in-order pipeline that sustains one instruction per clock, except for instruction and data cache misses. Each core has private instruction and data caches. The cores share a unified lockup-free L2 cache via a magic crossbar interconnect. Each L2 bank connects to a DRAM controller model, which models delay through a first-come, first-served queue with a constant service rate. Modeling the timing behavior of cache coherence traffic on realistic interconnects is a target for future work, though should fit easily within the current design framework.

Separating timing from function expands the range of systems RAMP Gold can model, and allows the effort expended on the functional model to be reused across many different target machines. For example, we can model the performance of a system with large caches by keeping only the cache metadata inside the FPGA. The functional model still fetches from its host instruction cache and performs memory accesses to its host data cache when the timing model schedules it to do so. Moreover, the flexibility of splitting timing and function allows us to configure RAMP Gold's timing models at runtime. To model different cache sizes, for example, we fix the maximum cache size at synthesis time, and at runtime we program configuration registers that determine how the cache tag RAMs are indexed and masked. Most timing model parameters can be set at runtime; among these are the size and associativity of the L1 and L2 caches, the number of L2 cache banks and their latencies, and DRAM bandwidth and latency. The current implementation of the timing model runs at 90 MHz on the Virtex-5 FPGA, and supports up to 12 MB of aggregate target cache, while using over 90% of the on-chip FPGA block RAM resources.

Synthesis of RAMP Gold takes about two hours on a mid-range workstation, resulting in 28% logic (LUT) and 90% BRAM utilization on a mid-size Virtex-5 FPGA. The low logic utilization is due in part to mapping computation to the built-in DSPs and by omitting bypass multiplexers. The high block RAM utilization is mainly due to the large target caches we support. More details on the RAMP Gold implementation can be found in [38].

4.2 Model Verification and Flexibility

RAMP Gold comprises about 36,000 lines of SystemVerilog with minimal third-party IP blocks. We liberally employ SystemVerilog assertions to aid in RTL debugging and verification. The functional model is verified against the SPARC V8 certification suite from SPARC International. Because it uses abstracted RTL, RAMP Gold requires the same simulator timing verification as SAME simulators, but the far greater performance eases the verification effort. We verify our timing models with custom microbenchmarks.

The timing model and its interface to the functional model are designed to be simple and extensible to facilitate rapid evaluation of alternative memory hierarchies and microarchitectures. Despite its extensive runtime configurability, the timing model comprises only 1000 lines of SystemVerilog. It is thus easy to understand and prototype new architectural ideas. For example, we implemented a version of a novel quality-of-service framework, Globally-Synchronized Frames [22], in about 100 lines of code and three hours of implementation effort.

4.3 Related FAME Work

RAMP Gold is inspired in part by other recent projects in the FAME community. Fort et al. [17] employed multithreading to improve utilization of soft processors with little area cost. Protoflex [12] is an FPGA-based full-system simulator without a timing model, and is designed to provide similar functionality to Simics [24] at FPGA-accelerated speeds. ProtoFlex employs host multithreading to simulate multiple SPARC V9 target cores with a single host pipeline but lacks a hardware floating-point unit as it targets commercial workloads like OLTP; its performance thus suffers on arithmetic-intensive parallel programs. HAsim [31] is a FAME Level 011 simulator that decouples target timing from functionality, but models a more complex out-of-order superscalar processor. A newer version of HAsim with host multithreading is under development. FAST [11, 10] is a hybrid FAME/SAME simulator which uses a speculative execution scheme to allow a software functional model to efficiently run in parallel with a decoupled timing model in an FPGA. RAMP Gold is the first multithreaded, decoupled FAME Level 111 simulator with a detailed multi-level memory hierarchy timing model.

5. EVALUATION: A MANYCORE OS SCHEDULING CASE STUDY

To demonstrate the capabilities of Multithreaded FAME, we experiment with the interaction between hardware partitioning mechanisms and operating system scheduling policy using RAMP Gold. We chose this case study [8, 13] because we feel it contains many important components of modern architecture research: We run a modern parallel benchmark suite, boot a research operating system, simulate manycore target architectures with multi-level memory hierarchy timing models, and add experimental hardware mechanisms to the target machine.

The additional simulation capacity of RAMP Gold enables us to move beyond simple benchmarking, and instead experiment with different operating system policies to see if the OS can effectively utilize these added mechanisms. We feel that our results illustrate the potential of FAME not only for parallel computer architecture research but also as an enabler of hardware and system software co-design.

The speedup in simulation time from FAME allows for a far more robust analysis than would have been possible using SAME, and the conclusions reached using the additional simulation capacity are qualitatively different from those that would be obtained using the slower SAME simulation capability.

5.1 Problem Statement

In the manycore era, operating systems face the *spatial resource allocation* problem of having to manage a growing number of on-chip resources shared by a growing number of concurrently running applications. Spatial resource allocation is challenging because applications can have diverse resource requirements, and the range of possible schedules grows combinatorially with applications and resources. Our proposal to help the scheduler make intelligent spatial scheduling decisions is to employ *predictive models* of application performance. The OS scheduler uses the model of each application's performance to predict which schedule will have the best overall system behavior (i.e., best performance or lowest energy). To make the case for model-based control of spatial resource scheduling, we need to learn if the performance models we create are accurate, which metrics the scheduler should use, and how far from optimal are the resulting schedules. Evaluating each issue requires seconds of simulated target time and/or hundreds of experiments. We thus need a simulator that can run at OS timescales with reasonable turnaround.

Furthermore, we believe architectural support for performance isolation can greatly improve the effectiveness of predictive modeling and scheduling, as well as improve application performance by reducing interference. To test this theory, we added hardware partitioning mechanisms to the target architecture.

5.2 Partitioning Mechanisms

Our allocation framework includes the following resources: the cores and their private caches, the shared last-level cache, and shared memory bandwidth. For each resource, we provide a mechanism to prevent applications from exceeding their allocated share. The OS assigns cores and their associated private resources to a specific application. For the shared last-level cache, we modify the OS page-coloring algorithm so that applications are never given a page from a different application's color allocation.

To partition off-chip memory bandwidth, we use Globally-Synchronized Frames (GSF)[22]. GSF provides strict Quality-of-Service guarantees for minimum bandwidth and the maximum delay of a point-to-point network—in our case the memory network—by controlling the number of packets that each core can inject per frame. We use a modified version of the original GSF design, which tracks allocations per application instead of per core, does not reclaim frames early, and does not allow applications use the excess band-

Attribute	Setting
CPUs	64 single-issue in-order cores @ 1 GHz
L1 Instruction Cache	Private, 32 KB, 4-way set-associative, 128-byte lines
L1 Data Cache	Private, 32 KB, 4-way set-associative, 128-byte lines
L2 Unified Cache	Shared, 8 MB, 16-way set-associative, 128-byte lines, inclusive, 4 banks, 10 ns latency
Off-Chip DRAM	2 GB, 4×3.2 GB/sec channels, 70 ns latency

Table 2: Target machine parameters simulated by RAMP Gold.

Name	Type	Parallelism	Working Set	Bandwidth Demand
Blackscholes	financial PDE solver	coarse data parallel	2.0 MB	minimal
Bodytrack	vision	medium data parallel	8.0 MB	grows with cores
Fluidanimate	animation	fine data parallel	64.0 MB	grows with cores
Streamcluster	data mining	medium data parallel	16.0 MB	high
Swaptions	financial simulation	coarse data parallel	0.5 MB	grows with cores
x264	media encoder	pipeline	16.0 MB	grows with cores
Tiny	synthetic	one thread does all work	1 KB	minimal
Greedy	synthetic	data parallel	16.0 MB	high

Table 3: Benchmark description. PARSEC benchmarks use `simlarge` input set sizes, except for x264 and fluidanimate, which use `simmedium` due to limited physical memory capacity. PARSEC characterizations are from [7].

width. These changes make GSF more suited to our study since we want to strictly bound the maximum bandwidth per application. Implementing GSF required some modifications to the target machine's memory controller in RAMP Gold to synchronize the frames and track application packet injections. Due to the functional/timing split in RAMP Gold, this modification was no more difficult than modifying a software simulator would have been.

5.3 Modeling and Scheduling Framework

To explore the relationship between model accuracy and model type for our problem space, we evaluate linear additive models, quadratic response surface models, and nonlinear models. The OS scheduler uses the models of each application to optimally allocate resources between a mix of concurrently running applications. The algorithm maximizes an objective function, which serves to convert model outputs into a measure of overall decision fitness. We evaluate three objective functions. A robust evaluation of this framework requires full cross validation of possible alternate schedules, which is computationally demanding.

5.4 Experimental Setup

Our experimental platform for this case study consists of five Xilinx XUP FPGA boards. Each board is programmed to simulate one instance of our target architecture. Table 2 lists the target machine parameters. We run six applications from the PARSEC benchmark suite [7], as well as two synthetic microbenchmarks. Table 3 summarizes the benchmarks. The performance models are built based on applications running alone on a partition of the machine but are tested against data collected from multiprogrammed scheduling scenarios. We simulated all possible allocations for each benchmark running alone, and then all possible schedules of allocations for 3 pairs of benchmarks running simultaneously, for a combined total of 68.5 trillion target core-cycles. (A core-cycle is 1 clock cycle of execution on 1 core; simulating a 64-core CMP for 1,000,000 cycles would be 64,000,000 core-cycles.)

5.5 Case Study Results

We found that predictive modeling has potential to successfully manage some applications, depending on the scheduler's objective function. For example, if the objective is to minimize energy, the approach works quite well. However, if the objective is to minimize the time it takes to complete both applications, the naive baselines, such as splitting the machine in half or time-multiplexing, often performed as well or significantly better than model-based allocation. Figure 2(a) presents an example of these results. More importantly, our conclusions about the value of model-based scheduling would have been different had we *not* simulated the entire execution of benchmarks, with large input sets, for all possible allocations.

Effect of Benchmark Input Set Size. We quantified the effect of benchmark configuration size by rerunning our experiments using either the PARSEC `simsmall` size input sets or only synthetic benchmarks. While we would expect different inputs or simpler benchmarks to produce slightly different results, Figure 2b reveals that these modifications significantly change the conclusion. For this particular scheduling problem, with both the small input set and synthetic benchmarks our scheduling technique is very close to optimal performance. However, for the larger input set the prediction-based schedule is 50% worse than optimal, and naively dividing the machine in half is always better. The reduced benchmarks improve the worst case while also easing the process of making good decisions, giving us an unwarranted confidence in the scheduler's abilities.

Effect of Testing All Possible Allocations. Full cross-validation of our scheduler requires collecting data on all possible schedules. We would otherwise have no idea what the optimal or pessimal scheduling decisions are, and thus no way to tell how well the scheduler is doing in comparison. The space of scheduling performance is complicated and discontinuous, so we are not guaranteed to capture true global optima if we validate by only testing against a sample of possible schedules.

Figure 3 illustrates how limited validation approaches may skew our interpretation of experimental results. Figure 3a

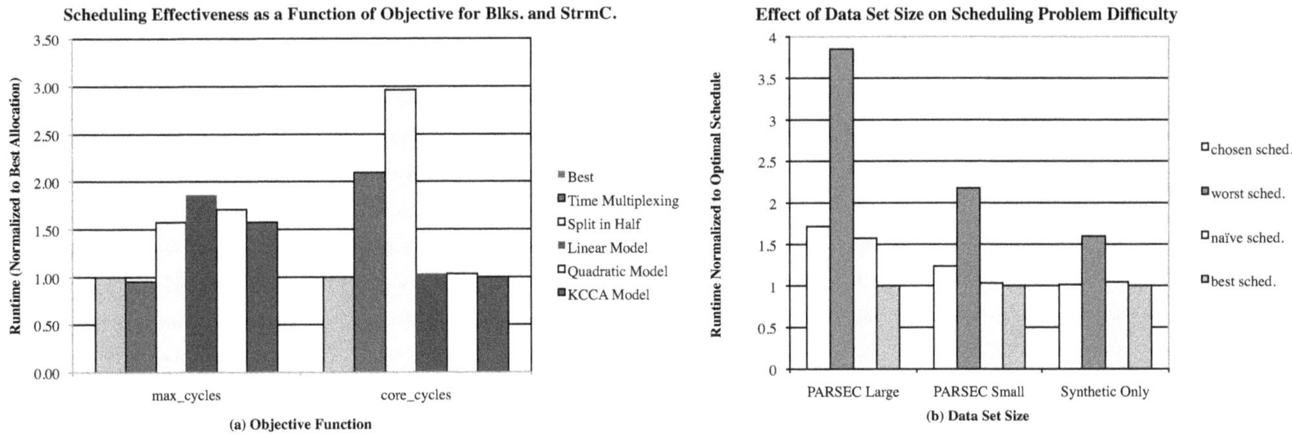

Figure 2: (a) The performance of various scheduling methodologies and objective functions for one scheduling problem, normalized to the globally optimal schedule's performance. The scheduler tries to minimize each objective function. (b) The effect of benchmark size on the difficulty of the scheduling problem. The average chosen schedule performance, global worst case and naive scheduling case are normalized to the globally optimal schedule's performance for each dataset. The scheduling decision is Blackscholes vs. Streamcluster, the objective function is to minimize runtime.

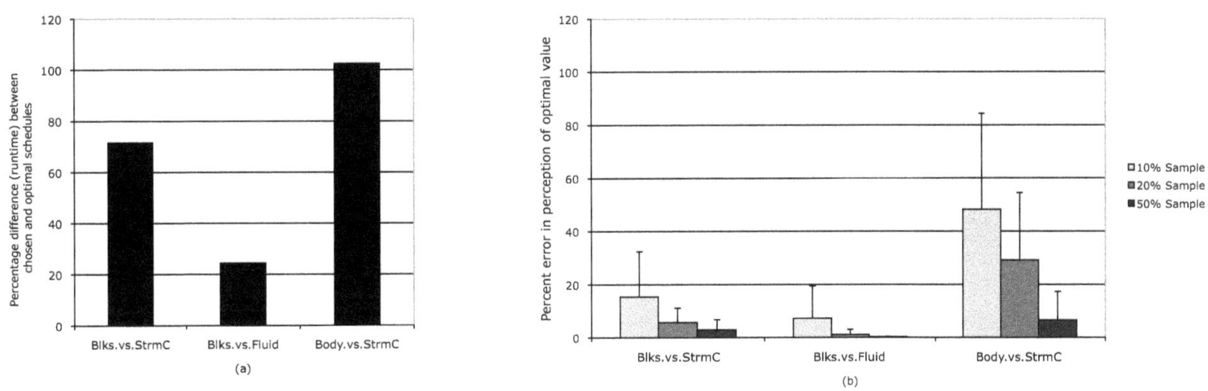

Figure 3: (a) The percentage difference in runtime between the average chosen schedule and the globally optimal schedule, for three scheduling problems. (b) The percentage error between the perceived optimal schedule for a given validation sample size and the true globally optimal schedule. Note that error in perception increases as sample size decreases, and can be a significant fraction of the percentage difference in runtime from (a).

plots the percentage difference in runtime between the average chosen schedule and the globally optimal schedule, for three scheduling problems. This difference illustrates how far our scheduler really is from finding the best schedule, but it can only be determined by evaluating the performance of all possible schedules.

In Figure 3b, we vary the number of schedules examined during validation, covering different subsets of the total possible schedules. For each validation sample set size, we take many different samples and report the percentage error in the average observed optima. The observed error varies because samples that are not inclusive of all possible schedules may miss optimal points, and smaller samples are more likely to exclude these important points. Note that the errors in Figure 3b can be a significant fraction of the true performance in Figure 3a for the smaller validation samples.

This data indicates that using reduced validation methods would have caused us to *overestimate* the quality of our scheduling solutions. As the perceived optimum degrades, our scheduler falsely appears to perform better. Only examining all possible schedules gave us an unbiased view of algorithmic and modeling quality. In conclusion, we could not have discovered the problem cases for our scheduling framework had we done a study with only reduced benchmarks or using only a small set of validation points. Gaining a more complete understanding of scheduler performance with new hardware was only possible by using FAME.

5.6 Simulator Speedup Results

To compare against RAMP Gold's performance, we run the PARSEC benchmarks inside Virtutech Simics [24], a popular SAME simulator. We run Simics with varying levels of architectural modeling detail: pure functional simulation, Simics `g-cache` timing modules, and the Multifacet GEMS [25] Ruby timing module.

We configure Simics to model the same case study target machine as closely as possible. However, both `g-cache` and GEMS Ruby modules implement timing for a MESI coher-

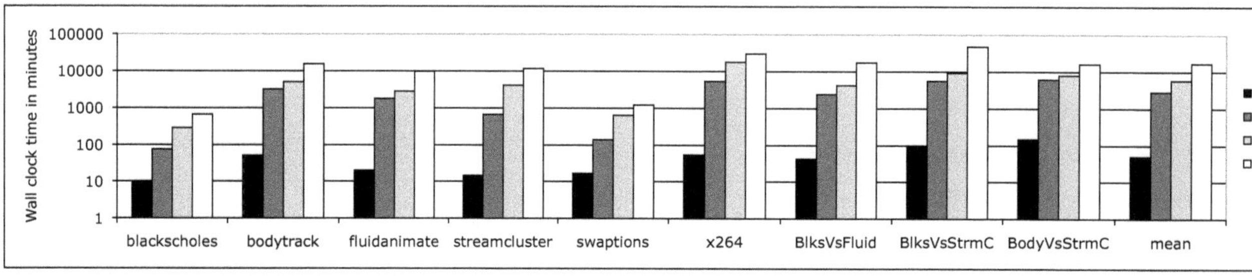

Figure 4: Wallclock time of RAMP Gold and Simics simulations. The target machine has 64 cores. Possible Simics configurations are functional modeling only, **g-cache** timing modules, and the GEMS Ruby module, with an interleave of 1 instruction. In the cases where two applications are run, each gets 1/2 of the partitionable hardware resources.

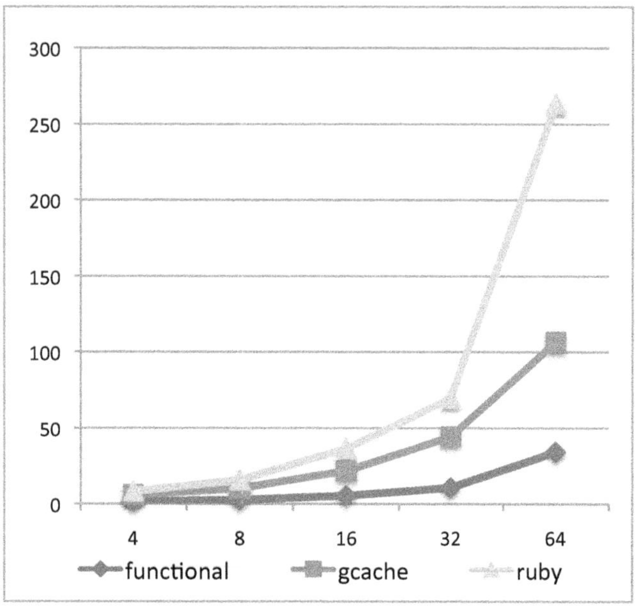

Figure 5: Geometric mean speedup of RAMP Gold over Simics across benchmarks. Possible Simics configurations are functional modeling only, **g-cache** timing modules, and the GEMS Ruby module, with an interleave of 1 instruction. The x-axis is target cores.

ence policy, whereas RAMP Gold does not at present do so. We configure Ruby to not simulate contention in the on-chip interconnection network (neither **g-cache** nor RAMP Gold do so presently). We are in the process of developing coherence timing models for RAMP Gold, and we believe these would have very little impact on simulation speed as they would run in parallel to the functional model.

We vary the number of target machine cores simulated in both RAMP Gold and Simics. The applications spawn as many threads as the target machine has cores, but the workload size is fixed. Simics was run on 2.2 GHz dual-socket dual-core AMD Opteron processors with 4 GB of DRAM. Reducing the frequency at which Simics interleaved different target processors offered a limited performance improvement.

The longest running Simics simulation of a single benchmark point takes over 192 hours (8 days), whereas the longest RAMP Gold simulation takes 66 minutes. Figure 4 plots the wall clock runtime of a 64-core target machine simulated by RAMP Gold and different Simics configurations across benchmarks and pairs of co-scheduled benchmarks. RAMP Gold is up to two orders of magnitude faster. Critically, this speedup allows the research feedback loop to be tens of minutes, rather than hundreds of hours.

RAMP Gold runtimes generally improve as the number of cores is increased because multithreading becomes more effective, whereas Simics' performance degrades super-linearly with the number of cores simulated. With 64-core target machines, RAMP Gold is even faster than Simics's functional simulation. Figure 5 shows the geometric mean speedup of FAME over SAME across the different benchmarks and for different SAME configurations. The maximum speedup is a factor of 806×.

The slowdowns incurred by Simics are due nearly entirely to host machine performance, as the benchmarks themselves scale in performance across more target cores equivalently on Simics and RAMP Gold. The fact that the slowdowns also correlate with the size of the benchmarks' inputs and working set suggests that host cache and TLB misses may present a major performance bottleneck. Unfortunately, Simics is closed-source, so we were not able to diagnose its poor performance more precisely.

In terms of our case study, we calculate that just the verification of the scheduling decisions' optimality would have taken over 73,000 hours (8.3 years) of wall clock time using Simics versus 257 hours with RAMP Gold. Table 4 includes estimates for the entire case study. These estimates are generous to SAME, as they do not include increased simulation time caused by decreased application performance due to limited simulated resource allocation sizes. This application slowdown was around 2–5× for RAMP Gold. Ironically, we were not able to run Simics long enough to calculate the actual slowdown, which is why we use estimates based on a sample of 2 billion instructions.

While the extreme SAME simulation overhead could have been partially mitigated by using a cluster of machines, the latency of individual simulations would remain unchanged. In our experience, long latencies are harmful to experimenter productivity, as they require waiting days or weeks (33 *days* worst case) for feedback on which design decisions proved worthwhile, which studies should be done next, or even whether a new mechanism is implemented correctly. We believe performing a case study as presented here, incorporating both novel software and hardware, and operating over realistic stretches of simulated time, would be completely untenable with SAME methods.

Case Study Component	FAME Total Runtime (hours)	Est. SAME Total Runtime (hours)	Median/Max FAME Latency (hours)	Median/Max SAME Latency (hours)
Model Sample Sets	49	2,848	0.5 / 2	44 / 196
Model Validation	145	16,150	0.5 / 2	44 / 196
Scheduling Validation	257	73,073	1 / 3	179 / 796
Misconfigured Experiments	82	8,612	1 / 3	179 / 796

Table 4: Comparison of case study simulation times with RAMP Gold (FAME) and Simics (SAME). Total hours could be concurrently divided across multiple simulator instances. SAME times are estimated based on observed wall clock times for 2B target cycles, and assuming unrestricted target machine resource allocations.

6. DISCUSSION

In our conversations with the broader architecture community, the use of FPGA-based simulation technology raises several major concerns.

The larger development effort of FAME versus SAME is perhaps the biggest valid concern. Simulator developers need to learn a hardware description language and FPGA CAD tools, and develop a highly concurrent hardware simulation model. In our experience, the inherent complexity of FAME simulators is somewhat greater than SAME simulators, but not vastly so. In any case, few researchers build simulators from scratch, and so the effort to modify an existing simulator is a more important measure. For many experiments, only the timing model needs to be changed, and the entire timing model for RAMP Gold is only around 1000 lines of System Verilog code. The RAMP Gold functional model is around 35,000 lines of System Verilog code, but much new functionality can be added by simply changing the microcode in the existing pipeline. The massively improved simulator performance is itself a significant boost to developer productivity, as many tasks (verification, software porting, calibration) require many simulation cycles. A much bigger problem than simulator complexity for developer productivity is the poor state of FPGA CAD tools, which are even worse than ASIC CAD tools. During the 2-year development of RAMP Gold, we encountered 78 formally tracked bugs in four tools from two companies, ranging from logic synthesis and simulation to formal verification. We can only hope the tools will improve in quality.

The cost of FPGA boards is another common concern, but when Multithreaded FAME techniques are used, the FPGA hardware is far more cost-effective than conventional clusters. For example, consider what our experiments would have cost had we run them in the cloud, which would be far cheaper than maintaining a large private cluster for most institutions. The five XUP boards we used were attached to a single workstation and cost \$3750 and took 257 total hours (11 XUP days) to run our case study, with a maximum latency of 3 hours for one experiment. Had we run the experiments on Amazon EC2/S3, we estimate the cost would have been about \$12,500 for the 73,000 hours (3000 CPU days) it would take to run the case study[2]. The cloud run costs a little over a factor of three more than our initial investment, yet this is only for one set of experiments. We can continue to use the XUP boards for our architecture research, amortizing this capital investment over 2–3 years and hundreds of research experiments. Additionally, the latency of individual experiments is not helped using a cluster, which means many of our simulations would still take longer than 33 days on EC2. FAME techniques dramatically *lower* the cost of large-scale simulations compared to SAME.

Improving the performance of SAME simulation via sampling is sometimes proposed as an alternative to FAME simulation. But serious questions remain for the practical application of sampling for many multiprocessor experiments. First, to greatly reduce simulation time, the sampling system has to support flexible microarchitecture-independent snapshots, which remain an open research problem for multiprocessors [6, 43]. Without snapshots, simulation time is dominated by the functional warming needed to fast-forward between sample points (ProtoFlex was developed, in part, to accelerate functional warming [12]). Second, for parallel systems, program behavior depends on microarchitectural details, for example, due to operating system scheduling, lock contention, or dynamic code adaptation, so detailed timing models are needed between sample points, reducing the speedup from sampling. Finally, it is not clear that fast, accurate sampling simulators are actually easier to develop and modify than a brute-force FAME simulator.

Obviously, not all architecture research projects need FAME simulators. For example, SAME simulators likely work well enough when trying to improve branch predictors or pipeline designs of small-scale multiprocessors. For experiments that do not require accurate timing models or many cores, SAME can be accelerated through the use of dynamic binary translation. However, we believe that many current computer architecture research challenges concern large core counts, detailed microarchitecture models, significant time durations, non-deterministic behavior, and dynamic software, in which case SAME is no longer tractable.

7. CONCLUSION

For many reasons, we believe the move to parallel computing means the research community needs a boost in simulation performance. To clarify the many efforts at using FPGAs to deliver that boost, we propose a four-level taxonomy for FPGA Architecture Model Execution (FAME). By estimating experiments per day per dollar, we show improvements in cost-performance by factors of 200,000 between the lowest and highest FAME levels. We use a research case study using RAMP Gold, which simulates 64 SPARC CPUs on a \$750 Xilinx Virtex5 board, to demonstrate the benefits of the highest FAME level. The 250× decrease in simulation time versus a Software Architecture Model Execution (SAME) simulator led to vastly different conclusions than had we been constrained by slower SAME simulation to fewer experiments with smaller input sets. We believe that the dramatic improvement in simulation latency

[2]We assume Amazon's High-CPU Medium Instances [4], which most closely match the machines on which we performed our SAME experiments; each instance costs \$0.17 per hour.

and throughput offered by FAME simulators opens the door for exciting research in computer architecture and hardware-software co-design.

ACKNOWLEDGEMENTS

We'd like to thank the many members of the RAMP community for their contributions to the various levels of the FAME methodology over the last five years. We especially thank SPARC International, Inc. for donating the SPARC v8 verification suite. Thanks to the ROS implementers for their assistance on the RAMP Gold port, and to Kevin Klues in particular for providing page coloring support to facilitate our case study. We'd also like to thank Doug Burger, Derek Chiou, John Davis, Joel Emer, Mark Hill, David Wood, James Hoe, Chuck Thacker, Kees Vissers, and the anonymous reviewers for their insightful feedback on drafts of this paper.

The RAMP collaboration was supported by funding from NSF grant number CNS-0551739. The evaluation study was funded by DARPA Award FA8650-09-C-7907. This research was also supported by Microsoft (Award #024263) and Intel (Award #024894) funding and by matching funding by U.C. Discovery (Award #DIG07-10227). Additional support comes from Par Lab affiliates National Instruments, NEC, Nokia, NVIDIA, Samsung, and Sun Microsystems. Special thanks to Xilinx for their continuing financial support and donation of FPGAs and development tools. We also appreciate the financial support provided by the Gigascale Systems Research Center (GSRC).

8. REFERENCES

[1] Incisive Enterprise Palladium Series with Incisive XE Software, http://www.cadence.com/rl/Resources/datasheets/incisive_enterprise_palladium.pdf.

[2] MicroBlaze Soft Processor Core, http://www.xilinx.com/tools/microblaze.htm, 2009.

[3] R. Alverson et al. The Tera Computer System. In *Proc. of the 4th Int'l Conference on Supercomputing*, 1990.

[4] Amazon Inc. *Amazon Elastic Compute Cloud (Amazon EC2)*. Amazon Inc., http://aws.amazon.com/ec2/#pricing, 2010.

[5] K. Asanović et al. A view of the parallel computing landscape. *Commun. ACM*, 52(10):56–67, 2009.

[6] K. Barr. *Summarizing Multiprocessor Program Execution with Versatile, Microarchitecture-Independent Snapshots*. PhD thesis, MIT, Sept 2006.

[7] C. Bienia et al. The PARSEC Benchmark Suite: Characterization and Architectural Implications. In *Proc. of the 17th Int'l Conference on Parallel Architectures and Compilation Techniques*, 2008.

[8] S. Bird. Software Knows Best: A Case for Hardware Transparency and Measurability. Master's thesis, EECS Department, University of California, Berkeley, May 2010.

[9] T. Brewer. Instruction set innovations for the Convey HC-1 computer. *IEEE Micro*, March/April 2010.

[10] D. Chiou, H. Angepat, N. P. Patil, and D. Sunwoo. Accurate Functional-First Multicore Simulators. *Computer Architecture Letters*, 8(2), July 2009.

[11] D. Chiou et al. FPGA-Accelerated Simulation Technologies (FAST): Fast, Full-System, Cycle-Accurate Simulators. In *MICRO*, 2007.

[12] E. Chung et al. ProtoFlex: Towards Scalable, Full-System Multiprocessor Simulations Using FPGAs. *ACM Trans. on Reconfigurable Technology and Systems*, 2009.

[13] J. Colmenares et al. Resource Management in the Tessellation Manycore OS. In *HotPar10*, Berkeley, CA, June 2010.

[14] N. Dave et al. Implementing a functional/timing partitioned microprocessor simulator with an FPGA. In *Proc. of the Workshop on Architecture Research using FPGA Platforms*, held at HPCA-12, Feb. 2006.

[15] J. Davis, C. Thacker, and C. Chang. BEE3: Revitalizing Computer Architecture Research. Technical Report MSR-TR-2009-45, Microsoft Research, Apr 2009.

[16] L. L. Dick et al. US Patent 5425036 - Method and apparatus for debugging reconfigurable emulation systems, http://www.patentstorm.us/patents/5425036.html.

[17] B. Fort et al. A Multithreaded Soft Processor for SoPC Area Reduction. In *FCCM '06: Proc. of the 14th Annual IEEE Symposium on Field-Programmable Custom Computing Machines*, 2006.

[18] G. Gibeling, A. Schultz, and K. Asanović. RAMP architecture and description language. In *2nd Workshop on Architecture Research using FPGA Platforms*, February 2006.

[19] L. Hammond, B. A. Nayfeh, and K. Olukotun. A single-chip multiprocessor. *Computer*, 30(9):79–85, 1997.

[20] K. Klues et al. Processes and Resource Management in a Scalable Many-core OS. In *HotPar10*, Berkeley, CA, June 2010.

[21] A. Krasnov et al. RAMP Blue: A Message-Passing Manycore System In FPGAs. In *Proc. of the Int'l Conference on Field Programmable Logic and Applications*, 2007.

[22] J. W. Lee, M. C. Ng, and K. Asanović. Globally-Synchronized Frames for Guaranteed Quality-of-Service in On-Chip Networks. In *ISCA*, 2008.

[23] R. Liu et al. Tessellation: Space-Time Partitioning in a Manycore Client OS. In *HotPar09*, Berkeley, CA, March 2009.

[24] P. S. Magnusson et al. Simics: A Full System Simulation Platform. *IEEE Computer*, 2002.

[25] M. M. K. Martin et al. Multifacet's general execution-driven multiprocessor simulator (GEMS) toolset. *SIGARCH Computer Architecture News*, 33(4):92–99, 2005.

[26] J. Miller et al. Graphite: A Distributed Parallel Simulator for Multicores. In *HPCA*, January 2010.

[27] S. Mukherjee et al. Wisconsin Wind Tunnel II: A Fast, Portable Parallel Architecture Simulator. *IEEE Concurrency*, 2000.

[28] N. Njoroge et al. ATLAS: A Chip-Multiprocessor with Transactional Memory Support. In *Proceedings of the Conference on Design Automation and Test in Europe (DATE), Nice, France, April 2007*, pages 1–6, 2007.

[29] V. S. Pai, P. Ranganathan, and S. V. Adve. RSIM Reference Manual. Version 1.0. Technical Report 9705, Department of Electrical and Computer Engineering, Rice University, July 1997.

[30] M. Pellauer et al. Quick performance models quickly: Closely-coupled partitioned simulation on FPGAs. In *ISPASS*, 2008.

[31] M. Pellauer et al. A-Port Networks: Preserving the Timed Behavior of Synchronous Systems for Modeling on FPGAs. *ACM Trans. on Reconfigurable Technology and Systems*, 2009.

[32] M. Pellauer et al. Soft Connections: Addressing the Hardware-Design Modularity Problem. In *DAC '09: Proc. of the 46th Annual Design Automation Conference*, 2009.

[33] S. Reinhardt et al. The Wisconsin Wind Tunnel: virtual prototyping of parallel computers. *SIGMETRICS Performance Evaluation Review*, 1993.

[34] M. Rosenblum et al. Using the SimOS machine simulator to study complex computer systems. *ACM Trans. on Modeling and Computer Simulation*, 1997.

[35] J. Shalf. private communication, June 2009.

[36] G. E. Suh, C. W. O'Donnell, and S. Devadas. Aegis: A Single-Chip Secure Processor. *IEEE Design and Test of Computers*, 24(6):570–580, 2007.

[37] S. Swanson et al. Area-Performance Trade-offs in Tiled Dataflow Architectures. In *ISCA*, 2006.

[38] Z. Tan et al. RAMP Gold: An FPGA-based Architecture Simulator for Multiprocessors. In *DAC '10: Proceedings of the 47th Annual Design Automation Conference*, 2010.

[39] C. Thacker. private communication, May 2009.

[40] C. Thacker. Beehive: A many-core computer for FPGAs, January 2010.

[41] J. Wawrzynek et al. RAMP: Research Accelerator for Multiple Processors. *IEEE Micro*, 27(2):46–57, 2007.

[42] M. Wehner, L. Oliker, and J. Shalf. Towards Ultra-High Resolution Models of Climate and Weather. *International Journal of High Performance Computing Applications*, 2008.

[43] T. Wenisch et al. SimFlex: Statistical Sampling of Computer System Simulation. *IEEE Micro*, July 2006.

[44] E. Witchel and M. Rosenblum. Embra: Fast and Flexible Machine Simulation. *SIGMETRICS Performance Evaluation Review*, 1996.

Evolution of Thread-Level Parallelism in Desktop Applications

Geoffrey Blake, Ronald G. Dreslinski, Trevor Mudge
University of Michigan, Ann Arbor
[blakeg,rdreslin,tnm]@umich.edu

Krisztián Flautner
ARM
krisztian.flautner@arm.com

ABSTRACT

As the effective limits of frequency and instruction level parallelism have been reached, the strategy of microprocessor vendors has changed to increase the number of processing cores on a single chip each generation. The implicit expectation is that software developers will write their applications with concurrency in mind to take advantage of this sudden change in direction. In this study we analyze whether software developers for laptop/desktop machines have followed the recent hardware trends by creating software for chip multi-processing. We conduct a study of a wide range of applications on Microsoft Windows 7 and Apple's OS X Snow Leopard, measuring *Thread Level Parallelism* on a high performance workstation and a low power desktop. In addition, we explore graphics processing units (GPUs) and their impact on chip multi-processing. We compare our findings to a study done 10 years ago which concluded that a second core was sufficient to improve system responsiveness. Our results on today's machines show that, 10 years later, surprisingly 2-3 cores are more than adequate for most applications and that the GPU often remains under-utilized. However, in some application specific domains an 8 core SMT system with a 240 core GPU can be effectively utilized. Overall these studies suggest that many-core architectures are not a natural fit for current desktop/laptop applications.

Categories and Subject Descriptors

C.4 [**Performance of Systems**]: Measurement techniques

General Terms

Measurement

Keywords

Benchmarking, Multi-core, Thread Level Parallelism, Desktop applications

ISCA'10, June 19–23, 2010, Saint-Malo, France.

1. INTRODUCTION

Ten years ago the idea of *chip multi-processing* was still being explored primarily in research labs with projects such as the Stanford Hydra [38] and the Compaq Piranha [29]. The first commercial chip multi-processor, the POWER4 [6] was still a few years away. Meanwhile, Intel and AMD were engaged in the megahertz war as chips from these two leading vendors were approaching 1GHz and looked to continue well beyond. Consumer PCs were almost exclusively built as uni-processor systems. Multi-processor systems were a niche product relegated to high performance workstations and, of course servers. At that time Flautner et al. [33] presented a study of *"Thread Level Parallelism"* (TLP) on interactive desktop applications for modest Symmetric Multi-Processor (SMP) workstations of 2-4 CPUs. These were still not chip multi-processors as each CPU was on its own die. The original work was performed to gauge whether multi-processors provided any advantages to desktop applications. They found that two processors improved responsiveness of general interactive programs and larger systems were beneficial only for domain specific applications like video encoding.

Approximately five years ago chip manufactures began to reach the limits of frequency scaling as a result of power constraints. At that point, Intel and AMD turned to making multi-core chips for the desktop market. These were dual-core chip multi-processors [7, 8]. Since then, chip multi-processors have become the flagship products for the two leading desktop chip makers [23, 25, 17], currently using upwards of eight cores per die. In addition low power chip-multiprocessors for small sub-notebooks have been created. Examples include Intel's Atom [12] with 2-cores, Intel's Consumer Ultra Low Voltage (CULV) [28] chips with 2-cores, and Qualcomm's Snapdragon processor with 2 ARM v7 ISA based cores [27]. Chip multi-processor systems are now poised to enter the mobile phone market to run applications on smart phones, e.g., TI's OMAP4 [21]. Historically mobile phone chips had one application core and many accelerators.

Current chip multi-processing systems are more complex than the original SMP systems studied 10 years ago. They may include simultaneous multi-threading (SMT) support, cores sharing caches on chip, multiple chips in a system, and advanced GPUs that function as offload engines for highly parallel general purpose code, such as those from AMD [9] and NVIDIA [11]. Future desktop/laptop chips in advanced development now include heterogenous chip-multiprocessors, for example AMD's Llano [15] and Intel's Sandy Bridge [24] architectures that integrate programmable GPU cores onto the die with several regular general purpose

CPU cores. Manufacturers are designing these systems with increasing numbers of cores expecting application developers to write code that makes profitable use of them. This belief that wide-spread parallel software will materialize is reminiscent of the movie "Field of Dreams", where the protagonist is compelled to build a baseball diamond in the middle of a corn-field by a mysterious voice that says: "If you build it, they will come".

Now that multi-processor systems are the norm rather than the exception, we present this study to determine to what extent the growth in number of cores has been accompanied by an increase in software parallelism. We repeat the experiments of Flautner et al. [34, 33] investigating a broad range of desktop applications under two desktop/laptop operating systems: Microsoft Windows 7 and Apple's OS X Snow Leopard. In addition to the original study, we look at the impact of SMT, GPUs and the effects of moving to a low power architecture by performing the same tests on an embedded processor based desktop. One of the outcomes of our study is to provide a ten year perspective on desktop multi-processing. Our goal is to answer the following questions:

- To what degree does the overall system leverage concurrency, and how has that changed from 10 years ago?
- What impact does SMT have on parallel performance?
- How are GPU's being used to improve system performance, and do opportunities exist to further exploit them?
- How does architectural sophistication and clock frequency impact TLP?

In the original study, Flautner et al. showed that desktop applications leveraged TLP very sparingly, and the majority of gains came from improving user perceived responsiveness with one additional core. We have also chosen TLP as a metric because it indicates how efficiently we are using parallel resources when at least one core needs to do work, and indicates how many cores would be needed to fully support the parallel portions of an application. In our study we find that the number of cores that can be profitably used now approaches 3. In addition we find that SMT can be beneficial, the GPU is often under-utilized (although it has potential for providing additional parallelism), and TLP is insensitive to processor speed.

The rest of the paper is organized as follows: In Section 2 we present background from the original work and discuss other related work. Section 3 describes our measurement environment and metrics. In Section 4 we present the benchmarks used. Section 5 presents and analyzes the results for the mainstream desktop. Section 6 presents our results for our experiments on the low power desktop. In Section 7 we discuss the implications of the results and present our concluding remarks in Section 8.

2. BACKGROUND AND RELATED WORK

We base our work on the original studies done by Flautner et al. [34, 33] in early 2000. The authors investigated whether a modest SMP system of 2 to 4 desktop processors offered advantages for interactive applications over a single processor. Their work was performed on the commodity operating systems of the time: Windows NT 4.0, Linux, and BeOS. They found that developers had programmed their applications with threads, but the behavior was still primarily single threaded. Only in a few domain specific applications, such as Adobe Photoshop for image manipulation, used more than two processors. The final conclusion was that the majority of benefit came from the increased responsiveness provided by two processors. This responsiveness came from running the graphical user interface (GUI) portion of the program concurrently with the processing back end.

Other studies have been done in a similar vein. Works from Zhou et al. [48], Lee et al. [43] Endo et al. [32] and Chen et al. [31] from the mid to late 1990's all looked at profiling applications in the desktop environment. They note that the workload characteristics of this environment is very different from server or scientific workloads, where accesses to memory and disk are more random and latency is a more important metric. More recent sources for desktop application evaluation has come from non-academic sources such as enthusiast web sites like XBit Labs [30], or TomsHardware.com. These sites provide insight into how desktop applications (primarily games) perform on modern hardware, and their results reflect the results of Flautner et al. in that a two processor system is sufficient for most applications.

Work by Hauser et al. [39] looks at the programming paradigms for threads used in interactive applications. They found that threads are used primarily to structure programs into a comprehensible organization rather than for performance. This was confirmed by Flautner et al. when they observed that the GUI thread was separate from the back end of the application. Work by Giacaman et al. [37] proposes the restructuring of desktop applications using threads to gain performance from modern chip multi-processors. Work in parallelizing web browsers for desktops and mobile devices was investigated by Jones et al. [42].

Other works by Hung et al. [40], Frachtenberg et al. [36, 35], Nguyen et al. [45] look at multiprocessor applications for the desktop from an Operating System (OS) perspective. They all seek to characterize these applications in order to improve OS schedulers to provide better quality of service. For example if the OS detected a multimedia playback application is in focus, it could give it priority over a background task in order to reduce frame drops seen by the user.

3. METHODOLOGY

For this study we required a system profiling method that would allow us to observe the entire system and measure how effectively threads were being used on a modern chip multi-processor. Statistics currently provided by the OS are insufficient in characterizing the effectiveness of chip-multiprocessing. For example, machine utilization is a poor metric for interactive applications due to the large periods of idle time. Statistics about the number of threads created or the number of threads active in a system, like those presented in Table 1, illustrate that programmers do program with threads, but these statistics offer no insight into whether the observed threads execute concurrently. In the following sub-sections we present our metrics, tracing utilities and system setup.

3.1 Metrics

The principle metrics we are interested in for this study are the GPU Utilization and Thread Level Parallelism (TLP).

Benchmark	Created	Avg Live
Handbrake 0.9	22511	24
Call of Duty 4	77	44
Photoshop CS4	82	75
Adobe Reader 9	239	24
Quicktime-HD	53	52
Firefox 3.5	522	38

Table 1: Summary of number of threads created and average that were being used by a benchmark from each category of applications tested.

Hardware	Software
2009 Mac Pro	OS X 10.6.2
2x Intel Xeon E5520	Snow Leopard
6GB RAM	Dual boot
NVIDIA GTX285 -or-	Windows 7
NVIDIA GT120	Enterprise
ASUS ASRock	Windows 7
1x Intel Atom 330	Enterprise
4GB RAM	
NVIDIA ION	
Intel X-25M SSD	

Table 2: Benchmark environment system setup

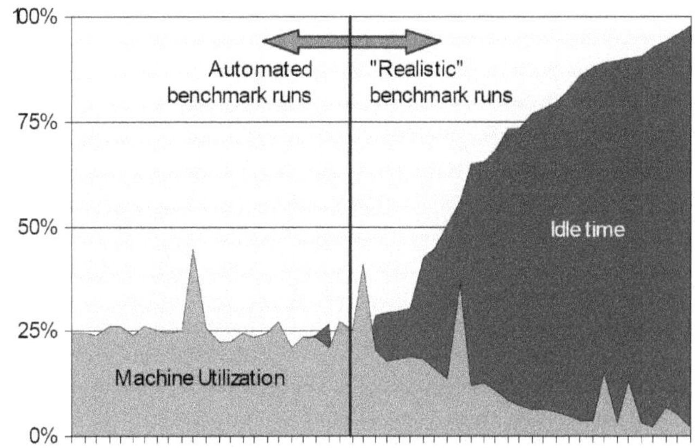

Figure 1: Figure qualitatively describing the utilization differences between automated desktop workloads and "realistic" runs performed by a user from [33]

GPU utilization is merely the average of GPU use over time. Thread Level Parallelism is a variation of machine utilization that factors out idle time and accurately describes usage of the parallel resources for the entire system.

Because there is a large amount of idle time in interactive applications, as illustrated in Figure 1, we use the metric Flautner et al. term as *TLP*. TLP is calculated by summing up c_i's that are the fraction of time that exactly $i = 0, ..., n$ (where n is the number of thread contexts in the machine) threads are executed concurrently. That number is then divided by fraction of non-idle time, $1 - c_0$, to get the TLP. TLP characterizes the average amount of concurrency exhibited by the program during its execution when at least one core is active. The formula for TLP is given in Equation 1.

$$TLP = \frac{\sum_{i=1}^{n} c_i i}{1 - c_0} \quad (1)$$

We have chosen TLP as our metric because it is an indication of efficiency in using the resources in a chip multiprocessor. A low TLP does not necessarily indicate that performance or responsiveness of the application is poor, it provides information about what portion of the machine is idle. Alternatively, it indicates the minimum number of processors needed to support an applications parallel workload. We seek not to measure the idle time, but how much of the system is utilized when at least one core is performing work. As more cores are added to a chip multi-processor, it is important to gauge how we are using them and TLP remains the best metric for determining this.

3.2 Trace Collection

We collect system wide traces of thread context switch activity and GPU utilization which are then processed to get the final TLP and GPU utilization statistics. We found that our collection techniques had minimal impact on our test system and therefore easily factored out of the final results. The details are presented in the following sub-sections.

3.2.1 Processor Context Switches

To profile whether threads are being used concurrently we use existing functionality in the two-targeted operating systems to track when a context switch happens on any processor. By tracing context switches we get very detailed information on how the parallel resources are used.

On OS X, we use DTrace [10], which was first implemented by Sun Microsystems in the Solaris OS. DTrace works by dynamically modifying the OS binary (and even user space binaries) with hook instructions at user specified points anywhere in the kernel. This gives us immense flexibility, but presents the problem of determining where to trace. We found two functions in the OS X kernel that provided us with sufficient information to trace all context switches in the system: `timer_switch` and `thread_dispatch`. The DTrace data we gather contains a *timestamp*, *CPUID*, *ProcessID*, *ThreadID* and *executing image* name.

On Windows we use Event Tracing for Windows(ETW) [41, 46]. It is similar to DTrace, but limited in comparison. Instead of tracing function calls by modifying the kernel binary like DTrace, it records specific events exposed and reported by the OS. This is less flexible than DTrace, but more intuitive as the events provided are well documented. We traced the `CSwitch`, `Thread` and `Process` events provided by the Windows kernel using ETW. These events gave us the same information as DTrace.

3.2.2 GPU Utilization

We also trace GPU usage, as they are now very capable general purpose chip multi-processors in their own right. To accomplish this we employ two similar methods.

On OS X we use the functionality in the Apple I/O Kit [19] interface to probe performance statistics present in the GPU driver. Because we were limited to a small set of statistics, and by the interface to the GPU driver, we could only measure GPU utilization by polling. For OS X we measured GPU utilization every 10 milliseconds to minimize the overhead from calling into the driver through the I/O Kit. We then used DTrace to instrument our executable that polled the GPU driver statistics to combine it with the CPU trace so we could correlate CPU and GPU activity.

In Windows we use the NVPerfKit [13] to collect similar statistics that were available in OS X. In the NVPerfkit, we gain access to the onboard GPU counters. We used the GPU idle cycle and clock cycle counters to derive GPU utilization. As in OS X, we could only poll the GPU (the polling frequency was again 10ms). Similarly to OS X, the binary that polled the GPU also registered with the Windows ETW subsystem. This provided an additional ETW event that we collect to enable correlation of GPU and CPU activity.

3.3 System Setup

The system setup we use is substantially different from the original work by Flautner et al. In the ten years that have passed, major advances in manufacturing technology and years of incremental improvements to the x86 architecture and GPUs have given us a system that is an order of magnitude faster than the original tested system. In 2000, a standard consumer system ran at around 1GHz and had a 3-way out-of-order processor (Intel Pentium III [4] or AMD Athlon [3]) with 256kB-512kB of last level cache. Our system runs at 2.26GHz, has four cores per chip, is 4-way out-of-order, has 8MB of last level cache and uses two chips. The amount of RAM commonly used then was about 256MB, whereas this system has 6GB. In terms of GPU, the increase is more astounding, NVIDIA's first GPU, the GeForce 256 [5] was a fixed graphics pipeline ASIC with 32MB of memory. NVIDIA's GTX285 is a fully programmable 240-core chip multi-processor with 1GB of onboard memory. We also test NVIDIA's GT120 [20] GPU which is a 32-core chip multi-processor. In ten years we have progressed from small 2-4 processor SMP machines running around 1GHz to very powerful many-core (100+ cores) heterogeneous machines.

In contrast to the very powerful desktop we tested, we also tested an Intel Atom based desktop system. We did so to gain insight into the effects on leveraged parallelism when the processor architecture looks more like the future chip-multiprocessors slated to be used in smart phones. The Atom is a 2-way superscalar in-order design that is reminiscent of the original Intel Pentium [2] processor. The Atom architecture also trends toward what academic researchers believe will represent future many-core chip-multiprocessors: a large number of simple processor tiles [18]. The Atom tested runs at 1.6Ghz, has 2 cores with 2-way SMT. The Intel Atom desktop also uses an NVIDIA ION low power GPU which has 16 fully programmable cores. In this study we were unable to report GPU numbers for the ION as it is currently unsupported by the NVPerfKit.

For software, we test Windows 7 Enterprise and OS X Snow Leopard on the Mac Pro. For the Atom machine, only Windows 7 Enterprise was available to test. We decided to use these desktop/laptop operating systems to be able to test a wide range of free and commercial programs that consumers would be likely to use. Our exact system specifications are shown in Table 2.

The three video cards we test are from NVIDIA and support CUDA [11] enabled applications. CUDA allows general purpose programs to offload kernels of execution to the GPU. The kernels can be any type of general purpose code that could benefit from massive parallelism offered by our tested GPUs that have 16, 32, and 240 cores respectively(for the ION, GT120 and GTX285). In our tests we study two CUDA enabled applications and evaluate real-world results obtained from using low-end GPUs and a high-end GPU.

Both systems we test also have 2-way SMT for each core that exposes up to 16 hardware thread contexts to the OS on the Mac Pro and 4 hardware contexts for the Atom. We also had the ability in both OS's to turn individual cores on and off to experiment with different core counts on the same setup. In Windows we could turn cores on and off at boot time, but only had SMT available when all eight cores were activated. In OS X we were able to try all combinations of cores and SMT support.

4. BENCHMARKS

We performed a variety of experiments for interactive programs on both the Windows and OS X operating systems. We tried to pick our benchmarks to have as much overlap as possible between Windows and OS X to provide insights to the effective use of TLP on modern day chip multi-processor machines. All the tests were carried out by hand where the user worked on the program with a strict set of timing, input, and usage constraints to allow for repeatable tests. No user interface (UI) automation tool we found was able to handle the nature of the interactive sessions because timings can experience subtle changes between runs—such as differing latencies for loading web pages or different play outcomes in game scenarios. Neither could any UI automation tool handle events such as frequently changing web content. Accordingly we elected to do the tests with a real user. Because of the possible impacts of human interaction and the variability in some of the benchmarks we ran each test a minimum of 5 times to obtain a measure of variance. The test results proved to be repeatable as the measured standard deviation was low. For the sake of brevity we briefly describe each benchmark, but each test is documented in detail at [26]. Unless otherwise noted, all benchmarks were tested on both operating systems.

4.1 3D Games

3D games have long been a driver for faster hardware. Game developers continually strive for more realistic graphics, artificial intelligence, physics, and immersive game play. Games were primarily single threaded until around 2005 when chip multi-processors were released on both PC and the current generation gaming consoles.

Activision Call of Duty 4: Modern Warfare- Is a tactical first person shooter (FPS) game that showcases high definition graphics with lots of enemies and background activity on screen. This game was originally developed for the Xbox360 and Playstation 3 game consoles which both use chip multi-processing.

2K Games Bioshock[1]**-** A slower paced action-adventure FPS game. This game was originally developed for the Xbox360 and Playstation 3.

EA Crysis[1]**-** Is a standard FPS from EA. It showcases advanced graphics, AI, and physics. It was originally developed for the PC.

4.2 Image Authoring

Image authoring has been known to use multiple processors effectively and a large amount of TLP was present in the original study. We test a 2D image authoring program and a 3D modeling program for these tests.

Adobe Photoshop CS4- Photoshop is an advanced image authoring and composition tool. We tested Photoshop by applying 5 hand picked filters in succession to a 20 megapixel photograph.

[1]Only available on Windows platform

Autodesk Maya 3D 2010- Maya 3D is a three-dimensional modeling tool. The test consisted of opening up a complex model, rotating, zooming and panning the workspace camera. Then the user smoothed the model and rendered the scene using the rasterizing renderer and the raytracing renderer.

4.3 Office

For the Office productivity tests we selected applications that are commonly used by users for basic office tasks.

Adobe Reader 9- We tested Adobe Reader 9 by opening up an eight megabyte PDF file, browsing and searching for phrases in it.

Microsoft Excel 2007/2008- Microsoft Excel was tested with a large 10,000 row spreadsheet to make commands like calculating the standard deviation take an appreciable amount of time. The test consisted of performing common operations on the data, such as calculations and plotting.

Microsoft PowerPoint 2007/2008- Microsoft PowerPoint was tested on a large presentation with a large amount of illustrations and animation. We performed common operations such as adding/deleting slides, previewing animations, inserting pictures and changing the slide formatting.

Microsoft Word 2007/2008- The Microsoft Word test involved adding/deleting text, changing format, and inserting/deleting/moving embedded images.

Microsoft Streets and Trips 2010[1]- Microsoft Streets and Trips is a full featured mapping and route planning application. The user was tasked with navigating the user interface briefly and planning a cross country trip to fifteen randomly selected cities in the United States.

4.4 Multimedia Playback

For multimedia playback we picked two media players that are popular and common across both platforms: iTunes and QuickTime player.

iTunes 9- The iTunes test consisted of searching and playing an MP3 files from a local database and also searching and playing videos from the same database.

QuickTime Player- We tested QuickTime by playing a 480p video and a 1080p high definition video encoded in the H.264/AVC format.

4.5 Video Authoring

Video authoring is becoming an increasingly popular application on the desktop as consumer grade camcorders can now shoot high definition video and transferring video to a user's machine for editing is as simple as putting the flash card in a reader. Video authoring is also important because users now want to transcode their personal videos to multiple different formats to put on YouTube.com or share on a DVD.

CyberLink PowerDirector v8[1]- PowerDirector v7 from CyberLink is a full featured video editor and production program. It also leverages CUDA for the video transcoding. For testing PowerDirector we imported some video clips and composed them into a short video complete with transitions and titles and rendered it with and without CUDA support.

Handbrake 0.9- Handbrake is an open source licensed video transcoder that can take many input formats and convert it to numerous other formats. It does not have any editing capability. We tested Handbrake by encoding a portion of a source DVD to a high profile H.264 format.

Elemental Badaboom[1]- Badaboom is another video transcoder. It uses CUDA to do the video transcoding. To test Badaboom we repeated the Handbrake test as it is a transcoder with no editing ability.

4.6 Web Browsing

In the past ten years web browsing has become a very common workload for desktop users so we do a variety of tests on multiple web browsers. Web browsers are now very complicated pieces of software, having to support many standards such as Flash, Java etc to display rich content. Because of this we perform four distinct types of tests to profile the selected browsers. All the tests take approximately 5 minutes to perform.

The first test (Tabs) has the user first watch a video on YouTube.com, then browse to ESPN.com, go to CNN.com, browse the BestBuy.com site, and finally play a flash game. Each new page is visited by creating a new tab in the browser. An additional test (Sequential) is to perform the Tabs test, but without using tabs and simply leaving the current site for the next in succession. The final two browser tests are to see the difference between sites with lots of active content like Java and Flash and one without much active content. One test was to browse ESPN.com, and the other to browse a Facebook.com profile. We test two browsers: Mozilla's Firefox 3.5, and Apple's Safari 4.0.

5. RESULTS: INTEL XEON SYSTEM

In this section we present our analysis of the data we collected from our experiments. We will cover overall results, present breakdowns for certain applications, and present an analysis of GPU usage characteristics.

5.1 Overall Results

A summary of all the 8 Core simulations with SMT support and the GTX285 GPU are presented in Table 3. The TLP data is summarized in three fields. The first field shows what percentage of total execution time (c_i) that exactly i=0, ...,n threads are executed concurrently, where n is the number of thread contexts in the machine. Correspondingly, c_0 specifies the amount of idle time experienced by the benchmark. The second field shows the measured amount of thread-level parallelism of the entire system averaged over at least 5 runs of the test. The third field reports the standard deviation. The small values indicate the tests are reproducible and insensitive to the variations induced by a real user. The fourth field presents GPU utilization percentages of the system. At the end of the table an average TLP and average GPU utilization is calculated for each of the benchmark categories.

The first thing to note is that every benchmark shows some portion of time with concurrent execution but in many cases this concurrent execution is a small percentage. Meaning programmers are writing applications with threads that can use a multi-processor machine. However, in many cases the applications do not have a high percentage of concurrent execution. For instance, in *Office* and *Web Browsing* the average TLP is between 1 and 2 for our test system. Some web tests show a surprising amount of concurrency with numbers above 2. Even for more compute intensive applications like *Games*, *Playback* and *Image Authoring* the average TLP,

[1]Only available on Windows platform

			Idle	8 Core SMT - System Wide TLP																		GPU		
	Application	OS	C0	C1	C2	C3	C4	C5	C6	C7	C8	C9	C10	C11	C12	C13	C14	C15	C16	TLP	σ	Utilization	Average TLP	Average GPU Utilization
Game	Bioshock	Windows	1%	57%	31%	7%	1%	2%	1%											1.6	0.05	75%	1.6	69%
	Call of Duty 4	Windows	0%	12%	35%	20%	14%	8%	7%	2%	1%									2.1	0.21	86%		
	Call of Duty 4	OS X	6%	77%	16%	1%														1.2	0.02	29%		
	Crysis	Windows	1%	72%	23%	4%	1%													1.4	0.07	84%		
Image Authoring	Maya3D 2010	Windows	55%	34%	6%	1%					1%								2%	2.4	0.53	18%	2.1	12%
	Maya3D 2010	Mac	57%	32%	5%	1%													1%	2.2	0.14	12%		
	Photoshop CS4	Windows	43%	43%	7%	1%					3%								1%	2.0	0.56	17%		
	Photoshop CS4	Mac	50%	38%	7%	1%	1%											1%	1%	1.9	0.19	1%		
Office	Adobe Reader 9	Windows	65%	25%	8%	1%														1.3	0.05	23%	1.2	11%
	Adobe Reader 9	OS X	70%	24%	6%															1.2	0.02	4%		
	Excel 2007	Windows	72%	23%	4%															1.2	0.02	10%		
	Excel 2008	OS X	57%	38%	5%															1.1	0.01	2%		
	PowerPoint 2007	Windows	69%	25%	5%	1%														1.2	0.03	16%		
	PowerPoint 2008	OS X	66%	30%	4%															1.1	0.01	7%		
	Streets & Trips 2010	Windows	68%	23%	7%	1%														1.4	0.01	14%		
	Word 2007	Windows	74%	22%	4%															1.2	0.04	16%		
	Word 2008	OS X	70%	27%	3%															1.1	0.01	3%		
Playback	iTunes 9	Windows	71%	23%	5%	1%														1.3	0.16	22%	1.5	22%
	iTunes 9	OS X	79%	18%	3%															1.2	0.02	5%		
	Quicktime 7.6	Windows	50%	38%	10%	2%														1.3	0.01	43%		
	Quicktime X	OS X	79%	14%	6%	1%														1.4	0.01	0%		
	Quicktime 7.6 - HD	Windows	66%	22%	5%	1%	1%				3%									2.1	0.06	40%		
	Quicktime X - HD	OS X	67%	13%	17%	3%														1.7	0.02	19%		
CUDA	Badaboom	Windows	54%	35%	9%	2%														1.3	0.03	95%	2.2	62%
	PowerDirector v8	Windows	42%	20%	12%	6%	5%	4%	3%	2%	3%	1%								3.2	0.52	28%		
Video Authoring	Handbrake 0.9	Windows	1%				1%	3%	9%	17%	22%	20%	14%	8%	4%	1%				8.4	0.02	8%	7.4	9%
	Handbrake 0.9	OS X	1%				1%	3%	8%	16%	21%	20%	15%	9%	4%	1%				9.0	0.44	0%		
	PowerDirector v8	Windows	27%	20%	11%	6%	4%	3%	2%	6%	8%	5%	5%	3%						4.8	0.15	18%		
Web Browsing	Firefox 3.5*	Windows	66%	24%	6%	1%					1%									1.5	0.05	24%	2.0	16%
	Firefox 3.5*	OS X	49%	33%	10%	3%	1%						1%	1%	1%	1%				2.2	0.12	10%		
	Safari 4.0*	Windows	50%	34%	11%	3%	1%				1%									1.6	0.06	24%		
	Safari 4.0*	OS X	50%	27%	10%	3%	1%	1%			1%	1%	1%	1%	1%	1%	1%			2.5	0.19	6%		

Table 3: Table of System TLP and GPU Utilization results. Concurrency values less than 1% are not displayed.

though higher, is still approximately 2. Only in the domain specific application of *Video Authoring* do we observe a high amount of TLP, in this case an average of approximately 7. Because of the average TLP being primarily just below or above 2, this leads to the conclusion that a small multi-processing machine of 2-3 cores is adequate for all but a few domain specific applications like *Video Authoring*. The following subsections will provide more detailed studies of the applications run on our test system.

In terms of GPU usage only a handful of applications, *Games* and *CUDA*, fully exploit the GPU with average utilizations near 70%. All the other benchmarks leave it primarily under-utilized, offering a wealth of resources for future parallel programmers. A more detailed discussion of the GPU can be found in Section 5.6.

5.2 Ten Year Perspective

A comparison of similar applications from the 2000 study and our study is presented in Figure 2. The biggest gains made in the past ten years has been in *Video Authoring*. This type of application has high computation requirements, and is inherently parallel, making it a prime target for parallelization. In fact, the ParallelMPEG decoder from the original study was only a research project at the time, but this type of code has now found itself in mainstream video players. On the other hand, some applications have shown only modest improvements, such as the *Web Browsing* and *Office* areas. For *Office* applications the major improvement has come from the virus scan interface of the system, successfully leveraging the additional cores, but in all cases it can be concluded that current single-threaded performance is adequate for *Office* applications. For *Web Browsing* it appears that there are benefits to be gained by moving to parallel code, but little progress has been made with TLP approaching 2 on average for these applications. There has been some improvement in 3D image rendering but it is offset in the *Image Authoring* applications by the decrease in 2D rendering (Photoshop). The decrease in both the Photoshop and Quicktime applications can be attributed to the gains of single core performance in terms of both frequency and architectural features.

5.3 OS Threading Support

OS X and Windows are two substantially different operating systems. OS X is derived from a combination of the BSD Unix [44] and Mach [47] operating systems. Because of its Unix heritage it natively supports the POSIX [1] threads (pthreads) interface for concurrency. Windows has a proprietary kernel and uses its own custom threading interface. These subtle differences mean that some applications, when written for one OS, may perform sub-optimally when ported to the other OS.

For all applications that run both in Windows and OS X a TLP comparison is made in Figure 3. The interesting trend to note is that OS X is better at *Video Authoring*, *Playback* and *Web Browsing*. The Quicktime and Safari applications are developed by Apple and tuned for OS X, which is a main contributor to why their performance is better in OS X and also use more features of the system. For instance, Quicktime X leverages the onboard video decode ASICs found on

Browser	Test	OS	Idle C0	C1	C2	C3	C4	C5	C6	C7	C8	C9	C10	C11	C12	C13	C14	C15	C16	TLP	σ	GPU Utilization	Average TLP	Average GPU Utilization
Firefox 3.5	Tabs	Windows	55%	29%	11%	3%	1%													1.7	0.06	29%	1.5	24%
	ESPN	Windows	67%	26%	5%	1%														1.4	0.04	23%		
	Facebook	Windows	77%	19%	3%															1.3	0.05	15%		
	Sequential	Windows	66%	24%	6%	1%					1%									1.7	0.05	28%		
	Tabs	OS X	29%	41%	15%	5%	1%					1%	1%	1%	1%	1%	1%	1%		2.7	0.13	13%	2.2	10%
	ESPN	OS X	60%	33%	6%	1%														1.6	0.13	7%		
	Facebook	OS X	71%	25%	4%															1.3	0.06	7%		
	Sequential	OS X	36%	33%	14%	5%	1%				1%	1%	2%	2%	3%	2%	1%			3.3	0.14	13%		
Safari 4.0	Tabs	Windows	37%	38%	16%	5%	1%	1%			1%									1.7	0.05	31%	1.6	24%
	ESPN	Windows	53%	34%	9%	2%	1%													1.5	0.07	20%		
	Facebook	Windows	64%	29%	6%	1%														1.3	0.09	16%		
	Sequential	Windows	45%	37%	12%	3%	1%				2%									1.7	0.02	30%		
	Tabs	OS X	26%	32%	18%	7%	3%	1%	1%	1%	1%	1%	2%	2%	2%	2%	1%			3.2	0.33	9%	2.5	6%
	ESPN	OS X	64%	26%	6%	1%														1.9	0.18	3%		
	Facebook	OS X	76%	20%	3%															1.4	0.10	2%		
	Sequential	OS X	34%	30%	15%	5%	2%	1%	1%	1%	1%	1%	1%	2%	2%	2%	2%			3.5	0.14	10%		

Table 4: Table of System TLP, and Graphics Utilization results for Web Browser workloads. Concurrency values less than 1% are not displayed.

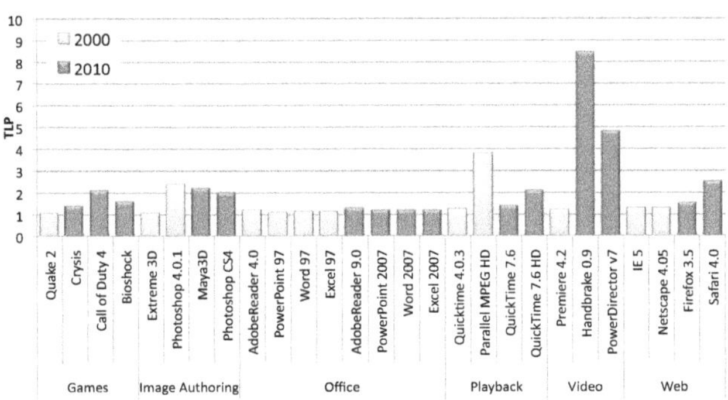

Figure 2: System TLP comparison for 2000 vs. 2010.

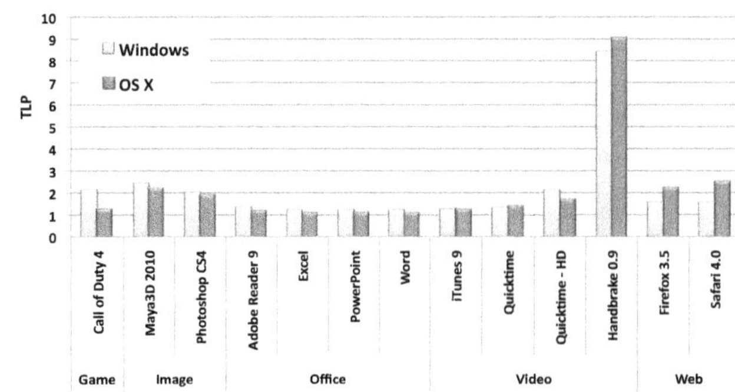

Figure 3: System TLP of 8 Cores w/ SMT on applications in both Windows and OS X.

current generation NVIDIA GPUs, as shown by 0% GPU utilization for the 480P resolution test. The Handbrake benchmark is an open source benchmark developed mostly on Linux and is tuned well to work using pthreads, which OS X supports natively and Windows emulates. On the other hand, *Games* and *Office* applications are initially developed for Windows, yielding better performance than on OS X. The port of these applications to OS X has not leveraged the parallelism realized in its Windows counterpart. For example, Call of Duty 4 has a TLP of 2 on Windows whereas the port to OS X exhibits significant single-thread behavior. In addition, the Windows *Office* applications gain in overall TLP by invoking the virus scan application in a separate thread. Overall, the trend is that applications show slight preference to one or the other OS, typically the one they were initially developed for.

With the introduction of Windows 7 and Mac OS X Snow Leopard, there has been considerable effort to push high level parallel programming initiatives and include them as integral parts of the OS. These initiatives include: DirectCompute [14] for Windows to leverage GPUs; OS X Snow Leopard supports OpenCL [22] for GPUs and introduces Grand Central Dispatch (GCD) [16] for the main multicore CPU. OpenCL and DirectCompute style parallel programming are targeted towards data-parallel applications like video transcoding, which as shown in this study is already taking advantage of such parallelism with CUDA and threads. GCD targets general applications such as web browsing, which while heavily threaded still exhibits primarily single threaded behavior. It remains to be seen whether these new programming initiatives will be used heavily in the future.

5.4 Core Scaling

The TLP performance as the system scales from 2 to 8 cores is another important trend to consider. Figures 4 and 5 show how TLP and GPU utilization changes over time for a subset of the benchmark run. First, the Handbrake application in Figure 4 illustrates the scalability of a highly parallel program which heavily utilizes the system. From the graph it can be seen that the TLP is at a maximum for most of the run on 2,4, and 8 core systems. When SMT is enabled on an 8 core system the resultant TLP fluctuates around 8. The theoretical maximum would be a TLP of 16, but in the case of Handbrake the algorithm used for the H.264 encoding has reached the peak of its scaling—it appears the code as written has bottlenecks that prevent scaling past 8-9 concurrent threads on average. This was confirmed by reading the developer notes present for Handbrake's H.264 encoder. It is also important to note that the transcoding rate of this application in frames-per-second (fps) scales up linearly with the number of cores until more than 8 thread contexts become available.

The second trend is illustrated by the Photoshop benchmark in Figure 5. In this case the benchmark is often filled with idle time as the user navigates menus, and configures

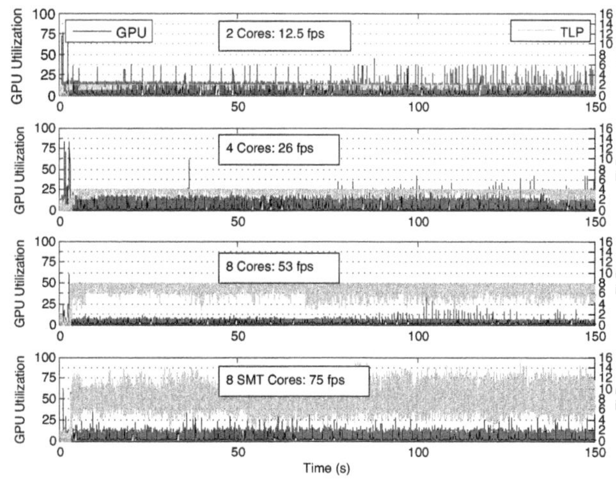

Figure 4: System TLP and GPU Utilization over time for the Handbrake benchmark in Windows for differing numbers of cores. Note as cores increase the benchmark takes almost full advantage showing good scalability for video transocde workloads.

filters. The plot shows the user performing several filter operations, these correspond to the peaks seen in the 8 core graph. In the 2 core system the runtime is long and the TLP is flat between 1 and 2. As the number of cores is increased the peaks where the filters are performed grow both higher, due to increased resources for the parallel part, and narrower, due to the decrease in runtime from the parallelism. Overall, this reduces the runtime to complete these filters and the shortened total execution time can be observed in the figure.

In summary, there are two trends that increased resources provide: 1) for non-interactive applications where the system can be fully utilized, application performance increases, in this case fps was increased; and 2) for interactive applications, the time a user waits for small tasks to complete—responsiveness of the application—can be improved and total execution time reduced.

5.5 Simultaneous Multi-Threading

The impact of SMT on parallelism is another important feature to evaluate when examining concurrent architectures for desktop applications. Figure 7 shows the resulting fps of the transcoding of the Handbrake benchmark in Windows, OS X, and OS X with SMT support. It also shows the performance of a CUDA offload application, Badaboom, that will be discussed in Section 5.6. The Handbrake benchmark transcoding rate increases with the addition of cores. The graph is not ideally linear due to the way the cores are interconnected. In particular, some cores share cache on-die while others need to communicate between chips in different sockets. In our SMT 4 core system all 8 thread contexts are on the same die and can communicate through the shared on-die cache. While our non-SMT 8 core system needs to communicate between the two sockets, increasing latency to complete the operations. This is illustrated in Figure 7 where the SMT 4 core system outperforms the non-SMT 8 core system. This shows that SMT is beneficial for parallel applications when cache can be shared and is fast to access.

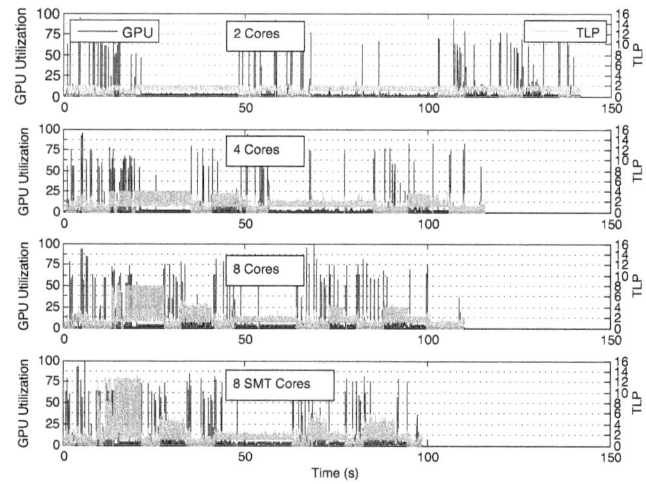

Figure 5: System TLP and GPU Utilization over time for the Photoshop benchmark in Windows for differing numbers of cores. Note that as cores increase, the peaks of the filtering operations become taller and narrower, yielding a shorter runtime. As SMT is enabled a large improvement is seen.

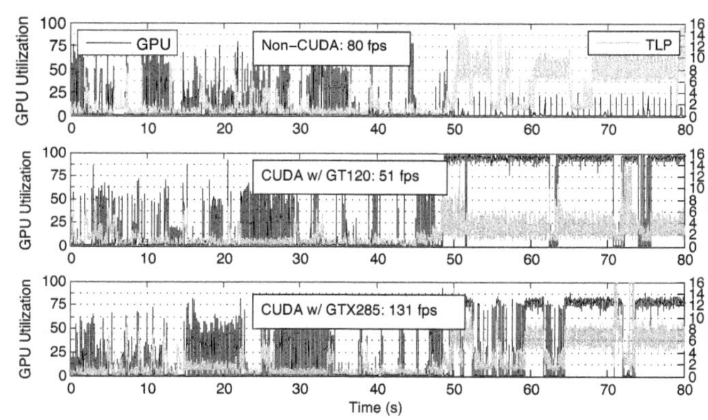

Figure 6: A time plot of a subsection of the PowerDirector benchmark, transcoding begins around 50s. The three plots show the non-CUDA enhanced version, and CUDA enhanced for a low-end GPU and a high-end GPU. Note the improvement in transcoding rate with CUDA enhancements on the high end graphics card.

5.6 Graphics

One of the main questions this work wanted to answer was: "Are GPU's being used to improve system performance, and what opportunities are there to further use them?" The following subsections will break down the measurements of our CUDA applications and typical GPU utilization. These will show there remains potential to leverage the additional computational resources of the GPU.

5.6.1 Graphics Offloading

CUDA support is a promising new programming technique where the goal is to offload highly parallel work to the GPU. For this study the PowerDirector and Badaboom benchmarks offer two video transcoding applications with CUDA support that can be compared to non-CUDA transcoders. First the transcoding rate, fps, of the Badaboom

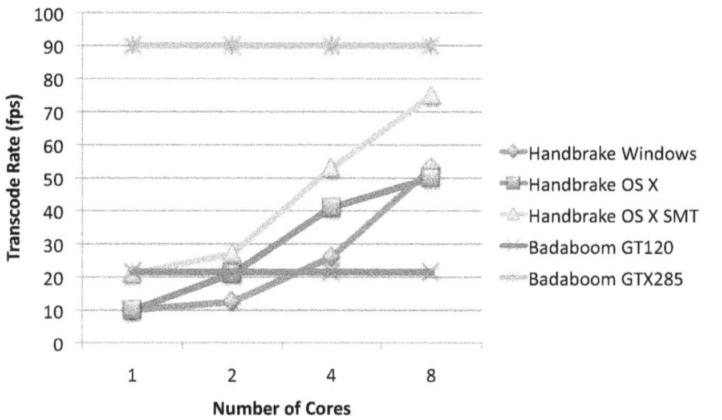

Figure 7: Transcoding Rate of Handbrake and CUDA Application Badaboom for 1 to 8 Cores. Illustrating the performance afforded by GPU offloading, and the impact of SMT on performance.

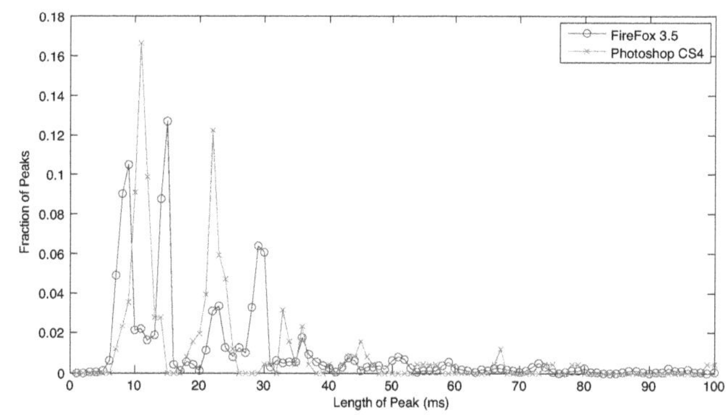

Figure 8: Frequency of GPU Utilization Peaks above 10% of various durations for the Firefox and Photoshop Benchmarks.

benchmark is shown in Figure 7. It is plotted both for the low-end graphics card, GT120, and the high-end graphics card, GTX285. From the graph it can be seen that the system (running the non-CUDA Handbrake application) easily outperforms a low-end graphics card for core counts greater than 2. However, a high end card is capable of transcoding at 125% the speed of even an 8 core system with SMT.

Figure 6 shows a time breakdown of the TLP and graphics utilization of the PowerDirector benchmark with and without CUDA support. The first thing to note is the transcoding rate achieved by each application, and the trends are similar to the Badaboom application. In terms of graphics utilization it can be seen that the non-CUDA version uses almost no graphics support during the transcoding phase of the application. When the GT120 is used with CUDA the graphics utilization reaches 100% and the transcoding becomes GPU limited. Once the graphics card is improved to the GTX285 the utilization of the GPU falls off and the TLP of the system increases to 8 leaving the transcoding once again core limited because the graphics card has enough resources to match the transcoding rate of the cores.

In conclusion CUDA is promising when high-end GPUs with many cores are available. For low-end GPUs, CUDA may not offer much improvement, and may even perform worse than a typical 2 or 4 core chip multi-processor.

5.6.2 Graphics Utilization

In Table 3 the GPU column presents the average utilization of the GPU for each benchmark. It is noteworthy that for most applications the GPU utilization is low. The majority of the time there are short spikes when the screen needs to be updated, e.g. moving a window. The typical spike in utilization for the Firefox benchmark in Windows is approximately 20ms in length and 40% utilization. Figure 8 shows a breakdown for the length of GPU utilization spikes higher than 10% for the Photoshop and Firefox applications. It shows that for these applications there is plenty of parallel resources being under-utilized in the GPU. If GPU offloading enhancements could be made for the benchmarks, there is significant opportunity to further utilize the GPU. There are, however, a couple of application classes, *Playback* and *Game*, where the GPU is already highly utilized and there are less opportunities for off-loading. The other area with high utilization is the *CUDA* applications, this is, of course, due to the fact that they are already leveraging off-load capabilities.

5.7 Web Browser Workload

A detailed breakdown of the individual web browser tests is presented in Table 4. The interesting observation from the results is that the sequential page access test actually observes a higher TLP than the tab based page access under OS X. The tab based approach is keeping alive pages, including some that are streaming content, and does exhibit higher TLP for that portion of the run. However, in the sequential version of the tests a garbage collection thread runs each time a site is navigated away from. This garbage collection thread is used to reduce the memory footprint of each web browser by cleaning up allocated memory and writing back cacheable items to the file cache, e.g., pictures. The information still resides in the system so it is faster to access compared to retrieving the site again over the network. The tab based version keeps the memory alive, and the tabs can be thought of as a user controlled cache of the sites likely to be revisited soon. Overall, web-browsing is a more CPU intensive application than it previously was 10 years ago. Then, it was primarily network dominated, but now network bandwidth is plentiful and the amount of content present takes appreciable cpu time to render. Behavior is still primarily single threaded, as indicated by the low TLP. Jones et al. [42] see the same behavior where the browser is CPU dominated instead of waiting idle for the network and are working towards developing methods to parallelize web browsing.

6. RESULTS: INTEL ATOM SYSTEM

We tested the Atom to see if decreasing the overall performance of the cores made an appreciable difference in the observed TLP. The hypothesis was: The Intel Xeon system has very high single thread performance therefore individual tasks may be completing quickly enough that they were not running concurrently. The Intel Atom's single thread performance compared to the Intel Xeon is very low and could lead to increases in TLP. This performance differential is seen in the Handbrake video transcoder, a single core of the Xeon processor can maintain a 10fps average encode rate

	Application	Idle C0	System TLP C1	C2	C3	C4	TLP	σ	Average TLP
Game	Bioshock	2%	25%	35%	27%	11%	2.2	0.04	2.0
	Call of Duty 4	1%	37%	27%	26%	10%	2.1	0.05	
	Crysis	0%	39%	44%	14%	2%	1.8	0.02	
Image Authoring	Maya3D 2010	20%	41%	13%	5%	21%	2.1	0.05	1.9
	Photoshop CS4	8%	59%	17%	6%	10%	1.6	0.11	
Office	Adobe Reader 9	40%	36%	19%	5%	1%	1.5	0.03	1.4
	Excel 2007	45%	40%	12%	2%		1.3	0.01	
	PowerPoint 2007	38%	42%	16%	4%	1%	1.4	0.01	
	Streets & Trips 2010	39%	34%	20%	5%	2%	1.6	0.02	
	Word 2007	35%	49%	13%	3%		1.3	0.01	
Playback	iTunes 9	24%	45%	24%	6%	1%	1.5	0.09	2.1
	Quicktime 7.6	4%	28%	39%	23%	6%	2.1	0.10	
	Quicktime 7.6 - HD	11%	19%	22%	22%	26%	2.6	0.01	
CUDA	Badaboom	68%	23%	9%	1%		1.3	0.04	2.0
	PowerDirector v8	8%	17%	20%	23%	32%	2.8	0.07	
Video Authoring	Handbrake 0.9	0%		2%	10%	88%	3.8	0.04	3.6
	PowerDirector v8	3%	8%	11%	19%	58%	3.3	0.04	
Web Browsing	Firefox 3.5*	25%	42%	19%	9%	5%	1.6	0.04	1.7
	Safari 4.0*	23%	35%	21%	12%	8%	1.8	0.08	

Table 5: Table of System TLP for the Intel Atom machine on Windows 7 only. Concurrency values less than 1% are not displayed.

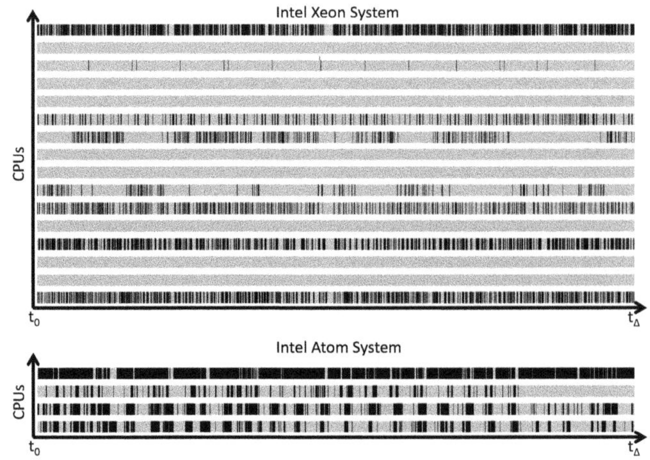

Figure 9: Trace of 1 second of execution for the *Call of Duty 4* benchmark for the Xeon and Atom systems on Windows 7. Black is active processing, and Gray is idle time. Each bar corresponds to a logical CPU visible to the OS.

while the Atom processor averages 3fps. Therefore a single Atom core is roughly 30% of the performance of a Xeon core.

The overall experiment results are presented in Table 5. The tests were carried out in the exact same manner as the tests reported in Table 3, but only numbers for Windows 7 are reported, OS X is not supported on the atom platform. We are also not able to report GPU statistics for the NVIDIA ION chip as the version of NVPerfKit we used did not support it.

The first major difference between the Atom results and the Xeon results is the marked decrease in *idle* time between the two platforms, except for *Games*. This further reinforces that the Atom's single thread performance is inferior to the Xeon. Further confirmation of this lack of performance was reported by the human tester as almost all the tests produced poor user experiences with long wait times.

The *Playback* test sees an increase in TLP to around 2 on average, but the *idle* time is very small on the Atom. The *Games* tests have TLP results that are almost identical between the two platforms. The similar TLP numbers indicate that the software is the main factor in the low amount of parallelism exposed. This can be seen in Figure 9 which shows an execution trace for both the Xeon and Atom on the Call of Duty 4 test. For both architectures, the amount of idle time is large with one main thread appearing to spawn multiple small tasks, which explains why the TLP is relatively low.

The *Office* tests show the same TLP as the Xeon tests with averages between 1 and 1.5. The idle times are surprising as they are much lower than the Xeon tests. This emphasizes that single-thread performance is still important. The tester noted that *Office* applications were particularly sluggish. Interestingly, the results for performing *Video Authoring* or *Image Authoring* on the Atom are the same as on the Xeon; these applications are able to successfully leverage all the contexts available.

The *Web Browsing* tests are again interesting. The idle time is less than one quarter of the execution time on the Atom whereas on the Xeon it was more than one half. This implies web browsing is more CPU limited than commonly perceived, as the network link used was low latency and high bandwidth. This is especially apparent the for *Tabs* and *Sequential* tests where the user is going to many content and feature rich sites. The idle time for these tests was close to zero, but the TLP only approached 2. This also indicates the software is the main cause of low TLP.

The Atom results show that low single-thread performance can have a small impact on the TLP observed. The Xeon did hide some TLP as it completed tasks very quickly compared to the Atom. But overall, this effect was small. The main observation was that the software is the main limiting factor, even on a "small" chip-multiprocessor with 2 cores and 4 hardware thread contexts.

7. DISCUSSION

Most modern designs have adopted multi-cores in an attempt to further increase performance. However, there has been surprisingly little increase in actual concurrency for desktop/laptop applications since the original study by Flautner et al. ten years ago. This is true in spite of the fact that programmers create a large number of threads in their programs. It appears that these threads exist primarily to structure code to be comprehensible and that desktop/laptop applications are mainly single threaded in behavior. This lack of parallelism in desktop applications such as games and web browsing may be inherent, but if it is not, then programmers must find significantly more parallelism to take advantage of future many-core chip multiprocessors. If the past is a predictor of the future, this seems unlikely.

In the scientific and server application domains, leveraging multi-processing is well understood and is backed by a large body of literature. As a product of this research and development, current architectures are well suited for these two areas. Multi-core SMP systems on a chip work very well for servers, and current GPUs work well for scientific applications that need abundant floating point performance. Unfortunately, as shown by our results, applications from the desktop/laptop space fit very poorly with these architectures because of their low TLP and GPU utilization. The only exception is applications like video transcoding which are very similar to scientific applications.

The apparent lack of progress in creating usable concurrency in the desktop/laptop application domain points to a lack of deeper understanding of the applications. To yield a more applicable design, architects should consider more relevant workloads, e.g. web browsing as benchmark choices. Future designs may require different characteristics from than those of server or scientific architectures to continue allowing increases in performance and energy efficiency. The tests with the Atom platform further indicate that software is the main factor in the lack of parallelism. The continued progression to larger chip-multiprocessors with less capable cores may be applicable for scientific computers and some servers, but seems less of a viable path to follow for desktop/laptop computers that value latency over throughput.

8. CONCLUSION

In the time since the original study, much has changed in the computing landscape. Architectures have become radically different and multi-processing is now the norm on the desktop from low power processors like the Intel Atom to the high performance Intel Xeon, offering up to hundreds of threads. On the other hand, as shown in the results, little has changed from the software perspective. In domain specific applications like video transcoding, many-core processors are being fully utilized, whether it be the general purpose cores with Handbrake, or the GPU with its hundreds of cores for Badaboom. However, in general purpose applications the average TLP 10 years later has shown only a modest improvement to ~2, and continuing to add cores to either the GPU or CPU may not be the answer for this application space. For the desktop/laptop environment multicore processor hardware is out-stripping software developers ability to keep up even for low performance systems like the Intel Atom. For 3D games, they seem to be able to use just over 2 processors. For web browsing, it can utilize multiple cores, though only up to about four as rendering a web page requires lots of threads to gather the content to render. In other areas like office productivity, multiple cores are hardly used as the level of parallelism has changed little in the last 10 years.

Our final conclusion is that software developers are still playing catch up, perhaps as a result of the relatively abrupt transition from high performance single-thread machines to chip multi-processors. In practice software developers use large numbers of threads in most applications in the desktop/laptop application space. However, they have not made appreciable steps in exploiting chip multi-processors, because the threads rarely run in parallel or the work distributed among threads is very unbalanced. This imbalance in work leads to Amdahl's effects resulting in the low TLP seen. Similar problems plague GPU vendors, because they are developing massive chip multi-processors with the majority of the silicon being left under-utilized. Developers have started to test the waters by writing multi-threaded applications that leverage both CPUs and GPUs, but have yet to take the plunge into the many-core chip multi-processing era. If many-core is to be the solution for future desktop/laptop applications, then programmers and algorithm designers must discover much greater levels of balanced parallelism. Our ten years perspective suggests this may be a significant challenge.

9. ACKNOWLEDGEMENTS

We would like to thank the anonymous reviewers for their suggestions and comments. This work was supported by ARM.

10. REFERENCES

[1] IEEE. Standard for Threads Interface to POSIX. P1003.1c, 1996.

[2] Intel Pentium Processor. http://datasheets.chipdb.org/Intel/x86/Pentium/24199710.PDF, 1997.

[3] AMD Athlon Processor Product Brief. http://www.amd.com/us-en/Processors/ProductInformation/0,,30_118_1260_759%5E1151,00.html, 1999.

[4] Intel Pentium III Processor. http://www.intel.com/design/intarch/pentiumiii/pentiumiii.htm, 1999.

[5] NVIDIA GeForce 256. http://www.nvidia.com/page/geforce256.html, 1999.

[6] Power4 system microarchitecture. http://www-03.ibm.com/systems/p/-hardware/whitepapers/power4.html, 2001.

[7] AMD Announces World's First 64-Bit, x86 Multi-Core Processors For Servers And Workstations At Second-Anniversary Celebration Of AMD Opteron Processor. *AMD News Room*, 2005.

[8] Intel Has Double Vision: First Multi-Core Silicon Production Begins. *Intel Press Room*, 2005.

[9] AMD "Close to Metal" Technology Unleashes the Power of Stream Computing . *AMD News Room*, 2006.

[10] DTrace User Guide. *Sun Microsystems Inc.*, 2006.

[11] NVIDIA Unveils CUDA - the GPU Computing Revolution Begins. *NVIDIA News Releases*, 2006.

[12] Intel Atom Processor. http://www.intel.com/products/processor/atom/specifications.htm, 2008.

[13] NVIDIA PerfKit. *Nvidia Developer Zone*, 2008.

[14] The Direct3D11 Compute Shader. Microsoft WINHEC Session GRA-T517, 2008.

[15] AMD Displays Llano Die: 4 x86 Cores, 480 Stream Processors. http://www.xbitlabs.com/news/cpu/display/20091111143547_AMD_Displays_Llano_Die_4_x86_Cores_480_Stream_Processors.html, 2009.

[16] Grand Central Dispatch:A better way to do multicore. Apple Inc. Technical Breif, 2009.

[17] Intel Previews Intel Xeon 'Nehalem-EX' Processor. *Intel Press Room*, 2009.

[18] International Technology Roadmap For Semiconductors - System Drivers. *Iternational Technology Roadmap for Semiconductors*, 2009.

[19] Leopard Reference Library. *Apple Inc. Developer Connection*, 2009.

[20] NVIDIA GeForce GT 120 (OEM Product). http://www.nvidia.com/object/product_geforce_gt_120_us.html, 2009.

[21] OMAP 4: Mobile applications platform. *Texas Instruments Product Bullentin*, 2009.

[22] OpenCL:Parallel Computing for Hetergeneous Devices. http://www.khronos.org/developers/library/overview/opencl_overview.pdf, 2009.

[23] AMD Sets the New Standard for Price, Performance, and Power for the Datacenter. *AMD Newsroom*, 2010.

[24] Intel Sandy Bridge. http://en.wikipedia.org/wiki/Intel_Sandy_Bridge_%28microarchitecture%29, 2010.

[25] Intel Spotlights New Extreme Edition Processor, Software Developer Resources at Game Conference. *Intel Press Room*, 2010.

[26] Interactive TLP Bench. http://itlpbench.eecs.umich.edu, 2010.

[27] The Snapdragon Platform. http://www.qctconnect.com/products/snapdragon.html, 2010.

[28] Ultra-Thin Notebooks: Powered by ultra-low-voltage Intel Core processors. http://www.intel.com/in/irdonline/ultra_low.htm, 2010.

[29] L. A. Barroso, K. Gharachorloo, R. McNamara, A. Nowatzyk, S. Qadeer, B. Sano, S. Smith, R. Stets, and B. Verghese. Piranha: a scalable architecture based on single-chip multiprocessing. In *ISCA '00: Proceedings of the 27th annual international symposium on Computer architecture*, pages 282–293, New York, NY, USA, 2000. ACM.

[30] A. Berillo. Multi-Core Processors in 3D Games. http://ixbtlabs.com/articles3/video/quadcore-p6.html, 2008.

[31] B. Chen, Y. Endo, K. Chan, D. M. A. Dias, A. Dias, M. Seltzer, and M. D. Smith. The measured performance of personal computer operating systems. *ACM Transactions on Computer Systems*, 14:3–40, 1995.

[32] Y. Endo, Z. Wang, J. B. Chen, and M. Seltzer. Using latency to evaluate interactive system performance. In *OSDI '96: Proceedings of the second USENIX symposium on Operating systems design and implementation*, pages 185–199, New York, NY, USA, 1996. ACM.

[33] K. Flautner, R. Uhlig, S. Reinhardt, and T. Mudge. Thread-level parallelism and interactive performance of desktop applications. *SIGARCH Comput. Archit. News*, 28(5):129–138, 2000.

[34] K. Flautner, R. Uhlig, S. Reinhardt, and T. Mudge. Thread-level parallelism of desktop applications. *Workshop on Multi-threaded Execution, Architecture and Compilation*, 2000.

[35] E. Frachtenberg. Process scheduling for the parallel desktop. In *ISPAN '05: Proceedings of the 8th International Symposium on Parallel Architectures,Algorithms and Networks*, pages 132–139, Washington, DC, USA, 2005. IEEE Computer Society.

[36] E. Frachtenberg and Y. Etsion. Hardware Parallelism: Are Operating Systems Ready? (Case Studies in Mis-Scheduling). *Workshop on the Interaction between Operating System and Computer Architecture*, 2006.

[37] N. Giacaman, O. Sinnen, N. Giacaman, and O. Sinnen. Inhibitors for desktop parallelisation, 2006.

[38] L. Hammond, B. A. Hubbert, M. Siu, M. K. Prabhu, M. Chen, and K. Olukotun. The stanford hydra cmp. *IEEE Micro*, 20(2):71–84, 2000.

[39] C. Hauser, C. Jacobi, M. Theimer, B. Welch, and M. Weiser. Using threads in interactive systems: a case study. *SIGOPS Oper. Syst. Rev.*, 27(5):94–105, 1993.

[40] L. D. Hung and S. Sakai. Dynamic estimation of task level parallelism with operating system support. In *ISPAN '05: Proceedings of the 8th International Symposium on Parallel Architectures,Algorithms and Networks*, pages 358–363, Washington, DC, USA, 2005. IEEE Computer Society.

[41] R. Isaacs, P. Barham, J. Bulpin, R. Mortier, and D. Narayanan. Request extraction in magpie: events, schemas and temporal joins. In *EW11: Proceedings of the 11th workshop on ACM SIGOPS European workshop*, page 17, New York, NY, USA, 2004. ACM.

[42] C. G. Jones, R. Liu, L. Meyerovich, K. Asanovic, and R. Bodik. Parallelizing the Web Browser. *First USENIX Workshop on Hot Topics in Parallelism*, 2009.

[43] D. C. Lee, P. J. Crowley, J.-L. Baer, T. E. Anderson, and B. N. Bershad. Execution characteristics of desktop applications on windows nt. *SIGARCH Comput. Archit. News*, 26(3):27–38, 1998.

[44] M. K. McKusick, K. Bostic, M. J. Karels, and J. S. Quarterman. *The design and implementation of the 4.4BSD operating system*. Addison Wesley Longman Publishing Co., Inc., Redwood City, CA, USA, 1996.

[45] T. D. Nguyen, R. Vaswani, and J. Zahorjan. Parallel application characterization for multiprocessor scheduling policy design. In *of Lectures Notes in Computer Science*, pages 105–118. Springer-Verlag, 1996.

[46] I. Park and R. Buch. Improve Debugging And Performance Tuning With ETW. *MSDN Magazine*, 2007.

[47] R. Rashid, R. Baron, R. Forin, D. Golub, and M. Jones. Mach: A system software kernel. In *In Proceedings of the 1989 IEEE International Conference, COMPCON*, pages 176–178. Press, 1989.

[48] M. Zhou and A. J. Smith. Analysis of personal computer workloads. In *MASCOTS '99: Proceedings of the 7th International Symposium on Modeling, Analysis and Simulation of Computer and Telecommunication Systems*, page 208, Washington, DC, USA, 1999. IEEE Computer Society.

Web Search Using Mobile Cores: Quantifying and Mitigating the Price of Efficiency

Vijay Janapa Reddi
Harvard University
vj@eecs.harvard.edu

Benjamin C. Lee
Stanford University
bcclee@stanford.edu

Trishul Chilimbi
Microsoft Research
trishulc@microsoft.com

Kushagra Vaid
Microsoft Corporation
kvaid@microsoft.com

ABSTRACT

The commoditization of hardware, data center economies of scale, and Internet-scale workload growth all demand greater power efficiency to sustain scalability. Traditional enterprise workloads, which are typically memory and I/O bound, have been well served by chip multiprocessors comprising of small, power-efficient cores. Recent advances in mobile computing have led to modern small cores capable of delivering even better power efficiency. While these cores can deliver performance-per-Watt efficiency for data center workloads, small cores impact application quality-of-service robustness, and flexibility, as these workloads increasingly invoke computationally intensive kernels. These challenges constitute the price of efficiency. We quantify efficiency for an industry-strength online web search engine in production at both the microarchitecture- and system-level, evaluating search on server and mobile-class architectures using Xeon and Atom processors.

Categories and Subject Descriptors

C.0 [**Computer Systems Organization**]: General—*System architectures*; C.4 [**Computer Systems Organization**]: Performance of Systems—*Design studies, Reliability, availability, and serviceability*

General Terms

Measurement, Experimentation, Performance

1. INTRODUCTION

Internet services are experiencing a paradigm shift in which computation and data migrates from clients to a cloud of distributed resources located in data centers. The commoditization of hardware, data center economies of scale, and Internet-scale workload growth all demand greater power efficiency to sustain scalability. Advances in chip multiprocessors comprised of small cores provide opportunities for power efficiency. Piranha and Niagara propose integrating simple cores to lower design effort and improve throughput, respectively [1, 7, 9]. These smaller cores deliver throughput with better power efficiency when compared to their low-latency, high-performance counterparts. Recent advances in mobile computing provide small cores with even greater power efficiency. Traditional enterprise and online transaction processing (OLTP) applications are amenable to execution on small cores because they are typically memory or I/O bound. Consequently, platform and overall system design, rather than microarchitectural design, determine whether the application's service requirements are met.

Emerging data center workloads increasingly invoke computationally intensive and performance-critical kernels, for which small cores may weaken service requirements and guarantees. Relative to the traditional sort, these workloads are comprised of computationally intensive and performance-critical kernels that have latency requirements as part of their service level agreement (SLA). Microarchitecture design for small cores will increasingly determine whether service requirements are satisfied for these emerging and more compute-prone workloads. Although small cores are advantageous for power efficiency and throughput computing, they are less capable of handling increases in computational intensity and might jeopardize application quality-of-service and latency constraints. These challenges constitute the price of efficiency from small cores.

We quantify the price of small-core power efficiency for industry-strength web search, Microsoft Bing. Unlike traditional enterprise workloads, our version of web search relies on machine learning kernels at its core, which significantly increases computation at index serving nodes in a way that contravenes conventional wisdom regarding small cores for enterprise workloads. We demonstrate the computational intensity of our search engine with respect to other workloads in Figure 1.[1] Our search engine experiences significantly more instruction level parallelism (ILP) and is the only workload in Figure 1 exhibiting an un-normalized IPC greater than one, which surpasses prior search engines that experience an IPC similar to traditional enterprise workloads [2, 3]. This demand for ILP indicates a need for more performance than is typically provided by simple, in-order cores. Consequently, the strategy of small cores for greater power efficiency has deep implications for our Internet-scale workload. We explore these implications and make the following contributions:

ISCA'10, June 19–23, 2010, Saint-Malo, France.

[1] All workloads are configured as per industry-standard settings[23] and are operating under typical load conditions, running natively on a 4-way superscalar processor (Table 1).

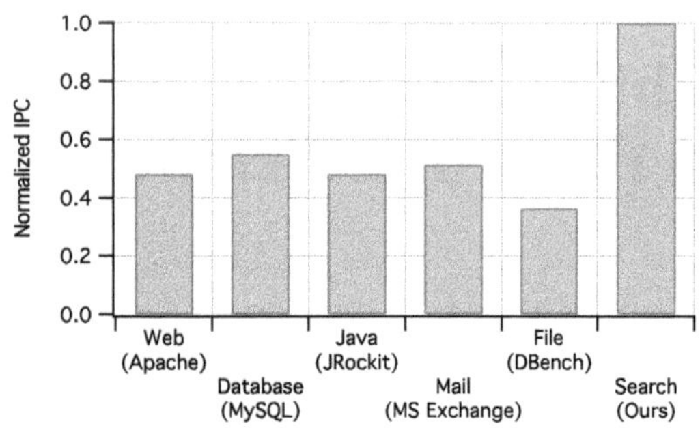

Figure 1: The computational needs of our search engine exceed that of traditional workloads with an un-normalized IPC noticeably greater than one.

- **Search:** We evaluate an online web search engine operating in an enterprise environment that uses machine learning kernels at the index serving nodes to service user queries. (Section 2)
- **Efficiency:** We compare the power efficiency of the server-class Xeon and mobile-class Atom microarchitectures for Search, relying on hardware counter data and multimeter power measurements. Search is 5× more efficient on Atom than on Xeon. (Section 3)
- **Price of Efficiency:** Search efficiency on Atom comes at the expense of robustness and flexibility. Quality-of-service guarantees become less robust as per query latency increases and becomes more variable. Computational intensity increases and microarchitectural bottlenecks impact search computation. (Section 4)
- **Mitigating the Price of Efficiency:** We address the price of efficiency through effective system design strategies, greater integration and enhanced microarchitectures. These strategies also address the total cost of ownership (TCO) at the data center level due to inefficiencies at the platform level, which translates to lower performance per dollar.

Collectively, the results in this paper contravene conventional wisdom with respect to small cores and data centers for online web search. The microprocessor industry offers a choice of two strategies to achieve the economies of scale necessary for this evolving workload: (1) start with big, high performance cores and improve efficiency or (2) start with small, low power cores and improve performance. We compare these two strategies and favor the latter for search.

2. SEARCH

Search is representative of a broad class of data center workloads that perform distributed and expensive computation. The workload requires thousands of processors to service queries under strict performance, flexibility and reliability guarantees. A single query might require tens of billions of processor cycles and access hundreds of megabytes of data [3]. Traditionally, parallel indexing affords substantial improvement in performance. However, as search engines continue to evolve and machine learning techniques become integral, per core performance is becoming more important again.

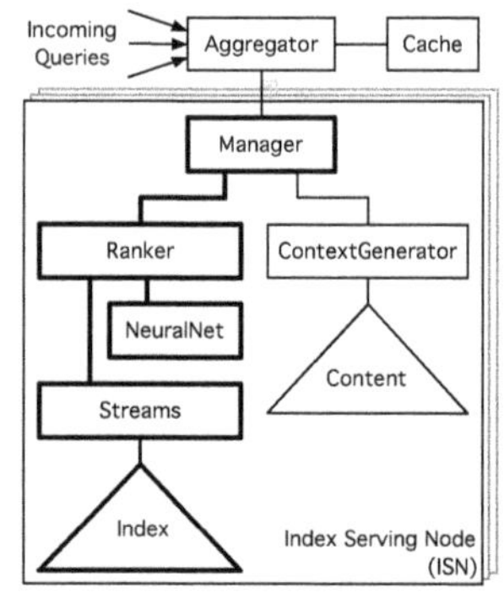

Figure 2: Overview of our specific Search instantiation. In this paper, we target the darkened subset within each index serving node (ISN).

2.1 Structure

Figure 2 outlines the structure of the search engine. Search queries enter the system through a top-level Aggregator. If the aggregator cannot satisfy a query from its set of frequently asked queries (i.e., Cache), it distributes the query to the Index Serving Nodes (ISNs). The ISNs operate in a distributed manner. Examining its subset of the document index, each node uses neural networks to identify and to return the top N most relevant pages and their dynamic ranks. Each ISN is responsible for ranking pages, as well as generating descriptions of relevant pages for the user [5].

Upon receiving a query, an ISN's Manager invokes the Ranker on the ISN's local subset of the index. The ranker parses the query and invokes Streams that use query features to identify a matching list of pages from query features. The ranker then uses statistical inference engines to compute a relevance score for each page in the matching list. Using these scores, the ranker identifies the top N results and passes these results to the aggregation layer, which in turn decides upon the set of results to return. After aggregating and sorting relevance scores, the aggregator requests captions from the ISNs. Each caption is comprised of a title, URL, and context snippets. Captions are generated by the ContextGenerator based on the content distributed to each particular ISN. Captions for the top N results across the ISNs are returned to the user in response to the query.

2.2 Requirements

Robustness. Search performance is quantified by a combination of Quality-of-Service (QoS), throughput, and latency. The application defines a QoS metric by the minimum percentage of queries handled successfully. For example, a QoS metric of θ percent requires a minimum of θ successful queries for every 100. The other 100-θ queries might time-out due to long latencies for expensive query features or might be dropped due to fully occupied queues. Given a QoS target constraint, we might consider a platform's sustainable throughput, which quantifies the maximum number of queries per second (QPS) that can arrive at a node without causing the node to violate the QoS constraint. If QPS exceeds the sustainable throughput, QoS degrades.

Query processing must also observe latency constraints. The average response time of queries must fall within a certain number of milliseconds, with additional constraints for the 90-th percentile of queries. Latency directly impacts relevance (i.e., documents corresponding to a specific query) by affecting the number of iterative refinements made to a search result. Given a latency constraint, the ranker checks for remaining time before, for example, checking the next tier in a tiered index. Lower query processing latencies allow for additional refinements to improve relevance.

Flexibility and Absolute Load. The search engine operates in a highly distributed system under a variety of loads and activity patterns. Not only must such a system be scalable, it must also be flexible to changes in activity. For example, activity patterns are often periodic and correlated with time of day. Moreover, even a modest spike in complex queries may generate sudden activity spikes measured in absolute terms, as complex queries cannot be broken down into simpler queries for redistribution across multiple nodes. Every ISN must handle its own incoming complex query load. Therefore, the underlying architecture must be robust enough to tolerate these *absolute* spikes and, ideally, would exhibit gradual rather than sharp QoS degradations as load increases. Architectures that exhibit gradual rather than sharp QoS degradations as load increases in absolute terms would provide greater flexibility with less disruption.

Reliability and Relative Load. Hardware failures are to be expected within large-scale data centers. To ensure reliability and robustness in the presence of failures, ISNs must operate with spare capacity to bear additional load when a fraction of index serving nodes fail, since work is then dynamically re-balanced across the remaining nodes. Each node experiences a fractional increase of a failed node's sustainable throughput, an activity spike measured in *relative* terms. Architectures that exhibit gradual and minimal QoS degradations as load increases in relative terms would provide greater reliability with less disruption.

3. EFFICIENCY

Search exercises the datapath as it uses inference engines (e.g., Neural Nets) to service queries. Therefore, the workload is traditionally run using high-end server processors. But in this section, we seek to understand the trade-offs between using high-end processors and small-core designs. After explaining our experimental infrastructure, we compare search running on Xeon versus Atom, quantifying the microarchitectural, power and cost efficiency across both designs in terms of delivered search application performance.

3.1 Experimental Setup and Methodology

Microarchitectural Extrema. Considering the spectrum of commodity x86 microprocessors, we observe high-performance, server-class microprocessors at one end and low-power, mobile-class processors at the other end. Table 1 summarizes the microarchitectures we consider.

The Xeon is representative of modern, high-performance microarchitectures. We consider the Harpertown, a dual-die, quad-core processor comprised of Penryn cores [8, 14]. This processor implements several power optimizations. Implemented at 45nm using high-K dielectric and metal gate transistors, the process technology reduces leakage power by 5-10× and switching power by 30 percent. Moreover, the L2 cache is organized into 1MB slices, allowing cache resizing in 1MB increments for power reduction. Dynamic voltage and frequency scaling supports system-driven power mitigation. Finally, we consider a particularly low-power Harpertown part, the L5420, which operates at 2.5 GHz. The choice of a power-optimized Harpertown provides an optimistic baseline, which favors server-class architectures.

	Xeon	Atom
	Harpertown	Diamondville
Processors	1	1
Cores	4	2
Process	45nm	45nm
Frequency	2.5GHz	1.6 GHz
Pipeline Depth	14 stages	16 stages
Superscalar Width	4 inst issue	2 inst issue
Execution	out-of-order	in-order
Reorder Buffer	96 entries	n/a
Load/Store Buffer	32/20 entries	n/a
Inst TLB	128-entry, 4-way	Unavailable
Data TLB	256-entry, 4-way	Unavailable
L1 Inst/Data Cache	32/32KB	32/24KB
L2 Cache (per die)	12MB, 24-way	1MB, 8-way
FSB	1066MHz	533 MHz

Table 1: Microarchitectural extrema. We evaluate search on Xeon-Harpertown [8, 14, 21] and Atom-Diamondville [10, 14] processors that represent endpoints in the spectrum of x86 commodity processors.

The Atom is representative of modern, low-power microarchitectures. We consider a dual-core Diamondville [10, 14]. Each core is designed to operate in the sub-1W to 2W range. Diamondville cores implement an in-order pipeline with power efficient instruction decode and scheduling algorithms. The Diamondville datapath is also narrower than that of a Harpertown, issuing only two instructions per cycle. Furthermore, the Atom design avoids specialized execution units and favors general-purpose logic that can provide multiple functionality. For example, the SIMD integer multiplier and floating point divider are used to execute instructions that would normally execute on separate, dedicated scalar equivalents [10]. Such strategies are intended to reduce power, but also may have implications for performance as will be described in Section 4.

Workload Setup. While search is a distributed activity across several nodes, in this paper we specifically target its activity within an ISN. We use the application currently in production and drive it with real queries from user activity. Of the search components illustrated in Figure 2, we specifically examine the darkened subset that ranks pages online and returns the sorted results to the aggregator.

The quality of search or the relevance of pages depends upon ISN performance. CPU activity at an ISN ranges between 60 to 70 percent, indicating ISNs are usually under heavy load. Consequently, an ISN's performance depends on the capabilities of the underlying microarchitecture, which motivates our evaluation of the leaf-nodes within search. We neglect the aggregator, as well as the caption generators. From hereon, we loosely refer to the term "search engine" as the parts we are investigating.

The ISN computes page ranks for forty thousand queries after warmup. Input queries are obtained from production runs. The query arrival rate is a parameter within our experiments. We sweep this rate to identify the maximum QPS an architecture can sustain without violating the QoS target. For each query, the ISN computes overall ranks for pages that match the query for a 1 GB production index, a subset of the global index distributed across several nodes.

The index fits in memory to eliminate page faults and minimize disk activity. In effect, we consider the first tier of a tiered index, which resides in memory. Subsequent tiers require accessing disk, but the tiers are organized such

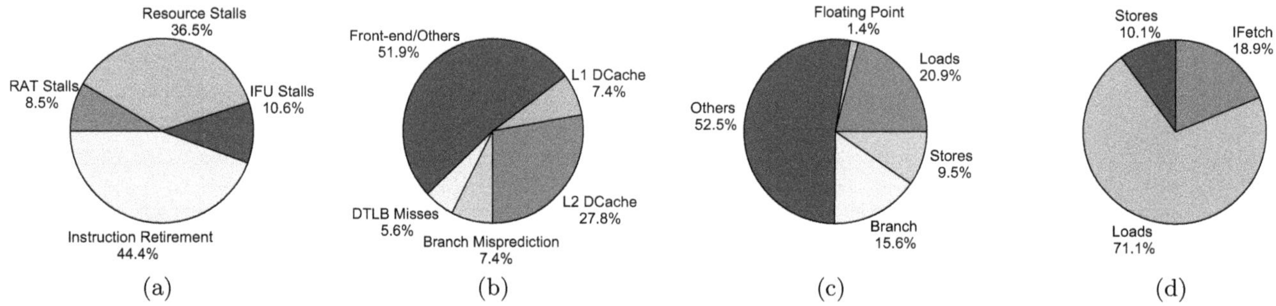

Figure 3: Microarchitectural synopsis of search on Xeon. (a) Execution versus stall time. (b) Breakdown of stall activity. (c) Instruction mix of search. (d) Sources of L2 cache accesses.

that this is extremely rare in practice. Therefore, it is the microarchitecture that determines application performance and not system-level configuration.

Additionally, to ensure fair comparison between Atom and Xeon, the total number of application threads servicing queries matches the number of hardware contexts available. More specifically, simultaneous multithreading (SMT) is enabled on Atom and results are normalized to a single Harpertown socket unless stated otherwise. System software (application and server OS) is also configured such that our setup is representative of a typical deployment strategy, allowing core-level comparison.

Microarchitectural and Power Measurements. We analyze the performance of the microarchitecture using details collected via VTune [13], a toolbox that provides us an interface to hardware counters on the Xeon and Atom. These counters provide detailed insight into microarchitectural activity as various parts of the search engine execute. To relate this microarchitectural activity to energy consumption, we quantify power dissipated by the processor at the voltage regulator module. We identify the 12V lines entering the regulator, apply a Hall-effect clamp ammeter (Agilent 34134A), and collect power measurements at 1KHz using a digital multimeter (Agilent 34411A).

3.2 Microarchitecture

Let X_θ be Xeon's sustainable throughput given the search application's quality of service target θ. Figure 3 illustrates microarchitectural events as search executes at X_θ queries per second on the Xeon. As shown in Figure 3(a), 55.6 percent of execution time is spent stalled for either the register alias table (RAT), the front end (IFU), or other resources (e.g., cache and memory). These stalls suggest the datapath is not fully utilized with only 44.4 percent of execution time spent retiring instructions due to structural conflicts in the front end (fetch or decode) or long latency memory instructions blocking instruction retirement. Figure 3(b) breaks down stall activity further.

Stalls during instruction fetch arise from branches and instruction cache effects. As illustrated in Figure 3(c), substantial branch activity of 15.6 branches per 100 instructions makes the branch predictor a bottleneck. Moreover, the datapath sees a seven cycle penalty when the number of in-flight speculative branches exceeds the capacity of the branch predictor (e.g., branch history table) [13]. Furthermore, the instruction fetch often stalls for L2 cache activity with 18.9 percent of L2 caches accesses attributed to instruction cache misses (Figure 3(d)).

Other resource stalls may be attributed to memory activity. According to Figure 3(c), a total of 30.4 percent of instructions either load or store data, which leads to pressure on the cache hierarchy. Consequently, Figure 3(d) shows that loads and stores account for 81.2 percent of all cache accesses. L2 cache activity often translates into memory requests with 67.0 percent of bus activity attributed to memory transactions (not shown). Application activity on Atom demonstrates similar behavior.

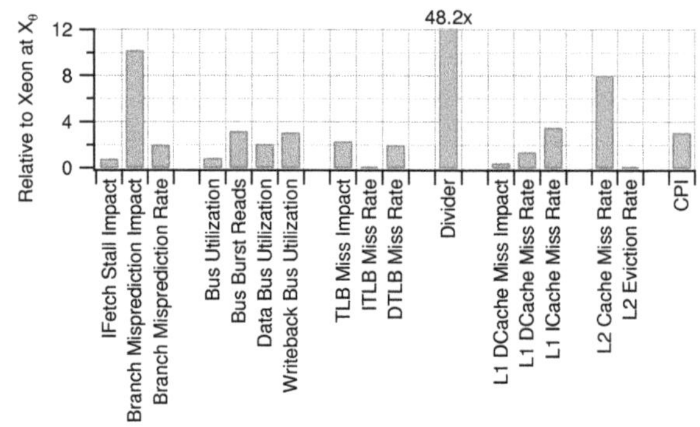

Figure 4: Atom with respect to Xeon.

Relative to Xeon, the Atom implements a simpler and deeper pipeline. As Figure 4 demonstrates, microarchitectural effects are aggravated in the low-power Atom. This data corresponds to Atom at A_θ, the Atom's sustainable throughput for quality-of-service target θ. The high frequency of branches and Atom's deeper pipeline depth leads to a 10× increase in performance penalties from mispredicted branches. Atom divide time is 48.2× greater than that of the Xeon. These performance effects may arise from the decision to favor generality over specialization for execution units. Specifically, "the use of specialized execution units is minimized. For example, the SIMD integer multiplier and Floating Point divider are used to execute instructions that would normally require a dedicated scalar integer multiplier and integer divider respectively." [10]

Moreover, on a per core basis, the Atom implements a much smaller cache hierarchy. According to Table 1, the Atom data and L2 caches are 25 and 66 percent smaller per core than their Xeon counterparts. This smaller cache hierarchy translates into 1.5× and 8.0× the number of data and L2 cache misses. Collectively, these microarchitectural effects lead to a 3× increase in cycles per instruction.

Table 2 compares throughput for search at its quality-of-service target θ. Let X_θ and A_θ be the sustainable throughput of the Xeon and Atom in queries per second (QPS). At the same θ, Xeon sustains 3.9× the throughput sustained by an Atom ($X_\theta = 3.9 \times A_\theta$). On a per core basis, each of

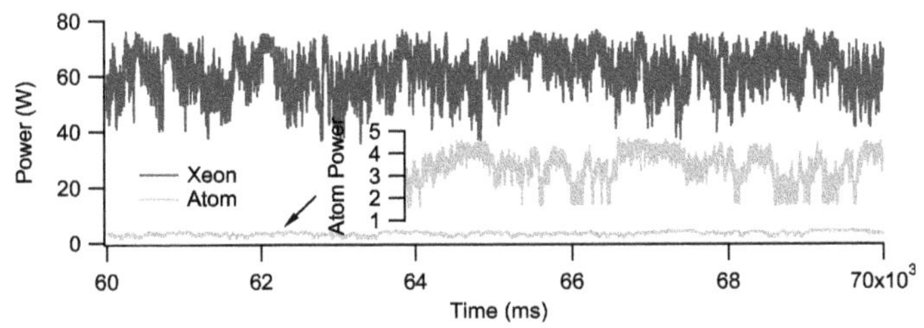

Figure 5: Xeon consumes ~62.5W, where as the low-power Atom consumes ~3.2W on average.

the four Xeon cores sustain 2.0× the throughput sustained by each of the two Atom cores. Sustainable throughput differs from absolute CPI because some processing is wasted on failed queries (time-outs), therefore system-level throughput gains can be less than microarchitectural gains.

3.3 Power

Figure 5 illustrates the power time series for both Xeon and Atom as search is running. The Xeon operates with an idle power component of 38.5W. The substantial idle power dissipated is particularly problematic given that the processor is stalled for 56.6 percent of its cycles. The Xeon exhibits a dynamic power range of 38.5 to 75W with a 95 percent difference between the idle and peak power. In contrast, Atom has a low idle power component of 1.4W with a 168 percent difference between idle and peak power. The Atom gets a drastic power reduction of 9.8× relative to Xeon. Atom's low idle power and large dynamic range is particularly attractive in the pursuit of energy proportional computing [4].

3.4 Performance

On a per core basis, the Atom is 5× more efficient than the Xeon. We compute performance and power efficiency as sustainable QPS per watt. Table 2 compares the Xeon and Atom over a variety of metrics. The power differentials (19.5× per processor, 9.8× per core) dominate the performance differentials (3.9× per processor, 1.9× per core). The large power cost of the Xeon is not justified by relatively modest increases in sustainable throughput.

Although this paper focuses primarily on power efficiency, we also mention area and price efficiency for comparison. Area efficiency is comparable between the two architectures, indicating the Xeon area overheads from dynamic instruction scheduling and out-of-order execution produce a linear improvement in throughput for search. However, Xeon price efficiency is 0.45× Atom price efficiency. Xeon prices are 8.4× Atom prices, but each Xeon sustains only 3.8× the number of queries per second. Note we consider price seen by the data center, not cost seen by processor manufacturers; manufacturers may target higher profit margins on server-class processors. Moreover, this analysis considers only equipment prices, not total cost of ownership. Peripheral components (e.g., motherboard, network interface card) will also impact the analysis. Section 5 will further assess the sensitivity of these effects.

4. PRICE OF EFFICIENCY

To understand the role of mobile-class architectures in data centers as workloads continue to emerge and evolve, we must identify and understand the price of exploiting small core efficiency. For search, we find quality-of-service becomes less robust as small cores are less capable of absorbing even modest increases in query load. Greater variance in the per query latency distribution indicates more queries experience higher latencies, which limit the time available to perform additional computation and improve search result relevance and ranking. Both quality-of-service and latency effects depend, in part, on the shifts in computational intensity and resource bottlenecks when using small cores.

4.1 Robustness

Quality-of-Service(QoS). Given a quality of service target θ, Xeon and Atom sustain a throughput X_θ and A_θ, respectively. We consider QoS guarantees robust if target θ is met despite fluctuations or temporary increases in query load. Robust QoS guarantees are a critical application requirement for search and data center applications. Robustness also determines the extent to which any one node can be utilized. If index server nodes can absorb activity spikes with little QoS degradation, they can operate closer to peak sustainable throughput.

For a given increase in query load, Figure 6 indicates robustness trends. The horizontal axis quantifies QPS normalized to Xeon's sustainable throughput X_θ. The vertical axis quantifies QoS in terms of the percentage of successfully processed queries. Xeon processes the additional queries more robustly. Degradations in quality-of-service are modest and gradual. Atom is unable to absorb a large number of additional queries and quickly violates its QoS target.[2]

Latency. Increasing query load not only degrades the success rate in a quality-of-service metric, it also increases the latency at which that service is delivered. The search algorithm uses multiple strategies to refine search results if the query latency has not yet exceeded a cutoff latency L_C. Figure 7 illustrates latency trends with latencies normalized to the cutoff latency L_C. Using a logarithmic vertical axis, the figure indicates super-exponential increases in mean latency as query load increases on both Xeon and Atom. At their respective sustainable throughputs, Atom's latency is nearly 3× greater than that of the Xeon ($0.33L_C$ versus $0.12L_C$).

Relevance. QoS and latency shortcomings have a direct impact on search query relevance, which refers to a user's utility from a set of search results. Search algorithms often have multiple strategies for refining their results. However, load and cutoff latency L_C determine room for refinement. In a tiered index, pages indexed in the first tier are always ranked but indices in subsequent tiers may only be ranked if L_C has not been exceeded. In such scenarios, lower per query latencies allow for multiple iterative refinements of search results to improve page relevance. Moreover, lower latencies provide opportunities to search algorithm designers for exploring latency-relevance trade-offs.

Since the average latency on Atom at A_θ is higher than on the Xeon at X_θ (see Figure 7), search on the Atom is unable to refine pages in a manner equivalent to the Xeon. Figure 8 shows how page relevance on the Atom compares to the Xeon at X_θ as load increases. The vertical axis compares matching pages returned by search on Xeon and Atom, defining baseline relevance with Xeon search results. For example, 100 percent means 100 percent of Atom queries return search results that perfectly match those from Xeon

[2]We study Xeon and Atom beyond sustainable throughput to characterize robustness. We do not assume sustainable operation under such loads.

	Per Processor			Per Core		
	Xeon	Atom	$\Delta_{X/A}$	Xeon	Atom	$\Delta_{X/A}$
Performance (QPS)	$3.86A_\theta$	A_θ	3.86×	$0.96A_\theta$	$0.5A_\theta$	1.93×
Power (W)	62.50	3.2	19.53×	15.63	1.60	9.77×
Power Efficiency (QPS/W, $\times 10^{-2}$)	$6.17A_\theta$	$31.25A_\theta$	0.20×	$6.17A_\theta$	$31.25A_\theta$	0.20×
Area (T, $\times 10^6$)	820	94	8.72×	n/a	n/a	n/a
Area (mm^2)	214	50	4.28×	n/a	n/a	n/a
Area Efficiency (QPS/mm^2, $\times 10^{-2}$)	$1.80A_\theta$	$2.00A_\theta$	0.90×	n/a	n/a	n/a
Price ($)	380	45	8.44×	95	22.50	4.22×
Price Efficiency (QPS/$, $\times 10^{-2}$)	$1.02A_\theta$	$2.22A_\theta$	0.45×	$1.02A_\theta$	$2.22A_\theta$	0.45×

Table 2: Search on Xeon versus Atom. Performance is quantified by sustainable throughput, which is the maximum number of queries arriving per second (QPS) that can be serviced successfully at the target quality-of-service θ. QPS is reported relative to Atom performance A_θ. Average power is used to compute efficiency. Area is reported per processor. Price is reported per unit purchased in orders of one thousand units.

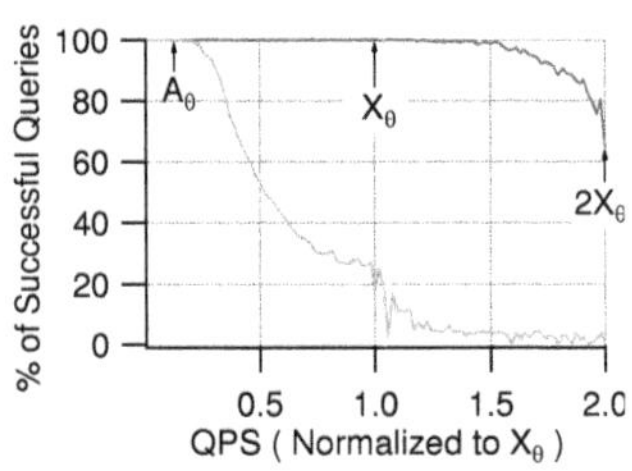

Figure 6: QoS on Xeon and Atom normalized to X_θ.

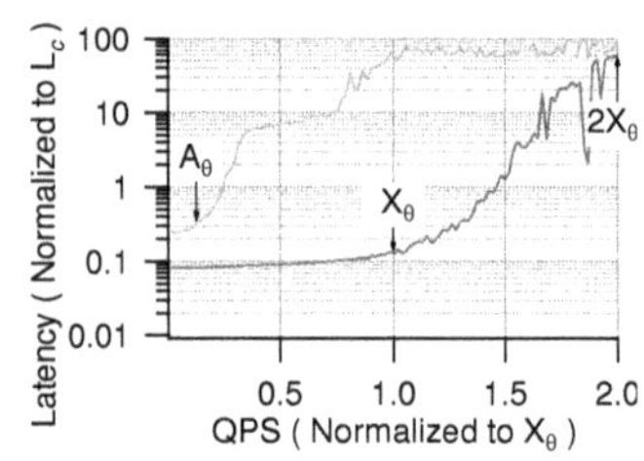

Figure 7: Latency on Xeon and Atom normalized to X_θ.

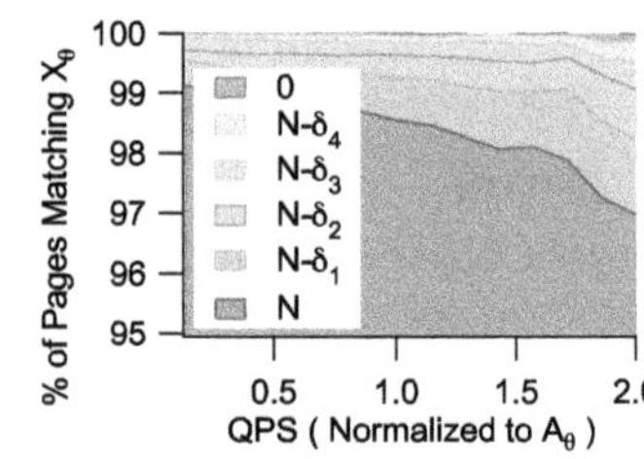

Figure 8: Bottlenecks on Atom limit the quality of page hits.

search. At 98 percent, the vertical axis indicates 2 percent of Atom queries produce different results relative to Xeon. A query's results match perfectly across architectures if the top N results match. The magnitude of the difference is quantified by $\delta_1 < \delta_2 < \delta_3 < \delta_4 < N$ where a reduced subset of $N - \delta_i$ of results match. In the worst case, none of the results match. This measure of relevance is highly conservative since it assumes Xeon defines the best relevance and any result mismatch degrades user perceived relevance. However, this metric facilitates the relevance analysis by quantifying search result differences.

Even considering the case when the load is at an absolute minimum on the Atom, approximately 1 percent of queries produce different results on Atom. Query latency on Atom at minimum load (e.g., 10 queries per second) is still higher than the latency on Xeon at X_θ (see Figure 7). Consequently, page refining algorithms have a third of the time to complete their work, leading to different search results from those on the Xeon. At A_θ about 1.5 percent of queries produce different results and the number of differing queries increases to 3 percent as load approaches $2A_\theta$.

4.2 Flexibility

A search engine frequently experiences user-generated activity spikes measured in absolute terms. Therefore, the underlying microarchitecture must be capable of adapting to rapid and significant shifts in search activity. This is especially the case in the presence of complex queries. Complex queries consist of multiple simpler queries that cannot be broken down and distributed across multiple nodes; each index serving node (ISN) must process the complex query. Even a modest spike in complex queries causes a significant absolute activity spike within an ISN. Therefore, nodes sensitive to activity spikes must be overprovisioned by operating below sustainable throughput to provide a safety margin. To understand this sensitivity, we evaluate how query latency

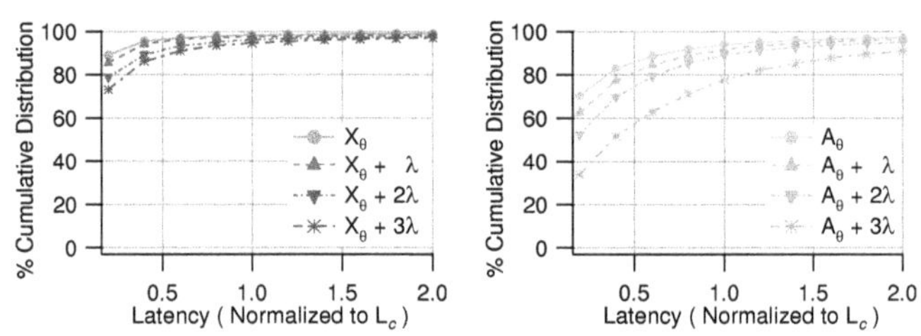

(a) Xeon (b) Atom

Figure 9: Query latency distribution. The experiment allows queries to exceed L_C and tracks the frequency in order to understand how the two processors handle sudden bursts in activity spikes.

distribution changes as load increases in the presence of different types of queries. We explain the behavior through microarchitectural effects.

Cutoff Latencies. Figure 9 illustrates the latency distribution with latencies normalized to the cutoff latency L_C. The experiment allows queries to exceed L_C and tracks the frequency to understand how the two processors handle sudden bursts in activity spikes. Processing queries at X_θ, 89.4 percent of queries are satisfied in less than $0.2L_C$, 98.2 percent of queries are satisfied before the cutoff latency L_C, and less than 1.0 percent of queries require more than $2L_C$. Moreover, on the Xeon, these trends are modestly sensitive to activity spikes, which we quantify using λ. For an increased load of $X_\theta + 3\lambda$, 82.7 and 96.4 percent of queries are still satisfied in less than $0.2L_C$ and L_C.

Atom per query latency exhibits much greater variation and sensitivity to activity spikes (Figure 9(b)). Processing queries at A_θ on the Atom, only 68.2 percent of queries are satisfied in less than $0.2L_C$. At 93.4 percent, the number of queries completing before L_C on the Atom is comparable to that on the Xeon. However, nearly 3.0 percent of queries

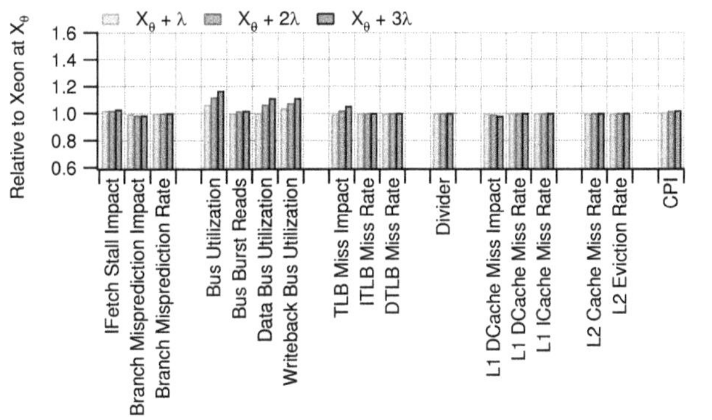

(a) Xeon

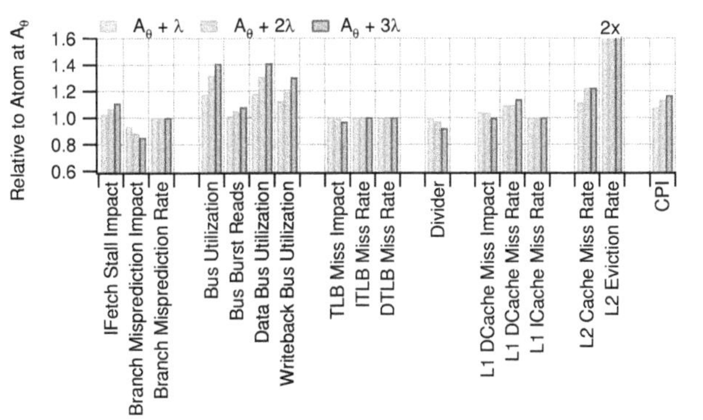

(b) Atom

Figure 10: Activity beyond sustainable query load.

require more than $2L_C$. Thus, compared to Xeon latency distributions, we observe a much larger spread in Atom's minimum and maximum per query latencies. Furthermore, Atom latency distributions are highly sensitive to activity spikes. For an increased load of $A_\theta + 3\lambda$, only 33.0 and 77.6 percent of queries are satisfied in less than $0.2L_c$ and L_C.

Figure 10 examines microarchitectural activity to provide deeper insight into the flexibility of the Xeon processor and the inflexibility of the Atom processor under load. Data is normalized with respect to activity on each processor at its sustainable throughput. Increases in query load minimally impacts the Xeon because next to added bus activity we see no other noticeable changes in Figure 10(a). However, query load increases of λ, 2λ and 3λ QPS beyond A_θ on the Atom degrades microarchitectural performance (CPI) by 7.5, 13.2, and 16.5 percent, respectively. These performance degradations arise primarily from increasing contention in the cache hierarchy. The small 1 MB, 8-way L2 cache becomes a constraint with L2 miss rate increasing by up to 22.2 percent and L2 eviction rate increasing by up to 100 percent. The increased eviction rate results in much higher bus utilization; writebacks increase linearly with the additional query load. As the memory subsystem becomes a bottleneck, the pipeline is more often stalled waiting for data. The divider utilization falls by 8 percent with an extra load of 3λ QPS.

Query Complexity. Atom processor's susceptibility to absolute load spikes is a function of query complexity. Query latency on the Atom takes a significant hit at throughput rates higher than A_θ because certain types of queries require more computation than others. Search criteria (e.g., language specification, conditional statements like ANDs, ORs etc.) determine query complexity, and how long it takes

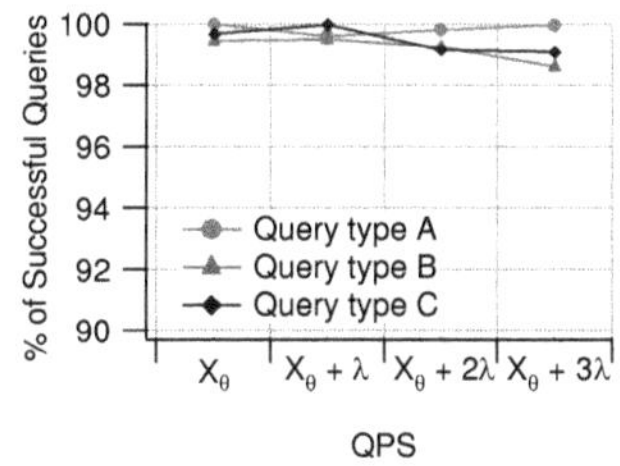

(a) Xeon

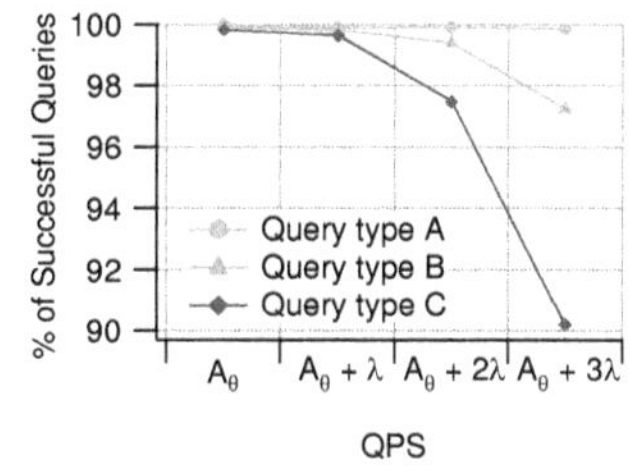

(b) Atom

Figure 11: QoS degradation by query complexity. Query type A has no search constraints. Query types B and C have increasing amounts of complexity, requiring more processing capability.

to process a query. Complex queries are broken down into simpler multiple individual queries within the ISN, so the "effective" query load is higher for complex queries.

To demonstrate how query complexity affects processor behavior and sustainable throughput, we isolate queries with different search criteria from the pool of mixed queries we use for all other evaluation and label them as query types A, B and C in Figure 11. Query type A has no complex search criteria, and is therefore fast to process. Query types B and C impose search criteria. Query type C contains many more constraints than type B, and thus requires even more processing.

Atom is able to sustain QoS equivalent to that of the Xeon for query type A even under high activity spikes (A_θ+3λ QPS) because of query simplicity. But the processor is unable to stay competitive for query types B and C as load increases beyond A_θ. At A_θ+3λ QPS the percentage of successful queries is only 90 percent when a stream of type C queries arrive back to back. These queries take longer to process, and consequently search queues begin to fill up and new incoming queries are dropped until search completes some pending queries or exceeds cutoff latencies . In contrast, Figure 11(a) shows Xeon does not suffer from this problem. Regardless of query complexity, Xeon is able to absorb activity spikes smoothly.

4.3 Reliability

Hardware or software-based failures are often threats in a data center. Therefore, we must understand how a homogeneous deployment of servers comprising of only Atom processors performs when load is re-balanced to accommodate failures. Load redistribution due to node failures leads to fractional or relative increases of sustainable throughput for a given processor. For instance, a processor will experience a relative load of 1.2θ when a hypothetical rack consisting of five systems experiences one system failure. Since the same absolute load is more evenly distributed across many more Atom ISNs, as compared to a data center full of Xeons, we find that on a per-node basis Atom achieves higher sustainable fail-over throughput compared to a Xeon.

Atom is more reliable for deploying search. To compare how QoS degrades due to fractional load increases across Atom and Xeon, we present the QoS data of each system normalized to its sustainable throughput in Figure 12. At loads slightly beyond sustainable throughput θ (1.0 QPS on the normalized axis), the Xeon latency trend line increases more sharply than that of the Atom. Atom QoS degrades to 95 percent at $2A_\theta$whereas Xeon QoS degrades to 64.5 per-

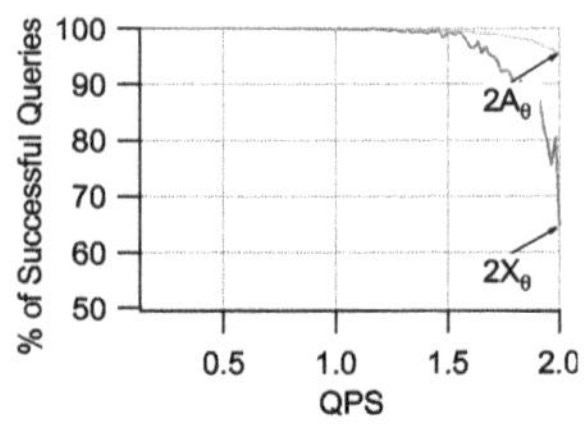

Figure 12: Comparing QoS normalized to each system's sustainable throughput.

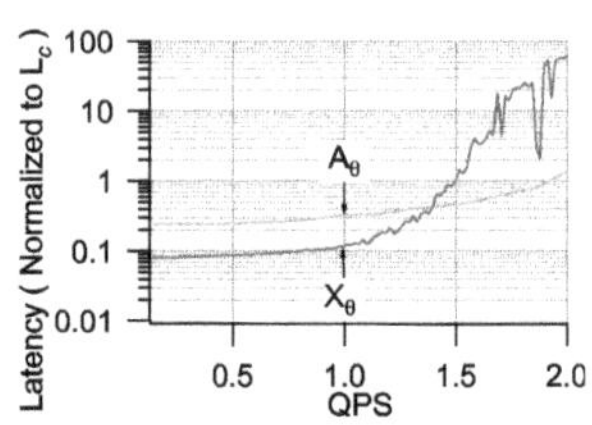

Figure 13: Comparing latency normalized to each system's sustainable throughput.

cent at $2X_\theta$. QoS degrades more gradually because the same fractional increase in load (e.g., 1.2×) on Atom corresponds to a smaller increase in the absolute number of queries on Xeon; $X_\theta$is larger than A_θ.

Xeon is unable to handle load increases robustly because of latency violations. Compare the latency on Xeon versus Atom with respect to each machine's sustainable throughput in Figure 13. Latency increases more gradually on the Atom than on the Xeon. Query latencies exceed L_C on the Xeon beyond $1.5X_\theta$. This means that even though the processor eventually locates pages corresponding to a query, the results are invalid because the aggregator terminates after L_C, assuming the ISN cannot produce the required pages. By comparison, latency on the Atom is still tolerable at $0.5L_C$ at A_θ, and thus its results are still valid.

Xeon is unable to scale to higher loads because the microarchitecture is saturated beyond $1.5X_\theta$. Figure 14 shows microarchitectural effects across the Xeon and Atom processors for relative load increases of 1.2×, 1.4×, 1.6×, 1.8×, and 2× beyond sustainable throughput. On Xeon, the processor's microarchitectural event activity plateaus from $1.6X_\theta$ onwards. Branch misprediction rates, bus utilization, TLB activity, cache activity all reach maximum levels. Therefore, the CPI increase is capped at ∼1.11x. While the Xeon system saturates at $1.6X_\theta$, Atom has more room for additional fail-over load, as indicated by increasing additional microarchitectural activity and CPI for the same relative loads.

Overall, these findings indicate that while Xeon is capable of sustaining higher throughput, it must run significantly under peak capacity to handle fail-overs, thus lowering throughput-per-watt further on top of already high power costs. As fail-over load per Atom server is smaller, and as its load is more distributed than in a data center comprising of fewer but higher capacity Xeons, Atom-based search is more reliable and energy-efficient. However, there are platform and system-level effects, in addition to flexibility sensitivity that impact any transition to Atoms.

5. MITIGATING THE PRICE OF EFFICIENCY

Strategies are necessary to mitigate the price of efficiency in using small cores for our web search. In this section, we propose holistic system-level strategies, as well as microarchitectural enhancements to individual cores to enhance robustness, flexibility and reliability guarantees.

5.1 Over-provisioning and Under-utilization

To improve QoS despite activity spikes, we might overprovision and underutilize Atom's. If we find an Atom node

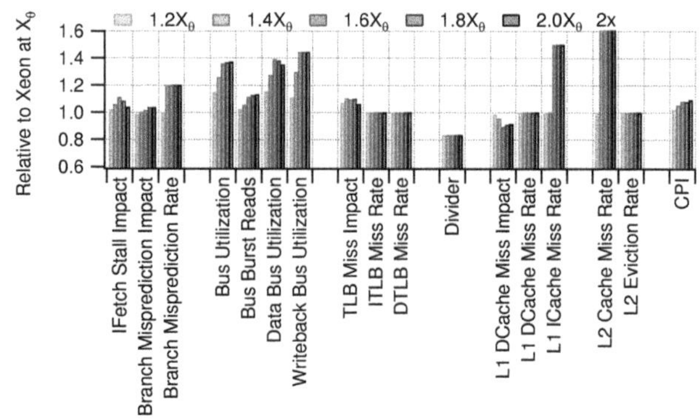

(a) Xeon

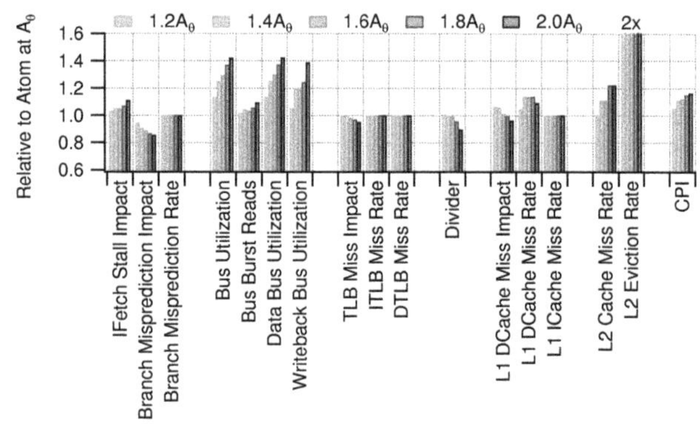

(b) Atom

Figure 14: Microarchitectural activity during load redistribution because of fail-overs.

cannot tolerate a λ increase in QPS in a robust manner, we simply utilize the node at $(1-\lambda/A_\theta)$ percent. While this reduces throughput, the power difference between Atom and Xeon processors still favors mobile processors. Overprovisioning, however, incurs significant power overheads and has implications for the total cost of ownership (TCO). We break down TCO into server costs, their average power consumption, and the associated infrastructure for cooling and power distribution to provide insight into the system-level costs of Xeons and Atoms. We also assess the sensitivity of Atom's efficiency advantages to system-level costs.

Platform Overheads. Although the Atom core itself typically dissipates anywhere between 1.5 to 4.5W when running search, peripheral components on the motherboard contribute another 20 to 30W to platform power. To be successful, multiprocessor integration is necessary to help reduce these overheads. Through system engineering, Atom processors can deliver better platform-level performance-per-watt, since multiprocessor integration will amortize peripheral penalties over a larger number of processors. Based on our peripheral component analysis in Table 3, Atom-Diamondvilles exhibit only 0.4× the platform-level cost and power efficiency of the Xeon. Although the Atom processor is itself much more power-efficient, system engineering and optimization is required to reduce the overheads of peripheral components, such as the motherboard, network interface card, memory, and storage.

To reduce platform overheads, an amortization strategy is needed to integrate more Atom cores into a single processor

	Xeon		Atom			
	Harpertown 4-core, 2-socket		Diamondville 2-core, 1-socket		Hypothetical 8-core, 2-socket	
	Cost ($)	Power (W)	Cost ($)	Power (W)	Cost ($)	Power (W)
Processor	760	125	45	3.2	760	25.6
Motherboard	200	30	80	30	200	30
Network Interface	0	5	0	5	0	5
Memory (4GB)	150	8	150	8	150	8
Storage (HDD)	100	10	100	10	100	10
Total Server Cost	1210	178	375	56.2	1210	78.6
Normalized Efficiency	1.0 QPS/$	1.0 QPS/W	0.4 QPS/$	0.4 QPS/W	1.0 QPS/$	2.3 QPS/W

Table 3: Peripheral component costs. Xeon motherboard cost and power is quoted for the Intel S5000PAL [12] and Atom is quoted for the Intel D945GCLF2 [6]. Memory data is reported from Micron power specifications [16]. Storage data is reported from Seagate data sheets [19]. Processor and motherboard cost of the hypothetical Atom is based on the Xeon-Harpertown. Its power corresponds to the Atom-Diamondville.

die. We compute the cost of building a two socket system consisting of Atom-Diamondville processors by evaluating the number of Atom cores that fit in the area budget of a Xeon processor. Four dual-core Atom-Diamondville processors fit into the area of a single socket Xeon-Harpertown processor (50 sq-mm into 214 sq-mm). This hypothetical scenario is based on industry trends towards multiple in-order x86 CPU cores [20]. We assume processor and motherboard costs for the multiprocessor-based Atom are equivalent to the Xeon-Harpertown platform. As manufacturing costs are driven by die area and not by the number of cores for a given die size, we assume the same processor cost. Similarly, because of socket compatibility, we assume motherboard cost is the same. System memory and storage costs are independent of processor specifics, and therefore equivalent across all three platforms.

To test the benefits of multiprocessor integration, we compare the costs of a two-socket Xeon-Harpertown platform, a single-socket Atom-Diamondville platform (representative of current experimental systems), and a dual-socket Atom-Hypothetical platform (representative of projected integration). By integrating up to eight Diamondville cores into a single chip and building a system with two sockets, amortization once again highlights Atom efficiency. As per our computed cost in Table 3, an integrated low-power multiprocessors would be competitive with a cost and power efficiency advantage of 1.03× and 2.3× over the Xeon. In summary, our analysis prompts us towards better system integration to enable successful overprovisioning, while achieving much better performance-per-watt for approximately the same performance-per-dollar.

Efficiency Sensitivity. Depending upon application robustness, flexibility and reliability characteristics on a platform, a certain degree of overprovisioning is necessary. However, overprovisioning degrades efficiency by reducing the operational load on the processor. Therefore, while Table 3 reports efficiency differences at maximum sustainable load on Xeon and Atoms, there are cost and power efficiency trade-offs that require careful consideration while underutilizing and overprovisioning processors.

We present overprovisioning analysis of search in Figure 15. At peak throughput utilization, or 0 percent overprovisioning, the integrated Atom-Hypothetical is 1.0× as cost efficient and 2.3× as power efficient as the Xeon-Harpertown (see Figure 15(a) and Figure 15(b), respectively). However, when considering flexibility requirements, Harpertown efficiency improves. For example, if search requires a tolerance

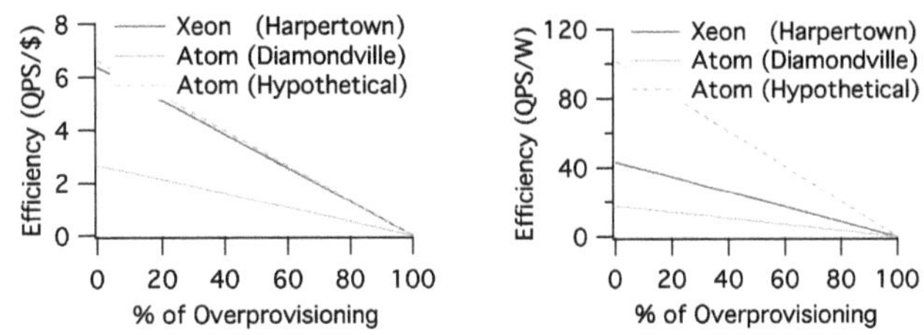

(a) QPS-per-Dollar (b) QPS-per-Watt

Figure 15: Efficiency sensitivity to overprovisioning when processors are underutilized for robustness, flexibility and reliability service requirements.

of λ QPS against activity spikes, the Harpertown requires only 7.4 percent overprovisioning, whereas every core within the hypothetical Atom requires a 28.6 percent margin. Consequently, cost and power efficiency of Harpertown with respect to the hypothetical Atom improves by 25 percent and 12 percent to 1.25× and 0.55×, respectively. Based on the sensitivity analysis in Figure 15, we invite readers to identify target utilization levels that best fit production-level robustness, flexibility and reliability requirements.

Capital and Operational Costs. To study the costs of managing Xeons versus Atoms at the scale of an entire data center, we quantify TCO in terms of aggregate sustainable throughput-per-TCO dollar. We assume search is running on either the Xeon or Atom processors. We evaluate the Atom-Diamondville and Atom-Hypothetical.

We use a publicly available cost model to estimate data center capital and operational costs [11]. The model assumes $200M facility costs based on 15MW of critical power with a data center power usage efficiency (PUE) of 1.7. The model amortizes power distribution and cooling infrastructure costs over fifteen years and the purchase cost of servers over three years. The total cost of operating and managing the data center is presented on a monthly basis. The model categorizes the TCO into the following: power (electricity bill for running all servers), servers (purchase cost), cooling and power distribution (data center infrastructure power cost) and others (miscellaneous costs). To maintain our focus on platform overheads and power efficiency only, we constrain our TCO analysis by omitting discussion about network, software licensing, and personnel costs, assuming they are uniform across all deployments.

Figure 16 proportionally illustrates TCO costs associated with using Atom processors instead of Xeon-Harpertowns.

In going from the Xeon-Harpertowns (Figure 16(a)) to the Atom-Diamondvilles (Figure 16(b)), we suffer a 56 percent loss in performance-per-dollar spent managing the data center. Despite spending the same amount of money purchasing servers (51.4 percent on the Xeons versus 51.1 percent on the Atom-Diamondvilles), we get lower aggregate throughput from the Atom-Diamondvilles.

The loss in efficiency is mainly because of power inefficiencies at the system-level, which limit the number of Atom systems per data center. For a fixed critical power budget of 15MW, the data center houses 84,269 Xeons, which is far fewer than the 267,857 Atom-Diamondvilles possible within that same power envelope. But the Xeons generate 59 percent more throughput than the Atom-Diamondvilles. To match that throughput, the data center requires 650,000 Atom-Diamondvilles, far exceeding the data center's critical power budget by a factor of 3×.

With better system integration, however, an Atom-based data center can achieve approximately 1.5× the throughput-per-TCO dollar of Xeons. Figure 16(c) illustrates better throughput-per-dollar improvement through sheer increase in pie size with respect to the Xeons. Notice that this is a significant improvement at the data center-level in contrast to the system-level where the difference between Xeon-Harpertown and Atom-Hypothetical is negligible (see Table 3). The larger advantage at the data center-level arises from issues like power and cooling distribution. For instance, a multiprocessor-based Atom consumes approximately 3× less power than Xeons, and therefore its cooling requirements are lower, which benefits data center density.

System integration achieves better value per dollar spent managing the data center. Consider the distribution changes between the slices corresponding to Figure 16(a) and Figure 16(c). In the hypothetical Atom, server purchase cost is a significant portion of the monthly TCO, increasing from 51.4 percent for Xeons to 70.5 percent for Atoms. Despite this increase, using Atoms is opportune for two reasons. First, aggregate throughput using multiprocessor-based Atoms increases by over 2.3×. Second, considering the same critical power envelope of the data center, we are able to accommodate many more servers that are delivering higher aggregate throughput. By better integration, we void the need to expand or build newer data centers with higher power budgets, since we are capable of exploiting existing infrastructure more effectively. Moreover, compared to the purchase cost of additional servers, the overall operational and management costs of Atoms increase by only 60 percent relative to the Xeons. These trends, combined with lower expenditures for power and cooling infrastructure, indicate investment value will improve by transitioning to small cores.

5.2 Microarchitectural Enhancements

While overprovisioning addresses robustness QoS concerns at the system level, achieving lower latency per query is still essential on the Atom, especially for flexibility requirements in the presence of complex query load. Otherwise, the quality of search results will deteriorate as explained in Figure 8. To effectively achieve lower latency, we require microarchitectural enhancements to the Atom core. In Section 3, we found the Atom experiences particular stress on the divider, branch predictor, and cache hierarchy. Enhancing the Atom core based on those findings implies designing small cores using unconventional strategies in which, for example, a light-

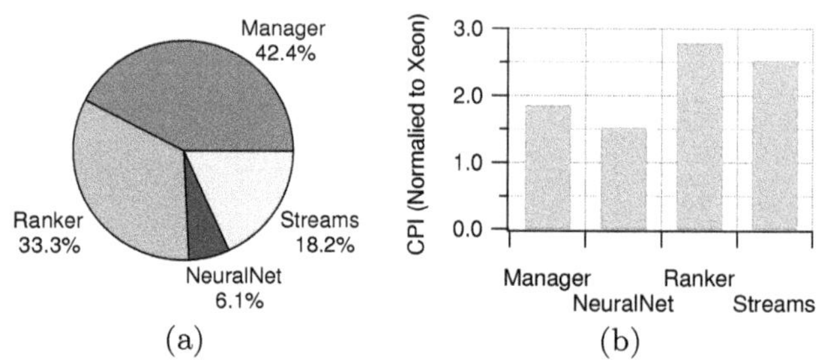

Figure 17: Search execution activity. (a) Execution time distribution across search phases. (b) Cycles-per-instruction (CPI) normalized to Xeon across the different phases of search computation on Atom.

weight datapath is paired with a disproportionately large cache hierarchy, at least for applications like search. These subtle modifications are likely to be more power efficient than transitioning to an out-of-order datapath.

To understand Atom bottlenecks and their root causes in the design, we must breakdown and analyze the different parts of search in isolation. Figure 17(a) illustrates that execution time is fairly distributed across all phases of search computation. This distribution gathered on a Xeon is identical to search on Atom. Additionally, Figure 17(b) suggests the most important functions exist throughout the phases of computation; all four major components of the search engine experience significant microarchitectural latency increases between 1.5× and 2.8× relative to Xeon performance. Atom performance degradation is broadly distributed and cannot be attributed to any one function or phase of computation.

Bottlenecks are limited to a few functions within each phase of search computation. We observe a significant overlap within the top 20 functions across both Xeon and Atom, indicating function importance depends more on the application and less on the architecture. Given the 20 most important functions and our knowledge of computation phases, we identify a representative function from each phase (Manager, NeuralNet, Ranker, and Streams). Figure 18 illustrates the microarchitectural events that affect the performance of those four representative functions. The events illustrate a broad range of performance limitations when adopting the small Atom cores. Just as no single function or single phase of computation accounts for Atom's performance limitations, no single microarchitectural event can be identified as the performance constraint.

Each function representing a different phase of search exercises different parts of the microarchitecture. Atom resources are constrained and particular stress is exerted on the divider, branch predictor, and cache hierarchy. The neural network stresses the divider and L2 cache. This function exhibits a 64× increase in division time, which seems to arise from a design decision regarding SIMD versus scalar dividers; scalar division is performed in a SIMD execution unit [10]. Atom's small 1MB, 8-way L2 cache leads to a 14× increase in L2 cache misses. The net effect is a 4.8× increase in CPI. In contrast, other parts of the ranker stress the branch predictor and L1 data cache. The performance impact of branch misprediction increases by 142× from a very low Xeon baseline. Such penalties may arise from the ranker's algorithmic components, which apply different strategies depending on the query and cutoff latencies. The

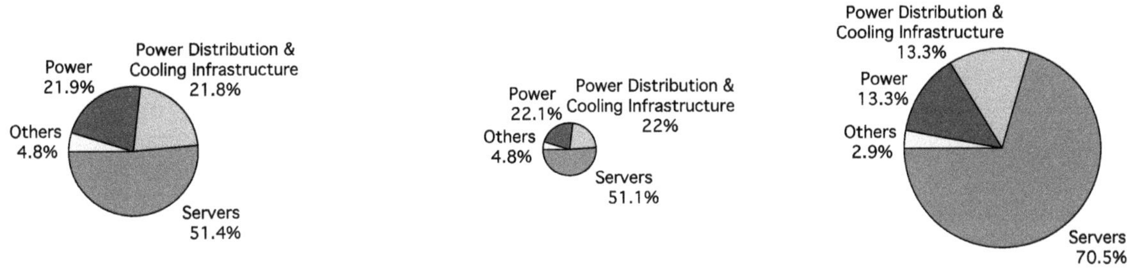

(a) Xeon (Harpertown) (b) Atom (Diamondville) (c) Atom (Hypothetical)

Figure 16: Total Cost of Operation (TCO) dollar. Each chart illustrates the breakdown of capital and operational expenses associated with sustainable throughput per monthly TCO dollar. With Xeon-based systems (a) as the baseline, pie charts (b) and (c) proportionally illustrate the return value per dollar spent managing the data center using either Atom-Diamondvilles, or our proposed integrated Atoms.

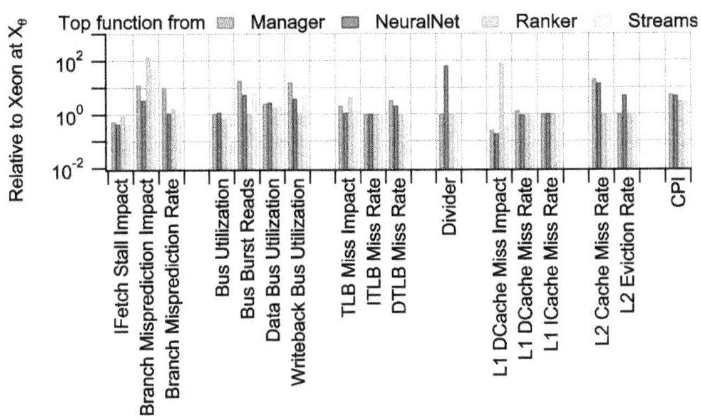

Figure 18: Identifying bottlenecks across phases of search using a representative functions.

impact of L1 data cache misses increases by 79× from a very low Xeon baseline. The net effect is a 2.9× increase in CPI.

Also stressing the branch predictor, streams manipulate an iterator data structure containing indices that match words within the query. Finding a particular element within the iterator requires non-trivial control flow, which exercises the branch predictor with a 49× penalty relative to Xeon. Therefore, CPI increases by 2.8×. Lastly, the manager coordinates the movement of index files to and from memory. The smaller L2 cache limits opportunities to exploit locality and produces a 14× increase in misses. The smaller cache also increases memory subsystem activity by 20 to 22×, thus causing a 4.6× increase in CPI. Overall, although we observe comparable performance degradations between 2.8× and 4.8× in representative functions across the four major phases of computation in search, the microarchitectural bottlenecks differ significantly.

Despite the near-term shortcomings, the ideal efficient microprocessor seems closer to the mobile-class end of the microarchitectural spectrum. For instance, reflecting back on the microarchitectural effects shown for activity spikes in Figure 10, we observe that the Xeon is significantly over-provisioned since activity spikes do not have any noticeable effect on the branch predictor, divider or the cache hierarchy. In migrating to simpler cores, some of that logic or area overhead can be redirected towards our proposal for (traditionally) disproportional structures like large caches and bus bandwidth for mobile cores to reduce latency.

5.3 Towards Heterogeneous Cores or Accelerated Multiprocessors

Looking further beyond microarchitectural enhancements, heterogeneous multiprocessors might provide accelerators to mitigate computational bottlenecks. Prior efforts have been made to combine large and small cores into a single chip multiprocessor (Section 6). However, when considering task-level division (Manager, NeuralNet, Ranker, Streams) across big and small cores, our analysis indicates that such a solution is inefficient for our version of web search.

Search has no single function or phase of computation that can be carved out to execute efficiently on a large core, such as the Xeon. Consider the four phases of computation (Manager, NeuralNet, Ranker, Streams) and their potential performance gains on Xeon (4.8×, 4.6×, 2.9×, 2.8×) from Figure 18. Furthermore, pessimistically assume the Atom operates at its measured peak (4.3W) and optimistically assume Xeon operates at its measured idle (38.5W). Thus, we derive the minimum power increase of 16.3× when performing computation on Xeon versus Atom; the power increase will always be larger in practice. Even in this optimistic scenario, the power differential of 16.3× dominates the performance differential of 2.8-4.8×.

Speeding up the Manager, NeuralNet, Ranker, and Streams with a Xeon core in an heterogeneous multiprocessor would lead to 0.29×, 0.17×, 0.18×, and 0.29× the Atom efficiency, indicating the difficulty of efficient acceleration with heterogeneous multiprocessors comprised of general-purpose architectures. While it may be possible to extract parallelism at a granularity finer than computational phases, doing so requires significant re-engineering of our production web search, which is a complicated and costly task. It might also be feasible to direct complex queries to Xeon instead of Atom, since Xeon can handle ISN-level internal absolute load spikes more gracefully than Atom (see Section 4.2). However, the cost to efficiency is high.

In the future, more efficient acceleration may arise from application-specific accelerators targeting computational kernels (e.g., neural network). Such accelerators may incur low power costs, while recovering performance lost by low-power, mobile-class architectures.

6. RELATED WORK

The landscape of data center workloads is changing. Ranganathan and Jouppi discuss the changing workload mix and usage patterns, motivating the need for integrated analysis of microarchitectural efficiency and application service-level agreements in their survey of enterprise information technology trends [17]. We complement their prior work by examining the role of power efficiency from small cores with in-depth microarchitectural analysis relating to application robustness, flexibility, and reliability constraints.

Power efficient data center design is an active area of research. Barroso et al. make the case for energy proportional computing in which data center components utilize energy proportional to the amount of computation [3]. Ranganathan et al. propose power management schemes across an ensemble of systems to mitigate costs associated with power and heat [18]. Efficient microarchitectures are integral components of such efforts and we further our understanding of microarchitectural effects in this work.

Piranha and Niagara make the case for small cores to improve design efficiency and throughput for memory and I/O bound workloads, such as transaction processing [1, 7, 9]. In contrast, we quantify limitations of small cores, specifically mobile processors, for more computationally intensive data center workloads, such as online web search. Lim et al. take a system view of warehouse-computing environments and propose unified systems, which transition from high-end server-class processors to mobile and embedded processors [15]. Similarly, Vasudevan et al., propose using fast arrays of wimpy nodes (FAWN) to achieve energy efficiencies in data intensive computing [22]. Both efforts emphasize low-power embedded processors for performance (queries per second) and power efficiency, using system power measured at the electrical socket. In contrast, we take a microarchitectural view of the differences between server- and mobile-class processors and measure, in addition to system power, core power by tracking current activity at the voltage regulator.

Making the case for chip multiprocessors, Barroso quantifies the economic price of high-performance, high-power platforms as compared to smaller cores [2]. While small cores reduce the economic price, they increase the application's perceived price of efficiency as we quantify in terms of quality-of-service robustness, flexibility, and reliability. As emerging data center workloads exercise the data path more extensively, the application perceived price of efficiency raises qualifications and caveats in the case for small cores in data centers. Once these limitations are understood, microprocessor and system architects can better navigate the inherent trade-offs between performance and power efficiency.

7. CONCLUSION

Emerging data center applications exercise the processor more significantly than traditional enterprise and online transaction processing (OLTP) applications. Thus, we deeply examine the role of small cores, specifically mobile processors, for an Internet-scale workload: web search. In particular, we study the challenges with respect to robustness flexibility and reliability of search. The price of efficiency has implications on system design, implementation and deployment strategies. For example, in the future, reducing platform power overheads associated with peripheral components is essential. In the longer term, microarchitectural enhancements, heterogeneous multiprocessors, or accelerators customized to mitigate bottlenecks may be instrumental in reducing the price of small core power efficiency.

8. ACKNOWLEDGMENTS

We are extremely grateful to several people for helping us with this research undertaking, including the reviewers. We would like to specifically thank Preet Bawa, William Casperson, Utkarsh Jain, Paul England, Mark Shaw, CJ Williams, Tanj Bennett, David Brooks, Qiang Wu, Dan Connors and Michael D. Smith. We are also grateful to the National Science Foundation under Grant #0937060 to the Computing Research Association for the CIFellows Project. Any opinions, findings, and conclusions or recommendations expressed in this material are those of the author(s) and do not necessarily reflect the view of the National Science Foundation or the Computing Research Association.

9. REFERENCES

[1] L. Barroso, K. Gharachorloo, R. McNamara, A. Nowatzyk, S. Qadeer, B. Sano, S. Smith, R. Stets, and B. Verghese. Piranha: A scalable architecture based on single-chip multiprocessing. In *ISCA'00*.

[2] L. A. Barroso. The price of performance: An economic case for chip multiprocessing. *Queue, ACM*, 2005.

[3] L. A. Barroso, J. Dean, and U. Holzle. Web search for a planet: The Google cluster architecture. *Micro, IEEE*, 2003.

[4] L. A. Barroso and U. Holzle. The case for energy-proportional computing. *Computer, IEEE*, 2007.

[5] S. Brin and L. Page. The anatomy of a large-scale hypertextual web search engine. In *WWW7*, 1998.

[6] I. Corporation. Technical product specification. *Intel Desktop Board D945GCLF2*, 2008.

[7] J. Davis, J. Laudon, and K. Olukotun. Maximizing CMP throughput with mediocre cores. In *PACT'05*.

[8] V. George, S. Jahagirdar, C. Tong, K. Smits, S. Damaraju, S. Siers, V. Naydenov, T. Khondker, S. Sarkar, and P. Singh. Penryn: 45-nm next generation intel core 2 processor. In *ASSCC'07*, 2007.

[9] L. Geppert. Sun's big splash: Niagara multiprocessor chip. *IEEE Spectrum'05*.

[10] G. Gerosa, S. Curtis, M. D'Addeo, B. Jiang, B. Kuttanna, F. Merchant, B. Patel, M. Taufique, and H. Samarchi. A sub-1W to 2W low-power IA processor for mobile internet devices and ultra-mobile pcs in 45nm hi-K metal gate CMOS. In *ISSCC'08*.

[11] J. Hamilton. Cost of power in large-scale data centers. In *http://perspectives.mvdirona.com*.

[12] Intel Corporation. Thermal/mechanical design guide. *Intel 5000 Series Chipset Memory Controller Hub (MCH)*, 2006.

[13] Intel Corporation. 45nm Intel Core 2 Duo Processor: BAClears. *Intel VTune Performance Analyzer 9.1 Help*, 2008.

[14] Intel Corporation. Volume 1 basic architecture. *Intel 64 and IA-32 Architectures: Software Developers Manual*, 2009.

[15] K. Lim, P. Ranganathan, J. Chang, C. Patel, T. Mudge, and S. Reinhardt. Understanding and designing new server architectures for emerging warehouse-computing environments. In *ISCA'08*.

[16] Micron. Technical note TN-47-04: Calculating memory system power for DDR2. In *www.micron.com*, 2006.

[17] P. Ranganathan and N. Jouppi. Enterprise IT trends and implications for architecture research. In *HPCA-11*, 2005.

[18] P. Ranganathan, P. Leech, D. Irwin, and J. Chase. Ensemble-level power management for dense blade servers. In *ISCA'06*.

[19] Seagate. Barracuda 7200.12 data sheet. In *www.seagate.com*, 2009.

[20] L. Seiler, D. Carmean, E. Sprangle, T. Forsyth, M. Abrash, P. Dubey, S. Junkins, A. Lake, J. Sugerman, R. Cavin, R. Espasa, E. Grochowski, T. Juan, and P. Hanrahan. Larrabee: a many-core x86 architecture for visual computing. *ACM Trans. Graph.*, 2008.

[21] R. Swinburne. Intel Core i7 - Nehalem architecture dive. In *www.bit-tech.net*, 2008.

[22] V. Vasudevan, J. Franklin, D. Anderson, A. Phanishayee, L. Tan, M. Kaminsky, and I. Morau. FAWNdamentally power-efficient clusters. In *HotOS-XII*, 2009.

[23] VMware. Vmmark benchmark. In *www.vmware.com/products/vmmark*, 2009.

The Impact of Management Operations on the Virtualized Datacenter

Vijayaraghavan Soundararajan and Jennifer M. Anderson
VMware, Inc.
3401 Hillview Ave.
Palo Alto, CA 94306
1 (650) 427-1706
{ravi,jennifer}@vmware.com

ABSTRACT

Virtualization has the potential to dramatically reduce the total cost of ownership of datacenters and increase the flexibility of deployments for general-purpose workloads. If present trends continue, the datacenter of the future will be largely virtualized. The base platform in such a datacenter will consist of physical hosts that run hypervisors, and workloads will run within virtual machines on these platforms. From a system management perspective, the virtualized environment enables a number of new workflows in the datacenter. These workflows involve operations on the physical hosts themselves, such as upgrading the hypervisor, as well as operations on the virtual machines, such as reconfiguration or reverting from snapshots. While traditional datacenter design has focused on the cost vs. capability tradeoffs for the end-user applications running in the datacenter, we argue that the *management workload* from these workflows must be factored into the design of the virtualized datacenter.

In this paper, we examine data from real-world virtualized deployments to characterize common management workflows and assess their impact on resource usage in the datacenter. We show that while many end-user applications are fairly light on I/O requirements, the management workload has considerable network and disk I/O requirements. We show that the management workload scales with the increasing compute power in the datacenter. Finally, we discuss the implications of this management workload for the datacenter.

Categories and Subject Descriptors

C.4 [*Computer Systems Organization*]: Performance of Systems

General Terms

Performance, Management, Measurement, Design.

Keywords

Virtual Machine management, cloud computing, datacenter management, management workload

ISCA'10 June 19–23, 2010, Saint-Malo, France.

1. INTRODUCTION

In a virtualized datacenter, applications are run in virtual machines (VMs) on top of physical hosts. Virtualization affords significant flexibility. As a result, many enterprises, hosting providers, and cloud vendors have shifted to a virtualization-based model for running applications and providing various services like email, web serving, and payroll [25]. This flexibility allows workflows that would be much more onerous in a physical environment. For example, one key feature of virtualization platforms is the ability to move a VM between physical hosts while the VM is running. When maintenance is required in a virtualized datacenter, one can simply migrate the VMs off the server to another with no application down-time. While this capability increases productivity and allows the operation to occur regularly with ease, it comes with a cost: this live migration exerts additional load on the datacenter's network infrastructure, potentially requiring higher-performance network components than would be required strictly by the needs of the applications running in the datacenter. Moreover, virtualization may change other decisions within the datacenter. For example to achieve the best performance for virtualized workloads, it is desirable to use the latest CPUs with hardware support for virtualization. Also, since hundreds of mission-critical VMs may be running per host, purchasing more reliable yet more expensive components may be most cost-effective overall. Each of these issues factors into the cost vs. capability tradeoffs inherent in datacenter design.

In this paper, we discuss various tradeoffs in the design of a datacenter for virtualized environments. We consider in particular an often-overlooked aspect of datacenter design: the management workload. The management workload stresses parts of the system that are historically under-utilized in typical datacenters, namely, the storage and network subsystems. The flexibility that virtualization brings to datacenter operations results in new types of management workflows and places new demands on datacenter designs. The load is fundamental to the workflows and is independent of the virtualization layer being used.

The contributions of this paper are as follows. First, we introduce data from real deployments and provide insight into various workflows in the virtual datacenter. Second, we present a sensitivity analysis of how requirements change as the datacenter scales. Finally, we discuss the impact of these operations on the design of a datacenter for virtualized environments.

The outline of the paper is as follows. In Section 2, we describe the virtualized datacenter in more detail. In Section 3, we characterize the management workload in the virtualized datacenters that we have profiled. In Section 4, we examine how the management workload scales with increased compute-power in the datacenter. In Section 5, we discuss the implications for datacenter design. In Section 6, we discuss related work. Finally, we summarize this work in Section 7.

2. THE VIRTUALIZED DATACENTER

A datacenter consists of physical hosts, storage and networking infrastructure, power/cooling hardware, and a management/monitoring framework for ongoing operation. The hosts are organized into racks. Power is routed to each rack, and each rack also includes some amount of storage and network hardware.

To allow multiple hosts to share data and to simplify backup, most datacenters utilize shared storage like Storage Area Networks (SANs) [11] or Network-attached storage (NAS). SANs export a block-device interface to each host, so that the device appears to be a local hard drive even if it resides in a different rack. Common SAN protocols include FibreChannel and iSCSI. FibreChannel SANs use special-purpose cabling and switches, whereas iSCSI [20] relies on standard IP networking infrastructure. A NAS exports file-level storage and also uses standard networking infrastructure. These devices are designed for high-bandwidth, low-latency shared access by large numbers of hosts.

In addition to shared storage, a significant component of a datacenter is the networking infrastructure. There are rack switches and core infrastructure switches that are used to allow connectivity in a datacenter. Often, a single networking infrastructure is used to multiplex both storage-based traffic (NAS and iSCSI traffic) as well as standard network traffic.

Datacenters also include a management framework in order to assess the health of the components of the datacenter. An administrator has tools to configure networking and storage, power-cycle hosts, or access the console of the hosts. Once machines have been provisioned and workloads have been set up in a production datacenter, a great deal of datacenter management consists of monitoring application service levels. Administrators must also monitor the hardware to check for failures and fix failures when they occur [9].

A virtualized datacenter consists of the same hardware components as a physical datacenter. However, in a virtualized datacenter, each host contains a hypervisor layer for running virtual machines on top of the physical hosts. In addition, the management framework is extended to include management and monitoring of both VMs and hosts.

Deploying new applications or adding new users can be time-consuming in non-virtualized environments because of the need to provision physical compute, storage, or networking resources. In a virtual environment, however, the virtualization layer allows such operations to occur much more frequently.

Consider an IT administrator who must configure a test and development setup for one group, and then must replicate the setup for a different group. In a physical environment, this may occur rarely because of the complexity of setting up a group of hosts and then duplicating the setup. In a virtual environment, however, simply performing a snapshot and cloning a group of VMs is sufficient to perform the same task. As a result, virtual environments see more provisioning or reconfiguration operations than physical environments.

Another task unique to virtualization is live migration of VMs [21]. In live migration, a VM is migrated from one physical host to another while it is running. Live migration can be used for maintenance cycles, for reducing power consumption by powering-off unneeded servers, or for load balancing of VMs across the physical hosts. Live migration can use significant network bandwidth, and additional NICs may be required simply to support the virtual management operations.

We refer to the ongoing operations in a virtualized datacenter that involve the maintenance and monitoring of the physical and virtual hosts as the *management workload.* Management workloads consist of critical operations whose completion time is of paramount importance. If a set of VMs must be provisioned before the start of a business day, the administrator must be able to accurately plan how long that will take, and must ensure that the task is completed in time.

Table 1: Resource Consumption for a Set of Common Applications.
On average, applications have modest resource requirements. For disk and networking, peaks are also within modest bounds.

Application	CPU Usage (%)		Avg. Memory Usage	Disk Bandwidth		Network Bandwidth	
	Average	Peak		Average	Peak	Average	Peak
Apache	5.7	32	4 GB	243 KBps	1.5 MBps	1.9 KBps	94.0 KBps
Cognos 8	1.1	3	2 GB	151 KBps	1.2 MBps	0.6 KBps	5.8 KBps
DB2	3.4	34	6 GB	498 KBps	31.0 MBps	5.2 KBps	170.0 KBps
Oracle	5.3	96	2 GB	286 KBps	19.0 MBps	5.0 KBps	665.0 KBps
SAS	7.2	90	2 GB	290 KBps	7.8 MBps	0.5 KBps	4.4 KBps
Siebel	5.8	27	8 GB	392 KBps	5.3 MBps	55.0 KBps	1.3 MBps
SQL 2000	5.3	64	2 GB	309 KBps	16.0 MBps	32.0 KBps	1.4 MBps
Windows 2003	3.0	70	4 GB	325 KBps	35.0 MBps	13.0 KBps	1.6 MBps

An important distinction between the management workload and the application workload is the type of resources used. From profiling numerous customer environments [27], we see that many applications have modest CPU, memory, network, and disk requirements, as shown in Table 1. These are average values over a wide range of servers. In addition, many organizations have some key applications (like databases) that can consume large amounts of network and disk bandwidth. The datacenter designer often explicitly over-provisions for these servers. Hot spots, when they occur, typically result in spikes in CPU usage, and disk and network remain modest. For example, the applications use at most ~500KBps disk bandwidth on average, with peaks up to 35MBps. The network requirements are at most 55 KBps on average, with peaks of a maximum 1.6MBps, well below the bandwidth available in commodity 1Gbps network cards. Despite the modest storage and networking requirements of many applications, administrators often order servers with multiple storage adapters (HBAs) and NICs. These resources are often used for management operations like backups or for lights-out management [13]. This indicates that on a per-host level, server administrators must factor in the resource usage of management operations. With virtualization, the number of applications consolidated onto a single host increases, and that the same sorts of factors start to apply at the rack and datacenter level.

3. MANAGEMENT OPERATIONS IN VIRTUALIZED DATACENTERS

We start with a question: what management operations do administrators perform in virtualized environments? To help answer this question, we collected detailed profiles of management workload activity from 17 enterprise datacenters running VMware's virtualization software [26].

Table 2 lists the most common operations found in the datacenters we profiled. Each datacenter is a different size, so the operations occur at different frequencies per datacenter. For each operation, we chose a single site and computed the average number of operations per day by taking the total number of operations performed and dividing by the number of days the management server was running. To illustrate the burstiness of management operations, we also examined the profiles to find the maximum number of times the operation was performed on a given day. Note that this peak number of operations is sometimes several orders of magnitude more than the average.

Many of the operations in Table 2 are self-explanatory, but for completeness, we define them here. *VM reconfigure* is reconfiguring the hardware for a VM (e.g., adding a NIC or adding a disk). *VM powerOn* and *powerOff* are powering on and off VMs, respectively, and *VM reset* is soft-resetting a VM (the equivalent of hitting the reset switch on a physical host). *Automated Live Migration* is load balancing performed in an automated manner [30] by moving VMs between hosts while the VMs are powered on. Live migration requires shared storage between the source and destination hosts. *Patch Install* involves installing a patch on a physical host (e.g., updating the hypervisor) or installing a patch in a VM (e.g., updating the guest OS with the latest security fixes). A *Create Snapshot* operation checkpoints the state of a VM. This allows a user to perform operations on the VM and then rollback to a known state in case of failure. A common use for snapshots is when installing the latest version of an application. The user snaphots the VM and then installs the software. If the installation succeeds, the snapshot can be removed and the user simply continues from the current state. If the software is buggy or crashes, however, the user can *revert* the snapshot, restoring the VM to the checkpointed state without the software installed. *Committing a snapshot* means writing to disk all of changes that occurred since the VM snapshot was taken, and removing the snapshot file. Finally, *VM clone* creates a replica of a powered-off VM. This is useful when duplicating a configuration, as mentioned earlier: for example, when a new employee joins a company, the standard desktop VM image can quickly be deployed to the employee's computer.

Table 2: Common Management Operations in Virtualized Datacenters. The average and peak number of operations per day at a given site are shown. Differences between average and peak frequency demonstrate the burstiness of management activity.

Operation	Average Number Per Day at Various Sites	Peak Per Day at Various Sites
VM reconfigure	2.3	699
Automated Live Migration	51	3156
VM powerOn	90	1576
VM powerOff	35	1535
VM reset	4.6	176
Patch Install	5.3	250
Create Snapshot	4.8	56
Snapshot Revert	7.0	101
Snapshot Commit	13	19
VM Clone	6.0	44

The customer data shows that even in production virtualized environments, there is some amount of ongoing management traffic. VM-related operations dominate the list, which makes sense since the number of VMs is typically much larger than the number of hosts. The data also illustrates some of the differences between expected management operations in a physical datacenter vs. a virtualized datacenter. For example, in some environments, VMs are powered on an average of 90 times in a day (and sometimes as often as 1500 times per day), and VMs are migrated over 50 times per day. Such activity is not found in datacenters without virtualization, as migrating applications that run directly on physical servers is much more involved than migrating VMs. In addition, physical hosts are seldom powered-on or powered-off except in case of failure or periodic maintenance.

3.1 Virtualized Datacenter Workflows

This aggregate data in Table 2 clearly shows significant day-to-day management activity and also illustrates the burstiness of such activity. The next step is to analyze the management workflows involved so that we can understand the context for these operations. In the subsequent sections, we explore these workflows in more detail.

3.1.1 Periodic Snapshot/Revert

Consider Figure 1, which shows the number of management operations (tasks) performed per day for a deployment over the period of one year. These management tasks consist of operations listed in Table 2 as well as other host- and VM-specific operations. We can see a periodic background load among some ambient management activity due to automated load balancing.

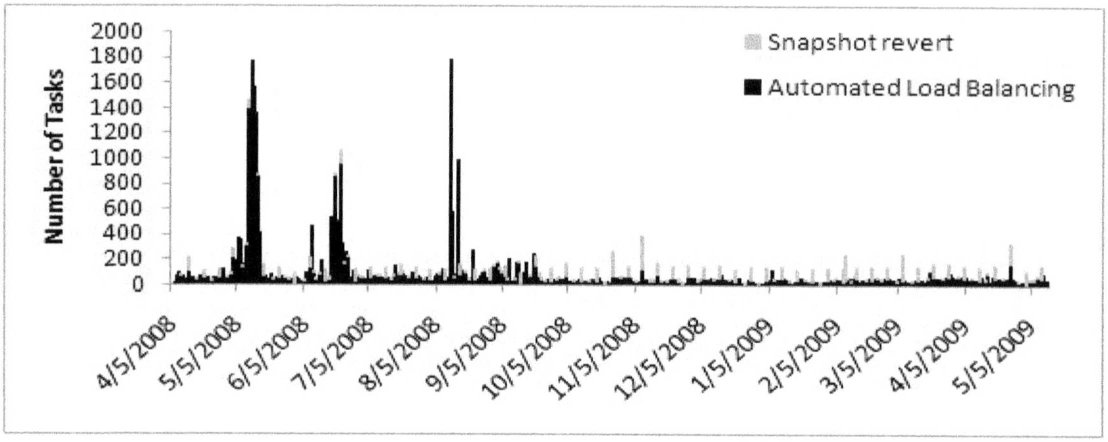

Figure 1: Management Traffic Demonstrating Snapshot/Revert over a One-Year Period. There are periodic spikes in snapshot/revert operations over the course of a year, mixed in with automated load balancing operations.

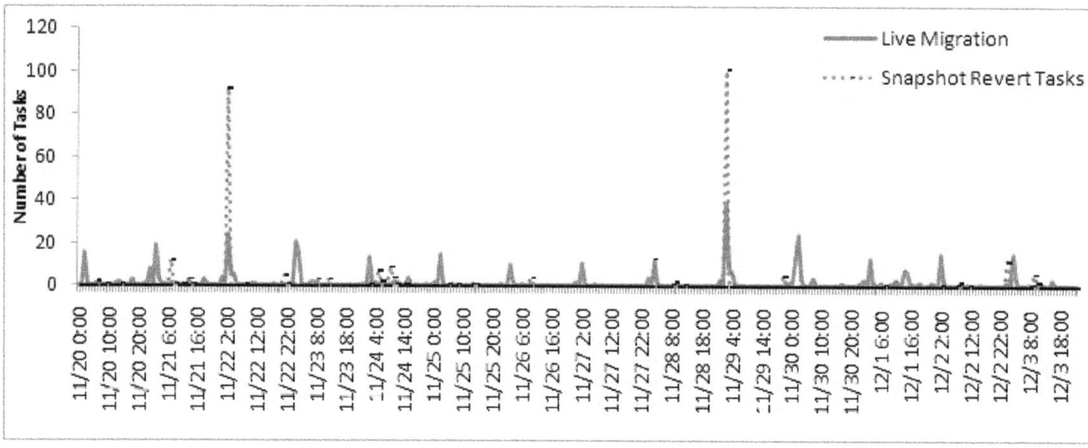

Figure 2: Management Traffic of Snapshot/Revert over a Two-Week Period. Snapshot/revert operations occur once per week to undo the changes during the week. Live migrations occur periodically to balance load due to application resource needs.

Looking more carefully at a selected two-week period in Figure 2, we see that there are small spikes daily around 2am and large spikes each Saturday at 2am (11/22 and 11/29). The tasks are subdivided into live migration tasks and snapshot revert tasks. In Figure 2, the weekly spikes at 2am are snapshot revert tasks, needed because this deployment is used for training purposes. This customer teaches a class. At the beginning of the week, the VM is snapshotted. Throughout the week, the students modify the state of the VM during the class. At the end of the week, the customer reverts the VMs back to the pre-class state, in preparation for the next week's class. This revert of snapshots occurs during a weekly maintenance window in one large burst.

The presence of automated migrations at 2am also indicates some nightly maintenance, most likely backups. These migrations sometimes happen at exactly the same time as the revert operations. Such overlapping of various management tasks can increase the burstiness of the management traffic, further complicating the resource usage issues in the management workload.

3.1.2 Host and VM Patching

Figure 3 illustrates another common management activity: patch management. We see spikes of "patch installation" routines occurring roughly once per month. For this customer, patching is a periodic maintenance event across the entire infrastructure. Once per month, the customer brings down various hosts and VMs and applies the latest patches. Because this occurs across the entire infrastructure, the total number of patch installs is very bursty, occurring 250 at a time for one day per month. On days with patch updates, the number of management tasks is significantly larger than on non-patch days.

3.1.3 After-Hours Maintenance

The previous examples have shown weekly and monthly spikes in management activity. Figure 4 shows a workflow with finer-grain activity, including nearly all of the operations listed in Table 2 plus some additional tasks.

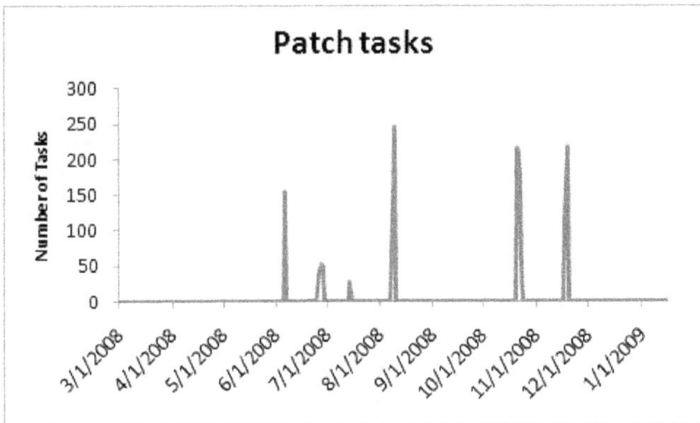

Figure 3: Patching Tasks during a 10-Month Period. Patching occurs approximately once per month, causing a burst in network and disk activity.

We see periodic spikes of activity after 6pm each night for a given two-week period. The majority of these tasks are powering on VMs and committing snapshots. In this case, an IT department was doing a rollout of new VMs and phasing out old ones. Numerous snapshots were taken so that new software could be tested and verified. Once verified, these changes could be committed. The maintenance window was after 6pm each night. At this time, the VM snapshots were committed, and other VMs were powered on and tested in the new environment. This *after-hours maintenance* workflow is fairly common in both physical datacenters and virtualized datacenters, though the operation mix is different between the two. For example, a virtualized datacenter will see snapshot/commit operations, whereas a physical datacenter may see nightly backups of various shared storage devices.

3.1.4 Boot Storm

One of the increasingly common uses of virtualization is "Virtual Desktop Infrastructure" (VDI), in which virtual desktops are hosted on physical machines in a datacenter and are accessed remotely through thin clients. VDI deployments are susceptible to so-called "boot-storms," in which all VMs are turned on at the start of the day as employees come to work. As a result, bursts of hundreds of power operations to VMs can occur daily. Because VDI deployments consist of large numbers of similar virtual machines, they are subject to other types of "storms" as well. For example, anti-virus storms can happen when the virtual machines perform nightly virus scans. Figure 5 shows the number of tasks vs. time in a VDI deployment. Note the burst in tasks around 9am, in which over 2500 tasks occur within 1 hour. Both of these examples (anti-virus storm and boot storm) further illustrate the bursty nature of management traffic.

3.1.5 Automated Live Migration

One of the big advantages of virtualization is automated resource management. An application is contained within a VM, and as the resource needs of the application grow or shrink, the VM can be migrated to other hosts to balance the load. Often, the balancing is done within a specified set of hosts (for example, within the same rack), and high-speed links are used between those hosts. VMware provides a facility known as *Distributed Resource Scheduling* (DRS) [30] for automated load balancing. We contrast these automated tasks with non-automated tasks, such as an administrator manually powering off a VM in order to add a new device or to reconfigure the virtual network connected to the VM.

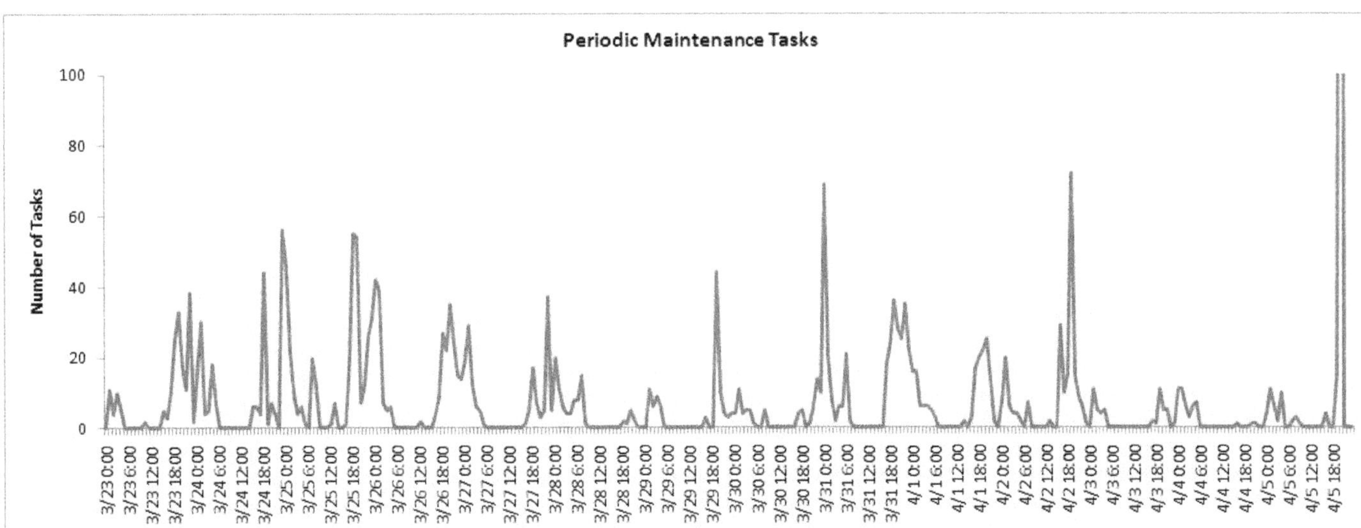

Figure 4: Management Activity Demonstrating After-Hours Maintenance over a Two-Week Period. The management activity at this site occurs after hours during the nightly maintenance window and is significantly higher than the activity during the day.

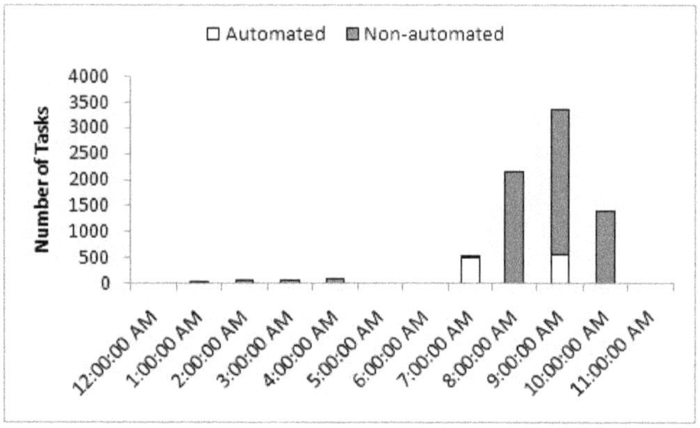

Figure 5: VDI Boot-storm Activity in a Test and Development Environment. Non-automated tasks include user-initiated booting of VMs, while automated tasks include live migration. There is a spike in VM booting at between 8am and 9am, when many users come in to work and power-on their VMs.

Figure 6 shows automated and non-automated tasks for one deployment over a two-week period. The automated tasks were largely live migrations. There are two notable regions. One is a spike in non-automated tasks on 7/31. In this case, a number of host reconfiguration operations were occurring, in preparation for a vast movement of VMs. This movement occurred a few days later on 8/4. In the background, over the entire two-week period we consistently see live migrations in response to application load. We find that a large number of enterprise-class customers enabled automated resource management in their infrastructures, providing an ambient level of management traffic that is specific to virtualized datacenters.

3.2 Multi-tenant Management Issues

All of the previous use cases have considered data from individual datacenters that hosted servers from single corporations. A multi-tenant environment is one in which multiple customers (or departments) share access to the same physical resources. For example, perhaps a provider is hosting Coke and Pepsi in the same virtualized datacenter. The hosting provider must guarantee performance isolation even in the face of unpredictable management traffic. For example, the hosting provider may end up with combinations of all of the workflows that we have seen. Consider Figure 2, with periodic peaks at 2am each Saturday morning and a correspondingly large amount of disk traffic at this time. Suppose this 2am traffic were occurring in Chicago while a VDI deployment from Europe experienced a 9am boot storm. This 9am spike would occur at the same time as the 2am spike in Chicago, and the combination could cause extreme stress on the storage subsystem.

Next, consider the case in which the previous traffic is combined with the nightly patching from Figure 3 or the periodic maintenance in Figure 4, or even the automated load balancing in Figure 6. All of these conflicting needs can stress the datacenter more than the application traffic itself, and various design questions arise. For example, shared storage is essential, but should hosts with conflicting management operations be placed in the same rack? How do we place VMs to avoid spikes that occur because of time zone issues? How do we provision the storage and networking to accommodate these bursts? How do we schedule management operations among customers with different demands? These issues demonstrate that considering the management workload is essential in a virtualized datacenter.

4. SCALING OF MANAGEMENT WORKLOAD

As shown in Table 1 many enterprise workloads have light IO requirements. In contrast, a management workload puts a non-trivial load on the IO subsystem. In this section, we discuss the management workload in more detail and perform a sensitivity analysis to see how the management workload scales with increasing compute density.

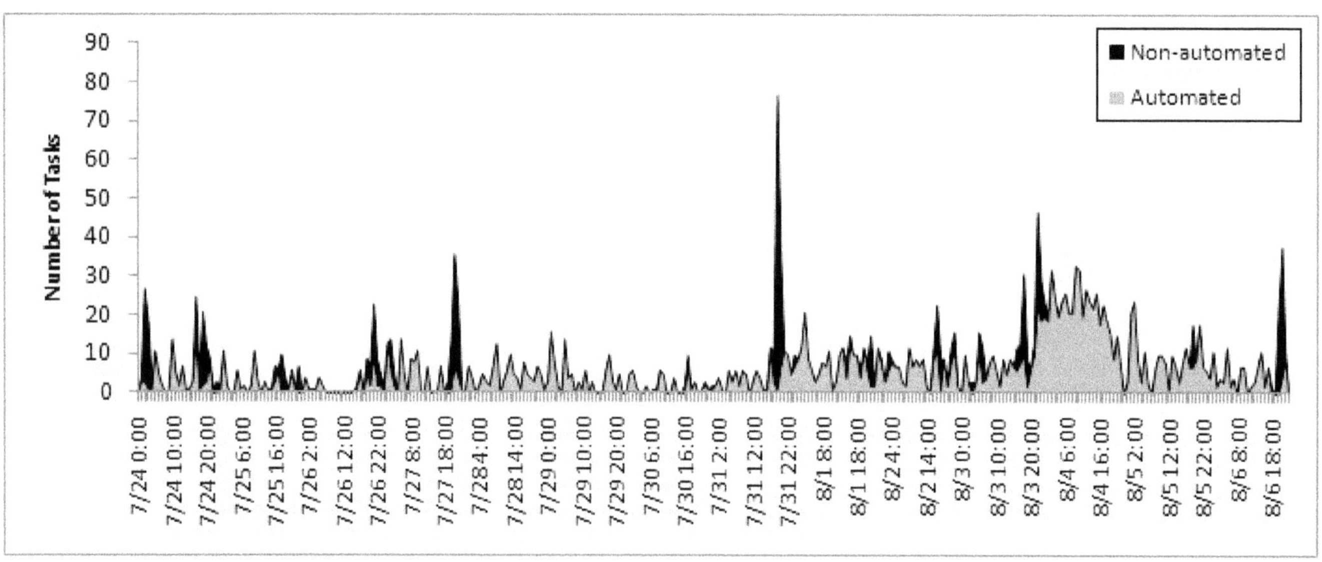

Figure 6: Automated Management Operations over a Two-Week Period. This customer site exhibits a large amount of automated operations (live migrations). The spike in non-automated activity on 7/31 reflects a number of manual host reconfigurations in preparation for a vast movement of VMs. This movement occurred in an automated way starting on 8/3.

4.1 Common Management Workload Patterns

Our customer data shows some common management workload patterns, each exerting a different background load in a virtualized datacenter. In Table 3, we summarize these patterns and indicate whether the load scales with the number of hosts or number of VMs, whether the pattern impacts disk or network, and whether the pattern impacts CPU or memory usage. We discuss this resource usage in more detail in the following sections.

The industry is tending toward larger number of cores per processor socket [3][15]. As the number of cores per socket increases, we will see corresponding increases in the numbers of cores per server, memory per server, and the number of VMs that can run on a server. With greater VM densities, we will see an increase in the management workload for a given datacenter size. In the next few sections, we analyze the resource usage under these various loads as we increase the number of hosts and VMs. The changing resource usage can impact various aspects of datacenter design.

4.2 Datacenter and Server Configurations

For our sensitivity analysis, we try to choose configurations that represent valid design points in the next few years. We focus on the number of hosts in a rack and the compute density in the rack. For the purposes of this study, we assume that the memory in the server is sufficient to meet the VM consolidation demands.

Racks in a datacenter come with a variety of power specifications that support a varying number of hosts. We assume configurations ranging from 10 hosts in a rack, representing the lower end of the power spectrum, to a very dense configuration of 40 hosts in a rack. For our default server building blocks, we use quad-socket servers with 8 cores per socket, for a total of 32 cores per host. Further, we apply a ratio of VMs to cores of 4:1, giving us 128 VMs per server. This assumption is reasonable based on statistics from customer data. Today, 1-way and 2-way VMs are the most common configurations, with only a small number of 4-way VMs. We summarize the various configurations in Table 4.

4.3 Workload Investigation

In this section we examine each of our workloads in turn. We discuss their scaling behavior and analyze their expected resource usage under the configurations listed in Table 4.

Table 3: Workflows and their Resource Usage in Virtualized Datacenters.

Workload Pattern	Host or VM scaling?	Disk or Network impact?	Impact on CPU/Memory usage?
Periodic Snapshot/revert	VMs	Disk	Memory
Host/VM Patching	Both	Both	Both
Boot Storm	VMs	Disk	Both
After-hours Maintenance	Both	Both	Both
Automated Load Balancing	VMs	Network	Both

Table 4: Datacenter and Server Configurations in Sensitivity Analysis.

Configuration	Number of hosts in rack	Cores in rack	VMs in rack
Small	10	320	1280
Medium	20	640	2560
Large	30	960	3840
Future	40	1280	5120

4.3.1 Periodic Snapshot/Revert

The first workload we consider is the periodic reversion of snapshots. To revert a snapshot, a host must read data from disk for each VM being reverted. This data is the memory state of the VM at the time of the snapshot, and its size is correlated with the size of the VM's memory. Reverting a large number of snapshots simultaneously can thus cause a large amount of disk traffic. If a host has 128 VMs, and each VM has a snapshot that is being reverted, then the host must support the disk traffic required for these 128 reverts. Given a time window for reverting snapshots of 30 minutes and 1GB VM memory size, then the host must support 1GB/30minutes = 555 KBps for each revert operation. Hosts running 128 VMs must therefore support (128 × 555 KBps) = 70 MBps of additional disk traffic for the half hour window. Comparing to the data in Table 1, we see that management traffic alone can exceed the disk traffic as the highest peaks for end-user applications. Figure 7 shows the overall rack storage bandwidth requirements for our configurations for the snapshot/revert management workload. We assume that the maintenance window for snapshot/revert is either 30 minutes or 1 hour, similar to what we have seen in practice.

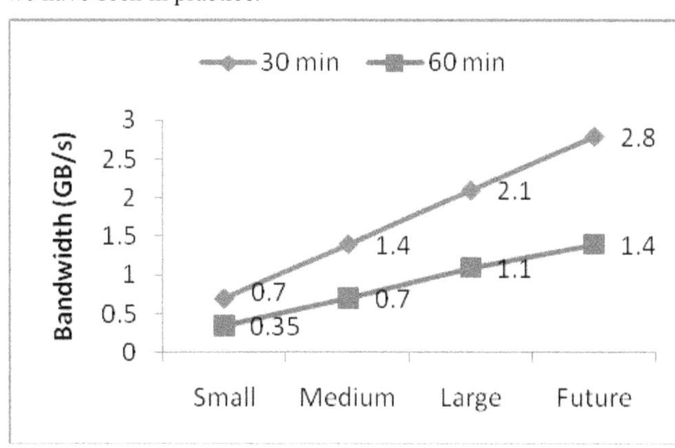

Figure 7: Per-Rack Storage Bandwidth Requirements for Snapshot/Revert Management Workload, 30-minute and 60-minute Maintenance Windows. For a 30-minute maintenance window and the 'Future' configuration with VMs of 1 GB memory size, the entire rack must support up to 2.8GBps of storage bandwidth above and beyond typical application needs.

The rack disk bandwidth requirement at the largest configuration and with the smallest revert window is 2.8 GBps. At first glance, this seems modest for the entire rack, and a typical high-end storage-array network (SAN) [11] can handle this bandwidth. However, 70 MBps must be sustained per host, which suggests that each host must have a 1 Gbps SAN HBA and be connected to a SAN switch with 1 Gbps ports in order to satisfy this particular load. The choice of SAN switch may limit the number of servers that can go in the rack. With the smallest configuration of 10 hosts and 128 VMs/host and a 1-hour revert window, the per-host bandwidth is halved to 35 MBps per host. This bandwidth requirement suggests a less-expensive SAN and less-expensive SAN switch (or perhaps even high-end local storage). Aside from the storage requirements, reverting a large number of snapshots at once can also cause memory pressure and CPU load on the server, in addition to the CPU and memory required to run applications.

In summary, the snapshot/revert workload stresses the per-host storage bandwidth. The system administrator and datacenter designer must work together to plan out the requirements: varying the maintenance window and limiting the number of VMs that are reverted at one time can help reduce the storage bandwidth requirements as well as the CPU and memory requirements. Choosing to place the storage within the rack or outside the rack will impact the choice of storage and storage switch as well as the inter-rack uplink storage bandwidth requirements.

4.3.2 Patching VMs and Hosts

The second workload we consider is patch management. Typically, patch management in a virtualized datacenter involves downloading a number of patches from a patch server to each of the patched hosts and VMs. In VMware's Virtual Update Manager [34], patching a host involves downloading a set of patches and rebooting the host until the patches are fully installed. Patching a VM requires the VM to remotely mount an ISO image that is located on the patch server. VM and host patches can be up to hundreds of MBs per month [34]. We assume 20 patches of 30 MB each, for a total patch size per VM of 600MB. Because the number of VMs is two orders of magnitude larger than the number of hosts, we will focus on VM patching.

Assuming the patch server resides outside of the rack, the remote mounting of the ISO image by the VMs requires network traffic from outside the rack to the VMs inside the rack. The length of the maintenance window and the number of VMs in the rack are needed to determine the amount of bandwidth required to handle this patching sequence. In Figure 8, we list the network bandwidth required from the patch server to the rack for our configurations, assuming maintenance windows from 1 hour to 8 hours. We assume that up to 48 VMs can be patched concurrently [34]. Since the number of VMs ranges from 1280 per rack to 5120 per rack (see Table 4), we make the simplifying assumption that it will take (1280/48) = 27 iterations for patching in the smallest configuration, (2560/48) = 54 iterations in the Medium configuration, 80 in the Large configuration, and 107 iterations in the Future configuration: during each iteration, we patch 48 VMs. Each iteration must be able to accommodate the bandwidth requirements for patching 48 VMs concurrently, and all iterations must complete in the maintenance window. For example, in the Large configuration, there are 80 iterations. For a 1-hour maintenance window, we have (1 hour/80 iterations) = 45s per iteration. Since each patch is 600 MB, (48 × 600 MB) = 28800 MB must be downloaded into a rack from the patch server. In a 45s iteration, this means the bandwidth into the rack must be at least (28800 MB/45s) = 640 MBps = 5.1 Gbps.

As Figure 8 shows, the bandwidth into the rack for this management operation alone ranges from 0.22 Gbps to 6.8 Gbps depending on the configuration. The choice of maintenance window is important: 0.22 Gbps into the rack suggests a commodity switch with 1 Gbps uplinks, while 6.8 Gbps suggests a more expensive switch with a higher-bandwidth uplink, or that the patch server should reside within the rack. Moreover, consider the disk bandwidth requirements at the patch server. For a patch server to provide 0.22 Gbps = 27 MBps is no problem: a local disk is fine. However, consider the patch server for the Future scenario and a 1-hour maintenance window. This patch server would need to provide 6.8 Gbps = 853 MBps. Clearly, this is impractical, and multiple patch servers are required in this case. It is also possible to optimize this by caching patches that apply to multiple VMs, avoiding a separate download per VM.

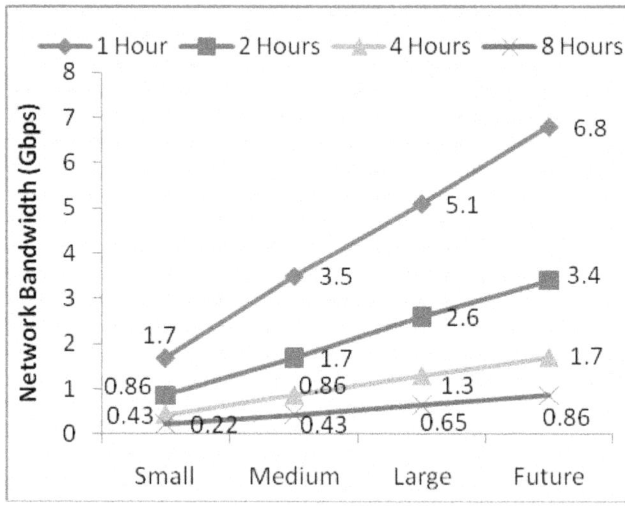

Figure 8: Per-Rack Network Bandwidth Requirements for Patch Maintenance Cycles Ranging from 1 Hour to 8 hours. We assume 48 VMs can be patched concurrently. The Future configuration requires 6.8Gbps of additional network bandwidth per rack to complete within a one-hour maintenance window.

To summarize, for this patch management workload, the bandwidth required into the rack is non-trivial, ranging from 0.22 Gbps to 6.8 Gbps, and depends on a variety of factors, including the number of hosts in the rack, the number of VMs per host, the size of the patches, and the length of the maintenance window. The datacenter administrator and designer have many choices to make, ranging from the location of the patch server (inside or outside the rack), the type of storage for the patch server, the type of switch to handle the management traffic, and the length of the maintenance window, and these tradeoffs can seriously impact the end-user.

4.3.3 Boot Storm

In the boot-storm workload, a large number of VMs are powered-on at once. When booting a VM, data is read from disk until the VM is able to run an OS and complete the boot sequence. In our setups, about 200 MB of data is read from disk before a VM can boot. Thus, if 500 VMs were powered-on at once, then this is an additional 500 × 200 MB = 100 GB of disk traffic that the rack must be able to handle. Moreover, booting such a large number of VMs at once stresses the memory system on each host and saturates the CPU. Windows operating systems zero out all of memory before start-up, so each host writes a significant amount of memory for each VM that is booted. This can be optimized a bit in the hypervisor by using a shared zero pages.

In Figure 9, we show the per-rack storage bandwidth requirements for various configurations for the boot-storm workload, assuming 200MB must be read for each VM. We look at boot-storm-windows of 15 minutes and 30 minutes, based on the performance requirements from typical customer deployments.

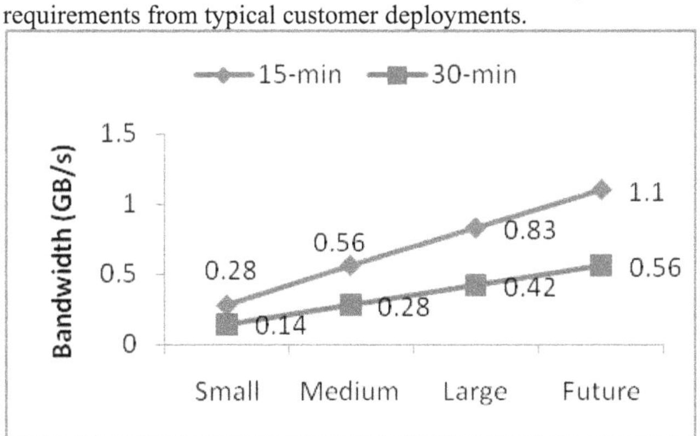

Figure 9: Per-Rack Storage Bandwidth Requirements, Boot-Storm Workload, 15-minute and 30-minute Boot-Storm Windows. A 15-minute window for completing boot-storms for thousands of VMs can incur over 1GBps of storage traffic.

The per-rack storage bandwidth required for the largest configuration and the smallest boot-storm window is 1.1 GBps, which may suggest a high-end SAN device for the entire rack. However, the per-host bandwidth in this case is (128 × 200 MB/15 minutes) = 28.4 MBps. This per-host bandwidth can be satisfied even with a simple local SCSI disk, though reliability concerns may suggest a backup strategy involving SAN or software redundancy [6][9]. Another option is a network-attached storage (NAS), which also would require the rack network switch to satisfy 1.1 GBps, or nearly 10 Gbps. This may require more than a simple commodity switch with four 1 Gbps uplinks.

4.3.4 After-Hours Maintenance

In some environments, we see a large number of management operations after hours, often in settings where rolling upgrades or rolling backups are taking place. These sorts of workloads can cause spikes in disk writes commensurate to the sizes of the VMs being backed up, which can be on the order of GBs per VM. The data we've collected suggests that after-hours maintenance tends to involve small numbers of concurrent operations. The most common operations we have seen include reconfiguring VMs, powering on VMs, cloning VMs, and creating snapshots or committing snapshots of VMs.

The number of concurrent operations varies with the size of the virtualized environment, and the load exerted on the system depends on the type of operation. Reconfiguring a VM is a fast operation with small resource requirements, so we will focus on the other operations instead. As noted before, power operations require loading approximately 200 MB per VM. Creating a snapshot of a running VM requires writing the contents of memory to disk and is proportional to the size of the VM's memory. Committing a snapshot requires merging the contents of a change log to disk, requiring reads from the change log and then writes to disk. In our experience, a rule of thumb for Windows VMs is that the amount of data read (and therefore the amount of data written to disk) is at least the size of the paging file in Windows. For a 2 GB VM, therefore, we would need to read 2 GB from the change log and write those 2 GB to disk.

In the environments we studied, the number of operations per VM is correlated with the size of the environment. In addition, maintenance operations tend to be bursty: they are initiated at once and allowed to complete before more are performed. During maintenance windows we see 20 operations per hour on average for the deployments we examined. Table 5 shows the minimum rack bandwidth required to do 20 or 40 concurrent operations in 30 minutes or 1 hour. To compute this, we take the number of concurrent operations, multiply by the size of data that must be transferred, and then divide by the time. For example, to clone 20 16 GB VMs, we must read up to (20 × 16 GB) = 320 GB and then write up to 320 GB, all in 1 hour, taking 0.18 GBps.

As the table suggests, the types of periodic maintenance operations that occur can impact the storage and bandwidth requirements. If periodic maintenance is a small number of power operations, then a simple 1 Gbps network is more than sufficient for the rack. If, however, a large number of clones must be done in a short amount of time, as in the 40-clone case for 16 GB VMs, then 0.36 GBps is required. If this clone is occurring via NAS, this requires more than 1 Gbps for the management network from that rack.

Table 5: Per-Rack Storage/Network Bandwidth Required for Concurrent Operations during a Maintenance Window.

Operation	30-minute window		1-hour window	
	# of Concurrent Operations		# of Concurrent Operations	
	20	40	20	40
Power on (200MB to boot)	2.2 MBps	4.4 MBps	1.1 MBps	2.2 MBps
Create Snapshot (2GB)	0.022 GBps	0.044 GBps	0.011 GBps	0.022 GBps
Commit Snapshot (2GB)	0.044 GBps	0.088 GBps	0.022 GBps	0.044 GBps
Clone VM (16 GB)	0.360 GBps	0.720 GBps	0.180 GBps	0.360 GBps

4.3.5 Automated Load Balancing

Automated load balancing heavily leverages live migration. Because this is a CPU-intensive operation, the CPU usage of the live-migration agent is typically capped to avoid saturating the CPU and slowing down applications running on the same host. Each live migration must transfer approximately the size of the VM's memory (not counting zero pages) between hosts. Most virtualized deployments utilize an entirely different network and separate NIC per host to accommodate live migration traffic [28].

In the environments we studied, the rate of automated live migration varied quite a bit, from 0 to 80 per hour. In Table 6, we show the intra-rack bandwidth required for varying rates of live migration per hour and varying amounts of data transferred. For example, for 20 live migrations per hour, with each live migration transferring 512 MB, the rack bandwidth required is (20 × 512MB/1 hour) = 23 Mbps.

As the table suggests, the bandwidth demands within the rack are quite modest. However, each host essentially requires a gigabit NIC to be devoted exclusively to live migration traffic.

Table 6: Rack Network Bandwidth Required for Live Migration.

Live migration rate (per hour)	Amount of memory transferred per live migration					
	512 MB	**1024 MB**	**2048 MB**	**4096 MB**	**8192 MB**	**16384 MB**
20	23 Mbps	46 Mbps	91 Mbps	182 Mbps	364 Mbps	728 Mbps
40	46 Mbps	91 Mbps	182 Mbps	364 Mbps	728 Mbps	1.5 Gbps
60	68 Mbps	137 Mbps	273 Mbps	546 Mbps	1.1 Gbps	2.2 Gbps
80	91 Mbps	182 Mbps	364 Mbps	728 Mbps	1.5 Gbps	2.9 Gbps

Consider the 2.9 Gbps case. If this rate of live migrations is seen with 10 hosts in a rack, then each host must be able to sustain 290 Mbps. Moreover, if VMs are located across racks for fault-tolerance purposes, the traffic demands will change. For example, if 80 concurrent live migrations of 16 GB VMs must occur at once, and the transfer is from one rack to another, then the rack-level switch must have multiple 1 Gbps uplinks. For traffic purely within the rack, a switch that uses 1 Gbps ports can likely be oversubscribed and still satisfy the bandwidth demands easily.

4.4 Summary

Table 7 summarizes the results of our study, showing the workload, the per-rack bandwidth required, and the resource (storage or network) that is the primary resource used. Of course, if NAS devices are used instead of SAN devices, then the bandwidth tradeoffs shift from storage to networking.

Table 7: Per-Rack Storage and Network Requirements for Management Workloads.

Workflow	Rack Bandwidth Requirement	Resource tradeoff
Periodic Snapshot/revert	0.35 GBps – 2.8 GBps	Storage
Host/VM Patching	0.22 Gbps – 6.8 Gbps	Network
Boot storm	0.14 GBps – 1.1 GBps	Storage
After-hours maintenance	2.2 MBps – 0.18 GBps	Storage/network
Automated Load Balancing	23 Mbps – 2.9 Gbps	Network

It is important to note that the basic mechanisms required to perform each of these workflows is expected to be similar regardless of virtualization platform. For example, live migration requires transferring memory over the network regardless of which hypervisor is used, and reverting a snapshot will require some method of reading memory for the VM from disk. Consequently, we expect that these results are applicable across any virtualized environments, and are not confined to the one used in the environments we profiled.

One natural question to ponder is what will happen as storage and network technology continues to improve. 10 Gbps is becoming the standard for networking and high-end storage arrays can support over 100 GBps in aggregate data bandwidth. Moreover, technologies like Cisco UCS [8] and InfiniBand [14] offer significant network and storage bandwidth through unified storage/network fabrics. In addition, as SSDs [16] continue to improve, they will be used to improve aggregate storage bandwidth. Although the per-host and per-rack bandwidth will improve, compute-density will also increase, and the management workload will scale as a result. Though the absolute numbers for management traffic are not staggering (2.9 Gbps for rack network bandwidth and 1 GBps for rack storage bandwidth), they do induce substantial traffic for critical operations that must fit within maintenance windows. Moreover, there is a direct relationship between cost and capability of components and the speed with which management operations can be completed. The datacenter designer must be aware of this tradeoff.

5. IMPLICATIONS FOR ARCHITECTS

Our study provides two major results for the computer architecture community: the definition of a management workload for virtualized datacenters, and a set of implications for datacenter design. We discuss these in more detail below.

5.1 Definition of the Management Workload

This paper describes a collection of common workflows in the virtualized datacenter and quantifies their impact. We bring attention to the fact that management operations comprise a unique *management workload.* This is a key step towards formulating a general-purpose management workload that architects can use for studying virtualized datacenters.

The virtualization management workload has different characteristics from the individual applications, such as databases and mail servers, running in the datacenter. Furthermore, the virtualized management workload also differs from parallelized high-performance computing applications and internet-scale applications like Google Search.

The virtualization management workload primarily stresses the disk and network subsystems in the datacenter. It is bursty by nature, and has hard latency requirements. Moreover, the bursts of management activity are not controlled by individual administrators, since a given datacenter may host virtual machines from multiple customers in multiple geographies each with different maintenance windows. Management operations are not typically checkpointed (as are large-scale parallel applications). Failures are not tolerated because users could lose all access to their machines, so efficient methods of fault containment, isolation, and recovery are necessary.

5.2 Virtualized Datacenter Design

This characterization of management operations in a virtualized datacenter also yields several implications for computer architects. The datacenter architect must factor in a "management budget" when constructing a datacenter. The choice of appropriate compute elements, racks, storage, networking, and power management is important to ensure good price-performance within a given power budget.

Starting at the processor level, there are some design tradeoffs for architects to consider. Virtualization deployments are benefiting to a great extent from the latest advances in processor design.

Applications running in virtual machines see improved performance with virtualization extensions. Both virtualized applications and management operations benefit from increased core counts (due to their concurrent nature), and larger caches. However, employing the latest processors both costs more money and consumes more power than older-generation processors or processors without virtualization extensions (like mobile processors). In addition, virtualized datacenters are designed to run legacy enterprise workloads, which expect reliable, server-grade hardware and do not tolerate frequent failures.

At the system level, the storage and network requirements for management operations (such as live migration or cloning a virtual machine) suggest a high-speed I/O bus coupled with multiple adapters. For example, multiple network adapters may be required for management operations (like live migration, fault-tolerance, or high-availability) in addition to the networking demands of the applications. A convergent fabric [17] can be a solution as long as the individual storage/network requirements do not overwhelm the convergent adapter on the node or the I/O bus.

Going beyond the individual server, our results show that the datacenter infrastructure and rack architecture are also impacted by management workloads. While there are benefits to maximizing the density of compute servers in a rack, the higher densities result in greater network and storage requirements for the management workload. This design motivates a hierarchical network/storage interconnect with high-bandwidth storage/networking within a rack feeding into global I/O interconnect. Now the scheduling of these management operations becomes important: it may be useful to consider the management required for a given virtual machine when placing it in a particular rack. For example, if a virtual machine is likely to be migrated frequently, then it will benefit from high intra-rack bandwidth rather than high inter-rack bandwidth. The choice of overall storage is important as well: NFS may be less expensive and sufficient for certain workloads, but the additional bandwidth and reduced latency of a SAN may be required for management workloads, since they stress both storage and networking. Increased numbers of low-cost storage elements throughout the datacenter may be more efficient than using fewer numbers of large storage arrays. For situations like patch management, a local patch store per rack is critical, so designing for rack-local storage and high intra-rack bandwidth is key. Solutions like RamClouds [22] can help reduce critical-path bandwidth requirements for networking and storage, but still require sophisticated solutions for persisting data in a timely manner.

Finally, we consider the issue of power management. Various solutions exist for dynamically varying the power delivery in a datacenter [1][23] or for rebalancing workloads to optimize power consumption [29]. Because the management workload potentially operates around the clock, the power budget must take it into account. For example, it is possible that distributing storage and networking throughout the datacenter may be more efficient than consolidating the storage/networking because the power is distributed more uniformly throughout the datacenter. More evaluation is needed before any conclusions can be drawn.

6. RELATED WORK

To the best of our knowledge, this is the first work that focuses on virtualized datacenters and specifically considers the impact of the management workload on virtualized datacenter operations.

While our work was done in the context of enterprise workloads running within a virtualized datacenter, many of our findings can be applied to cloud computing infrastructures such as Amazon EC2 [2] and Terremark [25] Such infrastructures are often virtualized. As multiple customers use a given set of datacenters, each user's management needs comprises a workload by itself, and the collection of management workloads is analogous to a cloud-computing workload.

Our work focuses on the management aspects of large-scale systems, but another important component is monitoring for errors or assessing system-wide performance. One of the challenges of monitoring is collecting large amounts of data and then correlating this data to events in the system, like network overloads or drive failures. Examples of such monitoring and reporting systems include Ganglia [19], Chukwa [7], and the Google System Health Infrastructure [24]. As compute densities increase, efficient monitoring for virtualized datacenters becomes more important. The management operations themselves require monitoring to determine whether they have completed or failed due to some system failure.

Some of our conclusions about diversity of hosts and storage subsystem and the need for adequately provisioning networks may differ from the design principles of warehouse-scale computers (WSCs) used by Google [6], Amazon [2] and Yahoo [35] to run their Internet services. One reason is that WSCs run different workloads from the datacenters we are considering. For example, most WSCs run internet-scale applications that have built-in mechanisms for dealing with hardware failures. In contrast, the datacenters we consider run enterprise applications, such as Exchange or SQL Server, that do not have built-in fault-resiliency. They typically rely on external (to the application) high-availability or fault-tolerance solutions. Such applications expect that the hardware is generally reliable and failures are uncommon. In such cases, more expensive hardware with more robust reliability guarantees is essential, and using cheaper components that can fail with impunity may not be an option. Essentially, the difference is between cloud-scale applications (like those that run in WSCs) vs. applications running in a cloud (like Exchange).

Previous work in cloud computing [5] has focused on similar workloads as WSCs: namely, cloud-scale applications (like MapReduce [10] or Hadoop [4]) vs. applications running in a cloud (like various instances of Microsoft Exchange). These cloud-scale applications have bursty behavior similar to our management workload, so similar techniques for balancing load or provisioning resources may be applicable to the management workload.

7. CONCLUSIONS

The datacenter of the future will make heavy use of virtualized infrastructure. Virtualization allows a more efficient use of hardware through server consolidation and also enables a range of new workflows that can reduce total cost of ownership and improve administrator productivity in the datacenter. While easing the day-to-day tasks of an administrator, however, virtualization also introduces a number of new considerations into the datacenter. In particular, the management operations constitute a workload over and above the actual applications that are running in VMs in the datacenter. Understanding of this management workload is critical for proper datacenter design.

In this paper we have examined data from a number of virtualized deployments and studied the management operations in each of those deployments. We have provided a characterization of the operations into various management workloads and studied their resource usage. We demonstrate five different management workloads present in the virtualized datacenter: snapshot/revert, VM patching, boot storm, after-hours maintenance, and automated live migration. The complexity of this management workload is likely to increase as more value-added virtualization features like high-availability [31], disaster recovery [32], and storage load balancing [12] become even more commonplace. We have found that in general, management operations have significant storage and networking requirements over and above that of most traditional user applications: over 1 GBps additional rack bandwidth required for management storage traffic and almost 3 Gbps additional rack bandwidth required for management network traffic. We find that burstiness is the rule, rather than the exception, in the virtualized management workload, and planning for this burstiness is essential for efficient datacenter operations: in particular, phasing management operations and choosing appropriate hardware can reduce the length of maintenance cycles from hours to minutes and minimize perturbations to the application load in the system. Finally, we show that the management workload scales as the computation power of servers increases and becomes even more critical with the increasing proliferation of massively multi-core processors.

8. ACKNOWLEDGMENTS

Our thanks to Jeremy Rodriguez, Devaki Kulkarni, Sunil Satnur, John Liang, Xuwen Yu, Sam McBride, Warakorn Thapanangkun, Bruce Herndon, Shicong Meng, Carl Waldspurger, Ben Verghese, Dan Scales, and Julie Brodeur for helpful comments on previous drafts of this paper. We would also like to thank our customers for graciously letting us use data collected from their environments.

9. REFERENCES

[1] Ahmad, F., et al. Joint Optimization of Idle and Cooling Power in Data Centers While Maintaining Response Time. In Proceedings of ASPLOS XV (Pittsburgh, PA, March 13-17, 2010). 243-256.

[2] Amazon EC2. http://aws.amazon.com/ec2.

[3] AMD Magny-Cours. http://www.amd.com/us/products/server/processors/6000-series-platforms/Pages/6000-series-platform.aspx

[4] Apache Hadoop. http://hadoop.apache.org/

[5] Armbrust, M., et al. Above the Clouds: A Berkeley View of Cloud Computing. University of California at Berkeley Technical Report No. UCB/EECS-2009-28.

[6] Barroso, L., et al. The Datacenter as a Computer: An Introduction to the Design of Warehouse-Scale Machines. Morgan and Claypool Publishers. 2009.

[7] Boulon, J., et al. Chukwa, a large-scale monitoring system. In Proceedings of CCA '08. Oct 2008

[8] Cisco. Unified Computing System. http://www.cisco.com/en/US/netsol/ns944/#~in_depth

[9] Dean, J. Designs, Lessons, and Advice from Building Large Distributed Systems. Keynote from LADIS 2009 (Big Sky, Montana, October 10-11, 2009).

[10] Dean, J., et al. MapReduce: Simplified Data Processing on Large Clusters. Communications of the ACM, vol. 51, no. 1 (2008), pp. 107-113.

[11] EMC. EMC Symmetrix DMX-3 950 specifications. http://www.emc.com/collateral/hardware/specification-sheet/c1153-dmx3-950-ss.pdf

[12] Gulati, A., et al. BASIL: Automated IO Load Balancing across Storage Devices. In Proceedings of USENIX FAST '10 (San Jose, CA, February 23-26, 2010). 169-182.

[13] HP. Lights-out management. http://h18000.www1.hp.com/products/servers/management/ilo/

[14] InfiniBand Trade Association. http://www.infinibandta.org/

[15] Intel Nehalem. http://www.intel.com/p/en_US/products/server/processor/xeon7000

[16] Intel. Solid State Drives. http://www.intel.com/design/flash/nand/mainstream/index.htm

[17] Leigh, K., et al, Fabric Convergence Implications on Systems Architecture. In Proceedings of HPCA '08 (Salt Lake City, UT, February 16-20, 2008). 15-26.

[18] Lim, K., et al, Understanding and Designing New Server Architectures for Emerging Warehouse-Computing Environments. In Proceedings of ISCA 2008 (Beijing, China, June 21-25, 2008). 315-236.

[19] Massie, M.,et al. The Ganglia Distributed Monitoring System: Design, Implementation, and Experience. In Parallel Computing Volume 30, Issue 7, pp 817- 840, 2004.

[20] NAS Devices. http://www.nasdevices.com

[21] Nelson, M., et al. Fast Transparent Migration for Virtual Machines. In Proceedings of USENIX '05 (Anaheim, CA, April 10-15, 2005). 391-394.

[22] Ousterhout, J., et al. The Case for RamClouds: Scalable High-Performance Storage Entirely in DRAM. In SIGOPS OSR. December, 2009.

[23] Pelley, S., et al. Power Routing: Dynamic Power Provisioning in the Data Center. In Proceedings of ASPLOS XV (Pittsburgh, PA, March 13-17, 2010). 231-242.

[24] Pinheiro, E., et al. Failure Trends in a Large Disk Drive Population. In Proceedings of FAST '07 (San Jose, CA, February 13-16, 2007). 17-28.

[25] Terremark. http://vcloudexpress.terremark.com/

[26] VMware. http://www.vmware.com

[27] VMware. Capacity Planner. http://www.vmware.com/products/capacity-planner/

[28] VMware. Communities Forum. http://communities.vmware.com/thread/67695

[29] VMware. VMware Distributed Power Management Concepts and Use. http://www.vmware.com/files/pdf/DPM.pdf

[30] VMware. VMware DRS. http://www.vmware.com/products/drs/

[31] VMware. VMware High-Availability. http://www.vmware.com/products/high-availability

[32] VMware. VMware Site Recovery Manager. http://www.vmware.com/products/site-recovery-manager

[33] VMware. VirtualCenter 1.0 Support. http://www.vmware.com/support/vc/doc/c11clonevm.html

[34] VMware. VMware Update Manager Performance and Best Practices. http://www.vmware.com/pdf/vum_1.0_performance.pdf

[35] Yahoo! http://www.yahoo.com

Energy Proportional Datacenter Networks

Dennis Abts
Google Inc.
Madison, WI
dabts@google.com

Michael R. Marty
Google Inc.
Madison, WI
mikemarty@google.com

Philip M. Wells
Google Inc.
Madison, WI
pwells@google.com

Peter Klausler
Google Inc.
Madison, WI
pmk@google.com

Hong Liu
Google Inc.
Mountain View, CA
hongliu@google.com

ABSTRACT

Numerous studies have shown that datacenter computers rarely operate at full utilization, leading to a number of proposals for creating servers that are *energy proportional* with respect to the computation that they are performing. In this paper, we show that as servers themselves become more energy proportional, the datacenter network can become a significant fraction (up to 50%) of cluster power. In this paper we propose several ways to design a high-performance datacenter network whose power consumption is more proportional to the amount of traffic it is moving— that is, we propose *energy proportional datacenter networks*.

We first show that a flattened butterfly topology itself is inherently more power efficient than the other commonly proposed topology for high-performance datacenter networks. We then exploit the characteristics of modern plesiochronous links to adjust their power and performance envelopes dynamically. Using a network simulator, driven by both synthetic workloads and production datacenter traces, we characterize and understand design tradeoffs, and demonstrate an 85% reduction in power — which approaches the ideal energy-proportionality of the network.

Our results also demonstrate two challenges for the designers of future network switches: 1) We show that there is a significant power advantage to having independent control of each unidirectional channel comprising a network link, since many traffic patterns show very asymmetric use, and 2) system designers should work to optimize the high-speed channel designs to be more energy efficient by choosing optimal data rate and equalization technology. Given these assumptions, we demonstrate that energy proportional datacenter communication is indeed possible.

Categories and Subject Descriptors

C.2.1 [**Network Architecture and Design**]: Network communications; Topology; B.4.3 [**Interconnections**]: Fiber optics; Topology

General Terms

Performance, Design

Keywords

Low-power networking, Datacenter networks, Interconnection networks

1. INTRODUCTION

The cost of power and its associated delivery and cooling are becoming significant factors in the total expenditures of large-scale datacenters. Barroso and Hölzle recently showed a mismatch between common server workload profiles and server energy efficiency [3]. In particular, they show that a typical Google cluster spends most of its time within the 10-50% CPU utilization range, but that servers are inefficient at these levels. They therefore make the call for *energy proportional computing systems* that ideally consume almost no power when idle and gradually consume more power as the activity level increases.

Servers and their processors are the obvious targets to improve energy proportionality because they are today's primary power consumers. Today's typical multi-tiered datacenter network consumes little power, relative to servers, because of its high degree of *over-subscription*. As an example of over-subscription, machines connected to the same rack switch (i.e., the first tier) have significantly more bandwidth to each other than to machines in other racks. The level of bandwidth over-subscription is typically an order of magnitude or more for each subsequent tier.

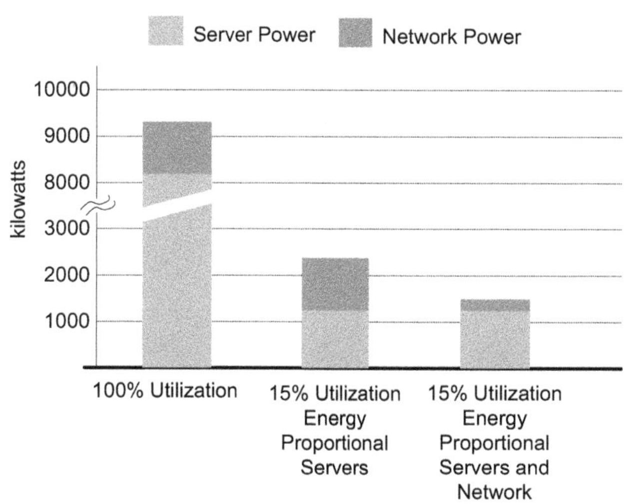

Figure 1: Comparison of server and network power

Going forward, there are many factors that will drive adoption of high-performance datacenter networks with much greater bisection bandwidth, thereby eliminating or reducing over-subscription. Greenberg et al. [7] argue that less over-subscription enables dynamic resource allocation across large pools of servers. Thus clusters can be virtualized and servers can achieve better utilization because communication-intensive jobs can be run anywhere rather than being constrained to a single tier or rack (i.e., rack affinity). Over-subscription can also couple the failure domains to the bandwidth domains. For example, if applications must schedule with rack affinity for bandwidth reasons, then the failure of a rack switch or power distribution unit can adversely affect service availability. Decoupling the failure domain from the available network bandwidth domain can enable greater opportunities for cluster-level file systems such as Lustre [24], GFS [6], Hadoop [5] and more. Barroso and Hölzle also suggest that even with abundant amounts of thread-level parallelism, the effects of Amdahl's Law can start to become a limitation without cost-effective, high port-count, high bandwidth networking [4]. We also see the emergence of faster storage technologies, like flash and phase-change memory, as another driver of increased cluster network bandwidth. A substantial increase in cluster bisection bandwidth, however, requires significantly more switching chips with faster, more power-consuming links. We therefore argue that network power will become a first-order operating expenditure in future datacenter networks.

Figure 1 illustrates the impact of network power in a target system we develop in Section 2, where we assume each of 32k servers consumes 250 watts at peak load. Even with a high-performance datacenter network based on a folded-Clos topology (i.e., fat trees) [2, 7, 17, 20] the network consumes only 12% of overall power at full utilization. But since servers typically operate at much lower levels of utilization, and are becoming more energy proportional, the network power cannot be ignored — much in the same way that Amdahl's arguments for performance demonstrate diminishing returns when focusing on only one part of the system. For instance, if the system is 15% utilized (servers and network) and the servers are fully energy-proportional, the network will then consume nearly 50% of overall power. At 15% load, making the network energy proportional results in a savings of 975,000 watts regardless of whether servers are energy proportional. Assuming an average industrial electricity rate of \$0.07 per kilowatt-hour [25], and a datacenter PUE of 1.6,[1] this results in a savings of approximately \$3.8M over a four year service life of the network!

Unfortunately, existing or proposed datacenter networks exhibit very little *dynamic range*. That is, the power consumed when the network is idle is still significant compared to the power consumed when the network is fully utilized. A primary reason is that high-speed channels are "always on" regardless of whether they are flowing data packets. The channels cannot be quickly deactivated and then reactivated without negotiation from both sides of the channel to establish data rate, symbol alignment, and lane alignment. Further exacerbating the problem is that deactivating a link appears as if the link is faulty to the routing algorithm, in which case packets must either be buffered or routed around the deactivated link. Buffering for extended periods of time is not feasible and will lead to packet discards or backpressure depending on the network's flow control mechanism. On the other hand, changing routes in many networks require coordination among all nodes to ensure that no newly injected traffic takes a path that would cross an inactive link.

[1]The PUE, or Power Usage Effectiveness, is the ratio of a datacenter's total power to the power actually used by computing equipment. We use a value of 1.6, which is the middle-point between industry-leading datacenters (1.2 [12]) and the EPA's 2007 survey (2.0 [26]).

Our goal is to provide a network that supports *energy proportional communication*. That is, the amount of energy consumed is proportional to the traffic intensity (offered load) in the network. We tackle this goal from multiple angles. First we demonstrate that a datacenter network based on the flattened butterfly topology results in a more power-efficient network and therefore lowers operational expenditures. With a solid foundation for a high-performance power-efficient network, we then add dynamic range by periodically estimating the future bandwidth needs of each link and reconfiguring its data rate to meet those requirements while consuming less power. Specifically, this paper makes the following contributions:

- We analytically demonstrate how a network based on the flattened butterfly topology consumes less power than a bandwidth-comparable and size-comparable folded-Clos (recently proposed for datacenter interconnects [2, 7, 20]). Our example demonstrates \$1.6M in energy savings over a four-year lifetime of the network.
- We develop techniques to make the datacenter network more energy proportional by increasing its *dynamic range*. We do so by exploiting properties of both the flattened butterfly topology and modern high-speed links that support multiple data rates.
- Using detailed event-driven simulation, we evaluate our energy-proportional communication schemes with traces taken from a production datacenter running web search applications. We show a $6\times$ reduction in power using the same topology, leading to a potential four-year energy savings of an *additional* \$2.4M in a full-scale network.
- Finally, based on our analysis, we propose opportunities for switch designers to further enable energy proportional networks, and we introduce the concept of *dynamic topologies*, where in addition to dynamically adjusting the data rate of existing links, those links are dynamically powered up and down, in effect creating a dynamically changing topology.

2. LOW-POWER, HIGHLY-SCALABLE TOPOLOGIES

In this section, we propose the flattened butterfly (FBFLY) topology as a cornerstone for energy-proportional communication in large-scale clusters with 10,000 servers or more. We will show why the topology, by itself, is lower in power than a comparable folded-Clos with equivalent bisection bandwidth and same number of hosts. While commonplace in high-performance computing interconnects, folded-Clos networks (aka fat trees [17]) are being proposed as a means to provide a datacenter network with little or no over-subscription [7, 9].[2] Not only does the flattened butterfly result in lower power at full utilization, but it is also more amenable to techniques to increase the dynamic range of network power, the topic of Section 3.

2.1 Background: Flattened Butterfly

The *flattened butterfly* (FBFLY) k-ary n-flat topology [15] takes advantage of recent high port count switches [16, 23] to create a scalable, yet low-diameter network. This is accomplished by making the deliberate tradeoff of fewer physical links compared to a

[2]In this paper, we do not consider traditional multi-tiered cluster networks, common in today's datacenters, because of their high degrees of over-subscription, leading to low performance for workloads that are not localized to a single rack or tier.

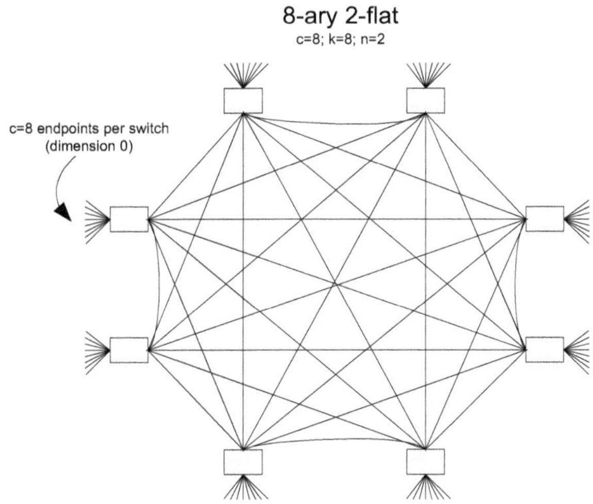

Figure 2: Logical diagram of an 8-ary 2-flat flattened butterfly topology.

folded-Clos, at the expense of increased routing complexity to load balance the available links. The FBFLY topology, for example, *requires* adaptive routing to load balance arbitrary traffic patterns, whereas a folded-Clos has multiple physical paths to each destination and very simple routing.

A flattened butterfly is a multi-dimensional direct network, in many ways like a torus (k-ary n-cube), where every switch in the network is connected to hosts as well as other switches. The biggest difference is that in a torus, each dimension is connected as a ring, and in an FBFLY, each dimension is fully connected. That is, within a FBFLY dimension all nodes connect to all others.

This interconnection is depicted in Figure 2, which shows 2-dimensional FBFLY (8-ary 2-flat) with $8 \times 8 = 64$ nodes and eight 15-port switch chips. Scaling the number of dimensions in a FBFLY consists, essentially, of taking this single 8-switch group, replicating it 8 times, and interconnecting each switch with its peer in the other 7 groups (i.e., each upper-left switch connects to the other 7 upper left switches in the other 7 groups). Doing so yields an 8-ary 3-flat with $8^3 = 512$ nodes, and 64 switch chips each with 22 ports. The flattened butterfly topology and packet traversal can also be explained with a simple metaphor. Consider a chessboard, with eight squares in each of two dimensions. Each square on the chessboard represents a switch that routes packets. Packets traverse the flattened butterfly in the same manner that a rook moves on a chessboard: on each turn (hop), we can move to an arbitrary square (switch) in a given dimension.

Though a FBFLY scales exponentially with the number of dimensions, you can also scale by increasing the radix. When possible, it is advantageous to build the highest-radix, lowest dimension FBFLY that scales high enough and does not exceed the number of available switch ports. This reduces the number of hops a packet takes as well as the number of links and switches in the system.

As you scale up a FBFLY, there are two properties of the topology that reduce both capital and operational expenditures: 1) the topology can take advantage of *packaging locality* in the sense that nodes which are in close physical proximity can be cabled with inexpensive copper cables, 2) it uses fewer optical transceivers and fewer switching chips than a comparable folded-Clos, and therefore consumes less power, as we show in Section 2.2.

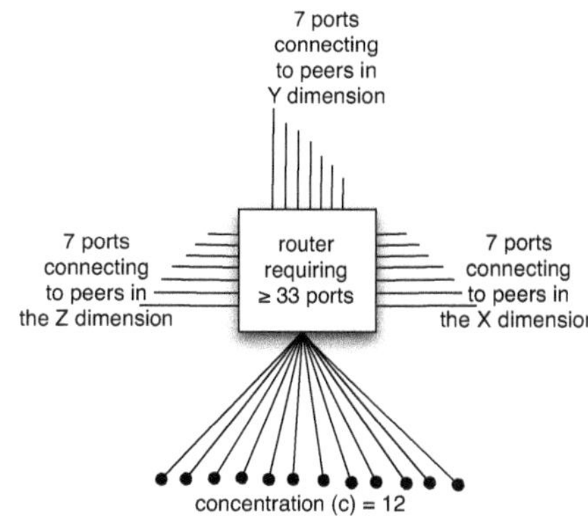

Figure 3: A 33-port router necessary to implement an 8-ary 4-flat with a concentration of 12 (over-subscription of 3:2).

2.1.1 *Over-subscription in Flattened Butterfly*

While we argue for high performance datacenter networks with little over-subscription, the technique remains a practical and pragmatic approach to reduce power (as well as capital expenditures), especially when the level of over-subscription is modest. Though the original work on the flattened butterfly topology did not describe it, over-subscription can easily be achieved, if desired, by changing the *concentration* (c), or number of terminal nodes, at each switch. For example, we could provide a concentration of 12 nodes per switch in an 8-ary 4-flat using a 33 ported router (see Figure 3) which would allow the network to scale to: ck^{n-1}, or $12 \times 8^3 = 6144$ nodes, instead of 4096 nodes with 8 nodes per switch. We express this using the tuple (c, k, n) to describe a k-ary n-flat with c nodes per switch. Nonetheless, our evaluation and topology comparison in this paper does not over subscribe the network in order to provide the maximum performance ceiling when operating at full power.

2.2 Topology Power Comparison

A datacenter network based on the flattened butterfly topology uses less hardware compared to a folded-Clos network of equivalent size and performance. This, by itself, results in a more power-efficient network and lower operating expenditures. To illustrate this power efficiency, we develop a baseline system with 32k server nodes and compare the first-order part counts between a flattened butterfly and folded-Clos. The number of switch chips, in particular, dominates the power consumption of the network. We also report the number of expensive optical transceivers required by the two topologies, since they tend to dominate the capital expenditure of the interconnect. A more detailed capital expenditure cost comparison between the two topologies can be found in [15].

For the purposes of this comparison, we make the following assumptions:

- A 36-ported switch (router node) where ports operate at 40 Gb/s,
- Each switch consumes 100 watts regardless of whether of what combination of "always on" links it is driving, e.g., electrical backplane, electrical cable, or optical,[3]
- Each host network interface controller (NIC) consumes 10 watts at full utilization, and
- The same switch chips are used throughout the interconnect.

[3]We arrive at 100 Watts by assuming each of 144 SerDes (one per lane per port) consume $\approx$0.7 Watts

Table 1: Comparing energy consumption of different topologies for fixed bisection bandwidth

Parameter Description	Folded Clos	FBFLY (8-ary 5-flat)
Number of hosts (N)	32k	32k
Bisection B/W (40 Gb/s links)	655 Tb/s	655 Tb/s
Number of electrical links	49,152	47,104
Number of optical links	65,536	43,008
Number of switch chips	**8,235**	**4,096**
Total power (W)	**1,146,880**	**737,280**
Power per bisection B/W (W/Gb/s)	1.75	1.13

The second assumption simplifies the comparison even though our data in Figure 5, showing the profile of an existing switch chip, uses 25% less power to drive an electrical link compared to an optical link. This represents a second-order effect in our comparison, and is actually disadvantageous for the flattened butterfly, since other factors come into play (such as packaging locality).

When comparing topologies, something must be held constant in order for the results to be meaningful— our comparison is based on a fixed bisection bandwidth. The number of ports per switch per switch necessary to build a k-ary n-flat FBFLY with concentration c is: $p = c + (k-1)(n-1)$. Thus a 32k node 8-ary 5-flat with $c = k = 8$ requires 36 ports. We assume that all short electrical links (<5m) will use passive copper cables, and anything longer requires an optical link. The comparable 3-stage folded-Clos is built from the same 36-ported switch. For the flattened butterfly, the first dimension, which interconnects all the switches within a local domain, can use short (<1m) electrical links. Similarly, all $c = k = 8$ links from the hosts to switch can be electrical. In general, this *packaging locality* allows for e electrical links: $e = (k-1) + c$, which make a significant fraction of the overall links:

$$f_e = \frac{(k-1)+c}{c+(k-1)(n-1)}$$

In this case $\frac{15}{36} \approx 42\%$ of the FBFLY links are inexpensive, lower-power, electrical links. However, for ease of comparison we assume that *all* links are the same power efficiency (which does not favor the FBFLY topology).

The total number of switches for the FBFLY is given by:

$$S_{FBFLY} = k^{n-1} = 8^4 = 4,096$$

For the folded-Clos, we use 27 36-port switches to build a 324-port non-blocking router chassis for stage-2 and stage-3 of a multi-staged folded-Clos network.[4] We assume that the backplane connections within the 324-port stage-2 and stage-3 switches are free. Thus the folded-Clos requires

$$S_{stage3}\left\lceil\frac{32k}{324}\right\rceil = 102, S_{stage2}\left\lceil\frac{32k}{324/2}\right\rceil = 203$$

chassis, and the total number of switch chips required for the folded-Clos is: $S_{Clos} = 27 \times (S_{tier3} + S_{tier2}) = 27 \times 305 = 8,235$. In this example 32k system build with 36-ported switches, there are 8,235 switches in the folded-Clos, however only ports on 8,192 switches are used.[5] The results are summarized in Table 1.

[4]We could also build a 648-ported chassis, which might reduce cost, but will require the same number of switch chips, and same total power according to our simple model.

[5]There are some unused ports which we do not count in the power analysis.

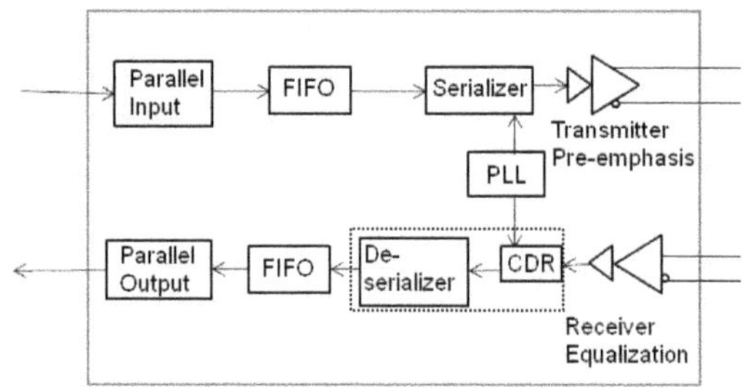

Figure 4: Example block diagram of a SerDes block.

Overall, as Table 1 shows, the cluster with the flattened butterfly interconnect uses 409,600 fewer watts than a folded-Clos with the same bisection bandwidth. Assuming an average industrial electricity rate of $0.07 per kW hour [25] and an average PUE of 1.6 [26], using the flattened butterfly topology alone results in over $1.6M of energy savings over a four-year lifetime of the cluster. Nonetheless, the "always on" nature of today's networks leaves a lot of cost savings on the table without additional mechanisms: Even the baseline FBFLY network consumes 737,280 watts resulting in a four year power cost of $2.89M.

We have considered other configurations, using different switch chips with more ports and more power demand, and the trends shown in Table 1 continue to hold for this scale of cluster.

3. ADDING DYNAMIC RANGE

The previous section showed that the flattened butterfly topology inherently consumes less power than a bandwidth- and size-comparable folded-Clos. In this section, we seek to further improve network power by making communication more energy-proportional to the amount of data being transmitted. We do this by dynamically tuning individual links to match the required performance while consuming as little power as possible.

3.1 Background: Plesiochronous Links

High-speed channels are typically constructed from several serialized *lanes* that operate at the same data rate, with a *physical unit* (phit) being striped across all the active lanes. Channels commonly operate *plesiochronously*, where the core logic in the router operates at a frequency different than that of the I/O channels. All I/O channels can themselves run asynchronously, where frequency may vary a small amount ($\approx \pm$100ppm) among all the ports. The physical layer (PHY) uses a serializer/deserializer (*SerDes*, see Figure 4), which accepts a phit of data and "squeezes" it onto a high-speed serial bit stream for transmission. On the other side of the channel, the SerDes receives the serial bit stream, where it reassembles the phit and passes it up to the *data-link* layer. Frequency differences

Table 2: InfiniBand support for multiple data rates.

InfiniBand data rate	Name	Data rate (Gb/s)
Single Data Rate	1× SDR	2.5 Gb/s
	4× SDR	10 Gb/s
Double Data Rate	1× DDR	5 Gb/s
	4× DDR	20 Gb/s
Quad Data Rate	1× QDR	10 Gb/s
	4× QDR	40 Gb/s

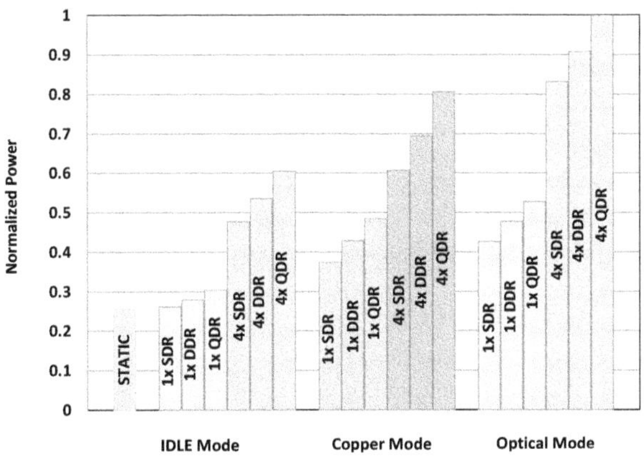

Figure 5: Dynamic range of an InfiniBand switch chip for both copper and optical links.

among ports and between ports and core router logic are absorbed by the input and output FIFOs of the SerDes.

The problem, in terms of power, is that these channels are *always on* regardless of whether they are flowing data packets, because they must still send *idle* packets to maintain byte and lane alignment across the multiple lanes. Even though they are always on, plesiochronous channels often do have *dynamic range*, in terms of their ability to vary their data rate and power consumption.

One good example of dynamic channel range is the InfiniBand architectural specification, which defines multiple operational data rates (see Table 2). Figure 5 illustrates the normalized dynamic range of an off-the-shelf InfiniBand switch available today, where it is possible to manually adjust the link rates corresponding to Table 2. The maximum link rate of 40 Gb/s is obtained with four lanes running at quad data rate (QDR) of 10 Gb/s each. However it is possible to operate the link with less lanes and at a lower data rate to reduce the power consumption of the always-on link. The dynamic range of this particular chip is 64% in terms of power, and 16X in terms of performance. Though we lack detailed dynamic power range numbers, the Cray YARC [23] switch has 64 ports that similarly can operate as 1×, 2×, or 3× lanes with each lane operating at a range of frequencies from 1.25–6.25 Gb/s. Thus each YARC link can transmit 1.25–18.75 Gb/s in each direction.

Both InfiniBand and YARC allow links to be configured for a specified speed and width, though the *reactivation time* of the link can vary from several nanoseconds to several microseconds. For example, when the link rate changes by 1×, 2×, and 4× (e.g., InfiniBand's SDR, DDR and QDR modes), the chip simply changes the receiving *Clock Data Recovery* (CDR) bandwidth and re-locks the CDR. Since most SerDes today use digital CDR at the receive path (Figure 4), the locking process for receiving data at a different data rates is fast, ≈50ns–100ns for the typical to worst case.

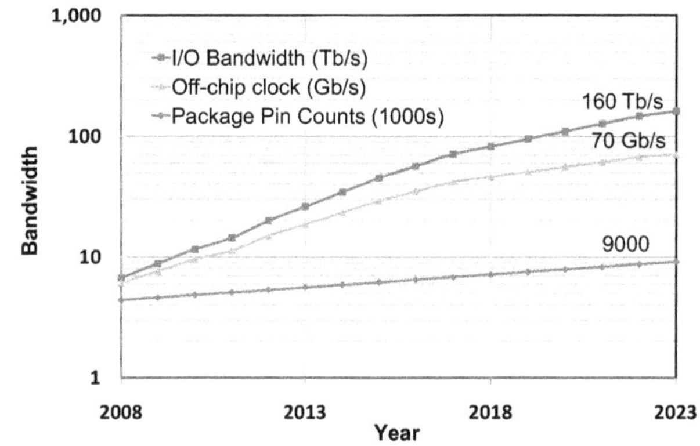

Figure 6: Bandwidth trends from International Roadmap for Semiconductors (ITRS).

Adding and removing lanes is a relatively slower process compared to link rate changes, but the process could be optimized within a few microseconds.

While there exists opportunity to improve the energy-efficiency of each channel [10], going forward we expect more I/Os per switch package, operating at higher data rates, further increasing chip power consumption (Figure 6).

3.2 Exploiting a Link's Dynamic Range

The previous section outlines how modern plesiochronous links already show dynamic range in their performance and power, but in current networks and switches, maximum link speed is typically something that must be manually configured. We propose adding additional switch mechanisms to exploit those capabilities by reconfiguring link speeds on-the-fly to match bandwidth (and power) with the traffic demand. In doing so, communication can be made more energy proportional without fundamentally changing the topology, traffic routes, or even performance of the network.

The essence of our proposal is to periodically estimate the future bandwidth needs of each link, and reconfigure its data rate to meet those requirements while consuming less power. However a couple pragmatic requirements arise when taking this approach: 1) this approach requires the ability to accurately predict the future bandwidth requirements of the link, and 2) it requires the ability to tolerate a link reactivation that is non-instantaneous.

Predicting future bandwidth demands can be done, in classic computer architecture fashion, by using recent history as a guide. This could be accomplished with the mechanisms already used for congestion sensing in adaptive routing [14, 23]. For example, credit-based link-level flow control can deliver *precise* information on the congestion of upstream receive buffers, or *channel utilization* can be used over some timescale as a proxy for congestion. However, because datacenter workloads are bursty over a wide range of timescales, care must be taken to avoid both averaging over too long of a timescale, and meta-instability arising from too-frequent reconfiguration.

A number of strategies can be employed to tolerate reactivation latency. One option is to remove the reactivating output port from the list of legal adaptive routes and drain its output buffer before reconfiguration. This scheme relies on sufficient path diversity within the topology so that traffic that might normally route to that port is able to be redirected to other paths.

A second option is to continue to allow traffic to be routed to the output port, and then either drop packets (in a lossy network), or supply back-pressure (in a loss-less network) when the output buffers fill up. Any packet routed to that port will incur an additional latency as the link reactivates, but if the reactivation is small, this latency is likely to be tolerated by the application. This scheme relies on the congestion-sensing and adaptivity mechanisms to automatically route around the link that is undergoing reconfiguration in order to avoid excessive back-pressure or packet loss.

A third option is to combine these two methods depending on the length of time the reactivation is expected to take.

Exploiting links' dynamic range is possible with other topologies, such as a folded-Clos. However, there are a couple of important factors that make a high-performance flattened butterfly a great fit. First, a FBFLY already relies on adaptive routing in order to balance the load and achieve high performance. These same mechanisms can be used to predict a link's future bandwidth demands. Second, in a FBFLY, the choice of a packet's route is inherently a *local* decision (though it must abide by global rules). This nicely matches our proposed strategy, where the decision of link speed is also entirely local to the switch chip.

3.3 Proposed Heuristics

With the inherent capabilities of the flattened butterfly topology, heuristics for power-optimizing links can range from simple to complex. We propose a simple mechanism where the switch tracks the utilization of each of its links over an *epoch*, and then makes an adjustment at the end of the epoch. We set a target utilization for each link, and if the actual utilization is less than the target, we detune the speed of the link to half the current rate, down to the minimum. If the utilization exceeds the target, then the link rate is doubled up to the maximum. The target utilization should not be set too high, because that will saturate the network and lead to excessive performance degradation. The epoch duration needs to be sized to amortize the time needed to reactivate the link, but still react quickly enough to bursty and dynamic traffic patterns.

We use link utilization over the previous epoch as the only input to our decision function. The reason we do not need to consider other common inputs for adaptive routing, such as output buffer occupancy or available credits, is that utilization effectively captures both: if we have data to send, and credits to send it, then the utilization will go up, and we should upgrade the speed of the link. If we either don't have data or don't have enough credits, utilization will fall, and there is no reason to keep the link at high speed.

When links are undergoing reactivation, we do not explicitly remove them from the set of legal output ports, but rather rely on the adaptive routing mechanism to sense congestion and automatically route traffic around the link.

3.3.1 Independent Channel Control

The routing algorithm views each unidirectional channel in the network as a routing resource. However, the physical and data-link layer may treat a *pair* of unidirectional channels, in opposing directions, as a combined entity (typically called the *link*). Thus, the load on the link may be *asymmetric*, i.e., one channel may have much higher load than the other, but the link pair must be reconfigured together to match the requirements of the channel with the highest load.

Although not a capability of current chips, we also propose and evaluate the ability to *independently* tune the data rates of the unidirectional channels of a link pair.

Based on the data in Figure 5 that reflects an existing switch chip, there is not much power saving opportunity for powering off links

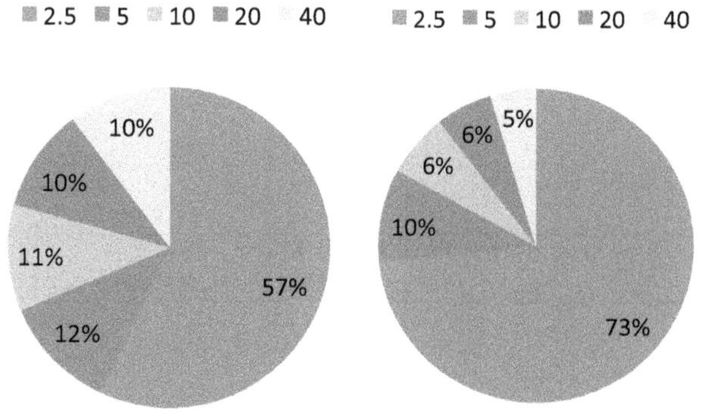

(a) Bidirectional link pair (b) Independent control

Figure 7: Fraction of time spent at each link speed (Gb/s).

entirely. Nonetheless, Section 5 discusses the opportunity to power off links if future switch chips offered a true "power off" state.

4. EVALUATION

Having identified a flattened butterfly as inherently lower-power, we focus the detailed evaluation of our dynamic range techniques on that topology alone, though the proposed mechanisms and policies described can also apply to other topologies.

4.1 Methodology

We evaluate an energy-proportional FBFLY using an in-house event-driven network simulator, which has been heavily modified to support future high-performance networks. We model a 15-ary 3-flat FBFLY (3375 nodes) with no over-subscription, so that every host, on a uniform random traffic pattern, can inject and receive at full line rate. Links have a maximum bandwidth of 40 Gb/s, and can be detuned to 20, 10, 5 and 2.5 Gb/s, similar to the InfiniBand switch in Figure 5. We model a network with credit-based, cut-through flow control, and adaptively route on each hop based solely on the output queue depth. Switches are both input and output buffered. We assume the same reactivation time, defaulting to a conservative value of $1\mu s$, no matter what mode the link is entering. We study the sensitivity to link activation time in Section 4.2.2.

We use three workloads for this study: one synthetic and two taken from traces of a production Google datacenter. *Uniform* is a uniform random workload, where each host repeatedly sends a 512k message to a new random destination. *Advert* is a trace from an advertising service, and *Search* is from a web search service. In both applications, distributed file system traffic (e.g., GFS [6]) accounts for a significant fraction of traffic. In order to model future applications which take advantage of such a high-performance network, the later two workloads have been significantly scaled up from the original traces, and application placement has been randomized across the cluster in order to capture emerging trends such as cluster virtualization. Though scaled up, these workloads share a common trait: they are very bursty at a variety of timescales, yet exhibit low *average* network utilization of 5–25%.

4.2 Results

In this section we describe results from our simulations. We compare results to a baseline full power system, as well as one with *ideal* energy proportionality.

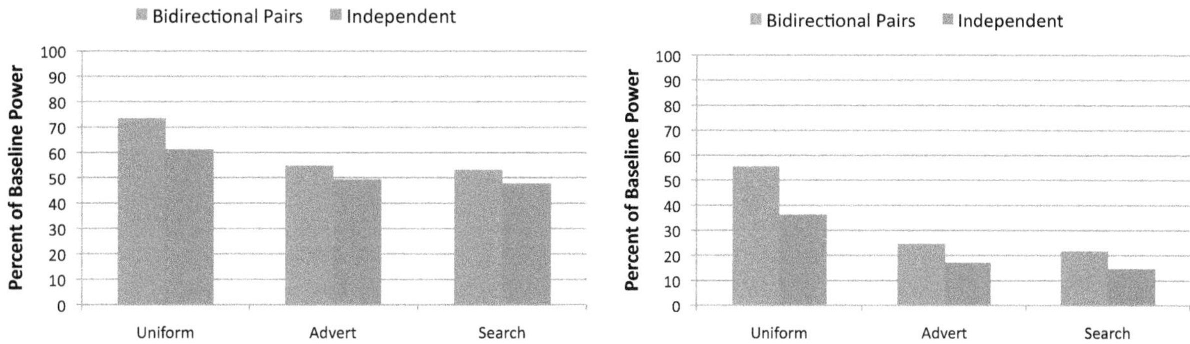

(a) Assuming optical channel power from Figure 5.

(b) Assuming ideally energy-proportional channels.

Figure 8: Network power when dynamically detuning FBFLY links

4.2.1 Power and Performance

Our first set of experiments explore the ability of our proposed heuristics to downgrade links to match the bandwidth required by the workload. Figure 7 shows the aggregate fraction of time links spend at different speeds for the *Search* workload. This figure assumes a $1\mu s$ reconfiguration time for the links, a $10\mu s$ epoch, and a 50% target channel utilization. We model both mechanisms described in Section 3.3 for reducing the speed and power of a link, where a bidirectional link-pair must be tuned to the same speed (Figure 7(a)), and the more flexible option, where a unidirectional channel can be tuned independently to different speeds (Figure 7(b)).

We first see that energy proportionality works: in a workload with low average utilization, most links spend a majority of their time in the lowest power/performance state.

We also see that the ability to independently control each unidirectional channel nearly halves the fraction of time spent at the faster speeds (10, 20, and 40 Gb/s), and commensurately increases the fraction of time spent at the slowest speed (2.5 Gb/s). This channel asymmetry arises in part due to workload characteristics. For example, depending on replication factor and the ratio of reads to writes, a file server in a distributed file system may respond to more reads (i.e., inject data into the network) than writes (i.e., receive data from the network), or vice versa. Perhaps surprisingly, the charts look very similar for the uniform random workload (not shown) even though the average channel utilization is very uniform. The reason is simply that the workload is bursty across the relatively short $10\mu s$ epoch.

Figure 8(a) shows the percent of power consumed by an energy proportional flattened butterfly network compared to a baseline FBFLY with all links operating at full bandwidth (40 Gb/s). We report power based on the amount of time each links spends at a given speed given the data from Figure 5. Because links spend a majority of their time in low-power mode, the power for the entire network approaches the relative power of that slowest mode ($\approx$42% of full power).

Figure 8(b) shows the same experiments as shown in Figure 8(a), except that we assume channels are ideally energy-proportional with offered load themselves. Thus a channel operating at 2.5 Gb/s uses only 6.125% the power of a channel operating at 40 Gb/s. We can see that together, energy proportional channels and the ability to independently tune each unidirectional channel provide a $6\times$ advantage in terms of network power for both advertising and search workloads.

The middle column of points in Figure 9(a) demonstrates the difference in performance when using an energy proportional FBFLY. This figure shows that the increase in mean latency, at a 50% target utilization and $1\mu s$ reactivation time, is only 10–$50\mu s$. Unlike many distributed scientific computations, typical datacenter applications can tolerate such small changes in latency. Though not shown, the additional mean latency with independent channel tuning is $75\mu s$ for the two datacenter application traces and $200\mu s$ for the uniform random workload.

A flattened butterfly network that always operated in the slowest and lowest power mode would consume 42% of the baseline power (or 6.1% assuming ideal channels). Our proposed energy proportional FBFLY comes within a few percent of that low power configuration in several cases. However, unlike all of the configurations above, ***a network that always operates in the slowest mode fails to keep up with the offered host load.***

An ideally energy proportional FBFLY network would include ideal channels and zero reactivation time. When a link had something to transmit, it does so at full speed (and power), and when it does not have something to transmit, it consumes no power. In other words, the energy consumed by the network would exactly equal the average utilization of all links in the network. On the baseline system, our three workloads have an average utilization, and hence ideal power relative to the baseline, of 23% for *Uniform*, 6% for *Search* and 5% for *Advert*. Using our proposed heuristics, ideal independent channels, and a conservative reconfiguration time of $1\mu s$, we can achieve relative power of 36%, 17%, and 15% of baseline, respectively— a remarkable feat considering the simplicity of our proposed heuristics.

4.2.2 Sensitivity to Target Link Utilization and Reconfiguration Latency

Target link utilization is an important factor when tuning link speeds. If set too low, then the network is missing out on opportunities to save power. If set too high, the network will be beyond saturation and performance will suffer. In Figure 9(a), we explore three values for target link utilization: 25, 50, and 75%. For the workload traces, the latency increases substantially more at 75% utilization than at 25%. Running with utilization much higher than 75% is not feasible for these workloads, because the network saturates. We don't show the power data when varying target utilization, though interestingly, there is very little difference for any of the workloads when using reactivation times of $1\mu s$ or less. The reason is, again, that these workloads are bursty: either they are sending data, and in (or transitioning to) high-power mode, or not

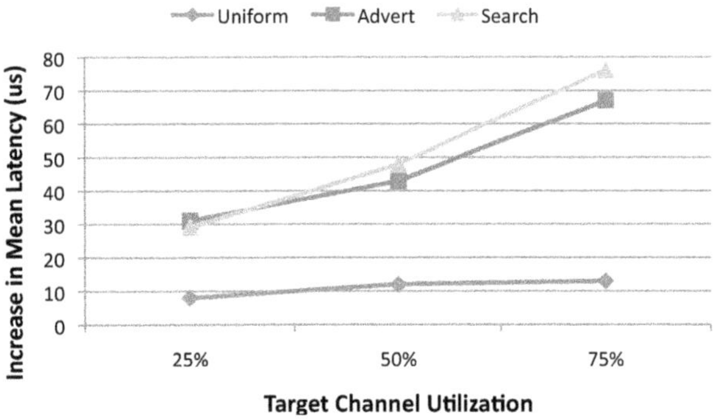

(a) Additional mean latency for a range of target channel utilization. Based on $1\mu s$ reactivation time and paired links.

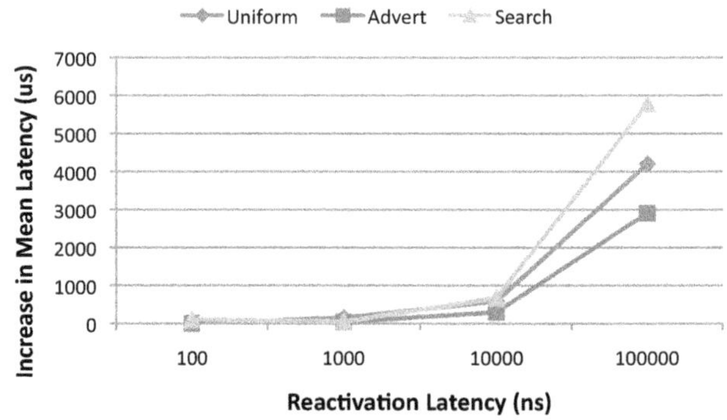

(b) Additional mean latency for a range of reactivation times. Based on 50% target utilization and paired links.

Figure 9: Sensitivity of target channel utilization and reactivation times

sending data and in (or transitioning to) the low-power mode. They don't spend much time in the intermediate modes when the reactivation times (and hence utilization measurement epoch) is small.

Finally, we report our results assuming a range of link reactivation penalties, from 100ns–$100\mu s$ in Figure 9(b). We set the epoch at $10\times$ the reactivation latency, which bounds the overhead of reactivation to 10%. Yet as the reactivation time rises to $10\mu s$, the increase in mean network latency approaches 1ms. With a $100\mu s$ reactivation, latency rises to several additional milliseconds, an overhead that can impact many different types of applications. Clearly our proposed techniques only become feasible when the reactivation time is less than $10\mu s$. Though we do not show a power graph, increasing the reactivation time (and hence utilization measurement epoch) does decrease the opportunity to save power. Especially for the *Uniform* workload, which is less bursty than the traces at larger timescales, the power savings completely disappear for $100\mu s$. For the two traces at 50% utilization, the reduction in power savings for $100\mu s$ is only 2–5%. Fortunately actual link reactivation time of modern links can be much lower, less than our default value of $1\mu s$, which shows significant power reductions.

The bottom line is that for an insignificant change in performance, an energy proportional flattened butterfly can deliver up to a $6.6\times$ reduction in power. If we extrapolate this reduction to our full-scale network presented in Section 2.2, the potential additional four-year energy savings is \$2.5M.

5. DISCUSSION AND FUTURE WORK

Although the results in the previous section are impressive, there is still room for significant reductions in network power.

5.1 Better Heuristics

With the flexibility of the flattened butterfly topology, we were able to apply a simple but effective heuristic to change the performance and power of individual links. However there remains opportunity to do even better: there is still a $3\times$ difference between our results and an ideally energy proportional network. With bursty workloads, it may be advantageous to immediately tune links to either their lowest or highest performance mode without going through the intermediate steps. A better algorithm might also take into account the difference in link resynchronization latency to account for whether the lane speed is changing, the number of lanes are changing, or both. Opportunities may also exist for more complex predictive models.

5.2 Dynamic Topologies

In this paper, we demonstrated energy proportional networking by dynamically changing the performance and power envelope of individual links. However we did not evaluate powering off a link for two reasons. First, we based our evaluation on the data from the switch chip characterized in Figure 5, which shows very little additional power savings in shutting off a link entirely. Second, powering off links fundamentally changes the topology and routing, which is not currently supported in our simulation environment. Yet a flattened butterfly is actually quite amenable to powering off links because routing decisions can be made locally. In contrast, powering off a link in the folded-Clos topology requires propagating routing changes throughout the entire network.

Though we do not evaluate it in detail, we wish to highlight a fertile area of future innovation: *dynamic topologies*, which could take advantage of future switch chips that offer a true power-off state. From a flattened butterfly, we can selectively disable links, thereby changing the topology to a more conventional mesh or torus. For example, we can disable links in the flattened butterfly topology to make it appear as a multidimensional *mesh*. As the offered demand increases, we can enable additional wrap-around links to create a *torus* with greater bisection bandwidth than the mesh at the expense of more power consumed by wrap-around links.[6] Additional links (which are cabled as part of the topology) are dynamically powered on as traffic intensity (offered load) increases. The notion of energy-proportional dynamic topology requires an energy-aware routing algorithm capable of placing new routes with live traffic. There are other subtleties to consider. For example, in a network with credit-based flow control, one direction of a link cannot operate without the other direction active in order to receive credits back.

5.3 Opportunities for Future Switch Chips

Independent of the wire protocols (e.g., ethernet, InfiniBand, proprietary, etc.) there are certain requirements that *enable* fine-grained energy proportional networks. Foremost is the ability to sense congestion at individual output links, and *dynamically* adapt around congestion that results from either hotspot traffic or power-optimized links. Adaptive routing techniques have been common

[6]Though constructing a torus with radix $k > 4$ requires additional virtual channels and awareness in the routing algorithm to avoid toroidal deadlocks.

to high-performance computing [13, 14, 22, 23] community. Our results indicate that using the same heuristics for adaptive routing can be applied to energy-proportional switching. The decision to change the data rate of a link can be made by hardware, firmware, or with an embedded processor as part of a managed switch.

Second, our results showed much more significant power-saving opportunities for links that are truly energy proportional. For example, a link configured for 2.5 Gb/s should ideally use only 6.25% the power of the link configured for 40 Gb/s. In contrast, Figure 5 shows that a switch chip today still consumes 42% the power when in the lower performance mode.

Third, we highlight the opportunity to allow individual channels, in a bidirectional link, to operate at different performance and power modes.

6. RELATED WORK

The area of large-scale interconnection networks has been a fertile area of research, however, the notion of *energy proportional* communication in large datacenter networks has remained an important and unexplored topic. Most of the research to date has focused on providing a more energy-efficient communication channel by optimizing the physical characteristics of the link [21].

Heller, et al., recently proposed ElasticTree [11] to save energy in datacenter networks. They do so by continuously monitoring datacenter traffic conditions at the system scale, and then determining which parts of the fabric can be powered off. Our work focuses on lower-power topologies and fine-grained techniques to reduce a link's power usage at the time-scale of nanoseconds or microseconds.

The ethernet ALR work [8] proposes similar ideas using ethernet, and evaluates them with an analytic model and simulation using synthetic traffic patterns. Our evaluation uses actual traces from a production datacenter. Since ethernet data rates vary by factors of 10 (e.g. 100 Mb/s, 1 Gb/s, 10 Gb/s) dynamic rate adapting typically requires link re-initialization, with reactivation latency in excess of 1ms, which adds an unacceptable delay for all the workloads evaluated.

Other approaches [18] have focused on the MPI run-time system to activate or deactivate links involved in the traffic pattern. This approach requires detailed knowledge of the traffic pattern *a priori*. Unfortunately, unlike high-performance computer (HPC) systems, datacenter networks run multiple workloads simultaneously, making the traffic pattern difficult or impossible to predict at the time of job scheduling. Our approach takes advantage of the congestion sensing heuristics used for adaptive routing and piggybacks on these techniques to sense traffic intensity, dynamically activating links as they are needed. Likewise, as the offered load is decreased, we sense the lower channel utilization and reduce the link speed to save power, similar to the approach of Mahadevan et al. [19] used for ethernet. However, rate adapting their ethernet channels takes 1–3 *seconds*. To tolerate several seconds of traffic disruption requires significant buffering and path diversity to mitigate performance impact during link rate adjustments.

The Hyper-X network, proposed by Ahn, et al., [1], also recognizes the benefits of a flattened butterfly topology for building highly scalable networks. They do not address power or energy efficiency in their work. Al-Fares, et al., [2] present a scheme to build a high-bandwidth datacenter network in a folded-Clos topology with commodity ethernet chips. They find that their network, composed of 1 Gb/s ethernet chips, uses considerably less power than a hierarchical network composed of high-end, power inefficient 10 Gb/s switches. Our topology comparison is independent of any particular switch chip. A switch with sufficient radix, routing, and congestion-sensing capabilities allows building a flattened butterfly topology, which uses half the number of switch chips of the folded-Clos. We then go even further by dynamically adjusting the power envelope of the network to increase its energy proportionality, an issue not tackled by Al-Fares et al. The VL2 datacenter network proposed by Greenberg, et al., [7] also uses the folded-Clos topology, as does Portland [20]. They do not address the issue of power.

7. CONCLUSIONS

As servers themselves become more energy proportional with respect to the computation that they are performing, the network becomes a significant fraction of cluster power. In this paper we propose several ways to build a cluster-scale network whose power consumption is more proportional to the amount of traffic it is transmitting.

As a first step, we compare the flattened butterfly and folded-Clos topologies and show that flattened butterfly alone is more energy-efficient resulting in a lower operating expense. Second, we show that the dynamic range for a commercial switch chip, which provides nearly 60% power savings compared to full utilization, can be used to dynamically reduce power. Detailed event-driven simulations of both synthetic workloads and production datacenter traces are used to characterize and understand design tradeoffs. By operating the network links at a data rate in proportion to the offered traffic intensity, an *energy proportional* datacenter network can further improve on the energy savings offered by the flattened butterfly topology. Modern switch chips capable of congestion sensing and adaptive routing already have the essential ingredients to make energy-proportional communication viable for large-scale clusters. Together, we show that our proposals can reduce operating expenses for a large-scale cluster by up to $3M over a four-year lifetime.

Our results also demonstrate two challenges for the designers of future switches: 1) We show that there is significant advantage to having independent control of each unidirectional channel comprising a network link, since these channels typically see asymmetric use, and 2) ideally, high-speed channel designs will evolve to be more energy proportional themselves, i.e., a link operating at 2.5 Gb/s should consume proportionately less power than a link operating at 40 Gb/s.

Acknowledgements

We are grateful to Urs Hölzle, Luiz Barroso, Chris Johnson, Bob Felderman, and Jim Laudon for supporting this work. We thank Florentina Popovici, Dan Gibson, and the anonymous reviewers for helpful feedback.

8. REFERENCES

[1] Jung Ho Ahn, Nathan Binkert, Al Davis, Moray McLaren, and Robert S. Schreiber. HyperX: topology, routing, and packaging of efficient large-scale networks. In *SC '09: Proceedings of the Conference on High Performance Computing Networking, Storage and Analysis*, pages 1–11. ACM, 2009.

[2] Mohammad Al-Fares, Alexander Loukissas, and Amin Vahdat. A scalable, commodity data center network architecture. In *SIGCOMM '08: Proceedings of the ACM SIGCOMM 2008 Conference on Data Communication*, 2008.

[3] Luiz André Barroso and Urs Hölzle. The case for energy-proportional computing. *Computer*, 40(12):33–37, 2007.

[4] Luiz André Barroso and Urs Hölzle. *The Datacenter as a Computer: An Introduction to Design of Warehouse-scale Machines*. Morgan Claypool, 2009.

[5] Borthakur, Dhruba. The Hadoop distributed file system: Architecture and design. `http://hadoop.apache.org/common/docs/r0.18.0/hdfs_design.pdf`.

[6] Sanjay Ghemawat, Howard Gobioff, and Shun-Tak Leung. The Google file system. In *19th ACM Symposium on Operating System Principles*, 2003.

[7] Albert Greenberg, James R. Hamilton, Navendu Jain, Srikanth Kandula, Changhoon Kim, Parantap Lahiri, David A. Maltz, Parveen Patel, and Sudipta Sengupta. Vl2: a scalable and flexible data center network. In *SIGCOMM '09: Proceedings of the ACM SIGCOMM 2009 Conference on Data Communication*, pages 51–62, 2009.

[8] Chamara Gunaratne, Kenneth Christensen, Bruce Nordman, and Stephen Suen. Reducing the energy consumption of ethernet with Adaptive Link Rate (ALR). *IEEE Trans. Comput.*, 57:448–461, April 2008.

[9] Chuanxiong Guo, Guohan Lu, Dan Li, Haitao Wu, Xuan Zhang, Yunfeng Shi, Chen Tian, Yongguang Zhang, and Songwu Lu. BCube: A high performance, server-centric network architecture for modular data centers. In *SIGCOMM '09: Proceedings of the ACM SIGCOMM 2009 Conference on Data Communication*, pages 63–74, 2009.

[10] H. Hatamkhani and Yang C-K.K. A study of the optimal data rate for minimum power of I/Os. In *IEEE Transactions on Circuits and Systems*, pages 1230–1234, 2006.

[11] Brandon Heller, Srini Seetharaman, Priya Mahadevan, Yiannis Yiakoumis, Puneet Sharma, Sujata Banerjee, and Nick McKeown. Elastictree: Saving energy in data cneter networks. In *Proceedings of the 7th USENIX Symposium on Networked System Design and Implementation (NSDI)*, pages 249-264. ACM, 2010.

[12] Google Inc. Efficient computingâ step 2: efficient datacenters. `http://www.google.com/corporate/green/datacenters/step2.html`.

[13] Nan Jiang, John Kim, and William J. Dally. Indirect adaptive routing on large scale interconnection networks. In *ISCA '09: Proceedings of the 36th annual International Symposium on Computer Architecture*, pages 220–231, 2009.

[14] John Kim, William J. Dally, and Dennis Abts. Adaptive routing in high-radix clos network. In *SC '06: Proceedings of the 2006 ACM/IEEE Conference on Supercomputing*, page 92, 2006.

[15] John Kim, William J. Dally, and Dennis Abts. Flattened butterfly: a cost-efficient topology for high-radix networks. In *ISCA '07: Proceedings of the 34th annual International Symposium on Computer Architecture*, pages 126–137, 2007.

[16] John Kim, William J. Dally, Brian Towles, and Amit K. Gupta. Microarchitecture of a high-radix router. In *ISCA '05: Proceedings of the 32nd Annual International Symposium on Computer Architecture*, pages 420–431, 2005.

[17] Charles E. Leiserson. Fat-trees: universal networks for hardware-efficient supercomputing. *IEEE Trans. Comput.*, 34(10):892–901, 1985.

[18] Jian Li, Lixin Zhang, Charles Lefurgy, Richard Treumann, and Wolfgang E. Denzel. Thrifty interconnection network for hpc systems. In *ICS '09: Proceedings of the 23rd International Conference on Supercomputing*, pages 505–506, 2009.

[19] Priya Mahadevan, Puneet Sharma, Sujata Banerjee, and Parthasarathy Ranganathan. Energy aware network operations. In *INFOCOM'09: Proceedings of the 28th IEEE International Conference on Computer Communications Workshops*, pages 25–30, 2009.

[20] Radhika Niranjan Mysore, Andreas Pamboris, Nathan Farrington, Nelson Huang, Pardis Miri, Sivasankar Radhakrishnan, Vikram Subramanya, and Amin Vahdat. Portland: a scalable fault-tolerant layer 2 data center network fabric. *SIGCOMM Comput. Commun. Rev.*, 39(4):39–50, 2009.

[21] Rambus Corporation. `http://www.rambus.com/us/patents/innovations/detail/low_power_multi_gbps.html`.

[22] S. Scott and G. Thorson. The Cray T3E Network: Adaptive Routing in a High Performance 3D Torus. In *Hot Interconnects 4*, Aug. 1996.

[23] Steve Scott, Dennis Abts, John Kim, and William J. Dally. The blackwidow high-radix clos network. In *ISCA '06: Proceedings of the 33rd annual International Symposium on Computer Architecture*, pages 16–28, 2006.

[24] Sun Microsystems. Lustre file system. `http://www.sun.com/software/products/lustre/`.

[25] U.S. Department of Energy. Average retail price of electricity. `http://www.eia.doe.gov/cneaf/electricity/epm/table5_6_a.html`.

[26] U.S. Environmental Protection Agency. Report to congress on server and datacenter energy efficiency. Public Law 109-431, August 2, 2007.

Improving the Future by Examining the Past

Charles P. Thacker
Microsoft Research

Abstract: During the last fifty years, the technology underlying computer systems has improved dramatically. As technology has evolved, designers have made a series of choices in the way it was applied in computers. In some cases, decisions that were made in the twentieth century make less sense in the twenty-first. Conversely, paths not taken might now be more attractive given the state of technology today, particularly in light of the limits the field is facing, such as the increasing gap between processor speed and storage access times and the difficulty of cooling today's computers.

In this talk, I'll discuss some of these choices and suggest some possible changes that might make computing better in the twenty-first century.

Categories & Subject Descriptors: C.0 Computer Systems Organization; General.

General Term: Design.

ISCA'10, June 19–23, 2010, Saint-Malo, France.
ACM 978-1-4503-0053-7/10/06.

The Rebirth of Neural Networks

Olivier Temam
INRIA

Abstract: After the hype of the 1990s, where companies like Intel or Philips built commercial hardware systems based on neural networks, the approach quickly lost ground for multiple reasons: hardware neural networks were no match for software neural networks run on rapidly progressing general-purpose processors, their application scope was considered too limited, and even progress in machine-learning theory overshadowed neural networks.

However, in the past few years, a remarkable convergence of trends and innovations is casting a new light on neural networks and could make them valuable components of future computing systems. Trends in technology call for architectures which can sustain a large number of defects, something neural networks are intrinsically capable of. Tends in applications, summarized in the recent RMS categorization, highlight a number of key algorithms which are eligible to neural networks implementations. At the same time, innovations in technology, such as the recent realization of a memristor, are creating the conditions for the efficient hardware implementation of neural networks. Innovations in machine learning, with the recent advent of Deep Networks, have revived interest in neural networks. Finally, recent findings in neurobiology carry even greater prospects, where detailed explanations of how complex functions, such as vision, can be implemented further open up the defect-tolerance and application potential of neural network architectures.

Categories & Subject Descriptors: C.1.0 Computer Systems Organization; PROCESSOR ARCHITECTURES, General.

General Term: Design.

ISCA'10, June 19–23, 2010, Saint-Malo, France.
ACM 978-1-4503-0053-7/10/06.

NoHype: Virtualized Cloud Infrastructure without the Virtualization

Eric Keller Jakub Szefer Jennifer Rexford Ruby B. Lee
Princeton University, Princeton, NJ, USA
{ekeller, szefer}@princeton.edu jrex@cs.princeton.edu rblee@princeton.edu

ABSTRACT

Cloud computing is a disruptive trend that is changing the way we use computers. The key underlying technology in cloud infrastructures is virtualization – so much so that many consider virtualization to be one of the key features rather than simply an implementation detail. Unfortunately, the use of virtualization is the source of a significant security concern. Because multiple virtual machines run on the same server and since the virtualization layer plays a considerable role in the operation of a virtual machine, a malicious party has the opportunity to attack the virtualization layer. A successful attack would give the malicious party control over the all-powerful virtualization layer, potentially compromising the confidentiality and integrity of the software and data of any virtual machine. In this paper we propose removing the virtualization layer, while retaining the key features enabled by virtualization. Our NoHype architecture, named to indicate the removal of the hypervisor, addresses each of the key roles of the virtualization layer: arbitrating access to CPU, memory, and I/O devices, acting as a network device (e.g., Ethernet switch), and managing the starting and stopping of guest virtual machines. Additionally, we show that our NoHype architecture may indeed be "no hype" since nearly all of the needed features to realize the NoHype architecture are currently available as hardware extensions to processors and I/O devices.

Categories and Subject Descriptors

C.1.0 [**Processor architectures**]: General; D.4.6 [**Operating systems**]: Security and protection—*invasive software*

General Terms

Design, Management, Security

Keywords

Cloud computing, Multi-core, Many-core, Security, Hypervisor, Virtualization, System architecture

1. INTRODUCTION

There is no doubt that "cloud computing" has tremendous promise. The end user of a service running "in the cloud" is unaware of how the infrastructure is architected – it just works. The provider of that service (the cloud customer in Fig. 1(a)) is able to dynamically provision infrastructure to meet the currene demand by leasing resources from a hosting company (the cloud provider). The cloud provider can leverage economies of scale to provide dynamic, on-demand, infrastructure at a favorable cost.

While there is debate over the exact definition, the main idea behind cloud computing, common to all approaches, is enabling a virtual machine to run on any server. Since there are many customers and many servers, the management of the infrastructure must be highly automated – a customer can request the creation (or removal) of a virtual machine and without human intervention a virtual machine is started (or stopped) on one of the servers. To take advantage of the economic benefits, the cloud providers use multi-tenancy, where virtual machines from multiple customers share a server.

Unfortunately, this multi-tenancy is the source of a major security concern with cloud computing as it gives malicious parties direct access to the server where their victim may be executing in the cloud. The malicious party can actively attack the virtualization layer. If successful, as many vulnerabilities have shown to be possible [1, 2, 3, 4, 5, 6], the attacker has an elevated level of execution capabilities on a system running other virtual machines. The malicious party can then inspect the memory, exposing confidential information such as encryption keys and customer data, or even modify the software a virtual machine is running. Even without compromising the hypervisor, multi-tenancy exposes side-channels that can be used to learn confidential information [7]. These security risks make companies hesitant to use hosted virtualized infrastructures [8].

In fact, if not for this security concern, running applications in the cloud can actually be *more* secure than when run in private facilities. Commonly cited are the economic benefits that the economies of scale provide to the cloud infrastructure providers [9]. There is a similar principle with regards to security that is, however, not often discussed. In many organizations, physical security is limited to a locked closet which stores the servers in the company's office. Since cloud providers are served out of large data centers, there are surveillance cameras, extra security personnel, and by the very nature of the environment, the access is much more controlled. That level of physical security is cost prohibitive for a single organization, but when spread out across many, it almost comes for free to the customer of the cloud. Similarly, in a private organization, network security of servers is commonly limited to a firewall. Cloud providers can install and maintain special intrusion detection (or prevention) systems which inspect packets for matches to known attacks that exploit bugs in commonly used software. As with physical security, these devices may be cost prohibitive for a single organization but can be provided by the cloud provider for a small cost.

Rather than attempting to make the virtualization layer more secure by reducing its size or protecting it with additional hardware [10], we instead take the position that the virtualization layer should be *removed altogether*. In this paper we propose getting rid of the virtualization layer (the hypervisor) running beneath each guest operating system (OS) in order to make running a virtual machine in the cloud as secure as running it in the customer's private facilities – and possibly even *more* secure. As a side benefit, removing the active hypervisor removes the 'virtualization tax' which is incurred when needing to invoke a hypervisor for many operations. We argue that today's virtualization technology is used as a convenience, but is not necessary for what cloud providers really want to achieve. We believe that the key capabilities are the automation, which eases management of the cloud infrastructure by enabling the provisioning of new virtual machines on-the-fly, and multi-tenancy, which allows the cloud provider to gain the financial benefits of sharing a server.

To remove the virtualization layer, we present the NoHype architecture, which addresses, and renders unnecessary, each of the responsibilities of today's hypervisors[1]. This architecture is an entire system solution combining processor technology, I/O technology, and software in order to realize the same capabilities enabled by today's virtualization in a cloud infrastructure, yet done without an active virtualization layer running under a potentially malicious guest operating system. The main components of the architecture revolve around resource isolation. The NoHype architecture automatically dedicates resources to each guest VM, and the guest VM has full control of these resource throughout its runtime on the physical machine. The important features of our architecture are:

- **One VM per Core** - Each processor core is dedicated to a single VM. This prevents interference between different VMs, mitigates side-channels which exist with shared resources (e.g., L1 cache), and simplifies billing, in terms of discrete *compute units*[2]. Yet, multi-tenancy is still possible as there are multiple cores on a chip.
- **Memory Partitioning** - Hardware-enforced partitioning of physical memory ensures that each VM can only access the assigned physical memory and only in a fair manner.
- **Dedicated Virtual I/O Devices** - I/O device modifications to support virtualization enables each VM to be given direct access to a dedicated (virtual) I/O device. The memory management facilities along with chipset support ensure that only the authorized VM can access the memory-mapped I/O and only at a given rate.

[1]We will use the term *hypervisor* to mean hypervisor, VMM (virtual machine monitor) or other similar virtualization technology.

[2]A *compute unit* is a definition of a unit of computational resources that the customer purchases, e.g.: 1GHz CPU core, 2GB of RAM and 160GB of disk space.

Removing the active virtualization layer brings significant security benefits. Doing so comes at the cost of not being able to (i) sell in extremely fine grain units (e.g., selling 1/8th of a core) and (ii) highly over-subscribe a physical server (i.e., sell more resources than are available). However, we do not see either of these as a serious limitation. As processors have increasingly many cores on them, the granularity of a single core will become finer with each multicore processor generation (e.g., a single core in a 4-core device is 25% of the system's compute power, in a 128-core device, it's less than 1% of the compute power and it is doubtful applications have such consistent load that expansion and contraction of compute units at a finer granularity than core units would even make sense). Also, attempting to over-subscribe a server is counter to the model of what cloud computing provides. As opposed to private infrastructures where the goal is to maximize utilization of the server by using techniques that adjust the allocation of resources across virtual machines based on current usage [11], in cloud computing the customer is promised the ability to use a certain amount of resources. The customer chooses the amount of resources it needs to match its application. If the customer needs some resources, it pays for them, if not, the cloud provider can assign them to another customer – but does not sell to another customer the resources already promised to a customer. That said, we do not require that the entire cloud infrastructure use the NoHype architecture – a provider may offer a discount to customers willing to forgo either the security benefits or the resource guarantees, enabling the provider to over-subscribe a sub-set of servers.

The NoHype name comes from the radical idea of removing the hypervisor. It also implies that it is not hype, but indeed implementable. In this paper, we also discuss currently available hardware and show that nearly all of what is needed to realize the NoHype architecture is available from computer hardware vendors. As such, we are proposing a commercially viable solution. This does not mean that the current architectures are ideal – we also wish to stimulate the architecture community to think along the lines of additional hardware features that extend the concepts behind NoHype to increase performance and achieve an even greater level of security.

The remainder of the paper is organized as follows. In Section 2 we discuss the security threats that arise from the use of virtualization and formulate our threat model. In Section 3 we discuss the role of the virtualization layer. In Section 4 we propose our NoHype architecture which removes the virtualization layer. We then discuss the security benefits of moving to a cloud infrastructure which uses NoHype in Section 5. Then in Section 6 we take a look at currently available hardware technology and assess the possibility of realizing the NoHype architecture. Finally, we wrap up with related work in Section 7 and conclude in Section 8.

2. SECURITY THREATS

The problem we are addressing with the NoHype architecture is that of multi-tenancy in a hosted (public) cloud environment. Essentially, the goal is to make running a virtual machine in the cloud as secure as running it in the customer's private facilities. In this section we briefly explain why this is not the case with today's virtualization-based cloud architecture. We also detail our threat model.

2.1 Concerns with Current Virtualization

Shown in Figure 1(a) is a diagram depicting the cloud customer's interaction with the cloud provider to control VM setup as well as an end user then using the service offered by the cloud customer. The cloud customer makes a request with a description of the VM (e.g., provides a disk image with the desired OS) to the cloud provider's *cloud manager*. The cloud manager chooses a server to host the VM, fetches the image from storage, and forwards the request to the control software running on the server to be handled locally. Once the cloud customer's VM is running, end users can begin using the cloud customer's service (end users can be external users, as in the case of web service, or internal customers, as in the case where the cloud is used to expand an internal IT infrastructure). Shown in Figure 1(b) is a generic diagram of one of the servers in today's infrastructures – consisting of a hypervisor along with several virtual machines. The virtual machine labeled "root context" is a special virtual machine which contains control software that interacts with the cloud manager and has elevated privileges that, for example, allow it to access devices and control the startup and shutdown of virtual machines. As such, it is considered part of the virtualization layer (along with the hypervisor)[3]. The virtual machines labeled VM1 and VM2 are the guest virtual machines running on the system and can be unmodified as the hypervisor provides the abstraction that they are running directly on the processor – in a hosted infrastructure, these would be the customer's virtual machines.

VM1 and VM2 should be completely isolated from one another. They should not be able to (i) inspect each other's data or software, (ii) modify each other's data or software, or (iii) affect the availability of each other (either by hogging resources or triggering extra work to be done by each other). As the virtualization layer is privileged software in charge of administering the physical system, a compromised virtualization layer can affect the running VMs. As it manages the virtual to physical mapping of memory addresses, confidential data may be exposed or the executable or data can be modified. As it manages the scheduling of VMs, a virtual machine can be interrupted (switching to the hypervisor's code) – exposing the current registers to inspection and modification, and control flow modification (e.g., by making the virtual machine return to a different location in the executable).

Unfortunately, securing the virtualization layer (hypervisor plus root context) is getting more difficult as hypervisors become more complex. Xen's hypervisor is about 100k lines of code and the dom0 kernel can be 1500k lines of code [12]. While the size of VMWare's solution is not publicly available, it is likely to match or exceed Xen's size. This complexity makes the current virtualization solutions difficult to verify and vulnerable to attacks – numerous vulnerabilities have already been shown in [1, 2, 3, 4, 5, 6, 7]. As the virtualization layer is complex, having many responsibilities as discussed in Section 3, we fully expect many new vulnerabilities to emerge.

To exploit one of these vulnerabilities, an attacker needs only to gain access to a guest OS and run software that can attack the hypervisor or root context (via the hypervisor) – since the guest OS interacts with both for many functions, there is a large attack surface. Getting access to a guest OS is simple as the malicious party can lease a VM directly from the cloud provider. Further, if the attacker is targeting a specific party (e.g., company A wanting to disrupt its competitor, company B), it can check whether its VM is located on the same physical server as the targeted victim's VM using network-based co-residence checks such as matching small packet round-trip times (between the attacker's VM and the victim's VM) and numerically close IP addresses [7].

To keep a guest VM from being able to exploit the vulnerabilities of the hypervisor, in the NoHype architecture we propose removing the hypervisor completely, as shown in Figure 1(c), by removing extraneous functionality not needed in the cloud computing scenario and by transferring some functionality to virtualization-aware hardware and firmware. We acknowledge that the hardware and firmware may not be completely free of bugs, however, we feel that the extensive testing and relatively non-malleable nature of the hardware and firmware configurations (when compared to software) makes it more difficult to attack. Of course, we will need to retain system management software used to start and stop VMs at the behest of the cloud manager. This software will be privileged, however to attack it will require going through the cloud manager first – guest VMs cannot directly invoke system management software in our NoHype architecture.

2.2 Threat Model

First, we assume the cloud provider is not malicious. The cloud provider's business model centers around providing the hosted infrastructure and any purposeful deviation from the stated service agreements would effectively kill its reputation and shut down its business. To that end, we assume that sufficient physical security controls are employed to prevent hardware attacks (e.g., probing on the memory buses of physical servers) through surveillance cameras and restricted access to the physical data center facilities.

Second, we make no assumptions about security of guest operating systems. The cloud provider can restrict what OS the customer can run, but even that OS can have security holes. Therefore, we simply assume customers can run whatever software they desire.

Third, the security and correctness of the cloud management software is out of scope for this paper – we assume it is secure. The cloud management software runs on dedicated servers and is the interface that the cloud customers use to request and relinquish resources. From this, we also assume the system management software (system manager shown in Figure 1(c) and core managers) running on each server is also secure as the only communication it has is with the cloud management software. The guest VMs are isolated from it (no shared memory, disk or network), and do not interact with it.

3. THE VIRTUALIZATION LAYER'S ROLE

We propose the NoHype architecture which removes the virtualization layer in the multi-tenant server setting. To

[3]Note that the functionality of the "root context" could be included in the hypervisor for performance benefits. That has no impact on our argument.

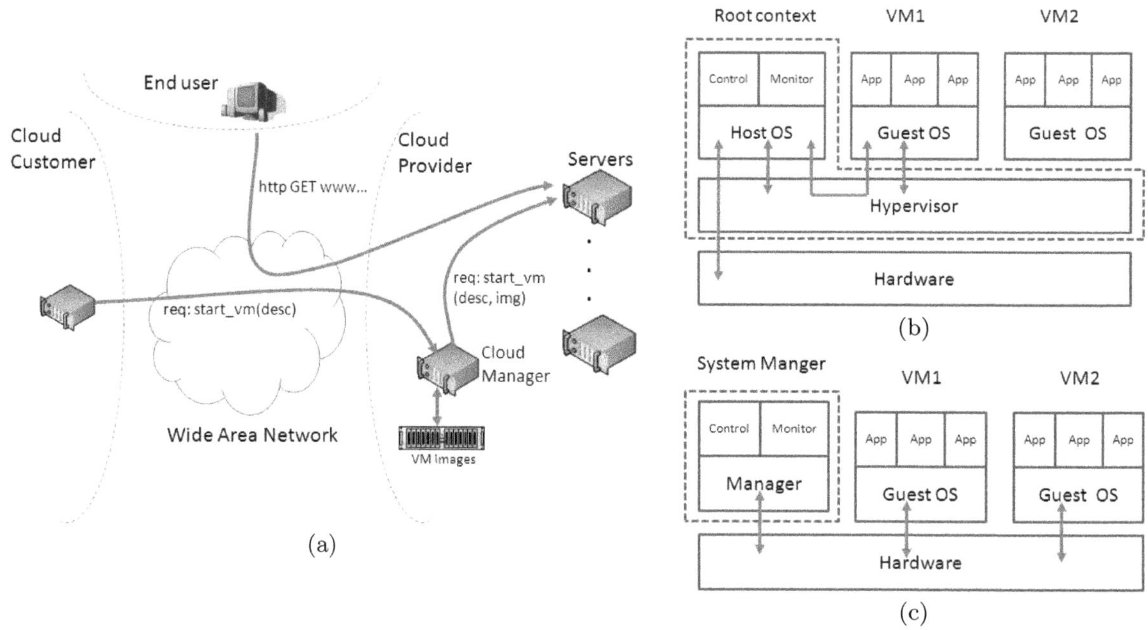

Figure 1: (a) High-level view of the cloud customer's interaction with the cloud provider's management to start a VM and the end user's interaction with the service offered by the cloud customer (a web service in this case). (b) Generic virtualization of one server – arrows indicate interaction between the guest OS and hypervisor, host OS and the hypervisor, guest OS and the host OS (via the hypervisor), and the host OS and the I/O devices. (c) A server in the NoHype architecture after the removal of the hypervisor: the direct interaction between VMs and management software is removed.

better understand the implications of this proposal, we need to first understand the role the virtualization layer plays in today's technology. Below, we discuss the many functions of today's virtualization layers (as used in cloud infrastructures).

Scheduling Virtual Machines : Since in today's typical virtualized environment, multiple virtual machines are running on a single processor, the hypervisor needs to arbitrate the access to the processor cycles. Much as an OS controls the CPU allocation of running processes, the hypervisor controls the CPU allocation of running virtual machines. Whenever a timer expires, I/O is performed, or a *VM exit* occurs, the hypervisor's scheduler routine is run to decide which VM to run next.

Memory Management : The hypervisor takes care of managing the physical memory available on the system. Memory is a limited resource which the hypervisor needs to arbitrate and share among the guest VMs. To help with the illusion that each guest VM has its own physical memory, the hypervisor presents each guest VM with its *guest physical memory*. In order to maximize utilization across all of the VMs, the hypervisor can coax one VM to page some memory to disk in order to be able to allocate that physical memory to another VM [11]. The hypervisor then maps the *guest physical memory* to the *host physical memory* which is the actual physical memory available. Through this remapping of memory, the hypervisor is able to achieve isolation between the guest VMs. Each VM thinks that it has some physical memory, the *guest physical memory*, and is only able to access that memory. This prevents VMs from accessing the memory of other VMs.

Emulating I/O Devices and Arbitrating Access to them : Access to the physical devices is essential as the I/O of the system is how a program interacts with the real world. Whether sending packets to a remote computer, or writing to storage, programs require I/O. As the machine is shared, the virtualization layer must arbitrate accesses to each device. Additionally, the virtualization layer can present a generic view of the underlying device rather than the actual device in order to enable a virtual machine to run on servers with equivalent but different devices. In this scenario, the root context virtual machine runs the real device drivers and emulates the generic device the VMs access.

Network Packet Processing (switching, NAT, and access control) : VM-to-VM communication is essential to enable communication between the services running inside the VMs. Since VMs can run on the same server, VM-to-VM communication may not need to go through the cloud provider's network. Because of this, modern virtualization technology typically runs a software Ethernet switch in the root context virtual machine with similar functionality as separate hardware switches would have [13].

Starting/Stopping/Migrating Virtual Machines : The hypervisor emulates the underlying hardware, giving each virtual machine the view that it is running on its own machine. Management software in the root context can interact with the hypervisor to create a new virtual machine and control the power to the virtual machine (e.g., power on or reset). The hypervisor emulates all of the aspects of the server, enabling the OS to run through its boot sequence. The management software provides an interface to a central cloud manager which controls the creation and placement of virtual machines based on requests from customers, typically through a web interface. The management software may also be involved in live migration – the process of moving a running VM from one physical server to another while maintaining the appearance that the VM is continuously active to those that are interacting with it.

4. NOHYPE ARCHITECTURE: REMOVING THE HYPERVISOR

Our NoHype architecture removes the virtualization layer yet retains the management capabilities needed by cloud infrastructures. To do this, recall the major functions of the virtualization layer: arbitrating access to memory, CPU, and devices, providing important network functionality, and controlling the execution of virtual machines. Our architecture, shown in Figure 2, addresses each of these issues in order to remove the virtualization layer. Note that the cloud architecture remains unchanged, where the servers in Figure 1(a) are now NoHype-enabled servers.

The main point is that each of the guest VMs runs directly on the hardware without an underlying active hypervisor. Of course we cannot remove management software completely – there is the need for a management entity that can start and stop a virtual machine based on requests from the cloud provider's management software. Unlike today's virtualization architectures, in the NoHype architecture, once a VM is started it runs uninterrupted and has direct access to devices. The guest OS does not interact with any management software which is on the server and there are no tasks that a virtualization layer must do while the VM is running. In the following sub-sections we will discuss each of the roles of a typical hypervisor, and how the NoHype architecture removes the need for it.

4.1 CPU: One VM per core

In the NoHype architecture, each core can run only one VM. That is, cores are not shared among different guest VMs, which removes the need for the active VM scheduling done by the hypervisor. As an added benefit, dedicating a core to a single VM eliminates the potential software cache-based side channel which exists when sharing an L1 cache [14, 15].

Dedicating a core to each VM may not seem reasonable, as many associate virtualization with maxing out resources on each physical server to run as many VMs on it as possible. However, we believe that is counter to (i) the trend in computing towards multi-core, and (ii) the cloud computing model. The trend in processors is to increase the number of cores on the chip with each generation (as opposed to using clock frequency as the main source of performance improvements). Already, 8-core devices are available today [16] and there are predictions of 16-core devices becoming available in the next few years [17][4]. With each generation, the number of VMs a server can support would grow with the number of cores and sharing of cores to support more VMs will not be necessary.

Furthermore, we view running extra VMs to fill in for idle VMs (i.e., over-subscribing) to be counter to the model of cloud computing. The cloud infrastructure is dynamic in nature and the number of virtual machines needed by the customer can be scaled with the demand of the application. Therefore, idleness is handled by the customer by shutting down some of its virtual machines, instead of the cloud provider over-subscribing. While such over-subscribing can be done at a discount for customers who do not value security, it may not be necessary for customers who demand Secure Cloud Computing, especially with tens or hundreds of cores in future many-core chips.

4.2 Memory: Hardware support for partitioning and enforcing fairness

Unlike the processor, which is already moving toward divisible units, memory is still a unified resource. In the NoHype architecture, we propose using partitioning of physical memory. Here, we capitalize on the fact that modern servers are supporting more and more RAM – 256GB is not unheard of [18].

The ideal way to partition memory is to give each guest OS a view of memory where the OS has a dedicated and guaranteed fraction of physical memory (the *guest physical memory*) on the host system. Each VM can be assigned a different amount as decided by the customer when requesting a new VM to be started – any 'underutilization' is within each VM based on the customer requesting, and paying for, more than was needed. Given a portion of the memory, the OS will then be able to manage its own memory as it does today (managing the mapping from virtual memory locations to physical memory locations and swapping pages to/from disk as needed). Hardware support in the processor then performs the mapping between the *guest physical memory* address and the *host physical memory* address and restricts memory operations to the assigned range. In Figure 2, this responsibility falls to the multi-core memory controller (MMC) and the hardware page table mechanisms (inside each core) which will have built-in support for performing these re-mappings.

Not only must access to memory be partitioned, it must be fair. In the context of multi-tenant servers, rather than optimizing for memory bus utilization, the MMC must be designed for providing fairness among each of the VMs. As there can only be one VM assigned to a core, the MMC can instead provide fairness among each of the cores. This greatly simplifies the MMC as it can be designed for the number of cores the device has, rather than the number of VMs that may run on the system (which in traditional virtualization is undetermined and variable, and can be many more times than the number of cores). Including fairness in the multi-core memory controller and running one VM per core creates a system where one cloud customer's VM is greatly limited in how it can affect the performance of other cloud customers' VMs.

4.3 Devices: Per-VM virtualized devices and rate-limited I/O

An additional aspect of the physical system that needs to be partitioned is the access to I/O devices. In today's virtualization, operating systems interact with virtualized devices in the virtualization layer. This hides the details of the actual device and also allows the hypervisor to arbitrate access to the real device. Therefore, when the guest operating systems tries to access a device, this causes a switch over to the hypervisor and then to the root context VM. In the NoHype architecture, each guest operating system is

[4] We're referring to server class processors. Network processors and other specialized chips have on the order of 100 cores already.

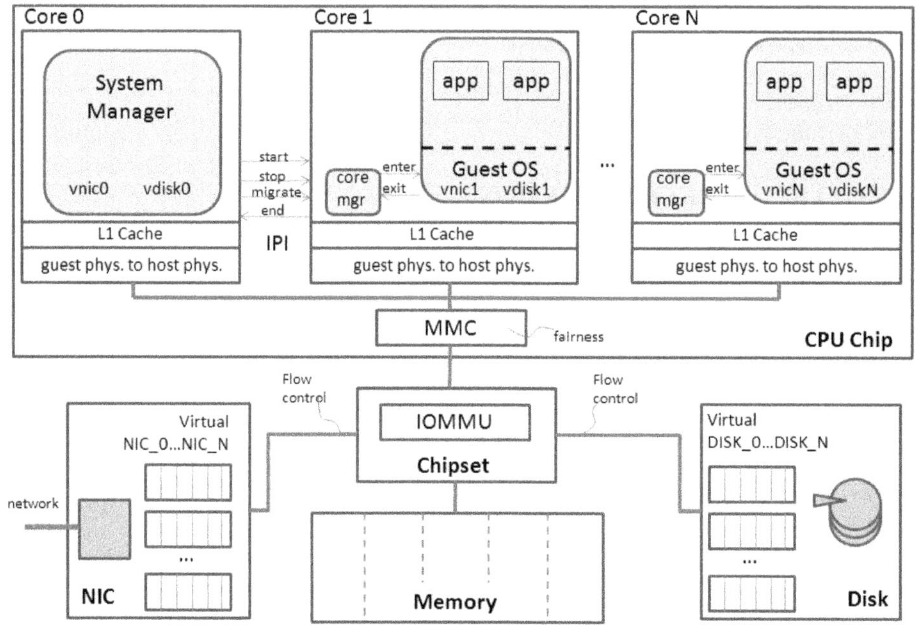

Figure 2: The NoHype system architecture.

assigned its own physical device and given direct access to it.

Of course, this relies on the assumption that there are enough devices to assign at least one per virtual machine. We believe that the view of multiple physical devices should be realized by the device itself supporting virtualization – that is, the device would be a single physical device, but tell the system that it is N separate devices. Each VM will interact only with the virtual device(s) assigned to it. As seen in Figure 2, a virtual device can have one or more queues dedicated to it. This forms the interface that is seen by the associated VM. The primary devices needed in a cloud computing scenario are the network interface card (NIC) and the disk. Other devices, such as graphics processing units (GPUs) could also be virtualized, thus removing a need for having N separate devices.

Providing this view requires some support in the MMC and I/O MMU[5]. For writes/reads to/from the device initiated by the cores, each device will be mapped to a different range in memory (as is done today) and each would be allowed to access only its memory ranges. This would enable the guest OS to interact directly (and only) with its assigned devices. From the device side, the I/O MMU would enforce the DMA to/from memory, so a device assigned to one core would only be able to access that core's memory range. For interrupts, since each VM will be assigned dedicated access to a given device, the interrupts associated with that device will be assigned to the guest virtual machine such that when an interrupt occurs, the guest OS handles it, not the virtualization layer.

One complication introduced by enabling direct access to devices is the bandwidth of the shared I/O bus (e.g., PCIe), is limited. When all device accesses go through the virtualization layer, the single piece of software can arbitrate access and prevent any single VM from overloading the shared bus. However, giving each VM the ability to access the devices directly means that there is no ability for software to prevent a VM from overloading the I/O bus. As such, in the NoHype architecture rate-limited access to each I/O bus is achieved via a flow-control mechanism where the I/O device controls the rate of transmission. Each VM's assigned device is configured with the rate at which the device can be accessed by the VM. The device uses this to limit the amount of data it sends over the peripheral bus and uses a feedback signal to limit the amount of data sent to it by the I/O MMU.

[5]I/O MMU - Input/Output Memory Management Unit is responsible for enforcing memory protection for transactions coming from I/O devices.

4.4 Networking: Do networking in the network, not on the server

In the NoHype architecture, we argue that the virtualization layer should be removed and instead its functionality should be provided through modifications to system components. For networking, this means that the Ethernet switches in the data center network should perform the switching and security functions, not a software switch in the virtualization layer. This is consistent with giving VMs direct access to the network interfaces – because they bypass the virtualization layer, the software Ethernet switch is also bypassed. Doing so has numerous benefits: (i) it simplifies management as it removes an extra type of switch and layer in the switch hierarchy, (ii) it frees up the processor on the server as it no longer has to perform, in software, Ethernet switching for an increasingly large number of VMs, and (iii) it allows the use of all of the features of the Ethernet switch, not just the ones also supported by the software switch.

Further, we argue that the software Ethernet switch is not doing anything special. Instead, it is merely used as an initial solution that enables using the Ethernet switches that are currently available. These switches are not designed for virtualized infrastructures, but instead designed for enterprise networks. For example, because of its history as a shared medium, Ethernet switches drop packets that would be forwarded out of the same port as they arrived – a situation which would occur in virtualized infrastructures when two communicating VMs are located on the same server. Integrating support into hardware Ethernet switches for capabilities such as allowing a packet to be forwarded out of the same port as it was received would eliminate the need for the software switch.

While one may argue that requiring packets to go to the dedicated Ethernet switch has performance limitations, we note that this is only the case for the special situation of communication between two VMs located on the same server. In the cloud environment, the customers intended use of VMs is not known to the cloud provider. Making assumptions about the amount of traffic between co-resident VMs is equivalent to attempting to over subscribe the system, which we argue is not a good idea as the customer is paying for guaranteed resource usage. By not over subscribing, the peripheral bus bandwidth and bandwidth from the NIC to the top-of-rack switches must be provisioned to be able to support the guaranteed traffic bandwidth. With the software Ethernet switch, latency will be reduced for co-resident VM communication. However, it incurs the extra latency of going through an extra, lower performance (since it's in software), switch for *all* other packets. Instead, by bypassing the software Ethernet switch we are providing better average latency. While the cloud provider could attempt to maximize this situation by placing the VMs from a given customer on a single server, doing so comes at the cost of increasing the impact that a single server failure will have on that customer.

4.5 Starting/Stopping/Migrating Virtual Machines: Decouple VM management from VM operation

In the NoHype architecture we removed the hypervisor, yet we still need the ability to start and stop virtual machines on demand. To do this, we decouple the VM management from the VM operation – the management code is active before a VM is started and after it is stopped, but during the life of the VM, the guest OS never interacts with the management code on the core, or on the server (i.e., with the system manager running on a separate core). When a server starts up, one core is randomly selected as the bootstrap processor, as is done in today's multi-core systems. The code that starts executing on that core is the trusted *NoHype system manager*[6]. The system manager initially starts up in hyper-privileged mode to setup the server. It is then responsible for accepting commands from the cloud manager software (via its network interface) and issuing commands to individual cores to start/stop guest VMs via the inter-processor interrupts (IPIs). The sending, and masking, of IPIs is controlled through memory-mapped registers of the core's local APIC[7]. The memory management can be used to restrict the access to these memory regions to only software running in hyper-privileged mode, and therefore preventing VMs from issuing or masking IPIs. Upon receiving an IPI, the core will jump to a predefined location to begin executing the core manager code to handle the VM management. Figure 3 summarizes the actual procedures for starting and stopping VMs, with detailed description in the following paragraphs.

Starting a VM: Before a VM is started, the system manager must receive a command from the cloud manager. The instructions to the cloud manager are issued by the customer who specifies how many VMs and of what type he or she wants. The cloud manger then provides both a description of the VM (e.g., amount of memory it is assigned) and the location of the disk image to the system manager. Next, the system manager maps the to-be-assigned VM's memory and disk into its space to allow the manager to access the resources and initialize them. The disk image is then downloaded by the manager and stored on the local disk and the memory assigned to the core allocated to this VM is zeroed out. This brings in the guest OS image into the VM. Next, the to-be-assigned VM's disk and memory are un-mapped from the system manager's space so it no longer has access to them. Finally a 'start' inter-processor interrupt (IPI) is issued to the core where the VM is to start. Upon receiving a start IPI the core comes online and starts executing code which is stored at a predefined location. The code that executes is the *core manager* which starts running in the hyper-privileged mode and initializes the core (sets up the memory mapping and maps the virtual NIC and disk devices). To start the guest OS, the core manager performs a *VM exit* which switches the core out of the hyper-privileged mode and starts the execution of the guest OS from the image now stored locally on the disk. On bootup the guest OS reads the correct system parameters (e.g. the amount of memory that it has been assigned) and starts execution.

Stopping a VM: A guest OS can exit when a stop command is issued by the system manager (e.g., the system manager receives a message from the cloud manager that the customer does not need the VM anymore or the instance-hour(s) purchased by the customer have been used up). In this situation, the system manager sends a 'stop' IPI to the core running the VM that is to be shut down. This interrupt causes the core to switch to the hyper-privileged mode and jump to a predefined code location in the core manager's code. Next, the core manager optionally zeros out the memory space assigned to the VM, and potentially the assigned disk space if the customer's VM uploads its data to some storage before termination. The core manager also optionally saves the disk image of the VM, depending on the Service Level Agreement (SLA) for continuing service of this VM at a later time. Finally, the core manager puts the core in sleep mode (to wait for the next start IPI) and the system manager notifies the cloud manager of completion.

Aborting a VM: A guest OS can be aborted when the guest OS performs an illegal operation (e.g., trying to access memory not assigned to it)[8]. An illegal operation will cause a trap, which in turn causes entrance into the hyper-privileged mode and execution of code located at a predefined location in the core manager. At this point, the core

[6]The whole system manager does not have to be trusted, but for clarity of presentation and space reasons we will not explore issues of trust of the system manager here and hence we make this simplifying statement.

[7]APIC is the Advanced Programmable Interrupt Controller.

[8]Illegal operations also include the use of some processor instructions, which may require the OS to be altered. For example, we do not support nested virtualization, so any attempts to do so by the OS would be illegal.

Start a VM
1. Cloud manager notifies system manager to start a VM
2. System manager maps the memory and disk of the to-be-assigned VM into the system manager's space
3. System manager downloads the disk image and stores it on a local disk and zeroes out the memory
4. After initialization, system manager un-maps the memory and disk from its space
5. System manager issues a 'start' IPI to the core
6. Core manager initializes memory and I/O mapping
7. Core manager exits to guest OS, starting the guest OS execution

Stop a VM
1. Cloud manager notifies system manager to stop a VM
2. System manager issues a 'stop' IPI to the core running the target VM
3. Core manager optionally saves the disk image of the VM, then clears the disk and memory
4. Core manager un-maps memory and I/O
5. Core manager puts the current core into idle state

Abort a VM
1. Enter core manager on an illegal operation
2. Core manager sends an 'end' IPI to the system manager
3. Core manager optionally clears disk and memory
4. Core manager un-maps memory and I/O
5. Core manager puts the current core into idle state
6. System manager notifies cloud manager

Figure 3: Outline of steps used to start, stop and abort a VM.

manager sends an 'end' IPI to the system manager to inform the system manager that the VM exited abnormally. Optionally, the core manager can zero out the memory and the disk to prevent data leaks. The memory and I/O is un-mapped. The core is then put into sleep mode (waiting for a start IPI) and the system manager notifies the cloud manager of the aborted VM's status change.

Live Migration of a VM: A live migration operation is initiated by the cloud manager, which instructs the system manager on the source server to migrate a particular VM to a given target server. In a simplistic implementation, the system manager would send a 'migrate' IPI to a core on which the VM is running. The interrupt handler located in the core manager would stop the execution of the VM, capture the entire state of the VM, and hash and encrypt it. The system manager would then take the state, send it to the target server where the system manager would send an IPI to the core manager, which would check the hash and decrypt the state, re start the new VM and continue execution.

Of course, this process can take a while and in order to minimize downtime, optimizations using iterative approaches have been developed [19]. In these approaches, a current snapshot is taken, but the VM is not stopped. When the state is done transferring, the difference from the current snapshot and the previous snapshot is sent. The process may be repeated until the difference is sufficiently small to minimize actual downtime. In NoHype, we have the memory management unit track which pages have been modified. This enables the system manager to periodically send an IPI to obtain only the differences (for the first time accessing it, the difference will be a comparison to when the VM started, so will be an entire snapshot). With this, we do not introduce a hypervisor which is actively involved. For each iteration, the system manager forwards any data to the target server – on the target server the system manager forwards data to the core manager, the core manager updates the memory, disk and other state it receives. The last step is for the core manager on the source server to send one last set of differences, shutting down the VM on the last 'migrate' IPI. After all the state is replicated on the target server, the system manager on the target sends a 'start' IPI to start the VM. It should be noted that while the downtime can be reduced from what would be seen with the simplistic approach, it cannot be eliminated altogether. In Xen, this may range from 60ms for an ideal application to 3.5s for a non-ideal case [19]. The nature of cloud computing makes it such that (i) how long the downtime will actually be for a given VM cannot be known, and (ii) the downtime the customer is willing to tolerate is not known. As such, an alternate approach would be to involve the customer in the process, enabling them to gracefully 'drain' any ongoing work or perform migration themselves [20].

For all four actions, during the runtime of the guest OS, the guest OS does not invoke either the core manager or the system manager. Even during a live migration, no action the guest OS performs causes any management software to run – each iteration is initiated by the system manager. Hence, the guest OS has no opportunity to directly corrupt these trusted software components. Interaction with the cloud manager is from servers external to the cloud infrastructure (i.e., the customer's server). Securing this interaction is not the focus of this paper.

5. SECURITY BENEFITS OF NOHYPE

Because of the numerous benefits that hosted cloud infrastructures provide, many organizations want to use the cloud. However, concerns over security are holding some of them back. The NoHype architecture targets these concerns, creating an architecture where customers are given comparable security to running their VMs in their own virtualized infrastructure – and even *improved* security when considering the extra physical security and protection against malware that cloud providers can provide.

To achieve a comparable level of security, no VM should be able to (i) affect the availability of another VM, (ii) access the data/software of another VM (either to read or modify), or (iii) learn confidential information through side channels. Note that this does not mean that the cloud customer is completely protected, as vulnerabilities in the cloud customer's own applications and operating system could still be present – end users can attack a vulnerable server independent of whether it is running in the cloud or not.

Availability : Availability can be attacked in one of three ways in current hypervisor-based virtualization architectures– (i) altering the hypervisor's scheduling of VMs, (ii) interrupting a core running a VM, or (iii) performing extraordinary amounts of memory or I/O reads/writes to gain a disproportionate share of the bus and therefore affect the performance of another VM. By dedicating a core to a single VM and removing the hypervisor from making any scheduling decisions, we eliminate the first attack. With hardware masking for inter-processor and device interrupts, there is no possible way to interrupt another VM, eliminating the second attack. Through additions to the mutli-core memory controller for providing fairness [21] and through the chipset to rate-limit access to I/O, we eliminate the third attack. As such, with the NoHype architecture, a VM has no ability to disrupt the execution of another VM.

Confidentiality/integrity of data and software : In order to modify or inspect another VM's software or data, one would need to have access to either registers or physical memory. Since cores are not shared and since there is no hypervisor that runs during the entire lifetime of the virtual machine, there is no possible way to access the registers. Memory access violations are also mitigated. Since the NoHype architecture enforces memory accesses in hardware, the only way a VM could access physical memory outside of the assigned range would be to alter the tables specifying the mapping of *guest physical* addresses to *host physical* addresses. To do so would require compromising the system manager software and altering the code performing the start/stop functions. This would first require compromising the cloud manager, which we assume is trusted, as the system manager only interacts with the cloud manager and the core managers, and is isolated from the guest VMs.

Side-channels : Side-channels exist whenever resources are shared among multiple pieces of software. Ignoring any side-channels that are based on physical analysis (e.g., examining power usage), which falls outside of our threat model, side-channels are typically based on the timing of operations (e.g., hits in caches are shorter than misses, so one can determine if a particular cache line was accessed by timing an access to a specific memory location). While completely eliminating side-channels is a near impossible feat for a shared infrastructure, reducing them to be of little use is possible. In the NoHype architecture, since L1 caches are not shared, some of the most damaging attacks to date have been eliminated (using cache-based side-channel attacks to infer a cryptographic key) [22]. Since NoHype provides fair access to memory [21] and rate-limited accesses to I/O, a bandwidth-based side channel is likely very limited in each of those cases as well.

6. CURRENT HARDWARE SUPPORT

In Section 4, we presented our NoHype architecture. In this section, we examine current technology and whether it is possible to actually realize NoHype. A lot of hardware extensions, both in the processors and in the devices, have been introduced in recent years which aid computing in the virtualized model. Interestingly, while these extensions are mostly designed to address the performance overhead, we are able to leverage these in the NoHype architecture that we propose. We will present extensions found in Intel products – similar solutions are available from AMD and NoHype should be implementable on AMD platforms as well.

6.1 Isolating Each Core

As multi-tenancy requires running multiple virtual machines on the same processor, they need to share the processor resources. In order to remove the need for the hypervisor to schedule each VM, the NoHype architecture assigns a single VM per core. To fully isolate each VM from other VMs, however, we need to be able to restrict a core running one VM from sending IPIs to other cores. This can be achieved through use of the advanced programmable interrupt controller (APIC). Modern x86 processors have an interrupt mechanism based on the APIC. As shown in Figure 4, each core has a local APIC and there is a single I/O APIC for the entire system.

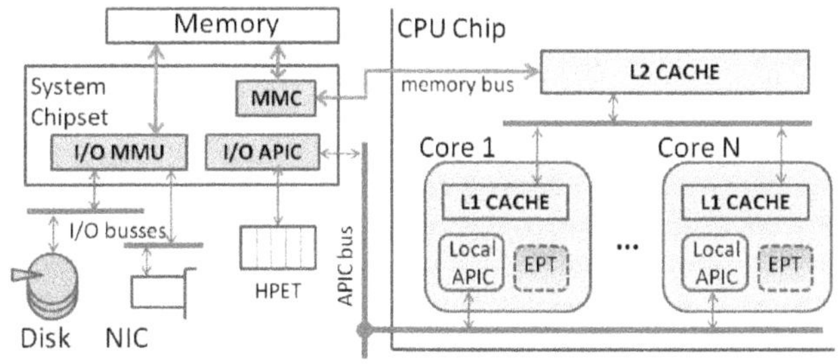

Figure 4: Selected parts of a modern x86 architecture which are relevant to NoHype.

The APIC can be used by a core to send an interrupt to another core. These IPIs[9] are generated by programming the interrupt command register (ICR) in the core's local APIC. By writing to this register, a message will be sent over the APIC bus with the destination field of the ICR indicating which core should receive the interrupt. While one VM can attempt to interrupt another VM with this mechanism, each core can mask out maskable interrupts that may be sent from other cores, to prevent them from interrupting the core.

6.2 Memory Partitioning

A key to isolating each virtual machine is making sure that each VM can access its own *guest physical memory* and not be allowed to access memory of other VMs. In order to remove the virtualization layer, we must have the hardware enforce the access isolation. Here, we capitalize on the paging protection available in modern processors, along with advances in providing these protections to each VM.

The Extended Page Tables (EPT) mechanism supported by VT-x technology from Intel can be used to enforce the memory isolation. The EPT logically adds another layer to the familiar virtual-to-physical memory translation page tables. The OS running on a core manages the translation from guest virtual to guest physical addresses, using the familiar mechanisms (e.g., CR3 register is used to set the page directory location). The EPT mechanisms are then used to translate from the guest physical to host physical address – the set of page tables which define this mapping are initialized by the core manager. Once initialized, the translation does not have to be modified throughout the lifetime of the OS instance running on a given core. A hardware page table walker uses the tables to automatically perform the translation. Access to a virtual address not currently in the guest physical memory will cause a page fault that is handled by the guest OS – a hypervisor layer is not needed. Access to memory outside of the guest physical address range pre-assigned to the VM will cause a new fault which is handled by the core manager, which causes the VM to be killed – as any action that would exit to a virtualization layer is assumed by NoHype architecture to be due to a misbehaving guest OS.

An open issue is the memory fairness and preventing cores

[9]The "processor" in "inter-processor interrupt" actually refers to a processor core.

from interfering with each other through use of the the memory subsystem. Currently, a processor core can hog the memory bandwidth, based on current memory controllers' scheduling algorithms which optimize overall memory performance, rather than being fair to all cores. We propose using a solution similar to one presented by Mutlu, et al., [21] whereby the memory controller is modified to help achieve a more fair sharing of memory bandwidth.

Another open issue is the optimal support for live migration that is completely transparent to the customer (involving the customer requires no support from the system). The simplistic *stop-and-copy* approach is fully supported. However, in order to use optimizations which iteratively copy differences during execution requires tracking dirty pages. Current processors do not support this, so software would be needed. In this case, each time a page is accessed, an exception would occur and be handled by the core manager which would simply mark a bit in a table. As this interaction is extremely limited (no information is passed and the required function is extremely simple), the vulnerability that is opened is very limited (though, still not ideal).

6.3 I/O Devices

The NoHype architecture relies on each virtual machine having direct access to its own physical device(s). Fortunately, I/O performance is an important factor in overall system performance, and as such, technologies are available to make this a reality.

6.3.1 Direct Access to I/O Devices

In the NoHype architecture the virtual machine must be able to access its own devices without going through the virtualization layer. This involves three aspects: (i) the VM being able to DMA to the device, (ii) the device being able to DMA to the VM, and (iii) the device being able to send an interrupt to the VM.

For the VM being able to DMA to the device, the memory partitioning discussed in Section 6.2 is the enabling technology. Each VM is assigned a device, with each device being assigned a memory mapped I/O range. The guest physical to host physical memory mapping enables VMs to directly interact with memory mapped I/O. The fact that the guest VM can only write to particular physical memory ranges, enforced by the hardware, means that each VM can write only to its device.

In the reverse direction, the I/O device sending data to the VM, requires support from the chipset which sits between the device and the system memory. Here the I/O MMU provides protection by creating multiple DMA protection domains. These domains are the memory regions that a given device is allowed to DMA into. This would correspond to the assigned physical memory that the VM was given. The chipset enforces this by using address-translation tables. When a device attempts to write to a memory location, the I/O MMU performs a lookup in its address-translation tables for access permission of that device. If the device is attempting to write to a location outside of the permitted range, the access is blocked.

The final aspect of interacting with devices without the involvement of the virtualization layer is the ability for interrupts from a device to be directly handled by the virtual machine associated with that device. For this, the MSI (Message Signaled Interrupts) and extension MSI-X specification [23] serve just this purpose. With MSI-X, a device can request an interrupt by writing to a particular memory address. The value written to that address indicates which interrupt is to be raised. By setting up the APIC tables, a given interrupt can be directed to a specific core on the processor (via its local APIC). The memory protection mechanisms can be used to block devices from writing certain memory locations, consequently limiting which device can interrupt which core.

6.3.2 I/O Device Virtualization

While it is possible to realize each VM having its own device by having multiple physical devices, as the number of cores (and therefore the number of VMs) grows, this will become impractical. The advantage we have here when considering the hosted cloud infrastructure setting is that there is only a small subset of devices that are actually of interest: the network interface card, the storage device, and a timer, but not, for example, a monitor or keyboard. Here, we can take advantage of a standard specified by PCI-SIG called single root I/O virtualization (SR-IOV). SR-IOV enables a single device to advertise that it is actually multiple devices, each with independent configuration and memory space.

To do this, the devices present two types of interfaces: one for configuration and the other for regular device access. The system software can use the configuration interface to specify how many virtual devices the physical device should act as and the options for each virtual device. Each virtual device is assigned a separate address range, enabling the system manager to map a virtual device to a particular virtual machine. The guest VM can then interact directly with the device through the regular device interface presented by the physical device. Only the system manager has the privileges to use the configuration interface and the VMs can only access the interfaces assigned to them.

Network: Intel has a network interface card that supports SR-IOV [24]. To distinguish between each of the virtual devices, the NIC has multiple queues on it. The NIC performs classification on the packets to direct each packet to the correct queue. Then, because of the memory partitioning, only the OS on the appropriate core can read directly from that virtual device, or write to it..

Storage: Unfortunately, there are currently no available storage devices which support the notion of virtual devices. LSI, however, recently announced a demonstration of an SR-IOV capable storage controller [25]. Additionally, more should be coming as disk drives already have a lot of functionality in the form of firmware on the drive itself – for example, reordering requests to optimize read/write performance. Furthermore, there are disk devices such as from Fusion-io which have a PCIe interface (and therefore can implement SR-IOV) and a programmable FPGA on board (and therefore can be upgraded). Until the LSI chip is integrated into disk drives or firmware is modified, multiple physical disk drives can be used. Server motherboards have already multiple SATA (Serial Advanced Technology Attachment) connections. When used in combination with network storage, this provides an acceptable, though not ideal, solution until SR-IOV enabled disk drives become available.

Timers: Timers are an essential part of operating systems and many programs which perform periodic tasks (such as scheduling processes). Each local APIC contains a 32-bit timer that is software configurable, and therefore provides each VM with its own timer. However, higher-precision timers require an external chip – the HPET (High Precision Event Timer). The HPET communicates with the I/O APIC, which as previously mentioned can be configured to deliver (timer) interrupts to a specific core via its local APIC. The HPET specification allows for up to 8 blocks of 32 timers and the HPET configuration is memory mapped – the map for each block can be aligned on a 4 kilobyte boundary so paging mechanisms can easily be used to restrict which core has access to which block of timers. In this way, the core can have full control over its timers which are not affected by other VMs.

Both the networking and disk devices' bandwidth usage need to be shared among the VMs. If a VM is able to use a disproportionately large amount of the I/O bandwidth, other VMs may be denied service very easily. Fortunately, the PCI Express (PCIe) interconnection network uses credit-based flow control. Each device has an input queue and senders consume tokens when sending packets. When the queue in the device associated with the sending core becomes full, the sender no longer has tokens for sending data. A device, e.g. the NIC, with virtual queues will take packets from the queues in round-robin fashion and return tokens to the sender. If a VM fills up its assigned queue, it will not be able to send more packets which will allow other VMs to regain their share of the bandwidth.

6.4 Virtualization aware Ethernet Switches

In the NoHype architecture, the networking is performed by networking devices and not by the software running on the server. This requires the Ethernet switches that are connected to the servers (e.g., the top-of-rack switches) to be virtualization aware. The switches need the abstraction that they have a connection to each virtual interface, rather than the single connection to the NIC shared across multiple virtual machines. As the market for virtualized infrastructures (not just hosted cloud infrastructures) is potentially very large, commercial Ethernet switch vendors are moving in this direction already. The Cisco Virtual Network Link (VN-link) [26] technology is supported in Cisco Nexus switches [13] where it is used to simplify the software switch and offload switching functionality to a physical switch, but this requires some changes to the Ethernet format. In contrast, HP has proposed Virtual Ethernet Port Aggregator (VEPA) [27], which does not require changes to the Ethernet format, but instead overcomes the limitation of not being able to forward a packet out of the same port it was received. Commercial availability of hardware switches which support VEPA are forthcoming, and Linux has support for VEPA for software based switches [28]. (not suitable for use in the data center, but useful for experimentation).

7. RELATED WORK

Virtual machine monitors and hypervisors have been studied extensively. Some of the work relating specifically to securing the virtualization layer in a server or "cloud" setting includes work by Santos, et al., [29] and sHype [30] from IBM. Santos, et al., presented a solution which uses the Terra hypervisor [31]. The sHype is a secure hypervisor architecture whose goal is to provide a secure foundation for server platforms. Rather than attempt to secure the virtualization layer, we instead removed it.

We should note that trusting the virtualization layer usually comes with the disclaimer that the virtualization layer must be minimal (i.e., minimizing the Trusted Computing Base, TCB). A number of projects have worked on minimizing the TCB (for example Flicker [32]) which attests to the importance of having the TCB as small as possible. None, however, went so far as to completely remove the hypervisor that actively runs under the OS, as we have.

Finally, hardware architectures have been proposed to enable running applications without trusting the operating system [33, 34, 35, 36, 10]. While these could perhaps be extended, or applied, to support running a trusted virtual machine on an untrusted hypervisor, we instead took an approach which proposes minimal changes to the processor core architecture along with modifications to system peripherals and software.

8. CONCLUSIONS

While cloud computing has tremendous promise there are concerns over the security of running applications in a hosted cloud infrastructure. One significant source of the problem is the use of virtualization, where an increasingly complex hypervisor is involved in many aspects of running the guest virtual machines. Unfortunately, virtualization is also a key technology of the cloud infrastructure enabling multi-tenancy and the ability to use highly automated processes to provision infrastructure. Rather than focus on making virtualization more secure, we remove the need for an active virtualization layer in the first place.

We presented the NoHype architecture which provides benefits on par with those of today's virtualization solutions without the active virtualization layer. Instead, our architecture makes use of hardware virtualization extensions in order to remove any need for a virtualization layer to run during the lifetime of a virtual machine. The extensions are used to flexibly partition resources and isolate guest VMs from each other. Key aspects of the architecture include (i) running one VM per core, (ii) hardware enforced memory partitioning, and (iii) dedicated (virtual) devices that each guest VM controls directly without intervention of a hypervisor. We also discussed the fact that current processor and I/O devices support much of the functionality required by the NoHype architecture. While there are clearly more architectural, implementation, software, performance and security issues to be resolved, we believe that the architecture is not hype but is a very viable architecture that can be implemented in the near future. We also hope that this paper will stimulate further research into many-core architectural features, at both the processor and system levels, that support using the many cores for security as in our NoHype architecture, rather than just for performance and power improvements.

9. ACKNOWLEDGMENTS

This work was supported in part by NSF CCF-0917134 and by research gifts from Intel and IBM. We would like to thank the anonymous ISCA reviewers, and also James Hamilton and Steven Ko for their feedback.

10. REFERENCES

[1] K. Kortchinsky, "Hacking 3D (and Breaking out of VMWare)," *BlackHat USA*, 2009.

[2] Anonymous, "Xbox 360 hypervisor privilege escalation vulnerability," 2007. http://www.h-online.com/security/news/item/Xbox-360-hack-was-the-real-deal-732391.html.

[3] "CVE-2007-4993: Xen guest root can escape to domain 0 through pygrub," 2007. http://cve.mitre.org/cgi-bin/cvename.cgi?name=CVE-2007-4993.

[4] "CVE-2007-5497: Vulnerability in XenServer could result in privilege escalation and arbitrary code executionr," 2007. http://support.citrix.com/article/CTX118766.

[5] R. Wojtczuk, "Subverting the Xen hypervisor," *BlackHat USA*, 2008.

[6] "CVE-2008-2100: VMware Buffer Overflows in VIX API Let Local Users Execute Arbitrary Code in Host OS." http://cve.mitre.org/cgi-bin/cvename.cgi?name=CVE-2008-2100.

[7] T. Ristenpart, E. Tromer, H. Shacham, and S. Savage, "Hey, you, get off of my cloud! Exploring information leakage in third-party compute clouds," in *Computer and Communications Security(CCS)*, 2009.

[8] F. Gens, "IT Cloud Services User Survey, pt.2: Top Benefits & Challenges," Oct. 2008. http://blogs.idc.com/ie/?p=210.

[9] A. Greenberg, J. Hamilton, D. A. Maltz, and P. Patel, "The cost of a cloud: Research problems in data center networks," *SIGCOMM Comput. Commun. Rev.*, vol. 39, no. 1, pp. 68–73, 2009.

[10] D. Champagne and R. B. Lee, "Scalable architectural support for trusted software," in *IEEE International Symposium on High-Performance Computer Architecture (HPCA)*, pp. 31–42, January 2010.

[11] C. A. Waldspurger, "Memory resource management in VMware ESX server," in *5th Symposium on Operating Systems Design and Implementation (OSDI)*, 2002.

[12] D. G. Murray, G. Milos, and S. Hand, "Improving Xen security through disaggregation," in *VEE '08: Proceedings of the fourth ACM SIGPLAN/SIGOPS international conference on Virtual execution environments*, 2008.

[13] "Cisco Nexus 1000V Series Switches," 2009. http://www.cisco.com/en/US/products/ps9902/index.html.

[14] Z. Wang and R. B. Lee, "New cache designs for thwarting software cache-based side channel attacks," in *34th International Symposium on Computer Architecture (ISCA)*, pp. 494 – 505, 2007.

[15] Z. Wang and R. B. Lee, "A novel cache architecture with enhanced performance and security," in *Proceedings of the 41st. Annual IEEE/ACM International Symposium on Microarchitecture (Micro-41)*, pp. 88–93, December 2008.

[16] "Intel Previews Intel Xeon Nehalem-EX Processor," 2009. http://www.intel.com/pressroom/archive/releases/20090526comp.htm.

[17] A. Shah, "AMD plans 16-core server chip: The Interlagos chip will be released in 2011," *Infoworld*, April 2009.

[18] "Dell PowerEdge R905 server product details," 2009. http://www.dell.com/us/en/enterprise/servers/pedge_r905/pd.aspx?refid=pedge_r905.

[19] C. Clark, K. Fraser, S. Hand, J. G. Hansen, E. Jul, C. Limpach, I. Pratt, and A. Warfield, "Live migration of virtual machines," in *2nd Symposium on Networked Systems Design and Implementation (NSDI)*, 2005.

[20] M. A. Kozuch, M. Kaminsky, and M. P. Ryan, "Migration without virtualization," in *12th Workshop on Hot Topics in Operating Systems (HotOS)*, 2009.

[21] O. Mutlu and T. Moscibroda, "Stall-time fair memory access scheduling for chip multiprocessors," in *MICRO 2007*, 2007.

[22] D. J. Bernstein, "Cache-timing attacks on AES," in *University of Illinois at Chicago Tech Report*, 2005. http://cr.yp.to/antiforgery/cachetiming-20050414.pdf.

[23] "PCI Local Bus Specification, 3.0 edition," 2004.

[24] "Intel 82599 10 gigabit ethernet controller," 2009. http://download.intel.com/design/network/prodbrf/321731.pdf.

[25] "LSI to Demonstrate Industry's First Single-Root I/O Virtualization Solution at Intel Developer Forum," 2009. http://www.lsi.com/news/product_news/2009/2009_09_22.html.

[26] "Cisco VN-Link: Virtualization-Aware Networking," 2010. http://www.cisco.com/en/US/solutions/collateral/ns340/ns517/ns224/ns892/ns894/white_paper_c11-525307_ps9902_Products_White_Paper.html.

[27] "Edge Virtual Bridging with VEB and VEPA," May 2009. http://www.ieee802.org/1/files/public/docs2009/new-hudson-vepa_seminar-20090514d.pdf.

[28] "Net/bridge: add basic VEPA support," June 2009. http://lwn.net/Articles/337547/.

[29] N. Santos, K. P. Gummadi, and R. Rodrigues, "Towards trusted cloud computing," in *Workshop On Hot Topics in Cloud Computing (HotCloud)*, 2009.

[30] IBM, "sHype - Secure Hypervisor." http://www.research.ibm.com/secure_systems_department/projects/hypervisor/.

[31] T. Garfinkel, B. Pfaff, J. Chow, M. Rosenblum, and D. Boneh, "Terra: A virtual machine-based platform for trusted computing," *SIGOPS Oper. Syst. Rev.*, vol. 37, no. 5, pp. 193–206, 2003.

[32] J. M. McCune, B. Parno, A. Perrig, M. K. Reiter, and H. Isozaki, "Flicker: An Execution Infrastructure for TCB Minimization," in *ACM European Conference in Computer Systems (EuroSys)*, 2008.

[33] G. E. Suh, C. W. O'Donnell, I. Sachdev, and S. Devadas, "Design and implementation of the AEGIS single-chip secure processor using physical random functions," in *Proc. ISCA*, June 2005.

[34] R. B. Lee, P. C. S. Kwan, J. P. McGregor, J. Dwoskin, and Z. Wang, "Architecture for protecting critical secrets in microprocessors," in *Proc. ISCA*, June 2005.

[35] D. Lie, C. Thekkath, M. Mitchell, P. Lincoln, D. Boneh, J. Mitchell, and M. Horowitz, "Architectural support for copy and tamper resistant software," in *Proc. ASPLOS*, November 2000.

[36] J. Dwoskin and R. B. Lee, "Hardware-rooted trust for secure key management and transient trust," in *ACM Conference on Computer and Communications Security (CCS)*, October 2007.

Modeling Critical Sections in Amdahl's Law and its Implications for Multicore Design

Stijn Eyerman Lieven Eeckhout
Ghent University, Belgium
Email: {seyerman,leeckhou}@elis.UGent.be

ABSTRACT

This paper presents a fundamental law for parallel performance: it shows that parallel performance is not only limited by sequential code (as suggested by Amdahl's law) but is also fundamentally limited by synchronization through critical sections. Extending Amdahl's software model to include critical sections, we derive the surprising result that the impact of critical sections on parallel performance can be modeled as a completely sequential part and a completely parallel part. The sequential part is determined by the probability for entering a critical section and the contention probability (i.e., multiple threads wanting to enter the same critical section).

This fundamental result reveals at least three important insights for multicore design. (i) Asymmetric multicore processors deliver less performance benefits relative to symmetric processors than suggested by Amdahl's law, and in some cases even worse performance. (ii) Amdahl's law suggests many tiny cores for optimum performance in asymmetric processors, however, we find that fewer but larger small cores can yield substantially better performance. (iii) Executing critical sections on the big core can yield substantial speedups, however, performance is sensitive to the accuracy of the critical section contention predictor.

Categories and Subject Descriptors

C.0 [**Computer Systems Organization**]: Modeling of computer architecture; C.4 [**Computer Systems Organization**]: Performance of Systems—*Modeling Techniques*

General Terms

Performance

Keywords

Analytical performance modeling, Amdahl's law, synchronization, critical sections

ISCA'10, June 19–23, 2010, Saint-Malo, France.

1. INTRODUCTION

Amdahl's law, in spite of its simplicity, has important consequences for the multicore or chip-multiprocessor (CMP) era [10]. The software model in Amdahl's law is simple though: it assumes either completely sequential code or completely parallel code. This paper augments Amdahl's software model with the notion of synchronization through critical sections. Assuming that part of the parallel code needs to be executed within critical sections and assuming that critical sections are entered at random times, we derive a simple analytical (probabilistic) model for how long it takes to execute a critical section (including the time waiting for the critical section to be released). This simple model reveals a novel and surprising insight: it shows that the time spent in critical sections can be modeled as a completely sequential part plus a completely parallel part. The sequential part is proportional to the probability for a critical section and the contention probability (multiple threads competing for the same critical section).

Augmenting Amdahl's law with this probabilistic model for critical sections reveals that parallel performance is not only limited by sequential code (as suggested by Amdahl's law) but is also fundamentally limited by synchronization. Although it is well understood that fine-grain synchronization and low contention rates lead to better performance, this paper is the first, to the best of our knowledge, to provide a theoretical underpinning.

This fundamental law has important implications for multicore design. For one, asymmetric multicore processors (with one big core for sequential code and many small cores for parallel code) offer smaller performance benefits relative to symmetric multicore processors than suggested by Amdahl's law. In some cases, asymmetric processors may even yield worse performance than symmetric processors, the reason being that contending critical sections are executed on the small cores rather than on the relatively larger cores in a symmetric multicore processor. Second, Amdahl's law suggests that optimum performance is achieved with many tiny cores in an asymmetric processor, however, we find it is beneficial to make these cores larger, and thus have fewer cores for the same hardware budget. Larger small cores speed up the execution of critical sections, thereby improving overall parallel performance (although there are fewer cores). Third, accelerating critical sections (ACS) [22] by migrating critical sections to the big core can yield substantial speedups, provided that a highly accurate critical section contention predictor is available. Naive ACS which migrates all critical sections to the big core results in false serialization which deteriorates performance, especially for low contention probabilities. The gap with perfect ACS, which executes only contending critical sections on the big core, is huge. Future research in ACS contention prediction is likely to yield substantial perfor-

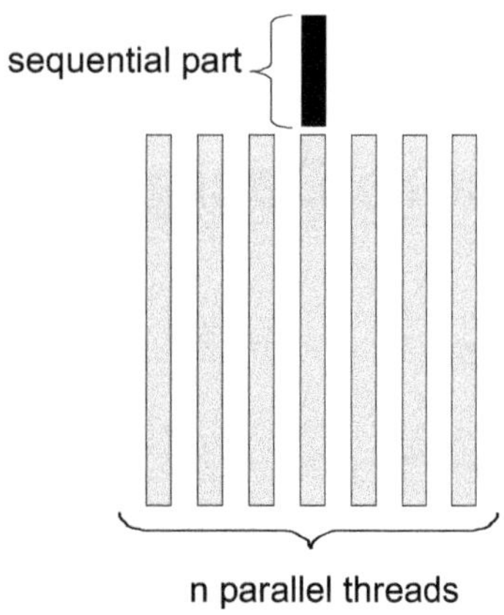

Figure 1: Amdahl's software model.

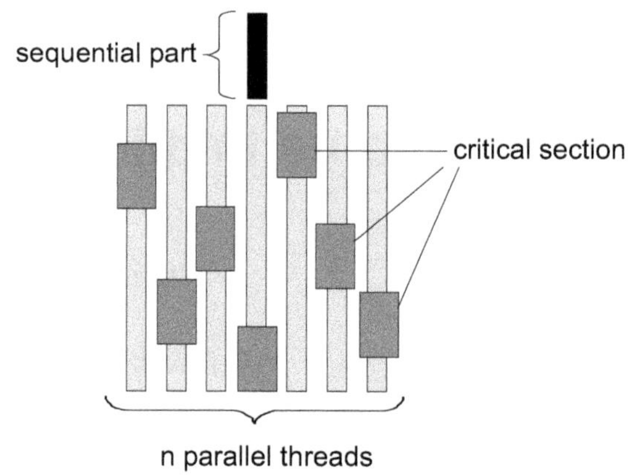

Figure 2: Amdahl's software model including critical sections.

mance benefits, and should focus on both eliminating false serialization and predicting contending critical sections.

2. AMDAHL'S LAW AND EXTENSIONS

We first briefly revisit Amdahl's law.

2.1 Amdahl's law

Define speedup as the original execution time divided by the enhanced execution time, and assume that a fraction f of a program's execution time is indefinitely parallelizable. Amdahl's law [1] then provides a formula for the speedup S that can be achieved by parallelizing the fraction f across n processors (see also Figure 1); the remaining fraction $(1 - f)$ is executed sequentially:

$$S = \frac{1}{(1-f) + \frac{f}{n}}. \qquad (1)$$

The significance of Amdahl's law for parallel computing is that it shows that the speedup is bound by a program's sequential part:

$$\lim_{n \to \infty} S = \frac{1}{1-f}. \qquad (2)$$

2.2 Amdahl's law for asymmetric CMPs

Asymmetric multicore processors have one or more cores that are more powerful than the others [2, 4, 6, 10, 13]. Amdahl's law suggests that only one core should get more resources; the others should be as small as possible. The reason is that the parallel part gets a linear speedup from adding cores; the sequential part gets only sublinear speedup, i.e., core performance increases sublinearly with resources [5]. Assume now that the parallel part is executed on the n small cores at performance of one; further, assume that the sequential part is executed on the big core which yields a speedup of p relative to small core execution. Hence, asymmetric multicore speedup is computed as [10]:

$$S = \frac{1}{\frac{1-f}{p} + \frac{f}{n+p}}. \qquad (3)$$

3. MODELING CRITICAL SECTIONS

Amdahl assumes a simple parallel software model: the program's execution time is either parallelizable or it is totally sequential. Amdahl's law does not take into account the impact of critical sections. We now extend Amdahl's law to model synchronization among parallel threads through critical sections.

Consider a program's sequential execution, and split it up in three fractions (see also Figure 2). We define f_{seq} as the totally sequential fraction of the program's execution that cannot be parallelized; this is the time required to spawn threads, distribute the data across the parallel threads, merge the data produced by the parallel worker threads, etc. Further, we define $f_{par,ncs}$ as the parallelizable fraction of the program's execution; this fraction is assumed to be indefinitely parallelizable, and does not need synchronization and is thus executed outside critical sections. Finally, we define $f_{par,cs}$ as the fraction of the program's execution time that can be parallelized but requires synchronization and is to be executed inside critical sections. If two or more threads compete for entering the same critical section at the same time, their execution will be serialized; if not, their execution can proceed in parallel. We define these fractions to sum up to one, i.e., $f_{seq} + f_{par,ncs} + f_{par,cs} = 1$, i.e., the fractions are all with respect to sequential execution.

3.1 Total execution time

We now compute what the execution time will be on a parallel machine. We therefore make a distinction between two cases, based on whether the total execution time can be approximated by the average per-thread execution time (i.e., all threads execute equally long, hence the total execution time can be approximated by the 'average' thread), or whether the total execution time is determined by the slowest thread (i.e., the time spent in critical sections is significant and the average thread is not representative for computing the total execution time).

3.1.1 Case #1: Execution time determined by average thread

The sequential part does not scale with parallelism ($T_{seq} \propto f_{seq}$); the parallel fraction executed outside critical sections on the other hand is indefinitely parallelizable ($T_{par,ncs} \propto f_{par,ncs}/n$). The difficulty now is to determine how long it will take to execute the parallel fraction due to critical sections ($T_{par,cs}$). For computing the average time spent in critical sections $T_{par,cs}$, we propose an analytical, probabilistic model.

We define the *probability for a critical section* during parallel execution P_{cs} as

$$P_{cs} = Pr[\textit{critical section} \mid \textit{parallel}] = \frac{f_{par,cs}}{f_{par,ncs} + f_{par,cs}} \qquad (4)$$

The probability for i threads out of n threads to be executing in critical sections is binomially distributed, assuming that critical sections are entered at random times — this is an example of a

Bernoulli experiment — hence:

$$Pr[\textit{i of n threads in critical section}] = \binom{n}{i} P_{cs}^{i} (1 - P_{cs})^{n-i} \quad (5)$$

We now define the *contention probability* P_{ctn}, or the probability for *two* critical sections to contend, i.e., both critical sections access the same shared memory state and hence they require serial execution, i.e., both critical sections are guarded by the same lock variable or both critical sections are executed within contending transactions.[1] Assuming that critical sections contend randomly, the probability for j threads out of these i threads to contend for the same critical section is also binomially distributed:

$$Pr[\textit{j of i threads contend for the same critical section}] = \binom{i}{j} P_{ctn}^{j} (1 - P_{ctn})^{i-j} \quad (6)$$

We are now ready to compute the average time spent in critical sections. Consider a thread entering a critical section. The probability for i out of the remaining $n-1$ threads to also enter a critical section is determined by Equation 5; the probability for j out of these i threads to contend with the given critical section is determined by Equation 6. If j other critical sections contend with the current critical section, then in total $j+1$ critical sections will serialize, and hence it takes $(j+1) f_{par,cs}/n$ time units to execute this critical section: $j \cdot f_{par,cs}/n$ time units for executing the other critical sections (while the given critical section waits for the critical section to be released), plus $f_{par,cs}/n$ time units to execute the given critical section (once the thread acquires the critical section). Putting it all together, the average time spent in a critical section is computed as:

$$T_{par,cs} \propto \sum_{i=0}^{n-1} \binom{n-1}{i} P_{cs}^{i} (1 - P_{cs})^{n-1-i} \cdot \sum_{j=0}^{i} \binom{i}{j} P_{ctn}^{j} (1 - P_{ctn})^{i-j} \cdot \frac{j+1}{n} \cdot f_{par,cs} \quad (7)$$

Exploiting the property $\sum_{i=0}^{n} \binom{n}{i} P^i (1-P)^{n-i} = nP$ (average of a binomial distribution), we can simplify this expression to the following equation:

$$T_{par,cs} \propto f_{par,cs} \cdot \left(P_{cs} P_{ctn} + (1 - P_{cs} P_{ctn}) \cdot \frac{1}{n} \right) \quad (8)$$

This expression reveals a novel, interesting and surprising insight: it shows that the average time spent in critical sections can be modeled as a completely sequential part plus a completely parallel part (see also Figure 3 for a graphical illustration). The sequential part is proportional to the probability for a critical section multiplied by the contention probability. The parallel part can be significant if the critical sections are small and show low contention probabilities.

Assuming that the total execution time of a parallel program can be approximated by the execution time of the 'average' thread, then the total execution time is proportional to

$$T \propto f_{seq} + f_{par,cs} P_{cs} P_{ctn} + \frac{f_{par,cs}(1 - P_{cs} P_{ctn}) + f_{par,ncs}}{n} \quad (9)$$

[1]For a parallel program with only one lock variable for all critical sections, $P_{ctn} = 1$ and hence all critical sections will serialize; P_{ctn} is smaller than one for fine-grained locking with multiple lock variables and/or through rarely contending transactions.

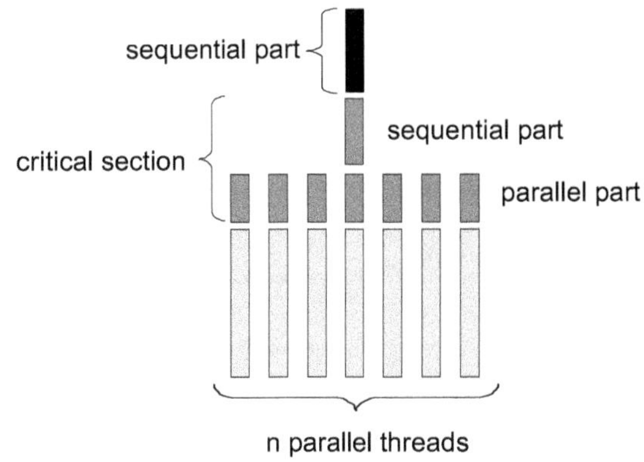

Figure 3: Critical sections can be modeled as a sequential part plus a parallel part.

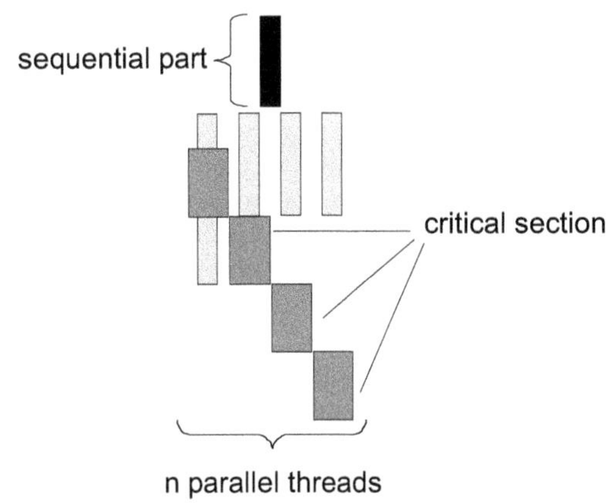

Figure 4: Example illustrating the case in which the total execution time is determined by the slowest thread.

3.1.2 *Case #2: Execution time determined by slowest thread*

The assumption that a parallel program's execution time equals the average per-thread execution time does not always hold true, especially in case the time spent in critical sections is high and/or contention probability is high — this is a case in which the total execution time is determined by the slowest thread, see Figure 4 for an example. We now derive a formula for the total execution time as the execution time of the slowest thread — we assume that the execution of the slowest thread is determined by the serialized execution of all the contending critical sections. The average execution time of the slowest thread is determined by three components: (i) the sequential part ($T_{seq} \propto f_{seq}$), (ii) the total time spent in contending critical sections which involves sequential execution ($T_{seq,cs} \propto f_{par,cs} P_{ctn}$), and (iii) the time spent executing parallel code including indefinitely parallel code and non-contending critical sections ($T_{par} \propto (f_{par,cs}(1 - P_{ctn}) + f_{par,cs})/2n$; given that we assume that critical section occur randomly, we need to add the factor 2 in the denominator, i.e., on average half the parallel code will be executed before the contending critical sections and half the parallel code will be executed after the contending critical sections). The total execution time then equals the average execution time of the slowest thread:

$$T \propto f_{seq} + f_{par,cs} P_{ctn} + \frac{f_{par,cs}(1 - P_{ctn}) + f_{par,ncs}}{2n} \quad (10)$$

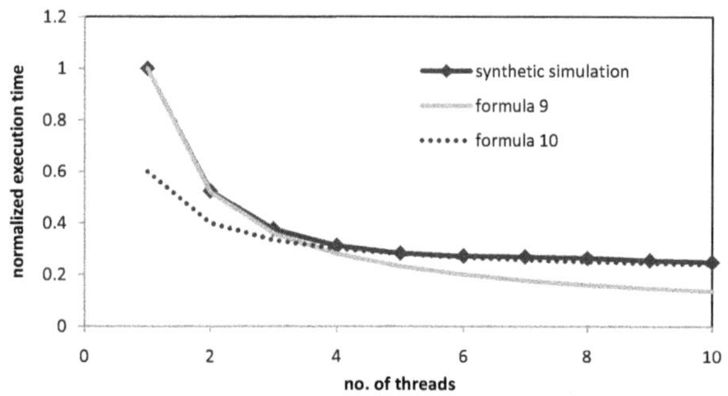

Figure 5: Validation of the analytical probabilistic model against a synthetic simulator.

3.1.3 Putting it together

We now have two expressions for the total execution time, each expression with its own set of assumptions. The former (case #1) assumes that the total execution time of the parallel program can be approximated by the average per-thread execution time; the latter (case #2) makes the observation that this assumption no longer holds true once the serialized execution of contending critical sections exceeds the average per-thread execution time. Hence, we conjecture the overall execution time can be computed as the maximum of these two expressions:

$$T \propto f_{seq} + \max\left(f_{par,cs}P_{cs}P_{ctn} + \frac{f_{par,cs}(1-P_{cs}P_{ctn}) + f_{par,ncs}}{n};\; f_{par,cs}P_{ctn} + \frac{f_{par,cs}(1-P_{ctn}) + f_{par,ncs}}{2n}\right) \quad (11)$$

Because this formula is fairly complicated and builds on assumptions and probabilistic theory, we validate the formula against a synthetic simulator that generates and simulates a synthetic parallel workload. The validation was done across a wide range of possible values for $f_{par,cs}$, $f_{par,ncs}$, P_{ctn} and n; the average absolute error across all of these experiments equals 3%. Figure 5 shows the execution time as a function of the number of threads n for $f_{par,cs} = 0.5$, $f_{par,ncs} = 0.5$ and $P_{ctn} = 0.5$. For a small number of threads, then formula 9 (case #1) is more accurate, and for a large number of threads then formula 10 (case #2) is more accurate and converges towards 0.25 which equals the $f_{par,cs} \cdot P_{ctn} = 0.5 \cdot 0.5 = 0.25$. This graph illustrates that the max operator is a reasonable approximation.

3.2 Extending Amdahl's law

Integrating the above in Amdahl's law yields the following result for $n \to \infty$:

$$\lim_{n\to\infty} S = \frac{1}{f_{seq} + \max(f_{par,cs}P_{cs}P_{ctn}; f_{par,cs}P_{ctn})} = \frac{1}{f_{seq} + f_{par,cs}P_{ctn}} \quad (12)$$

This is a novel fundamental law for parallel performance: it shows that parallel speedup is not only limited by the sequential part (as suggested by Amdahl's law) but is also fundamentally limited by synchronization. In other words, the larger the time spent in critical sections, the lower the maximum speedup. Similarly, the larger the contention probability, the lower the maximum speedup. Although it is intuitively well understood that fine-grained critical sections and low contention rates lead to better performance, this paper is the first to provide a theoretical underpinning for this insight. It shows that parallel performance is fundamentally limited by synchronization, and more specifically, critical section size and their contention probability.

4. IMPLICATIONS FOR CMP DESIGN

The above fundamental finding has important implications for multicore design, especially in the context of asymmetric multicore processors.

4.1 Asymmetric multicores

One compelling argument for asymmetric multicore processors is that the sequential fraction of a program's execution can be executed on the big core whereas the parallel work can be done on the small cores [2, 3, 4, 10, 15]. Given Amdahl's law, this may yield substantially higher speedups compared to symmetric multicore processors.

Critical sections however limit the potential benefit from asymmetric multicore processors, because the parallel part of the program's execution time is not indefinitely parallelizable. Instead there is a sequential part due to critical sections that will be executed on the small cores. Assuming n small cores with performance of one, along with a big core that yields a speedup of p compared to the small cores, the execution time on an asymmetric processor is:

$$T \propto \frac{f_{seq}}{p} + \max\left(f_{par,cs}P_{cs}P_{ctn} + \frac{f_{par,cs}(1-P_{cs}P_{ctn}) + f_{par,ncs}}{n+p};\; f_{par,cs}P_{ctn} + \frac{f_{par,cs}(1-P_{ctn}) + f_{par,ncs}}{2(n+p)}\right) \quad (13)$$

The key insight from this equation is that the sequential part due to critical sections has an even bigger (relative) impact on performance for an asymmetric multicore processor than is the case for a symmetric multicore processor. This is because the sequential fraction of the execution time is sped up on the asymmetric processor (by a factor p) relative to the symmetric processor which is not the case for the sequential fraction due to critical sections (compare Equation 13 against Equation 11). The impact of sequential execution of critical sections increases further with increasing probability for a critical section and contention probability.

This, in its turn, has an important implication on how to design an asymmetric multicore processor. For asymmetric multicore processors, the original Amdahl's law suggests that the maximum speedup is achieved with the small cores being as small as possible. Tiny cores imply that more cores can be put on the die, which yields a linear performance speedup for parallel code; larger cores (and thus fewer cores) do not yield as much performance benefit because of sublinear core performance improvements with resources [5]. Now, the new Amdahl's law for asymmetric processors (Equation 13) which includes the effect of critical sections, suggests that the small cores in asymmetric processors should be sufficiently large (and not be as small as possible as suggested by Amdahl's law) because they will be executing the sequential part of the critical sections. In other words, it is important that critical sections be executed fast so that other threads can enter their critical sections as soon as possible.

To verify this intuition, we now consider a simple design problem in which we have a total number of 256 base core equivalents

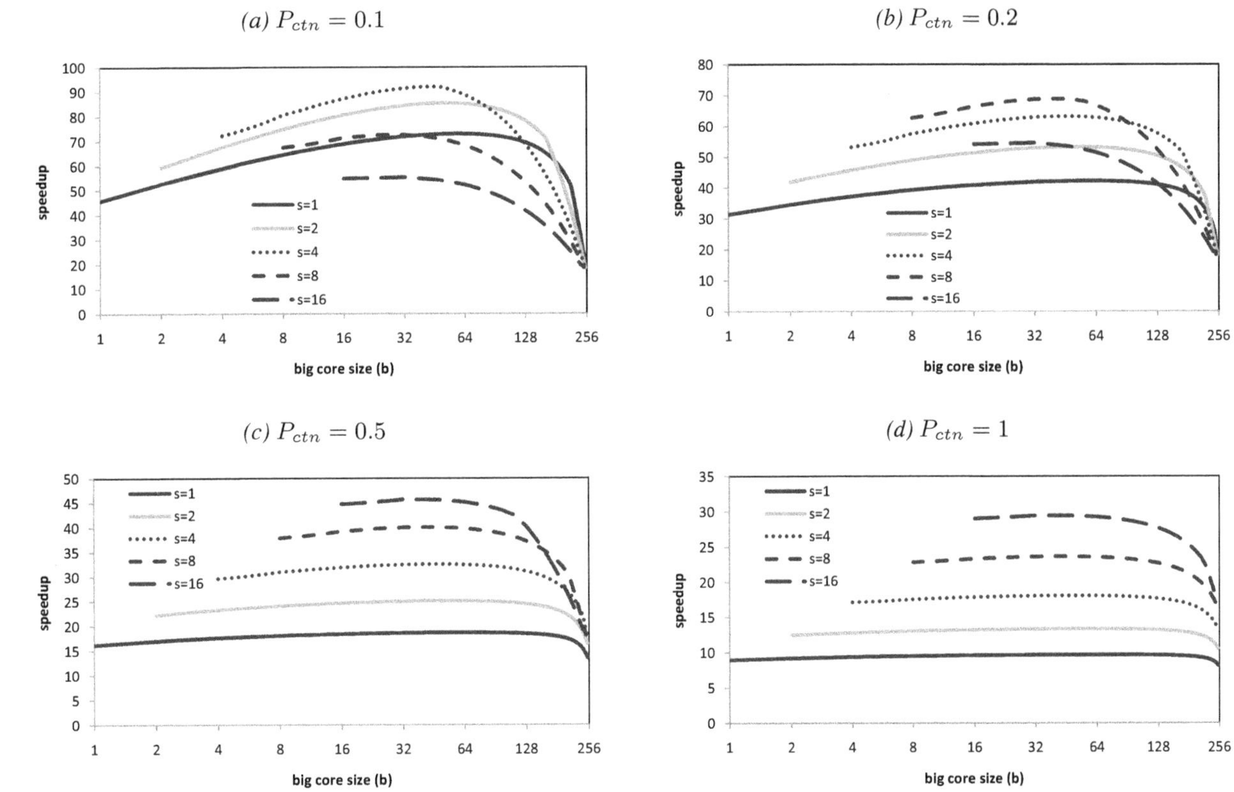

Figure 6: Speedup for an asymmetric processor as a function of the big core size (b) and small core size (s) for different contention rates, assuming a total number of 256 BCEs.

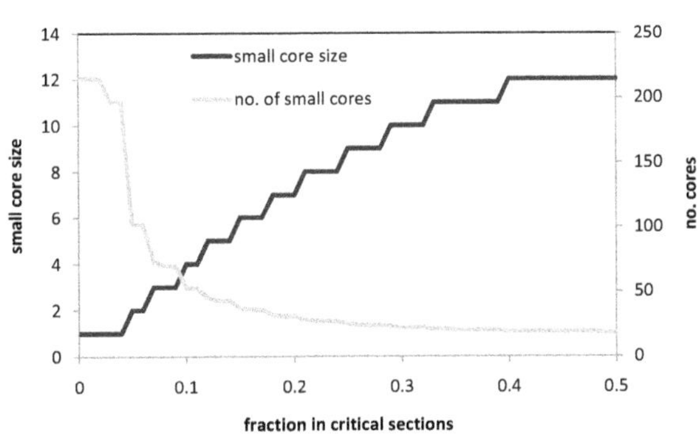

Figure 7: Optimum number of small cores and their size as a function of the fraction of time spent in critical sections, assuming $P_{ctn} = 0.1$.

(BCEs), following the approach taken by Hill and Marty [10]. We now divide these BCEs among the big core (b BCEs) and the small cores (s BCEs per core). Figure 6 shows the attainable speedup as a function of the size of the big core (b) and the size of the small cores (s); we assume a square-root relationship between resources (number of BCEs) and performance [5] (also known as Pollack's law). For low contention rates, small cores yield the best speedup (see Figure 6(a)). However, for higher contention rates, larger cores yield the best performance. For example, for a contention rate of 20% (Figure 6(b)), optimum performance is achieved for a large core of size 40 BCEs and 27 small cores of size 8 BCEs. Figure 7 further confirms this finding and shows the optimum number of small cores and their size as a function of $f_{par,cs}$, or the fraction of the program's execution in critical sections. The larger the fraction spent in critical sections, the larger the small cores should be, and (hence) the fewer small cores there need to be for optimum performance.

4.2 Accelerating critical sections

A solution to mitigate the large impact of critical sections on parallel performance, is to execute the critical sections on the big core in an asymmetric multicore processor. The basic idea is that if critical sections are released earlier, other threads can enter the critical section faster. This technique is called Accelerating Critical Sections (ACS) [22].

4.2.1 *Naive ACS*

Naive ACS would execute all critical sections serially on the large core, which yields the following execution time:

$$T \propto \frac{f_{seq} + f_{par,cs}}{p} + \frac{f_{par,ncs}}{n+p}. \tag{14}$$

Compared to Equation 13, we observe that the sequential part due to synchronization is sped up by a factor p, however, the parallel part gets slowed down by a factor $(n+p)/p$. Naive ACS may lead to serialized execution of non-contending critical sections (false serialization) which potentially has a detrimental effect on performance.

4.2.2 *Perfect ACS*

Perfect ACS, which would yield optimum ACS performance, would execute only the sequential part due to synchronization (i.e., the contending critical sections) on the big core; the parallel part (including the non-contending critical sections) would still be executed on the small cores. The execution time under perfect ACS equals:

$$\begin{aligned} T \propto & \frac{f_{seq}}{p} + \\ & \max\Big(\frac{f_{par,cs}P_{cs}P_{ctn}}{p} + \frac{f_{par,cs}(1-P_{cs}P_{ctn}) + f_{par,ncs}}{n+p}; \\ & \frac{f_{par,cs}P_{ctn}}{p} + \frac{f_{par,cs}(1-P_{ctn}) + f_{par,ncs}}{2(n+p)}\Big) \end{aligned} \tag{15}$$

Perfect ACS is hard (if not impossible) to achieve because it requires a predictor that perfectly predicts whether critical sections will contend (and thus need to be serialized and executed on the big core).

4.2.3 *Selective ACS*

Suleman et al. [22] also recognized that in order to mitigate false serialization, one needs to predict whether critical sections will contend or not — this is called Selective ACS. Predicting whether critical sections will contend or not is non-trivial, and mispredictions have significant impact on performance. Predicting that a critical section will contend and needs to be executed on the big core, which eventually does not contend — a false positive — results in false serialization. Predicting that a critical section will not contend and execute that critical section on a small core, which eventually results in a contention — a false negative — unnecessarily prolongs the critical section's execution. Assuming a contention predictor with sensitivity α (ability to predict true positives) and specificity β (ability to predict true negatives), the execution time under selective ACS is given by (define $P_{cf} = P_{cs}P_{ctn}$):

$$\begin{aligned} T \propto & \frac{f_{seq}}{p} + \\ & \max\Big(\frac{f_{par,cs}(\alpha P_{cf} + (1-\beta)(1-P_{cf}))}{p} + \\ & (1-\alpha)f_{par,cs}P_{cf} + \frac{f_{par,cs}\beta(1-P_{cf}) + f_{par,ncs}}{n+p}; \\ & \frac{f_{par,cs}(\alpha P_{ctn} + (1-\beta)(1-P_{ctn}))}{p} + \\ & (1-\alpha)f_{par,cs}P_{ctn} + \frac{f_{par,cs}\beta(1-P_{ctn}) + f_{par,ncs}}{2(n+p)}\Big) \end{aligned} \tag{16}$$

Note that for $\alpha = 1$ and $\beta = 0$, selective ACS equals naive ACS; for $\alpha = 0$ and $\beta = 1$, selective ACS equals a conventional asymmetric multicore processor (see Equation 13); perfect ACS means $\alpha = 1$ and $\beta = 1$. We will evaluate ACS performance and its dependence on specificity and sensitivity as part of the next section.

4.3 High-level CMP design space exploration

Having obtained the above formulas, we can now perform a high-level design space exploration for multicore processors in which we compare symmetric multicore processors and asymmetric multicore processors against naive, perfect ACS and selective ACS, while varying the number of cores, their size and the fraction of the program's execution time spent in critical sections. We will vary the fraction of the time spent in critical sections and their contention rates, and reason about which processor architecture yields the best performance. Similar as before, we assume 256 BCEs and a square-root relationship between resources (number of BCEs) and core-level performance [5]. We consider the following processor architectures:

- **Symmetric multicore.** The symmetric multicore processor is optimized for maximum speedup, i.e., we optimize the number of cores (and their size) for optimum speedup.
- **Asymmetric multicore with tiny cores.** The asymmetric multicore processor has tiny small cores (single-BCE with performance of one). We optimize the big core for optimum speedup. This corresponds to the asymmetric processor assumed by Hill and Marty [10], and is the optimum asymmetric processor according to the original Amdahl's law.
- **Asymmetric multicore with optimized cores.** Both the big core and the small cores are optimized for optimum performance. The small cores are potentially larger than a single BCE in order to execute serialized critical sections faster.
- **Naive ACS.** The big core is optimized for optimum performance; the optimum small core size is one BCE. All critical sections are executed on the big core.
- **Perfect ACS.** Same as for naive ACS, however, only the contending critical sections are serialized on the big core; the non-contending critical sections are executed in parallel on the small cores.

Figure 8 shows the speedup for each of these processor architectures for different contention rates (different graphs show different contention rates) and different fractions of the time spent in critical sections ($f_{par,cs}$ on the horizontal axes). One percent of the code is completely sequential ($f_{seq} = 0.01$). We derive some interesting insights.

Asymmetric versus symmetric multicore processors. The benefit of asymmetric processing over symmetric processing is limited by critical sections (see the symmetric and asymmetric ($s = 1$) curves in Figure 8). In the absence of critical sections, asymmetric processors offer a substantial performance benefits over symmetric processors, see the leftmost points on the graphs ($f_{par,cs} = 0$) — these points correspond to the data presented by Hill and Marty [10]. However, as the time spent in critical sections and their contention rate increases, the relative benefit from asymmetric multicore processing decreases. For large critical sections and high contention rates, symmetric multicore processors even yield worse performance compared to asymmetric processors with tiny small cores. The reason is that the contending critical sections serialize on the small single-BCE cores in the asymmetric processor; on a symmetric processor, the critical sections are executed on relatively larger cores.

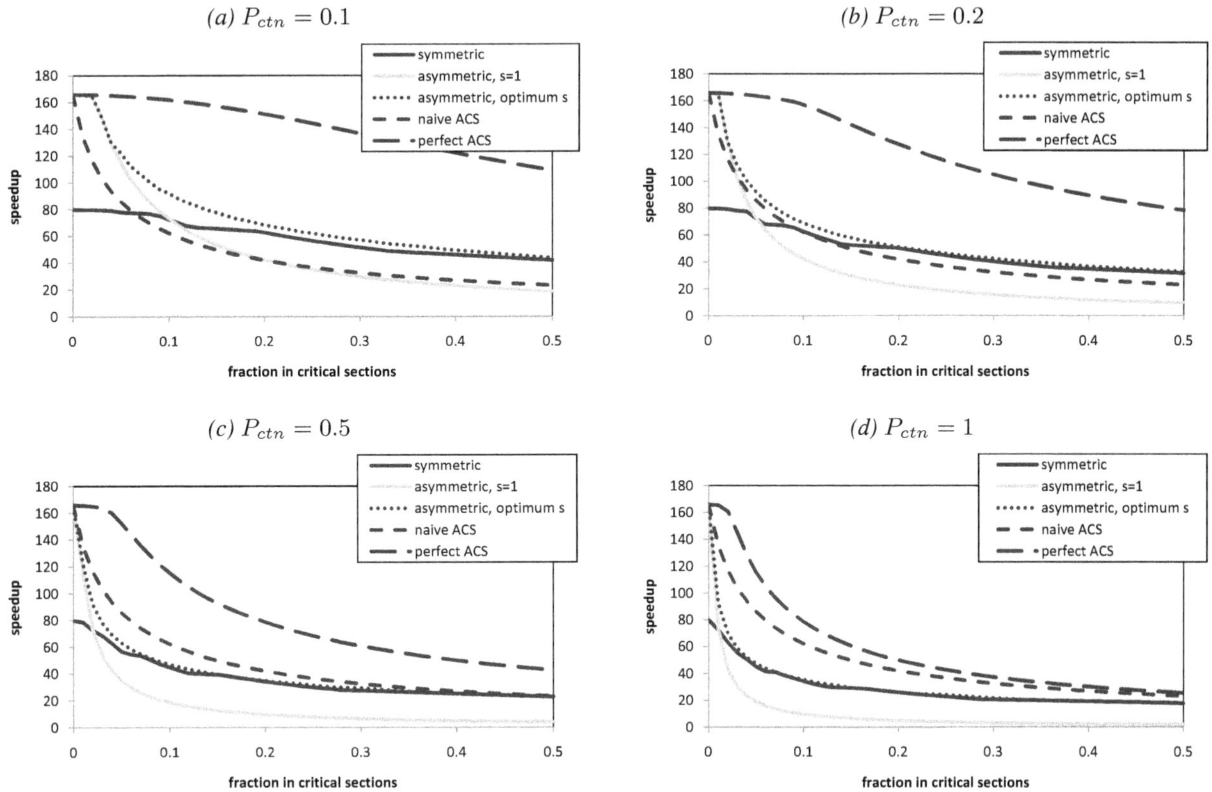

Figure 8: High-level design space exploration across symmetric, asymmetric and ACS multicore processors while varying the fraction of the time spent in critical sections and their contention rates. Fraction spent in sequential code equals 1%.

Because critical sections serialize on the small cores, it is beneficial to increase the small core size to be larger than a single BCE. By optimizing the big core and small core sizes, one can optimize asymmetric multicore processor performance to achieve the best of both worlds and achieve at least as good performance as symmetric processors and asymmetric processors with single-BCE small cores (see the asymmetric curve with optimum s in Figure 8).

Naive ACS. Naive ACS serializes all critical sections on the big core, even though these critical sections may not contend with each other (false serialization). Naive ACS performance quickly deteriorates for even small increases in the time spent in critical sections, see left part of the graphs ($0 < f_{par,cs} < 0.1$). Naive ACS performs worse than an asymmetric processor with optimum small core size for low contention rates (see $P_{ctn} = 0.1$), however, for larger contention rates, naive ACS performs better than asymmetric (and symmetric) processors. This is because naive ACS executes all critical sections on the big core, whereas the asymmetric and symmetric processors execute these critical sections on relatively small cores.

Huge gap between naive and perfect ACS. There is a huge gap between naive and perfect ACS for low contention probabilities (see $P_{ctn} = 0.1$ and $P_{ctn} = 0.2$). Perfect ACS predicts whether or not critical sections will contend; if they do contend, the critical sections are executed on the big core; if not, they are executed in parallel on the small cores. This suggests that significant performance benefits are to be gained from improving ACS contention predictors — a good avenue for future work. However, for higher contention probabilities, this gap becomes smaller (see $P_{ctn} = 0.5$ and $P_{ctn} = 1$), and naive ACS is likely to achieve most of the benefits of perfect ACS.

Selective ACS. Figure 9 shows speedup as a function of the ACS contention predictor's specificity and sensitivity, and fraction in critical sections $f_{par,cs}$ on the horizontal axis. The important insight here is that for selective ACS to yield speedup compared to naive ACS, the contention predictor's sensitivity is more important than its specificity. (ACS with $\alpha = 0.98$ and $\beta = 0.50$ yields better performance than naive ACS across all critical section sizes.) Hence, the ability to predict contending critical sections (that will be executed on the big core) is more important than eliminating false serialization (i.e., executing non-contending critical sections on the small cores). Optimizing and balancing both sensitivity and specificity yields even better performance (see the curve with $\alpha = 0.85$ and $\beta = 0.85$ in Figure 9), especially for smaller fractions of time spent in critical sections.

5. LIMITATIONS

Arguably, the synchronization model presented in this paper has its limitations. For one, it is limited to critical sections only and does not tackle other forms of synchronization. Further, it assumes that the parallel workload is homogeneous, i.e., all threads execute the same code and exhibit the same probability for a critical section and the same contention probability. We also assume that the critical sections are entered at random times. The original Amdahl's law and its extension for multicore hardware also has its limitations, as discussed by Hill and Marty [10]. Some researchers even question the validity of Amdahl's law, see for example [7, 19]. However, and more importantly though, the goal of the model is not to present accurate quantitative performance numbers and predictions, but to provide insight and intuition, and stimulate discussion and future work.

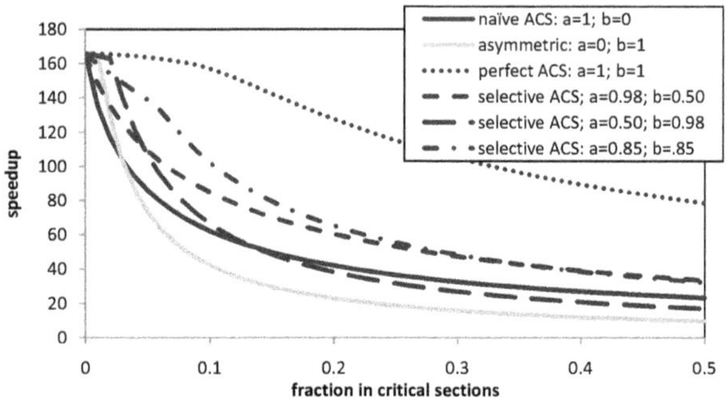

Figure 9: Speedup as a function of the ACS contention predictor's specificity and sensitivity. Fraction spent in sequential code equals 1%, and the contention probability equals 0.2.

6. RELATED WORK

6.1 Asymmetric processors

Asymmetric processors have been proposed to improve performance by many researchers, see for example [10, 15, 18]. As suggested by Amdahl's law, the big core executes the sequential part whereas the parallel part is executed on the small cores. None of these prior works incorporated the notion of critical sections though. However, when incorporated in Amdahl's law, critical sections significantly change the view on asymmetric processors in a number of ways — as described extensively in this paper.

6.2 Other architecture paradigms

The insights from this paper could also inspire other architecture paradigms. For example, multicore processors with each core supporting simultaneous multithreading (SMT) [24] could benefit from a critical section contention predictor in a similar way as we discussed for ACS on asymmetric multicores. The thread entering a predicted contending critical section could be given more or even all fetch slots by the SMT fetch policy (i.e., throttle the other threads), so that the critical section can execute faster and is not slowed down by other co-executing threads. Core fusion [11] can benefit in a similar way: the critical section contention predictor can predict when to fuse multiple small cores to form a more powerful core at runtime. Also, a conflict contention predictor would enable applying core-level DVFS [12] on a multicore processor to contending critical sections which would optimize performance (execute the critical sections faster) while limiting power consumption (by not boosting non-contending critical sections).

6.3 Feedback-driven threading

Suleman et al. [23] propose feedback-driven threading, a framework for dynamically controlling the number of threads during runtime. They propose a simple analytical model to derive the optimum number of threads. The model proposed for applications that are bounded by synchronization is similar to the model discussed in Section 3.1.2 which assumes that the total execution time is determined by the slowest thread and the serialized execution of the contending critical sections.

6.4 Reducing impact of critical sections

Reducing the impact of critical sections on parallel performance is a very active field of research. It is well known that fine-grain synchronization (i.e., small critical sections) generally lead to better performance than coarse-grain synchronization (i.e., large critical sections) — at the cost of significant programming effort. The critical section model presented in this paper provides a theoretical underpinning for this well-known insight: critical section size relates to the probability for a critical section P_{cs} and has a substantial impact on parallel performance.

Several recent enhancements reduce contention (P_{ctn}) compared to lock-based critical sections. Techniques such as transactional memory (TM) [8, 17, 9], speculative lock elision [20], transactional lock removal [21] and speculative synchronization [14] execute critical sections speculatively without acquiring the lock, and if they do not access the same shared data, they are committed successfully.

6.5 Workload characterization

Stanford's TCC group proposed and characterized the STAMP TM benchmark suite [16]. They found that several of these benchmarks spend a substantial amount of time in critical sections (transactions) — this relates to P_{cs} in our model. Only 2 of the 8 benchmarks spend less than 20% in transactions, one benchmarks spends around 40% of its time in transactions, and the remaining 5 benchmarks spend over 80% and up to 100% in transactions. The paper does not report contention probabilities, but instead reports the number of retries per transaction: depending on the TM system, some benchmarks exhibit anything between zero retries (no contention) up to 10 retries per transaction. We thus believe that the values assumed in this paper for P_{cs} and P_{ctn} are reasonably realistic.

7. CONCLUSION

This paper augments Amdahl's law with the notion of critical sections. A simple analytical (probabilistic) model reveals that the impact of critical sections can be split up in a completely sequential and a completely parallel part. This leads to a new fundamental law: parallel performance is not only limited by the sequential part (as suggested by Amdahl's law) but is also fundamentally limited by critical sections. This result provides a theoretical underpinning for research efforts towards fine-grain synchronization and low contention rates.

This fundamental result has important implications for asymmetric multicore processor design. (i) The performance benefit of asymmetric multicore processors may not be as high as suggested by Amdahl's law, and may even be worse than symmetric multicore processors for workloads with many and large critical sections and high contention probabilities. (ii) The small cores should not be tiny as suggested by Amdahl's law, but should instead be larger to execute critical sections faster. (iii) Accelerating critical sections through execution on the big core may yield substantial speedups, however, performance is very sensitive to the critical section contention predictor.

8. ACKNOWLEDGEMENTS

We thank Aater Suleman, Mark Hill and the anonymous reviewers for their constructive and insightful feedback. Stijn Eyerman is supported through a postdoctoral fellowship by the Research Foundation–Flanders (FWO). Additional support is provided by the FWO projects G.0232.06, G.0255.08, and G.0179.10, and the UGent-BOF projects 01J14407 and 01Z04109.

9. REFERENCES

[1] G. M. Amdahl. Validity of the single-processor approach to achieving large-scale computing capabilities. In *Proceedings*

of the American Federation of Information Processing Societies Conference (AFIPS), pages 483–485, 1967.

[2] M. Annavaram, E. Grochowski, and J. Shen. Mitigating Amdahl's law through EPI throttling. In *Proceedings of the International Symposium on Computer Architecture (ISCA)*, pages 298–309, June 2005.

[3] K. Asanovic, R. Bodik, B. C. Catanzaro, J. J. Gebis, P. Husbands, K. Keutzer, D. A. Patterson, W. L. Plishker, J. Shalf, S. W. Williams, and K. A. Yelick. The landscape of parallel computing research: A view from berkeley. Technical Report UCB/EECS-2006-183, EECS Department, University of California, Berkeley, Dec. 2006.

[4] S. Balakrishnan, R. Rajwar, M. Upton, and K. Lai. The impact of performance asymmetry in emerging multicore architectures. In *Proceedings of the International Symposium on Computer Architecture (ISCA)*, pages 506–517, June 2005.

[5] S. Borkar. Thousand core chips — a technology perspective. In *Proceedings of the Design Automation Conference (DAC)*, pages 746–749, June 2007.

[6] M. Gschwind, H. P. Hofstee, B. Flachs, M. Hopkins, Y. Watanabe, and T. Yamazaki. Synergistic processing in Cell's multicore architecture. *IEEE Micro*, 26(2):10–24, March/April 2006.

[7] J. L. Gustafson. Reevaluating Amdahl's law. *Communications of the ACM*, 31(5):532–533, May 1988.

[8] L. Hammond, V. Wong, M. Chen, B. D. Carlstrom, J. D. D. an B. Hertzberg, M. K. Prabhu, H. Wijaya, C. Kozyrakis, and K. Olukotun. Transactional memory coherence and consistency. In *Proceedings of the International Symposium on Computer Architecture (ISCA)*, pages 102–113, June 2004.

[9] M. Herlihy and J. Moss. Transactional memory: Architectural support for lock-free data structures. In *Proceedings of the International Symposium on Computer Architecture (ISCA)*, pages 289–300, June 1993.

[10] M. D. Hill and M. R. Marty. Amdahl's law in the multicore era. *IEEE Computer*, 41(7):33–38, July 2008.

[11] E. Ipek, M. Kirman, N. Kirman, and J. F. Martinez. Core fusion: Accommodating software diversity in chip multiprocessors. In *Proceedings of the International Symposium on Computer Architecture (ISCA)*, pages 186–197, June 2007.

[12] W. Kim, M. S. Gupta, G.-Y. Wei, and D. Brooks. System level analysis of fast, per-core DVFS using on-chip switching regulators. In *Proceedings of the International Symposium on High-Performance Computer Architecture (HPCA)*, pages 123–134, Feb. 2008.

[13] R. Kumar, K. I. Farkas, N. P. Jouppi, P. Ranganathan, and D. M. Tullsen. Single-ISA heterogeneous multi-core architectures: The potential for processor power reduction. In *Proceedings of the ACM/IEEE Annual International Symposium on Microarchitecture (MICRO)*, pages 81–92, Dec. 2003.

[14] J. F. Martinez and J. Torrellas. Speculative synchronization: Applying thread-level speculation to explicitly parallel applications. In *Proceedings of the International Conference on Architectural Support for Programming Languages and Operating Systems (ASPLOS)*, pages 18–29, Oct. 2002.

[15] D. Menasce and V. Almeida. Cost-performance analysis of heterogeneity in supercomputer architectures. In *Proceedings of the International Conference on Supercomputing (ICS)*, pages 169–177, Nov. 1990.

[16] C. C. Minh, J. Chung, C. Kozyrakis, and K. Olukotun. STAMP: Stanford transactional applications for multi-processing. In *Proceedings of the IEEE International Symposium on Workload Characterization (IISWC)*, pages 35–46, Sept. 2008.

[17] K. E. Moore, J. Bobba, M. J. Moravan, M. D. Hill, and D. A. Wood. LogTM: Log-based transactional memory. In *Proceedings of the International Symposium on High Performance Computer Architecture (HPCA)*, pages 254–265, Feb. 2006.

[18] T. Y. Morad, U. C. Weiser, A. Kolodny, M. Valero, and A. Ayguade. Performance, power efficiency and scalability of asymmetric cluster chip multiprocessors. *IEEE Computer Architecture Letters*, 5(1):14–17, Jan. 2006.

[19] J. M. Paul and B. H. Meyer. Amdahl's law revisited for single chip systems. *International Jounal of Parallel Programming*, 35(2):101–123, Apr. 2007.

[20] R. Rajwar and J. R. Goodman. Speculative lock elision: Enabling highly concurrent multithreaded execution. In *Proceedings of the International Symposium on Microarchitecture (MICRO)*, pages 294–305, Dec. 2001.

[21] R. Rajwar and J. R. Goodman. Transactional lock-free execution of lock-based programs. In *Proceedings of the International Conference on Architectural Support for Programming Languages and Operating Systems (ASPLOS)*, pages 5–17, Oct. 2002.

[22] M. A. Suleman, O. Mutlu, M. K. Qureshi, and Y. N. Patt. Accelerating critical section execution with asymmetric multi-core architectures. In *Proceedings of the International Conference on Architectural Support for Programming Languages and Operating Systems (ASPLOS)*, pages 253–264, Mar. 2009.

[23] M. A. Suleman, M. K. Qureshi, and Y. N. Patt. Feedback-driven threading: Power-efficient and high-performance execution of multi-threaded workloads on CMPs. In *Proceedings of the International Conference on Architectural Support for Programming Languages and Operating Systems (ASPLOS)*, pages 277–286, Mar. 2008.

[24] D. M. Tullsen, S. J. Eggers, J. S. Emer, H. M. Levy, J. L. Lo, and R. L. Stamm. Exploiting choice: Instruction fetch and issue on an implementable simultaneous multithreading processor. In *Proceedings of the 23rd Annual International Symposium on Computer Architecture (ISCA)*, pages 191–202, May 1996.

Resistive Computation: Avoiding the Power Wall with Low-Leakage, STT-MRAM Based Computing

Xiaochen Guo Engin İpek Tolga Soyata

University of Rochester
Rochester, NY 14627 USA
{xiguo, ipek, soyata}@ece.rochester.edu

ABSTRACT

As CMOS scales beyond the 45nm technology node, leakage concerns are starting to limit microprocessor performance growth. To keep dynamic power constant across process generations, traditional MOSFET scaling theory prescribes reducing supply and threshold voltages in proportion to device dimensions, a practice that induces an exponential increase in subthreshold leakage. As a result, leakage power has become comparable to dynamic power in current-generation processes, and will soon exceed it in magnitude if voltages are scaled down any further. Beyond this inflection point, multicore processors will not be able to afford keeping more than a small fraction of all cores active at any given moment. Multicore scaling will soon hit a power wall.

This paper presents *resistive computation*, a new technique that aims at avoiding the power wall by migrating most of the functionality of a modern microprocessor from CMOS to spin-torque transfer magnetoresistive RAM (STT-MRAM)—a CMOS-compatible, leakage-resistant, non-volatile resistive memory technology. By implementing much of the on-chip storage and combinational logic using leakage-resistant, scalable RAM blocks and lookup tables, and by carefully re-architecting the pipeline, an STT-MRAM based implementation of an eight-core Sun Niagara-like CMT processor reduces chip-wide power dissipation by 1.7× and leakage power by 2.1× at the 32nm technology node, while maintaining 93% of the system throughput of a CMOS-based design.

Categories and Subject Descriptors

B.3.1 [**Memory Structures**]: Semiconductor Memories; C.1.4 [**Processor Architectures**]: Parallel Architectures

General Terms

Design, Performance

Keywords

Power-efficiency, STT-MRAM

ISCA'10, June 19–23, 2010, Saint-Malo, France.

1. INTRODUCTION

Over the past two decades, the CMOS microprocessor design process has been confronted by a number of seemingly insurmountable technological challenges (e.g., the memory wall [4] and the wire delay problem [1]). At each turn, new classes of systems have been architected to meet these challenges, and microprocessor performance has continued to scale with exponentially increasing transistor budgets. With more than two billion transistors integrated on a single die [27], power dissipation has become the current critical challenge facing modern chip design. On-chip power dissipation now exhausts the maximum capability of conventional cooling technologies; any further increases will require expensive and challenging solutions (e.g., liquid cooling), which would significantly increase overall system cost.

Multicore architectures emerged in the early 2000s as a means of avoiding the power wall, increasing parallelism under a constant clock frequency to avoid an increase in dynamic power consumption. Although multicore systems did manage to keep power dissipation at bay for the past decade, with the impending transition to 32nm CMOS, they are starting to experience scalability problems of their own. To maintain constant dynamic power at a given clock rate, supply and threshold voltages must scale with feature size, but this approach induces an exponential rise in leakage power, which is fast approaching dynamic power in magnitude. Under this poor scaling behavior, the number of active cores on a chip will have to grow much more slowly than the total transistor budget allows; indeed, at 11nm, over 80% of all cores may have to be dormant at all times to fit within the chip's thermal envelope [16].

This paper presents *resistive computation*, an architectural technique that aims at developing a new class of power-efficient, scalable microprocessors based on emerging resistive memory technologies. Power- and performance-critical hardware resources such as caches, memory controllers, and floating-point units are implemented using spin-torque transfer magnetoresistive RAM (STT-MRAM)—a CMOS- compatible, near-zero static-power, persistent memory that has been in development since the early 2000s [12], and is expected to replace commercially available magnetic RAMs by 2013 [13]. The key idea is to implement most of the on-chip storage and combinational logic using scalable, leakage-resistant RAM arrays and lookup tables (LUTs) constructed from STT-MRAM to lower leakage, thereby allowing many more active cores under a fixed power budget than a pure CMOS implementation could afford.

By adopting hardware structures amenable to fast and efficient LUT-based computing, and by carefully re-architecting the pipeline, an STT-MRAM based implementation of an eight-core, Sun Niagara-like CMT processor reduces leakage and total power at 32nm by 2.1× and 1.7×, respectively, while maintaining 93% of the system throughput of a pure CMOS implementation.

2. BACKGROUND AND MOTIVATION

Simultaneously to power-related problems in CMOS, DRAM is facing severe scalability problems due to precise charge placement and sensing hurdles in deep-submicron processes. In response, the industry is turning its attention to *resistive memory technologies* such as phase-change memory (PCM), memristors (RRAM), and spin-torque transfer magnetoresistive RAM (STT-MRAM)—memory technologies that rely on resistivity rather than charge as the information carrier, and thus hold the potential to scale to much smaller geometries than charge memories [13]. Unlike the case of SRAM or DRAM, resistive memories rely on non-volatile, resistive information storage in a cell, and thus exhibit near-zero leakage in the data array.

2.1 STT-MRAM

STT-MRAM [13,20,31–33] is a second generation MRAM technology that addresses many of the scaling problems of commercially available toggle-mode magnetic RAMs. Among all resistive memories, STT-MRAM is the closest to being a CMOS-compatible *universal memory* technology as it offers read speeds as fast as SRAM [39] (< 200ps in 90nm), density comparable to DRAM ($10F^2$), scalable energy characteristics [13], and infinite write endurance. Functional array prototypes [14, 20, 31], CAM circuits [37], and simulated FPGA chips [39] using STT-MRAM have already been demonstrated, and the technology is under rapid commercial development, with an expected industry-wide switch from toggle-mode MRAM to STT-MRAM by 2013 [13]. Although MRAM suffers from relatively high write power and write latency compared to SRAM, its near-zero leakage power dissipation, coupled with its fast read speed and scalability makes it a promising candidate to take over as the workhorse for on-chip storage in sub-45nm processes.

Memory Cells and Array Architecture. STT-MRAM relies on magnetoresistance to encode information. Figure 1 depicts the fundamental building block of an MRAM cell, the magnetic tunnel junction (MTJ). An MTJ consists of two ferromagnetic layers and a tunnel barrier layer, often implemented using a magnetic thin-film stack comprising $Co_{40}Fe_{40}B_{20}$ for the ferromagnetic layers, and MgO for the tunnel barrier. One of the ferromagnetic layers, the *pinned layer*, has a fixed magnetic spin, whereas the spin of the electrons in the *free layer* can be influenced by first applying a high-amplitude current pulse through the pinned layer to polarize the current, and then passing this spin-polarized current through the free layer. Depending on the direction of the current, the spin polarity of the free layer can be made either parallel or anti-parallel to that of the pinned layer.

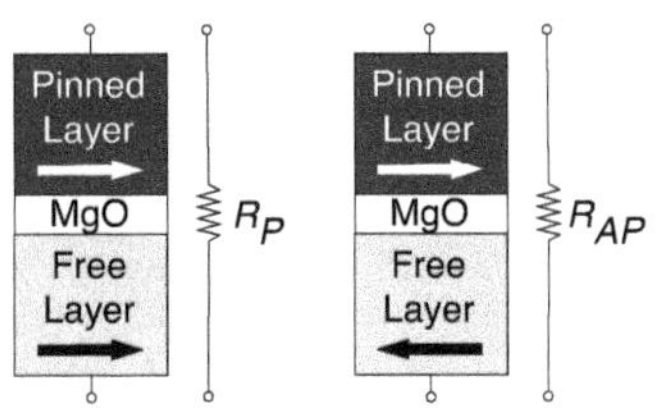

Figure 1: Illustrative example of a magneto-tunnel junction (MTJ) in (a) low-resistance parallel and (b) high-resistance anti-parallel states.

Applying a small bias voltage (typically 0.1V) across the MTJ causes a tunneling current to flow through the MgO tunnel barrier without perturbing the magnetic polarity of the free layer. The magnitude of the tunneling current—and thus, the resistance of the MTJ—is determined by the polarity of the two ferromagnetic layers: a lower, *parallel resistance* (R_P in Figure 1-a) state is experienced when the spin polarities agree, and a higher, *antiparallel resistance* state is observed when the polarities disagree (R_{AP} in Figure 1-b). When the polarities of the two layers are aligned, electrons with polarity anti-parallel to the two layers can travel through the MTJ easily, while electrons with the same spin as the two layers are scattered; in contrast, when the two layers have anti-parallel polarities, electrons of either polarity are largely scattered by one of the two layers, leading to much lower conductivity, and thus, higher resistance [6]. These low and high resistances are used to represent different logic values.

The most commonly used structure for an STT-MRAM memory cell is the 1T-1MTJ cell that comprises a single MTJ, and a single transistor that acts as an access device (Figure 2). Transistors are built in CMOS, and the MTJ magnetic material is grown over the source and drain regions of the transistors through a few (typically two or three) additional process steps. Similarly to SRAM and DRAM, 1T-1MTJ cells can be coupled through wordlines and bitlines to form memory arrays. Each cell is read by driving the appropriate wordline to connect the relevant MTJ to its bitline (BL) and source line (SL), applying a small bias voltage (typically $0.1V$) across the two, and by sensing the current passing through the MTJ using a current sense amplifier connected to the bitline. Read speed is determined by how fast the capacitive wordline can be charged to turn on the access transistor, and by how fast the bitline can be raised to the required read voltage to sample the read-out current. The write operation, on the other hand, requires activating the access transistor, and applying a much higher voltage (typically Vdd) that can generate enough current to modify the spin of the free layer.

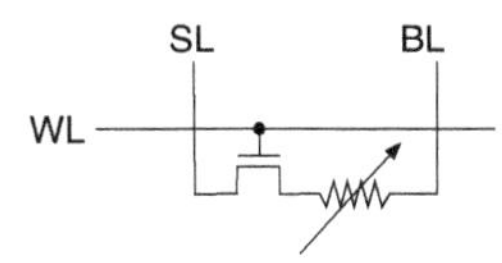

Figure 2: Illustrative example of a 1T-1MTJ cell.

An MTJ can be written in a thermal activation mode through the application of a long, low-amplitude current pulse (>10ns), under a dynamic reversal regime with intermediate current pulses (3-10ns), or in a precessional switching regime with a short (<3ns), high-amplitude current pulse [12]. In a 1T-1MTJ cell with a fixed-size MTJ, a tradeoff exists between switching time (i.e., current pulse width) and cell area. In precessional mode, the required current density $J_c(\tau)$ to switch the state of the MTJ is inversely proportional to switching time τ

$$J_c(\tau) \propto J_{c0} + \frac{C}{\tau}$$

where J_{c0} is a process-dependent intrinsic current density parameter, and C is a constant that depends on the angle of the magnetization vector of the free layer [12]. Hence, operating at a faster switching time increases energy-efficiency: a 2× shorter write pulse requires a less than 2× increase in write current, and thus, lower write energy [8, 20, 26]. Unfortunately, the highest switching speed possible with a fixed-size MTJ is restricted by two fundamental factors: (1) the maximum current that the cell can can support during an $R_{AP} \rightarrow R_P$ transition cannot exceed R_{AP}/Vdd since the cell has to deliver the necessary switching current over the MTJ in its high-resistance state, and (2) a higher switching current requires the access transistor to be sized larger so that it can source the required current, which increases cell area [1] and hurts read energy and delay due to higher gate capacitance.

Figure 3 shows 1T-1MTJ cell switching time as a function of cell area based on Cadence-Spectre analog circuit simulations of a single cell at the 32nm technology node, using ITRS 2009 projections on MTJ parameters (Table 1),

[1]The MTJ is grown above the source and drain regions of the access transistor and is typically much smaller than the transistor itself; consequently, the size of the access transistor determines cell area.

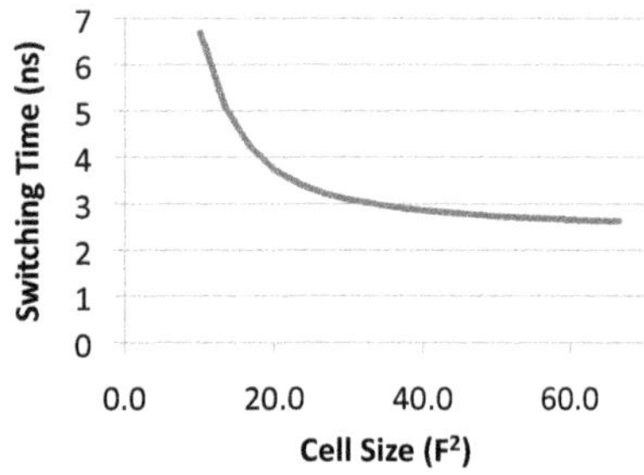

Figure 3: 1T-1MTJ cell switching time as a function of cell size based on Cadence-Spectre circuit simulations at 32nm.

and the BSIM-4 predictive technology model (PTM) of an NMOS transistor [38]; results presented here are assumed in the rest of this paper whenever cell sizing needs to be optimized for write speed. As the precise value of intrinsic current density J_{c0} is not included in ITRS projections, J_{c0} is conservatively assumed to be zero, which requires a 2× increase in switching current for a 2× increase in switching speed. If feature size is given by F, then at a switching speed of 6.7ns, a 1T-1MTJ cell occupies $10F^2$ area—a 14.6× density advantage over SRAM, which is a $146F^2$ technology. As the access transistor's $\frac{W}{L}$ ratio is increased, its current sourcing capability improves, which reduces switching time to 3.1ns at a cell size of $30F^2$. Increasing the size of the transistor further causes a large voltage drop across the MTJ, which reduces the drain-source voltage of the access transistor and pushes the device into deep triode, and ultimately limits its current sourcing capability. As a result, switching time reaches an asymptote at 2.6ns, which is accomplished at a cell size of $65F^2$.

Parameter	Value
Cell Size	$10F^2$
Switching Current	$50\mu A$
Switching Time	$6.7ns$
Write Energy	$0.3pJ/bit$
MTJ Resistance (R_{LOW}/R_{HIGH})	$2.5k\Omega$ / $6.25k\Omega$

Table 1: STT-MRAM parameters at 32nm based on ITRS'09 projections.

2.2 Lookup-Table Based Computing

Field programmable gate arrays (FPGAs) adopt a versatile internal organization that leverages SRAM to store truth tables of logic functions [35]. This not only allows a wide variety of logic functions to be flexibly represented, but also allows FPGAs to be re-programmed almost indefinitely, making them suitable for rapid product prototyping. With technology scaling, FPGAs have gradually evolved from four-input SRAM-based truth tables to five- and six-input tables, named lookup tables (LUT) [7]. This evolution is due to increasing IC integration density—when LUTs are created with higher numbers of inputs, the area they occupy increases exponentially; however, place-and-route becomes significantly easier due to the increased functionality of each LUT. The selection of LUT size is technology dependent; for example, Xilinx Virtex-6 FPGAs use both five- and six-input LUTs, which represent the optimum sizing at the 40nm technology node [35].

This paper leverages an attractive feature of LUT-based computing other than reconfigurability: since LUTs are constructed from memory, it is possible to implement them using a leakage-resistant memory technology such as STT-MRAM, for dramatically reduced power consumption. Like other resistive memories, MRAM dissipates near-zero leakage power in the data array; consequently, power density can be kept under check by reducing the supply voltage with each new technology generation. (Typical MRAM read voltages of 0.1V are reported in the literature [20].) Due to its high write power, the technology is best suited to implementing hardware structures that are read-only or are seldom written. Previous work has explored the possibility of leveraging MRAM to design L2 caches [30,34], but this work is the first to consider the possibility of implementing much of the combinational logic on the chip, as well as microarchitectural structures such as register files and L1 caches, using STT-MRAM.

3. FUNDAMENTAL BUILDING BLOCKS

At a high-level, an STT-MRAM based resistive microprocessor consists of storage-oriented resources such as register files, caches, and queues; functional units and other combinational logic elements; and pipeline latches. Judicious partitioning of these hardware structures between CMOS and STT-MRAM is critical to designing a well-balanced system that exploits the unique area, speed, and power advantages of each technology. Making this selection correctly requires analyzing two broad categories of MRAM-based hardware units: those leveraging RAM arrays (queues, register files, caches), and those leveraging look-up tables (combinational logic, functional units).

3.1 RAM Arrays

Large SRAM arrays are commonly organized into hierarchical structures to optimize for area, speed, and power tradeoffs [3]. An array comprises multiple independent banks that can be simultaneously accessed through separate address and data busses to improve throughput. To minimize wordline and bitline delays and to simplify decoding complexity, each bank is further divided into subbanks sharing address and data busses; unlike the case of banks, only a single subbank can be accessed at a time (Figure 4). A subbank consists of multiple independent mats sharing an address line, each of which supplies a different portion of a requested data block on every access. Internally, each mat comprises multiple subarrays. Memory cells within each subarray are organized as *rows* × *columns*; a decoder selects the cells connected to the relevant wordline, whose contents are driven onto a set of bitlines to be muxed and sensed by column sensing circuitry; the sensed value is routed back to the data bus of the requesting bank through a separate reply network. Different organizations of a fixed-size RAM array into different numbers of banks, subbanks, mats, and subarrays yield dramatically different area, speed, and power figures [22].

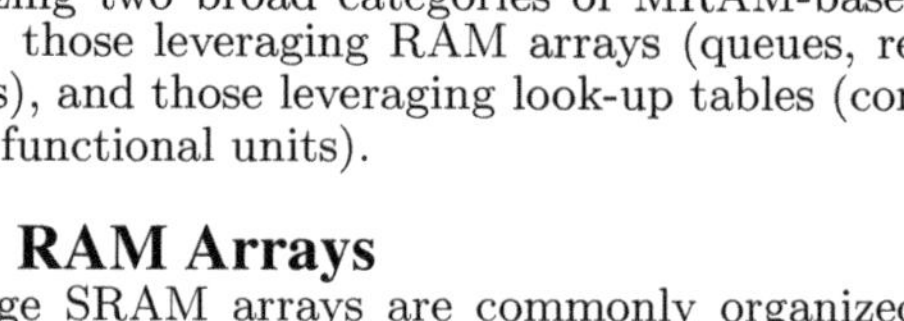

Figure 4: Illustrative example of a RAM array organized into a hierarchy of banks and subbanks [22].

MRAM and SRAM arrays share much of this high-level structure with some important differences arising from the size of a basic cell, from the loading on bitlines and wordlines, and from the underlying sensing mechanism. In turn, these differences result in different leakage power, access energy, delay, and area figures. Since STT-MRAM has a smaller cell size than SRAM ($10F^2$ vs $146F^2$), the length of the bitlines and wordlines within a subarray can be made shorter, which reduces bitline and wordline capacitance and resistance, and improves both delay and energy. In addition, unlike the case of 6T-SRAM where each cell has two access transistors, a 1T-1MTJ cell has a single access device whose size is typically smaller than the SRAM access transistor; this reduces the amount of gate capacitance on wordlines, as well as the drain capacitance attached to bitlines, which lowers energy and delay. The smaller cell size of STT-MRAM implies that subarrays can be made smaller, which shortens the global H-tree interconnect that is responsible for a large share of the overall power, area, and delay. Importantly, unlike the case of SRAM where each cell comprises a pair of cross-coupled inverters connected to the supply rail, STT-MRAM does not require constant connection to Vdd within a cell, which reduces leakage power within the data array to virtually zero.

Handling Long-Latency Writes. Despite these advantages, STT-MRAM suffers from relatively long write latencies compared to SRAM (Section 2.1). Leveraging STT-MRAM in designing frequently accessed hardware structures requires (1) ensuring that critical reads are not delayed by long-latency writes, and (2) long write latencies do not result in resource conflicts that hamper pipeline throughput.

One way of accomplishing both of these goals would be to choose a heavily multi-ported organization for frequently written hardware structures. Unfortunately, this results in an excessive number of ports, and as area and delay grow with port count, hurts performance significantly. For example, building an STT-MRAM based architectural register file that would support two reads and one write per cycle with fast, $30F^2$ cells at 32nm, 4GHz would require two read ports and 13 write ports, which would increase total port count from 3 to 15. An alternative option would be to go to a heavily multi-banked implementation without incurring the overhead of extreme multiporting. Unfortunately, as the number of banks are increased, so does the number of H-tree wiring resources, which quickly overrides the leakage and area benefits of using STT-MRAM.

Instead, this paper proposes an alternative strategy that allows high write throughput and read-write bypassing without incurring an increase in the wiring overhead. The key idea is to allow long-latency writes to complete locally within each sub-bank without unnecessarily occupying global H-tree wiring resources. To make this possible, each subbank is augmented with a *subbank buffer*—an array of flip-flops (physically distributed across all mats within a subbank) that latch in the data-in and address bits from the H-tree, and continue driving the subarray data and address wires throughout the duration of a write while bank-level wiring resources are released (Figure 5). In RAM arrays with separate read and write ports, subbank buffers drive the write port only; reads from other locations within the array can still complete unobstructed, and it also becomes possible to read the value being written to the array directly from the subbank buffer.

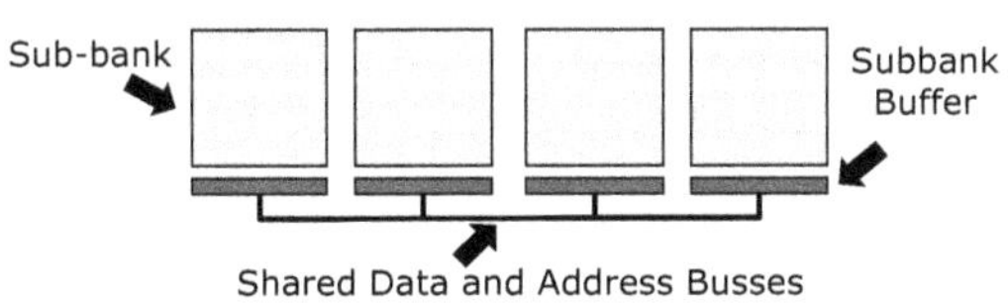

Figure 5: Illustrative example of subbank buffers.

Subbank buffers also make it possible to perform differential writes [18], where only bit positions that differ from their original contents are modified on a write. For this to work, the port attached to the subbank buffer must be designed as a read-write port; when a write is received, the subbank buffer (physically distributed across the mats) latches in the new data and initiates a read for the original contents. Once the data arrives, the original contents and the new contents are bitwise XOR'ed to generate a mask indicating those bit positions that need to be changed. This mask is sent to all relevant subarrays as the enable signals for the bitline drivers along with the actual data—in this way, it becomes possible to perform differential writes without incurring additional latency and energy on the global H-tree wiring. Differential writes can reduce the number of bit flips, and thus write energy, by significant margins, and can make STT-MRAM based implementation of heavily written arrays practical.

3.2 Lookup Tables

Although large STT-MRAM arrays dissipate near-zero leakage power in the subarrays, the leakage power of the peripheral circuitry can be appreciable and in fact dominant as the array size is reduced. With smaller arrays, opportunities to share sense amplifiers and decoding circuitry across multiple rows and multiple columns is significantly lower. One option to combat this problem would be to utilize very large arrays to implement lookup tables of logic functions; unfortunately, both access time and the area overhead deteriorate with larger arrays.

Rather than utilizing an STT-MRAM array to implement a logic function, we rely on a specialized STT-MRAM based lookup table employing differential current-mode logic (DCML). Recent work in this area has resulted in fabricated, two-input lookup tables [8] at 140nm, as well as a non-volatile full-adder prototype [26]. Figure 6 depicts an example three-input LUT. The circuit needs both complementary and pure forms of each of its inputs, and the LUT produces complementary outputs—when multiple LUTs are cascaded in a large circuit, there is no need to generate additional complementary outputs.

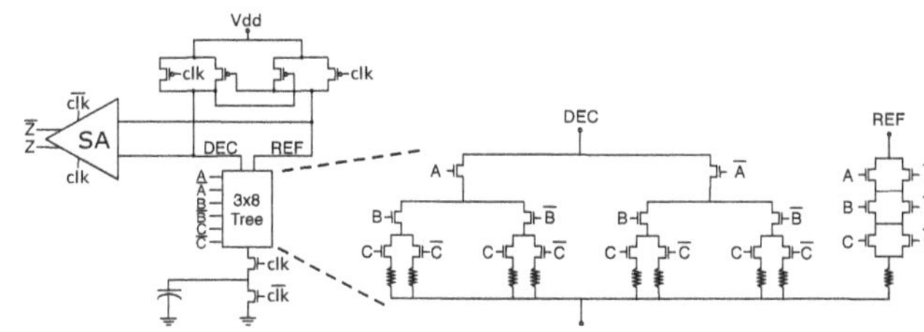

Figure 6: Illustrative example of a three-input lookup table.

This LUT circuit, an expanded version of what is proposed in [8], utilizes a dynamic current source by charging and discharging the capacitor shown in Figure 6. The capacitor is discharged during the $\overline{clk}$ phase, and sinks current through the 3×8 decode tree during the clk phase. Keeper PMOS transistors charge the two entry nodes of the sense amplifier (SA) during the $\overline{clk}$ phase and sensing is performed during the clk phase. These two entry nodes, named DEC and REF, reach different voltage values during the sensing phase (clk) since the sink paths from DEC to the capacitor vs. from REF to the capacitor exhibit different resistances. The reference MTJ needs to have a resistance between the low and high resistance values; since ITRS projects R_{LO} and R_{HIGH} values of $2.5k\Omega$ and $6.25k\Omega$ at 32nm, $4.375k\Omega$ is chosen for R_{REF}.

Although the MTJ decoding circuitry is connected to Vdd at the top and dynamically connected to GND at the bottom, the voltage swing on the capacitor is much smaller than Vdd, which dramatically reduces access energy. The output of this current mode logic operation is fed into a sense amplifier, which turns the low-swing operation into a full-swing complementary output.

In [8], it is observed that the circuit can be expanded to higher numbers of inputs by expanding the decode tree. However, it is important to note that expanding the tree beyond a certain height reduces noise margins and makes the LUT circuit vulnerable to process variations, since it becomes increasingly difficult to detect the difference between high and low MTJ states due to the additional resistance introduced by the transistors in series. As more and more transistors are added, their cumulative resistance can become comparable to MTJ resistance, and fluctuations among transistor resistances caused by process variations can make sensing challenging.

3.2.1 *Optimal LUT Sizing for Latency, Power, and Area*

Both the power and the performance of a resistive processor depend heavily on the LUT sizes chosen to implement combinational logic blocks. This makes it necessary to develop a detailed model to evaluate latency, area, and power tradeoffs as a function of STT-MRAM LUT size. Figure 7 depicts read energy, leakage power, read delay, and area as a function of the number of LUT inputs. LUTs with two to six inputs (4-64 MTJs) are studied, which represent realistic LUT sizes for real circuits. As a comparison, only five- and six-input LUTs are utilized in modern FPGAs (e.g., Xilinx Virtex 6) as higher sizes do not justify the increase in latency and area for the marginal gain in flexibility when implementing logic functions. As each LUT stores only one bit of output, multiple LUTs are accessed in parallel with the same inputs to produce multi-bit results (e.g., a three-bit adder that produces a four-bit output).

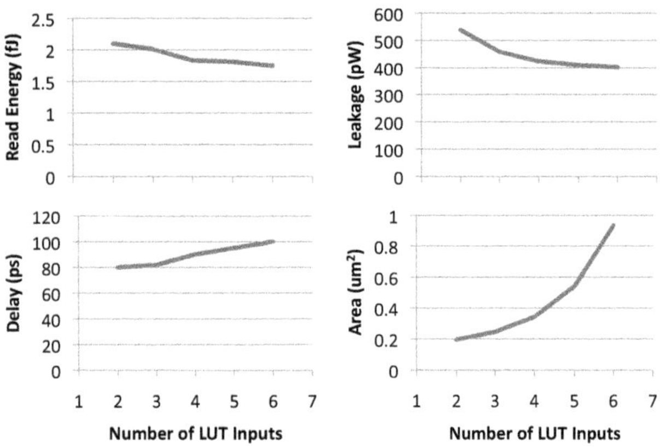

Figure 7: **Access energy, leakage power, read delay, and area of a single LUT as a function of the number of LUT inputs based on Cadence-Spectre circuit simulations at 32nm.**

Read Energy. Access energy decreases slightly as LUT sizes are increased. Although there are more internal nodes—and thus, higher gate and drain capacitances–to charge with each access on a larger LUT, the voltage swing on the footer capacitor is lower due to the increased series resistance charging the capacitor. As a design choice, it is possible to size up the transistors in the decode tree to trade off power against latency and area. The overall access energy goes down from 2fJ to 1.7fJ as LUT size is increased from two to six for the minimum-size transistors used in these simulations.

Leakage Power. Possible dominant leakage paths for the LUT circuit are: (1) from Vdd through the PMOS keeper transistors into the capacitor, (2) from Vdd through the footer charge/discharge NMOS to GND, and (3) the sense amplifier. Lower values of leakage power are observed at higher LUT sizes due to higher resistance along leakage paths (1) and (2), and due to the stack effect of the transistors in the 3×8 decode tree. However, similarly to the case of read energy, sizing the decoder transistors appropriately to trade-off speed against energy can change this balance. As LUT size is increased from two to six inputs, leakage power reduces from 550pW to 400pW.

Latency. Due to the increased series resistance of the decoder's pull-down network with larger LUTs, the RC time constant associated with charging the footer capacitor goes up, and latency increases from 80 to 100ps. However, LUT speed can be increased by sizing the decoder transistors higher, at the expense of larger area, and a higher load capacitance for the previous stage driving the LUT. For optimal results, the footer capacitor must also be sized appropriately. A higher capacitance allows the circuit to work with a lower voltage swing at the expense of increased area. Lower capacitance values cause higher voltage swings on the capacitor, thereby slowing down the reaction time of the sense amplifier due to the lower potential difference between the DEC and REF nodes. A 50fF capacitor was used in these simulations.

Area. Although larger LUTs amortize the leakage power of the peripheral circuitry better, and offer more functionality without incurring a large latency penalty, the area overhead of the lookup table increases exponentially with the number of inputs. Every new input doubles the number of transistors in the branches; as LUT size is increased from two to six inputs, the area of the LUT increases fivefold. Nevertheless, a single LUT can replace approximately 12 CMOS standard cells on average when implementing such complex combinational logic blocks as a floating-point unit (Section 4.5) or a memory controller's scheduling logic (Section 4.6.4); consequently, analyses shown later in the paper assume six-input LUTs unless otherwise stated.

3.2.2 Case Study: Three-bit Adder using Static CMOS, ROM, and STT-MRAM LUT Circuits

To study the power and performance advantages of STT-MRAM LUT-based computing on a realistic circuit, Table 2 compares access energy, leakage power, area, and delay figures obtained on three different implementations of a three-bit adder: (1) a conventional, static CMOS implementation, (2) a LUT-based implementation using the STT-MRAM (DCML) LUTs described in Section 3.2, and (3) a LUT-based implementation using conventional, CMOS-based static ROMs. Minimum size transistors are used in all three cases to keep the comparisons fair. Circuit simulations are performed using Cadence AMS (Spectre) with Verilog-based test vector generation; we use 32nm BSIM-4 predictive technology models (PTM) [38] of NMOS and PMOS transistors, and the MTJ parameters presented in Table 1 based on ITRS'09 projections. All results are obtained under identical input vectors, minimum transistor sizing, and a 370K temperature. Although simulations were also performed at $16nm$ and $22nm$ nodes, results showed similar tendencies to those presented here, and are not repeated.

Parameter	STT-MRAM LUT	Static CMOS	ROM-Based LUT
Delay	100ps	110ps	190ps
Access Energy	7.43fJ	11.1fJ	27.4fJ
Leakage Power	1.77nW	10.18nW	514nW
Area	$2.40 \mu m^2$	$0.43 \mu m^2$	$17.9 \mu m^2$

Table 2: **Comparison of three-bit adder implementations using STT-MRAM LUTs, static CMOS, and a static CMOS ROM. Area estimates do not include wiring overhead.**

Static CMOS. A three-bit CMOS ripple-carry adder is built using one half-adder (HAX1) and two full-adder (FAX1) circuits based on circuit topologies used in the OSU standard cell library [29]. Static CMOS offers the smallest area among all three designs considered, since the layout is highly regular and only 70 transistors are required instead of 348, which is the case of the STT-MRAM LUT-based design. Leakage is $5.8\times$ higher than MRAM since the CMOS implementation has a much higher number of leakage paths than an STT-MRAM LUT, whose subthreshold leakage is confined to its peripheral circuitry.

STT-MRAM LUTs. A three-input half-adder requires four STT-MRAM LUTs, one for each output of the adder (three sum bits plus a carry-out bit). Since the least significant bit of the sum depends only on two bits, it can be calculate using a two-input LUT. Similarly, the second bit of the sum depends on a total of four bits, and can be implemented using a four-input LUT. The most significant bit and the carry-out bit each depend on six bits, and each of them requires a six-input LUT. Although results presented here are based on unoptimized, minimum-size STT-MRAM LUTs, it is possible to slow down the two- and four-input LUTs to save access energy by sizing their transistors. The results presented here are conservative compared to this best-case optimization scenario.

An STT-MRAM based three-bit adder has $1.5\times$ lower access energy than its static CMOS counterpart due to its energy-efficient, low-swing, differential current-mode logic implementation; however, these energy savings are achieved at the expense of a $5.6\times$ increase in area. In a three-bit adder, a six-input STT-MRAM LUT replaces three CMOS standard cells. Area overhead can be expected to be lower when implementing more complex logic functions that require the realization of many minterms, which is when LUT-based computation is most beneficial; for instance, a single six-input LUT is expected to replace 12 CMOS standard cells on average when implementing the FPU (Section 4.5) and the memory controller scheduling logic (Section 4.6.4).

The most notable advantage of the STT-MRAM LUT over static CMOS is the 5.8× reduction in leakage. This is due to the significantly smaller number of leakage paths that are possible with an STT-MRAM LUT, which exhibits subthreshold leakage only through its peripheral circuitry. The speed of the STT-MRAM LUT is similar to static CMOS: although CMOS uses higher-speed standard cells, an STT-MRAM LUT calculates all four bits in parallel using independent LUTs.

CMOS ROM-Based LUTs. To perform a head-on comparison against a LUT-based CMOS adder, we build a 64×4 static ROM circuit that can read all three bits of the sum and the carry-out bit with a single lookup. Compared to a 6T-SRAM based, reconfigurable LUT used in an FPGA, a ROM-based, fixed-function LUT is more energy efficient, since each table entry requires either a single transistor (in the case of a logic 1) or no transistors at all (in the case of a logic 0), rather than the six transistors required by an SRAM cell. A 6-to-64 decoder drives one of 64 wordlines, which activates the transistors on cells representing a logic 1. A minimum sized PMOS pull-up transistor and a skewed inverter are employed to sense the stored logic value. Four parallel bitlines are used for the four outputs of the adder, amortizing dynamic energy and leakage power of the decoder over four output bits.

The ROM-based LUT dissipates 290× higher leakage than its STT-MRAM based counterpart. This is due to two factors: (1) transistors in the decoder circuit of the ROM represent a significant source of subthreshold leakage, whereas the STT-MRAM LUT uses differential current-mode logic, which connects a number of access devices in series with each MTJ on a decode tree, without any direct connections between the access devices and Vdd, and (2) the ROM-based readout mechanism suffers from significant leakage paths within the data array itself, since all unselected devices represent sneak paths for active leakage during each access. The access energy of the ROM-based LUT is 3.7× higher than the STT-MRAM LUT, since (1) the decoder has to be activated with every access, and (2) the bitlines are charged to Vdd and discharged to GND using full-swing voltages, whereas the differential current-sensing mechanism of the STT-MRAM LUT operates with low-swing voltages.

The ROM-based LUT also runs 1.9× slower than its STT-MRAM based counterpart due to the serialization of the decoder access and cell readout: the input signal has to traverse through the decoder to activate one of the wordlines, which then selects the transistors along that wordline. Two thirds of the delay is incurred in the decoder. Overall, the ROM-based LUT delivers the worst results on all metrics considered due to its inherently more complex and leakage-prone design.

3.2.3 *Deciding When to Use LUTs*

Consider a three-bit adder which has two three-bit inputs and four one-bit outputs. This function can be implemented using four six-input LUTs, whereas the VLSI implementation requires only three standard cells, resulting in a $\frac{stdcell}{LUT}$ ratio of less than one. On the other hand, an unsigned multiplier with two three-bit inputs and a six-bit output requires six six-input LUTs or 36 standard cells, raising the same ratio to six. As the size and complexity of a Boolean function increases, thereby requiring more minterms after logic minimization, this ratio can be as high as 12 [5]. This is due not only to the increased complexity of the function better utilizing the fixed size of the LUTs, but also to the sheer size of the circuit allowing the boolean minimizer to amortize complex functions over multiple LUTs. As this ratio gets higher, power consumption and leakage advantage of LUT based circuits improve dramatically. This observation that LUT-based implementations work significantly better for large and complex circuits is one of our guidelines for choosing which parts of a microprocessor should be implemented using LUTs vs. conventional CMOS.

4. STRUCTURE AND OPERATION OF AN STT-MRAM BASED CMT PIPELINE

Figure 8 shows how hardware resources are partitioned between CMOS and STT-MRAM in an example CMT system with eight single-issue in-order cores, and eight hardware thread contexts per core. Whether a resource can be effectively implemented in STT-MRAM depends on both its size and on the expected number of writes it incurs per cycle. STT-MRAM offers dramatically lower leakage and much higher density than SRAM, but suffers from long write latency and high write energy. Large, wire-delay dominated RAM arrays—L1 and L2 caches, TLBs, memory controller queues, and register files—are implemented in STT-MRAM to reduce leakage and interconnect power, and to improve interconnect delay. Instruction and store buffers, PC registers, and pipeline latches are kept in CMOS due to their small size and relatively high write activity. Since LUTs are never written at runtime, they are used to implement such complex combinational logic blocks as the front-end thread selection, decode, and next-PC generation logic, the floating-point unit, and the memory controller's scheduling logic.

An important issue that affects both power and performance for caches, TLBs, and register files is the size of a basic STT-MRAM cell used to implement the subarrays. With $30F^2$ cells, write latency can be reduced by 2.2× over $10F^2$ cells (Section 2.1) at the expense of lower density, higher read energy, and longer read latency. Lookup tables are constructed from dense, $10F^2$ cells as they are never written at runtime. The register file and the L1 d-cache use $30F^2$ cells with 3.1ns switching time as the 6.7ns write occupancy of a $10F^2$ cell has a prohibitive impact on throughput. The L2 cache and the memory controller queues are implemented with $10F^2$ cells and are optimized for density and power rather than write speed; similarly, TLBs and the L1 i-cache are implemented using $10F^2$ cells due to their relatively low miss rate, and thus, low write probability.

4.1 Instruction Fetch

Each core's front-end is quite typical, with a separate PC register and an eight-deep instruction buffer per thread. The i-TLB, i-cache, next-PC generation logic, and front-end thread selection logic are shared among all eight threads. The i-TLB and the i-cache are built using STT-MRAM arrays; thread selection and next-PC generation logic are implemented with STT-MRAM LUTs. Due to their small size and high write activity, instruction buffers and PC registers are left in CMOS.

4.1.1 *Program Counter Generation*

Each thread has a dedicated, CMOS-based PC register. To compute the next sequential PC with minimum power and area overhead, a special 6 × 7 "add one" LUT is used rather than a general-purpose adder LUT. A 6 × 7 LUT accepts six bits of the current PC plus a carry-in bit to calculate the corresponding six bits of the next PC and a carry-out bit; internally, the circuit consists of two-, three-, four-, five-, and six-input LUTs (one of each), each of which computes a different bit of the seven bit output in parallel.

The overall next sequential PC computation unit comprises five such 6 × 7 LUTs arranged in a carry-select configuration (Figure 9). Carry out bits are used as the select signals for a chain of CMOS-based multiplexers that choose either the new or the original six bits of the PC. Hence, the delay of the PC generation logic is four multiplexer delays, plus a single six-input LUT delay, which comfortably fits

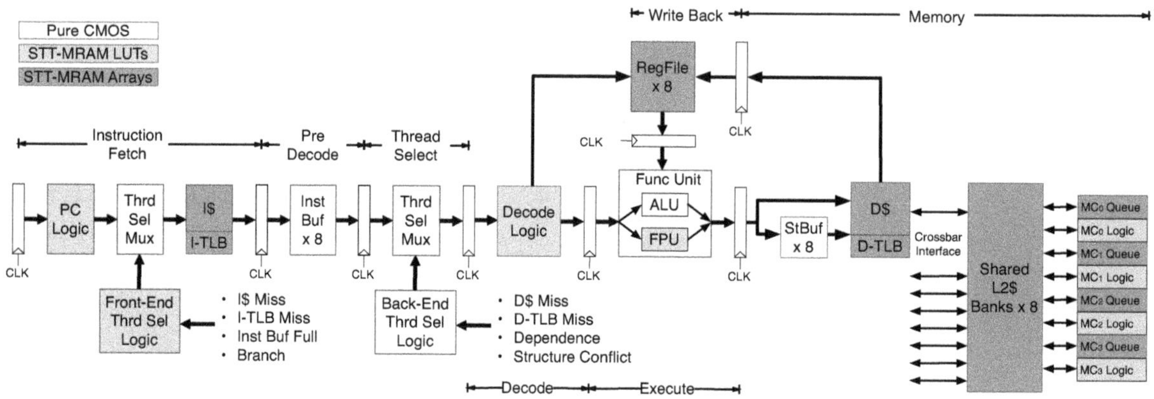

Figure 8: Illustrative example of a resistive CMT pipeline.

within a 250ps clock period in PTM-based circuit simulations (Section 6).

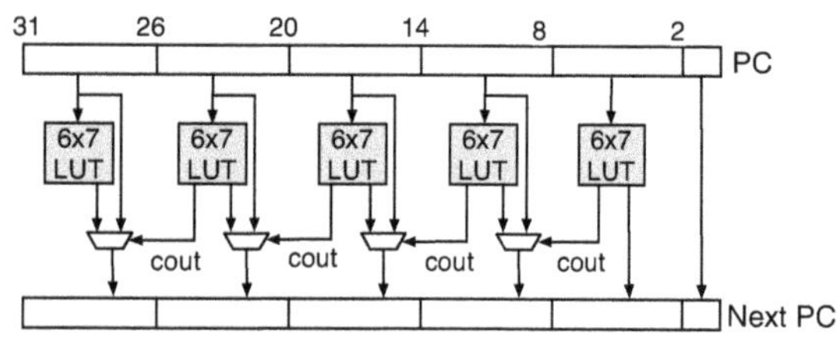

Figure 9: Next PC generation using five add-one LUTS in a carry-select configuration.

4.1.2 *Front-End Thread Selection*

Every cycle, the front-end selects one of the available threads to fetch in round-robin order, which promotes fairness and facilitates a simple implementation. The following conditions make a thread unselectable in the front-end: (1) an i-cache or an i-TLB miss, (2) a full instruction buffer, or (3) a branch or jump instruction. On an i-cache or an i-TLB miss, the thread is marked unselectable for fetch, and is reset to a selectable state when the refill of the i-cache or the i-TLB is complete. To facilitate front-end thread selection, the ID of the last selected thread is kept in a three-bit CMOS register, and the next thread to fetch from is determined as the next available, ublocked thread in round-robin order. The complete thread selection mechanism thus requires an 11-to-3 LUT, which is built from 96 six-input LUTs sharing a data bus with tri-state buffers—six bits of the input are sent to all LUTs, and the remaining five bits are used to generate the enable signals for all LUTs in parallel with the LUT access. (It is also possible to optimize for power by serializing the decoding of the five bits with the LUT access, and by using the enable signal to control the LUT clk input.)

4.1.3 *L1 Instruction Cache and TLB*

The i-cache and and the i-TLB are both implemented in STT-MRAM due to their large size and relatively low write activity. Since writes are infrequent, these resources are each organized into a single subbank to minimize the overhead of the peripheral circuitry, and are built using $10F^2$ cells that reduce area, read energy, and read latency at the expense of longer writes. The i-cache is designed with a dedicated read port and a dedicated write port to ensure that the front-end does not come to a complete stall during refills; this ensures that threads can still fetch from the read port in the shadow of an ongoing write. To accommodate multiple outstanding misses from different threads, the i-cache is augmented with an eight-entry refill queue. When a block returns from the L2 on an i-cache miss, it starts writing to the cache immediately if the write port is available; otherwise, it is placed in the refill queue while it waits for the write port to free up.

Parameter	SRAM (32KB)	STT-MRAM (32KB)	STT-MRAM (128KB)
Read Delay	397ps	238ps	474ps
Write Delay	397ps	6932ps	7036ps
Read Energy	35pJ	13pJ	50pJ
Write Energy	35pJ	90pJ	127pJ
Leakage Power	75.7mW	6.6mW	41.4mW
Area	$0.31mm^2$	$0.06mm^2$	$0.26mm^2$

Table 3: Instruction cache parameters.

It is possible to leverage the 14.6× density advantage of STT-MRAM over SRAM by either designing a similar-capacity L1 i-cache with shorter wire delays, lower read energy, and lower area and leakage, or by designing a higher-capacity cache with similar read latency and read energy under a similar area budget. Table 3 presents latency, power, and area comparisons between a 32KB, SRAM-based i-cache; its 32KB, STT-MRAM counterpart; and a larger, 128KB STT-MRAM configuration that fits under the same area budget [2]. Simply migrating the 32KB i-cache from SRAM to STT-MRAM reduces area by 5.2×, leakage by 11.5×, read energy by 2.7×, and read delay by one cycle at 4GHz. Leveraging the density advantage to build a larger, 128KB cache results in more modest savings in leakage (45%) due to the higher overhead of the CMOS-based peripheral circuitry. Write energy increases by 2.6 − 3.6× over CMOS with 32KB and 128KB STT-MRAM caches, respectively.

4.2 Predecode

After fetch, instructions go through a predecode stage where a set of predecode bits for back-end thread selection are extracted and written into the CMOS-based instruction buffer. Predecode bits indicate if the instruction is a member of the following equivalence classes: (1) a load or a store, (2) a floating-point or integer divide, (3) a floating-point add/sub, compare, multiply, or an integer multiply, (4) a brach or a jump, or (5) any other ALU operations. Each flag is generated by inspecting the six-bit opcode, which requires a total of five six-input LUTs. The subbank ID of the destination register is also extracted and recorded in the instruction buffer during the predecode stage to faciliate back-end thread selection.

4.3 Thread Select

Every cycle, the back-end thread selection unit issues an instruction from one of the available, unblocked threads. The goal is to derive a correct and balanced issue schedule that prevents out-of-order completion; avoids structural hazards and conflicts on L1 d-cache and register file subbanks; maintains fairness; and delivers high throughput.

[2]The experimental setup is described in Section 5.

4.3.1 *Instruction Buffer*

Each thread has a private, eight-deep instruction buffer organized as a FIFO queue. Since buffers are small and are written every few cycles with up to four new instructions, they are implemented in CMOS as opposed to STT-MRAM.

4.3.2 *Back-End Thread Selection Logic*

Every cycle, back-end thread selection logic issues the instruction at the head of one of the instruction buffers to be decoded and executed. The following events make a thread unschedulable: (1) an L1 d-cache or d-TLB miss, (2) a structural hazard on a register file subbank, (3) a store buffer overflow, (4) a data dependency on an ongoing long-latency floating-point, integer multiply, or integer divide instruction, (5) a structural hazard on the (unpipelined) floating-point divider, and (6) the possibility of out-of-order completion.

A load's buffer entry is not recycled at the time the load issues; instead, the entry is retained until the load is known to hit in the L1 d-cache or in the store buffer. In the case of a miss, the thread is marked as unschedulable; when the L1 d-cache refill process starts, the thread transitions to a schedulable state, and the load is replayed from the instruction buffer. On a hit, the load's instruction buffer entry is recycled as soon as the load enters the writeback stage.

Long-latency floating-point instructions and integer multiplies from a single thread can be scheduled back-to-back so long as there are no dependencies between them. In the case of an out-of-order completion possibility—a floating-point divide followed by any other instruction, or any floating-point instruction other than a divide followed by an integer instruction—, the offending thread is made unschedulable for as many cycles as needed for the danger to disappear.

Threads can also become unschedulable due to structural hazards on the unpipelined floating-point divider, on register file subbank write ports, or on store buffers. As the register file is built using $30F^2$ STT-MRAM cells with 3.1ns switching time, the register file subbank write occupancy is 13 cycles at 4GHz. Throughout the duration of an on-going write, the subbank is unavailable for a new write (unless it is the same register that is being overwritten), but the read ports remain available; hence, register file reads are not stalled by long-latency writes. If the destination subbank of an instruction conflicts with an ongoing write to the same bank, the thread becomes unschedulable until the target subbank is available. If the head of the instruction buffer is a store and the store buffer of the thread is full, the thread becomes unschedulable until there is an opening in the store buffer.

In order to avoid starvation, a least recently selected (LRS) policy is used to pick among all schedulable threads. The LRS policy is implemented using CMOS gates.

4.4 Decode

In the decode stage, the six-bit opcode of the instruction is inspected to generate internal control signals for the following stages of the pipeline, and the architectural register file is accessed to read the input operands. Every decoded signal propagated to the execution stage thus requires a six-input LUT. For a typical, five-stage MIPS pipeline [15] with 16 output control signals, 16 six-input LUTs suffice to accomplish this.

4.4.1 *Register File*

Every thread has 32 integer registers and 32 floating-point registers, for a total of 512 registers (2kB of storage) per core. To enable a high-performance, low-leakage, STT-MRAM based register file that can deliver the necessary write throughput and single-thread latency, integer and floating-point register from all threads are aggregated in a subbanked STT-MRAM array as shown in Figure 10. The overall register file consists of 32 subbanks of 16 registers each, sharing a common address bus and a 64-bit data bus. The register file has two read ports and a write port, and the write ports are augmented with subbank buffers to allow multiple writes to proceed in parallel on different subbanks without adding too much area, leakage, or latency overhead (Section 3.1). Mapping each thread's integer and floating-point registers to a common subbank would significantly degrade throughput when a single thread is running in the system, or during periods where only a few threads are schedulable due to L1 d-cache misses. To avert this problem, each thread's registers are are striped across consecutive subbanks to improve throughput and to minimize the chance of a subbank write port conflict. Double-precision floating-point operations require reading two consecutive floating-point registers starting with an even-numbered register, which is accomplished by accessing two consecutive subbanks and driving the 64-bit data bus in parallel.

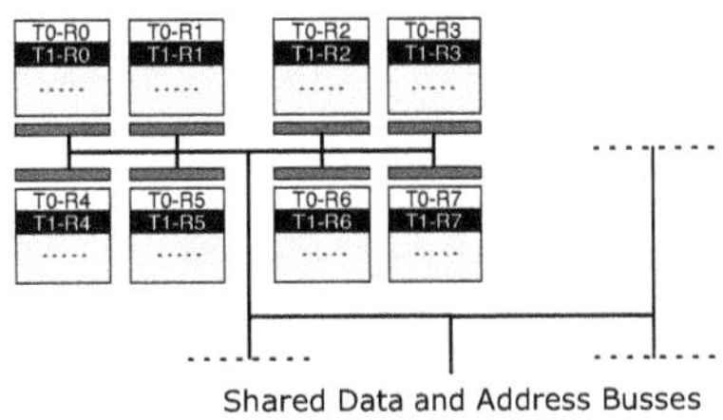

Figure 10: Illustrative example of a subbanked register file.

Table 4 lists area, read energy, and leakage power advantages that are possible by implementing the register file in STT-MRAM. The STT-MRAM implementation reduces leakage by 2.4× and read energy by 1.4× over CMOS; however, energy for a full 32-bit write is increased by 22.2×. Whether the end result turns out to be a net power savings depends on how frequently the register file is updated, and on how effective differential writes are on a given workload.

Parameter	SRAM	STT-MRAM
Read Delay	137ps	122ps
Write Delay	137ps	3231ps
Read Energy	0.45pJ	0.33pJ
Write Energy	0.45pJ	10.0pJ
Leakage Power	3.71mW	1.53mW
Area	$0.038mm^2$	$0.042mm^2$

Table 4: Register file parameters.

4.5 Execute

After decode, instructions are sent to functional units to complete their execution. Bitwise logical operations, integer addition and subtraction, and logical shifts are handled by the integer ALU, whereas floating-point addition, multiplication, and division are handled by the floating-point unit. Similar to Sun's Niagara-1 processor [17], integer multiply and divide operations are also sent to the FPU rather than a dedicated integer multiplier to save area and leakage power. Although the integer ALU is responsible for 5% of the baseline leakage power consumption, many of the operations it supports (e.g., bitwise logical operations) do not have enough circuit complexity (i.e., minterms) to amortize the peripheral circuitry in a LUT-based implementation. Moreover, operating an STT-MRAM based integer adder (the power- and area-limiting unit in a typical integer ALU [28]) at single-cycle throughput requires the adder to be pipelined in two stages, but the additional power overhead of the pipeline flip-flops largely offsets the benefits of transitioning to STT-MRAM. Consequently, the integer ALU is left in CMOS. The FPU, on the other hand, is responsible for a large fraction of the per-core leakage power and dynamic access energy, and is thus implemented with STT-MRAM LUTs.

Floating-Point Unit. To compare ASIC- and LUT-based implementations of the floating-point unit, an industrial FPU design from Gaisler Research, the GRFPU [5], is taken as a baseline. A VHDL implementation of the GRFPU synthesizes to 100,000 gates on an ASIC design flow, and runs at 250MHz at 130nm; on a Xilinx Virtex-2 FPGA, the unit synthesizes to 8,500 LUTs, and runs at 65MHz. Floating-point addition, subtraction, and multiplication are fully pipelined and execute with a three-cycle latency; floating-point division is unpipelined and takes 16 cycles.

To estimate the required pipeline depth for an STT-MRAM LUT-based implementation of the GRFPU to operate at 4GHz at 32nm, we use published numbers on configurable logic block (CLB) delays on a Virtex-2 FPGA [2]. A CLB has a LUT+MUX delay of 630ps and an interconnect delay of 1 to 2ns based on its placement, which corresponds to a critical path of six to ten CLB delays. For STT-MRAM, we assume a critical path delay of eight LUTs, which represents the average of these two extremes. Assuming a buffered six-input STT-MRAM LUT delay of 130ps and a flip-flop sequencing overhead ($t_{setup} + t_{C \to Q}$) of 50ps, and conservatively assuming a perfectly-balanced pipeline for the baseline GRFPU, we estimate that the STT-MRAM implementation would need to be pipelined eight times deeper than the original to operate at 4GHz, with floating-point addition, subtraction, and multiplication latencies of 24 cycles, and an unpipelined, 64-cycle floating-point divide latency. When calculating leakage power, area, and access energy, we account for the overhead of the increased number of flip-flops due to this deeper pipeline (flip-flop power, area, and speed are extracted from 32nm circuit simulations of the topology used in the OSU standard cell library [29]). We characterize and account for the impact of loading on an STT-MRAM LUT when driving another LUT stage or a flip-flop via Cadence-Spectre circuit simulations.

To estimate pipeline depth for the CMOS implementation of the GRFPU running at 4GHz, we first scale the baseline 250MHz frequency linearly from 130nm to 32nm, which corresponds to an intrinsic frequency of 1GHz at 32nm. Thus, conservatively ignoring the sequencing overhead, to operate at 4GHz, the circuit needs to be pipelined 4× deeper, with 12-cycle floating-point addition, subtraction, and multiplication latencies, and a 64-cycle, unpipelined floating-point divide. Estimating power for CMOS (100,000 gates) requires estimating dynamic and leakage power for an average gate in a standard-cell library. We characterize the following OSU standard cells using circuit simulations at 32nm, and use their average to estimate power for the CMOS-based GRFPU design: INVX2, NAND2X1, NAND3X1, BUFX2, BUFX4, AOI22X1, MUX2X1, DFFPOSX1, and XNORX1.

Table 5 shows the estimated leakage, dynamic energy, and area of the GRFPU in both pure CMOS and STT-MRAM. The CMOS implementation uses 100, 000 gates whereas the STT-MRAM implementation uses 8,500 LUTs. Although each CMOS gate has lower dynamic energy than a six-input LUT, each LUT can replace 12 logic gates on average. This 12× reduction in unit count results in an overall reduction of the total dynamic energy. Similarly, although each LUT has higher leakage than a CMOS gate, the cumulative leakage of 8,500 LUTs reduces leakage by 4× over the combined leakage of 100, 000 gates. Area, on the other hand, is comparable due to the reduced unit count compensating for the 5× higher area of each LUT and the additional buffering required to cascade the LUTs. (Note that these area estimates do not account for wiring overheads in either the CMOS or the STT-MRAM implementations.) In summary, the FPU is a good candidate to place in STT-MRAM since its high circuit complexity produces logic functions with many minterms that require many CMOS gates to implement, which is exactly when a LUT-based implementation is advantageous.

Parameter	CMOS FPU	STT-MRAM FPU
Dynamic Energy	36pJ	26.7pJ
Leakage Power	259mW	61mW
Area	$0.22mm^2$	$0.20mm^2$

Table 5: FPU parameters. Area estimates do not include wiring overhead.

4.6 Memory

In the memory stage, load and store instructions access the STT-MRAM based L1 d-cache and d-TLB. To simplify the scheduling of stores and to minimize the performance impact of contention on subbank write ports, each thread is allocated a CMOS-based, eight-deep store buffer holding in-flight store instructions.

4.6.1 Store Buffers

One problem that comes up when scheduling stores is the possibility of a d-cache subbank conflict at the time the store reaches the memory stage. Since stores require address computation before their target d-cache subbank is known, thread selection logic cannot determine if a store will experience a port conflict in advance. To address this problem, the memory stage of the pipeline includes a CMOS-based, private, eight-deep store buffer per thread. So long as a thread's store buffer is not full, the thread selection logic can schedule the store without knowing the destination subbank. Stores are dispatched into and issued from store buffers in FIFO order; store buffers also provide an associative search port to support store-to-load forwarding, similar to Sun's Niagara-1 processor. We assume relaxed consistency models where special synchronization primitives (e.g., memory fences in weak consistency, or acquire/release operations in release consistency) are inserted into store buffers, and the store buffer enforces the semantics of the primitives when retiring stores and when forwarding to loads. Since the L1 d-cache supports a single write port (but multiple subbank buffers), only a single store can issue per cycle. Store buffers, and the L1 refill queue contend for access to this shared resource, and priority is determined based on a round-robin policy.

4.6.2 L1 Data Cache and TLB

Both the L1 d-cache and the d-TLB are implemented using STT-MRAM arrays. The d-cache is equipped with two read ports (one for snooping, and one for the core) and a write port shared among all subbanks. At the time a load issues, the corresponding thread is marked unschedulable and recycling of the instruction buffer entry holding the load is postponed until it is ascertained that the load will not experience a d-cache miss. Loads search the store buffer of the corresponding thread and access the L1 d-cache in parallel, and forward from the store buffer in the case of a hit. On a d-cache miss, the thread is marked unschedulable, and is transitioned back to a schedulable state once the data arrives. To accommodate refills returning from the L2, the L1 has a 16-deep, CMOS-based refill queue holding incoming data blocks. Store buffers and the refill queue contend for access to the two subbanks of the L1, and are given access using a round-robin policy. Since the L1 is written frequently, it is optimized for write throughput using $10F^2$ cells. L1 subbank buffers perform internal differential writes to reduce write energy.

Parameter	SRAM (32KB)	STT-MRAM (32KB, $30F^2$)	STT-MRAM (64KB, $30F^2$)
Read Delay	344ps	236ps	369ps
Write Delay	344ps	3331ps	3399ps
Read Energy	60pJ	31pJ	53pJ
Write Energy	60pJ	109pJ	131pJ
Leakage Power	78.4mW	11.0mW	31.3mW
Area	$0.54mm^2$	$0.19mm^2$	$0.39mm^2$

Table 6: L1 d-cache parameters.

Table 6 compares the power, area, and latency characteristics of two different STT-MRAM based L1 configurations to a baseline, 32KB CMOS implementation. A capacity-equivalent, 32KB d-cache reduces access latency from two clock cycles to one, and cuts down the read energy by 1.9× due to shorter interconnect lengths possible with the density advantage of STT-MRAM. Leakage power is reduced by 7.1×, and area is reduced by 2.8×. An alternative, 64kB configuration requires 72% of the area of the CMOS baseline, but increases capacity by 2×; this configuration takes two cycles to read, and delivers a 2.5× leakage reduction over CMOS.

4.6.3 L2 Cache

The L2 cache is designed using $10F^2$ STT-MRAM cells to optimize for density and access energy rather than write speed. To ensure adequate throughput, the cache is equipped with eight banks, each of which supports four subbanks, for a total of 32. Each L2 bank has a single read/write port shared among all subbanks; unlike the L1 d-cache and the register file, L2 subbanks are not equipped with differential writing circuitry to minimize leakage due to the CMOS-based periphery.

Table 7 compares two different STT-MRAM L2 organizations to a baseline, 4MB CMOS L2. To optimize for leakage, the baseline CMOS L2 cache uses high-Vt transistors in the data array, whereas the peripheral circuitry needs to be implemented using low-Vt, high-performance transistors to maintain a 4GHz cycle time. A capacity-equivalent, 4MB STT-MRAM based L2 reduces leakage by 2.0× and read access energy by 63% compared to a CMOS baseline. Alternatively, it is possible to increase capacity to 32MB while maintaining lower area, but the leakage overhead of the peripheral circuitry increases with capacity, and results in twice as much leakage as the baseline.

Parameter	SRAM (4MB)	STT-MRAM (4MB)	STT-MRAM (32MB)
Read Delay	2364ps	1956ps	2760ps
Write Delay	2364ps	7752ps	8387ps
Read Energy	1268pJ	798pJ	1322pJ
Write Energy	1268pJ	952pJ	1477pJ
Leakage Power	6578mW	3343mW	12489mW
Area	$82.33mm^2$	$32.00mm^2$	$70.45mm^2$

Table 7: L2 cache parameters.

4.6.4 Memory Controllers

To provide adequate memory bandwidth to eight cores, the system is equipped with four DDR2-800 memory controllers. Memory controller read and write queues are implemented in STT-MRAM using $10F^2$ cells. Since the controller needs to make decisions only every DRAM clock cycle (10 processor cycles in our baseline), the impact of write latency on scheduling efficiency and performance is negligible.

The controller's scheduling logic is implemented using STT-MRAM LUTs. To estimate power, performance, and area under CMOS- and MRAM-based implementations, we use a methodology similar to that employed for the floating-point unit. We use a DDR2-800 memory controller IP core developed by HiTech [11] as our baseline; on an ASIC design flow, the controller synthesizes to 13,700 gates and runs at 400MHz; on a Xilinx Virtex-5 FPGA, the same controller synthesizes to 920 CLBs and runs at 333MHz. Replacing CLB delays with STT-MRAM LUT delays, we find that an STT-MRAM based implementation of the controller would meet the 400MHz cycle time without further modifications.

Table 8 compares the parameters of the CMOS and STT-MRAM based implementations. Similarly to the case of the FPU, the controller logic benefits significantly from a LUT based design. Leakage power is reduced by 7.2×, while the energy of writing to the scheduling queue increases by 24.4×.

Parameter	CMOS	STT-MRAM
Read Delay	185ps	154ps
Write Delay	185ps	6830ps
Read Energy	7.1pJ	5.6pJ
Write Energy	7.1pJ	173pJ
MC Logic Energy	30.0pJ	1.6pJ
Leakage Power	41.4mW	5.72mW
Area	$0.097mm^2$	$0.051mm^2$

Table 8: Memory controller parameters. Area estimates do not include wiring overhead.

4.7 Write Back

In the write-back stage, an instruction writes its result back into the architectural register file through the write port. No conflicts are possible during this stage since the thread selection logic schedules instructions by taking register file subbank conflicts into account. Differential writes within the register file reduce write power during write backs.

5. EXPERIMENTAL SETUP

We use a heavily modified version of the SESC simulator [25] to model a Niagara-like in-order CMT system with eight cores, and eight hardware thread contexts per core. Table 9 lists the microarchitectural configuration of the baseline cores and the shared memory subsystem.

Processor Parameters	
Frequency	4 GHz
Number of cores	8
Number of SMT contexts	8 per core
Front-end thread select	Round Robin
Back-end thread select	Least Recently Selected
Pipeline organization	Single-issue, in-order
Store buffer entries	8 per thread
L1 Caches	
iL1/dL1 size	32kB/32kB
iL1/dL1 block size	32B/32B
iL1/dL1 round-trip latency	2/2 cycles(uncontended)
iL1/dL1 ports	1 / 2
iL1/dL1 banks	1 / 2
iL1/dL1 MSHR entries	16/16
iL1/dL1 associativity	direct mapped/2-way
Coherence protocol	MESI
Consistency model	Release consistency
Shared L2 Cache and Main Memory	
Shared L2 cache	4MB, 64B block, 8-way
L2 MSHR entries	64
L2 round-trip latency	10 cycles (uncontended)
Write buffer	64 entries
DRAM subsystem	DDR2-800 SDRAM [21]
Memory controllers	4

Table 9: Parameters of baseline.

For STT-MRAM, we experiment with two different design points for L1 and L2 caches: (1) configurations with capacity equivalent to the CMOS baseline, where STT-MRAM enjoys the benefits of lower interconnect delays (Table 10-Small), and (2) configurations with larger capacity that still fit in under same area budget as the CMOS baseline, where STT-MRAM benefits from fewer misses (Table 10-Large). STT-MRAM memory controller queue write delay is set to 27 processor cycles. We experiment with an MRAM-based register file with 32 subbanks and a write delay of 13 cycles each, and we also evaluate the possibility of leaving the register file in CMOS.

To derive latency, power, and area figures for STT-MRAM arrays, we use a modified version of CACTI 6.5 [23] augmented with $10F^2$ and $30F^2$ STT-MRAM cell models. We use BSIM-4 predictive technology models (PTM) of NMOS and PMOS transistors at 32nm, and perform circuit simulations using Cadence AMS (Spectre) mixed signal analyses with Verilog-based input test vectors. Only high performance transistors were used in all circuit simulations. Temperature is set to 370K in all cases, which is a meaningful thermal design point for the proposed processor operating at 4GHz [24].

For structures that reside in CMOS in both the baseline and the proposed architecture (e.g., pipeline latches, store buffers), McPAT [19] is used to estimate power, area, and latency.

6. EVALUATION

6.1 Performance

Figure 11 compares the performance of four different MRAM-based CMT configurations to the CMOS baseline. When the register file is placed in STT-MRAM, and the L1 and L2 cache capacities are made equivalent to CMOS, performance degrades by 11%. Moving the register file to CMOS improves performance, at which point the system achieves 93% of the baseline performance. Enlarging both L1 and L2 cache capacities under the same area budget reduces miss rates but loses the latency advantage of the smaller caches; this configuration outperforms CMOS by 2% on average.

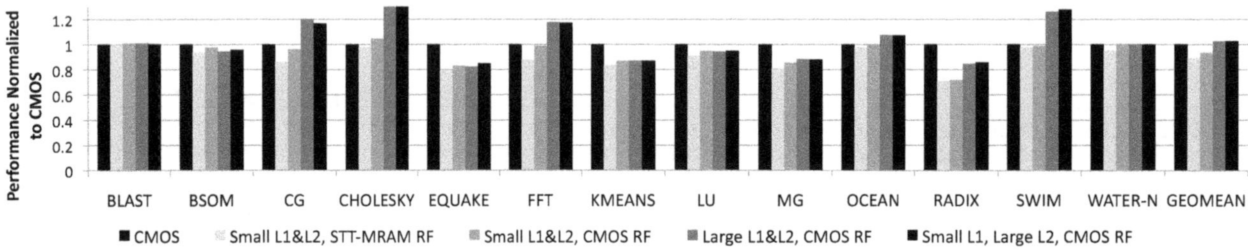

Figure 11: Performance

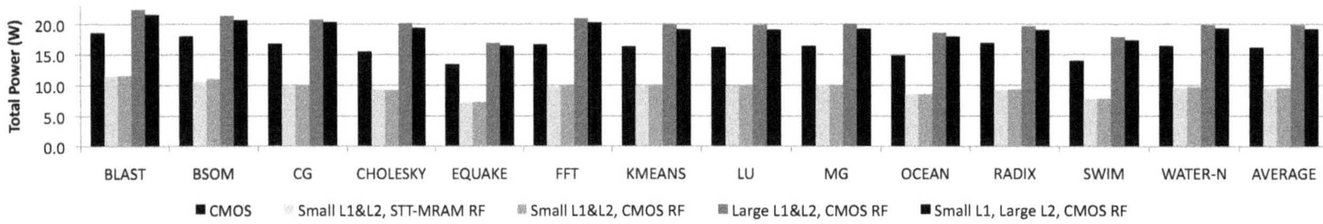

Figure 12: Total Power

	Small	Large
iL1/dL1 size	32kB/32kB	128kB/64kB
iL1/dL1 latency	1/1 cycles	2/2 cycles
L1s write occupancy	13 cycles	13 cycles
L2 size	4MB	32MB
L2 latency	8 cycles	12 cycles
L2 write occupancy	24 cycles	23 cycles

Table 10: STT-MRAM caches parameters

Benchmark	Description	Problem size
Data Mining		
BLAST	Protein matching	12.3k sequences
BSOM	Self-organizing map	2,048 rec., 100 epochs
KMEANS	K-means clustering	18k pts., 18 attributes
NAS OpenMP		
MG	Multigrid Solver	Class A
CG	Conjugate Gradient	Class A
SPEC OpenMP		
SWIM	Shallow water model	MinneSpec-Large
EQUAKE	Earthquake model	MinneSpec-Large
Splash-2 Kernels		
CHOLESKY	Cholesky factorization	tk29.O
FFT	Fast Fourier transform	1M points
LU	Dense matrix division	512 x 512to16 x 16
RADIX	Integer radix sort	2M integers
Splash-2 Applications		
OCEAN	Ocean movements	514×514 ocean
WATER-N	Water-Nsquared	512 molecules

Table 11: Simulated applications and their input sizes.

Optimizing the L2 for fewer misses (by increasing capacity under a the same area budget) while optimizing the L1s for fast hits (by migrating to a denser, STT-MRAM cache with same capacity) delivers similar results.

In general, performance bottlenecks are application dependent. For applications like CG, FFT and WATER, the MRAM-based register file represents the biggest performance hurdle. These applications encounter a higher number of subbank conflicts than others, and when the register file is moved to CMOS, their performance improves significantly. EQUAKE, KMEANS, MG, and RADIX are found sensitive to floating-point instruction latencies as they encounter many stalls due to dependents of long-latency floating-point instructions in the 24-cycle, STT-MRAM based floating-point pipeline. CG, CHOLESKY, FFT, RADIX, and SWIM benefit most from increasing cache capacities under the same area budget as CMOS, by leveraging the density advantage of STT-MRAM.

6.2 Power

Figure 12 compares total power dissipation across all five systems. STT-MRAM configurations that maintain the same cache sizes as CMOS reduce total power by 1.7× over CMOS. Despite their higher performance potential, configurations which increase cache capacity under the same area budget increase power by 1.2× over CMOS, due to the significant amount of leakage power dissipated in the CMOS-based decoding and sensing circuitry in the 32MB L2 cache. Although a larger L2 can reduce write power by allowing for fewer L2 refills and writes to memory controllers' scheduling queues, the increased leakage power consumed by the peripheral circuitry outweighs the savings on dynamic power.

Figure 13 shows the breakdown of leakage power across different components for all evaluated systems. Total leakage power is reduced by 2.1× over CMOS when cache capacities are kept the same. Systems with a large L2 cache increase leakage power by 1.3× due to the CMOS-based periphery. The floating-point units, which consume 18% of the total leakage power in the CMOS baseline, benefit significantly from an STT-MRAM based implementation. STT-MRAM based L1 caches and TLBs together reduce leakage power by another 10%. The leakage power of the memory controllers in STT-MRAM is negligible, whereas in CMOS it is 1.5%.

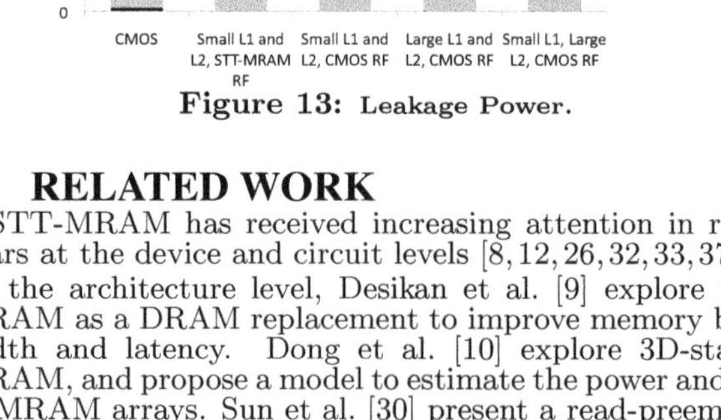

Figure 13: Leakage Power.

7. RELATED WORK

STT-MRAM has received increasing attention in recent years at the device and circuit levels [8,12,26,32,33,37,39]. At the architecture level, Desikan et al. [9] explore using MRAM as a DRAM replacement to improve memory bandwidth and latency. Dong et al. [10] explore 3D-stacked MRAM, and propose a model to estimate the power and area of MRAM arrays. Sun et al. [30] present a read-preemptive write technique which allows an SRAM-MRAM hybrid L2 cache to get performance improvements and power reductions. Zhou et al. [40] apply an early write termination technique at the circuit level to reduce STT-MRAM write energy. Wu et al. [34] propose a data migration scheme to a hybrid cache architecture to reduce the number of writes to resistive memories. Xu et al. [36] propose a circuit technique, which sizes transistors smaller than the worst case size required to generate the switching current to improve density. Most of this earlier work on MRAM considers it as a DRAM or SRAM cache replacement in the system and none of them discusses how to use resistive memories to build combinational logic.

8. CONCLUSIONS

In this paper, we have presented a new technique that reduces leakage and dynamic power in a deep-submicron microprocessor by migrating power- and performance-critical hardware resources from CMOS to STT-MRAM. We have evaluated the power and performance impact of implementing on-chip caches, register files, memory controllers, floating-point units, and various combinational logic blocks using magnetoresistive circuits, and we have explored the critical issues that affect whether a RAM array or a combinational logic block can be effectively implemented in MRAM. We have observed significant gains in power-efficiency by partitioning on-chip hardware resources among STT-MRAM and CMOS judiciously to exploit the unique power, area, and speed benefits of each technology, and by carefully re-architecting the pipeline to mitigate the performance impact of long write latencies and high write power.

We believe this paper is part of an exciting new trend toward leveraging resistive memories in effecting a significant leap in the performance and efficiency of computer systems.

9. ACKNOWLEDGMENTS

The authors would like to thank Yanwei Song, Ravi Patel, Sheng Li, and Todd Austin for useful feedback.

10. REFERENCES

[1] V. Agarwal, M. Hrishikesh, S. Keckler, and D. Burger. Clock rate vs. IPC: End of the road for conventional microprocessors. In *International Symposium on Computer Architecture*, Vancouver, Canada, June 2000.

[2] ALTERA. Stratix vs. Virtex-2 Pro FPGA performance analysis, 2004.

[3] B. Amrutur and M. Horowitz. Speed and power scaling of SRAMs. 2000.

[4] D. Burger, J. R. Goodman, and A. Kagi. Memory bandwidth limitations of future microprocessors. In *International Symposium on Computer Architecture*, Philedelphia, PA, May 1996.

[5] E. Catovic. GRFPU-high performance IEEE-754 floating-point unit. http://www.gaisler.com/doc/grfpu_dasia.pdf.

[6] C. Chappert, A. Fert, and F. N. V. Dau. The emergence of spin electronics in data storage. *Nature Materials*, 6:813–823, November 2007.

[7] M. D. Ciletti. *Advanced Digital Design with the Verilog HDL*. 2004.

[8] D. Suzuki *et al.* Fabrication of a nonvolatile lookup table circuit chip using magneto/semiconductor hybrid structure for an immediate power up field programmable gate array. In *Symposium on VLSI Circuits*, 2009.

[9] R. Desikan, C. R. Lefurgy, S. W. Keckler, and D. C. Burger. On-chip MRAM as a high-bandwidth, low-latency replacement for DRAM physical memories. In *IBM Austin Center for Advanced Studies Conference*, 2003.

[10] X. Dong, X. Wu, G. Sun, H. Li, Y. Chen, and Y. Xie. Circuit and mircoarchitecture evaluation of 3D stacking magnetic RAM (MRAM) as a universal memory replacement. In *Design Automation Conference*, 2008.

[11] HiTech. DDR2 memory controller IP core for FPGA and ASIC. http://www.hitechglobal.com/IPCores/DDR2Controller.htm.

[12] Y. Huai. Spin-transfer torque MRAM (STT-MRAM) challenges and prospects. *AAPPS Bulletin*, 18(6):33–40, December 2008.

[13] ITRS. *International Technology Roadmap for Semiconductors: 2009 Executive Summary*. http://www.itrs.net/Links/2009ITRS/Home2009.htm.

[14] K. Tsuchida *et al.* A 64Mb MRAM with clamped-reference and adequate-reference schemes. In *Proceedings of the IEEE International Solid-State Circuits Conference*, 2010.

[15] G. Kane. *MIPS RISC Architecture*. 1988.

[16] U. R. Karpuzcu, B. Greskamp, and J. Torellas. The bubblewrap many-core: Popping cores for sequential acceleration. In *International Symposium on Microarchitecutre*, 2009.

[17] P. Kongetira, K. Aingaran, and K. Olukotun. Niagara: A 32-way multithreaded sparc processor. *IEEE Micro*, 25(2):21–29, 2005.

[18] B. Lee, E. Ipek, O. Mutlu, and D. Burger. Architecting phase-change memory as a scalable dram alternative. In *International Symposium on Computer Architecture*, Austin, TX, June 2009.

[19] S. Li, J. H. Ahn, R. D. Strong, J. B. Brockman, D. M. Tullsen, and N. P. Jouppi. McPAT: An integrated power, area, and timing modeling framework for multicore and manycore architectures. In *International Symposium on Computer Architecture*, 2009.

[20] M. Hosomi and H. Yamagishi and T. Yamamoto and K. Bessha *et al.* A novel nonvolatile memory with spin torque transfer magnetization switching: Spin-RAM. In *IEDM Technical Digest*, pages 459–462, 2005.

[21] Micron. *512Mb DDR2 SDRAM Component Data Sheet: MT47H128M4B6-25*, March 2006. http://download.micron.com/pdf/datasheets/dram/ddr2/512MbDDR2.pdf.

[22] N. Muralimanohar, R. Balasubramonian, and N. Jouppi. Optimizing NUCA organizations and wiring alternatives for large caches with CACTI 6.0. Chicago, IL, Dec. 2007.

[23] N. Muralimanohar, R. Balasubramonian, and N. P. Jouppi. NAS parallel benchmarks. Technical report, NASA Ames Research Center, March 1994. Tech. Rep. RNR-94-007.

[24] U. G. Nawathe, M. Hassan, K. C. Yen, A. Kumar, A. Ramachandran, and D. Greenhill. Implementation of an 8-core, 64-thread, power-efficient sparc server on a chip. *IEEE Journal of Solid-State Circuits*, 43(1):6–20, January 2008.

[25] J. Renau, B. Fraguela, J. Tuck, W. Liu, M. Prvulovic, L. Ceze, S. Sarangi, P. Sack, K. Strauss, and P. Montesinos. SESC simulator, January 2005. http://sesc.sourceforge.net.

[26] S. Matsunaga *et al.* Fabrication of a nonvolatile full adder based on logic-in-memory architecture using magnetic tunnel junctions. *Applied Physics Express*, 1(9), 2008.

[27] S. Rusu *et al.* A 45nm 8-Core Enterprise Xeon Processor. In *Proceedings of the IEEE International Solid-State Circuits Conference*, pages 56–57, Feb. 2009.

[28] Sanu K. Mathew and Mark A. Anders and Brad Bloechel *et al.* A 4-GHz 300-mW 64-bit integer execution ALU with dual supply voltages in 90-nm CMOS. *IEEE Journal of Solid-State Circuits*, 40(1):44–51, January 2005.

[29] J. E. Stine, I. Castellanos, M. Wood, J. Henson, and F. Love. Freepdk: An open-source variation-aware design kit. In *International Conference on Microelectronic Systems Education*, 2007. http://vcag.ecen.okstate.edu/projects/scells/.

[30] G. Sun, X. Dong, Y. Xie, J. Li, and Y. Chen. A novel 3D stacked MRAM cache architecture for CMPs. In *High-Performance Computer Architecture*, 2009.

[31] T. Kawahara *et al.* 2 Mb SPRAM (spin-transfer torque RAM) with bit-by-bit bi-directional current write and parallelizing-direction current read. *IEEE Journal of Solid-State Circuits*, 43(1):109–120, January 2008.

[32] T. Kishi and H. Yoda and T. Kai *et al.* Lower-current and fast switching of a perpendicular TMR for high speed and high density spin-transfer-torque MRAM. In *IEEE International Electron Devices Meeting*, 2008.

[33] U. K. Klostermann *et al.* A perpendicular spin torque switching based MRAM for the 28 nm technology node. In *IEEE International Electron Devices Meeting*, 2007.

[34] X. Wu, J. Li, L. Zhang, E. Speight, R. Rajamony, and Y. Xie. Hybrid cache architecture with disparate memory technologies. In *International Symposium on Computer Architecture*, 2009.

[35] Xilinx. *Virtex-6 FPGA Family Overview*, November 2009. http://www.xilinx.com/support/documentation/data_sheets/ds150.pdf.

[36] W. Xu, Y. Chen, X. Wang, and T. Zhang. Improving STT MRAM storage density through smaller-than-worst-case transistor sizing. In *Design Automation Conference*, 2009.

[37] W. Xu, T. Zhang, and Y. Chen. Spin-transfer torque magnetoresistive content addressable memory (CAM) cell structure design with enhanced search noise margin. In *International Symposium on Circuits and Systems*, 2008.

[38] W. Zhao and Y. Cao. New generation of predictive technology model for sub-45nm design exploration. In *International Symposium on Quality Electronic Design*, 2006. http://ptm.asu.edu/.

[39] W. Zhao, C. Chappert, and P. Mazoyer. Spin transfer torque (STT) MRAM-based runtime reconfiguration FPGA circuit. In *ACM Transactions on Embedded Computing Systems*, 2009.

[40] P. Zhou, B. Zhao, J. Yang, and Y. Zhang. Energy reduction for STT-RAM using early write termination. In *International Conference on Computer-Aided Design*, 2009.

Security Refresh: Prevent Malicious Wear-out and Increase Durability for Phase-Change Memory with Dynamically Randomized Address Mapping

Nak Hee Seong Dong Hyuk Woo Hsien-Hsin S. Lee
School of Electrical and Computer Engineering
Georgia Institute of Technology
Atlanta, GA 30332
{nhseong, dhwoo, leehs}@ece.gatech.edu

ABSTRACT

Phase change memory (PCM) is an emerging memory technology for future computing systems. Compared to other non-volatile memory alternatives, PCM is more matured to production, and has a faster read latency and potentially higher storage density. The main roadblock precluding PCM from being used, in particular, in the main memory hierarchy, is its limited write endurance. To address this issue, recent studies proposed to either reduce PCM's write frequency or use wear-leveling to evenly distribute writes. Although these techniques can extend the lifetime of PCM, most of them will not prevent deliberately designed malicious codes from wearing it out quickly. Furthermore, all the prior techniques did not consider the circumstances of a compromised OS and its security implication to the overall PCM design. A compromised OS will allow adversaries to manipulate processes and exploit side channels to accelerate wear-out.

In this paper, we argue that a PCM design not only has to consider normal wear-out under normal application behavior, most importantly, it must take the worst-case scenario into account with the presence of malicious exploits and a compromised OS to address the durability and security issues simultaneously. In this paper, we propose a novel, low-cost hardware mechanism called Security Refresh to avoid information leak by constantly migrating their physical locations inside the PCM, obfuscating the actual data placement from users and system software. It uses a dynamic randomized address mapping scheme that swaps data using random keys upon each refresh due. The hardware overhead is tiny without using any table. The best lifetime we can achieve under the worst-case malicious attack is more than six years. Also, our scheme incurs around 1% performance degradation for normal program operations.

Categories and Subject Descriptors

B.3 [**Memory Structures**]: Semiconductor Memories;
B.6.1 [**Design Styles**]: Memory control and access

ISCA'10, June 19–23, 2010, Saint-Malo, France.

General Terms

Design, Experimentation, Performance, Security

Keywords

Phase Change Memory, Security, Wear Leveling, Dynamic Address Remapping

1. INTRODUCTION

Phase change memory (PCM) has emerged as one potential memory technology for improving the performance of the overall system memory hierarchy. A PCM cell is made of phase-change material based on chalcogenide alloy typically composed of **Ge**, **Sb**, and **Te**. The material has two distinct phases — a high electrical resistive amorphous phase and a low resistive crystalline phase. The crystalline phase can be reached by heating the material above the crystallization temperature while it can be switched into the amorphous phase by melting and quickly quenching it. A data bit can be stored in either states, which are non-volatile. Compared to floating-gate flash memory, PCM has much shorter latency and longer write endurance. These advantages make it a perfect candidate as the alternative to flash memory devices. On the other hand, the density of current PCM is higher than that of DRAM [1]. Also, PCM promises better scalability with process technology scaling. Moreover, if we can utilize its multi-level cell feature [15], the density will be even greater. Recently, researchers have studied the trade-off of using PCM as the main memory [9, 14] or even as the last level cache [22]. Although its latency is currently several times higher than DRAM latency, these studies showed that its benefit gained from its high density can outweigh the degradation of access time by employing a deeper memory hierarchy [15] or having a hybrid memory architecture with mixed usage of other memory technologies [14, 22].

The primary roadblock for using PCM as part of the main memory is its much lower write endurance compared to DRAM. The current write endurance of a PCM cell is around 10^8 although the number is projected to be increased to 10^{15} in 2022 according to ITRS [1]. Several recent studies attempted to address this issue by either reducing PCM's write frequency or using wear-leveling techniques to evenly distribute PCM writes. Although these techniques can extend the lifetime of PCM under normal operations of typical applications, we found that most of them fail to prevent an adversary from writing malicious code deliberately designed to wear out and fail PCM. For instance, the schemes to reducing write frequency, such as *data comparison write* [23] and *Flip-N-*

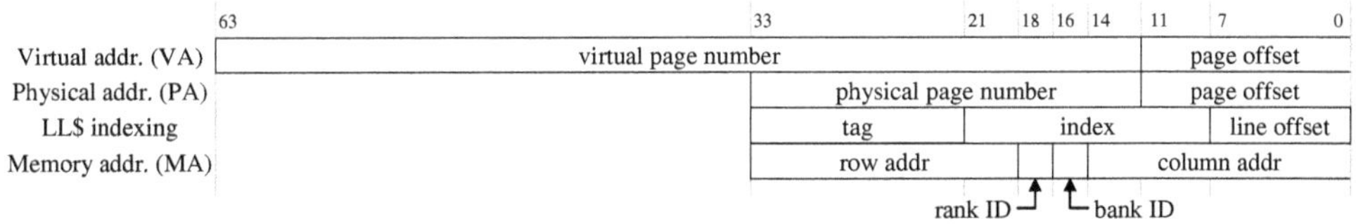

Figure 1: The Addressing Scheme of the Baseline Architecture

Write [3] do not prevent an adversary from wiggling the memory bits of the same PCM location and wearing them out. Similarly, the prior wear-leveling schemes are also vulnerable due to the inherent weaknesses caused by static randomization, coarse-grained shuffling, and regular shuffling pattern as we will detail later. Furthermore, all the prior art did not consider the circumstances when the underlying OS is compromised and its security implication to PCM design. A compromised OS, (*e.g.*, via simple buffer overflow) will allow adversaries to manipulate all processes and exploit side channels easily, which accelerates the wear-out of targeted PCM blocks and renders a dysfunctional system. For example, a compromised OS can thrash or turn off all caches, disabling the shield from PCM. Moreover, if the compromised OS allows a malicious process to obtain and assemble useful information leaked from side channels (*e.g.*, timing attacks [7, 20] to deduce shuffling pattern in a wear-leveling scheme), the wear-leveling scheme will not stop adversaries from tracking, pinpointing, and wearing out target PCM blocks. Note that attacking a system with side channels using time [7, 20], power [8], electromagnetic emission [2], architectural vulnerability [18, 25], etc., has been successfully demonstrated in many systems including the Xbox [4]. Designing PCM without careful consideration for all these implications will lead to critical data loss in PCM, rendering incorrect computing or transaction results, eventually leading to dire financial consequences.

In this paper, we argue that PCM designs not only have to consider wear-out under normal execution of typical applications, most importantly, they must take the worst-case scenarios into account with the presence of malicious exploits and a compromised OS. Such design consideration will address durability and security issues of a PCM system simultaneously. After demonstrating and analyzing the attack models that exploit the weakness of prior proposals, we will show that we need dynamic runtime randomization with low-cost hardware implementation to improve wear-out vulnerability and to prevent construction of useful knowledge gleaned from side channels. To achieve this goal, in this paper, we propose *Security Refresh*. Similar to the concept of protecting charge leak from DRAM, Security Refresh, a low-cost hardware embedded inside PCM, prevents information leak by constantly migrating physical locations of PCM data (thus refresh) and obfuscating the actual data placement from users and system software. The contributions of our paper are as follows:

- We demonstrate that security is a separate yet more serious issue from simply extending durability in PCM design.
- We analyze the vulnerability of prior studies and provide their respective, practical attack models to wear out PCM within a reasonable amount of time.
- We propose a dynamic, low-cost wear-leveling scheme called *Security Refresh* to battle intentional, malicious wear-out and present the implementation trade-off from the security and durability standpoint.

The rest of this paper is organized as follows. Section 2 describes prior proposals and their vulnerabilities with their corresponding attack models. Section 3 introduces Security Refresh. Section 4 discusses the implementation trade-off. Section 5 proposes two-level Security Refresh scheme. Section 6 evaluates different configurations of our scheme. We conclude in Section 7.

2. VULNERABILITY OF PRIOR WEAR-OUT MANAGEMENT SCHEMES

Recently, several architectural techniques were proposed to prolong the limited write endurance of PCM. They can be classified into two groups: the methods to eliminating redundant writes [3, 9, 14, 23, 24] and the ones to evenly wearing out the entire memory space [14, 15, 24]. Among all the prior schemes, the most recent proposal, randomized Region Based Start-Gap (RBSG) [15], is the only proposal that considers the security problem. In this paper, we will demonstrate that these prior schemes including the randomized RBSG scheme are vulnerable to well-designed malicious attacks. In our analysis, we evaluate their vulnerabilities using a baseline architecture similar to the one used in a recent study [15]. Basically, we assume that an off-chip DRAM is used as a last-level cache backed up with PCM used as the actual main memory. The interface between the DRAM cache and PCM is a DDR3-1600 like 64-bit bus. The 16GB PCM consists of four ranks while each rank contains four banks with 32K rows in each bank.[1] Furthermore, we assume that the write endurance of PCM is 10^8, and its read and write latencies are 150ns and 450ns, respectively.

To clarify the terminology used in this paper, Figure 1 depicts the layers of address translation and mapping from virtual address all the way down to the low level physical memory location. Note that a memory controller usually maps a given physical address (PA) into a memory address (MA) that consists of a rank ID, a bank ID, a row address, and a column address for indexing the main memory. In the following discussion, we also assume that a memory controller interleaves consecutive row addresses across different banks, a common mechanism to enhance bank-level parallelism.

2.1 Vulnerability of PCM Without Protection

The simplest way to attack a durability-oblivious PCM is to repeatedly write to a fixed location. To force cache misses for PCM accesses, it is obvious that one can deliberately cook up a program that continuously write to nine different addresses mapped to the same set of the 8-way cache with `s` sets in our baseline [21]. The first eight instructions inside a loop sequentially write to `a[i]`, `a[i+1*s]`, to `a[i+7*s]` filling up one cache set followed by the subsequent eight instructions that write to `a[i]` to `a[i+6*s]` and then to `a[i+7*b*s]`, where b is a large value to guarantee `a[i+ 7*s]` and `a[i+7*b*s]` do not hit in the same memory page (*i.e.*, row buffer hit) but located in the same PCM bank. After these two write sequences (16 writes) in the loop, we perform a *memory fence* operation to ensure addresses will not collapse in an internal buffer but go to external memory directly. As such, this simple code will generate conflict misses between `a[i+7*s]` and

[1] A conventional 2GB DDR3 SDRAM DIMM is composed of 8 banks, each of which contains 32K 8KB rows. Considering PCM's scalability and multi-bit potential, we assume four times larger row size.

`a[i+7*b*s]` and create two row buffer misses all the time to update two different PCM locations.

In this attack model, it takes at least $2 \times (l_w + l_r)$ seconds to write two separate cache lines into PCM including the time (l_w) to bring two lines into the cache and the time (l_r) to write two dirty lines back to PCM. Given a modern PCM cell can endure no more than 10^8 writes, the lifetime of the baseline PCM without any architectural durability enhancement will be $2 \times (l_w + l_r) \times 10^8$, *i.e.*, about two minutes (= $2 \times (450ns + 150ns) \times 10^8$).

2.2 Vulnerability of Prior Redundant Write Reduction Techniques

We now examine the redundant write reduction schemes. To eliminate them, Lee *et al.* [9] and Qureshi *et al.* [14] proposed to maintain fine-grained dirty bits as a part of the cache line state to enable partial writes. These methods require additional partial dirty bits across all cache hierarchy. On the other hand, Yang *et al.* [23] and Zhou *et al.* [24] proposed *data comparison and write* schemes, which replace a write operation with a read-compare-write operation to eliminate silent stores [10] to PCM. Unfortunately, these methods still suffer from the same types of malicious wear-out attacks in Section 2.1 as an adversary can always write complementary values to the same PCM cells. More recently, Cho and Lee [3] leveraged the bus-invert coding idea [19] and proposed to add a single bit per PCM word to indicate if a stored word is inverted or not. With this additional state bit, a PCM chip can write data in an inverted form if the inverted value reduces the number of bit-flips when writing new data. However, this method is still subject to malicious attacks. For example, an attacker can use the same malicious code but repeatedly write 0x00 and 0x01 in turn, which will never activate Flip-N-Write and eventually wear out a bit in each byte. In summary, the lifetime of a target location in PCM in these systems will still be two minutes.

2.3 Vulnerability of Prior Wear-Leveling Techniques

Unlike the techniques described in Section 2.2, wear-leveling schemes extend the lifetime of PCM by evenly distributing the locally concentrated writes across the entire PCM space. Transparent to the users, these techniques periodically change the mapping between the physical address and the physical PCM location. Although such periodic mapping schemes can reduce the system's vulnerability to brute-force type of attacks, they are still vulnerable to deliberately-designed attacks, especially when the OS is compromised, as we will discuss in the following sections.

2.3.1 Row Shifting and Segment Swapping

Zhou *et al.* [24] proposed an integrated wear-leveling mechanism with two techniques: a fine-grained wear-leveling called *Row Shifting* and a coarse-grained one called *Segment Swapping*. Row Shifting rotates a physical PCM row one byte at a time for a given shift interval based on the number of writes to the row. On the other hand, the *Segment Swapping* scheme swaps the most frequently written segment with one of the less frequently written segments by monitoring the number of writes to each segment. A segment (1MB) contains several rows (32KB). Nevertheless, this wear-leveling has two main drawbacks: the overhead of a hardware address mapping table and a sorting network required for picking a less frequently written segment, both preventing the use of small segments. Thus, the authors used a large 1MB segment [24].

Unfortunately, such a coarse-grained segment allows an adversary to fail a system easily. For example, if the OS has already been compromised (*e.g.*, via buffer overflow), an attacker can allocate all the first physical pages of each of the 1MB PCM segments to the malicious program. Once the malicious program can access these 16K pages, it can execute a loop that writes the first byte of these pages one by one. Once the malicious program iterates this loop n times where n is the row shift interval, it should write the second byte of these pages (instead of the first byte) to attack the same physical cells even after a row is shifted. The attacker can continue such attack until PCM cells fail. Note that an attacker can also wear out these 16K pages in parallel using a distributed attack model with multiple threads on a multi-core processor [21]. This means that overall execution time of this process will be eventually limited by the bank-level parallelism of PCM, not by computation. Consequently, a group of PCM cells will fail after the following period: $(2 \times \#\text{ of segments} \times \frac{\text{(line-fill latency+write-back latency)}}{\#\text{ of possible writes in parallel}}$ $\times$PCM write endurance), where 2 accounts for the worst-case latency due to potentially unsynchronized rotation between the malicious code and actual hardware. For a system with 16 GB 16-bank PCM, PCM cells will fail within 2048 minutes.

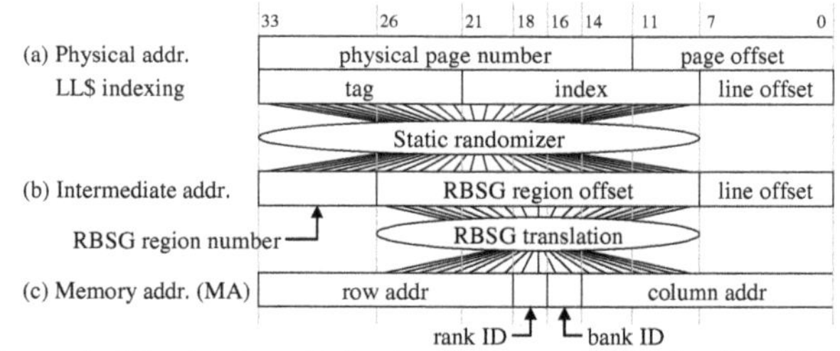

Figure 2: The Address Indexing Scheme of Randomized RBSG

2.3.2 Randomized Region Based Start-Gap

In contrast to a table-based translation scheme, Qureshi *et al.* proposed *randomized Region Based Start-Gap (randomized RBSG)* wear-leveling method by using an algebraic mapping between physical addresses and memory addresses [15], which is also the first work that discussed security threat to PCM. As shown in Figure 2(a) and (b), a physical address issued from the cache is translated into an intermediate address through an *Address-Space Randomization* method based on *Feistel Network* or a *Random Invertible Binary Matrix*. Note that such a randomization function is only updated once when the system is booted. In this section, we assumed that the unit of translation is one PCM row, which the original paper suggested as the unit of translation when we use an open-row policy. We chose such a design because it allows a memory controller to exploit data locality within a row similar to a conventional memory subsystem. Note that our attack model is not limited to a system that uses an open-row policy as will be elaborated later.

On the other hand, the intermediate address space is partitioned into several segments called RBSG regions. Each RBSG region has an extra storage line that allows us to evenly wear out the entire memory space within a region by rotating each line one by one. Furthermore, each RBSG region has a *Start pointer* that points to a memory line with the lowest *physical address* in the region and a *Gap pointer* that points to an empty line in the region. These two pointers along with another algebraic function called *Region Based Start-Gap (RBSG)* are used to further translate RBSG region offset bits (Figure 2(b)) into an actual physical location. Note that our baseline architecture (Figure 1) assumes that the rank ID and the bank ID are located between the row address and the column address like a conventional memory addressing scheme.

Figure 3 illustrates an example of RBSG translation. In this example, one RBSG region contains four memory lines across two banks. When the number of writes in this region exceeds a certain

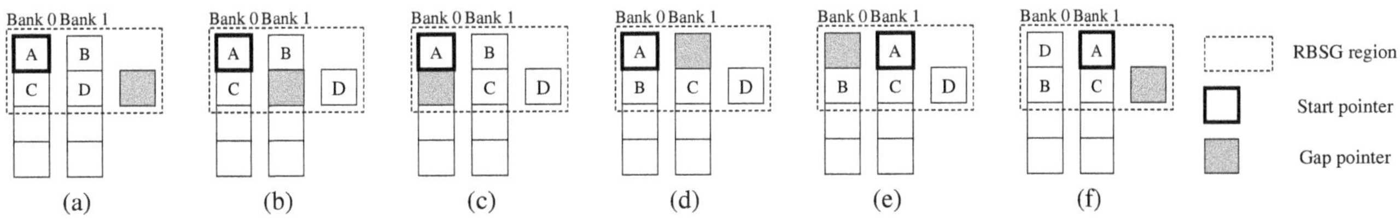

Figure 3: An Example of RBSG Translation for One Rotation Phase

threshold, ψ, indicated by an overflowed write counter, the memory line (D) adjacent to the Gap pointer in this region is shifted into the extra space while the Gap pointer will point to where the migrated memory line used to be (Figure 3(b)). Once the write counter overflows again, the memory line (C) adjacent to the Gap pointer is shifted following the same direction to the empty space. Afterward, the Gap pointer points to the empty slot (Figure 3(c)). Such migration continues for every ψ and finally reaches the state in Figure 3(f) when all four memory lines are rotated by one from the initial state (Figure 3(a)). The Start pointer is updated to indicate the current PCM location of the lowest physical address (A) in this RBSG region. This RBSG scheme enables wear-leveling without using a large table.

However, we found that a deliberately-contrived malicious code can still fail such systems by exploiting side channels given the OS is compromised. Such an attack is made possible (1) because the randomly shuffled address mappings remain unchanged once booted and (2) because the migration of their scheme performs linear shifting, which is deterministic. How a malicious process identifies consecutive physical addresses in a region is shown below.

We calculated a ψ value and the corresponding region size for our baseline architecture as recommended by the original paper [15]. To limit write overhead less than 1%, we set ψ to 100 as proposed in the original paper. This configuration leads the region size to be 16GB because the original paper recommended the maximum number of lines, K, in each region to meet the following condition: $K < \frac{\text{(PCM Write endurance)}}{\psi}$. Now, we will explain our attack model as follows:

Step 1: Finding a set of physical addresses mapped to the same bank. First, the malicious process picks an arbitrary physical address b_0. For every memory line a_x, timing attacks [7] are applied to see if b_0 is in the same bank of an a_x. The rationale is simple — if the measured data access time to two back-to-back accesses a_1 and b_0 is longer than that to another back-to-back accesses a_2 and b_0, we can conclude that a_1 and b_0 are located within the same bank while a_2 and b_0 are accessed in parallel from different banks. (In a system with a closed row policy, our attack model is still valid because it uses latency differences caused by the bank-level parallelism.) Note that a compromised OS can schedule only the malicious process to perform such profiling. Using this attack, the malicious process find all the lines in the same bank with b_0. We call this set of memory lines T_0. Similarly, by choosing another arbitrary physical address b_1 in the complementary set of the T_0 and measuring data access time for every memory line a_y in T_0^c, another set of memory lines, T_1, will be revealed. By repeating this measuring sequence, the malicious process finally can classify all physical memory lines according to their bank locations within 1.33 seconds.

Step 2: Forcing one memory line to migrate to an adjacent bank. After that, the malicious process shifts one memory line by writing a randomly chosen physical address, v_0, 100 times. This causes one memory line shifted to an adjacent bank like the previous example. This step takes a negligibly small amount of time.

Step 3: Finding a memory line that is migrated to the adjacent bank. Then, the malicious process repeats the measuring sequence (Step 1) and figures out the physical address p_0 of the shifted memory line by comparing the current bank sets with the previous bank sets. Obviously, this step takes another 1.33 seconds.

Step 4: Forcing one more line to migrate to the adjacent bank. Now, we update v_0 again 100 times. Because the Gap Pointer points to the old location of p_0 after Step 3, these 100 writes of Step 4 will force another line, p_1, to be migrated to the old location of p_0.

Step 5: Finding a memory line that is migrated to the old location of p_0. Then, the malicious process again repeats the measuring sequence (Step 3) to find out a new physical address p_1 that is newly migrated to the old location of p_0. This step again takes 1.33 seconds. After this step, we can detect that p_1 will always take a previous location of p_0 upon one rotation because of the deterministic migration pattern of the randomized RBSG scheme.

Step 6: Attacking a specific PCM line. The final step is to fail the memory line indicated by the physical address p_0. The malicious process can attack the memory line until the entire region is rotated by one. After the rotation, the physical address p_1 will be mapped to the same PCM cells. Thus, the malicious process can still attack the same PCM cells by repeatedly updating p_1 for another rotation period. After these two rotation phases, the target PCM cells will fail because of the following reason. According to the original paper, a physical address is mapped to one memory line for $\psi \times K$ writes before this physical address is migrated to another memory line. In particular, $\psi \times K$ is large enough to consume one half of the lifetime of one physical cell, thus two rotation phases are good enough to fail the system. We found that Step 6 can be completed within 62.9 seconds.

Note that up to this point, we did not account for *delayed write factor* (DWF), which is proposed by the original RBSG paper to enhance security. The DWF basically delays a write request until the predefined number of writes to different addresses are queued in the write queue. If we assume the DWF to be 16 as in the original paper, we found that our side-channel attack needs to figure out 32 physical addresses adjacently located in the region, because a memory line can be written $\frac{\psi \times K}{\text{DWF}}$ times for one rotation period. Consequently, it takes around 17.5 minutes to fail one PCM memory line.[2] In sum, our side-channel attack exploits the deterministic mapping pattern of the randomized RBSG to fail PCM cells efficiently.

So far, we mainly exploited the fact that a region is spread across bank boundaries following a conventional addressing scheme as explained previously. If a region is located inside a bank, then our current side-channel attack model cannot identify the exact mapping from a physical address to a memory line. However, the side-channel attack performed in Step 1 can still reveal all phys-

[2]In the case of a system using a closed row policy, the memory line size can be as small as the last-level cache line size. In this case, an attacker can fail the system within 13 minutes.

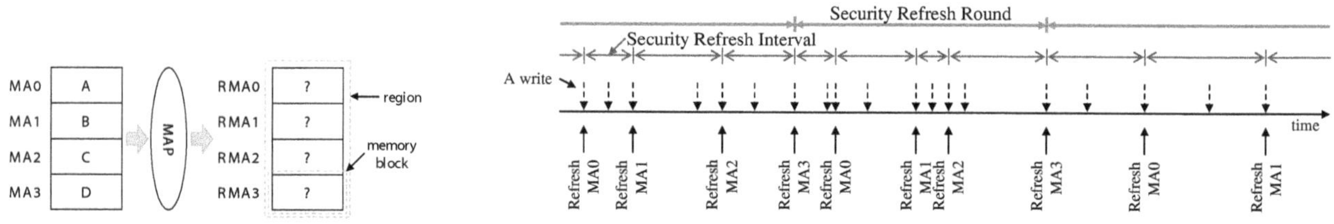

(a) A Region and A Memory Block

(b) Security Refresh Interval and Round

Figure 4: Security Refresh Terminology

ical addresses mapped to the same bank. After figuring out a set of physical addresses mapped to the same bank, we can perform a brute-force attack similar to the attack used in Section 2.3.1. This takes around 23 days to fail all memory lines in the bank. This is mainly because the number of memory lines in the bank is at most 2^{15} when we use a 32KB memory line for an open-row scheduling policy.

Another recent research work by Seznec [17] submitted concurrently with our paper demonstrated that a common birthday paradox attack (BPA) can be used to attack RBSG rather efficiently. The BPA works in the following context: if one randomly selects any element among M elements and repeat this experiment until the same element is selected twice, the expected number of trials until the second occurrence is surprisingly small. According to his analysis, the BPA can fail an architecture with the randomized RBSG scheme within a reasonable amount of time. When a region is located inside a bank, we found that our side-channel attack model can further accelerate Seznec's attack model because our attack method done in Step 1 can help an attacker to figure out all memory lines mapped to a single bank, effectively shrinking the number of elements, M.

3. SECURITY REFRESH

As mentioned earlier, prior studies mainly focused on extending the lifetime of a PCM-based system that runs conventional applications but failed to protect the system against deliberately-crafted malicious attacks. A malicious application can exploit the properties of a durability solution to destruct a PCM portion easily. Although durability and security seem to be two separate issues in PCM design, they share a common goal and should be addressed at the same time. In this paper, we argue that a correct, usable PCM design should consider the worst-case wear-out under malicious attacks such as side channel exploits to make PCM practical and commercially viable. In general, if PCM can sustain malicious attacks, they should simultaneously address the durability issue. To circumvent these intentional exploits, we must keep adversaries from inferring an actual physical PCM location. Furthermore, the address space must be shuffled *dynamically* over time to avoid useful information leaked through side-channels.

3.1 Security Refresh Controller

First, we define one more address space, the *Refreshed or Remapped Memory Address (RMA)*, inside a PCM bank to dissociate a memory address (MA) (defined in Figure 1) from the actual data location. After receiving an access command (in MA) from the memory controller, each PCM bank re-calculates its own internal row and column address (in RMA). To allow such mapping, in this work, we propose *Security Refresh*. Similar to DRAM refresh that prevents charge leaking from a DRAM cell, our Security Refresh prevents address information leaked from PCM accesses by dynamically randomizing mapping between MAs and RMAs. On the other hands, rather than refreshing based on time in DRAM cell, our Security Refresh scheme refreshes a PCM region based on usage, *i.e.*, the number of writes. Our Security Refresh is controlled by *Security Refresh Controller* (SRC), which is embedded inside the PCM bank. The SRC not only remaps an MA into an RMA but also periodically changes the mapping between these two address domains with extremely low-overhead hardware. The rationale and advantages of employing an SRC inside a PCM bank are as follows:

- To obfuscate the address information regarding the actual physical data placement from applications, the (compromised) OS, and the memory controller.
- To obfuscate potential side-channel leakage, if any.
- To prohibit any physical tampering, *e.g.*, memory bus probing.
- To allow a memory controller to exploit bank-level parallelism for better scheduling.
- To provide high efficiency without disturbing the off-chip bus during data shuffling and swapping.
- To enable a high-bandwidth data swapping mechanism without being constrained by limited, off-chip pin bandwidth.
- To allow PCM vendors to protect their product without relying on a third-party such as the OS or the memory controller.

3.2 Basics of Distributed Security Refresh

Since our proposed SRC will be implemented inside each PCM bank that will likely be manufactured with a process optimized for PCM cell density, the hardware overhead for the SRC should be kept low to make it practical. Furthermore, as demonstrated previously, information can leak through side channels. A sufficient amount of such information allows an adversary to assemble useful knowledge and devise a side-channel attack for target PCM locations. Simply hiding internal memory addresses alone will not address this issue properly. Thus, we need to constantly update the address mapping to obfuscate any relationship among information leaked from side channels.

Before explaining our algorithm, we first introduce our nomenclature in Figure 4. First of all, we treat one PCM bank as one region. As shown in Figure 4(a), one region is composed of many memory blocks (To simplify, we show only four in the figure). A memory block should be no smaller than a cache line in order to keep address lookup simple. For every r writes ($r = 2$ in Figure 4(b)), the SRC will "refresh" a memory block by potentially remapping it to a new PCM location using a randomly generated key. We will detail our algorithm in Section 3.3.[3] We call this number of writes, r, which denotes the *security refresh interval* analogous to DRAM's refresh rate. The refresh operations continue for all memory blocks in each region. A complete iteration of refreshing every single memory block in a region is called a *se-*

[3]We differentiate these two terms: refresh and remapping. A refresh will be evaluated upon the due of a security refresh interval, however, as we will show later, it may or may not lead to an address remapping in PCM space.

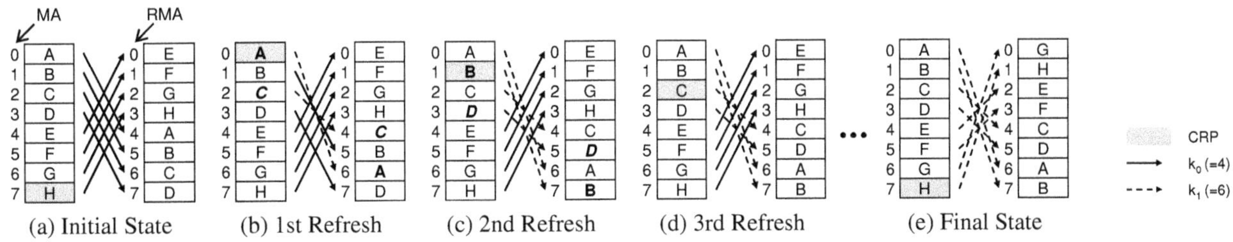

Figure 5: An Example of One Complete Security Refresh Round

curity refresh round, similar to DRAM's refresh period. To begin another security refresh round, the SRC will generate a new random key and use it together with the key from its previous refresh round.

3.3 Security Refresh Algorithm

Now we use an example to walk through our algorithm followed by its formal definition and description. Figure 5 depicts an example of one security refresh round. From Figure 5(a) to (e), we start from an initial state with eight successive security refreshes for eight memory blocks in one PCM region. In each sub-figure, the left column shows MAs (memory addresses) of these blocks with their data in capital letters while the right column shows the RMAs (refreshed memory addresses) and the actual data placement in PCM. We explain each sub-figure in the following.

1. Figure 5(a) shows the initial state in which all eight RMAs were generated by XORing their corresponding MAs with a key k_0 where $k_0 = 4$. For example, the memory address MA0 (000) XOR k_0 (100) is mapped to RMA4 (100) in the physical PCM. Also note that, Figure 5(a) has reached the end of a security refresh round as all the MAs have been refreshed with k_0. Upon each security refresh, the candidate MA to be refreshed is pointed by a register called *Current Refresh Pointer (CRP)* shown as a shaded box in the figure. The CRP is incremented after each security refresh.

2. Upon the next security refresh (Figure 5(b)), a new security refresh round will be initiated because CRP has reached the first MA of a region. Consequently, a new key ($k_1 = 6$) will be generated by a hardware random number generator in the SRC for refreshing all MAs in the current round. At this point, MA0 is refreshed and remapped from RMA4 to RMA6. Since the data (A) of MA0 is now moved to RMA6 where the data (C) of MA2 used to be. Hence, C should be evicted from RMA4 and stored somewhere else. Interestingly, due to the nature of XOR, MA2 will actually be mapped to RMA4 using the new key ($2 \oplus k_1 = 4$), *i.e.,* the RMA of MA0 from the previous round ($0 \oplus k_0 = 4$). This security refresh, essentially, swaps data between MA0 and MA2 in their PCM locations. We call this interesting property the *pairwise remapping property*, which will be defined and proved formally later. Note that the SRC will be responsible for reading and writing two memory blocks to physically swap the data between them.

3. Similarly, in the next security refresh (Figure 5(c)), data for MA1 and MA3 (a victim evicted by MA1) in PCM are swapped between RMA5 and RMA7.

4. In Figure 5(d), MA2 pointed by CRP is supposed to be remapped after its security refresh. However, it has been swapped previously (Figure 5(b)) in the current security refresh round. Thus, we will not swap again but simply increment the CRP pointer. To test whether an MA has already been swapped in the current round can easily be done by exploiting the pairwise remapping property. All we need to do is to XOR the current candidate MA with the key used in the prior refresh round and the key used in the current round. If the outcome is smaller than CRP, it indicates the memory block has been swapped in the current round. For instance in Figure 5(d), we XOR MA2 with 4 (k_0) and 6 (k_1) giving a result of 0 ($2 \oplus 4 \oplus 6 = 0$). Since it is smaller than CRP (=2), it indicates that MA2 has been swapped in the current refresh round. We will show the formal proof later in this section.

5. The next five memory blocks are refreshed in the same manner. After the eighth security refresh in the current round, CRP will wrap around and reach MA0 again, completing the current security refresh round (Figure 5(e)). Upon the next refresh, a new key, k_2, will be generated and a new round starts using k_1 and k_2. k_0 will no longer be needed. Note that, for each refresh round, only the most recent two keys are needed.

Now, we formally explain the pairwise remapping property, which allows us to exchange a pair of memory blocks only with two keys. For our address remapping, assume that we use a binary operation, $\oplus$, closed on a set S, which satisfies the following properties for all x, y, and z, the elements of S where S is a set of possible addresses in a PCM region.

- Associative Property: $(x \oplus y) \oplus z = x \oplus (y \oplus z)$.
- Commutative Property: $x \oplus y = y \oplus x$.
- Self-Inverse Property: $x \oplus x = e$, where e is an identity element so that $x \oplus e = x$.

Basically, we find an RMA for a given MA by simply performing this binary operation between MA and a randomly generated key (k) of the same length *i.e.,* $MA \oplus k = RMA$. Here, we define several notations used in this proof as shown in Table 1.

Table 1: Notations Used in the Proof

k_p	A previous key generated in the previous security refresh round
k_c	A current key generated in the current security refresh round
A_m	An MA to be refreshed in the current refresh
A_{r_p}	An RMA to which A_m was mapped with k_p (*i.e.,* $A_{r_p} = A_m \oplus k_p$)
A_{r_c}	An RMA to which A_m will be mapped with k_c (*i.e.,* $A_{r_c} = A_m \oplus k_c$)
B_m	An MA mapped to A_{r_c} with k_p, thus to be evicted by A_m
B_{r_p}	An RMA to which B_m was mapped with k_p (*i.e.,* $B_{r_p} = B_m \oplus k_p$)
B_{r_c}	An RMA to which B_m will be mapped with k_c (*i.e.,* $B_{r_c} = B_m \oplus k_c$)

According to associative and self-inverse properties, when A_m newly occupies A_{r_c}, B_m can be easily detected by performing $\oplus$ operation between A_{r_c} and k_p because $A_{r_c} \oplus k_p = (B_m \oplus k_p) \oplus k_p = B_m$. More interestingly, the new location (B_{r_c}) that B_m should be mapped to with k_c is the old location (A_{r_p}) that A_m used to be mapped to with k_p because $B_{r_c} = B_m \oplus k_c =$

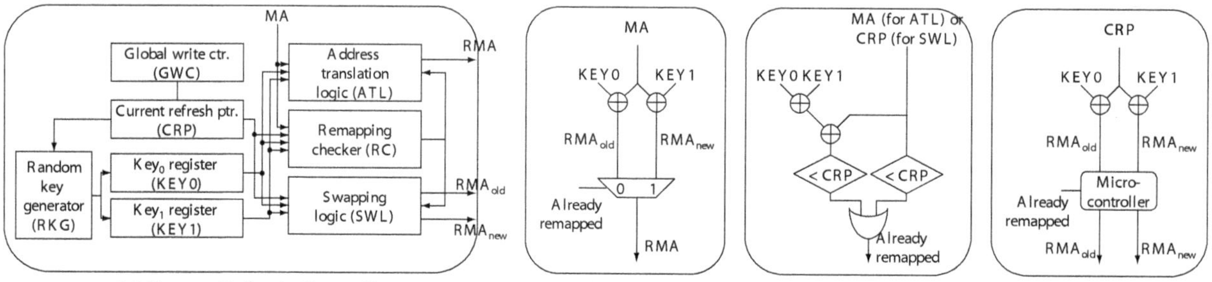

(a) Secure Refresh Controller (b) ATL (c) RC (d) SWL

Figure 6: Secure Refresh Controller

$(A_{r_c} \oplus k_p) \oplus k_c = ((A_m \oplus k_c) \oplus k_p) \oplus k_c = A_m \oplus k_p = A_{r_p}$. In short, we can simultaneously map a pair of MAs into their new RMA locations by simply swapping the physical data of their old PCM blocks. Consequently, the actual swapping operations in a security refresh round will be done by one half of all security refresh operations. The simplest function that satisfies all three properties is an eXclusive-OR although we have proved that any function satisfying the above three properties can be used as the refresh/remapping function. For the rest of this paper, we use XOR.

3.4 Key Selection for Address Translation

To correctly find the data location in PCM, we need to translate the given MA to its current RMA using the right key. It seems that the most straightforward way to find the right key is to add one bit in SRC for each MA to indicate whether it needs to be translated using the key in previous refresh round or the current key. Even though 1-bit per block seems small, for a 1GB PCM region with 16KB memory blocks, we will need 8KB (=2^{16} bits) extra space. In fact, hardware overhead for maintaining translation information of each block is the main reason why the prior table-based approach [24] cannot support fine-granularity segments.

Fortunately, in our scheme, the pairwise remapping property along with the use of the linearly increasing CRP value property allows us to determine the right key without any table. In particular, when a memory controller wants to read from or write to an MA C_m, we need to use the current key (k_c) in the following two cases, otherwise, the key in previous refresh round (k_p) should be used.

- If C_m is less than the value of CRP, we should use the current key (k_c) since C_m has already been refreshed in the current security refresh round.
- If $C_m \oplus k_p \oplus k_c$ is less than the value of CRP, we should use the current key, too. This is not very intuitive, so we will describe it with a formal method. What we want to detect in this condition is whether C_m was a victim that is evicted when another MA, D_m, is remapped to the old RMA value of C_m, *i.e.*, $C_m \oplus k_p$. As explained in Section 3.3, we can reconstruct D_m by simply performing an XOR operation between the RMA value and the current key, which is $(C_m \oplus k_p) \oplus k_c$. If we compare D_m against the value of CRP, we can detect whether C_m was a victim that is already remapped when D_m was remapped.

3.5 Implementing Security Refresh Controller

The main additional hardware for supporting Security Refresh is the Security Refresh Controller (SRC) (Figure 6(a)) per region. Each SRC consists of four registers, a random key generator (RKG), address translation logic (ATL), remapping checker (RC), swapping logic (SWL), and two swap buffers. The four registers required are: (1) KEY0 register to store a prior key ($\log_2 n$ bits where n is the number of memory blocks in a region), (2) KEY1 register to store a current key, (3) a global write counter (GWC) to count the total number of writes to a region for triggering security refresh, and (4) the current refresh pointer (CRP) that points to the next MA to be refreshed. A new key is generated by RKG in-between two security refresh rounds using thermal noise generated by undriven resistors in the SRC [5]. These keys can never be accessed or leave outside the PCM chip.

The ATL (Figure 6(b)) performs address translation. It essentially maps an MA from the memory controller to a corresponding RMA. As explained earlier, the translation process needs to understand whether a given MA has been remapped in the current round. This algorithm is implemented in the RC (Figure 6(c)), which consists of only two bitwise XOR gates, two comparators, and one OR gate. Additionally, the RC is also responsible for finding an address to be remapped. Upon every security refresh, the RC provides the same output to the SWL (Figure 6(d)) so that SWL can decide whether the MA should be remapped or not. And if needed, the SWL performs a swap operation with a pair of swap buffers.

3.6 Memory Controller Design Issues

In a conventional DRAM-based system, a memory controller understands whether a given memory request will hit in a row buffer or not. Consequently, it can schedule its commands so that the return data of those commands will not conflict in a memory bus. However, in our proposed PCM system that obfuscates internal address information, the memory controller cannot schedule the external PCM bus alone like a conventional DRAM memory controller. To utilize the bus more efficiently, we envision that future PCM chips should be actively involved in bus arbitration. For example, a PCM chip can send a data ready signal to the memory controller once the requested data are brought into a row buffer. Based on this ready signal, the memory controller can utilize the bus more intelligently. However, detailed PCM memory controller design issues are outside of the scope of this paper.

3.7 Testability

As mentioned earlier, our Security Refresh scheme is embedded inside PCM to avoid leaking useful information. However, it is also important to make the memory module testable when our scheme is applied. To suppress randomized address remapping due to Security Refresh so the physical data locations can be determined, we can set both the key registers KEY0 and KEY1 to zero in test mode. Also, to make the access latency deterministic, the refresh asserting signal from the GWC should be masked. By doing the above, we can use existing test methods to test the memory cell array, the address decoding logic, and the data path. Lastly, a scan chain along with an isolation ring can be used to test the SRC it-

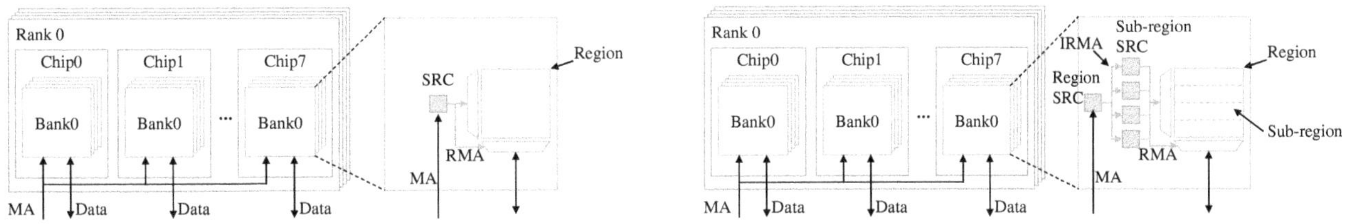

(a) One-Level Security Refresh (b) Two-Level Security Refresh

Figure 7: One-Level vs. Two-Level Security Refresh (Four Ranks, Four Banks per Rank)

self. Note that this test mode must be disabled to forbid potential side-channel attacks.

4. IMPLEMENTATION TRADE-OFF OF SECURITY REFRESH

So far, we have discussed how Security Refresh works and its advantage from the standpoint of malicious wear-out. However, there are several trade-offs in the PCM design space. For example, if the total number of writes required to start a new security refresh round is larger than the PCM write endurance limit, an adversary could wear a PCM block out before a new refresh round is triggered (**robustness**). On the other hand, extra PCM writes are induced for swapping two blocks upon remapping. Frequent swaps may unnecessarily increase the total number of PCM writes even for normal applications (**write overhead**), leading to performance degradation (**performance penalty**). Thus, we must carefully examine these design trade-offs of Security Refresh to maximize its robustness while minimizing the write overheads and its performance penalty. To quantify the trade-off, we used simple analytical models to estimate robustness and write overhead. From our analysis, we made the following observations:

1. A larger region distributes localized writes across a larger memory space.
2. A large region requires a shorter refresh interval to increase the frequency of randomized mapping changes. Otherwise, if one refresh round is too long, it may inadvertently leave a mapping unchanged for too long as well, making potential side channel attacks possible.
3. A shorter refresh interval will, nonetheless, inflict higher write overheads due to its more frequent swapping, which can lead to higher performance penalty.

Given the first observation, we first evaluated a region size as large as a PCM bank as illustrated in Figure 7(a). Note that the reason why we did not evaluate multiple banks in a PCM chip as a region is to allow a memory controller to exploit bank-level parallelism for better scheduling. As explained in our second and third observations, we found that the write overhead of a bank-sized region is undesirably high in this one-level scheme of Figure 7(a), which motivates us to investigate other techniques to mitigate them.

5. TWO-LEVEL SECURITY REFRESH

To address the issues of write overheads and performance penalty while still taking advantage of a large region size, in this paper, we propose a hierarchical, two-level Security Refresh scheme as illustrated in Figure 7(b). In lieu of using a very small refresh interval that increases write overheads, we break up a region into multiple, smaller sub-regions. Each sub-region contains its own *Sub-region SRC* to perform address remapping itself based on an inner-level refresh interval. In addition, an outer-level *Region SRC* is employed to distribute writes across the entire region with its own refresh interval. The rationale behind our two-level Security Refresh scheme is that, given a refresh interval, a small sub-region effectively triggers address remapping more frequently because of a smaller number of memory blocks within each sub-region. On the other hand, an outer-level SRC occasionally remaps an MA of a given memory block across sub-regions. This additional level effectively enlarges a region size as will be detailed later.

So far, we have laid out a logical basis for the two-level Security Refresh scheme. Now, we will explain how a security refresh of each level is performed and how it maintains the integrity of its own address remapping. Each individual Security Refresh level can be regarded as an independent layer. In other words, each level performs the Security Refresh algorithm with its own register values and settings, and the Security Refresh algorithm guarantees the integrity of the address remapping as mentioned in Section 3.3. Even at the same level, different regions can have different settings such as their memory block sizes and refresh intervals, though they are preset in a manufacturing phase for the maximum lifetime and the hardware feasibility.

Figure 7(b) depicts a block diagram of the two-level Security Refresh embedded in a PCM bank. Basically, the two-level Security Refresh works in a recursive fashion. An outer-level Security Refresh controller (*i.e.*,, Region SRC) accepts a demand memory request from the memory controller as its input. The Region SRC remaps a memory address (MA) of the demand request to an intermediate remapped memory address (IRMA). Meanwhile, if the demand request is a write that triggers a new refresh, the Region SRC performs the demand write request and then generates a swap operation that consists of two read requests and two write requests for two IRMAs. Note that the region size of the outer-level Security Refresh is the size of a bank. Consequently, every r_o writes to a given bank (where r_o is the security refresh interval of the outer-level Security Refresh) will trigger one new refresh operation in the bank. Furthermore, in order to keep the integrity of its address remapping, the outer SRC should halt other requests until the swap is completed. The demand request or the swap requests generated by the outer SRC are forwarded to their own corresponding sub-regions according to a sub-region index field (Figure 8) in their IRMAs.

On the other hand, each sub-region operates the Security Refresh algorithm with its own sub-region SRC. The sub-region SRC takes a request from the Region SRC, which can be either a demand request or a swap request generated by the Region SRC. The sub-region SRC will use the IRMA of those requests to find a corresponding RMA, which is the actual physical cell location inside the sub-region. Meanwhile, if the request from the Region

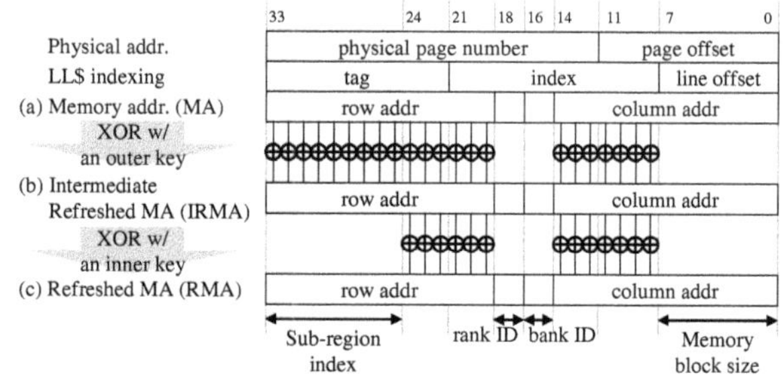

Figure 8: Two-Level Security Refresh (Within a bank)

SRC triggers an inner-level, sub-region refresh, the sub-region SRC atomically performs a swap operation of two RMAs inside the sub-region. Consequently, every r_i writes to a given sub-region (where r_i is the security refresh interval of the inner-level sub-region Security Refresh) will trigger one new refresh operation in the sub-region. Also note that when the first write request of a swap operation from the Region SRC triggers a sub-region refresh, the second write request of the outer-level swap operation is performed after the completion of the inner-level refresh to guarantee the integrity of the address remapping in the sub-region.

Figure 8 shows an example of address remapping from MA to IRMA through the outer-level Security Refresh and that from IRMA to RMA through the inner-level Security Refresh. In this example, each 1GB bank is divided into 512 sub-regions while the memory block sizes for both region and sub-region are 256B. As shown, nine MSBs from a row address is used as a sub-region index. In other words, a row in one PCM bank is virtually partitioned into 512 sub-regions. Basically, in each sub-region, the inner-level SRC will perform the operations of Security Refresh as explained Section 3. Similarly, the Region SRC will perform the same operation across the entire bank. Note that the Region SRC may swap two memory blocks that belong to different sub-regions because the sub-region index is a part of output values of the XOR operation. Such swapping between distinct sub-regions triggered by Region SRC allows us to distribute localized writes across the entire bank without using a large region at the inner-level.

6. EVALUATION

6.1 Robustness and Write Overhead

To evaluate the robustness, we evaluated the average lifetime for both our single-level and two-level Security Refresh mechanisms by exercising as many writes as the system can possibly take. As mentioned in Section 2.3.2, birthday paradox attacks (BPA) [6] based on a randomized function could fail wear-leveling schemes employing randomization with a high probability. To evaluate the vulnerability of Security Refresh against BPA, we implemented our mechanisms, iteratively simulated each configuration, and calculated the average lifetime under a pinpoint attack that writes to one single logical non-cacheable address by toggling its data bits. Note that this attack method has the same effect with BPA because our Security Refresh remaps all memory addresses with a new random key for every refresh round. Throughout this subsection, we assume the same baseline architecture used in Section 2.

6.1.1 Single-Level Security Refresh

Figure 9 shows the average lifetime of the single-level Security Refresh. Here, we varied the memory block size from 256B to 8KB and the refresh interval from 1 to 128. We keep the same 1GB bank size for PCM with four banks and four ranks used in Section 2. The read and write latencies are 150ns and 450ns, respectively. As shown, for a given memory block size, as we refresh more frequently with a shorter refresh interval, our system is more robust. Unfortunately, such benefit comes at the cost of higher write overhead, which is calculated by $\frac{\text{the number of additional writes}}{\text{the total number of writes to PCM}}$. Note that, the extra write overheads were all accounted for when calculating the average lifetime. For example, if our refresh interval is one, the write overhead is 50%. Such additional writes can accelerate the wear-out, but we found that the additional latency caused by these additional writes effectively delays the attack as well, resulting in a longer lifetime. (Note that our lifetime result here accounts for additional latency of performing those additional writes.)

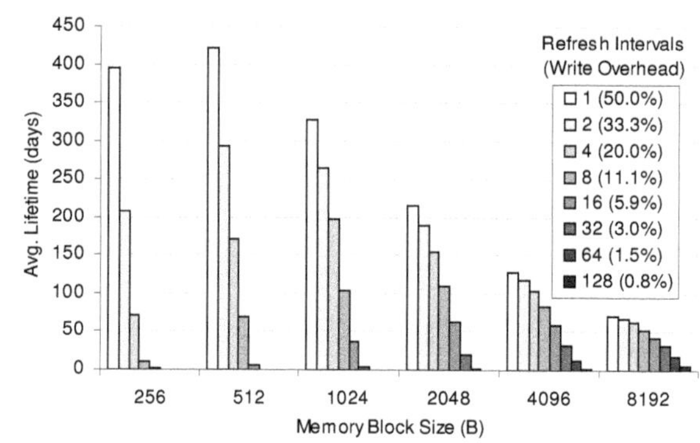

Figure 9: Single-Level Robustness

On the other hand, given a fixed region size, if a smaller memory block is used, we get more blocks in a region. As a result, the probability of a randomly selected block mapped to the same physical cell decreases, thus robustness is increased. However, a smaller memory block often negatively affects robustness because, given a fixed refresh interval and a fixed region size, more blocks in a region increases the required number of writes to trigger a new security refresh round. In other words, the frequency of generating a new random key is reduced. These trade-offs are manifested in Figure 9. As shown, the average lifetime tends to increase as we reduce the memory block size down to 512B, then it decreases when we further reduce it to 256B. Note that for blocks smaller than 256B (the cache line size of the last-level cache) may require multiple PCM accesses to retrieve a single cache line, thus we did not simulate such configurations.

Overall, we found that the longest lifetime, 422 days, is achieved when we use 512B as the memory block size. This, however, may not satisfy the current average server's replacement cycle which is usually three to four years [13, 12].

6.1.2 Two-Level Security Refresh

Figure 10 shows the average lifetime of our two-level Security Refresh scheme when the refresh interval of an outer-level Security Refresh is 128. In this evaluation, we use the same memory block size, 256B, for both inner and outer levels. Since the last-level cache line size is 256B, it is likely that the datapath of the baseline PCM, with respect to power and performance, will be optimized for 256B as well. Furthermore, we found that the PCM with a memory block size of 256B under two-level Security Refresh demonstrated reasonably long lifetimes. Therefore, we only present results with 256B memory blocks.

To study the sensitivity, we varied the number of sub-regions and the inner-level refresh interval. Note that we did not simulate

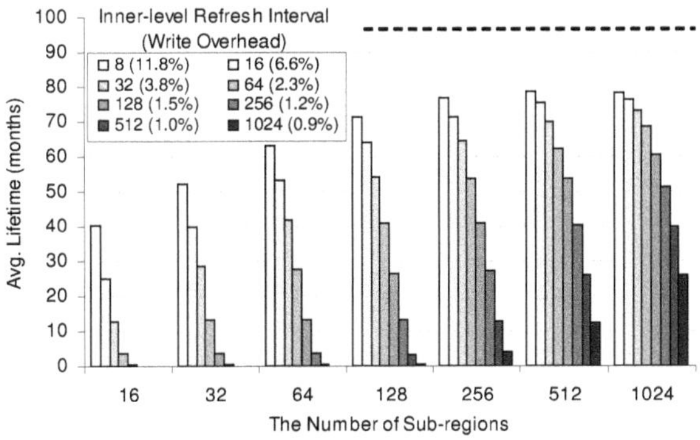

Figure 10: Two-Level Robustness vs. Sub-regions

extremely short inner-level refresh intervals simply because they incur too much write overhead. As shown in the figure, we found that the configuration with 512 sub-regions and refreshing memory blocks every eight writes inside a sub-region can sustain around 78.8 months. This achieves 81.2% of the lifetime of the perfect wear-leveling scheme, which is 97.1 months with the same block size. It is noteworthy that this average lifetime is very pessimistic as we assume that an attacker can monopolize the entire system resources to perform a pinpoint attack continuously for 78.8 months.

Figure 11 shows the average lifetime of the two-level Security Refresh scheme with 64 or higher outer-level refresh intervals. The results suggest that the average lifetime is more sensitive to the inner-level refresh interval than the outer-level. This is explained by the following. Since a sub-region (inner level) contains fewer memory blocks, a shorter refresh interval will provide better wear-leveling.

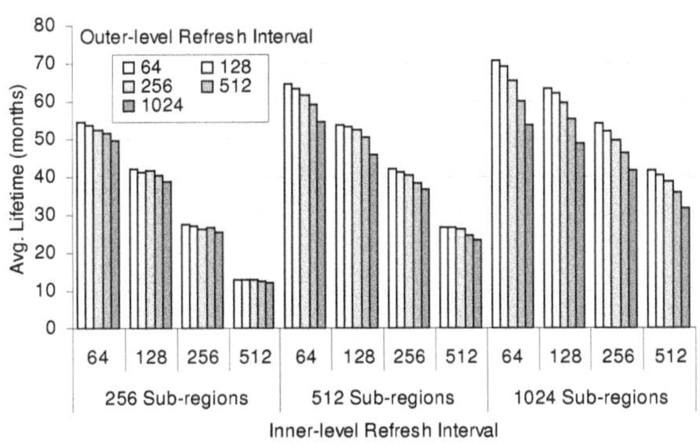

Figure 11: Two-Level Robustness vs. Refresh Intervals

6.2 Hardware Overhead

In this subsection, we describe the hardware cost of our Security Refresh. To calculate the size of registers required to implement the single-level Security Refresh, we need a detailed configuration. First, assume that a 4GB PCM rank is composed of eight PCM chips as in a conventional SDRAM DIMM while each chip consists of four banks. Then, to build a 16GB PCM system, we need 32 PCM chips. If an SRC is in charge of a PCM bank, 128 SRCs exist in the 16GB PCM system. When a memory block size is 256B and SRC's refresh rate is 64, each SRC consists of three 22-bit registers for KEY0, KEY1, and CRP, and a 6-bit register for GWC. Since eight chips are accessed in parallel to serve a 256B request, each chip has a pair of 32B swap buffers per bank. In sum, the total register size required for a chip is 292B ($= 4banks \times (3 \times 22bit + 6bit + 2 \times 32Byte)$).

In case of the two-level Security Refresh, each sub-region also has a dedicated inner-level SRC. To model the area overhead, we assume the followings: 1) an outer region is divided into n sub-regions, 2) the outer region and each inner sub-region contains 2^p and 2^q memory blocks, respectively, and 3) their refresh intervals are 2^x and 2^y, respectively, then the total hardware cost per outer region without considering swap buffers can be calculated like $(x + 3 \times p) + n \times (y + 3 \times q)$ bits. On the other hand, swap buffers can be shared in the same level because a bank allows only one request to access its PCM cell array at a time, which serializes all requests. This serialization property, along with the atomicity of the inner refresh, allows all sub-regions to share physical swap buffers. That is, each level needs one pair of swap buffers.

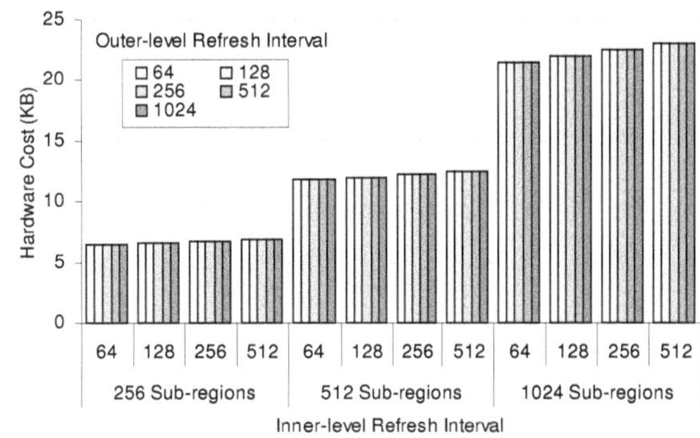

Figure 12: Two-Level Hardware Cost per Chip (512MB PCM Cells)

Figure 12 shows the hardware cost of those configurations used in Section 6.1.2. The hardware cost grows exponentially as the number of sub-regions increases. Thus, if more than 5 years of attack endurance is required, dividing a bank into 512 sub-regions can satisfy this requirement with around 12KB of the hardware cost. (Note that these configurations can sustain for 64.5, 63.3, and 61.5 months as indicated in Figure 11.) It is the trade-off between the cost and higher security requirement due to worst-case or malicious wear-out. Unlike the conventional DRAM process, PCM fabrication process is compatible with CMOS, thus those hardware overhead will not be significant.

6.3 Wear-Leveling

In this section, we study how well writes generated by an attack are distributed across the memory space. To count the number of writes for each memory block, we use PIN [11]. In this simulation, we use the two-level Security Refresh scheme with four 1GB PCM banks, each divided into 512 subregions. Each PCM bank is one region. Furthermore, we use the same memory block size (256B) for both the region and the subregion while the refresh interval for Region SRC (outer level) is 128 writes. To study the sensitivity of inner-level refresh intervals, we use three different inner-level refresh intervals — 32, 64, and 128 writes.

Figure 13 shows the accumulated number of writes (including swap write overhead in our scheme) for a given pinpointed physical address (134518272) for 10^8 times and 10^{11} times. The y-axis of this chart plots the *accumulated* number of writes across the memory addresses on the x-axis. To read the number of writes to a particular PCM address A, one has to obtain the values of A and (A-1) on y-axis in this chart and take a subtraction. As shown in Figure 13(a), without any wear-leveling scheme, all 10^8 writes hit the same location. With our two-level Security Refresh, these writes are distributed across the entire memory space. The more linear a curve is, the more evenly distributed the writes are. Based

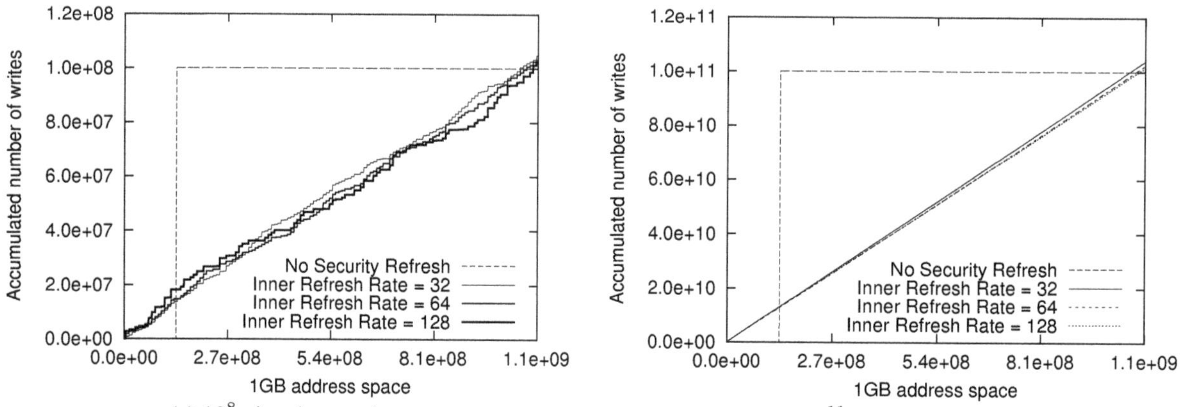

(a) 10^8 pinpoint attacks

(b) 10^{11} pinpoint attacks

Figure 13: Accumulated Number of Writes over the Memory Space

on this, as shown in Figure 13(a), we found that a finer-grained swap interval tends to lead to a more balanced wear-out distribution. Not surprisingly, as the number of writes is increased to 10^{11}, they are even better distributed as shown in Figure 13(b).

The figures also show how many writes are additionally generated due to the swap operations during refreshes. For example, in Figure 13(a), the difference between the final accumulated number (on the right) and 10^8 tick on y-axis represents the extra writes contributed by swap operations. The percentage increase of writes for the three different inner-level refresh intervals are 3.8%, 2.3% and 1.5%, respectively.

6.4 Performance Impact

Finally, we evaluate the performance impact of our Security Refresh scheme using SESC [16] with 26 SPEC2006 benchmark programs. Similar to previous studies [14, 15], our system employs an 8MB L3 DRAM cache for hiding PCM's relatively long read latency. Also, we modeled a memory controller that exploits bank-level parallelism and arbitrates requests to improve PCM row buffer hits. We used a two-level Security Refresh scheme with the same configuration in Section 6.3 to compare against a baseline without any wear-leveling technique.

As shown in Figure 14, the performance of most of the benchmark programs is barely affected with our Security Refresh for the three inner-level refresh intervals experimented. The two exceptional cases are 433.milc and 459.GemsFDTD, which contain not only many PCM writes but also many PCM reads. As such, the latency of the reads is often increased due to the swapping operations for Security Refresh. However, the geometric means of IPC variations are found to be −1.2%, −0.7%, and −0.5% when we use 32, 64, and 128 as our inner-level refresh interval, respectively. Not surprisingly, such trend is analogous to our write overhead of those configurations, 3.8%, 2.3%, and 1.5%.

Furthermore, note that our scheme allows the memory controller to utilize data locality at a row buffer due to the nature of bitwise XOR operations. In particular, as shown in Figure 8, our remapping method uses a bitwise operation without shuffling address bit positions. This means that one MA row address is mapped to one RMA row address, which allows the memory controller to utilize spatial locality inside a row for better scheduling. Furthermore, the bitwise remapping allows us to send a row address of MA to a PCM chip separately from a column address of the MA similar to conventional DRAM memory commands. As a result, even though a refresh often closes a row opened by a previous demand request, our simulation results show that the row hit rates decrease by only 0.4%, 0.3%, and 0.2%, for the three inner-level refresh intervals we simulated, respectively. Overall, the performance impact with our Security Refresh scheme is negligible.

7. CONCLUSION

In this paper, we argue that a robust PCM design must take both security and durability issues into account simultaneously. More importantly, it must be able to circumvent the scenarios of intentional, malicious attacks with the presence of a compromised OS and potential information leak from side channels. By analyzing prior durability techniques at architectural level, we demonstrated practical attacking models to wear out and fail PCM blocks. For example, prior redundant write reduction techniques do not obfuscate addresses, making a victim memory block easy to target. Some wear-leveling technique performs address randomization, however, the mapping was static at boot time, leaving open side channels for adversaries to glean and assemble useful information.

To address these shortcomings, we propose *Security Refresh*, a novel, low-cost hardware-based wear-leveling scheme that performs dynamic randomization for placing PCM data. Security Refresh relies on an embedded controller inside each PCM to prevent adversaries from tampering the bus interface or aggregating meaningful information via side channels. Furthermore, we evaluated the implementation trade-off of Security Refresh and quantified the reliability for a two-level Security Refresh mechanism. Given a 1GB PCM bank with 512 sub-regions at the inner-level, our two-level security refresh can endure more than 5 years with a 256B memory block using 128 and 64 writes for the outer- and inner-level refresh intervals. In addition, we also applied pinpoint attacks to understand the wear-out distribution using Security Refresh. We found that as the number of pinpoint writes to the same memory address is increased, our technique will distribute the data placement more uniformly, improving durability. Finally, we analyzed the performance impact of Security Refresh with normal applications (SPEC2006) and showed the average IPC degradation is below 1.2%.

8. ACKNOWLEDGMENT

This research is supported in part by an NSF grant CCF-0811738, NSF CAREER Award (CNS-0644096), and Samsung Electronics Global Scholarship program. The authors would like to thank Moinuddin Qureshi and Doug Burger for their constructive suggestions

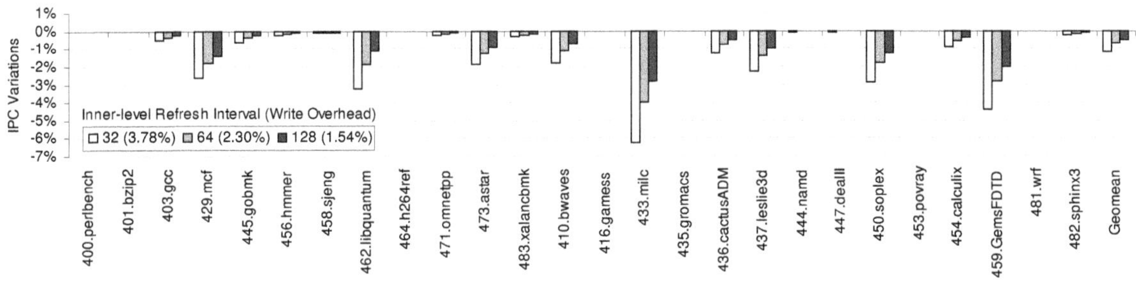

Figure 14: Relative IPC

and technical discussions that highly improved the quality of this paper.

9. REFERENCES

[1] International Technology Roadmap for Semiconductors, Emerging Research Devices, 2007.

[2] D. Agrawal, B. Archambeault, J. R. Rao, and P. Rohatgi. The EM Side-Channels. In *Cryptographic Hardware and Embedded Systems*, 2002.

[3] S. Cho and H. Lee. Flip-N-Write: A Simple Deterministic Technique to Improve PRAM Write Performance, Energy and Endurance. In *Proceedings of the International Symposium on Microarchitecture*, 2009.

[4] A. Huang. *Hacking the Xbox: An Introduction to Reverse Engineering*. No Starch Press, 2003.

[5] B. Jun and P. Kocher. The Intel Random Number Generator. Technical report, Cryptography Research, Inc., 1999.

[6] M. Klamkin and D. Newman. Extensions of the birthday surprise. *Journal of Combinatorial Theory*, 3(3):279–282, 1967.

[7] P. C. Kocher. Timing Attacks on Implementations of Diffie-Hellman RSA, DSS, and Other Systems. In *Advances in Cryptology*, 1996.

[8] P. C. Kocher, J. Jaffee, and B. Jun. Differential Power Analysis. In *Cryptography Research*, 1999.

[9] B. Lee, E. Ipek, O. Mutlu, and D. Burger. Architecting Phase Change Memory as a Scalable DRAM Alternative. In *Proceedings of the International Symposium on Computer Architecture*, 2009.

[10] K. M. Lepak and M. H. Lipasti. On the Value Locality of Store Instructions. In *Proceedings of the International Symposium on Computer Architecture*, 2000.

[11] C.-K. Luk, R. Cohn, R. Muth, H. Patil, A. Klauser, G. Lowney, S. Wallace, V. J. Reddi, and K. Hazelwood. Pin: Building Customized Program Analysis Tools with Dynamic Instrumentation. In *Proceedings of the ACM SIGPLAN Conference on Programming Language Design and Implementation*, 2005.

[12] S. Madara. The Future of Cooling High Density Equipment. 2007 IBM Power and Cooling Technology Symposium.

[13] L. Price and G. McKittrick. Setting the Stage: The "New Economy" Endures Despite Reduced IT Investment. In *Digital Economy*, 2002.

[14] M. Qureshi, V. Srinivasan, and J. Rivers. Scalable High Performance Main Memory System Using Phase-Change Memory Technology. In *Proceedings of the International Symposium on Computer Architecture*, 2009.

[15] M. K. Qureshi, J. Karidis, M. Fraceschini, V. Srinivasan, L. Lastras, and B. Abali. Enhancing Lifetime and Security of Phase Change Memories via Start-Gap Wear Leveling. In *Proceedings of the International Symposium on Microarchitecture*, 2009.

[16] J. Renau, B. Fraguela, J. Tuck, W. Liu, M. Prvulovic, L. Ceze, S. Sarangi, P. Sack, K. Strauss, and P. Montesinos. SESC simulator, 2005. http://sesc.sourceforge.net.

[17] A. Seznec. A Phase Change Memory as a Secure Main Memory. *IEEE Computer Architecture Letters*, 99(RapidPosts), 2010.

[18] W. Shi and H.-H. S. Lee. Authentication Control Point and its Implications for Secure Processor Design. In *Proceedings of the International Symposium on Microarchitecture*, 2006.

[19] M. R. Stan and W. P. Burleson. Bus-Invert Coding for Low-Power I/O. *IEEE Transactions on VLSI*, 3(1), 1995.

[20] Z. Wang and R. B. Lee. New cache designs for thwarting software cache-based side channel attacks. In *Proceedings of the International Symposium on Computer Architecture*, 2007.

[21] D. H. Woo and H.-H. S. Lee. Analyzing Performance Vulnerability due to Resource Denial of Service Attack on Chip Multiprocessors. In *Workshop on Chip Multiprocessor Memory Systems and Interconnects*, 2007.

[22] X. Wu, J. Li, L. Zhang, E. Speight, R. Rajamony, and Y. Xie. Hybrid Cache Architecture with Disparate Memory Technologies. In *Proceedings of the International Symposium on Computer Architecture*, 2009.

[23] B.-D. Yang, J.-E. Lee, J.-S. Kim, J. Cho, S.-Y. Lee, and B.-G. Yu. A Low Power Phase-Change Random Access Memory using a Data-Comparison Write Scheme. In *Proceeding of IEEE International Symposium on Circuit and Systems*, 2007.

[24] P. Zhou, B. Zhao, J. Yang, and Y. Zhang. A Durable and Energy Efficient Main Memory Using Phase Change Memory Technology. In *Proceedings of the International Symposium on Computer Architecture*, 2009.

[25] X. Zhuang, T. Zhang, H.-H. S. Lee, and S. Pande. Hardware Assisted Control Flow Obfuscation for Embdedded Processors. In *Proceedings of International Conference on Compilers, Architecture, Synthesis for Embedded System*, 2004.

IVEC: Off-Chip Memory Integrity Protection for Both Security and Reliability

Ruirui Huang and G. Edward Suh
Cornell University
Ithaca, NY 14853, USA
{huang,suh}@csl.cornell.edu

ABSTRACT

This paper proposes a unified off-chip memory integrity protection scheme, named IVEC. Today, a system needs two independent mechanisms in order to protect the memory integrity from both physical attacks and random errors. Integrity verification schemes detect malicious tampering of memory while error correcting codes (ECC) detect and correct random errors. IVEC enables both detection of malicious attacks for security and correction of random errors for reliability at the same time by extending the integrity verification techniques. Analytical and experimental studies show that IVEC can correct single-bit errors and even multi-bit errors from one DRAM chip within a cache block read without any additional ECC bits, when the integrity verification is also required for security, effectively removing the memory and bandwidth overheads (12.5%) of typical ECC schemes. Alternatively, with parity bits, IVEC can provide even stronger error correction capabilities comparable to the traditional chip-kill correct, still with less overheads. For both cases, IVEC can use standard non-ECC DIMMs.

Categories and Subject Descriptors

B.3.4 [**Memory Structures**]: Reliability, Testing and Fault Tolerance—*Error-Checking*

General Terms

Design, Reliability, Security

Keywords

fault tolerance, error correction, error detection, memory systems, security, reliability

1. INTRODUCTION

Recently, there have been significant efforts to build secure and reliable computing devices through architectural enhancements. For security, researchers have proposed "secure processor" techniques in order to protect against both software attacks and physical attacks. At the same time, many techniques have been developed for reliability as the technology scaling expects to increase both transient and permanent faults in hardware. In a high level, both security and reliability deal with unintended errors in computing devices. Yet, most of today's techniques only target either security or reliability separately, perhaps due to differences in fault/attack models. This paper investigates the potential synergy between security and reliability and shows that it is indeed possible to benefit from handling the two types of errors together. For off-chip memory, integrity verification that is designed for security can be extended for reliability with minimal costs and replace traditional Error Correcting Code (ECC).

The integrity verification mechanism in secure processors is designed to detect any unauthorized change in off-chip memory content. As we expand the use of computing devices, many systems are physically exposed to potential attackers; users may not be able to fully trust data center operators in cloud computing, embedded devices often operate in an open field, mobile devices may be lost or stolen, and device owners may be motivated to break the system security in cases such as copyright protection violation. In such environments, an attacker can physically tamper with the off-chip memory by either changing critical data or reading confidential information. As an example, the security of Xbox was broken by reading a secret key from an off-chip bus [13]. The integrity verification checks that a value from off-chip memory is the most recent one that was written by the processor at the memory address. If any error is detected, a processor aborts the program in order to prevent further damages. As devices continue to expand in the physical world, such hardware protection techniques for off-chip memory are likely to become more popular. In fact, IBM recently introduced a technology named SecureBlue that includes off-chip encryption and integrity verification. SecureBlue is reported to be in production for one IBM client already [4].

In order to tolerate random transient errors, today's computer systems often have Error Correcting Code (ECC) for both on-chip and off-chip memory. Systems typically use a Single-Error-Correction and Double-Error-Detection (SEC-DED) code, which requires 8 additional parity bits per 64-bit chunk. The code guarantees detection of all 1-bit or 2-bit errors and correction of all 1-bit errors. As a result, a system can continue its operation under a small number of bit flips in memory. On the other hand, the SEC-DED ECC provides no guarantee beyond 2-bit errors within a 64-bit chunk; an error may be detected, correctly corrected, or incorrectly corrected. To handle multi-bit errors, a technique called chip-kill correct [5] is widely used. The chip-kill correct can correct up to 4 adjacent bits at once, and hence can handle a complete failure of a x4 DRAM chip [17].

This paper investigates whether protecting memory from hardware faults can be simplified in secure processors when the integrity verification is also required for security. Intuitively, the integrity verification mechanism provides a stronger error detection capability than the traditional ECC because security must consider *any* changes including malicious tampering when ECC only handles random errors. This suggests that the error detection aspect of ECC is redundant if the integrity verification already exists.

However, today's integrity verification techniques cannot simply replace ECC. In general, there are a couple of inherent differences between today's security techniques and hardware fault tolerance techniques. First, security protection techniques tend to protect a smaller portion of a system compared to corresponding reliability techniques. For example, the integrity verification is only concerned with off-chip memory because it is much more difficult to tamper with on-chip memory. On the other hand, ECC is often applied to both on-chip and off-chip memory as both are equally vulnerable to hardware errors. Therefore, security techniques can only help a subset of reliability techniques when both protect the same components. This paper focuses on combining the off-chip integrity verification with off-chip ECC.

Another important difference between security and reliability lies in their responses to an error. Today's security mechanisms including the integrity verification often focus only on error detection and do not attempt to recover from errors. While availability is important for security as well, the recovery is extremely difficult, if not impossible, when an adversary physically controls a system. For example, there is no way to "correct" errors when an attack can arbitrarily change memory content. On the other hand, error correction is common for reliability mechanisms that enable a system to continue its operation under random errors. Therefore, the integrity verification must be augmented with error correction in order to replace ECC.

Unfortunately, the error correction in today's integrity verification is not straightforward due to its use of complex cryptographic signatures, often called hash or MAC. Unlike ECC where error locations can be mathematically obtained from parity bits, cryptographic primitives for integrity verification do not reveal where errors may be. In fact, if they do, such mathematical properties will be a security vulnerability in cryptography. Therefore, in the integrity verification, we need a different way to identify error locations. At the same time, unlike parity bits in ECC, cryptographic primitives do not consider errors in hashes or MACs, which requires a way to correct errors in them. Finally, we must ensure that the integrity verification is still secure even after the addition of error correction.

In this paper, we extend the integrity verification to correct errors by *searching* for error locations when an integrity check fails. We call this enhanced integrity verification IVEC (Integrity Verification with Error Correction). For example, to correct a single-bit error, IVEC tries to flip one bit at a time until the integrity check passes. Obviously, the naïve brute-force search does not scale for multi-bit errors. To handle multi-bit errors more efficiently, this paper presents intelligent search algorithms based on typical error patterns and selective use of parity bits. Essentially, our approach converts the error correction into a search problem. To correct errors in hashes/MACs, IVEC exploits a tree structure in common integrity verification schemes.

This paper also shows that IVEC can still ensure a proper level of security against malicious changes in memory. To break the integrity verification scheme, an attack must find a different value that produces the same signature (hash/MAC) as the authentic one in memory - this is often called a collision. The IVEC scheme slightly lowers the security of the baseline integrity verification mechanism because an attack only needs to be close enough to a collision instead of being an exact collision. Fortunately, however, our analysis shows that the lowered security is still sufficient for typical hash/MAC lengths.

Overall, the IVEC scheme enables efficient protection of off-chip memory from both security attacks and random errors without paying unnecessary memory and bandwidth overheads twice. IVEC can handle single-bit upsets and simple multi-bit errors within a single read without any ECC bits. With a small number of additional parity bits, IVEC offers a correction capability that is comparable to the chip-kill correct even for wide DRAMs. Thanks to its security protection, IVEC also provides a much stronger error detection capability than ECC. While the error correction takes longer in our approach than traditional ECC, experimental results suggest that the overall performance overhead is negligible even under pessimistic error rates. The paper also shows that the parity bits can be efficiently managed in regular memory space without requiring expensive ECC DIMMs because the parity bits are only used for correcting errors. In addition to reducing the ECC overheads for secure processors, IVEC also enables dynamic trade-offs between the error correction strengths and the error correction latency.

The rest of the paper is organized as follows. Section 2 discusses attack and fault models that IVEC aims to cover. Section 3 describes current integrity verification techniques for security, and Section 4 proposes IVEC. Section 5 discusses the hardware implementation details of IVEC. Section 6 evaluates IVEC for its error detection and correction capabilities as well as the performance and memory bandwidth impacts. Section 7 discusses related work in the area, and Section 8 concludes the paper.

2. ATTACK AND FAULT MODELS

2.1 Security Model

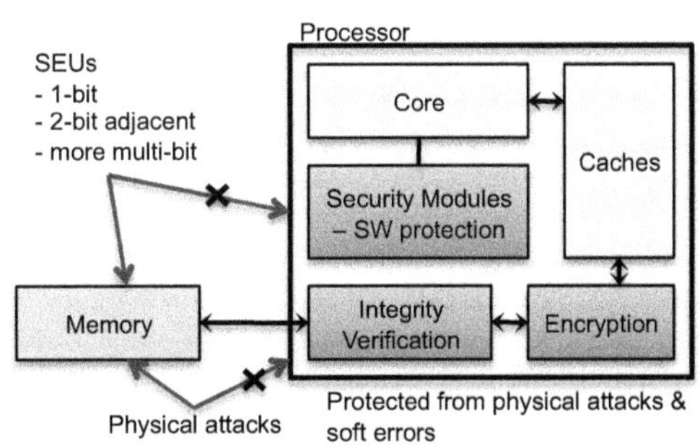

Figure 1: IVEC attack and fault models.

Figure 1 illustrates a security model that is commonly assumed for secure processors. Put briefly, a secure processor is trusted and protected from physical attacks, so that its internal state cannot be tampered with or observed directly by physical means. Therefore, an attacker cannot read or modify on-chip state. On the other hand, all components outside the processor chip, including external memory and peripherals, are assumed to be insecure. They may be observed and tampered with at will by an adversary.

The integrity verification protects the integrity of off-chip memory from physical attacks. In general, attackers may *replay*, *relocate*, or *substitute* the off-chip state. In *replay attacks*, attackers replace a new value with an old value from the same location. The processor needs to be able to check the freshness of each state in order to detect a replay attack. In *relocation attacks*, attackers move a valid value from one location to another. The processor should be able to verify the location (address) where each state is saved. Finally, *substitution attacks* replace a state with an arbitrary value.

Secure processors typically have additional protection mechanisms to ensure the integrity and the confidentiality of the whole systems. For example, encryption protects the confidentiality of off-chip memory from physical attacks, the security kernel and hardware memory isolation such as paging protect against software attacks, and attestation detects unauthorized changes in software. This paper only focuses on extending off-chip memory integrity protection.

2.2 Fault Model

Memory errors can be categorized as soft and hard errors. Soft errors (also called transient errors) are caused by random single event upsets (SEUs) that are often caused by ions or electro-magnetic radiation striking. Hard errors, which corrupt bits in memory because of a physical defect, often occur in a repeatable manner. For reliability, IVEC aims to detect and correct both transient errors and hard errors in off-chip memory. Similar to the security model, our fault model assumes that on-chip components are properly protected from hardware errors using other techniques such as ECC. As a result, the on-chip registers and caches are error-free. Errors are introduced when a value is read from off-chip memory.

In today's memory technologies, most memory systems used in servers are at least protected by SEC-DED ECC [12], which is typically applied to a 64-bit block with 8 additional parity bits. However, the SEC-DED ECC can only reliably correct single-bit errors. To handle multi-bit errors, a chip-kill correct technique [5] is used in high-end servers. The chip-kill correct is based on the assumption that multi-bit errors are likely to affect only one DRAM chip, and can tolerate up to an entire x4 DRAM chip failure in a memory system. For x4 DRAM chips, the chip-kill correct technique distributes bits from each DRAM chip to a different ECC word so that a multi-bit error from one chip translates to one-bit errors in multiple ECC words [17]. To ensure this property, a typical chip-kill correct technique for x4 DRAMs reads a 256-bit (4 times 64) data block from 64 DRAM chips on 4 DIMMs. In this paper, we use the term *read-block* for such a data block where each DRAM chip contributes only once. If a cache block is larger than the read-block, multiple reads from each DRAM chip are needed to read one cache block. In recent chip-kill correct implementations such as the Sun UltraSPARC-T1/T2[31] and the AMD Opteron [1], a 128-bit read-block is used. We note that the IVEC scheme can be used with various length read-block configurations.

In this paper, our discussion is focused on 256-bit read-blocks. Recent studies show that multi-bit error correction is becoming more important. For example, a real-world study from Google [29] reports that the chip-kill correct technique reduces uncorrectable errors by up to 10 times compared to the traditional ECC.

The IVEC scheme aims to address both single-bit errors and multi-bit errors from one DRAM chip, similar to the chip-kill correct model. To further investigate the trade-off in the error correction capability, Table 1 defines four fault models at a cache block granularity, which is the protection granularity for integrity verification. Note that the fault models assume that there are multiple read-blocks per cache block. If not, the last three models are identical. Typical chip-kill correct techniques [29, 17] can correct errors in up to 4 adjacent bits and are comparable to the MCME model.

3. INTEGRITY VERIFICATION

This section describes integrity verification algorithms, which ensure that the values stored in off-chip memory have not been changed. When describing the algorithms, this paper uses a term *block* as the minimum memory block that is verified by the integrity checking. If a word within a block is read by a processor, the entire block is brought into the processor and its integrity is checked. In this paper, blocks for integrity verification are identical to the L2 cache blocks.

3.1 Cryptographic Primitives

Integrity verification techniques typically use one of the two cryptographic primitives as basic building blocks: a cryptographic hash function or a message authentication code (MAC). Here, we briefly introduce the two primitives. A cryptographic hash of a message is a fixed length fingerprint of the message. One of the key properties of a cryptographic hash function is that it is hard to find two distinct inputs that produce the same hash. This property is called collision-resistance. The collision-resistance enables a hash function to protect the integrity of data if the hash can be trusted. For example, a file that is downloaded from a website can be checked by recomputing its hash if the correct hash is known. Because it is infeasible to find another file that produces the same hash, an adversary cannot change the file without changing the hash.

A message authentication code (MAC) is a keyed hash function where the hash depends on a secret key so that only parties with the correct key can compute a valid MAC. Unlike hashes that must be trusted, the secret key enables MACs to be either sent over untrusted networks or stored in an untrusted storage. As the name suggests, MACs are often used to authenticate a message sent over networks. A sender computes the MAC of a message and sends it along with the message. Later, a receiver recomputes the MAC of the received message and compares it with the attached MAC. If the MACs match, the receiver knows that the message is from the sender with the valid secret key.

There are many instantiations of the cryptographic hash and MAC. The standard hash functions are SHA-1 [23] and SHA-256 [24]. Both hash functions process 512 bits at a time and take 80 rounds of operations per 512-bit block. SHA-1 produces 160-bit hashes and SHA-256 produces 256-bit hashes. However, both hash outputs can be truncated to produce a shorter hash. For the MAC, HMAC [14] is the most widely used implementation today and takes two hash-

Fault Model	Definition
SBE	Single-Bit-Error: Single bit error in a cache block.
SCSE	Single-Chip-Single-Error: Multi-bit error from a single DRAM chip in one read-block.
SCME	Single-Chip-Multi-Error: Multi-bit errors from a single DRAM chip in multiple read-blocks.
MCME	Multi-Chip-Multi-Error: Multi-bit errors in any one DRAM chip in each read-block.

Table 1: Fault models. Each earlier fault model is a subset of the latter models.

ing operations. To avoid the long latency of the hash functions (80 rounds), GMAC [7] has recently been proposed as one of NIST recommendations. GMAC uses the Advanced Encryption Standard (AES), which has only 10 to 14 rounds, as the underlying building block. GMAC can also be easily combined with encryption.

3.2 Hash/MAC Trees

To protect the integrity of off-chip memory without requiring an excessive amount of trusted on-chip memory, virtually all integrity verification techniques rely on Hash trees (or Merkle trees), which were originally developed for untrusted storage [20]. Figure 2 illustrates this hash tree algorithm applied to the off-chip memory verification. The protected data blocks are located at the leaves of a tree. Each internal hash is computed over a block below. The root hash of the tree is stored in secure on-chip memory where it cannot be tampered with while others are stored in off-chip memory.

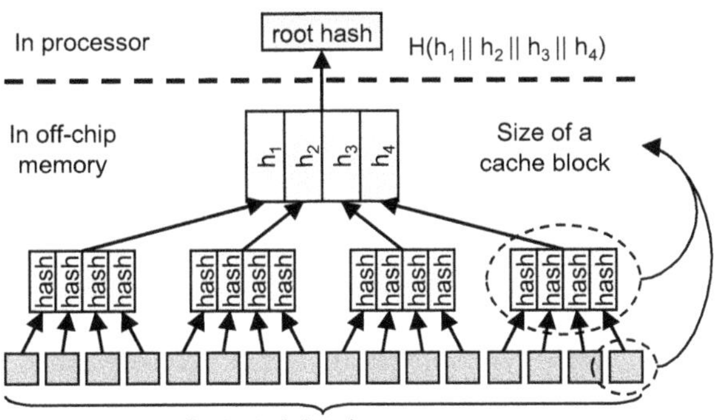

Figure 2: A 4-ary hash tree assuming that one block can contain four hashes. For example, a 64-B block can contain four 128-bit (16-B) hashes.

In the figure, one block can contain four hashes, which results in a 4-ary hash tree (one parent hash covers four children hashes or one data block). For example, a 64-B block can have four 128-bit hashes. The arity of a tree can be increased by either increasing the L2 cache block size or reducing the length of a hash. To check the integrity of a block in the tree, the processor (i) reads the block, (ii) computes the hash of the block, (iii) checks that the resultant hash matches the parent hash, and (iv) checks the integrity of the block containing the parent hash. The steps are repeated all the way to the root of the tree. The root does not need to be checked as it is stored in on-chip memory. To update a block, the processor (i) reads the block and checks its integrity, (ii) modifies the block, (iii) recomputes the parent hash, and (iv) updates the parent with the new hash. Again, these steps are repeated to update the whole path from the block to the root.

With a balanced k-ary tree, the number of blocks to be checked on each memory access is $log_k(N)$, where N is the number of blocks in the verified memory space. Unfortunately, this logarithmic bandwidth overhead of the hash tree can be significant. For example, a previous study [8] showed that applying the hash tree to protect 4-GB memory can slow down the system by as much as factor of ten.

3.3 Cached Hash Trees

The bandwidth overhead of using a hash tree can be dramatically reduced by caching the internal hash blocks on-chip with regular data. The processor trusts data stored in the cache, and can access it directly without any checking. Therefore, instead of checking the entire path from the block to the root of the tree, the processor checks the path from the block to the first hash it finds in the cache.

The internal hash blocks can be cached either in the existing L2 cache with other data blocks or in a separate cache dedicated to the hash blocks. For a high performance processor with a large L2 cache, sharing the existing cache is likely to be a better choice because it provides a large cache for hashes without significantly increasing the logic area. On the other hand, embedded processors with only L1 caches should have a dedicated hash cache because sharing an L1 cache will result in a significant performance degradation.

Previous work [8] showed that the cached hash tree reduces the performance overheads of the integrity verification down to around 25% on average. Additional optimizations have been proposed to further reduce the overheads. Using GMAC in place of a hash function lowers the overheads to around 5% even with encryption [33] and Bonsai Merkle Trees report the overhead of 2% using small trees [27].

3.4 Security

To break the integrity verification scheme, an adversary needs to change a protected block in a way that its hash or MAC does not change, essentially finding a collision in the hash/MAC. Note that even though an attacker can change the protected block and its parent hash/MAC together at the leaves of the Merkle tree, one must eventually find a collision for the root hash/MAC that is stored on-chip.

Attacks	Applicability			Security Level
	Hash	HMAC	GMAC	
Brute force search	Yes	Yes	Yes	2^m
On-line birthday attack	Yes	Yes	No	$2^{m/2}$
Off-line birthday attack	Yes	No	No	$2^{m/2}$

Table 2: Security of the integrity verification schemes with m-bit hashes/MACs.

As shown in Table 2, an attacker can try to find a collision in a few different ways depending on the cryptographic primitives used in the integrity verification. Note that we do not consider attempts to mathematically break the cryptographic functions here. To find a collision with a particular memory block, an attacker needs to try one possible value at a time (brute-force search) by either computing a hash by himself or changing the block in the target system. For such a brute-force attack, the collision probability is $1/2^m$ given an m-bit hash/MAC function. In this scenario, an attacker is expected to try 2^m different values before finding a collision, and even 64-bit hashes or MACs are considered strong enough. Even if an attacker can try a few billion values per second, finding a collision will take over a thousand years.

Alternatively, an attacker can try to find a collision by constructing a table with a large number of hashes/MACs and their input values. In this scenario, the birthday problem in the probability theory shows that one can expect a collision within the table if there are $2^{\frac{m}{2}}$ entries. In the on-line birthday attack, an attacker constructs the table by observing all hashes or MACs that a processor produces. For hashes, attackers can also construct a table by computing hashes off-line by themselves. Once $2^{\frac{m}{2}}$ different values are in the table, an attacker can expect to find a collision. If the hash or MAC includes an address as well as data, then attacker needs to see $2^{\frac{m}{2}}$ values per cache block. If the birthday attack is possible, the hash or MAC needs to be at least 128 bits because 64-bit hashes can be broken only after 4 billion table entries.

However, the birthday attack is not always possible. For example, a GMAC-based scheme uses a counter value, which is unique for each MAC and whose integrity is protected separately. Therefore, even if a collision for a MAC is known, an attacker must also replace the counter value without being detected. This proposition requires another collision in the counter values, whose probability is only $1/2^m$.

4. IVEC

In this section, we propose our approach of extending an existing off-chip memory integrity verification scheme to perform memory error correction. To explain the key ideas, this section describes the IVEC algorithms based on the simple cached hash tree. However, the algorithms are easily applicable to other integrity verification schemes as well. For example, the IVEC can be implemented with MACs by simply replacing hashes in the algorithm with MACs. Section 5 discusses the details of applying IVEC to a state-of-the-art integrity verification based on GMAC [33].

4.1 Error Detection

The basic idea of the integrity verification scheme is to compute and store the hash of a memory block on a write. When the block is read back, the hash of the loaded block is re-computed and compared with the stored hash value. If a block in memory is tampered by an adversary, the change gets detected by an inconsistent hash value. Conceptually, from the physical perspective, there is no difference between data corruptions from random errors and corruptions from malicious attacks. Therefore, the integrity verification for security can also detect random errors.

In the integrity verification, a hash value is shorter than the memory block that is protected by the hash. As an example, hashes are often 64 or 128 bits while cache blocks are 512 bits. Hence, a hash function may map two or more input values to the same hash value, which is referred to as hash collision. As a result, the error detection in integrity verification is probabilistic and the false negative rate - the probability of not detecting an error - is determined by the hash collision rate. Fortunately, the false negative rate is extremely low even with typical hash lengths. Strong hash or MAC functions such as SHA-1 [23] and GMAC [7] uniformly distribute hashes in its output space. Therefore, the expected collision rate is inverse exponentially related to the hash output length: $1/2^m$ for m-bit hashes or MACs.

4.2 Error Correction as a Search

While the integrity verification scheme can be used for memory error detection, the existing integrity verification schemes cannot correct errors in a corrupted memory block. Here, we describe the IVEC error correction strategy, which searches for possible error locations. The discussion assumes that hashes (or MACs) are error-free and only considers one memory block and its hash. The next subsection removes this assumption by extending the error correction to a tree structure. IVEC scheme can handle all four previously defined fault models, and offer the flexibility to dynamically correct the target fault model of the system.

4.2.1 *Error Correction without Parity*

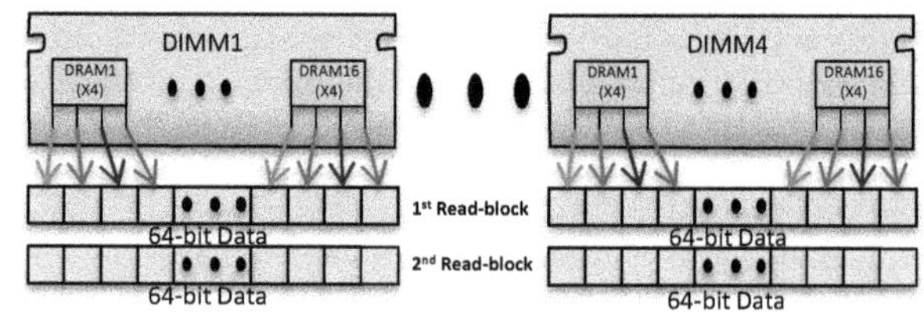

Figure 4: A cache block read from DRAM DIMMs.

The error correction can be viewed as finding erroneous bits within a cache block. Once the error locations are known, those bits can be simply flipped to correct errors. Therefore, if we assume that the hash can *detect* any errors with a very high probability, we can correct errors by performing a search. As an example, for a single-bit error (SBE), we can try to flip one bit at a time, and check if the new value passes the integrity verification. In theory, if we exhaustively search through all possibilities, we can correct any error. However, in practice, the search space quickly explodes as the number of bit flips increases. To keep the search manageable, the IVEC algorithm restricts the search space based on the fault model and hardware configurations.

Figure 4 illustrates how a cache block is read from DRAMs assuming the configuration used by typical chip-kill correct: 4 DIMMs with 16 DRAM chips each ignoring ECC bits. In this configuration, a 64-byte cache block corresponds to two 32-byte memory read-blocks and each DRAM chip produces 4 adjacent bits. For our multi-bit fault models based on chip-kill correct (Table 1), the error search can be restricted to bit positions from one DRAM chip; bits from different DRAM chips in a read-block cannot have errors simultaneously.

Figure 3 describes the baseline error correction algorithm. The algorithm takes a cache block, its hash and the desired fault model as inputs and returns either a corrected block, if a block that matches the hash can be found, or a correction fail signal. As shown in the figure, the algorithm searches the error space based on the fault model, starting from more likely cases. The algorithm tries single-bit errors (SBE), multi-bit errors from a single DRAM chip in one read-block (SCSE), multi-bit errors from a single DRAM chip in both read-blocks (SCME), and multi-bit errors in any one DRAM chip in each read-block (MCME) in order. Our analysis in Section 6 shows that this baseline algorithm is efficient enough for the SBE and SCSE models in x4 DRAMs, but becomes rather expensive for stronger fault models.

4.2.2 *Error Correction with Parity*

This subsection extends the baseline error correction using additional parity bits, which reduces the error correction

Error Correction Operation without Parity

error_correct_np(Block, CorrectHash, FaultModel):

1. For (i=0; i<BLOCK_SIZE; i++)
   (a) Flip a bit in Block[i].
   (b) If hash(Block) == CorrectHash, return Block.

2. If FaultModel == SCSE then
   For (i=0; i<BLOCK_SIZE; i+=CHIP_WIDTH)
   (a) Try possible errors in Block[i:i+CHIP_WIDTH-1].
   (b) If hash(Block) == CorrectHash, return Block.

3. If FaultModel == SCME then
   For (i=0; i<READ_BLOCK_SIZE; i+=CHIP_WIDTH).
   (a) Try possible errors in Read_Block_1[i:i+CHIP_WIDTH-1] and Read_Block_2[i:i+CHIP_WIDTH-1].
   (b) If hash(Block) == CorrectHash, return Block.

4. If FaultModel == MCME then
   For (i=0; i<READ_BLOCK_SIZE; i+=CHIP_WIDTH)
   (a) For each error pattern in Read_Block_1[i:i+CHIP_WIDTH-1]
   (b) For (j=0; j<READ_BLOCK_SIZE; j+=CHIP_WIDTH).
      i. Try errors in Read_Block_2[j:j+CHIP_WIDTH-1]
      ii. If hash(Block) == CorrectHash, return Block.

Figure 3: Baseline Error Correction Algorithm. The algorithm assumes that each Block consists of two Read_Block. Block[n] indicates n^{th} bit of Block, and Block[n:m] indicate n^{th} to m^{th} bit in Block. Read_Block_k represents Block[(k-1)·READ_BLOCK_SIZE:k·READ_BLOCK_SIZE-1].

search space and significantly improve multi-bit error correction. Figure 5 illustrates how the additional parity bits are used. As shown, there are 4 parity bits for each read-block, and each covers one bit from every DRAM chip. For example, P1 is a parity bit that covers every DRAM chips' left most bit in the first read-block. We can correct up to a complete chip failure in each read-block while using parity bits to guide our search. We note that the corresponding parity bits from two read-blocks can be combined into one for the SBE and SCSE fault models where only one read-block may have errors.

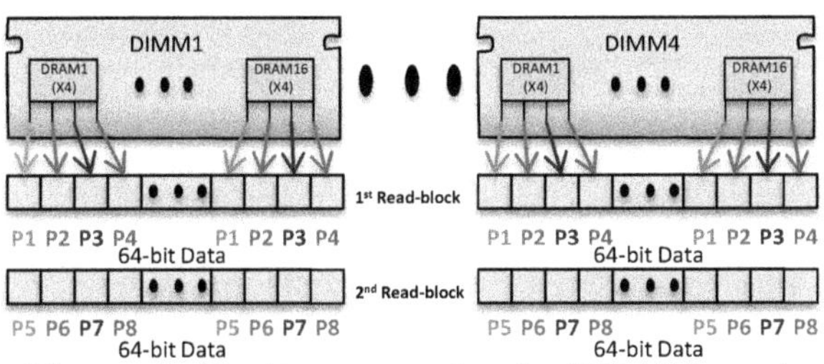

Figure 5: Parity protection in DRAM reads.

Figure 6 describes the error correction algorithm with parity bits. In the algorithm, a sub-block is defined as bits in a read-block that are protected by one parity bit. A parity error indicates that a particular sub-block has an odd-bit error. In our fault models, at most one DRAM chip in each read-block would be erroneous. As each parity bit in our scheme only covers one bit from each chip, a parity error indicates a 1-bit flip within a sub-block. Also, the fault models imply that all errors in a read-block are from the same DRAM chip and thus the same location in each erroneous sub-block. For example, parity upsets in Parity[1][1] and Parity[2][1] (Parity[i][j] is defined in Figure 6) indicate that the first and second bits of one chip in the first read-block have errors. Therefore, the search algorithm simply needs to identify which DRAM chip is erroneous.

The algorithm can be easily extended to work with more or fewer parity bits. More parity bits further reduce the search space. For example, if the number of parity bits is doubled, the search space of each sub-block is reduced by a factor of two respectively. The algorithm can also work with fewer parity bits even though the search space would grow exponentially if each parity bit covers more than one bits from each DRAM chip. We further evaluate the implication of various parity bit configurations in Section 6.

While not shown in the algorithm, the search can be further optimized even without increasing the parity bits. A recent study by Google [29] reports that DRAMs that recently had errors are much more likely to have errors again. Therefore, the search algorithm can store a list of DRAM chips with recent errors and start its search from them in order to reduce the average error correction latency. For example, in case of a complete chip failure, the search algorithm can always start with the faulty chip and thus reduce error correction latency significantly.

4.3 Integration with Hash/MAC Trees

So far, we have discussed error correction for one block when its hash is error-free. Here, we discuss how IVEC is integrated with the Merkle tree structure in integrity verification schemes. Figure 7 shows the read operation on IVEC. Most of the operations are identical to the cached hash tree in Section 3.3 except for Step 6. When an integrity check fails, IVEC tries to correct errors by calling either error_correct_np() or error_correct_parity(). The error correction functions require a hash that is error-free. This property is ensured by calling tree_read(HashAddress) before the error correction. If there is an error in the parent hash, it will be corrected before the error correction for a child. The root hash is stored on-chip and should be error-free. The write operation in IVEC is the same as the cached hash tree except for updating parity bits if they exist.

4.4 IVEC Parity Management in DRAMs

The baseline IVEC scheme completely eliminates the need for ECC bits when the integrity verification exists. Therefore, the baseline scheme can simply use non-ECC DIMMs. The parity scheme, on the other hand, requires a small number of parity bits on top of the integrity verification. In a naïve approach, the parity bits can be stored in additional bits in ECC DIMMs. However, this approach requires special DIMMs with fewer ECC bits in order to benefit from the small number of parity bits. Instead, we propose to store parity bits in regular memory space in the same way that the integrity verification stores its meta-data. The parity bits are protected in the same way that data and hashes/MACs, are. Therefore, before an error correction operation is performed on data or hashes, the associated parity bits are read, checked and possibly corrected first using the same algorithms shown in this section.

This configuration allows the IVEC schemes to utilize non-ECC DIMMS even with parity bits, and also exploits the inherent decoupling between error detection and correction. Because hashes/MACs detect errors, IVEC only uses the parity bits in a rare case when there is an error. Therefore, without an error, the parity bits do not need to be read from memory on a read. On an L2 write-back, the parity bits for the evicted block are updated. This optimization reduces

Error Correction Operation with Parity

error_correct_parity(Block, Parity, CorrectHash, FaultModel):

1. Check parity bits
   (a) $\texttt{NumUpset}_j$=the number of parity errors in read-block j.
   (b) ParityUpset[i][j]=1 if $\texttt{SubBlock}_{ij}$ has a parity error.
2. If $\texttt{NumUpset}_j$ == 0 for all j
   Indicates errors in multiple DRAM chips in a read-block, return unsuccessful.
3. If FaultModel == (SBE||SCSE||SCME) then
   For (n = 0; n<SB_SIZE; n++)
   (a) Flip $\texttt{SubBlock}_{ij}$[n] if ParityUpset[i][j] ==1.
   (b) If hash(Block) == CorrectHash, return Block.
4. If FaultModel == MCME then
   For (n = 0; n<SB_SIZE; n++)
   (a) Flip $\texttt{SubBlock}_{i1}$[n] if ParityUpset[i][1] ==1.
   (b) For (m = 0; m<SB_SIZE; m++)
      i. Flip $\texttt{SubBlock}_{i2}$[m] if ParityUpset[i][2] ==1.
      ii. If hash(Block) == CorrectHash, return Block.

Parity and SubBlock Definition

1. $\texttt{SubBlock}_{ij}$ = i^{th} bit from each chip in read-block j.
2. Parity[i][j] = a parity bit for $\texttt{SubBlock}_{ij}$.
   SB_SIZE is the number of bits in a sub-block.
   SB_SIZE = BLOCK_SIZE/PARITY_LENGTH.

Figure 6: Error Correction Algorithm with Parity.

To Read an IVEC Protected Block from Memory

tree_read(Address):

1. Check an on-chip cache. Return Block on a hit.
2. Read Block from Address in memory.
3. Compute Hash' = hash(Block).
4. Read the parent hash of the Block.
   (a) If the parent is the root, Hash = RootHash.
   (b) else
      i. HashAddress = get_hash_address(Address).
      ii. Hash = tree_read(HashAddress).
5. Check if Hash == Hash', if so return Block.
6. If not, call error_correct(Block, Hash, FaultModel).
   (a) If error_correct() returns Unsuccessful, raise an exception.
   (b) else return Block.

Figure 7: IVEC algorithm for a read.

the memory bandwidth usage for parity bits, which leads to lower power consumption and performance overheads.

5. HARDWARE IMPLEMENTATION

This section discusses the implementation details of IVEC. Our implementation is based on a previously proposed integrity verification scheme [33], which uses GMAC as its MAC function. We refer to this baseline scheme as GMAC-Tree. The integrity verification aspect of our IVEC implementation is essentially identical to GMAC-Tree. IVEC only differs in its error correction operations when the integrity verification fails. Here, we briefly summarize the common GMAC-Tree operations and discuss the additional hardware that is required for IVEC compared to GMAC-Tree. We note that GMAC-Tree is chosen as a representative scheme. The IVEC implementation can be easily adapted to other integrity verification schemes.

In addition to a secret key and an input string to protect, GMAC requires another constant that is unique for each MAC. For this purpose, the GMAC-Tree scheme [33] maintains a counter per memory block, which is incremented on each write to the corresponding block. The counter concatenated with a block's address provides the unique constant for GMAC. As an optimization, GMAC-Tree uses split-counters where an 7-bit counter is maintained per block to reduce overheads and a 64-bit counter is used per page to avoid overflows. The counters are cached on-chip for performance. Our IVEC implementation adopts the same split-counter design. The GMAC-Tree paper provides more details on the baseline integrity verification [33].

The use of a counter in GMAC enables efficient operations both for integrity verification and error correction. The GMAC computation consists of three operations: an AES encryption of a counter value, Galois field (GF) multiplications with XORs on a memory block, and an XOR of the two results. As shown in Figure 8, the AES operation can be performed in parallel to reading a memory block if a counter value exists in a cache, which is the common case. In this

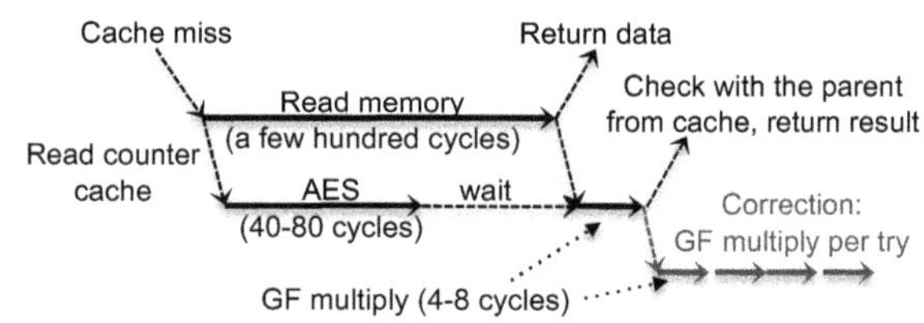

Figure 8: GMAC-based IVEC operations.

case, only the GF multiplication and XORs need to be done after the block arrives from memory, which adds only an 8 cycle latency for a 512-bit block even with conservative estimates [33]. Moreover, the AES result does not change when IVEC re-computes the MAC for error correction. As a result, each error correction try requires only the GF multiplication and XORs.

The integrity verification schemes commonly optimize performance by allowing a processor to use a block from memory before the integrity check completes (see Figure 8). To ensure security, the processor delays the commit (retire) of the load instruction until the check is done. If the check fails, the processor flushes the pipeline and re-executes from the failed load after an error correction. To avoid the hardware complexity, it is also possible to simply delay memory reads and wait for integrity checks. The previous study shows even this conservative approach only results in a 6% slowdown with GMAC-Tree [33].

The IVEC scheme needs to store meta-data such as MACs, counters, and optional parity bits in off-chip memory. As discussed in the previous section, we store parity bits in the standard memory space along with other meta-data. Therefore, the IVEC scheme can be implemented using non-ECC DIMMs without requiring special DIMMs with additional parity bits. The meta-data are stored in a part of the physical memory in a way that the IVEC unit can compute the addresses of the parent MAC, the counter, and the parity bits from a memory block's physical address. This approach is the same as other integrity verification schemes. The MAC tree protects the counters, data, and parity bits (if used) as leaf nodes to ensure their integrity. The root MAC and counter are stored on-chip.

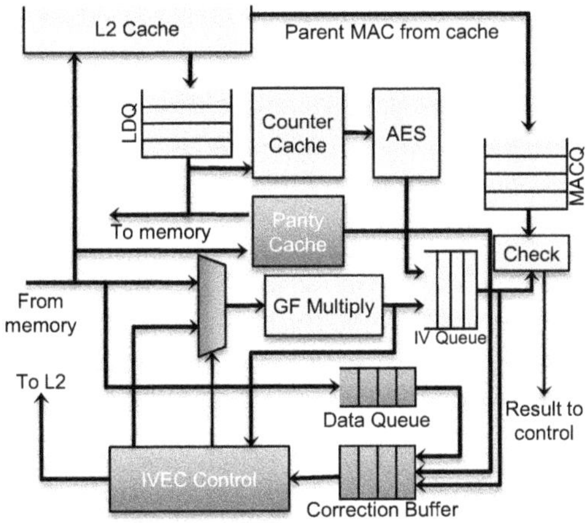

Figure 9: The hardware block diagram. The dark (blue) modules indicate additional modules necessary for IVEC.

Figure 9 shows the high-level block diagram of the IVEC implementation. The light (yellow) blocks indicate the ones that already exist in the baseline GMAC-Tree scheme. The dark (blue) blocks indicate the new blocks for IVEC. On an L2 read miss, the access is queued in a load queue (LDQ), which initiates a read from memory. At the same time, the parent MAC gets loaded from the L2 cache to a MAC queue (MACQ), and the counter is loaded from the counter cache for an AES encryption. When a memory block arrives, the GF multiply result is computed and queued in the IV queue along with the AES result for the integrity check.

IVEC only adds a few small modules to GMAC-Tree. First, a data queue stores a block from memory while its integrity is being checked. Second, the correction buffer stores information for memory blocks whose integrity check failed. The buffer entry includes the AES result, the memory block, the parent MAC, parity bits, and an identifier or an address. The depth of the buffer needs to match the height of the MAC tree to correct errors from the root to a leaf in the worst case. A parity cache is used to load parity bits on an error detection, and to store parity bits on an L2 write-back operation. Alternatively, the parity bits can share the L2 cache similar to the way MACs are stored in L2. Section 6 studies both design options and the impact of different parity cache sizes. Finally, the IVEC control unit is a simple FSM to try the error correction. Note that the GMAC computation can simply reuse the existing GF multiply unit. Given that the area overhead of the integrity verification is dominated by the AES unit and the counter cache, the overhead of IVEC is quite small. Even with 128-bit MACs and 512-bit blocks, the additional buffer space for IVEC excluding the parity cache will be less than 16KB.

6. EVALUATION

This section evaluates various aspects of the IVEC scheme including its effectiveness such as the security and the error detection and correction capabilities, and the overheads in memory space, performance, and memory bandwidth usage. The evaluation focuses on five IVEC configurations, IVEC with no parity (IVEC-NP), IVEC with 4-bit parity per block (IVEC-P4), IVEC with 8-bit parity per block (IVEC-P8), IVEC with 16-bit parity per block (IVEC-P16) and IVEC with 32-bit parity per block (IVEC-P32). IVEC-NP represents the baseline that can handle the SBE and SCSE fault models with minimal overheads, while IVEC-P4 can handle the SBE and SCSE fault models more efficiently than IVEC-NP. IVEC-P8, IVEC-P16, and IVEC-P32 present the schemes to handle the worst-case fault model (MCME) for x4, x8, and x16 DRAMs, respectively.

Detection Rate	Miscorrection Rate	Correction Latency
$1-\frac{1}{2^m}$	$1-(1-\frac{1}{2^m})^k$	$k \cdot h$

Table 3: IVEC error detection and correction

6.1 Analytical Study

This subsection presents analytical studies on various aspects of the IVEC scheme, including the detection and correction rates, mis-correction rate, correction latency, and security. Table 3 summarizes the analysis results using the following parameters: n for the memory block size in bits, m for the hash length in bits, h for the hash latency in cycles, p for the number of parity bits per block, and k for the worst-case number of correction attempts in the IVEC scheme.

Detection Rate: The integrity verification scheme should detect memory errors unless a hash collision occurs. For a strong m-bit hash or MAC function, the expected collision rate is $1/2^m$ and the detection rate is simply $1-1/2^m$. We note that if the optional parity bits are checked on every read, they can be used to further guarantee the error detection under our fault model.

Miscorrection Rate: The mis-correction rate is the probability that a value after a successful correction operation is incorrect. A mis-correction happens when a hash collision occurs on a correction attempt with an incorrect value. Therefore, the maximum mis-correction rate happens when IVEC tries the maximum number of correction attempts and at least one has a collision. This probability is computed by subtracting the probability of all attempts being collision-free from one.

Correction Latency: The correction latency is the number of cycles that a successful correction takes. Here, we assume that the hash computation dominates the latency of a correction attempt. Under this assumption, the worst-case latency can be calculated as the product of the maximum number of correction attempts and the latency of each hash computation. The average latency will be roughly one half of the worst-case latency under the uniform random distribution of errors.

Security: The error correction attempts lower the security against a brute-force attack (see Table 2) because an attacker only needs to find one collision in any correction attempt. Therefore, the probability of success for an attack can be as high as $1-(1-\frac{1}{2^m})^{(k+1)}$. Essentially, the probability is the same as the worst-case mis-correction rate except the addition of 1 in the exponent for the initial integrity check.

However, the lowered security is still enough to prevent brute-force attacks. Also, IVEC does not affect the security against birthday attacks (see Section 3.4 for detailed discussion). For example, even with a short 64-bit MAC ($m=64$) and the worst-case fault model (MCME), an attacker needs to physically change memory more than 2^{54} times assuming

Parity	SBE			SCSE			SCME			MCME		
	x4	x8	x16	x4	x8	x16	x4	x8	x16	x4	x8	x16
None	512	512	512	2432	2^{14}	2^{21}	2^{14}	2^{21}	2^{36}	2^{20}	2^{26}	2^{40}
4 bits	128	128	128	128	1920	2^{19}	960	2^{17}	2^{32}	2^{16}	2^{22}	2^{36}
8 bits	64	64	64	64	64	2^{14}	64	8160	2^{28}	4096	2^{18}	2^{32}
16 bits	32	32	32	32	32	32	32	32	2^{20}	1024	1024	2^{24}
32 bits	16	16	16	16	16	16	16	16	16	256	256	256

Table 4: The maximum number of correction attempts under typical IVEC configurations. The table assumes 64-byte cache blocks and 32-byte read-blocks.

	ECC	IV (64b/54b)	IV+ECC (64b/54b)	IVEC-NP	IVEC-P4	IVEC-P8	IVEC-P16	IVEC-P32
Overheads	12.50%	16.32% / 13.72%	28.82% / 26.22%	16.36%	17.42%	18.48%	20.61%	24.88%

Table 5: Memory space overhead of various protection schemes assuming 64-bit MACs and 512-bit blocks.

x4 (or x8) DRAMs with 16-bit parity ($p = 16$). The security of IVEC is even less of a concern for a longer MAC or a weaker fault model. The correction attempts do not affect the security against birthday attacks because there is no way for an attacker to check if a hash is *close* to a collision; attackers still need to find an exact collision.

Maximum Correction Attempts: The mis-correction rate, the security, and the correction latency are all determined largely by the maximum number of correction attempts, which reflects the search space for IVEC. The search space again depends on the fault model, the DRAM width, and the number of parity bits. Table 4 summarizes the maximum number of correction attempts (k) for typical DRAM widths and parity sizes under our fault models. As shown in the table, the IVEC scheme with no parity (IVEC-NP) can handle either single-bit errors (SBE) in any DRAM configurations or multi-bit errors from one chip in one read-block (SCSE) in x4 DRAMs with reasonable correction attempts (less than 2.5K). On the other hand, IVEC-NP's search space quickly grows for stronger fault models and wider DRAMs. For such configurations, a small number of parity bits can be added to reduce the search space. IVEC can handle multi-bit errors with no greater than 4096 searches for the MCME model and with no greater than 64 searches for all other three fault models, if the parity bits are two times the DRAM width.

Experimental Validation: We further validated the above analytical results by running functional simulations with real-world hash and MAC functions. For this purpose, we implemented the IVEC algorithms in C using SHA-1 and GMAC with different number of parity bits. Each configuration was tested by injecting a random error pattern under each fault model 100 million times. Given 64-bit hash/MACs ($m = 64$) and 64-byte cache blocks ($n = 512$), we did not observe any undetected errors or mis-correction for any IVEC configurations. Experiments showed a small mis-correction rate for a very short hash/MAC (16 bits), which was expected from the analytical study.

6.2 Memory Space Overhead

Table 5 presents the overall memory space overheads of SEC-DED ECC, the baseline integrity verification scheme (IV), the integrity verification with ECC (IV+ECC), and various IVEC configurations. The ECC scheme has a 12.5% overhead to store 8 parity bits for each 64 data bits. Even though the baseline integrity verification scheme also uses a 64-bit MAC per 512-bit block, it has a higher overhead (16.32%) due to additional counters and tree structures [33]. IV+ECC shows the case where IV and ECC are combined in a naïve way. Given that IVEC provides a slightly lower level of security against brute-force attacks compared to IV with the same length MACs, the table shows memory overheads of IV and IV+ECC for both typical 64-bit MACs and 54-bit MACs. The 54-bit MACs are deduced from the security level of IVEC-P16 with x4 or x8 DRAM chips under the MCME model. The overheads for 54-bit MACs are presented simply for a comparison. In practice, MACs needs to be a multiple of a word (32 bits) to match a standard memory system.

The memory space overhead of IVEC-NP is only 0.04% more than the baseline IV. IVEC uses slightly more memory to protect all counter values, while the baseline IV only protects counters related to data. Therefore, IVEC-NP saves 12.1% of memory compared to IV+ECC. Even with parity bits, IVEC uses noticeably less memory space compared to IV+ECC because it only requires a small number of parity bits.

6.3 Performance Simulation Methods

To evaluate the performance and off-chip bandwidth usage of IVEC, we use detailed simulations. The simulation infrastructure is built with the Pin binary instrumentation tool [18] and the TAXI performance simulator [32]. The Pin tool runs a program and sends execution traces so that the TAXI simulator performs a cycle-by cycle micro-architecture simulation that models the processing core and the memory hierarchy. The performance simulations use benchmarks from the SPEC CPU2000 suite [11]. For each benchmark, we use a reference input set and its early single simulation points respectively [26]. Table 6 summarizes the simulation parameters. The size of the parity cache was selected as a fraction of the L2 cache size based on the ratio between the parity bits and a L2 cache block.

Component	Parameters
Core	3 GHz, 4-issue out-of-order
Caches	L1 I/D: 64KB/64KB 2-ways 2 cycle latency, L2: 2-MB unified, 8-ways, 14 cycle latency
DRAM	4GB, Latency: 50 ns, Bandwidth: 8 GB/s
IV Checks	Split Counter GMAC Merkle Tree, 64-bit GMAC
AES	128-bit, 80 cycle latency
GF Multiply	8 cycle latency
Counter cache	32KB, 8-ways, 2 cycle latency
Parity cache	32KB (IVEC-P4), 64KB (IVEC-P8), 128KB (IVEC-P16), 256KB (IVEC-P32), 8 ways, 2 cycle latency

Table 6: Simulation parameters.

In the performance evaluations, the baseline represents the GMAC-Tree scheme with split counters [33]. The baseline was chosen to have the integrity verification because IVEC is mainly designed for systems that already require integrity verification for security. Our performance study shows the instruction-per-cycle (IPC) that is normalized to the baseline configuration, and focuses on evaluating the overheads of the IVEC scheme compared to the conventional integrity verification. The average performance overhead of the baseline is reported to be less than 5% when compared with a system without any protection [33].

6.4 Performance

There are two potential sources of the performance overheads for IVEC compared to the baseline integrity verification scheme: error correction latency and off-chip bandwidth usage from parity updates. However, the correction latencies only come into effect when there is an error on a memory read. During the normal operation, the error correction does not add any additional overhead. The soft-error rate (SER) for modern DRAM cells is reported to be 100 to 1000FIT/MB [30]. For 4GB memory, this SER translates to about an error every 10^{11} seconds. Given that the worse-case error correction takes tens of thousands of cycles in the IVEC configurations that we study, the performance overhead from error correction will be negligible. We note that in a case where the SER is several orders of magnitude higher than the current SER, the slower error correction of IVEC will become more visible.

Because our IVEC implementation maps parity bits to regular memory space without using special DIMMs, the additional parity accesses may interfere with processor's memory accesses. Figure 10(a) shows the performance of various IVEC configurations normalized to the baseline integrity verification scheme. Here, simulations assume that there is no memory error. Note that the performance of IVEC-NP is not shown in the graph because it is identical to the baseline. As shown in the figure, the performance overheads from additional parity accesses are less than 0.5% in the worst case. Figure 10(b) shows the IVEC-P16 scheme with various parity cache sizes, and also the the alternative hardware design where parity bits share the L2 cache similar to the way MACs are stored in L2. Overall, the performance overhead increases with smaller parity cache sizes, most apparent in the memory intensive benchmarks such as `equake`. The shared L2 configuration also increases the performance overhead on average.

6.5 Memory Bandwidth Usage

This subsection studies the bandwidth usage of IVEC compared to the baseline integrity verification. While the performance impact of additional bandwidth consumption for parity bits has been studied in the previous subsection, the bandwidth usage is also a measure of the DRAM power consumption. Again, the off-chip bandwidth usage of IVEC-NP is almost identical to that of the baseline integrity verification. Therefore, IVEC-NP saves roughly 12.5% of off-chip traffic compared to the case where a traditional ECC is simply added to the integrity verification.

Table 7 shows the baseline memory bandwidth and Figure 11 shows the bandwidth usage overhead for different IVEC configurations. Overall, as the number of parity bits increases, the overhead of bandwidth traffic increases accordingly. In Figure 11(a), the bandwidth overheads are always less than the traditional ECC's 12.5%. The average bandwidth overhead is at most 3.2% even for the IVEC-P32 case, which is considerably lower than ECC's. In Figure 11(b), a larger parity cache helps to reduce the bandwidth traffic, since it would improve the miss rate of the cache. The shared L2 configuration shows comparable overhead to the default 128KB parity cache size for IVEC-P16.

6.6 Strengths and Limitations

Overall, the experiments illustrate two key advantages of IVEC compared to implementing the integrity verification and ECC separately. For simple fault models such as single-bit errors (SBE) or multi-bit errors from one chip in one read-block (SCSE), IVEC can provide error correction capabilities with negligible memory and bandwidth overheads beyond the baseline integrity verification (IVEC-NP). Alternatively, with parity bits, IVEC can handle a fault model (MCME) that is comparable to the chip-kill correct coverage, still with significant memory and bandwidth savings. For x4 DRAMs, IVEC-P8 has 2.1% memory overheads for parity bits and 0.9% bandwidth overheads. In addition, IVEC provides the flexibility to dynamically change the desired error protection level by controlling the search space.

IVEC also has a couple of limitations. First, the scheme is mainly useful for systems where both physical security and reliability are important. IVEC is more expensive than a simple ECC if only 1-bit correction is necessary without security. However, we believe that both physical security and reliability will become increasingly important for future computing devices. Second, while the overall performance overhead is negligible, each error correction is much slower in IVEC compared to ECC. Therefore, the current IVEC design is not well suited for real-time systems with tight deadlines.

7. RELATED WORK

This section summarizes the existing integrity verification and ECC schemes. The section also covers an existing technique that combine security and reliability concerns.

Memory Integrity Verification: To protect the integrity of off-chip memory without relying on an excessive amount of trusted on-chip memory, almost all integrity verification techniques rely on the tree structure. The original Merkle tree algorithm was proposed for untrusted storage in general [20]. Gassend et al. first proposed to apply the Merkle tree to protect off-chip memory with caching [8]. A split counter mode memory encryption and integrity verification is proposed using GMAC to further improve the integrity verification latency and overheads [33]. Bonsai Merkle tree [27] improves the performance and makes the integrity verification more OS friendly by using smaller Merkle trees to only authenticate counters. The IVEC scheme can be applied to any of the previous integrity verification schemes based on trees.

ECC: The SEC-DED ECC is originally introduced by Hamming [10]. Hsiao [12] proposed a class of optimal SEC-DED codes that simplifies the decoding logic. SEC-DED codes has also been further extended to detect single byte errors [3, 9] or correct 2-bit errors in adjacent bits [6] with the same number of bits. To handle multi-bit errors that SEC-DEC code cannot cover, researchers have proposed double-error-correcting triple-error-detecting (DEC-TED) codes [15, 2]. However, DEC-TED codes need 15 bits for each 64-bit data block with more complex encoding and decoding, almost doubling the memory overhead of SEC-DEC codes. The encoding and decoding latencies both double while the area increases by 3x for encoder and 5x for decoder [22]. Overall, although there are numerous extensions which im-

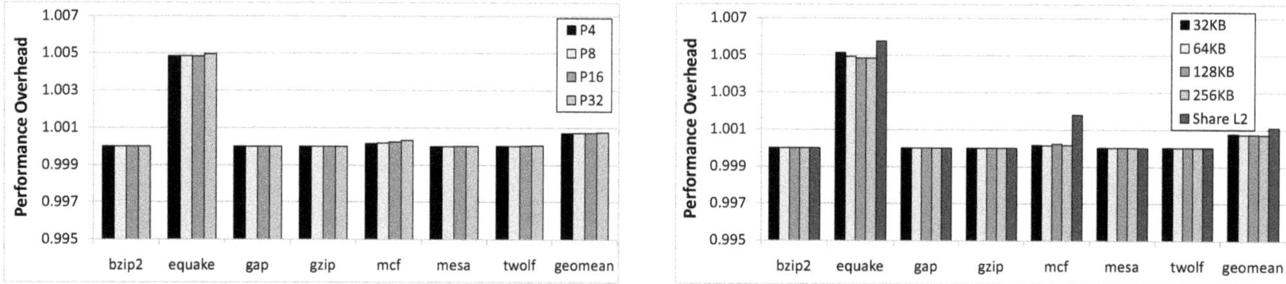

(a) Baseline parity cache configuration.

(b) IVEC-P16 for various parity cache sizes.

Figure 10: Normalized performance of IVEC configurations. The performance of IVEC-NP is identical to the baseline performance.

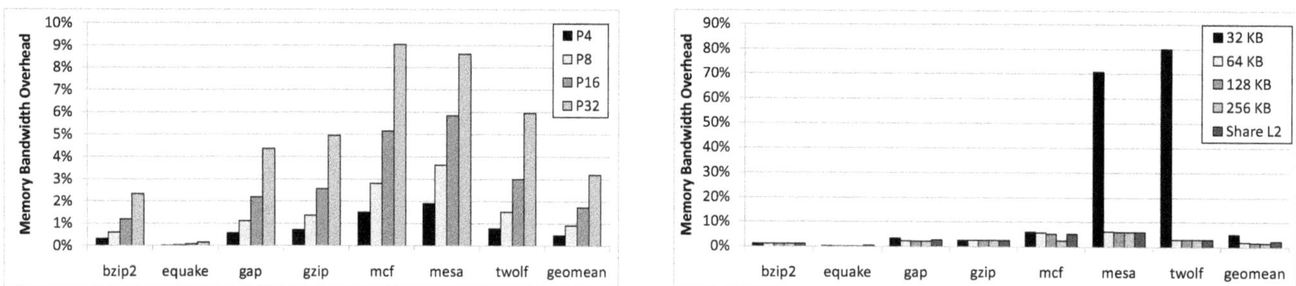

(a) Normalized Bandwidth.

(b) IVEC-P16 with various parity cache sizes.

Figure 11: The bandwidth usage for IVEC. IVEC-NP has identical bandwidth usage as the baseline IV.

	bzip2	equake	gap	gzip	mcf	mesa	twolf
Bandwidth	$3.78{\cdot}10^{8}$	$2.12{\cdot}10^{10}$	$5.06{\cdot}10^{8}$	$5.47{\cdot}10^{7}$	$2.20{\cdot}10^{9}$	$2.24{\cdot}10^{8}$	$1.85{\cdot}10^{8}$

Table 7: The average memory bandwidth usage (bits/S) for the baseline configuration.

prove upon the SEC-DED ECC, the SEC-DED code still remains the most popular choice in the industry due to its simple encoding and decoding and low overhead in terms of speed, area, and power consumption.

Chip-kill Correct Physical bit interleaving can also be used to address multi-bit error protection [25, 19]. A widely used technique is called chip-kill correct [5, 17], which can correct up to 4 adjacent bits at once, and hence can handle a complete failure within a x4 DRAM chip. The chip-kill correct can also handle a complete failure within a x8 DRAM chip when using a different SEC-DED code that handles 4 adjacent bit errors [5]. The chip-kill correct mechanism is observed to reduce the uncorrectable error rate by up to 10 times when compared to the traditional ECC in a real world study [29]. IVEC with a small number of parity bits can handle a fault model (MCME) that is comparable to chip-kill correct. Also, IVEC's "chip-kill" protection can be applied even for wide DRAM chips (x8, x16) where traditional chip-kill correct cannot be efficiently applied.

Tiered ECC: To improve the power and latency overheads of ECC, Sadler et al. proposed to decouple error-detection from error-correction so that a low-cost code can be used for detection while traditional ECC is used only for infrequent correction [28]. A similar idea is also used to reduce the power consumption of on-chip ECC by power-gating the ECC portion of clean cache lines [16], and to store expensive error correction code in memory while only maintaining detection code on-chip for caches [34]. A recent study uses virtualized two-tiered error protection code to provide chip-kill correct like protection using existing DRAM and packaging technology [35]. IVEC uses the same idea to optimize its parity bits. In our case, the hashes/MACs for integrity verification serve as a detection code, and the parity bits are used for correction.

Reliability and Security Engine: The Reliability and Security Engine (RSE) aims to solve security and reliability concerns together [21]. RSE is a common processor-level framework that embeds hardware-implemented modules which monitors the processor pipeline for both security and reliability checks. While the idea of combining security and reliability is the same with IVEC, RSE is applicable to a completely different domain.

8. CONCLUSION

This paper proposes to extend the integrity verification with error correction capability. By removing the error detection aspect of ECC, which is redundant when the integrity verification exists, the proposed IVEC scheme enables efficient protection of off-chip memory from both security attacks and random errors. For example, IVEC can correct single-bit errors or multi-bit errors from one DRAM chip in one read-block without any additional ECC bits. Moreover, with parity bits, IVEC can handle a stronger fault model (MCME) that is comparable to chip-kill correct, still with much less memory and bandwidth overheads than the traditional SEC-DED ECC. The analytical and experimental studies show that IVEC can be applied with minimal overheads and without compromising the security. Overall, we believe that the IVEC scheme can eliminate the overhead of traditional SEC-DED ECC for off-chip memory when a system requires integrity verification for physical security.

9. ACKNOWLEDGMENT

We thank anonymous reviewers for their feedback. This work was partially supported by the National Science Foundation under grants CNS-0746913, CNS-0708788 and SA4897-10808PG, by the Air Force Office of Scientific Research under Grant FA9550-09-1-0131, and an equipment donation from Intel Corporation. Any opinions, findings, and conclusions or recommendations expressed in this material are those of the author(s) and do not necessarily reflect the views of NSF, AFOSR, or Intel.

10. REFERENCES

[1] AMD. BIOS and kernel developer's guide for AMD NPT family 0Fh processors, July 2007. http://support.amd.com/us/Processor_TechDocs/32559.pdf.

[2] E. R. Berlekamp. *Algebraic Coding Theory, Revised Edition.* 1984.

[3] C. L. Chen. Error-correcting codes with byte error-detection capability. *IEEE Trans. Comput.*, 32(7):615–621, 1983.

[4] CNNMoney.com. IBM launches new security technology, 2006. http://money.cnn.com/2006/04/10/technology/IBM_security/.

[5] T. J. Dell. A white paper on the benefits of chipkill-correct ECC for PC server main memory. *IBM Microelectronics*, 1997.

[6] A. Dutta and N. A. Touba. Multiple bit upset tolerant memory using a selective cycle avoidance based SEC-DED-DAEC code. *VLSI Test Symposium, IEEE*, 2007.

[7] M. Dworkin. Recommendation for block cipher modes of operation: Galois/counter mode(GCM) and GMAC, November 2007.

[8] B. Gassend, G. E. Suh, D. Clarke, M. van Dijk, and S. Devadas. Caches and merkle trees for efficient memory integrity verification. In *Proceedings of* 9th *International Symposium on High Performance Computer Architecture (HPCA)*, 2003.

[9] M. Hamada and E. Fujiwara. A class of error control codes for byte organized memory systems -sbec-(sb+s)ed codes-. *IEEE Trans. Comput.*, 46(1):105–109, 1997.

[10] R. W. Hamming. Error detecting and correcting codes. *Bell Systems Technical Journal*, 29(2):147–163, 1950.

[11] J. L. Henning. SPEC CPU2000: Measuring CPU performance in the new millennium. *IEEE Computer*, July 2000.

[12] M. Y. Hsiao. A class of optimal minumum odd-weightcolumn SEC-DED codes. *IBM Journal of Research and Developement*, 14(4):395–401, 1970.

[13] A. Huang. Keeping secrets in hardware: The microsoft Xbox^{TM} case study. In *CHES*, volume 2523 of *Lecture Notes in Computer Science*, 2002.

[14] H. Krawczyk, M. Bellare, and R. Canetti. RFC 2104: HMAC: Keyed-Hashing for Message Authentication, Feb. 1997.

[15] P. K. Lala. An adaptive double error corrrection scheme for semiconductor memory systems. *Digital Processes*, 4, 1978.

[16] L. Li, V. Degalahal, N. Vijaykrishnan, M. Kandemir, and M. Irwini. Soft error and energy consumption interactions: A data cache perspective. *Proceedings of International Symposium on Low Power Electronics and Design (ISLPED)*, August 2004.

[17] D. Locklear. Chipkill correct memory architecture. *Dell Enterprise Systems Group technology brief*, August 2000.

[18] C.-K. Luk, R. Cohn, R. Muth, H. Patil, A. Klauser, G. Lowney, S. Wallace, V. J. Reddi, and K. Hazelwood. Pin: Building customized program analysis tools with dynamic instrumentation. In *Proceedings of the 2005 Conference on Programming Language Design and Implementation International (PLDI)*, June 2005.

[19] J. Maiz, S. Hareland, K. Zhang, and P. Armstrong. Characterization of multi-bit soft error events in advanced SRAMs. In *IEEE International Electron Devices Meeting*, 2003.

[20] R. C. Merkle. Protocols for public key cryptography. In *IEEE Symposium on Security and Privacy*, 1980.

[21] N. Nakka, Z. Kalbarczyk, R. K. Iyer, and J. Xu. An architectural framework for providing reliability and security support. In *Proceedings of the 2004 International Conference on Dependable Systems and Networks (DSN)*, 2004.

[22] R. Naseer and J. Draper. Parallel double error correcting code design to mitigate multi-bit upsets in SRAMs. *Solid-State Circuits Conference*, 2008.

[23] NIST. FIPS PUB 180-1: Secure Hash Standard, April 1995.

[24] NIST. FIPS PUB 180-2: Secure Hash Standard, August 2002.

[25] K. Osada, K. Yamaguchi, Y. Saitoh, and T. Kawahara. SRAM immunity to cosmic-ray-induced multierrors based on analysis of an induced parasitic bipolar effect. *Solid-State Circuits, IEEE Journal of*, 39(5):827–833, May 2004.

[26] E. Perelman, G. Hamerly, and B. Calder. Picking statistically valid and early simulation points. In *Proceedings of the* 12th *International Conference on Parallel Architectures and Compilation Techniques (PACT)*, 2003.

[27] B. Rogers, S. Chhabra, M. Prvulovic, and Y. Solihin. Using address independent seed encryption and Bonsai merkle trees to make secure processors OS- and performance-friendly. In *Proceedings of the* 40th *Annual IEEE/ACM International Symposium on Microarchitecture*, 2007.

[28] N. N. Sadler and D. J. Sorin. Choosing an error protection scheme for a microprocessor's L1 data cache. In *Proceedings of International Conference on Computer Design (ICCD)*, 2006.

[29] B. Schroeder, E. Pinheiro, and W. Weber. DRAM errors in the wild: a large-scale field study. *In ACM SIGMETRICS*, pages 193–204, 2009.

[30] C. W. Slayman. Cache and memory error detection, correction, and reduction techniques for terrestrial servers and workstations. *IEEE Transactions on Devices and Materials Reliability*, 5(3), 2005.

[31] Sun Microsystems Inc. OpenSPARC T2 System-On-Chip (SOC) microarchitecture specification, May 2008.

[32] S. Vlaovic. TAXI: Trace analysis for x86 interpretation. In *Proceedings of the 2002 IEEE International Conference on Computer Design*, 2002.

[33] C. Yan, D. Englender, M. Prvulovic, B. Rogers, and Y. Solihin. Improving cost, performance, and security of memory encryption and authentication. In *Proceedings of the* 33rd *International Symposium on Computer Architecture (ISCA)*, June 2006.

[34] D. Yoon and M. Erez. Memory mapped ECC: Low-cost error protection for last level caches. *Proceedings of 36th International Symp Computer Architecture (ISCA)*, June 2009.

[35] D. H. Yoon and M. Erez. Virtualized and flexible ecc for main memory. In *Proceedings of the* 15th *Architectural Support for Programming Languages and Operating Systems (ASPLOS)*, 2010.

Sentry: Light-Weight Auxiliary Memory Access Control*

Arrvindh Shriraman
Department of Computer Science
University of Rochester
ashriram@cs.rochester.edu

Sandhya Dwarkadas
Department of Computer Science
University of Rochester
sandhya@cs.rochester.edu

ABSTRACT

Light-weight, flexible access control, which allows software to regulate reads and writes to any granularity of memory region, can help improve the reliability of today's multi-module multi-programmer applications, as well as the efficiency of software debugging tools. Unfortunately, access control in today's processors is tied to support for virtual memory, making its use both heavy weight and coarse grain. In this paper, we propose Sentry, an auxiliary level of virtual memory tagging that is entirely subordinate to existing virtual memory-based protection mechanisms and can be manipulated at the user level. We implement these tags in a complexity-effective manner using an M-cache (metadata cache) structure that only intervenes on L1 misses, thereby minimizing changes to the processor core. Existing cache coherence states are repurposed to implicitly validate permissions for L1 hits. Sentry achieves its goal of flexible and light-weight access control without disrupting existing inter-application protection, sidestepping the challenges associated with adding a new protection framework to an existing operating system.

We illustrate the benefits of our design point using 1) an Apache-based web server that uses the M-cache to enforce protection boundaries among its modules and 2) a watchpoint-based tool to demonstrate low-overhead debugging. Protection is achieved with very few changes to the source code, no changes to the programming model, minimal modifications to the operating system, and with low overhead incurred only when accessing memory regions for which the additional level of access control is enabled.

Categories and Subject Descriptors: B.3.2 [Memory Structures]: Design Styles—Shared memory; C.0 [General]: Hardware/Software interfaces; C.1.2 [Processor Architectures]: Multiprocessors; D.2.0 [Software Engineering]: General — Protection mechanisms

General Terms: Performance, Design, Reliability, Security

Keywords: Access control, Cache coherence, Multiprocessors, Memory protection, Sentry, Protection domains, Safety.

*This work was supported in part by NSF grants CCF-0702505, CNS-0411127, CNS-0615139, CNS-0834451, and CNS-0509270; NIH grants 5 R21 GM079259-02 and 1 R21 HG004648-01; and equipment support from Sun Microsystems Laboratories.

ISCA'10, June 19–23, 2010, Saint-Malo, France.

1. INTRODUCTION

Modern software are complex artifacts consisting of millions of lines of code written by many developers. Developing correct, high performance, and reliable code has thus become increasingly challenging. The prevalence of multi-core processors has increased the burden on software developers. Fine-grain intra- and inter-thread interactions via memory make it difficult for developers to track, debug, and regulate the accesses arising from the various software modules. Architectural features for *access control* that enable software to track and regulate accesses will help develop more robust and fault tolerant applications.

As one example, Figure 1 presents a high-level representation of the developers' view of Apache [31]. The system designers specify a software interface that defines the set of functions and data that are private and/or exported to other modules. For the sake of programming simplicity and performance, current implementations of Apache run all modules in a single process and rely on adherence to the module interface to protect modules. Unfortunately, a bug or safety problem in any module could potentially (and does) violate the interface and affect the whole application.

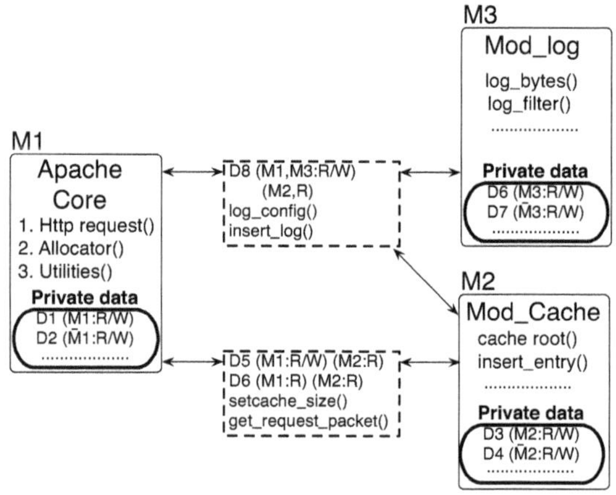

Figure 1: Example of software modules in Apache. M1,M2,M3 — modules, D1...D8 — data elements. Dashed lines indicate data and functions shared between modules. Tuple D: (M:P) indicates module M has permission P on the memory location D. R - Read only ; R/W - Read or Write

There are two key aspects in regulating the accesses to a specific datum: (1) the domain, referring to the environment or module, that a thread performing the access is executing in; and (2) the access privileges, the set of permissions available to a domain for the object [10]. Access control is used to enforce the permissions specified for the domain and object. An instance of the use of flexible access control is enforcing the rule that a plug-in should not have access to the application's data or another plug-in's data, while the application could have unrestricted access to all data. Access control can also be used for program debugging in order to efficiently intercept accesses and detect violations of specific invariants, such as accesses to uninitialized or unallocated locations, dangling references, unexpected write values, etc. Tracking memory bugs is an intensive task and it is especially complicated in module-based applications where memory is accessed at many different sites.

Access control mechanisms in current general-purpose processors consist of either operating system (OS) page protection bits or a limited number of word-granularity watchpoint registers (4 on the x86). The former is restricted to providing page-granularity protection while the latter's usefulness is handicapped by the small number of watchpoint registers. Unfortunately, the protection targets in most realistic applications are often more fine-grain, at the granularity of a few words. Also another consideration in protection usage is "thread-awareness", which would need to allow different application threads to be regulated differently for the same location and also allow the same thread to have different access permissions to different locations. Finally, hardcoding the number of protection levels and semantics has lead to restricted use of the mechanism. Overall, existing systems do not satisfy modular software's demands for flexible memory protection.

Currently, flexible access control typically relies on software instrumentation tools, which can cause significant slowdown (e.g., 22—60× [14, 27]). Recent work [6] has reduced the overheads by focusing on the integrity of data (no unsafe writes) and compromising the safety (permit unsafe reads). Software-based access control also need synchronization to ensure the atomicity of metadata operations and data access in multi-threaded workloads. Recent hardware proposals for fine-grain access control such as employed by Mondrian [24] seek to provide a flexible protection framework. However, such a design also introduces additional permission tag structures within the highly optimized processor pipeline. The permission tags are accessed on every memory operation, which results in extra work and energy consumption. Finally, they add new layers of protection to replace OS processes and require every application, regardless of its desire for flexible access control, to use the new interface.

In this paper, we investigate *Sentry*, a hardware framework that enables software to enforce protection policies at runtime. The core developer annotates the program to define the policy and then the system ensures the privacy and integrity of a module's private data (no external reads or writes), the safety of inter-module shared data (by enforcing permissions specified by the application), and adherence to the module's interface (controlled function call points).

We propose a light-weight, multi-purpose access control mechanism that is independent of and subordinate to (enforced after) the page protection in the Translation-Lookaside-Buffer (TLB). We implement Sentry using a permissions metadata cache (*M-cache*) that intercepts only L1 misses and resides entirely outside the processor core. It reuses the L1 cache coherence states in a novel manner to enforce permissions and elide checks on L1 hits. Permission metadata checks thus require between 1 and 10% (depending on workload) of the energy required by the in-processor option. Since the M-cache is on the L1-miss path it places fewer constraints on the pipeline cycle compared to per-access in-processor checks [24]. Finally, the M-cache also exploits cache coherence to implicitly invalidate cached metadata on permission changes (no need for heavyweight software shootdowns).

From the software's perspective, Sentry is a pluggable access control mechanism for application-level fine-grain protection. It works as a supplement (not a replacement) to OS process-based protection and this leads to three main advantages. First, Sentry incurs space and performance overhead only when additional fine-grain protection is needed as otherwise existing page-based access control can be used. Second, the software runtime that manages the intra-application protection can reside entirely at the user level and can operate without much OS intervention, making the system both efficient and attractive to mainstream OS vendors. Third, within the same system, applications using the Sentry protection framework can co-exist with applications that do not use Sentry's services. We demonstrate that Sentry can realize various intra-application protection models with simple permissions annotations and does not require any changes to the programming model or language.

We used Sentry to enforce a protection model for the Apache web server. We primarily safeguard the core web server's data from extension modules by ensuring that modules do not violate the specified interface. We achieved this without requiring any changes to the programming model, with minimal source code annotations, and moderate performance overheads ($\simeq$13%). We note that our efforts to compare against process-based protection (i.e., enclose the module in a separate process and use RPC for web server to module communication) were frustrated by the programming model and cumbersome non-shared-memory interface. We also validate the suitability of Sentry when employed for a watchpoint-based memory debugger. We estimate that its overheads are comparable to proposed debugging hardware (6%) and are much lower than proposed fine-grain protection hardware (half the overhead) or software approaches.

Section 2 presents the design of the M-cache hardware and describes the M-cache operations. Section 3 describes the various Sentry protection models and the support needed from software. Section 4 demonstrates the applications and evaluates Sentry's performance overheads. Section 5 discusses related work and we conclude in Section 6.

2. SENTRY: AUXILIARY MEMORY ACCESS CONTROL

Access control must essentially provide a way for software to express permissions to a given location for the active threads. Hardware is expected to intercept the accesses, check them against the expressed permissions, and raise an exception if the thread does not have the appropriate permissions. Current processors typically implement a physical memory hierarchy through which an access traverses looking for data. Accesses can be intercepted at any level in the memory hierarchy: within the processor core, in the L1 miss path (this paper), or any other level.

Why not within the processor?

Most protection schemes (e.g., Mondrian [24], Loki [26], TLB) adopt the logically simple option of intercepting all memory accesses within the processor. However, this requires additional structures in highly optimized stages of the processor pipeline. Since the access control hardware is consulted in parallel with L1 access on every load and store, the hardware design is constrained by the need to stay within the 1-2 cycle L1 access latency. High-performance transistor technology will likely be employed, leading to a noticeable energy and area budget.

Access Control on L1 misses

In Sentry, we have chosen to place the access checks on the L1 miss path to avoid processor core modifications. The L1 miss rate in most applications is a small percentage of the total accesses (1-4% for PARSEC, 4-9% for SPLASH2, 16% for Apache). Since the checks occur only on L1 misses and in parallel with L2 accesses (which can take 30—40 cycles), we have a longer time window to complete the checks and can trade performance for energy. Employing energy-optimized transistor technology [13] can save leakage and dynamic power. We found that all things equal (granularity of protection, number of entries), the L1 miss path option consumes only 1—10% of the power of an approach implementing the checks within the processor. Placing the access control hardware any further down (say on the L2 miss path) complicates the processor interface (for example, when propagating exceptions back to software). Furthermore, protection changes which require invalidation of in-cache data causes higher overhead, since an eviction at the higher cache level incurs higher penalty.

Our design choice to intercept L1 misses implies that the smallest protection granularity we support is an L1 cache line. Sub-cache-line granularity can be supported at the cost of either additional bits in the L1 or software disambiguation. To accommodate L1 cache line granularity monitoring (typically 16 - 64 bytes), the memory allocator can be modified to create cache-line-aligned regions with the help of software annotations (compiler or programmer). Software can also further disambiguate an access exception in order to implement word granularity monitoring if necessary.

2.1 Metadata Hardware Cache (M-Cache)

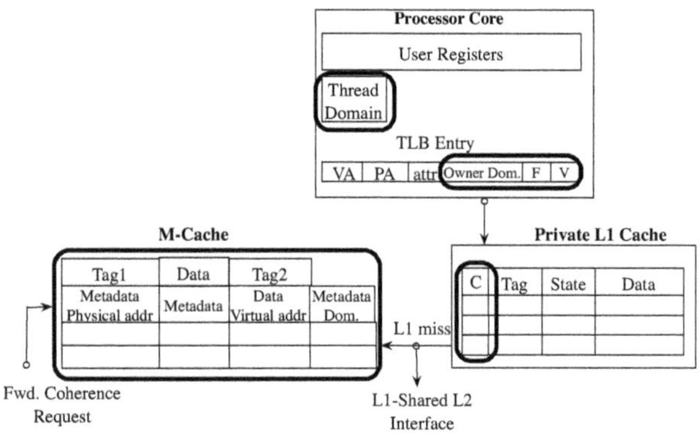

Figure 2: M-cache Mechanism. Dark lines enclose add-ons. Dom.: Domain.

In Sentry, we maintain the invariant that a thread is allowed to access the L1 cache without requiring any checks i.e., L1 accesses are implicitly validated. To implement this we include a new hardware metadata cache (M-cache) that controls whether data is allowed into the L1.

Figure 2 shows the M-cache positioned in the L1 miss path outside the processor core. Each entry in the M-cache provides permission metadata for a specific virtual page. The per-page metadata varies based on the intended protection model (see Section 3). In general, it is a bitmap data structure that encodes 2 bits of access permission (read-only, read/write, no access, execute) per cache line. Note that these are auxiliary to the OS protection scheme since the access has to pass the TLB checks before getting to the memory system. This ensures that the M-cache's policies don't interfere with the OS protection scheme. An M-cache entry is tagged on the processor side using the virtual address (VA) of the page requiring the permission check. Using virtual addresses allows user-level examination and manipulation of the M-cache entries and avoids the need to purge the M-cache on a page swap. The M-cache also contains a network-side tag consisting of the physical address of the metadata (MPA) to ensure entries are invalidated if the metadata is changed (more details in Section 2.4). The domain id fields included in the processor register, TLB entry, and M-cache, implement the concept of protection domains (we discuss this in more detail in Section 3). Table 1 lists the ISA interface of the M-cache.

Dual tags

The dual tagging of the M-cache does introduce an interesting challenge. We need to ensure that when the entry in one of the tag arrays is invalidated (VA due to processor action or MPA due to network message), the corresponding entry in the other tag array is also cleaned up. One option is to use a fully associative MPA tag array, but this is expensive in terms of both energy and area. Assuming limited associativity, the VA, the data address using the access control metadata, and the MPA, the metadata word's physical address, may index into different positions in their respective tag arrays. To solve this issue, we include forward and back pointers similar to those proposed by Goodman [7] — a VA tag (with which the metadata is associated) includes a pointer (set index and way position) to the corresponding entry in the MPA array and the MPA tag entry includes a back pointer. The dual tagging could result in additional conflict evictions due to collisions in the VA and MPA mappings.

2.2 When is the access checked?

Sentry creates permissions metadata only when an application requires fine-grain or user-level access control. To achieve this, we use an unused bit in the page-table entry to encode an "F" bit (Fine-grain). If the software doesn't need the checks, it leaves the 'F' bit unset and hardware bypasses the M-cache for accesses to the page. [1] If the bit is set, on an L1 miss, the M-cache is indexed using the virtual address of the access to examine the metadata. The virtual address needed by the M-cache lookup is available at the load-store unit for the L1 miss. Once a cache block is loaded into the processor's L1 cache, we use coherence's MESI states to transparently enforce permissions (i.e., cache hits don't check the M-cache). Without involving any modifications to the coherence protocol, M or E can support read/write permissions, S can enforce read-only, and I can check any permission type. An attempt to access data without the appropriate coherence state will result in an L1 miss, which checks the M-cache.

Data persistence in caches does introduce a challenge; data fetched into the L1 by one thread continues to be visible to other threads on the processor. Essentially, if two threads have different access permissions, the L1 hits could circumvent the access control mechanism. Consider two threads T1 and T2, which the application has dictated to have read-write and read-only rights to location A. T1 runs on a processor, stores A, and caches it in the "M" state. Subsequently, the OS switches in T2 to the same processor. Now, if T2 was allowed to write A, the permission mechanism would be circumvented. To ensure complexity-effectiveness, we need to guard against this without requiring that all L1 hits check the M-cache. We employ two bits, a "V" (Verify) bit in the page-table to indicate whether the page has different permissions for different threads and "C" (checked) bit in the cache tag, which indicates if the cache block has already been verified (1 yes, 0 no). All accesses (hit or miss) check permissions if the TLB entry's "V" bit is set and the "C" bit in the L1 cache tag is unset, indicating first access within the thread context. Once the first access verifies permissions, the "C" bit is set. This ensures that subsequent L1 hits to the cache line need not access the M-cache. The "C" bit of all cached lines is flash-cleared on context switches.

Exception Trigger

When an access does not have appropriate rights, the hardware triggers a permission exception, which occurs logically before the access. These exceptions are entirely at the user level and can use

[1] We also use this technique to prevent accesses on the permissions metadata from having to look for metadata.

Registers	
`%mcache_handlerPC:`	address of handler to be called on a user-space alert
`%Domain1_Handler:`	address of handler to be called within user-level supervisor (see Section 3.3)
`%mcache_faultPC:`	PC of faulting instruction
`%mcache_faultAddress:`	virtual address that experienced the access exception
`%mcache_faultInstructionType:`	read, write, or execute
`%mcache_faultType:`	M-cache miss or permission exception
`%mcache_entry:`	per-page permissions metadata; 2 bits / cache line to represent Read-only, Read/Write, Execute, and No access)
`%mcache_index`	index into the M-cache
Instructions	
`get_entry vaddr,%mcache_index`	get an entry for vaddr and store its index in `%mcache_index`
`inv_entry vaddr,%mcache_index`	evict vaddr's metadata from M-cache and return its position in %mcache_index
`LD vaddr, %mcache_index`	load vaddr into M-cache position pointed to by `%mcache_index`
`LL vaddr, %mcache_index`	Load Linked version of the above
`LD_MPA vaddr,%mcache_index`	load physical address of cache block corresponding to vaddr into MPA
`ST %mcache_index,%mcache_entry`	store the data in `%mcache_entry` into the M-cache entry pointed to by `%mcache_index`
`SC %mcache_index,%mcache_entry`	Store-Conditional version of the above
`switch_call %R1, %R2`	Effects a subroutine call to the address in %R1 and changes thread domain to that specified in %R2 (see Section 3.3)

Table 1: M-cache Interface. The %Domain1_Handler register and switch_call instruction are discussed in detail in Section 3.3.

the same stack, privilege level, and address space as the thread making the access. Our design reuses the exception mechanism on modern processors. The M-cache response marks the instruction as an exception point in the reorder buffer. The permissions checks are enforced at instruction retirement, at which time the exception type is checked and a software handler is triggered, if needed. The permission check, which is performed by looking up either the L1 cache state on a hit or the M-cache metadata on a miss, has potential impact only at the back end of the pipeline in the case of a miss. Pipeline critical paths and thereby cycle time consequently remain unaffected. Note that permission violations can be detected at the execution stage and the line will be brought into the appropriate state if it doesn't have permissions. (e.g., read-only permissions means line is in "S" state, no permissions means the line is not allocated).

On a permission exception, the M-cache provides the following information in registers: the program counter of the instruction that failed the check (%mcache_faultPC) , the address accessed (%mcache_faultAddress), and the type of instruction (%mcache_faultInstructionType). There are separate sets of registers for kernel and user-mode exceptions.

2.3 How is the M-cache filled?

The M-cache entries can be indexed and written under software control similar to a software TLB. Allowing software to directly write M-cache entries (1) allows maintenance of the metadata in virtual memory regions using any data structure and (2) permits flexibility in setting permission policies. The former decouples the metadata size from the limitations of the hardware M-cache size, allowing the protection metadata to grow arbitrarily under software control and to be structured to suit the specific applications' need. Hardware never updates the M-cache entries and it is expected that software already has a consistent copy. Hence, any evictions from the M-cache are silently dropped (no writebacks). Since no controller is required to handle refills or eviction, the implementation is simplified.

The ISA extensions (see Table 1) required are similar to the software-loaded TLB found across many RISC architectures (e.g., SPARC, Alpha, MIPS). There are separate load and store instructions that access the metadata using an index into the M-cache. In addition, to fill the MPA (not typically found in the TLB) we use an instruction (LD_MPA) that specifies the virtual address of the physical address for which a tag needs to be set up in the MPA.[2]

[2]Hardware also sets up pointer to the virtual address tags so that invalidations can cleanup entries consistently in both tag arrays (see Section 2.1).

M-Cache Fill Routine()

```
/*X: Virtual address of data */
1. get_entry X,%mcache_index
2. LL X,%mcache_index
3. P = get_permissions(X)
4. LD P,%mcache_entry
5. LD_MPA P,%mcache_index
6. SC %mcache_index,%mcache_entry
7. if failed(SC) goto 1;
```

Figure 3: Pseudocode for inserting a new M-cache entry.

The MPA is used by the hardware to ensure the entry is invalidated if the metadata changes, i.e., when a store occurs anywhere in the system to the MPA address. Typically, the metadata is maintained in the virtual address space of the application. Figure 3 shows the pseudo code for the insert routine: lines 1 — 2 get an entry from the M-cache and set up the virtual address of the data to be protected, lines 3 — 5 set up the permissions metadata in the corresponding entry, and the final two instructions 6 — 7 try to update the metadata in the M-cache entry. An exception event between 1 — 6 (e.g., context switch) will cause line 7 to fail which restarts the routine.

2.4 Changing Permissions

The permissions metadata structure is in virtual memory space and this allows software to directly access and modify it. When changes to the access permissions (metadata) are made, we need to ensure that subsequent accesses to the data locations check the new permissions metadata. For example, assume there are two threads T1 and T2 on processors P1 and P2 that have write permissions on location A. If T1 decides to downgrade permissions to read-only, we need to ensure that (1) the old metadata entry in P2's M-cache is invalidated and (2) since P2 could have cached a copy of A in its L1 before the permissions changed, this copy is also invalidated. Both actions are necessary to ensure that P2 obtains new permissions on the next access. We deal with these in order.

Shooting down M-cache entries

This operation is simplified by the MPA field in the M-cache, which is used by hardware to ensure coherence of the cached metadata. These set of tags snoop on coherence events and any metadata updates result in invalidation of the corresponding M-cache entry. Hence all software has to do is update the metadata and the resulting coherence operations triggered will clean up all M-cache entries. The most straightforward option uses the physical address of the metadata as the MPA tag for the M-cache entry, but in essence software can set up any address. It is even valid and useful to have multiple M-cache entries managed by the same physical address. For example, locations X and Y could each have an entry in the M-cache where the VA is tagged with the page addresses of X and Y while both their corresponding MPA entries could be tagged with MPA P. When P is written, a lookup in the MPA array would match two entries each with a back pointer to the corresponding VA entries of X and Y, which can then be invalidated — an efficient bulk invalidation scheme. Most previously proposed permission lookaside structures (e.g., TLB, Mondrian [24]) typically use interprocessor interrupts and sophisticated algorithms to shootdown the entry [19].

Checks of future accesses

Sentry moves permission checks to the L1 miss path and allows L1 hits to proceed without any intervention. Hence, when permissions are downgraded, the appropriate data blocks need to be evicted from all the L1 caches to ensure future accesses trigger permission checks. To cleanup the blocks from all L1s, software can perform prefetch-exclusives, which will result in invalidation of the cache blocks at remote L1s, and follow this by evicting the cache line from the local L1 (e.g., using PowerPC's dcb-flush instruction). A final issue to consider is that the cleanup races with other concurrent accesses from processors and the system needs to ensure that these accesses get the new permissions. To solve this problem, software must order the permission changes (including cleaning up remote M-cache entries) before the L1 cache cleanup so that subsequent accesses will reload the new permissions.

3. SENTRY PROTECTION MODELS

The protection framework in most previously proposed systems is dependent on hiding the protection metadata from manipulation by user-level applications. For example, the TLB, Mondrian, and Loki [24, 26] are all exclusively managed by low-level operating system software. To utilize the protection framework, every application in the system must cross protection boundaries via well-defined (system call) interfaces and abstractions to convey the application's protection policy to system software.

Our objective is to support low-cost and flexible protection models, with an emphasis on application-controlled intra-process protection. Hence, Sentry supplements the existing process-based protection provided by the TLB. It leaves the process-based protection untouched and permits relocation of the software routines that manage the M-cache to the user level (within each application itself). This eliminates the challenge of porting a new protection framework to the OS and reduces the risk of one application's policy affecting another application. Each application can independently choose whether to use the Sentry framework or not.

3.1 Foundations for Sentry Protection Models

A key concept in realizing protection is the *protection domain* — the context of a thread that determines the access permissions to each data location [10]. Every executing thread at any given instant belongs to exactly one protection domain and multiple threads can belong to the same protection domain. Furthermore, a thread can dynamically transition between different protection domains if the system policy permits it. Sentry uses integer values to identify protection domains. Domain 0 is reserved for the operating system while domain 1 and larger identifiers are used by applications. Within a process, different application domains must carry different identifiers, but domains in different processes may share the same identifier. Sentry is focused on intra-application protection and the M-cache entries are flushed on address space (process) context switches.

There are three fields that allow the hardware to recognize and restrict accesses based on domains: a per-thread `%Thread_Domain` register, a per-entry `Metadata_Domain` field in the M-cache, and a per-entry `Owner_Domain` field in the TLB (all illustrated earlier in Figure 2). `%Thread_Domain` is a new CPU register that identifies the protection domain of the currently executing thread. `Metadata_Domain` is a per-entry field in the M-cache identifying the protection domain that the entry's access permission information applies to. On an M-cache check, the `%Thread_Domain` register and the access address are both used to index into the M-cache. The M-cache entry with matching `Metadata_Domain` and virtual address tag is identified and its access permission information is then checked. The M-cache entries for a particular protection domain can be thought of as a capability list — they specify the data access permissions for a thread running in the domain. The ability to dynamically change a thread's protection domain gives software the flexibility to perform permissions changes over large regions without changing per-entry permissions.

The privilege of filling M-cache entries must be carefully regulated. If the M-cache were allowed to be modified by any domain, then a thread would be able to grant itself arbitrary permissions to any location. We introduce a per-entry `Owner_Domain` field in the TLB, which identifies the domain that "owns" the page corresponding to that entry. Only a thread in the page's owner domain or the exception handler in domain 1 can fill the M-cache for the locations in that page. The hardware enforces this by guaranteeing that an M-cache entry can be filled only when the `%Thread_Domain` register matches the target page's `Owner_Domain` [3] or when the `%Thread_Domain` is 1. Note that ownership is maintained at a coarser page granularity while the access control mechanism is managed at cache line granularity.

Domain 1 serves as an application-level supervisor, with the main thread of execution at the time of process creation being assigned to this domain. Specifically, Domain 1 enjoys the following privileges:

1. *Page Ownership :* Domain 1 controls page (both code and data) ownership; all requests for ownership change must be directed to the operating system via Domain 1.
2. *Thread Domain :* Domain 1 handles the tasks of adding, removing, and changing the domain of a thread during its lifetime.
3. *M-cache updates by non-owner domains :* M-cache exceptions (e.g., no metadata entry) triggered on accesses to non-owner locations (addresses owned by a different domain) are handled by Domain 1.
4. *Cross-Domain Calls :* Domain 1 ensures cross-domain calls (code that is in pages owned by a different domain) can occur only at specific entry points (according to application-specified policies registered with Domain 1).

In the following subsections we describe a few example protection models that can be realized using Sentry. We start from the simple case of one protection domain per process. Even in this degenerate case, we show Sentry's versatility in supporting low-cost watchpoints and protection of memory shared across OS processes. We then present a *compartment* model that can isolate various software modules and improve the safety of an application.

[3] The page table entry for the filled address needs to be in the TLB when filling the M-cache. If needed, we ensure that an M-cache fill instruction (see Table 1) triggers a TLB reload for the filled address.

3.2 One Domain Per Process

In this model, the existing process-based protection domain boundaries are inherited without any further refinement. Sentry's primary benefit is to support flexible cache-line granularity access control. All threads within a process belong to protection domain 1. The domain identifiers 0 and 1 differentiate between operating system and application. Sentry supports two modes of access control. The mode is determined by each page's owner domain (0 or 1) loaded into the TLB's `Owner_Domain` field. In the first mode (`Owner_Domain` is 1), the application threads retain ownership of all the pages, the privileges of filling the M-cache content, and handling permission exceptions. In the second mode (`Owner_Domain` is 0), only the operating system can perform these tasks.

The application-managed model incurs much less overhead than the OS-managed model. For instance, the cost of permission exception handling appears as an unconditional jump in the instruction stream (tens of cycles). In comparison, an OS-level exception incurs the cost of a privilege switch (hundreds of cycles), which requires switching privilege levels and saving registers. The application-managed model is useful for supporting cache-line-grain watchpoints. Reads and writes to specific locations can be trapped by setting appropriate M-cache permissions. The low-cost, cache-line-grain watchpoints can help with detecting various buffer overflow and stack smashing attacks, as well as with debugging code [15,29]. This model has weak protection semantics since any part of the application can modify the M-cache.

In the OS-managed model, low-level system software directly manages the M-cache contents. This allows for a controlled sharing of cache-line granularity regions between processes. For example, in remote procedure calls (RPCs), the argument stack can be mapped between an RPC client and server process with different permissions (currently, a page granularity is used [1], incurring significant space or copy overhead). Sentry can be used to implement a safe kernel-user shared memory region without the need to ensure page alignment and can eliminate expensive memory copies between the operating system and applications.

3.3 Intra-Process Compartments

This model supports multiple protection domains within a single process. A real-world use of this model is the Apache application (see Figure 1) that supports various features (like caching pages fetched from the disk) in modules loaded into the web server's address space. The core set of developers set an interface between independently developed modules; isolating these modules into separate domains and enforcing the interface between them (data and functions) can improve reliability and safety.

In the compartment model, each domain owns a set of data and executable code regions. Threads in a protection domain can set up the permissions, execute code, and access the data owned by the domain. The domain can set up a handler to process M-cache misses and fill the M-cache.

Cross-Domain Data Accesses and Code Executions

Threads in a protection domain may need to access data that is not owned by the domain and we call these *cross-domain data accesses*. For instance, a web server module accesses some request data structure from the core application in order to apply output filters. Threads in a domain may also want to call functions that are not owned by the domain and we call these *cross-domain calls*. Individual domains may set up specific permissions for authorizing non-owner accesses and they must be carefully checked for safety.

One of our key design objectives is to minimize the role of the operating system and allow much of the management tasks to be performed directly by the application. This affords the most flexibility in terms of application-specific protection policies. It also incurs low management cost, since it keeps application-specific policies out of critical operating system components. Domain 1 in each process is designated as the user-level supervisor. Domain 1 is responsible for coordinating cross-domain data accesses and code invocation. It is implicitly given the ownership role for all memory in the process address space that the OS does not care about, and has the rights to fill M-cache content and handle M-cache permission exceptions. Domain 1 can also dynamically change the domain (anything other than domain 0) of a running thread by modifying the `%Thread_Domain` register. Given its privileges, domain 1 guards its own data and code against unauthorized accesses by owning those pages.

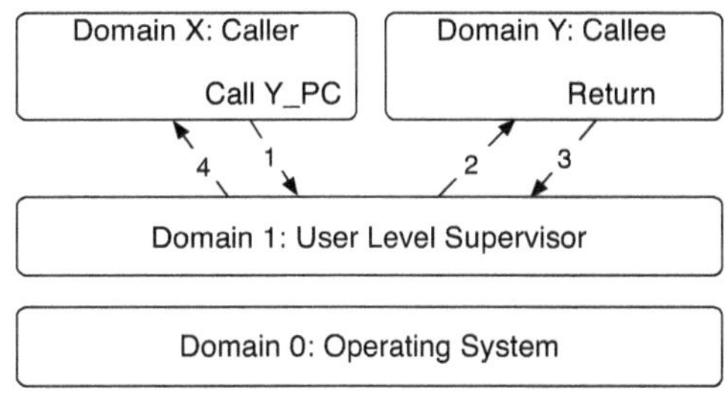

Steps of a cross-domain call when a thread in domain X invokes a function whose code is owned by domain Y:

1. Domain X tries to jump into a code region that it does not own. The hardware intercepts the call by recognizing a mismatch between the `%Thread_Domain` register and the `Owner_Domain` field in the TLB entry associated with the target instruction. The target instruction `Y_PC` is saved. The hardware then effects an exception into the `%Domain1_Handler` while simultaneously changing the current domain to domain 1.

2. If the target address has been registered as a cross-domain call, the domain 1 exception handler marshals the arguments on the stack, grants the appropriate data access permissions to the callee domain, and invokes the function through a special `switch_call` instruction. The instruction jumps into `Y_PC` and changes the protection domain context (`%Thread_Domain`) to Y.

3. On return, the function tries to jump back to the caller. Since the return target is owned by domain X, an exception is triggered into domain 1 and the return target address is saved.

4. Domain 1 finally executes `switch_call` back to X.

Figure 4: Cross-domain call execution flow.

Non-owner data accesses that trigger M-cache miss exceptions (i.e., no M-cache entry) need to be handled carefully. The thread itself lacks the privilege to set up the metadata. Hence, these operations are handled by domain 1. The address to this exception handler in domain 1 is located in a CPU register (`%Domain1_Handler`), which is managed exclusively by domain 1. On a non-owner M-cache exception, hardware changes the domain context (i.e., %Thread_Domain register) to domain 1 and traps to the `%Domain1_Handler`. Based on application specific policies, the domain 1 exception handler can let the non-owner data access progress (finish or raise an exception) by filling the appropriate M-cache entry. When the miss handler has finished its operations, domain 1 reverts back to the original domain context to continue execution. Subsequent accesses to the same location (from the non-owner domain) can proceed without interruption.

Cross-domain calls are registered with domain 1. A cross-domain call and its return are redirected and managed by domain 1 in a four-step process illustrated in Figure 4. The indirection through domain 1 for cross-domain calls does impose a minor performance penalty. Unlike earlier work that speeds up cross-address space calls by using shared-memory segments [1], our cross-domain call remains in the same address space and the complete execution flow utilizes the same stack. This allows us to achieve efficiencies comparable to a function call.

4. EVALUATIONS

Our base hardware is a 16-core chip (1 GHz clock frequency), which includes private L1 instruction and data write-back caches (32KB, 4-way, 1 cycle) and a banked, shared L2 (8MB, 8-way, 30 cycle), with a memory latency of 300 cycles. The cores are connected to each other using a 4×4 mesh network (3 cycle link latency, 64 byte links). The L2 is organized on one side of this mesh and the cores interface with the 16-banked L2 over a 4×16 crossbar switch. The L1s are kept coherent with the L2 using a MESI directory protocol. This coherence protocol is based on the SGI ORIGIN 3000 3-hop scheme with silent evictions. Our infrastructure is based on the full-system GEMS-Simics framework. We faithfully emulate the Sentry hardware/software interface and model the latency penalty of the software handlers from within the simulator. We simulate all memory references made by the handler and use instruction counts to estimate the latency of non-memory instructions.

We begin by evaluating the M-cache implementation (area and latency) cost and basic management costs (software and hardware). We then evaluate the use of Sentry for three applications: Apache, remote procedure call (RPC), and memory debugging. Via the Apache and RPC benchmarks, we demonstrate the flexibility, usability, and performance efficiency of utilizing Sentry to implement application-level protection. In evaluating Sentry for debugging, we compare its performance overheads against MemTracker [21] and Mondrian [24].

4.1 M-cache Implementation

Area, Latency, and Energy

The M-cache area implications are a function of its size and organization. All known cache and TLB optimizations apply (banking, associativity, etc.). Most importantly, the M-cache intercepts only L1 misses, thereby reducing its impact on the processor critical path. While dual-tagged, each tag array is single-ported. The virtual tag is accessed only from the processor side (for checking permissions and filling M-cache entries) and the MPA is accessed only from the network side (for snoop-based coherence). We used CACTI 6 [13] to estimate cycle time for a 256-entry M-cache (4KB, 4 way, 16 bytes per entry) that provides good coverage (fine-grain permissions for a 1MB working set). We estimate that in 65 nm high-performance technology (ITRS HP), the M-cache can be indexed within 0.5ns (1 processor cycle using our parameters). Furthermore, since the M-cache is located outside the processor core and is accessed in parallel with a long latency L1 miss we can trade latency for energy benefits. If we use the low power transistor technology in CACTI (ITRS LOP) , the access latency increases by 2-3$\times$ (to $\sim$3 cycles) compared to high-performance transistor technology (ITRS HP). There is a significant energy reduction: an M-cache with ITRS LOP consumes 1% of the leakage power and

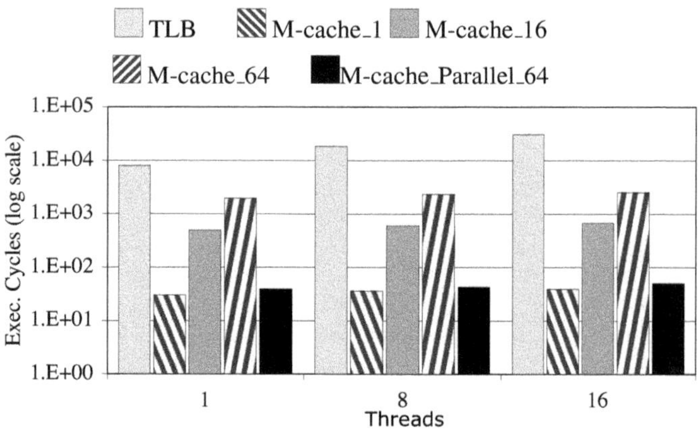

Figure 5: TLB vs. M-cache. M-cache_N measures execution cycles for changing permissions on N cache lines. L1 handles stores in order. In M-cache_Parallel_64, the L1 can sustain 64 concurrent misses.

33% of the dynamic access power of an M-cache employing ITRS HP. On average (geometric mean), across the PARSEC, SPLASH2, and Apache workloads, the M-cache with ITRS LOP consumes 0.029nJ, 0.037nJ, and 0.27nJ respectively per operation; in comparison a TLB with the same number of entries consumes 3nJ.

Operation cost

There are two main management costs associated with any hardware protection mechanism: (1) the cost of switching to the privilege level that can manipulate it and (2) the cost of maintaining the coherence of the cached copies of the metadata. The M-cache can be managed entirely at user level. In addition, the metadata physical address (MPA) tag allows the M-cache to exploit coherence to propagate metadata invalidations to remote processors. This simplifies the software protocol required to manage the M-cache and improves performance compared to existing protection mechanisms that use the interprocessor interrupt mechanism.

We compare the cost of changing the metadata associated with the M-cache against the cost of manipulating page-attribute protection bits in the TLB. We set up a microbenchmark that creates K threads (varied from 1—16) on the machine, and every 10,000 instructions a random thread is picked to make permission changes. To test the TLB, we change permissions for a page, and to test the M-cache we change permissions for N cache lines within a page. Overall, modifying permissions with the M-cache is 10—100$\times$ faster than TLB shootdowns (see Figure 5). The dominant cost with the M-cache is that of purging the data from the L1 caches (see Section 2.4). The routine needs to prefetch the data cache blocks in exclusive mode in order to invalidate all L1s, and this typically results in coherence misses. In our design, each L1 cache allows only one outstanding miss and hence the invalidation of each cache line directly appears on the critical path. The latency of the permission change is directly proportional to the number of cache blocks that are invalidated (M-cache_1, M-cache_16 and M-cache_64 bars). We also evaluate performance when 64 outstanding L1 prefetches are allowed (M-cache_Parallel_64) and show that overlapping the latency of multiple misses is sufficient to significantly reduce permission change cost.

Teller et al. [19] discuss hardware support to keep TLBs coherent and recently, concurrent with our work, UNITD [16] explored the performance benefits of coherent TLBs. Both these works mainly seek to reduce the overheads of conventional OS TLB management routines while Sentry employs coherence to enable user-level software routines to manage the M-cache.

4.2 Compartmentalizing Apache

In this section, we use Sentry's intra-process compartment protection model (see Section 3.3) to enforce a safety contract between a web server (Apache) and its modules. Apache includes support for a standard interface to aid module development; the "Apache Portable Runtime" (APR) [31] exports many services including support for memory management, access to Apache's core data structures (e.g., file stream), and access to intercept fields in the web request. Apache's modules are typically run in the same address space as the core web server in the interest of efficiency and the desire to maintain a familiar programming model (conventional procedure calls between Apache and the module). A module therefore has uninhibited access to the web server's data structures, resulting in the system's safety relying on the module developers' discipline.

Our goal is to (1) isolate each module's code and data in a separate domain and ensure that the APR is enforced. This protects the web server's data and ensure that modules can access the web server's data only through the exported routines; and (2) achieve this isolation with simple annotations in the source code without requiring any source revisions. While the definition of a module may be abstract, here we use the term to refer to the collection of code that the developers included to extend the functionality of the web server. To enable protection, Sentry annotates the source to perform the following tasks: (1) specify the ownership (domain) of code and data regions, (2) assign permissions to the various data regions for the different domains, and (3) assign domains to pre-forked threads that wait for requests. To simplify our evaluation, we set up the core Apache code (all folders other than module/) to directly execute in domain 1 and emulate all the actions required by domain 1 (those that would be provided in the form of a library) for cross-domain calls from within the simulator. The only modifications required to Apache's source code were the instructions that set up the domains and permissions.

The modules we compartmentalized are `mod_cache` and `mod_mem_cache`, which work in concert to provide a caching engine that stores pages in memory that were previously fetched from disk. "mod_cache" consists of two parts: (1) module-Apache interface (`mod_cache.c`) and (2) the cache implementation (`cache_cache.c[.h]`,`cache_hash.c[.h]`, and `cache_pqueue.c[.h]`). "mod_cache" also needs to interface with a storage engine, for which we use `mod_mem_cache` (`cache_storage.c`, `mod_mem_cache.c`). We compiled the modules into the core web server and compartmentalized the storage engine (mod_mem_cache) into domain 2 and the cache engine (mod_cache) into domain 3, respectively.

Compartmentalizing Code

Our primary goal was to enforce the APR interface and ensure that module domains cannot call into non-APR functions. First, we compiled in the modules and did a static object code analysis to determine the module boundaries. We then added routines to the core Apache web server that (1) registered the APR code regions as owned by Apache and set up read-write permissions for Apache (domain 1) and read-only permissions for the modules and (2) declared the individual module code regions as owned by the appropriate domains. The modules expose only a subset of the functions to other modules (e.g., the storage module exports the `cache_create_entity()` to the cache module as read-only while it hides the internal `cleanup_cache_mem`, which is used for internal memory management). The module's entire code is accessible to the Apache web server. Finally, the pre-forked worker threads are started in domain 1. When the threads call into a module's routines, the exception handler in domain 1 transitions the thread to the appropriate domain if the call is made to the module's exported APR. Non-APR calls from the module would be caught by Sentry.

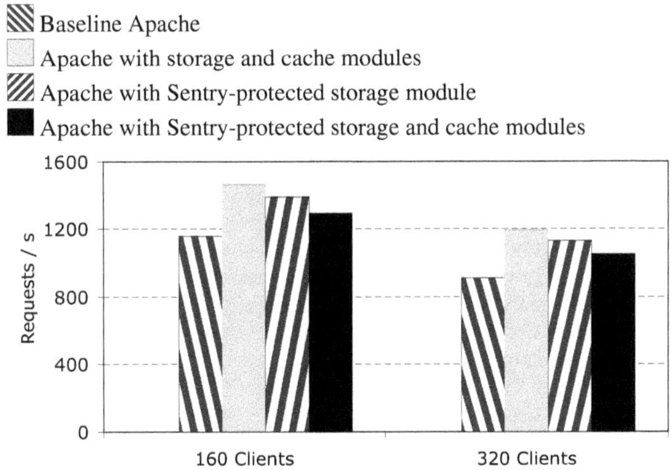

Figure 6: Performance of Sentry-protected Apache with compartmentalized modules.

Since memory ownership is assigned at the page granularity, we have to ensure that code from two different modules or the core web server are not linked into the same page. While current compilers do not provide explicit support for page alignment, it is fortunate that our compiler (gcc) allows code generated from an individual source file to remain contiguous in the linked binary. Given the contiguity of each module's code segment, we added appropriate padding in the form of no-ops (`asm volatile nops`) to the end of the source (.h and .c files) to page align each module.

Compartmentalizing Data

Assigning ownership to data regions proved to be a simpler task. The core web server and modules all use the APR provided memory allocator (`srclib/apr/memory/unix/apr_pools.c`). With this allocator, it was possible to set up different pools of memory regions and request allocation from a specific pool. We specified separate pools for each of the domains: Apache web server (domain 1), mod_mem_cache module (domain 2), and mod_cache module (domain 3). We then assigned ownership of the pool to the domain that it served. The allocator itself is part of the APR interface (domain 1). The permissions rules we set up were (1) Apache's core (domain 1) can read/write all memory in the program, (2) each module can read/write any memory in their pool, and (3) a module has read-only access to some specific variables exported by other external modules — this is where fine-grain permission assignment was useful. In some cases, a variable exported by a module (read-only for remote domains) was located in the same page as a local variable (no permissions). For example, the cache object in the storage engine (mem_cache_object) contained two different sets of fields, those that described the page being cached (e.g., html headers) and those that described the actual storage (e.g., position in the cache). The former needs to be readable from the cache engine, while the latter should be inaccessible.

Performance Results

We now estimate the overheads of compartmentalizing the modules in Apache. In this experiment, we pre-compiled modules into the core kernel, disabled logging, and used POSIX mutexes for synchronization. The specific configuration we used is *-with-mpm=worker -enable-proxy -disable-logio -enable-cgi -enable-*

cgid -enable-suexec –enable-cache. We configured the Surge client for two different loads: 10 or 20 threads per processor (total of 160 or 320 threads) and set the think time to 0ms. Our total webpage database size was 1GB with the file sizes following a Zipf distribution (maximum file size of 10 MB). We warmed up the software data structures (e.g., OS buffer cache) for 50,000 requests and measured performance for 10,000 requests. Sentry permits incremental adoption of compartment-based protection. In our experiments we protect apache's modules in two stages: we first moved `mod_mem_cache` into a separate domain leaving `mod_cache` within domain 1 (along with the core webserver). Subsequently, we moved both `mod_mem_cache` and `mod_cache` out of domain 1, each into a separate domain.

Figure 6 shows relative performance. Sentry protection imposes an overhead of $\simeq$13% when compartmentalizing both `mod_cache` and `mod_mem_cache` and a $\simeq$6% when compartmentalizing just the `mod_mem_cache`. The primary overheads with Sentry are the execution of the handlers required to set up data permissions in the M-cache and the indirection through domain 1 needed for cross-domain calls. Approximately 20% of the functions invoked by the module are APR routines, which involve a domain crossing. We believe the overhead is acceptable given the safety guarantees and the level of programmer effort needed.

Process-based Protection vs. Sentry

To evaluate the protection schemes afforded by OS process-based protection, we develop mod_case (a module that changes the case of ASCII characters in the webpage) using process-based protection and compare it against Sentry's compartment model. To employ process-based protection we needed to make significant changes to the programming model and reorganize the code and data. We had to implement a mod_case specific shim (implemented as an Apache module) that communicates with mod_case through IPC (inter-process communication), requiring a shared-memory segment. All interaction between Apache and mod_case passes through the shim, which converts the function calls between Apache and mod_case into IPC. Although Apache's APR helps with setting up shared-memory segments between the shim and the mod_case process, the shim and the module still needed to write explicit memory routines (for each interface function) to copy from and to the shared argument passing region. The conversion of even this simple module to use IPC was frustrated by the inability to pass data pointers directly between the processes and the need to use a specific interface between the shim and the module itself. As Figure 7 shows, the process-based protection adds significant overhead (33%) compared to Sentry (7%). To summarize, we believe the programming rigidity, need to customize the interface for individual modules, and performance overheads are major barriers to adoption of process-based protection.

We briefly compare Sentry's cross domain calls against existing IPC mechanisms. Despite considerable work to reduce the cost of IPC [1, 8, 12], it is still 10^3 slower than an intra-process function call. In contrast, Sentry focuses on functions calls between protection domains established within a process. They have lower overheads since they share the OS process context and crossing domains does not involve address-space switches. The indirection through the user-level supervisor domain 1 adds 2 call instructions (to jump from caller→ to domain 1 and then into callee) and 9 instructions to align the parameters to a cache line boundary and set appropriate permissions to the stack for the callee domain (i.e., permissions to access only the parameters and its own activation records). The overhead at runtime varies between 20 and 30 cycles (compared to 5 cycles required for a typical function call).

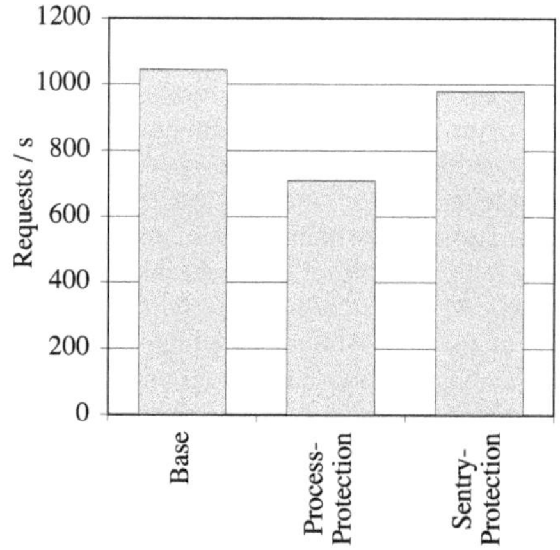

Figure 7: Comparing process-based protection with Sentry. Base: Apache with mod_case.

4.3 Lightweight Remote Procedure Call

RPC is a form of inter-process communication where the caller process invokes a handler exported by a callee process. We first describe the scheme used to implement RPC in current OS kernels (e.g., Solaris): (1) The caller copies arguments into a memory buffer and generates a trap into the OS. (2) The OS copies the buffer content into the address space of the callee. It then context switches into the callee. (3) To return, the callee traps into the kernel, which unblocks the caller process. The main overhead is due to the four privilege switches (two from user→kernel space and two from kernel→user space) and the memory copy required. Earlier proposals [1] have optimized RPC by using a shared memory segment (i.e., `shmem()`) to directly pass data between the caller and callee process. The minimum size of the shared memory segment is a page and a copy is still needed from the argument location to the shared page. More recently, Mondrian [24] postulated that word granularity permission and translation can eliminate the argument passing region.

We use the M-cache to provide fine-grain access control of the locations that need to be passed from the the caller to the callee process and eliminate the copying entirely. The caller process must align the arguments to a cache line boundary and request the kernel to map the argument memory region into the callee's address space (requiring a user-kernel and kernel-user crossing). We experiment with a client that makes RPC calls to a server periodically (every 30,000 cycles). The server is passed a 2 KB random alphabet string that it reverses while switching the case of characters. We compare the cost of argument passing using several approaches — Sentry, the implementation in the Solaris RPC library, and an optimized implementation that uses page sharing [1]. Our results indicate that completely eliminating the copying provides a ($\sim$9–10$\times$) speedup compared to the optimized page sharing approach. The unoptimized RPC implementation has 10^3–10^4 $\times$ higher latency.

4.4 Debugger: Sentry-Watcher

We developed Sentry-Watcher, a C library that applications call into for watchpoint support. A watchpoint is usually set by the programmer to monitor a specific region of the memory and when an access occurs to this region, it raises an exception. Sentry-Watcher employs the one-domain per process model and operates in the application mode (permissions metadata and M-cache managed by a library in the application space). It exports a simple interface: `insert_watchpoint()`, `delete_watchpoint()`, and `set_handler()`, with which the programmer can specify the range to be monitored, type of accesses to check, and the handler to trigger.

Apart from fine granularity watchpoints, there are three additional benefits with Sentry-Watcher: (1) it supports flexible thread-specific monitoring, allowing different threads to set up different permissions to the same location [4], (2) it supports multi-threaded code efficiently since the hardware watchlist can be propagated in a consistent manner across multiple processors at low overhead (also supported by MemTracker [21]), and (3) it effectively virtualizes the watchpoint metadata and allows an unbounded number of watchpoints.

Benchmark	Mallocs/1s	Heap Size	Heap Access %	Bug Type
BC	810K	60KB	75%	BO
Ncom	2	8B	0.6%	SS
Gzip	0	0	0%	BO,IV
GO	10	294B	1.9%	BO
Man	350K	210KB	89%	BO,SS
Poly	890	11KB	27%	BO
Squid	178K	900KB	99.5%	ML

B-Bytes, KB-Kilobytes, MB-Megabytes
BO-Buffer Overflow SS-Stack Smash, ML-Memory Leak, IV-Invariant Violation. Squid is multi-threaded.

Table 2: Application Characteristics

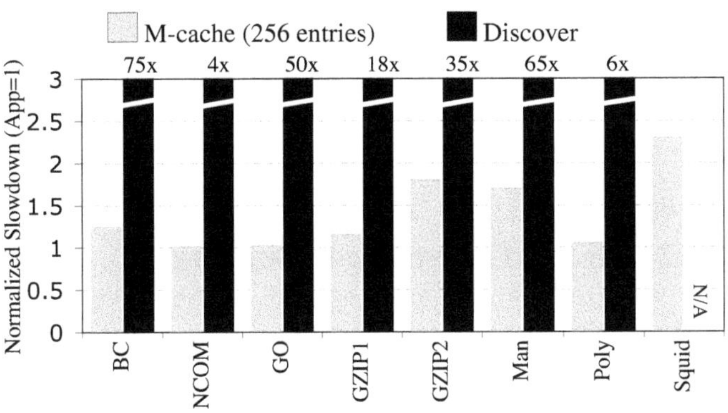

Figure 8: Sentry-Watcher vs. Binary instrumentation. N/A - Discover is not compatible with multi-threaded code. Gzip1 detects Buffer-Overflow bugs. Gzip2 detects memory leak, buffer overflow, and stack smash bugs.

Debugging Examples

Generic unbounded watching of memory can help widen the scope of debugging. Here, we use the system to detect four types of bugs: (1) Buffer Overflow — this occurs when a process accesses data beyond the allocated region. To detect it we pad all heap buffers with an additional cache line and watch the padded region. (2) Stack Smashing — A specific case of buffer overflow where the overflow occurs on a stack variable and manages to modify the return address; we watch the return addresses on the stack. Dummy arguments need to be passed to the functions to set up the appropriate padding and eliminate false positives. (3) Memory Leak — We monitor all heap allocated objects and update a per-location timestamp on every access. Any location with a sufficiently old access timestamp is classified as a potential memory leak. (4) Invariant Violation—Monitor application-specific variables and check specified assertions. We demonstrate the prototype on the benchmark suite provided with iWatcher [29] — Table 2 describes the benchmark properties. We compare the performance of Sentry-Watcher against Discover (a SPARC binary instrumentation tool [32]). Sentry-Watcher is evaluated on our simulator. Discover is set up on the Sun T1000. Compared to the binary instrumentation technique, Sentry-Watcher provides 6–75× speedup. Sentry still incurs noticeable overhead compared to the original applications—varying between 3–50% for most applications. At worst, we encounter up to ~2× overhead on the memory-leak detector experiments, which instrument all heap accesses (see Squid in Figure 8).

[4] Since all threads run in the same domain, this would require a flush of the M-cache on a thread switch.

Comparing with Other Hardware

To understand the performance overheads of Sentry-Watcher, we further compared it against the performance of MemTracker [21], a hardware mechanism tuned for debugging, and Mondrian [24], a fine- and variable-grain flexible protection mechanism placed within the processor pipeline.

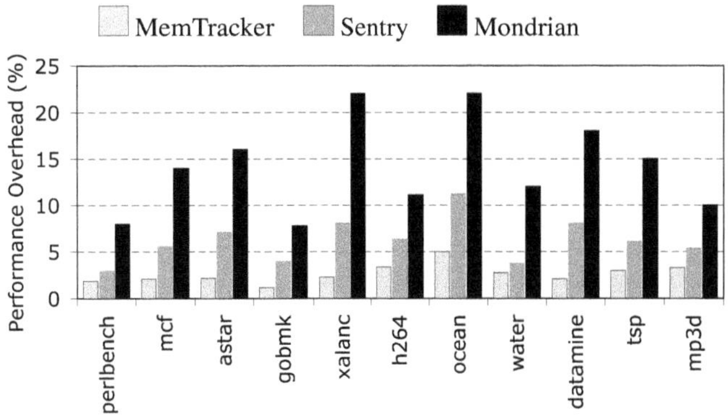

Figure 9: Effect of software handlers and cost of manipulating metadata in the OS.

In MemTracker, a software-programmable hardware controller maintains the metadata, fetching and operating on it in parallel with the data access. To emulate the controller's operations, we assign a 0 cycle penalty for all operations other than the initial setup of the metadata. This is an optimistic assumption since typically metadata misses in MemTracker also add to the overhead. In Mondrian, setting up or changing the metadata require privilege mode switches into and out of the operating system kernel. To estimate the cost of a fast privilege switch, we measure the latency of an optimized low overhead call (e.g., `gethrtimer()`) on three widely available microarchitectures (SPARC, x86, and PowerPC). We observed 280 cycles (SPARC), 312 cycles (x86) and 450 cycles(PowerPC). To emulate Mondrian, we add a penalty of 300 cycles to every permission exception and metadata modification; we assign a 0 cycle penalty to metadata operations. To limit the number of variables, we keep the metadata cache size fixed across all the systems (256 entries). For this comparison, we implemented the debugger tool discussed by the MemTracker paper [21], which checks for heap errors, buffer overflow, and stack smashing. The workloads we use are from the SPECCPU 2006 suite [21]. We also include the SPLASH2 benchmarks to verify that our findings are valid for multi-threaded workloads. Figure 9 shows that the overhead of Sentry-Watcher averages 6.2%, compared to the idealized MemTracker's 2.6% and Mondrian's 14%. Since MemTracker requires a hardware controller to fetch and manipulate the metadata while we leave all such operations in software, we believe that our system is more complexity-effective.

5. RELATED WORK

5.1 Access Control for Data Protection

Access control mechanisms are commonly exploited to protect data against inappropriate accesses from buggy programs or malicious attacks. Most modern processors and operating systems associate a protection domain (or a process) with a separate, linear page-based address space. Multiple threads in a process typically see the same access permission to a location. With the coupling of the protection domain and address space, an inter-domain communication requires operating system intervention and pointer swizzling [23]. Furthermore, domains are assigned at process creation and persist for a process' lifetime. OS processes are widely used in fault isolation applications to sandbox software components [25]. Unfortunately, processes also impose complete isolation between sandboxes and the programmer has to use custom library interfaces to enable data sharing.

Efforts were made to separate protection from the address space using a protection lookaside buffer [9] and page tagging labels and protection identifiers (in HP's PA-RISC [22]). These designs are confined to a page or larger granularity and cannot provide the fine granularity of control over protection needed by current modular software. While x86 segmentation hardware [4] allows variable granularity, the number of segment registers available is small. Moreover, the PA-RISC and x86 hardware hardcode the relationship among domains. Sentry is highly flexible and allows each application to choose its protection model independently.

Several approaches specifically target protection within the operating system but they lack the flexibility to support application-level protection. For instance, SPIN takes advantage of type-safe languages in constructing safe OS extensions [2]. The required use of certain type-safe languages can restrict general application development. As another example, Nooks uses lightweight processes and page protection to guard the kernel against device driver bugs [18]. Unfortunately, when data is shared between domains, these schemes require the programmer to use custom wrapper libraries to enable the protection framework to capture and marshal the accesses.

Capability systems [3,5,11,17] augment object reference pointers to include information on access control. The capabilities shared between threads are marshaled by the OS and can support generalized protection models. Typical capability implementations change the layout of memory and fatten pointers. Software developers need to be aware of the modified layout and typically need code rewrites, which lessens their appeal. More importantly, the relatively large management cost for a capability (e.g., when revoking access rights) makes it ill-suited to protecting fine-grain data elements. Typically, capability-protected objects are external resources such as files, or memory segments at large granularity.

Recently, Mondrian [24] decoupled protection from a conventional paging framework and implemented it using segments. An application's address space is described by a collection of variable-sized segments, each capable of supporting word granularity. This flexibility comes at the cost of additional hardware and operating system modifications. This work replaces the existing protection framework (TLB) with a new permissions-lookaside-buffer (PLB) that checks all accesses in the pipeline and needs add-ons (e.g., sidecar registers) to reduce the performance overheads. Furthermore, it introduces new layers in the operating system to implement all protection (intra-process and inter-process) based on the PLB approach. This requires every application to communicate its policy to the low-level supervisor.

Loki [26] adopted a different tagging strategy, choosing to tag physical memory with labels that further map to a set of permission rules. Loki allows system software to translate application security policies into memory tags. Threads must have the corresponding entry in the permissions cache in order to be granted access permission. If the threads need to be segregated into separate domains, then this would require software support to convert inter-thread function calls into cross-domain call gates. Permission cache modifications must be performed within the operating system. Permission revocation in the case of page swapping would require a sweep of all process/thread's permissions caches.

Our Approach

While we share the goals of Mondrian and Loki to allow more flexible protection models, Sentry employs an auxiliary protection architecture that supplements existing mechanisms on commodity platforms. Specifically, Sentry's hardware is implemented entirely outside the processor core, is subordinate to the existing TLB mechanism, and intercepts only L1 misses. Sentry uses coherence states to implicitly verify all L1 hits, which saves the energy and performance overhead of checking the metadata for a large fraction of the accesses. Further, it also maintains coherence of the protection metadata across multiple processors, simplifying software management (no need for interprocessor interrupts to ensure consistency of the metadata). Finally, no changes are made to the existing process-based protection and the intra-process protection models may be implemented at the user level. Compared to Mondrian and Loki, Sentry reduces the changes required to the core hardware and operating system software. It enables flexible, low-cost protection within individual applications. Finally, it incurs space or time overhead only when auxiliary intra-application protection is needed.

5.2 Access Control for Debugging

When used for debugging applications, the space and performance overheads are directly proportional to the number of locations being watched. Prior proposals mainly focus on reducing the overhead of intercepting memory operations and manipulating some debugger-specific metadata. This capability is sufficient to detect a variety of memory bugs [14].

Hardware proposals seek to eliminate the performance overheads of software-based debugging by intercepting and checking accesses in a transparent manner. A common feature of all these works is that they intercept all loads and stores in the processor pipeline. They also share the metadata among different threads, which makes it difficult to set up thread-specific access control. The major differences among these systems is the hardware state bits used to track the watchpoint metadata: bloom filters [20], additional cache-tag bits [30], ECC bits [15,29], or separate lookaside structures [21]; which have varying levels of false positives and coverage characteristics. They also vary in whether the hardware semantics are hardcoded for a specific tool [28] or support a general-purpose state machine [21].

Our Approach

The M-cache mechanism proposed in this paper is a more complexity-effective implementation since it resides entirely outside the processor core and intercepts only L1 cache misses. It uses cache coherence to enable low-cost maintenance of the metadata scattered across multiple processors (without requiring hardware controllers to coordinate data and metadata movement [21]). Furthermore, it supports thread-specific monitoring, allowing different threads to have different permissions to the same location.

6. CONCLUSIONS

Light-weight and flexible data protection is highly desirable for the improved reliability and debugging support of modular software. Sentry provides a protection framework using virtual memory tagging that is completely subordinate to the existing OS-TLB framework. The main hardware component, the metadata cache (M-cache), implements permission checks entirely outside the processor core. It intervenes only on L1 misses, transparently reusing the L1 coherence states to enforce permissions on hits. Compared to previously proposed protection hardware that intercepts all accesses in the pipeline, the M-cache is a complexity-effective design that provides significant energy reduction (consuming 1—10% of the energy of the in-core approach).

Sentry realizes intra-application protection models with predominantly user-level software, requires very little OS intervention, and makes no changes to process-based protection. We developed an intra-application compartment protection model and used it to isolate the modules of a popular web server application (Apache), thereby protecting the core web server from buggy modules. Our evaluation demonstrated that Apache's module interface can be enforced at low overhead ($\simeq$13%), with few application annotations, and in an incremental fashion. Finally, the user-level management of Sentry also supports low-overhead, fine-grain watchpoints. We developed a memory debugger to demonstrate that Sentry's flexibility and overheads are comparable to previously proposed hardware-based debuggers. We show that user-level management (as opposed to OS-level management) is an important design choice to limit the overheads in such applications.

7. REFERENCES

[1] B. N. Bershad, T. E. Anderson, E. D. Lazowska, and H. M. Levy. Lightweight Remote Procedure Call. *ACM Trans. on Computer Systems*, 8(1):37-55, Feb. 1990. Originally presented at the *12th ACM Symp. on Operating Systems Principles*, Dec. 1989.

[2] B. N. Bershad, S. Savage, P. Pardyak, E. . Sirer, M. Fiuczynski, D. Becker, S. Eggers, and C. Chambers. Extensibility, Safety and Performance in the SPIN Operating System. In *Proc. of the 15th ACM Symp. on Operating Systems Principles*, Dec. 1995.

[3] N. P. Carter, S. W. Keckler, and W. J. Dally. Hardware Support for Fast Capability-Based Addressing. In *Proc. of the 6th Intl. Conf. on Architectural Support for Programming Languages and Operating Systems*, Oct. 1994.

[4] T. Chiueh, G. Venkitachalam, and P. Pradhan. Integrating Segmentation and Paging Protection for Safe, Efficient and Transparent Software Extensions. In *Proc. of the 17th ACM Symp. on Operating Systems Principles*, Dec. 1999.

[5] S. Colley, G. Cox, K. Lai, J. Rattner, and R. Swanson. The Object-Based Architecture of the Intel 432. In *Proc. of the IEEE COMPCON Spring '81*, Feb. 1981.

[6] U. Erlingsson, M. Abadi, M. Vrable, M. Budiu, and G. Necula. XFI: software guards for system address spaces. In *Proc. of the 7th Symp. on Operating Systems Design and Implementation*, 2006.

[7] J. R. Goodman. Coherency for Multiprocessor Virtual Address Caches. In *Proc. of the 2nd Intl. Conf. on Architectural Support for Programming Languages and Operating Systems*, Oct. 1987.

[8] F. Kaashoek, D. Engler, G. Ganger, H. Briceno, R. Hunt, D. Mazières, T. Pinckney, R. Grimm, and K. Mackenzie. Application Performance and Flexibility on Exokernel Systems. In *Proc. of the 16th ACM Symp. on Operating Systems Principles*, Oct. 1997.

[9] E. J. Koldinger, J. S. Chase, and S. J. Eggers. Architectural Support for Single Address Space Operating Systems. In *Proc. of the 5th Intl. Conf. on Architectural Support for Programming Languages and Operating Systems*, Oct. 1992.

[10] B. W. Lampson. Protection. In *Proc. of the 5th Princeton Symp. on Information Sciences and Systems*, pages 437-443, Mar. 1971. Reprinted in *ACM SIGOPS Operating Systems Review 8*:1 (Jan. 1974), pp. 18-24.

[11] H. M. Levy. *Capability-Based Computer Systems*. Digital Press, Bedford, MA, 1984.

[12] J. Liedtke. Improving IPC by Kernel Design. In *Proc. of the 14th ACM Symp. on Operating Systems Principles*, Dec. 1993.

[13] N. Muralimanohar, R. Balasubramonian, and N. Jouppi. Optimizing NUCA Organizations and Wiring Alternatives for Large Caches With CACTI 6.0. In *Proc. of the 40th Intl. Symp. on Microarchitecture*, Dec. 2007.

[14] N. Nethercote and J. Seward. Valgrind: A Framework for Heavyweight Dynamic Binary Instrumentation. In *Proc. of the SIGPLAN 2007 Conf. on Programming Language Design and Implementation*, June 2007.

[15] F. Qin, S. Lu, and Y. Zhou. SafeMem: Exploiting ECC-Memory for Detecting Memory Leaks and Memory Corruption During Production Runs. In *Proc. of the 10th Intl. Symp. on High Performance Computer Architecture*, Feb. 2005.

[16] B. F. Romanescu, A. R. Lebeck, D. J. Sorin, and A. Bracy. UNified Instruction/Translation/Data (UNITD) Coherence: One Protocol to Rule Them All. In *Proc. of the 16th Intl. Symp. on High Performance Computer Architecture*, Jan. 2010.

[17] J. S. Shapiro, J. M. Smith, and D. J. Farber. EROS: a Fast Capability System. In *Proc. of the 17th ACM Symp. on Operating Systems Principles*, Charleston, SC, Dec. 1999.

[18] M. M. Swift, B. N. Bershad, and H. M. Levy. Improving the Reliability of Commodity Operating Systems. In *Proc. of the 19th ACM Symp. on Operating Systems Principles*, Oct. 2003.

[19] P. J. Teller, R. Kenner, and M. Snir. TLB Consistency on Highly-Parallel Shared-Memory Multiprocessors. In *Proc. of the 21st Hawaii Intl. Conf. on System Sciences*, Jan. 1988.

[20] J. Tuck, W. Ahn, L. Ceze, and J. Torrellas. SoftSig: software-exposed hardware signatures for code analysis and optimization. In *Proc. of the 13th Intl. Conf. on Architectural Support for Programming Languages and Operating Systems*, Mar. 2008.

[21] G. Venkataramani, B. Roemer, Y. Solihin, and M. Prvulovic. MemTracker: Efficient and Programmable support for Memory Access Monitoring and Debugging. In *Proc. of the 13th Intl. Symp. on High Performance Computer Architecture*, Feb. 2007.

[22] J. Wilkes and B. Sears. A Comparison of Protection Lookaside Buffers and the PA-RISC Protection Architecture. HLP-92-55, Hewlett Packard Laboratories, Mar. 1992.

[23] P. R. Wilson. Pointer Swizzling at Page Fault Time: Efficiently and Compatibly Supporting Huge Address Spaces on Standard Hardware. In *Proc. of the Intl. Workshop on Object Orientation in Operating Systems*, Sept. 1992.

[24] E. Witchel, J. Cates, and K. Asanović. Mondrian Memory Protection. In *Proc. of the 10th Intl. Conf. on Architectural Support for Programming Languages and Operating Systems*, Oct. 2002.

[25] B. Yee, D. Sehr, G. Dardyk, J. B. Chen, R. Muth, T. Ormandy, S. Okasaka, N. Narula, and N. Fullagar. Native Client: A Sandbox for Portable, Untrusted x86 Native Code. In *IEEE Symposium on Security and Privacy*, May 2009.

[26] N. Zeldovich, H. Kannan, M. Dalton, and C. Kozyrakis. Hardware Enforcement of Application Security Policies. In *Proc. of the 8th Symp. on Operating Systems Design and Implementation*, Dec. 2008.

[27] Q. Zhao, R. M. Rabbah, S. P. Amarasinghe, L. Rudolph, and W.-F. Wong. How to Do a Million Watchpoints: Efficient Debugging Using Dynamic Instrumentation. In *Springer-Verlag*, 2008.

[28] P. Zhou, W. Liu, F. Long, S. Lu, F. Qin, Y. Zhou, S. Midkiff, and J. Torrellas. AccMon: Automatically Detecting Memory-Related Bugs via Program Counter-based Invariants. In *Proc. of the 37th Intl. Symp. on Microarchitecture*, Dec. 2004.

[29] P. Zhou, F. Qin, W. Liu, Y. Zhou, and J. Torrellas. iWatcher: Efficient Architecture Support for Software Debugging. In *Proc. of the 31st Intl. Symp. on Computer Architecture*, June 2004.

[30] UFO: A General-Purpose User-Mode Memory Protection Technique for Application Use UIUCDCS-R-2007-2808, Jan 2007.

[31] Apache Project. In *http://Apr.apache.org/*.

[32] Cool Tools. In *http://cooltools.sunsource.net/*.

Elastic Cooperative Caching: An Autonomous Dynamically Adaptive Memory Hierarchy for Chip Multiprocessors

Enric Herrero[1] eherrero@ac.upc.edu

José González[2] pepe.gonzalez@intel.com

Ramon Canal[1] rcanal@ac.upc.edu

[1]Dept. d'Arquitectura de Computadors, Universitat Politècnica de Catalunya

[2]Larrabee Architecture Group, Intel Barcelona

ABSTRACT

Next generation tiled microarchitectures are going to be limited by off-chip misses and by on-chip network usage. Furthermore, these platforms will run an heterogeneous mix of applications with very different memory needs, leading to significant optimization opportunities. Existing adaptive memory hierarchies use either centralized structures that limit the scalability or software based resource allocation that increases programming complexity.

We propose Elastic Cooperative Caching, a dynamic and scalable memory hierarchy that adapts automatically and autonomously to application behavior for each node. Our configuration uses elastic shared/private caches with fully autonomous and distributed repartitioning units for better scalability. Furthermore, we have extended our elastic configuration with an Adaptive Spilling mechanism to use the shared cache space only when it can produce a performance improvement. Elastic caches allow both the creation of big local private caches for threads with high reuse of private data and the creation of big shared spaces from unused caches. Local data allocation in private regions allows to reduce network usage and efficient cache partitioning allows to reduce off-chip misses.

The proposed scheme outperforms previous proposals by a minimum of 12% (on average across the benchmarks) and reduces the number of offchip misses by 16%. Plus, the dynamic and autonomous management of cache resources avoids the reallocation of cache blocks without reuse which results in an increase in energy efficiency of 24%.

Categories and Subject Descriptors: B.3.2 [Memory Structures]: Design Styles-*Cache memories*; C.1.4 [Processor Architectures]: Parallel Architectures-*Distributed architectures*

General Terms: Design, Experimentation, Performance.

Keywords: Chip multiprocessors, memory hierarchy, elastic cooperative caching, tiled microarchitectures.

1. INTRODUCTION

Chip multiprocessors are now widely used and, due to the limited parallelism of most commercial applications, are expected to run multiple heterogeneous workloads simultaneously. In this environment the behavior of each of these applications can be very different and therefore lead to different cache requirements. Recent studies [16] show that cache partitioning has a significant performance impact in runtime execution and that dynamic configurations can adapt to the program's time-varying phase behavior and improve performance.

One example of the optimization opportunities that adaptive configurations can exploit is the simultaneous execution of streaming and cache bound applications. For instance, audio and video streaming are commonly executed simultaneously with text editors, web browsers or antivirus in desktop computers. In general, streaming applications do not take advantage of the upper levels of the memory hierarchy and introduce a high amount of data in the caches that is not going to be reused. This inefficiency is aggravated in shared caches by the eviction of blocks from other applications that could be eventually reused. Therefore, it is interesting to have a memory hierarchy that provides some kind of intelligent control to distribute resources fairly and take advantage of the differences among applications. Ideally, the reallocation of resources should be managed autonomously through hardware arbiters to avoid adding extra complexity to the software layer. In addition, next generation memory hierarchies should provide the elasticity to offer the low latency advantages of private caches and the low off-chip miss rate of shared caches. Future tiled microarchitectures also need scalable structures to allow increased levels of parallelism.

Prior work has been done to distribute cache resources dynamically either by software or hardware. Organizations with software allocation [4, 13, 21] increase the programming complexity and, in some cases, use centralized structures that limit the scalability. On the other hand, organizations with hardware allocation either use snooping mechanisms [9] or have a centralized structure, like the last-level cache [23, 24] or the directory [12], that limit the scalability. In addition, most existing solutions do not consider applications with shared data since resources are divided among threads without considering if replication is desirable.

To solve the scalability issues of existing solutions, we propose the Elastic Cooperative Caching (ElasticCC). ElasticCC uses distributed cache partitioning units able to operate autonomously with local information, allowing the redistribution of cache resources without centralized structures or intensive communication among nodes. In our configuration, Shared/Private caches are used in each node together with its own repartitioning unit. Shared regions of all caches create a big shared cache to store evicted blocks from the most active private regions and try to reduce the number of off-chip misses. On the other hand, private regions allow big local private caches when all applications have similar cache requirements. The hardware overhead of the proposed solution is minimal and it does not require software support. Furthermore, we have extended our dynamic configuration with Adaptive Spilling, a technique to improve the usage of the shared cache space.

The proposed scheme outperforms previous proposals such as the Distributed Cooperative Caching and the Adaptive Selective Replication, achieving an average speed-up of 27% and 12% respectively. At the same time, it reduces the number of off-chip misses by 19% and 16% due to the more efficient cache allocation and it increases energy-efficiency by 71% and 24% due to the reallocation avoidance of non-reused cache blocks.

This paper makes the following contributions:

- We introduce Elastic Cooperative Caching, a distributed cache partitioning mechanism that allows autonomous, scalable, and elastic cache behavior based on application needs for next generation tiled microarchitectures.
- We present the first distributed cache repartitioning mechanism able to operate only with local information.
- We propose a mechanism to further optimize the reallocation of evicted blocks in the shared cache space that is also scalable and relies only on local information.

2. BACKGROUND

There is extensive prior research on the memory hierarchy of chip multiprocessors. This work can be divided between static and dynamic resource partition mechanisms.

In static resource partition mechanisms [2, 3, 6, 11, 14, 19, 25, 28] all threads have the same priority and the amount of cache assigned to each thread is changed through the coherence protocol and replacement mechanisms. These organizations either have inter-thread interferences (e.g. Cache-intensive threads may degrade performance of other applications by replacing their blocks) or are not able to give all the cache space to a single thread if the others are not using the cache. This is logical if we consider that the cache space is statically mapped to threads, and can lead to a non-optimal usage of resources in unbalanced workloads.

If we want to optimize cache allocation to reduce off-chip misses, a repartitioning mechanism is desirable to be able to change the cache size assigned to every thread. Dynamic resource partition mechanisms dynamically modify the amount of memory that is assigned to every node and eliminate inter-thread cache conflicts by allocating independent partitions of resources. These resources can be divided in banks, sets or ways and require an arbitration mechanism that can be software or hardware based.

Software-based dynamic configurations delegate resource allocation to the OS. Most of these organizations divide resources in independent sections to be able to provide QoS [4, 13, 21, 10]. Virtual Private Caches [21] divide resources in ways and implement a hardware arbiter to dynamically distribute the unallocated space in accordance to a fairness policy. In the Cooperative Cache Partitioning [4] resources are not only partitioned spatially, but also in time. They apply Multiple Time-sharing Partitions to expand the cache capacity of some threads at a given time and increase throughput. Iyer [13] studies different mechanisms to allow QoS in the memory hierarchy. However, it is focused on the distribution of a unified shared last-level cache. Liu et al. present the Shared Processor-Based Split L2 [17], a cache configuration that also allows software-based distribution of cache resources. The purpose of this configuration is not to provide QoS but to be able to select private or shared caches depending on the application. This organization is limited by a snoop based protocol to access cache data that requires broadcast messages to all cache banks. Finally, R-NUCA proposes a variable block mapping depending on the kind of data; allocating private data close to the requesting node and replicating shared read-only blocks. However, it requires OS support and works at a page-level granularity. These configurations are limited by centralized structures in some cases and by a software-based arbitration that increases programming complexity.

Hardware-based dynamic organizations [9, 12, 23, 24], on the other hand, are able to implement the repartitioning policy in hardware, reducing the programming complexity. They are based on performance counters to measure the benefit of increasing the cache size for each thread. Adaptive Set Pinning [24] divides resources of a last level cache through sets by granting the replacement ownership to a thread. This ownership is varied dynamically to optimize the cache usage. Extra small private caches are required to allocate blocks of threads that don't have the ownership of the corresponding set. In the case of the NUCA Substrate [12], a centralized directory and a shared pool of small cache banks with different degrees of sharing is proposed. Dynamic mapping allows data to be stored in multiple banks but requires a tag check of all the possible destinations. The Dynamic Spill-Receive (DSR) [22], on the other hand, uses private L2 caches to allocate evicted blocks from other caches if a performance improvement is expected. The ability to reallocate or accept evicted blocks is decided through set dueling using miss information of all caches. Therefore, for a given cache, miss information of all caches must be provided for the tested sets to decide its behavior. This makes this technique interesting for a small number of nodes but unfeasible for a large number of them due to the communication overhead that this would entail. And finally, several works [9, 23] have appeared recently that adapt the cache size through the column caching technique [5]. Column caching is a cache partitioning mechanism that restricts the available number of sets when allocating a block, therefore enabling the cache to be partitioned. In the case of Utility-Based Cache Partitioning (Utility) [23] a single last-level cache is partitioned and assigned among threads. On the other hand, in the Adaptive Shared/Private NUCA (ASP-NUCA) [9] a cache for each node is divided into shared and private cache space according to thread requirements.

Cache partitioning is controlled by the repartitioning unit, depicted in Figure 1 for ASP-NUCA. Repartitioning in ASP-NUCA is based on the expected reduction in misses for each thread. This technique, also used in the Utility-Based Cache Partitioning [23], stores the tags of the evicted blocks on a

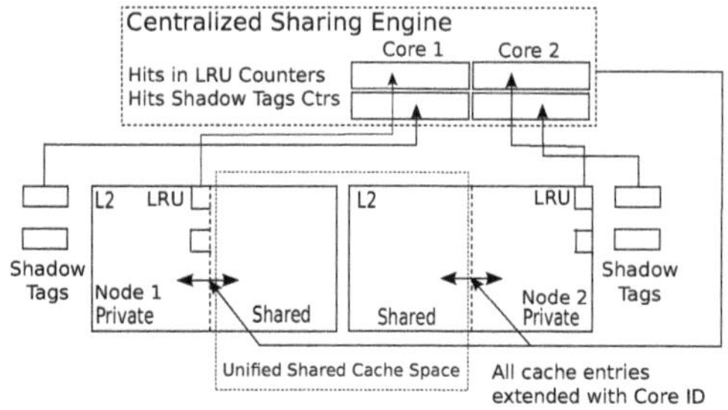

Figure 1: Adaptive Shared/Private NUCA Repartitioning Unit.

replacement in the private region. These tags are known as shadow tags. On a cache miss, the shadow tag is checked to detect the potential benefit of increasing the cache size. On the other hand, on a hit in the LRU block the second counter is updated to detect the potential degradation of reducing the cache size.

ASP-NUCA uses all the shared cache space as a centralized shared cache where all nodes can store as many blocks as indicated by a variable set for each of them. To be able to track the number of blocks from each core, ASP-NUCA also requires a CoreID field for each cache entry. When a block needs to be allocated in the shared region all shared partitions are checked to count the number of allocated blocks for that core. If there are less than allowed, the LRU block from all shared partitions is evicted. If not, the LRU block from that core is evicted.

The usage of shadow tags in all sets implies a significant hardware overhead and, therefore, only a few sets are monitored (6%). Even after doing this reduction the hardware overhead of ASP-NUCA is: a CoreID field in all cache entries, a shadow tag for the 6% of all cache sets, and two counters per node.

In addition to that, ASP-NUCA never changes the amount of private and shared cache space since every time that a private region in one node is increased, it is also decreased in another node. Therefore, this method is not optimal when all nodes execute independent tasks and big private caches would be desirable for each of them or when all threads share the data and a big shared cache would be better.

As we have seen, none of these techniques is suitable for large tiled microarchitectures because they require either a centralized cache or a centralized repartitioning unit that limits the scalability.

3. TAXONOMY OF APPLICATIONS

The design of dynamic memory hierarchies requires the implementation of policies to distribute cache resources. Applications can benefit from cache memory up to a certain point and the allocation mechanism must know the individual needs of each of them. In this section we study the behavior of applications in order to analyze the potential performance benefit of reallocating cache resources.

Figure 2 shows a characterization of the SpecOMP benchmarks for varying number of ways and sizes. It is important to note that application behavior is highly dependent on the section of code being executed and the cache size. We have evaluated the SpecOMP benchmark set with 8 nodes, private 16kb-4way L1s and private L2s of varying size and associativity.[1] Size is incremented with the addition of extra ways to evaluate the benefits in way-partitioned caches. Execution is started in each benchmark's most important parallel regions once all data structures are initialized. Three different parameters are shown in Figure 2; normalized performance compared to the 8way 256kb configuration, number of misses per instruction, and the sharing relation. Each row uses different graph scales to allow a better clarity in application behavior variations. Sharing relation shows the average number of nodes that share a block before its eviction and indicates if threads have independent data sets. Therefore, this parameter shows the potential savings in cache space a shared cache would provide by reducing replication.

Previous studies of dynamic cache repartitioning [23] have divided applications in three categories; low utility, high utility and saturating utility. However, after evaluating all applications we have detected that these categories do not consider the amount of sharing, which is important for an efficient cache partitioning.

Therefore we have divided the benchmarks into four categories:

Saturating Utility: These type of applications are characterized by having a small working set that fits in the cache. Therefore, granting more cache space to them has no impact on their performance. These applications are characterized by improving performance with each increase of cache size until the working set fits in it. If extra cache space is provided performance is not affected (e.g. Equake).

Low Utility: This category is for benchmarks with low temporal locality that make an intensive use of the memory hierarchy but do not have reuse. These applications are especially harmful for competing benchmarks that would benefit from more cache space. They are characterized by not improving performance when we increase cache sizes (e.g. Gafort).

Shared High Utility: In these applications, there are several threads that share a large number of blocks. Therefore, to optimize cache usage replication should be reduced for shared blocks reducing private regions. Replication in highly reused blocks, however, is still granted by L1 caches. These applications are characterized by a high sharing (e.g. Ammp).

Private High Utility: Finally, Private High Utility applications are those that benefit from larger levels of memory hierarchy but do not share data between threads. They are characterized by always improving performance when cache size is increased and by low data sharing among nodes (e.g. Swim).

Table 1 shows the classification of the SpecOMP benchmarks in the previously defined categories with tested benchmarks in bold. A multiprogrammed benchmark set is used to see the influence of memory intensive benchmarks over applications with lower cache requirements. We have selected benchmarks from each category to study the behavior of our dynamic configurations under all possible combinations.

4. ELASTIC COOPERATIVE CACHING

In this section we describe the Elastic Cooperative Caching (ElasticCC), a distributed and dynamic memory hierarchy that adapts autonomously to application behavior. We have

[1]Further details of the simulation environment can be found in Section 4.

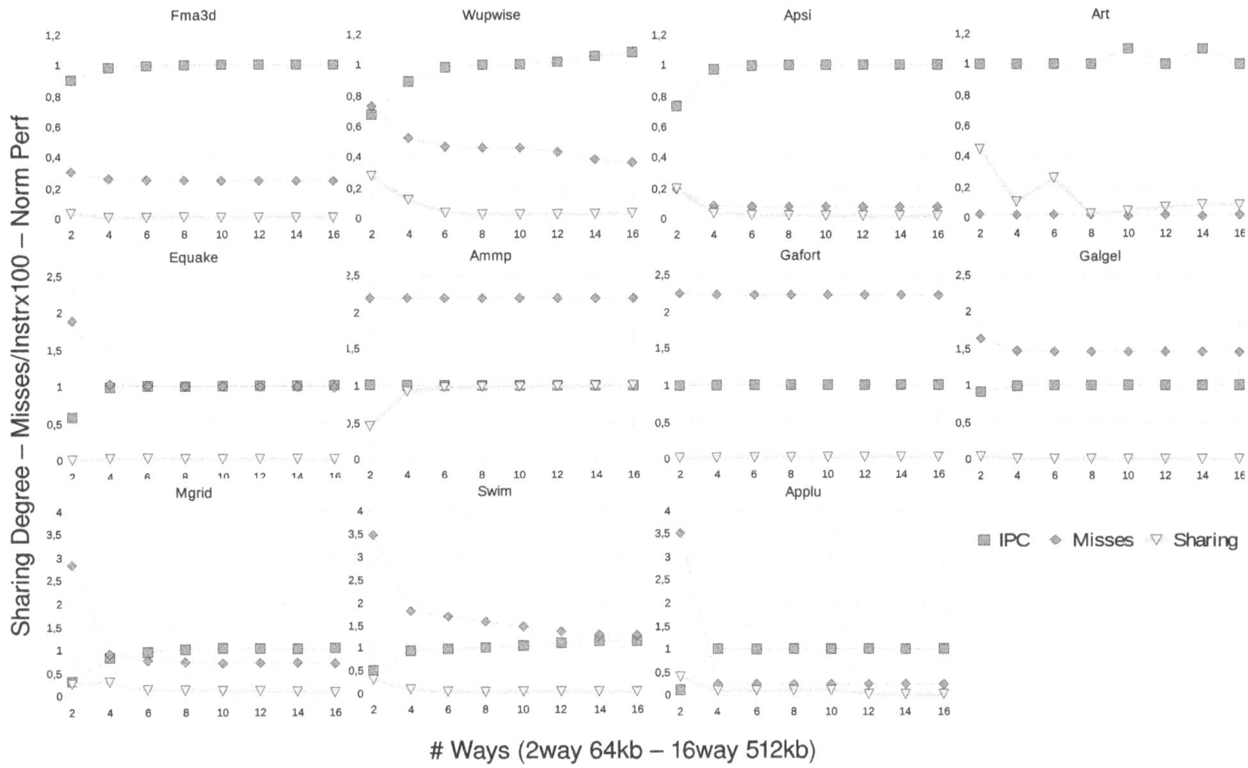

Figure 2: Spec OMP 2001 benchmark characteristics for different L2 sizes.

Type	Benchmark
Saturating Utility	Applu, **Apsi**, **Art**, **Equake**, Fma3d
Low Utility	**Gafort**, Galgel
Shared High Utility	**Ammp**
Private High Utility	Mgrid, **Swim**, Wupwise

Table 1: Benchmark Classification

focused on designing a scalable solution suited for next generation tiled microarchitectures.

4.1 Memory Coherence

To be able to have a scalable memory hierarchy organization it is important that all parts can be distributed to avoid bottlenecks. Therefore, in this paper we use the Distributed Coherence Engines (DCEs) [11] to grant coherence in the ElasticCC and in the evaluated version of Adaptive Selective Replication. DCEs are directory caches responsible for maintaining coherence for a portion of the address space. These directories can be distributed across the chip and have been used in the ElasticCC and in the evaluated distributed version of Adaptive Selective Replication.

Figure 3 shows the working principle of DCEs. When a request from a given node has missed in local L1 and L2 caches the request is forwarded to the DCE where the block address is mapped. If the requested block is located in another cache the DCE will forward the request to that node so the data is transfered to the requester.

Distributed Cooperative Caching (DCC) and ElasticCC also use the N-Chance forwarding mechanism [7] to reduce

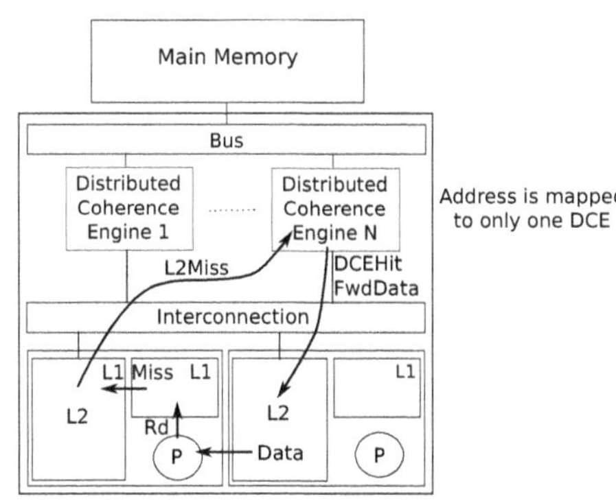

Figure 3: DCE working example.

off-chip misses. This mechanism reallocates evicted cache blocks in neighboring caches when the block is the last on-chip copy. Forwarding (also known as spilling) is handled by the DCE since it stores sharers information and also is able to avoid coherence races during the transmission. Spilling can be repeated N times for a given block. Since replication control is already enforced by the coherence protocol, in this paper N is set to 1 like in [3] and [11]. Therefore, if the spilled block is evicted again, it is evicted from the chip.

4.2 ElasticCC Structure

The ElasticCC framework consists of several independent L2 cache memories that are logically divided into a shared and a private region that compete for the cache space. Private regions store all the evicted blocks from the local L1 and

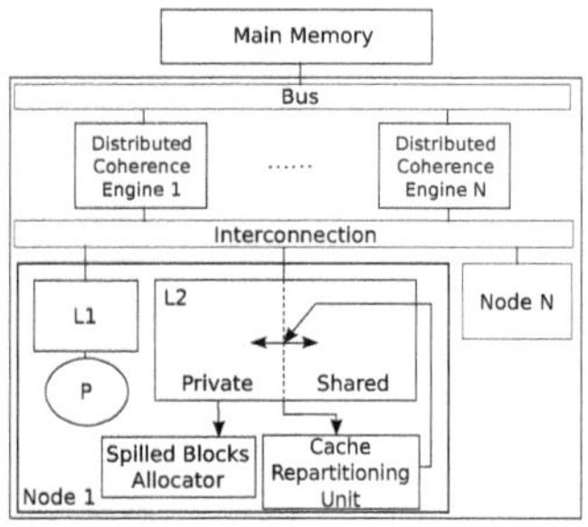

Figure 4: ElasticCC Node Structure.

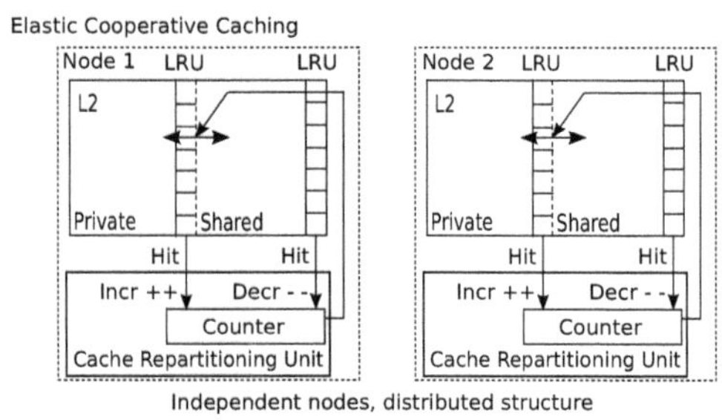

Figure 5: ElasticCC Repartitioning Unit.

shared regions store spilled blocks from neighboring caches. This allows the creation of big local private caches if all applications have similar cache requirements and a big shared cache if only a few take advantage of extra cache space. ElasticCC also adjusts the level of replication by repartitioning caches. Shared data is replicated when requested in the corresponding private regions but is never replicated in the shared region since it stores only unique blocks. Therefore, bigger private regions allow a higher replication and bigger shared regions limit it. To achieve the separation between private and shared cache space we have used the column caching technique proposed by Chiou [5] that allows separation and dynamic repartitioning without having to invalidate any block.

The extra hardware required for each node is a Repartitioning Unit and a Spilled Block Allocator, described in detail in the next subsections. The Cache Repartitioning Unit is responsible for dynamically adjusting the amount of cache that is going to be private or devoted to spilled blocks. Since not all nodes have the same shared cache space, the Spilled Block Allocator is responsible for deciding to which node a locally evicted block is spilled. This part is also important because more blocks should be spilled to the nodes with more shared space and less to the ones highly used by the local node. Figure 4 shows the structure of the proposed configuration.

4.3 Cache Repartitioning Unit

Our Cache Repartitioning Unit, depicted in Figure 5, adjusts the proportion of private and shared space locally for every L2 cache, avoiding centralized structures that limit the scalability. As can be seen, the hardware overhead of the repartitioning unit is minimal. The Repartitioning Unit only needs one counter per node that is incremented with Private LRU block hits and decremented with Shared LRU block hits.

Our cache repartitioning is done every fixed number of cycles and the decision is based on the number of hits on the Least Recently Used (LRU) blocks of the shared and the private parts of the cache. If the resulting value of the counter exceeds an Upper Threshold (UT) then the size of the private region is increased. If the value does not reach a Lower Threshold (LT) then the size of the shared region is increased. For all the middle values the size is not changed to avoid oscillatory states. Repartitioning is done at a given number of cycles to match program phases behavior and thresholds are control registers set at boot time.

```
If Private_LRU_Hit then
   Increase Counter
EndIf
If Shared_LRU_Hit then
   Decrease Counter
EndIf
If Repartition_Cycle then
   If Counter > Upper_Threshold then
      Add_Private_Way
      Send Repartition_Info_Msg
   ElseIf Counter < Lower_Threshold then
      Add_Shared_Way
      Send Repartition_Info_Msg
   EndIf
   Clear Counter
EndIf
```

Figure 6: Cache Repartitioning Algorithm.

Figure 6 shows the cache repartitioning algorithm, where hits in the LRU blocks of the private region increase a counter and hits in the LRU blocks of the shared region decrease it. Because we use LRU hits to decide to change the cache size, we can increase the private size of the cache even when the working set already fits in it. However, this is only going to happen when the shared region is not used since in the other cases the LRU hits in the shared region will compensate the counter value.

Repartitioning does not require the eviction of all cache blocks of the reassigned way since this would degrade performance unnecessarily. Once a cache is repartitioned partition sizes are updated and this information is used by the replacement mechanism. Therefore, new blocks will gradually replace the ones belonging to the other partition. Private and Shared portions must always have at least 1 way to simplify the coherence protocol and avoid race conditions. Therefore, partitioning only affects the replacement and allocation mechanisms. For accesses, the L2 cache can be seen as a normal shared cache, directly accessed by the local processor or indirectly accessed by other nodes through the DCEs. This organization also means that in-flight coherence messages of blocks being shifted among regions are not going to be affected.

4.4 Spilled Block Allocator

The second important part of the Elastic Cooperative Caching is the distribution of spilled blocks across the chip. Due to the dynamic behavior of caches some nodes can be mostly private and without cache space for spilled blocks and other nodes can be completely shared. Therefore it is important to have a Spilled Block Allocator in each node to distribute spilled blocks efficiently.

Type	Working Set size	Sharing	Local Reuse	Private Cache size	Spilling
Saturating Utility	Small	H/L	H/L	Small	No
Low Utility	Big	Low	Low	Small	No
Shared High Utility	Big	High	H/L	Small	Yes
Private High Utility	Big	Low	High	Big	Yes

Table 2: Application Types Behavior

Every time that a cache is repartitioned, a message is broadcast to all nodes with the partitioning information. This information is later used by the Spilled Block Allocator to distribute data among caches in a more efficient way: sending more evicted blocks to caches with more shared space. Since this mechanism is only used to balance the amount of spilled blocks among nodes, and the maximum size variation on each repartitioning is going to be a single way, we allow the use of stale information when caches are repartitioned. Thus, it is possible to separate the repartitioning information from the critical paths and broadcast it in a low priority network channel.

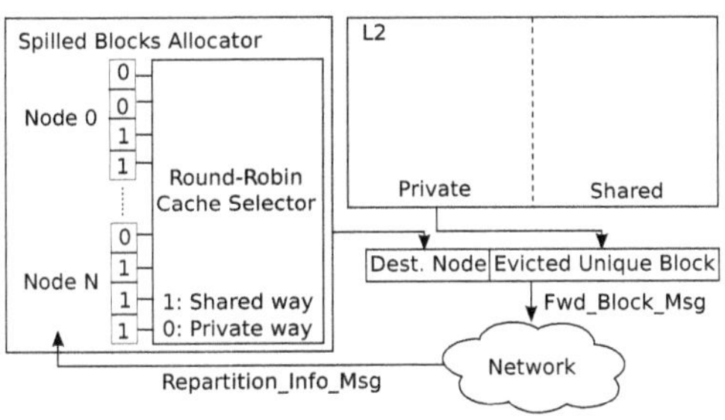

Figure 7: Spilled Block Allocator.

The proposed Spilled Block Allocator depicted in Figure 7 uses a Round-Robin arbiter with a bit vector containing the cache partitioning information of each way of each cache. The bit vector is updated every time that a message with partitioning information is received, with a bit representing the shared or private state of each way. When a block is evicted from the local private partition the arbiter selects the next shared way and spills the block to the corresponding node. Therefore, all shared ways are used equally and in circular order and nodes with more shared space receive more spilled blocks.

4.5 Adaptive Spilling mechanism

Elastic Cooperative Caching, as shown in previous sections, distributes available cache space to reduce the number of off-chip misses. Spilling, however, is done regardless of application properties. This may cause interferences between applications in the shared cache space. We propose an extension to the Elastic Cooperative Caching that takes advantage of its fully distributed organization and decides locally (i.e. autonomously) whether spilling is needed or not depending on the type of application.

Table 2 shows the most important characteristics of each of the application categories defined in section 2 and the last two columns show the desired behavior of our system. Low Utility applications, for example, minimize private regions due to their low reuse but still are able to use the shared region. Since this type of applications may have a very high number of misses, the shared cache is going to be filled by blocks that are not going to be reused. The desired behavior in this case would be to forbid spilling. It can be seen that only High Utility applications benefit from the shared cache space. Therefore, our Adaptive Spilling mechanism detects high utility applications and allows them to use the shared cache space while making it unavailable to others.

We will allow spilling, then, for both Private and Shared High Utility applications, but our mechanisms detect each of these applications differently. Private High Utility applications are detected through block reuse. Since applications with high reuse will have a high number of private ways, spilling is allowed when 75% of the cache (6 ways) is private. For Shared High Utility applications, sharing is detected by monitoring cache-to-cache transfers. The spilling decision is done on a per-block basis, allowing us to spill only the truly shared blocks. To track the sharing history of data, one bit is added to each entry of the DCE and is set when there is a cache-to-cache transfer (1= Block was shared, 0= Block was never shared). This bit is later used to detect the corresponding utility type together with the size of the private and shared regions. Our studies have shown that if a block was shared only once it is worth while to spill that block. This information is stored in the DCEs because it provides a global view of the sharing history of the block and avoids the influence of variations in the L2 cache size. The hardware overhead of this improvement is 64 Bytes of extra memory per DCE, which is negligible.

5. EXPERIMENTAL SETUP

We have evaluated our proposed framework with Simics [18], a full-system execution-driven simulator extended with the GEMS [20] toolset that provides a detailed memory hierarchy model. We have added a power model to the simulator based on Orion [27] and Cacti [26] to evaluate the energy efficiency of our proposal. Our configuration uses simple cores with small primary caches to improve the aggregate thread throughput by a high number of processors [8]. Table 3 shows the values for the most important configuration parameters.

Previously selected benchmarks of the SPECOMP2001 workload set have been simulated with the reference input sets and in pairs, each of them executing 8 threads.

The Elastic Cooperative Caching framework has been compared against traditional organizations such as shared or private last level cache. As we have seen, existing cache partitioning techniques rely on a centralized cache or a centralized repartitioning unit with information from all caches that works very well for a small number of nodes. However, for a high number of cores, the scalability of these techniques is very limited. For instance, ASP-NUCA has a max number of blocks in a set for the private and the shared partition. This means that for replacements in the shared region, all

Parameter	Value
Number Processors	16
Instr Window/ROB	16/48 entries
Branch Predictor	YAGS
Technology	70 nm
Frequency	4 GHz
Voltage	1.1 V
Block size	64 bytes
L1 I/D Cache	16 KB, 4-way
L2 Cache	256 KB, 8-way
DCE Size	8192 entries
Network Type	Mesh with 2 VNC
Hop Latency	3 cycles
Link BW	16 bytes/cycle
Memory Bus Latency	250 cycles

Table 3: Configuration Parameters

shared partitions are considered as a unique cache. Therefore a distributed version of this technique would require snooping all nodes on every cache replacement, potentially saturating the network. Therefore we consider it more fair to compare ElasticCC to scalable state-of-the-art cache organizations like the Adaptive Selective Replication [2] and the Distributed Cooperative Caching [11].

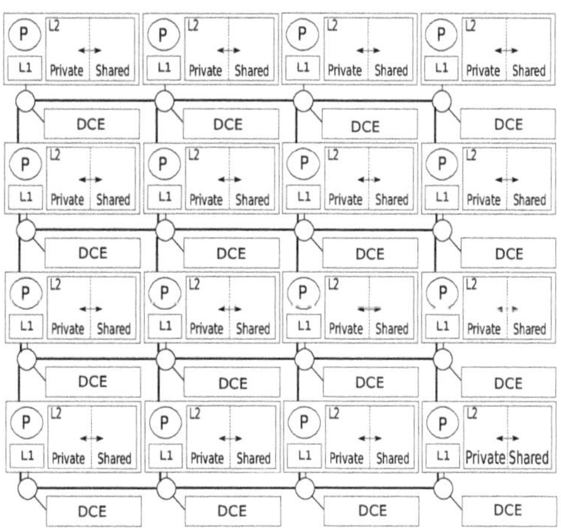

Figure 8: ElasticCC Memory Structure.

Since our work is intended for large tiled microarchitectures we have used Distributed Coherence Engines (DCEs) [11] to grant coherence in the ASR technique and in the ElasticCC to avoid centralized directories or snoop based protocols. To the best of the authors knowledge, this is the first time a realistic distributed version of the ASR technique is implemented and evaluated. Network interconnect also plays an important role in the overall performance [15]. Therefore, we have used a mesh interconnect to have a scalable solution. Figure 8 shows the memory structure of ElasticCC with one DCE per node. In all the tested configurations two levels of cache are used, as well as a MOESI protocol to grant coherence between nodes. All simulations use a local and private L1 cache and a shared/private L2 cache for every processor. Evaluated configurations are:

Shared Memory. This configuration assumes a Non-Uniform Cache Access (NUCA) architecture. L2 cache is physically distributed across the nodes and logically unified. Addresses are mapped to cache banks in an interleaved way to try to distribute requests in the network. L1 and L2 caches are inclusive and the L2 also includes the directory information for the allocated entries. On an L1 miss, the L2 bank corresponding to the address is accessed. If the block is located in another L1 in read-only mode, then it is replicated in the requesting node L1. Otherwise, the owner is invalidated without having to access the off-chip directory. This configuration tries to optimize cache usage and reduce off-chip accesses.

Private Memory. In this design, an L2 cache bank is assigned to every processor. On an L2 cache miss, memory must be accessed to check if the block is shared and to retrieve the data. This configuration makes little usage of the on-chip network and tries to optimize the access latency by placing all cache blocks in the local L2.

Distributed Cooperative Caching. (DCC) [11] This configuration has been used as a baseline, therefore, results are normalized over it. With this configuration it is possible to see the influence of interferences produced by the usage of a common cache space for private and spilled blocks. It uses 1 DCE for each node/processor with 2 R/W ports and 8-way associativity.

Adaptive Selective Replication. (ASR) [2] We have evaluated a distributed version of the ASR technique where coherence is granted through DCEs. This configuration uses 8 K entry 8 way NLHBs and 512 entry 8 way VTBs for each node.

Elastic Cooperative Caching. (ElasticCC) We have evaluated our dynamic proposal with a Cache Repartitioning Unit updated every 100k cycles and with a high threshold of 5 and a low threshold of 0. Thresholds are determined empirically. Since there is no previous information available on the behavior of applications, caches are initialized with 4 private and 4 shared ways.

ElasticCC + Adaptive Spilling. (ElasticCC+AS) This configuration evaluates the Elastic Cooperative Caching extended with the Adaptive Spilling mechanism, which only allows spilling when the private region occupies 75% of the cache (6 ways) or when the evicted block was shared. Thresholds for the Repartitioning Unit are the same as the previous configuration.

Ideal. Finally, a configuration that shows how much performance is possible to extract by increasing the cache size is evaluated. This configuration doubles the cache space in each node by using half private half shared 16 way 512kb L2 caches. In this case the shared/private division is static and grants 8 ways to each region. This situation emulates a configuration where there is -at the same moment- the maximum private and maximum shared space (i.e. twice the capacity of the evaluated cache).

6. RESULTS

6.1 Performance and Energy Efficiency

In this section, the Elastic Cooperative Caching is evaluated and compared to existing memory hierarchy configurations. Figure 9(a) shows the performance of the studied configurations normalized to Distributed Cooperative Caching, the power/performance relation that measures the energy efficiency of the proposed solutions, and the number of off-chip misses per instruction.

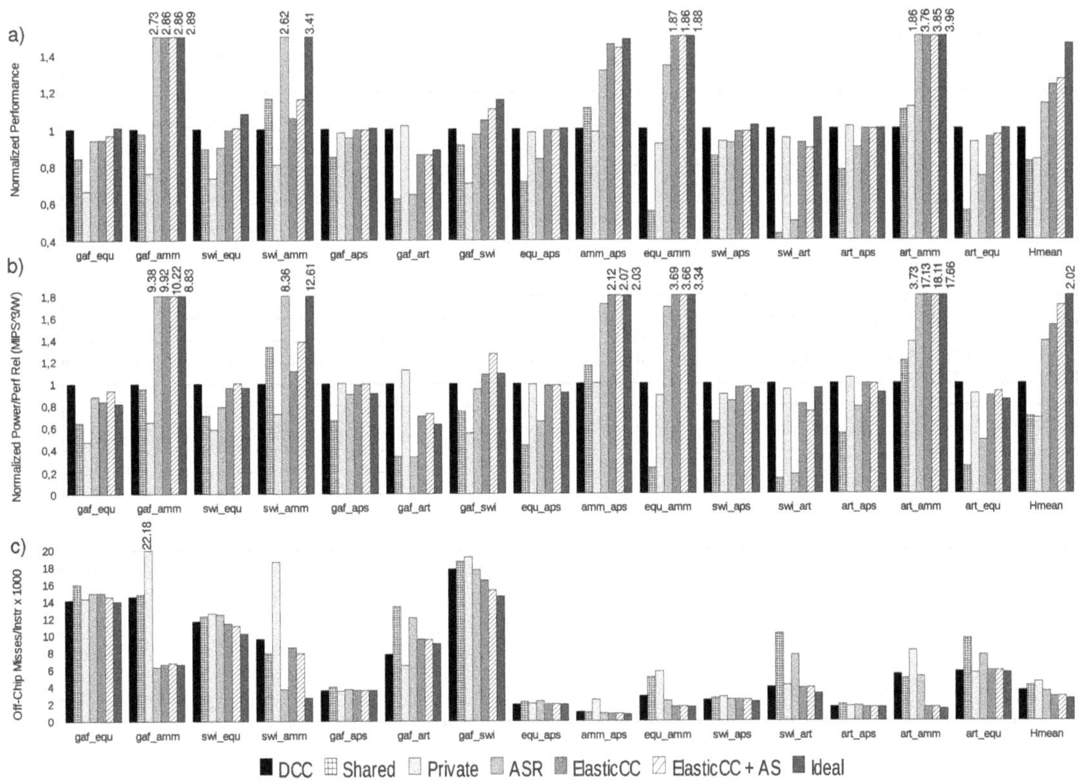

Figure 9: Normalized performance, Normalized energy efficiency and Off-Chip misses per Instr.

The performance graph shows that the Elastic Cooperative Caching outperforms the Distributed Cooperative Caching by an average of 27%, by 12% over the distributed version of Adaptive Selective Replication, by 52% over private caches, and by 53% over a distributed shared cache. Performance improvement in dynamic configurations is highly dependent on the characteristics of all the applications being executed simultaneously. Performance improvements can only come from High Utility benchmarks and in the other cases the adaptive mechanism must find the lowest amount of dedicated resources that does not degrade performance.

It can be seen that the Elastic Cooperative Caching is able to improve the performance of High Utility benchmarks when they are able to benefit from the extra cache space of neighboring applications. In some cases, it achieves almost the same performance as the Ideal configuration that has twice the cache space. The only configuration where performance is not similar to the ideal configuration is the one executing two High Utility benchmarks (Swim-Ammp), where ASR gets better performance. In this case both benchmarks benefit from the larger cache space and none of them leaves unused cache space. ElasticCC, however, outperforms ASR in all other cases thanks to its ability to repartition caches.

From the High Utility applications, Ammp is the one that improves its performance in a more significant way. This application is known for sharing a lock variable that leads to increased invalidations and cache misses[1]. Elastic Cooperative Caching is able to keep this data in the caches by avoiding replication of shared blocks and this leads to a high reduction in the number of off-chip cache misses. On the other hand, Swim requires much more cache space to improve its performance. Therefore, in this case, performance improvements depend much more on the other application that is executing simultaneously. However, when executing with a Low Utility benchmark (Gafort-Swim), it is able to increase performance by 10%.

The energy efficiency of Elastic Cooperative Caching is showed in Figure 9(b). Results in $MIPS^3/W$ are normalized over the DCC configuration. ElasticCC+AS shows a 71% improvement over DCC and 24% over ASR. The more effective usage of shared regions with Adaptive Spilling can be seen in this graph. ElasticCC+AS improves the energy efficiency by 12% over ElasticCC without Adaptive Spilling. This improvement is produced by more effective spilling that reduces the network traffic and the avoids unnecessary reallocations of blocks without reuse.

Finally, Figure 9(c) shows the number of off-chip misses per instruction for each configuration. As expected the more efficient use of caches of ElasticCC brings an average reduction of 18.6% over DCC and 16.4% over ASR.

6.2 Dynamic behavior of ElasticCC

To see how the Elastic Cooperative Caching adapts to application behavior Figure 10 shows the average partitioning of the caches through the execution of the applications. Results show that the Repartitioning Unit is able to detect the application behavior and adapt cache sizes accordingly. The Low Utility application (Gafort) is granted in all cases less than 4 ways. The number of private ways assigned depends on the neighbor application. Therefore, when the second application is a Private High Utility one (Gafort-Swim), private ways are even reduced to less than 2. On the other

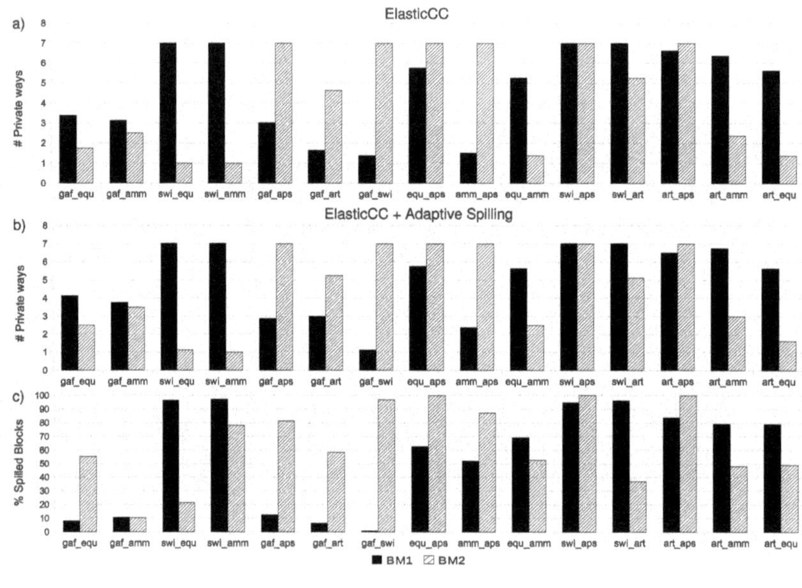

Figure 10: Average number of private ways per benchmark in ElasticCC and ElasticCC + AS and percentage of spilled blocks per benchmark in ElasticCC + AS compared to ElasticCC.

hand, the Private High Utility application (Swim) always uses all the available cache space and ends with 7 private ways. Finally, in the case of the Shared High Utility application (Ammp), it is possible to see that the amount of private cache is reduced to reduce replication and keep a bigger number of different cache blocks on-chip.

Although cache repartitioning is done correctly, the usage of the shared space is not optimized since Low Utility applications are going to corrupt it. Therefore a configuration with Adaptive Spilling also has been tested. Figure 10(b) shows the average final state for this configuration and also the percentage of evicted blocks that have been spilled to the shared cache. Caches are adapted to application behavior as well as without Adaptive Spilling but in this case private regions are slightly larger. This increase is compensated by the much more restrictive usage of shared regions. It is interesting to observe how the Adaptive Spilling is able to filter data that is not going to be reused. Figure 10(c) shows the percentage of spilled blocks. Spilling for the Low Utility application (Gafort) is significantly cut down in all cases compared with the ElasticCC alone where all evicted blocks are spilled. This reduction increases the available cache space for other applications.

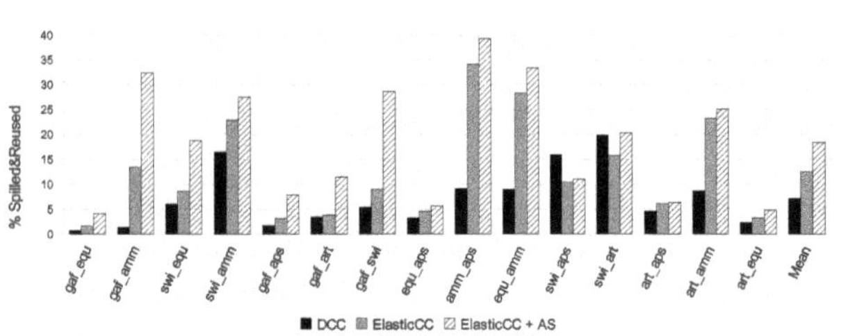

Figure 11: Percentage of spilled blocks that are reused.

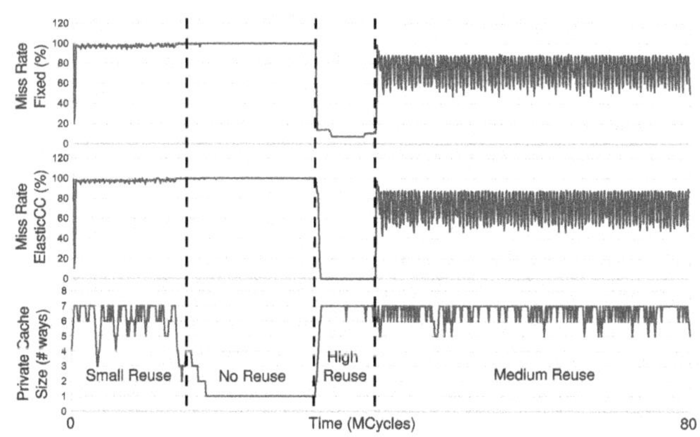

Figure 12: Cache behavior for thread 1 of Equake.

The effectiveness of Adaptive Spilling can bee seen in Figure 11 where the percentage of spilled blocks that are reused is shown. Elastic Cooperative Caching clearly increases the efficiency of spilling compared to Distributed Cooperative Caching. Reuse is increased on average from 7.1% to 12.5%, avoiding unnecessary reallocations of blocks without reuse. Adaptive Spilling is able to further increase this reuse up to 18.4%. This translates to fewer unnecessary messages across the network and improves the energy efficiency of the proposed configuration.

Finally, Figure 12 shows the temporal behavior of the elastic Shared/private cache of the node executing thread 1 of Equake for the Gafort-Equake combination. The plot shows the miss rate of the private region for a fixed version with half private-half shared cache and for ElasticCC. When the local thread makes no reuse at all, the shared cache space is increased so other nodes can take advantage. On the other hand, when reuse is high, the cache behaves as private to reduce cache misses. An finally, when reuse is small or medium, the behavior depends on other threads requirements. Since Gafort is an application with low reuse, very few blocks are going to be reallocated in the shared space and the cache is kept mostly private. In addition, Figure 12 shows that when reuse is small the cache is more likely to repartition than when we have a medium reuse. It can be seen that ElasticCC is not only capable of detecting differences among applications but also variations within the same application, adjusting cache size accordingly.

7. CONCLUSIONS

A dynamic and scalable memory hierarchy is necessary for next generation tiled microarchitectures. Elastic Cooperative Caching is shown to be a good candidate due to its autonomy, distributed organization and adaptivity to applications. Its repartitioning unit is the first to allow independent resource allocation based on local information, making it suitable for tiles with a high number of cores. The proposed scheme is able to detect the different cache requirements among applications and distribute cache resources accordingly without software support. Furthermore, the sensitivity of the repartitioning unit is able to detect changes in the execution phase of an application and adapt the system to the new situation. ElasticCC achieves a speedup of 27% over Distributed Cooperative Caching, 12% over Adaptive Selective Replication, 52% over private caches, and 53% over a distributed shared cache. More effective cache allocation is responsible for this improvement since it leads to a 19% reduction of off-chip misses compared to DCC and 16% compared to ASR. Furthermore, the dynamic management of cache resources avoids the energy overhead of reallocating not-reused cache blocks and consequently increases energy efficiency by 71% over the DCC configuration and 24% over the ASR configuration.

8. ACKNOWLEDGEMENTS

This work has been supported by the Generalitat de Catalunya under grant 2009SGR1250, and the Spanish Ministry of Education and Science under grant TIN2007-61763. We would like to thank Dean Tullsen and Marc Lupon for their comments on this work.

9. REFERENCES

[1] V. Aslot and R. Eigenmann. Quantitative performance analysis of the spec ompm2001 benchmarks. *Scientific Programming*, 11(2):105–124, 2003.

[2] B. Beckmann, M. Marty, and D. Wood. Asr: Adaptive selective replication for cmp caches. *MICRO-39: 39th IEEE/ACM Int. Symp. on Microarchitecture*, Dec. 2006.

[3] J. Chang and G. S. Sohi. Cooperative caching for chip multiprocessors. In *ISCA '06: 33rd Int. Symp. on Computer Architecture*, pages 264–276, 2006.

[4] J. Chang and G. S. Sohi. Cooperative cache partitioning for chip multiprocessors. In *ICS '07: 21st Int. Conf. on Supercomputing*, pages 242–252, 2007.

[5] D. Chiou. Extending the reach of microprocessors: Column and curious caching. *PhD Thesis, Massachusets Institute of Technology*, 1999.

[6] Z. Chishti, M. Powell, and T. Vijaykumar. Distance associativity for high-performance energy-efficient non-uniform cache architectures. *MICRO-36: 36th IEEE/ACM Int. Symp. on Microarchitecture*, pages 55–66, 3-5 Dec. 2003.

[7] M. Dahlin, R. Wang, T. Anderson, and D. Patterson. Cooperative caching: Using remote client memory to improve file system performance. *OSDI '94: 1st Conf. on Operating Systems Design and Impl.*, pages 267–280, Nov. 1994.

[8] J. Davis, J. Laudon, and K. Olukotun. Maximizing cmp throughput with mediocre cores. *PACT '05: 14th Int. Conf. on Parallel Architectures and Compilation Techniques*, pages 51–62, 17-21 Sept. 2005.

[9] H. Dybdahl and P. Stenstrom. An adaptive shared/private nuca cache partitioning scheme for chip multiprocessors. *HPCA '07: 13th Int. Symp. on High Performance Computer Architecture*, pages 2–12, 10-14 Feb. 2007.

[10] N. Hardavellas, M. Ferdman, B. Falsafi, and A. Ailamaki. Reactive nuca: near-optimal block placement and replication in distributed caches. In *ISCA '09: 36th Int. Symp. on Computer architecture*, pages 184–195, New York, NY, USA, 2009. ACM.

[11] E. Herrero, J. Gonzalez, and R. Canal. Distributed cooperative caching. *PACT '08: 17th Int. Conf. on Parallel Architectures and Compilation Techniques*, 25-29 Oct. 2008.

[12] J. Huh, C. Kim, H. Shafi, L. Zhang, D. Burger, and S. Keckler. A nuca substrate for flexible cmp cache sharing. In *ICS '05: 19th Int. Conf. on Supercomputing*, pages 31–40, 2005.

[13] R. Iyer. Cqos: a framework for enabling qos in shared caches of cmp platforms. In *ICS '04: 18th Int. Conf. on Supercomputing*, pages 257–266, New York, NY, USA, 2004.

[14] N. D. E. Jerger, L.-S. Peh, and M. H. Lipasti. Virtual tree coherence: Leveraging regions and in-network multicast trees for scalable cache coherence. *MICRO-41: 41st IEEE/ACM Int. Symp. on Microarchitecture*, 8-12 Nov. 2008.

[15] R. Kumar, V. Zyuban, and D. M. Tullsen. Interconnections in multi-core architectures: Understanding mechanisms, overheads and scaling. In *ISCA '05: 32nd Int. Symp. on Computer Architecture*, pages 408–419, Washington, DC, USA, 2005. IEEE Computer Society.

[16] J. Lin, Q. Lu, X. Ding, Z. Zhang, X. Zhang, and P. Sadayappan. Gaining insights into multicore cache partitioning: Bridging the gap between simulation and real systems. In *HPCA '08: 14th Int. Symp. on High Performance Computer Architecture*, pages 367–378, Feb. 2008.

[17] C. Liu, A. Sivasubramaniam, and M. Kandemir. Organizing the last line of defense before hitting the memory wall for cmps. In *HPCA '04: 10th Int. Symp. on High Performance Computer Architecture*, page 176, Washington, DC, USA, 2004. IEEE Computer Society.

[18] P. Magnusson, M. Christensson, J. Eskilson, D. Forsgren, G. Hallberg, J. Hogberg, F. Larsson, A. Moestedt, and B. Werner. Simics: A full system simulation platform. *Computer*, 35(2):50–58, 2002.

[19] M. Martin, M. Hill, and D. Wood. Token coherence: decoupling performance and correctness. *ISCA '03: 30th Int. Symp. on Computer Architecture*, pages 182–193, 9-11 June 2003.

[20] M. Martin, D. J. Sorin, B. Beckmann, M. Marty, M. Xu, A. Alameldeen, K. Moore, M. Hill, and D. Wood. Multifacet's general execution-driven multiprocessor simulator (gems) toolset. *SIGARCH Comput. Archit. News*, 33(4):92–99, 2005.

[21] K. J. Nesbit, J. Laudon, and J. E. Smith. Virtual private caches. In *ISCA '07: 34th Int. Symp. on Computer architecture*, pages 57–68, New York, NY, USA, 2007. ACM.

[22] M. Qureshi. Adaptive spill-receive for robust high-performance caching in cmps. *HPCA '09: 15th Int. Symp. on High Performance Computer Architecture*, 14-18 Feb. 2009.

[23] M. Qureshi and Y. Patt. Utility-based cache partitioning: A low-overhead, high-performance, runtime mechanism to partition shared caches. *MICRO-39: 39th IEEE/ACM Int. Symp. on Microarchitecture*, pages 423–432, Dec. 2006.

[24] S. Srikantaiah, M. Kandemir, and M. J. Irwin. Adaptive set pinning: managing shared caches in chip multiprocessors. In *ASPLOS XIII: 13th Int. Conf. on Architectural Support for Programming Languages and Operating Systems*, pages 135–144, New York, NY, USA, 2008. ACM.

[25] K. Strauss, X. Shen, and J. Torrellas. Uncorq: Unconstrained snoop request delivery in embedded-ring multiprocessors. *MICRO-40: 40th IEEE/ACM Int. Symp. on Microarchitecture*, Dec. 2007.

[26] D. Tarjan, S. Thoziyoor, and N. Jouppi. Cacti 4.0. Technical report, HP Labs Palo Alto, June 2006.

[27] H.-S. Wang, X. Zhu, L.-S. Peh, and S. Malik. Orion: a power-performance simulator for interconnection networks. *MICRO-35: 35th IEEE/ACM Int. Symp. on Microarchitecture*, pages 294–305, 2002.

[28] M. Zhang and K. Asanovic. Victim replication: maximizing capacity while hiding wire delay in tiled chip multiprocessors. *ISCA '05: 32nd Int. Symp. on Computer Architecture*, pages 336–345, June 2005.

Cohesion*: A Hybrid Memory Model for Accelerators

John H. Kelm, Daniel R. Johnson, William Tuohy, Steven S. Lumetta, Sanjay J. Patel

University of Illinois at Urbana-Champaign
Urbana, IL 61801

ABSTRACT

Two broad classes of memory models are available today: models with hardware cache coherence, used in conventional chip multiprocessors, and models that rely upon software to manage coherence, found in compute accelerators. In some systems, both types of models are supported using disjoint address spaces and/or physical memories. In this paper we present Cohesion, a hybrid memory model that enables fine-grained temporal reassignment of data between hardware-managed and software-managed coherence domains, allowing a system to support both. Cohesion can be used to dynamically adapt to the sharing needs of both applications and runtimes. Cohesion requires neither copy operations nor multiple address spaces.

Cohesion offers the benefits of reduced message traffic and on-die directory overhead when software-managed coherence can be used and the advantages of hardware coherence for cases in which software-managed coherence is impractical. We demonstrate our protocol using a hierarchical, cached 1024-core processor with a single address space that supports both software-enforced coherence and a directory-based hardware coherence protocol. Relative to an optimistic, hardware-coherent baseline, a realizable Cohesion design achieves competitive performance with a 2× reduction in message traffic, 2.1× reduction in directory utilization, and greater robustness to on-die directory capacity.

Categories and Subject Descriptors

C.1.4 [**Computer Systems Organization**]: Processor Architectures—*Parallel Architectures*

General Terms

Design, Performance

Keywords

Accelerator, Computer Architecture, Cache Coherence

*In linguistics, cohesion is the assemblage of ideas into a coherent discourse.

ISCA'10, June 19–23, 2010, Saint-Malo, France.

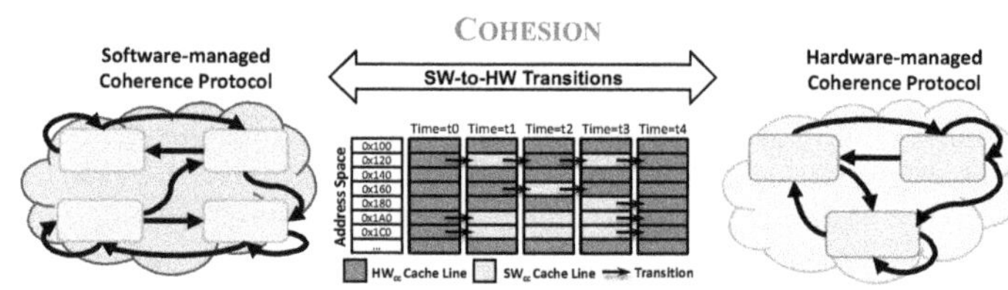

Figure 1: Cohesion enables migrating data between coherence domains without copying.

1. INTRODUCTION

Chip multiprocessors (CMP) supporting four to 32 hardware threads are available commercially [11, 24, 28, 38], and compute accelerators, such as graphics processing units (GPUs), already support 1000's of concurrent hardware threads [30]. However, the memory systems of these two dominant multicore systems, general-purpose CMPs and domain-specific GPUs, indicate a clear divergence. While CMPs continue to espouse strict memory consistency models with a single address space and hardware cache coherence, GPUs support relaxed memory orderings, multiple address spaces, and software-managed coherence. As CMP core counts increase, a tension grows between the desire to support programming paradigms that rely upon the existence of a hardware-coherent address space and the difficulty of scaling hardware cache coherence.

In this paper we present Cohesion, a hybrid memory model that bridges the gap between weak, easily scalable models found in accelerators and strict, more difficult to scale models founds in CMPs. Cohesion uses a hybrid hardware/software coherence scheme, as illustrated in Figure 1. When possible, Cohesion performs coherence management in software at coarse granularity, or avoids it completely. For accesses that would otherwise be prohibitively expensive in a weaker model, Cohesion incorporates hardware-supported coherence regions. Cohesion achieves scalability by taking advantage of the lack of fine-grained sharing in many scalable parallel applications, applying hardware coherence techniques when advantageous and deferring to software-managed coherence when possible, such as in the cases of private, immutable, and read-shared data.

The three key benefits of Cohesion are (1) a system with a single address space that supports a variety of *coherence domains*, which are regions of memory for which coherence guarantees are provided collectively by the memory model,

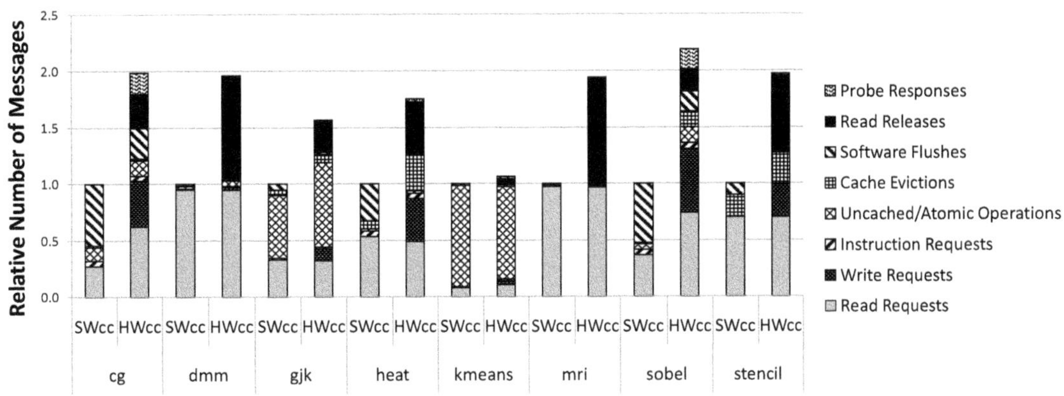

Figure 2: Number of messages sent by the local caches shared by eight cores (L2) to the global shared last-level cache (L3) for SW_{cc} and optimistic HW_{cc}. Results normalized to SW_{cc}.

(2) the ability to perform temporal reallocation between coherence domains without copies, and (3) fine granularity—interleaving data managed using a software protocol and a hardware protocol at the granularity of a cache line. The goal of COHESION is to enable scalability by reducing reliance upon hardware mechanisms without sacrificing the conventional shared memory programming model.

COHESION incorporates two components, one software and one hardware, and comprises a protocol for transitioning between the two. The software component leverages programmer knowledge of data usage, including immutable data and private data such as stacks. It is also useful for shared data with coarse-grained dependences separated by barriers, which is a common programming idiom in accelerator software [6, 19, 23, 31]. The software interface is a set of library routines that can be optimized for the underlying architecture, but do not rely on compiler support. The second part of COHESION is a hardware mechanism that allows software to indicate to hardware what regions of memory must be tracked by a hardware coherence protocol. The unifying mechanism is a protocol that allows regions of memory to transition between coherence domains at synchronization points in the code. The protocol allows for consistent behavior as coherence management of cache blocks transitions dynamically between hardware and software control.

2. MOTIVATION

We motivate COHESION by demonstrating that software-managed and hardware-managed coherence both have overheads that can be mitigated by a hybrid memory model. We also motivate COHESION from a programmability and optimization perspective. We find a compelling use case in heterogeneous processors with general-purpose and accelerator cores with a shared address space. In such a design, in which the coherence needs and capabilities vary by core, a hybrid approach may be beneficial by reducing the need for data marshalling and the cost of data copies.

2.1 The Case for Software Cache Coherence

A software-managed coherence protocol embedded in the compiler [1, 25], runtime [3, 5], or programming model [18, 23] avoids the overheads of hardware coherence management. No memory is required for directories [2, 8] or duplicate tags [4, 24]. No design effort is expended implementing and verifying the coherence protocol. For the network, there is less traffic and relaxed design constraints. Furthermore, fine-grained software protocols can eliminate false sharing.

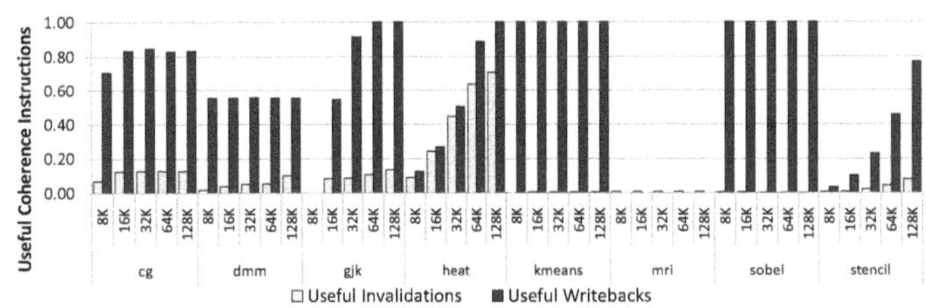

Figure 3: Fraction of software invalidations and writebacks issued that are performed on valid lines in the local cache (L2) with varied sizing. We eagerly write back dirty output data and lazily invalidate read-only input data. Operations performed to invalid lines are an inefficiency of SW_{cc}.

We simulated a 1024-core system running multi-threaded kernels (Section 4.1) that use a barrier-based task queue programming model. Figure 2 shows the messaging overhead for an optimistic implementation of hardware coherence (HW_{cc}). For this experiment, we assume a complete full-map on-die directory with infinite capacity that eliminates directory evictions and broadcasts. The software-managed protocol (SW_{cc}) uses explicit flush and invalidation instructions inserted by software to manage coherence. Figure 3 evaluates the efficiency of issued flush and invalidate instructions under SW_{cc} by counting the number of such instructions that operate on valid lines in the cache. The methodology is discussed further in Section 4.

Figure 2 shows significantly increased message traffic across all benchmarks for HW_{cc} except for `kmeans`, which is dominated by atomic read-modify-write histogramming operations. The additional messages come primarily from two sources: write misses and read release/invalidation operations. For SW_{cc}, software is responsible for tracking ownership. For a non-inclusive cache hierarchy [4, 11] per-word dirty/valid bits are maintained in cache. Writes can be issued as write-allocates under SW_{cc} without waiting on a directory response. Also, under HW_{cc} silent evictions are not supported and thus read releases are issued to the directory when a clean line is evicted from a local cache (L2). For SW_{cc}, there is no need to send any message, and the invalidation occurs locally. Even if a protocol without read releases were used, HW_{cc} would still show significant message overhead for invalidation cache probes; the implications of a protocol without read releases are discussed in Section 3.2.

SW_{cc} has the ability to mass invalidate shared read data, signaling many invalidations with only a few messages. To coordinate this action, a global synchronization event such as a barrier is used. The equivalent operation in hardware requires sending potentially many invalidation messages exactly when a state transition or eviction is needed. Such an invalidation mechanism lengthens the critical path for coherence actions, increases contention for the network, and requires greater capacity from the network to handle the invalidation traffic. SW_{cc} can eliminate false sharing since multiple write sharers that access disjoint sets of words on a line will not generate coherence probes that would otherwise cause the line to ping-pong between sharers in HW_{cc}.

2.2 The Case for Hardware Cache Coherence

Hardware cache coherence provides a number of programmability benefits. HW_{cc} can enforce strict memory models whereby hardware ensures that all reads receive the latest write to a word in memory, which makes it easier to reason about sharing in some applications. HW_{cc} enables speculative prefetching and data migration. Shared memory applications can be ported to a HW_{cc} design without a full rewrite, albeit with possibly degraded performance.

SW_{cc} is a *push* mechanism; explicit actions must occur to make data modified by one sharer visible to other sharers. On the other hand, HW_{cc} is a *pull* mechanism allowing a requester to locate the latest copy of data on-demand. The implication is that SW_{cc} protocols may be more conservative than necessary, pushing all data that *may* be read by another core to a globally-visible point, e.g., memory or a globally shared last-level cache. Furthermore, the additional traffic required for read release messages under HW_{cc} makes up a significant portion of message traffic, these messages are not on the critical path for a waiting access, whereas an invalidation sent by the directory is.

SW_{cc} reduces instruction stream efficiency since it introduces explicit cache many flush instructions which show up as additional software flush messages in Figure 2. Under a software protocol with deferred coherence actions, the state of lines must be tracked in memory, which can be less efficient than maintaining a small number of bits with each cache tag—the conventional method for tracking coherence state. Furthermore, flush instructions are wasted, as the lines they target may have already been evicted from the cache by the time the SW_{cc} actions occur. We quantify this effect in Figure 3, which depicts the number of SW_{cc} actions that are performed on lines valid in the L2. Indeed, many of the coherence instructions issued dynamically are superfluous, operating on lines not present in the cache.

2.3 A Hybrid Memory Model

Supporting multiple coherence implementations enables software to dynamically select the appropriate mechanism for blocks of memory. Supporting incoherent regions of memory allows more scalable hardware by reducing the number of

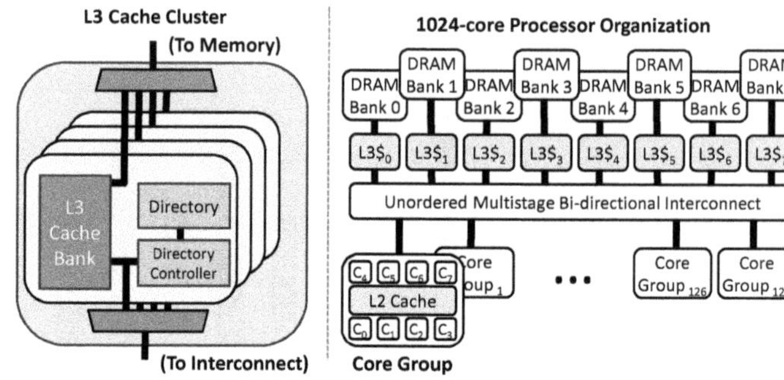

Figure 4: Baseline processor architecture.

shared lines, resulting in fewer coherence messages and less directory overhead for tracking sharer state. Furthermore, having coherence as an option enables tradeoffs to be made regarding software design complexity and performance. A hybrid memory model provides the runtime with a mechanism for managing coherence needs across applications, even if modified applications do not need data to transition between SW_{cc} and HW_{cc} frequently,

From the perspective of system software, HW_{cc} has many benefits. HW_{cc} allows for migratory data patterns not easily supported under SW_{cc}. Threads that sleep on one core and resume execution on another must have their local modified stack data available, forcing coherence actions at each thread swap under SW_{cc}. Likewise, task-based programming models [12, 36] are aided by coherence. HW_{cc} allows children tasks to be scheduled on their parent, incurring no coherence overhead, or stolen by another core, which allows data to be pulled using HW_{cc}.

Systems-on-a-chip, which incorporate accelerators and general-purpose cores, are available commercially [42] and are a topic of current research [44]. The assortment of cores makes supporting multiple memory models on the same chip attractive. A hybrid approach allows for cores without HW_{cc} support, such as accelerator cores, to cooperate with cores that do have HW_{cc} support and interface with coherent general-purpose cores. While a single address space is not a requirement for heterogeneous systems, as demonstrated by the Cell processor [14] and GPUs [30], it may aid in portability and programmability by extending the current shared memory model to future heterogeneous systems. A hybrid approach allows for HW_{cc} to be leveraged for easier application porting from conventional shared memory machines and easier debugging for new applications. SW_{cc} can then be used to reduce the stress on the hardware coherence mechanisms to improve performance.

2.4 Summary

Hardware-managed and software-managed cache coherence offer both advantages and disadvantages for applications and system software. We list many of the tradeoffs in Table 1. A hybrid memory model such as COHESION leverages the benefits of each while mitigating the negative effects of the respective models. The key benefits from SW_{cc} are reduced network and directory costs. The key benefits from HW_{cc} derive from its ability to share data without explicit software actions, which, as we demonstrate, can be costly in terms of message overhead and instruction stream efficiency. A

	Programmability	Network Constraints	On-die Storage
HW_{cc}	Conventional CMP shared-memory paradigm; supports fine-grained, irregular sharing without relying on compiler or programmer for correctness	Potential dependences handled by hardware instead of extra instructions and coherence traffic	Optimized for HW_{cc}: when HW_{cc} desired, coherence data stored efficiently
SW_{cc}	Used in accelerators; provides programmer/compiler control over sharing	Eliminates probes/broadcasts for independent data, e.g., stack, private, immutable data	Optimized for SW_{cc}: minimal hardware overhead beyond hardware-managed caches
COHESION	Supports HW_{cc} and SW_{cc}; clear performance optimization strategies allowing $SW_{cc} \Leftrightarrow HW_{cc}$ transitions	SW_{cc} used to eliminate traffic for coarse-grain/regular sharing patterns; HW_{cc} for unpredictable dependences	Reduces pressure on HW_{cc} structures; enables hardware design optimizations based on HW_{cc} and SW_{cc} needs

Table 1: Tradeoffs for HW_{cc}, SW_{cc}, and COHESION.

hybrid approach can enable scalable hardware-managed coherence by supporting HW_{cc} for the regions of memory that require it, using SW_{cc} for data that does not. In comparison to a software-only approach, a hybrid memory model makes coherence management an optimization opportunity and not a correctness burden.

3. DESIGN

COHESION provides hardware support and a protocol to allow data to migrate between coherence domains at runtime, with fine granularity, and without the need for copy operations. The default behavior for COHESION is to keep all of memory coherent in the HW_{cc} domain. Software can alter the default behavior by modifying tables in memory that control how the system enforces coherence. No hardware coherence management is applied to data that are not shared, or can have coherence handled at a coarse granularity by software, using the SW_{cc} domain. The rest of this section describes the protocols and hardware support that enable on-the-fly coherence domain changes.

3.1 Baseline Architecture

Figure 4 shows a diagram of the 1024-core accelerator we use as a baseline. It is a variant of the Rigel architecture [22]. The processor has a single address space and three levels of cache. Each core is a simple, in-order processor with private L1 instruction and data caches and a RISC-like instruction set. Eight cores form a *cluster* and share a unified L2 cache. A single multi-banked shared last-level L3 cache serves as the point of coherence for the chip.

The interconnect between the cores and the L2 is a pipelined two-lane split-phase bus. The interconnect between the clusters and the L3 cache banks has two levels. The first level is a tree interconnect that combines the traffic of sixteen clusters. The root of each tree is connected to a crossbar that connects to L3 cache banks. Each four banks of L3 have an independent GDDR memory channel. Table 3 lists timing and sizing parameters for the design.

3.2 Hardware Coherence Protocol

The hardware protocol is represented on the right side of Figure 6. Data in the HW_{cc} domain uses an MSI protocol. An exclusive state is not used due to the high cost of exclusive to shared downgrades for read-shared data. Owned state is omitted since we use the L3 to communicate data and the directory to serialize accesses, removing much of the benefit of sourcing shared data from another L2.

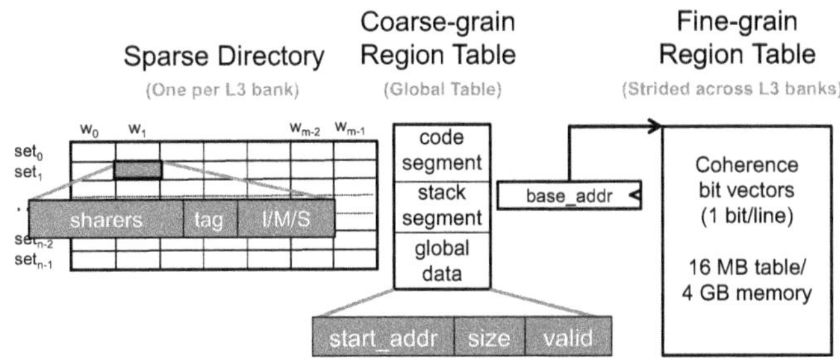

Figure 5: COHESION architecture.

For overall runtime experiments, a limited directory scheme [2] (Dir_4B) is used due to its lower storage overhead. Other experiments use a full-map scheme [8], which we use to provide a lower bound on the performance impact and message overhead of pure hardware coherence. We employ sparse directories [15, 34] where the directory only holds directory entries for lines present in at least one L2. Note that the directory storage overhead is worse for CMPs than multi-socket systems since the overhead grows linearly in the number of sharers, i.e., cores, and not sockets. Therefore, memory bandwidth does not scale with directory size as in multi-socket multiprocessors with directories. Duplicate tags [4] were not chosen due to their high required associativity (2048 ways) and difficulty supporting a multi-banked last-level cache which may require replicating the duplicate tags across L3 banks.

The baseline architecture is non-inclusive between L2 and L3 caches. The directory is inclusive of the L2s and thus may contain entries for lines not in the L3 cache. L2 evictions notify the directory and, if the sharer count drops to zero, the entry is deallocated from the directory. Entries evicted from the directory have all sharers invalidated.

One bank of the directory is attached to each L3 cache bank. All directory requests are serialized through a home directory bank, thus avoiding many of the potential races in three-party directory protocols [27]. Associating each L3 bank with a slice of the directory allows the two mechanisms to be collocated, reducing the complexity of the protocol implementation compared to a design where a directory access may initiate a request to a third party structure, such as another L2 cache as in Origin [27] or an L3 bank that is across the network.

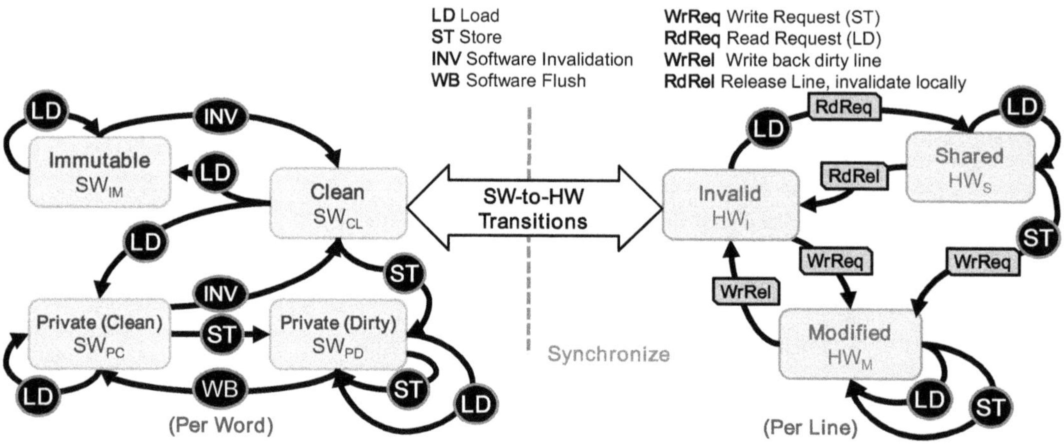

Figure 6: COHESION as a protocol bridge. Software-managed coherence is shown on the left, the hardware coherence protocol on the right. COHESION allows for blocks of memory to transition between the two.

3.3 Software Coherence Protocol

Our software coherence protocol is the Task Centric Memory Model [23] modified to support hybrid coherence, as shown on the left side of Figure 6. The protocol leverages the bulk-synchronous [41] (BSP) compute pattern. BSP comprises phases of mostly data-parallel execution followed by communication, with barriers separating each phase. The software protocol makes use of the fact that most data is not read-write shared across tasks between two barriers and most inter-task communication occurs across barriers. Other software protocols for managing coherence could be used, but we restrict ourselves to BSP for simplicity of illustration and its applicability to existing scalable programming models.

The software protocol provides a set of state transitions, which are initiated explicitly by software or implicitly by hardware, that allow for a programmer or compiler to reason about coherence for a block of data. The motivation for designing such a protocol is that in a system that uses cached memory for communication, but without hardware coherence, there is the potential for hardware to implicitly move data into a globally visible location. These implicit actions are uncontrollable by software and thus the SW_{cc} protocol, and by extension COHESION, must take them into account.

3.4 COHESION: A Hybrid Memory Model

COHESION achieves hybrid coherence by tracking the coherence domain to which regions of memory belong and orchestrating coherence domain transitions. As shown in Figure 5, the system is composed of a directory for tracking currently shared HW_{cc} lines, a coarse-grain region table for tracking common large regions of memory that are SW_{cc}, and a fine-grain region table that is used for tracking the rest of memory that may transition between HW_{cc} and SW_{cc}. One bit of state per line, the *incoherent bit*, is added to the L2 cache to track which cached lines are not HW_{cc}. A compressed hardware structure, such as the structure used in [43], was considered to move all tracking information on-die. However, we find a bitmap cached at the L3 to be a sufficient approach. If additional L3 latency for table accesses becomes a concern, the dense structure of the table is amenable to on-die caching.

The directory is queried when a request arrives at the L3. If the line is a directory hit, the line is in HW_{cc} and the response is handled by the directory. If the line is accessible to the requester, the L3 is accessed in the next cycle and the response is returned to the requesting L2. A directory hit with an L3 miss results in the directory access blocking. A response is generated when the fill from memory occurs. A directory miss results in the region tables being examined.

The coarse-grain region table is a small on-die structure that contains a map of address ranges that are in the SW_{cc} domain and is accessed in parallel with the directory. The three regions used most frequently are for code, private stacks, and persistent globally immutable data. When an access misses in the directory and the address maps into one of these ranges, the L3 cache controller responds with the data. The message includes a bit signalling to the L2 that an incoherent access has occurred. When the response arrives, the L2 sets the incoherent bit in the L2 cache tag for the line. Under SW_{cc}, if the line is invalidated by software or evicted while in the clean state, the line is simply dropped and no message is sent from the L2 to the L3.

The fine-grained region table is queried for all other accesses. The table may be cached in the L3 since the L3 is outside of the coherence protocol, which only applies between the L2 caches. We map all of memory using one bit per cache line, 16 MB total. To reduce the footprint of the table, a subset of memory could be designated as the COHESION-enabled region. A fine-grained region table lookup must access the L3. A minimum of one cycle of delay is incurred by fine-grained lookups and more under contention at the L3 or if an L3 cache miss for the table occurs. If the bit in the table is set, the L3 responds with the data and sends the incoherent bit along with the message. If the bit is cleared, an entry for the corresponding line is placed into the directory. The line is returned to the requester and thereafter is kept hardware coherent. Should a directory eviction occur followed by a future access to the table, the directory entry will be reinserted.

API Call	Description
`void * malloc(size_t sz)`	Allocate memory on coherent heap. Data is always in HW_{cc} domain. Standard libc implementation.
`void free(void * hwccptr)`	Deallocate object pointed to by `hwccptr`. Standard libc implementation.
`void * coh_malloc(size_t sz)`	Allocate memory on the incoherent heap. Data is allowed to transition coherence domains. Initial state is SW_{cc} and the data is not present in any private cache.
`void coh_free(void * swccptr)`	Deallocate object pointed to by ptr.
`void coh_SWcc_region(void * ptr, size_t sz)`	Make region ptr part of the SW_{cc} domain. Data may be HW_{cc} or SW_{cc} data.
`void coh_HWcc_region(void * ptr, size_t sz)`	Make region ptr part of the HW_{cc} domain. Data may be HW_{cc} or SW_{cc} data.

Table 2: Programmer-visible software API for COHESION.

The region tables are set up by the runtime at initialization. The bootstrap core allocates a 16MB region for the fine-grained region table, zeroes it, and sets a machine specific register to the base address of the table in physical memory. The process is akin to setting up a hardware-walked page table. To toggle the coherence domain of a line, the runtime uses atomic instructions, `atom.or` and `atom.and`, that bypass local caches and perform bitwise operations at the L3 to set or clear bits in the table, respectively. Atomic read-modify-write operations are necessary to avoid races between concurrent updates to the table.

Calculating an address to modify an entry in the table requires special consideration. The table is distributed across the L3 banks in our design. To remove the need for one L3 bank to query another L3 bank on a table lookup, we map the slice of the table covering one L3 bank into the same L3 bank it maps into. Since the address space is strided across L3 banks, the target address that we want to update in the table must be hashed before being added to the table base address[1]. Since the hash function is dependent upon the number of L3 banks, we choose to add an instruction to perform the hashing. The `hybrid.tbloff` instruction takes the target address and produces a word offset into the table that can be added to the base address before accessing the table from hardware. Adding such an instruction makes COHESION microarchitecture-agnostic since the number and size of L3 banks and the stride pattern can be changed without modifying software.

3.5 Software Interface to COHESION

In this section we discuss the application programming interface (API) to COHESION. The API calls are listed in Table 2. For this work we make two simplifying assumptions. First, we assume there is a single application running on the system. Second, we assume a single 32-bit address space where physical addresses match virtual addresses. The architecture we propose could be virtualized to support multiple applications and address spaces concurrently by using per-process region tables.

The COHESION region tables are initialized by the runtime when the application is loaded. The coarse-grain SW_{cc} regions are set for the code segment, the constant data region, and the per-core stack region. The code segment and constant data address ranges are found in the ELF header for the application binary. Our architecture does not support self-modifying code so HW_{cc} is not required for cached instructions. Variable-sized stacks are possible by treating the stack region as a SW_{cc} heap, but fixed-sized stacks were found to be sufficient for our current implementation. There are two heaps in our implementation: a conventional C-style heap that is kept coherent and another that is not kept HW_{cc} by default. The *incoherent heap* is used for data that may transition coherence domains during execution. Note that the minimum sized allocation on the incoherent heap is 64 bytes, or two cache lines, so that the metadata for the allocation can be kept coherent. Current libc implementations support 16-32 byte minimum allocations, so we believe 64 bytes to be reasonable.

3.6 Coherence Domain Transitions

A transition between SW_{cc} and HW_{cc} is initiated by word-aligned, uncached read-modify-write operations performed by the runtime to the fine-grained region table. The issuing core blocks until the transition is completed by the directory for the purposes of memory ordering. If a request for multiple line state transitions occurs, the directory serializes the requests line-by-line. All lines that may transition between coherence domains are initially allocated using the incoherent heap in our implementation and the initial state of these lines is SW_{cc}. The runtime can transition SW_{cc} (HW_{cc}) lines to be HW_{cc} (SW_{cc}) by clearing (setting) the state bits in the fine-grained region table.

The directory controller is responsible for orchestrating the $HW_{cc} \Leftrightarrow SW_{cc}$ transitions. The directory snoops the address range for the fine-grained region table and on an access that changes coherence domain of a line, the directory performs the actions described below to transition between SW_{cc} and HW_{cc}. The request is completed by sending an acknowledgement to the issuing core. Handling the transitions at the directory allows for requests for a line to be serialized across the system. Coherence domain transitions for a single line thus occur in a total order across the system with all other coherent and non-coherent accesses at the L3 being partially ordered by the transitions.

$HW_{cc} \Rightarrow SW_{cc}$ **Transitions** To move a line out of the hardware coherent domain requires removing any directory state associated with the line, updating the table, and putting the line in a consistent state known to software. Figure 7(a) shows the potential states a line can be in when software initiates a $HW_{cc} \Rightarrow SW_{cc}$ transition. Each of the states corresponds to a possible state allowed by the MSI directory protocol. After a transition is complete, the line is not

[1]DRAM row stride is used. $addr_{[10..0]}$ map to the same memory controller and $addr_{[13..11]}$ are used to stride across controllers. The hashing function for an eight controller configuration uses $addr_{[9..5]}$ to index into the word, and the table word offset address is: $addr_{[31..24]} \circ addr_{[13..11]} \circ addr_{[23..14]} \circ addr_{[10]} << 2$.

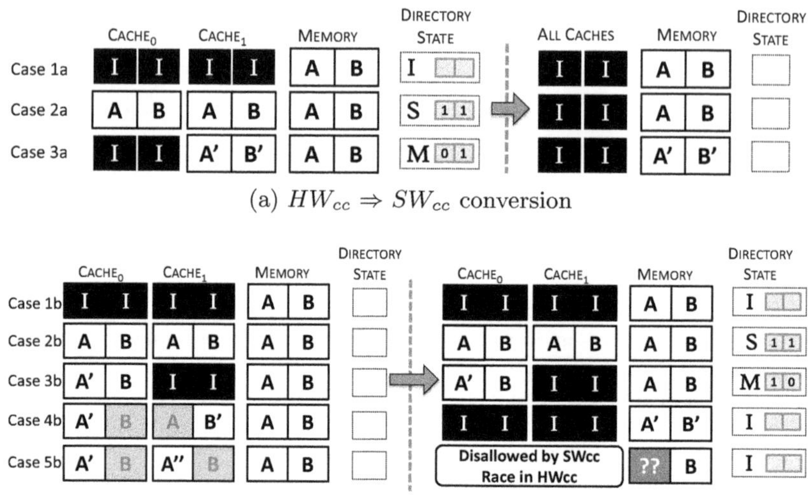

(a) $HW_{cc} \Rightarrow SW_{cc}$ conversion

(b) $SW_{cc} \Rightarrow HW_{cc}$ conversion

Figure 7: Potential system states on a $SW_{cc} \Leftrightarrow HW_{cc}$ conversion. Memory and L3 are interchangeable. Each block shown has two words. A and B are the initial values. On the left side of the figure, A', A", and B' denote distinct modified values in the local cache. Grayed blocks are potentially valid, but are not accessed by software. The right side of the figure shows the system state after the state transition occurs.

present in any L2 and the current value is present in the L3 cache or in memory.

For Case 1a of Figure 7(a), the directory controller queries the directory and finds the entry not present indicating that there are no sharers. Therefore, no action must be taken other than to set the bit in the region table. Case 2a has the line in the shared state with one or more sharers. The directory performs a directory eviction that invalidates all sharers of the line. When all acknowledgements are received, the directory entry is removed, the bit is set in the region table, and the response is returned to the core requesting the transition. When a line is in the modified state, shown in Case 3a, a newer version of the data exists in some L2. The directory sends a writeback request to the owner. When the response arrives, the L3 is updated, the table is modified, and a response is sent to the requester.

$SW_{cc} \Rightarrow HW_{cc}$ **Transitions** The left half of Figure 7(b) shows the potential states that a line may be in for two L2 caches when a line is under SW_{cc}. Since the directory has no knowledge of the line state, a transition to HW_{cc} initiates a broadcast clean request sent from the directory. When the line is found in an L2 in the clean state, the incoherent bit is cleared, i.e., the line is now susceptible to cache probes, but the line is not evicted from the L2. Clean lines send an acknowledgement message to the directory which adds the L2 to the list of sharers. If the line is not found in the L2, a negative acknowledgement is sent to the directory. Figure 7(b), Cases 1b and 2b demonstrate transitions for lines that are not modified.

If a dirty line is found, shown in Cases 3b and 4b, the L2 sends the directory a notification. If there are any read sharers, the directory sends messages forcing all readers to invalidate the line and the owners to write back the dirty copies. If the line is dirty in only one cache, the sharer is upgraded to owner at the directory and no writeback occurs, saving bandwidth. If multiple writers are found, writeback requests are sent to all L2s holding modified lines and invalidations are sent to all L2s holding clean lines. Our architecture maintains per-word dirty bits with the cache lines allowing the L3 to merge the result of multiple writers if the write sets are disjoint. When either operation is complete, the line is not present in any L2 and the L3/memory holds the most recent copy of the line.

The system can always force a $SW_{cc} \Rightarrow HW_{cc}$ transition to make caches consistent, such as between task swaps, but the data values may not be safe. It is possible for buggy software to modify the same line in two L2 caches concurrently when under the control of SW_{cc}, Figure 7(b), Case 5b. This state represents a hardware race. To safely clean the state of a word, the runtime can always turn on coherence and then zero the value. It will cause the dirty values in the separate caches to be thrown away and the zeroed value to persist. For debugging, it may be useful to have the directory signal an exception with its return message to the requesting core.

4. EVALUATION

Two benefits of using COHESION are a reduction in message traffic and a reduction in the on-die directory storage overhead compared to HW_{cc}. COHESION shows performance comparable to pure HW_{cc}, despite optimistic assumptions for the pure model, and a large improvement over HW_{cc} with a realistic on-die directory.

4.1 Methodology

We simulate the architecture described in Section 3.1. We use an execution-driven simulation of the design and run each benchmark for at least one billion instructions. We model cores, caches, interconnects, and memory controllers. The cycle-accurate DRAM model uses GDDR5 timings.

We evaluate four design points: SW_{cc}, optimistic HW_{cc}, HW_{cc} with realistic hardware assumptions, and COHESION with the same realistic hardware assumptions. The hardware configuration for SW_{cc} is equivalent to our baseline described in Section 3.1, but with no directory and all sharing

Parameter	Value	Unit	Parameter	Value	Unit	Parameter	Value	Unit
Cores	1024	–	Line Size	32	bytes	Directory Size (realistic)	16K	$\frac{entries}{L3\ bank}$
Memory BW	192	GB/s	Core Freq.	1.5	GHz	Directory Assoc. (realistic)	128	ways
DRAM Channels	8	–	DRAM Type	GDDR5	–	Directory Size (optimistic)	∞	$\frac{entries}{L3\ bank}$
L1I Size	2	KB	L1I Assoc.	2	way	Directory Assoc. (optimistic)	Full	–
L1D Size	1	KB	L1D Assoc.	2	way	L2 Ports	2	R/W
L2 Size	64	KB	L2 Assoc.	16	way	L3 Ports	1	R/W
L2 Size (Total)	8	MB	L2 Latency	4	clks	L3 Latency	16+	clks
L3 Size	4	MB	L3 Assoc.	8	way	L3 Banks	32	–

Table 3: Timing parameters for the baseline architecture.

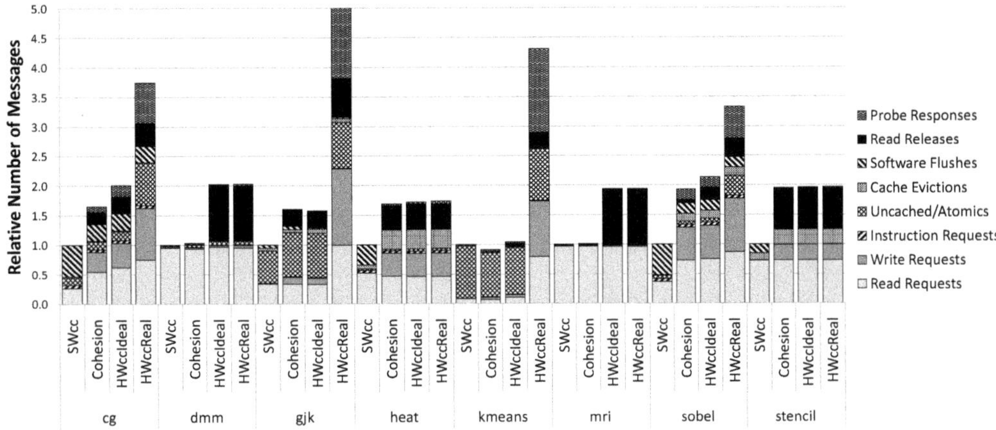

Figure 8: L2 output message counts for SW_{cc}, COHESION, HW_{cc} with a full on-die full-map directory, and HW_{cc} with a 128-way sparse directory on-die normalized to SW_{cc}.

handled by software. For SW_{cc} writes occur at the L2 with no delay and evictions performed to clean data happen without creating any network traffic. The optimistic HW_{cc} case removes all directory conflicts by making the on-die directory infinitely sized and fully-associative. The behavior is equivalent to a full-map directory in memory [8], but with zero cost access to the directory. The HW_{cc} realistic case comprises a 128-way sparse directory at each L3 cache bank. The COHESION configuration uses the same hardware as the realistic HW_{cc} configurations.

The applications that we evaluate are optimized kernels extracted from scientific and visual computing applications. The SW_{cc} variants have explicit invalidate and writeback instructions in the code at task boundaries. The COHESION variants have such instructions when SW_{cc} is used and none for data in the HW_{cc} domain. The COHESION API, as shown in Table 2, is used to allocate the SW_{cc} and non-coherent data on the incoherent heap. The HW_{cc} versions eliminate programmed coherence actions in the benchmark code. The benchmarks are written using a task-based, barrier-synchronized work queue model. The kernels include conjugate gradient linear solver (`cg`), dense matrix multiply (`dmm`), collision detection (`gjk`), 2D stencil (`heat`), k-means clustering (`kmeans`), medical image reconstruction (`mri`), edge detection (`sobel`), and 3D stencil (`stencil`).

4.2 Message Reduction

Figure 8 shows the number of messages sent by the L2s to the directory, normalized to SW_{cc}. There is a reduction in messages relative to the HW_{cc} configurations across all benchmarks. The `kmeans` benchmark is the only benchmark where SW_{cc} shows higher message counts than COHESION. This reduction is due to optimizations that reduce the number of uncached operations issued by the benchmark by relying upon HW_{cc} under COHESION. For some benchmarks, the number of messages are nearly identical across COHESION and optimistic HW_{cc} configurations, such as `heat` and `stencil`. We see potential to remove many of these messages by applying further, albeit more complicated, optimization strategies using COHESION. We leave more elaborate coherence domain remapping strategies to future work.

4.3 Directory Entry Savings

Figures 9a and 9b show the normalized runtime for different directory sizes under HW_{cc} and COHESION, respectively, compared to an infinite-sized directory. We make directories fully associative to isolate the influence of capacity. Figure 9a demonstrates the rapid drop off in performance for shrinking directory sizes. In Figure 9b we show that COHESION reduces the performance sensitivity with respect to directory sizing across all benchmarks. Figure 9c shows the mean and maximum number of directory entries used by COHESION and the optimistic HW_{cc} baseline. We average samples taken every 1000 cycles. We classify the entries as to whether they map to code, which is negligible, private stack data, or heap allocations and static global data. The HW_{cc} data in Figure 9c is a proxy for the on-die working set of the benchmarks since all lines cached in an L2 have allocated directory entries and all uncached lines are removed from the directory when the L2 sharer count drops to zero. The data also illustrates the degree of read sharing since the ratio of directory entries to valid L2 cache lines is smaller

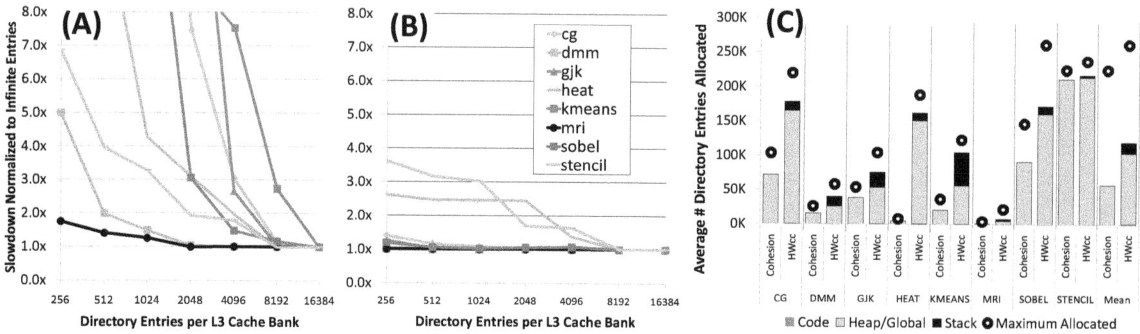

Figure 9: Slowdown for different directory sizes is shown for (A) HW_{cc} and (B) COHESION. Note that performance falls off precipitously in HW_{cc}. (C) shows the time-average (sampled every 1000 cycles) and maximum number of directory entries allocated for for both COHESION and HW_{cc} when directories have unbounded size and associativity.

when there are more sharers. The implication of more read sharing is that smaller directories are needed.

Across all benchmarks, COHESION provides a reduction in average directory utilization of 2.1×. For some benchmarks, simply keeping the stack incoherent achieves most of the benefit, but on average, the stack alone only represents 15% of the directory resources. Code makes up a trivial portion of the directory entries since our benchmarks have large data sets. These results show that most of the savings comes from using COHESION to allocate globally shared data on the incoherent heap, thus avoiding coherence overhead for that data.

4.4 Directory Area Estimates

To quantify the area savings COHESION could provide, we evaluate the on-die area costs for HW_{cc} by comparing the number of bits necessary for each scheme. The 128 L2 caches have a capacity of 2048 lines each, resulting in 256K 32-byte lines on-die, and 8 MB total. A full-map directory requires 128 bits for sharer data and 2 bits of state for each line. For a sparse scheme, 16 additional tag bits are also be required. A limited scheme with four pointers (Dir_4B) requires 28 bits per entry for sharer state and 2 bits for coherence state. The sparse directory structure is set-associative and banked to mitigate the effects port conflicts and load imbalance across L3 banks. The overhead for a full-map directory is 9.28 MB (113% of L2) and a limited scheme is 2.88 MB (35.1% of L2).

Duplicate tags [4] require 21 bits for each L2 tag. Since the directories are distributed across L3 banks, it may be necessary to replicate duplicate tag entries across banks, which leads to a 1× to 8× overhead. Duplicate tags require require 736KB * $N_{replicas}$. While a single set of duplicate tags would result in only 736 KB (8.98% of L2) overhead, the structure would still be 2048-way associative and need to service up to 32 requests per cycle on behalf of the L3 cache banks.

Clearly, none of these optimistic options is attractive for a practical design. However, COHESION has the potential to reduce hardware overhead by building smaller directories, or fewer replicas and ports for duplicate tags, compared to a pure HW_{cc} system, making known techniques more scalable and attractive. Our results indicate that a greater than 2× reduction in directory utilization is possible, which could yield 5% to 55% reduction in L2 overhead for directory storage on-die.

4.5 Application Performance

Figure 10 shows the run time of our benchmarks normalized to COHESION. As the results demonstrate, two benchmarks perform better and two slightly worse with COHESION relative to SW_{cc} and optimistic HW_{cc}, while the others show insignificant differences. Compared to realistic hardware assumptions, COHESION delivers many times better performance. These benefits come from reduced message traffic (Section 4.2) and a reduction in the number of flush operations issued by the SW_{cc} configurations, many of which may be unnecessary, as shown in Figure 3.

The negative performance difference between COHESION and optimistic HW_{cc} is less than 5% for `gjk` and `mri` and could be improved to parity with optimistic HW_{cc} using more complex coherence domain transitions not evaluated in this work. Moreover, neither benchmark is limited by coherence costs, but rather by task scheduling overhead due to task granularity in the case of `gjk` and execution efficiency for `mri` due to its high arithmetic intensity. The `kmeans` benchmark has a large number of atomic operations that can conflict with SW_{cc} coherence actions and lead to decreased performance due to queuing effects in the network. In some cases, HW_{cc} has the effect of dispersing the coherence actions in time, thus reducing the effect of queuing delays.

4.6 Summary

COHESION reduces the number of messages sent compared to a purely hardware coherent configuration, thus reducing demand on the network. COHESION is able to reduce the pressure on the directory, thus reducing the resources needed by the directory to achieve similar performance to a purely hardware coherent design. While we find an increase in the total number of messages injected when converting regions from the SW_{cc} domain to the HW_{cc} domain, we show improved performance due to the reduction in time spent issuing coherence management instructions under SW_{cc} and the timeliness of HW_{cc} messages. Overall, COHESION provides increased performance, reduced network demands, and less directory pressure for most workloads compared to SW_{cc} or HW_{cc} alone.

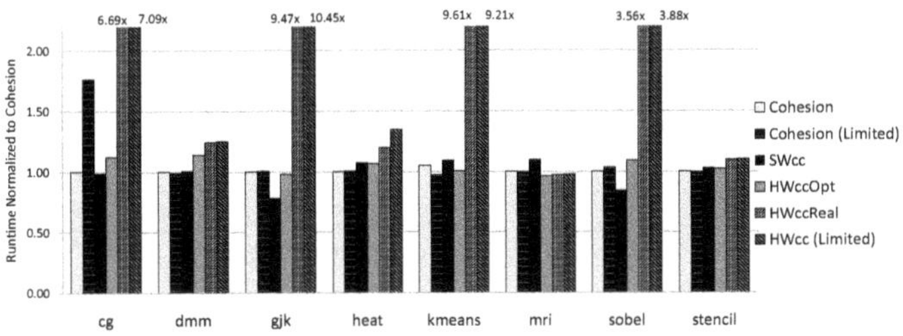

Figure 10: Relative performance for COHESION with a full-map directory, COHESION with a Dir_4B directory, SW_{cc}, optimistic HW_{cc}, and $HW_{cc}$with a full-map and Dir_4B 128-way sparse directory. All results normalized to COHESION with a full-map directory.

There is an interplay between message count, directory utilization, and execution time. Reducing the dependence on the directory by minimizing the number of lines tracked by HW_{cc} allows for fewer on-die directory resources to be provisioned and can avoid pathological cases due to directory set aliasing and capacity issues. However, doing so may lead to more messages being injected, thus reducing performance unless network capacity is increased. The programming effort is increased beyond developing an application using HW_{cc} alone as the developer must partition data accesses into SW_{cc} and HW_{cc} domains. Therefore, the tradeoff is between the level of achieved performance and the amount of programming effort required.

5. RELATED WORK

In this section, we put COHESION into context with previous work in scalable hardware-managed and software-managed coherence.

Hardware Schemes.

Snoopy coherence protocols [13] rely upon ordered networks and broadcasts to maintain consistency across caches, but are difficult to scale. Directory schemes [8] provide a scalable alternative, but full implementations suffer from high memory overhead. Limited directories [2] and sparse directories [15] can aid in reducing memory overhead with the potential cost of extra messages.

Coarse-grain coherence tracking [7] and RegionScout [33] both propose mechanisms to reduce coherence traffic in broadcast-based systems by managing coherence at a coarser granularity than a line. While these techniques can reduce storage costs, both mechanisms impose restrictions on alignment and sizing of coherence regions and may lead to increased message traffic; both are situations we wish to avoid with COHESION. Token coherence [32] attempts to increase scalability of coherence by associating a fixed number of tokens with each line and requiring a core to posses at least one token to read and all tokens to write. Token coherence requires additional messages for token requests avoided in COHESION by using software-coherence for known-private regions. Moreover, Raghavan [35] adds a directory to reduce broadcast occurrences, but still requires all lines to be tracked by the on-die directory.

Modern accelerator hardware, such as Cell [14] and NVIDIA Tesla [30], provide a variety of access modes to data located in different physical address spaces, but require explicit software management of data movement. Leverich et al. [29] demonstrate the benefit of software management of data movement on hardware cached platforms, which COHESION can facilitate with the added precision of variable coherence regions.

Software/Hybrid Schemes.

Distributed shared memory (DSM) provides the illusion of a single coherent address space across processors at a coarse grain using virtual memory and a runtime system in the case of TreadMarks [3] and at a fine grain using compiler support such as in Shasta [40]. While these approaches could trivially support incoherence due to their distributed memory architecture, they synthesized coherence when needed fully in software. Cooperative Shared Memory [18] uses software hints to reduce the complexity and cost of hardware supported coherence. Software-assisted hardware schemes, such as LimitLESS [9], trap to software when the number of sharers supported by hardware is exceeded. CSM and LimitLESS suffer from high round-trip latency between directory and cores in a hierarchically cached system and require all data to be tracked by the coherence protocol, resulting in unnecessary traffic for some data.

Several previous works on distributed memory multiprocessors investigate hybrid schemes that combine message passing with hardware-managed coherent shared memory. FLASH [26] and Typhoon [37] utilized programmable protocol controllers that support customized protocols. User-Level Shared Memory in Typhoon made fine-grained access control a key component of customizing protocols. COHESION provides a mechanism to allow such customization without a separate protocol controller. Munin [5] used parallel program access patterns to provide different consistency guarantees to different classes of data. Multiphase Shared Arrays [10] provide a means for the programmer to specify access modes for array data and to change the mode for different program phases. COHESION on an integrated shared memory multiprocessor captures these features with modest hardware and an intuitive programming model that does not require a message passing component.

The ability to change the strictness of regions of memory is available in a limited form on x86 processors with write combining [21] and PowerPC allows for pages to be set incoherent [20]. Both mechanisms work at page granularity and require operating system support. A hybrid x86 system with a consistent programming model for GPU and CPU cores using a subset of the address space has been proposed [39]. Unlike COHESION, that work does not investigate dynamic transitions between different coherence domains. Furthermore, while [39] focuses solely on a host-accelerator model with one CPU core, COHESION is demonstrated using 1024 cooperating cores.

WildFire [16] used operating system support to transition between line-level ccNUMA shared memory and a form of COMA known as Coherent Memory Replication (CMR). CMR and ccNUMA pages trade off coherence space overhead for coherence message overhead since all lines in the system were tracked by hardware and CMR pages require replication of coherence state. Copy operations are required by replication under CMR, which are eliminated by COHESION. Unlike WildFire, COHESION provides symmetric access to the last-level cache, analogous to memory in DSM systems, and does not present a tradeoff between state and message overheads; it reduces both when using SW_{cc}.

Reactive NUCA [17] uses operating system remapping of page-sized regions on a distributed NUCA multicore. The analysis in [17] shows that different regions of memory possess different coherence needs, an opportunity for hybrid coherence, and illuminates many of the tradeoffs in scaling distributed versus shared cache architectures. In contrast to COHESION, the work evaluates mostly server and multiprogrammed workloads scaling to eight or sixteen cores, while we target the class of visual computing applications that tend to have higher degrees of read-sharing and more structured sharing patterns [6, 19, 23, 31] and are shown to scale to 100+ cores.

6. CONCLUSION

In this paper we present COHESION, a memory model that allows applications to combine the benefits of software and hardware coherence schemes into one unified model. We show the opportunity for message reduction and area reduction provided by a hybrid scheme relative to hardware-only cache coherence. We present a design for the hardware required to support a hybrid memory model and the protocol that the software and directory must follow to safely transition between coherence domains.

Our evaluation demonstrates that hardware coherence results in an increased number of network messages, even for data-parallel kernels. Even with optimistic hardware assumptions, hardware coherence provides poor performance for some benchmarks and can lead to thrashing behavior under more realistic hardware assumptions, resulting in significant slowdown. We find that, using COHESION, we can reduce the number of messages and thus increase performance while relaxing the design requirements for the network.

Lastly, we find that having both hardware-managed coherence and software-managed coherence as options enables developers to optimize portions of an application in a targeted way. Developers focus on data structure organization and matching coherence needs to the data access patterns across phases of execution instead of reasoning about code paths that interact and reorganizing data layouts for each phase of computation. Furthermore, we see potential for using a hybrid approach for integrating host processors and accelerators under one memory model. Ultimately, COHESION makes explicit coherence management for accelerators an optimization opportunity and not a correctness burden.

7. ACKNOWLEDGEMENTS

The authors acknowledge the support of the Focus Center for Circuit & System Solutions (C2S2 and GSRC), two of the five research centers funded under the Focus Center Research Program, a Semiconductor Research Corporation Program. The authors thank the Trusted ILLIAC Center at the Information Trust Institute for their contribution of use of their computing cluster.

8. REFERENCES

[1] S. V. Adve, V. S. Adve, M. D. Hill, and M. K. Vernon. Comparison of hardware and software cache coherence schemes. *SIGARCH Comput. Archit. News*, 19(3):298–308, 1991.

[2] A. Agarwal, R. Simoni, J. Hennessy, and M. Horowitz. An evaluation of directory schemes for cache coherence. In *ISCA '88: Proceedings of the 15th Annual International Symposium on Computer Architecture*, pages 280–298, Los Alamitos, CA, USA, 1988. IEEE Computer Society Press.

[3] C. Amza, A. L. Cox, S. Dwarkadas, P. Keleher, H. Lu, R. Rajamony, W. Yu, and W. Zwaenepoel. Treadmarks: Shared memory computing on networks of workstations. *Computer*, 29(2), 1996.

[4] L. A. Barroso, K. Gharachorloo, R. McNamara, A. Nowatzyk, S. Qadeer, B. Sano, S. Smith, R. Stets, and B. Verghese. Piranha: a scalable architecture based on single-chip multiprocessing. In *ISCA '00: Proceedings of the 27th Annual International Symposium on Computer Architecture*, pages 282–293, New York, NY, USA, 2000. ACM.

[5] J. K. Bennett, J. B. Carter, and W. Zwaenepoel. Munin: distributed shared memory based on type-specific memory coherence. In *PPoPP'90*, pages 168–176, New York, NY, USA, 1990. ACM.

[6] C. Bienia, S. Kumar, J. P. Singh, and K. Li. The PARSEC benchmark suite: Characterization and architectural implications. Technical Report TR-81108, Princeton University, January 2008.

[7] J. F. Cantin, M. H. Lipasti, and J. E. Smith. Improving multiprocessor performance with coarse-grain coherence tracking. In *ISCA '05: Proceedings of the 32nd Annual International Symposium on Computer Architecture*, pages 246–257, Washington, DC, USA, 2005. IEEE Computer Society.

[8] L. M. Censier and P. Feautrier. A new solution to coherence problems in multicache systems. *IEEE Trans. Comput.*, 27(12):1112–1118, 1978.

[9] D. Chaiken, J. Kubiatowicz, and A. Agarwal. LimitLESS directories: A scalable cache coherence scheme. In *ASPLOS-IV: Proceedings of the fourth international conference on Architectural support for programming languages and operating systems*, pages 224–234, New York, NY, USA, 1991. ACM.

[10] J. DeSouza and L. V. Kalé. MSA: Multiphase specifically shared arrays. In *Proceedings of the 17th International Workshop on Languages and Compilers for Parallel Computing*, West Lafayette, Indiana, USA, September 2004.

[11] J. Dorsey, S. Searles, M. Ciraula, S. Johnson, N. Bujanos, D. Wu, M. Braganza, S. Meyers, E. Fang, and R. Kumar. An integrated quad-core opteron processor. In *Solid-State Circuits Conference, 2007. ISSCC 2007. Digest of Technical Papers. IEEE International*, pages 102–103, Feb. 2007.

[12] M. Frigo, C. E. Leiserson, and K. H. Randall. The implementation of the cilk-5 multithreaded language. *SIGPLAN Not.*, 33(5), 1998.

[13] J. R. Goodman. Using cache memory to reduce processor-memory traffic. In *ISCA'83*, Los Alamitos, CA, USA, 1983.

[14] M. Gschwind. Chip multiprocessing and the cell broadband engine. In *Proceedings of the 3rd conference on Computing frontiers*, pages 1–8. ACM, 2006.

[15] A. Gupta, W. Weber, and T. Mowry. Reducing memory and traffic requirements for scalable directory-based cache coherence schemes. In *In International Conference on Parallel Processing*, pages 312–321, 1990.

[16] E. Hagersten and M. Koster. Wildfire: A scalable path for smps. In *HPCA '99: Proceedings of the 5th International Symposium on High Performance Computer Architecture*, page 172, Washington, DC, USA, 1999. IEEE Computer Society.

[17] N. Hardavellas, M. Ferdman, B. Falsafi, and A. Ailamaki. Reactive nuca: near-optimal block placement and replication in distributed caches. In *ISCA '09: Proceedings of the 36th Annual International Symposium on Computer Architecture*, pages 184–195, New York, NY, USA, 2009. ACM.

[18] M. D. Hill, J. R. Larus, S. K. Reinhardt, and D. A. Wood. Cooperative shared memory: software and hardware for scalable multiprocessors. *ACM Trans. Comput. Syst.*, 11(4), 1993.

[19] C. J. Hughes, R. Grzeszczuk, E. Sifakis, D. Kim, S. Kumar, A. P. Selle, J. Chhugani, M. Holliman, and Y.-K. Chen. Physical simulation for animation and visual effects: parallelization and characterization for chip multiprocessors. In *Proceedings of the 34th Annual International Symposium on Computer Architecture*, 2007.

[20] IBM Staff. *PowerPC Microprocessor 32-bit Family: The Programming Environments*, February 2000.

[21] Intel Corporation. *Intel 64 and IA-32 Architectures Software Developer's Manual, Volume: 1*, November 2008.

[22] J. H. Kelm, D. R. Johnson, M. R. Johnson, N. C. Crago, W. Tuohy, A. Mahesri, S. S. Lumetta, M. I. Frank, and S. J. Patel. Rigel: An architecture and scalable programming interface for a 1000-core accelerator. In *Proceedings of the International Symposium on Computer Architecture*, pages 140–151, June 2009.

[23] J. H. Kelm, D. R. Johnson, S. S. Lumetta, M. I. Frank, and S. J. Patel. A task-centric memory model for scalable accelerator architectures. In *Proceedings of the International Conference on Parallel Architectures and Compilation Techniques*, pages 77–87, September 2009.

[24] P. Kongetira, K. Aingaran, and K. Olukotun. Niagara: A 32-way multithreaded sparc processor. *IEEE Micro*, 25(2):21–29, 2005.

[25] A. Krishnamurthy, D. E. Culler, A. Dusseau, S. C. Goldstein, S. Lumetta, T. von Eicken, and K. Yelick. Parallel programming in Split-C. In *SC'93*, 1993.

[26] J. Kuskin, D. Ofelt, M. Heinrich, J. Heinlein, R. Simoni, K. Gharachorloo, J. Chapin, D. Nakahira, J. Baxter, M. Horowitz, A. Gupta, M. Rosenblum, and J. Hennessy. The stanford flash multiprocessor. In *ISCA '98: 25 years of the International Symposia on Computer Architecture (selected papers)*, pages 485–496, New York, NY, USA, 1998. ACM.

[27] J. Laudon and D. Lenoski. The SGI Origin: a ccNUMA highly scalable server. *SIGARCH Comput. Archit. News*, 25(2):241–251, 1997.

[28] H. Q. Le, W. J. Starke, J. S. Fields, F. P. O'Connell, D. Q. Nguyen, B. J. Ronchetti, W. M. Sauer, E. M. Schwarz, and M. T. Vaden. IBM POWER6 microarchitecture. *IBM J. Res. Dev.*, 51(6):639–662, 2007.

[29] J. Leverich, H. Arakida, A. Solomatnikov, A. Firoozshahian, M. Horowitz, and C. Kozyrakis. Comparing memory systems for chip multiprocessors. In *ISCA'07*, pages 358–368, 2007.

[30] E. Lindholm, J. Nickolls, S. Oberman, and J. Montrym. NVIDIA Tesla: A unified graphics and computing architecture. *IEEE Micro*, 28(2):39–55, 2008.

[31] A. Mahesri, D. Johnson, N. Crago, and S. J. Patel. Tradeoffs in designing accelerator architectures for visual computing. In *Proceedings of the International Symposium on Microarchitecture*, 2008.

[32] M. M. K. Martin, M. D. Hill, and D. A. Wood. Token coherence: decoupling performance and correctness. In *ISCA '03: Proceedings of the 30th Annual International Symposium on Computer Architecture*, pages 182–193, New York, NY, USA, 2003. ACM.

[33] A. Moshovos. RegionScout: Exploiting coarse grain sharing in snoop-based coherence. In *ISCA '05: Proceedings of the 32nd Annual International Symposium on Computer Architecture*, pages 234–245, Washington, DC, USA, 2005. IEEE Computer Society.

[34] B. W. O'Krafka and A. R. Newton. An empirical evaluation of two memory-efficient directory methods. In *ISCA '90: Proceedings of the 17th Annual International Symposium on Computer Architecture*, pages 138–147, New York, NY, USA, 1990. ACM.

[35] A. Raghavan, C. Blundell, and M. M. K. Martin. Token tenure: Patching token counting using directory-based cache coherence. In *MICRO '08: Proceedings of the 2008 41st IEEE/ACM International Symposium on Microarchitecture*, pages 47–58, Washington, DC, USA, 2008. IEEE Computer Society.

[36] J. Reinders. *Intel Threading Building Blocks: Outfitting C++ for Multi-core Processor Parallelism.* O'Reilly, 2007.

[37] S. K. Reinhardt, J. R. Larus, and D. A. Wood. Tempest and typhoon: user-level shared memory. In *ISCA '94: Proceedings of the 21st Annual International Symposium on Computer Architecture*, pages 325–336, Los Alamitos, CA, USA, 1994. IEEE Computer Society Press.

[38] S. Rusu, S. Tam, H. Muljono, J. Stinson, D. Ayers, J. Chang, R. Varada, M. Ratta, and S. Kottapalli. A 45nm 8-core enterprise xeon processor. In *Solid-State Circuits Conference - Digest of Technical Papers, 2009. ISSCC 2009. IEEE International*, pages 56–57, Feb. 2009.

[39] B. Saha, X. Zhou, H. Chen, Y. Gao, S. Yan, M. Rajagopalan, J. Fang, P. Zhang, R. Ronen, and A. Mendelson. Programming model for a heterogeneous x86 platform. In *PLDI '09: Proceedings of the 2009 ACM SIGPLAN conference on Programming language design and implementation*, Dublin, Ireland, Jun 2009. ACM.

[40] D. J. Scales, K. Gharachorloo, and C. A. Thekkath. Shasta: a low overhead, software-only approach for fine-grain shared memory. In *ASPLOS'96*, 1996.

[41] L. G. Valiant. A bridging model for parallel computation. *Communications of the ACM*, 33(8), 1990.

[42] S. J. Vaughn-Nichols. Vendors draw up a new graphics-hardware approach. *Computer*, 42(5):11–13, 2009.

[43] E. Witchel, J. Cates, and K. Asanović. Mondrian memory protection. In *ASPLOS-X: Proceedings of the 10th international conference on Architectural support for programming languages and operating systems*, pages 304–316, New York, NY, USA, 2002. ACM.

[44] H. Wong, A. Bracy, E. Schuchman, T. M. Aamodt, J. D. Collins, P. H. Wang, G. Chinya, A. K. Groen, H. Jiang, and H. Wang. Pangaea: a tightly-coupled ia32 heterogeneous chip multiprocessor. In *PACT '08: Proceedings of the 17th international conference on Parallel architectures and compilation techniques*, pages 52–61, New York, NY, USA, 2008. ACM.

Data Marshaling for Multi-core Architectures

M. Aater Suleman† Onur Mutlu§ José A. Joao† Khubaib† Yale N. Patt†

†The University of Texas at Austin
{suleman, joao, khubaib, patt}@hps.utexas.edu

§Carnegie Mellon University
onur@cmu.edu

ABSTRACT

Previous research has shown that Staged Execution (SE), i.e., dividing a program into segments and executing each segment at the core that has the data and/or functionality to best run that segment, can improve performance and save power. However, SE's benefit is limited because most segments access *inter-segment data*, i.e., data generated by the previous segment. When consecutive segments run on different cores, accesses to inter-segment data incur cache misses, thereby reducing performance. This paper proposes *Data Marshaling (DM)*, a new technique to eliminate cache misses to inter-segment data. DM uses profiling to identify instructions that generate inter-segment data, and adds only 96 bytes/core of storage overhead. We show that DM significantly improves the performance of two promising Staged Execution models, Accelerated Critical Sections and producer-consumer pipeline parallelism, on both homogeneous and heterogeneous multi-core systems. In both models, DM can achieve almost all of the potential of ideally eliminating cache misses to inter-segment data. DM's performance benefit increases with the number of cores.

Categories and Subject Descriptors: C.0 [General]: System architectures;
General Terms: Design, Performance.
Keywords: Staged Execution, Critical Sections, Pipelining, CMP.

1. INTRODUCTION

Previous research has shown that execution models that *segment* a program and run each segment on its best suited core (the core with the data and/or the functional units needed for the segment) unveil new performance opportunities. Examples of such models include Accelerated Critical Sections [41], producer-consumer pipelines, computation spreading [13], Cilk [10], and Apple's Grand Central Dispatch [5]. We collectively refer to these models as *Staged Execution (SE).*[1] In SE, when a core encounters a new segment, it ships the segment to the segment's *home core* (i.e., the core most suited for the segment's execution). The home core buffers the execution request from the *requesting core* and processes it in turn.

While SE can improve locality [41, 11, 18], increase parallelism [43], and leverage heterogeneous cores [4], its performance benefit is limited when a segment accesses *inter-segment* data, i.e., data generated by the previous segment. Since each segment runs on a different core, accesses to inter-segment data generate cache misses, which reduces performance. Unfortunately, hardware prefetching is ineffective for inter-segment data because the data access patterns are irregular and fewer cache lines need to be transferred than required to train a hardware prefetcher.

To reduce cache misses for inter-segment data, we propose a mechanism to identify and send the inter-segment data required by a segment to its home core. We call it *Data Marshaling (DM)*, a term borrowed from the network programming community where data required by a remote procedure call is sent to the remote core executing that procedure. However, the implementations of the two mechanisms are fundamentally different, as would be expected due to their dissimilar environments, as shown in Section 7.3.

We use a key observation to design DM: *the generator set, i.e., the set of instructions that generate inter-segment data stays constant throughout the execution.* The compiler uses profiling to identify the generator set and the hardware marshals the data written by these instructions to the home core of the next segment. This approach has three advantages. First, since the generator instructions are statically known, DM does not require any training. Second, the requesting core starts marshaling the inter-segment cache lines as soon as the execution request is sent to the home core, which makes data transfer timely. Third, since DM identifies inter-segment data as *any* data written by a generator instruction, DM can marshal any arbitrary sequence of cache lines. DM requires only a modest 96 bytes/core storage, one new ISA instruction, and compiler support.

DM is a general framework and can be applied to reduce inter-segment data misses in *any* SE paradigm. In this paper, we show how DM can improve the performance of the promising Accelerated Critical Section (ACS) paradigm [41] and the traditional producer-consumer pipeline paradigm. ACS accelerates the critical sections by running them on the large core of an Asymmetric Chip Multiprocessor (ACMP). DM can marshal the inter-segment data needed by the critical section to the large core. Our evaluation across 12 critical-section-intensive applications shows that DM eliminates almost all inter-segment data misses in ACS. Overall, DM improves performance by 8.5% over an aggressive baseline with ACS and a state-of-the-art prefetcher, at an area budget equivalent to 16 small cores. In a producer-consumer pipeline, cores are allocated to pipeline stages and each work-quantum moves from core to core as it is processed. In this case, DM can marshal the data produced at one stage to the next stage. Our evaluation across 9 pipelined workloads shows that DM captures almost all performance potential possible from eliminating inter-segment data misses and improves performance by 14% at an area budget of 16 cores. Section 6 discusses other uses of DM, such as task-parallel workloads [21, 10, 5] and systems with specialized accelerators.

Contributions: This paper makes two main contributions:

- We propose Data Marshaling (DM) to overcome the performance degradation due to misses for inter-segment data by identifying and marshaling the required data to the home core. DM is a flexible and general framework that can be useful in many different execution paradigms. DM uses profiling and requires only 96-byte/core storage.

[1] We borrow the term *Staged Execution* from the operating systems [27] and database [18] communities.

ISCA'10, June 19–23, 2010, Saint-Malo, France.

- We design and evaluate two applications of Data Marshaling: Accelerated Critical Sections and producer-consumer pipeline parallelism. We show that in both cases DM can eliminate almost all performance loss due to inter-segment data misses.

2. BACKGROUND

2.1 Staged Execution

The central idea of Staged Execution (SE) is to split a program into code *segments* and execute each segment where it runs the best, i.e., its **home core**. The criteria commonly used to choose a segment's home core include performance criticality, functionality, and data requirements, e.g. critical sections which are on the critical path of the program are best run at the fastest core [41]. Mechanisms to choose the home core are beyond the scope of this paper and are discussed in other work on SE [41, 11, 13, 17].

Implementation: Each core is assigned a work-queue which stores the segments to be processed by the core. Every time the core completes a segment, it dequeues and processes the next entry from the work-queue. If the work-queue is empty, the core waits until a request is enqueued or the program finishes.

The program is divided into *segments*, where each segment is best suited for a different core. Each segment, except the first, has a *previous-segment* (the segment that executed before it). Similarly, each segment, except the last, has a *next-segment* (the segment that will execute after it). At the end of each segment is an *initiation routine* for its next-segment. The **initiation routine** enqueues a request for execution of the next-segment at the next-segment's home core. The core that runs the initiation routine to request a segment's execution is the segment's **requesting core**.

Example: Figure 1(a) shows a code with three segments: S0, S1, and S2. S0 is S1's previous-segment and S2 is S1's next-segment. At the end of S0 is S1's initiation routine and at the end of S1 is S2's initiation routine. Figure 1(b) shows the execution of this code on a CMP with three cores (P0-P2) with the assumption that the home cores of S0, S1, and S2 are P0, P1, and P2 respectively. After completing S0, P0 runs S1's initiation routine, which inserts a request for the execution of S1 in P1's work-queue. Thus, P0 is S1's requesting core. P1 dequeues the entry, executes segment S1, and enqueues a request for S2 in P2's work-queue. Processing at P2 is similar to the processing at P0 and P1.

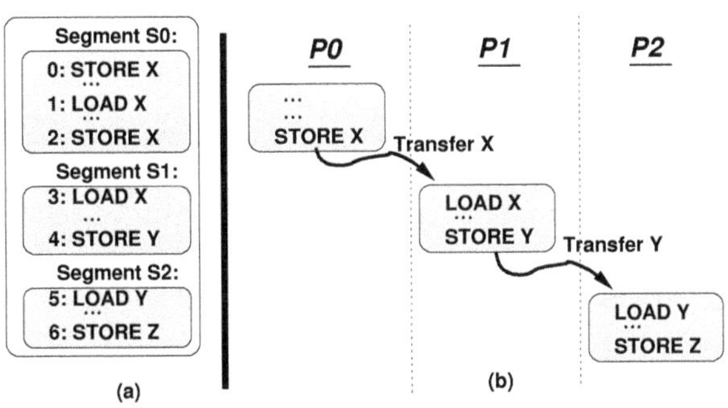

Figure 1: (a) Source code, (b) Execution in SE.

2.2 Problem: Locality of Inter-Segment Data

We define the **Inter-Segment Data** of a segment as *the data the segment requires from its previous segment.* In Figure 1, X is S1's inter-segment data as X is produced by S0 and consumed by S1. Locality of inter-segment data is high in models where consecutive segments run on the same core: the data generated by the first segment remains in the local cache until the next segment can use it. However, in SE, accesses to inter-segment data incur cache misses and the data is transferred from the requesting core to the home core via cache coherence. In Figure 1, P1 incurs a cache miss to transfer X from P0's cache and P2 incurs a cache miss to transfer Y from P1's cache. These cache misses limit SE's performance.

3. DATA MARSHALING

Data Marshaling (DM) aims to reduce cache misses to inter-segment data. In DM, the requesting core identifies the inter-segment data and marshals it to the home core when it ships a segment to the home core.

3.1 Key Insight

We first define new terminology. We call the last instruction that modifies the inter-segment data in a segment a *generator*. For example, in Figure 1(a), the *STORE* on line 2 is X's generator since there are no other stores to X between this STORE and the initiation of S1. The LOAD on line 1 is *not* a generator because it does not modify X and the STORE on line 0 is *not* a generator since there is a later STORE (the one on line 2) to X. We generalize our definition of generators to cache lines by redefining a generator as *the last instruction that modifies a cache line containing inter-segment data before the next segment begins.*

We call the set of all generator instructions, i.e. generators of all the cache lines containing inter-segment data, the *generator-set*. We observed that the generator-set of a program is often small and does not vary during the execution of the program and across input sets (see Section 4.5.1 for details). This implies that any instruction that has once been identified as a generator stays a generator. Thus, a cache line written by a generator is very likely to be inter-segment data required by the following segment, hence, a good candidate for data marshaling. Based on this observation, we assume that *every cache line written by an instruction in the generator-set is inter-segment data and will be needed for the execution of the next segment.* We call the set of inter-segment data cache lines generated by a segment its *marshal-set*. DM adds all cache lines written by generators to the marshal-set. When a core finishes the initiation routine of the next segment, all cache lines that belong to the marshal-set are transferred to the next-segment's home core.

We only marshal data between consecutive segments for two reasons: 1) it achieves most of the potential benefit since 68% of the data required by a segment is written by the immediately preceding segment, and 2) in most execution paradigms, the requesting core only knows the home core of the next segment, but not the home cores of the subsequent segments.

3.2 Overview

The functionality of DM can be partitioned into three parts:

Identifying the generator-set: DM identifies the generator-set at compile-time using profiling.[2] We define the *last-writer* of a cache line to be the last instruction that modified a cache line. Thus, *a line is inter-segment data if it is accessed inside a segment but its last-writer is a previous segment instruction.* Since the generator-set is stable, we assume that last-writers of all inter-segment data are generators. Thus, every time DM detects an inter-segment cache line, it adds the cache line's last-writer to the generator-set (unless it is already in the generator-set). The compiler conveys the identified generator-set to the hardware using new ISA semantics.

Recording of inter-segment data: Every time an instruction in the generator-set is executed, its destination cache line is predicted to be inter-segment data and added to the marshal-set.

[2] We use profiling because a static analysis may not be able to identify all generators without accurate interprocedural pointer alias analysis. However, if an efficient static analysis is developed, the proposed ISA and hardware will be able to fully leverage it.

Marshaling of inter-segment data: All elements of the marshal-set are transferred, i.e. marshaled, to the home core of the next-segment when the next segment is initiated.

For example, DM for the code shown in Figure 1 works as follows. DM detects X to be inter-segment data, identifies the STORE on line 2 to be X's last-writer, and adds it to the generator-set. When P0 executes the STORE on line 2 again, DM realizes that it is a generator and adds the cache line it modifies to the marshal-set. When P0 runs the initiation routine for S1, DM marshals all cache lines in the marshal-set to P1. Consequently, when S1 executes at P1, it (very likely) will incur a cache hit for X.

DM requires support from the compiler, ISA, and hardware.

3.3 Profiling Algorithm

The profiling algorithm runs the application as a single thread and instruments all memory instructions.[3] The instrumentation code takes as input the PC-address of the instrumented instruction and the address of the cache line accessed by that instruction. Figure 2 shows the profiling algorithm. The algorithm requires three data structures: 1) a *generator-set* that stores the identified generators, 2) a *current-last-writer* table that stores the last-writer of each cache line modified in the current segment, and 3) a *previous-last-writer* table that stores the last-writer of each cache line modified in the previous segment.

On every memory access:
If cache-line not present in segment's accessed lines and
last-writer is from previous segment
Add last-writer to generator-set
On every store:
Save address of store in current-last-writer
At the end of segment:
Deallocate previous-last-writer
current-last-writer becomes previous-last-writer
Allocate and initialize current-last-writer

Figure 2: The profiling algorithm.

For every memory access, the algorithm checks whether or not the line was modified in the previous segment by querying the previous-last-writer table. If the line was not modified in the previous segment, the line is ignored. If the cache line was modified in the previous segment, the last-writer of the line (an instruction in the previous segment) is added to the generator-set. When an instruction modifies a cache line, the profiling algorithm records the instruction as the last-writer of the destination cache line in the current-last-writer table. At the end of each segment, the lookup table of the previous segment is discarded, the current segment lookup table becomes the previous segment lookup table, and a new current segment lookup table is initialized. After the program finishes, the generator-set data structure contains all generators.

3.4 ISA Support

DM adds two features to the ISA: a GENERATOR prefix and a MARSHAL instruction. The compiler marks all generator instructions by prepending them with the GENERATOR prefix. The MARSHAL instruction is used to inform the hardware that a new segment is being initiated. The instruction takes the home core ID of the next-segment as its only argument. When the initiation routine initiates a segment at a core, it executes the MARSHAL instruction with that core's ID.[4] When the MARSHAL instruction executes, the hardware begins to marshal all cache lines in the marshal-set to the core specified by HOME-ID.

[3]We also evaluated a thread-aware version of our profiling mechanism but its results did not differ from the single-threaded version.

[4]The runtime library stores a segment-to-core mapping which is populated by executing a CPUID instruction on each core.

3.5 Data Marshaling Unit

Each core is augmented with a Data Marshaling Unit (DMU), which is in-charge of tracking and marshaling the inter-segment data to the home core. Figure 3(a) shows the integration of the DMU with the core. Its main component is the *Marshal Buffer*, which stores the addresses of the cache lines to be marshaled. The Marshal Buffer is combining, i.e. multiple accesses to the same cache line are combined into a single entry, and circular, i.e. if it becomes full its oldest entry is replaced with the incoming entry.

Figure 3(b) shows the operation of the DMU. When the core retires an instruction with the GENERATOR prefix, it sends the physical address of the cache line written by the instruction to the DMU. The DMU enqueues the address in the *Marshal Buffer*. When the core executes the MARSHAL instruction, it asserts the MARSHAL signal and sends the HOME-ID to the DMU. The DMU starts marshaling data to the home core. For each line address in the Marshal Buffer, the DMU accesses the local L2 cache to read the coherence state and data. If the line is in shared state or if a cache miss occurs, the DMU skips that line. If the line is in exclusive or modified state, the DMU puts the line in a temporary state that makes it inaccessible (similar to [30]) and sends a *DM Transaction* (see Section 3.6) containing the cache line to the home core. The home core installs the marshaled line in its fill buffer and responds with an ACK, signaling the requesting core to invalidate the cache line. If the fill buffer is full, the home core responds with a NACK, signaling the requesting core to restore the original state of the cache line.

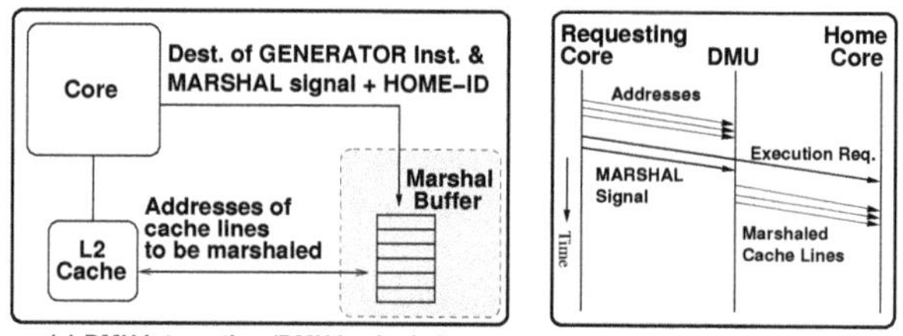

(a) DMU integration (DMU is shaded) (b) DMU functionality

Figure 3: Data Marshaling Unit.

Note that DM marshals lines into L2 caches (not L1). This reduces contention for cache ports between the core and DMU. Moreover, L2, being bigger, is less prone to cache pollution. However, this also implies that DM does not save L1 misses. We find that the performance benefit of marshaling into the L2 outweighs its cost.

3.6 On-Chip Interconnect Support

The interconnect supports one new *DM transaction*, which is sent by the DMU to a remote core via the directory/ordering-point. Each DM transaction is a point-to-point message containing the address and data of a marshaled cache line, and requires the same interconnect support (wires, routing, etc.) as a cache-to-cache transfer, which is available in existing CMPs.

3.7 Handling Interrupts and Exceptions

An interrupt or exception can modify the virtual-to-physical address mapping, thereby making the contents of the Marshal Buffer invalid. Since DM does not impact correctness, we simply flush the contents of the Marshal Buffer at an interrupt or exception.

3.8 Overhead

DM can significantly improve performance by reducing inter-segment cache misses. However, it also incurs some overhead:

- DM adds the GENERATOR prefix to all generator instructions. This only marginally increases the I-cache footprint, since the average size of the generator-set is only 55 instructions.
- DM adds a MARSHAL instruction to each segment. This overhead is low because the MARSHAL instruction: (1) does not

read/write any data, and (2) executes only once per segment, which often consists of thousands of instructions.

- The DMU can contend with the core for cache ports. This overhead is no different from the baseline, where the inter-segment data cache-to-cache transfer requests contend for the cache.
- DM augments each core with a Marshal Buffer. The storage overhead of this buffer is only 96 bytes/core (16 6-byte entries, each storing the physical address of a cache line). Section 4.5.8 shows the sensitivity of performance to Marshal Buffer size.

In summary, the overhead of DM is low. We now discuss the use of DM in different execution paradigms.

4. ACCELERATED CRITICAL SECTIONS

Data Marshaling is beneficial in any execution paradigm that uses the basic principle of Staged Execution. In this section we describe the application of DM to improve a recently proposed SE paradigm: Accelerated Critical Sections (ACS) [41].

4.1 Background

Critical Sections: Accesses to shared data are encapsulated inside critical sections to preserve mutual exclusion. Only one thread can execute a critical section at any given time, while other threads wanting to execute the same critical section must wait, thereby reducing performance. Furthermore, contention for critical sections increases with more threads, thereby reducing application scalability. This contention can be reduced if critical sections execute faster. When threads are waiting for the completion of a critical section, reducing the execution time of the critical section significantly affects not only the thread that is executing it but also the threads that are waiting for it.

Suleman et al. [41] proposed *Accelerated Critical Sections (ACS)* to reduce execution time of critical sections. ACS leverages the Asymmetric Chip Multiprocessor (ACMP) architecture [39, 19, 31], which provides at least one large core and many small cores on the same chip. ACS executes the parallel threads on the small cores and leverages the large core(s) to speedily execute Amdahl's serial bottleneck as well as critical sections.

ACS introduces two new instructions, CSCALL and CSRET, which are inserted at the beginning and end of a critical section respectively. When a small core executes a CSCALL instruction, it sends a *critical section execution request (CSCALL)* to the large core P0 and waits until it receives a response. P0 buffers the CSCALL request in the *Critical Section Request Buffer (CSRB)* and starts executing the requested critical section at the first opportunity. When P0 executes a CSRET, it sends a *critical section done (CSDONE)* signal to the requesting small core, which can then resume normal execution.

ACS is an instance of Staged Execution (SE) where code is split into two types of segments: critical-section segments that run at the large core, and non-critical-section segments that run at the small cores. Every critical-section segment is followed by a non-critical-section segment and vice-versa. Every non-critical-section segment terminates with a CSCALL and every critical-section segment terminates with a CSRET instruction. A CSCALL instruction initiates a critical-section segment and enqueues it at the large core's work-queue (the CSRB). A CSRET instruction initiates a non-critical-section segment at the small core.

4.2 Private Data in ACS

By executing all critical sections at the same core, ACS keeps the shared data (protected by the critical sections) and the lock variables (protecting the critical section) at the large core, thereby improving locality of shared data. However, every time the critical section accesses data generated outside the critical section (i.e. thread-private data), the large core incurs cache misses to transfer this data from the small core. This data is inter-segment data: it is generated in the non-critical-section segment and accessed in the critical-section segment. Marshaling this data to the large core can reduce cache misses at the large core, thereby accelerating the critical-section even more. Note that marshaling the inter-segment data generated by the critical-section segment and used by the non-critical-section segment only speeds up the non-critical section code, which is not critical for overall performance. We thus study marshaling private data from the small core to the large core. Since private data and inter-segment data are synonymous in ACS, we use them interchangeably.

4.3 Data Marshaling in ACS

Employing DM in ACS requires two changes. First, the compiler identifies the generator instructions by running the profiling algorithm in Section 3.3, treating critical sections and the code outside critical sections as two segments. Second, the library inserts the MARSHAL instruction right before every CSCALL instruction. The argument to the MARSHAL instruction, the core to marshal the data to, is set to the ID of the large core.

4.4 Evaluation Methodology

Table 1 shows the configuration of the simulated CMPs, using our in-house cycle-level x86 simulator. We use simulation parameters similar to [41]. All cores, both large and small, include a state-of-the-art hardware prefetcher, similar to the one in [42].

Table 1: Configuration of the simulated machines.

Small core	2-wide, 2GHz, 5-stage, in-order
Large core	4-wide, 2GHz, 2-way SMT, 128-entry ROB, 12-stage, out-of-order; 4x the area of small core
Interconnect	64-byte wide bi-directional ring, all queuing delays modeled, minimum cache-to-cache latency of 5 cycles
Coherence	MESI on-chip distributed directory similar to SGI Origin [28], cache-to-cache transfers, # of banks = # of cores, 8K entries/bank
Prefetcher	Aggressive stream prefetcher [42] with 32 stream buffers, can stay 16-lines ahead, prefetches into cores' L2 caches
Caches	Private L1I and L1D: 32KB, write-through, 1-cycle, 4-way. Private L2: 256KB, write-back, 6-cycle, 8-way (1MB, 8-cycle, 16-way for large core). Shared L3: 8MB, 20-cycle, 16-way
Memory	32 banks, bank conflicts and queuing delays modeled. Precharge, activate, column access latencies are 25ns each
Memory bus	4:1 CPU/bus ratio, 64-bit wide, split-transaction
Area-equivalent CMPs. Area is equal to N small cores. We vary N from 1 to 64.	
ACMP	1 large core and N-4 small cores; large core runs serial part, 2-way SMT on large core and small cores run parallel part, conventional locking (Maximum number of concurrent threads = N-2)
ACS	1 large core and N-4 small cores; (N-4)-entry CSRB at the large core, large core runs the serial part, small cores run the parallel part, 2-way SMT on large core runs critical sections using ACS (Max. concurrent threads = N-4)
IdealACS	Same as ACS except all cache misses to private data on the large core are *ideally* turned into cache hits. Note that this is an *unrealistic* upper bound on DM.
DM	Same as ACS with support for Data Marshaling

Unless specified otherwise: 1) all comparisons are done at equal area budget, equivalent to 16 small cores, 2) the number of threads for each application is set to the number of available contexts.

Workloads: Our evaluation focuses on 12 critical-section-intensive workloads shown in Table 2. We define a workload to be critical-section-intensive if at least 1% of the instructions in the parallel portion are executed within critical sections. The benchmark `maze` solves a 3-D puzzle using a branch-and-bound algorithm. Threads take different routes through the maze, insert new possible routes in a shared queue and update a global structure to indicate which routes have already been visited. `iplookup`, `puzzle`, `webcache` and `pagemine` are similar to the benchmarks with the same names used in [40].

Table 2: Simulated workloads.

Workload	Description	Source	Profile Input	Evaluation Input	# of disjoint critical sections	What is Protected by CS?
is	Integer sort	NAS suite [6]	n = 16K	n = 64K	1	buffer of keys to sort
pagemine	Data mining kernel	MineBench [32]	2K pages	10Kpages	1	global histogram
puzzle	15-Puzzle game	[40]	3x3-easy	3x3	2	work-heap, memoization table
qsort	Quicksort	OpenMP SCR [15]	4K elements	20K elements	1	global work stack
sqlite	sqlite3 [2] database engine	SysBench [3]	insert-test	OLTP-simple	5	database tables
tsp	Traveling salesman problem	[26]	7 cities	11 cities	2	termination condition, solution
maze	3D-maze solver		128x128 maze	512x512 maze	2	visited nodes
nqueen	N-queens problem	[22]	20x20 board	40x40 board	534	task queue
iplookup	IP packet routing	[45]	500 queries	2.5K queries	# of threads	routing tables
mysql-1	MySQL server [1]	SysBench [3]	insert-test	OLTP-simple	20	meta data, tables
mysql-2	MySQL server [1]	SysBench [3]	insert-txn	OLTP-complex	29	meta data, tables
webcache	Cooperative web cache	[40]	10K queries	100K queries	33	replacement policy

4.5 Evaluation

We evaluate DM on four metrics. First, we show that the generator-set stays stable throughout execution. Second, we show the coverage, accuracy, and timeliness of DM followed by an analysis of DM's effect on L2 cache miss rate inside critical sections. Third, we show the effect of DM on the IPC of the critical program paths. Fourth, we compare the performance of DM to that of the baseline and ideal ACS at different number of cores.

4.5.1 Stability of the Generator-Set

DM assumes that the generator-set, the set of instructions which generate private data, is small and stays stable throughout execution. To test this assumption, we measure the stability and size of the generator set. Table 3 shows the size and variance of the generator-set in 12 workloads. Variance is the average number of differences between intermediate generator-sets (computed every 5M instructions) and the overall generator-set, divided by the generator-set's size. In all cases, variance is less than 7% indicating that the generator-set is stable during execution. We also evaluated the stability of the generator-set on different input sets and found that the generator-set is constant across input sets.

Table 3: Size and variance of the generator-set.

Workload	is	pagemine	puzzle	qsort	tsp	maze	nqueen	sqlite	iplookup	mysql-1	mysql-2	webcache	amean
Size	3	10	24	23	34	49	111	23	27	114	277	7	58.5
Variance (%)	0.1	0.1	0.1	0.9	3.0	2.2	4.9	4.2	4.3	6.4	6.3	1.2	-

4.5.2 Coverage, Accuracy, and Timeliness of DM

We measure DM's effectiveness in reducing private data misses using three metrics: coverage, accuracy, and timeliness. **Coverage** is the fraction of private data cache lines identified by DM. **Accuracy** is the fraction of marshaled lines that are actually used at the large core. **Timeliness** is the fraction of useful marshaled cache lines that reach the large core before they are needed. Note that a marshaled cache line that is in transit when it is requested by the large core is not considered timely according to this definition, but it can provide performance benefit by reducing L2 miss latency.

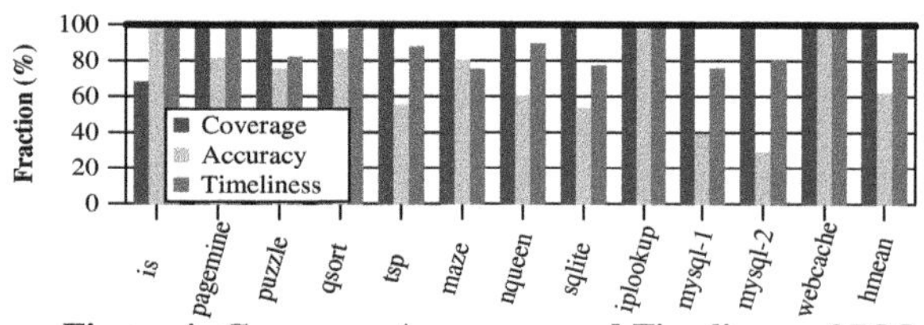

Figure 4: Coverage, Accuracy, and Timeliness of DM.

Figure 4 shows the coverage of DM. DM is likely to detect all private lines because it optimistically assumes that every instruction that once generates private data always generates private data. We find that DM covers 99% of L2 cache misses to private data in all workloads except `is`. The private data in `is` is 117 cache lines, which fills up the Marshal Buffer, and thus several private lines are not marshaled (see Section 4.5.8).

Figure 4 also shows the accuracy of DM. Recall our assumption that every cache line written by any of the generator instructions is private data. This assumption is optimistic since a generator's destination cache line may or may not be used by a critical section depending on control-flow inside the critical section. For example, the critical sections in the irregular database-workloads `mysql-1` and `mysql-2` have a larger number of data-dependent control flow instructions, which leads to a lower accuracy of DM. Despite our optimistic assumption, we find that a majority (on average 62%) of the cache lines marshaled are useful. Moreover, note that marshaling non-useful lines can cause cache pollution and/or interconnect contention, but only if the number of marshaled cache lines is high. We find this not to be the case. Table 4 shows the number of cache lines marshaled per critical section for every workload. In general, we found that transferring *only* an average of 5 cache lines, 62% of which are useful on average, causes a minimal amount of cache pollution and/or interconnect contention.

Table 4: Number of cache lines marshaled per critical section.

Workload	is	pagemine	puzzle	qsort	tsp	maze	nqueen	sqlite	iplookup	mysql-1	mysql-2	webcache	amean
Lines	**16**	9.0	5.6	1.8	3.6	1.8	2.8	8.5	2.9	9.8	15.4	1.8	5.0

Figure 4 also shows DM's timeliness. We find that 84% of the useful cache lines marshaled by DM are timely. Since coverage is close to 100%, timeliness directly corresponds to the reduction in private data cache misses. DM reduces 99% of the cache misses for private data in `pagemine` where timeliness is the highest. In `pagemine`, the main critical section performs reduction of a temporary local histogram (private data) into a persistent global histogram (shared data). `pagemine`'s private data is 8 cache lines: 128 buckets of 4-bytes each. Since the critical section is long (212 cycles on the large core) and contention at the large core is high, DM gets enough time to marshal all the needed cache lines before they are needed by the large core. DM's timeliness is more than 75% in all workloads.

4.5.3 Cache Miss Reduction Inside Critical Sections

Table 5 shows the L2 cache misses per kilo-instruction inside critical sections (CS-MPKI) for ACS with no prefetcher (ACS-NP), ACS with prefetcher (ACS) and DM. ACS is only marginally better (11%) than ACS-NP, showing that an aggressive hardware prefetcher is ineffective for inter-segment data misses. When DM is employed, the arithmetic mean of CS-MPKI reduces by **92%** (from 8.92 to 0.78). The reduction is only 52% in `is` because DM has low coverage. We conclude that DM largely reduces L2 cache misses inside critical sections.

Table 5: MPKI inside critical sections.

Workload	is	pagemine	puzzle	qsort	tsp	maze	nqueen	sqlite	iplookup	mysql-1	mysql-2	webcache	amean	hmean
ACS-NP	13.4	15.6	4.7	25.6	0.8	22.6	18.5	0.8	1.0	5.3	11.5	0.9	10.0	1.8
ACS	3.0	15.6	4.7	25.5	0.8	22.5	16.9	0.8	1.0	5.0	10.9	0.9	8.9	1.6
DM	1.4	0.2	0.5	0.2	0.9	2.2	1.3	0.4	0.4	0.5	1.2	0.1	0.8	0.4

4.5.4 *Speedup in Critical Sections*

DM's goal is to accelerate critical section execution by reducing cache misses to private data. Figure 5 shows the retired critical-section-instructions per-cycle (CS-IPC) of DM normalized to CS-IPC of baseline ACS. In workloads where CS-MPKI is low or where L2 misses can be serviced in parallel, DM's improvement in CS-IPC is not proportional to the reduction in CS-MPKI. For example, in `webcache`, DM reduces CS-MPKI by almost 6x but the increase in CS-IPC is only 5%. This is because CS-MPKI of `webcache` is only 0.85, which has a small effect on performance since these misses are serviced by cache-to-cache transfers.

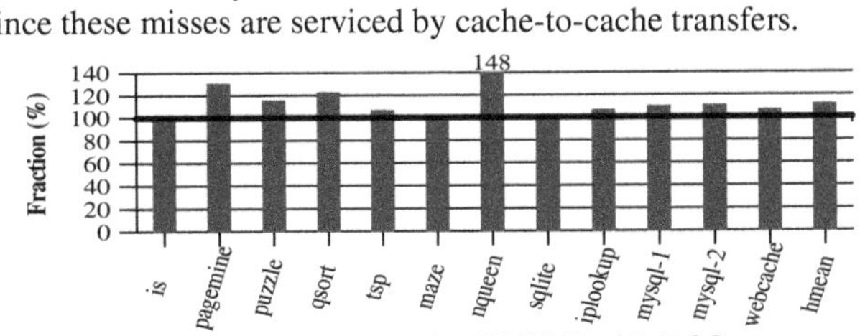

Figure 5: Increase in CS-IPC with DM.

In workloads where CS-MPKI is higher, such as in `pagemine`, `puzzle`, `qsort`, and `nqueen`, DM speeds up critical section execution by more than 10%. Most notably, `nqueen's` critical sections execute 48% faster with DM. Note that in none of the workloads do critical sections execute slower with DM than in ACS. On average, critical sections execute 11% faster with DM. Thus, in benchmarks where there is high contention for critical sections, DM will provide a high overall speedup, as we show next.

4.5.5 *Performance*

DM increases the IPC of critical sections, thereby reducing the time spent inside critical sections. For highly-contended critical sections, reducing the time spent inside the critical section substantially increases overall performance. Moreover, as the number of available cores on a chip increases (which can increase the number of concurrent threads), contention for critical sections further increases and DM is expected to become more beneficial. We compare ACMP, ACS, and DM at area budgets of 16, 32 and 64.

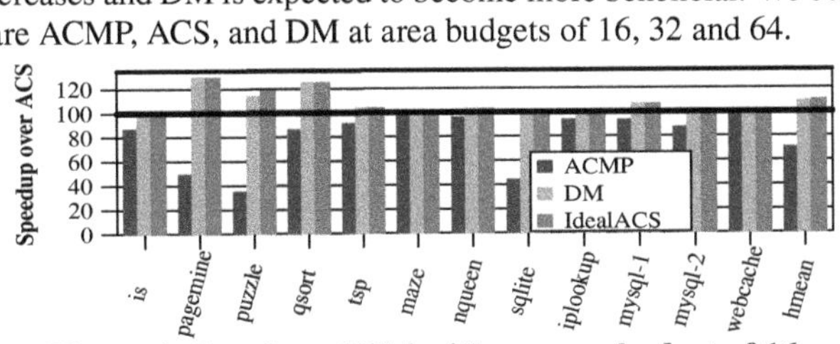

Figure 6: Speedup of DM with an area-budget of 16.

Area budget of 16: Figure 6 shows the speedup of ACMP, DM, and IdealACS normalized to the baseline ACS. DM outperforms ACS on all workloads, by 8.5% on average. Most prominently, in `pagemine`, `puzzle`, and `qsort`, DM outperforms ACS by more than 10% due to large increases in CS-IPC. In other benchmarks such as `tsp` and `nqueen`, DM performs 1-5% better than ACS. Note that DM's performance improvement strongly tracks the increase in critical section IPC shown in Figure 5. There is one exception, `nqueen`, where the main critical section updates a FIFO work-queue that uses very fine-grain locking. Thus, contention for the critical sections is low and, even though DM speeds up the critical sections by 48%, overall performance improvement is only 2%. In all other workloads, faster critical sections lead to higher overall performance. DM's performance is within 1% of the IdealACS for all workloads. Thus, *DM achieves almost all the performance benefit available from eliminating cache misses to private data.*

Note that DM is able to provide an overall speedup of 8.5% by accelerating the execution of *only* the large core by 11% (as shown in Figure 5). This is because when critical sections are on the critical path of the program, accelerating *just* the critical sections by any amount provides an almost-proportional overall speedup without requiring acceleration of all threads.

Larger area budgets (32 and 64): Figure 7 shows that DM's average performance improvement over ACS increases to 9.8% at area budget 32. Most prominently, in `pagemine` DM's improvement over ACS increases from 30% to 68%. This is because `pagemine` is completely critical-section-limited and any acceleration of critical sections greatly improves overall speedup. DM's performance is again within 1% of that of IdealACS, showing that DM achieves almost all potential benefit.

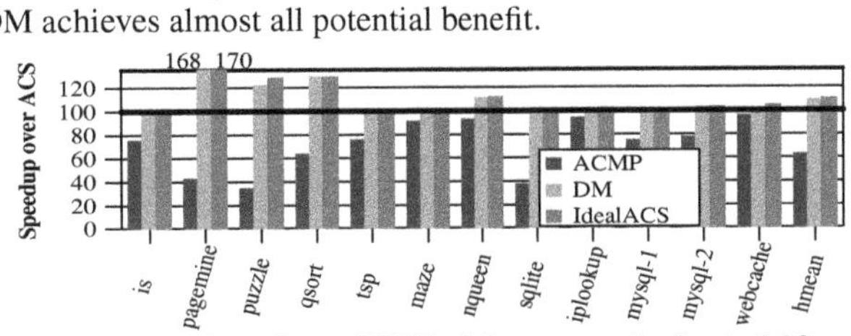

Figure 7: Speedup of DM with an area-budget of 32.

As the chip area further increases to 64, DM's improvement over ACS continues to increase (Figure 8). On average, DM provides 13.4% performance improvement over ACS and is within 2% of its upper bound (IdealACS). We conclude that DM's benefits are likely to increase as systems scale to larger number of cores.

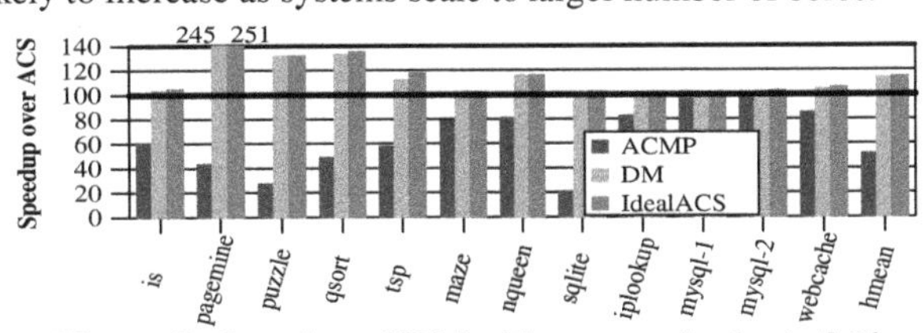

Figure 8: Speedup of DM with an area-budget of 64.

At best-threads: The best-threads of a workload is the minimum number of threads required to minimize its execution time. We also evaluated DM's speedup with best-threads normalized to ACS with best-threads for an area budget of 16. Our results show that even if we use oracle information to pick the best number of threads, which penalizes DM since DM performs better at a higher thread count, DM improves performance by 5.3% over ACS.

4.5.6 *Sensitivity to Interconnect Hop Latency*

DM's performance improvement over ACS can change with the interconnect hop latency between caches for two reasons. First, increasing the hop latency increases the cost of each on-chip cache miss, increasing the performance impact of misses to private data and making DM more beneficial. Second, increasing the hop latency increases the time to marshal a cache line, which can reduce DM's timeliness, reducing its benefit. We evaluate ACS and DM using hop latencies of 2, 5, and 10 cycles. On average, the speed up of DM over ACS increases from 5.2% to 8.5% to 12.7% as hop latency increases from 2 to 5 to 10. We conclude that DM is even more effective in systems with longer hop latencies, e.g. higher frequency CMPs or SMPs.

4.5.7 *Sensitivity to L2 Cache Size*

Private data misses are communication misses that cannot be avoided by increasing cache capacity. Thus, DM, which reduces communication misses, stays equally beneficial when L2 cache size increases. In fact, DM's benefit might increase with larger caches due to three reasons: 1) enlarging the cache reduces capacity and conflict misses, increasing the relative performance impact of communication misses and techniques that reduce such misses; 2) increasing the L2 size of the large core increases the likelihood that a marshaled cache line will not be evicted before it is used, which increases DM's coverage and timeliness; 3) increasing the small core's L2 capacity increases the amount of private data that stays resident at the small cores' L2 caches and thus can be marshaled, which can increase DM's coverage.

Table 6: Sensitivity of DM to L2 Cache Size.

L2 Cache Size (KB)	128	256	512	1024	2048
ACS vs. ACS 256KB (%)	-5.4	0.0	2.1	2.9	3.1
DM vs. ACS 256KB (%)	-11.4	8.5	10.6	11.3	12.0

Table 6 shows the average speedup across all benchmarks for ACS and DM for small-core L2 cache sizes from 128KB to 2048KB. Note that the cache of the large core is always 4x as large as the cache of a small core. The performance benefit of DM over ACS slightly increases as cache size increases from 256KB to 2048KB. In fact, DM with a 256KB L2 cache outperforms ACS with a 2MB L2 cache. However, with a 128KB L2 cache, DM performs worse than ACS. This is because marshaling private data into a small L2 cache at the large core causes cache pollution, evicting shared data or marshaled data of other critical sections not yet executed, and leading to longer-latency L2 cache misses, serviced by the L3. We conclude that DM's performance benefit either increases or stays constant as L2 cache size increases.

4.5.8 *Sensitivity to Size of the Marshal Buffer*

The number of entries in the Marshal Buffer limits the number of cache lines DM can marshal for a critical section segment. We experimented with different Marshal Buffer sizes and found that 16 entries (which we use in our main evaluation) suffice for all workloads except `is`. Since `is` requires the marshaling of 117 cache lines on average, when we use a 128-entry Marshal Buffer, CS-MPKI in `is` is reduced by 22% and performance increases by 3.8% compared to a 16-entry Marshal Buffer.

5. PRODUCER-CONSUMER PIPELINE

Pipeline parallelism is a commonly used approach to split the work in a loop among threads. In pipeline parallelism, each iteration of a loop is split into multiple work-quanta where each work-quantum executes in a different pipeline stage. Each stage is allocated one or more cores. Pipeline parallelism is another instance of Staged Execution: each iteration of a loop is split into code segments (pipeline stages) which run on different cores.

Figure 9(a) shows a code example of two pipeline stages: S1 and S2, running on cores P1 and P2, respectively. S1 computes and stores the value of a variable X (lines 1-2) and then enqueues a request to run S2 at core P2 (line 3). Note that X is used by S2 (line 4). P2 may process the computation in S2 immediately or later, depending on the entries in its work-queue.

5.1 DM in Pipelines

Processing of a pipeline stage often requires data that was generated in the previous pipeline stage. Since each stage executes at a different core, such inter-segment or inter-stage data must be transferred from core to core as the work-quantum is processed by successive pipeline stages. For example, in the pipeline code in Figure 9(a), variable X is inter-segment data as it is generated in S1 (line 2) and used by S2 (line 4). When S2 runs on P2, P2 incurs a cache miss to fetch X from P1.

(a) Code of a pipeline.	(b) Modified code with DM.
Pipeline Stage S1: 1: .... 2: store X 3: Enqueue a request at S2's home core	*Pipeline Stage S1:* 1: .... ;Compute X 2: **GENERATOR store X** 3: Enqueue a request at S2's home core ;S2's initiation 4: **MARSHAL <S2's home core>**
Pipeline Stage S2: 4: Y = ... X	*Pipeline Stage S2:* 5: Y = ... X ... ;Compute Y using X ....

Figure 9: Code example of a pipeline.

DM requires two code changes. First, the compiler must identify the generator instructions and prepend them with a GENERATOR prefix. Second, the compiler/library must insert a MARSHAL instruction in the initiation routine. Figure 9(b) shows the code in Figure 9(a) with the modifications required by DM. Since X is inter-segment data, the compiler identifies via profiling the store instruction on line 2 as a generator and prepends it with the GENERATOR prefix. Furthermore, the MARSHAL instruction is inserted in the initiation routine (line 4).

When P1 (the core assigned to S1) runs the store on line 2, the hardware inserts the physical address of the cache line being modified into P1's Marshal Buffer. When the MARSHAL instruction on line 4 executes, the Data Marshaling Unit (DMU) marshals the cache line containing X to P2's L2 cache. When S2 runs on P2, it incurs a cache hit for X, which likely reduces execution time.

5.2 Evaluation Methodology

We simulate a symmetric CMP with all small cores with the parameters shown in Table 1. We simulate three different configurations: Baseline (a baseline CMP without DM), Ideal (an idealistic but impractical CMP where all inter-segment misses are turned into hits), and DM (a CMP with support for DM). The Ideal scheme, which unrealistically eliminates all inter-segment misses, is an upper bound of DM's performance. We evaluate DM on 16-core and 32-core CMPs, but not on a 64-core CMP because a majority of our workloads do not scale to 64 threads. Table 7 shows the simulated workloads. A MARSHAL instruction was inserted in the initiation routine of each workload. The core-to-stage allocation is proportional to execution times, e.g. if two stages execute in 500 and 1000 cycles (on a single core), we assign the latter twice as many cores as the former. All comparisons are at equal-area of 16 small cores unless otherwise stated.

5.3 Evaluation

We evaluate coverage, accuracy, timeliness, inter-segment data MPKI, and overall performance of DM. We also show DM's sensitivity to relevant architectural parameters.[5]

5.3.1 *Coverage, Accuracy, and Timeliness*

Figure 10 shows DM's coverage, i.e., the fraction of inter-segment data cache lines identified by DM. Coverage is over 90% in all workloads except `dedupD`, `image`, and `mtwist` where the inter-segment data per segment exceeds the size of the Marshal Buffer (16) and not all inter-segment data is marshaled.

Figure 10 also shows the accuracy of DM, i.e., the fraction of

[5]We validated that the generator-sets are stable during execution and across input sets for pipeline workloads, but we do not show the results due to space constraints.

Table 7: Workload characteristics.

Workload	Description (No. of pipeline stages)	Major steps of computation	Profile Input	Evaluation Input
black	BlackScholes Financial Kernel [33] **(6)**	Compute each option's call/put value	0.25M opts	1M opts
compress	File compression using bzip2 algorithm **(5)**	Read file, compress, re-order, write	0.5MB image	4MB text file
dedupE	De-duplication (Encoding) [8] **(7)**	Read, find anchors, chunk, compress, write	simsmall	simlarge
dedupD	De-duplication (Decoding) [8] **(7)**	Read, decompress, check-cache, write	simsmall	simlarge
ferret	Content based search [8] **(8)**	Load, segment, extract, vector, rank, out	simsmall	simlarge
image	Image conversion from RGB to gray-scale **(5)**	Read file, convert, re-order, write	10M pixels	100M pixels
mtwist	Mersenne-Twister PRNG [33] **(5)**	Read seeds, generate PRNs, box-muller	path= 20M	path= 200M
rank	Rank string similarity with an input string **(3)**	Read string, compare, rank	100K strings	800K strings
sign	Compute the signature of a page of text **(7)**	Read page and compute signature	100K pages	1M pages

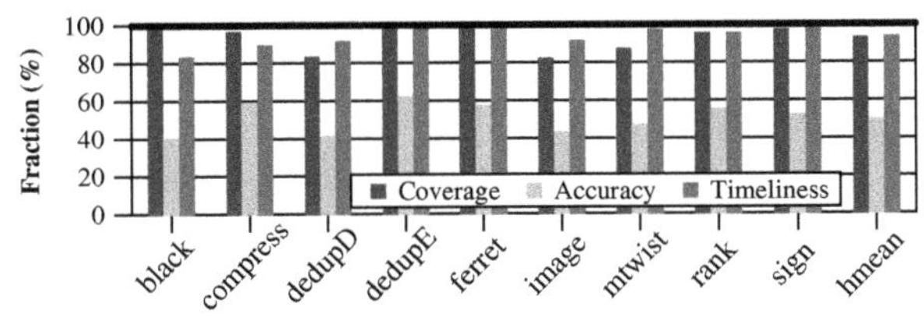

Figure 10: Coverage, Accuracy, and Timeliness of DM.

marshaled lines that are actually used by the home core. DM's accuracy is low, between 40% and 50%, because stages contain control flow. However, the increase in interconnect transactions/cache pollution for DM is negligible because the number of cache lines marshaled per segment is small: the average is 6.8 and the maximum is 16 (the size of the Marshal Buffer).

Figure 10 also shows DM's timeliness, i.e., the percentage of useful cache lines identified by DM that reach the remote home core before their use. Timeliness is high, more than 80% in all cases, for two reasons: (1) segments often wait in the home core's work-queue before their processing, giving DM enough time to marshal the lines, (2) transferring the few lines that are marshaled per segment requires a small number of cycles.

5.3.2 *Reduction in Inter-Segment Cache Misses*

Table 8 shows the L2 MPKI of inter-segment data in baseline-NP (baseline with no prefetcher), baseline and DM. The prefetcher reduces the average MPKI by only 9%. DM reduces the MPKI significantly more in all cases. Most noticeable is `sign` where DM reduces the MPKI from 30.3 to 0.9. In `sign`, the main inter-segment data is a 256-character page signature array (4 cache lines). Since DM's profiling algorithm marks the instruction that stores the array as a generator, DM saves all cache misses for the array. Similarly, DM almost completely eliminates inter-segment data misses in `ferret` and `dedupE`. DM reduces the harmonic and arithmetic mean of MPKI by 81% and 69% respectively.

Table 8: L2 Misses for Inter-Segment Data (MPKI). We show both amean and hmean because hmean is skewed due to `dedupE`. Note: MPKI of inter-segment data in Ideal is 0.

Workload	black	compress	dedupD	dedupE	ferret	image	mtwist	rank	sign	amean	hmean
baseline-NP	15.2	7.8	49.5	0.7	4.9	67.6	59.4	4.2	31.3	26.6	4.57
baseline	14.2	7.7	47.5	0.4	4.4	55.6	51.4	4.1	30.3	24.0	2.76
DM	2.8	1.7	33.0	0.0	0.1	20.4	7.4	0.3	0.9	7.4	0.53

5.3.3 *Performance*

Execution time of a pipelined program is always dictated by its slowest stage. Thus, DM's impact on overall performance depends on how much it speeds up the slowest stage. Figure 11 shows the speedup of Ideal and DM over the baseline at 16 cores. On average, DM provides a 14% speedup over the baseline, which is 96% of the potential. DM improves performance in all workloads. DM's improvement is highest in `black` (34% speedup) because DM reduces inter-segment misses by 81% and as a result speeds up the slowest stage significantly. DM's speedup is less (5% lower) than the Ideal speedup in `black` because accesses to inter-segment data are in the first few instructions of each stage and consequently the marshaled cache lines are not always timely. DM's speedup is lower in `dedupE` and `ferret` because these workloads only incur a small number of inter-segment misses and DM's potential is low (Ideal speedup is only 5% for ferret).

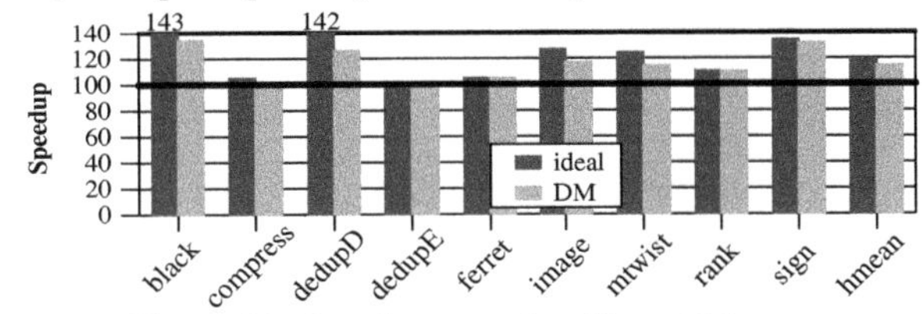

Figure 11: Speedup over baseline at 16 cores.

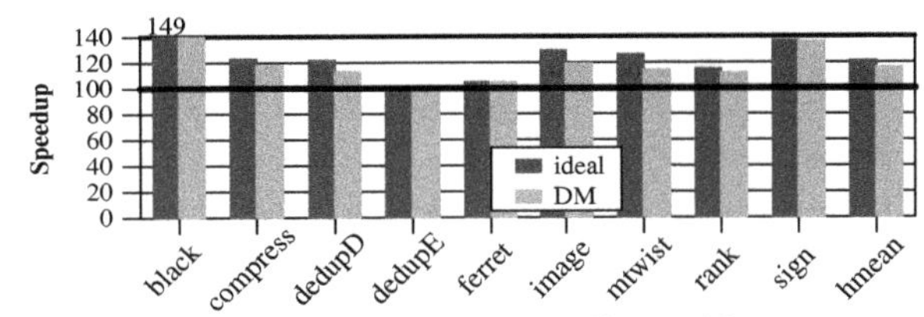

Figure 12: Speedup over baseline at 32 cores.

32-core results: Figure 12 shows the speedup of Ideal and DM over the baseline with 32 cores. DM's speedup increases for all workloads compared to 16 cores. Most significant is the change in `compress`, from 1% to 18%, because the slowest stage in `compress` changes between 16 and 32 cores. At 16 threads, `compress`'s slowest stage is the stage that compresses chunks of input data. This stage is compute-bound and does not offer a high potential for DM. However, the compression stage is scalable, i.e., its throughput increases with more cores. At 32 cores, the compression stage's throughput is more than the non-scalable re-order stage (the stage which re-orders chunks of compressed data before writing them to the output file). Unlike the compression stage which is compute-bound, the re-order stage is bounded by cache misses for inter-segment data, ergo, a higher potential for DM and thus the higher benefit. On average, at 32 cores, DM improves performance by 16%, which is higher than its speedup at 16 cores (14%). In summary, DM is an effective technique that successfully improves performance of pipelined workloads, with increasing benefit as the number of cores increases.

Performance at best-threads: We also evaluate pipelined workloads with the minimum number of threads required to maximize performance. Since a majority of our workloads saturate between 16 and 32 threads, our results at best-threads resemble those at 32-threads, i.e., DM provides a 16% speedup over the baseline.

5.3.4 *Sensitivity to Interconnect Hop Latency*

We find that the speedup of DM increases with hop latency (refer to Section 4.5.6 for reasons). We evaluated DM with hop latencies of 2, 5, and 10 cycles and find that it provides speedups of 12.4%, 14%, and 15.1% over the baseline, respectively.

5.3.5 Sensitivity to L2 Cache Size

DM's benefit increases with cache size for pipeline workloads as well (see Section 4.5.7 for reasons). DM's speedup over the baseline is 4.6%, 14%, 14.8%, 15.3%, and 15.4% for cache sizes of 128KB, 256KB, 512KB, 1MB, and 2MB, respectively.

5.3.6 Sensitivity to Size of the Marshal Buffer

We find that a 16-entry Marshal Buffer is sufficient for all workloads except `dedupD`, `image`, and `mtwist`. The number of inter-segment cache lines per segment in these workloads is greater than 16. For example, the primary inter-segment data structure in image, an array of 150 32-bit RGB pixels, spans 32-cache lines. Table 9 shows the performance of DM with varying Marshal Buffer sizes in these three workloads. In each case, performance saturates once there are enough entries to fit all inter-segment cache lines (32, 32, and 128 for dedupD, image, and mtwist respectively). In summary, while there are a few workloads that benefit from a larger Marshal Buffer, a 16-entry buffer suffices for most workloads.

Table 9: Speedup (%) for different Marshal Buffer sizes.

# of entries	16	32	64	128	256
dedupD	26	40	40	40	40
image	17	24	24	24	24
mtwist	14	18	21	22	22

6. DM ON OTHER PARADIGMS

We have shown two concrete applications of DM: ACS and pipeline parallelism. DM can also be applied to any paradigm that resembles SE, for example:

- Remote special-purpose cores, e.g., encryption or video encoding engines, which are often used to accelerate code segments. DM can be used to marshal data to such accelerators.
- Task-parallelism models such as Cilk [10], Intel TBB [21] and Apple's Grand Central Dispatch [5]. DM can marshal the input arguments of the task to the core that will execute the task.
- Computation Spreading [13], which improves locality by always running the operating system code on the same set of cores. DM can marshal the data to and from these cores.
- Thread Motion [35], which migrates threads among cores to improve power-performance efficiency. DM can be extended to reduce cache misses due to thread migration.
- The CoreTime OS scheduler [11], which assigns data objects to caches and migrates threads to increase locality. DM can marshal any extra data required by the thread (e.g., portions of its stack).

DM can also enable new execution paradigms. DM lowers the cost of data-migration, the single most important overhead associated with remote execution of code segments. DM can thus enable remote execution in scenarios where it was previously infeasible. Examples include remote execution of fine-grain tasks for increasing parallelism, sharing of rarely-used functional units between cores for saving chip area, and new core specialization opportunities for increased performance and power-efficiency.

In summary, DM is applicable to widely-used current paradigms, and can potentially enable new paradigms.

7. RELATED WORK

The main contribution of this paper is a novel solution to a major limitation of the Staged Execution paradigm: the large increase caused by it in cache misses to inter-segment data. Data Marshaling has related work in the areas of hardware prefetching and OS/compiler techniques to improve locality.

7.1 Hardware Prefetching

Hardware prefetchers can be broadly classified as prefetchers that target regular (stride/stream) memory access patterns (e.g., [24, 42]) and those that target irregular memory access patterns (e.g., [23, 14, 37, 16]). Prefetchers that handle only regular data cannot capture misses for inter-segment data because inter-segment cache lines do not follow a regular stream/stride pattern and are scattered in memory. Prefetchers that handle irregular data (as well as stride/stream based prefetchers) are also not suited for prefetching inter-segment data because the number of cache misses required for training such prefetchers is often more than all of the inter-segment data (an average of 5 in ACS and 6.8 in pipeline workloads). Thus, by the time prefetching begins, a majority of the cache misses have already been incurred.

DM does not have these disadvantages. DM requires minimal on-chip storage, can marshal any arbitrary sequence of inter-segment cache lines, and starts marshaling as soon as the next code segment is shipped to its home core, without requiring any training. Note that our baseline uses an aggressive stream prefetcher [42] and the reported improvements are on **top** of this aggressive prefetcher.

7.2 Reducing Cache Misses

Yang et al. [29] show that pushing (vs. pulling) cache lines to the core can save off-chip cache misses for linked data structures. In contrast, DM saves on-chip misses for any sequence of inter-segment data. Bhattacharjee et al. [7] schedule tasks to maximize cache locality in TBB [21], another example of SE. DM can further help by eliminating the remaining cache misses. Hossain et al. [20] propose DDCache where the producer pushes a cache line to all the sharers of the line when one of the sharers requests the line. DDCache is orthogonal to DM as it only improves locality of shared data, while DM improves locality of private (inter-segment) data.

Other proposals improve shared data locality by inserting software prefetch instructions before the critical section [44, 36]. Such a scheme cannot work for inter-segment data because prefetch instructions must be executed at the home core as part of the next code segment and very close to the actual use of the data, likely making the prefetches untimely. Recent cache hierarchy designs (e.g., [34]) aim to provide fast access to both shared and private data. They can further benefit from DM to minimize cache-to-cache transfers. Proposals to accelerate thread migration [12, 38] are orthogonal and can be combined with DM. Other mechanisms [46, 25] reduce cache line access latency by migrating cache lines closer to the cores that are accessing them. Such schemes cannot reduce inter-segment data misses because –like prefetching– they do not marshal the data proactively and also require training.

7.3 Other Related Work

Remote Procedure Calls (RPC) [9], used in networking, require the programmers to "marshal" the input data with the RPC request. This is similar to DM, which marshals inter-segment data to the home core of the next code segment. However, unlike RPC, DM is solely for performance (i.e., not required for correct execution), does not require programmer input, and is applicable to instances of Staged Execution that do not resemble procedure calls.

8. CONCLUSION

We propose *Data Marshaling (DM)* to improve the reduced locality of inter-segment data in Staged Execution (SE), thereby overcoming a major limitation of SE. DM identifies and marshals the inter-segment data needed by a segment before or during the segment's execution. We show in detail two applications of DM. First, we use DM to marshal the thread-private data to remotely executing critical sections in the Accelerated Critical Section (ACS) mechanism. Our evaluation with 12 critical-section-intensive workloads shows that DM reduces the average execution time by 8.5% compared to an equal-area (16 small cores) baseline ACMP with support for ACS. Second, we use DM for workloads with pipeline parallelism to marshal the data produced in one pipeline stage to the next stage. Our evaluation with 9 pipelined workloads shows that DM improves performance by 14% on a 16-core CMP and 16% on a 32-core CMP. We find that DM's performance is within 5% of an ideal mechanism that eliminates all inter-segment data misses using oracle information, showing that DM achieves almost all of its performance potential. We describe a variety of other possible applications of DM, and conclude that DM is a promising approach that can successfully recover performance loss due to cache misses incurred for inter-segment data in Staged Execution paradigms.

ACKNOWLEDGMENTS

We thank members of the HPS research group, and the anonymous reviewers for their suggestions. We thank the Cockrell Foundation, Intel, and CMU CyLab for their support and the Texas Advanced Computing Center (TACC) for providing HPC resources. M. Aater Suleman was supported by an Intel PhD Fellowship.

REFERENCES

[1] MySQL database engine 5.0.1. http://www.mysql.com, 2008.

[2] SQLite database engine version 3.5.8. 2008.

[3] SysBench: a system performance benchmark v0.4.8. 2008.

[4] M. Annavaram, E. Grochowski, and J. Shen. Mitigating Amdahl's law through EPI throttling. In *ISCA-32*, 2005.

[5] Apple. Grand Central Dispatch. Tech. Brief, 2009.

[6] D. H. Bailey et al. NAS parallel benchmarks. Technical Report RNR-94-007, NASA Ames Research Center, 1994.

[7] A. Bhattacharjee and M. Martonosi. Thread criticality predictors for dynamic performance, power, and resource management in chip multiprocessors. In *ISCA*, 2009.

[8] C. Bienia et al. The PARSEC benchmark suite: Characterization and architectural implications. In *PACT*, 2008.

[9] A. D. Birrell and B. J. Nelson. Implementing remote procedure calls. *ACM TOCS*, 2(1):39–59, 1984.

[10] R. D. Blumofe et al. Cilk: an efficient multithreaded runtime system. In *PPoPP*, 1995.

[11] S. Boyd-Wickizer et al. Reinventing scheduling for multicore systems. In *HotOS-XII*, 2009.

[12] J. A. Brown and D. M. Tullsen. The shared-thread multiprocessor. In *ICS*, 2008.

[13] K. Chakraborty, P. M. Wells, and G. S. Sohi. Computation spreading: Employing hardware migration to specialize CMP cores on-the-fly. In *ASPLOS-XII*, 2006.

[14] R. Cooksey et al. A stateless, content-directed data prefetching mechanism. In *ASPLOS*, 2002.

[15] A. J. Dorta et al. The OpenMP source code repository. In *Euromicro*, 2005.

[16] E. Ebrahimi et al. Techniques for bandwidth-efficient prefetching of linked data structures in hybrid prefetching systems. *HPCA*, 2009.

[17] M. Gordon et al. Exploiting coarse-grained task, data, and pipeline parallelism in stream programs. In *ASPLOS*, 2006.

[18] S. Harizopoulos and A. Ailamaki. StagedDB: Designing database servers for modern hardware. *IEEE Data Eng. Bull.*, June 2005.

[19] M. Hill and M. Marty. Amdahl's law in the multicore era. *IEEE Computer*, 41(7), 2008.

[20] H. Hossain et al. DDCache: Decoupled and delegable cache data and metadata. In *PACT*, 2009.

[21] Intel. Source code for Intel threading building blocks.

[22] Intel. Getting Started with Intel Parallel Studio, 2009.

[23] D. Joseph and D. Grunwald. Prefetching using Markov predictors. In *ISCA*, 1997.

[24] N. P. Jouppi. Improving direct-mapped cache performance by the addition of a small fully-associative cache and prefetch buffers. In *ISCA-17*, 1990.

[25] C. Kim et al. An adaptive, non-uniform cache structure for wire-delay dominated on-chip caches. In *ASPLOS*, 2002.

[26] H. Kredel. Source code for traveling salesman problem (tsp). http://krum.rz.uni-mannheim.de/ba-pp-2007/java/index.html.

[27] J. R. Larus and M. Parkes. Using cohort scheduling to enhance server performance. In *USENIX*, 2002.

[28] J. Laudon and D. Lenoski. The SGI Origin: A ccNUMA Highly Scalable Server. In *ISCA*, 1997.

[29] C. lin Yang and A. R. Lebeck. Push vs. pull: Data movement for linked data structures. In *ICS*, 2000.

[30] M. R. Marty. *Cache coherence techniques for multicore processors*. PhD thesis, 2008.

[31] T. Morad et al. Performance, power efficiency and scalability of asymmetric cluster chip multiprocessors. *Comp Arch Letters*, 2006.

[32] R. Narayanan et al. MineBench: A benchmark suite for data mining workloads. In *IISWC*, 2006.

[33] NVIDIA Corporation. CUDA SDK code samples, 2009.

[34] M. K. Qureshi. Adaptive spill-receive for robust high-performance caching in CMPs. *HPCA*, 2009.

[35] K. K. Rangan et al. Thread motion: Fine-grained power management for multi-core systems. In *ISCA*, 2009.

[36] P. Ranganathan et al. The interaction of software prefetching with ILP processors in shared-memory systems. *ISCA*, 1997.

[37] S. Somogyi et al. Spatio-temporal memory streaming. *ISCA*, 2009.

[38] R. Strong et al. Fast switching of threads between cores. *SIGOPS Oper. Syst. Rev.*, 43(2), 2009.

[39] M. A. Suleman et al. ACMP: Balancing hardware efficiency and programmer efficiency. Technical Report TR-HPS-2007-001, Univ. of Texas at Austin, 2007.

[40] M. A. Suleman et al. An asymmetric multi-core architecture for accelerating critical sections. Technical Report TR-HPS-2008-003, Univ. of Texas at Austin, 2008.

[41] M. A. Suleman et al. Accelerating critical section execution with asymmetric multi-core architectures. *ASPLOS*, 2009.

[42] J. M. Tendler et al. POWER4 system microarchitecture. *IBM Journal of Research and Development*, 46(1):5–26, 2002.

[43] W. Thies et al. Streamit: A language for streaming applications. In *11th Conf. on Compiler Construction*, 2002.

[44] P. Trancoso and J. Torrellas. The impact of speeding up critical sections with data prefetching and forwarding. In *ICPP*, 1996.

[45] M. Waldvogel, G. Varghese, J. Turner, and B. Plattner. Scalable high speed IP routing lookups. In *SIGCOMM*, 1997.

[46] M. Zhang and K. Asanovic. Victim replication: Maximizing capacity while hiding wire delay in tiled chip multiprocessors. In *ISCA*, 2005.

Debunking the 100X GPU vs. CPU Myth: An Evaluation of Throughput Computing on CPU and GPU

Victor W Lee[†], Changkyu Kim[†], Jatin Chhugani[†], Michael Deisher[†], Daehyun Kim[†], Anthony D. Nguyen[†], Nadathur Satish[†], Mikhail Smelyanskiy[†], Srinivas Chennupaty[*], Per Hammarlund[*], Ronak Singhal[*] and Pradeep Dubey[†]

victor.w.lee@intel.com

[†]Throughput Computing Lab, Intel Corporation

[*]Intel Architecture Group, Intel Corporation

ABSTRACT

Recent advances in computing have led to an explosion in the amount of data being generated. Processing the ever-growing data in a timely manner has made throughput computing an important aspect for emerging applications. Our analysis of a set of important throughput computing kernels shows that there is an ample amount of parallelism in these kernels which makes them suitable for today's multi-core CPUs and GPUs. In the past few years there have been many studies claiming GPUs deliver substantial speedups (between 10X and 1000X) over multi-core CPUs on these kernels. To understand where such large performance difference comes from, we perform a rigorous performance analysis and find that after applying optimizations appropriate for both CPUs and GPUs the performance gap between an Nvidia GTX280 processor and the Intel Core i7 960 processor narrows to only 2.5x on average. In this paper, we discuss optimization techniques for both CPU and GPU, analyze what architecture features contributed to performance differences between the two architectures, and recommend a set of architectural features which provide significant improvement in architectural efficiency for throughput kernels.

Categories and Subject Descriptors

C.1.4 [**Processor Architecture**]: Parallel architectures
; C.4 [**Performance of Systems**]: Design studies
; D.3.4 [**Software**]: Processors—*Optimization*

General Terms

Design, Measurement, Performance

Keywords

CPU architecture, GPU architecture, Performance analysis, Performance measurement, Software optimization, Throughput Computing

ISCA'10, June 19–23, 2010, Saint-Malo, France.

1. INTRODUCTION

The past decade has seen a huge increase in digital content as more documents are being created in digital form than ever before. Moreover, the web has become the medium of choice for storing and delivering information such as stock market data, personal records, and news. Soon, the amount of digital data will exceed exabytes (10^{18}) [31]. The massive amount of data makes storing, cataloging, processing, and retrieving information challenging. A new class of applications has emerged across different domains such as database, games, video, and finance that can process this huge amount of data to distill and deliver appropriate content to users. A distinguishing feature of these applications is that they have plenty of data level parallelism and the data can be processed independently and in any order on different processing elements for a similar set of operations such as filtering, aggregating, ranking, etc. This feature together with a processing deadline defines *throughput computing applications*. Going forward, as digital data continues to grow rapidly, throughput computing applications are essential in delivering appropriate content to users in a reasonable duration of time.

Two major computing platforms are deemed suitable for this new class of applications. The first one is the general-purpose CPU (central processing unit) that is capable of running many types of applications and has recently provided multiple cores to process data in parallel. The second one is the GPU (graphics processing unit) that is designed for graphics processing with many small processing elements. The massive processing capability of GPU allures some programmers to start exploring general purpose computing with GPU. This gives rise to the GPGPU field [3, 33].

Fundamentally, CPUs and GPUs are built based on very different philosophies. CPUs are designed for a wide variety of applications and to provide fast response times to a single task. Architectural advances such as branch prediction, out-of-order execution, and super-scalar (in addition to frequency scaling) have been responsible for performance improvement. However, these advances come at the price of increasing complexity/area and power consumption. As a result, main stream CPUs today can pack only a small number of processing cores on the same die to stay within the power and thermal envelopes. GPUs on the other hand are built specifically for rendering and other graphics applications that have a large degree of data parallelism (each pixel on the screen can be processed independently). Graphics applications are also latency tolerant (the processing of each pixel can be delayed as long as frames are processed at interactive rates). As a result, GPUs can trade off single-thread performance for increased parallel processing. For instance,

GPUs can switch from processing one pixel to another when long latency events such as memory accesses are encountered and can switch back to the former pixel at a later time. This approach works well when there is ample data-level parallelism. The speedup of an application on GPUs is ultimately limited by the percentage of the scalar section (in accordance with Amdahl's law).

One interesting question is the relative suitability of CPU or GPU for throughput computing workloads. CPUs have been the main workhorse for traditional workloads and would be expected to do well for throughput computing workloads. There is little doubt that today's CPUs would provide the best single thread performance for throughput computing workloads. However, the limited number of cores in today's CPUs limits how many pieces of data can be processed simultaneously. On the other hand, GPUs provide many parallel processing units which are ideal for throughput computing. However, the design for graphics pipeline lacks some critical processing capabilities (e.g., large caches) for general purpose workloads, which may result in lower architecture efficiency on throughput computing workloads.

This paper attempts to correlate throughput computing characteristics with architectural features on today's CPUs and GPUs and provides insights into why certain throughput computing kernels perform better on CPUs and others work better on GPUs. We use a set of kernels and applications that have been identified by previous studies [6, 10, 13, 44] as important components of throughput computing workloads. We highlight the importance of platform-specific software optimizations, and recommend an application-driven design methodology that identifies essential hardware architecture features based on application characteristics.

This paper makes the following contributions:

- We reexamine a number of claims [9, 19, 21, 32, 42, 45, 47, 53] that GPUs perform 10X to 1000X better than CPUs on a number of throughput kernels/applications. After tuning the code for **BOTH** CPU and GPU, we find the GPU only performs 2.5X better than CPU. This puts CPU and GPU roughly in the same performance ballpark for throughput computing.
- We provide a systematic characterization of throughput computing kernels regarding the types of parallelism available, the compute and bandwidth requirements, the access pattern and the synchronization needs. We identify the important software optimization techniques for efficient utilization of CPU and GPU platforms.
- We analyze the performance difference between CPU and GPU and identify the key architecture features that benefit throughput computing workloads.

This paper is organized as follows: Section 2 discusses the throughput computing workloads used for this study. Section 3 describes the two main compute platforms – CPUs and GPUs. Section 4 discusses the performance of our throughput computing workloads on today's compute platforms. Section 5 provides a platform-specific optimization guide and recommends a set of essential architecture features. Section 6 discusses related work and Section 7 concludes our findings.

2. THE WORKLOAD: THROUGHPUT COMPUTING KERNELS

We analyzed the core computation and memory characteristics of recently proposed benchmark suites [6, 10, 13, 44] and formulated the set of *throughput computing kernels* that capture these characteristics. These kernels have a large amount of data-level parallelism, which makes them a natural fit for modern multi-core architectures. Table 1 summarizes the workload characterization. We classify these kernels based on (1) their compute and memory requirements, (2) regularity of memory accesses, which determines the ease of exploiting data-level parallelism (SIMD), and (3) the granularity of tasks, which determines the impact of synchronization. These characteristics provide insights into the architectural features that are required to achieve good performance.

1. SGEMM (both dense and sparse) is an important kernel that is an integral part of many linear algebra numerical algorithms, such as linear solvers. SGEMM is characterized by regular access patterns and therefore maps to SIMD architecture in a straightforward manner. Threading is also simple, as matrices can be broken into sub-blocks of equal size which can be operated on independently by multiple threads. SGEMM performs $O(n^3)$ compute, where n is the matrix dimension and has $O(n^2)$ data accesses. The ratio of compute to data accesses is $O(n)$, which makes SGEMM a compute-bound application, when properly blocked.

2. MC or Monte Carlo randomly samples a complex function, with an unknown or highly complex analytical representation, and averages the results. We use an example of Monte Carlo from computational finance for pricing options [34]. It simulates a random path of an underlying stock over time and calculates a payoff from the option at the end of the time step. It repeats this step many times to collect a large number of samples which are then averaged to obtain the option price. Monte Carlo algorithms are generally compute-bound with regular access patterns, which makes it a very good fit for SIMD architectures.

3. Conv or convolution is a common image filtering operation used for effects such as blur, emboss and sharpen. Its arithmetic computations are simple multiply-add operations and its memory accesses are regular in small neighborhood. Each pixel is calculated independently, thus providing ample parallelism at both SIMD and thread level. Though its compute-to-memory characteristic varies depending on the filter size, in practice, it usually exhibits high compute-to-memory ratio. Its sliding-window-style access pattern gives rise to a memory alignment issue in SIMD computations. Also, multi-dimensional convolutions incur non-sequential data accesses, which require good cache blocking for high performance.

4. FFT or Fast Fourier Transform is one of the most important building blocks for signal processing applications. It converts signals from time domain to frequency domain, and vice versa. FFT is an improved algorithm to implement Discrete Fourier Transform (DFT). DFT requires $O(n^2)$ operations and FFT improves it to $O(n \log n)$. FFT algorithms have been studied exhaustively [26]. Though various optimizations have been developed for each usage model/hardware platform, their basic behavior is similar. It is composed of $\log n$ stages of the butterfly computation followed by a bit-reverse permutation. Arithmetic computations are simple floating-point multiply-adds, but data access patterns are non-trivial pseudo-all-to-all communication, which makes parallelization and SIMDification difficult. Therefore, many studies [7] have focused on the challenges to implement FFT on multi-core wide-SIMD architectures well.

5. SAXPY or Scalar Alpha X Plus Y is one of the functions in the Basic Linear Algebra Subprograms (BLAS) package and is a combination of scalar multiplication and vector addition. It has a regular access pattern and maps well to SIMD. The use of TLP requires only a simple partitioning of the vector. For long vectors that do not fit into the on-die storage, SAXPY is bandwidth bound.

Kernel	Application	SIMD	TLP	Characteristics
SGEMM (**SGEMM**) [48]	Linear algebra	Regular	Across 2D Tiles	Compute bound after tiling
Monte Carlo (**MC**) [34, 9]	Computational Finance	Regular	Across paths	Compute bound
Convolution (**Conv**) [16, 19]	Image Analysis	Regular	Across pixels	Compute bound; BW bound for small filters
FFT (**FFT**) [17, 21]	Signal Processing	Regular	Across smaller FFTs	Compute/BW bound depending on size
SAXPY (**SAXPY**) [46]	Dot Product	Regular	Across vector	BW bound for large vectors
LBM (**LBM**) [32, 45]	Time Migration	Regular	Across cells	BW bound
Constraint Solver (**Solv**) [14]	Rigid body physics	Gather/Scatter	Across constraints	Synchronization bound
SpMV (**SpMV**) [50, 8, 47]	Sparse Solver	Gather	Across non-zero	BW bound for typical large matrices
GJK (**GJK**) [38]	Collision Detection	Gather/Scatter	Across objects	Compute Bound
Sort (**Sort**) [15, 39, 40]	Database	Gather/Scatter	Across elements	Compute bound
Ray Casting (**RC**) [43]	Volume Rendering	Gather	Across rays	4-8MB first level working set, over 500MB last level working set
Search (**Search**) [27]	Database	Gather/Scatter	Across queries	Compute bound for small tree, BW bound at bottom of tree for large tree
Histogram (**Hist**) [53]	Image Analysis	Requires conflict detection	Across pixels	Reduction/synchronization bound
Bilateral (**Bilat**) [52]	Image Analysis	Regular	Across pixels	Compute Bound

Table 1: Throughput computing kernels characteristics. The referred papers contains the best previous reported performance numbers on CPU/GPU platforms. Our optimized performance numbers are at least on par or better than those numbers.

For very short vectors, SAXPY spends a large portion of time performing horizontal reduction operation.

6. LBM or Lattice Boltzmann method, is a class of computational fluid dynamics. LBM uses the discrete Boltzmann equation to simulate the flow of a Newtonian fluid instead of solving the Navier Stokes equations. In each time step, for a D3Q19 lattice, LBM traverses the entire 3D fluid lattice and for each cell computes new distribution function values from the cell's 19 neighbors (including self). Within each time step, the lattice can be traversed in any order as values from the neighbors are computed from the previous time step. This aspect makes LBM suitable for both TLP and DLP. LBM has $O(n)$ compute and requires $O(n)$ data, where n is the number of cells. The working set consists of the data of the cell and its 19 neighbors. The reuse of these values is substantially less than convolution. Large caches do not improve the performance significantly. The lack of reuse also means that the compute to bandwidth ratio is low; LBM is usually bandwidth bound.

7. Solv or constraint solver is a key part of game physics simulators. During the execution of the physical simulation pipeline, a collision detection phase computes pairs of colliding bodies, which are then used as inputs to a constraint solving phase. The constraint solver operates on these pairs and computes the separating contact forces, which keeps the bodies from inter-penetrating into one another. The constraints are typically divided into batches of independent constraints [14]. SIMD and TLP are both exploited among independent constraints. Exploiting SIMD parallelism is however challenging due to the presence of gather/scatter operations required to gather/scatter object data (position, velocity) for different objects. Ideally, the constraint solver should be bandwidth bound, because it iterates over all constraints in a given iteration and the number of constraints for realistic large scale destruction scenes exceeds the capacity of today's caches. However, practical implementations suffer from synchronization costs across sets of independent constraints, which limits performance on current architectures.

8. SpMV or sparse matrix vector multiplication is at the heart of many iterative solvers. There are several storage formats of sparse matrices, compressed row storage being the most common. Computation in this format is characterized by regular access patterns over non-zero elements and irregular access patterns over the vector, based on column index. When the matrix is large and does not fit into on-die storage, a well optimized kernel is usually bandwidth bound.

9. GJK is a commonly used algorithm for collision detection and resolution of convex objects in physically-based animations/simulations in virtual environments. A large fraction of the run-time is spent in computing support map, i.e., the furthest vertex of the object along a given direction. Scalar implementation of GJK is compute bound on current CPUs and GPUs and can exploit DLP to further speedup the run-time. The underlying SIMD is exploited by executing multiple instances of the kernel on different pairs of objects. This requires gathering the object data (vertices/edges) of multiple objects into a SIMD register to facilitate fast support map execution. Hence the run-time is dependent on support for an efficient gather instruction by the underlying hardware. There also exist techniques [38] that can compute support map by memoizing the object into a lookup table, and performing lookups into these tables at run-time. Although still requiring gathers, this lookup can be performed using texture mapping units available on GPUs to achieve further speedups.

10. Sort or radix sort is a multi-pass sorting algorithm used in many areas including databases. Each pass sorts one digit of the input at a time, from least to most significant. Each pass involves data rearrangement in the form of memory scatters. On CPUs, the best implementation foregoes the use of SIMD and implements a scatter oriented rearrangement within cache. On GPUs, where SIMD use is important, the algorithm is rewritten using a 1-bit sort primitive, called split [39]. The split based code, however, has more scalar operations than the buffer code (since it works on a single bit at a time). The overall efficiency of SIMD use relative to optimized scalar code is therefore not high even for split code. The number of bits considered per pass of radix sort depends on the size of the local storage. Increasing cache sizes will thus improve performance (each doubling of the cache size will increase the number of bits per pass by one). Overall, radix sort has $O(n)$ bandwidth and compute requirements (where n is the number of elements to be sorted), but is usually compute bound due to the inefficiency of SIMD use.

11. RC or Ray Casting is an important visual application, used to visualize 3D datasets, such as CT data used in medical imaging. High quality algorithms, known as ray casting, cast rays through the volume, performing compositing of each voxel into a corresponding pixel, based on voxel opacity and color. Tracing multiple rays using SIMD is challenging, because rays can access non-contiguous memory locations, resulting in incoherent and irregular memory accesses. Some ray casting implementations perform a decent amount of computation, for example, gradient shading. The first level working set due to adjacent rays accessing the same volume data is reasonably small. However, the last level working set can be as large as the volume itself, which is several gigabytes of data.

12. Search or in-memory tree structured index search is a commonly used operation in various fields of computer science, especially databases. For CPUs, the performance depends on whether the trees can fit in cache or not. For small trees (tree sizes smaller than the last-level cache (LLC)), the search operation is compute bound, and can exploit the underlying SIMD to achieve speedups. However, for large trees (tree sizes larger than the LLC), the last few levels of the tree do not fit in the LLC, and hence the run-time for search is bound by the available memory bandwidth. As far as the GPUs are concerned, the available high-bandwidth exceeds the required bandwidth even for large trees, and the run-time is compute bound. The run-time of search is proportional to the tree depth on the GTX280.

13. Hist or histogram computation is an important image processing algorithm which hashes and aggregates pixels from the continuous stream of data into a smaller number of bins. While address computation is SIMD friendly, SIMDification of the aggregation, however, requires hardware support for conflict detection, currently not available on modern architectures. The access pattern is irregular and hence SIMD is hard to exploit. Generally, multi-threading of histogram requires atomic operation support. However, there are several parallel implementations of histogram which use privatization. Typically, private histograms can be made to fit into available on-die storage. However, the overhead of reducing the private histograms is high, which becomes a major bottleneck for highly parallel architectures.

14. Bilat or bilateral filter is a common non-linear filter used in image processing for edge-preserving smoothing operations. The core computation has a combination of a spatial and an intensity filter. The neighboring pixel values and positions are used to compute new pixel values. It has high computational requirements and the performance should scale linearly with increased flops. Typical image sizes are large; TLP/DLP can be exploited by dividing the pixels among threads and SIMD units. Furthermore, the bilateral filter involves transcendental operations like computing exponents, which can significantly benefit from fast math units.

3. TODAY'S HIGH PERFORMANCE COMPUTE PLATFORMS

In this section, we describe two popular high-performance compute platforms of today: (1) A CPU based platform with an Intel Core i7-960 processor; and (2) A GPU based platform with an Nvidia GTX280 graphics processor.

3.1 Architectural Details

First, we discuss the architectural details of the two architectures, and analyze the total compute, bandwidth and other architectural features available to facilitate throughput computing applications.

3.1.1 Intel Core i7 CPU

The Intel Core i7-960 CPU is the latest multi-threaded multi-core Intel-Architecture processor. It offers *four* cores on the same die running at a frequency of 3.2GHz. The Core i7 processor cores feature an out-of-order super-scalar microarchitecture, with newly added 2-way hyper-threading. In addition to scalar units, it also has 4-wide SIMD units that support a wide range of SIMD instructions [24]. Each core has a separate 32KB L1 for both instructions and data, and a 256KB unified L2 data cache. All four cores share an 8MB L3 data cache. The Core i7 processor also features an on-die memory controller that connects to three channels of DDR memory. Table 2 provides the peak single-precision and double-precision FLOPS for both scalar and SSE units, and also the peak bandwidth available per die.

3.1.2 Nvidia GTX280 GPU

The Nvidia GTX280 is composed of an array of multiprocessors (a.k.a. SM). Each SM has 8 scalar processing units running in lockstep[1], each at 1.3 GHz. The hardware SIMD structure is exposed to programmers through thread warps. To hide memory latency, GTX280 provides hardware multi-threading support that allows hundreds of thread contexts to be active simultaneously. To alleviate memory bandwidth, the card includes various on-chip memories – such as multi-ported software-controlled 16KB memory (referred to as *local shared buffer*) and small non-coherent read-only caches. The GTX280 also has special functional units like the texture sampling unit, and math units for fast transcendental operations. Table 2 depicts the peak FLOPS and the peak bandwidth of the GTX280[2].

3.2 Implications for Throughput Computing Applications

We now describe how the salient hardware features on the two architectures differ from each other, and their implications for throughput computing applications.

Processing Element Difference: The *CPU core* is designed to work well for a wide range of applications, including single-threaded applications. To improve single-thread performance, the CPU core employs out-of-order super-scalar architecture to exploit instruction level parallelism. Each CPU core supports scalar and SIMD operations, with multiple issue ports allowing for more than one operation to be issued per cycle. It also has a sophisticated branch predictor to reduce the impact of branch misprediction on performance. Therefore, the size and complexity of the CPU core limits the number of cores that can be integrated on the same die.
In comparison, the processing element for GPU *or SM* trades off fast single thread performance and clock speed for high throughput. Each SM is relatively simple. It consists of a single fetch unit and eight scalar units. Each instruction is fetched and executed in parallel on all eight scalar units over four cycles for 32 data elements (a.k.a. a *warp*). This keeps the area of each SM relatively small, and therefore more SMs can be packed per die, as compared to the number of CPU cores.

Cache size/Multi-threading: CPU provides caches and hardware prefetchers to help programmers manage data implicitly. The caches are transparent to the programmer, and capture the most frequently used data. If the working set of the application can fit into the on-die caches, the compute units are used more effectively. As a result, there has been a trend of increasing cache sizes in recent years. Hardware prefetchers provide additional help to reduce memory latency for streaming applications. Software prefetch instructions are also supported to potentially *reduce* the latency incurred with irregular memory accesses. In contrast, GPU provides for a large number of light-weight threads to hide memory latency. Each *SM* can support up to 32 concurrent warps per multi-processor. Since all the threads within a warp execute the same instruction, the warps are switched out upon issuing memory requests. To capture repeated access patterns to the same data, GTX280 provides for a few local storages (shared buffer, constant cache and texture cache). The size

[1]We view 8 scalar units as SIMD lanes, hence 8-element wide SIMD for GTX280.

[2]The peak single-precision SIMD Flops for GTX280 is 311.1 and increases to 933.1 by including fused multiply-add and a multiply operation which can be executed in SFU pipeline.

	Num. PE	Frequency (GHz)	Num. Transistors	BW (GB/sec)	SP SIMD width	DP SIMD width	Peak SP Scalar FLOPS (GFLOPS)	Peak SP SIMD Flops (GFLOPS)	Peak DP SIMD Flops (GFLOPS)
Core i7-960	4	3.2	0.7B	32	4	2	25.6	102.4	51.2
GTX280	30	1.3	1.4B	141	8	1	116.6	311.1/933.1	77.8

Table 2: Core i7 and GTX280 specifications. BW: local DRAM bandwidth, SP: Single-Precision Floating Point, DP: Double-Precision Floating Point.

of the local shared buffer is just 16KB, and much smaller than the cache sizes on CPUs.

Bandwidth Difference: Core i7 provides a peak external memory bandwidth of 32 GB/sec, while GTX280 provides a bandwidth of around 141 GB/sec. Although the ratio of peak bandwidth is pretty large (~4.7X), the ratio of bytes per flop is comparatively smaller (~1.6X) for applications not utilizing fused multiply add in the SFU.

Other Differences: CPUs provide for fast synchronization operations, something that is not efficiently implemented on GPUs. CPUs also provide for efficient in-register cross-lane SIMD operations, like general shuffle and swizzle instructions. On the other hand, such operations are emulated on GPUs by storing the data into the shared buffer, and loading it with the appropriate shuffle pattern. This incurs large overheads for some throughput computing applications. In contrast, GPUs provide support for gather/scatter instructions from memory, something that is not efficiently implemented on CPUs. Gather/Scatter operations are important to increase SIMD utilization for applications requiring access to non-contiguous regions of memory to be operated upon in a SIMD fashion. Furthermore, the availability of special function units like texture sampling unit and math units for fast transcendental helps speedup throughput computing applications that spend a substantial amount of time in these operations.

4. PERFORMANCE EVALUATIONS ON CORE I7 AND GTX280

This section evaluates the performance of the throughput computing kernels on the Core i7-960 and GTX280 processors and analyzes the measured results.

4.1 Methodology

We measured the performance of our kernels on (1) a 3.2GHz Core i7-960 processor running the SUSE Enterprise Server 11 operating system with 6GB of PC1333 DDR3 memory on an Intel DX58SO motherboard, and (2) a 1.3GHz GTX280 processor (an eVGA GeForce GTX280 card with 1GB GDDR3 memory) in the same Core i7 system with Nvidia driver version 19.180 and the CUDA 2.3 toolkit.

Since we are interested in comparing the CPU and the GPU architectures at the chip level to see if any specific architecture features are responsible for the performance difference, we did not include the data transfer time for GPU measurements. We assume the throughput computing kernels are executed in the middle of other computations that create data in GPU memory before the kernel execution and use data generated by the kernel in GPU memory. For applications that do not meet our assumption, transfer time can significantly degrade performance as reported by Datta in [16]. The GPU results as presented here are an upper bound of what will be seen in actual applications for these algorithms.

For both CPU and GPU performance measurements, we have optimized most of the kernels individually for each platform. For some of the kernels, we have used the best available implementation that already existed. Specifically, evaluations of **SGEMM**, **SpMV**, **FFT** and **MC** on GTX280 have been done using code from

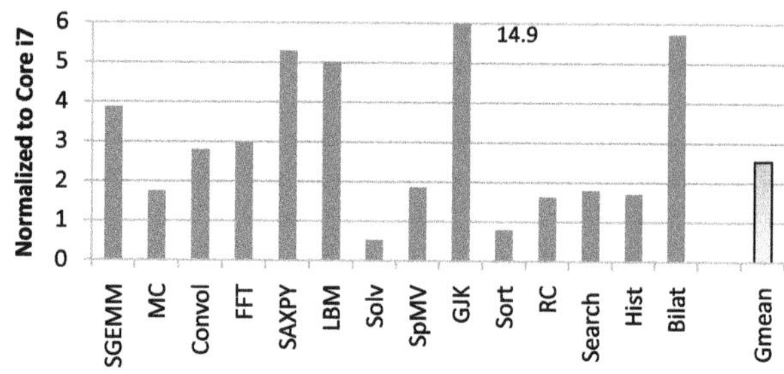

(a) Relative Performace

Figure 1: Comparison between Core i7 and GTX280 Performance.

[1, 8, 2, 34], respectively. For the evaluations of **SGEMM**, **SpMV** and **FFT** on Core i7, we used Intel MKL 10.0. Table 3 shows the performance of throughput computing kernels on Core i7 and GTX280 processor with the appropriate performance metric shown in the caption. *To the best of our knowledge, our performance numbers are at least on par and often better than the best published data.* We typically find that the highest performance is achieved when multiple threads are used per core. For Core i7, the best performance comes from running 8 threads on 4 cores. For GTX280, while the maximum number of warps that can be executed on one GPU *SM* is 32, a judicious choice is required to balance the benefit of multithreading with the increased pressure on registers and on-chip memory resources. Kernels are often run with 4 to 8 warps per core for best GPU performance.

4.2 Performance Comparison

Figure 1 shows the relative performance between GTX280 and Core i7 processors when data transfer time for GTX280 is not considered. Our data shows that GTX280 only has an average of 2.5X performance advantage over Core i7 in the 14 kernels tested. Only **GJK** achieves a greater than 10X performance gap due to the use of the texture sampler. **Sort** and **Solv** actually perform better on Core i7 . Our results are far less than previous claims like the 50X difference in pricing European options using Monte Carlo method [9], the 114X difference in LBM [45], the 40X difference in FFT [21], the 50X difference in sparse matrix vector multiplication [47] and the 40X difference in histogram computation [53], etc.

There are many factors that contributed to the big difference between previous reported results and ours. One factor is what CPU and GPU are used in the comparison. Comparing a high performance GPU to a mobile CPU is not an optimal comparison as their considerations for operating power, thermal envelop and reliability are totally different. Another factor is how much optimization is performed on the CPU and GPU. Many studies compare optimized GPU code to unoptimized CPU code and resulted in large difference. Other studies which perform careful optimizations to CPU and GPU such as [27, 39, 40, 43, 49] report much lower speedup similar to ours. Section 5.1 discusses the necessary software optimizations for improving performance for both CPU and GPU platforms.

Apps.	SGEMM	MC	Conv	FFT	SAXPY	LBM	Solv	SpMV	GJK	Sort	RC	Search	Hist	Bilat
Core i7-960	94	0.8	1250	71.4	16.8	85	103	4.9	67	250	5	50	1517	83
GTX280	364	1.4	3500	213	88.8	426	52	9.1	1020	198	8.1	90	2583	475

Table 3: Raw performance measured on the two platforms. From the left, metrics are Gflops/s, billion paths/s, million pixels/s, Gflops/s, GB/s, million lookups/s, FPS, Gflops/s, FPS, million elements/s, FPS, million queries/s, million pixels/s, million pixels/s.

4.3 Performance Analysis

In this section, we analyze the performance results and identify the architectural features that contribute to the performance of each of our kernels. We begin by first identifying kernels that are purely bounded by one of the two fundamental processor resources - bandwidth and compute. We then identify the role of other architectural features such as hardware support for irregular memory accesses, fast synchronization and hardware for performing fixed function computations (such as texture and transcendental math operations) in speeding up the remaining kernels.

4.3.1 Bandwidth

Every kernel requires some amount of external memory bandwidth to bring data into the processor. The impact of external memory bandwidth on kernel performance depends on two factors: (1) whether the kernel has enough computation to fully utilize the memory accesses; and (2) whether the kernel has a working set that fits in the on-die storages (either cache or buffers). Two of our kernels, **SAXPY** and **LBM** have large working sets that require global memory accesses without much compute on the loaded data - they are *purely bandwidth bound*. These kernels will benefit from increased bandwidth resources. The performance ratios for these two kernels between GTX280 and Core i7 are 5.3X and 5X respectively. These results are inline with the ratio between the two processors' peak memory bandwidth (which is 4.7X).

SpMV also has a large working set and very little compute. However, the performance ratio for this kernel between GTX280 and Core i7 is 1.9X, which is about 2.3X lower than the ratio of peak bandwidth between the two processors. This is due to the fact that the GTX280 implementation of SpMV keeps both vector and column index data structures in GDDR since they do not fit in the small on-chip shared buffer. However, in the Core i7 implementation, the vectors always fit in cache and the column index fits in cache for about half the matrixes. On average, the GPU bandwidth requirement for SpMV is about 2.5X the CPU requirement. As the result, although the GTX280 has 4.7X more bandwidth than Core i7 , the performance ratio is only 1.9X.

Our other kernels either have a high compute-to-bandwidth ratio or working sets that fit completely or partially in the on-die storage, thereby reducing the impact of memory bandwidth on performance. These categories of kernels will be described in later sections.

4.3.2 Compute Flops

The computational flops available on a processor depend on single-thread performance, as well as TLP due to the presence of multiple cores, or DLP due to wide vector (SIMD) units. While most applications (except the bandwidth-bound kernels) can benefit from improved single-thread performance and thread-level parallelism by exploiting additional cores, not all of them can exploit SIMD well. We identify **SGEMM**, **MC**, **Conv**, **FFT** and **Bilat** as being able to exploit all available flops on both CPU and GPU architectures. Figure 1 shows that **SGEMM**, **Conv** and **FFT** have GTX280-to-Core i7 performance ratios in the 2.8-4X range. This is close to the 3-6X single-precision (SP) flop ratio of the GTX280 to Core i7 architectures (see Table 2), depending on whether kernels can utilize fused multiply-adds or not.

The reason for not achieving the peak compute ratio is because GPUs do not achieve peak efficiency in the presence of shared buffer accesses. Volkov et al. [48] show that GPUs obtain only about 66% of the peak flops even for **SGEMM** (known to be compute bound). Our results match their achieved performance ratios. **MC** uses double precision arithmetic, and hence has a performance ratio of 1.8X, close to the 1.5X double-precision (DP) flop ratio. **Bilat** utilizes fast transcendental operations on GPUs (described later), and has a GTX280 to Core i7 performance ratio better than 5X. The algorithm used for **Sort** critically depends on the SIMD width of the processor. A typical radix sort implementation involves reordering data involving many scalar operations for buffer management and data scatters. However, scalar code is inefficient on GPUs, and hence the best GPU sort code uses a SIMD friendly split primitive. This has many more operations than the scalar code - and is consequently **1.25X slower** on the GTX280 than on Core i7.

Seven of our fourteen kernels have been identified as bounded by compute or bandwidth resources. We now describe the other architectural features that have a performance impact on the other seven kernels.

4.3.3 Cache

As mentioned in the section 4.3.1, on-die storage can alleviate external memory bandwidth pressure if all or part of the kernel's working set can fit in such storage. When the working set fits in cache, most kernels are compute bound and the performance will scale with increasing compute. The five kernels that we identify as compute bound have working sets that can be tuned to fit in any reasonably sized cache without significant loss of performance. Consequently, they only rely on the presence on some kind of on-chip storage and are compute bound on both CPUs and GPUs.

There are kernels whose working set cannot be easily tuned to any given cache size without loss of performance. One example is radix sort, which requires a working set that increases with the number of bits considered per pass of the sort. The number of passes over the data, and hence the overall runtime, decreases as we increase cache size. On GPUs with a small local buffer of 16 KB shared among many threads, we can only sort 4 bits in one pass - requiring 8 passes to sort 32-bit data. On Core i7, we can fit the working set of 8 bits in L2 cache; this only requires 4 passes - a 2X speedup. This contributes to **Sort** on Core i7 being **1.25X faster** than GTX280. Another interesting example is index tree search (**Search**). Here, the size of the input search tree determines the working set. For small trees that fit in cache, search on CPUs is compute bound, and in fact is **2X faster** than GPU search. For larger trees, search on CPUs is bandwidth bound, and becomes **1.8X slower** than GPUs. GPU search, in contrast, is always compute bound due to ISA inefficiencies (i.e., the unavailability of cross-lane SIMD operations).

Another important working set characteristic that determines kernel performance is whether the working set scales with the number of threads or is shared by all threads. Kernels like **SGEMM**, **MC**, **Conv**, **FFT**, **Sort**, **RC**, and **Hist** have working sets that scale with the number of threads. These kernels require larger working sets for GPUs (with more threads) than CPUs. This may not have any performance impact if the kernel can be tiled to fit into a cache of an arbitrary size (e.g. **SGEMM** and **FFT**). However, tiling can only be done to an extent for **RC**. Consequently, **RC** becomes bandwidth bound on GPUs, which have very small amount of on-die storages, but is not bandwidth bound on CPUs (instead being affected by gathers/scatters, described later), and the performance ratio on GTX280 to Core i7 is only 1.6X, far less than bandwidth and compute ratios.

4.3.4 Gather/Scatter

Kernels that are not bandwidth bound can benefit with increasing DLP. However, the use of SIMD execution units places restrictions on kernel implementations, particularly in the layout of the data. Operands and results of SIMD operations are typically required to be grouped together sequentially in memory. To achieve the best performance, they should be placed into an address-aligned structure (for example for 4-wide single-precision SIMD, the best performance will be when the data is 16-byte aligned). If the data does not meet these layout restrictions, programmers must convert the data layout of kernels. This generally involves gather/scatter operations, where operands are gathered from multiple locations and packed together into a tight grouping, and results are scattered from a tight grouping to multiple locations. Performing gather/scatter in software can be expensive.[3] Thus, efficient hardware support for gather/scatter operations is very important.

A number of our kernels rely on the availability of gather/scatter operations. For example, **GJK** spends a large fraction of its runtime in computing the support map. This requires gathering the object data (vertices/edges) of multiple objects into a SIMD register to facilitate fast support map execution. Another example is **RC**, which requires gathering volume data across the rays. Frequent irregular memory accesses result in large number of gather operations. Up to 10% of the dynamic instructions are gather requests.

On Core i7, there is no hardware gather/scatter support. Consequently, **GJK** and **RC** do not utilize SIMD efficiently. For example, **RC** sees very incremental benefit from SSE between 0.8X and 1.2X, due to large overhead of software gather. **GJK** also sees minimal benefits from SSE. On GTX280, support for gather/scatter is offered for accesses to the local buffer and GDDR memory. Local shared buffer supports simultaneous gather/scatter accesses to multiple banks. The GDDR memory controller coalesces requests to the same line to reduce the number of gather/scatter accesses. This improved gather/scatter support leads to an improvement of **GJK** performance on the GTX280 over the Core i7 . However, gather/scatter support only has a small impact (of 1.2X) on **RC** performance because the accesses are widely spread out to memory, requiring multiple GDDR accesses even with coalescing support – it therefore becomes limited by GPU memory bandwidth. Consequently, the ratio of GTX280 to Core i7 performance for **RC** is only 1.6X, slightly better than the scalar flop ratio of 1.5X.

4.3.5 Reduction and Synchronization

Throughput computing kernels achieve high performance through thread-level (multiple cores and threads) and/or data-level (wide vector) parallelism. Reduction and synchronization are two operations that do not scale with increasing thread count and data-level parallelism. Various optimization techniques have been proposed to reduce the need of reduction and to avoid synchronization. However, the synchronization overhead is still dominant in some kernels such as **Hist** and **Solv**, and will become an even bigger performance bottleneck as the number of cores/threads and the SIMD width increase.

The performance of **Hist** is mainly limited by atomic updates. Although Core i7 supports a hardware lock increment instruction, 28% of the total run-time is still spent on atomic updates. Atomic update support on the GTX280 is also very limited. Consequently, a privatization approach where each thread generates a local histogram was implemented for both CPU and GPU. However, this implement does not scale with increase core count because the reduction overhead increases with the number of cores. Also, the lack of cross-SIMD lane operations like reduction on GPUs leads to large instruction overhead on GTX280. Thus, **Hist** is only 1.8X faster on GTX280 than on Core i7, much lower than the compute and bandwidth ratios (~5X). As was mentioned in Section 2, mapping **Hist** to SIMD requires support for conflict detection which is not currently available on modern architectures. Our analysis of ideal conflict detection hardware, capable of detecting an arbitrary number of conflicting indices within the same SIMD vector, improves histogram computation by up to 3X [29].

In **Solv**, a batch of independent constraints is executed simultaneously by multiple cores/threads, followed by a barrier before executing the next batch. Since resolving a constraint requires only small amount of computation (on the order of several hundred instructions), the task granularity is small. As a result, the execution time is dominated by the barrier overhead. On Core i7, barriers are implemented using atomic instructions. While it is possible to implement barrier operations entirely on GPU [48], this implementation does not guarantee that previous accesses to all levels of memory hierarchy have completed. CPUs provide a memory consistency model with the help of a cache coherence protocol. Due to the fact that cache coherence is not available on today's GPUs, assuring memory consistency between two batches of constraints requires launching the second batch from the CPU host, which incurs additional overhead. As a result, the barrier execution time of GTX280 is order of magnitude slower than on Core i7, resulting in an overall **1.9X slow down** in performance for GTX280 when compared to Core i7 for the constraint solver.

4.3.6 Fixed Function

Bilat consists of *transcendental operations* like computing exponential and power functions. However, for image processing purpose, high accuracy version of these functions are not necessary. Current CPUs use algebraic expressions to evaluate such expressions up to the required accuracy, while modern GPUs provide hardware to speedup the computation. On Core i7 , a large portion of run-time (around 66%) is spent in transcendental computation. On GTX280, due to the presence of fast transcendental hardware, it achieves a 5.7X performance ratio compare to Core i7 (much more than the peak compute ratio of around 3X). Speeding up transcendental on Core i7 (for example, as on GTX280) would improve **Bilat** performance by around 2X, and the resultant GPU-to-CPU performance ratio would be around 3X, which is closer to the peak compute ratio. **MC** is another kernel that would benefit from fast transcendental on CPUs.

Modern GPUs also provide for other fixed function units like the texture sampling unit, which is a major component of rendering algorithms. However, by reducing the linear-time support-map computation to constant-time texture lookups, **GJK** collision detection algorithm can exploit the **fast texture lookup** capability of GPUs, resulting in an overall 14.9X speedup on GTX280 over Core i7.

5. DISCUSSION

The platform-specific software optimization is critical to fully

[3]For 4-wide SIMD on Core i7, a compiler generated gather sequence will take 20 instructions and even a hand optimized assembly sequence will still take 13 instructions.

utilize compute/bandwidth resources for both CPUs and GPUs. We first discuss these software optimization techniques and derive a number of key hardware architecture features which play a major role in improving performance of throughput computing workloads.

5.1 Platform Optimization Guide

Traditionally, CPU programmers have heavily relied on increasing clock frequencies to improve performance and have not optimized their applications to fully extract TLP and DLP. However, CPUs are evolving to incorporate more cores with wider SIMD units, and it is critical for applications to be parallelized to exploit TLP and DLP. In the absence of such optimizations, CPU implementations are sub-optimal in performance and can be orders of magnitude off their attainable performance. For example, the previously reported **LBM** number on GPUs claims 114X speedup over CPUs [45]. However, we found that with careful multithreading, reorganization of memory access patterns, and SIMD optimizations, the performance on both CPUs and GPUs is limited by memory bandwidth and the gap is reduced to only 5X. Now we highlight the key platform-specific optimization techniques we learned from optimizing the throughput computing kernels.

CPU optimization: First, most of our kernels can linearly scale with the number of cores. Thus multithreading provides 3-4X performance improvement on Core i7. Second, CPUs heavily rely on caches to hide memory latency. Moreover, memory bandwidth on CPUs is low as compared to GPUs. Blocking is one technique which reduces LLC misses on CPUs. Programmers must be aware of the underlying cache hierarchy or use auto-tuning techniques to obtain the best performing kernels [18, 35]. Many of our kernels, **SGEMM**, **FFT**, **SpMV**, **Sort**, **Search**, and **RC** use cache blocking. **Sort**, for best performance, requires the number of bits per pass to be tuned so that its working set fits in cache. **RC** blocks the volume to increase 3D locality between rays in a bundle. We observe that cache blocking improves the performance of **Sort** and **Search** by 3-5X. Third, we found that reordering data to prevent irregular memory accesses is critical for SIMD utilization on CPUs. The main reason is that CPUs do not have gather/scatter support. **Search** performs explicit SIMD blocking to make memory accesses regular. **Solv** performs a reordering of the constraints to improve memory access patterns. Other kernels, such as **LBM** and **RC** convert some of the data structures from array-of-structure to structure-of-array format to completely eliminate gather operations. For example, the performance of **LBM** improves by 1.5X from this optimization.

GPU optimization: For GPUs, we found that global inter-thread synchronization is very costly, because it involves a kernel termination and new kernel call overhead from the host. **Hist** minimizes global synchronization by privatizing histograms. **Solv** also performs constraint reordering to minimize conflicts among neighboring constraints, which are global synchronization points. Another important optimization for GPUs was the use of the local shared buffer. Most of our kernels use the shared buffer to reduce bandwidth consumption. Additionally, our GPU sort uses the fact that buffer memory is multi-banked to enable efficient gathers/scatters of data.

5.2 Hardware Recommendations

In this section we capitalize on the learning from Section 4.3 to derive a number of key processor features which play major role in improving performance of throughput computing applications.

High compute flops and memory bandwidth: High compute flops can be achieved in two ways - by increasing core count or increasing SIMD width. While increasing core count provides higher performance benefits, it also incurs high area overhead. Increasing SIMD width also provides higher performance, and is more area-efficient. Our observation is confirmed by the trend of increasing SIMD width in computing platforms such as Intel architecture processor with AVX extension [23], Larrabee [41] and next generation Nvidia GT GPUs [30]. Increasing SIMD width will reach a point of diminishing return. As discussed in Section 4.3.4, irregular memory accesses can significantly decrease SIMD efficiency. The cost to fix this would offset any area benefit offered by increase SIMD width. Consequently, the future throughput computing processor should strike the right balance between SIMD and MIMD execution.

With the growth of compute flops, high memory bandwidth is critical to achieve scalable performance. The current GPUs leverage high-end memory technology (e.g., graphics DDR or GDDR) to support high compute throughput. This solution limits the memory capacity available in a GPU platform to an amount much smaller than the capacities deployed in CPU-based servers today. Furthermore, increasing memory bandwidth to match the compute has pin-count and power limitations. Instead, one should explore emerging memory technologies such as 3D-stacking [12] or cache compression [5].

Large cache: As shown in Section 4.3.3, caches provide significant benefit for throughput computing applications. An example proof of our viewpoint is that GTX280 has limited on-die memories and around 40% of our benchmarks will lose the opportunity to benefit from increasing compute flops. The size of the on-die storage should match the working set of target workloads for maximum efficiency. Some workloads have a working set that only depends on the dataset and does not change with increasing core count or thread count. For today's datasets, 8MB on-die storage is sufficient to eliminate 90% of all accesses to external memory. As the data footprint is likely to increase tomorrow, larger on-die storage is necessary for these workloads to work well. Other workloads have working set scales with the number of processing threads. For these workloads, one should consider their per thread on-die storage size requirement. For today's dataset, we found most per thread working sets can be as small as a few KB to as large as 256KB. The per thread working sets are unlikely to change in the future as they are already set to scale with increased thread count.

Gather/Scatter: 42% percent of our benchmarks can exploit SIMD better with an efficient gather/scatter support. Our simulation-based analysis projects a 3X performance benefit for **SpMV** and **RC** with idealized gather operations. Idealized gather operation can simultaneously gather all elements into SIMD register in the same amount of time to load one cache line. This may require significant hardware and be impractical to build as it may require a large number of cache ports. Therefore, this represents the upper bound of the gather/scatter hardware potential. Cheaper alternatives exist. One alternative is to use multi-banking - an approach taken by GTX280. On GTX280, its local shared memory allows 16 simultaneous accesses to 16 banks in a single cycle, as long as there are no bank conflicts. However, this data structure is explicitly managed by the programmer. Another alternative is to take advantage of cache line locality by gathering - i.e. to extract all elements required the same gather from a single load of the required cache line. This approach requires shuffle logic to reorder the data within a cache line before writing into the target register. Shuffle logic is already available in general-purpose CPUs for permutation operations within SIMD registers. Our analysis shows that many throughput computing kernels have large amounts of cache line locality. For example, **Solv** accesses on average 3.6 cache lines within each 8-wide gather request. **RC** accesses on average

5 cache lines within each 16-wide gather request. Lastly, future throughput computing processors should provide improved easy-of-programming support for gather/scatter operations.

Efficient synchronization and cache coherence: Core i7 allows instructions like increment and compare&exchange to have an atomic lock prefix. GTX280 also has support for atomic operations, but only through device memory. In both CPUs and GPUs, the current solutions are slow, and more importantly do not scale well with respect to core count and SIMD width. Therefore, it is critical to provide efficient synchronization solutions in the future.

Two types of synchronizations are common in throughput computing kernels: reductions and barriers. First, reductions should provide atomicity between multiple threads and multiple SIMD lanes. For example, **Hist** loses up to 60% of SIMD efficiency because it cannot handle inter-SIMD-lane atomicity well. We recommend hardware support for atomic vector read-modify-write operations [29], which enables conflict detection between SIMD lanes as well as atomic memory accesses across multiple threads, thus achieving 54% performance improvement on four cores with 4-wide SIMD. Second, faster barrier and coherent caches become more important as core count increases and task size gets smaller. For example, in **Solv**, the average task size is only about 1000 cycles, while a barrier takes several hundred cycles on CPUs and several micro-seconds on GPUs. We recommend hardware support for fast barriers to amortize small task size and cache coherence to guarantee memory consistency between barrier invocations. In addition, we also believe that hardware accelerated task queues will improve synchronization performance even more (68% to 109% [28]).

Fixed function units: As shown in Section 4.3.6, **Bilat** can be sped up by 2X using fast transcendental operations. Texture sampling units significantly improve the performance of **GJK**. In fact, a large class of image processing kernels (i.e., video encoding/decoding) can also exploit such fixed function units to accelerate specialized operations at very low area/power cost. Likewise, Core i7 introduced a special purpose CRC instruction to accelerate the processing of CRC computations and the upcoming 32nm version will add encryption/decryption instructions that accelerate key kernels by 10X [36]. Future CPUs and GPUs will continue this trend of adding key primitives for developers to use in accelerating the algorithms of interest.

6. RELATED WORK

Throughput computing applications have been identified as one of the most important classes of future applications [6, 10, 13, 44]. Chen et al. [13] describe a diverse set of emerging applications, called RMS (Recognition, Mining, and Synthesis) workloads, and demonstrate that its core kernel functions exist in applications across many different domains. The PARSEC benchmark discusses emerging workloads and their characteristics for CMPs [10]. The Berkeley View report illustrates 13 kernels to design and evaluate throughput computing models [6]. The UIUC's Parboil benchmark tailors to capture the strengths GPUs [44]. In this paper, we share the vision that throughput computing will significantly impact future computing paradigms, and analyze the performance of a representative subset of kernels from these workload suites on common high-performance architectures.

Multi-core processors are a major architectural trend in today's general-purpose CPUs. Various aspects of multi-core architectures such as cache/memory hierarchy [11], on-chip interconnect [4] and power management [37] have been studied. Many parallel kernels have also been ported and optimized for multi-core systems, some of which are similar to the kernels discussed in this paper [15, 17, 50]. However, these efforts concentrate on (1) overcoming parallel scalability bottlenecks, and (2) demonstrating multi-core performance over a single-core of the same type.

General-purpose computation on graphics hardware (GPGPU) has been an active topic in the graphics community. Extensive work has recently been published on GPGPU computation; this is summarized well in [3, 33]. A number of studies [8, 9, 19, 20, 21, 25, 27, 34, 40, 43, 53] discuss similar throughput computing kernels as in this paper. However, their focus is to map non-graphic applications to GPUs in terms of algorithms and programming models

Analytical models of CPUs [51] and GPUs [22] have also been proposed. They provide a structural understanding of throughput computing performance on CPUs and GPUs. However, (1) each discusses either CPUs or GPUs only, and (2) their models are very simplified. Further, they try to verify their models against real silicons, rather than to provide in-depth performance comparison between CPUs and GPUs.

This paper provides an architectural analysis of CPUs and GPUs. Instead of simply showing the performance comparison, we study how architectural features such as core complexity, cache/buffer design, and fixed function units impact throughput computing workloads. Further, we provide our recommendation on what architecture features to improve future throughput computing architectures. To the best of our knowledge, this is the first paper that evaluates CPUs and GPUs from the perspective of architecture design. In addition, this paper also presents a fair comparison between performance on CPUs and GPUs and dispels the myth that GPUs are 100x-1000x faster than CPUs for throughput computing kernels.

7. CONCLUSION

In this paper, we analyzed the performance of an important set of throughput computing kernels on Intel Core i7-960 and Nvidia GTX280. We show that CPUs and GPUs are much closer in performance (2.5X) than the previously reported orders of magnitude difference. We believe many factors contributed to the reported large gap in performance, such as which CPU and GPU are used and what optimizations are applied to the code. Optimizations for CPU that contributed to performance improvements are: multithreading, cache blocking, and reorganization of memory accesses for SIMDification. Optimizations for GPU that contributed to performance improvements are: minimizing global synchronization and using local shared buffers are the two key techniques to improve performance. Our analysis of the optimized code on the current CPU and GPU platforms led us to identify the key hardware architecture features for future throughput computing machines – high compute and bandwidth, large caches, gather/scatter support, efficient synchronization, and fixed functional units. We plan to perform power efficiency study on CPUs and GPUs in the future.

8. REFERENCES

[1] CUDA BLAS Library. http://developer.download.nvidia.com/ compute/cuda/2_1/toolkit/docs/ CUBLAS_Library_2.1.pdf, 2008.

[2] CUDA CUFFT Library. http://developer.download.nvidia.com/ compute/cuda/2_1/toolkit/docs/ CUFFT_Library_2.1.pdf, 2008.

[3] General-purpose computation on graphics hardware. http://gpgpu.org/, 2009.

[4] D. Abts, N. D. Enright Jerger, J. Kim, D. Gibson, and M. H. Lipasti. Achieving predictable performance through better memory controller placement in many-core cmps. In *ISCA '09: Proceedings of the 36th annual international symposium on Computer architecture*, 2009.

[5] A. R. Alameldeen. *Using compression to improve chip multiprocessor performance*. PhD thesis, Madison, WI, USA, 2006. Adviser-Wood, David A.

[6] K. Asanovic, R. Bodik, B. C. Catanzaro, J. J. Gebis, P. Husbands, K. Keutzer, D. A. Patterson, W. L. Plishker, J. Shalf, S. W. Williams, and K. A. Yelick. The landscape of parallel computing research: A view from berkeley. *Technical Report UCB/EECS-183*, 2006.

[7] D. H. Bailey. A high-performance fft algorithm for vector supercomputers-abstract. In *Proceedings of the Third SIAM Conference on Parallel Processing for Scientific Computing*, page 114, Philadelphia, PA, USA, 1989. Society for Industrial and Applied Mathematics.

[8] N. Bell and M. Garland. Implementing sparse matrix-vector multiplication on throughput-oriented processors. In *SC '09: Proceedings of the 2009 ACM/IEEE conference on Supercomputing*, 2009.

[9] C. Bennemann, M. Beinker, D. Egloff, and M. Gauckler. Teraflops for games and derivatives pricing. http://quantcatalyst.com/download.php?file=DerivativesPricing.pdf.

[10] C. Bienia, S. Kumar, J. P. Singh, and K. Li. The PARSEC benchmark suite: characterization and architectural implications. In *PACT '08: Proceedings of the 17th international conference on Parallel architectures and compilation techniques*, pages 72–81, New York, NY, USA, 2008. ACM.

[11] S. Biswas, D. Franklin, A. Savage, R. Dixon, T. Sherwood, and F. T. Chong. Multi-execution: multicore caching for data-similar executions. *SIGARCH Comput. Archit. News*, 37(3):164–173, 2009.

[12] B. Black, M. Annavaram, N. Brekelbaum, J. DeVale, L. Jiang, G. H. Loh, D. McCaule, P. Morrow, D. W. Nelson, D. Pantuso, P. Reed, J. Rupley, S. Shankar, J. Shen, and C. Webb. Die stacking (3d) microarchitecture. In *MICRO 39: Proceedings of the 39th Annual IEEE/ACM International Symposium on Microarchitecture*, pages 469–479, Washington, DC, USA, 2006. IEEE Computer Society.

[13] Y. K. Chen, J. Chhugani, P. Dubey, C. J. Hughes, D. Kim, S. Kumar, V. W. Lee, A. D. Nguyen, M. Smelyanskiy, and M. Smelyanskiy. Convergence of recognition, mining, and synthesis workloads and its implications. *Proceedings of the IEEE*, 96(5):790–807, 2008.

[14] Y.-K. Chen, J. Chhugani, C. J. Hughes, D. Kim, S. Kumar, V. W. Lee, A. Lin, A. D. Nguyen, E. Sifakis, and M. Smelyanskiy. High-performance physical simulations on next-generation architecture with many cores. *Intel Technology Journal*, 11, 2007.

[15] J. Chhugani, A. D. Nguyen, V. W. Lee, W. Macy, M. Hagog, Y.-K. Chen, A. Baransi, S. Kumar, and P. Dubey. Efficient implementation of sorting on multi-core simd cpu architecture. *PVLDB*, 1(2):1313–1324, 2008.

[16] K. Datta, M. Murphy, V. Volkov, S. Williams, J. Carter, L. Oliker, D. Patterson, J. Shalf, and K. Yelick. Stencil computation optimization and auto-tuning on state-of-the-art multicore architectures. In *SC '08: Proceedings of the 2008 ACM/IEEE conference on Supercomputing*, pages 1–12, Piscataway, NJ, USA, 2008. IEEE Press.

[17] F. Franchetti, M. Püschel, Y. Voronenko, S. Chellappa, and J. M. F. Moura. Discrete Fourier transform on multicore. *IEEE Signal Processing Magazine, special issue on "Signal Processing on Platforms with Multiple Cores"*, 26(6):90–102, 2009.

[18] M. Frigo, Steven, and G. Johnson. The design and implementation of fftw3. In *Proceedings of the IEEE*, volume 93, pages 216–231, 2005.

[19] L. Genovese. Graphic processing units: A possible answer to HPC. In *4th ABINIT Developer Workshop*, 2009.

[20] N. Govindaraju, J. Gray, R. Kumar, and D. Manocha. Gputerasort: high performance graphics co-processor sorting for large database management. In *SIGMOD '06: Proceedings of the 2006 ACM SIGMOD international conference on Management of data*, pages 325–336, NY, USA, 2006. ACM.

[21] N. K. Govindaraju, B. Lloyd, Y. Dotsenko, B. Smith, and J. Manferdelli. High performance discrete fourier transforms on graphics processors. In *SC '08: Proceedings of the 2008 ACM/IEEE conference on Supercomputing*, pages 1–12, Piscataway, NJ, USA, 2008. IEEE Press.

[22] S. Hong and H. Kim. An analytical model for a gpu architecture with memory-level and thread-level parallelism awareness. *SIGARCH Comput. Archit. News*, 37(3):152–163, 2009.

[23] Intel Advanced Vector Extensions Programming Reference.

[24] Intel. SSE4 Programming Reference. 2007.

[25] C. Jiang and M. Snir. Automatic tuning matrix multiplication performance on graphics hardware. In *PACT '05: Proceedings of the 14th International Conference on Parallel Architectures and Compilation Techniques*, pages 185–196, Washington, DC, USA, 2005. IEEE Computer Society.

[26] J. R. Johnson, R. W. Johnson, D. Rodriquez, and R. Tolimieri. A methodology for designing, modifying, and implementing fourier transform algorithms on various architectures. *Circuits Syst. Signal Process.*, 9(4):449–500, 1990.

[27] C. Kim, J. Chhugani, N. Satish, E. Sedlar, A. Nguyen, T. Kaldewey, V. Lee, S. Brandt, and P. Dubey. FAST: Fast Architecture Sensitive Tree Search on Modern CPUs and GPUs. In *ACM SIGMOD*, 2010.

[28] S. Kumar, C. J. Hughes, and A. Nguyen. Carbon: architectural support for fine-grained parallelism on chip multiprocessors. In *ISCA '07: Proceedings of the 34th annual international symposium on Computer architecture*, pages 162–173, New York, NY, USA, 2007. ACM.

[29] S. Kumar, D. Kim, M. Smelyanskiy, Y.-K. Chen, J. Chhugani, C. J. Hughes, C. Kim, V. W. Lee, and A. D. Nguyen. Atomic vector operations on chip multiprocessors. In *ISCA '08: Proceedings of the 35th International Symposium on Computer Architecture*, pages 441–452, Washington, DC, USA, 2008. IEEE Computer Society.

[30] N. Leischner, V. Osipov, and P. Sanders. Fermi Architecture White Paper, 2009.

[31] P. Lyman and H. R. Varian. How much information. http://www2.sims.berkeley.edu/research/projects/how-much-info-2003/, 2003.

[32] NVIDIA. NVIDIA CUDA Zone. http://www.nvidia.com/object/cuda_home.html, 2009.

[33] Owens, D. John, Luebke, David, Govindaraju, Naga, Harris, Mark, Kruger, Jens, Lefohn, E. Aaron, Purcell, and J. Timothy. A survey of general-purpose computation on graphics hardware. *Computer Graphics Forum*, 26(1):80–113, March 2007.

[34] V. Podlozhnyuk and M. Harris. Monte Carlo Option Pricing. http://developer.download.nvidia.com/compute/cuda/sdk/website/projects/MonteCarlo/doc/MonteCarlo.pdf.

[35] M. Püschel, J. M. F. Moura, J. Johnson, D. Padua, M. Veloso, B. Singer, J. Xiong, F. Franchetti, A. Gacic, Y. Voronenko, K. Chen, R. W. Johnson, and N. Rizzolo. SPIRAL: Code generation for DSP transforms. *Proceedings of the IEEE, special issue on "Program Generation, Optimization, and Adaptation"*, 93(2):232– 275, 2005.

[36] R. Ramanathan. Extending the world.s most popular processor architecture. *Intel Whitepaper*.

[37] K. K. Rangan, G.-Y. Wei, and D. Brooks. Thread motion: fine-grained power management for multi-core systems. *SIGARCH Comput. Archit. News*, 37(3):302–313, 2009.

[38] R. Sathe and A. Lake. Rigid body collision detection on the gpu. In *SIGGRAPH '06: ACM SIGGRAPH 2006 Research posters*, page 49, New York, NY, USA, 2006. ACM.

[39] N. Satish, M. Harris, and M. Garland. Designing efficient sorting algorithms for manycore GPUs. In *IPDPS*, pages 1–10, 2009.

[40] N. Satish, C. Kim, J. Chhugani, A. Nguyen, V. Lee, D. Kim, and P. Dubey. Fast Sort on CPUs and GPUs: A Case For Bandwidth Oblivious SIMD Sort. In *ACM SIGMOD*, 2010.

[41] L. Seiler, D. Carmean, E. Sprangle, T. Forsyth, M. Abrash, P. Dubey, S. Junkins, A. Lake, J. Sugerman, R. Cavin, R. Espasa, E. Grochowski, T. Juan, and P. Hanrahan. Larrabee: a many-core x86 architecture for visual computing. *ACM Trans. Graph.*, 27(3):1–15, August 2008.

[42] M. Silberstein, A. Schuster, D. Geiger, A. Patney, and J. D. Owens. Efficient computation of sum-products on gpus through software-managed cache. In *Proceedings of the 22nd ACM International Conference on Supercomputing*, pages 309–318, June 2008.

[43] M. Smelyanskiy, D. Holmes, J. Chhugani, A. Larson, D. Carmean, D. Hanson, P. Dubey, K. Augustine, D. Kim, A. Kyker, V. W. Lee, A. D. Nguyen, L. Seiler, and R. A. Robb. Mapping high-fidelity volume rendering for medical imaging to cpu, gpu and many-core architectures. *IEEE Trans. Vis. Comput. Graph.*, 15(6):1563–1570, 2009.

[44] The IMPACT Research Group, UIUC. Parboil benchmark suite. http://impact.crhc.illinois.edu/parboil.php.

[45] J. Tolke and M. Krafczyk. TeraFLOP computing on a desktop pc with GPUs for 3D CFD. In *International Journal of Computational Fluid Dynamics*, volume 22, pages 443–456, 2008.

[46] N. Univ. of Illinois. Technical reference: Base operating system and extensions , volume 2, 2009.

[47] F. Vazquez, E. M. Garzon, J.A.Martinez, and J.J.Fernandez. The sparse matrix vector product on GPUs. Technical report, University of Almeria, June 2009.

[48] V. Volkov and J. Demmel. LU, QR and Cholesky Factorizations using Vector Capabilities of GPUs. Technical Report UCB/EECS-2008-49, EECS Department, University of California, Berkeley, May 2008.

[49] V. Volkov and J. W. Demmel. Benchmarking GPUs to tune dense linear algebra. In *SC '08: Proceedings of the 2008 ACM/IEEE conference on Supercomputing*, pages 1–11, Piscataway, NJ, USA, 2008. IEEE Press.

[50] S. Williams, L. Oliker, R. Vuduc, J. Shalf, K. Yelick, and J. Demmel. Optimization of sparse matrix-vector multiplication on emerging multicore platforms. In *SC '07: Proceedings of the 2007 ACM/IEEE conference on Supercomputing*, pages 1–12, New York, NY, USA, 2007. ACM.

[51] S. Williams, A. Waterman, and D. Patterson. Roofline: an insightful visual performance model for multicore architectures. *Commun. ACM*, 52(4):65–76, 2009.

[52] W. Xu and K. Mueller. A performance-driven study of regularization methods for gpu-accelerated iterative ct. In *Workshop on High Performance Image Reconstruction (HPIR)*, 2009.

[53] Z. Yang, Y. Zhu, and Y. Pu. Parallel Image Processing Based on CUDA. In *International Conference on Computer Science and Software Engineering*, volume 3, pages 198–201, 2008.

Using Hardware Vulnerability Factors to Enhance AVF Analysis

Vilas Sridharan and David R. Kaeli
ECE Department
Northeastern University
Boston, MA 02115
{vilas, kaeli}@ece.neu.edu

ABSTRACT

Fault tolerance is now a primary design constraint for all major microprocessors. One step in determining a processor's compliance to its failure rate target is measuring the Architectural Vulnerability Factor (AVF) of each on-chip structure. The AVF of a hardware structure is the probability that a fault in the structure will affect the output of a program. While AVF generates meaningful insight into system behavior, it cannot quantify the vulnerability of an individual system component (hardware, user program, etc.), limiting the amount of insight that can be generated. To address this, prior work has introduced the Program Vulnerability Factor (PVF) to quantify the vulnerability of software. In this paper, we introduce and analyze the Hardware Vulnerability Factor (HVF) to quantify the vulnerability of hardware.

HVF has three concrete benefits which we examine in this paper. First, HVF analysis can provide insight to hardware designers beyond that gained from AVF analysis alone. Second, separating AVF analysis into HVF and PVF steps can accelerate the AVF measurement process. Finally, HVF measurement enables runtime AVF estimation that combines compile-time PVF estimates with runtime HVF measurements. A key benefit of this technique is that it allows software developers to influence the runtime AVF estimates. We demonstrate that this technique can estimate AVF at runtime with an average absolute error of less than 3%.

Categories and Subject Descriptors

C.4 [**Performance of Systems**]: Fault Tolerance

General Terms

Reliability

Keywords

Reliability, Fault Tolerance, Architectural Vulnerability Factor

ISCA'10, June 19–23, 2010, Saint-Malo, France.

1. INTRODUCTION

Fault tolerance is a primary design constraint for all major microprocessors. Chip vendors typically set a failure rate target for each design and strive to maximize performance subject to this constraint. To validate that a design meets the failure rate target, vendors perform extensive pre- and post-silicon analysis. This analysis measures the rate at which faults occur in a system as well as whether a given fault will cause a system failure (an *error*).

Some faults do not result in an error; these faults are said to be *masked.* Fault masking in a system can be quantified using the *Architectural Vulnerability Factor*, or AVF. The AVF of a hardware structure is the fraction of faults in that structure that affect correct program operation [11]. AVF is both simple to understand and easy to measure: *ACE Analysis* is a method to derive an upper bound on AVF using performance simulation. Therefore, recent research in the area of transient faults has used ACE Analysis to observe AVF behavior and propose novel applications for AVF [3] [9] [19] [23].

AVF is not without its limitations, however. In particular, AVF exploits very little of the abstraction that is present in modern computer systems. AVF provides device-level abstraction: it models multiple underlying hardware devices (e.g., SRAMs, latches) as basic memory elements. However, AVF provides for none of the abstractions at the higher levels of the system stack, such as the Instruction Set Architecture (ISA) or Application Binary Interface (ABI), that have been key drivers of modern computer architecture.

Some researchers have started to develop fault frameworks capable of exploiting these higher levels of abstraction. For example, Sridharan and Kaeli introduced the *Program Vulnerability Factor* (PVF) to quantify the portion of AVF that is attributable to a user program [21]. This allows a software designer to measure the microarchitecture-independent vulnerability of a program during its design phase.

Prior work does not, however, provide a method to quantify the non-PVF components of AVF, nor does it provide a method to re-compute AVF from PVF. In this paper, we introduce the *Hardware Vulnerability Factor* (HVF) to address these limitations. HVF quantifies the hardware portion of AVF, independent of program-level masking effects. AVF can then be calculated as the product of HVF and PVF.

Computing HVF has three concrete benefits which we examine in this paper. First, using HVF analysis (in conjunction with AVF analysis) provides insight to hardware designers beyond that gained by AVF analysis alone. Second, separating AVF analysis into HVF and PVF steps can accelerate the AVF measurement process. Our results show a 2x reduction in simulation time with no loss of accuracy. Finally, runtime monitoring of HVF enables runtime estimation of AVF by combining HVF measurements with compile-time PVF estimates. A key benefit of this technique, relative to earlier AVF estimation techniques, is that it allows software developers to influence the runtime AVF estimates. We demonstrate that our technique estimates AVF with an average absolute error of less than 3%.

The rest of this paper is organized as follows. Section 2 provides background and discusses related work. Section 3 introduces the *System Vulnerability Stack*, our framework to separate AVF into hardware and software components. Section 4 demonstrates the use of HVF to provide insight to hardware designers about hardware behavior. Section 5 examines the use of HVF (in conjunction with PVF traces) to accelerate AVF modeling during processor design. Finally, Section 6 presents our technique to use HVF and PVF to estimate AVF at runtime.

2. BACKGROUND AND RELATED WORK

Mukherjee et al. introduced the *Architectural Vulnerability Factor* (AVF) and *ACE Analysis* as a means to estimate a processor's failure rate from transient faults early in the design cycle [11]. The AVF of a hardware structure is the probability that a fault in that structure will result in a visible error in the final output of a program. The authors call bits required for correct operation *ACE bits*; bits not required for correct operation are *unACE bits*. The AVF of a hardware structure is the fraction of bits in the structure that are ACE. For hardware structure H with size B_H, its AVF over a period of N cycles can be expressed as follows:

$$AVF_H = \frac{\sum_{n=0}^{N} (ACE\ bits\ in\ H\ at\ cycle\ n)}{B_H \times N} \quad (1)$$

AVF quantifies full-system vulnerability. Some previously-introduced metrics can quantify the vulnerability of individual system components such as devices or user programs. The most relevant of these metrics is the *Program Vulnerability Factor* (PVF), which computes the vulnerability of a user program [21]. PVF can be computed across ISA-defined architectural resources (e.g., the architectural register file) and uses the dynamic instruction stream to measure time. The PVF of an architectural resource is the probability that a fault in that resource will result in a visible error in the final output of the program. For architectural resource R with size B_R, its PVF over a period of I instructions can be expressed as follows[1]:

$$PVF_R = \frac{\sum_{i=0}^{I} (Activated\ and\ exposed\ faults\ in\ R\ at\ instruction\ i)}{B_R \times I} \quad (2)$$

Other related work includes Seifert and Tam's *Timing Vulnerability Factor* (TVF) [16]. TVF quantifies device-level fault masking but does not extend to other system layers. Sanda et al. report experimental AVFs of a Power6 processor in *machine derating* and *application derating* components, but do not provide a method for *a priori* calculation of vulnerability [15]. Finally, Weaver et al. calculate DUE AVF (Detected Unrecoverable Error AVF), which excludes architectural sources of unACEness such as logical masking, and is similar to HVF in some respects [25]. DUE AVF incorporates structure-specific information about error handling, however, and is not guaranteed to match up with the non-PVF components of AVF. Furthermore, HVF and DUE AVF serve different purposes: HVF can guide decisions about redundancy, while DUE AVF uses existing redundancy to calculate a structure's DUE rate.

[1]Note that we formulate PVF using terminology from Section 3 of this paper.

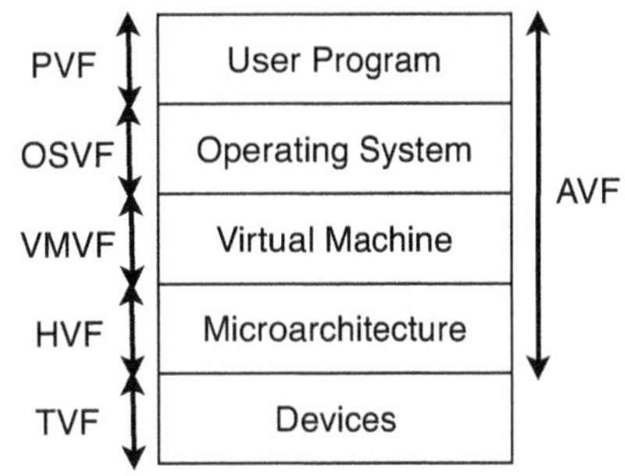

Figure 1: We calculate a vulnerability factor at every layer of the system. A bit is assigned a vulnerability at every layer to which it is visible. If it is vulnerable at every layer of the system, it is vulnerable to the system (i.e., its AVF is 1).

3. THE SYSTEM VULNERABILITY STACK

In this section, we introduce the *System Vulnerability Stack*, our method to separate AVF into individual vulnerability factors measured at each level of the system stack. We first introduce the basic concepts of the stack. We then explain how we use the stack to compute HVF, and how to re-compute AVF from its individual components.

3.1 Definitions and Concepts

We define a *fault* as a raw failure event such as a single-bit flip in a hardware structure. In this work, we refer to faults using the notation (b, n): b is the location of the fault (e.g., the bit in which it occurs), and n is the time of the fault (e.g., the cycle at which it occurs).

The basic underpinning of the vulnerability stack is the calculation of a vulnerability factor for each layer of the system stack (see Figure 1). A layer's vulnerability factor is the fraction of faults that cause incorrect operation of that layer. We define incorrect operation of a system layer as any disruption of the interface being implemented by that layer; we refer to this as an *error* in the layer. For instance, a hardware error is defined as any deviation in the semantics of the ISA being implemented. This includes faults that are propagated to ISA-visible state such as an architectural register, faults that entirely halt ISA function (e.g., a core deadlock), and any other behaviors that corrupt ISA state or disrupt program execution.

Not all faults in a system can cause an error in every system layer. For instance, a fault in a free physical register cannot cause a user program error without first propagating to program state. To determine the set of potential faults that can cause an error within a given system layer, we use the concept of *bit visibility*. A *visible bit* is a bit that is observable (accessible) by a particular system layer. For instance, a bit in a free physical register is visible to the microarchitecture, but not to a user program. A bit in a valid cache line, on the other hand, is visible to both the microarchitecture and the user program. For a fault to cause an error within a given system layer, it must occur within a bit visible to that layer. Therefore, a program-visible fault can occur only in a bit that is visible to the architected state of the program. On a given system, the set of bits visible to an upper layer of the stack (e.g., the user program) is a subset of the bits visible to a lower level of the stack (e.g., the microarchitecture).

There are three possible consequences of a visible fault within a system layer. First, the fault can propagate to an interface implemented by the layer, thus becoming visible to another system layer. For instance, a microarchitecture-visible fault that propagates to ISA-visible state becomes visible to the user program. This fault has been *exposed* to the user program.

Second, a visible fault can create an error without being exposed to another system layer. For instance, a fault in an instruction scheduler unit might cause the unit to deadlock, freezing the system. This fault is not exposed to the user program, but still causes an error in the microarchitecture[2]. We refer to this fault as *activated* within the microarchitecture.

Finally, a visible fault that is neither activated within a layer nor exposed to another layer will not cause an error. We refer to these faults as *masked.*

A fault is either exposed, activated, or masked within every system layer to which it is visible. At a given layer, only exposed faults are made visible to higher system layers. For instance, masked and activated faults within the hardware are not visible to the operating system or user program. It is possible for a fault to be both activated within a layer and exposed to the next layer. However, we assume without loss of generality that an activated fault is not also exposed; that is, it is not visible to any higher system layers.

A fault's ACEness to the system will be determined by the highest layer to which it is exposed. If the fault is activated within that layer, it is ACE to the system. If the fault is masked within that layer, it is unACE to the system.

Two examples can help to illustrate the way the vulnerability stack treats a typical system. First, consider a bit in a free physical register whose contents will be overwritten when the register is mapped to an architected register. A fault in this bit will be masked within the microarchitecture and will not be visible to any higher system layers. Therefore, this fault will be unACE to the system.

Second, consider a bit in a register that is used as a load address. Further, assume that the load is dynamically-dead (i.e., its result is never used) [5]. A microarchitecture-visible fault in this bit will be exposed to the next layer of the system, typically the operating system. Assume the operating system does not examine the address, but allows the load to proceed normally. Thus, the OS exposes the fault to the user program. Finally, since the load is dynamically-dead, the fault is masked within the user program. As a result, the bit is unACE to the system.

Now instead assume that the operating system first performs a bounds check on the address and crashes the system on an out-of-range address. If the fault causes the address to be out-of-range, the fault will be exposed to the OS by the hardware, activated within the operating system, and not visible to the user program. Therefore, in this case the bit will be ACE to the system.

To compute the vulnerability of a system layer, activated and exposed faults are assigned a vulnerability factor (VF) of 1, while masked faults are assigned a VF of 0. In the next section, we show how to use these definitions to calculate the vulnerability of the hardware layer.

[2]Although this fault is not visible to the user program, the resulting error obviously still affects the program.

3.2 Computing Hardware Vulnerability

The *Hardware Vulnerability Factor* (HVF) of a hardware structure is the fraction of faults in the structure that are either activated within the hardware layer or exposed to a higher layer. The HVF of hardware structure H with size B_H over N cycles can be represented as follows:

$$HVF_H = \frac{\sum_{n=0}^{N} (\textit{Activated and exposed faults in H at cycle n})}{B_H \times N} \quad (3)$$

A hardware-visible fault is exposed to the user program if it will corrupt committed state. In a register file, for example, a fault within a physical register with a valid architectural mapping will be exposed to the user program. In instruction-based structures (e.g., Issue Queue, Reorder Buffer), faults are often exposed if they occur in an entry that eventually commits, or if the fault causes the instruction to incorrectly overwrite committed state. For instance, a fault in the destination register address of a squashed instruction is exposed if the faulty address points to an architected register and causes the instruction to overwrite a committed register value.

Whether a fault within a particular bit is activated is highly dependent on the details of the microarchitecture. For instance, a fault in a valid bit of an instruction scheduler might always be activated, while a fault in a valid bit of a load buffer might be activated only when the corresponding entry is occupied.

3.3 Computing System Vulnerability

The system vulnerability (AVF) of a bit is the product of its vulnerability factors in all system layers to which it is visible. In this section, we compute the AVF of a register in a system that consists of a microarchitecture and a user program. For simplicity, we assume that the VFs of all software layers of the system (e.g., virtual machine, user program) are captured as part of the PVF value.

Figure 2 shows a sequence of machine instructions and the corresponding events in physical register $P1$ of the microarchitecture. During cycles 4-6 and 12, $P1$ is not mapped to an architectural register, and a microarchitecture-visible fault during these cycles will be masked. Therefore, the HVF of all bits of $P1$ is 0. In the remaining cycles, $P1$ is mapped to architectural registers $R1$ and $R2$, and a microarchitecture-visible fault during these cycles will be exposed to the user program. In these cycles, the HVF of all bits of $P1$ is 1.

If a program-visible fault in $R1$ or $R2$ is masked by the user program, the bit is assigned a PVF of 0. For instance, a fault during cycle 14 will be masked if it does not change the result of the compare operation in cycle 15. PVF uses dynamic instructions to mark time. Therefore, the PVF

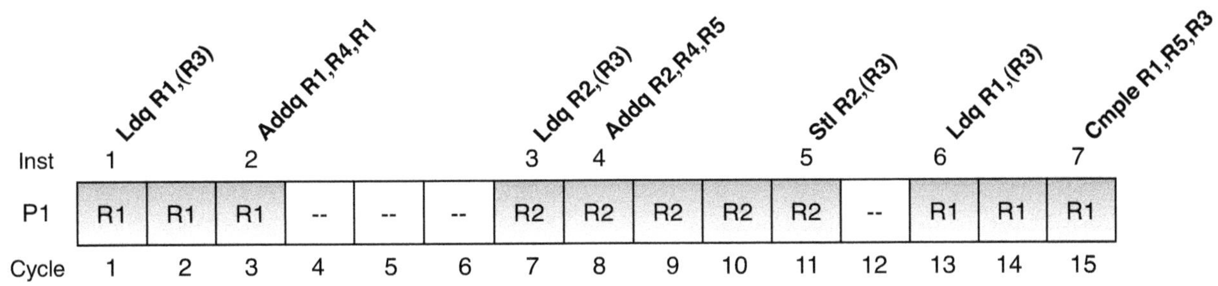

Figure 2: Physical register P1 is mapped to architectural registers R1 and R2 over 15 cycles. A microarchitecture-visible fault during cycles 4-6 and 12 will be masked in hardware. A fault during cycles 1-3, 7-11, and 13-15 will be exposed to the user program, creating a program-visible fault. The AVF of register P1 is a function of the HVF of P1 and the PVF of R1 and R2.

assigned to bit b of $P1$ during cycle n is the PVF of the architectural state a_b contained in b at the time (instruction) i_n, the instruction that consumes the value stored in $P1$ during cycle n. For example, in cycle 10, the AVF of $P1$ is the PVF of $R2$ at time 5 (instruction $Stl\ R2,(R3)$).

We can calculate the AVF of bit b in register $P1$ just using PVF values:

$$\begin{aligned} AVF_{b,1-15} = \frac{1}{15} \times (&PVF_{R1_b,i_1} + PVF_{R1_b,i_2} + PVF_{R1_b,i_3} + \\ &PVF_{R2_b,i_7} + PVF_{R2_b,i_8} + PVF_{R2_b,i_9} + \\ &PVF_{R2_b,i_{10}} + PVF_{R2_b,i_{11}} + PVF_{R2_b,i_{13}} + \\ &PVF_{R1_b,i_{14}} + PVF_{R1_b,i_{15}}) \end{aligned}$$

We can replace $R1_b$ and $R2_b$ in the equation above with a_b, the architectural state assigned to b. Then we can compute $AVF_{b,1-15}$ by multiplying the HVF and PVF values assigned to b during each cycle, and summing over all 15 cycles:

$$AVF_{b,1-15} = \frac{1}{15} \sum_{n=1}^{15} HVF_{b,n} \times PVF_{a_b,i_n}$$

More generally, we can compute the AVF of a hardware structure H with size B_H over N cycles as:

$$AVF_{H,N} = \frac{1}{N \times B_H} \sum_{b=1}^{B_H} \sum_{n=1}^{N} HVF_{b,n} \times PVF_{a_b,i_n} \quad (4)$$

3.4 Multi-Exposure Faults

Some faults that are exposed by the hardware to a user program will cause multiple program-visible faults when corrupted; we call these *multi-exposure faults.* Figure 3 gives an example: a fault within the Physical Source Register Index field of the IQ will cause an incorrect source operand to be fetched for the computation, resulting in up to 64 program-visible faults in the destination register.

The presence of multiple faults can change the behavior of a fault. Therefore, the PVF of a bit calculated using a single-fault model cannot be used to compute the AVF of a bit with a multi-exposure fault. Instead, we must calculate the AVF of a bit b with a multi-exposure fault as follows:

$$AVF_{b,N} = \frac{1}{N} \sum_{n=1}^{N} HVF_{b,n} \times PVF_{A_{b,n}} \quad (5)$$

In this equation, $A_{b,n}$ is the set of all program-visible faults resulting from a microarchitecture-visible fault in bit b at cycle n. $PVF_{A_{b,n}}$ is 1 if and only if the set of program-visible faults $A_{b,n}$ causes the program to produce incorrect

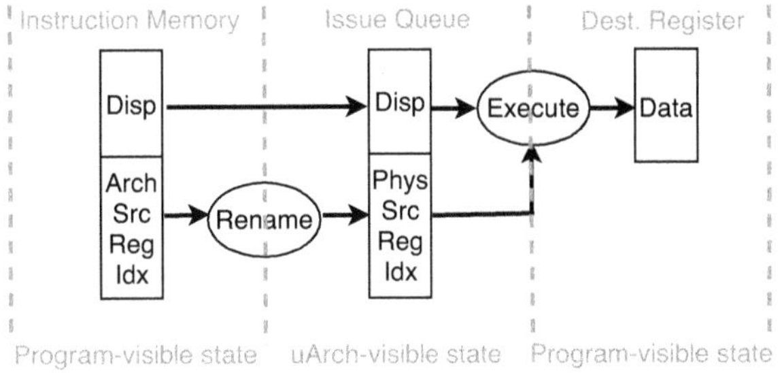

Figure 3: A single microarchitecture-visible fault that causes multiple program-visible faults is a *multi-exposure fault.* For instance, a fault in a bit in the Physical Source Register Index in the Issue Queue can cause multiple program-visible faults (e.g., in the destination register). To precisely calculate the AVF of a multi-exposure fault requires evaluating the impact of all the program-visible faults simultaneously.

output. Calculating a precise value for $PVF_{A_{b,n}}$ requires modeling multiple simultaneous program-visible faults. This is tractable for a small set of faults, but is not feasible to evaluate in general.

In practice, there are many cases where we can conclusively determine the PVF of a multi-exposure fault. For example, a bit in the Physical Source Register Index field of the IQ will have a PVF of 0 (i.e., a fault in this bit will be masked within the user program) if the destination register is dead, logically masked by a subsequent instruction, or otherwise not needed for program correctness. In this work, unless we can conclusively prove that a multi-exposure fault is masked within the user program, we treat the bit as activated within the hardware.

4. USING HVF FOR PROCESSOR DESIGN

Currently, architects use AVF to guide decisions such as where or when to add redundancy. For runtime reliability techniques (e.g., IQ squashing [25] or dynamic RMT [23]), this is appropriate. However, using AVF alone to evaluate the impact of design-time microarchitectural decisions (e.g., structure sizing) is suboptimal because AVF is not sensitive to operations that are masked at a program level, which can obscure changes in hardware behavior.

Figure 4 presents an illustrative example. The figure shows the behavior of four physical registers, P1 through P4, over 10 cycles, using two different scheduling algorithms. In Figure 4a, each register is written at cycle 0, and a sequence of reads occurs in cycles 4, 6, 8, and 10. We assume that the reads of $P2$, $P3$, and $P4$ do not affect program output due to logical masking later in the program's execution (i.e., the reads are dead). Since $P1$ is only ACE for 4 cycles, the AVF of $P1$-$P4$ over these 10 cycles is 10%.

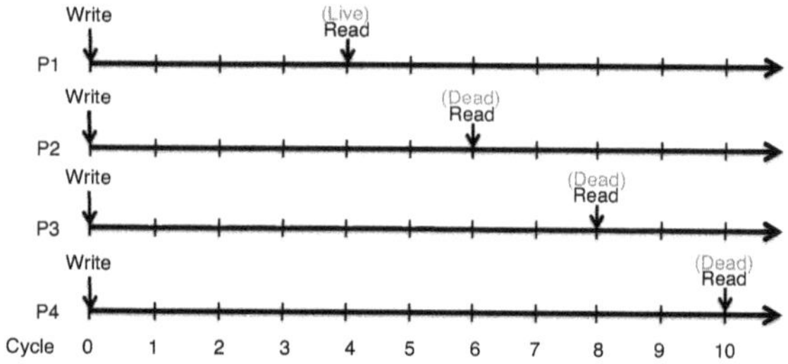

(a) Baseline

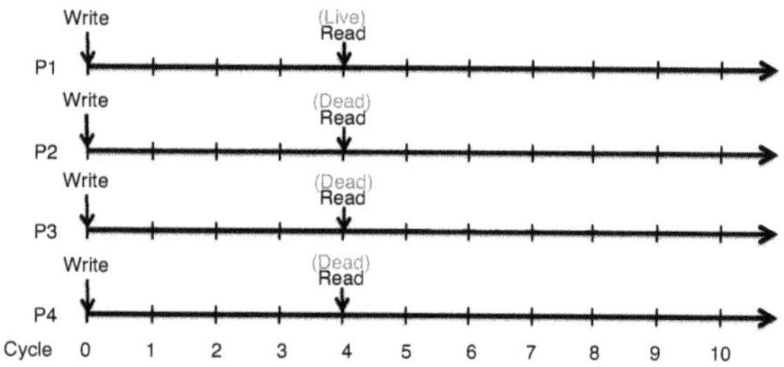

(b) Scheduler Change

Figure 4: The behavior of four physical registers over 10 cycles. In the baseline case, the registers have an HVF of 70% and an AVF of 10%. After a change to the scheduling algorithm, the registers have an HVF of 40% and an AVF of 10%. In this case, AVF does not capture the significant change to register behavior caused by the scheduler change. In contrast, the change in HVF will alert the designer to a change in potential vulnerability behavior.

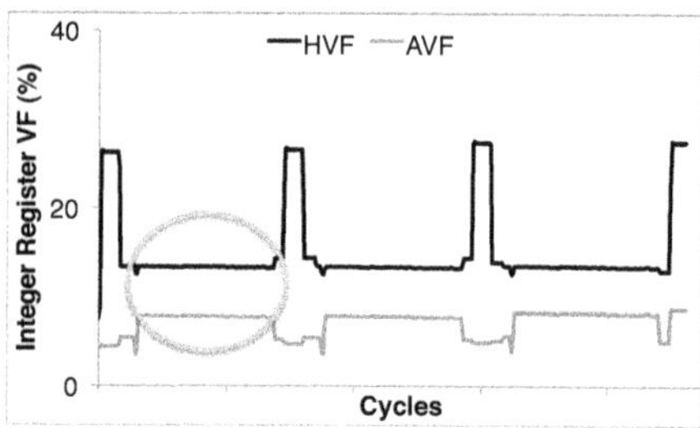

(a) equake

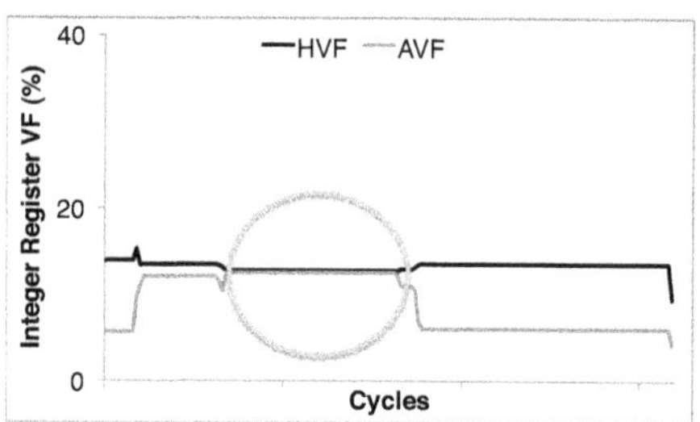

(b) mgrid

Figure 5: The AVF and HVF of the register file for *equake* and *mgrid*. The circled areas indicate regions of similar register behavior, with similar HVFs (15%). Due to program masking, however, *equake* has a much lower AVF (8%) than mgrid (15%). If *equake* is run during processor design, a designer using only AVF will underestimate the potential vulnerability of this behavior. Therefore, it is important to understand the causes of high HVF in a hardware structure.

Now assume we make a change to the instruction scheduler, which results in the behavior indicated by Figure 4b. We wish to examine the vulnerability impact of this design change. Unfortunately, the AVF of Figure 4b is still 10%, since the design change only altered the behavior of dead reads.

In the field, a different workload (or the same workload with different input data) may execute the same sequence of operations, but a different subset of the reads may be dead, resulting in a change in AVF. In this case, a designer would like to know that the scheduler change will have a potential impact on vulnerability. Unfortunately, AVF is not sensitive to the placement of dead reads, and does not provide insight into this behavior change.

If, instead, the designer also measured the HVF of the registers, he/she would see that the HVF in Figure 4a is 70%, while the HVF in Figure 4b is 40%. This change in HVF alerts the designer to the significant change in behavior. This is an example of a situation in which HVF gives us insight into potential vulnerability changes that AVF does not. Therefore, we suggest that HVF is a useful metric to examine in conjunction with AVF.

A similar real-world example is presented in Figure 5, which shows the AVF and HVF of *equake* and *mgrid*. In the circled regions, the two workloads perform a similar series of register operations. This is reflected in their similar HVFs of approximately 15%. However, due to program masking characteristics, the AVF of *equake* is only 8%, while the AVF of *mgrid* is 15%. If a hardware designer runs *equake* in simulation, he/she will significantly underestimate the potential AVF of this register behavior in the field. Thus, it is important to understand behaviors that cause high HVF, regardless of the AVF of a particular workload.

Finally, a comparison to performance evaluation is also instructive. Assume we have a workload whose goal is to maximize transactions executed per cycle (TPC). There are two components to TPC: the transactions-per-instruction rate (TPI), and the number of instructions per cycle (IPC). Increases in both TPI and IPC will increase TPC, but IPC is the only metric within the control of a hardware designer. Therefore, microarchitects focus on improving IPC during processor design. Similarly, when looking to maximize reliability, HVF is the only metric within the control of the hardware designer, and microarchitects should focus on improving HVF during processor design. (Note that, just as the ultimate goal of performance evaluation is to improve TPC, our ultimate goal is to improve AVF.)

4.1 Measuring HVF

Both activated and exposed faults can be identified using fault injection or ACE Analysis, in either a performance model or in RTL. In this work, we measure the HVF of a hardware structure using a modified version of ACE Analysis: we assume that all faults are activated unless we can prove they are exposed to another layer or masked. Determining that a fault is exposed to another layer is, at maximum, as difficult as determining that a bit is ACE during AVF computation. Determining that a fault is exposed is often quicker than determining it is ACE since a value need only be tracked until it is visible to the architected state.

We examine the HVF of the Issue Queue (IQ), Reorder Buffer (ROB), Load Buffer (LDB), Store Buffer (STB), and Integer Register File (RF). Within each structure, we split each entry into multiple subfields and measure the HVF of each subfield independently. For example, an Issue Queue entry contains several fields, including a destination register

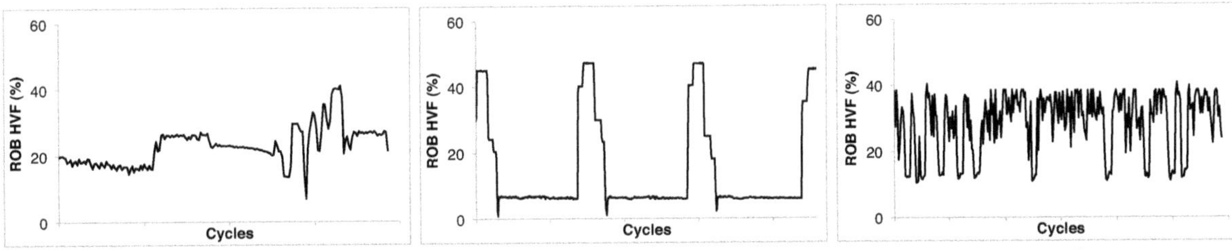

(a) ammp (b) equake (c) mcf

Figure 6: The HVF of a hardware structure is the fraction of faults that are activated within the layer or exposed to another layer. The HVF behavior of microarchitectural structures such as the Reorder Buffer varies substantially across benchmarks, increasing when the structure is full of correct-path instructions, and decreasing when the structure is empty or contains mostly wrong-path instructions.

Parameter	Value
Issue / Commit Width	8 instructions
IQ / ROB / LDB / STB	64 / 192 / 32 / 32 entries
Physical Registers	256 Int. / 256 FP
L1 I-Cache	32 kB, 2 cycle access 2-way SA
L1 D-Cache	64 kB, 2 cycle access, WB 2-way SA, allocate-on-miss
L2 Cache	2 MB, 10 cycle access, WB 8-way SA, allocate-on-miss
Memory Latency	200 cycles

Table 1: Simulated machine parameters used in this paper.

address and control information for the functional units. We measure the HVF of each field separately and calculate a weighted average to compute IQ HVF.

Figure 6 plots the HVF of the Reorder Buffer for three typical benchmarks from the SPEC2000 suite. The dramatic changes in HVF represent shifts in system behavior. Typically, the high HVF phases are the result of memory stalls or other events that cause the structure to fill with correct-path instructions. Low HVF phases (e.g., in *equake*) will result when the structure is relatively empty (e.g., as a result of low fetch bandwidth due to instruction cache misses). Low HVF can also be caused by a high incidence of flushes (e.g., from mispredicted branches) when the structure contains mostly wrong-path instructions.

4.2 Using HVF for Design Exploration

In this section, we present the results of a microarchitecture exploration study performed using HVF. For all experiments, we use the detailed CPU model in the M5 simulator modeling an Alpha 21264-like CPU [2]; our baseline system configuration is shown in Table 1. All experiments were run using the SPEC CPU2000 benchmarks at the single early simulation points given by Simpoint analysis [12]. We use a 100M-instruction warmup window and a 100M-cycle cooldown window for all simulations [3].

Assume that the goal of our study is to choose the optimal number of store buffer entries for our microarchitecture, subject to performance and reliability constraints. Therefore, we vary the number of store buffer entries while monitoring the HVF of several large structures and the average CPI of the workloads. Figure 7 shows the results averaged over all benchmarks. A 32-entry Store Buffer increases performance by approximately 2% over a 16-entry Store Buffer (STB). However, this is accompanied by a 16%, 25%, and 30% increase in the HVF of the Load Buffer (LDB), Reorder Buffer (ROB), and Issue Queue (IQ), respectively. In addition, the HVF decrease in the Store Buffer (from 7.2% to 3.2%) is offset by the 4x increase in its size. Therefore, by choosing a 16-entry Store Buffer, we can derive most of the performance benefit of a 32-entry Store Buffer but substantially improve overall reliability.

In general, our experiments have shown that the AVF of microarchitectural structures with architectural equivalents (such as register files) shows low correlation to HVF, while the AVF of structures with no architectural equivalent (e.g., issue queue, reorder buffer) shows good correlation to HVF.

4.3 Using Occupancy to Approximate HVF

Previous studies have shown that a structure's AVF increases with its occupancy, leading to a high correlation between AVF and structure occupancy [6] [19] [23]. These studies have demonstrated reasons for this correlation based on performance statistics (events such as memory stalls that lead to high occupancy also tend to increase AVF), but no study has demonstrated the component(s) of AVF that are responsible for the correlation. We expect that the correlation between occupancy and AVF is due to a correlation between occupancy and HVF, and that significant deviations in the AVF/occupancy relationship are due to program-specific (PVF) effects.

Figure 8 shows that committed instruction occupancy is a good but conservative predictor of HVF in the ROB and IQ. The correlation coefficients between HVF and occupancy are high (greater than 0.97 for all benchmarks). However, the IQ HVF is approximately 65% of the IQ occupancy on average; for certain benchmarks, the HVF is only 50% of the average occupancy. This result has an important implication for AVF measurements in complex hardware structures. Many techniques provide an upper bound on AVF by using the simplifying assumption that all bits in an entry are ACE if any bit within the entry is ACE (e.g., [8] [9] [19]). (Generally, this is due to infrastructure limitations which result in occupancy being used as a heuristic for HVF.) While an upper bound on AVF is often desirable in design settings, our results indicate that a more detailed implementation is needed if the goal is to provide an accurate estimate, rather than a bound, for AVF.

5. BOUNDING AVF AT DESIGN TIME

The previous section discussed the use of HVF during the processor design cycle for activities such as microarchitectural exploration. When attempting to determine a processor's soft error rate, however, designers will want to measure the AVF of the processor, including workload effects. In this section, we discuss how to use HVF to improve AVF simulation during processor design. Note that all HVF and PVF measurements are performed using full ACE Analysis (i.e., not calculated using heuristics).

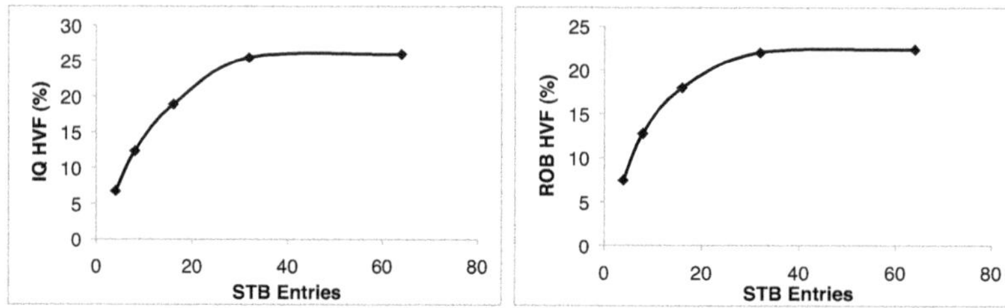

(a) Issue Queue (b) ROB

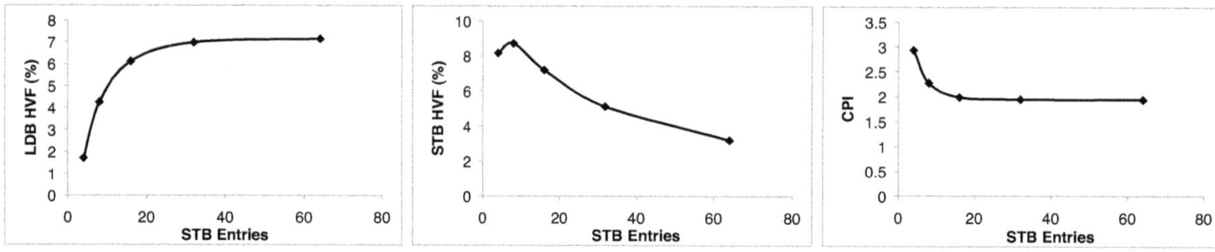

(c) Load Buffer (d) Store Buffer (e) CPI

Figure 7: Microarchitectural exploration using HVF. We vary the size of the Store Buffer (STB) and compute the average HVF of the IQ, ROB, LDB, and STB, and the CPI across all benchmarks in the SPEC CPU2000 suite. Increasing the Store Buffer from 16 to 32 entries provides a 2% performance boost at the cost of a 25% increase in vulnerability.

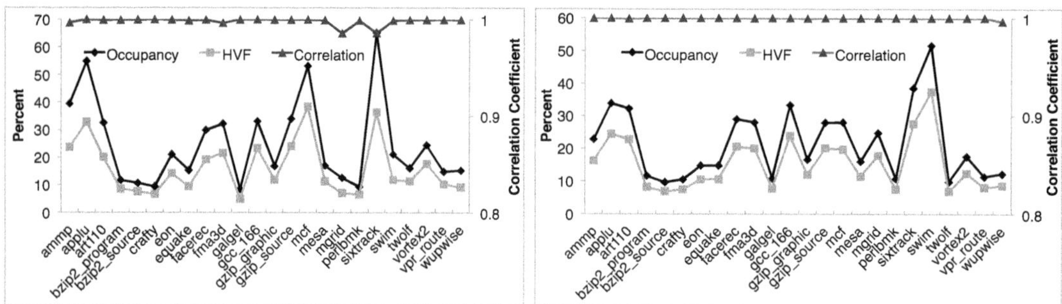

(a) IQ (b) ROB

Figure 8: The relationship between HVF and committed instruction occupancy across benchmarks for the IQ and ROB. HVF is, on average, 65% of occupancy in the IQ and 72% of occupancy in the ROB. However, we find correlation coefficients between HVF and occupancy (using 100 samples per Simpoint) to be greater than 0.97 across all benchmarks. This indicates that committed instruction occupancy is a good but conservative heuristic for HVF.

We simulate AVF using a two-step process. First, we perform PVF simulation of a program and save the results in a *PVF trace*. This step happens offline (i.e., not on the critical path of a processor design) in architecture-only simulation (e.g., using Pin [10]). Second, during the hardware design phase, we perform HVF simulation of the microarchitecture. For a given instruction or data value, we determine its HVF and then retrieve the corresponding PVF value from the trace. The simulator then multiplies the two values to determine the AVF of the value in question.

Since benchmarks are typically used over multiple chip generations, PVF traces can be re-used over multiple processor designs. This also allows us to increase the accuracy of PVF analysis without increasing simulation time during processor design. For instance, we assess effects such as transitive logic masking, which take significant simulation time, that are often omitted from AVF simulation [11].

Our methodology resulted in an approximately 2x reduction in the time required for AVF simulation relative to standard ACE analysis. The speedup is due to two factors. First, we no longer need to perform PVF calculations (e.g., dynamic-dead analysis) during microarchitectural simulation. Second, we drastically reduce the amount of state that the simulator needs to track. Standard ACE analysis defers analysis of an event until after the corresponding instruction has been analyzed in a post-commit window which can be tens of thousand instructions in length [11]. This requires the simulator to maintain large event history buffers within each hardware structure. Our methodology defers analysis of an event only until after HVF analysis, which typically completes soon after the corresponding instruction commits. This significantly reduces the average size of the history buffers and yields a much smaller memory footprint for the simulator itself. Our experiments show an approximately 3x reduction in memory usage for each simulation.

5.1 Capturing PVF Traces

The primary difficulty with offline PVF analysis is capturing PVF traces such that they can be easily mapped to simulation state during HVF simulation. To do this, we exploit the fact that ACE Analysis monitors events (e.g., reads and writes) in each structure. A bit within the structure is ACE if it is read by an event that affects the outcome of the program (a *live event*). A bit is unACE if it is not read; or if it is read only by *dead events*.

During PVF simulation, we assign a unique ID to each in-

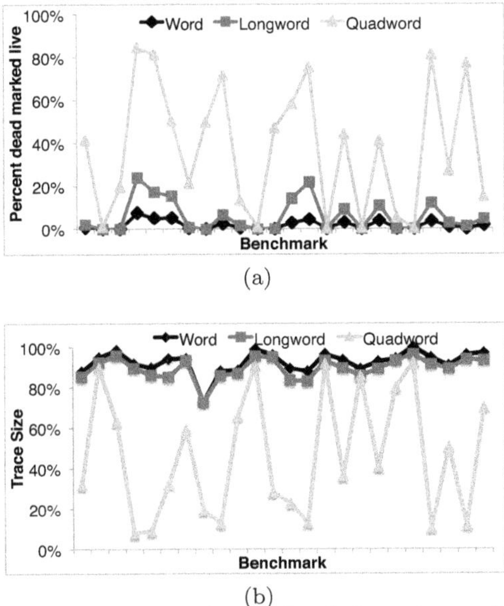

Figure 9: PVF traces can be used to help estimate AVF during hardware design. There is a tradeoff between the accuracy of PVF analysis and the size of PVF traces. For example, changing the granularity at which we perform PVF analysis from 1 to 8 bytes decreases the number of dead events identified, but significantly reduces the trace size. We show results for PVF analysis at different granularities: word (2 byte), longword (4 byte), and quadword (8 byte), normalized to byte granularity.

struction. If an instruction generates a dead event, we record its ID in the trace along with identifying information such as the type of event, the register or memory target, and the deadness of each byte within the event. During HVF simulation, we recreate the ID of each instruction and check the trace for any dead events associated with that instruction. If an instruction generates a microarchitecturally-live event, we apply the deadness value from the trace to determine the event's liveness to the system. We use the resulting liveness value to make ACE/unACE determinations within each hardware structure.

Increasing the accuracy of PVF simulation will lead to more dead events and a larger trace, but will also lead to a better estimate of PVF. Figure 9 presents an example of one such tradeoff: the granularity at which events are recorded in the trace. Reducing the granularity of the analysis decreases trace size at the expense of accuracy. (In this work, we record traces at a byte granularity.)

5.2 Results

Dead events in a PVF trace arise from effects such as static and dynamically dead instructions, transitively dead instructions, static and dynamic logical masking, and transitive logical masking. Figure 10 shows that, on average, 57% of dead events in our PVF traces are the result of dead instructions, while 33% and 9% of dead events result from first-level and transitive logical masking, respectively. Interestingly, this breakdown is not reflected in the contribution to AVF of each of these sources. For example, in the IQ, dead instructions reduce the AVF bound by 24% on average, while first-level and transitive logic masking combined provide only a 1% further reduction. Mukherjee et al. found a similar result; they showed that first-level logic masking had a 1% impact on the AVF of the execution units [11]. Our results extend these findings to all structures that we tested and to both first-level and transitive logic masking.

Figure 11 shows the impact of using PVF traces with HVF simulation to bound AVF. In all cases, incorporating PVF information significantly reduces the AVF estimate achieved using HVF-only simulation. Accounting for PVF yields a 62% reduction in the AVF bound for the register file, primarily due to the effects of dead and ex-ACE register values. In the other structures, the use of PVF traces also results in significant reductions in the AVF bound: 25% for the IQ, 27% and 30% for the Load and Store Buffers, and 22% for the ROB.

6. ESTIMATING AVF AT RUNTIME

Sections 4 and 5 demonstrated that HVF can be used to improve the hardware design cycle. Previous work has shown that PVF can be used during software design to statically reduce program vulnerability [21]. In this section, we demonstrate that the vulnerability stack can also be used to *dynamically* impact system reliability at runtime. In particular, we demonstrate how to combine compile-time PVF estimates with runtime HVF estimates to monitor AVF at runtime. A runtime AVF monitor can allow a system to tune its redundancy capabilities, enabling protection when AVF is high and disabling it when AVF is low (e.g., [23]). AVF monitoring can be used in conjunction with redundancy techniques (e.g., [1], [7], [13]) to provide highly-effective redundancy with low overhead.

Previous runtime AVF estimation techniques fall into two basic categories: training-based predictors [4] [6] [23]; and runtime-only predictors [9] [19]. The training-based predictors use a set of training benchmarks to determine a relationship between AVF and hardware statistics that can be measured at runtime. For instance, Walcott et al. use linear regressions to generate a microarchitecture-specific predictor equation that allows AVF estimation based on statistics that are easily measurable at runtime [23]. Similarly, Duan et al. use Boosted Regression Trees to correlate AVF with processor statistics and extend this to predict correlations across microarchitectural changes [6].

Runtime-only predictors, on the other hand, attempt to measure (or bound) AVF directly at runtime. For instance, the predictor proposed by Soundararajan et al. uses the ROB's instruction occupancy to bound its AVF [19]. Another technique, proposed by Li et al., uses simulated fault injection tracked via *error bits* attached to each hardware structure [9]. If a fault propagates to a pre-defined failure point, the injection is said to result in an error. The system computes AVF as the number of errors divided by the number of injections.

6.1 Methodology

Our key observation is that none of the predictors discussed above include any mechanism for the programmer to influence the AVF computation; they all require hardware designers to predict software reliability behavior. To do this, hardware designers generally rely on the behavior of typical software. For instance, the predictor proposed by Li et al. assumes a fault is ACE if it propagates to memory. This assumption falls apart in many software applications that deviate from the norm. For example, gaming and multimedia applications are memory-intensive yet extremely fault-tolerant [17] [22]. As a result, every predictor discussed so far will likely overestimate the AVF of these applications.

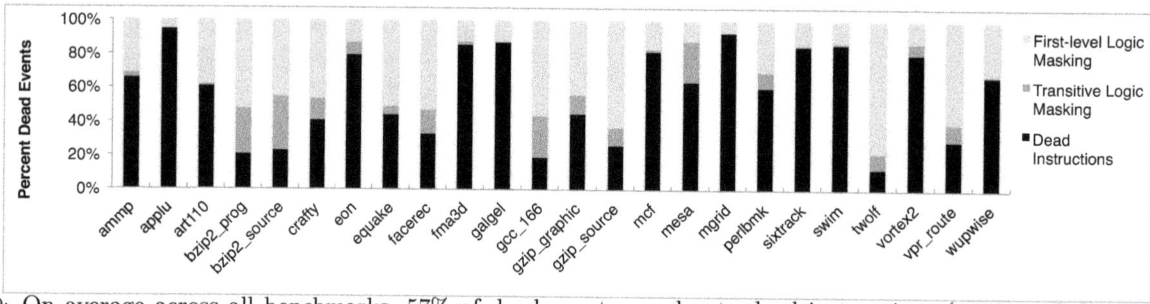

Figure 10: On average across all benchmarks, 57% of dead events are due to dead instructions (static and dynamic), while 33% and 9% of dead events are due to first-level and transitive logic masking, respectively. Since PVF analysis is performed offline, we can perform expensive analyses such as detection of transitive logic masking without increasing simulation time during hardware design.

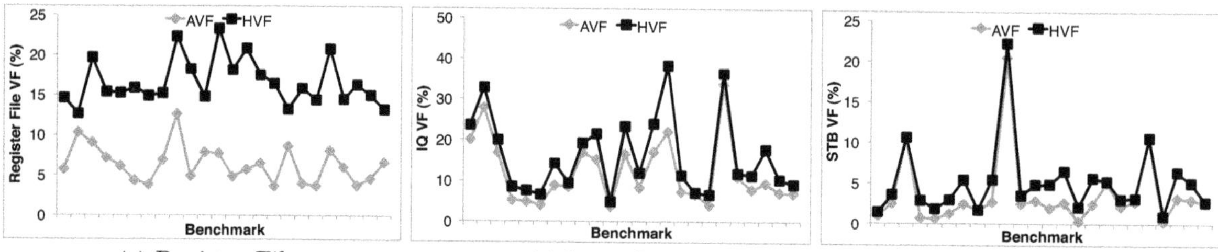

(a) Register File (b) Issue Queue (c) Store Buffer

Figure 11: Incorporating PVF traces tightens the AVF bound by 60% in the register file, 25% in the Issue Queue, and 30% in the Store Buffer. Results for the ROB and Load Buffer are similar to those of the IQ and Store Buffer.

Similarly, software-based redundancy techniques such as SWIFT [14], PLR [18], or SRMT [24] will not be recognized by any of the hardware-based predictors. In fact, these techniques typically increase processor utilization. This will likely lead to higher AVF estimates than for the same application without redundancy. The problem is further complicated if a mix of redundant and non-redundant code is executing on the same system.

The vulnerability stack addresses this problem by separating the analysis of program behavior (PVF) from hardware behavior (HVF). We can calculate HVF estimates in hardware at runtime, but allow each program to supply its own PVF estimates. This allows each program to specify its level of fault tolerance to the system in a microarchitecture-independent format. Finally, the system can combine the HVF and PVF estimates to generate an overall AVF estimate.

To communicate PVF estimates to hardware, we propose a set of registers called the *Program Vulnerability State* (PVS). These registers are used by software to communicate PVF estimates of architectural resources to the system. We implement one PVS register for the integer register file and one for the floating-point register file, and one for instruction-based structures to store the fraction of dead instructions in the dynamic instruction stream. Since ECC protection is standard on most memory-based structures, we omit any memory-based registers.

6.2 PVF Prediction via Software Profiling

Our prior work has shown that in the SPEC CPU2006 suite, changes in a program's execution profile are the primary reason for PVF changes due to different input data, and that the PVF of a single basic block is relatively insensitive to input data [20]. This implies that computing PVF based on representative training data will generate accurate runtime PVF estimates. In this work, we adopt this methodology as it requires a programmer to generate PVF estimates just once at compile time.

To generate PVF predictions, we profile each benchmark in the SPEC 2000 suite using the *train* input data set. Based on this training run, we generate an average PVF value for each function in the program's call graph; we then instrument the program to record these values into the PVS registers at runtime.

Figure 12 shows the accuracy of the training runs for the SPEC CFP2000 benchmarks. The only benchmark where input data has a significant effect on a function's PVF is *mesa*, where the *ref* input shows a lower PVF in several short-lifetime functions. This is likely solvable by using a more extensive training data set, but we leave a detailed examination of this effect for future work. Results for the SPEC CINT2000 benchmarks are similar; the only benchmark that shows significant PVF differences is *gcc*, where the *propagate_block* function's PVF increases from 59% in the *train* data to 72% in the *ref* data. Again, we expect this to be solvable with more extensive training or by profiling at a granularity smaller than a function. We note that, despite these prediction inaccuracies, our runtime predictor yields acceptable AVF estimates for both *gcc* and *mesa*.

Loading and storing PVS registers at each function boundary requires two memory operations per function per PVS register. However, we can apply profile-time optimizations to reduce the runtime overhead. First, we only update the PVS registers if the absolute difference in PVF between old and new predictions is more than 3%. Second, we omit predictions for short-lifetime functions to avoid adding overhead to short function executions. Finally, in certain code regions that exhibit a round-robin calling pattern between three or more functions, we use one average prediction for all functions in the call chain. Using our optimizations, we reduce the overhead of PVS updates to an average of 6.2 extra memory operations per million instructions.

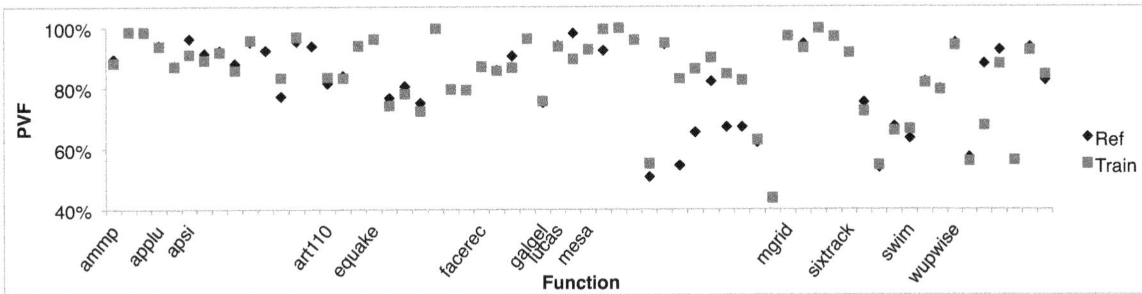

Figure 12: The x-axis plots functions that comprise over 90% of the execution of the first Simpoint of the SPEC CFP2000 benchmarks' *ref* inputs. The y-axis plots the fraction of dead instructions using both the *train* and *ref* input sets. Within a function, the difference in PVF between input sets is less than 4% except for short-lifetime functions in *mesa* and *wupwise*.

6.3 HVF Monitor Unit

To estimate HVF at runtime, we implement an *HVF Monitor Unit* (HMU) for each structure. At a fixed 512-cycle interval, the HMU chooses a random entry within the structure. If the specified entry generates an *HVF trigger* during the next 512-cycle interval, the structure sets a bit within the ROB entry for the corresponding instruction. At commit, a centralized *AVF Calculation Unit* (ACU) reads these added ROB bits. If the bit for a given structure is set, a 3-bit *HVF Counter* is incremented. When the counter overflows, it is reset and the value from the appropriate PVS register is fetched, right-shifted by 3 bits, and added to an *AVF Counter* for the structure. Every 2^{20} cycles, the *AVF Counter* value is divided by the total number of samples (2048) to yield an AVF estimate for the previous interval.

We choose our interval sizes to allow a new AVF prediction every 1 million cycles, similar to previous work [9]. By choosing power-of-two interval sizes, we implement all arithmetic operations as either bit-shifts or integer addition.

The core logic in the HMU and ACU is similar for all structures and can easily be replicated across structures; only the HVF trigger varies from structure to structure. The trigger event in the Issue Queue is an instruction issue, the trigger in the ROB is an instruction commit, and the trigger in the LDB is a read of the load address. Each structure typically has just one HVF trigger, limiting the complexity of monitoring these events.

In terms of hardware overhead, each structure requires the HMU logic and related state; a bit within each ROB entry; a set of basic counters in the ACU; and the logic required to calculate AVF (which is used infrequently and can be shared across all structures). The overhead of our technique is similar to that of other proposed techniques (e.g., [9]).

We expect that using only one HMU per hardware structure will sometimes result in a high estimate of HVF because the estimate will converge to committed instruction occupancy. As discussed in Section 4, this is a loose bound on HVF. The estimate can be improved by treating individual fields within a structure as independent structures with separate HMUs. For example, the IQ's displacement field stores instruction-carried constants such as load/store offsets and arithmetic immediate values, and can be evaluated separately from the rest of the IQ.

6.4 Results

We implement our baseline HVF predictor (one HMU per structure) in the Reorder Buffer, Load Buffer, and Issue Queue. In addition, we implement two additional predictors in the Issue Queue. Predictor *IQ-3* uses 3 HMUs in the IQ: one each for the Displacement field and Branch Control field (which is used only for control instructions), and a third for the remainder of the fields. We identified the displacement and branch control fields as the most likely to benefit from separate measurement. Similarly, predictor *IQ-All* splits the IQ into 8 sub-structures. Obviously, *IQ-All* has high hardware overhead, but we include these results to demonstrate the potential of the technique.

We run our experiments on the first Simpoint of the *ref* input data set for each benchmark. We evaluate our AVF predictor on two relevant metrics: the ability of the predictor to follow time-varying changes in AVF; and the mean absolute error of our AVF estimates to the actual AVF. Actual AVF is measured on a per-field basis as described in Section 4.1.

Figure 13 visually depicts a representative set of results of the baseline predictor. The predictor is highly responsive to time-varying changes in AVF. However, it is obvious that the predictor can have a high error (e.g., the IQ and LDB when running *applu*). Table 2 confirms this result; the mean absolute error (MAE) for many benchmarks is over 10%, which we deem unacceptably high[3]. Our data show that these large errors are due almost entirely to HVF overestimates, and can be corrected by using multiple HMUs per structure.

The results for the *IQ-3* and *IQ-All* predictors are shown in Figure 14 and Table 3. As expected, *IQ-3* substantially improves its HVF estimates over the baseline predictor, which translates into better AVF predictions. *IQ-3* has a 3.6% average MAE across all benchmarks and only one benchmark has an MAE higher than 8%. *IQ-All* further improves the estimate and reduces the average MAE to just 2.7%. Furthermore, only one benchmark has an MAE higher than 6%.

An interesting result is that a few benchmarks have a higher MAE with the *IQ-All* predictor than with *IQ-3*. As discussed in Section 6.2, *gcc*'s training input underestimates the *ref* input's PVF. This underestimate is offset by an HVF overestimate in the *Baseline* and *IQ-3* predictors, but not in *IQ-All*. In *mcf* and *swim*, predictor *IQ-3* slightly overestimates HVF, while predictor *IQ-All* underestimates HVF by a slightly higher magnitude, resulting in a slightly higher MAE. However, the magnitude of the MAE for these benchmarks is still within those reported by prior work [9]. Based on these results, we suggest that predictor *IQ-3* achieves a good balance between overhead and accuracy.

[3]Because AVF is reported as a percent, absolute errors carry a unit of percent. For example, an actual AVF of 10% and an estimated AVF of 15% implies a mean absolute error (MAE) of 5%.

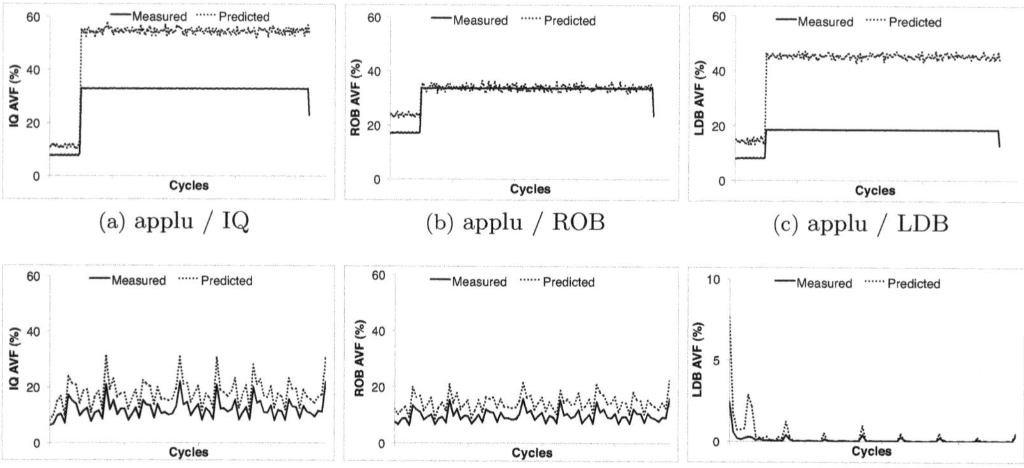

(a) applu / IQ (b) applu / ROB (c) applu / LDB

(d) vortex2 / IQ (e) vortex2 / ROB (f) vortex2 / LDB

Figure 13: A visual depiction of the results from Table 2 for the Issue Queue, Reorder Buffer, and Load Buffer, for the first 100M-instruction Simpoint of *applu* and *vortex2*. Our predictor closely follows the time-varying behavior of AVF in every benchmark. However, the predictor has a high MAE for certain benchmark / structure pairs (e.g., *applu* IQ and LDB).

Benchmark	IQ	ROB	LDB	Benchmark	IQ	ROB	LDB
ammp	18.6	5.7	7.1	lucas	9.2	3.0	0.1
applu	19.6	1.6	24.4	mcf	6.5	5.3	0.1
apsi	5.4	1.9	6.5	mesa	6.2	4.3	5.9
art110	7.1	8.6	6.7	mgrid	3.2	6.2	12.0
crafty	0.4	0.5	0.5	perlbmk_makerand	3.3	4.1	3.4
eon_rushmeier	6.3	3.0	1.0	sixtrack	24.1	1.8	10.4
equake	6.0	4.0	9.5	swim	0.9	2.3	23.9
facerec	10.0	3.3	1.6	twolf	3.8	3.7	2.3
galgel	5.3	6.5	12.9	vortex2	6.0	4.7	0.2
gcc_166	2.9	1.8	4.9	vpr_route	5.3	4.7	0.9
gzip_graphic	2.0	1.8	18.2	wupwise	4.1	3.1	1.7

Table 2: Mean Absolute Errors (MAE) (in %) of the predicted AVF relative to the actual (measured) AVF. Our predictor often has a high MAE because the HMU treats each entry as a single field (similarly to other techniques [9]), which results in HVF overestimates. This highlights the need for more accurate HVF assessment in complex structures such as the IQ.

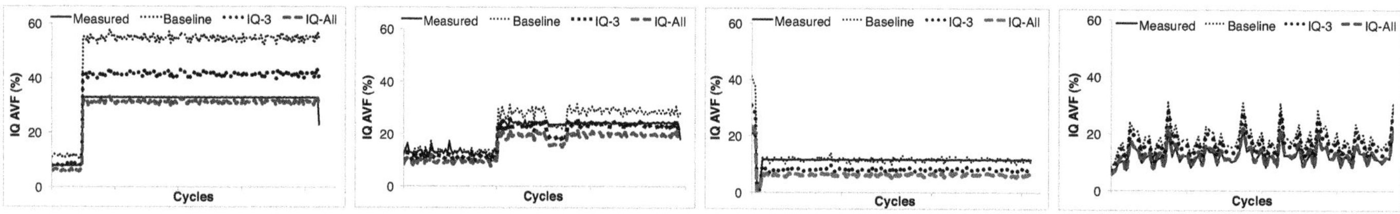

(a) applu (b) gcc_166 (c) swim (d) vortex2

Figure 14: Predicted and measured AVFs of the *Baseline*, *IQ-3*, and *IQ-All* predictors. Most benchmarks (e.g.,*applu*, *vortex2*) and see a steady improvement of AVF estimates. For a few benchmarks (*gcc_166*, *swim*, and *mcf*), *IQ-3* performs slightly better than *IQ-All* due to PVF or HVF underprediction as discussed in Section 6.4. However, all *IQ-All* AVF predictions still have an absolute error of less than 6%, with an average absolute error of less than 3%.

Benchmark	Baseline	IQ-3	IQ-All	Benchmark	Baseline	IQ-3	IQ-All
ammp	18.6	8.5	2.5	lucas	9.2	4.2	4.4
applu	19.6	7.7	1.5	mcf	6.5	2.1	5.4
apsi	5.4	1.9	0.9	mesa	6.2	3.2	0.7
art110	7.1	6.1	6.6	mgrid	3.2	2.3	3.0
crafty	0.4	0.8	1.5	perlbmk_makerand	3.3	2.0	0.7
eon_rushmeier	6.3	3.4	0.5	sixtrack	24.1	6.8	4.5
equake	6.0	3.8	3.0	swim	0.9	3.5	5.2
facerec	10.0	4.9	4.0	twolf	3.8	1.4	0.7
galgel	5.3	3.0	1.6	vortex2	6.0	3.8	0.7
gcc_166	2.9	1.6	4.6	vpr_route	5.3	2.5	0.7
gzip_graphic	2.0	2.7	3.7	wupwise	4.1	2.6	2.2

Table 3: Mean Absolute Errors (in %) of improved predictors that treat each IQ entry as multiple structures. *Baseline* is the IQ predictor from Table 2, with 1 HMU. *IQ-3* uses 3 HMUs in the IQ, and *IQ-All* uses 8 HMUs, one for each field in the IQ. As expected, *IQ-3* requires less hardware than *IQ-All* but delivers much better AVF estimates than *Baseline*.

7. CONCLUSIONS AND FUTURE WORK

In this paper, we introduced the Hardware Vulnerability Factor, one component of the System Vulnerability Stack. We demonstrated that HVF is useful during the hardware design process. HVF can be used to provide greater insight to microarchitectural design decisions and to accelerate AVF simulation, allowing hardware designers to more quickly and accurately assess a processor's vulnerability. Finally, we proposed a technique to enable the runtime monitoring of AVF using pre-calculated PVF and online HVF estimates. The key benefit of this technique is to enable software designers to influence runtime AVF calculations.

In general, the vulnerability stack presents many further opportunities for exploration and optimization. For example, we have not yet explored VM and OS-level vulnerability, although these are important components of many modern computer systems. Furthermore, techniques to dynamically predict PVF may improve the task of runtime AVF estimation. Finally, because the vulnerability stack isolates the system-level effects of a transient fault from its (device-level) causes, we believe that portions of the vulnerability stack may eventually be used to model the effects of other hardware faults.

Overall, we believe that HVF and the System Vulnerability Stack represent an important step forward in our understanding of system vulnerability. The stack can empower a much broader community (e.g., software and OS designers) to more fully participate in the design of fault-tolerant systems, and has the potential to significantly expand the scope of fault tolerance research and enable the design of more robust systems at lower cost.

Acknowledgments

The authors would like to thank Arijit Biswas and Michael D. Powell for their comments on the original manuscript and the anonymous reviewers for their feedback on the final version. This work was supported in part by a Fellowship provided by the Northeastern University Provost's Office.

8. REFERENCES

[1] N. Aggarwal, N. P. Jouppi, P. Ranganathan, J. Smith, and K. Saluja. Reducing overhead for soft error coverage in high availability systems. In *Workshop on System Effects of Logic Soft Errors (SELSE-4)*, Austin, TX, April 2008.

[2] N. Binkert, R. Dreslinski, L. Hsu, K. Lim, A. Saidi, and S. Reinhardt. The M5 simulator: Modeling networked systems. *IEEE Micro*, 26(4):52–60, July-Aug. 2006.

[3] A. Biswas, P. Racunas, R. Cheveresan, J. Emer, S. S. Mukherjee, and R. Rangan. Computing architectural vulnerability factors for address-based structures. In *International Symposium on Computer Architecture (ISCA-32)*, 2005.

[4] A. Biswas, N. Soundararajan, S. S. Mukherjee, and S. Gurumurthi. Quantized AVF: A means of capturing vulnerability variations over small windows of time. In *Workshop on System Effects of Logic Soft Errors (SELSE-5)*, 2009.

[5] J. A. Butts and G. Sohi. Dynamic dead-instruction detection and elimination. In *International Conference on Architectural Support for Programming Languages and Operating Systems (ASPLOS-10)*, 2002.

[6] L. Duan, B. Li, and L. Peng. Versatile prediction and fast estimation of architectural vulnerability factor from processor performance metrics. In *Int'l Symposium on High Performance Computer Architecture (HPCA-15)*, 2009.

[7] M. A. Gomaa and T. N. Vijaykumar. Opportunistic transient-fault detection. In *International Symposium on Computer Architecture (ISCA-32)*, 2005.

[8] X. Li, S. Adve, P. Bose, and J. Rivers. Softarch: an architecture-level tool for modeling and analyzing soft errors. *International Conference on Dependable Systems and Networks (DSN '05)*, 2005.

[9] X. Li, S. V. Adve, P. Bose, and J. A. Rivers. Online estimation of architectural vulnerability factor for soft errors. In *International Symposium on Computer Architecture (ISCA-35)*, 2008.

[10] C.-K. Luk, R. Cohn, R. Muth, H. Patil, A. Klauser, G. Lowney, S. Wallace, V. J. Reddi, and K. Hazelwood. Pin: building customized program analysis tools with dynamic instrumentation. In *Conference on Programming Language Design and Implementation (PLDI '05)*, 2005.

[11] S. S. Mukherjee, C. Weaver, J. Emer, S. K. Reinhardt, and T. Austin. A systematic methodology to compute the architectural vulnerability factors for a high-performance microprocessor. In *International Symposium on Microarchitecture (MICRO-36)*, 2003.

[12] E. Perelman, G. Hamerly, and B. Calder. Picking statistically valid and early simulation points. In *International Conference on Parallel Architectures and Compilation Techniques (PACT-12)*, 2003.

[13] V. K. Reddy, E. Rotenberg, and S. Parthasarathy. Understanding prediction-based partial redundant threading for low-overhead, high- coverage fault tolerance. In *Int'l Conf. on Arch. Support for Prog. Langs. and Op. Sys. (ASPLOS-12)*, 2006.

[14] G. A. Reis, J. Chang, N. Vachharajani, R. Rangan, and D. I. August. SWIFT: Software implemented fault tolerance. In *International Symposium on Code Generation and Optimization (CGO '05)*, 2005.

[15] P. N. Sanda, J. W. Kellington, P. Kudva, R. Kalla, R. B. McBeth, J. Ackaret, R. Lockwood, J. Schumann, and C. R. Jones. Soft-error resilience of the IBM POWER6 processor. *IBM Journal of Research and Development*, 52(3):275–284, 2008.

[16] N. Seifert and N. Tam. Timing vulnerability factors of sequentials. *Device and Materials Reliability, IEEE Transactions on*, 4(3):516–522, Sept. 2004.

[17] J. W. Sheaffer, D. P. Luebke, and K. Skadron. The visual vulnerability spectrum: characterizing architectural vulnerability for graphics hardware. In *SIGGRAPH/EUROGRAPHICS Symposium on Graphics Hardware (GH '06)*, 2006.

[18] A. Shye, J. Blomstedt, T. Moseley, V. J. Reddi, and D. A. Connors. PLR: A software approach to transient fault tolerance for multicore architectures. *IEEE Transactions on Dependable and Secure Computing*, 6(2):135–148, 2009.

[19] N. K. Soundararajan, A. Parashar, and A. Sivasubramaniam. Mechanisms for bounding vulnerabilities of processor structures. In *International Symposium on Computer Architecture (ISCA-34)*, 2007.

[20] V. Sridharan and D. R. Kaeli. The effect of input data on program vulnerability. In *Workshop on System Effects of Logic Soft Errors (SELSE-5)*, 2009.

[21] V. Sridharan and D. R. Kaeli. Eliminating microarchitectural dependency from architectural vulnerability. In *International Symposium on High Performance Computer Architecture (HPCA-15)*, 2009.

[22] A. Sundaram, A. Aakel, D. Lockhart, D. Thaker, and D. Franklin. Efficient fault tolerance in multi-media applications through selective instruction replication. In *Workshop on Radiation Effects and Fault Tolerance (WREFT '08)*, 2008.

[23] K. R. Walcott, G. Humphreys, and S. Gurumurthi. Dynamic prediction of architectural vulnerability from microarchitectural state. In *International Symposium on Computer Architecture (ISCA-34)*, 2007.

[24] C. Wang, H. seop Kim, Y. Wu, and V. Ying. Compiler-managed software-based redundant multi-threading for transient fault detection. In *International Symposium on Code Generation and Optimization (CGO '07)*, 2007.

[25] C. Weaver, J. Emer, S. S. Mukherjee, and S. K. Reinhardt. Techniques to reduce the soft error rate of a high-performance microprocessor. In *International Symposium on Computer Architecture (ISCA-31)*, 2004.

Necromancer: Enhancing System Throughput by Animating Dead Cores

Amin Ansari Shuguang Feng Shantanu Gupta Scott Mahlke

Advanced Computer Architecture Laboratory
University of Michigan, Ann Arbor, MI 48109
{ansary, shoe, shangupt, mahlke}@umich.edu

ABSTRACT

Aggressive technology scaling into the nanometer regime has led to a host of reliability challenges in the last several years. Unlike on-chip caches, which can be efficiently protected using conventional schemes, the general core area is less homogeneous and structured, making tolerating defects a much more challenging problem. Due to the lack of effective solutions, disabling non-functional cores is a common practice in industry to enhance manufacturing yield, which results in a significant reduction in system throughput. Although a faulty core cannot be trusted to correctly execute programs, we observe in this work that for most defects, when starting from a valid architectural state, execution traces on a defective core actually coarsely resemble those of fault-free executions. In light of this insight, we propose a robust and heterogeneous core coupling execution scheme, Necromancer, that exploits a functionally dead core to improve system throughput by supplying hints regarding high-level program behavior. We partition the cores in a conventional CMP system into multiple groups in which each group shares a lightweight core that can be substantially accelerated using these execution hints from a potentially dead core. To prevent this *undead* core from wandering too far from the correct path of execution, we dynamically resynchronize architectural state with the lightweight core. For a 4-core CMP system, on average, our approach enables the coupled core to achieve 78.5% of the performance of a fully functioning core. This defect tolerance and throughput enhancement comes at modest area and power overheads of 5.3% and 8.5%, respectively.

Categories and Subject Descriptors

B.8.1 [**Performance and Reliability**]: Reliability, Testing, and Fault-Tolerance

General Terms

Design, Reliability, Performance

Keywords

Manufacturing defects, Heterogeneous core coupling, Execution abstraction

1. INTRODUCTION

The rapid growth of the silicon process over the last decade has substantially improved semiconductor integration levels. However, this aggressive technology scaling has lead to a host of reliability challenges such as manufacturing defects, wear-out, and parametric variations [10, 9]. These threats can affect correct program execution, one of the most significant aspects of any computer system [4]. Traditionally, hardware reliability was only a concern for high-end systems (e.g., HP Tandem Nonstop and IBM eServer zSeries) for which applying high-cost redundancy solutions such as triple modular redundancy (*TMR*) was acceptable. Nevertheless, hardware reliability has already become a major issue for mainstream computing, where the usage of high-cost reliability solutions is not acceptable [24].

One of the main challenges for the semiconductor industry is manufacturing defects, which have a direct impact on yield. From each process generation to the next, microprocessors become more susceptible to manufacturing defects due to higher sensitivity of materials, random particles attaching to the wafer surface, and sub-wavelength lithography issues such as exposure tool optimization, cleaning technology, and resist process optimization [18]. Thus, in order to maintain an acceptable level of manufacturing yield, a substantial investment is required [32]. Traditionally, modern high-performance processors are declared as functional if all parts of the design are fault-free, or if they can operate correctly by tolerating failures. However, since manufacturing defects can cause a significant yield loss, semiconductor companies have recently started to manufacture parts that have been over-designed to hedge against defects. For instance, to improve yield, IBM did this with the Cell Broadband Engine that sometimes only had 7 out of the 8 processing elements activated [34].

Based on the latest ITRS report [19], for current and near future CMOS technology, one manufacturing defect per five $100mm^2$ dies can be expected. Fortunately, a large fraction of die area is devoted to memory structures, in particular caches, which can be protected using existing techniques such as row/column redundancy, 2D-ECC [21], ZerehCache [3], Bit-Fix [38], and sub-block disabling [1]. With appropriate protection mechanisms in place for caches, the processing cores become the major source of defect vulnerability on the die. Consequently, we try to tackle hard-faults in the non-cache parts of the processing core. Due to the inherent irregularity of the general core area, it is well-known that handling defects in the non-cache parts is challenging [27]. A common solution is core disabling [2]. However, the industry is currently dominated by Chip Multi-Processor (*CMP*) systems with only a modest number of high-performance cores (e.g., Intel Core 2), systems which cannot afford to lose a core due to manufacturing defects. The other extreme of the solution spectrum lies fine-grained micro-architectural redundancy [32, 12, 35]. Here, broken micro-architectural structures, such as ALUs, are isolated or replaced to maintain core functionality. Unfortunately, since the majority of the core logic is non-redundant, the fault coverage from these approaches is very limited – less than 10% for an Intel processor [27].

In this work, we propose Necromancer (*NM*) to tackle manufacturing defects in current and near future technology nodes. NM enhances overall system throughput and mitigates the performance loss caused by defects in the non-cache parts of the core. To accomplish this, we first relax the correct execution constraint on a faulty core – the *undead core* – since it cannot be trusted to faithfully execute programs. Next, we leverage high level execution information (*hints*) from the undead core to accelerate the execution of an *animator core*. The animator core is an additional core, introduced by NM, that is an older generation of the baseline cores in the CMP with less resources and the same instruction set architecture (*ISA*). The main rationale behind our approach is the fact that, for most defect instances, the execution flow of the program on the undead core *coarsely resembles* the fault-free program execution on the animator core – when starting from the same architectural state (i.e., program counter (*PC*), architectural registers, and memory). Moreover, in the animator core, these hints are only treated as performance enhancers and do not influence execution correctness. In NM, we rely on intrinsically robust hints and effective hint disabling to ensure the animator core is not mislead by unprofitable hints. Dynamic inter-core state resynchronization is also employed to update the undead core with valid architectural state whenever it strays too far from the correct execution path. To increase our design efficiency, we share each small animator core among multiple cores. Our scheme is unique in the sense that it keeps the undead core on a semi-correct execution path, ultimately enabling the animator core to achieve a performance close to the performance of a live (fully-functional) core. In addition, NM does not noticeably increase the design complexity of the baseline cores and can be easily applied to current and near future CMP systems to enhance overall system throughput.

2. UTILITY OF AN UNDEAD CORE

We motivate the NM design by demonstrating the high-level rationale behind it. To this end, we provide evidence that supports the following two statements: **(1)** Although an aggressive out-of-order (*OoO*) core with a hard-fault in the non-cache area cannot be trusted to perform its normal operation, it can still provide useful execution hints in most cases. **(2)** By exploiting hints from the undead core, the animator core can typically achieve a significantly higher performance.

2.1 Effect of Hard-Faults on Program Execution

Prior work has studied the effect of a single-event upset, or a transient fault, on program execution for high-performance microprocessors. Using fault-injection, it has been shown that transient faults are often masked, easier to categorize, and have a temporal effect on program behavior [37]. On the other hand, the effect of hard-faults on program execution is hard to study since each hard-fault can result in a complicated intertwined behavior. For example, a hard-fault can cause multiple data corruptions that finally mask each others effect. Moreover, hard-faults are persistent and their effect does not go away. As a result, hard-faults can dramatically corrupt program execution. In order to illustrate the negative impact of hard-faults on program execution, we study the average number of instructions that can be committed before observing an architectural state mismatch. This result, for 5000 area-weighted hard-fault injection experiments across SPEC-CPU-2K benchmarks, is depicted in Figure 1. Details of the Monte Carlo engine, statistical area-weighted fault injection infrastructure, target system, and benchmark suite can be found in Section 5.1. For these experiments, we have a golden execution which compares its architectural state with the faulty execution every cycle and as soon as a mismatch is detected, it stops the simulation and reports the number of committed instructions up to that point. For instance, looking at 188.amp, 26% of the injected hard-faults cause an architectural state mismatch to happen in less than 100 committed instructions. Since 176.gcc more uniformly stresses different core resources, it shows a higher vulnerability to hard-faults. As this figure shows, more than 40% of the injected hard-faults can cause an immediate – < 10K – architectural state mismatch. Thus, a faulty core cannot be trusted to provide correct functionality even for short periods of program execution.

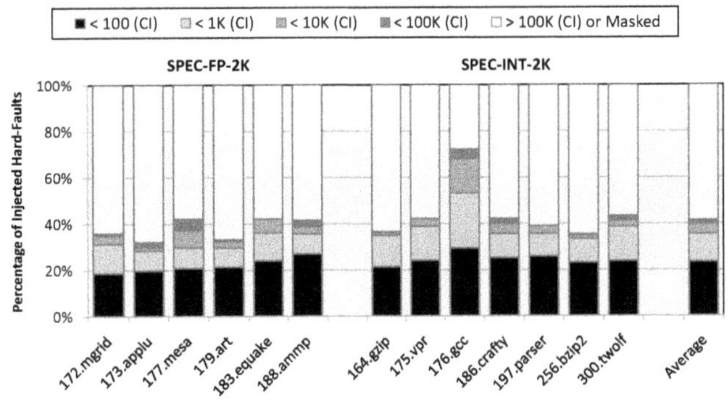

Figure 1: Distribution of injected hard-faults that manifest as architectural state mismatches across different latencies – in terms of the number of committed instructions (*CI*).

2.2 Relaxing Correctness Constraints

As just discussed, program execution on a dead core cannot be trusted. Here, we try to determine the quality of program execution on a dead core when relaxing the absolute correctness constraints. In other words, we are interested in knowing for what expected level of correctness, a dead core can practically execute large chunks of a program. Based on 5K injected hard-faults, Figure 2 depicts how many instructions can be committed in a dead core before it gets considerably off the correct execution path. In order to have a practical system, the dead core should be able to execute the program over reasonable time periods before its execution becomes ineffectual. Here, we define a similarity index (*SI*) that measures the similarity between the PC of committed instructions in the dead core and a golden execution of the same program. This SI is calculated every 1K instructions and whenever it becomes less than a pre-specified threshold, we stop the simulation and record the number of committed instructions. For instance, a similarity index of 30% for PC values means, that during each 1K instruction window, 30% of PCs hit exactly the same instruction cache line in both the golden execution and program execution on the dead core. Figure 2 shows the number of committed instructions for three different SI thresholds. For instance, considering SI threshold of 90%, on average only 12% of the hard-faults renders the program execution on a dead core ineffectual before at least 10K instructions get committed. Hence, even for an SI threshold of 90%, in more than 85% of cases, the dead core can successfully commit at least 100K instructions before its execution differs by more than 10%.

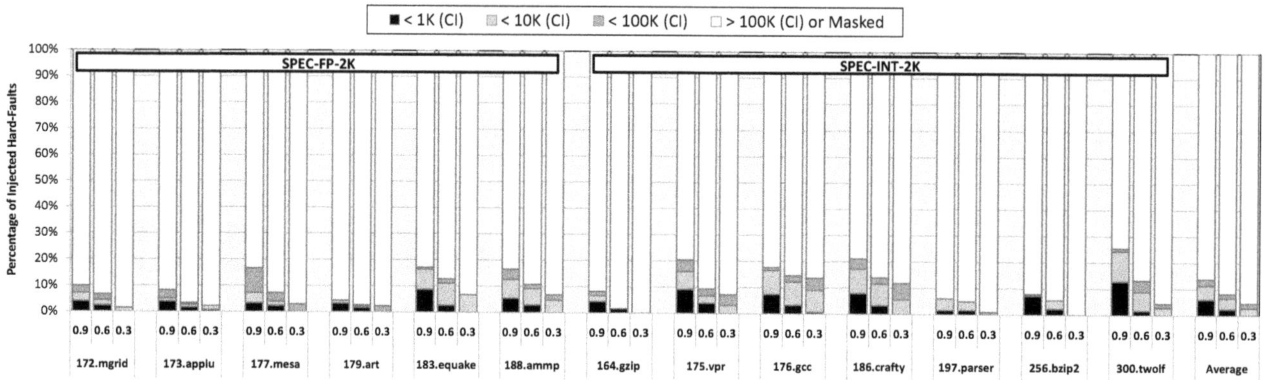

Figure 2: Number of instructions that are committed (*CI*) before an injected hard-fault results in a violation of a pre-specified similarity index threshold. For this purpose, 5K hard-faults were injected while considering three different similarity index thresholds (90%, 60%, and 30%).

2.3 Opportunities for Acceleration

Since the execution behavior of a dead core coarsely matches the intact program execution for long time periods, we can take advantage of the program execution on the dead core to accelerate the execution of the same program on another core. This can be done by extracting useful information from the execution of the program on the dead core and sending this information (hints) to the other core (the animator core), running the same program. We allow the *undead core* to run without requiring absolutely correct functionality. The undead core is only responsible to provide helpful hints for the animator core. This symbiotic relation between the two cores enables the animator core to achieve a significantly higher performance. When the hints lose their effectiveness, we resynchronize the architectural state of the two cores. Since an architectural state resynchronization, between two cores in a CMP system, takes about 100 cycles [27] and resynchronization in more than 85% of cases happens after at least 100K committed instructions, the overhead associated with resynchronization is small.

For the purpose of evaluation and since we want to have a single ISA system, based on the availability of the data on the power, area, and other characteristics of microprocessors, we use an EV6 (DEC Alpha 21264 [20]) for the baseline cores. On the other hand, for the animator core, we select a simpler core like the EV4 (DEC Alpha 21064) or EV5 (DEC Alpha 21164) to save on the overheads of adding this extra core to the CMP system. In order to evaluate the efficacy of the hints, in Figure 3, we show the performance boost for the aforementioned DEC Alpha cores using perfect hints (*PHs*) – perfect branch prediction and no L1 cache miss. Here, we have also considered the EV4 (OoO), an OoO version of the 2-issue EV4, as a potential option for our animator core. As can be seen, by employing perfect hints, the EV4 (OoO) can outperform the 6-issue OoO EV6 in most cases; thus, demonstrating the possibility of achieving a performance close to the performance of a live core through the NM system. Nevertheless, achieving this goal is quite challenging due to the presence of defects, different sources of imperfection in hints, and inter-core communication issues.

3. FROM TRADITIONAL COUPLING TO ANIMATION

In a CMP system, prior work has shown two cores can be coupled together to achieve higher single-thread performance. Since the overall performance of a coupled core system is bounded by the slower core, these two cores were traditionally identical to sustain an acceptable level of single-thread performance. However, in order to accelerate program execution, one of these coupled cores must progress through the program stream faster than the other. In order to do so, three methods have been proposed:

- In Paceline [16], the core that runs ahead (*leader*) and the core that receives execution hints (*checker*) from the leader core operate at different frequencies. Paceline cuts the frequency safety margin of the leader core and continuously compares the architectural state (excluding memories) of the two cores. When a mismatch happens, the frequency of the leader is adjusted, L1 state match is enforced, and finally the checkpoint interval is rolled back for re-execution.
- Slipstream processors [28] and Master/Slave speculative parallelization [41] need two different versions of the same program. In these schemes, the leader core runs a shorter version of the program based on the removal of ineffectual instructions while the checker core runs the unmodified program.
- Finally, Flea-Flicker two pass pipelining [6] and Dual-Core Execution [40] allow the leader core to return an invalid value on long-latency operations and proceed.

Although these schemes have widely varying implementation details, they share some common traits. In these schemes, the leader core tries to get ahead and sends hints that can accelerate checker core execution. These two cores are connected through one/several first-in first-out (*FIFO*) hardware queues to transfer hints and retired instructions along with their PCs. The checker core takes advantage of program execution on the leader core in 3 ways. First, the checker core receives pre-processed instruction and data streams. Second, during the program execution in the leader core, most branch mispredictions get resolved. Third, the program execution in the leader core automatically initiates L2 cache prefetches for the checker core.

A straight-forward extension of these ideas to animate a dead core seems plausible. However, NM encounters major difficulties when trying to fit the dead core into this execution model. Here, we briefly describe the two main challenges, leaving discussions of the proposed microarchitectural solutions for subsequent sections.

Fine-Grained Variations: One of the main sources of problems is the presence of defects in the dead core. Due to the presence of defects, the *undead core* might execute/commit more or less number of instructions, causing variations in the similarity of program executions between the two cores. For instance, in many cases, the undead core can take the wrong direction on an IF statement and get back to the right execution path afterwards, thereby preventing

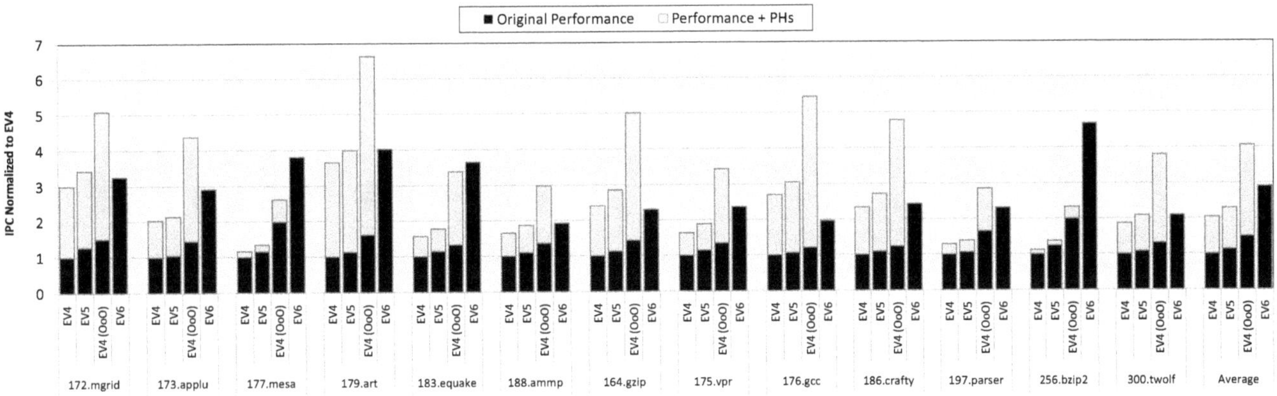

Figure 3: IPC of different DEC Alpha microprocessors, normalized to EV4's IPC. In most cases, by providing perfect hints for the simpler cores (EV4, EV5, and EV4 (OoO)), these cores can achieve a performance comparable to that achieved by a 6-issue OoO EV6.

a perfect data or instruction stream for the animator core. This necessitates employing generic hints that are more resilient to these local abnormalities. Moreover, the number of times that each PC is visited cannot be used to synchronize the two cores. A mechanism is required to help the animator core identify the proper time for pulling the hints off the communication queue. Given the variation in the usefulness of the hints, in order to enhance the efficiency of the animator core, fine-grained hint disabling can be leveraged. For instance, if the last K branch prediction hints for a particular PC were not useful, branch prediction for this particular PC can be handled by the animator core's branch predictor.

Global Divergences: When the undead core gets completely off the correct execution path, hints become useless, and it needs to be brought back to a valid execution point. For this purpose, the architectural state of the animator core can be copied over to the undead core. Although exact state matching, by checkpointing the register file, has been used in prior work [16], it is not applicable for animating a dead core since architectural state mismatches occur so frequently. Therefore, we need coarse-grained online monitoring of the effectiveness of the hints over a large time period to decide whether the undead core should be resynchronized with the animator core. Moreover, resynchronizations should be cheap and relatively infrequent to avoid a noticeable impact on the overall performance of the animator core. One possible approach for maintaining correct memory state, suggested by Paceline, is to re-fetch the cache-lines that are accessed during the last checkpointed interval into the L1 cache of the leader core [16]. However, since this might happen often for a dead core, we need a low-cost resynchronization approach that does not require substantial book keeping.

4. NM ARCHITECTURE

The main objective of NM is to mitigate system throughput loss due to manufacturing defects. For this purpose, it leverages a robust and flexible heterogeneous core coupling execution technique which will be discussed in the rest of this section. Given a group of cores, we introduce an animator core, an older generation with the same ISA, that is shared among these cores for defect tolerance purposes. In this section, we describe the architectural details for a coupled pair of dead and animator cores. The high-level NM design for a CMP system with more cores will be discussed in the next section. In Section 2, we showed that the faulty core – the undead core – cannot be trusted to run even a short part of the program. However, as we relaxed the exact architectural state match and looked at the global execution pattern, the undead core can execute a moderate portion of the program before a resynchronization is required. By executing the program on the undead core, NM provides hints to accelerate the animator core without requiring multiple versions of the same program. In other words, the undead core is used as an external run-ahead engine for the animator core that has been added to the CMP system. We believe NM is a valuable solution for improving the system throughput of the current and near future mainstream CMP systems without notably influencing design complexity.

4.1 High-Level NM System Description

Figure 4 illustrates the high-level NM heterogeneous coupled core design. As discussed in Section 2, for the purpose of evaluation, we use 6-issue OoO EV6 for the baseline cores and a 2-issue OoO EV4 as our animator core. In our design, most communications are unidirectional from the undead core to the animator core with the exception of the resynchronization and hint disabling signals. Thus, a single queue is used for sending the hints and cache fingerprints to the animator core. The hint gathering unit attaches a 3-bit tag to each queue entry to indicate its type. When this queue gets full and the undead core wants to insert a new entry, it stalls. To preserve correct memory state, we do not allow the dirty lines of the undead core's data cache to be written back to the shared L2 cache. As a result, a dirty data cache-line of the undead core is simply dropped whenever it requires replacement. Exception han-

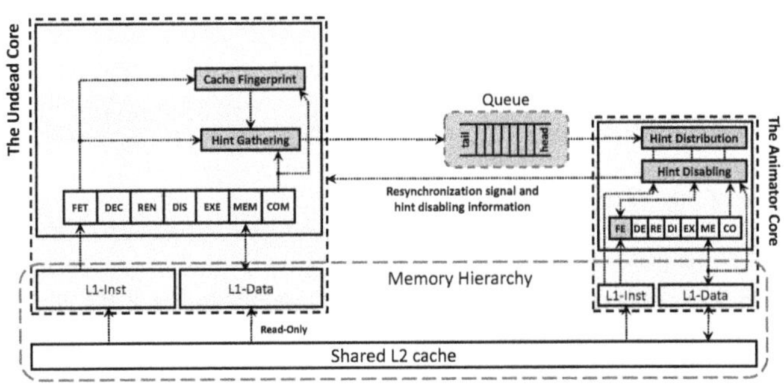

Figure 4: The high-level architecture of NM is shown in this figure and modules that are modified or added to the underlying cores are highlighted (not drawn to scale).

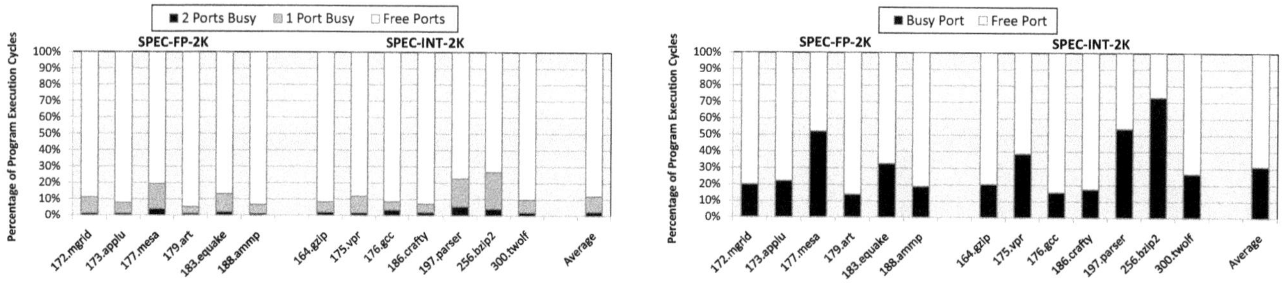

(a) Port activity for the animator core's L1-data cache

(b) Port activity for the animator core's L1-instruction cache

Figure 5: Port activity breakdown for local caches of the animator core. Here, we show the percentage of cycles that each cache port is either busy or free. For our animator core, the data cache has 2 ports while the instruction cache has a single port.

dling is also disabled at the undead core since the animator core maintains the precise state.

As discussed in Section 2, the animator core with perfect hints has the potential of surpassing the average performance of a live core. Nonetheless, the performance of the undead core can be a bottleneck for the NM system since: **a.** In many cases (Figure 3), performance of a baseline core is worse than the performance of the animator core with perfect hints. **b.** After each resynchronization, the undead core needs to warm-up the branch predictor and local caches. Therefore, we allow the undead core to proceed on the data cache L2 misses, without waiting for the several hundred cycles needed to receive data back from main memory. We simply return zero since L2 misses are not common and also value prediction would not be beneficial. This has a large impact on the performance of the undead core, potentially shortening the resynchronization period. Given the ability to eliminate stalls on L2 misses and also semi-perfect hints from the undead core, NM can *potentially* achieve even a higher performance than that of a live core. Nevertheless, providing even semi-perfect hints is challenging due to defects in the undead core, queue size, limited performance of the undead core, queue delay, and natural fluctuations in program behavior.

NM uses a heterogeneous core coupling program execution with a pruned core that has a significantly smaller area compared to a baseline core. In NM, we do not rely on overclocking the undead core or having multiple versions of the same program. Furthermore, it is a hardware-based approach that is transparent to the workload and operating system (*OS*). It also does not require register file checkpointing for performing exact state matching between two cores. Instead, we employ a fuzzy hint disabling approach based on the continuous monitoring of the hints effectiveness, and initiating resynchronizations when appropriate. Hint disabling also helps to enhance performance and save on communication power for program phases in which the undead core cannot get ahead of the animator core. Apart from that, the undead core might occasionally get off the correct execution path (e.g., taking the wrong direction on an IF statement) and return to the correct path afterwards – Y-branches [36]. In order to make the hints more robust against microarchitectural differences between two cores and also variations in the number/order of executed instructions, we leverage the number of committed instructions for hint synchronization and attach this number to every queue entry as an *age tag*. Moreover, we introduce the *release window* concept to make the hints more robust in the presence of aforementioned variations. For a particular hint type, the release window helps the animator core to determine the right time to utilize a hint. For instance, assuming the data cache (*D-cache*) release window is 100, and 1000 instructions have already been committed in the animator core, D-cache hints with age tags ≤ 1100 can be pulled off the queue and applied.

4.2 Hint Gathering and Distribution

Program execution on the undead core automatically warms-up the shared L2 cache without requiring communication between two cores. However, other hints – i.e., L1 data cache, L1 instruction cache, and branch prediction hints – need to be sent through the queue to the animator core. The hint gathering unit in the undead core is responsible for gathering hints and cache fingerprints, attaching the age and 3-bit type tags, and finally inserting them into the queue. On the other side, the hint distribution unit receives these packets and compares their age tag with the local number of committed instructions plus the corresponding release window sizes.

Every cycle, the hint gathering unit looks over the committed instructions for data and instruction cache (*I-cache*) hints. In fact, the PC of committed instructions and addresses of committed loads and stores are considered as I-cache and D-cache hints, respectively. On the animator core side, the hint distribution unit treats the incoming I-cache and D-cache hints as prefetching information to warm-up its local caches. For the animator core, Figure 5 depicts the utilization of two D-cache ports and a single I-cache port. Given the pipelined cache access for all high-performance processors, as can be seen for D-cache, both ports are busy for less than 5% of cycles. Therefore, we leverage the original cache ports for applying our D-cache hints. However, since hints can only *potentially* help the program execution, priority of the access should always be given to the normal operation of the animator core. On the other hand, the I-cache port is busy for more than 50% of cycles for 3 benchmarks and is free only if the instruction fetch queue (*IFQ*) is full. Moreover, since the I-cache operation is critical for having a sustainable performance, we add an extra port to this cache in the animator core.

In order to provide branch prediction hints, the hint gathering unit looks at the branch predictor (*BP*) updates and every time the BP of the undead core gets updated, a hint will be sent through the queue. In the animator core side, the default BP – for EV4 – is a simple bimodal predictor. We firstly add an extra bimodal predictor (*NM BP*) to keep track of incoming branch prediction hints. Furthermore, we employ a hierarchical tournament predictor to decide for a given PC, whether the original or NM BP should take over. During our design space exploration, the size of these structures will be determined – Section 5.2. As mentioned earlier, we introduced release window size to get the hints just before they are needed. However, due to the variations in the number of executed instructions on the undead core, even the release window cannot guarantee the perfect timing of the hints. In such a scenario, for a subset of instructions, the tournament predictor can give an ad-

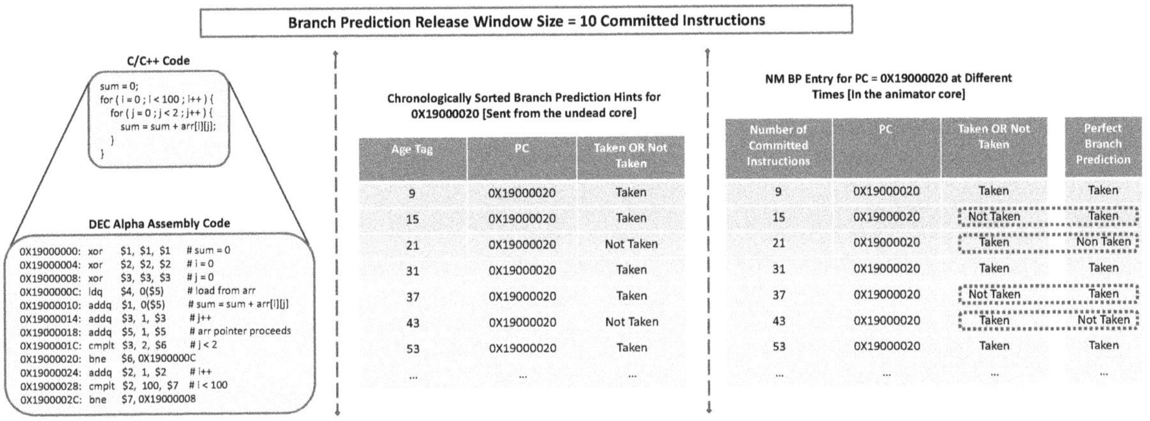

Figure 6: A code example in which the NM BP performs poorly and switching to the original BP of the animator core is required. The code simply calculates the summation of a 2D-array elements which are stored in a row-based format. It should be noted that the branch prediction release window size is normally set so that the branch prediction accuracy for the entire execution gets maximized. As can be seen, hints are received by the animator core at improper times, resulting in low branch prediction accuracy.

vantage to the original BP of the animator core to avoid any performance penalty. Having this in mind, Figure 6 shows a simple example in which the NM BP can only achieve 33% branch prediction accuracy. This is mainly due to the existence of a tight inner loop – number of instructions in the loop body is less than BP release window size – with a low trip count. Switching to the original BP can enhance the overall branch prediction accuracy for this code region.

Another aspect of the NM dual core execution is the potential of hints on the speculative execution paths. If a speculative path turns to be a correct path, instructions on this path will eventually be committed and the corresponding hints will be sent to the animator core. On the other hand, for a wrong path, although sending hints can potentially accelerate the execution of speculative paths on the animator core, this acceleration can only decrease the efficiency of our hints for the correct paths. For instance, if the animator core executes a wrong path faster, it will bring more useless data to its local D-cache which causes prefetched data for non-speculative paths to be dropped out of D-cache. Therefore, it is clear that sending hints for speculative paths can merely hurt the performance of the NM system.

4.3 Reducing Communication Overheads

In order to reduce the queue size, communication traffic needs to be limited to more beneficial hints. Consequently, in the hint gathering unit, we use two content addressable memories (*CAM*s) with several entries to discard I-cache and D-cache hints that were recently sent. Eliminating redundant hints also minimizes the resource contention on the animator core side. For this purpose, these two CAMs keep track of the last N – number of CAM entries – committed load/store addresses in the undead core. In addition to sending less number of hints, queue size can be reduced by sending less bits per hint. Saving on the number of bits can be done in several ways: sending only the block related bits of address for I-cache and D-cache hints, ignoring hints on the speculative paths, and for branch prediction hints, only sending lower bits of the PC that are used for updating branch history table of the NM BP.

Given a design with multiple communication queues, the undead core stalls when at least one queue is full and it wants to insert a new entry to that queue. The other queues that are not full during these stalls remain underutilized; thus, using a single aggregated queue guarantees a higher utilization, which reduces the area overhead, number of stalls, and overheads of interconnection wires. On the other hand, since a single queue is used, multiple entries might need to be sent to or received from the queue at the same cycle. This can be solved by grouping together several hints with the same age tag and sending them as a single packet over the queue. This requires a small buffer in the hint distribution unit to handle the case that hints have non-identical release windows sizes.

4.4 Hint Disabling Mechanisms

Hints can be disabled when they are no longer beneficial for the animator core. This might happen because of several reasons. First, the program execution on the undead core gets off the correct execution path due to the destructive impact of defects. Second, in certain phases of the program, performance of the animator core might be close to its ideal case, attenuating the value of hints. Lastly, at certain parts of the program, due to the intertwined behavior of the NM system, the animator core might not be able to get ahead of the undead core. In all these scenarios, hint disabling helps in four ways:

- It avoids occupying resources of the animator core with ineffective hints that does not buy any performance benefit.
- The queue fills up less often which means less number of stalls for the undead core.
- Disabling hint gathering and distribution saves power and energy in both sides.
- It serves as an indicator of when the undead core has strayed far from the correct path of execution (i.e., when hints are frequently disabled) and resynchronization is required.

The hint disabling unit is responsible for realizing when each type of hint should get disabled. In order to disable cache hints, the cache fingerprint unit generates high-level cache access information based on the committed instructions in the last disabling time interval – e.g., last 1K committed instructions. These fingerprints are sent through the queue and compared with the animator core's cache access pattern. Based on a pre-specified threshold value for the similarity between access patterns, the animator core decides whether the cache hint disabling should happen. In addition, when a hint gets disabled, that hint remains disabled during a time period called the back-off period. More precisely, the cache fingerprint unit retains two tables for keeping track of non-speculative I-cache and D-cache accesses in the last disabling time interval. Figure 7(a) illustrates an example of cache disabling. Considering D-cache hints, the corresponding table has only several entries – 8 entries in our example – and each entry will be incremented for a commit-

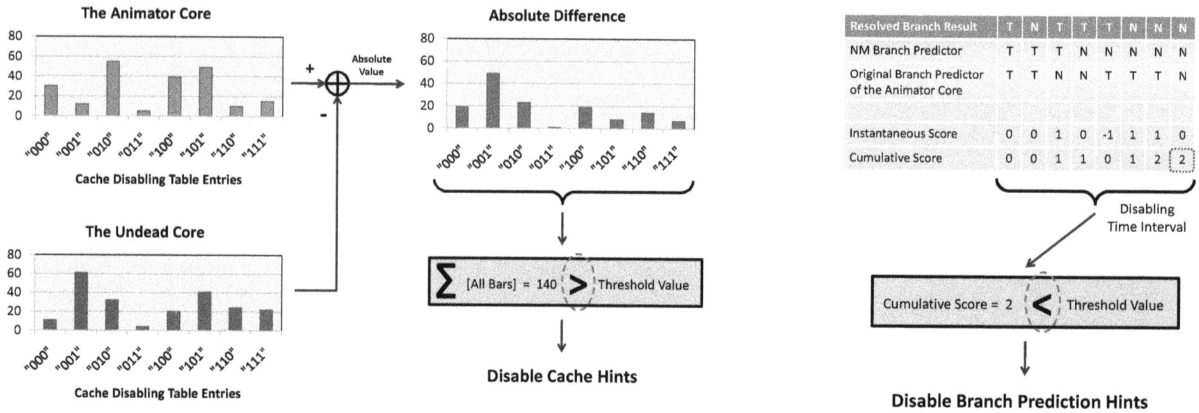

(a) Disabling cache hints (b) Disabling branch prediction hints

Figure 7: Two high-level examples of cache and branch prediction hint disabling mechanisms. Here, values on the X-axes of the plots correspond to eight entries of the cache disabling table.

ted load/store, whenever the LSBs of the address match the rank order of that entry. Therefore, the cache disabling table maintains a high-level distribution of addresses that are accessed during the last interval. At the end of each interval, the table contents will be sent over the queue to the animator core and entries will be cleared for the next interval. Given a similar cache access distribution at the animator core's side, for evaluating similarity between two distributions, $(V_1, V_2, ..., V_{16})$ for the undead core and $(S_1, S_2, ..., S_{16})$ for the animator core, we calculate $K = \sum_{i=1}^{16} |S_i - V_i|$. Then, if K (140 in our example) is less than a pre-specified threshold, a signal will be sent to the undead core to stop gathering that particular hint for the back-off period.

Disabling branch prediction hints can solely be done by the animator core. Apart from prioritizing the original BP of the animator core for a subset of PCs, the NM BP can be also employed for global disabling of the branch prediction hints. For this purpose, we continuously monitor the performance of the NM BP and if this performance – compared to the original BP – is worse than a pre-specified threshold for the last disabling time interval, we disable branch prediction hints. As Figure 7(b) depicts, for branch prediction hint disabling, we use a score-based scheme with a single counter. For every branch that the original and NM BPs either both correctly predict or both mispredict no action should be taken. Nonetheless, for the branches that the NM BP correctly predicts and the original BP does not, the score counter is incremented by one. Similarly, for the ones that NM BP mispredicts but the original BP correctly predicts, the score counter is decremented. Finally, at the end of each disabling time interval, if the score counter (2 in our example) is less than a certain threshold, the branch prediction hints will be disabled for the back-off period. For performing infrequent disabling-related computations, we add a 4-bit ALU to the hint disabling unit.

4.5 Resynchronization

Since the undead core might get off the correct execution path, a mechanism is required to take it back to a valid architectural state. In order to do so, we use resynchronization between the two cores during which the animator core's PC and architectural register values get copied to the undead core. According to [27], for a modern processor, the process of copying PC and register values between cores takes on the order of 100 cycles. Moreover, all instructions in the undead core's pipelines are squashed, the rename table is reset, and the D-cache content is also invalidated for "resynchronizing" the memory state.

Resynchronization should happen when the undead core gets off the correct execution path and it can no longer provide useful hints for the animator core. The simplest policy is to resynchronize every N committed instructions where N is a constant number like 100K. However, as we will show in Section 5.2, a more dynamic resynchronization policy can achieve a higher overall speed-up for the NM system. We take advantage of the hint disabling information to identify when resynchronization should happen. An aggressive policy is to resynchronize every time a hint gets disabled. However, such a policy results in too many resynchronizations in a short time which clearly reduces the efficiency of our scheme. Another potential policy is to resynchronize only if at some point in time all or at least two of the hints get disabled. Later in Section 5.2, we will compare some of these potential resynchronization policies.

4.6 NM Design for CMP Systems

So far, we described the NM heterogeneous coupled core execution approach and its architectural details. Here, NM for CMP systems will be discussed. Figure 8 illustrates the NM design for a 16-core CMP system with 4 clusters modeled after the Sun Rock processor. Each cluster contains 4 cores which share a single animator core, shown in the call-out. In order to maintain scalability of the NM design, we employ the aforementioned 4-core cluster design as the building block. Although a single animator core might be shared among more cores, it introduces long interconnection wires that should travel from one corner of the die to another.

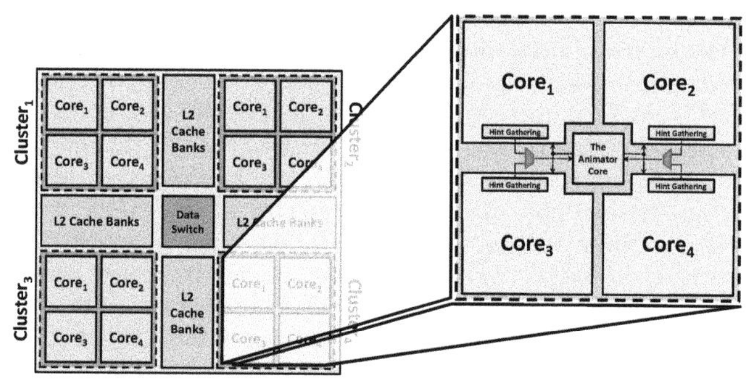

Figure 8: The high-level NM design for a large CMP system with 16 cores, modeled after the Sun Rock processor, which has 4 cores per cluster. The details of NM core coupling can be found in Figure 4.

Therefore, given the low area overhead of NM for a 4-core CMP (5.3% as will be discussed in Section 5.2), the proposed building block preserves design scalability. On the other hand, since many dies are fault-free, in order to avoid disabling the animator cores, these cores can be leveraged for accelerating the operation of live cores. One possibility is to use the animator cores to exploit Speculative Method-Level Parallelism by spawning an extra thread and moving it to the animator core to execute the method call. The original thread executes the code that follows the method's return by leveraging a return value predictor. This is based on the observation that inter-method dependency violations are infrequent. However, evaluation of the latter is beyond the scope of this work.

For a heterogeneous CMP system, the problem is slightly more difficult due to the inherent diversity of the cores. Therefore, sharing an animator core between multiple cores might not be possible since those cores have different computational capabilities. A potential solution is to partition the CMP system to groups of cores in which each group contains cores with similar characteristics and performance. Therefore, each group can share an animator core with different specifications. An alternative is to partition the cores to groups such that in each group, we have several large cores and a small core – all from the original set of heterogeneous cores. In each group, the smaller core should have the capability of operating as a conventional core or as an animator core when there is a defect in one of the larger cores in its own group. These dual purpose cores are a suitable fit for many heterogeneous CMP systems that come with a bunch of simpler cores such as the IBM Cell processor.

In our design, since the animator core is shared among multiple cores, it is reasonable to shift the overheads to the animator core side to avoid replicating of the same module in the baseline cores. For instance, most of the similarity matching structures for hint disabling are located on the animator core side. Furthermore, since the undead core runs significantly ahead of the animator core in the program stream, the communication queue should also be closer to the animator core to reduce the timing overhead of accessing the queue and checking the age tags. Finally, disabling hints, when they are no longer beneficial, allows the undead core to avoid gathering and sending the hints which saves power/energy on both sides.

5. EVALUATION

In this section, we describe experiments performed to quantify the potential of NM in enhancing the system throughput.

5.1 Experimental Methodology

In order to model NM's heterogeneous coupled core execution, we heavily modified SimAlpha, a validated cycle accurate microarchitectural simulator based on SimpleScalar [5]. We run two different versions of the simulator, implementing the undead and animator cores, and use inter process communication (*IPC*) to model the information flow between two cores (e.g., L2 warm-up, hints, and cache fingerprints). As mentioned earlier, a 6-issue OoO EV6 and a 2-issue OoO EV4 are chosen as our baseline and animator cores, respectively. The configuration of these two coupled cores and the memory system is summarized in Table 1. We simulate the SPEC-CPU-2K benchmark suite cross-compiled for DEC Alpha and fast-forwarded to an early SimPoint [31].

To study the effect of manufacturing defects on the NM system, we developed an area-weighted, Monte Carlo fault injection engine. During each iteration of Monte Carlo simulation, a microarchitectural structure is selected and a random single stuck-at fault is injected into the timing simulator. Table 2 summarizes the fault locations used in our experiments. Since every transistor has the same probability of being defective, hard-fault injections should be distributed across microarchitectural structures in proportion to their area. Therefore, for each fault injection experiment, we inject 5000 hard-faults while artificially prioritizing structures that have larger area. These stuck-at faults are injected one by one in the course of each individual experiment. As a result, at any point in time, there is a single stuck-at fault in the undead core. Given an operational frequency of 600MHz [22] for EV6 in $0.35\mu m$, scaling to a $90nm$ technology node would result in a frequency of $2.3GHz$ at 1.2V. This frequency is a pessimistic value for the animator core and NM can clearly achieve even better overall performance if the animator core were allowed to operate at a higher frequency. Nevertheless, since the amount of work per pipeline stage remains relatively consistent across Alpha microprocessor generations [22], for a given supply voltage level and a technology node, the peak operational frequency of these different cores are essentially the same.

Dynamic power consumption for both cores is evaluated using Wattch [13] and leakage power is evaluated with HotLeakage [39]. Area for our EV6-like core – excluding the I/O pads, interconnection wires, the bus-interface unit, L2 cache, and control logic – is derived from [22]. In order to derive the area for the animator core,

Table 1: The target NM system configuration.

Parameter	The animator core	A baseline core
Fetch/issue/commit width	2 per cycle	6 per cycle
Reorder buffer entries	32	128
Load/store queue entries	8/8	32/32
Issue queue entries	16	64
Instruction fetch queue	8 entries	32 entries
Branch predictor	tournament (bimodal + NM BP)	tournament (bimodal + 2-level)
Branch target buffer size	256 entries, direct-map	1024 entries, 2-way
Branch history table	1024 entries	4096 entries
Return address stack	-	32 entries
L1 data cache	8KB direct-map, 3 cycles latency, 2 ports	64KB, 4-way, 5 cycles latency, 4 ports
L1 instr. cache	4KB direct-map, 2 cycles latency, 2 ports	64KB, 4-way, 5 cycles latency, 1 port
L2 cache	2MB Unified, 8-way, 15 cycles latency	
Main memory	250 cycles access latency	

Table 2: Fault injection locations and their corresponding pipeline stages along with stage-level area break-down for EV6.

Pipeline Stage	Area Break-down	Fault Location
Fetch	14.3%	Program counter
		Branch target buffer
		Instruction fetch queue
Decode	15.6%	Input latch of decoder
Rename	5.1%	Rename alias table
Dispatch	24.1%	Integer register file
		Floating point register file
		Reorder buffer
Backend	40.8%	Integer ALU
		Integer multiplier
		Integer divider
		Floating point ALU
		Floating point multiplier
		Floating point divider
		Load/store queue

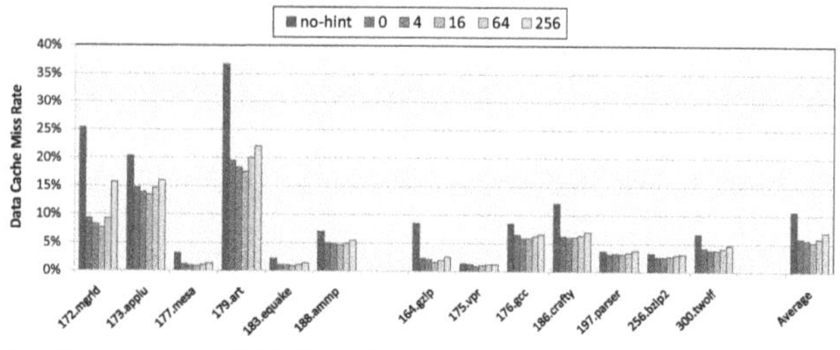

(a) Effect of the NM D-cache release window size on the data cache miss rate of the animator core.

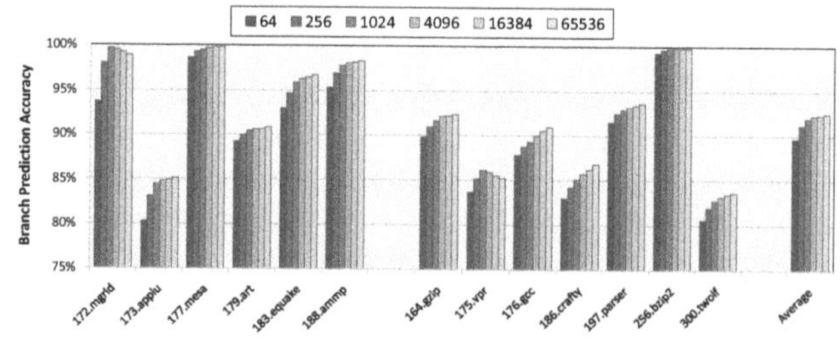

(b) Effect of the branch history table size of the NM BP on the overall branch prediction accuracy of the animator core.

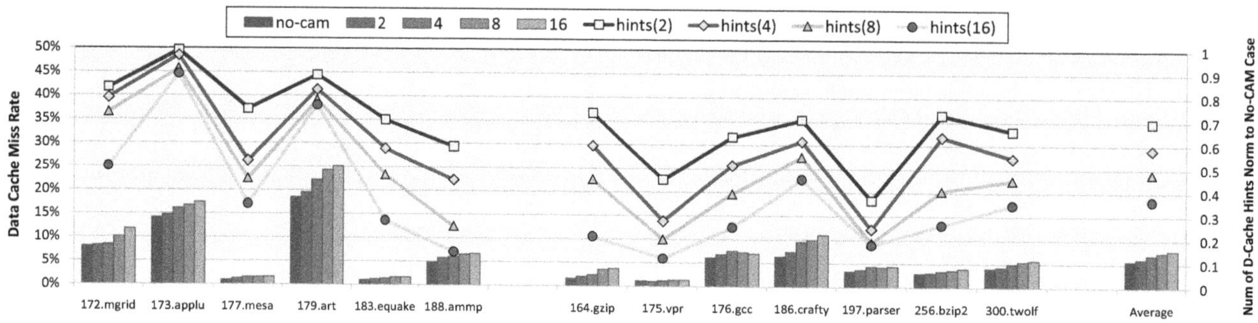

(c) Effect of CAM size that are used for reducing the number of D-cache hints – generated in the undead core – on the data cache miss rate of the animator core. Here, the lines show the number of data cache hints should be sent to the animator core per cycle, normalized to the the case without any CAM.

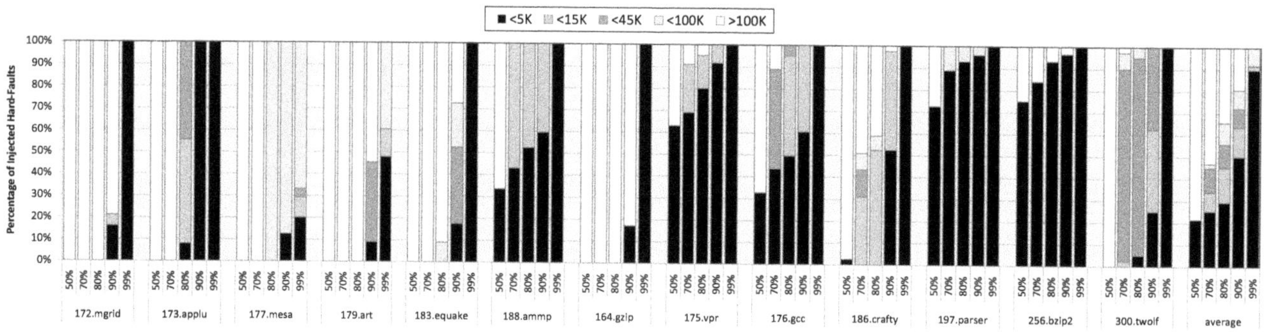

(d) Number of instructions committed in the animator core before the branch prediction hint is disabled for different pre-specified branch prediction hint disabling thresholds (i.e., 50%, 70%, 80%, 90%, and 99% similarities).

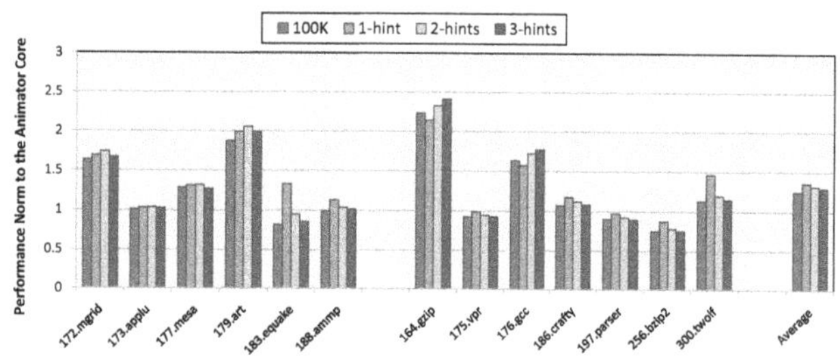

(e) Effect of different resynchronization policies on the overall speed-up of the NM coupled cores normalized to the performance of the baseline animator core.

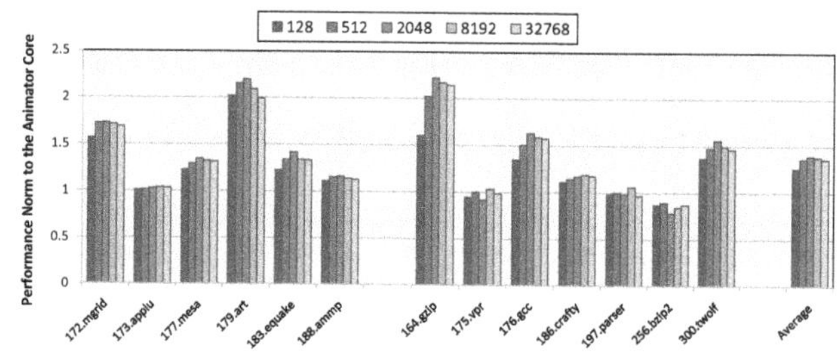

(f) Effect of communication queue size on the overall speed-up of the NM coupled cores normalized to the performance of the baseline animator core.

Figure 9: Design space exploration for the NM system described in Table 1.

we start from the publicly available area break-down for the EV6 and resize every structure based on the size and number of ports. Furthermore, CACTI [26] is used to evaluate the delay, area, and power of the on-chip caches. Overheads for the SRAM memory structures that we have added to the design, such as the NM branch prediction table, are evaluated with the SRAM generator module provided by the 90*nm* Artisan Memory Compiler. Moreover, the Synopsys standard industrial tool-chain, with a TSMC 90*nm* technology library, is used to evaluate the overheads of the remaining miscellaneous logic (e.g., MUXes, shift registers, and comparators). Finally, the area for interconnection wires between the coupled cores is estimated using the same methodology as in [23], with intermediate wiring pitch taken from the ITRS road map [19].

5.2 Experimental Results

In this section, we evaluate different aspects of the NM design

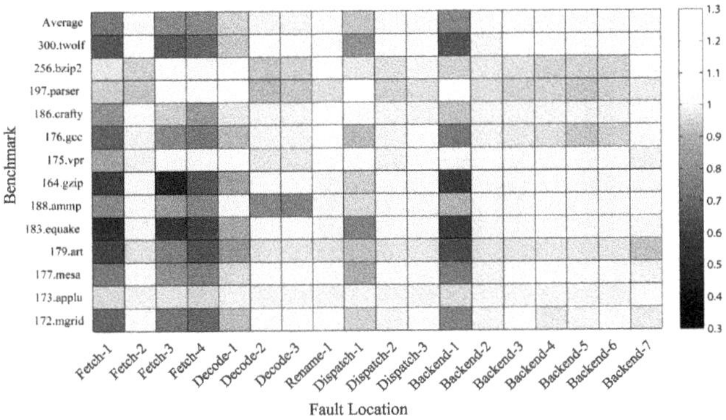

Figure 10: Variations in the speed-up of the animator core for different hard-fault locations across SPEC-CPU-2K benchmarks. To only highlight the impact of hard-fault locations, in each row, results are normalized to the average speed-up that can be achieved by the NM coupled cores for that particular benchmark.

such as design space, achievable speed-up in the presence of defects, performance impact of different hard-fault locations, area and power overheads, and finally throughput enhancement.

Design Space Exploration: Here, we fix the architectural parameters that are involved in the NM design. Since there is a variety of parameters (both hardware and policy), due to space considerations, we only present a subset of the exploration for parameters with the most interesting behaviors. During the exploration, we initially assign a nominal value to each of the parameters and as we select a proper value for each parameter, we use the updated value for the reminder of the experiments. Figure 9 depicts this design space exploration for a pruned set of NM parameters. In Figure 9(a), the release window size is varied between 0 to 256 committed instructions while monitoring the data cache miss rate of the animator core. As can be seen, there is an optimal window size (i.e., 16 committed instructions) that maximizes prefetching efficiency, given the variations in the number of committed instructions on the undead core. The D-cache miss rate, even before optimizing other parameters, is reduced from 10.7% to 5.3%. Figure 9(b) illustrates the effect of reducing the branch history table (*BHT*) size of the NM BP on the branch prediction accuracy of the animator core. To save area, we limit the BHT size to 1024 entries, causing less than 0.5% reduction in the achievable branch prediction accuracy.

The size of the D-cache hint CAM is a double-edged sword and its impact on the D-cache miss rate and communication traffic is shown in Figure 9(c). Increasing the CAM size, reduces the communication traffic and queue size. However, this aggravates the efficiency of D-cache hints. The reason is that sending more up-to-date hints increases the likelihood that data is present in the local D-cache of the animator core when it is needed. Nevertheless, using a CAM with 2 entries can reduce the number of transmitted D-cache hints by more than 30% while affecting the D-cache miss rate by less than 0.5%. Next, Figure 9(d) illustrates the effect of varying the threshold for disabling branch prediction hints. For each injected hard-fault and benchmark, we record the number of instructions committed before the branch prediction hint is disabled. Results of this process are depicted for 5 different threshold values (i.e., 50%, 70%, 80%. 90%, and 99% similarities). For high similarity requirements, such as 99%, the branch prediction hints are mostly disabled even before 5K instruction are committed in the animator core. Consequently, we select 70% similarity so that the hint disabling does not occur too frequently while still receiving occasional feedback about the effectiveness of the hints during program execution.

Finally, Figures 9(e) and (f) show the impact of different resynchronization policies and communication queue sizes on the achievable speed-up by NM, respectively. In these two plots, speed-ups are normalized to the performance of a baseline animator core. We consider 4 candidates for the resynchronization policy, consisting of one static and 3 dynamic polices. For the static policy, resynchronization occurs periodically after committing 100K instructions while for the dynamic policies, the number of disabled hints determines whether resynchronization is required. Since we aggressively exploit the hints by rarely disabling them, the resynchronization policy that is invoked on the first disabled hint achieves a better speed-up. Finally, the sensitivity to the communication queue size is presented in Figure 9(f). Although it seems that a larger queue is always better, an extremely large queue enables the undead core to get too far ahead of the animator core, polluting the L2 cache with unprofitable prefetches.

The values for the remaining parameters were identified in a similar fashion: I-cache release window size (4 committed instructions), branch prediction release window size (4 committed instructions), I-cache hint CAM size (2 entries), branch prediction hint disabling threshold (70% similarity), D-cache hint disabling threshold (70% similarity), I-cache hint disabling threshold (80% similarity), D-cache hint disabling table size (32 entries), and I-cache hint disabling table size (32 entries). Given these parameter values, on average, NM can achieve 39.5% speed-up over the baseline animator core. In our simulation, we set the queue delay to 15 cycles – same as L2 cache; however, since the NM coupled core design is highly pipelined, it has a minimal sensitivity to the queue delay. For instance, even setting this delay to 45 cycles, only affects the final speed-up by less than 1%.

Performance Impact of Different Hard-Fault Locations: In order to highlight the impact of a fault location on the achievable speed-up by the NM system, Figure 10 depicts the performance breakdown results for the fault locations described in Table 2. Results in each row of this plot is normalized to the average speed-up that can be achieved by the NM coupled core for that particular benchmark. This was done to eliminate the advantage/disadvantage that comes from the inherent benchmark suitability for core coupling. As can be seen, hard-faults in some locations are more harmful than others. These locations consist of the PC, integer ALU, and instruction fetch queue. Another interesting observation is that, for a benchmark like 197.parser, reaction to defects can significantly differ from other benchmarks. We conclude two main points from this plot. First, on average, there are only a few fault locations that can drastically impact the NM speed-up gain. Second, for a given fault location, different benchmarks show various degrees of susceptibility; thus, heterogeneity across the benchmarks running on a CMP system helps NM to achieve a higher speed-up by having a more suitable workload assigned to the coupled cores.

Summary of Benefits and Overheads: Figure 11(a) demonstrates the amount of speed-up that can be achieved by the NM coupled cores for CMP systems with different numbers of cores. As can be seen, NM achieves a higher overall speed-up as the number of cores increases. For a 16-core system, on average, the coupled cores can achieve the performance of a live core, essentially providing the appearance of a fully-functional 6-issue baseline core with a 2-issue animator core. This is because NM achieves different speed-ups based on the defect type, location, and the workload running on the system. Here, we assume full utilization, which means there is always one job per core. Hence, for larger CMPs, with more heterogeneity across the benchmarks running on the system,

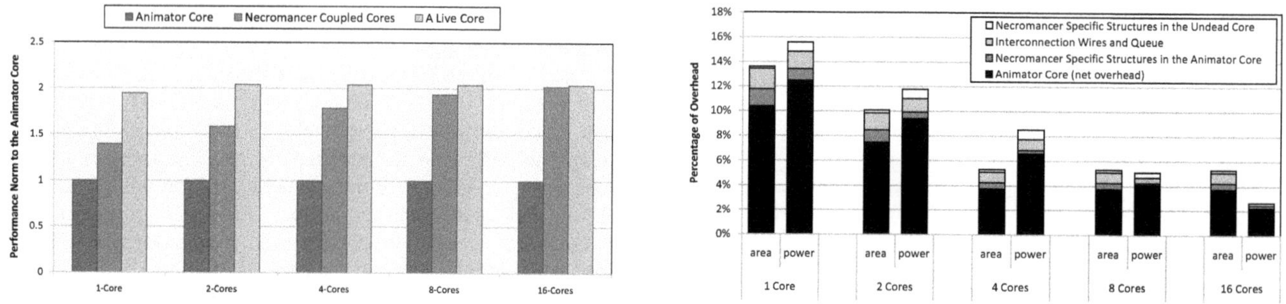

(a) Performance of the baseline animator core, NM coupled cores, and a live core normalized to the average performance of a baseline animator core. Due to the higher heterogeneity across the benchmarks for a CMP system with more cores, NM can achieve a higher overall speed-up.

(b) Break-down of NM area and power overheads for CMP systems with different numbers of cores. As can be seen, the overheads that are imposed by the the baseline animator core is typically the major component, which gets amortized as the number of cores grows.

Figure 11: Summary of benefits and overheads of our scheme for CMP systems with different number of cores.

there is more opportunity for NM to exploit. The speed-up evaluation was done by conducting a Monte Carlo simulation with 1000 iterations. In each iteration, we select one benchmark for each core, while allowing replication in the selected benchmarks.

Figure 11(b) shows the breakdown of area and power overheads for our scheme. Here, we assume a single core system has 2MB L2 while assuming 1MB shared L2 per core for CMP systems. As can be seen, the area overhead gradually shrinks as the number of cores grows since the cost of the animator core is amortized among more cores. Nevertheless, since we simply replicate the 4-core building block to construct CMPs with more than 4 cores, the area overhead remains the same. In terms of power overhead, two points should be noted. First, based on our target defect rate, for CMPs with more than 4 cores, other animator cores remain disabled and do not contribute to the power consumption. Next, as the speed-up results show, for CMPs with less than 8 cores, the undead core remains ahead of the animator core and it needs to stall when the queue gets full. During stall times, the undead core does not consume dynamic power which is accounted for in the net overhead of the animator core – Figure 11(b).

Finally, as discussed earlier, based on the expected defect rate for current and near future CMOS technologies, on average one defect per five manufactured $100mm^2$ dies should be expected. In the case of a defect in one of the original cores, we apply our scheme. On the other hand, if any of the animator cores, communication queues, or NM specific modules like the hint gathering unit are faulty, we simply disable the animator core and the rest of the system can continue their normal operation.

6. RELATED WORK

Manufacturing defects can cause transistors in different parts of a microprocessor to get corrupted. Prior work on defect tolerance mostly focused on on-chip caches since there is less homogeneity in the non-cache parts of a core, making defect tolerance a more challenging issue. Typically, for high-end server systems designed with reliability as a first-order design constraint (e.g., HP Tandem NonStop [7], Teramac [15], and the IBM eServer zSeries [7]), coarse-grained replication has been employed [8, 33]. Configurable Isolation [2] is a high availability chip multiprocessor architecture for partitioning cores to multiple fault domains which allows independent redundant executions. However, dual and triple modular redundant systems incur significant overheads in terms of area and power which is not generally acceptable for mainstream computing. An easy solution is to disable the faulty cores – to avoid yield loss – which clearly causes a significant reduction in the system throughput and sale price [2]. This simple core disabling approach has been taken by microprocessor vendors, such as IBM, Intel, AMD, and Sun Microsystems, to maintain an acceptable level of manufacturing yield.

Core Cannibalization [29] and StageNet [17] suggest breaking each core into pipeline stages and allowing one core to borrow stages from other cores through interconnection networks. Introduction of these interconnection networks in the processor pipeline presents performance, power consumption, and design complexity challenges. Finer-grained redundancy maintenance has been used by Bulletproof [14] and sparing of array structures [11]. In the same vein, Shivakumar et. al. [32] proposed a method to disable non-functional microarchitectural components (e.g., execution units) and faulty entries in small array structures (e.g., register file). Rescue is mainly a microarchitectural design-for-test (*DFT*) technique which can map out faulty pipeline units that have spares [30]. However, as shown in [27], these schemes have a limited applicability due to the small amount of microarchitectural redundancy that exists in a modern high-performance processor.

Architectural Core Salvaging [27] is a high-level low-cost architectural proposals which uses thread migration between the cores to guarantee the correct execution. To avoid incorrect execution, for each instruction, it assesses whether the fault location might be exercised by the corresponding *opcode*. Thus, without using extra redundancy, it is only applicable to defects in about 10% of core area. DIVA [4] was proposed for dynamic verification of complex high-performance microprocessors. It employs a checker pipeline that re-runs the same instruction stream for ensuring correct program execution. Given the fact that DIVA is not a defect tolerant scheme, as shown in [4], a "catastrophic" core processor failure results in about 10X slow-down. Detour [25] is a completely software-based approach which leverages binary translation for handling defects in execution units and register files. Apart from limited defect types that can be handled, a binary translation layer cannot typically be applied to high-performance x86 cores [27].

7. CONCLUSION

Since manufacturing defects directly impact yield in nanoscale CMOS technologies, to maintain an acceptable level of manufacturing yield, these defects need to be addressed properly. Non-cache parts of a core are less structured and homogeneous; thus, tolerating defects in the general core area has remained a challenging problem. In this work, we presented Necromancer, an architectural scheme to enhance the system throughput by exploiting dead cores. Although a dead core cannot be trusted to perform program execution, for most defect incidences, its execution flow – when starting from a valid architectural state – coarsely matches the intact program behavior for a long time period. Hence, Necromancer does not rely on correct program execution on a dead core; instead, it only expects this undead core to generate effective execution hints to accelerate the animator core. In order to increase Necromancer efficacy, we use microarchitectural techniques to provide intrinsically robust hints, effective hint disabling, and dynamic inter-core state resynchronization. For a 4-core CMP system, on average, our approach enables the coupled core to achieve 78.5% of the performance of a live core. This defect tolerance and throughput enhancement comes at modest area and power overheads of 5.3% and 8.5%, respectively. We believe NM is a valuable and low-cost solution for tolerating manufacturing defects and improving the throughput of the current and near future mainstream CMP systems.

8. ACKNOWLEDGMENTS

We thank the anonymous referees for their valuable comments and suggestions. This research was supported by National Science Foundation grants CCF-0916689 and CCF-0347411 and by ARM Limited.

9. REFERENCES

[1] J. Abella, J. Carretero, P. Chaparro, X. Vera, and A. González. Low vccmin fault-tolerant cache with highly predictable performance. In *Proc. of the 42nd Annual International Symposium on Microarchitecture*, page To appear, 2009.

[2] N. Aggarwal, P. Ranganathan, N. P. Jouppi, and J. E. Smith. Configurable isolation: building high availability systems with commodity multi-core processors. In *Proc. of the 34th Annual International Symposium on Computer Architecture*, pages 470–481, 2007.

[3] A. Ansari, S. Gupta, S. Feng, and S. Mahlke. Zerehcache: Armoring cache architectures in high defect density technologies. In *Proc. of the 42nd Annual International Symposium on Microarchitecture*, 2009.

[4] T. Austin. Diva: a reliable substrate for deep submicron microarchitecture design. In *Proc. of the 32nd Annual International Symposium on Microarchitecture*, pages 196–207, 1999.

[5] T. Austin, E. Larson, and D. Ernst. Simplescalar: An infrastructure for computer system modeling. *IEEE Transactions on Computers*, 35(2):59–67, Feb. 2002.

[6] R. D. Barnes, E. N. Nystrom, J. W. Sias, S. J. Patel, N. Navarro, and W. W. Hwu. Beating in-order stalls with "flea-flicker" two-pass pipelining. In *Proc. of the 36th Annual International Symposium on Microarchitecture*, page 387, 2003.

[7] W. Bartlett and L. Spainhower. Commercial fault tolerance: A tale of two sytems. *IEEE Transactions on Dependable and Secure Computing*, 1(1):87–96, 2004.

[8] D. Bernick, B. Bruckert, P. D. Vigna, D. Garcia, R. Jardine, J. Klecka, and J. Smullen. Nonstop advanced architecture. In *International Conference on Dependable Systems and Networks*, pages 12–21, June 2005.

[9] K. Bernstein. Nano-meter scale cmos devices (tutorial presentation), 2004.

[10] S. Borkar. Designing reliable systems from unreliable components: The challenges of transistor variability and degradation. *IEEE Micro*, 25(6):10–16, 2005.

[11] F. A. Bower, P. G. Shealy, S. Ozev, and D. J. Sorin. Tolerating hard faults in microprocessor array structures. In *Proc. of the 2004 International Conference on Dependable Systems and Networks*, page 51, 2004.

[12] F. A. Bower, D. J. Sorin, and S. Ozev. A mechanism for online diagnosis of hard faults in microprocessors. In *Proc. of the 38th Annual International Symposium on Microarchitecture*, pages 197–208, 2005.

[13] D. Brooks, V. Tiwari, and M. Martonosi. A framework for architectural-level power analysis and optimizations. In *Proc. of the 27th Annual International Symposium on Computer Architecture*, pages 83–94, June 2000.

[14] K. Constantinides, S. Plaza, J. Blome, B. Zhang, V. Bertacco, S. Mahlke, T. Austin, and M. Orshansky. Bulletproof: A defect-tolerant CMP switch architecture. In *Proc. of the 12th International Symposium on High-Performance Computer Architecture*, pages 3–14, Feb. 2006.

[15] W. Culbertson, R. Amerson, R. Carter, P. Kuekes, and G. Snider. Defect tolerance on the teramac custom computer. In *Proc. of the 5th IEEE Symposium on FPGA-Based Custom Computing Machines*, pages 116–123, 1997.

[16] B. Greskamp and J. Torrellas. Paceline: Improving single-thread performance in nanoscale cmps through core overclocking. In *Proc. of the 16th International Conference on Parallel Architectures and Compilation Techniques*, pages 213–224, 2007.

[17] S. Gupta, S. Feng, A. Ansari, J. Blome, and S. Mahlke. The stagenet fabric for constructing resilient multicore systems. In *Proc. of the 41st Annual International Symposium on Microarchitecture*, pages 141–151, 2008.

[18] T. Higashiki. Status and future lithography for sub hp32nm device. In *2009 Lithography Workshop*, 2009.

[19] ITRS. International technology roadmap for semiconductors 2008, 2008. http://www.itrs.net/.

[20] R. E. Kessler. The alpha 21264 microprocessor. *IEEE Micro*, 19(2):24–36, 1999.

[21] J. Kim, N. Hardavellas, K. Mai, B. Falsafi, and J. C. Hoe. Multi-bit Error Tolerant Caches Using Two-Dimensional Error Coding. In *Proc. of the 40th Annual International Symposium on Microarchitecture*, 2007.

[22] R. Kumar, K. I. Farkas, N. P. Jouppi, P. Ranganathan, and D. M. Tullsen. Single-ISA Heterogeneous Multi-Core Architectures: The Potential for Processor Power Reduction. In *Proc. of the 36th Annual International Symposium on Microarchitecture*, pages 81–92, Dec. 2003.

[23] R. Kumar, N. Jouppi, and D. Tullsen. Conjoined-core chip multiprocessing. In *Proc. of the 37th Annual International Symposium on Microarchitecture*, pages 195–206, 2004.

[24] M.-L. Li, P. Ramachandran, U. R. Karpuzcu, S. K. S. Hari, and S. V. Adve. Accurate microarchitecture-level fault modeling for studying hardware faults. In *Proc. of the 15th International Symposium on High-Performance Computer Architecture*, pages 105–116, 2009.

[25] A. Meixner, M. Bauer, and D. Sorin. Argus: Low-cost, comprehensive error detection in simple cores. *IEEE Micro*, 28(1):52–59, 2008.

[26] N. Muralimanohar, R. Balasubramonian, and N. P. Jouppi. Optimizing nuca organizations and wiring alternatives for large caches with cacti 6.0. In *IEEE Micro*, pages 3–14, 2007.

[27] M. D. Powell, A. Biswas, S. Gupta, and S. S. Mukherjee. Architectural core salvaging in a multi-core processor for hard-error tolerance. In *Proc. of the 36th Annual International Symposium on Computer Architecture*, page To Appear, June 2009.

[28] Z. Purser, K. Sundaramoorthy, and E. Rotenberg. A study of slipstream processors. In *Proc. of the 33rd Annual International Symposium on Microarchitecture*, pages 269–280, 2000.

[29] B. F. Romanescu and D. J. Sorin. Core cannibalization architecture: Improving lifetime chip performance for multicore processor in the presence of hard faults. In *Proc. of the 17th International Conference on Parallel Architectures and Compilation Techniques*, 2008.

[30] E. Schuchman and T. N. Vijaykumar. Rescue: A microarchitecture for testability and defect tolerance. In *Proc. of the 32nd Annual International Symposium on Computer Architecture*, pages 160–171, 2005.

[31] T. Sherwood, E. Perelman, G. Hamerly, and B. Calder. Automatically characterizing large scale program behavior. In *Tenth International Conference on Architectural Support for Programming Languages and Operating Systems*, pages 45–57, New York, NY, USA, 2002. ACM.

[32] P. Shivakumar, S. Keckler, C. Moore, and D. Burger. Exploiting microarchitectural redundancy for defect tolerance. In *Proc. of the 2003 International Conference on Computer Design*, page 481, Oct. 2003.

[33] L. Spainhower and T. Gregg. IBM S/390 Parallel Enterprise Server G5 Fault Tolerance: A Historical Perspective. *IBM Journal of Research and Development*, 43(6):863–873, 1999.

[34] E. Sperling. Turn down the heat...please, 2006. http://www.edn.com/article/CA6350202.html.

[35] J. Srinivasan, S. V. Adve, P. Bose, and J. A. Rivers. Exploiting structural duplication for lifetime reliability enhancement. In *Proc. of the 32nd Annual International Symposium on Computer Architecture*, pages 520–531, June 2005.

[36] N. J. Wang, M. Fertig, and S. J. Patel. Y-branches: When you come to a fork in the road, take it. In *Proc. of the 12th International Conference on Parallel Architectures and Compilation Techniques*, pages 56–65, 2003.

[37] N. J. Wang, J. Quek, T. M. Rafacz, and S. J. Patel. Characterizing the Effects of Transient Faults on a High-Performance Processor Pipeline. In *International Conference on Dependable Systems and Networks*, page 61, June 2004.

[38] C. Wilkerson, H. Gao, A. R. Alameldeen, Z. Chishti, M. Khellah, and S.-L. Lu. Trading off cache capacity for reliability to enable low voltage operation. *Proc. of the 35th Annual International Symposium on Computer Architecture*, 0:203–214, 2008.

[39] C. Zhang, F. Vahid, and W. Najjar. A highly configurable cache architecture for embedded systems. *ACM SIGARCH Computer Architecture News*, 31(2):136–146, 2003.

[40] H. Zhou. Dual-core execution: Building a highly scalable single-thread instruction window. In *Proc. of the 14th International Conference on Parallel Architectures and Compilation Techniques*, pages 231–242, 2005.

[41] C. Zilles and G. Sohi. Master/slave speculative parallelization. In *Proc. of the 35th Annual International Symposium on Microarchitecture*, pages 85–96, Nov. 2002.

Leveraging the Core-Level Complementary Effects of PVT Variations to Reduce Timing Emergencies in Multi-Core Processors

Guihai Yan
a) Key Laboratory of Computer System and Architecture, Institute of Computing Technology, Chinese Academy of Sciences (CAS), China
b) Graduate University of CAS
yan_guihai@ict.ac.cn

Xiaoyao Liang
NVIDIA Corporation
USA
xliang@nvidia.com

Yinhe Han, Xiaowei Li
a) Key Laboratory of Computer System and Architecture, Institute of Computing Technology, Chinese Academy of Sciences (CAS), China
b) Graduate University of CAS
{yinhes, lxw}@ict.ac.cn

ABSTRACT

Process, Voltage, and Temperature (PVT) variations can significantly degrade the performance benefits expected from next nanoscale technology. The primary circuit implication of the PVT variations is the resultant timing emergencies. In a multi-core processor running multiple programs, variations create spatial and temporal unbalance across the processing cores. Most prior schemes are dedicated to tolerating PVT variations individually for a single core, but ignore the opportunity of leveraging the complementary effects between variations and the intrinsic variation unbalance among individual cores. We find that the notorious delay impacts from different variations are not necessary aggregated. Cores with mild variations can share the violent workload from cores suffering large variations. If operated correctly, variations on different cores can help mitigating each other and result in a variation-mild environment. In this paper, we propose Timing Emergency Aware Thread Migration (TEA-TM), a delay sensor-based scheme to reduce system timing emergencies under PVT variations. Fourier transform and frequency domain analysis are conducted to provide the insights and the potential of the PVT co-optimization scheme. Experimental results show on average TEA-TM can help save up to 24% throughput loss, at the same time improve the system fairness by 85%.

Categories and Subject Descriptors

B.8.1 [**Performance and Reliability**]: Reliability, Testing, and Fault-Tolerance; C.1.4 [**Processor Architectures**]: Parallel Architectures

General Terms

Reliability, Experimentation, Design

Keywords

Timing emergency, PVT variations, complimentary effects, delay sensor, thread migration

1. INTRODUCTION

CMOS technology scaling has been and will continue to be the main driving force in quest for performance in the computing industry by integrating smaller and faster transistors onto a single chip. The scaling trend, however, is greatly threatened by the ever-increasing parameter variations. Parameter variations induce delay violations in the system, which can eat up the performance gain from technology scaling [1]. Parameter variations can be classified into process, voltage, and temperature variations (PVT) [2]. Manufacturing and process imperfections cause process variation which makes each transistor slightly different in their delay and power profile. Voltage variation occurs when large current switch happens in the microprocessor that leads to supply voltage fluctuations through parasitic power delivery network. Temperature variation is mostly due to the imbalanced power consumption in a chip, which leads to different intra- or inter-core temperature. The primary circuit impact of PVT variations is the resultant delay violation or timing emergency (i.e. part of the microarchitecture circuit cannot meet the operating frequency). The traditional solution for the problem is to over-design the system based on the worst-case scenario. However, with the variations growing, the worst-case principle of design may cause too much design overhead and fabrication cost.

Recently, researchers have started to look for alternative solutions for PVT variations. Liang et al. proposed voltage interpolation [3] [4] and Teodorescu et al. proposed fine-grain body bias tuning at the microarchitecture level for mitigating the delay impact of process variation [5]. Powell et al. proposed pipeline damping [6] and Gupta et al. proposed delayed commit and rollback scheme for reducing or tolerating voltage variation [7]. Skadron et al. conducted some of the early work on processor temperature variation [8] and Donald et al. surveyed many different techniques for controlling the variation [9]. However, prior schemes are dedicated to tolerating PVT variations individually, but ignore the opportunity for leveraging the complementary effects between these variations. Since not all the variations affect circuit delay at the same time and to the same direction, we find that the delay impacts from different types of variations are not necessary aggregated. Moreover, the nature of parameter variations create intrinsic imbalance in variation tolerability across different cores in the processor. If operated correctly, these variations can help compensate each other across cores and thereby result in a variation mild environment.

In this paper, we propose a new approach to mitigate the impact of PVT variations. Our approach, called Timing Emergency Aware Thread Migration (TEA-TM), aims to address the "real" timing emergencies which endanger the reliability of the processors. Our scheme is purely based on the circuit delay values measured by distributed delay sensors, waiving the need for any other sensing schemes such as temperature or voltages sensors. With the delay measured in individual cores, Fast Fourier Transform (FFT) is conducted and simple frequency analysis will provide the strength of each variation source (P, V, and T), deduced from the magnitude of corresponding frequency components on the frequency spectrum. The DC and low frequency components typically represent for process and temperature variations, while the high frequency components stand for the voltage variation. Optimizations are performed to smooth out the total variation strength across cores by exchanging their high frequency components through thread migration (TM). In time domain, this is equivalent to migrate voltage-violent threads to process- and temperature-mild cores which lead to overall reductions in timing emergencies. Since frequency analysis is hard to achieve in real-time, we discuss alternative algorithms with their hardware complexity and effectiveness. Overall, we make three contributions:

- Unlike the previous schemes targeting to PVT variations individually, TEA-TM seeks to leverage the spatial and temporal complementary effects between variations and across different cores. PVT variations have different space and time span that provides unique opportunity to cancel/mitigate their circuit impact — delay variation. Our results show migrating voltage-violent thread to process- and temperature-mild cores can greatly reduce the overall occurrence of timing emergencies.
- Unlike the previous schemes requiring different sensors for different variations, our scheme only relies on delay sensors, which provides the most faithful information for timing emergency. We can deduce the strength of different variations by performing simple frequency analysis. This solution is scaling friendly since we can apply the same method to new variation sources without deploying new types of sensors in the future.
- We present an analysis method from frequency domain perspective. Using this method, we can provide insights on how to leverage the complementary effects between variations and how to decide the optimal thread migration intervals. In addition, this paper shows that the frequency analysis can be a powerful tool for computer architects in dealing with variation-related issues.

The rest of the paper is organized as follows: Section 2 presents background information. Section 3 discusses the frequency and time domain perspective of the scheme. Section 4 presents the design challenges and the detailed design implementation. Section 5 presents the experiment setup, followed by simulation results in Section 6. Section 7 provides the related work and Section 8 concludes this paper.

2. BACKGROUND

2.1 PVT Variations

Process Variation. Chip manufacturing imperfections introduce process variation which makes transistors slightly differ in their delay characteristic. At system level, process variation leads to different maximum operating frequency for processing cores on a single die [10]. This phenomenon can also be interpreted as different cores have different tolerability to delay variation if they are configured at the same frequency. In other words, process-mild cores (i.e. faster cores) are able to tolerate more delay fluctuations. This unbalanced "tolerability" provides a new optimization opportunity especially for the future many-core architectures. Process variation is static and determined at the chip fabrication time. In a frequency domain analysis, it engenders DC component on the spectrum as explained in Section 3.

Voltage Variation. Voltage variation mainly results from program variability. Different application activity requires different amount of current. Variation in current demand transfers to voltage fluctuations through two physical mechanisms: IR-drop and Inductive Noise (a.k.a. Ldi/dt problem). The presence of parasitical capacitance and inductance makes a robust power delivery subsystem extremely difficult to implement. Voltage variation also affects circuit delay and causes delay unbalance among processing cores. Unlike the process and temperature variations, voltage variation is usually fast changing and represents high frequency components in frequency analysis.

Temperature Variation. The average and peak temperature of a processor core is highly application-specific [9]. Even for the same program, different phase of the application will generate different power consumption and temperature. In a multi-core processor, this creates temperature imbalance among cores which provides another optimization opportunity. Circuit delay is highly temperature-related [11]. Typically, a processing core can run faster with lower temperature. In other words, temperature-mild cores (i.e. cooler cores) are able to tolerate larger delay fluctuations. Temperature variation is usually slow time-varying and shows up to be low frequency components on the spectrum in frequency analysis.

The common impact of the three variations to multi-core processors is the delay variation observed among individual cores. But the negative delay impacts of the three variations are not necessary aggregated. Some application threads tend to be voltage-violent (note that "voltage violent" is not necessarily associated with higher power/temperature, and vice versa) and they cause large voltage fluctuations. If they happen to be running on slow or hot cores, the aggregated effect will make the cores very susceptible to timing errors. The chance of timing violations, however, can be greatly reduced if we migrate such threads to faster or cooler cores beforehand. Most of the prior works focus on measuring real-time temperature or voltage. Instead, we focus on measuring the real circuit delay. Since timing violation is the ultimate impact of temperature and voltage fluctuations, focusing directly on circuit delay brings the most reliable and confident design choice. In this paper, we will study the joint delay impact of the three variations, focus on leveraging the complimentary effect and propose a co-optimization scheme to reduce the timing emergencies.

2.2 Delay Sensors

One key concept of this paper is to infer the impact of PVT variations purely through circuit delay measurement, unlike the prior schemes [7][9] depending on slow temperature and voltage sensors. This brings three benefits to our scheme: 1) delay sensors naturally take the process variation into account; 2) delay sensors are much faster than thermal or voltage sensors, which is critical in triggering timely thread migration; 3) delay sensors save us the additional cost for adding temperature, voltage and other types of sensors.

Real-time delay values are provided by distributed delay

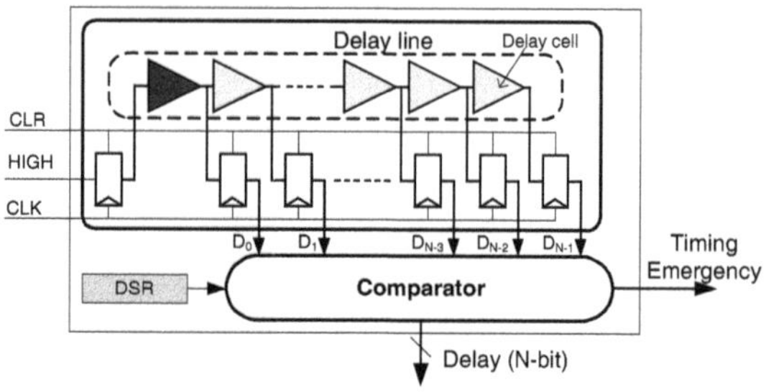

Figure 1: Conceptual delay sensor design

sensors. These sensors serve as canary circuits and the delay values measured represent critical circuit delays of the surrounding region. The measurements are highly reliable since the delay sensors share the same process corner, ambient temperature and voltage supply network with the critical paths in the same core. The key element of a delay sensor is Time-to-Digital Converter (TDC), as Figure 1 shows. TDC [12][13] is an appropriate and well-studied device for delay measurement. The measured resolution can easily reach 5ps with 90nm technology [13].

The basic working principle of delay sensors is describe as follows: At the effective edge of CLK, the signal 'HIGH' is triggered to propagate through the delay line. At the end of the cycle, the delay propagation is stamped by a series of flip-flops, represented as thermometer code: $D_0D_1 \cdots D_{N-1}$. Delay signature register (DSR) is used to store delay thresholds which are used for comparing against the sampled delay for emergency detection.

2.3 Thread Migration

Our scheme relies on thread migration (TM) which has been proved necessary for multi-core processors [14]. Not only can TM be engaged for thermal management [15], but also help steer the applications running in a more power-efficient way on multi-core processors [16]. Every migration involves transferring some states such as architectural registers, from one core to the other. The performance penalty imposed by migration largely depends on the target multi-core architectures. For light-weight cores with limited speculative capabilities, the migration penalty is much less than heavy-weight cores with aggressive speculation.

The performance penalty for heavy-weight cores can also be amortized well if the TM interval is kept above a threshold. Comprehensive case study [14] shows that for a multi-core processor with private L1 and shared L2 cache, TM interval of 2.5M instructions (0.825ms at 3GHz) or more makes the performance penalty negligible. Even with TM interval at 640K instructions (0.21ms at 3GHz), the worst-case overhead is no more than 15%. We will prove in this paper that this TM interval lines up well on the frequency spectrum between the slow varying process/temperature variations and the fast changing voltage variation. The optimum TM interval in our scheme only imposes marginal performance penalty. This serves as the basic rationale behind our TEA-TM scheme.

2.4 Rollback Recovery

Our scheme can reduce timing emergencies but cannot completely eliminate timing violations. Rollback recovery scheme [17][18] is applied when the circuit undergoes true timing errors. The architectural states of all active cores are check-pointed at the magnitude of tens of millisecond. Whenever an error is detected, the architecture states will be rolled back to the most recent check-point and re-run. This means

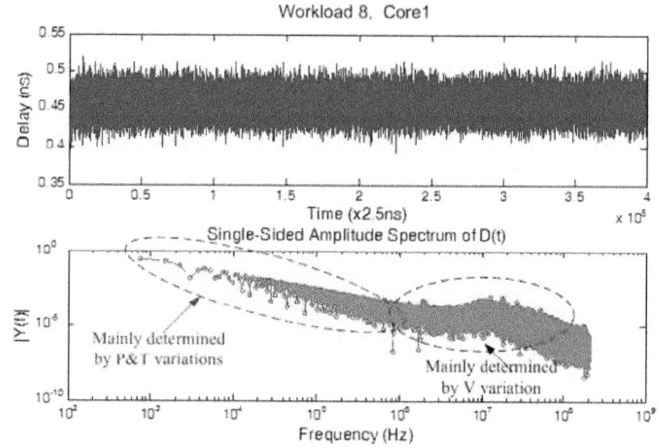

Figure 2: Frequency analysis of D(t)

an error can impose hundreds of millions cycles overhead under the worst-case. In this paper, we assume each core in the processor has individual checkpoint and rollback logic, just as previous proposed ReVive architecture [17].

3. FREQUENCY AND TIME DOMAIN PERSPECTIVE OF PVT VARIATIONS

In this section, we will discuss PVT variations at both frequency and time domain. Fourier Transform is performed on the sampled delay values and frequency analysis provides clear insight on how our proposed TEA-TM scheme can help to mitigate the delay variation.

3.1 Characterizing Timing Emergency under PVT Variations

At any time t, the critical delay $D(t)$ is determined by the real-time on-site variations. The variations include time-independent process variation P, slow-varying temperature variation $T(t)$ and fast-changing voltage variation $V(t)$, which is shown in Eq.(1).

$$D(t) = f(P, V(t), T(t)) \tag{1}$$

We define the designed nominal voltage as V_{spec}, nominal temperature as T_{spec}, and the designed nominal delay as D_{spec}. At any time, the delay variation $\Delta D(t)$ is defined as the difference between the critical delay and the nominal delay $\Delta D(t) \triangleq D_t - D_{spec}$. It can be further decomposed into the impact of the three variations respectively using a linear model [11] shown in Eq.(2), where α, β, γ are experience constants.

$$\Delta D(t) = D(t) - D_{spec} = \alpha P + \beta(V(t) - V_{spec}) + \gamma(T(t) - T_{spec}) \tag{2}$$

We further defined timing emergency occurs when $\Delta D(t)$ is larger than a predetermined threshold D_{TH}. This happens if the delay variation becomes big enough and generates timing violations in the circuit. The Emergency Level (EL) is defined as the total number of timing emergencies per every 100 millions cycles. Higher EL means more delay violations which may lead to larger performance loss.

To conduct Discrete Fourier Transform (DFT), we sample $D(t)$ by delay sensors and obtain discrete delay values $D(n)$. Eq.(3) shows Fourier Transform, where $\omega = 2\pi \times frequency$. $Y(e^{j\omega})$ is called the frequency spectrum of $D(n)$. The strength of each frequency component is expressed with the $|Y(e^{j\omega})|$.

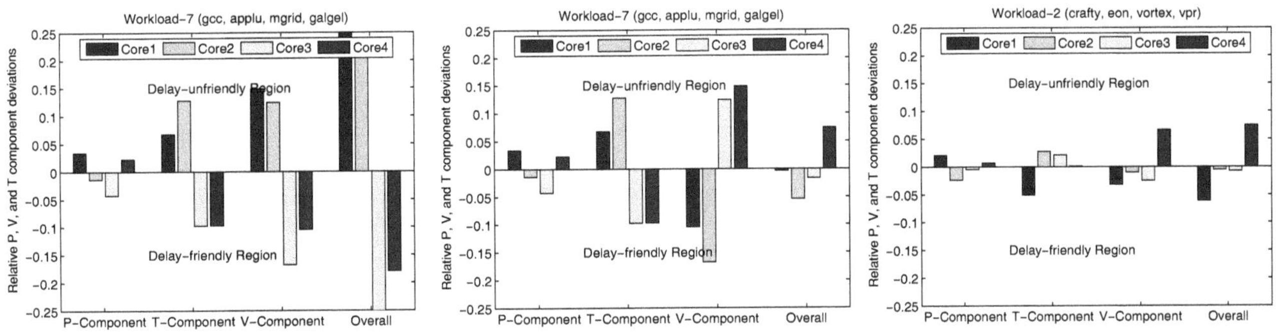

(a) Large potential, but without optimization (b) Large potential, with optimization (c) Little optimization potential

Figure 3: Relative frequency spectrum deviations of P, V, and T components in 1ms execution interval on a 2GHz quad-core processor. The boundary frequencies for P-Component: 0-100Hz, T-Component: 100Hz-1MHz, V-Component: 1MHz-250MHz.

$$Y(e^{j\omega}) = \sum_{n=-\infty}^{\infty} D(n)e^{-j\omega n} \quad (3)$$

3.2 Frequency Domain Analysis

Timing variation is determined by voltage variation (V component), temperature (T component), and process variations (P component). From frequency domain, qualitatively, P component clearly represents the DC component, T component contributes to low-frequency components due to millisecond thermal constant of silicon material, while V component dominates the high-frequency components due to its much faster circuit switching activities.

Figure 2 shows the critical delay fluctuation in a microprocessor for 1ms. We conduct FFT on the delay values, and show the corresponding frequency spectrum in the below subfigure, where both the frequency and amplitude are plotted in logarithmic scale. The amplitude in the spectrum stands for the strength of variation components. Given that the typical silicon and copper thermal constants are about 2ms, the frequency components ranging from 0 to 1MHz should be mainly contributed by the P and T component. In contrast, the high-frequency components from 1MHz to 250MHz are mainly contributed by the V component, though the frequency boundaries are not necessarily exact.

To clearly expose the impacts of the P, V, and T component of each core on a multi-core processor running different applications, we further investigate the frequency spectrum of two quad-core processors running different workloads. To highlight the core-to-core variations, we plot each core's PVT components relatively to their nominal case in Figure 3. The positive deviation implies the variation component increases circuit delay, hence delay-unfriendly, while the negative deviation implies the variation components help reduce circuit delay, hence delay-friendly. We also plot the overall variation strength which is the sum of the three variation components in each core.

To reduce timing emergencies and delay variation, a direct way is to reduce the overall variations strength on each core, which is not easy since the variations are either fabrication or application related. Unless we can change fabrication process or program flow, those variations cannot be reduced. More observations find the overall variation strength differs significantly from core to core. This unbalance provides us the unique opportunity to smooth out the overall variation strength across different cores. As shown in Figure 3(a), Core1 suffers large overall variation strength that will incur lots of timing emergencies. The overall variation strength of core4 is negative showing large delay tolerability. If we can exchange the V component of core4 and core1 on the spectrum, it will result in the overall variation strength shown in Figure 3(b), and both cores now become variation mild. The similar situation applies to Core2 and Core3. To switch V component among cores is relatively easy by existing thread migration technique, since V component is mostly thread-dependant. Although T component is also thread-dependant and should not be affected by thread migration, setting up TM frequency (or TM interval) in between the V and T components will only switch the V component and leave T component intact because the two components locate in different frequency regions.

From the frequency domain analysis, we can draw two important conclusions:

- **Optimization Potential:** The unbalanced variation strength on each core can be smoothed out through thread migration. By exchanging V components, each core can obtain the best P, T and V combination that results in smaller overall variation strength and less timing emergencies. But the potential of the scheme is core and application specific. For example in Figure 3(c), there is not much room to optimize however we switch the V components. Our scheme leverages the intrinsic unbalance among cores. It cannot work if all cores are equally timing risky. Since PVT variations naturally create unbalance in the system, our scheme works for most cases as shown in Section 6.
- **Optimization Strategy:** Knowing the individual P, V, and T component is critical to guide specific optimization strategy. As in Figure 3(b), we switch the V components between Core1/Core4 and Core2/Core3 respectively to keep their low variation strength level. The rational behind the spectrum grafts lies in the spectrum separation. P and T component resides at low-frequency region with the center frequency around 300KHz, while the V component mainly stays in high-frequency region with center frequency around 25MHz. To effectively leverage the complementary effects between T and V, the TM frequency has to be properly set without affecting T component. In another word, we want to keep TM frequency higher than T component to achieve frequency separation. T component is determined by the millisecond thermal constant, which indicates the TM interval to be smaller than millisecond. We will show later in this paper that we can safely set TM intervals that meet the frequency separation while incurs little performance overhead.

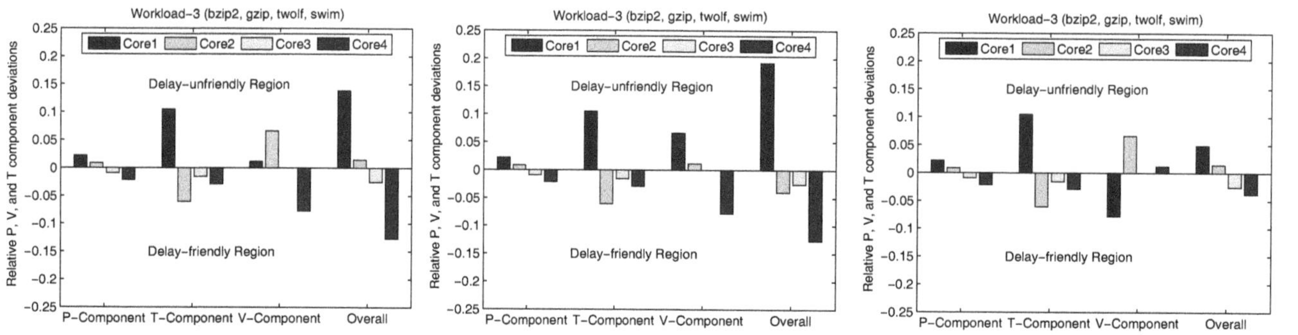

(a) Original deviation breakdown (b) Thermal-oriented optimization (c) Timing Emergency-oriented optimization

Figure 4: Thermal-oriented optimization vs. Timing Emergency-oriented optimization

TEA-TM is not a thermal management scheme, though many previous thermal-related schemes use the thread migration technique as well [15]. The basic principle of thermal management for a multi-core processor is to exchange the thread on the hottest core with that on the coolest one, expecting to balance the temperature distribution. But from the timing emergency perspective, such thermal-oriented operation can be misleading. Figure 4 shows the reason. Originally, Core1 is the hottest and Core2 is the coolest. To reduce the timing emergency in the traditional thermal management scheme, Core1 and Core2 will exchange their threads. Figure 4(b) shows the overall variation strength of Core1 after the migration. Unfortunately, the variation strength of Core1 increases significantly because the thread on Core2 happens to be voltage violent at the migration moment, which causes even more timing emergencies in Core1. The fundamental reason behind that is the thermal-oriented migration schemes disregard the V components. In contrast, according to our TEA-TM scheme, exchanging the threads between Core1 and Core4 can yield lower overall timing emergencies, as Figure 4(c) shows.

Hence, TEA-TM scheme is not a simply extension from existing thermal management schemes. Temperature based migration is not always helpful if we cannot setup a proper migration strategy based on the frequency separation of variation sources. Simply migrating hot thread with mild voltage to a cool core may not be optimal. Migrating cool thread with violent voltage to a hot core may introduce more timing emergencies. This discovery differentiates our work from others.

3.3 Time Domain Explanation

We explain the scheme at the time-domain as shown in Figure 5. Core1 has relatively low temperature, but Core3 has higher temperature after a period of execution. Moreover, thread running on Core3 exhibits to be more voltage-violent than the thread running on Core1. Obviously, Core 3 will experience more timing emergencies than Core1. After we exchange their threads, both cores will be relatively relaxed in timing. The idea can be simply explained as to switch the voltage-violent threads to process- and temperature-mild cores to average out the variation impact. PVT variations affect the circuit delay with different time and space span so that their circuit effects may not always aggregate. If the system can detect the real-time P and T conditions of all the cores and V conditions of all the threads, optimizations can be applied to alleviate the total variation impact of the system.

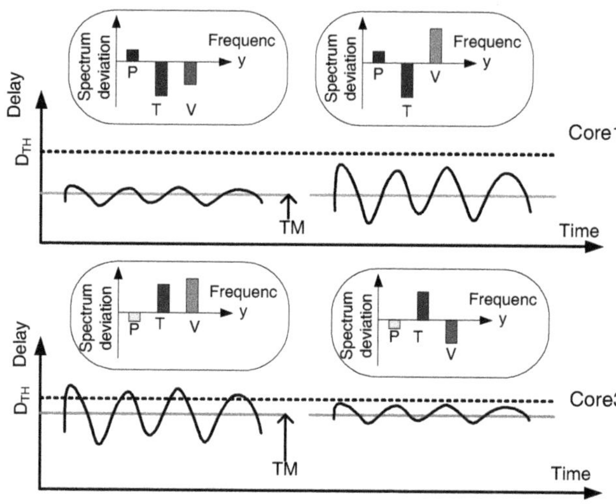

Figure 5: Time-domain explanation of TEA-TM

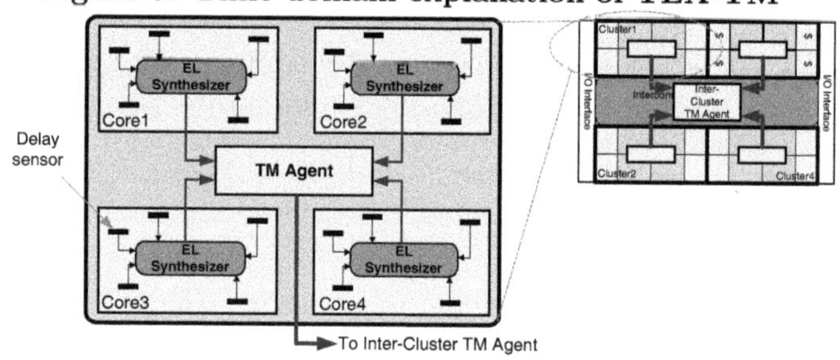

Figure 6: The Framework of TEA-TM

4. IMPLEMENTATION OF TEA-TM

This section discusses three major challenges encountered from implementing TEA-TM and presents several techniques and algorithms to solve them.

Without loss of generality, the implementation assumes a quad-core processor, as shown in Figure 6, which can also be thought of as a typical cluster for future many-core systems [19]. The TM Agent is responsible for generating TM control signals. Multiple delay sensors are deployed into each core to provide accurate and real-time critical delay values. Although these delay sensors faithfully reflect EL, the "raw" delay information is still not enough to guide specific TM strategy. We need to extract corresponding variation strength of P, V, and T components. This brings the first design challenge.

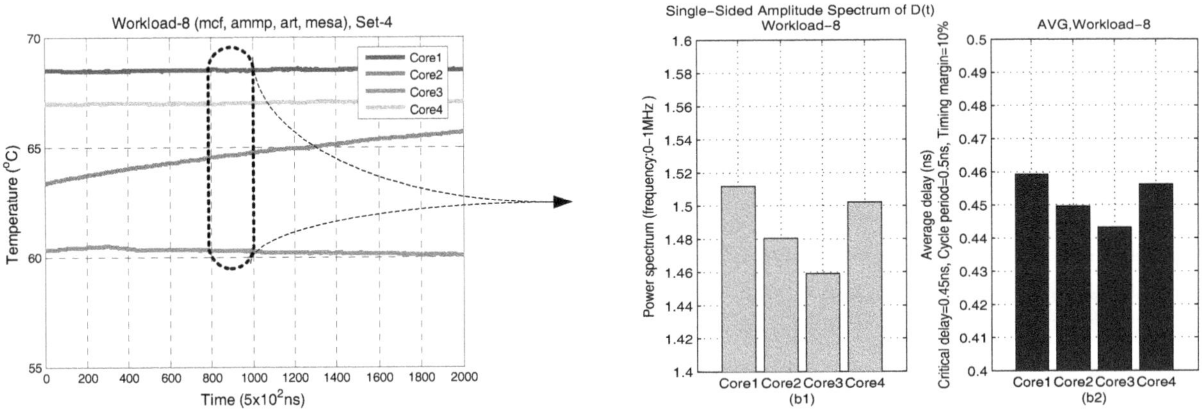

(a) Temperature for four cores (b) Correlation between temperature and the mean of delay

Figure 7: Using mean of delay values to inter temperature

4.1 Challenge 1: Infer PVT component from Delay Values

Although the frequency analysis in Section 3 can clearly provide the variation strength or each component, the computation and associated storage requirement makes the real-time FFT prohibitively complicated. To reduce the hardware cost, we seek an alternative solution.

Considering that the scheme actually does not need to discriminate between P and T components, because the slow-varying T and static P affect the processor core in almost equivalent manner in a TM interval. We refer P and T component to a unified PT component and discuss how to extract it through delay values.

• **Use mean delay to infer PT component.** Because P and T variations reside in low frequency region (<1MHz), while the delay values cover many random samples with spectrum span up to 250MHz, the arithmetic mean value of all the delay samples serves as a good approximation to reflect the low frequency PT component. To prove this argument, we conduct the following experiment as Figure 7(a) shows. We extract the thermal trace for a quad-core processor running four SPEC2000 benchmarks. In this experiment, we only consider T component since P is simply a DC constant for each core. Within the rectangular period indicated by the dotted lines, Core1 is the hottest, followed by Core4, Core2, and Core3. We conduct FFT on the circuit delay values for the same period. We plot the total variation strength of PT component (below 1MHz) for each core on Figure 7(b1). Comparing to the temperatures of the four cores shown in 7(a), we find that the temperature of each cores is well correlated with the their PT component.

Furthermore, we find that using the mean delay to approximate PT component is very effective. Figure 7(b2) shows the average delay of the same period. We find that the average delay is also well correlated with the core temperature. This greatly simplifies the hardware to extract PT component of each core since calculating the mean delay only needs an accumulator and shifters. This simplification greatly facilitates cost-efficient implementation of TEA-TM.

• **Infer V component.** As pointed out in Section 3, TEA-TM needs two types of information. The variation conditions of the cores are mostly dictated by low-frequency PT component, which can be directly calculated from mean delay. The variation conditions of the thread are mainly related to the high-frequency V components, which cannot be obtained through simple mathematics — this bring us the second challenges. We will propose a greedy approach to avoid the explicit dependence on V component in our TEA-TM scheme in following subsection.

4.2 Challenge 2: On-the-fly TEA-TM Decision Making

Unlike the TM for thermal management where the agents responsible for making TM decisions operate at milliseconds, our TM decision making agent has to finish at small time span requiring more efficient algorithms.

The basic policy is to migrate the most voltage-violent thread to the most process- and temperature-mild cores, as Section 3 explains. However, we cannot directly calculate the V component explained in Section 4.1. We observed that a core associated with small PT component and high EL typically has large V component and tend to be running a voltage-violent thread. In contrast, a core with large PT component but low EL typically has small V component. This observation motivates a decision making policy based on EL and PT component only, and thereby obviating the need for calculating the exact V component.

Consider M cores c_1, c_2, ..., c_M and N threads p_1, p_2, ..., p_N, $N \leq M$. Assume at the start of the kth TM interval, the predicted PT components of the M cores are $PT_1(k)$, $PT_2(k)$, ..., $PT_M(k)$, respectively, and the predicted EL of the N threads are $EL_1(k)$, $EL_2(k)$, ..., $EL_N(k)$. Without loss of generality, we assume that before migration, thread p_i is assigned to c_i, $i = 1, 2, \ldots, N$.

We propose two heuristics to guide the decision making procedure.

• **Urgent First Policy (UFP):** We rank the N threads according to their EL, and sort them with location index $L_{EL} = [a_1, a_2, \ldots, a_N]$. The thread with highest EL is assigned to a_1. For example, $a_1 = 2$ means Thread 2 (p_2) has the highest EL. We also prioritize the M cores according to their PT, and sort them in $L_{PT} = [b_1, b_2, \ldots, b_M]$. The most PT-violent core is assigned to b_1. For example, $b_1 = 3$ means Core 3 (c_3) has the highest EL. The specific relocation strategy can be expressed as migrating thread a_1 to core b_M, thread a_2 to the core b_{M-1}, and so on.

This heuristic is not always optimum because it may waste some cores' tolerability. Assume thread a_1 has the highest EL mainly due to high temperature, but not voltage fluctuation. Switching this thread to PT-mild cores may not be optimum in terms of the overall EL reduction, since the PT-mild core

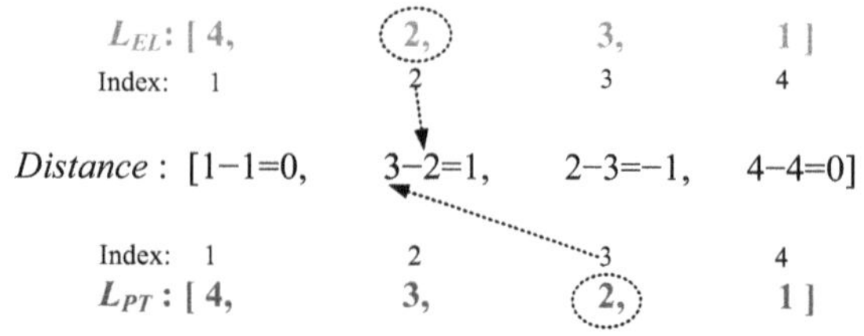

Figure 8: Example: Distance calculation for DUFP

should have been assigned to a voltage-violent thread. This is mostly due to the fact that we cannot directly calculate V component but use EL as an indicator instead.

• **Distance Driven Urgent First Policy (DUFP):** To overcome the disadvantage of UFP, we propose DUFP to further improve the effectiveness. Here, we present an example to clarify the policy. Assume we have $L_{EL} = [4, 2, 3, 1]$ and $L_{PT} = [4, 3, 2, 1]$. In this case, p_4 has the highest EL indicating largest V component. But p_4 is running on c_4 and c_4 has highest EL. This means p_4 might not be the most voltage-violent thread since the high EL might be due to the high PT component on this core. To consider this factor, we define *distance* between L_{EL} and L_{PT}.

For example, c_2 takes the third place in L_{PT}, while p_2 takes the second place in L_{EL}. The distance is calculated as $3-2 = 1$ as shown in Figure 8. Similarly, we can calculate the distance of the other cores. The larger distance implies that the thread is likely to be more voltage-violent, and should be assigned to a PT-mild core. If two cores have the same distance, the thread running on the core with higher EL gets priority. This results in a TM pattern for the next interval as follows:

- Thread 2 will migrate to Core 1;
- Thread 4 will migrate to Core 2;
- Thread 1 will migrate to Core 3;
- Thread 3 will migrate to Core 4.

As for a comparison, the TM pattern of UFP policy for the same case is shown below:

- Thread 4 will migrate to Core 1;
- Thread 2 will stay on Core 2;
- Thread 1 will migrated to Core 4;
- Thread 3 will stay on Core 3.

4.3 Challenge 3: On-the-fly Variation Prediction

The objective of TEA-TM is to reduce the timing emergencies in the future. According to our decision-making heuristics, we need to predict the EL and PT component of the next TM interval based on their historical values. We use a linear prediction mechanism to fulfill this purpose.

The theory of linear prediction is fundamental to many signal processing applications. Least-square method is commonly applied in the linear regression to identify the parameters of the process models [20][21].

Our problem can be expressed as

$$Z(k) = \sum_{i=1}^{M} a_i \times Z(k-i) \tag{4}$$

We predict $Z(k)$ using a linear combination of M most recent past samples. The integer M is called the prediction order. Some training samples are necessary to determine the parameters a_i, i=1,2,..., M. Assuming T training samples

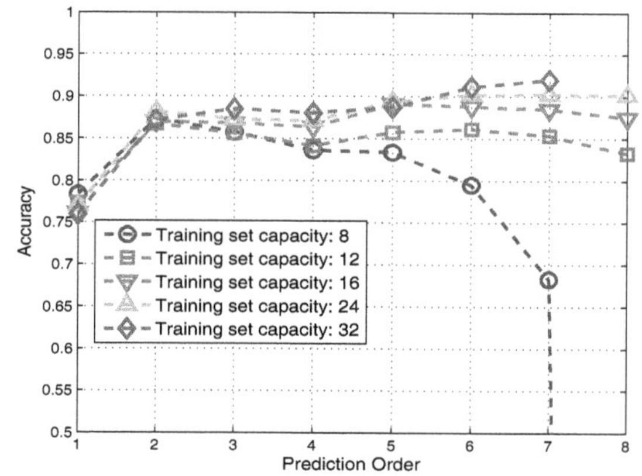

Figure 9: Accuracy vs. Prediction Order and Sample Capacity

are available, i.e $Z(b_1)$, ..., $Z(b_T)$. The following equation can be obtained:

$$Y = XA, \tag{5}$$

where

$$A = [a_1, a_2, \ldots, a_M]^T \tag{6}$$

$$X = \begin{bmatrix} Z(b_1-1) & Z(b_1-2) & \cdots & Z(b_1-M) \\ Z(b_2-1) & Z(b_2-2) & \cdots & Z(b_2-M) \\ \vdots & \vdots & \ddots & \vdots \\ Z(b_T-1) & Z(b_T-2) & \cdots & Z(b_T-M) \end{bmatrix},$$

and

$$Y = [Z(b_1), Z(b_2), \ldots, Z(b_T)]^T.$$

If X^TX is non-singular, the least-squares estimator can be calculated by

$$A = (X^TX)^{-1}X^TY. \tag{7}$$

When X^TX is singular, $A = \mathbf{1}$ is adopted. The parameter A can be updated with the newly available training samples.

The prediction accuracy is affected by two parameters: prediction order and training size. Our experimental results show that neither high nor low prediction order yields the best prediction accuracy. Figure 9 shows the results of using the simplest one order predictor —a typical "last-value" predictor for EL prediction. The accuracy on average is between 75% and 80%. Two-order predictor can reach up to 87%. Higher orders do not necessarily perform better, probably because the high-order predictors involve too many states that can hurt some locality. Moreover, Figure 9 indicates that higher-order predictors need larger training samples. Overall, a five-order predictor is good enough for EL prediction achieving 90% accuracy.

For PT prediction, one order predictor is sufficient since the P component never changes, and the T component can be thought as unchanged for small TM intervals.

4.4 Hardware Cost

All the implementation above is cost-efficient. We assume the processor has already equipped with the capability of thread migration and rollback checking. Besides delay sensors, we don't need any other sensors. For each delay sensor in the core, two accumulators are implemented: one for recording the EL and the other for calculating the mean delay. We implemented the five-order EL prediction logic with

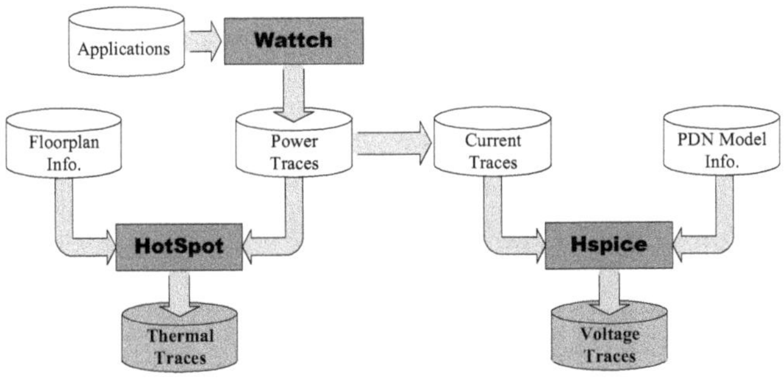

Figure 10: Experiment methodology

Table 1: Processor core configuration

Parameter	Configuration
Clock Frequency	2GHz
Fetch/Issue/Commit	4
Issue Queue/ROB	20/80
Load/Store Queues	64
Functional Units	4-Int/1-cycle latency, 4-FP/7-cycle
Branch Predictor	8K Hybrid Bimodal
L1 I-Cache/D-Cache	64KB, 64B blocks 2-way/4-way, 1-cycle
L2 Cache	2MB, 256B blocks, 8-way, 12-cycle

16 training sets and the DUFP logic in Verilog. The netlist synthesized with Synopsys Design Compiler only consists of several thousands of logic gates. Overall, the hardware cost is negligible.

5. EXPERIMENTAL METHODOLOGY

Figure 10 shows our experimental framework. For each workload, the power traces are generated by Wattch [22]. With a Alpha21246-like floorplan information, we use HotSpot [8] to generate the temperature traces. To get the voltage traces, we first convert the power traces to current traces under a constant voltage level. To get the voltage variation of each core, we use the current traces as stimuli for stressing power delivery network. We use Hspice simulation to expose accurate voltage fluctuations (the simulation time of each workload is about 45 minutes on a 2.33GHz 8-core Xeon workstation).

5.1 Processor Configuration and Workloads

We extend a homogeneous two-core processor used in [14] to a quad-core processor. The processor cores are based on modified SimpleScalar simulator [23]. Each core has private L1 data and instruction caches and L2 caches are shared. Both the L1 data and L2 caches are write-back and write-allocate. The baseline processing core configurations are listed in Table 1.

We use ten mixed workloads from SPEC CPU2000 benchmarks, as Table 2 shows. The workload combinations are similar to that used in [9]. We use SimPoint [24] to sample the simulation intervals based on standard single simulation points configuration. We assign the ten workloads to ten different quad-core processors with each processor suffering different process variation.

5.2 Power Delivery Network

The power delivery networks (PDN) for the modern processors are hierarchically organized. We take a quad-core processor, resembling to Intel Xeon 5500 series processor, as the PDN of our processor. Figure 11(a) illustrates the recommended PDN design for Intel Xeon Processors [25]. The

Table 2: Mixed workloads for quad-core processor

No.	Benchmarks	Property (INT/FP)
1	gcc, gzip, mcf, vpr	int, int, int, int
2	crafty, eon, vortex, vpr	int, int, int, int
3	bzip2, gzip, twolf, swim	int, int, int, fp
4	vortex, vpr, eon , lucas	int, int, int, fp
5	gcc, eon, art, equake	int, int, fp, fp
6	gzip, twolf, ammp, lucas	int, int, fp, fp
7	gcc, applu, mgrid, galgel	int, fp, fp, fp
8	mcf, ammp, art, mesa	int, fp, fp, fp
9	art, lucas, mgrid, swim	fp, fp, fp, fp
10	ammp, applu, mesa, equake	fp, fp, fp, fp

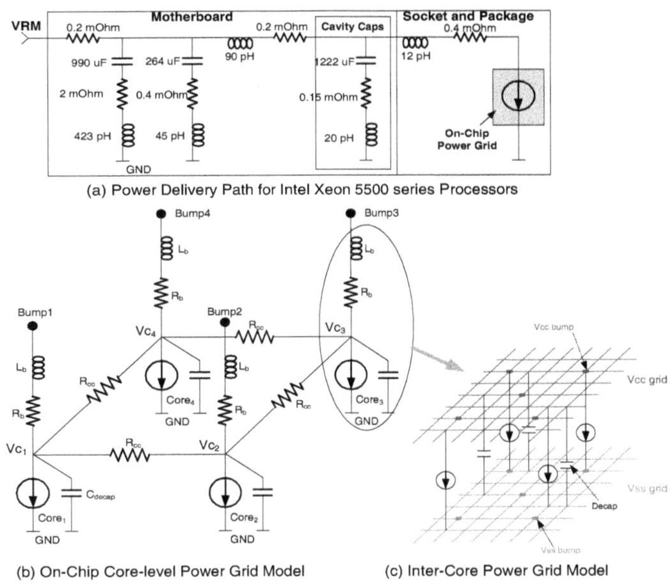

Figure 11: Intel Xeon processor 5500 series-based power delivery impedance model path [25]

power budget is 130W (peak 150W) at the highest voltage level of 1.35V, which is close to the spec of our simulated processors. We use a lumped power grid model for the quad-core processor, as Figure 11(b) shows. To highlight the intra-core power supply interactions and keep the simulation short, we use the following simplification: 1) each core was modeled with a time-varying current source and a decoupling capacitance C_{decap}; 2) the intra-core current paths are modeled with a resistor R_{cc}; 3) multiple voltage bumps serve as the voltage supplier to the cores, through a bump inductor L_b and resistor $R_b = 0.1mOhm$. In our PDN model, $C_{decap} = 400nF$, $R_{cc} = 10mOhm$, $L_b = 0.1nH$, which comply with a typical 500-pin flip-chip package.

5.3 Relations between PVT Variations and Circuit Delay

As shown in Eq.(2), we need to obtain experience constants for PVT and delay relations. We conducted a detailed Hspice simulation on ISCAS85 Benchmarks circuits. Figure 12 shows HSPICE results for c880, a representative ISCAS85 circuit. We implemented the circuit using the high-performance version of PTM models [26], with 32nm technology. The simulation results indicate that within the temperature range of 25–105^oC, the delay linearly increase by about 1.7 picosecond per degree centigrade (1.7ps/^oC). The linear relationship also holds for voltage variation (0.55ps/mV). Similar linear trend is also applicable for process variation [27].

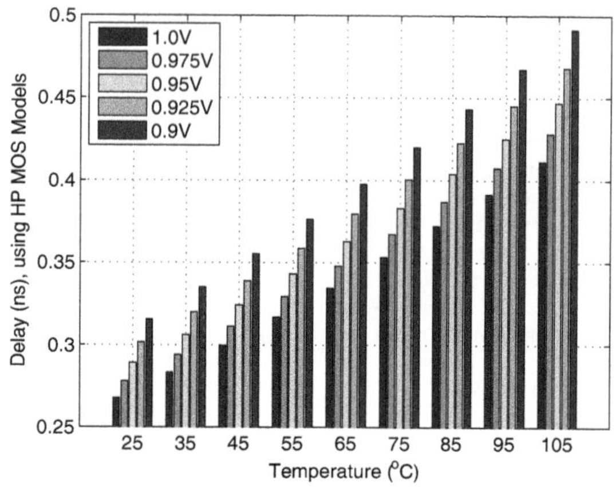

Figure 12: Delay vs (Temperature and Voltage)

Table 3: Parameters used in simulations

Parameters	Values
Timing Threshold	10% cycle period
Process Variation (σ/μ)	1%
Voltage Specification (V_{spec})	1.05V
Temperature Specification (T_{spec})	341K
Frequency	2GHz
Simulation Time	8 million cycles
Wattch Sampling Interval	10 cycles/sample
Hotspot sampling Interval	1K cycles/sample

5.4 Parameter Definitions

Table 3 lists the set of adopted parameters. We assume optimistic 1% process variation and we believe this static variation is relatively easy to compensate using other techniques. Nevertheless, larger process variation can actually improve the effectiveness of our scheme, since larger process variation introduces more unbalance across the cores. The thermal constant is estimated as follows: chip thickness 0.5mm; silicon thermal conductivity $100W/m \cdot K$, copper thermal conductivity $400W/m \cdot K$; silicon thermal capacitance $1.75 \times 10^6 J/m^3 \cdot K$; copper thermal capacitance $3.55 \times 10^6 J/m^3 \cdot K$. The chip's thermal constant should be between 2.2ms and 4.4ms [8].

5.5 Metrics

Higher EL implies higher failure rate and higher performance loss. We assume the performance loss is positively correlated with both EL and IPC for a given thread i, as shown in Eq.(8).

$$P_{loss,i} = \eta \times EL_i \times IPC_i \quad (8)$$

where η is a constant. Based on $P_{loss,i}$, we use relative metric to evaluate the effectiveness of TEA-TM.

Throughput Loss: We define the total Throughput Loss (TL) with N threads running in the processor as the sum of the performance loss of each thread.

$$TL = \sum_{i=1}^{N} P_{loss,i} \quad (9)$$

We define Relative Throughput Loss (RTL) as Eq.(10).

$$RTL = \frac{TL^{\text{w/o TEA-TM}} - TL^{\text{w/ TEA-TM}}}{TL^{\text{w/o TEA\_TM}}} \quad (10)$$

Fairness: TEA-TM leverages the variation and delay unbalance naturally resides in processor cores and always tries to balance them, thereby brings the benefit of fairness across

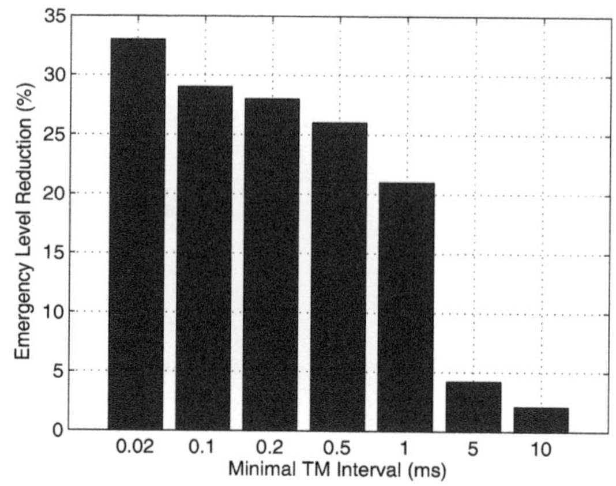

Figure 13: Impact of TM interval on average EL reduction

cores. We use the standard deviation based-metric to evaluate the fairness, defined as

$$Fairness = \frac{1}{\left(\frac{1}{N}\sum_{i=1}^{N}(P_{loss,i} - \overline{P_{loss}})^2\right)^{\frac{1}{2}}} \quad (11)$$

where, $\overline{P_{loss}} = \frac{1}{N}\sum_{i=1}^{N} P_{loss,i}$.

Based on that, we have the Relative Fairness (RF) improvement for the TEA-TM:

$$RF = \frac{Fairness^{\text{w/ TEA-TM}} - Fairness^{\text{w/o TEA-TM}}}{Fairness^{\text{w/o TEA-TM}}} \quad (12)$$

6. SIMULATION RESULTS

6.1 Timing Emergency Reduction

First, we want to investigate the potential of the scheme to reduce EL. The effectiveness is closely related to TM intervals, assuming perfect EL prediction accuracy. In the frequency domain analysis, we have pointed out that TEA-TM only want to switch the high-frequency V component across cores but keeps the low-frequency PT component intact. This means a high TM frequency (or short TM interval) is beneficial for frequency separation. In time domain, this means to find a relatively short TM interval during which the process and temperature cannot change much but the voltage can fluctuate a lot. Figure 13 shows the average EL reduction of ten workloads. We find the EL reduction can reach up to 30% when TM interval is 0.02ms, and is still above 20% with TM interval of 1ms. The effectiveness quickly diminishes with TM increasing to 5-10ms. The result agrees well with the thermal constant (2ms) where TM interval larger than 2ms can no longer separate the V and PT component.

Although a TM interval of 0.02ms can provide the best improvement, this is the ideal case without considering the overhead of thread migration. Previous study shows such frequent TM (60K cycles for 3GHz) can result in about 30% throughput loss [14]. In the later discussion, we adopt a TM interval between 0.1 and 1ms.

Figure 14 shows the EL improvement for 10 workloads. For most cases, TEA-TM reduces the overall EL by a significant amount. However, the potential is workload-specific. The poorest case is for workload 2 — only marginal improvement achieved. This is because all of the threads in workload 2 are high-IPC threads and therefore very power-intensive. This results in high temperature in every core so that there are

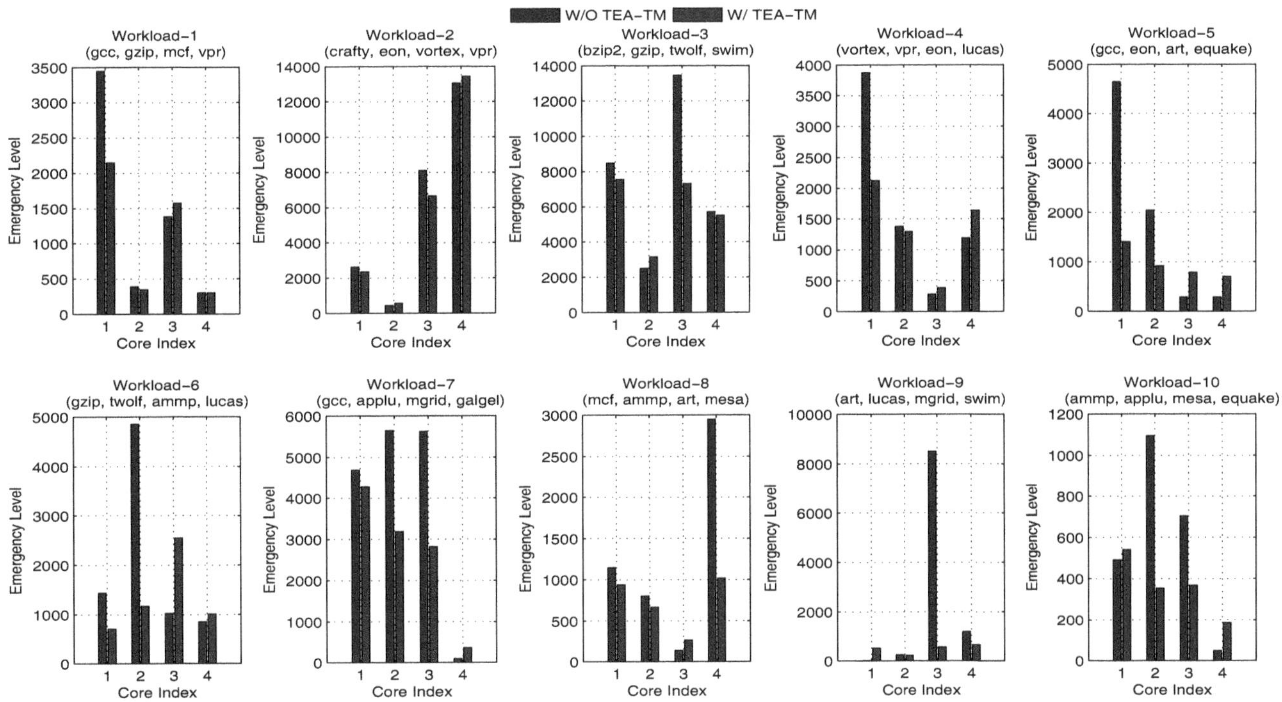

Figure 14: Potential of EL improvement under perfect EL prediction, TM interval: 0.2ms

no mild-cores left for optimization. For other workloads the potential is significant since there are always some mild-cores in the system for tolerating voltage-violent threads.

All the above potential investigation assumes perfect EL prediction with 100% accuracy. We also want to study the impact of imperfect EL prediction. Two types of predictors are evaluated: the simple "last-value" predictor which provides about 80% accuracy and a five-order, 16 training capacity predictor which provides 90% accuracy. Figure 15 shows the percentage EL reduction for different EL prediction accuracies. Even with simpler predictor, we can still achieve meaningful EL reduction from 15% to 25%. The simplest "last-value" predictor can still provide 20% EL reduction with TM interval of 0.2ms. The predictor is barely a register which proves TEA-TM is very cost-effective in hardware overhead. Even a 90% accurate, five-order, 16 training capacity predictor doesn't cost much hardware. Another implication is accuracy matters more for larger TM intervals. Compared with 100% accuracy predictor, the "last-value" predictor degrades about 35% in EL reduction for 1ms TM interval, while it only degrade 26% for 0.1ms TM interval. Therefore, it would be worthy of paying more hardware for accurate predictor when deploying large TM intervals in TEA-TM.

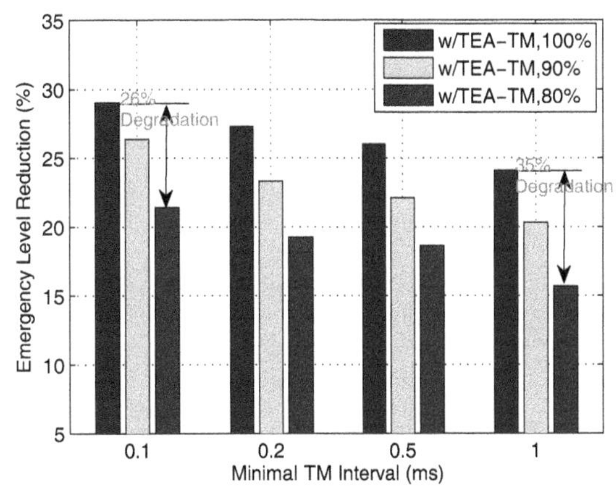

Figure 15: Impact of EL prediction accuracy on average EL reduction

6.2 Relative Throughput Loss Reduction and Fairness

A more strict metric for evaluating the scheme is to use Relative Throughput Loss (RTL) rather than EL since RTL includes the thread IPC information. In this section, we study the RTL reduction of three TM decision-making policies: UFP, DUFP, and Oracle (the hypothetical TM decision-making policy based on predicted EL and requiring post data processing and exhaustive search).

Figure 16 shows that TEA-TM can reduce 22% RTL on average with the simplest UFP policy under 90% EL prediction accuracy. Switching to the more complicated DUFP policy adds marginal 3% RTL reduction on average (but for some workloads such as 8 and 10, DUFP can provide decent 7% improvement). Compared with the 35% RTL reduction for oracle policy, there is still much headroom to improve. The large discrepancy between the oracle and the proposed policies lies in the fact that we cannot directly obtain V component. Both policies try to infer V component through EL which can be directly calculated through delay values. Although EL correlates closely with V component, it always carry errors due to other factors. Meanwhile, we find the RTL reduction changes little with different EL prediction accuracies. The RTL reduction only changes from 23% with perfect predictor to 21% with simplest predictor. These observations imply that TM decision making policy is the bottleneck in the current TEA-TM scheme. Developing sophisticated heuristics is more critical than pushing prediction accuracy to higher level.

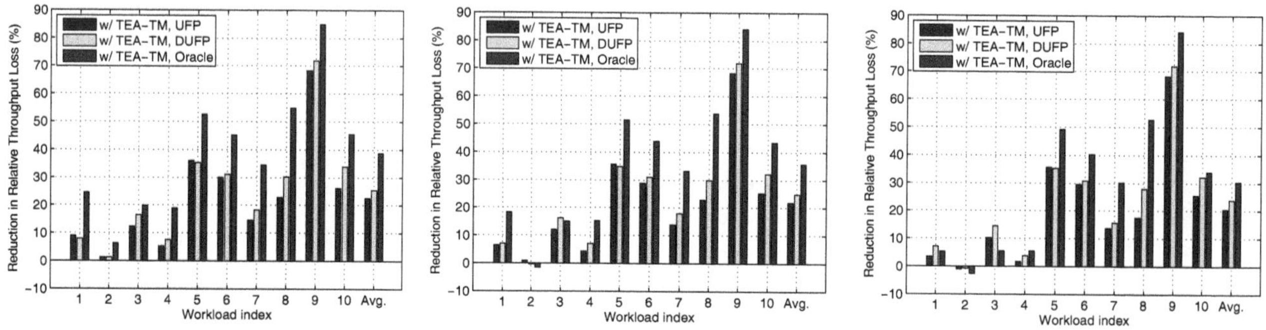

(a) EL prediction accuracy: 100% (b) EL prediction accuracy: 90% (c) EL prediction accuracy: 80%

Figure 16: Reduction in Relative Throughput Loss. TM Interval: 0.2ms

For workload 2 in Figure 16(b) and (c), TEA-TM generates negative results, even with the Oracle TM policy. This is first because the optimization potential for the workload 2 is very limited. The high IPC of the benchmarks make all the cores equally bad thus eliminates the opportunity for TEA-TM. Also the imperfect predictor may lead to incorrect or unnecessary thread migrations and introduce additional performance overhead. Therefore for the workloads with limited potential, temporary disabling TEA-TM will be a preferred option.

Fairness: Variations naturally introduce EL unbalance among cores. TEA-TM tries to balance the EL across cores through thread migration. In another word, the fairness of the system can be improved. As shown in Figure 14, take the workload 9 for example, the EL of core 3 is eight times larger than the other three cores without TEA-TM. This happens due to a violent thread running on a slow and hot core. If we apply TEA-TM, the burden of running violent thread is shared across the other three mild cores, resulting in all cores' EL kept below a small value. This balance in EL will translate into the fairness of the whole system, as Figure 17 shows. With the UFP and DUFP policy, TEA-TM offers up to 80% fairness improvement on average. For some extreme case such as workload 9, the fairness improvement can be around 400%. The oracle policy can improve 350% fairness on average. In other words, TEA-TM is a fairness-improving scheme which can greatly help smooth the EL unbalance in a multi-core processor. Variations create process, temperature, and voltage unbalance which ultimately lead to delay and timing unfairness in a multi-core architecture. TEA-TM in turn serves as a perfect candidate for such architectures under variations.

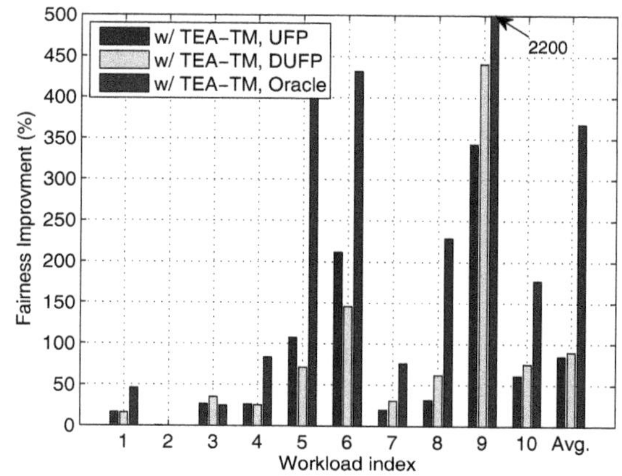

Figure 17: Fairness Improvement. TM Interval: 0.2ms, EL prediction accuracy: 90%

7. RELATED WORK

Timing Variation. The implication of device variability on the full-chip timing is discussed in details in [28][10][2] Sarangi et al. studied the possibility of utilizing processors with variation-induced timing errors [29] by trade off the error rate with performance, power, and hardware cost. Gupta et al. also recognized that PVT variations together determine the ultimate timing variation and proposed to use microarchitectural-level recovery mechanism to approach average case design [30]. Razor [31] scheme is another archetype of using delayed error detection to help improve the chips' power efficiency. Unlike their approach, we take the advantage of complementary effects in multi-core processors and only use judicious TM to maximize the tolerability to timing errors.

Process Variation. Variable latency techniques for structures such as caches, register files, and pipeline stages can address device variability by tuning architectural latencies [27][32]. Voltage interpolation and fine-grain body bias have also been proposed to mitigate the delay impact of process variation [4][5]. Considering that process variation results in different power profile across cores, the researches proposed to allocate the applications to the cores with lower power consumption, thereby maximizing the power efficiency [33][16]. These approaches, however, is oblivious to temperature and voltage variations and miss the opportunity to leverage the complementary effects to relax the optimization for process variation.

Voltage Variation. A novel voltage variation modeling algorithm was proposed in [34]. Powell et al. proposed the "Pipeline Damping" approach [6] to restrain the rate of current change, thereby indirectly limiting the voltage variation. Mohamood et al. designed an inductive noise controller [35] to alleviate the voltage variation. Recently, Reddi et al. found the voltage emergency can be predicted by monitoring the execution patterns [36], thereby dispensing the voltage sensors which are "notorious" for large response latency. Gupta et al. proposed a "DeCoR" architecture to reactively handle the power noise by engaging a checkpointing and rollback mechanism [7]. Gupta et al. also proposed a software assisted approach [37] to predict voltage emergency through program signatures. These approaches only strive to defend voltage integrity and may be not sufficient to deal with timing emergency as we discussed in Section 2.

Temperature Variation. A temperature model was proposed in [8] and the HotSpot tool motivates many researches on temperature management. Many dynamic thermal management schemes were surveyed in [38][9] [39][40]. Puttaswamy et al. studied the thermal issues in 3D microarchitectures [41]. However, due to the intrinsic thermal sensor latency, the existing thermal management scheme cannot effectively exploit the relatively fine-grained voltage-mild/-violent phase characteristics of a thread due to large operation interval. Although a temperature-balanced situation could be indirectly beneficial to reduce timing emergencies, the aid is probably too far to be helpful.

8. CONCLUSIONS

We proposed TEA-TM, a novel scheme to reduce timing emergencies resulted from PVT variations. Unlike the prior solutions that strive to keep individual P, V, and T in check, TEA-TM leverages the core-level complementary effect between PVT variations. We find that migrating the voltage-violent threads to temperature- and process-mild cores can create variation-mild environment, thereby reducing timing emergency rate. We further offer insights on how the PVT variations can be co-optimized from frequency and time domain perspective. These insights guide to an efficient TEA-TM implementation which only relies on delay sensors. The experimental results show on average TEA-TM can help save up to 24% throughput loss, at the same time improving the fairness by 85% compared with the processor without TEA-TM.

9. ACKNOWLEDGMENTS

The work was supported in part by National Basic Research Program of China (973) under grant No. 2005CB321604, in part by National Natural Science Foundation of China (NSFC) under grant No.(60806014, 60831160526, 60633060, 60921002), and in part by Hi-Tech Research and Development Program of China (863) under grant No.2009AA01Z126.

10. REFERENCES

[1] ITRS, "Process Intergration, Devices, and Structures," 2007 Edition.

[2] O.S. Unsal, J.W. Tschanz, K. Bowman, V. De, X. Vera, A. Gonzalez, and O. Ergin, "Impact of Parameter Variations on Circuits and Microarchitecture," *IEEE Micro*, pp. 30–39, 2006.

[3] X. Liang, D. Brooks, and G.Y. Wei, "A Process-Variation-Tolerant Floating-Point Unit with Voltage Interpolation and Variable Latency," *ISSCC*, pp. 404–405, 2008.

[4] X. Liang, G.Y. Wei, and D. Brooks, "ReVIVaL: A Variation-Tolerant Architecture Using Voltage Interpolation and Variable Latency," *ISCA*, pp. 191–202, 2008.

[5] R. Teodorescu, J. Nakano, A. Tiwari, and J. Torrellas, "Mitigating Parameter Variation with Dynamic Fine-Grain Body Biasing," *Micro*, pp. 27–42, 2007.

[6] M.D. Powell, and T.N. Vijaykumar, "Pipeline damping: a microarchitectural technique to reduce inductive noise in supply voltage," *ISCA*, pp. 72–83, 2003.

[7] M. S. Gupta, K. Rangan, M. D. Smith, G.Y. Wei, and D. M. Brooks, "DeCoR: A Delayed Commit and Rollback Mechanism for Handling Inductive Noise in Processors," *HPCA*, pp. 381–392, 2008.

[8] K. Skadron, M.R. Stan, W. Huang, S. Velusamy, K. Sankaranarayanan, and D. Tarjan, "Temperature-Aware Microarchitecture," *ISCA*, pp. 2–13, 2003.

[9] J. Donald, and M. Martonosi, "Techniques for Multicore Thermal Management: Classification and New Exploration," *ISCA*, pp. 78–88, 2006.

[10] K.A. Bowman, S.G. Duvall, and J.D. Meindl, "Impact of die-to-die and within-die parameter fluctuations on the maximum clock frequency distribution for gigascale integration," *JSSC*, vol. 37, pp. 183–190, Feb. 2002.

[11] B. Lasbouygues, R. Wilson, N. Azemard, and P. Maurine, "Timing Analysis in Presence of Supply Voltage and Temperature Variations," *ISPD*, pp. 10–16, 2006.

[12] R. B. Staszewski, S. Vemulapalli, P. Vallur, J. Wallberg, and P. T. Balsara, "1.3 V 20 ps time-to-digital converter for frequency synthesis in 90-nm CMOS," *IEEE Trans. on Circuits and Systems II*, pp. 220–224, 2006.

[13] S. Henzler, S. Koeppe, W. Kamp, H. Mulatz, and D. Schmitt-Landsiedel, "90nm 4.7ps-Resolution 0.7-LSB Single-Shot Precision and 19pJ-per-Shot Local Passive Interpolation Time-to-Digital Converter with On-Chip Characterization," *ISSCC*, pp. 548–549, 2008.

[14] T. Constantinou, Y. Sazeides, P. Michaud, D. Fetis, and A. Seznec, "Performance implications of single thread migration on a chip multi-core," *ACM SIGARCH Computer Architecture News*, vol. 33, no. 4, pp. 80–91, 2005.

[15] P. Michaud, A. Seznec, D. Fetis, Y. Sazeides, and T. Constantinou, "A Study of Thread Migration in Temperature-Constrained Multicores," *ACM Trans. Archit. Code Optim.*, vol. 4, no. 2, pp. 1–28, 2007.

[16] K.K. Rangan, G.Y. Wei, and D. Brooks, "Thread Motion: Fine-Grained Power Management for Multi-Core Systems," *ISCA*, pp. 302–313, 2009.

[17] M. Prvulovic, Z. Zhang, J. Torrellas, "ReVive: cost-effective architectural support for rollback recovery in shared-memory multiprocessors," *ISCA*, pp. 111–122, 2002.

[18] D.J. Sorin, M.M.K. Martin, M.D. Hill, D.A. Wood, "SafetyNet: Improving the Availability of Shared Memory Multiprocessors with Global Checkpoint/Recovery," *ISCA*, pp. 123–134, 2002.

[19] M. Tremblay and S. Chaudhry, "A Third-Generation 65nm 16-Core 32-Thread Plus 32-Scout-Thread CMT SPARC Processor," *ISSCC*, pp. 82–83, 2008.

[20] P. P. Vaidyanathan, *The Theory of Linear Prediction.* Morgan & Claypool Publishers series, 2008.

[21] X. Chen, "Recursive least-squares method with membership functions," *International Conference on Machine Learning and Cybernetics*, pp. 1962–1966, 2004.

[22] D. Brooks, V. Tiwari, and M. Martonosi, "Wattch: a framework for architectural-level power analysis and optimizations," *ISCA*, pp. 83–94, 2000.

[23] D. Burger, and T. Austin, "The SimpleScalar Tool Set, Version 2.0," *Computer Sciences Department, University of Wisconsin-Madison, Technical Report 1342*, 1997.

[24] T. Sherwood, E. Perelman, G. Hamerly, and B. Calder, "Automatically Characterizing Large Scale Program Behavior," *ASPLOS*, pp. 45–57, 2002.

[25] Intel, "Voltage Regulator Module (VRM) and Enterprise Voltage Regulator-Down (EVRD) 11.1," *Design Guidelines*, March 2009.

[26] W. Zhao, and Y. Cao, "New generation of Predictive Technology Model for sub-45nm early design exploration," *IEEE Trans. on Electron Devices*, vol. 53, pp. 2816–2823, Nov. 2006. http://www.eas.asu.edu/~ptm.

[27] X. Liang, and D. Brooks, "Mitigating the Impact of Process Variations on Processor Register Files and Execution Units," *Micro*, pp. 504–514, 2006.

[28] S. Borkar, T. Karnik, S. Narendra, J. Tschanz, A. Keshavarzi, and V. De, "Parameter Variations and Impact on Circuits and Microarchitecture," *DAC*, pp. 338–342, 2003.

[29] S. Sarangi, B.Greskamp, A. Tiwari, and J. Torrellas, "EVAL: Utilizing Processors with Variation-Induced Timing Errors," *Micro*, pp. 423–434, 2008.

[30] M.S. Gupta, J.A. Rivers, P. Bose, G.Y. Wei, and D. Brooks, "Tribeca: Design for PVT Variations with Local Recovery and Fine-grained Adaptation," *Micro*, pp. 435–446, 2009.

[31] S. Das, D. Roberts, S. Lee, S. Pant, D. Blaauw, T. Austin, K. Flautner, and T. Mudge, "A Self-Tuning DVS Processor Using Delay-Error Detection and Correction," *JSSC*, vol. 41, pp. 792–804, Apr. 2006.

[32] A. Tiwari, S. R. Sarangi, and J. Torrellas, "ReCycle: Pipeline Adaptation to Tolerate Process Variation," *ISCA*, pp. 323–334, 2007.

[33] R. Teodorescu, and J. Torrellas, "Variation-Aware Application Scheduling and Power Management for Chip Multiprocessors," *ISCA*, pp. 363–374, 2008.

[34] E. Grochowski, D. Ayers, and V. Tiwari, "Microarchitectural Simulation and Control of di/dt-induced Power Supply Voltage Variation," *HPCA*, pp. 7–16, 2002.

[35] F. Mohamood, M.B. Healy, S.K. Lim, and H.S. Lee, "A FloorplanAware Dynamic Inductive Noise Controller for Reliable 2D and 3D Microprocessors," *Micro*, pp. 3–14, 2006.

[36] V.J. Reddi, M.S. Gupta, G. Holloway, M.D. Smith, G.Y. Wei, and D. Brooks, "Voltage Emergency Prediction: A Signature-Based Approach To Reducing Voltage Emergencies," *HPCA*, pp. 18–29, 2009.

[37] M. S. Gupta, K. K. Rangan, M. D. Smith, G.Y. Wei, and D. Brooks, "Towards a software approach to mitigate voltage emergencies," *ISLPED*, pp. 123–128, 2007.

[38] D. Brooks, and M. Martonosi, "Dynamic Thermal Management for High-Performance Microprocessors," *HPCA*, pp. 171–182, 2001.

[39] W. Wu, L. Jin, J. Yang, P. Liu, Sheldon X.-D. Tan, "Efficient power modeling and software thermal sensing for runtime temperature monitoring," *ACM Trans. Des. Autom. Electron. Syst.*, vol. 12, no. 3, pp. 1–29, 2007.

[40] I. Yeo, C.C. Liu, and E.J. Kim, "Predictive dynamic thermal management for multicore systems," *DAC*, pp. 734–739, 2008.

[41] K. Puttaswamy, and G. H. Loh, "Thermal Herding: Microarchitecture Techniques for Controlling Hotspots in High-Performance 3D-Integrated Processors," *HPCA*, pp. 193–204, 2007.

Relax: An Architectural Framework for Software Recovery of Hardware Faults

Marc de Kruijf, Shuou Nomura, Karthikeyan Sankaralingam
Vertical Research Group
University of Wisconsin – Madison
{dekruijf, nomura, karu}@cs.wisc.edu

ABSTRACT

As technology scales ever further, device unreliability is creating excessive complexity for hardware to maintain the illusion of perfect operation. In this paper, we consider whether exposing hardware fault information to software and allowing software to control fault recovery simplifies hardware design and helps technology scaling.

The combination of emerging applications and emerging many-core architectures makes software recovery a viable alternative to hardware-based fault recovery. Emerging applications tend to have *few I/O and memory side-effects*, which limits the amount of information that needs checkpointing, and they allow *discarding individual sub-computations* with small qualitative impact. Software recovery can harness these properties in ways that hardware recovery cannot.

We describe Relax, an architectural framework for software recovery of hardware faults. Relax includes three core components: (1) an ISA extension that allows software to mark regions of code for software recovery, (2) a hardware organization that simplifies reliability considerations and provides energy efficiency with hardware recovery support removed, and (3) software support for compilers and programmers to utilize the Relax ISA. Applying Relax to counter the effects of process variation, our results show a 20% energy efficiency improvement for PARSEC applications with only minimal source code changes and simpler hardware.

Categories and Subject Descriptors

C.0 [**Computer Systems Organization**]: General—*Hardware/Software Interfaces*; C.4 [**Computer Systems Organization**]: Performance of Systems—*Fault Tolerance*

General Terms

Design, Performance, Reliability

1. INTRODUCTION

As CMOS technology scales, individual transistor components will soon consist of only a handful of atoms. At these sizes, transistors are extremely difficult to control in terms of their individual power and performance characteristics, their susceptibility to soft errors caused by particle strikes, the rate at which their performance degrades over time, and their manufacturability – concerns commonly referred to as *variability*, *soft errors*, *wear-out*, and *yield*, respectively. Already, the illusion that hardware is perfect is becoming hard to maintain at the VLSI circuit design, CAD, and manufacturing layers. Moreover, opportunities for energy efficiency are lost due to the conservative voltage and frequency assumptions necessary to overcome unpredictability.

This trend towards increasingly unreliable hardware has led to an abundance of work on hardware fault detection [21, 25, 27, 33, 36] and recovery [3, 8, 32, 38]. Additionally, researchers have explored architectural pruning [26] and timing speculation [12, 14, 15] as ways to mitigate chip design and manufacturing constraints. However, in all cases these proposals have focused on conventional applications running on conventional architectures, with a typical separation of hardware and software concerns.

In this paper, we observe two complementary trends in emerging applications and architectures that favor a new overall architectural vision: hardware faults recovered in software. Below, we explain these trends, articulate the challenges in designing an architecture with software recovery, and finally describe our proposed framework, Relax.

Emerging applications – applications that continue to drive increases in chip performance – include computer vision, data mining, search, media processing, and data-intensive scientific applications. Many of these applications have two distinct characteristics that make them interesting from a reliability perspective. First, and a key observation unique to this work, is that many have *few memory side-effects* at the core of their computation. In particular, state-modifying I/O operations are rare and memory operations are primarily loads, because the compute regions of these applications perform reductions over large amounts of data. Second, for many emerging applications, a perfect answer is not attainable due to the inherent computational complexity of the problem and/or noisy input data. Therefore, they employ approximation techniques to maximize the qualitative "usefulness" of their output. This suggests that these applications might be *error tolerant*, which has been observed in prior work as well [6, 11, 22, 23, 42]. In this paper, we specifically explore the phenomenon that the application can *discard* computations in the event of an error.

The concurrent architecture trend is that massively multicore architectures are emerging to meet the computational

ISCA'10, June 19–23, 2010, Saint-Malo, France.

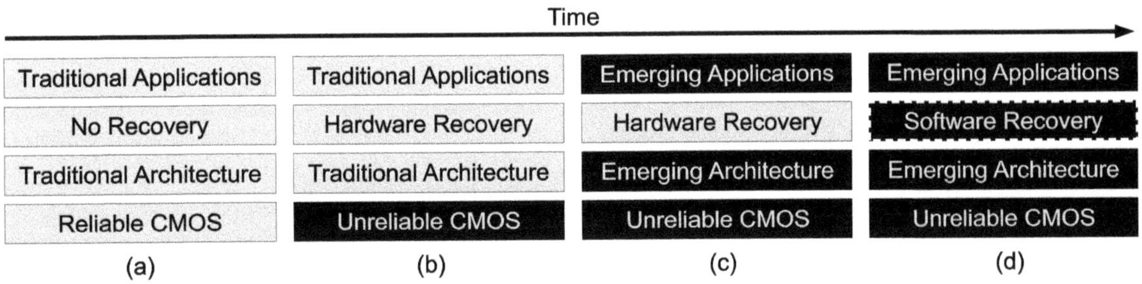

Figure 1: The evolution of hardware, architecture, and applications in the context of Relax.

demands of emerging applications [13, 16, 19]. These architectures often employ simple, in-order cores to maximize throughput and energy efficiency with little or no support for speculative execution or buffering. Hence, the paradigm that hardware misspeculation-recovery mechanisms can be repurposed for error recovery does not apply for these architectures. The valuable chip real estate that would otherwise be devoted to hardware recovery resources could be better spent elsewhere if software recovery were efficient.

Overall, the combination of limited side-effects and error tolerance that exists in large portions of emerging applications renders hardware recovery inflexible, unnecessarily conservative, and too expensive for emerging many-core architectures. Figure 1 shows the evolutionary path to software recovery considering these trends in hardware, architecture, and applications. Historically, traditional applications running on traditional superscalar processor architectures built with perfect CMOS devices required no recovery (Figure 1(a)). Even with imperfect CMOS, these applications still work best utilizing hardware recovery when running on traditional processor architectures (Figure 1(b)). However, with emerging applications running on emerging many-core architectures, hardware recovery introduces the inefficiencies we have described (Figure 1(c)). In the future, while hardware substrates will be unreliable, we require mechanisms that provide flexibility to software and keep the architecture simple. An architecture that exposes hardware errors to allow software recovery enables synergy between applications and architectures as shown in Figure 1(d).

The design of a system architecture that allows such software recovery of hardware faults involves many important questions and challenges. The first and most obvious question is whether changes to the ISA are necessary. To answer this question, we refer to prior studies that show application tolerance to arbitrary instruction-level errors is very poor [6, 11, 23, 22, 42]. Operations relating to control flow and memory accesses are failure prone and constitute a large percentage of application operations. For an architecture to allow reasonably fine-grained software recovery without ISA changes, it would be necessary for the hardware to somehow distinguish these "critical" operations from the "non-critical" operations as it executes code. To date, no one has been able to propose an efficient way to do this. Hence, ISA support appears necessary.

The next logical question concerns what form ISA support should take. Software recovery of hardware faults has been proposed before in the context of software detection, using compiler-automated triple-modular redundancy (TMR) [8]. TMR makes sense when the overhead of detection is already very high, as is the case with comprehensive software detection. However, it is expensive and does not allow the application to exploit error tolerance. A more efficient solution that allows an application to choose its own form of recovery is closer to ideal.

Yet still more questions follow: How might the application writer express software recovery in the application? How can applications be designed to behave predictably when errors occur non-deterministically? Are there ways in which the software development process can be automated or assisted? What should be the hardware organization – should all cores have no recovery support, or just some cores? Are there special considerations for the hardware microarchitecture?

In this paper, we propose a holistic architectural framework, called Relax, that provides specific answers to each of these questions. We divide Relax into three core components: (1) an ISA extension, (2) hardware support to implement the Relax ISA, and (3) software support for applications to use the Relax ISA. We discuss each component in a separate section:

- **ISA extension:** In Section 2, we describe the Relax ISA extension, which enables software to register a fault handler for a region of code. The extension allows applications to encode behavior similar to the *try/catch* behavior found in modern programming languages. The ISA behavior is intuitive to programmers, and the compiler and hardware combine to make guarantees about the state of the program as the region is executed. We also provide a rigorous definition of the ISA's semantics.

- **Hardware support:** We cover the hardware support for Relax in Section 3. The Relax ISA's semantics allow hardware design simplification and provide energy efficiency by relaxing the reliability constraints of the hardware. We describe support for fault detection and discuss hardware organizations that support Relax. We show that mechanisms such as aggressive voltage scaling, frequency overclocking, and turning off recovery mechanisms provide adaptive support for Relax. We also consider statically heterogeneous architectures, where cores are constructed with different reliability guarantees at design time.

- **Software support:** In Section 4, we develop a C/C++ language-level recovery construct to expose the Relax ISA extension to developers. We propose two key ideas: *relax blocks* to mark regions that may experience a hardware fault, and optional *recover blocks* to specify recovery code if a fault occurs. Our results indicate promise for alternative forms of application support as well, such as automated support through compiler static analysis or profile-guided compilation.

To support Relax, we develop performance models to guide the development of "relaxed" applications. The models, discussed in Section 5, determine the efficiency of Relax based on application and architecture characteristics and can be used to compute the achievable efficiency improvements for a given application, recovery behavior, and architecture combination. We evaluate Relax in Sections 6 and 7, where we apply our language construct and Relax compiler to real applications, and simulate how Relax enables energy efficiency gains using process variation as a case study. We discuss directions for future work in Section 8, related work in Section 9, and finally we conclude in Section 10.

2. ISA SUPPORT

In this section, we discuss the ISA component of the Relax framework. In Section 2.1, we describe the Relax ISA extension and briefly introduce our language-level construct, which we use to illustrate how high-level recovery behavior is mapped onto the ISA. In Section 2.2 we describe the ISA semantics in detail.

2.1 ISA & Compiler Support

We sketch a simple C function example to motivate and explain software recovery, and use this example to introduce Relax's ISA extension. Code Listing 1 shows a simple C function and how it is augmented with Relax support and compiled to a sequence of instructions. Listing 1(a) shows the simple summation function and Listing 1(b) shows this function augmented to use Relax. The function uses our *relax/recover* construct, which is analogous to the *try/catch* construct of high-level languages that support exceptions. For the purposes of the example, the next paragraph provides a brief overview of the construct. Section 4 gives more details and uses.

In Code Listing 1(b), all code except the return statement is wrapped in a *relax block*. Code inside a relax block is susceptible to failure, where a hardware fault detected inside the block constitutes failure. The optional variable `rate` specifies a relax block's probability of failure. Without it, the hardware dictates this probability independent of the application. In some situations, this variable is important to make reasonable guarantees about the quality of an application's output. If a failure occurs, control transfers to the *recover block*. In this case, the recover block contains a retry statement, which causes re-execution of the relax block.

To support this behavior through the ISA, Code Listing 1(c) shows the assembly code for this function with the Relax additions highlighted. For readability, we use symbolic register names rather than numbered registers. A single instruction (`rlx`) communicates the start and end of relax blocks to the hardware. When used to enter a relax block, the `rlx` instruction optionally reads a general purpose register containing the desired failure rate, as well as the offset of the PC address to the recovery block, to which the hardware automatically transfers control on failure. The same instruction with a PC offset of 0 signals the end of the relax block. Within the relax block, the execution semantics of the hardware are relaxed. A rigorous definition of what this means follows in Section 2.2.

Compiler support for Relax is relatively straightforward. The compiler sets up the recovery block and adds compensating code to save or recover state if necessary. In the case of the example function, the function has no side-effects and therefore has no state, beyond its input state, that needs to be restored in the event of a failure. If a failure occurs inside the function, it is sufficient to simply jump back to the beginning of the function, as Code Listing 1(c) demonstrates, with the guarantee that the input registers have not been overwritten. The compiler transparently enforces this guarantee simply by knowing that such a control path exists, thereby effectively implementing a software checkpoint. The checkpoint is extremely lightweight: the compiler only saves state that is strictly required. In this case, the two inputs, `list` and `len`, must either be saved to the program stack or must occupy available registers. Five physical registers are needed to store all the live variables in this function. If five are available, Relax adds no software overhead.

2.2 ISA Semantics

Relax allows instructions to commit potentially erroneous state, while the compiler ensures that this state is either discarded or overwritten after the fault is discovered and recovery is initiated. For the compiler to ensure recovery from the fault, the resulting error must be a *Locally Correctable Error* (LCE), as defined by Sridharan et al. [39]. Hence, the error must be spatially and temporally contained, which forces the following hardware constraints:

1. Errors must be spatially contained to the target resources of a relax block's execution. In other words, an instruction must not commit corrupted state to a register or memory location not written to by other instructions in the relax block. For stores, this means that a store must not commit if its destination address is corrupt, or if the store is reached through erroneous control flow. A simple (but high overhead) way to handle this is to stall on the error detection logic prior to committing a store. For other instructions that write only to registers, a tight coupling between the detection logic of the destination register datapath and the instruction commit logic enables rapid resolution of writes to incorrect destination registers.
2. The contents of memory locations must not spontaneously change, e.g. due to a particle strike. Relax depends on traditional mechanisms such as ECC to protect memories, caches, and registers from soft errors. Other errors that cannot be temporally contained to the scope of a relax block, such as most faults in the cache coherence or cache writeback logic, are also not recoverable by Relax.
3. Arbitrary control flow is not allowed. Control flow must follow the program's static control flow edges. Note that faulty control *decisions* are still acceptable since the static control flow is not violated.
4. Hardware exceptions must not trigger until hardware detection ensures that the exception is not the result of an undetected hardware fault.
5. Specifically under retry behavior (as in the example of Code Listing 1), an instruction may not store to a volatile address: on re-execution, the store might write to a different address and the initial store is then an irreversible data corruption. Atomic read-modify-write operations, such as an atomic increment, are also problematic to handle under retry behavior without violating the atomicity constraint. For this reason, relax blocks using retry may not currently contain any atomic read-modify-write operations.

Code Listing 1 A simple summation function (a) modified to use Relax (b) and the assembly output produced by the compiler (c). For (c), the Relax additions are in bold. The RECOVER label can be folded away but is included for clarity.

```
int sum(int *list, int len) {
  int sum = 0;
  for (int i = 0; i < len; ++i) {
    sum += list[i];
  }
  return sum;
}
```

(a)

```
int sum(int *list, int len) {
  relax (rate) {
    int sum = 0;
    for (int i = 0; i < len; ++i) {
      sum += list[i];
    }
  } recover { retry; }
  return sum;
}
```

(b)

```
ENTRY:
  rlx ${rate}, RECOVER  # Relax on
  mv  0 -> $sum
  ble $len, 0, EXIT
LOOP_PREHEADER:
  mv  0 -> $i
LOOP:
  sll $i, 2 -> $tmp
  ld  [$list + $tmp] -> $tmp
  add $sum, $tmp -> $sum
  add $i, 1 -> $i
  blt $i, $len, LOOP
EXIT:
  rlx 0    # Relax off
  ret $sum
RECOVER:  # Relax automatically off
  jmp ENTRY
```

(c)

```
    RECOVER:
√     rlx ${1/rate}, RECOVER
√     mv  0 -> $sum
√     ble $len, 0, EXIT
X     mv  0 -> $i
      sll $i, 2 -> $tmp
?     ld  [$list + $tmp] -> $tmp
```

Figure 2: An example of Relax's execution behavior.

Execution may leave a relax block once the hardware detection guarantees error-free execution. In the event of an error, the hardware must trigger recovery at some point before execution leaves the relax block.

An example that illustrates Relax's ISA semantics in action is shown in Figure 2. It uses the instruction stream from Code Listing 1(c). The `rlx`, `mv`, and `ble` instructions all complete and commit successfully but a fault occurs executing the second `mv` that is initially undetected and so the instruction commits as normal. Next, the result of the `sll` instruction is pipeline bypassed to the `ld` instruction. When the `ld` executes it triggers a page fault exception due to its corrupted input address. Before the exception is handled, the hardware waits for the detection to catch up. The fault from the `mv` is detected and execution jumps back to the `RECOVER` label.

3. HARDWARE SUPPORT

In this section, we present the hardware component of Relax. The Relax ISA's main hardware benefits are design simplification and energy efficiency, while the key hardware requirement is fault detection. We first discuss Relax's hardware benefits, followed by the hardware detection support. We conclude with a description of the overall hardware organization.

3.1 Hardware Simplification

Relax provides sevaral hardware benefits. First, the hardware need not provide support for buffering, checkpointing, or rollback for software-recoverable errors. Second, complicated techniques to combat parameter variations and wearout, such as fine-grained body biasing [40], are less useful under Relax because, by design, variations are more tolerable. Finally, Relax reduces hardware design complexity because design margins to account for silicon uncertainity can be relaxed. This also potentially improves energy efficiency, as it allows hardware to be designed for correct and efficient operation under common case conditions, but with possible failures under dynamically worst case conditions. The overall result is hardware that is error-prone, but is easier to design and potentially more energy efficient. In Section 7, we consider timing faults from process variations and show how Relax provides energy efficiency and design complexity benefits.

3.2 Hardware Detection

Relax requires support for low-latency fault detection in hardware. Two viable alternatives are Argus [25] and redundant multi-threading (RMT) [27]. Argus provides comprehensive error detection specifically targeted at simple cores, and RMT runs two copies of a program on separate hardware threads and compares their outputs to detect faults. In addition, Razor [12] describes support for adaptive failure rate monitoring for timing faults. Relax requires a similar mechanism to ensure the fault rate remains stable if the `rlx` instruction's target fault rate input is specified.

3.3 Hardware Organization

While hardware that implements Relax everywhere and has no recovery support at all is the ideal, it is disruptively different from existing hardware and requires complete software support. Other configurations that partially implement Relax can be incrementally built into existing hardware organizations. In this section, we consider in detail three such organizations with both relaxed hardware

Relaxed Hardware Implementation	Recover Cost	Transition Cost
Fine-grained tasks	5	5
DVFS	5	50
Architectural core salvaging	50	0

Table 1: Parameters for three alternative relaxed hardware designs.

and normal hardware, where relax blocks execute on relaxed hardware and other code executes on normal hardware.

Whether hardware is relaxed or not can be configured either statically or dynamically. In the static case, two types of cores are used: relaxed cores and normal cores. Relax blocks are off-loaded to relaxed cores and other code executes on normal cores. The relaxed cores can use less design guardband and do not need any hardware recovery mechanism. In the dynamic case, circuit techniques like voltage scaling or frequency over-clocking are used to execute relaxed blocks with improved overall efficiency and/or hardware recovery support can be adaptively disabled.

The type of hardware organization affects the performance of Relax. In particular, two costs dictated by the hardware are important: (1) the cost in cycles to detect and initiate recovery, and (2) the cost in cycles to transition into and out of relax blocks. Table 1 gives estimates for these two costs for three different hardware alternatives we examine.

The first alternative is a statically configured architecture with support for fine-grained parallelism, where relax blocks are enqueued on a neighboring, unreliable core with low latency (e.g. Carbon [19]). The cost to recover is the cost of a pipeline flush, approximated at 5 cycles for a simple in-order core, and the cost to transition is the time to enqueue a task, which we estimate at 5 cycles. The second alternative is a dynamically configured architecture that uses dynamic frequency and voltage scaling (DVFS) to enter and exit relax blocks (e.g. Paceline [14]). The cost to recover is again just the cost of a pipeline flush, and we approximate the cost of DVFS at 50 cycles, which the work of Kim et al. suggests is reasonable for on-chip DVFS [17]. Finally, we consider an organization where hardware recovery is adaptively disabled and a thread swap occurs with a neighboring core in the event of a fault (e.g. Architectural Core Salvaging [31]). We assume the cost of a thread swap to recover is 50 cycles, with no cost to transition. We revisit the values in Table 1 when we discuss performance models in Section 5.

4. SOFTWARE SUPPORT

In this section, we use the recovery construct introduced in Section 2.1 to demonstrate how Relax enables the implementation of flexible and efficient recovery policies in software through a series of example use cases. Our use cases derive from the code shown in Code Listing 2, adapted from the x264 video encoding application. The listing shows a C function returning the *sum of absolute differences* over the array inputs `left` and `right`. It provides an example of a computation that is well suited for software-level recovery.

Although this example is taken from x264, many modern, computationally-intensive applications employ computation such as this, i.e. reduction, at the core of their execution. x264 uses a two-dimensional version of this function to search for a predicted frame macroblock's most similar

Code Listing 2 The *sum of absolute differences* code example that is the basis for all use cases.

```
int sad(int *left, int *right, int len) {
  int sum = 0;
  for (int i = 0; i < len; ++i)
    sum += abs(left[i] - right[i]);
  return sum;
}
```

reference frame macroblock. The function measures similarity by performing a pixel by pixel comparison over two macroblocks. A high similarity presents redundancy that can be exploited to minimize the amount of information encoded. The overall process is called motion estimation, which allows for better data compression. The four use cases we explore each perform a different type of recovery over this function. We consider two high-level recovery behaviors: retry (Re) and discard (Di), furthermore distinguished by their granularities: coarse-grained (Co) and fine-grained (Fi). Table 2 illustrates the resulting taxonomy.

Use Case 1: Coarse-Grained Retry (CoRe). Relax and recover blocks can be used to implement coarse-grained retry (CoRe) as shown in the upper-left quadrant of Table 2. This case is the same as shown for the example presented in Section 2.1. Just like the `sum` function, the `sad` function has no memory side-effects and therefore execution can simply jump back to the beginning of the function if a fault occurs, provided the inputs are still available. The Relax compiler performs a control flow analysis over the relax block, sets up the recovery code, and adds compensating code to save or recover state if necessary.

Use Case 2: Coarse-Grained Discard (CoDi). Three difficulties with CoRe are that it (1) potentially requires saving and restoring software state, (2) requires a retry mechanism that can deflect recurring failures, and (3) can hurt performance predictability. For error-tolerant applications, particularly those with real-time constraints, a potentially better alternative is to simply abort the function and return a value that indicates the function output should be disregarded. The code in the upper-right quadrant of Table 2 explores this alternative. In the case of x264, returning a maximum integer value effectively tells the application to disregard this macroblock pair and continue looking. Similar to CoRe, this use case operates at a coarse granularity.

Use Case 3: Fine-Grained Retry (FiRe). Another alternative to CoRe is to retry at a finer granularity to minimize the amount of wasted work on failure. This can be done simply by moving the relax block into the loop as shown in the lower-left quadrant of Table 2. In this case, each individual accumulation is retried on failure. Since the last instruction of the relax block is the accumulation onto `sum`, the old value of `sum` can be immediately overwritten as the block terminates.

Use Case 4: Fine-Grained Discard (FiDi). For functions that allow approximate output, individual accumulation values can be discarded as shown in the lower-right quadrant of Table 2. Note that there is only a single relax block and no recover block. The resulting behavior is as if there was a recover block that was empty (omitting it en-

Coarse-grained, Retry

```
int sad(int *left, int *right, int len) {
  relax (rate) {
    int sum = 0;
    for (int i = 0; i < len; ++i)
      sum += abs(left[i] - right[i]);
  } recover { retry; }
  return sum;
}
```

Use Case 1 (CoRe)

Coarse-grained, Discard

```
int sad(int *left, int *right, int len) {
  relax (rate) {
    int sum = 0;
    for (int i = 0; i < len; ++i)
      sum += abs(left[i] - right[i]);
  } recover { return INT_MAX; }
  return sum;
}
```

Use Case 2 (CoDi)

Fine-grained, Retry

```
int sad(int *left, int *right, int len) {
  int sum = 0;
  for (int i = 0; i < len; ++i)
    relax (rate) {
      sum += abs(left[i] - right[i]);
    } recover { retry; }
  return sum;
}
```

Use Case 3 (FiRe)

Fine-grained, Discard

```
int sad(int *left, int *right, int len) {
  int sum = 0;
  for (int i = 0; i < len; ++i)
    relax (rate) {
      sum += abs(left[i] - right[i]);
    }
  return sum;
}
```

Use Case 4 (FiDi)

Table 2: Our four use cases classified by granularity and recovery behavior.

hances readability). Without the recover block, the variable sum has two possible values at the end of the relax block: either it has been updated with the new value, or it is unchanged. This achieves the desired behavior: on failure, the accumulation value is discarded.

5. APPLICATION DEVELOPMENT

Relax provides hardware energy efficiency improvements by removing the need for hardware recovery support while still allowing hardware faults to occur. However, there are software overheads associated with Relax. In the case of retry behavior, there is the potential cost of saving and restoring state, and also the overhead of the wasted time spent executing failed relax block executions. In the case of discard behavior, failed relax block executions reduce the application's output quality (e.g. image sharpness). To compensate, the application must be configured at a higher quality setting (e.g. more iterations) to achieve the same output quality. This introduces execution time overhead.

In this section, we develop a set of analytical models to help developers reason about the various efficiency considerations. One of the key outcomes of our models is that, depending on application, recovery behavior (e.g. retry vs. discard), and architecture characteristics, we can determine the specific fault rate that maximizes overall efficiency. The models are extended from the probabilistic models for the performance overhead of backward error recovery developed by De Kruijf et al. [9]. We refer the reader to a technical report for details on how we extended the models for Relax [10]. We focus on energy efficiency and specifically energy-delay product (EDP), although our methodology can be trivially extended to other metrics.

Model for Retry Behavior. Our model for retry behavior uses four primary inputs: *cycles*, the execution time in cycles of a relax block, *recover*, the cost in cycles to initiate recovery, *transition*, the cost of transitions into and out of relax blocks, and *rate*, the per-cycle error rate. Using basic probability theory we define a function to compute the overheads due to re-execution triggered by faults. We combine this with a hardware efficiency function that maps a hardware fault rate to the energy efficiency of the hardware

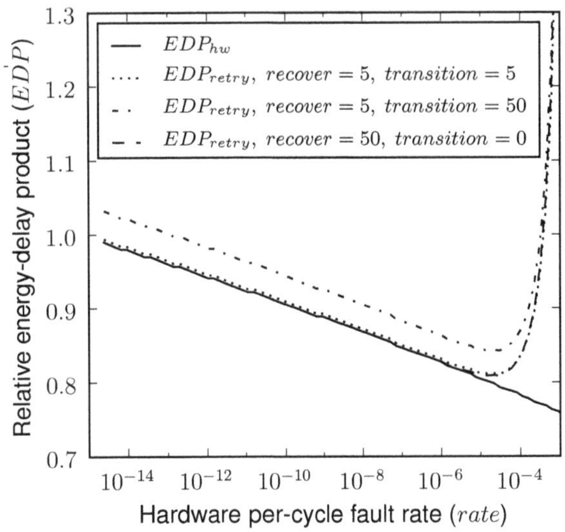

Figure 3: A mapping from fault rate to EDP for different architectural parameters.

relative to hardware that does not allow any faults. We call this function EDP_{hw}. The functions combine to produce a final function that maps a fault rate to the energy-delay of the whole system. We call this function EDP_{retry}. Solving for the derivative of this equation set to zero yields the fault rate that minimizes overall EDP.

For a relax block where *cycles* is roughly 1170, Figure 3 shows a graph evaluating the three hardware organizations from Table 1, using the hardware-specific values for *recover* and *transition* given in columns 2 and 3. We assume there is no overhead to save or restore software state, which we find to be realistic in practice. The solid curve shows a hypothetical EDP_{hw} mapping, which represents the ideal case. The dashed curve considers architectural core salvaging[1], the dotted curve considers fine-grained tasks, and the dash-

[1]For architectural core salvaging, the thread swap on failure effectively doubles the fault rate, since the neighboring core must abort as well. This is not modeled.

dotted curve considers DVFS. The figure shows that, for these three hypothetical design points, Relax provides an approximately 22.1%, 21.9%, and 18.8% optimal EDP reduction for each, respectively. The optimal fault rates are in the range $1.5e^{-5}$ to $3.0e^{-5}$ faults per cycle.

Model for Discard Behavior. The challenge with discard behavior is that an application's output quality depends on the fault rate. We add a new function that maps a combination of an application's input quality setting and the hardware fault rate to the application's output quality. That is, for a target output quality q_o and an input quality setting q_i, $quality(q_i, rate) = q_o$. Then, the constraint $quality(q_i, rate) = quality(q_{i_{base}}, 0)$ for input qualities q_i and $q_{i_{base}}$ ensures that output quality remains constant with Relax (left-hand side) relative to without Relax (right-hand side). We then, extend the retry models with this function to create $EDP_{discard}$. Our technical report presents a detailed discussion of determining the quality function for a given application and relax block, and give examples on how to apply it to the Relax framework [10].

6. EVALUATION METHODOLOGY

While several phenomena can cause faults to occur in the hardware, we evaluate one specific case here. The scenario we consider is Relax in the context of process variations where the hardware is designed to ignore these variations, resulting in some timing faults. This section discusses our evaluation methodology and the next section presents experimental results.

We implemented language support for relax and recover blocks in C/C++ programs using the LLVM compiler infrastructure [20]. We apply the compiler to applications and simulate them using instruction-level fault injection to estimate the potential energy efficiency gains of Relax when coupled with hardware that runs more efficiently in the presence of faults. In Section 6.1 we describe our methodology for evaluating applications using discard behavior specifically. In Section 6.2 we describe our fault injection methodology and in Section 6.3 we discuss performance metrics. Finally, in Section 6.4 we derive a hardware efficiency function to model the impact of allowing errors due to process variations on hardware energy efficiency.

6.1 Evaluating Discard Behavior

Prior work evaluating application-level error tolerance has employed application-specific quality metrics to assess the degree of output quality deterioration [6, 11, 22, 23]. These studies attempt to hold execution time relatively constant while using the error rate to vary output quality. The difficulty with this approach is that it is fundamentally hard to quantify and evaluate variations in output quality.

We provide a novel solution to this problem by taking the converse approach of holding output quality constant while using the error rate to vary execution time. For each application using discard behavior, we define a function that maps an input quality setting and a fault rate to an output quality, and we use it to adjust the input quality setting as we adjust the fault rate to hold output quality constant. The function is the *quality* function discussed at the end of Section 5, and it allows an apples-to-apples comparison across applications. We provide more detail in our technical report [10].

6.2 Fault Injection

To perform detailed quality analysis for discard behavior as described above, we required a simulation framework that would allow us to run relaxed applications to completion on large, representative input data. To meet this challenge, we developed an LLVM instrumentation pass to perform instruction-level fault injection for rapid simulation. We chose LLVM because its virtual ISA closely matches both the x86 and SPARC V9 instruction sets [2], while instrumenting LLVM bytecode is straightforward and flexible. For fault injection, each LLVM instruction inside a relax block is surrounded by code that probabilistically injects an error into the output of that instruction. Although we inject only single-bit errors, the nature of the error is in practice not relevant since corrupted output is ultimately either discarded or overwritten, and hence is never used.

If an error occurs in the address computation of a store instruction, the store does not commit and execution immediately jumps to the recovery destination. If an error occurs in any other instruction, the instruction commits and execution continues as normal, but a recovery flag is set to indicate that an error occurred. When control reaches the end of the relax block, execution jumps to the recovery destination if the recovery flag is set. This behavior is consistent with the ISA semantics described in Section 2.2.

6.3 Performance Metrics

We use execution cycles to measure performance overheads and energy efficiency improvements. To compute execution cycles we record the number of dynamic LLVM instructions executed (not including instructions added for fault instrumentation) and multiply by the CPL (cycles per LLVM instruction) of the relax block. We similarly divide the per-instruction fault rate by the the CPL to compute the per-cycle fault rate.

The validity of using CPL to produce cycle-accurate performance numbers depends on our ability to assert that CPL does not change when relax blocks are augmented with retry or discard behavior. Below, we explain why the two factors that might affect CPL, *instruction mix* and *memory latency*, are not adversely affected by these behaviors. First, all relax blocks we consider have a largely homogeneous instruction mix. Therefore, partial execution of a relax block has a CPL very close to the overall CPL of the block, and certainly averaged over many millions of executions, the CPL will tend towards the CPL of the whole block. Second, for memory latency, we note that retry behavior will re-execute over data that is already cached, and therefore our measured CPL will be an *overestimate*, while for discard behavior, any early termination will place more weight on up-front loads that bring in potentially uncached compute data, yielding an *underestimate*. We accept the overestimating factor and our results for retry behavior are therefore conservative. For discard behavior, we observe that none of our applications are structured with up-front loads since the relax blocks are in all cases iterating over simple array structures. We assert that the overestimating effect is therefore negligible.

6.4 Hardware Efficiency Model

De Kruijf et al. extend the VARIUS model [35] for process variations to provide estimates for the efficiency of hardware allowing timing faults for the OpenRISC core design [9]. The resulting model outputs the relative energy efficiency

Application Name	Function Name	Function % Exec. Time
barneshut	RecurseForce	>99.9
bodytrack	InsideError	21.9
canneal	swap_cost	89.4
ferret	isOptimal	15.7
kmeans	euclid_dist_2	83.3
raytrace	IntersectTriangleMT	49.4
x264	pixel_sad_16x16	49.2

Table 4: Application functions and percentage of execution time inside each function.

of a given processor design as the error rate is varied. We applied the methodology developed by De Kruijf et al. to develop our hardware efficiency function, which we use in our evaluation to model hardware that runs more efficiently in the presence of timing faults induced by process variations. Details of the function's derivation are in our technical report [10].

7. RESULTS

This section presents results using and evaluating the Relax framework. In Section 7.1 we show evidence for the *error tolerance* phenomenon by identifying applications from the PARSEC benchmark suite that are tolerant to discarded computations. We then show in Section 7.2 the results applying our language constructs to each of these applications. We show that relax block regions account for large portions of application execution times, and that the phenomenon of *limited memory side-effects* allows Relax to work with essentially no software overhead. Finally, using our efficiency mapping driven by process variations, we evaluate energy-delay improvement using Relax in Section 7.3. Overall, our results show that 20% improvement in energy efficiency is common, and the optimal fault rate is highly application dependent, varying by several orders of magnitude.

7.1 Evidence for Error Tolerance

We identified seven applications from the PARSEC benchmark suite [7] employing approximation techniques. However, two applications, fluidanimate and streamcluster, did not have an easily identifiable input quality parameter, which was needed to evaluate discard behavior. Since this was merely an artifact of their implementation, we replaced them with more straightforward alternatives from the same application domain. We replaced fluidanimate with barneshut, a physics application from the Lonestar Benchmark Suite [18], and streamcluster with kmeans, a clustering application from NU-MineBench [29].

Table 3 shows the details for each application. Columns 1-3 show the application name, benchmark suite, and application domain, respectively. Columns 4-5 concern evaluation of discard behavior only, and show the input quality parameter used to configure output quality and the quality evaluator used to evaluate output quality, respectively.

7.2 Application Relaxation

The seven applications were modified to implement the four use cases described in Section 4. For each application, we modified only a single, dominant function to use Relax. More functions exist, but evaluating all of them was beyond the scope of this work. Table 4 identifies each application's function and the percentage of execution time spent inside the function. Percentages were measured using the Google Performance Tools CPU profiler [1] running applications natively on a 2.53 GHz Core 2 Duo processor and include time spent in external library calls.

Six of the seven applications were evaluated for all four use cases FiRe, CoRe, FiRe, and FiDi. Barneshut could only support the two fine-grained use cases FiRe and FiDi. Table 5 shows detailed statistics for each application. Columns 2-5 show the length of each relax block in cycles. Columns 6 and 7 show the percentage of executed LLVM instructions affected by Relax for each use case. Combined with the data from Table 4, we see that for three applications more than 70% of the application is relaxed, for two others roughly 50% is relaxed, and for the last two less than 20% is relaxed. Columns 8 and 9 show the number of C/C++ source code lines modified or added. In all cases, the number of changes is very low. Relax blocks do not appear to obstruct code readability and are in most cases straightforward to implement. Finally, columns 10 through 11 show the number of register spills needed to set up a software checkpoint for retry behavior. The numbers assume an architecture with 16 general purpose integer registers and 16 floating point registers. In all cases, there is no software checkpointing overhead; the functions are side-effect free, and simple enough that there is insufficient register pressure to force additional register spills to save input state. Even with register pressure, the number of extra registers needed is between zero and two.

7.3 Execution Time and Energy Efficiency

Figure 4 shows execution time and energy-delay product (EDP) for each application and use case relative to execution without Relax. The triangles plot fault rate versus execution time and the stars plot fault rate versus EDP. EDP is measured applying our hardware efficiency function to the square of the execution time. The figure also shows the results predicted by our models developed in Section 5; the dotted curves plot the fault rate versus predicted execution time and the solid curves plot the fault rate versus predicted EDP. The x-axis ranges are centered around the predicted optimal fault rate. We model hardware with fine-grained task support, presented earlier as the first entry in Table 1, and hence model the hardware costs to initiate recovery and transition in and out of relax blocks at 5 cycles each.

For retry behavior, the results show that a 20% reduction in EDP is common for CoRe, and that CoRe tends to perform better than FiRe. In some cases, execution time with FiRe is very high, as with kmeans and x264. For these applications the fine-grained relax block size is only 4 cycles, and the 5 cycle cost to transition in and out of the relax block forces high overheads.

For discard behavior, we see two flavors of results: *ideal* and *insensitive*. The graphs are annotated with these labels. In the *ideal* cases, changing the input quality setting and/or injecting errors into the application affects behavior in a way that is very regular and consistent. As a result, the discard behavior results for CoDi and FiDi closely mirror those for CoRe and FiRe. The two differences are that (1) in some cases discard behavior cannot support a fault rate quite as high as retry behavior, and (2) the resulting data are slightly more noisy. However, discard behavior will still be the more desirable alternative when performance predictability is more important than output predictability, as

Application Name	Benchmark Suite	Application Domain	Input Quality Parameter	Quality Evaluator
barneshut (fluidanimate)	Lonestar (PARSEC)	Physics modeling	Distance before approximation	SSD[a] over body positions, relative to maximum quality output
bodytrack	PARSEC	Computer vision	Number of simultaneous body particles	Application-internal likelihood estimate
canneal	PARSEC	Optimization: local search	Number of iterations	Change in output cost, relative to maximum quality output
ferret	PARSEC	Image search	Maximum number of iterations	SSD[a] over top 10 ranking, relative to maximum quality output
kmeans (streamcluster)	NU-MineBench (PARSEC)	Data mining: clustering	Number of iterations	Application-internal validity metric
raytrace	PARSEC	Real-time rendering	Rendering resolution	PSNR of upscaled image, relative to high resolution output
x264	PARSEC	Media encoding	Motion estimation search depth	Encoded output file size relative to maximum quality output

[a]SSD = Sum of squared differences

Table 3: The seven applications modified to use Relax.

Application Name	Relax Block Length in Cycles				Percentage of Function Relaxed		Source Lines Modified		Checkpoint Size (Register Spills)	
	CoRe	CoDi	FiRe	FiDi	CoRe / CoDi	FiRe / FiDi	CoRe / CoDi	FiRe / FiDi	CoRe	FiRe
barneshut	N/A	N/A	98	98	N/A	70.6	N/A	6	N/A	0
bodytrack	775	812	25	25	76.3	47.8	2	2	0	0
canneal	2837	2837	115	115	99.8	62.0	2	8	0	0
ferret	4024	4077	12	11	99.6	72.3	2	4	0	0
kmeans	81	81	4	4	99.5	65.8	2	2	0	0
raytrace[a]	2682	2682	136	136	96.5	67.7	2	6	0	0
x264[a]	1174	1174	4	4	99.9	76.2	2	2	0	0

[a]SSE is emulated for x264 and raytrace

Table 5: Details for each application's function and the various use cases implemented.

might be the case with a real-time ray tracer or an online data clustering algorithm.

The *insensitive* discard behavior cases are bodytrack and x264. For bodytrack, the algorithm effectively only has two outputs: either the tracked body position is close, or it is off because the algorithm has lost a handle on the body position. For the quality settings we used, the algorithm did not lose the body position at fault rates of less than $1e^{-3}$ for CoDi and $2e^{-2}$ for FiDi. Hence, any lower fault rate setting produced effectively equivalent output quality, and, due to the nature of discard behavior, the execution time of the program was shortened by the faults and EDP improved. For x264, the reasons are slightly different. For x264 with the reference input we used, it was very difficult to affect the output quality by adjusting the input quality at all. Even at the lowest setting, with a 40% reduction in execution time, the change in output quality was still only extremely minor. Although our *quality* function was able to capture sufficient variation for FiDi, the range was too narrow for CoDi. Even for FiDi, the function was very noisy. We expect that different data input might lead to different results.

8. FUTURE WORK

The Relax framework presents many interesting directions for future work. We discuss a few of them below.

Architecture Exploration. In this paper, we considered the Relax framework in the context of some hypothetical hardware organizations and their associated parameters. The design of completely relaxed hardware would allow a detailed exploration of the trade-offs involved in implementing the Relax ISA. While we believe the ISA provides hardware simplicity, this design exercise would show how effective it truly is. Other topics for future work include considering phenomena beyond merely process variations, and also extending Relax to encompass faults occurring outside the processor core, which would yield a complete, chip-level recovery framework for hardware faults.

Compiler-Automated Retry Behavior. The key requirement for retry behavior on a region is idempotency, which is guaranteed by the absence of read-modify-write sequences. If, for example, a compiler creates a software checkpoint at the end of each read-modify-write sequence, Relax can be active throughout an entire application's execution. The key read-modify-write sequences to consider are load-store pairs targeting the same global or heap memory location; register spills and refills to and from the program stack are automatically handled by the compiler to preserve idempotency.

Binary Support for Retry Behavior. Applying Relax to static binaries when source code is not available is an-

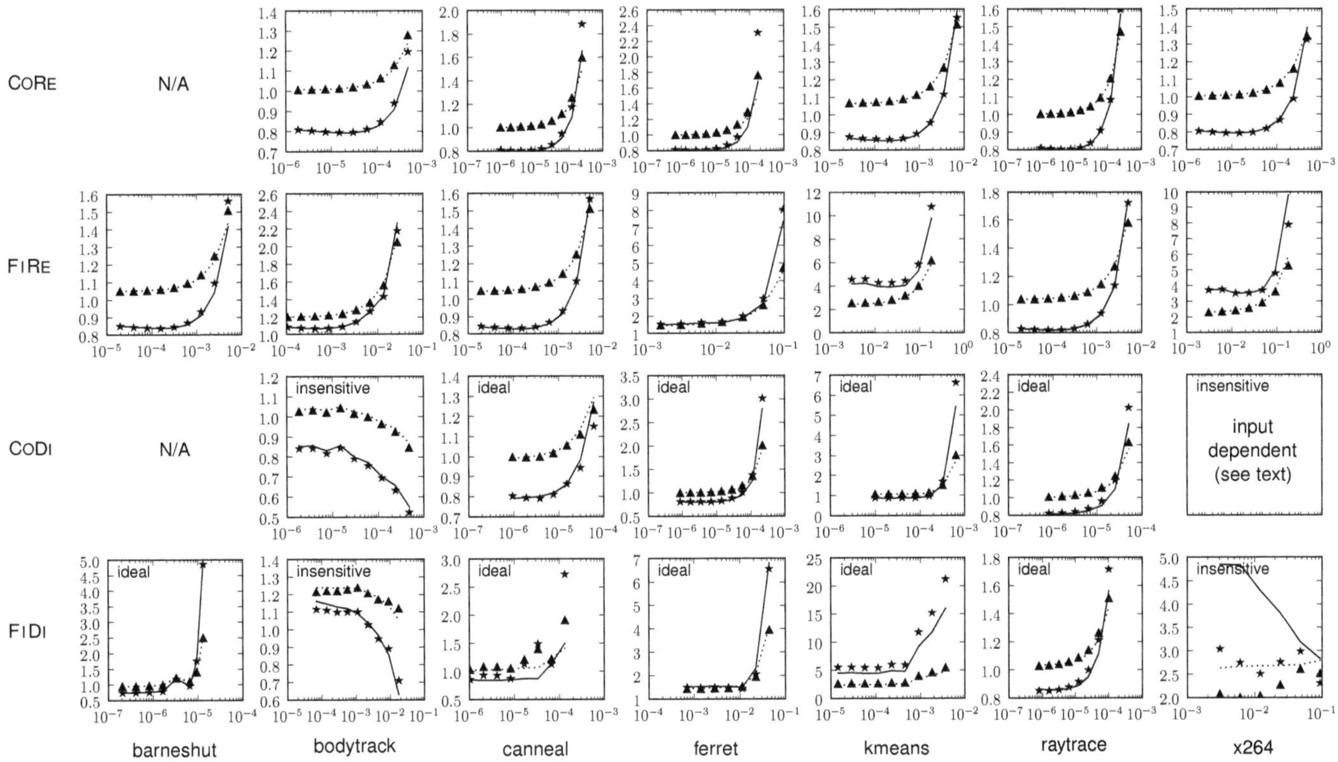

Figure 4: Solid curves plot analytically predicted fault rate (x-axis) versus EDP (y-axis) for each application and use case combination, with empirical data shown using stars. Dashed curves plot fault rate versus execution time only, with empirical data shown using triangles.

other interesting direction for future work. Dynamic binary instrumentation using tools like Pin [24] can be used to dynamically identify good relax block candidates. Static program analysis techniques [5] can also be used to identify idempotent regions in binaries.

Support for Discard Behavior. Discard behavior can be hard to reason about, in part because it exhibits non-determinism. Furthermore, unintentional non-determinism can easily lead to bugs that are very hard to track down. Language support to annotate intentional non-determinism could be used by a compiler or static analysis tool to identify potential bugs in the program. This and other tools to help reason about the efficacy and impact of discard behavior is an important topic for future work.

Nesting Support. Nesting relax blocks inside other relax blocks is a promising idea. The behavior for nested relax blocks should be a straightforward extension of the normal behavior: execution inside relax blocks is relaxed even when nested inside another relax block, and failures cause control to transfer to the end of the innermost relax block. Architecturally, the only requirement to implement this behavior is micro-architectural support for a stack-like structure to store the stack of failure destination addresses, akin to the Return Address Stack (RAS) in modern microprocessors.

9. RELATED WORK

We discuss related work in error recovery, full-system solutions to hardware errors, and application error tolerance.

Error Recovery. Sorin provides a complete treatment of error recovery solutions [37]. He describes two primary approaches to error recovery: *backward error recovery* (BER) and *forward error recovery* (FER). Relax provides BER under retry behavior, and a restricted form of FER under discard behavior. We consider each separately below.

For BER, Relax is distinct from other mechanisms in that it is both software based and has a small sphere of recoverability. Other software approaches have larger spheres of recoverability [30, 41] which comes at a substantial cost to performance. Hardware approaches have both large [32, 38] and small [3, 28] spheres of recoverability. However, hardware checkpoints consume substantial chip resources, and may not even be feasible when dealing with highly error-prone environments, where the checkpointing logic and storage itself cannot be made relatively immune to errors. Relax's fine-grained recovery in software is a good fit for an anticipated future with high fault rate systems running emerging applications that have few memory side-effects and can recover in software with low overhead.

On the FER side, the main competing approach is triple-modular redundancy (TMR). With discard behavior, Relax does not add any redundancy to implement FER, but rather allows the programmer to exploit the redundancy inherent in the application.

Full-System Solutions. Table 6 classifies other full-system proposals for managing error-prone hardware. SWAT [21, 34] uses lightweight symptom- and invariant-based detection techniques combined with heavyweight hardware checkpoints to recover from failure. SWAT optimizes for the

	Recovery	
Detection	Hardware	Software
Hardware	RSDT[4] SWAT [21, 34]	**Relax**
Software	SWAT [21, 34]	Liberty [8, 33]

Table 6: A taxonomy of full-system solutions.

modern-day common case of failure-free execution with a primary focus on reducing detection overhead while latency is not a concern as long as recovery remains possible. Our work is distinct from SWAT in anticipating a future where, for efficiency reasons, failure is much more common, and we shift priorities accordingly. Additionally, Relax is a software recovery framework that utilizes hardware detection, in contrast to SWAT's hybrid hardware-software detection with hardware recovery.

The Resilient-System Design Team (RSDT) attempts to manage faults entirely in hardware by adding mechanisms for testing, monitoring, and adaptive recovery [4]. While effective for general-purpose computing systems, this approach is overly restrictive for emerging applications with few side-effects and ignores application error tolerance.

Finally, the Liberty Research Group proposes transparent software-based detection and recovery through compiler instrumentation [8, 33]. This software-only approach can be readily deployed in commodity hardware but has high performance overheads.

Application Error Tolerance. A variety of studies have attempted to quantify application tolerance to errors [6, 11, 22, 23, 42]. In contrast to Relax, they allow errors to affect program state rather than discard them. However, the general findings are that control flow and memory operations, which together constitute a large percentage of these applications, remain intolerant to errors. As a result, these studies ultimately advocate for various forms of detection and/or recovery. The only technique that incorporates neither detection or recovery involves manually identifying "soft" computations and allowing only the backwards slice of these computations to fail [23]. These instructions can in some cases account for more than half of an application's dynamic instruction stream, but in general the technique by itself does not scale well beyond fault rates of more than $1e^{-6}$, and even this technique would still require changes to the ISA and compiler for the software to communicate information on what is a soft computation to the hardware. The evident conclusion is that arbitrary and uncontrolled failure is not generally feasible.

10. CONCLUSION

As CMOS technology scales, hardware reliability is becoming a primary design constraint. While languages, ISAs, and microarchitectures continue to maintain the illusion of the transistor as a perfect switch, VLSI circuits, CAD, and manufacturing layers of the silicon stack are under tremendous pressure to maintain this illusion. Emerging applications provide an opportunity to mitigate these CMOS scaling constraints by relaxing the burden of fault recovery on hardware.

This paper presented the Relax framework, which relaxes architectural semantics to help simplify CMOS scaling by removing the illusion of perfect hardware. Specifically, we proposed a handful of simple extensions to the programming language, compiler, ISA, and microarchitecture levels that simplify hardware design by enabling efficient software-level recovery of hardware faults. We constructed a spectrum of language models combining retry and discard behaviors with coarse and fine recovery granularities to enable flexible application handling of errors.

We showed that PARSEC applications are easily relaxed for more than 70% of their execution with only a handful of source-line modifications required, and that significant further opportunity exists. Applying the framework to allow timing errors due to process variations, we show that, applications are up to 20% more energy-efficient. Most importantly, the correctness requirements of hardware are reduced. Overall, the Relax framework enables flexible and efficient handling of hardware reliability through multiple levels of the system stack, instead of placing all the burden on hardware alone.

11. ACKNOWLEDGMENTS

We thank the anonymous reviewers and the Vertical group for comments and the Wisconsin Condor project and UW CSL for their assistance. Many thanks to Mark Hill and Guri Sohi for several discussions that helped refine this work. Support for this research was provided by NSF CAREER award #0845751 and Toshiba corporation.

12. REFERENCES

[1] Google performance tools. http://code.google.com/p/google-perftools/.

[2] V. Adve, C. Lattner, M. Brukman, A. Shukla, and B. Gaeke. LLVA: A low-level virtual instruction set architecture. In *MICRO '03*, pages 205–216.

[3] H. Akkary, R. Rajwar, and S. Srinivasan. Checkpoint processing and recovery: Towards scalable large instruction window processors. In *MICRO '03*, pages 423–434.

[4] T. Austin, V. Bertacco, S. Mahlke, and Y. Cao. Reliable systems on unreliable fabrics. *IEEE Design & Test of Computers*, 25(4):322–332, 2008.

[5] G. Balakrishnan, R. Gruian, T. W. Reps, and T. Teitelbaum. Codesurfer/x86-a platform for analyzing x86 executables. In R. Bodík, editor, *CC*, volume 3443 of *Lecture Notes in Computer Science*, pages 250–254. Springer, 2005.

[6] J. Bau, R. Hankins, Q. Jacobson, S. Mitra, B. Saha, and A. Adl-Tabatabai. Error resilient system architecture (ERSA) for probabilistic applications. In *SELSE '07*.

[7] C. Bienia, S. Kumar, J. P. Singh, and K. Li. The PARSEC benchmark suite: Characterization and architectural implications. In *PACT '08*, pages 72–81.

[8] J. Chang, G. A. Reis, and D. I. August. Automatic instruction-level software-only recovery. In *DSN '06*, pages 83–92.

[9] M. de Kruijf, S. Nomura, and K. Sankaralingam. A unified model for timing speculation: Evaluating the impact of technology scaling, CMOS design style, and fault recovery mechanism. In *DSN '10*.

[10] M. de Kruijf, S. Nomura, and K. Sankaralingam. Design, modeling, and evaluation of the Relax

architectural framework. Technical Report TR-1672, University of Wisconsin-Madison, Department of Computer Sciences, 2010.

[11] M. de Kruijf and K. Sankaralingam. Exploring the synergy of emerging workloads and silicon reliability trends. In *SELSE '09*.

[12] D. Ernst, N. S. Kim, S. Das, S. Pant, R. Rao, T. Pham, C. Ziesler, D. Blaauw, T. Austin, K. Flautner, and T. Mudge. Razor: A low-power pipeline based on circuit-level timing speculation. In *MICRO '03*, pages 7–18.

[13] V. Govindaraju, P. Djeu, K. Sankaralingam, M. Vernon, and W. R. Mark. Toward a multicore architecture for real-time ray-tracing. In *Proceedings of the 41st International Symposium on Microarchitecture*, pages 176–187, 2008.

[14] B. Greskamp and J. Torrellas. Paceline: Improving single-thread performance in nanoscale CMPs through core overclocking. In *PACT '07*, pages 213–224.

[15] B. Greskamp, L. Wan, U. Karpuzcu, J. Cook, J. Torrellas, D. Chen, and C. Zilles. Blueshift: Designing processors for timing speculation from the ground up. In *HPCA '09*, pages 213–224.

[16] J. H. Kelm, D. R. Johnson, M. R. Johnson, N. C. Crago, W. Tuohy, A. Mahesri, S. S. Lumetta, M. I. Frank, and S. J. Patel. Rigel: An architecture and scalable programming interface for a 1000-core accelerator. In *ISCA '09*, pages 140–151.

[17] W. Kim, M. Gupta, G.-Y. Wei, and D. Brooks. System level analysis of fast, per-core DVFS using on-chip switching regulators. In *HPCA '08*, pages 213–224.

[18] M. Kulkarni, K. Pingali, B. Walter, G. Ramanarayanan, K. Bala, and L. P. Chew. Optimistic parallelism requires abstractions. In *PLDI '07*, pages 211–222.

[19] S. Kumar, C. J. Hughes, and A. Nguyen. Carbon: architectural support for fine-grained parallelism on chip multiprocessors. In *ISCA '07*, pages 162–173.

[20] C. Lattner and V. Adve. LLVM: A compilation framework for lifelong program analysis & transformation. In *CGO '04*, pages 75–88.

[21] M. Li, P. Ramachandran, S. K. Sahoo, S. V. Adve, V. S. Adve, and Y. Zhou. Understanding the propagation of hard errors to software and implications for resilient system design. In *ASPLOS '08*, pages 265–276.

[22] X. Li and D. Yeung. Application-level correctness and its impact on fault tolerance. In *HPCA '07*, pages 181–192.

[23] X. Li and D. Yeung. Exploiting soft computing for increased fault tolerance. In *Workshop on Architectural Support for Gigascale Integration*, 2006.

[24] C.-K. Luk, R. Cohn, R. Muth, H. Patil, A. Klauser, G. Lowney, S. Wallace, V. J. Reddi, and K. Hazelwood. Pin: building customized program analysis tools with dynamic instrumentation. In *PLDI '05*, pages 190–200.

[25] A. Meixner, M. E. Bauer, and D. J. Sorin. Argus: Low-cost comprehensive error detection in simple cores. *IEEE Micro*, 28(1):52–59, 2008.

[26] F. Mesa-Martinez and J. Renau. Effective optimistic-checker tandem core design through architectural pruning. In *MICRO '07*, pages 236–248.

[27] S. Mukherjee, M. Kontz, and S. Reinhardt. Detailed design and evaluation of redundant multi-threading alternatives. In *ISCA '02*, pages 99–110.

[28] O. Mutlu, J. Stark, C. Wilkerson, and Y. Patt. Runahead execution: an alternative to very large instruction windows for out-of-order processors. In *HPCA '03*, pages 129–140.

[29] R. Narayanan, B. Ozisikyilmaz, J. Zambreno, G. Memik, and A. Choudhary. Minebench: A benchmark suite for data mining workloads. In *ISWC '06*, pages 182–188.

[30] J. S. Plank, K. Li, and M. A. Puening. Diskless checkpointing. *IEEE Trans. on Parallel and Distributed Systems*, 9(10):972–986, 1998.

[31] M. D. Powell, A. Biswas, S. Gupta, and S. S. Mukherjee. Architectural core salvaging in a multi-core processor for hard-error tolerance. In *ISCA '09*, pages 93–104.

[32] M. Prvulovic, Z. Zhang, and J. Torrellas. ReVive: Cost-effective architectural support for rollback recovery in shared-memory multiprocessors. In *ISCA '02*, pages 111–122.

[33] G. A. Reis, J. Chang, N. Vachharajani, R. Rangan, D. I. August, and S. S. Mukherjee. Software-controlled fault tolerance. *ACM Trans. on Architecture and Code Optimization*, 2(4):366–396, 2005.

[34] S. Sahoo, M.-L. Li, P. Ramachandran, S. Adve, V. Adve, and Y. Zhou. Using likely program invariants to detect hardware errors. In *DSN '08*, pages 70–79, 2008.

[35] S. Sarangi, B. Greskamp, R. Teodorescu, J. Nakano, A. Tiwari, and J. Torrellas. VARIUS: A model of process variation and resulting timing errors for microarchitects. *IEEE Trans. on Semiconductor Manufacturing*, 21(1):3–13, 2008.

[36] J. C. Smolens, B. T. Gold, B. Falsafi, and J. C. Hoe. Reunion: Complexity-effective multicore redundancy. In *MICRO '06*, pages 223–234.

[37] D. J. Sorin. *Fault Tolerant Computer Architecture.* Morgan & Claypool, 2009.

[38] D. J. Sorin, M. M. K. Martin, M. D. Hill, and D. A. Wood. SafetyNet: improving the availability of shared memory multiprocessors with global checkpoint/recovery. In *ISCA '02*, pages 123–134.

[39] V. Sridharan, D. A. Liberty, and D. R. Kaeli. A taxonomy to enable error recovery and correction in software. In *Workshop on Quality-Aware Design*, 2008.

[40] J. Tschanz, J. Kao, S. Narendra, R. Nair, D. Antoniadis, A. Chandrakasan, and V. De. Adaptive body bias for reducing impacts of die-to-die and within-die parameter variations on microprocessor frequency and leakage. *IEEE Journal of Solid-State Circuits*, 37(11):1396–1402, 2002.

[41] Y.-M. Wang, Y. Huang, K.-P. Vo, P.-Y. Chung, and C. Kintala. Checkpointing and its applications. In *FTCS '95*, page 22.

[42] V. Wong and M. Horowitz. Soft error resilience of probabilistic inference applications. In *SELSE '06*.

Author Index

www.ingramcontent.com/pod-product-compliance
Ingram Content Group UK Ltd.
Pitfield, Milton Keynes, MK11 3LW, UK
UKHW051415290926
15471UKWH00009B/1619